•

Praise for INDIA AFTER GANDHI

'Finally, here is a history of democratic India that is every bit as sweeping as the country itself . . . [A] magisterial work'
EDWARD LUCE, *Financial Times*

'A formidable undertaking . . . As comprehensive, balanced and elegantly crafted as any reasonable reader could expect'
PHILIP ZIEGLER, *Spectator*

'[A] dazzling book'
London Review of Books

'Guha is a scholar of astounding energy and ingenuity, and his book triumphantly dismisses an often-made plea: that India's contemporary history cannot be written because (as a result of government pigheadedness) the sources are not available. He seems to have visited every archive from Alabama to Allahabad, Calcutta to California, delving into a sea of private correspondence, news reports, pamphlet ephemera, as well as state papers. The result is a fascinating, kaleidoscopic narrative'
Daily Telegraph

'Guha has given democratic India the rich, well-paced history it deserves'
Washington Post

'Combining academic rigour with the readability of a thriller, *India After Gandhi* is a breathtaking survey'
Time Out Mumbai

INDIA
AFTER GANDHI

RAMACHANDRA GUHA

INDIA
AFTER GANDHI

The History of the
World's Largest Democracy

10th ANNIVERSARY EDITION
UPDATED AND EXPANDED

ecco
An imprint of HarperCollinsPublishers

Photo credits:
The Hindu – 1, 4, 8, 9, 29, 32, 33, 35, 36, 38, 39, 41, 42, 43, 45, 47.
Nehru Memorial Museum and Library – 2, 3, 12, 17, 19, 20, 21
Henri Cartier-Bresson/Magnum Photos – 5.
Press Information Bureau – 6, 13, 14, 22, 23, 26, 27, 28, 30, 31, 37.
Ananda Bazaar Patrika – 7, 11, 24, 25, 34, 44.
R. K. Laxman – 10. Author's collection – 15, 16, 18.
Prashant Panijar/*Outlook* – 40. AFP – 46. Getty Images – 48, 49.

HarperCollins books may be purchased for educational, business, or sales promotional use. For information, please email the Special Markets Department at SPsales@harpercollins.com.

Originally published in 2007 by Macmillan. Originally published in India in 2008 by Picador India, an imprint of Macmillan.

FIRST ECCO PAPERBACK EDITION PUBLISHED 2008.
SECOND ECCO PAPERBACK EDITION PUBLISHED 2019.

Library of Congress Cataloging-in-Publication Data has been applied for.

ISBN 978-0-06-297806-6 (pbk.)

19 20 21 22 23 LSC 10 9 8 7 6 5 4 3 2 1

For
Ira, Sasha and Suja:
lights on my coast

India is a pluralist society that creates magic with democracy, rule of law and individual freedom, community relations and [cultural] diversity. What a place to be an intellectual! . . . I wouldn't mind being born ten times to rediscover India.

ROBERT BLACKWILL, departing US ambassador, in 2003

Nobody could be more conscious than I am of the pitfalls which lie in the path of the man who wants to discover the truth about contemporary India.

NIRAD CHAUDHURI,
The Autobiography of an Unknown Indian (1950)

A Note on Place Names

In recent years, the names of several towns and cities in India have been modified or changed – thus Bombay has become Mumbai, Madras has become Chennai and Calcutta has become Kolkata. Likewise, the Bangladeshi capital, Dhaka, was for much of the period covered by this book known as Dacca, while the Chinese capital, Beijing, was until the 1980s referred to as Peking. The usage in this book conforms to historical convention rather than linguistic precision. For example, the capital of Maharashtra is referred to as Bombay until we come to the time when its name was officially changed to Mumbai.

Contents

Preface to the Second Edition

THIS BOOK WAS NOT my idea. In November 1997, a British publisher I had not heard of contacted me in Bangalore (as it then was). He had read an essay of mine in the Oxford historical journal, *Past and Present*, and wished to meet me. He was in Delhi soon; would I be there too?

As it turned out, I had a meeting in Delhi the week the publisher was in town. We met in his hotel, in a large airy atrium that served as a coffee shop. His name was Peter Straus, and he ran Picador, where he published, among other writers, V. S. Naipaul and Michael Ondaatje. He was carrying a copy of the *Past and Present* issue with my article in it. What, he asked, was the project I was working on now?

I pointed to the journal in his hands. I was, I told him, developing the essay he had read (on the social history of sport in colonial India) into a book. Would I consider abandoning that project, asked Peter Straus, and write a history of independent India instead?

This second question left me speechless. The scale and scope of the book he was suggesting seemed beyond my ambitions, and my training. I had begun writing occasionally for the press, but I still saw myself as principally an academic historian, who wrote for his peers and for university students. The books I had previously written had been on topics I had chosen myself: a social history of peasant protest in the Himalaya, two co-authored books on environmental conflicts, a biography of the maverick anthropologist Verrier Elwin. All had been published by university presses, and all had been highly focused, bounded by theme and/or region. How could I write, for a general readership, a single-volume history of a country as large and as diverse as India?

I am not normally at a loss for words, either in conversation or in print. Now, as I stayed silent, the visiting publisher asked some more questions. Was it not the case that historians of India stopped their narratives at 1947? Now that the nation had observed the fiftieth anniversary of its founding, would not a look back at its complicated and tumultuous history be a subject worthy of scholarly analysis? Would not such a book interest younger Indians, not to speak of the world at large? Did I not (as the article in *Past and Present* showed) greatly enjoy reading unpublished letters and manuscripts, as well as newspapers on microfilm?

To all these questions I nodded assent. So then, said the publisher, I agreed that such a history needed to be written. Why not research and write it myself? Why not at least think about it?

We left it at that. A month later, Peter Straus rang me in Bangalore, and asked whether I had given the idea further thought. I had, indeed, and sensed its appeal. He then told me to send a formal proposal, which I did, whereupon a contract was signed in March 1998, with a delivery date specified for March 2002, or four years later.

Now the job had to be done, the research begun. Where would I start? As I explain in the prologue to the first edition, had I been a historian of Europe or of a European country, commissioned to write a history of his country or continent since the end of World War II, I would have ordered five hundred books from the library – scholarly studies on politics, culture, law, economic policy and social change, with biographies of major or significant politicians thrown in. And, with these in hand, I would have attempted a work of synthesis.

In India, such secondary works were not available, for contemporary history as a branch of history had not yet been born. I had therefore to assemble the relevant primary materials on my own. The National Archives had plenty of state records on the colonial period, but precious few for the period since 1947. Fortunately, there was the Nehru Memorial Museum and Library (NMML), which had the private papers of hundreds of influential and important Indians. The NMML also had a superb collection of newspapers and journals on microfilm.

I spent many enjoyable months at the NMML, looking through its extraordinarily rich collection of (mostly unused) materials on the post-1947 period. The endnotes to this book provide more details on the numerous collections I consulted. Among them, the two that were perhaps most revealing were the papers of C. Rajagopalachari, the great friend-turned-critic of Jawaharlal Nehru, and of P. N. Haksar, Indira Gandhi's closest political confidant between 1967 and 1974.

The NMML also housed the old newspapers through which I tracked or fleshed out major events and controversies, the records of the Indian Parliament, as well as runs of left- and right-wing (as well as centrist) journals that conveyed the flavour and intensity of the many and various political debates of the period. This archive-cum-library was the bedrock of my research, but I also found vaulable materials in archives elsewhere in India and in the United Kingdom.

Those who read my newspaper columns know that I am a man of strong opinions. However, when it comes to my scholarly work I try to let the research do the talking. No writer can entirely hide or suppress his biases, but I did want to write this book in as non-ideological a manner as possible. I was seeking to interpret, not to judge. I wished to narrate, in as rich detail as I could, the conflict-ridden history of this unnatural nation and unlikely democracy. I also wanted the book to be comprehensive in scope – to deal with politics and economics, religion and language, caste and gender, although the confines of a single book and the limitations of an individual scholar surely mean that my reach has exceeded my grasp.

I was writing this book in the first decade of the twenty-first century, when, as India's economy grew, there was much talk of our becoming a superpower. The materials I was finding in the archives told an altogether different story. As the new nation struggled with the residues of Partition, with the problems posed by the settlement of refugees and the integration of the princely states, as both Hindu fundamentalism and a Communist insurgency gathered pace, few thought India would survive. For how could democracy and pluralism take root in this desperately poor, deeply divided and culturally heterogeneous country?

In the early years of independence, many obituaries of the new nation were written, confident anticipations that the Indian Republic would descend into civil war, balkanize into many parts, experience mass famine, or become a military dictatorship. In subsequent decades they continued to be written; whenever two monsoons failed in succession, or a prime minister died, or a major riot took place, some (professedly) serious Western writer would conclude that the project of a united and democratic India had failed.

But it didn't. That India survived despite the massive challenges it faced made me appreciate, even more than I had previously, the qualities of our first generation of political leaders – Nehru, Patel, Ambedkar, Rajagopalachari and their ilk – and the courage with which they confronted these challenges and the sagacity with which they overcame them. Perhaps no nation was born in more adverse circumstances; perhaps no new nation had such a remarkable concatenation of leaders to see it through the difficulties it faced in its early years. Had they not been there, or had they not acted as they did, those predictions of doom would surely have come to pass.

I admired these leaders, but this could not be a triumphalist book. For while India may have survived, throughout its history as a nation deep fissures persisted. I had to write about the question of Kashmir, yet in the course of my research I found that, even before the Kashmiris, a section of the Nagas had rejected Indian sovereignty. The conflict in Nagaland provided a counterpoint to the conflict in Kashmir, the two ends of the Indian Himalaya where so many people were not reconciled to being citizens of the Republic. Meanwhile, I had also to research and write about the vulnerability of Dalits, Muslims and tribals, three social groups who have struggled long and hard, if with decidedly mixed results, to achieve equal status with upper-caste Hindus.

I enjoyed the research enormously. The notebooks piled up (I had not then acquired a laptop), each filled in from beginning to end, the set covering a large shelf of my study in Bangalore. Other shelves contained out-of-print books and pamphlets acquired from second-hand bookstores around the world, relevant to my research. But how could I begin to make sense of, how would I structure, this mountain of material I had assembled?

It took me an unconscionably long time to think through a viable framework for the book, to design and decide upon the themes each chapter would cover, the order in which the chapters themselves would appear. Meanwhile, the deadline I had signed up for had come and gone. I had opened a folder on my desktop in which the drafts of the chapters I was writing were placed, one by one. The folder was called 'Mythical History Book', for I had no idea if, or ever, I would complete it. However, I eventually did, a full four years after the formal deadline had passed, when I finally sent Peter Straus a folder renamed 'History Book Revised'.

The book was submitted very late. It was also far longer than the publisher had hoped or bargained for. A friend who knew the American mind (and market) intimately told me that on no account should I exceed five hundred pages. A friend with domain knowledge about the United Kingdom thought that for a book of this kind four hundred pages would be an optimum length. Indians themselves were not known for being partial to large tomes, unless these were fictional (or mythical). The conventional wisdom was against me, but fortunately my editors could cut only 5,000 words from my draft, so a mastodon of 900 pages was the result.

The first edition of *India after Gandhi* was published in 2007. However, for all that it covered, and for all its length, the book could not remotely hope to have analysed all that was important or significant in the life of India or Indians. Fortunately, there has since been a rapid growth of interest in contemporary history, with many young scholars, Indian and foreign, writing fine dissertations and books on specific aspects of the history of India since Independence.

It is now ten years since *India after Gandhi* appeared. In this time the Republic has witnessed two general elections; the fall of the Congress and the rise of Narendra Modi; a major anti-corruption movement; more violence against women, Dalits, and religious minorities; a wave of prosperity for some states, regions and classes but the persistence of poverty for others; comparative peace in Nagaland but more (and perhaps greater than ever before) discontent in Kashmir; and much else. To take account of all this, I have prepared this revised and expanded edition, which brings the narrative up to the present. I have re-organized Section Five chronologically (in the earlier edition this last section followed a thematic approach), added two chapters based entirely on new material, and rewritten the epilogue.

All the books I have written (or will write) have been on my own initiative. Except this one. I am deeply grateful to a visionary publisher for giving me the chance to write the history of my country, and for doing so when he did. For I could not have written this book in my thirties, when I did not have the experience, or in my fifties, when I may not have had the energy.

Ramachandra Guha   Bengaluru   21 August 2016

Prologue

Unnatural Nation

I

Because they are so many, and so various, the people of India are also divided. It appears to have always been so. In the spring of 1827 the poet Mirza Asadullah Khan Ghalib set out on a journey from Delhi to Calcutta. Six months later he reached the holy Hindu city of Banaras. Here he wrote a poem called 'Chirag-i-Dair' (Temple Lamps), which contains these timeless lines:

> Said I one night to a pristine seer
> (Who knew the secrets of whirling Time),
> 'Sir, you well perceive,
> That goodness and faith,
> Fidelity and love
> Have all departed from this sorry land.
> Father and son are at each other's throat;
> Brother fights brother. Unity
> and Federation are undermined.
> Despite these ominous signs
> Why has not Doomsday come?
> Why does not the Last Trumpet sound?
> Who holds the reins of the Final Catastrophe?'[1]

Ghalib's poem was composed against the backdrop of the decline of the Mughal Empire. His home territory, the Indo-Gangetic plain, once ruled by a single monarch, was now split between contending chiefdoms and armies. Brother was fighting brother; unity and federation were being undermined. But even as he wrote, a new (and foreign) power was asserting its influence across the land in the form of the British, who were steadily acquiring control of the greater part of the subcontinent.

Then in 1857 large sections of the native population rose up in what the colonialists called the Sepoy Mutiny and Indian nationalists later referred to as the First War of Indian Independence.

Some of the bloodiest fighting was in Ghalib's home town, Delhi – still nominally the capital of the Mughals and in time to become the capital of the British Raj as well. His own sympathies were divided. He was the recipient of a stipend from the new rulers, yet a product of Mughal culture and refinement. He saw, more clearly than the British colonialist did then or the Indian nationalist does now, that it was impossible here to separate right from wrong, that horrible atrocities were being committed by both sides. Marooned in his home, he wrote a melancholy account of how 'Hindustan has become the arena of the mighty whirlwind and the blazing fire'. 'To what new order can the Indian look with joy?' he asked.[2]

An answer to this question was forthcoming. After the events of 1857 the Crown took over control of the Indian colonies. A sophisticated bureaucracy replaced the somewhat ad-hoc and haphazard administration of the old East India Company. New districts and provinces were created. The running of the state was overseen by the elite cadre of the Indian Civil Service supported by departments of police, forests, irrigation, etc. Much energy (and money) was spent on building a railway network that criss-crossed the land. This contributed enormously to the unity of British India, as well as to its stability, for now the rulers could quickly move troops to forestall any repeat of 1857.

II

By 1888 the British were so solidly established in India that they could anticipate, if not a thousand-year Raj, at least a rule that extended well beyond their own lifetimes. In that year a man who had helped put the Raj in place gave a series of lectures in Cambridge which were later published in book form under the simple title *India*. The man was Sir John Strachey. Strachey had spent many years in the subcontinent, ultimately becoming a member of the Governor General's Council. Now in retirement in England, he set his Indian experience against the background of recent political developments in Europe.

Large chunks of Strachey's book are taken up by an administrative history of the Raj; of its army and civil services, its land and taxation policies, the peculiar position of the 'native states'. This was a primer for those who might work in India after coming down from Cambridge. But there was also a larger theoretical argument to the effect that 'India' was merely a label of convenience, 'a name which we give to a great region including a multitude of different countries'.

In Strachey's view, the differences between the countries of Europe were much smaller than those between the 'countries' of India. 'Scotland is more like Spain than Bengal is like the Punjab.' In India the diversities of race, language and religion were far greater. Unlike in Europe, these 'countries' were not nations; they did not have a distinct political or social identity. This, Strachey told his Cambridge audience, 'is the first and most essential thing to learn about India – that there is not, and never was an India, or even any country of India possessing, according to any European ideas, any sort of unity, physical, political, social or religious'.

There was no Indian nation or country in the past; nor would there be one in the future. Strachey thought it 'conceivable that national sympathies may arise in particular Indian countries', but 'that they should ever extend to India generally, that men of the Punjab, Bengal, the North-western Provinces, and Madras, should ever feel that they belong to one Indian nation, is impossible. You might with as much reason and probability look forward to a time when a single nation will have taken the place of the various nations of Europe.'[3]

Strachey's remarks were intended as a historical judgement. At the time, new nations were vigorously identifying themselves within Europe on the basis of a shared language or territory, whereas none of the countries that he knew in India had displayed a comparable national awakening. But we might also read them as a political exhortation, intended to stiffen the will of those in his audience who would end up in the service of the Raj. For the rise of every new 'nation' in India would mean a corresponding diminution in the power and prestige of Empire.

Ironically, even as he spoke Strachey's verdict was being disputed by a group of Indians. These had set up the Indian *National* Congress, a representative body that asked for a greater say for natives in the running of their affairs. As the name suggests, this body wished to unite Indians across the divisions of culture, territory, religion, and language, thus to construct what the colonialist thought inconceivable – namely, a *single* Indian nation.

Very many good books have been written on the growth of the Indian National Congress, on its move from debating club through mass movement to political party, on the part played by leaders such as Gokhale, Tilak and (above all) Gandhi in this progression. Attention has been paid to the building of bridges between linguistic communities, religious groupings and castes. These attempts were not wholly successful, for low castes and especially Muslims were never completely convinced of the Congress's claims to be a truly 'national' party. Thus it was that when political independence finally came in 1947 it came not to one nation, but two – India and Pakistan.

This is not the place to rehearse the history of Indian nationalism.[4] I need only note that from the time the Congress was formed right up to when India was made free – and divided – there were sceptics who thought that Indian nationalism was not a natural phenomenon at all. There were, of course, British politicians and thinkers who welcomed Indian self-rule and, in their own way, aided its coming into being. (One of the prime movers of the Indian National Congress was a colonial official of Scottish parentage, A. O. Hume.) Yet there were many others who argued that, unlike France or Germany or Italy, there was here no national essence, no glue to bind the people and take them purposively forward. From this perspective stemmed the claim that it was only British rule that held India and the Indians together.

Among those who endorsed John Strachey's view that there could never be an independent Indian nation were writers both famous and obscure. Prominent in the first category was Rudyard Kipling, who had spent his formative years in – and was to write some of his finest stories about – the subcontinent. In November 1891 Kipling visited Australia, where a journalist asked him about the 'possibility of self-government in India'. 'Oh no!' he answered: 'They are 4,000 years old out there, much too old to learn that business. Law and order is what they want and we are there to give it to them and we give it them straight.'[5]

Where Kipling laid emphasis on the antiquity of the Indian civilization, other colonialists stressed the immaturity of the Indian mind to reach the same conclusion: namely, that Indians could not govern themselves. A cricketer and tea planter insisted, after forty years there, that

> [c]haos would prevail in India if we were ever so foolish to leave the natives to run their own show. Ye gods! What a salad of confusion, of bungle, of mismanagement, and far worse, would be the instant result.
>
> These grand people will go anywhere and do anything *if led by us*.

Themselves they are still infants as regards governing or statesmanship. And their so-called leaders are the worst of the lot.[6]

Views such as these were widely prevalent among the British in India, and among the British at home as well. Politically speaking, the most important of these 'Stracheyans' was undoubtedly Winston Churchill. In the 1940s, with Indian independence manifestly round the corner, Churchill grumbled that he had not become the King's first minister in order to preside over the liquidation of the British Empire.

A decade previously he had tried to rebuild a fading political career on the plank of opposing self-government for Indians. After Gandhi's 'salt *satyagraha*' of 1930 in protest against taxes on salt, the British government began speaking with Indian nationalists about the possibility of granting the colony dominion status. This was vaguely defined, with no timetable set for its realization. Even so, Churchill called the idea 'not only fantastic in itself but criminally mischievous in its effects'. Since Indians were not fit for self-government, it was necessary to marshal 'the sober and resolute forces of the British Empire' to stall any such possibility.

In 1930 and 1931 Churchill delivered numerous speeches designed to work up, in most unsober form, the constituency opposed to independence for India. Speaking to an audience at the City of London in December 1930, he claimed that if the British left the subcontinent, then 'an army of white janissaries, officered if necessary from Germany, will be hired to secure the armed ascendancy of the Hindu'. Three months later, speaking at the Albert Hall on 'Our Duty to India' – with his kinsman the Duke of Marlborough presiding – Churchill argued that 'to abandon India to the rule of the Brahmins [who in his opinion dominated the Congress Party] would be an act of cruel and wicked negligence'. If the British left, he predicted, then the entire gamut of public services created by them – the judicial, medical, railway and public works departments – would perish, and 'India will fall back quite rapidly through the centuries into the barbarism and privations of the Middle Ages'.[7]

III

A decade and a half after Winston Churchill issued these warnings, the British left India. A time of barbarism and privation did ensue, the blame for which remains a matter of much dispute. But then some sort of order was restored. No Germans were necessary to keep the peace. Hindu ascendancy, such as it was, was maintained not by force of arms but through regular elections based on universal adult franchise.

Yet, throughout the sixty years since India became independent, there has been speculation about how long it would stay united, or maintain the institutions and processes of democracy. With every death of a prime minister has been predicted the replacement of democracy by military rule; after every failure of the monsoon there has been anticipated countrywide famine; in every new secessionist movement has been seen the disappearance of India as a single entity.

Among these doomsayers there have been many Western writers who, after 1947, were as likely to be American as British. Notably, India's existence has been a puzzle not just to casual observers or commonsensical journalists; it has also been an anomaly for academic political science, according to whose axioms cultural heterogeneity and poverty do not make a nation, still less a democratic one. That India 'could sustain democratic institutions seems, on the face of it, highly improbable', wrote the distinguished political scientist Robert Dahl, adding: 'It lacks all the favourable conditions.' 'India has a well-established reputation for violating social scientific generalizations', wrote another American scholar, adding: 'Nonetheless, the findings of this article furnish grounds for skepticism regarding the viability of democracy in India.'[8]

The pages of this book are peppered with forecasts of India's imminent dissolution, or of its descent into anarchy or authoritarian rule. Here, let me quote only a prediction by a sympathetic visitor, the British journalist Don Taylor. Writing in 1969, by which time India had stayed united for two decades and gone through four general elections, Taylor yet thought that

> the key question remains: can India remain in one piece – or will it fragment? . . . When one looks at this vast country and its 524 million people, the 15 major languages in use, the conflicting religions, the many races, it seems incredible that one nation could ever emerge.
>
> It is difficult to even encompass this country in the mind – the great Himalaya, the wide Indo-Gangetic plain burnt by the sun and savaged by the fierce monsoon rains, the green flooded delta of the east, the great cities like Calcutta, Bombay and Madras. It does not, often, seem like

one country. And yet there is a resilience about India which seems an assurance of survival. *There is* something which can only be described as an Indian spirit.

I believe it no exaggeration to say that the fate of Asia hangs on its survival.[9]

The heart hoped that India would survive, but the head worried that it wouldn't. The place was too complicated, too confusing – a nation, one might say, that was *un*natural.

In truth, ever since the country was formed there have also been many Indians who have seen the survival of India as being on the line, some (the patriots) speaking or writing in fear, others (the secessionists or revolutionaries) with anticipation. Like their foreign counterparts, they have come to believe that this place is far too diverse to persist as a nation, and much too poor to endure as a democracy.

IV

In the last decade of the last century I became a resident of Ghalib's native city. I lived, however, not in the old walled town where his family *haveli*, or mansion, still stands, but in New Delhi, built as an imperial capital by the British. As in the poet's day, Indian was fighting Indian. On my way to work I had to pass through Rajpath (formerly Kingsway), the road whose name and location signal the exercise of state power. For about a mile, Rajpath runs along flat land; on either side are spacious grounds meant to accommodate the thousands of spectators who come for the annual Republic Day parade. The road then ascends a hill and reaches the majestic sandstone buildings known as the North and South Blocks, which house the offices of the Government of India. The road ends in the great house where the Viceroy of British India once lived.

By the time I moved to New Delhi the British had long departed. India was now a free and sovereign republic. But not, it seemed, an altogether happy one. The signs of discord were everywhere. Notably on Rajpath, where the grounds meant to be empty except on ceremonial days had become a village of tents, each with colourful placards hung outside it. One tent might be inhabited by peasants from the Uttarakhand Himalaya, seeking a separate province; a second by farmers from Maharashtra, fighting for a higher price for their produce; a third by residents of the southern Konkan coast, urging that their language be given official recognition by inclusion in the Eighth Schedule of the Constitution of India.

The people within these tents and the causes they upheld were ever changing. The hill peasants might be replaced by industrial workers protesting retrenchment; the Maharashtra farmers by Tibetan refugees asking for Indian citizenship; the Konkani speakers by Hindu monks demanding a ban on cow slaughter.

In the early nineties, these tents were summarily dismantled by a government worried about the impression made on foreign visitors by such open expression of dissent. Rajpath was vacated of encroachments and the lawns restored to their former glory. But the protesters regrouped, and relocated. They now placed themselves a mile to the north-west, next to the Jantar Mantar observatory in Connaught Place. Here they were away from the eyes of the state, but directly in view of the citizens who daily passed through this busy shopping district. In 1998 the police decided this would not do either. The shanties were once again demolished, but, as a newspaper report had it, 'as far as the authorities are concerned, only the venue has changed – the problem persists. The squatters are merely to be shifted to an empty plot at the Mandir Marg–Shankar Road crossing, where they are likely to draw less attention.'[10]

When I lived in Delhi, in the 1990s, I wished I had the time to walk on Rajpath every day from the first of January to the thirty-first of December, chronicling the appearance and disappearance of the tents and their residents. That would be the story of India as told from a single street, and in a single year. The book that is now in your hands follows a different method. Its narrative extends over six decades, from 1947 to the present. However, like the book that I once intended to write – based on a year spent walking up and down Rajpath – this too is a story, above all, of social conflicts, of how these arise, how they are expressed, and how their resolution is sought.

These conflicts run along many axes, among which we may – for the moment – single out four as pre-eminent. First, there is *caste*, a principal identity for many Indians, defining whom they might marry, associate with and fight against. 'Caste' is a Portuguese word that conflates two Indian words: *jati*, the endogamous group one is born into, and *varna*, the place that group occupies in the system of social stratification mandated by Hindu scripture. There are four *varnas*, with the former

'Untouchables' constituting a fifth (and lowest) strata. Into these *varnas* fit the 3,000 and more *jatis*, each challenging those, in the same region, that are ranked above it, and being in turn challenged by those below.

Then there is *language*. The Constitution of India recognizes twenty-two languages as 'official'. The most important of these is Hindi, which in one form or another is spoken by upwards of 400 million people. Others include Telugu, Kannada, Tamil, Malayalam, Marathi, Gujarati, Oriya, Punjabi, Bengali and Assamese, each of which is written in a distinct script and boasts many millions of native speakers. Naturally, national unity and linguistic diversity have not always been seen to be compatible. Indians speaking one tongue have fought with Indians who speak another.

A third axis of conflict is *religion*. A vast majority of the billion-plus Indians are Hindus. But India also has the second largest population of Muslims in the world – about 140 million (only Indonesia has more). In addition there are substantial communities of Christians, Sikhs, Buddhists and Jains. Since faith is as fundamental a feature of human identity as language, it should scarcely be a surprise that Indians worshipping one variation of God have sometimes quarrelled with Indians worshipping another.

The fourth major axis of conflict is *class*. India is a land of unparalleled cultural diversity but also, less appealingly, of massive social disparities. There are Indian entrepreneurs who are fabulously wealthy, owning huge homes in London and New York. Yet fully 26 per cent of the country's population, about 300 million individuals, are said to live below the official poverty line. In the countryside there are deep inequalities in landholding; in the city, wide divergences in income. Not unexpectedly, these asymmetries have fuelled many movements of opposition.

These axes of conflict operate both singly and in tandem. Sometimes a group professing a particular faith also speaks a separate language. Often the low castes are the subordinate classes as well. And to these four central axes one should perhaps add a fifth that cuts right across them: that of *gender*. Here, again, India offers the starkest contrasts. A woman served as prime minister for a full fifteen years, yet in some parts of India female infanticide is still very common. Landless labourers are paid meagre wages, the women among them the lowest of all. Low castes face social stigma, the women among them most of all. And the holy men of each religion tend to assign their women an inferior position in both this world and the next. As an axis of discrimination, gender is even more pervasive than the others, although it has not so often expressed itself in open and collective protest.

As a laboratory of social conflict the India of the twentieth century is – for the historian – at least as interesting as the Europe of the nineteenth. In both the conflicts were produced by the conjunction of two truly transformative processes of social change: industrialization and the making of modern nation-states. In India the scope for contention has been even greater, given the diversity of competing groups across religion, caste, class and language. Conflicts are also more visible in the subcontinent since, unlike nineteenth-century Europe, contemporary India is a democracy based on adult suffrage, with a free press and a largely independent judiciary. At no other time or place in human history have social conflicts been so richly diverse, so vigorously articulated, so eloquently manifest in art and literature, or addressed with such directness by the political system and the media.

One way of summarizing the history of independent India – and the contents of this book – would be through a series of 'conflict maps'. One might draw a map of India for each decade, with the conflicts then prevalent marked in various colours depending on their intensity: blue for those that democratically advance the interests of a particular group; red for those that more aggressively, yet still non-violently, ask for a major change in the law; black for those that seek the destruction of the Indian state by armed insurrection.

Reading these maps chronologically, one would find major variations across the decades, with red areas becoming black, black areas becoming red, and blue and red areas becoming white, that being the colour of those parts of India where there appears to be no major conflict at all. These maps would present a vivid kaleidoscope of changing colours. But amid all the changes the discerning observer would also notice that two things remain constant. The first is that the shape of the map does not change through all its iterations. This is because no part of India has successfully *left* India. The second is that at no time do the blue, red and black areas, taken together, anywhere approximate the extent of the white areas of the map. Even in what were once known as its 'dangerous decades', much more than 50 per cent of India was comfortably at peace with itself.

The press nowadays – broadsheet and tabloid, pink and white, Indian and Western – is chock full of stories of India's economic success, this reckoned to be so much at odds with its past history of poverty and deprivation. However, the real success story of modern India lies not in the domain of economics but in that of politics. The saluting of India's 'software boom' might be premature. We do not yet know whether this will lead to a more general prosperity among the masses. But that India is still a single nation after sixty testing years of independence, and that it is still largely democratic – these are facts that should compel our deeper attention. A recent statistical analysis of the relationship between democracy and development in 135 countries found that 'the odds against democracy in India were extremely high'. Given its low levels of income and literacy, and its high levels of social conflict, India was 'predicted as [a] dictatorship during the entire period' of the study (1950–90). Since, in fact, it was a democracy practically the entire period studied, there was only one way to characterize India, namely as 'a major outlier'.[11]

To explain this anomaly, this paradox, one needs perhaps to abandon the methods of statistical social science – in which India will always be the exception to the rule – in favour of the more primitive techniques of the narrative historian. The forces that divide India are many. This book pays due attention to them. But there are also forces that have kept India together, that have helped transcend or contain the cleavages of class and culture, that – so far, at least – have nullified those many predictions that India would not stay united and not stay democratic. These moderating influences are far less visible; it is one aim of this book to make them more so. I think it premature now to identify them; they will become clearer as the narrative proceeds. Suffice it to say that they have included individuals as well as institutions.

V

'[The] period of Indian history since 1947', writes the political theorist Sunil Khilnani, 'might be seen as the adventure of a political idea: democracy.' Viewed thus, independent India appears as the 'third moment in the great democratic experiment launched at the end of the eighteenth century by the American and French revolutions'. Each of these experiments 'released immense energies; each raised towering expectations; and each has suffered tragic disappointments'. While the Indian experiment is the youngest, says Khilnani, 'its outcome may well turn out to be the most significant of them all, partly because of its sheer human scale, and partly because of its location, a substantial bridgehead of effervescent liberty on the Asian continent'.[12]

As an Indian, I would like to think that democracy in India will turn out to be 'more significant' than comparable experiments in the West. As a historian, I know only that it is much less studied. There are hundreds, perhaps thousands, of books on the French and American revolutions: biographies of their leaders famous and obscure, studies of the social background of those who participated in them, assessments of their deepening or degradation in the decades and centuries that followed. By contrast, the works by historians on any aspect of Indian democracy can be counted on the fingers of one hand – or, if one is more open-minded, two.

The educationist Krishna Kumar writes that 'for Indian children history itself comes to an end with Partition and Independence. As a constituent of social studies, and later on as a subject in its own right, history runs right out of content in 1947 . . . All that has happened during the last 55 years may filter through the measly civics syllabus, popular cinema and television; history as formally constituted knowledge of the past does not cover it.'[13]

If, for Indian children, history comes to an end with Independence and Partition, this is because Indian adults have mandated it that way. In the academy, the discipline of history deals with the past, while the disciplines of political science and sociology deal with the present. This is a conventional and in many ways logical division. The difficulty is that in the *Indian* academy the past is defined as a single, immovable date: 15 August 1947. Thus, when the clock struck midnight and India became independent, history ended, and political science and sociology began.

In the decades since 1947, the present has moved on. Political scientists studied the first general election of 1952, and then the next one held five years later. Social anthropologists wrote accounts of Indian villages in the 1950s, and then some more in the 1960s. The past, however, has stayed fixed. By training and temperament, historians have restricted themselves to the period before Independence. A vast literature grew – and is still growing – on the social, cultural, political and economic consequences of British colonialism. An even more vast literature grew – and it too is still growing – on the forms, functions, causes and consequences of the opposition to colonial rule. Leading that opposition was the social reformer, spiritualist, prophet and political agitator Mohandas Karamchand Gandhi.

Gandhi was, and remains, greatly admired by some and cordially detested by others. Much the same could be said of the monumental edifice he opposed, the British Raj. The British finally left India in August 1947; Gandhi was assassinated by a fellow Indian a bare five and a half months later. That the demise of the Raj was followed so quickly by the death of its most celebrated opponent has had a determining influence on the writing of history. One cannot say whether, if Gandhi had lived on much longer, historians would have shown greater interest in the history of free India. As it turned out, by custom and convention Indian history is seen as 'ending' on 15 August 1947 – although biographers of the Mahatma are allowed a six-month extension. Thus many fine, as well as controversial, books have been written on the last intense, conflict-filled years of British India. That great institution, the British Raj, and that great individual, Mahatma Gandhi, continue to be of absorbing interest to historians. But the history of *independent* India has remained a field mostly untilled. If history is 'formally constituted knowledge of the past', then for the period since 1947 this knowledge practically does not exist.

And yet, as this book shows, the first years of freedom were as full of dramatic interest as the last years of the Raj. The British had formally handed over power, but authority had to be created anew. Partition had not put an end to Hindu–Muslim conflict, nor Independence to class and caste tension. Large areas of the map were still under the control of the Maharajas; these had to be brought into the Indian Union by persuasion or coercion. Amidst the wreckage of a decaying empire a new nation was being born – and built.

Of his recent history of postwar Europe, Tony Judt writes that 'a book of this kind rests, in the first instance, on the shoulders of other books'. He notes that 'for the brief sixty-year period of Europe's history since the end of the Second World War – indeed, for this period above all – the secondary literature in English is inexhaustible'.[14] The situation in India is all too different. Here the gaps in our knowledge are colossal. The Republic of India is a union of twenty-eight states, some larger than France. Yet not even the bigger or more important of these states have had their histories written. In the 1950s and 60s India pioneered a new approach to foreign policy, and to economic policy and planning as well. Authoritative or even adequate accounts of these experiments remain to be written. India has produced entrepreneurs of great vision and dynamism – but the stories of the institutions they built and the wealth they created are mostly unwritten. Again, there are no proper biographies of some of the key figures in our modern history: such as Sheikh Abdullah or Master Tara Singh or M. G. Ramachandran, 'provincial' leaders each of whose province is the size of a large European country.

Unlike a history of postwar Europe, a history of postwar India cannot simply rest on the shoulders of other books on more specialized subjects. In matters great and small it must fill in the blanks using materials picked up by the author. My first mentor, a very wise old civil servant named C. S. Venkatachar, once told me that every work of history is 'interim', to be amplified, amended, contested, and overthrown by works written in its wake. Despite the range of subjects it covers, this book cannot hope to have treated any of them comprehensively. Individual readers will have their own particular grouses; some might complain, for instance, that I have not said enough here about tribals, others that I should have written even more pages on Kashmir.

My own hopes for this book are best expressed in the words of Marc Bloch, writing about another country in another time:

> I could liken myself to an explorer making a rapid survey of the horizon before plunging into thickets from which the wider view is no longer possible. The gaps in my account are naturally enormous. I have done my best not to conceal any deficiencies, whether in the state of our knowledge in general or in my own documentation . . . When the time comes for my own work to be superseded by studies of deeper penetration, I shall feel well rewarded if confrontation with my false conjectures has made history learn the truth about herself.[15]

VI

The great Cambridge historian F. W. Maitland liked to remind his students that 'what is now in the past was once in the future'. There could be no better maxim for the historian, and especially the historian of the recent past, who addresses an audience with very decided views on the subjects about which he presumes to inform them. An

American historian of the Vietnam War is read by those who have mostly made up their minds on whether the war was just or not. A French historian of the student movement of 1968 knows that his readers shall have forceful, if mutually contradictory, opinions about that particular upsurge.

Those who write contemporary history know that the reader is not a passive vessel to receive the text placed before him or her. The reader is also a citizen, a *critical citizen*, with individual political and ideological preferences. These preferences direct and dictate the reader's view of the past, and of leaders and lawmakers most particularly. We live with the consequences of decisions taken by modern politicians, and often presume that an alternate politician – someone modelled on oneself – would have taken better or wiser decisions.

The further back we go in time, the less of a problem this is. Historians of the eighteenth century seek to interpret and understand that time, and so, following them, do their readers. A biographer of Jefferson or Napoleon can count on more *trusting* readers – they do not presume to know the things those men did, or wish they should have done them differently. Here, the reader is usually happy to be led and guided by the expert. But the biographer of John F. Kennedy or Charles de Gaulle is not so fortunate. Some, perhaps many, potential readers already know the 'truth' about these men, and are less willing to hear alternative versions of it, even if they are backed up by copious footnotes.

Contemporary historians thus face a challenge from their readers which their more backward-looking colleagues avoid. But there is also a second, and perhaps less commonly acknowledged, challenge. This is that *the historian too is a citizen*. The scholar who chooses to write on the Vietnam War already has strong views on the topic. The scholar who writes on the American Civil War would have less strong views, and one who writes on the Revolutionary War weaker views still. For the historian as well as the citizen, *the closer one gets to the present, the more judgemental one tends to become.*

In writing this book I have tried to keep Maitland's maxim always in front of me. I have been driven by curiosity rather than certainty, by the wish to understand rather than the desire to pass judgement. I have sought to privilege primary sources over retrospective readings, thus to interpret an event of, say, 1957 in terms of what was known in 1957 rather than in 2007. This book is, in the first instance, simply an attempt to tell the modern history of one-sixth of humankind. It is an account, as well as analysis, of the major characters, controversies, themes and processes in independent India. However, the manner of the story's telling has been driven by two fundamental ambitions: to pay proper respect to the social and political diversity of India, and to unravel the puzzle that has for so long confronted scholar and citizen, foreigner as well as native – namely, why is there an India at all?

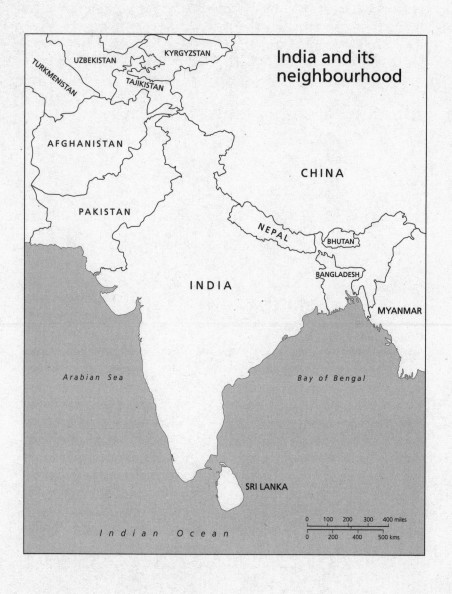

India and its neighbourhood

PART ONE

PICKING UP THE PIECES

1

FREEDOM AND PARRICIDE

The disappearance of the British Raj in India is at present, and must for a long time be, simply inconceivable. That it should be replaced by a native Government or Governments is the wildest of wild dreams . . . As soon as the last British soldier sailed from Bombay or Karachi, India would become the battlefield of antagonistic racial and religious forces . . . [and] the peaceful and progressive civilisation, which Great Britain has slowly but surely brought into India, would shrivel up in a night.

J. E. WELLDON, former Bishop of Calcutta, 1915

I have no doubt that if British governments had been prepared to grant in 1900 what they refused in 1900 but granted in 1920; or to grant in 1920 what they refused in 1920 but granted in 1940; or to grant in 1940 what they refused in 1940 but granted in 1947 – then nine-tenths of the misery, hatred, and violence, the imprisonings and terrorism, the murders, flogging, shootings, assassinations, even the racial massacres would have been avoided; the transference of power might well have been accomplished peacefully, even possibly without Partition.

LEONARD WOOLF, 1967

I

FREEDOM CAME TO INDIA on 15 August 1947, but patriotic Indians had celebrated their first 'Independence Day' seventeen years before. In the first week of January 1930 the Indian National Congress passed a resolution fixing the last Sunday of the month for countrywide demonstrations in support of *purna swaraj*, or complete independence. This, it was felt, would both stoke nationalist aspirations and force the British seriously to consider giving up power. In an essay in his journal *Young India*, Mahatma Gandhi set out how the day should be observed.

'It would be good', said the leader, 'if the declaration [of independence] is made by whole villages, whole cities even . . . It would be well if all the meetings were held at the identical minute in all the places.'

Gandhi suggested that the time of the meeting be advertised in the traditional way, by drum-beats. The celebrations would begin with the hoisting of the national flag. The rest of the day would be spent 'in doing some constructive work, whether it is spinning, or service of "untouchables", or reunion of Hindus and Mussalmans, or prohibition work, or even all these together, which is not impossible'. Participants would take a pledge affirming that it was 'the inalienable right of the Indian people, as of any other people, to have freedom and to enjoy the fruits of their toil', and that 'if any government deprives a people of these rights and oppresses them, the people have a further right to alter it or abolish it'.[1]

The resolution to mark the last Sunday of January 1930 as Independence Day was passed in the city of Lahore, where the Congress was holding its annual session. It was here that Jawaharlal Nehru was chosen President of the Congress, in confirmation of his rapidly rising status within the Indian national movement. Born in 1889, twenty years after Gandhi, Nehru was a product of Harrow and Cambridge who had become a close protégé of the Mahatma. He was intelligent and articulate, knowledgeable about foreign affairs, and with a particular appeal to the young.

In his autobiography Nehru recalled how 'Independence Day came, January 26th, 1930, and it revealed to us, as in a flash, the earnest and enthusiastic mood of the country. There was something vastly impressive about the great gatherings everywhere, peacefully and solemnly taking the pledge of independence without any speeches or exhortation.'[2] In a press statement that he issued the day after, Nehru 'respectfully congratulate[d] the nation on the success of the solemn and orderly demonstrations'. Towns and villages had 'vied with each other in showing their enthusiastic adherence to independence'. Mammoth gatherings were held in Calcutta and Bombay, but the meetings in smaller towns were well attended too.[3]

Every year after 1930, Congress-minded Indians celebrated 26 January as Independence Day. However, when the British finally left the subcontinent, they chose to hand over power on 15 August 1947. This date was selected by the Viceroy, Lord Mountbatten, as it was the second anniversary of the Japanese surrender to the Allied Forces in the Second World War. He, and the politicians waiting to take office, were unwilling to delay until the date some others would have preferred – 26 January 1948.

So freedom finally came on a day that resonated with imperial pride rather than nationalist sentiment. In New Delhi, capital of the Raj and of free India, the formal events began shortly before midnight. Apparently, astrologers had decreed that 15 August was an inauspicious day. Thus it was decided to begin the celebrations on the 14th, with a special session of the Constituent Assembly, the body of representative Indians working towards a new constitution.

The function was held in the high-domed hall of the erstwhile Legislative Council of the Raj. The room was brilliantly lit and decorated with flags. Some of these flags had been placed inside picture frames that until the previous week had contained portraits of British viceroys. Proceedings began at 11 p.m. with the singing of the patriotic hymn 'Vande Matram' and a two-minute silence in memory of those 'who had died in the struggle for freedom in India and elsewhere'. The ceremonies ended with the presentation of the national flag on behalf of the women of India.

Between the hymn and the flag presentation came the speeches. There were three main speakers that night. One, Chaudhry Khaliquzzaman, was chosen to represent the Muslims of India; he duly proclaimed the loyalty of the minority to the newly freed land. A second, the philosopher Dr Sarvepalli Radhakrishnan, was chosen for his powers of oratory and his work in reconciling East and West: appropriately, he praised the 'political sagacity and courage' of the British who had elected to leave India while the Dutch stayed on in Indonesia and the French would not leave Indo-China.[4]

The star turn, however, was that of the first prime minister of free India, Jawaharlal Nehru. His speech was rich in emotion and rhetoric, and has been widely quoted since. 'At the stroke of the midnight hour, when the world sleeps, India will awake to life and freedom,' said Nehru.[5] This was 'a moment which comes but rarely in history, when we step out from the old to the new, when an age ends, and when the soul of a nation, long suppressed, finds utterance'.

This was spoken inside the columned Council House. In the streets outside, as an American journalist reported, bedlam had broken loose. Hindus, Muslims, and Sikhs were happily celebrating together . . . It was Times Square on New Year's Eve. More than anyone else, the crowd wanted Nehru. Even before he was due to appear, surging thousands had broken through police lines and flowed right to the doors of the Assembly building. Finally, the heavy doors were closed to prevent a probably souvenir-hunting tide from sweeping through the Chamber. Nehru, whose face reflected his happiness, escaped by a different exit and after a while the rest of us went out.

No event of any importance in India is complete without a goof-up. In this case, it was relatively minor. When, after the midnight session at the Constituent Assembly, Jawaharlal Nehru went to submit his list of cabinet ministers to the governor general, he handed over an empty envelope. However, by the time of the swearing-in ceremony the missing piece of paper was found. Apart from Prime Minister Nehru, it listed thirteen other ministers. These included the nationalist stalwarts Vallabhbhai Patel and Maulana Abul Kalam Azad, as well as four Congress politicians of the younger generation.

More notable perhaps were the names of those who were not from the Congress. These included two representatives of the world of commerce and one representative of the Sikhs. Three others were lifelong adversaries of the Congress. These were R. K. Shanmukham Chetty, a Madras businessman who possessed one of the best financial minds in India; B. R. Ambedkar, a brilliant legal scholar and an 'Untouchable' by caste; and Syama Prasad Mookerjee, a leading Bengal politician who belonged (at this time) to the Hindu Mahasabha. All three had collaborated with the rulers while the Congress men served time in British jails. But now Nehru and his colleagues wisely put aside these differences. Gandhi had reminded them that 'freedom comes to India, not to the Congress', urging the formation of a Cabinet that included the ablest men regardless of party affiliation.[6]

The first Cabinet of free India was ecumenical in ways other than the political. Its members came from as many as five religious denominations (with a couple of atheists thrown in for good measure), and from all parts of India. There was a woman, Rajkumari Amrit Kaur, as well as two Untouchables.

On 15 August the first item on the agenda was the swearing-in of the Governor General, Lord Mountbatten, who until the previous night had been the last viceroy. The day's programme read:

8.30 a.m.   Swearing in of governor general and ministers at Government House

9.40 a.m.   Procession of ministers to Constituent Assembly

9.50 a.m.   State drive to Constituent Assembly

9.55 a.m.   Royal salute to governor general

10.30 a.m. Hoisting of national flag at Constituent Assembly

10.35 a.m. State drive to Government House

6.00 p.m.   Flag ceremony at India Gate

7.00 p.m.   Illuminations

7.45 p.m.   Fireworks display

8.45 p.m.   Official dinner at Government House

10.15 p.m. Reception at Government House

It appeared that the Indians loved pomp and ceremony as much as the departing rulers. Across Delhi, and in other parts of India, both state and citizen joyously celebrated the coming of Independence. Three hundred flag-hoisting functions were reported from the capital alone. In the country's commercial hub, Bombay, the city's mayor hosted a banquet at the luxurious Taj Mahal hotel. At a temple in the Hindu holy town of Banaras, the national flag was unfurled by, significantly, a Muslim. In the north-eastern hill town of Shillong, the governor presided over a function where the flag was hoisted by four young persons – two Hindu and Muslim boy / girl pairings – for 'symbolically it is appropriate for young India to hoist the flag of the new India that is being born'.

When the first, so to say fantastical, Independence Day was observed on 26 January 1930 the crowds were 'solemn and orderly' (as Nehru observed). But, in 1947, when the real day of Independence came, the feelings on display were rather more elemental. To quote a foreign observer, everywhere, 'in city after city, lusty crowds have burst the bottled-up frustrations of many years in an emotional mass jag. Mob sprees have rolled from mill districts to gold coasts and back again . . . [T]he happy, infectious celebrations blossomed in forgetfulness of the decades of sullen resentment against all that was symbolized by a sahib's sun-topi.'

The happenings in India's most populous city, Calcutta, were characteristic of the mood. For the past few years the city had been in the grip of a cloth shortage, whose signs now miraculously disappeared in a 'rash of flags that has broken out on houses and buildings . . ., on cars and bicycles and in the hands of babes and sucklings'. Meanwhile, in Government House, a new Indian governor was being sworn in. Not best pleased with the sight was the private secretary of the departing British governor. He complained that 'the general motley character of the gathering from the clothing point of view detracted greatly from its dignity'. There were no dinner jackets and ties on view: only loincloths and white Gandhi caps. With 'the throne room full of unauthorized persons', the ceremony was 'a foretaste of what was to come' after the British had left India. Its nadir was reached when the outgoing governor of Bengal, Sir Frederick Burrows, had a white Gandhi cap placed on his head as he made to leave the room.

II

In Delhi there was 'prolonged applause' when the president of the Constituent Assembly began the meeting by invoking the Father of the Nation – Mohandas Karamchand Gandhi. Outside, the crowds shouted 'Mahatma Gandhi ki jai'. Yet Gandhi was not present at the festivities in the capital. He was in Calcutta, but did not attend any function or hoist a flag there either. The Gandhi caps were on display at Government House with neither his knowledge nor permission. On the evening of the 14th he was visited by the chief minister of West Bengal, who asked him what form the celebrations should take the next day. 'People are dying of hunger all round,' answered Gandhi. 'Do you wish to hold a celebration in the midst of this devastation?'[7]

Gandhi's mood was bleak indeed. When a reporter from the leading nationalist paper, the *Hindustan Times*, requested a message on the occasion of Independence, he replied that 'he had run dry'. The British Broadcasting Corporation asked his secretary to help them record a message from the one man the world thought really represented India. Gandhi told them to talk to Jawaharlal Nehru instead. The BBC were not persuaded: they sent the emissary back, adding, as inducement, the fact that this message would be translated into many languages and broadcast around the globe. Gandhi was unmoved, saying: 'Ask them to forget I know English.'

Gandhi marked 15 August 1947 with a twenty-four-hour fast. The freedom he had struggled so long for had come at an unacceptable price. Independence had also meant Partition. The last twelve months had seen almost continuous rioting between Hindus and Muslims. The violence had begun on 16 August 1946 in Calcutta and spread to the Bengal countryside. From there it moved on to Bihar, then on to the United Provinces and finally to the province of Punjab, where the scale of the violence and the extent of the killing exceeded even the horrors that had preceded it.

The violence of August–September 1946 was, in the first instance, instigated by the Muslim League, the party which fuelled the movement for a separate state of Pakistan. The League was led by Mohammad Ali Jinnah, an austere, aloof man, and yet a brilliant political tactician. Like Nehru and Gandhi, he was a lawyer trained in England. Like them, he had once been a member of the Indian National Congress, but he had left the party because he felt that it was led by and for Hindus. Despite its nationalist protestations, argued Jinnah, the Congress did not really represent the interests of India's largest minority, the Muslims.

By starting a riot in Calcutta in August 1946, Jinnah and the League hoped to polarize the two communities further, and thus force the British to divide India when they finally quit. In this endeavour they richly succeeded. The Hindus retaliated savagely in Bihar, their actions supported by local Congress leaders. The British had already said that they would not transfer power to any government 'whose authority is directly denied by large and powerful elements in the Indian national life'.[8] The bloodshed of 1946–7 seemed to suggest that the Muslims were just such an element, who would not live easily or readily under a Congress government dominated by Hindus. Now 'each communal outbreak was cited as a further endorsement of the two-nation theory, and of the inevitability of the partition of the country'.[9]

Gandhi was not a silent witness to the violence. When the first reports came in from rural Bengal, he set everything else aside and made for the spot. This 77-year-old man walked in difficult terrain through slush and stone, consoling the Hindus who had much the worse of the riots. In a tour of seven weeks he walked 116 miles, mostly barefoot, addressing almost a hundred village meetings. Later he visited Bihar, where the Muslims were the main sufferers. Then he went to Delhi, where refugees from the Punjab had begun to pour in, Hindus and Sikhs who had lost all in the carnage. They were filled with feelings of revenge, which Gandhi sought to contain, for he was fearful that it would lead to retributory violence against those Muslims who had chosen to stay behind in India.

Two weeks before the designated day of Independence the Mahatma left Delhi. He spent four days in Kashmir and then took the train to

Calcutta, where, a year after it began, the rioting had not yet died down. On the afternoon of the 13th he set up residence in the Muslim dominated locality of Beliaghata, in 'a ramshackle building open on all sides to the crowds', to see whether 'he could contribute his share in the return of sanity in the premier city of Calcutta'.

Gandhi decided simply to fast and pray on the 15th. By the afternoon news reached him of (to quote a newspaper report) 'almost unbelievable scenes of fraternity and rejoicing' in some of the worst affected areas of Calcutta. 'While Hindus began erecting triumphal arches at the entrance of streets and lanes and decorating them with palm leaves, banners, flags and bunting, Muslim shopkeepers and householders were not slow in decorating their shops and houses with flags of the Indian Dominion'. Hindus and Muslims drove through the streets in open cars and lorries, shouting the nationalist slogan 'Jai Hind', to which 'large, friendly crowds of both communities thronging the streets readily and joyfully responded'.[10]

Reports of this spontaneous intermingling seem to have somewhat lifted the Mahatma's mood. He decided he would make a statement on the day, not to the BBC, but through his own preferred means of communication, the prayer meeting. A large crowd – of 10,000 according to one report, 30,000 according to another – turned up to hear him speak at the Rash Bagan Maidan in Beliaghata. Gandhi said he would like to believe that the fraternization between Hindus and Muslims on display that day 'was from the heart and not a momentary impulse'. Both communities had drunk from the 'poison cup of disturbances'; now that they had made up, the 'nectar of friendliness' might taste even sweeter. Who knows, perhaps as a consequence Calcutta might even 'be entirely free from the communal virus for ever'.

That Calcutta was peaceful on 15 August was a relief, and also a surprise. For the city had been on edge in the weeks leading up to Independence. By the terms of the Partition Award, Bengal had been divided, with the eastern wing going to Pakistan and the western section staying in India. Calcutta, the province's premier city, was naturally a bone of contention. The Boundary Commission chose to allot it to India, sparking fears of violence on the eve of Independence.

Across the subcontinent there was trouble in the capital of the Punjab, Lahore. This, like Calcutta, was a multireligious and multicultural city. Among the most majestic of its many fine buildings was the Badshahi mosque, built by the last of the great Mughal emperors, Aurangzeb. But

Lahore had also once been the capital of a Sikh empire, and was more recently a centre of the Hindu reform sect, the Arya Samaj. Now, like all other settlements in the Punjab, its fate lay in the hands of the British, who would divide up the province. The Bengal division was announced before the 15th, but announcement of the Punjab 'award' had been postponed until after that date. Would Lahore and its neighbourhood be allotted to India, or to Pakistan?

The latter seemed more likely, as well as more logical, for the Muslims were the largest community in the city. Indeed, a new governor had already been appointed for the new Pakistani province of West Punjab, and had moved into Government House in Lahore. On the evening of the 15th he threw a party to celebrate his taking office.

As he later recalled, this 'must have been the worst party ever given by anyone . . . The electric current had failed and there were no fans and no lights. The only light which we had was from the flames of the burning city of Lahore about half a mile away. All around the garden, there was firing going on – not isolated shots, but volleys. Who was firing at who, no one knew and no one bothered to ask.'[11]

No one bothered to ask. Not in the governor's party, perhaps. In Beliaghata, however, Mahatma Gandhi expressed his concern that this 'madness still raged in Lahore'. When and how would it end? Perhaps one could hope that 'the noble example of Calcutta, if it was sincere, would affect the Punjab and the other parts of India'.

III

By November 1946 the all-India total of deaths in rioting was in excess of 5,000. As an army memo mournfully observed: 'Calcutta was revenged in Noakhali, Noakhali in Bihar, Bihar in Garmukteshwar, Garmukteshwar in ????'[12]

At the end of 1946 one province that had escaped the rioting was the Punjab. In office there were the Unionists, a coalition of Muslim, Hindu and Sikh landlords. They held the peace uncertainly, for ranged against them were the militant Muslim Leaguers on the one side and the no less militant Sikh political party, the Akali Dal, on the other. Starting in January, episodic bouts of violence broke out in the cities of Punjab. These accelerated after the first week of March, when the Unionists were forced out of office. By May the epicentre of violence had shifted decisively from the east of India to the north-west. A statement submitted to the House of Lords said that 4,014 people were killed in riots in India between 18 November 1946 and 18 May 1947. Of these, as many as 3,024 had died in the Punjab alone.[13]

There were some notable similarities between Bengal and Punjab, the two provinces central to the events of 1946–7. Both had Muslim majorities, and thus were claimed for Pakistan. But both also contained many millions of Hindus. In the event, both provinces were divided, with the Muslim majority districts going over to East or West Pakistan, while the districts in which other religious groups dominated were allotted to India.

But there were some crucial differences between the two provinces as well. Bengal had a long history of often bloody conflict between Hindus and Muslims, dating back to (at least) the last decades of the nineteenth century. By contrast, in the Punjab the different communities had lived more or less in peace – there were no significant clashes on religious grounds before 1947. In Bengal large sections of the Hindu middle class actively sought Partition. They were quite happy to shuffle off the Muslim-dominated areas and make their home in or around the provincial capital. For several decades now, Hindu professionals had been making their way to the west, along with landlords who sold their holdings and invested the proceeds in property or businesses in Calcutta. By contrast, the large Hindu community in the Punjab was dominated by merchants and moneylenders, bound by close ties to the agrarian classes. They were unwilling to relocate, and hoped until the end that somehow Partition would be avoided.

The last difference, and the most telling, was the presence in the Punjab of the Sikhs. This third leg of the stool was absent in Bengal, where it was a straight fight between Hindus and Muslims. Like the Muslims, the Sikhs had one book, one formless God, and were a close-knit community of believers. Sociologically, however, the Sikhs were closer to the Hindus. With them they had a *roti-beti rishta* – a relationship of inter-dining and inter-marriage – and with them they had a shared history of persecution at the hands of the Mughals.

Forced to choose, the Sikhs would come down on the side of the Hindus. But they were in no mood to choose at all. For there were substantial communities of Sikh farmers in both parts of the province. At the turn of the century, Sikhs from eastern Punjab had been asked by the British to settle areas in the west, newly served by irrigation.

In a matter of a few decades they had built prosperous settlements in these 'canal colonies'. Why now should they leave them? Their holy city, Amritsar, lay in the east, but Nankana Saheb (the birthplace of the founder of their religion) lay in the west. Why should they not enjoy free access to both places?

Unlike the Hindus of Bengal, the Sikhs of Punjab were slow to comprehend the meaning and reality of Partition. At first they doggedly insisted that they would stay where they were. Then, as the possibility of division became more likely, they claimed a separate state for themselves, to be called 'Khalistan'. This demand no one took seriously, not the Hindus, not the Muslims, and least of all the British.

The historian Robin Jeffrey has pointed out that, at least until the month of August 1947, the Sikhs were 'more sinned against than sinning'. They had been 'abandoned by the British, tolerated by the Congress, taunted by the Muslim League, and, above all, frustrated by the failures of their own political leadership . . .'[14] It was the peculiar (not to say tragic) dilemma of the Sikhs that best explains why, when religious violence finally came to the Punjab, it was so accelerated and concentrated. From March to August, every month was hotter and bloodier than the last. Nature cynically lent its weight to politics and history, for the monsoon was unconscionably late in coming in 1947. And, like the monsoon, the boundary award was delayed as well, which only heightened the uncertainty.

The task of partitioning Bengal and the Punjab was entrusted to a British judge named Sir Cyril Radcliffe. He had no prior knowledge of India (this was deemed an advantage). However, he was given only five weeks to decide upon the lines he would draw in both east and west. It was, to put it mildly, a very difficult job. He had, in the words of W. H. Auden, to partition a land 'between two people fanatically at odds / with their different diets and incompatible gods', with 'the maps at his disposal . . . out of date', and 'the Census Returns almost certainly incorrect'.[15]

Radcliffe arrived in India in the first week of July. He was assigned four advisers for the Punjab: two Muslims, one Hindu, and one Sikh. But since these fought on every point, he soon dispensed with them. Still, as he wrote to his nephew, he knew that 'nobody in India will love me for the award about the Punjab and Bengal and there will be roughly 80 million people with a grievance who will begin looking for me. I do not want them to find me . . .'[16]

On 1 August a Punjab Boundary Force was set up to control the violence. The force was headed by a major general, T. W. ('Pete') Rees, a Welshman from Abergavenny. Under him were four advisers of the rank of brigadier: two Muslims, one Hindu, and one Sikh. In his first report Rees predicted that the boundary award 'would please no one entirely. It may well detonate the Sikhs'.[17] This was said on 7 August; on the 14th, the commander-in-chief of the British Indian Army, Field Marshal Sir Claude Auchinleck, observed that 'the delay in announcing the award of the Border Commission is having a most disturbing and harmful effect. It is realised of course that the announcement may add fresh fuel to the fire, but lacking the announcement, the wildest rumours are current, and are being spread by mischief makers of whom there is no lack.'[18]

The rains still held off, and the temperature was a hundred degrees in the shade. This was especially trying to Muslims, both soldiers and civilians, observing the dawn-to-dusk fast on the occasion of Ramzan, which that year fell between 19 July and 16 August. Rees asked his Muslim driver why the monsoon had failed, and he replied, 'God too is displeased'.

The boundary award was finally announced on 16 August. The award enraged the Muslims, who thought that the Gurdaspur district should have gone to Pakistan instead of India. Angrier still were the Sikhs, whose beloved Nankana Sahib now lay marooned in an Islamic state. On both sides of the border the brutalities escalated. In eastern Punjab bands of armed Sikhs roamed the countryside, seeking out and slaying Muslims wherever they were to be found. Those who could escaped over the border to West Punjab, where they further contributed to the cycle of retribution and revenge. Muslims from Amritsar and around streamed into the (to them) safe haven of Lahore. The 'stories of these Refugees, oriental and biblical in exaggeration, are indeed founded on very brutal fact, and they do not lack handless stumps etc., which they can and do parade before their fellow Muslims in Lahore and further west . . .'

According to Pete Rees's own figures, from March to the end of July, the casualties in the Punjab were estimated at 4,500 civilians dead and 2,500 wounded. But in the month of August alone, casualties as reported officially by the troops were estimated at 15,000 killed, and Rees admitted that the actual figure 'may well have been two or three times the number'.

The Indian prime minister, Jawaharlal Nehru, was deeply worried about the Punjab troubles and their wider repercussions. In the last fortnight of August he visited the province three times, talking to people on either side of the border and taking aerial sorties. Nehru did not think that there was 'anything to choose between the brutality of one side or the other. Both sides have been incredibly inhuman and barbarous'.[19] The adjective that Rees himself used for the savagery was 'pre-medieval'. In truth, it was also medieval and modern. For the arms used by the rioters 'varied from primitive axe, spear, and club to the most modern tommy-gun and light machine-gun'.

On 2 September the Punjab Boundary Force was disbanded. It had not been especially effective anyway. It was hampered by the problem of dual authority: by having to report to civilian officers in the absence of martial law. With the exit of the Punjab Boundary Force, responsibility for law and order was now vested in the governments of India and Pakistan. The riots continued, as did the two-way exodus. West Punjab was being cleansed of Hindus and Sikhs, East Punjab being emptied of Muslims. The clinical even-handedness of the violence was described by the Punjab correspondent of the respected Madras-based weekly *Swatantra*. He wrote of seeing

> an empty refugee special steaming into Ferozepur Station late one afternoon. The driver was incoherent with terror, the guard was lying dead in his van, and the stoker was missing. I walked down the platform – all but two bogeys were bespattered with blood inside and out; three dead bodies lay in pools of blood in a third-class carriage. An armed Muslim mob had stopped the train between Lahore and Ferozepur and done this neat job of butchery in broad daylight.
>
> There is another sight I am not likely to easily forget. A five-mile-long caravan of Muslim refugees crawling at a snail's pace into Pakistan over the Sutlej Bridge. Bullock-carts piled high with pitiful chattels, cattle being driven alongside. Women with babies in their arms and wretched little tin trunks on their heads. Twenty thousand men, women and children trekking into the promised land – not because it is the promised land, but because bands of Hindus and Sikhs in Faridkot State and the interior of Ferozepur district had hacked hundreds of Muslims to death and made life impossible for the rest.[20]

Ten million refugees were on the move, on foot, by bullock-cart, and by train, sometimes travelling under army escort, at other times trusting to fate and their respective gods. Jawaharlal Nehru flew over one refugee convoy which comprised 100,000 people and stretched for ten miles. It was travelling from Jullundur to Lahore, and had to pass through Amritsar, where there were 70,000 refugees from West Punjab 'in an excited state'. Nehru suggested bulldozing a road around the town, so that the two convoys would not meet.[21]

This was without question the greatest mass migration in history. 'Nowhere in known history ha[d] the transfer of so many millions taken place in so few days'. They fled, wrote an eyewitness,

> through heat and rain, flood and bitter Punjab cold. The dust of the caravans stretched low across the Indian plains and mingled with the scent of fear and sweat, human waste and putrefying bodies. When the cloud of hate subsided the roll of the dead was called and five hundred thousand names echoed across the dazed land – dead of gunshot wounds, sword, dagger and knife slashes and others of epidemic diseases. While the largest number died of violence, there were tired, gentle souls who looked across their plundered gardens and then lay down and died. For what good is life when reason stops and men run wild? Why pluck your baby from the spike or draw your lover from the murky well?[22]

The trouble in the province was made worse by the noticeably partisan attitude of the governor of West Punjab, Sir Francis Mudie. He was 'inveterate against the Congress'. Mudie thought he 'could govern himself. Thus he thwarts his Cabinet, above all in their attempts to bridge the gulf between West and East Punjab, and therefore between Pakistan and India'. Tragically, no Pakistani politician was willing to take on religious fanaticism. Whatever their private thoughts, they were unwilling to speak out in public. As for Pakistan's new governor general, Mohammad Ali Jinnah, he was headquartered in the coastal city of Karachi (the country's capital), and had 'only visited Lahore in purdah and most carefully guarded'. This timidity was in striking contrast to the brave defence of their minorities by the two pre-eminent Indian politicians. Indeed, as a British observer wrote, 'Nehru's and Gandhi's stock has never been so high with the Muslims of West Punjab'.[23]

Meanwhile, trouble had flared up once more in Bengal. There were reports of fresh rioting in Noakhali. In Calcutta itself the peace was broken in Gandhi's own adopted locality of Beliaghata. Here, on 31 August, a Hindu youth was attacked by Muslims. Retaliatory violence followed and spread. By dusk on 1 September more than fifty people lay dead. That night, Gandhi decided he would go on a fast. 'But how can you fast against the *goondas* [hooligans]?' asked a friend. Gandhi's answer, according to an eyewitness, ran as follows: 'I know I shall be able to tackle the Punjab too if I can control Calcutta. But if I falter now, the conflagration may spread and soon. I can see clearly two or three [foreign] Powers will be upon us and thus will end our short-lived dream of independence.' 'But if you die the conflagration will be worse,' replied the friend. 'At least I won't be there to witness it,' said Gandhi. 'I shall have done my bit.'[24]

Gandhi began his fast on 2 September. By the next day Hindu and Muslim *goondas* were coming to him and laying down their arms. Mixed processions for communal harmony took place in different parts of the city. A deputation of prominent politicians representing the Congress, the Muslim League and the locally influential Hindu Mahasabha assured Gandhi that there would be no further rioting. The Mahatma now broke his fast, which had lasted three days.

The peace held, prompting Lord Mountbatten to remark famously that one unarmed man had been more effective than 50,000 troops in Punjab. But the Mahatma and his admirers might have treasured as much this tribute from the *Statesman*, a British-owned paper in Calcutta that had long opposed him and his politics: 'On the ethics of fasting as a political instrument we have over many years failed to concur with India's most renowned practitioner of it . . . But never in a long career has Mahatma Gandhi, in our eyes, fasted in a simpler, worthier cause than this, nor one calculated for immediate effective appeal to the public conscience.'[25]

On 7 September, having spent four weeks in Beliaghata, Gandhi left for Delhi. He hoped to proceed further, to the Punjab. However, on his arrival in the capital he was immediately confronted with tales of strife and dispossession. The Muslims of Delhi were frightened. Their homes and places of worship had come under increasing attack. Gandhi was told that no fewer that 137 mosques had been destroyed in recent weeks. Hindu and Sikh refugees had also forcibly occupied Muslim homes. As a Quaker relief worker reported, 'the Muslim population of Delhi of all classes – civil servants, businessmen, artisans, tongawallahs, bearers – had fled to a few natural strongholds' – such as the Purana Qila, the great high-walled fort in the middle of the city, and the tomb of the Mughal emperor Humayun. In the Purana Qila alone there were 60,000 refugees, huddled together in tents, 'in the corners of battlements and in the open, together with their camels and tongas and ponies, battered old taxis and luxury limousines'.[26]

Gandhi now put his Punjab programme on hold. He visited the camps in the capital and outside it. In the plains around Delhi lived a farming community called Meos, Muslims by faith, but who had adopted many of the practices and rituals of their Hindu neighbours. In the madness of the time this syncretism was forgotten. Thousands of Meos were killed or driven out of their homes, whether these lay in Indian territory or in the princely states of Alwar and Bharatpur.[27]

Through September and October, writes his biographer D. G. Tendulkar, Gandhi 'went round hospitals and refugee camps giving consolation to distressed people'. He 'appealed to the Sikhs, the Hindus and the Muslims to forget the past and not to dwell on their sufferings but to extend the right hand of fellowship to each other, and to determine to live in peace . . .' He 'begged of them all to bring about peace quickly in Delhi, so that he might be able to proceed to both East and West Punjab'. Gandhi said 'he was proceeding to the Punjab in order to make the Mussalmans undo the wrong that they were said to have perpetrated there [against the Hindus and the Sikhs]. But he could not hope for success, unless he could secure justice for the Mussalmans in Delhi.'[28]

Gandhi also spoke at a camp of the Rashtriya Swayamsevak Sangh. Founded by a Maharashtrian doctor in 1925, the RSS was a cohesive and motivated body of Hindu young men. Gandhi himself was impressed by their discipline and absence of caste feeling, but less so by their antagonism to other religions. He told the RSS members that 'if the Hindus felt that in India there was no place for any one except the Hindus and if non-Hindus, especially Muslims, wished to live here, they had to live as the slaves of the Hindus, they would kill Hinduism'. Gandhi could see that the RSS was 'a well-organized, well-disciplined body'. But, he told its members, 'its strength could be used in the interests of India or against it. He did not know whether there was any truth in the allegations [of inciting communal hatred] made against the Sangha. It was for the Sangha to show by their uniform behaviour that the allegations were baseless.'[29]

Unlike Gandhi, Jawaharlal Nehru was not inclined to give the Sangh the benefit of doubt. 'It seems to me clear', he told his home minister, Vallabhbhai Patel, 'that the RSS have a great deal to do with the disturbances not only in Delhi but elsewhere. In Amritsar their activities have been very obvious'. Nehru's feelings about the RSS stemmed from his deeper worries about the communal situation. He thought that there was 'a very definite and well-organized attempt of certain Sikh and Hindu fascist elements to overturn the government, or at least to break up its present character. It has been something more than a communal disturbance. Many of these people have been brutal and callous in the extreme. They have functioned as pure terrorists.'[30]

The worry was the greater because the fanatics were functioning in 'a favourable atmosphere as far as public opinion was concerned'. In Delhi, especially, the Hindu and Sikh refugees from Pakistan were baying for blood. But the prime minister insisted that India must be a place where the Muslims could live and work freely. An Englishman on the governor general's staff wrote in his diary of how 'to see Nehru at close range during this ordeal is an inspiring experience. He vindicates one's faith in the humanist and the civilised intellect. Almost alone in the turmoil of communalism, with all its variations, from individual intrigue to mass madness, he speaks with the voice of reason and charity.'[31]

At the initiative of Gandhi and Nehru, the Congress now passed a resolution on 'the rights of minorities'. The party had never accepted the 'two-nation theory'; forced against its will to accept Partition, it still believed that 'India is a land of many religions and many races, and must remain so'. Whatever be the situation in Pakistan, India would be 'a democratic secular State where all citizens enjoy full rights and are equally entitled to the protection of the State, irrespective of the religion to which they belong'. The Congress wished to 'assure the minorities in India that it will continue to protect, to the best of its ability, their citizen rights against aggression'.[32]

However, the Rashtriya Swayamsevak Sangh was actively sceptical of this viewpoint. Its *sarsanghchalak*, or head, was a lean, bearded science graduate named M. S. Golwalkar. Golwalkar was strongly opposed to the idea of a secular state that would not discriminate on the basis of religion. In the India of his conception,

> The non-Hindu people of Hindustan must either adopt Hindu culture and language, must learn and respect and hold in reverence the Hindu religion, must entertain no idea but of those of glorification of the Hindu race and culture . . . in a word they must cease to be foreigners, or may stay in the country, wholly subordinated to the Hindu nation, claiming nothing, deserving no privileges, far less any preferential treatment – not even citizens' rights.[33]

On Sunday 7 December 1947 the RSS held a large rally at the Ramlila
Grounds in the heart of Delhi. The main speech was by M. S. Golwalkar.
As the *Hindustan Times* reported, Golwalkar denied that the RSS aimed
at the establishment of a Hindu Raj, but nevertheless insisted: 'We
aim at the solidarity of the Hindu society. With this ideal in view, the
Sangh will march forward on its path, and will not be deterred by any
authority or personality.'[34]

The authorities being alluded to were the Congress Party and the
government of India; the personalities, Nehru and Gandhi, towards
whom there was much hostility among those sections of the refugees
sympathetic to the RSS. Gandhi had his meetings disrupted by refugees who
objected to readings from the Quran, or who shouted slogans asking
why he did not speak of the sufferings of those Hindus and Sikhs still
living in Pakistan. In fact, as D. G. Tendulkar writes, Gandhi 'was equally
concerned with the sufferings of the minority community in Pakistan.
He would have liked to be able to go to their succour. But with what
face could he now go there, when he could not guarantee full redress
to the Muslims in Delhi?'

With attacks on Muslims continuing, Gandhi chose to resort to
another fast. This began on 13 January, and was addressed to three
different constituencies. The first were the people of India. To them he
simply pointed out that if they did not believe in the two-nation theory,
they would have to show in their chosen capital, the 'Eternal City' of
Delhi, that Hindus and Muslims could live in peace and brotherhood.
The second constituency was the government of Pakistan. 'How long',
he asked them, 'can I bank upon the patience of the Hindus and the
Sikhs, in spite of my fast? Pakistan has to put a stop to this state of affairs'
(that is, the driving out of minorities from their territory).

Gandhi's fast was addressed, finally, to the government of India.
They had withheld Pakistan's share of the 'sterling balance' which the
British owed jointly to the two dominions, a debt incurred on account
of Indian contributions during the Second World War. This amounted
to Rs550 million, a fair sum. New Delhi would not release the money
as it was angry with Pakistan for having recently attempted to seize the
state of Kashmir. Gandhi saw this as unnecessarily spiteful, and so he
made the ending of his fast conditional on the transfer to Pakistan of
the money owed to it.

On the night of 15 January the government of India decided to release
the money owed to the government of Pakistan. The next day more than

1,000 refugees signed a declaration saying they would welcome back the displaced Muslims of Delhi and allow them to return to their homes. But Gandhi wanted more authoritative assurances. Meanwhile, his health rapidly declined. His kidney was failing, his weight was dropping and he was plagued by nausea and headache. The doctors issued a warning of their own: 'It is our duty to tell the people to take immediate steps to produce the requisite conditions for ending the fast without delay.'

On 17 January a Central Peace Committee was formed under the leadership of the president of the Constituent Assembly, Rajendra Prasad. Other Congress Party members were among its members, as were representatives of the RSS, the Jamiat-ul-Ulema and Sikh bodies. On the morning of the 18th they took a joint declaration to Gandhi which satisfied him enough to end his fast. The declaration pledged 'that we shall protect the life, property and faith of Muslims and that the incidents which have taken place in Delhi will not happen again'.[35]

Would the 'miracle of Calcutta' be repeated in Delhi? The leaders of the militant groupings seemed chastened by Gandhi's fast. But their followers remained hostile. On previous visits to Delhi Gandhi had stayed in the sweepers colony; this time, however, he was put up at the home of his millionaire follower G. D. Birla. Even while his fast was on, bands of refugees marched past Birla House, shouting, 'Let Gandhi die'. Then, on 20 January, a Punjabi refugee named Madan Lal threw a bomb at Gandhi in Birla House while he was leading a prayer meeting. It exploded at some distance from him; luckily no one was hurt.

Gandhi was undaunted by the attempt on his life. He carried on meeting people, angry refugees included. On 26 January he spoke at his prayer meeting of how that day was celebrated in the past as Independence Day. Now freedom had come, but its first few months had been deeply disillusioning. However, he trusted that 'the worst is over', that Indians would work collectively for the 'equality of all classes and creeds, never the domination and superiority of the major community over a minor, however insignificant it may be in numbers or influence'. He also permitted himself the hope 'that, though geographically and politically India is divided into two, at heart we shall ever be friends and brothers helping and respecting one another and be one for the outside world'.

Gandhi had fought a lifelong battle for a free and united India; and yet, at the end, he could view its division with detachment and equanimity. Others were less forgiving. On the evening of 30 January he was shot dead by a young man at his daily prayer meeting. The assassin, who surrendered afterwards, was a Brahmin from Poona named Nathuram Godse. He was tried and later sentenced to death, but not before he made a remarkable speech justifying his act. Godse claimed that his main provocation was the Mahatma's 'constant and consistent pandering to the Muslims', 'culminating in his last pro-Muslim fast [which] at last goaded me to the conclusion that the existence of Gandhi should be brought to an end immediately'.[36]

IV

Gandhi's death brought forth an extraordinary outpouring of grief. There were moving tributes from Albert Einstein, who had long held Gandhi to be the greatest figure of the twentieth century, and from George Orwell, who had once thought Gandhi to be a humbug but now saw him as a saint. There was a characteristically flippant reaction from George Bernard Shaw – 'It shows you how dangerous it is to be good' – and a characteristically petty one from Mohammad Ali Jinnah, who said that the death of his old rival was a loss merely to 'the Hindu community'.

However, the two most relevant public reactions were from Gandhi's two most distinguished, not to say most powerful, followers, Vallabhbhai Patel and Jawaharlal Nehru. Patel, who was now home minister in the government of India, was a fellow Gujarati who had joined Gandhi as far back as 1918. He was a superb organizer and strategist who had played a major role in making the Congress a national party. In the Indian Cabinet, he was second only to the prime minister, Jawaharlal Nehru. Nehru had come to Gandhi a couple of years later than Patel, and could converse with him in only two of his three languages (Hindi and English). But he had a deep emotional bond with the Mahatma. Like Patel he generally called Gandhi 'Bapu', or 'Father'. But he was, in many ways, the favourite son (dearer by far than the four biological children of the Mahatma), and also his chosen political heir.

Now, in an India caught in the throes of civil strife, both men told the nation that while their master had gone, his message remained. Speaking on All-India Radio immediately after Gandhi's death, Patel appealed to the people not to think of revenge, but 'to carry the message of love and non-violence enunciated by Mahatmaji. It is a shame for us that the greatest man of the world has had to pay with his life for the sins which we have committed. We did not follow him when he was alive; let us at least follow his steps now he is dead.'[37] Speaking at Allahabad after immersing Gandhi's ashes in the Ganga, Nehru observed that 'we have had our lesson at a terrible cost. Is there anyone amongst us now who will not pledge himself after Gandhi's death to fulfil his mission . . . ?' Indians, said Nehru, had now 'to hold together and fight that terrible poison of communalism that has killed the greatest man of our age'.[38]

Nehru and Patel both called for unity and forgiveness, but as it happened the two men had recently been involved in a bitter row. In the last fortnight of December Nehru had planned to visit the riot-hit town of Ajmer. At the last minute he called off his trip and sent his personal secretary instead. Patel took serious offence. He felt that since the Home Ministry had sent its own enquiry team to Ajmer, the tour of the prime minister's underling implied a lack of faith. Nehru explained that he had been forced to cancel his own visit because of a death in the family, and had thus sent his secretary – mostly so as not to disappoint those who had expected him to come. But in any case, as the head of government he had the right to go wherever he wished whenever he wished, or to send someone else to deputize for him. Patel answered that in a cabinet system the prime minister was merely the first among equals; he did not stand above and dominate his fellow ministers.

The exchange grew progressively more contentious, and at one stage both men offered to resign. Then it was agreed that they would put their respective points of view before Gandhi. Before a suitable time could be found the Mahatma began his final fast. The next week Patel was out of Delhi, but the matter lay very much on his mind, and on Nehru's. Indeed, on 30 January Gandhi met Patel just before the fateful prayer meeting and asked that he and Nehru sort out their differences. He also said he would like to meet both of them the next day.

Three days after Gandhi's assassination Nehru wrote Patel a letter which said that 'with Bapu's death, everything is changed and we have to face a different and more difficult world. The old controversies have ceased to have much significance and it seems to me that the urgent need of the hour is for all of us to function as closely and co-operatively as possible . . .' Patel, in reply, said he 'fully and heartily reciprocate[d] the sentiments you have so feelingly expressed . . . Recent events had made me very unhappy and I had written to Bapu . . . appealing to him to relieve me, but his death changes everything and the crisis that has overtaken us must awaken in us a fresh realisation of how much we have achieved together and the need for further joint efforts in our griefstricken country's interests.'[39]

Gandhi could not reconcile, in life, Hindu with Muslim, but he did reconcile, through his death, Jawaharlal Nehru with Vallabhbhai Patel. It was a patch-up of rather considerable consequence for the new and very fragile nation.

2

THE LOGIC OF DIVISION

It was India's historic destiny that many human races and cultures should flow to her, finding a home in her hospitable soil, and that many a caravan should find rest here . . . Eleven hundred years of common history [of Islam and Hinduism] have enriched India with our common achievements. Our languages, our poetry, our literature, our culture, our art, our dress, our manners and customs, the innumerable happenings of our daily life, everything bears the stamp of our joint endeavour . . . These thousand years of our joint life have moulded us into a common nationality . . . Whether we like it or not, we have now become an Indian nation, united and indivisible. No fantasy or artificial scheming to separate and divide can break this unity.

MAULANA ABUL KALAM AZAD,
Congress Presidential Address, 1940

The problem in India is not of an intercommunal but manifestly of an international character, and must be treated as such . . . It is a dream that Hindus and Muslims can evolve a common nationality, and this misconception of one Indian nation has gone far beyond the limits, and is the cause of most of our troubles, and will lead India to destruction, if we fail to revise our actions in time. The Hindus and Muslims belong to two different religious philosophies, social customs, and literature. They neither intermarry, nor interdine together, and indeed they belong to two different civilizations which are based mainly on conflicting ideas and conceptions. Their aspects on and of life are different.

M. A. JINNAH,
Muslim League Presidential Address, 1940

I

DID INDIA HAVE TO be partitioned? When the British left, could they not have left a single country behind? Ever since 1947 such questions have been asked. And in the process of being answered, they bring forth the supplementary question – *Why* was India partitioned?

The nostalgia for an undivided India has been mostly manifest among people on the Indian side of the border. But there has sometimes been a sense of loss displayed in what has become Pakistan too. Indeed, on 15 August 1947 itself, a veteran Unionist politician wrote of how he wished he

> could do anything to save the unity of the Punjab . . . It is heartbreaking to see what is happening . . . It is all due to the policy of liquidating and quitting before any real agreement has been arrived at . . . The fixing of a date for transference of power ruled out any adjustment and vivisection was the only course left . . . We will have to start afresh [but] there is hardly any hope of building things on old lines as communal hatred and mutual destruction are now uppermost in everybody's mind.[1]

Why could not the unity of Punjab, or of India, be saved? There have been three rather different answers on offer. The first blames the Congress leadership for underestimating Jinnah and the Muslims. The second blames Jinnah for pursuing his goal of a separate country regardless of human consequences. The third holds the British responsible, claiming that they promoted a divide between Hindus and Muslims to perpetuate their rule.[2]

All three explanations, or should one say accusations, carry an element of truth. It is true that Nehru and Gandhi made major errors of judgement in their dealings with the Muslim League. In the 1920s Gandhi ignored Jinnah and tried to make common cause with the mullahs. In the 1930s Nehru arrogantly and, as it turned out, falsely, claimed that the Muslim masses would rather follow his socialist credo than a party based on faith. Meanwhile, the Muslims steadily moved over from the Congress to the League. In the 1930s, when Jinnah was willing to make a deal, he was ignored; in the 1940s, with the Muslims solidly behind him, he had no reason to cut a deal at all.

It is also true that some of Jinnah's political turns defy any explanation other than that of personal ambition. He was once known as an 'ambassador of Hindu–Muslim unity' and a practitioner of constitutional politics. Even as he remade himself as a defender of Islam and Muslims, in his personal life he ignored the claims of faith. (He liked his whisky and, according to some accounts, his ham sandwiches too.)[3] However, from the late 1930s he assiduously began to stoke religious passions. The process was to culminate in his calling for Direct Action Day, the day that set in train the bloody trail of violence and counter-violence that made Partition inevitable.

Finally, it is also true that the British did welcome and further the animosities between Hindus and Muslims. In March 1925, by which time the anti-colonial struggle had assumed a genuinely popular dimension, the secretary of state for India wrote to the viceroy: 'I have always placed my highest and most permanent hopes upon the eternity of the Communal Situation.'[4] Within England the growth of liberal values placed a premium on the sovereignty of the individual; but in the colonies the individual was always seen as subordinate to the community. This was evident in government employment, where care was taken to balance numbers of Muslim and Hindu staff, and in politics, where the British introduced communal electorates, such that Muslims voted exclusively for other Muslims. Most British officials were predisposed to prefer Muslims, for, compared with Hindus, their forms of worship and ways of life were less alien. Overall, colonial policy deepened religious divisions, which helped consolidate the white man's rule.

The short-sightedness of Congress, Jinnah's ambition, Britain's amorality and cynicism – all these might have played their part, but at least by the early 1940s Partition was written into the logic of Indian history. Even if the British had not encouraged communal electorates, the onset of modern electoral politics would have encouraged the creation of community vote banks. Muslims were increasingly persuaded to think of themselves as, indeed, 'Muslims'. As late as 1927 the Muslim League had a mere 1,300 members. By 1944 it had more than half a million in Bengal alone (Punjab had 200,000). Muslims of all classes flocked to the League. Artisans, workers, professionals, businessmen – all rallied to the call of 'Islam in Danger', fearing the prospect, in a united India, of a 'Brahmin Bania Raj'.[5]

The call for Pakistan was first made formally by the Muslim League in March 1940. The Second World War had kept the question of Pakistan (as of Indian independence more generally) on hold. After the war a Labour government came to power in Great Britain. Unlike the

Conservatives, the Labour Party 'regarded itself as morally committed to speed up the process of independence for India'. On the subject of India, Prime Minister Clement Attlee showed 'a decisiveness and passion unusual during his career'.[6]

Some leading Labour politicians had close ties to Congress. These included Sir Stafford Cripps, who in the beginning of 1946 was sent as part of a three-member Cabinet Mission to negotiate the terms of Indian independence. Cripps, and other Labour leaders, would have liked to leave behind a united India for the Congress to govern and guide. But a note prepared for the Mission in December 1945 showed how unlikely this would be. Its author was Penderel Moon, a Fellow of All Souls and sometime member of the Indian Civil Service. Moon pointed out that 'there is more likelihood of obtaining Hindu consent to Division than Muslim consent to Union'. From the British point of view, 'to unite India against Muslim wishes would necessarily involve force. To divide India against Hindu wishes would *not* necessarily involve force; and at worst the force required is likely to be less. The Hindus of Madras, Bombay, U. P, and C. P. may loudly lament their brethren in Bengal and the Punjab being torn from the embrace of Mother India, but they are not likely to have the will or the power to undertake a Crusade on their behalf.'[7]

The next few months bore out the cold wisdom of these remarks. Early in 1946 elections were held to the various provincial assemblies. These were conducted on a franchise restricted by education and property. About 28 per cent of the adult population was eligible to vote – but this, in a land the size of British India, still amounted to some 41 million people.[8]

The world over, the rhetoric of modern democratic politics has been marked by two rather opposed rhetorical styles. The first appeals to hope, to popular aspirations for economic prosperity and social peace. The second appeals to fear, to sectional worries about being worsted or swamped by one's historic enemies. In the elections of 1946 the Congress relied on the rhetoric of hope. It had a strongly positive content to its programme, promising land reforms, workers' rights, and the like. The Muslim League, on the other hand, relied on the rhetoric of fear. If they did not get a separate homeland, they told the voters, then they would be crushed by the more numerous Hindus in a united India. The League sought, in effect, a referendum on the question of Pakistan. As Jinnah put it in a campaign speech, 'Elections are the beginning of the end. If the Muslims decide to stand for Pakistan in the coming elections half the battle would have been won. If we fail in the first phase of our war, we shall be finished.'

The leader's message was energetically carried by the cadres. In Bihar the provincial Muslim League asked the voters to 'judge whether the bricks of votes should be used in the preparation of a fort of "Ram Raj" or for the construction of a building for the independence of Muslims and Islam'. A League election poster in Punjab offered some meaningful pairs of contrasts: *din* (the faith) versus *dunya* (the world); *zamir* (conscience) versus *jagir* (property); *haqq-koshi* (righteousness) versus *sufedposhi* (office). In each case, the first item stood for Pakistan, the second for Hindustan.

League propaganda also urged voters to overcome sectarian divisions of caste and clan. 'Unite on Islam – Become One', declared one poster. The Muslims were asked to act and vote as a single *qaum*, or community. A vital role was played by student volunteers, who traversed the countryside canvassing votes from house to house.

The election results were a striking vindication of the League's campaign. Across India, in province after province, the Congress did exceedingly well in the general category, but the Muslim seats were swept by the League, fighting on the single issue of a separate state for Muslims. In the province of Bengal, for example, the League won 114 out of 119 seats reserved for Muslims; since the strength of the assembly was 250, it required little effort to cobble together a majority. In the United Provinces the Congress won 153 seats out of a total of 228, and so formed the government. But within this larger victory there was a significant defeat, for of the 66 Muslim seats on offer in the United Provinces the League won a resounding 54. Even more striking were the results in the southern province of Madras, which even the most devoted follower of Jinnah would not claim for a prospective Pakistan. Here the Congress won 165 out of 215 seats, but the League won all 29 seats reserved for Muslims. Overall, in the general constituencies, the Congress won 80.9 per cent of the votes, whereas in the seats reserved for Muslims the League garnered 74.7 per cent.

After the results had come in, the League's paper, *Dawn*, proclaimed that 'Those who have been elected this time to the Legislatures have been charged by the voters with the duty . . . of winning Pakistan. Within and outside the Provincial and Central Assemblies and Councils that and that alone is now the "priority job". The time for decision is over; the time for action has come.'

This was written on 7 April 1946. Three days later Jinnah convened a meeting in Delhi of the 400 legislators elected on the Muslim League ticket. This convention reiterated the call for an independent Pakistan. However, in early May Jinnah attended a conference in Simla, where attempts were being made by the Cabinet Mission to find a unitary solution. Through the next two months various drafts were passed round, allowing for one nation-state but with provinces having the option to leave if they so desired. The Congress and the League could not agree on the conditions under which provinces would join or leave the projected union. Another sticking point was Jinnah's contention that the Congress could not nominate a Muslim as one of its representatives to the talks.[9]

Jinnah bargained hard, knowing now that he had Muslim popular sentiment behind him. By the end of June 1946 it was clear that no settlement could be reached. The Cabinet Mission returned to London. The League leaders met on 29 July and affirmed that 'the time has now come for the Muslim nation to resort to direct action in order to achieve Pakistan and assert their just rights and to vindicate their honour and to get rid of the present slavery under the British and contemplated future of Caste Hindu domination'.

Two weeks later was Direct Action Day, and the beginning of the end of the dream of United India.

II

Gandhi was not alone in choosing to mark the day of Independence for India, 15 August 1947, as a day of mourning rather than celebration. Across the border in Pakistan, where independence had come a day earlier, the poet Faiz Ahmad Faiz wrote of

> This leprous daybreak, dawn night's fangs have mangled –
> This is not that long-looked for break of day,
> Not that clear dawn in quest of which those comrades
> Set out, believing that in heaven's wide void
> Somewhere must be the stars' last halting-place,
> Somewhere the verge of night's slow-washing tide,
> Somewhere the anchorage for the ship of heartache.[10]

The lament here was not so much for the fact of Partition, as for its bloody costs. For at least by the end of 1945, and possibly earlier, some form of Pakistan seemed inevitable. It could not now be stopped by Congress magnanimity or a sudden show of modesty on the part of Jinnah. But the poet's lament impels us to ask one further question – if Partition had to happen, did it necessarily have to cause so much loss of life?

To answer this, we need to briefly rehearse the events of the last six months of the Raj. On 20 February 1947 the Labour government in London announced that the British would quit India by June 1948, and that the viceroy, Lord Wavell, would be replaced. On 22 March the new viceroy, Lord Mountbatten, assumed office. Over the next few weeks he discussed the terms of the British withdrawal with the relevant parties. He found that most Congress leaders were coming round to the inevitability of Partition. They saw that the 'immediate independence of the major part of India was preferable to the postponement of the independence of the whole of India'.[11] Gandhi made a last-ditch effort to save unity by asking Jinnah to head the first government of free India. But this offer did not have the backing of Congress, and Jinnah did not accept it in any case.

On 2 May the viceroy's chief of staff, Lord Ismay, was sent to London with a plan for Partition. He obtained Cabinet approval, but the plan had to be redrafted several times on his return, so as to satisfy both Congress and the League. (At one stage Jinnah, brazen to the last, asked for an 800-mile-long corridor through India to link the eastern and western wings of Pakistan.) The revised plan was taken by Mountbatten to the British Cabinet.

All this took the better part of a month. On 3 June Mountbatten, back from London, announced the Partition plan on All-India Radio. He was followed on the microphone by Nehru, Jinnah and Baldev Singh (speaking for the Sikhs). The next morning the viceroy addressed a press conference in the Legislative Assembly building. It was here that he suggested, for the first time, that the British would leave not by June 1948 but by the middle of August 1947, that is, in less than ten weeks.

The decision so dramatically to shorten the time frame of the British withdrawal was taken by Mountbatten himself. His biographer, Philip Ziegler, justified the decision as follows:

Once the principle of partition had been accepted, it was inevitable that communalism would rage freely. The longer the period before the transfer of power, the worse the tension and the greater the threat that violence would spread. Today it was the Punjab, tomorrow Bengal, Hyderabad, or any of the myriad societies in the sub-continent where Hindu and Muslim lived cheek by jowl. Two hundred thousand [dead] could have become two million, even twenty million.[12]

In fact, even while Ziegler wrote (in 1985), the toll of the Partition violence was estimated at a million dead; some later scholars have suggested the figure is closer to 2 million. How many would it have been if the British had left, as planned, in June 1948? In a blistering attack on Mountbatten's reputation, Andrew Roberts accuses him of softness and vacillation – 'whenever he had to exhibit toughness, Mountbatten took the most invertebrate line possible' – of being unwilling to crack down effectively on communal violence and, more specifically, of understaffing the Punjab Boundary Force and not supplying it with air cover. *Contra* Ziegler, Roberts is convinced that the 'overhasty withdrawal' led 'to more rather than fewer deaths'.[13]

Some contemporary observers also felt that the decision to undo in two months flat an empire built over two centuries was poorly conceived. In the summer of 1947 the man occupying the hottest of hot seats was the governor of the still undivided Punjab, Sir Evan Jenkins. In early May Jenkins wrote to Mountbatten urging him to 'reconsider the terms of any early announcement embodying a solution of the Indian political problem. In the Punjab we are going to be faced with a complete refusal of the communities to co-operate on any basis at all. It would clearly be futile to announce a partition of the Punjab which no community would accept.'[14] The decision was made regardless, and the governor was left with the task of maintaining law and order while the Punjab was divided. On 30 July he wrote to Mountbatten again, explaining that the prospect of Independence with Partition evoked anger rather than enthusiasm. The Muslims had hoped for the whole of the Punjab, whereas the Sikhs and Hindus were fearful that they would lose Lahore, 'It would be difficult enough', archly commented the governor, 'to partition within six weeks a country of 30 million people which has been governed as a unit for 98 years, even if all concerned were friendly and anxious to make progress.'[15]

Jenkins did in fact ask several times for more troops and for a 'Tactical Reconnaissance Squadron'. One reason there were too few troops available to deal with rioters was that they were busy guarding the paranoid rulers, who were convinced that British civilians would be attacked as soon as the decision to leave was made public. This feeling was widespread among all sections of Europeans in India: among officers, priests, planters, and merchants. In the summer of 1946, a young English official wrote to his family that 'we shall virtually have the whole country against us (for long enough at all events to wipe out our scattered European population) before the show becomes, as inevitably it will, a communal scrap between Hindus and Muslims'.[16]

To make the protection of British lives the top priority was pretty much state policy. In February 1947 the governor of Bengal said that his 'first action in the event of an announcement of a date for withdrawal of British power . . . would be to have the troops "standing to" and prepare for a concentration of outlying Europeans at very short notice as soon as hostile reactions began to show themselves'.[17] In fact, in the summer of 1947 white men and women were the safest people in India. No one was interested in killing them.[18] But their insecurity meant that many army units were placed near European settlements instead of being freed for riot control elsewhere.

The instinct of self-preservation also lay behind the decision to postpone the Punjab boundary award until after the date of Independence. On 22 July, after a visit to Lahore, Lord Mountbatten wrote to Sir Cyril Radcliffe asking him to hurry things up, for 'every extra day' would lessen the risk of disorder. The announcement of the boundary award *before* Independence would have allowed movements of troops to be made in advance of the transfer of power. The governor of Punjab was also very keen that the award be announced as soon as it was finalized. As it happened, Radcliffe was ready with the award on 9 August itself. However, Mountbatten now changed his mind, and chose to make the award public only after the 15th. His explanation for the delay was strange, to say the least: 'Without question, the earlier it was published, the more the British would have to bear responsibility for the disturbances which would undoubtedly result.' By the same token, 'the later we postponed publication, the less would the inevitable odium react upon the British'.[19]

As a rule, one must write of history only as it happened, not how it might have happened. Would a more extended time frame – an announcement in April 1947 that the British would quit in a year's time – have allowed for a less painful process of division? Would more active troop deployments and an earlier announcement of the Radcliffe award have led to less violence in the Punjab? Perhaps. Or perhaps not. As it turned out, the most appropriate epitaph on the last days of the Raj was provided by the Punjab official who told a young social worker from Oxford: 'You British believe in fair play. You have left India in the same condition of chaos as you found it.'[20]

While the debates continue to rage about the causes of Partition, somewhat less attention has been paid to its consequences. These were quite considerable indeed – as this book will demonstrate. The division of India was to cast a long shadow over demography, economics, culture, religion, law, international relations, and party politics.

3

APPLES IN THE BASKET

The Indian States are governed by treaties . . . The Indian States, if they do not join this Union, will remain in exactly the same situation as they are today.

SIR STAFFORD CRIPPS, British politician, 1942

We shall have to come out in the open with [the] Princes sooner or later. We are at present being dishonest in pretending we can maintain all these small States, knowing full well in practice we shall be unable to.

LORD WAVELL, Viceroy of India, 1943

I

FEW MEN HAVE BEEN so concerned about how history would portray them as Lord Mountbatten, the last viceroy and governor general of India. As a veteran journalist once remarked, Mountbatten appeared to act as 'his own Public Relations Officer'.[1] An aide of Mountbatten was more blunt, calling his boss 'the vainest man alive'. The viceroy always instructed photographers to shoot him from six inches above the eyeline because his friend, the actor Cary Grant, had told him that this way the wrinkles didn't show. When Field Marshal Montgomery visited India, and the press clamoured for photos of the two together, Mountbatten was dismayed to find that Monty wore more medals than himself.[2]

Altogether, Mountbatten had a personality that was in marked contrast to that of his predecessor, Lord Wavell. A civil servant who worked under Wavell noticed that 'vanity, pomposity and other such weaknesses never touched him', another way of saying that he did not look to, or care about, how history would judge him.[3] Yet it is Wavell who should get most of the credit for initiating the end of British rule in India. While sceptical of the political class, he was, despite the reserve which he displayed to them, deeply sympathetic to Indian aspirations.[4] It was he who set in motion the discussions and negotiations at the end of the war, and it was he who pressed for a clear timetable for withdrawal. But it was left to his flamboyant successor to make the last dramatic gestures that announced the birth of the two new nations.

After Mountbatten left India he worked hard to present the best possible spin on his tenure as viceroy. He commissioned or influenced a whole array of books that sought to magnify his successes and gloss his failures. These books project an impression of Mountbatten as a wise umpire successfully mediating between squabbling schoolboys, whether India and Pakistan, the Congress and the Muslim League, Mahatma Gandhi and M. A. Jinnah, or Jawaharlal Nehru and Vallabhbhai Patel.[5] His credit claims are taken at face value, sometimes absurdly so, as in the suggestion that Nehru would not have included Patel in his Cabinet had it not been for Mountbatten's recommendation.[6]

Curiously, Mountbatten's real contribution to India and Indians has been rather underplayed by his hagiographers. This was his part in solving a geopolitical problem the like of which no newly independent state had ever faced (or is likely to face in the future). For when the British departed the subcontinent they left behind more than 500 distinct pieces of territory. Two of these were the newly created nations of India and Pakistan; the others comprised the assorted chiefdoms and states that made up what was known as 'princely India'. The dissolution of these units is a story of extraordinary interest, told from a partisan point of view half a century ago in V. P. Menon's *Integration of the Indian States*, but not elsewhere or since.[7]

II

The princely states were so many that there was even disagreement as to their number. One historian puts it at 521; another at 565. They were more than 500, by any count, and they varied very widely in terms of size and status. At one end of the scale were the massive states of Kashmir and Hyderabad, each the size of a large European country; at the other end, tiny fiefdoms or *jagirs* of a dozen or less villages.

The larger princely states were the product of the *longue durée* of Indian history as much as of British policy. Some states made much of having resisted the waves of Muslim invaders who swept through north

India between the eleventh and sixteenth centuries. Others owed their very history to association with these invaders, as for instance the Asaf Jah dynasty of Hyderabad, which began life in the early eighteenth century as a vassal state of the great Mughal Empire. Yet other states, such as Cooch Behar in the east and Garhwal in the Himalayan north, were scarcely touched by Islamic influence at all.

Whatever their past history, these states owed their mid-twentieth-century shape and powers – or lack thereof – to the British. Starting as a firm of traders, the East India Company gradually moved towards a position of overlordship. They were helped here by the decline of the Mughals after the death of Aurangzeb in 1707. Indian rulers were seen by the Company as strategic allies, useful in checking the ambitions of their common enemy, the French. The Company forced treaties on these states, which recognized it as the 'paramount power'. Thus, while legally the territories the various Nawabs and Maharajas ruled over were their own, the British retained to themselves the right to appoint ministers and control succession, and to extract a large subsidy for the provision of administrative and military support. In many cases the treaties also transferred valuable areas from the Indian states to the British. It was no accident that, except for the states comprising Kathiawar and two chiefdoms in the south, no Indian state had a coastline. The political dependence was made more acute by economic dependence, with the states relying on British India for raw materials, industrial goods, and employment opportunities.[8]

The larger native states had their own railway, currency and stamps, vanities allowed them by the Crown. Few had any modern industry; fewer still modern forms of education. A British observer wrote in the early twentieth century that, taken as a whole, the states were 'sinks of reaction and incompetence and unrestrained autocratic power sometimes exercised by vicious and deranged individuals'.[9] This, roughly, was also the view of the main nationalist party, the Congress. From the 1920s they pressed the state rulers to at least match the British in allowing a modicum of political representation. Under the Congress umbrella rested the All-India States Peoples Conference, to which in turn were affiliated the individual *praja mandals* (or peoples' societies) of the states.

Even in their heyday the princes got a bad press. They were generally viewed as feckless and dissolute, over-fond of racehorses and other men's wives and holidays in Europe. Both the Congress and the Raj thought that they cared too little for mundane matters of administration. This

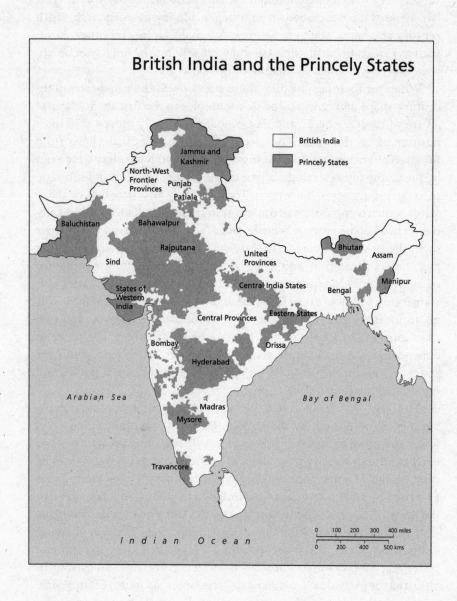

British India and the Princely States

British India

Princely States

Jammu and Kashmir

North-West Frontier Provinces

Punjab

Patiala

Baluchistan

Bahawalpur

Rajputana

Sind

Bhutan

Assam

United Provinces

Central India States

Manipur

Bengal

States of Western India

Central Provinces

Eastern States

Bombay

Orissa

Hyderabad

Arabian Sea

Bay of Bengal

Madras

Mysore

Travancore

Indian Ocean

0 100 200 300 400 miles

0 200 400 500 kms

was mostly true, but there were exceptions. The maharajas of Mysore and Baroda both endowed fine universities, worked against caste prejudice and promoted modern enterprises. Other maharajas kept going the great traditions of Indian classical music.

Good or bad, profligate or caring, autocratic or part-democratic, by the 1940s all the princes now found themselves facing a common problem: their future in a free India. In the first part of 1946 British India had a definitive series of elections, but these left untouched the princely states. As a consequence there was a 'growing antipathy towards princely governments'.[10] Their constitutional status, however, remained ambiguous. The Cabinet Mission of 1946 focused on the Hindu–Muslim or United India versus Pakistan question; it barely spoke of the states at all. Likewise the statement of 20 February 1947, formally announcing that the Raj was to end, also finessed the question. On 3 June the British announced both the date of their final withdrawal and the creation of two dominions – but this statement also did not make clear the position of the states. Some rulers began now 'to luxuriate in wild dreams of independent power in an India of many partitions'.[11]

Now, just in time, came the wake-up calls.

III

In 1946–7 the president of the All-India States Peoples Conference was Jawaharlal Nehru. His biographer notes that Nehru 'held strong views on this subject of the States. He detested the feudal autocracy and total suppression of popular feeling, and the prospect of these puppet princes . . . setting themselves up as independent monarchs drove him into intense exasperation.'[12] The prospect was encouraged by the officials of the Political Department, who led the princes to believe that once the British had left they could, if they so wished, stake their claims to independence.

On their part, the princes disliked and even feared Nehru. Fortunately the Congress had assigned the problem of the states to the pragmatic administrator Vallabhbhai Patel. Through the spring of 1947 Patel threw a series of lunch parties, where he urged his princely guests to help the Congress in framing a new constitution for India. This they could do by sending delegates to the Constituent Assembly, whose deliberations had begun in Delhi in December 1946. At the same time Patel wrote to the more influential *dewans* (chief ministers), urging them to ask their rulers to come to terms with the party which would now rule India.[13]

One of the first princes to come over to Patel's side was the Maharaja of Bikaner. His *dewan* was K. M. Pannikar, a widely respected historian who, more clearly than other people, could see that the 'Vasco da Gama epoch of Asian history'[14] was swiftly coming to an end. The forces of nationalism were irresistible; if one did not compromise with them, one would be swept away. Accordingly, in the first week of April 1947 Bikaner issued a public appeal to his fellow princes to join the Constituent Assembly. Their entry into the Assembly, he said, would 'make quite clear to everyone that the Indian Princes are not only working for the good of their States and for their mother country but are above all patriotic and worthy sons of India'.[15]

The first chiefdom to join the Constituent Assembly, back in February, had in fact been the state of Baroda. After Bikaner's appeal a dozen more states joined, many of them from Rajasthan. Pannikar and Bikaner had 'led the Rajput princes in a fresh act of traditional obeisance to Delhi, where in place of Mogul or British, a Pandit now rules. They have made a compact with Congress – probably, from their point of view, rightly.'[16]

Several states in Rajasthan, Bikaner included, would share a border with Pakistan; this, and ancient memories of battles with Muslim kings, predisposed them to an early compromise with Congress. But other states in the hinterland were less sure how far Delhi's writ would run after the British left. Might not the situation revert to that of the eighteenth century, when the peninsula was divided up among dozens of more or less sovereign states?

On 27 June a new States Department was set up by the government of India. This replaced the old Political Department, whose pro-princes, anti-Congress tenor had caused so much mischief.[17] Patel would be the minister in charge. As his secretary he chose V. P. Menon, a small, alert and ferociously intelligent Malayali from Malabar. Unusually for a man in his position, Menon had come from the ranks. Far from being a member of the elite Indian Civil Service – as other secretaries to government were – he had joined the government of India as a clerk and steadily worked his way up. He had been reforms commissioner and constitutional adviser to successive viceroys, and had played a key role in drafting the Indian Independence Bill.

His peers in the ICS derisively called him 'babu Menon', in reference to his lowly origins. In fact, as British Raj gave way to Congress Raj, there could have been no better man to supervise this most tricky aspect of the transition. Menon's first act was to urge the British government not to support fanciful claims to independence. 'Even an inkling that H.M.G. would accord independent recognition', he told London, 'would make infinitely difficult all attempts to bring the States and the new Dominions together on all vital matters of common concern.'[18]

Menon was also ideally placed to mediate between his old boss, Mountbatten, and his new boss, Vallabhbhai Patel. Between them they worked on a draft Instrument of Accession whereby the states would agree to transfer control of defence, foreign affairs and communications to the Congress government. On 5 July Patel issued a statement appealing to the princes to accede to the Indian Union on these three subjects and join the Constituent Assembly. As he put it, the 'alternative to co-operation in the general interest' was 'anarchy and chaos'. Patel appealed to the princes' patriotism, asking for their assistance in raising 'this sacred land to its proper place among the nations of the world'.[19]

On 9 July Patel and Nehru both met the viceroy, and asked him 'what he was going to do to help India in connection with her most pressing problem – relations with the [princely] States'. Mountbatten agreed to make this matter 'his primary consideration'. Later that same day Gandhi came to meet Mountbatten. As the viceroy recorded, the Mahatma 'asked me to do everything in my power to ensure that the British did not leave a legacy of Balkanisation and disruption on the 15th August by encouraging the States to declare their independence . . .'[20]

Mountbatten was being urged by the Congress trinity to bat for them against the states. This he did most effectively, notably in a speech to the Chamber of Princes delivered on 25 July, for which the viceroy had decked out in all his finery, rows of military medals pinned upon his chest. He was, recalled an adoring assistant, 'in full uniform, with an array of orders and decorations calculated to astonish even these practitioners in Princely pomp'.[21]

Mountbatten began by telling the princes that the Indian Independence Act had released 'the States from all their obligations to the Crown'. They were now technically independent, or, put another way, rudderless, on their own. The old links were broken, but 'if nothing can be put in its place, only chaos can result' – a chaos that 'will hit the States first'.

He advised them to forge relations with the new nation closest to them. As he brutally put it, 'you cannot run away from the Dominion Government which is your neighbour any more than you can run away from the subjects for whose welfare you are responsible'.

The Instrument of Accession the princes were being asked to sign would cede away defence – but in any case, said Mountbatten, the states would, by themselves, 'be cut off from any source of supplies of up-to-date arms or weapons'. It would cede away external affairs, but the princes could 'hardly want to go to the expense of having ambassadors or ministers or consuls in all these foreign countries'. And it would also cede away communications, but this was 'really a means of maintaining the life-blood of the whole sub-continent'. The Congress offer, said the viceroy, left the rulers 'with great internal authority' while divesting them of matters they could not deal with on their own.[22]

Mountbatten's talk to the Chamber of Princes was a *tour de force*. In my opinion it ranks as the most significant of all his acts in India. It finally persuaded the princes that the British would no longer protect or patronize them, and that independence for them was a mirage.

Mountbatten had prefaced his speech with personal letters to the more important princes. Afterwards he continued to press them to sign the Instrument of Accession. If they did so before 15 August, said the viceroy, he might be able to get them decent terms with the Congress. But if they did not listen, then they might face an 'explosive situation' after Independence, when the full might of nationalist wrath would turn against them.[23]

By 15 August virtually all the states had signed the Instrument of Accession. Meanwhile the British had departed, never to return. Now the Congress went back on the undertaking that if the princes signed up on the three specified subjects, 'in other matters we would scrupulously respect their autonomous existence'.[24] The *praja mandals* grew active once more. In Mysore a movement was launched for 'full democratic government' in the state. Three thousand people courted arrest.[25] In some states in Kathiawar and Orissa, protesters took possession of government offices, courts and prisons.[26]

Vallabhbhai Patel and the Congress Party cleverly used the threat of popular protest to make the princes fall in line. They had already *acceded*; now they were being asked to *integrate*, that is to dissolve their states as independent entities and merge with the Union of India. In exchange they would be allowed to retain their titles and offered an annual allowance in perpetuity. If they desisted from complying, they faced the threat of uncontrolled (and possibly uncontrollable) agitation by subjects whose suppressed emotions had been released by the advent of Independence.[27]

Through the latter part of 1947 V. P. Menon toured India, cajoling the princes one by one. His progress, wrote the *New York Times* correspondent in New Delhi,

> could be measured from the ensuing series of modest newspaper items, each series running about like this:
> First, a small headline, 'Mr V. P. Menon Visits State of Chhota Hazri';
> Then, in the Governor-General's daily Court Circular, a brief notice, 'H. H. the Maharajah of Chhota Hazri has arrived';
> And soon, a banner headline, 'CHHOTA HAZRI MERGED'.[28]

As this account makes clear, the groundwork was done by Patel and V. P. Menon; but the finishing touch was applied by Mountbatten, a final interview with whom was sometimes a necessary concession to princely vanity. The governor general also visited the more important chiefdoms, where he saluted their 'most wise and Statesmanlike decision' to link up with India.[29]

Mountbatten dealt with the symbolism of the princes' integration with India; V. P. Menon with the substance. In his book, Menon describes in some detail the tortuous negotiations with the rulers. The process of give and take involved much massaging of egos: one ruler claimed descent from Lord Rama, another from Sri Krishna, while a third said his lineage was immortal, as it had been blessed by the Sikh Gurus.

In exchange for their land each ruler was offered a 'privy purse', its size determined by the revenue earned by the state. The bigger, more strategically placed states had to be given better deals, but relevant too were such factors as the antiquity of the ruling dynasty, the religious halo which might surround it, and their martial traditions. Apart from an annual purse, the rulers were allowed to retain their palaces and other personal properties and, as significantly, their titles. The Maharaja of Chhota Hazri would still be the Maharaja of Chhota Hazri, and he could pass on the title to his son as well.[30]

To reassure the princes, Patel sought to include a constitutional guarantee with regard to the privy purses. But, as V. P. Menon pointed out, the pay-off had been trifling compared to the gains. In addition to securing the political consolidation of India, the integration of the states was, in economic terms, a veritable steal. By Menon's calculation, while the government would pay out some Rs150 million to the princes, in ten years' time the revenue from their states would amount to at least ten times as much.[31]

Acquiring the territory of the states was followed by the scarcely less difficult job of administrative integration. In most states, the land revenue and judicial systems were archaic, and there was no popular representation of any kind. The Ministry of States transferred officials trained in British India to put the new systems in place. It also oversaw the swearing-in of interim ministries prior to the holding of full-fledged elections.

Patel and Menon took more than one leaf out of the British book. They played 'divide-and-rule', bringing some princes on side early, unsettling the rest. They played on the childlike vanities of the maharajas, allowing them to retain their titles and sometimes giving them new ones. (Thus several maharajas were appointed governors of provinces.) But, like the British in the eighteenth century, they kept their eye firmly on the main chance: material advantage. For, as Patel told the officials of the states ministry, 'we do not want their women and their jewellery – we want their land'.[32]

In a mere two years, over 500 autonomous and sometimes ancient chiefdoms had been dissolved into fourteen new administrative units of India. This, by any reckoning, was a stupendous achievement. It had been brought about by wisdom, foresight, hard work and not a little intrigue.

IV

When Vallabhbhai Patel had first discussed the states problem with Mountbatten, he had asked him to bring in 'a full basket of apples' by the date of Independence. Would he be satisfied with a bag of 560 instead of the full 565, wondered the viceroy. The Congress strongman nodded his assent.[33] As it turned out, only three states gave trouble before 15 August, and three more after that date.

Travancore was the first state to question the right of the Congress to succeed the British as the paramount power. The state was strategically placed, at the extreme southern tip of the subcontinent. It had the most highly educated populace in India, a thriving maritime trade, and newly discovered reserves of monazite, from which is extracted thorium, used in the production of atomic energy and atomic bombs. The *dewan* of Travancore was Sir C. P. Ramaswamy Aiyar, a brilliant and ambitious lawyer who had been in his post for sixteen years. It was commonly believed that he was the real ruler of the state, whose maharaja and maharani were like putty in his hands.

As early as February 1946 Sir C. P. had made clear his belief that, when the British left, Travancore would become a 'perfectly independent unit', as it had been before 1795, when it first signed a treaty with the East India Company. In the summer of 1947 he held a series of press conferences seeking the co-operation of the people of Travancore in his bid for independence. He reminded them of the antiquity of their ruling dynasty and of Travancore's sinking of a Dutch fleet back in the year 1741 (this apparently the only naval defeat ever inflicted by an Asian state on a European power). This appeal to a past redolent in regional glory was meant to counter the pan-Indian nationalism of the present. For the Congress had a strong presence in the state, as did the Communist Party of India. Still, the *dewan* insisted that from 15 August 1947 'Travancore will become an independent country'. 'There was no particular reason', he defiantly added, 'why she should be in a worse position than Denmark, Switzerland, and Siam.'

Interestingly, Travancore's bid for independence was welcomed by Mohammad Ali Jinnah. On 20 June he sent Sir C. P. a wire indicating that Pakistan was 'ready to establish relationship with Travancore which will be of mutual advantage'. Three weeks later the *dewan* wrote to the Madras government informing them that Travancore was taking steps to 'maintain herself as an independent entity'. It was, however, ready to sign a treaty between the 'independent Sovereign State' of Travancore and the 'Dominion Governments' of both India and Pakistan.

On 21 July the *dewan* of Travancore had an appointment to meet the viceroy in Delhi. The previous evening he met a senior British diplomat and told him that he hoped to get recognition from his government. If India refused to supply Travancore with textiles, he asked, would the United Kingdom step in? Sir C. P. had, it seems, been encouraged in his ambitions by politicians in London, who saw an independent Travancore as a source of a material crucial to the coming Cold War. In fact, the Travancore government had already signed an agreement with the UK government for the supply of monazite. In London, the minister of supply advised his government to avoid making any statement that would 'give the Indian Dominions leverage in combating Travancore's claim for independence'. Since the state had the 'richest known deposit of monazite sand', said the minister, from the British point of view 'it would be an advantage if Travancore retained political and economic independence, at least for the time being.'

On the 21st Sir C. P. had his scheduled interview with Mountbatten. They were together for more than two hours, which time the *dewan* used to launch an excoriating attack on Gandhi, Nehru and the Congress. After he 'had worked off his emotional upset', the viceroy 'let him go and sent V. P. Menon to work on him'. Menon urged him to sign the Instrument of Accession, but the *dewan* said he would prefer to negotiate a treaty with India instead.

Sir C. P. returned to Travancore, his mind still apparently firm on Independence. Then, while on his way to a music concert on 25 July, he was attacked by a man in military shorts, knifed in the face and body and taken off for emergency surgery. (The would-be assassin turned out to be a member of the Kerala Socialist Party.) The consequences were immediate, and from the Indian point of view, most gratifying. As the viceroy put it in his weekly report to London, 'The States Peoples organisation turned the heat on and Travancore immediately gave in'. From his hospital bed Sir C. P. advised his maharaja to 'follow the path of conciliation and compromise' which he, 'being autocratic and overdecisive', had not himself followed. On 30 July the maharaja wired the viceroy of his decision to accede to the Indian Union.[34]

A second state that wavered on the question of accession was Bhopal. This lay in central India, and had the not unusual combination of a mostly Hindu population and a Muslim ruler. Since 1944 the Nawab of Bhopal had served as chancellor of the Chamber of Princes. He was known to be a bitter opponent of the Congress, and correspondingly close to Jinnah and the Muslim League. When, after the war, the British made clear their intention to leave India, the prospect filled the Nawab with despair. He saw this as 'one of the greatest, if not the greatest, tragedies that has ever befallen mankind'. For now the 'States, the Moslems, and the entire mass of people who relied on British justice . . . suddenly find themselves totally helpless, unorganised and unsupported'. The only course left to the Nawab now was to 'die in the cause of the Moslems of the world'.

These lines are from a letter of November 1946, written to the political adviser to Lord Wavell. Four months later Wavell was replaced as viceroy by Mountbatten, who, as it happens, was an old polo-playing buddy of the Nawab of Bhopal. Their friendship went back twenty-five years; Mountbatten once claimed that the Nawab was his 'second-best friend in India'.[35] But it was soon clear that they now stood in different camps. In mid-July 1947 Mountbatten wrote to Bhopal, as he had to all other princes, advising him to accede to India. He got a long and self-confessedly 'sentimental' letter in reply. This began by professing 'unbroken and loyal friendship' with the Crown of England; a link now being broken by the unilateral action of HMG. And to whom had they delivered Bhopal and his colleagues? The hated party of Gandhi and Nehru. 'Are we', asked Bhopal angrily, 'to write out a blank cheque and leave it to the leaders of the Congress Party to fill in the amount?'

From accusations of betrayal the letter then issued a warning. In India, said the Nawab, the main bulwarks against the 'rising tide of Communism' were men of property. The Congress had already stated their intention to liquidate landlords. To that party's left stood the Communist Party of India, which controlled the unions of transport workers; if they so chose, the communists could paralyse and starve the subcontinent. 'I tell you straight', said Bhopal to his friend, 'that unless you and His Majesty's Government support the States and prevent them from disappearing from the Indian political map, you will very shortly have an India dominated by Communists . . . If the United Nations one day find themselves with 450 million extra people under the heel of Communist domination they will be quite justified in blaming Great Britain for this disaster, and I naturally would not like your name associated with it.'

Bhopal hinted that he, like Travancore, would declare his independence; in any case he would not attend the meeting of the Chamber of Princes scheduled for 25 July. On the 31st Mountbatten wrote back to Bhopal inviting him once more to sign the Instrument of Accession. He reminded him of what he had said in the speech: that no ruler could 'run away' from the dominion closest to him. And he shrewdly turned the argument about communism on its head. Yes, he told Bhopal, there was indeed a Red threat, but it would be best met if the Congress and the princes joined hands. For men like Patel were 'as frightened of communism as you yourself are. If only they had support from all other stable influences such as that of the Princely Order, it might be possible for them to ward off the communist danger.'[36]

By this time Bhopal had received reports of the meeting of 25 July. He had heard of the terrific impression his old friend had made, and also of the increasing tide of accessions by his fellow princes. And so he capitulated, asking only for a small sop to his pride. Would the viceroy press Patel to extend the deadline by ten days, so that his accession would be announced *after* 15 August instead of before? That, said Bhopal, 'would enable me to sign our death warrant with a clear conscience'. (In the event, Patel said he could not make any exceptions; instead Mountbatten offered to Bhopal that if he would sign the Instrument of Accession on 14 August, he would keep it under lock and key and hand it over to Patel only after the 25th.)[37]

A case more curious still was that of Jodhpur, an old and large state with a Hindu king as well as a largely Hindu population. At a lunch hosted by Mountbatten in mid-July, the young Maharaja of Jodhpur had joined the other Rajput princes in indicating his willingness to accede to India. But soon afterwards someone – it is not clear who – planted the idea in his head that since his state bordered Pakistan, he might get better terms from that dominion. Possibly at Bhopal's initiative, a meeting was arranged between him and Jinnah. At this meeting the Muslim League leader offered Jodhpur full port facilities in Karachi, unrestricted import of arms and supply of grain from Sindh to his own famine-stricken districts. In one version, Jinnah is said to have handed the maharaja a blank sheet and a fountain pen and said, 'You can fill in all your conditions.'

If Jodhpur had defected to Pakistan, this would have opened up the possibility that states contiguous to it – such as Jaipur and Udaipur – would do likewise. However, K. M. Pannikar got wind of the plan and asked Vallabhbhai Patel to intervene. Patel contacted Jodhpur and promised him free import of arms too, as well as adequate grain. Meanwhile, his own nobles and village headmen had told the maharaja that he could not really expect them to be at ease in a Muslim state. The ruler of an adjoining state, Jaisalmer, also asked him what would happen if he joined Pakistan and a riot broke out between Hindus and Muslims. Whose side would he then take?

And so the Maharaja of Jodhpur also came round, but not before a last-minute theatrical show of defiance. When presented with the Instrument of Accession in the anteroom of the viceroy's office, Jodhpur took out a revolver and held it to the secretary's head, saying, 'I will not accept your dictation.' But in a few minutes he cooled down and signed on the line.[38]

V

Among the states that had not signed up by 15 August was Junagadh, which lay in the peninsula of Kathiawar in western India. This, like Bhopal, had a Muslim Nawab ruling over a chiefly Hindu population. On three sides Junagadh was surrounded by Hindu states or by India, but on the fourth – and this distinguished it from Bhopal – it had a long coastline. Its main port, Veraval, was 325 nautical miles from the Pakistani port city (and national capital) of Karachi. Junagadh's ruler in 1947, Mohabat Khan, had one abiding passion: dogs. His menagerie included 2,000 pedigree canines, including sixteen hounds specially deputed to guard the palace. When two of his favourite hounds mated, the Nawab announced a public holiday. On their 'marriage' he expended three lakh (300,000) rupees, or roughly a thousand times the average annual income of one of his subjects.

Within the borders of Junagadh lay the Hindu holy shrine of Somnath, as well as Girnar, a hilltop with magnificent marble temples built by, and for, the Jains. Both Somnath and Girnar attracted thousands of pilgrims from other parts of India. The forests of Junagadh were also the last refuge of the Asiatic lion. These had been protected by Mohabat Khan and his forebears, who discouraged even high British officials from hunting them.[39]

In the summer of 1947 the Nawab of Junagadh was on holiday in Europe. While he was away, the existing *dewan* was replaced by Sir Shah Nawaz Bhutto, a leading Muslim League politician from Sindh who had close ties to Jinnah.[40] After the Nawab returned, Bhutto pressed him to stay out of the Indian Union. On 14 August, the day of the transfer of power, Junagadh announced that it would accede to Pakistan. This it was legally allowed to do, although geographically it made little sense. It also flew in the face of Jinnah's 'two-nation' theory, since 82 per cent of Junagadh's population was Hindu.

Pakistan sat on the Nawab's request for a few weeks, but on 13 September it accepted the accession. It seems to have done this in the belief that it could then use Junagadh as a bargaining counter to secure Jammu and

Kashmir. That state too had not acceded to either dominion by 15 August. It had a Hindu maharaja and a majority Muslim population: in structural terms, it was a Junagadh in reverse.

The acceptance by Pakistan of Junagadh's accession enraged the Indian leaders. Touched in a particularly 'tender spot' was Vallabhbhai Patel, who came from the same region and spoke the same language (Gujarati) as the residents of Junagadh.[41] His first response was to secure the accession of two of Junagadh's tributary states, Mangrol and Babariawad. Their Hindu chiefs claimed that they had the right to join India; the Nawab of Junagadh denied this, claiming that as his vassals they had to seek his consent first. The Indian government went with the vassals, and sent in a small military force to support them.

In the middle of September V. P. Menon went to Junagadh to negotiate with the Nawab, but the ruler would not see him, feigning illness. Menon had to make do with meeting the *dewan* instead. He told Sir Shah Nawaz that from both cultural and geographical points of view Junagadh really should join India. Sir Shah Nawaz did not dispute this, but complained that local feelings had been inflamed by the 'virulent writings in the Gujarati Press'. He said that he personally would favour the issue being decided by a referendum.[42]

Meanwhile, a 'provisional government of Junagadh' was set up in Bombay. This was led by Samaldas Gandhi, a nephew of the Mahatma, and a native of the kingdom. This 'government' became the vehicle of popular agitation within Junagadh. In panic, the Nawab fled to Karachi, taking a dozen of his favourite dogs with him. The *dewan* was left holding the baby. On 27 October Sir Shah Nawaz wrote to Jinnah that, while 'immediately after accession [to Pakistan], His Highness and myself received hundreds of messages chiefly from Muslims congratulating us on the decision, today our brethren are indifferent and cold. Muslims of Kathiawar seem to have lost all their enthusiasm for Pakistan.'

Ten days later Sir Shah Nawaz informed the Indian government that he would like to hand over the administration of Junagadh. The formal transfer took place on 9 November. Back in Delhi, however, Mountbatten was cross that he had not been consulted before the territory was taken over. Partly to placate him, but also to establish its own legitimacy, the Indians then organized a plebiscite. A referendum held on 20 February 1948 resulted in 91 per cent of the electorate voting for accession to India.[43]

VI

The state of Hyderabad also had a Muslim ruler and a mostly Hindu population; but it was a prize greater by far than Bhopal or Junagadh. The state ran right across the Deccan plateau, in the centre of the subcontinent. Its area was in excess of 80,000 square miles, and its population more than 16 million, these distributed among three linguistic zones: Telugu, Kannada and Marathi. Hyderabad was surrounded by Central Provinces in the north, by Bombay in the west, and by Madras in the south and east. Although landlocked, it was self-sufficient in food, cotton, oilseed, coal and cement. Petrol and salt, however, had to be imported from British India.

Hyderabad began life as a Mughal vassal state in 1713. Its ruler was conventionally known as the Nizam. Eighty-five per cent of its population was Hindu, but Muslims dominated the army, police and civil service. The Nizam himself owned about 10 per cent of the land of the state; much of the rest was controlled by large landowners. From his holdings the ruler earned Rs25 million a year in rent, while another Rs5 million were granted him from the state treasury. There were some very rich nobles, but the bulk of the Muslims, like the bulk of the Hindus, worked as factory hands, artisans, labourers and peasants.[44]

In power in 1946–7 was the seventh Nizam, Mir Usman Ali, who had ascended to the throne as far back as 1911. He was one of the richest men in the world, but also one of the most miserly. He rarely wore new clothes, his preferred mode of dress being an unironed pyjama and shirt and a faded fez. He 'generally drove in an old, rattling, tin-pot of a car, a 1918 model; he never offered any kind of hospitality to a visitor'.[45]

This Nizam was determined to hang on to more than his personal wealth. What he wanted for his state, when the British left, was independence, with relations forged directly between him and the Crown. To help him with his case he had employed Sir Walter Monckton, a King's Counsel and one of the most highly regarded lawyers in England. (Among Monckton's previous clients was King Edward VIII, whom he had advised during his abdication.) For the Englishman's services the Nizam was prepared to pay a packet: as much as 90,000 guineas a year, it was rumoured. In a meeting with the viceroy, Monckton 'emphasized that His Exalted Highness would have great difficulty in taking any course likely to compromise his independent sovereignty'. When Mountbatten suggested that Hyderabad should join the Constituent Assembly, the Nizam's lawyer answered that if India pressed too hard his client might 'seriously consider the alternative of joining Pakistan'.[46]

The Nizam's ambitions, if realized, would virtually cut off the north of India from the south. And, as the constitutional expert Reginald Coupland pointed out, 'India could live if its Moslem limbs in the north-west and north-east were amputated, but could it live without its midriff?' Sardar Patel put it more directly, saying that an independent Hyderabad constituted a 'cancer in the belly of India'.[47]

In this face-off between the Nizam and the government of India, each side had a proxy of its own. The Indians had the Hyderabad State Congress, formed in 1938, which pressed hard for representative government within the state. The Nizam had the Ittihad-ul-Muslimeen, which wished to safeguard the position of Muslims in administration and politics. Another important actor was the Communist Party of India, which had a strong presence in the Telengana region of the state.

In 1946–7 all three voices grew more strident. The State Congress demanded that Hyderabad fall into line with the rest of India. Its leaders organized street protests, and courted arrest. Simultaneously, the Ittihad was being radicalized by its new leader, Kasim Razvi, an Aligarh-trained lawyer and a passionate believer in the idea of 'Muslim pride'. Under Razvi the Ittihad had promoted a paramilitary body called the 'Razakars', whose members marched up and down the roads of Hyderabad, carrying swords and guns.[48]

In the countryside, meanwhile, there was a rural uprising led and directed by the communists. Across Telengana large estates were confiscated and redistributed to land-hungry peasants. The insurrectionists first seized all holdings in excess of 500 acres, bringing the limit down successively to 200 and then 100 acres. They also abolished the institution of forced labour. In the districts of Nalgonda, Warangal and Karimnagar the communists ran what amounted to a parallel government. More than 1,000 villages were 'practically freed from the Nizam's rule'.[49]

On 15 August the national flag was hoisted by Congress workers in different parts of Hyderabad state. The offenders were arrested and taken off to jail.[50] On the other side the Razakars grew more truculent. They affirmed their support for the Nizam's declaration of independence, and printed and distributed handbills which proclaimed: 'Free Hyderabad for Hyderabadis' and 'No pact with the Indian Union'.[51]

The Nizam's ambitions were encouraged by the Conservative Party in Britain. Sir Walter Monckton was himself a prominent Tory and he had written to his party leaders to support his client's case. Monckton claimed the Congress practised a kind of 'power politics' that was an 'exact replica of those in which Hitler and Mussolini indulged'. Since Mountbatten was hand-in-glove with Nehru and Patel, it was up to the Tories to 'see to it that if this shameful betrayal of our old friends and allies cannot be prevented, at least it does not go uncastigated before the conscience of the world'.[52]

To see the Nizam's Hyderabad as Poland and the Congress as the equivalent to Hitler's Nazis boggles the imagination. Even Winston Churchill allowed himself to be persuaded of the analogy, perhaps because he had a longstanding dislike for Mahatma Gandhi. Speaking in the House of Commons, Churchill argued that the British had a 'personal obligation . . . not to allow a state, which they had declared a sovereign state, to be strangled, starved out or actually overborne by violence'. The party's rising star, R. A. Butler, weighed in on Churchill's side, saying that Britain should press for the 'just claims of Hyderabad to remain independent'.[53]

The Nizam, and more so the Razakars, also drew sustenance from the support to their cause from Pakistan. Jinnah had gone so far as to tell Lord Mountbatten that if the Congress 'attempted to exert any pressure on Hyderabad, every Muslim throughout the whole of India, yes, all the hundred million Muslims, would rise as one man to defend the oldest Muslim dynasty in India'.[54]

The Nizam now said he would sign a treaty with India, but not an Instrument of Accession. In late November 1947 he agreed to sign a 'Standstill Agreement', under which the arrangements forged between Hyderabad and the British Raj would be continued with its successor government. This bought both parties time; the Nizam to reconsider his bid for independence, the Indians to find better ways of persuading him to accede.

Under this agreement, the Nizam and the Indian government deputed agents to each other's territory. The Indian agent was K. M. Munshi, a trusted ally of Vallabhbhai Patel. In November the Nizam had appointed a new *dewan*, Mir Laik Ali, who was a wealthy businessman and a known Pakistan sympathizer. Laik Ali offered some Hindu representation in his government, but it was seen by the State Congress as a case of too little, too late. In any case, by now the real power had passed on to the

Razakars and its leader, Kasim Razvi. By March 1948 the membership of the Ittihad had reached a million, with a tenth of these being trained in arms. Every Razakar had taken a vow in the name of Allah to 'fight to the last to maintain the supremacy of Muslim power in the Deccan'.[55]

In April 1948 a correspondent of *The Times* of London visited Hyderabad. He interviewed Kasim Razvi, and found him to be a 'fanatical demagogue with great gifts of organization. As a "rabble-rouser" he is formidable, and even in a *tête-à-tête* he is compelling.'[56] Razvi saw himself as a prospective leader of a Muslim state, a sort of Jinnah for the Hyderabadis, albeit a more militant one. He had a portrait of the Pakistan leader prominently displayed in his room. Razvi told an Indian journalist that he greatly admired Jinnah, adding that 'whenever I am in doubt I go to him for counsel which he never grudges giving me'.

Pictures of Razvi show him with a luxuriant beard. He looked 'rather like an oriental Mephistopheles'.[57] His most striking feature was his flashing eyes, 'from which the fire of fanaticism exudes'. He had contempt for the Congress, saying 'we do not want Brahmin or Bania rule here'. Asked which side they would take if Pakistan and India clashed, Razvi answered that Pakistan could take care of itself, but added: 'Wherever Muslim interests are affected, our interest and sympathy will go out. This applies of course to Palestine as well. Even if Muslim interests are affected in hell, our heart will go out in sympathy.'[58]

The Razakars saw the Delhi–Hyderabad battle in Hindu–Muslim terms. The Congress, on the other hand, saw it as a clash between democracy and autocracy. In truth, it was a bit of both. Caught in the cross-fire were the citizens of Hyderabad, for whom the months after August 1947 were a time of deep insecurity.[59] Some Hindus began fleeing to the adjoining districts of Madras. Meanwhile, Muslims from the Central Provinces were flocking to Hyderabad. Mostly illiterate, these Muslims had heard fearful reports of attacks on their co-religionists in Bengal and Punjab. But they did not seem to realize that in Hyderabad too they would be a minority. Perhaps, as an independent observer put it, 'these emigrating Muslims have more trust in the Nizam's troops and Arabs to protect them than in the Union provincial administration'. In turn, these CP Muslims were said to have thrown out Hindus from their houses in Hyderabad, aided by the Nizam's men. It was even claimed that there was a plan to make Muslims a majority in the state: apparently, Hindu localities of cities such as Aurangabad, Bidar and Hyderabad had come to 'present a deserted appearance'.[60]

Through the spring and summer of 1948 the tension grew. There were allegations of gun-running from Pakistan to Hyderabad – in planes flown by British mercenaries – and of the import of arms from eastern Europe. The prime minister of Madras wrote to Patel saying he found it difficult to cope with the flood of refugees from Hyderabad. K. M. Munshi sent lurid reports of the Nizam's perfidy, of his 'fixed idea' of independence, of his referring to the government of India as 'the scoundrels of Delhi', of 'the venomous propaganda being carried out day and night through speeches, Nizam's radio, newspapers, dramas etc., against the Indian Union'.[61]

For the moment, the Indians temporized. In June 1948 V. P. Menon and Laik Ali held a series of meetings in Delhi. Menon asked that the state introduce representative government, and promise a plebiscite on accession. Various exceptions were proposed to protect the Nizam's dignity; these included the retention of troops. None was found acceptable. Meanwhile, the respected former *dewan* of Hyderabad, Sir Mirza Ismail, attempted to mediate. He advised the Nizam not to take the Hyderabad case to the United Nations (which Laik Ali had threatened to do), to get himself out of the clutches of the Razakars and to accede to India. Hyderabad, he told His Exalted Highness, 'must realize the weakness of its own position'.[62]

On 21 June 1948 Lord Mountbatten resigned from office of governor general. Three days previously he had written to the Nizam urging him to compromise, and go down in history 'as the peace-maker of South India and as the Saviour of your State, your dynasty, and your people'. If he stuck to his stand, however, he would 'incur the universal condemnation of thinking people'.[63] The Nizam chose not to listen. But, with Mountbatten gone, it became easier for Patel to take decisive action. On 13 September a contingent of Indian troops was sent into Hyderabad. In less than four days they had full control of the state. Those killed in the fighting included forty-two Indian soldiers and two thousand-odd Razakars.

On the night of the 17th, the Nizam spoke on the radio, his speech very likely written for him by K. M. Munshi. He announced a ban on the Razakars and advised his subjects to 'live in peace and harmony with the rest of the people in India'. Six days later he made another broadcast, where he said that Razvi and his men had taken 'possession of the state' by 'Hitlerite' methods and 'spread terror'. He was, he claimed, 'anxious to come to an honourable settlement with India but this group . . . got me to reject the offers made by the government of India from time to time . . .'[64]

Whether by accident or design, the Indian action against Hyderabad took place two days after the death of Pakistan's governor general. Jinnah had predicted that a hundred million Muslims would rise if the Nizam's state was threatened. That didn't happen, but in parts of Pakistan feelings ran high. In Karachi a crowd of 5,000 marched in protest to the Indian High Commission. The high commissioner, an old Gandhian, came out on the street to try to pacify them. 'You cowards,' they shouted back, 'you have attacked us just when our Father has died.'[65]

Back in June, a senior Congress leader had told the Nizam that if he made peace with the Union, His Exalted Highness of Hyderabad might even become 'His Excellency the Ambassador of the whole of India at Moscow or Washington'.[66] In the event that offer was not made, perhaps because his dress, or his style of entertainment, or both, did not behove a diplomatic mission. But he was rewarded for his final submission by being made *rajpramukh*, or governor, of the new Indian state of Hyderabad.

Two years after the end of the *ancien régime*, the Bombay journalist K. A. Abbas visited Hyderabad. He found that in the window of the hundred-year-old photo studio of Raja Deendayal, pictures of the city's 'liberator', Colonel J. N. Chaudhuri of the Indian Army, had eclipsed portraits of the Nizam. Now, in Hyderabad, the white Congress cap was 'the head-gear of the new ruling class, and inspire[d] the same awe as the conical Asafjahi dastaar (ready-to-wear turban) did before the police action'.[67]

VII

In August 1947 an experienced British official who had served in the subcontinent published an article with the portentous title 'India and the Future'. British India had just been divided into two new nations, but, the writer asked, 'will the division stop there?' Or would the subcontinent break up 'into innumerable, small, warring States'? Pakistan seemed inherently unstable; there was every chance of its north-western parts becoming an independent 'Pathanistan'. Nor was India necessarily more stable. Thus 'many competent observers believe that [the province of] Madras will ultimately secede into virtual independence'. As for the princely states, the smaller and more vulnerable ones would have no option but to join India. But 'the big States of the South, however, notably Hyderabad, Mysore and Travancore – are in an altogether different position. They could, if necessary, preserve an independent existence, and the recent threats of the Congress Party are not likely to deter them from deciding this matter solely on consideration of their own advantage.'

The 'ultimate pattern of India', concluded this prophet, 'is likely to consist of three or four countries in place of British India, together with a Federation of South Indian States. This will be, approximately speaking, a return to the pattern of sixteenth century India . . .'[68]

Given the odds, and the opposition, the integration of these numerous and disparate states was indeed a staggering achievement. The job was so smoothly and comprehensively done that Indians quite quickly forgot that this was once not one country but 500. In 1947 and 1948 the threat of disintegration was very real, what with 'honey-combs of intrigue' such as Bhopal and Travancore and 'strategic points of assault' such as Hyderabad. But a mere five years after the last maharaja had signed away his land, Indians had 'come to take integrated India so much for granted that it requires a mental effort today even to imagine that it could be different'.[69]

The position of the Indian princes in the Indian polity 'afforded no parallel to or analogy with any institution known in history'. Yet, through 'peaceful and cordial negotiations' the chiefdoms had dissolved themselves, and become 'hardly distinguishable from the other democratic units comprising the [Indian] Union'.

The words are from a booklet issued by the government of India in 1950. The self-congratulation was merited. Whereas the British-directed partition of India had exacted such a heavy toll, these 500 'centres of feudal autocracy' had, with little loss of life, been 'converted into free and democratic units of the Indian Union'. The 'yellow dots on the map' that marked these chiefdoms had now 'disappeared. Sovereignty and power have been transferred to the people'. 'For the first time', the booklet went on, 'millions of people, accustomed to living in narrow, secluded groups in the States, became part of the larger life of India. They could now breathe the air of freedom and democracy pervading the whole nation.'

This being an official booklet, the credit for the job was naturally given to the man in charge. 'What the British pro-consuls failed to achieve after two centuries of ceaseless efforts', wrote the publicists, 'Sardar Vallabhbhai Patel accomplished through his persuasive appeal to the nobler feelings of the Princely Order.'[70]

Patel's guiding hand was indeed wise and sure; another Congress politician, even (or especially) Nehru, might not have supervised the princes' extinction with such patience and foresight. But he could scarcely have done the job without V. P. Menon, who made hundreds of trips to the chiefdoms, chipping away at their rulers. In turn, Menon could have done little without the officials who effected the actual transition, creating the conditions for financial and social integration with the rest of India.

In truth, both politicians and bureaucrats had as their indispensable allies the most faceless of all humans: the people. For some decades, the people of the princely states had been clamouring in numbers for the rights granted to the citizens of British India. Many states had vigorous and active *praja mandals*. The princes were deeply sensible of this; indeed, without the threat of popular protest from below, they would not have ceded power so easily to the Indian government.

In the unification of India Vallabhbhai Patel had plenty of helpers. Most of them are now unknown and unhonoured. One who is not completely forgotten is V. P. Menon, who was both the chief draughtsman of princely integration as well as its first chronicler. Let us listen now to the lesson he drew from the process:

> To have dissolved 554 States by integrating them into the pattern of the Republic; to have brought order out of the nightmare of chaos whence we started, and to have democratized the administration in all the erstwhile States, should steel us to the attainment of equal success in other spheres.[71]

We shall, in time, turn our attention to those 'other spheres' of nation-building. But we have first to investigate the case of the princely state that gave the Indian Union the most trouble of all. This particular apple stayed perilously placed on the rim of the basket; never in it, but never out of it either.

4

A Valley Bloody and Beautiful

My love of the mountains and my kinship with Kashmir especially drew
me to them, and I saw there not only the life and vigour and beauty of the
present but also the memoried loveliness of ages past . . . When I think
of India, I think of many things . . . [but] above all, of the Himalayas,
snow-capped, or some mountain valley in Kashmir in the spring, covered
with new flowers, and with a brook bubbling and gurgling through it.
                                                    Jawaharlal Nehru, 1946

I

There were more than 500 princely states that joined the Indian
Union. Of these the most important was, and is, the state of Jammu
and Kashmir. At 84,471 square miles it was even larger than Hyderabad.
However, its population of just over 4 million was more thinly spread.
The state was marked by a great deal of cultural heterogeneity. There
were five main regions. The province of Jammu, abutting Punjab, had
low hills and large areas of arable land. Before Partition the Muslims
were in a slight majority (53 per cent), but with the wave of panic
migrations that year Jammu came to be dominated by Hindus. In
contrast, the Valley of Kashmir, which lay to Jammu's north, had a
substantial Muslim majority. The Valley was, by common consent, one
of the most beautiful parts of India, its lakes and slopes visited in the
summer by wealthy tourists from Delhi and the Punjab. It was also
home to a body of sophisticated craftsmen working with silk, wool,
wood and brass, making exquisite artefacts that were exported to all
parts of India and beyond. In both Jammu and the Valley there was also
a fair sprinkling of Sikhs.

To the Valley's east lay the high mountains of Ladakh, bordering
Tibet, and peopled mostly by Buddhists. Further west lay the thinly

populated tracts of Gilgit and Baltistan. The people here were mostly Muslim, but from the Shia and Ismaili branches of Islam, rather than (as was the case in the Valley) from the dominant Sunni tradition.

These disparate territories were brought under a single state only in the nineteenth century. The unifiers were a clan of Dogra Rajputs from Jammu who conquered Ladakh in the 1830s, acquired the vale of Kashmir (hereafter 'the Valley') from the British in the 1840s and moved into Gilgit by the end of the century. And thus the state of Jammu and Kashmir (hereafter 'Kashmir') came to share borders with Afghanistan, Chinese Sinkiang and Tibet. Only a very narrow tract of Afghan territory separated it from the Soviet Union.[1]

Its location gave the state a strategic importance quite out of proportion to its population. This importance increased after 15 August 1947, when Kashmir came to share borders with both the new dominions. The anomaly of a Hindu ruling a mostly Muslim population was compounded by an accident of geography: unlike the other disputed chiefdoms, such as Junagadh and Hyderabad, Kashmir was contiguous with both India *and* Pakistan.

The Maharaja of Kashmir in 1947 was Hari Singh. Having ascended the throne in September 1925, he spent much time at the racecourse in Bombay, and much time hunting in the vast and plentifully stocked jungles of his domain. In one other respect he was typical of his ilk. As his fourth and youngest queen complained, he 'never meets the people – that's the trouble. He just sits surrounded by fawning courtiers and favourites, and never really gets to know what is going on outside.'[2]

For much of his rule, the maharaja's *bête noire* was a Muslim from the Valley named Sheikh Muhammad Abdullah. Born in 1905, the son of a shawl merchant, Abdullah graduated with a master's degree in science from the Aligarh Muslim University. Despite his qualifications he was unable to find a government job in Kashmir, for the state administration was dominated by Hindus. Abdullah began to question 'why Muslims were being singled out for such treatment. We constituted the majority and contributed the most towards the State's revenues, still we were continually oppressed . . . Was it because a majority of Government servants were non-Muslims? . . . I concluded that the ill-treatment of Muslims was an outcome of religious prejudice.'[3]

Denied a job by the state, Abdullah became a schoolteacher instead. He started a reading club and spoke out on behalf of his fellow subjects. His was an inspiring presence: he stood 6' 4" tall and was a witty and compelling orator. Although he smoked the odd cigarette he did not drink. He visited the mosque every Friday, and had a deep knowledge of the Quran.[4]

In the summer of 1931 Abdullah was chosen as part of a delegation of Muslims that hoped to place their case before the maharaja.[5] Before they could meet with him, an activist named Abdul Qadir was arrested and put on trial. This led to a clash between protesters and the police in which twenty-one people died. This was followed by a wave of communal violence in the Valley, in which many Hindu shops were looted and burnt.

The next year, 1932, an All-Jammu Kashmir Muslim Conference was formed to give shape to the growing opposition to the maharaja. Among its leading lights were Sheikh Abdullah and Ghulam Abbas, a lawyer from Jammu. Six years later, Abdullah took the lead in transforming the organization into a 'National Conference', which would also include Hindus and Sikhs. The new body asked for representative government based on universal suffrage.

At about this time Abdullah also made the acquaintance of Jawaharlal Nehru. They hit it off instantly. Both were impulsive and had strong views, but fortunately these were the same – a commitment to Hindu–Muslim harmony and to socialism. The National Conference grew closer to the Indian National Congress, alienating some of its members, most notably Ghulam Abbas, who left the party and sought to organize Kashmiri Muslims on their own. This was the beginning of a bitter rivalry with Sheikh Abdullah, a feud which was as much personal as it was ideological.

In the mid-1940s Abdullah was winning this popularity contest hands-down. He was, recalled one contemporary, 'greatly loved by the people of Kashmir at the time'.[6] He had been in and out of jail since 1931, and in 1946 he was incarcerated once more after he asked the Dogra dynasty to 'quit Kashmir' and hand over power to the people. In the ensuing unrest more than twenty people died. The maharaja declared martial law and had the Sheikh sentenced to three years' imprisonment for 'sedition'. This particularly angered Jawaharlal Nehru, who dashed to the state in his friend's defence. Nehru was prevented from entering by the maharaja's men, who stopped him at the border and sent him back to British India.[7]

Now that it was clear that the British would soon leave the subcontinent, Hari Singh's prime minister, Ramchandra Kak, encouraged

him to think of independence for his state. On 15 July 1946 the maharaja
stated that the Kashmiris would 'work out our own destiny without
dictation from any quarter which is not an integral part of the State'.[8]
In November the British Resident in Srinagar observed that the

> Maharaja and Kak are seriously considering the possibility of Kashmir
> not joining the [Indian] Union if it is formed. On a previous occasion
> Kak hinted to me that Kashmir might have to stay out of the Union in
> view of the antagonism likely to be displayed by a Congress Central
> Government towards Kashmir. The Maharaja's attitude is, I suspect, that
> once Paramountcy disappears Kashmir will have to stand on its own
> feet, that the question of loyalty to the British Government will not
> arise and that Kashmir will be free to ally itself with any power – not
> excluding Russia – she chooses.[9]

The idea of independence had taken strong hold over the maharaja. He
loathed the Congress, so he could not think of joining India. But if
he joined Pakistan the fate of his Hindu dynasty might be sealed.[10]

In April 1947 a new viceroy took over in New Delhi. As it turned out,
he was an old acquaintance of Maharaja Hari Singh; they had served
together on the Prince of Wales's staff back when the prince visited
India in 1921–2. In the third week of June 1947, after the decision was
taken to divide India, Lord Mountbatten set off for Kashmir, 'largely
to forestall Nehru or Gandhi from doing so'.[11] He wanted to make his
own assessment of where the state might be going. In Srinagar, the
viceroy met Kak and advised him to tell the maharaja to accede to
either dominion – but to accede. The prime minister defiantly answered
that they intended to stay independent.[12] The viceroy then fixed a
private meeting with the maharaja. On the appointed day, the last of
Mountbatten's visit, Hari Singh stayed in bed with an attack of colic,
this most probably a ruse to avoid what would certainly have been an
unpleasant encounter.[13]

Nehru now told Mountbatten that 'your visit to Kashmir was from
my particular point of view not a success'; he wanted to go and break
the political deadlock himself. Gandhi also wished to go. Hari Singh,
expectedly, wanted neither.[14] In the event, Nehru was busy with other
matters, so the Mahatma went instead. At the maharaja's request he
addressed no public meetings during his three days in Srinagar. But

he met delegations of workers and students, who demanded Abdullah's release and Prime Minister Kak's dismissal.[15]

On 15 August, Jammu and Kashmir had not acceded to either India or Pakistan. It offered to sign a 'standstill agreement' with both countries which would allow the free movement of peoples and goods across borders. Pakistan signed the agreement, but India said it would wait and watch. However, in the middle of September the rail service between Sialkot in West Punjab and Jammu was suspended, and lorry traffic carrying goods for the state was stopped on the Pakistan side of the border.[16]

As relations with Pakistan deteriorated, the maharaja sacked two prime ministers in quick succession. First Kak was replaced with a soldier named Janak Singh; then he in turn gave way to a former judge of the Punjab High Court, Mehr Chand Mahajan, who had better relations with the Congress bosses. Of these, the two top ones were crucial: the prime minister, Jawaharlal Nehru (who was himself an ethnic Kashmiri), and the home minister and minister of states, Vallabhbhai Patel. Notably, while Nehru always wanted Kashmir to be part of India, Patel was at one time inclined to allow the state to join Pakistan. His mind changed on 13 September, the day the Pakistan government accepted the accession of Junagadh. For 'if Jinnah could take hold of a Hindu-majority State with a Muslim ruler, why should the Sardar not be interested in a Muslim-majority State with a Hindu ruler?'[17]

On 27 September 1947 Nehru wrote a long letter to Patel about the 'dangerous and deteriorating' situation in the state. He had heard that Pakistan was preparing to send infiltrators 'to enter Kashmir in considerable numbers'. The maharaja and his administration could hardly meet the threat on their own, hence the need for Hari Singh to 'make friends with the National Conference so that there might be this popular support against Pakistan'. Releasing Abdullah, and enlisting the support of his followers, would also help 'bring about the accession of Kashmir to the Indian Union'.[18]

On 29 September Sheikh Abdullah was released from prison. The next week, in a speech at the great Hazratbal mosque in Srinagar, Abdullah demanded a 'complete transfer of power to the people in Kashmir. Representatives of the people in a democratic Kashmir will then decide whether the State should join India or Pakistan'. A popular government in Kashmir, he added, 'will not be the government of any one community. It will be a joint government of the Hindus, the Sikhs and the Muslims. That is what I am fighting for.'[19]

Pakistan naturally expected Kashmir, with its Muslim majority, to join it. India thought that the religious factor was irrelevant, especially since the leading political party, the National Conference, was known to be non-sectarian. By early October, as Patel wrote to Nehru, there was no 'difference between you and me on matters of policy relating to Kashmir': both wanted accession.[20] What were the feelings of the Kashmiris themselves? Shortly after Abdullah's release, the British commander of the state forces noted that 'the vast majority of the Kashmiris have no strong bias for either India or Pakistan'. However, while there was 'no well-organized body in Kashmir advocating accession to Pakistan', the 'National Conference has been pro-Congress and anti-Pakistan'.[21]

As for Maharaja Hari Singh, he still clung to the dream of independence. On 12 October the deputy prime minister of Jammu and Kashmir said in Delhi that 'We intend to keep on friendly relations with both India and Pakistan. Despite constant rumours, we have no intention of joining either India or Pakistan . . . The only thing that will change our mind is if one side or the other decides to use force against us . . . The Maharaja has told me that his ambition is to make Kashmir the Switzerland of the East – a State that is completely neutral.'[22]

II

The only thing that will change our mind is if one side or the other decides to use force against us. Two weeks after these words were spoken a force of several thousand armed men invaded the state from the north. On 22 October they crossed the border that separated the North-West Frontier Provinces from Kashmir and briskly made their way towards the capital, Srinagar.

Most of these raiders were Pathans from what was now a province of Pakistan. This much is undisputed; what is not so certain is *why* they came and *who* was helping them. These two questions lie at the heart of the Kashmir dispute; sixty years later, historians still cannot provide definitive answers to them. One reason for this was that the northern extremity of Kashmir was both obscure and inaccessible. No railways or roads penetrated these high mountains. No anthropologists had come here, nor any journalists either. There are thus no independent eye-witness accounts of what came to be known as the 'tribal invasion of Kashmir'.

There are, however, plenty of loaded accounts, biased in one direction or the other. At the time, and later, Indians believed that the tribals were pushed across the border by Pakistan, who also supplied them with rifles and ammunition. The Pakistanis disclaimed any involvement in the invasion – they insisted that it was a 'spontaneous' rushing of Pathan Muslims to the aid of co-religionists persecuted by a Hindu king and a Hindu administration.[23]

There was, indeed, discontent in one part of Kashmir. This was the district of Poonch, which lay to the west of Srinagar. Until 1936 Poonch had been ruled by a subsidiary clan of the Dogra ruling family, but in that year the district came directly under the control of the maharaja in Srinagar. The loss of autonomy hurt, as did the new taxes imposed by the king. There were cesses on individual goats, sheep and cattle and a tax on entering the forest. Hardest hit were the pastoralists of Poonch, almost all of whom were Muslim.[24]

During the Second World War many Muslims from Poonch served in the British Indian Army. They came back, as demobilized soldiers tend to do, as highly conscious political beings. The rule of the Maharaja of Kashmir had already been challenged in the Valley by Sheikh Abdullah and his party. To that was now added the independent challenge of the men of Poonch.

On 14 August several shops and offices in Poonch had flown Pakistani flags, indicating that their allegiance lay to that country, and not to the still unaffiliated state of Kashmir. In the following weeks clashes between Dogra troops and local protesters were reported. By the beginning of September dozens of Poonch men had equipped themselves with rifles obtained from 'informal sources in Pakistan'. They had also established a base in the Pakistani town of Murree; here were collected arms and ammunition to be smuggled across the border to Kashmir. Pakistani accounts acknowledge that both the prime minister, Liaqat Ali Khan, and a senior Punjab Muslim League leader, Mian Iftikharuddin, knew and sanctioned assistance to the Poonch rebels. Overseeing the operation was Akbar Khan, a colonel in the Pakistan Army. Khan had collected 4,000 rifles from army supplies and diverted them for use in Kashmir. More fancifully, he had adopted the nom de guerre 'General Tariq', after a medieval Moorish warrior who had fought the Christians in Spain.[25]

Within Poonch, Muslim officials and soldiers had left their jobs in the state administration and joined the rebels. So, by the end of September, there were intimations of a serious conflict between a dissenting district and the government of Maharaja Hari Singh. But, although there were clashes here and there, there was no major eruption, no head-on battle. Poonch bordered West Punjab; Pakistani cities such as Rawalpindi were easily reached from there. However, the North-West Frontier Province is some distance to the west. Did the raiders from that province hear of the brewing insurrection in Poonch? Or were they planning to come anyway?

For these questions too one cannot supply uncontested answers. All we know for certain is that after the Pathan raiders crossed the border on 22 October they made remarkably swift progress in their march southwards. 'The principal characteristics of the tribal invasion', writes the historian Michael Brecher, 'were the surprise tactics of the tribesmen, the absence of the most rudimentary defence by the Kashmir State Army, and the pillage, loot and rapine of the tribesmen inflicted on Hindus and Muslims alike.' Or, as a British social worker familiar with Kashmir laconically put it, the invading Pathans had sensed 'an opportunity of gaining both religious merit and rich booty'.

Once in Kashmir the tribesmen moved quickly down the Jhelum valley. Their first stop was the town of Muzaffarabad, on the Kishanganga, just seven miles from the border. A battalion of the Jammu and Kashmir Infantry was stationed here, but it was split down the middle, with half the men, Muslims from Poonch, now asserting their disenchantment with the maharaja. The garrison fell, but not before a few men escaped and phoned Srinagar to tell them what had happened. This allowed the acting commandant of the state forces, Brigadier Rajinder Singh, to gather a couple of hundred men and rush towards Uri, a town that lay roughly halfway between Srinagar and Muzaffarabad.

The raiders were on their way to Uri too. Brigadier Rajinder Singh got there first, and as a precaution blew up the bridge that linked the town to the north. This held up the invaders for forty-eight hours, but they were eventually able to cross the river and decimate the brigadier's men. From Uri they made their way to Mahuta, the site of the power station that supplied electricity to the Valley. There they turned off the switches, plunging Srinagar into darkness.[26]

It should not surprise us that estimates of the number of invaders vary. Some said that they were as few as 2,000, others that they were as many as 13,000. We do know that they had rifles and grenades, and that they travelled in lorries. Their incursion into Kashmir was openly encouraged by the prime minister of the North-West Frontier Provinces, Abdul Qayyum. The British governor, Sir George Cunningham, turned a blind eye. So did the British officers who then served with the Pakistan army. As Jinnah's American biographer observes, 'trucks, petrol, and drivers were hardly standard tribal equipment, and British officers as well as Pakistani officials all along the northern Pakistan route they traversed knew and supported, even if they did not actually organize and instigate, the violent October operation by which Pakistan seems to have hoped to trigger the integration of Kashmir into the nation'.[27]

After taking the Mahuta power station on the 24th, the raiders headed down the open road to Srinagar. En route lay the town of Baramula. Here, for the first time, we can draw upon actual eyewitness accounts of what happened. A British manager of a timber firm in Baramula saw the raiders come, 'well supplied with lorries, petrol, and ammunition. They also have both two- and three-inch mortars.'

This manager was relieved of the Rs1,500 he had just drawn from the bank. The next target was the Convent of St Joseph. Here the visitors smashed the machinery in the hospital and shot and wounded the mother superior. A colonel who lived in the compound was killed outright. According to one report, the nuns were then lined up to be shot, but an Afridi who had studied in a convent school in Peshawar stopped his men from applying the finishing touches.[28]

'There can be no doubt that for those in the way, Pathans on the warpath are bad news.' So writes one historian of the Kashmir dispute, Alastair Lamb. He tells us that, apart from the attack on the convent, the Pathans also burnt shops owned by Hindus and Sikhs. Lamb says they did 'what might be expected from warriors engaged on what they saw as a *jihad*, a holy war'.[29] However, at Baramula the greed of the tribesmen conclusively triumphed over religious identity. For here they 'invaded the houses of the peace-loving Kashmiri Moslems as well. They looted and plundered the latter's houses and raped their young girls. Shrieks of terror and agony of those girls resounded across the town of Baramula.'[30]

The incidents at Baramula were a strategic and propaganda disaster for the invaders. They showed that 'once the first fanaticism of jehad had passed, there was left only the incentive of loot'. There was now a 'stampede to stuff the lorries full of the spoils of the Kashmir bazaars and send them back to their homes in Waziristan'.[31] By stopping to steal and rape, the raiders had lost sight of their principal objective: the capture of Srinagar. And by attacking Muslims as well as Hindus, they had undermined their case that they were fighting a holy war. It was especially damaging that among those they killed were apolitical Christian priests doing 'good works', and that a British correspondent was around to take down the testimony of those who survived.[32]

On 24 October, when the tribesmen were en route from Uri to Baramula, Maharaja Hari Singh wired the Indian government for military assistance. The next morning the government's Defence Committee met in New Delhi, and decided to depute V. P. Menon for an on-spot inspection. Menon flew to Srinagar later that day; when he landed at the airport he was 'oppressed by the stillness of a graveyard all around. Over everything hung an atmosphere of impending calamity.' He went straight to M. C. Mahajan's house and learnt that the raiders were in Baramula, less than fifty miles away. He also met the maharaja, and advised him to move to the safety of Jammu.

On the morning of the 26th Menon flew back to Delhi, accompanied by the prime minister of Kashmir. Another meeting of the Defence Committee was convened. In attendance, apart from Mountbatten, Nehru and Patel, was Sheikh Abdullah, who happened to be in Delhi that day. Both he and Mahajan urged that India immediately send troops to push back the invaders. Mountbatten suggested, however, that it would be best to secure Hari Singh's accession to India before committing any forces to his defence.

Menon flew now to Jammu, where the Maharaja had taken refuge. On arrival at the palace he 'found it in a state of utter turmoil with valuable articles strewn all over the place'. The maharaja was asleep, recovering from the all-night drive from Srinagar. He was woken, and agreed to accede at once. Menon took the signed Instrument of Accession back with him to Delhi.[33]

At dawn on the 27th the first plane left Delhi for Srinagar with troops and arms aboard. In all twenty-eight Dakotas flew to Srinagar that day. In the days following, more than a hundred planes took off from Delhi for the Valley, carrying soldiers and supplies and bringing back refugees and the wounded.[34]

Some of the planes that flew to Srinagar on the 27th belonged to the army or air force. Others were commandeered by the government of India from private airlines. As one officer who flew in one of these passenger planes recalled, 'the luxury fittings were ripped out, comfortable chairs pulled out of their fixtures, and within minutes fully armed troops clambered aboard – as many as could fit in'. They flew over the Punjab, seeing 'long strings of refugee caravans below them', with 'an odd house or village still smouldering'. They landed in Srinagar airport to 'the sound of small-arms and machine-gun fire'.[35]

With his troops in the Valley the Indian prime minister breathed a sigh of relief. 'If we had vacillated and delayed by a day', wrote Nehru to his sister, 'Srinagar might have been a smoking ruin. We got there in the nick of time.' He thought that they had succeeded 'in warning off Pakistan from Kashmir. We have agreed that the future of Kashmir must be determined by the people. Meanwhile, Sheikh Abdullah is being entrusted with the formation of a Ministry. For my part, I do not mind if Kashmir becomes more or less independent, but it would have been a cruel blow if it had become just an exploited part of Pakistan.'[36]

The view from the other side was all too different. The news that Indian troops had landed in Srinagar infuriated the governor general of Pakistan. Jinnah first fortified himself with several brandies and then ordered his generals to march their troops into Kashmir.[37] His British commander-in-chief refused to follow the order. So, for the moment, the Pakistani troops kept out of the conflict, although their officers remained in close contact with the raiders.

When the Indian troops landed in Srinagar the maharaja had already left. There was not much sign of his administration, either. The police were nowhere in sight; substituting for them were volunteers of the National Conference, who stood guard at street corners and bridges and generally supervised the movement of men and goods. A journalist who had covered the Punjab violence confessed that he was 'not prepared for the incredible sights of amity and indeed fraternity that I saw in Srinagar. Hindus and Sikhs moved about with complete unselfconsciousness among Muslims who constituted the vast majority of the population of the town; they marched shoulder to shoulder with them down Srinagar's streets as volunteers engaged in a common task.'[38] Another reporter recalled the happy relationship between the National Conference and the army, as symbolized in the drives taken together by Sheikh Abdullah and the divisional commander, Major General Thimayya.[39]

As the Indians prepared to push back the raiders, Lord Mountbatten flew to Lahore on a peace mission. On 1 November 1947 he had a contentious meeting with Jinnah, in which he was told that if India gave up its claim to Kashmir, Pakistan would relinquish its claim on that other disputed state, Junagadh. Jinnah described Kashmir's accession to India as based on 'fraud and violence'. Mountbatten suggested that the violence had come from raiders who were Pakistani citizens; he knew for a fact that Maharaja Hari Singh wanted independence, and had been forced to accede to India only after his state was attacked. Jinnah countered by saying that the maharaja had brought this upon himself by his ill treatment of Muslims in Poonch.[40]

In Kashmir, meanwhile, the Indian army had thrown a protective ring around Srinagar. There were now 4,000 troops in position, armed with machine guns. The safety of the city had been secured.[41] And with Srinagar no longer vulnerable, the Indians began to clear other parts of the Valley of infiltrators. Baramula was taken on 8 November, and four days later Mahuta was captured, just in time to save the power station from being blown up. The town of Uri fell the next day.[42]

With the onset of winter, the military operations were temporarily suspended. Attention now returned to the internal affairs of Kashmir. Mahajan was still prime minister, but he was being actively assisted by National Conference leaders. On 11 November Nehru wrote to Hari Singh asking him to place 'full confidence' in Sheikh Abdullah, that is to formally make him head of the administration instead of Mahajan. The 'only person who can deliver the goods in Kashmir is Sheikh Abdullah', insisted Nehru. 'He is obviously the leading popular personality in Kashmir. The way he has risen to grapple with the crisis has shown the nature of the man. I have a high opinion of his integrity and general balance of mind. He has striven hard and succeeded very largely in keeping communal peace. He may make any number of mistakes in minor matters, but I think he is likely to be right in regard to major decisions.'[43]

Mahatma Gandhi was equally impressed with the Sheikh. In the last week of November 1947 Abdullah visited Delhi, where he accompanied Gandhi to a meeting held on the birthday of the founder of the Sikh faith, Guru Nanak. As Gandhi told the gathering:

> You see Sheikh Abdullah Saheb with me. I was disinclined to bring him with me, for I know that there is a great gulf between the Hindus and the Sikhs on one side, and the Muslims on the other. But the Sheikh Saheb, known as the Lion of Kashmir, although a pucca Muslim, has won the hearts of both, by making them forget that there is any difference

between the three . . . Even though in Jammu, recently, the Muslims were killed by the Hindus and Sikhs, he went to Jammu and invited the evil-doers to forget the past and repent over the evil they had done. The Hindus and the Sikhs listened to him. Now the Muslims and the Hindus and the Sikhs . . . are fighting together to defend the beautiful valley of Kashmir.[44]

For Gandhi as well as Nehru the Sheikh had become a symbol of secularism, a practitioner of inter-faith harmony whose deeds in Kashmir were a stirring refutation of the two-nation theory. On the other hand, the Pakistani prime minister, Liaqat Ali Khan, contemptuously dismissed Abdullah as a 'quisling'. On 27 November Khan met with Nehru in Delhi, with Mountbatten playing the role of umpire. When a plebiscite was suggested as a way out of the impasse, Khan stated that first 'an entirely new administration should be set up in Kashmir, which the people of Pakistan would accept as impartial'.[45]

By now, Nehru was of the opinion that India must come to some 'rapid and more or less final decisions about Kashmir with the Pakistan Government'. For continuing military operations would mean 'grave difficulties and suffering for the people of the State'. In a letter to Maharaja Hari Singh, the Indian prime minister outlined the various forms a settlement could take. There could be a plebiscite for the whole state, to decide which dominion it would join. Or the state could survive as an independent entity, with its defence guaranteed by both India and Pakistan. A third option was of a partition, with Jammu going to India and the rest of the state to Pakistan. A fourth option had Jammu and the Valley staying with India, with Poonch and beyond being ceded to Pakistan. Nehru himself inclined to this last alternative. He saw that in Poonch 'the majority of the population is likely to be against the Indian Union'. But he was loath to give up the vale of Kashmir, a National Conference stronghold whose population seemed to be inclined towards India. From the Indian point of view, said Nehru to the maharaja,

it is of the most vital importance that Kashmir should remain within the Indian Union . . . But however much we may want this, it cannot be done ultimately except through the goodwill of the mass of the population. Even if military forces held Kashmir for a while, a later consequence might be a strong reaction against this. Essentially, therefore, this is a problem of psychological approach to the mass of the people and of making them feel they will be benefited by being in the Indian Union. If the average Muslim feels that he has no safe or secure place in the Union, then obviously he will look elsewhere. Our basic policy must keep this in view, or else we fail.[46]

This letter of Nehru's is much less well known than it should be. Excluded (for whatever reason) from his own *Selected Works*, it lies buried in the correspondence of Vallabhbhai Patel, to whom he had sent a copy. It shows that, contrary to received wisdom, the Indian prime minister was quite prepared to compromise on Kashmir. Indeed, the four options he outlined in December 1947 remain the four options being debated today.

III

On 1 January 1948 India decided to take the Kashmir issue to the United Nations. This was done on the advice of the governor general, Lord Mountbatten. Since Kashmir had acceded to it, India wanted the UN to help clear the northern parts of what it said was an illegal occupation by groups loyal to Pakistan.[47]

Through January and February the Security Council held several sittings on Kashmir. Pakistan, represented by the superbly gifted orator Sir Zafrullah Khan, was able to present a far better case than India. Khan convinced the delegates that the invasion was a consequence of the tragic riots across northern India in 1946–7; it was a 'natural' reaction of Muslims to the sufferings of their fellows. He accused the Indians of perpetrating 'genocide' in East Punjab, forcing 6 million Muslims to flee to Pakistan. The Kashmir problem was recast as part of the unfinished business of Partition. India suffered a significant symbolic defeat when the Security Council altered the agenda item from the 'Jammu and Kashmir Question' to the 'India–Pakistan Question'.

Pakistan now suggested the withdrawal of all armed forces in the state, and the holding of a plebiscite under an 'impartial interim administration'. Ironically, Pakistan had rejected the idea of a plebiscite in the case of Junagadh. Jinnah's position then was that the will of the ruler would decide which dominion a princely state would join. India instead referred the matter to the will of the people. Having done this in Junagadh, they could not now so easily duck the question in

Kashmir. However, the Indian government insisted a plebiscite could be conducted under a National Conference administration whose leader, Sheikh Abdullah, was the 'most popular political leader in the State'.[48]

So said the Sheikh himself, when he spoke at the United Nations on 5 February 1948. His language, recalled one observer, 'was blunt, direct, and devoid of diplomatic language'. 'There is no power on earth which can displace me from the position which I have [in Kashmir]', he told the Security Council. 'As long as the people are behind me I will remain there.'[49]

A striking feature of the UN discussions on Kashmir was the partisanship of the British. Their representative, Philip Noel-Baker, vigorously supported the Pakistani position. The British bias was deeply resented by the Indians. Some saw it as a hangover from pre-Independence days, a conversion for support to the Muslim League to support for Pakistan. Others thought it was in compensation for the recent creation of the state of Israel, after which there was a need to placate Muslims worldwide. A third theory was that in the ensuing struggle with Soviet Russia, Pakistan would be the more reliable ally. It was also better placed, with easy access to British air bases in the Middle East.[50]

In the first week of March 1948, the editor of the *Sunday Times* wrote to Noel-Baker that, 'in the world struggle for and against Communism, Kashmir occupies a place more critical than most people realise. It is the one corner at which the British Commonwealth physically touches the Soviet Union. It is an unsuspected soft spot, in the perimeter of the Indian Ocean basin, on whose inviolability the whole security of the Commonwealth and indeed world peace depend.'[51]

By now, Nehru bitterly regretted going to the United Nations. He was shocked, he told Mountbatten, to find that 'power politics and not ethics' were ruling an organization which 'was being completely run by the Americans', who, like the British, 'had made no bones of [their] sympathy for the Pakistan case'.[52] Within the Cabinet, pressure grew for the renewal of hostilities, for the throwing out of the invaders from northern Kashmir. But was this militarily feasible? A British general with years of service in the subcontinent warned that

Kashmir may remain a 'Spanish Ulcer'. I have not found an Indian familiar with the Peninsular War's drain on Napoleon's manpower and treasure: and I sometimes feel that Ministers are loath to contemplate

such a development in the case of Kashmir – I feel they still would prefer
to think that the affair is susceptible of settlement, in a short decisive
campaign, by sledge-hammer blows by vastly superior Indian forces
which should be 'thrown' into Kashmir.[53]

Meanwhile, in March 1948 Sheikh Abdullah replaced Mehr Chand
Mahajan as the prime minister of Jammu and Kashmir. Then, in the
middle of May, when the snows had melted, the war recommenced.
An infantry brigade advanced north and west from Uri. It took
the town of Tithwal, but met with sharp resistance en route to the key
town of Muzaffarabad.[54]

On the other side of an ever-shifting line of control, Pakistan had
sponsored a government of Azad (Free) Kashmir. They had also created
an Azad Kashmir army, manned by men from these parts of the state,
helped and guided by Pakistan army officers. These forces were skilful in
their use of the terrain. In the late summer of 1948 they took the towns
of Kargil and Dras, and threatened the capital of Ladakh, Leh, which
is at an altitude of 11,000 feet. However, an Indian air force squadron
was successful in bringing supplies to Leh. It was also the air force that
brought relief to the town of Poonch, in the west, whose surroundings
were under the control of the raiders.[55]

The two armies battled on through the later months of 1948. In
November both Dras and Kargil were recaptured by the Indians, making
Leh and Ladakh safe for the moment. In the same month the hills around
Poonch were also cleared. However, the northern and western parts of
Kashmir were still in the control of Pakistan. Some Indian commanders
wanted to move on, and asked for the redeployment of three brigades
from the plains. Their request was not granted. For one thing, winter
was about to set in. For another, the offensive would have required not
merely troop reinforcements, but also massive air support.[56] Perhaps it
was as well that the Indian Army halted its forward movement. For, as a
scholar closely following the Kashmir question commented at the time,
'either it must be settled by partition or India will have to walk into West
Punjab. A military decision can *never* be reached in Kashmir itself.'[57]

At the United Nations a Special Commission had been appointed for
Kashmir. Its members made an extensive tour of the region, visiting
Delhi, Karachi and Kashmir. In Srinagar they were entertained by
Sheikh Abdullah at the famous Shalimar Gardens. Later, Abdullah had
a long talk with one of the UN representatives, the Czech diplomat and

The Kashmir Conflict, c.1947–8

- - - - Cease-fire Line

AFGHANISTAN

USSR

PAKISTAN

Khyber Pass

Durand Line

Peshawar

Chitral

Rawalpindi

Murree

Chhamb

Sialkot

Lahore

Gurdaspur

Amritsar

Pathankot

INDIA

Jammu

Akhnur

Muzzaffarabad

Uri Poonch

Baramula

Srinagar

Anantnag

Banihal Pass

Zanskar

JAMMU AND KASHMIR

Zoji La Pass

Kargil

Leh

Tankse

Ladakh

Rupshu

Ladakh Range

Nanga Parbat

Gilgit

NORTHERN AREAS

Skardu

BALTISTAN

HUNZA

Karakoram Range

Mintaka

Karakoram Pass

AKSAI CHIN
(under Chinese
administration)

0
50
100
150
200
250 miles

0
50
100
150 miles

scholar Josef Korbel. The prime minister dismissed both a plebiscite and independence, arguing that the 'only solution' was the partition of Kashmir. Otherwise, said Abdullah, 'the fighting will continue; India and Pakistan will prolong the quarrel indefinitely, and our people's suffering will go on'.

In Srinagar Korbel went to hear Abdullah speak at a mosque. The audience of 4,000 listened 'with rapt attention, their faith and loyalty quite obvious in their faces. Nor could we notice any police, so often used to induce such loyalty.' The Commission then visited Pakistan, where they found that it would not consider any solution which gave the vale of Kashmir, with its Muslim majority, to India.[58]

IV

By March 1948 Sheikh Abdullah was the most important man in the Valley. Hari Singh was still the state's ceremonial head – now called 'sadr-i-riyasat' – but he had no real powers. The government of India completely shut him out of the UN deliberations. Their man, as they saw it, was Abdullah. Only he, it was felt, could 'save' Kashmir for the Union.

At this stage Abdullah himself was inclined to stress the ties between Kashmir and India. In May 1948 he organized a week-long 'freedom' celebration in Srinagar, to which he invited the leading lights of the Indian government. The events on the calendar included folk songs and poetry readings, the remembrance of martyrs and visits to refugee camps. The Kashmiri leader commended the 'patriotic morale of our own people and the gallant fighting forces of the Indian Union'. 'Our struggle', said Abdullah, 'is not merely the affair of the Kashmir people, it is the war of every son and daughter of India.'[59]

On the first anniversary of Indian independence Abdullah sent a message to the leading Madras weekly, *Swatantra*. The message sought to unite north and south, mountain and coast, and, above all, Kashmir and India. It deserves to be printed in full:

Through the pages of SWATANTRA I wish to send my message of fraternity to the people of the south. Far back in the annals of India the south and north met in the land of Kashmir. The great Shankaracharya came to Kashmir to spread his dynamic philosophy

but here he was defeated in argument by a Panditani. This gave rise
to the peculiar philosophy of Kashmir – Shaivism. A memorial to the
great Shankaracharya in Kashmir stands prominent on the top of
the Shankaracharya Hill in Srinagar. It is a temple containing the Murti
of Shiva.

More recently it was given to a southerner to take the case of
Kashmir to the United Nations and, as the whole of India knows, with
the doggedness and tenacity that is so usual to the southerner, he
defended Kashmir.

We in Kashmir expect that we shall continue to receive support
and sympathy from the people of the south and that some day when
we describe the extent of our country we shall use the phrase 'from
Kashmir to Cape Comorin'.[60]

The Madras journal, for its part, responded by printing a lyrical paean to
the union of Kashmir with India. 'The blood of many a brave Tamilian,
Andhra, Malayalee and Coorgi', it said, 'has soaked into the fertile soil of
Kashmir and mixed with the blood of the Kashmiri patriots, cementing
for ever the unity of the North and the South.' Sheikh Abdullah's Id
perorations, noted the journal, were attentively heard by many Muslim
soldiers from Kerala and Tamil Nadu. In Uri, sixty miles from Srinagar,
there was a grave of a Christian soldier from Travancore, which had the
Vedic swastika and a verse from the Quran inscribed on it. There could
be 'no more poignant and touching symbol of the essential oneness
and unity of India'.[61]

Whether or not Abdullah was India's man, he certainly was not
Pakistan's. In April 1948 he described that country as 'an unscrupulous
and savage enemy'.[62] He dismissed Pakistan as a theocratic state and
the Muslim League as 'pro-prince' rather than 'pro-people'. In his view,
'Indian and not Pakistani leaders . . . had all along stood for the rights
of the States' people'.[63] When a diplomat in Delhi asked Abdullah what
he thought of the option of independence, he answered that it would
never work as Kashmir was too small and too poor. Besides, said the
Sheikh, 'Pakistan would swallow us up. They have tried it once. They
would do it again.'[64]

Within Kashmir Abdullah gave top priority to the redistribution of
land. Under the maharaja's regime, a few Hindus and fewer Muslims
had very large holdings, with the bulk of the rural population serving

as labourers or as tenants-at-will. In his first year in power Abdullah transferred 40,000 acres of surplus land to the landless. He also outlawed absentee ownership, increased the tenant's share from 25 per cent to 75 per cent of the crop and placed a moratorium on debt. His socialistic policies alarmed some elements in the government of India, especially as he did not pay compensation to the dispossessed landlords. But Abdullah saw this as crucial to progress in Kashmir. As he told a press conference in Delhi, if he was not allowed to implement agrarian reforms, he would not continue as prime minister of Jammu and Kashmir. Asked what he would do if reactionary elements got the upper hand in the central government, Abdullah answered: 'Don't think I will desert you, even if you desert me. I will resign and join those people in the Indian Union who will also fight for economic betterment of the poor.'[65]

At this press conference Abdullah also made some sneering remarks about Maharaja Hari Singh. He pointed out that the maharaja had run away from Srinagar when it was in danger. In April 1949 Abdullah won a major victory when Hari Singh was replaced as sadr-i-riyasat by his eighteen-year-old son, Karan Singh. The next month Abdullah and three other National Conference men were chosen to represent Kashmir in the Constituent Assembly in Delhi, in a further affirmation of the state's integration with India.[66] That summer the Valley opened itself once more for tourists. As a sympathetic journalist put it, 'every tourist who goes to Kashmir this summer will be rendering as vital a service to Kashmir – and to India – as a soldier fighting at the front'.[67]

In the autumn came a visitor more important than a million tourists – Jawaharlal Nehru. Nehru and Abdullah took a leisurely two-hour ride down Srinagar's main thoroughfare, the river Jhelum. As their barge rode on, commented the correspondent of *Time* magazine, 'hundreds of *shikaras* (gondolas) milled around; their jampacked passengers wanted a good look, and they pelted Nehru with flowers'. Thousands watched the procession from the river banks, firing crackers from time to time. 'Carefully coached schoolchildren' shouted slogans in praise of Nehru and Abdullah. Seizing the chance, merchants had hung out their wares, alongside banners which advertised 'best Persian and Kashmiri carpets'.

'All the portents', concluded *Time*, were that 'India considered that the battle for Kashmir had been won – and that India intended to keep the prize.'[68]

V

The battle for Kashmir was, and is, not merely or even mostly a battle for territory. It is, as Josef Korbel put it half a century ago, an 'uncompromising and perhaps uncompromisable struggle of two ways of life, two concepts of political organization, two scales of values, two spiritual attitudes'.[69]

On one side was the idea of India; on the other side, the idea of Pakistan. In the spring of 1948 the British journalist Kingsley Martin visited both countries to see how Kashmir looked from each. Indians, he found, were utterly convinced of the legality of the state's accession, and bitter in their condemnation of Pakistan's help to the raiders. To them the religion of the Kashmiris was wholly irrelevant. The fact that Abdullah was the popular head of an emergency administration was 'outstanding proof that India was not "Hindustan" and that there are Muslims who have voluntarily chosen to come to an India which, as Nehru emphasised, should be a democracy in which minorities can live safely and freely'.

When Martin crossed the border he found 'how completely different the situation looks from the Pakistan angle'. Most people he met had friends or relatives who had died at the hands of Hindus and Sikhs. The dispute for the Pakistanis started with the rebellion in Poonch, which in India had been 'largely and undeservedly forgotten'. In Karachi and Lahore the people were 'completely sympathetic' to the raiders from the Frontier who, in their eyes, were fighting 'a holy war against the oppressors of Islam'.[70] Martin's conclusions were endorsed by the veteran Australian war correspondent Alan Moorehead. On a visit to Pakistan he too found that the Kashmir conflict was looked upon 'as a holy Moslem war . . . Some of them, I have seen, talk wildly of going on to Delhi. Everywhere recruiting is going on and there is much excitement at the success of the Moslems.'[71]

The fragility of the Pakistani state and its ideology was personalized in the ambivalent identities of its main leaders. The governor general, M. A. Jinnah, was a Gujarati who had married a Parsi. The prime minister, Liaqat Ali Khan, was an aristocrat from the United Provinces who was married to a Christian. Neither was, in any sense of the term, a practising Muslim. The top civil servants of Pakistan were, like Jinnah and Liaqat, 'mohajirs', migrants whose ancestral homes lay on the Indian side of the border. The ruling class had no roots in what was now their state.

This, one suspects, made them even more fervent in their desire to make Kashmir part of Pakistan.

However, the new Indian nation-state was not so robust either. Its insecurity was manifest in its anointing, as a secular hero, of a Muslim officer who had died fighting in Kashmir. True, unlike the Pakistani army, the Indian army was drawn from men of all religions. Among its senior commanders were a Sikh, a Parsi and two Coorgs, these last from a south Indian hill community that likes to see itself as 'not-Hindu'. Yet the commander who was to be venerated most was a Muslim. This man, Brigadier Usman, was educated in Allahabad and Sandhurst, and chose to stay with India at the time of Partition. It was claimed that Pakistan had dubbed him a 'kaffir', and that the Azad Kashmir government had put a price of Rs50,000 on his head, dead or alive.

In January–February 1948 Brigadier Usman and his men repulsed a fierce attack on Nowshera. In July of that year he died in action. An Indian journalist wrote of his death that 'a precious life, of imagination and unswerving patriotism, has fallen a victim to communal fanaticism. Brigadier Usman's brave example will be an abiding source of inspiration for Free India.'[72] His death was publicly mourned by Congress leaders, from Jawaharlal Nehru downwards. The tributes that poured in praised not merely his bravery but also his character: he was, the Indian public was told, an army officer who was withal 'a vegetarian, a non-smoker, and a teetotaller'. His body was brought back from Kashmir to Delhi and buried with full military honours. His grave was placed next to that of Dr M. A. Ansari, a legendary Nationalist Muslim of the previous generation.[73] One might say that Brigadier Usman was to the Indian army what Sheikh Abdullah was to Indian politics, the symbol of its putatively inclusive secularism, the affirmation of it being, if it was anything at all, the Other of a theologically dogmatic and insular Pakistan.

Both sides had invested men and money in the battle for Kashmir. More crucially, they had invested their respective ideologies of nationhood. The clash of these ideologies was captured in a debate on the future of Kashmir organized by a leading Bombay weekly, the *Current*. The protagonists were both young journalists – both Muslim, but one Indian, the other Pakistani. Both were asked to answer the question: which way would the Kashmiris vote if the United Nations did succeed in holding a plebiscite?

Speaking on India's behalf was the gifted novelist and scriptwriter Khwaja Ahmad Abbas. One-fourth of Kashmir's population, he said, were squarely behind Sheikh Abdullah and his National Conference – these were the politically conscious, 'progressive' elements. Another quarter were just as resolutely opposed to the Sheikh – these consisted of those 'fully indoctrinated by the Pakistan ideology'. Half the voters were undecided – they could go either way. These were attracted to the person of Abdullah, but also 'susceptible to the cry of Islam in Danger'. When the day of reckoning came, Abbas thought that the memories of the raiders' brutalities and the appeal of the progressive ideology of secularism would tilt the balance in favour of India. However, if India 'wanted to make absolutely sure of a comfortable and convincing majority', then the maharaja and his dynasty had to be removed, and the Sheikh allowed to implement fully his economic programme.[74]

The next week Abbas was answered by a Karachi-based journalist named Wares Ishaq. He thought that the pull of religion would ensure a Pakistani victory in any plebiscite in Kashmir. Islam, he argued, was not just a religion, but a culture and a way of life. There was only one circumstance in which the Kashmiris would disregard the call of the faith – if India actually lived up to its claim of being a secular state. However, after the death of Mahatma Gandhi, the position of minorities was fraught with danger. In particular, wrote Ishaq, the lifting of the ban on the Hindu chauvinist body, the Rashtriya Swayamsevak Sangh, 'has finally convinced Muslims all over India, and specially in Kashmir, that their position in India will always be that of a downtrodden minority'. Thus, when the crunch came, the bulk of the Kashmiris would vote to join 'the Islamic comity of nations'.[75]

VI

One might say of the conflict of 1947–8 that it had only losers. The indecision – with neither nation succeeding in acquiring the whole of the state – hurt both sides then, and it hurts them now. Hence the prevalence and persistence of conspiracy theories. On the Indian side the finger is pointed at the British governor general, who dragged the case to the UN, and at the British general in command of the Indian army, who is believed to have stopped his troops from going into northern Kashmir.[76] But the Pakistanis blame Mountbatten too; they think he conspired with Sir Cyril Radcliffe to gift the district of Gurdaspur to the Indians, so as to allow them a road into Kashmir.[77] And they chastise their own government for not helping the raiders even more. As a senior civil servant lamented in 1998:

> [T]he only chance of Pakistan obtaining Kashmir was by a blitzkrieg, combining the call of jihad, speed, and surprise, to present the enemy with a fait accompli before it could recover from the shock. The tribal invasion was well conceived as the only means to counter the Indian designs and compensate for Pakistan's military weakness . . . The one single element which decided the issue against Pakistan was the faulty leadership of the tribal horde . . . This was the only mistake, and a decisive one at that, for which those who organized the invasion . . . should bear responsibility.[78]

This book will return to Kashmir at regular intervals. But let me end this investigation of the dispute's origins with some prophetic statements made at the time. The quotes below come from observers speaking not in 1990 or 2000, but in the very early years of the conflict.[79]

> Kashmir is the one great problem that may cause the downfall of India and Pakistan (Henry Grady, United States Ambassador to India, January 1948).

> So long as the dispute over Kashmir continues it is a serious drain on the military, economic and, above all, on the spiritual strength of these two great countries (General A. G. L. McNaughton, UN mediator, February 1950).

> So vital seems its possession for economic and political security to Pakistan that her whole foreign and defence policy has largely revolved around the Kashmir dispute . . . Far more than the Punjab massacres, which, though horrible, were short lived, it is the Kashmir dispute which has poisoned every aspect of Indo-Pakistan relations (Richard Symonds, British social worker and author, 1950).

> Kashmir is one situation you could never localize if it should flare up. It would influence the whole Muslim world. [It is] potentially the most dangerous in the world (Ralph Bunche, senior UN official, February 1953).

5

REFUGEES AND THE REPUBLIC

Refugees are [being] sent all over India. They will scatter communal hatred on a wide scale and will churn up enormous ill-will everywhere. Refugees have to be looked after, but we have to take steps to prevent the infection of hatred beyond the necessary minimum which cannot be prevented.

C. RAJAGOPALACHARI, governor of Bengal, 4 September 1947

May the blood that flowed from Gandhiji's wounds and the tears that flowed from the eyes of the women of India everywhere they learnt of his death serve to lay the curse of 1947, and may the grisly tragedy of that year sleep in history and not colour present passions.

C. RAJAGOPALACHARI, 20 March 1948

I

IN THE INDIAN IMAGINATION Kurukshetra occupies a special place. It was the venue for the bloody battles described in the epic Mahabharata. According to the epic, the fighting took place on an open plain north-west of the ancient city of Indraprastha (now known as Delhi). The plain was called Kurukshetra, a name it retains to this day.

Several thousand years after the Mahabharata was composed, the place of its enactment became the temporary home of the victims of another war. This, too, was fought between closely related kin: India and Pakistan, rather than Pandava and Kaurava. Many of the Hindus and Sikhs fleeing West Punjab were directed by the government of India to a refugee camp in Kurukshetra. A vast city of tents had grown up on the plain, to house waves of migrants, sometimes up to 20,000 a day. The camp was initially planned for 100,000 refugees, but it came to accommodate three times that number. As an American observer wrote, 'the army worked miracles to keep the tents rising ahead of the last refugees'. The new inhabitants of Kurukshetra consumed 100 tons of flour daily, along with large quantities of salt, rice, lentils, sugar and cooking oil – all provided free of charge by the government. Helping the state in their effort was a network of Indian and foreign social workers, the United Council for Relief and Welfare (UCRW).

The refugees had to be housed and fed, but also clothed and entertained. With winter approaching, the 'Government soon recognized that the evenings and nights were hardest to bear'. So the UCRW commandeered a bunch of film projectors from Delhi, and set them up in Kurukshetra. Among the movies shown were Disney specials featuring Mickey Mouse and Donald Duck. With large cloth screens allowing for two-way projection, crowds of up to 15,000 could watch a single show. This 'two-hour break from reality', commented a social worker, 'was a lifesaver. The refugees forgot their shock experiences and misery for two golden hours of laughter. Yes, they who had been bruised and beaten, were homeless and wounded, could laugh. Here was hope.'[1]

Kurukshetra was the largest of the nearly 200 camps set up to house refugees from West Punjab. Some refugees had arrived before the date of transfer of power; among them prescient businessmen who had sold their properties in advance and migrated with the proceeds. However, the vast majority came after 15 August 1947, and with little more than the clothes on their skin. These were the farmers who had 'stayed behind till the last moment, firmly resolved to remain in Pakistan if they could be assured of an honourable living'. But when, in September and October, the violence escalated in the Punjab, they had to abandon that idea. The Hindus and Sikhs who were lucky enough to escape the mobs fled to India by road, rail, sea and on foot.[2]

Camps such as Kurukshetra were but a holding operation. The refugees had to be found permanent homes and productive work. A journalist visiting Kurukshetra in December 1947 described it as a city in itself, with 300,000 people, all 'sitting idle like mad'. 'The one thought that dominates the peasant-refugees of Kurukshetra', he wrote, is ' "Give us some land. We will cultivate it". That is what they shouted. These land-hungry peasants told us that they did not very much care where land was given to them provided [it] was cultivable. Their passion for land appeared to be elemental.'[3]

As it happened, a massive migration had also taken place the other way, into Pakistan from India. Thus, the first place to resettle the refugees was on land vacated by Muslims in the eastern part of the Punjab. If the transfer of populations had been 'the greatest mass migration' in history, now commenced 'the biggest land resettlement operation in the world'. As against 2.7 million hectares abandoned by Hindus and Sikhs in West Punjab, there were only 1.9 million hectares left behind by Muslims in East Punjab. The shortfall was made more acute by the fact that the areas in the west of the province had richer soils, and were more abundantly irrigated. Indeed, back in the late nineteenth century, hundreds of Sikh villages had migrated *en masse* to the west to cultivate land in the newly created 'canal colonies'. There they had made the desert flourish, but one fine day in 1947 they were told that their garden now lay in Pakistan. So, in a bare two generations, these dispossessed Sikhs found themselves back in their original homes.

To begin with, each family of refugee farmers was given an allotment of four hectares, regardless of its holding in Pakistan. Loans were advanced to buy seed and equipment. While cultivation commenced on these temporary plots, applications were invited for permanent allotments. Each family was asked to submit evidence of how much land it had left behind. Applications were received from 10 March 1948; within a month, more than half a million claims had been filed. These claims were then verified in open assemblies consisting of other migrants from the same village. As each claim was read out by a government official, the assembly approved, amended, or rejected it.

Expectedly, many refugees were at first prone to exaggeration. However, every false claim was punished, sometimes by a reduction in the land allotted, in extreme cases by a brief spell of imprisonment. This acted as a deterrent; still, an officer closely associated with the process estimated that there was an overall inflation of about 25 per cent. To collect, collate, verify and act upon the claims a Rehabilitation Secretariat was set up in Jullundur. At its peak there were about 7,000 officials working here; they came to constitute a kind of refugee city of their own. The bulk of these officials were accommodated in tents, the camp serviced by makeshift lights and latrines and with temporary shrines, temples for Hindus and *gurdwaras* for Sikhs.

Leading the operations was the director general of rehabilitation, Sardar Tarlok Singh of the Indian Civil Service. A graduate of the London School of Economics, Tarlok Singh used his academic training to good effect, making two innovations that proved critical in the successful settlement of the refugees. These were the ideas of the 'standard acre' and the 'graded cut'. A 'standard acre' was defined as that amount of land which could yield ten to eleven *maunds* of rice. (A *maund* is about 40 kilograms.) In the dry, unirrigated districts of the east, four physical acres comprised one 'standard' acre, whereas in the lush canal colonies, a real acre of land more or less equalled its standard counterpart.

The concept of the standard acre innovatively took care of the variations in soil and climate across the province. The idea of the 'graded cut', meanwhile, helped overcome the massive discrepancy between the land left behind by the refugees and the land now available to them – a gap that was close to a million acres. For the first ten acres of any claim, a cut of 25 per cent was implemented – thus one got only 7.5 acres instead of ten. For higher claims the cuts were steeper: 30 per cent for 10 – 30 acres, and on upwards, till those having in excess of 500 acres were 'taxed' at the rate of 95 per cent. The biggest single loser was a lady named Vidyawati, who had inherited (and lost) her husband's estate of 11,500 acres, spread across thirty-five villages of the Gujranwala and Sialkot districts. In compensation, she was allotted a mere 835 acres in a single village of Karnal.

By November 1949 Tarlok Singh and his men had made 250,000 allotments of land. These refugees were then distributed equitably across the districts of East Punjab. Neighbours and families were resettled together, although the re-creation of entire village communities proved impossible. Refugees were invited to protest against their allotments; close to 100,000 families asked for a review. A third of these objections were acted upon; as a result, 80,000 hectares changed hands once again.

In exchange for their well-watered lands in the west, these refugees were given impoverished holdings in the east. With the implementation of graded cuts, they had less of it as well. But with characteristic ingenuity and enterprise they set to work, digging new wells, building new houses, planting their crops. By 1950 a depopulated countryside was alive once again.[4]

Yet a sense of loss persisted. The economy could be rebuilt, but the cultural wrongs of Partition could never be undone – not in, or by, either side. The Sikhs once more had land to cultivate, but they would never get back much-loved places of worship. These included the *gurdwara* in Lahore where lay buried their great warrior-chieftain, Ranjit Singh, as well as Nankana Sahib, the birthplace of the founder of the faith, Guru Nanak.

In April 1948 the editor of the Calcutta *Statesman* visited Nankana Sahib, where he met the handful of Sikhs permitted by Pakistan to stay on as guardians of the shrine. A few months later the journalist visited the centre of the Ahmadiya sect of Islam, the town of Qadian, which lay in the Indian Punjab. The great tower of the Ahmadiya mosque was visible from miles around, but within its precincts there now lived only 300 of the faithful. Otherwise, the town had been taken over by 12,000 Hindu and Sikh refugees. In both Qadian and Nankana Sahib there was 'the conspicuous dearth of daily worshippers, the aching emptiness, the sense of waiting, of hope and . . . of faith fortified by humbling affliction'.[5]

II

The bulk of the migrants from West Punjab were farmers; but there were also many who were artisans, traders and labourers. To accommodate them the government built brand-new townships. One, Faridabad, lay twenty miles south of the nation's capital, Delhi. Among the groups active here was the Indian Cooperative Union (ICU), an organization headed by Kamaladevi Chattopadhyaya, a socialist and feminist who had been closely associated with Mahatma Gandhi.

The residents of Faridabad were mostly Hindu refugees from the North-West Frontier Province. A social worker named Sudhir Ghosh encouraged them to construct their own homes. However, the government wished to build the houses through its Public Works Department (PWD), notorious for its sloth and corruption, widely known both as the 'Public Waste Department' and as 'Plunder Without Danger'. In protest a group of refugees besieged the prime minister's house in Delhi. They were a 'nuisance' to Nehru, who encountered them as he went to work every morning, but at least they made him 'think furiously of the problems' facing the refugees. In a typically Indian compromise, the refugees were allowed to build about 40 per cent of the houses, with the PWD constructing the rest.

In Faridabad, the ICU organized co-operatives and self-help groups, setting up shops and small production units. To power these, and to light up the homes, a diesel plant was erected at short notice. This plant lay in a shed in Calcutta, where it had come as part of German war reparations. No one wanted it in that city, so it was sent to Faridabad instead. Sudhir Ghosh located the German engineer who had built the plant in Hamburg, and persuaded him to come to India. The engineer came, but to his dismay no cranes were available to erect it. So he trained the Faridabad men to operate 15-tonne jack screws, which helped raise the equipment inch-by-inch. In ten months the plant was ready. In April 1951 Nehru himself came to commission it, and as he 'pressed the button, the lights came on and lifted the spirits of all in Faridabad. The township had power in its hands to fashion its industrial future.'[6]

Meanwhile, thousands of refugees had made their homes in Delhi itself. Till 1911 that city had been Muslim in character and culture. In that year, the British shifted their capital there from Calcutta. After 1947 New Delhi became the seat of the government of free India. Urdu-speaking Muslims went away to Pakistan, many unwillingly, while Punjabi-speaking Hindus and Sikhs arrived in their place. They set up house, and shop, wherever they could. In the middle of the city lay Connaught Circus, a majestic shopping arcade designed by R. T. Russell. Had Russell ever seen what became of his creation, he would perhaps have been 'spinning in his grave like a dervish'. In 1948 and 1949, 'stalls and push-carts of every size and shape' had been set up along the pavements. Thus, 'what was once a shaded walk where the shopper could stroll at leisure, inspecting the goods on offer and not meeting an insistent salesman, unless he or she went into a store, has become pandemonium . . . All in all, the exclusive shopping district of New Delhi, which in pre-independence days catered to the élite and wealthy, is now just a glorified bazaar.'[7]

Almost half a million refugees came to settle in Delhi after Partition. They flooded the city, 'spreading themselves out wherever they could. They thronged in camps, schools, colleges, temples, gurdwaras, dharamshalas, military barracks, and gardens. They squatted on railway platforms, streets, pavements, and every conceivable space.' In time, these squatters built houses on land allotted to them to the west and south of Lutyens's Delhi. Here rose colonies that to this day are dominated by Punjabis: nagars or townships named after Patel, Rajendra (Prasad) and Lajpat (Rai), Hindu Congress leaders they particularly admired.

Like their counterparts settled on the farms of East Punjab, the refugees in Delhi displayed much thrift and drive. In time they came to gain 'a commanding influence in Delhi', dominating its trade and commerce. Indeed, a city that was once a Mughal city, then a British city, had by the 1950s emphatically become a Punjabi city.[8]

III

Like Delhi, the city of Bombay also had its culture and social geography transformed by Partition. By July 1948 there were half a million refugees in the city, these arriving from Sindh, Punjab and the Frontier. The refugees further intensified what was already the most acute of Bombay's problems: the housing shortage. Almost a million people were now sleeping on the pavements. Slums were growing apace. In crowded tenements, people lived fifteen or twenty to a room.[9]

One journalist claimed that the total losses of Sindh refugees were Rs4,000–5,000 million, since back home they had owned large amounts of land, dominated the public services and controlled business and trade. Whereas the Punjabi refugees now had East Punjab as their own, to fulfil there 'the essentials of an independent corporate existence and the attributes of an autonomous Government', the Sindhis had nothing similar on which to rebuild.[10] Some looked beseechingly or angrily to the state; others took matters into their own hands. Thus, in Bombay, it was 'a sight to see even little Sindhi boys hawking pieces of cloth in the thoroughfares of the city. They have got salesmanship in their blood. That is why the Gujaratis and Maharashtrians have not taken kindly to the Sindhi invader. Even little urchins from the backwoods of Sind are able to make a living by selling trinkets in suburban trains.'[11]

There were five refugee camps in Bombay. Their condition left much to be desired. The Kolwada camp had 10,400 people living in barracks. The average space allotted to each family was thirty-six square feet. There were only twelve water taps in the entire camp, no doctors, only one school and no electricity. The place was run in dictatorial fashion by a man named Pratap Singh. In April 1950 a minor riot broke out when some tenants refused to pay rent, protesting their living conditions. Pratap Singh had them served with an eviction order, and when they resisted, called in the police. In the ensuing affray a young man was killed. The journalist reporting the story appropriately called the residents of the camp 'inmates'; as he noted, 'other inmates [were] huge cat-sized ugly rats, bugs, mosquitoes, and snakes'.[12]

The refugees from Sindh spread themselves across the towns and cities of western India. Apart from Bombay, there were substantial communities in Pune and Ahmedabad. A social psychologist visiting them in the autumn of 1950 found the Sindhis deeply dissatisfied. The 'complaints of crowded, filthy quarters, inadequate water, insufficient rations, and above all, insufficient support from the government, are almost universal'. A refugee in Ahmedabad said that 'we are eating stuff which we used to throw away in Pakistan for the birds to eat'. Others complained of ill treatment by the local Gujaratis, and were particularly hostile towards the Muslims. And they fulminated against the Indian state, although they exonerated Nehru himself. 'Our government is useless,' they said. 'All are thieves collected together. Only Pandit [Nehru] is all right; the rest are all worthless and self-serving. The Pandit himself says what he can do; the rest of the machinery does not work.'[13]

IV

The influx of refugees also transformed the landscape of India's third great metropolis, Calcutta. Before Partition, the more prosperous Hindu families of eastern Bengal had begun moving with their assets to the city. After Partition the immigration was chiefly of working-class and farming families. Unlike in the Punjab, where the exodus happened in one big rush, in Bengal it was spread out. However, in the winter of 1949–50 there was a wave of communal riots in East Pakistan which forced many more Hindus across the border. In previous years about 400,000 refugees came into West Bengal; in 1950 the number jumped to 1.7 million.

Where did these people seek refuge? Those who could, stayed with relatives. Others made a home on the city's railway stations, where their beds, boxes and other accessories lay spread out on the platform. Here 'families lived, slept, mated, defecated and ate on the concrete amidst flies, lice, infants and diarrhoea. Victims of cholera would lie exhausted staring at their vomit, women were kept busy delousing each other, beggars begged.' Still others lived on the street, 'with the stray cattle, like the stray cattle, drinking gutter-water, eating garbage, sleeping on the curb . . .'[14]

So wrote the *Manchester Guardian* correspondent in India. In truth, the refugees were a good deal less passive than this description suggests.

Early in 1948 a 'large number of refugees, disgusted with their miserable existence at Sealdah station, occupied the Lake military barracks, Jodhpur military barracks, the Mysore House and other large unoccupied houses and military barracks at Shahpur, Durgapur, Ballygunge Circular Road and Dharmatala. Almost overnight these deserted houses swarmed with refugee men, women and children. These were deliberate acts of trespass.'[15]

Where some refugees took possession of empty houses, others colonized vacant land along roads and railway lines, as well as freshly cleared shrub jungle and recently drained marshes. The squatters 'would stealthily enter these plots at night, and under cover of darkness rapidly put up makeshift shelters. They would then refuse to leave, while offering in many instances to pay a fair price for the land.'[16]

It was the government of West Bengal that willy-nilly forced the refugees to take the law into their own hands. For one thing, there had been no massive migration in the other direction – as there had been in the Punjab – leaving untended fields and farms for the refugees to be settled in. For another, the government liked to believe – or hope – that this influx was temporary, and that when things settled down the Hindus would return to their homes in the east. Buttressing this belief was the claim that the Bengalis were somehow less 'communal-minded' than the Punjabis. Here, the Muslim spoke the same language and ate the same food as his Hindu neighbour; thus he might more readily continue to live cheek-by-jowl with him.

This latter argument was vigorously rejected by the refugees themselves. For them there was no going back to what they saw as an Islamic state. They found support for their views in the person of the historian Sir Jadunath Sarkar, arguably the most influential Bengali intellectual of his generation. Addressing a mammoth public meeting of refugees, held on 16 August 1948, Sir Jadunath compared the migration of East Bengal Hindus to the flight of French Huguenots in the time of Louis XIV. He urged the people of West Bengal to absorb and integrate the migrants, thus to nourish their culture and economy. With the help of the refugees, said the historian, 'we must make our West Bengal what Palestine under Jewish Rule will be, a light in darkness, an oasis of civilisation in the desert of medieval ignorance and obsolete theocratic bigotry'.[17]

In September 1948 an All-Bengal Refugee Council of Action was formed. Marches and demonstrations were organized demanding that the refugees be given fair compensation and citizenship rights. The leaders of the movement aimed to throw 'regimented bands of refugees in the streets of Calcutta and to maintain a relentless pressure on the Government . . . Processions, demonstrations and meetings, traffic jams, brickbats and teargas shells and *lathis* [bamboo sticks used by the police as weapons] coming down in showers, burning tramcars and buses, and occasional firings – these became the hallmark of the city.'[18]

Displaced from their homes by forces outside their control, refugees everywhere are potential fodder for extremist movements. In Delhi and the Punjab it was the radical Hindu organization, the Rashtriya Swayamsevak Sangh, that very early on got a foothold among the migrants. In Bengal the RSS's sister organization, the Hindu Mahasabha, also worked hard at giving a religious colour to the problem. The Bengali Hindus, they said, 'have been made sacrificial goats in the great Yajna of India's freedom'. In asking them to return to East Pakistan, the government was guilty of 'appeasement' and of abetting 'genocide'. While the state asked them to submit, what the refugees needed was a stiff dose of 'the virility of man'. 'One only wishes', wrote one angry Hindu in March 1950, that 'a Shivaji or a Rana Pratap emerged from their ranks'.[19]

This invocation of medieval Hindu warriors who had fought Muslim kings found more takers in Delhi and the Punjab. In Bengal, however, it was the communists who most successfully mobilized the refugees. It was they who organized the processions to government offices, and it was they who orchestrated the forcible occupation of fallow land in Calcutta, land to which the refugees 'had no sanction other than organized strength and dire necessity'. Thus in different parts of the city grew numerous impromptu settlements, 'clusters of huts with thatch, tile or corrugated-iron roofs, bamboo-mat walls and mud floors, built in the East Bengal style'.[20]

By early 1950 there were about 200,000 refugees in these squatter colonies. In the absence of state support, the refugees 'formed committees of their own, framed rules for the administration of the colonies and organised themselves into a vast united body'.[21] A 'South Calcutta Refugee Rehabilitation Committee' claimed to represent 40,000 families who, in their respective colonies, had constructed a total of 500 miles of road, sunk 700 tube wells and started 45 high schools as well as 100 primary schools – all at their own expense and through their own initiative. The Committee demanded that the government make these colonies 'legal' by formally bringing them under the Calcutta Municipality, that it similarly regularize private plots and school buildings, and help develop markets and arrange loans.[22]

Those who spoke for these migrants frequently complained about the preferential treatment given to the Punjabi refugees. A team of Bengali social workers visiting north India found the camps there 'of a superior kind'. The houses were permanent, with running water and adequate sanitation; whereas in West Bengal the refugees had to make do with 'decaying bamboo hutments' where 'lack of privacy and of kitchen space is notorious'. Cash and clothing allowances were also higher in the north.[23]

On the whole, the resettlement process was far less painful in the Punjab. By the early 1950s the refugees in the north had found new homes and new jobs. But in the east the insecurity persisted. So long as the Bengali refugees remained 'unsettled and unemployed', wrote one correspondent in July 1954, 'economic and political discontent will grow; the Communists will succeed in exploiting their grievances'.[24]

V

Unquestionably the main victims of Partition were women: Hindu, Sikh, and Muslim. As the respected Sindhi Congress politician Choitram Gidwani put it, 'in no war have the women suffered so much'. Women were killed, maimed, violated and abandoned. After Independence the brothels of Delhi and Bombay came to be filled with refugee women, who had been thrown out by their families after what someone else had done to them – against their will.[25]

In the summer of 1947, as the violence in the Punjab spread from village to village, Hindus and Sikhs in the east of the province abducted and kept Muslim women. On the other side the compliment – if it may be called that – was returned, with young Hindu and Sikh girls seized by Muslim men. However, after the dust had settled down and the blood dried, the governments of India and Pakistan agreed that these captured women must be returned to their original families.

On the Indian side, the operation to recover abducted women was led by Mridula Sarabhai and Rameshwari Nehru. Both came from aristocratic homes and both had sturdily nationalist credentials. Their work was encouraged and aided by Jawaharlal Nehru, who took a deep personal interest in the process. In a radio broadcast to the refugees, the prime minister spoke especially 'to those women who are the victims of all these hardships'. He assured them that 'they should not feel that we have any hesitation whatsoever in bringing them back or that we have any doubts about their virtue. We want to bring them back with affection because it had not been their fault. They were forcefully abducted and we want to bring them back respectfully and keep them lovingly. They must not doubt that they will come back to their families and be given all possible help.'[26]

The abducted women were tracked down singly, case by case. When a person had been located, the police would enter the village at sunset, after the men had returned from the fields. An 'informer' would lead them to the home of the abductor. The offender would usually deny that the woman in his possession had been seized. After his objections were overcome – sometimes by force – the woman would be taken away, at first to a government camp, and then across the border.[27]

By May 1948 some 12,500 women had been found and restored to their families. Ironically, and tragically, many of the women did not want to be rescued at all. For after their seizure they had made some kind of peace with their new surroundings. Now, as they were being reclaimed, these women were deeply unsure about how their original families would receive them. They had been 'defiled' and, in a further complication, many were pregnant. These women knew that even if they were accepted, their children – born out of a union with the 'enemy' – would never be. Often, the police and their accomplices had to use force to take them away. 'You could not save us then,' said the women, 'what right have you to compel us now?'[28]

VI

Compounding the refugee crisis were serious shortages of food. After the end of the war imports of grain were steadily on the rise, increasing from 0.8 million tons (mt) in 1944 to 2.8 mt four years later. On the eve of Independence a politician travelling through the district of East Godavari found men and women surviving on tamarind seeds, palmyra fruits, and the bark of the *jeelugu* tree – these boiled together into gruel, eating which led to bloated stomachs, diarrhoea and sometimes death.

The following year the rains failed in the western province of Gujarat, leading to acute water and fodder scarcity. Wells and river beds ran dry, and cattle and goats died of hunger and disease.[29]

In some places farmers were starving; in other places they were restive. In the uncertainty following the Indian takeover of Hyderabad, the communists moved swiftly to assume control of the Telengana region. They were aided by a pile of .303 rifles and Mark V guns left behind by the retreating Razakars. The communists destroyed the palatial homes of landlords and distributed their land to tillers of the soil. Dividing themselves into several *dalams*, or groups, each responsible for a number of villages, the communists asked peasants not to pay land revenue, and enforced law and order themselves.[30] In districts such as Warangal and Nalgonda, their work at getting rid of feudalism won the Reds much support. A Congress politician visiting the area admitted that 'every housewife silently rendered valuable assistance to the communists. Innocent looking villagers extended active sympathy to [them].'[31]

Their successes in Hyderabad had encouraged the communists to think of a countrywide peasant revolution. Telengana, they hoped, would be the beginning of a Red India. The party unveiled its new line at a secret conference held in Calcutta in February 1948. The mood was set by a speaker who said that the 'heroic people of Telengana' had shown the way 'to freedom and real democracy'; they were the 'real future of India and Pakistan'. If only the communist cadres could 'create this spirit of revolution among the masses, among the toiling people, we shall find reaction collapsing like a house of cards'.[32]

At the Calcutta meeting, the party elected a new general secretary, with P. C. Joshi giving way to B. T. Ranadive. By character, Ranadive was solemn and studious, unlike the playful and likeable Joshi. (Both, notably, were upper-caste Hindus – as was typical of communist leaders of the day.)[33]

Joshi was a friend of Nehru who urged 'loyal opposition' to the ruling Congress Party. He argued that after the murder of Gandhi the survival of free India was at stake. He supervised the production of a party pamphlet whose title proclaimed, *We Shall Defend the Nehru Government* (against the forces of Hindu revivalism). Ranadive, however, was a hardliner who believed that India was controlled by a bourgeois government that was beholden to the imperialists. Now, in a complete about-turn, the party described Nehru as a lackey of American imperialism. The pamphlet printed by the former general secretary was pulped. Joshi himself was demoted to a status of an ordinary member and a whole series of charges were levelled against him. He was dubbed a reformist who had encouraged the growth of 'anti-revolutionary' tendencies in the party.[34]

The new line of the Communist Party of India held that Nehru's government had joined the Anglo-American alliance in an 'irreconcilable conflict' with the 'democratic camp' led by the Soviet Union. The scattered disillusionment with the Congress was taken by B. T. Ranadive as a sign of a 'mounting revolutionary upsurge'. From his underground hideout he called for a general strike and peasant uprisings across the country. Communist circulars urged their cadres to 'fraternize with the revolutionary labourers in the factories and the students in the streets', and to 'turn your guns and bayonets and fire upon the Congress fascists'. The ultimate aim was to 'destroy the murderous Congress government'.[35]

Ranadive and his men took heart from the victory of the communists in China. In September 1949, shortly after Mao Zedong had come to power, Ranadive wrote him a letter of congratulation, saying that 'the toiling masses of India feel jubilant over this great victory. They know it hastens their own liberation. They are inspired by it to fight more determinedly and courageously their battle for ending the present regime [in India] and establishing the rule of People's Democracy.'[36] The Indian communists were also egged on by Russian theoreticians, who believed that 'the political regime established in India is similar in many respects to the anti-popular, reactionary regime which existed in Kuomintang China'.[37] The Soviet embassy in Delhi itself had a large staff, such that (in the words of a senior civil servant) the Indian 'communist movement [was] receiving first-class direction on the spot'.[38]

The communists had declared war on the Indian state. The government responded with all the force at its command. As many as 50,000 party men and sympathizers were arrested and detained. In Hyderabad the police arrested important leaders of communist *dalams*, although Ravi Narayan Reddy, 'the father of the Communist movement in Deccan, [was] still at large'. The military governor, J. N. Chaudhuri, launched a propaganda war against the communists. Telugu pamphlets dropped on the villages announced that the Nizam's private Crown lands would be distributed to the peasantry. Theatrical companies touring the villages presented the government case through drama and pantomime.

In one play, Chaudhuri was portrayed as a Hindu deity; the communists, as demons.[39]

The propaganda and the repression had its effect. The membership of the party dropped from 89,000 in 1948 to a mere 20,000 two years later. The government's counter-offensive had exposed the 'lack of popular empathy it experienced for its unbridled revolutionism'. It appears the party had grossly underestimated the hold of the Congress over the Indian people.[40]

Even as the communists were losing their influence, a band of extremists was gathering strength on the right. This was the Rashtriya Swayamsevak Sangh. After the murder of Mahatma Gandhi in January 1948, the RSS was banned by the government. Although not directly involved in the assassination, the organization had been active in the Punjab violence, and had much support among disaffected refugees. Their worldview was akin to Nathuram Godse's, and it was widely rumoured that RSS men had privately celebrated his killing of the Mahatma. Writing to the Punjab government two weeks after Gandhi's death, Nehru said that 'we have had enough suffering already in India because of the activities of the R.S.S. and like groups . . . These people have the blood of Mahatma Gandhi on their hands, and pious disclaimers and disassociation now have no meaning.'[41]

So the RSS was banned, and its cadres arrested. However, after a year the government decided to make the organization legal once more. Its head, M. S. Golwalkar, had now agreed to ask his men to profess loyalty to the Constitution of India and the national flag, and to restrict the Sangh's activities 'to the cultural sphere abjuring violence or secrecy'. The RSS chief promised the home minister, Vallabhbhai Patel, that 'while rendering help to the people in distress, we have laid our emphasis on promoting peace in the country'. Patel himself had mixed feelings about the RSS. While deploring their anti-Muslim rhetoric he admired their dedication and discipline. In lifting the ban on the Sangh, he advised them 'that the only way for them is to reform the Congress from within, if they think the Congress is going on the wrong path'.[42]

After the RSS was made legal, Golwalkar made a 'triumphal' speaking tour across the country, drawing 'mammoth crowds'. The Sangh, wrote one observer, 'has emerged from its recent ordeal with a mass support that other parties, not excluding the Congress, might well envy and guard against, while it is yet time, unless they wish to see the country delivered to a Hindu irredentism that will lead it to certain disaster'. The RSS was the Hindu answer to the Muslim League, 'imbued with aggressively communal ideas, and with the determination that there must be no compromise with the ideal of a pure and predominant Hindu culture in Bharat-Varsh'.[43]

Like the communist B. T. Ranadive, Golwalkar was an upper-caste Maharashtrian. Both men were relatively young – in their early forties – and both commanded the loyalty of hundreds of cadres a good deal younger than themselves. The RSS and the communists likewise drew upon the energy and idealism of youth, and upon its fanaticism too. In the early years of Indian independence, these two groups were the most motivated opponents of the ruling Congress Party.

At the helm of the Congress was the Prime Minister, Jawaharlal Nehru. In confronting the radicals of left and right, Nehru faced two major handicaps. First, he was a moderate, and the middle ground is generally not conducive to the kind of stirring rhetoric that compels men to act. Second, he and his colleagues were far older than their political rivals. In 1949 Nehru himself was sixty, an age at which a Hindu male is supposed to retire from the workaday world and take *sanyas*.

Nehru saw the RSS as the greater of the two threats. Others in his government, notably Vallabhbhai Patel, disagreed. Intriguingly, M. S. Golwalkar had written to Patel offering help in battling the common enemy – the communists. 'If we utilize the power of your government and the cultural strength of our organization', he wrote, 'we will be able to get rid of the [Red] menace very soon.'[44] This idea of a joint front appealed to Patel; indeed, it may have been one reason he contemplated absorbing the RSS within the Congress.

In the event, members of the RSS were not admitted into the Congress. But Golwalkar remained at large, free to propagate his views to those who chose to hear them. In the first week of November 1949, the RSS chief addressed a crowd of 100,000 in Bombay's Shivaji Park. A reporter in attendance described him as 'a man of medium height with a sunken chest, long uncut and unkempt hair and a flowing beard'. He looked for all the world like a harmless Hindu ascetic, except that 'the black piercing eyes deep in the sockets gave the [RSS] Chief the typical look of a black magician about to pull out a blood-curdling trick.' Before he spoke, Golwalkar was presented with garlands by clubs specializing in body-building and the martial arts. The speech itself 'waxed hot' on the virtues of Hindu culture. As the reporter put it:

'He had a cure-all for the ills of the nation: Make Golwalkar the Führer of All India'.[45]

A week later Jawaharlal Nehru came to speak in Bombay. The venue was the same as for Golwalkar: Shivaji Park, that oasis of green grass in the heart of the densely packed, middle-class, chiefly Marathi-speaking housing colonies of central Bombay. Nehru used the same microphone as Golwalkar, this supplied by the Motwane Chicago Telephone and Radio Company. But his message was emphatically different, for he spoke of the need to maintain social peace within India as well as peace between warring nations abroad.

Nehru's talk was delivered on his sixtieth birthday, 14 November 1949. He could not have wished for a better present: the abundant affection of his countrymen. The prime minister was due to arrive in Bombay at 4.30 p.m. An hour before his plane landed at Santa Cruz airport, 'people started closing their shops and stopped working so that they might be able to see Pandit Nehru. They jammed the sidewalks and the streets long before the open maroon car carrying Panditji sped by. As he passed by a tumultuous waving and rejoicing was noticed.'

An hour later, after a wash and a change, Nehru arrived at Shivaji Park. Here, 'a record crowd [had] stampeded the vast maidan grounds to hear him. More than six lakhs [600,000] assembled that memorable evening. There was one seething mass of humanity; men, women and children who had come . . . to hear him for they still had faith in his leadership and ability to show the way in these hard and trying times ahead of us.'[46]

A hundred thousand people had come to hear Golwalkar espouse the idea of a Hindu theocratic state for India. But in this Maharashtrian stronghold, six times as many came to cheer the prime minister's defence of democracy against absolutism, and secularism against Hindu chauvinism. In this contest between competing ideas of India, Jawaharlal Nehru was winning hands down; for the time being, at any rate.

VII

Like the integration of the princely states, the rehabilitation of refugees was a political problem unprecedented in nature and scope. The migrants into India from Pakistan, wrote one of their number, were 'like the fallen autumn leaves in the wind or bits of stray newspaper flying hither and thither in the blown dust'. For 'those who have come away safe in limb and mind are without any bearings and without any roots'.[47]

The refugees who came into India after Independence numbered close to 8 million. This was greater than the populations of small European countries such as Austria and Norway, and as many as lived in the colossal continent of Australia. These people were resettled with time, cash, effort and, not least, idealism.

There was indeed much heroism and grandeur in the building of a new India. There were also errors and mistakes, loose ends that remained untied. There was pain and suffering in the extinguishing of the princely order, and there was pain and suffering in the resettlement of the refugees. Yet both tasks were, in the end, accomplished.

Notably, the actors in this complicated and tortuous process were all Indian. This, at least on the British side, was completely unanticipated. A former governor of Bengal had written in 1947 of how

> The end of British political control in India will not mean the departure of the British, as individuals, from India. It will not be possible for many years ahead for India to do without a large number of British individuals in government service. They will remain under contract to the Government of India and to the governments of the Provinces and States in a wide range of administrative, legal, medical, police and professional and technical appointments. It will be many years before India will be able to fill, from amongst her own sons, all the many senior positions under the government that the administration of her 400 million people makes necessary.[48]

In the event, that help was not asked for, nor was it needed. Admittedly, the rulers had left behind a set of functioning institutions: the civil service and the police, the judiciary and the railways, among others. At Independence, the government of India invited British members of the ICS to stay on; with but the odd exception, they all left for home, along with their colleagues in the other services. Thus it came to be that the heroes remembered in these pages were all Indians – whether politicians like Nehru and Patel, bureaucrats like Tarlok Singh and V. P. Menon, or social workers like Kamaladevi Chattopadhyaya and Mridula Sarabhai. So too were the countless others who were unnamed then and continue to be unknown now: the officials who took in and acted upon applications for land allotment, the officials who built the houses and ran the hospitals and schools, the officials who sat in courts and secretariats. Also overwhelmingly Indian were the social workers who cajoled, consoled and cared for the refugees.

An American architect who worked in India in the early years of Independence has written with feeling of the calibre and idealism of those around him. 'The number and kinds of people I've seen,' wrote Albert Mayer, 'their ability, outlook, energy, and devotion; the tingling atmosphere of plans and expectation and uncertainty; and yet the calm and self-possession – what it adds up to is being present at the birth of a nation.'[49]

In the history of nation-building only the Soviet experiment bears comparison with the Indian. There too, a sense of unity had to be forged between many diverse ethnic groups, religions, linguistic communities and social classes. The scale – geographic as well as demographic – was comparably massive. The raw material the state had to work with was equally unpropitious: a people divided by faith and riven by debt and disease.

India after the Second World War was much like the Soviet Union after the First. A nation was being built out of its fragments. In this case, however, the process was unaided by the extermination of class enemies or the creation of gulags.

6

IDEAS OF INDIA

In Governance is realised all the forms of renunciation; in Governance is united all the sacraments; in Governance is combined all knowledge; in Governance is centred all the Worlds.

The Mahabharata

Constitutional morality is not a natural sentiment. It has to be cultivated. We must realize that our people have yet to learn it. Democracy in India is only a top-dressing on an Indian soil, which is essentially undemocratic.

B. R. AMBEDKAR

I

WITH 395 ARTICLES AND 12 schedules the constitution of India is probably the longest in the world. Coming into effect in January 1950, it was framed over a period of three years, between December 1946 and December 1949. During this time its drafts were discussed clause by clause in the Constituent Assembly of India. In all, the Assembly held eleven sessions, whose sittings consumed 165 days. In between the sessions the work of revising and refining the drafts was carried out by various committees and sub-committees.

The proceedings of the Constituent Assembly of India were printed in eleven bulky volumes. These volumes – some of which exceed 1,000 pages – are testimony to the loquaciousness of Indians, but also to their insight, intelligence, passion and sense of humour. These volumes are a little-known treasure-trove, invaluable to the historian, but also a potential source of enlightenment to the interested citizen. In them we find many competing ideas of the nation, of what language it should speak, what political and economic systems it should follow, what moral values it should uphold or disavow.

II

From the early 1930s the Congress had insisted that Indians would frame their own constitution. In 1946 Lord Wavell finally gave in to the demand. The members of the Assembly were chosen on the basis of that year's provincial elections. However, the Muslim League chose to boycott the early sittings, making it effectively a one-party forum.

The first meeting of the Constituent Assembly was held on 9 December 1946. A sense of anticipation was in the air. The leading Congress members, such as Nehru and Patel, sat on the front benches. But to demonstrate that it was not merely a Congress Party show, known opponents such as Sarat Bose of Bengal were given seats alongside them. A nationalist newspaper noted that 'nine women members were present, adding colour' to a scene dominated by Gandhi caps and Nehru jackets.[1]

Apart from the members sent by the provinces of British India, the Constituent Assembly also had representatives of the princely states, sent as these states joined the Union one by one. Eighty-two per cent of Assembly members were also members of the Congress. However, since the party was itself a broad church they held a wide range of views. Some were atheists and secularists, others 'technically members of the Congress but spiritually members of the RSS and the Hindu Mahasabha'.[2] Some were socialists in their economic philosophy, others defenders of the rights of landlords. Aside from the diversity within it, the Congress also nominated independent members of different caste and religious groups and ensured the representation of women. It particularly sought out experts in the law. In the event 'there was hardly any shade of public opinion not represented in the Assembly'.[3]

This expansion of the social base of the Assembly was in part an answer to British criticism. Winston Churchill in particular had poured scorn on the idea of a Constituent Assembly dominated by 'one major community in India', the caste Hindus. In his view the Congress was not a truly representative party, but rather a mouthpiece of 'actively organised and engineered minorities who, having seized upon power by force, or fraud or chicanery, go forward and use that power in the name of vast masses with whom they have long since lost all effective connection'.[4]

The process was made more participatory by asking for submissions from the public at large. There were hundreds of responses, a sampling of which gives a clue to the interests the law-makers had to take account of. Thus the All-India Varnashrama Swarajya Sangh (based in Calcutta) asked that the constitution 'be based on the principles laid down in ancient Hindu works'. The prohibition of cow-slaughter and the closing down of abbatoirs was particularly recommended. Low-caste groups demanded an end to their 'ill treatment by upper-caste people' and 'reservation of separate seats on the basis of their population in legislature, government departments, and local bodies, etc.'. Linguistic minorities asked for 'freedom of speech in [the] mother tongue' and the 'redistribution of provinces on linguistic basis'. Religious minorities asked for special safeguards. And bodies as varied as the District Teachers Guild of Vizianagaram and the Central Jewish Board of Bombay requested 'adequate representation . . . on all public bodies including legislatures etc.'.[5]

These submissions testify to the baffling heterogeneity of India, but also to the precocious existence of a rights culture among Indians. They were many; they were divided; above all, they were vocal. The Constitution of India had to adjudicate among thousands of competing claims and demands. The task was made no easier by the turmoil of the times. The Assembly met between 1946 and 1949, against a backdrop of food scarcity, religious riots, refugee resettlement, class war and feudal intransigence. As one historian of the process has put it, 'Fundamental Rights were to be framed amidst the carnage of Fundamental Wrongs'.[6]

III

The Constituent Assembly had more than 300 members. In his magisterial history of the Indian Constitution, Granville Austin identifies twenty as being the most influential. Of these, as many as twelve had law degrees, including the Congress stalwarts Jawaharlal Nehru, Vallabhbhai Patel and Rajendra Prasad.

Nehru's first major speech in the Assembly was on 13 December 1946, when he moved the Objectives Resolution. This proclaimed India as an 'independent sovereign republic', guaranteeing its citizens 'justice, social, economic and political; equality of status; of opportunity, and before the law; freedom of thought, expression, belief, faith, worship, vocation, association and action, subject to law and public morality' – all this while assuring that 'adequate safeguards shall be provided for minorities, backward and tribal areas, and depressed and other backward classes . . .' In moving the resolution, Nehru invoked the spirit of Gandhi and the 'great past of India', as well as modern precedents such as the French, American and Russian revolutions.[7]

Nine months later Nehru spoke again in that columned hall, at the midnight hour, when he asked Indians to redeem their tryst with destiny. In between, on 22 July 1947, he had moved a resolution proposing that the national flag of India be a 'horizontal tricolour of saffron, white and dark green in equal proportion', with a wheel in navy blue at the centre. On this occasion Nehru led a chorus of competitive patriotism, with each subsequent speaker seeking to see in the colours of the flag something special about his own community's contribution to India.[8]

The speeches of symbolic importance were naturally made by Nehru. Just as naturally, the bulk of the back-room work was done by Vallabhbhai Patel. A consummate committee man, he played a key role in the drafting of the various reports. It was Patel, rather than the less-patient Nehru, who worked at mediating between warring groups, taking recalcitrant members with him on his morning walks and making them see the larger point of view. It was also Patel who moved one of the more contentious resolutions: that pertaining to minority rights.[9]

The third Congress member of importance was the president of the Assembly, Rajendra Prasad. He was nominated to the office on the day after the Assembly was inaugurated and held it with dignity until the end of its term. His was an unenviable task, for Indians are better speakers than listeners, and Indian politicians especially so. Prasad had to keep the peace between quarrelsome members and (just as difficult) keep to the clock men who sometimes had little sense of what was trifling and what significant.

Outside this Congress trinity the most crucial member of the Assembly was the brilliant low-caste lawyer B. R. Ambedkar. Ambedkar was law minister in the Union government; and also chairman of the Drafting Committee of the Indian Constitution. Serving with him were two other formidable minds: K. M. Munshi, a Gujarati polymath who was a novelist and lawyer as well as freedom fighter, and Alladi Krishnaswami Aiyar, a Tamil who for fifteen years had served as advocate general to the Madras presidency.

To these six men one must add a seventh who was not a member of the Assembly at all. This was B. N. Rau, who served as constitutional adviser to the government of India. In a long career in the Indian Civil Service Rau had a series of legal appointments. Using his learning and experience, and following a fresh study-tour of Western democracies, Rau prepared a series of notes for Ambedkar and his team to chew upon. Rau, in turn, was assisted by the chief draughtsman, S. N. Mukherjee, whose 'ability to put the most intricate proposals in the simplest and clearest legal form can rarely be equalled'.[10]

IV

Moral vision, political skill, legal acumen: these were all brought together in the framing of the Indian Constitution. This was a coming together of what Granville Austin has called the 'national' and 'social' revolutions respectively.[11] The national revolution focused on democracy and liberty – which the experience of colonial rule had denied to all Indians – whereas the social revolution focused on emancipation and equality, which tradition and scripture had withheld from women and low castes.

Could these twin revolutions be brought about by indigenous methods? Some advocated a 'Gandhian constitution', based on a revived *panchayati raj* system of village councils, with the village as the basic unit of politics and governance. This was sharply attacked by B. R. Ambedkar, who held that 'these village republics have been the ruination of India'. Ambedkar was 'surprised that those who condemn Provincialism and communalism should come forward as champions of the village. What is the village but a sink of localism, a den of ignorance, narrow-mindedness and communalism?'[12]

These remarks provoked outrage in some quarters. The socialist H. V. Kamath dismissed Ambedkar's attitude as 'typical of the urban highbrow'. The peasant leader N. G. Ranga said that Ambedkar's comments only showed his ignorance of Indian history. 'All the democratic traditions of our country has [sic] been lost on him. If he had only known the achievements of the village panchayats in Southern India over a period of a millennium, he would not have said those things.'[13]

However, the feisty female member from the United Provinces, Begum Aizaz Rasul, 'entirely agreed' with Dr Ambedkar. As she saw it, the 'modern tendency is towards the rights of the citizen as against any corporate body and village *panchayats* can be very autocratic'.[14]

Ultimately it was the individual, rather than the village, that was chosen as the unit. In other respects, too, the constitution was to look towards Euro-American rather than Indian precedents. The American presidential system was considered and rejected, as was the Swiss method of directly electing Cabinet ministers. Several members argued for proportional representation (PR), but this was never taken very seriously. Another former British colony, Ireland, had adopted PR, but when the constitutional adviser, B. N. Rau, visited Dublin, Eamon de Valera himself told him that he wished the Irish had adopted the British 'first-past-the-post' system of elections and the British cabinet system. This, he felt, made for a strong government. In India, where the number of competing interest groups was immeasurably larger, it made even more sense to follow the British model.[15] The lower house of Parliament, as well as the lower houses of the provinces, were to be chosen on the basis of universal adult franchise. After much discussion Parliament, as well as most provinces, decided also to have a second chamber to act as a check on the excesses of democratic zeal. Its members were chosen through indirect election, in the case of the Upper House of Parliament by the state legislatures.

While the Cabinet was headed by a prime minister, the head of state was a president elected by a college comprising the national and provincial legislatures. The president would be the commander-in-chief of the armed forces, and had the power to refer bills back to Parliament. This was a position of 'great authority and dignity', but, like those of the British monarchy, one with 'no real power'.[16] (In the provinces a governor nominated by the 'centre' (as central government was coming to be known) played a role comparable to the president's.) The constitution provided for an independent election commission, and an independent comptroller general of accounts. To protect the judiciary from party politics, judges were to be appointed by the president in consultation with the chief justice, while their salaries were not decided by Parliament but charged directly to the Treasury. The Supreme Court in Delhi was seen both as the guardian of the social revolution and as the guarantor of civil and minority rights. It was endowed with broad appellate jurisdiction – any civil or criminal case could be referred to it so long as it involved an interpretation of the constitution.

The constitution mandated for a complex system of fiscal federalism. In the case of some taxes (for instance customs duties and company taxes) the centre retained all the proceeds; in other cases (such as income taxes and excise duties) it shared them with the states; in still other cases (e.g. estate duties) it assigned them wholly to the states. The states, meanwhile, could levy and collect certain taxes on their own: these included land and property taxes, sales tax, and the hugely profitable tax on bottled liquor.

These financial provisions borrowed heavily from the Government of India Act of 1935. The 'conscience of the constitution',[17] meanwhile, was contained in Parts III and IV, which outlined a series of fundamental rights and directive principles. The fundamental rights, which were enforceable in a court of law, derived from the obligations of the state not to encroach upon or stifle personal liberty, and to protect individuals and groups from arbitrary state action. The rights defined included freedom and equality before the law, the cultural rights of minorities, and the prohibition of such practices as untouchability and forced labour.[18] The directive principles, which were not justiciable, derived from the positive obligations of the state to provide for a more fulfilling life for the citizen. They were a curious amalgam of contending pulls. Some principles were a concession to the socialist wing of the Congress, others (such as the ban on cow-slaughter) to the party's conservative faction.[19]

To the unprejudiced eye the constitution was an adaptation of Western principles to Indian ends. Some patriots did not see it that way. They claimed that it was Indians who had invented adult suffrage. T. Prakasam spoke about an inscription on a 1,000-year-old Conjeevaram temple which talked of an election held with leaves as ballot papers and pots as ballot boxes.[20] This kind of chauvinism was not the preserve of the south alone. The Hindi scholar Raghu Vira claimed that ancient India was 'the originator of the Republican system of government', and 'spread this system to the other parts of the world'.[21]

Those who had looked closely at the provisions of the constitution could not thus console themselves. Mahavir Tyagi was 'very much disappointed [to] see nothing Gandhian in this Constitution'.[22] And K. Hanumanthaiya complained that while freedom fighters like himself had wanted 'the music of *Veena* or *Sitar*', what they had got instead was 'the music of an English band'.[23]

V

The Constitution of India sought both to promote national unity and to facilitate progressive social change. There was a fundamental right to propagate religion, but the state reserved to itself the right to impose legislation oriented towards social reform (such as a uniform civil code). The centre had the powers, through national planning, to redistribute resources away from richer provinces to poorer ones. The right of due process was not allowed in property legislation, another instance in which the social good as defined by the state took precedence over individual rights. Land-reform laws were on the anvil in many provinces, and the government wanted to close the door to litigation by disaffected moneylenders and landlords.

Fundamental rights were qualified and limited by needs of social reform, and also by considerations of security and public order. There were provisions for rights to be suspended in times of 'national emergency'. And there was a clause allowing for 'preventive detention' without trial. A veteran freedom fighter called this 'the darkest blot on this constitution'. Having spent ten years of his own life in 'dungeons and condemned cells in the days of our slavery under the British', he knew 'the tortures which detention without trial means and I can never reconcile myself to it'.[24]

The constitution showed a certain bias towards the rights of the Union of India over those of its constituent states. There was already a unitary system in place, imposed by the colonial power. The violence of the times gave a further push to centralization, now seen as necessary both to forestall chaos and to plan for the country's economic development.

The constitution provided for three areas of responsibility: union, state and concurrent. The subjects in the first list were the preserve of the central government while those in the second list were vested with the states. As for the third list, here centre and state shared responsibility. However, many more items were placed under exclusive central control than in other federations, and more placed on the concurrent list too than desired by the provinces. The centre also had control of minerals and key industries. And Article 356 gave it the power to take over a state administration on the recommendation of the governor.[25]

Provincial politicians fought hard for the rights of states, for fewer items to be put on the concurrent and union lists. They asked for a greater share of tax revenues and they mounted an ideological attack on the principle itself. A member from Orissa said that the constitution had 'so centralised power, that I am afraid, due to its very weight, the Centre is likely to break'. A member from Mysore thought that what was proposed was a 'unitary' rather than 'federal' constitution. Under its provisions 'democracy is centred in Delhi and it is not allowed to work in the same sense and spirit in the rest of the country'.[26]

Perhaps the most eloquent defence of states' rights came from K. Santhanam of Madras. He thought that the fiscal provisions would make provinces 'beggars at the door of the Centre'. In the United States, both centre and state could levy 'all kinds of tax', but here, crucial sources of revenue, such as the income tax, had been denied the provinces. Besides, the Drafting Committee had tried 'to burden the Centre with all kinds of powers which it ought not to have'. These included 'vagrancy', which had been taken away from the states list and put on the concurrent list. 'Do you want all India to be bothered about vagrants?' asked Santhanam sarcastically. As he put it, rather than place an excessive load on the Union government, 'the initial responsibility for the well-being of the people of the provinces should rest with the Provincial Governments'.[27]

The next day a member from the United Provinces answered these charges. Hearing Santhanam, he wondered whether it was not 'India's age-old historical tendency of disintegrating that was speaking through these stalwarts'. A strong centre was an absolute imperative in these 'times of stress and strain'. Only a strong centre would 'be in a position to think and plan for the well-being of the country as a whole'.[28]

Members of the Drafting Committee vigorously defended the unitary bias of the constitution. In an early session B. R. Ambedkar told the House that he wanted 'a strong united centre (*hear, hear*) much stronger than the centre we had created under the Government of India Act of 1935'.[29] And K. M. Munshi argued for the construction of 'a federation with a centre as strong as we can make it'.[30] In some matters Munshi was close to being a Hindu chauvinist; but here he found himself on the same side as the Muslims. For the horrific communal violence of 1946 and 1947 bore witness to the need for a strong centre. In the words of Kazi Syed Karimuddin, 'everybody is not Pandit Jawaharlal Nehru' (in respect of his commitment to inter-religious harmony). There were 'weak and vacillating executives in all the Provinces', said the *kazi*. Thus 'what we want today is a stable Government. What we want today is a patriotic

Government. What we want today is a strong Government, an impartial and unbending executive, that does not bow before popular whims.'[31]

VI

Much attention was paid by the Assembly to the rights of the minorities. The first extended discussion of the subject took place a bare ten days after Partition. Here, a Muslim from Madras made a vigorous plea for the retention of separate electorates. 'As matters stand at present in this country', said B. Pocker Bahadur, it was 'very difficult' for non-Muslims 'to realise the needs and requirements of the Muslim community'. If separate electorates were abolished, then important groups would be left feeling 'that they have not got an adequate voice in the governance of the country'.[32]

The home minister, Sardar Patel, was deeply unsympathetic to this demand. Separate electorates had in the past led to the division of the country. 'Those who want that kind of thing have a place in Pakistan, not here,' thundered Patel to a burst of applause. 'Here, we are building a nation and we are laying the foundations of One Nation, and those who choose to divide again and sow the seeds of disruption will have no place, no quarter, here, and I must say that plainly enough.'[33]

There were, however, some Muslims who from the start were opposed to separate electorates. These included Begum Aizaz Rasul. It was 'absolutely meaningless' now to have reservation on the basis of religion, said the begum. Separate electorates were 'a self-destructive weapon which separates the minorities from the majority for all time'. For the interests of the Muslims in a secular democracy were 'absolutely identical' with those of other citizens.[34]

By 1949 Muslim members who had at first demanded separate electorates came round to the begum's point of view. They sensed that reservation for Muslims 'would be really harmful to the Muslims themselves'. Instead, the Muslims should reconstitute themselves as voting blocs, so that in constituencies where they were numerous, no candidate could afford to ignore them. They could even come to 'have a decisive voice in the elections'; for 'it may be that an apparently huge majority may at the end . . . find itself defeated by a single vote'. Therefore, 'the safety of the Muslims lies in intelligently playing their part and mixing themselves with the Hindus in public affairs'.[35]

A vulnerable minority even more numerous than the Muslims were the women of India. The female members of the Assembly had come through the national movement and were infected early with the spirit of unity. Thus Hansa Mehta of Bombay rejected reserved seats, quotas or separate electorates. 'We have never asked for privileges,' she remarked. 'What we have asked for is social justice, economic justice, and political justice. We have asked for that equality which alone can be the basis of mutual respect and understanding and without which real co-operation is not possible between man and woman.'[36] Renuka Roy of Bengal agreed: unlike the 'narrow suffragist movement[s]' of 'many so-called enlightened nations', the women of India strove for 'equality of status, for justice and for fair play and most of all to be able to take their part in responsible work in the service of their country'. For 'ever since the start of the Women's Movement in this country, women have been fundamentally opposed to special privileges and reservations'.[37]

The only voice in favour of reservation for women was a man's. This was strange; stranger still was the logic of his argument. From his own 'experience as a parliamentarian and a man of the world', said R. K. Chaudhuri,

> I think it would be wise to provide for a women's constituency. When a woman asks for something, as we know, it is easy to get it and give it to her; but when she does not ask for anything in particular it becomes very difficult to find out what she wants. If you give them a special constituency they can have their scramble and fight there among themselves without coming into the general constituency. Otherwise we may at times feel weak and yield in their favour and give them seats which they are not entitled to.[38]

VII

There would be no reservation for Muslims and women. But the constitution did recommend reservation for Untouchables. This was in acknowledgement of the horrific discrimination they had suffered, and also a bow towards Mahatma Gandhi, who had long held that true freedom, or *swaraj*, would come only when Hindu society had rid itself of this evil. It was also Gandhi who had made popular a new term for 'Untouchables', which was 'Harijans', or children of God.

The constitution set aside seats in legislatures as well as jobs in government offices for the lowest castes. It also threw open Hindu temples to all castes, and asked for the abolition of untouchability in society at large. These provisions were very widely welcomed. Muniswamy Pillai of Madras remarked that 'the fair name of India was a slur and a blot by having untouchability . . . [G]reat saints tried their level best to abolish untouchability but it is given to this august Assembly and the new Constitution to say in loud terms that no more untouchability shall stay in our country.'[39]

As H. J. Khandekar of the Central Provinces pointed out, Untouchables were conspicuously under-represented in the upper echelons of the administration. In the provinces, where they might constitute up to 25 per cent of the population, there was often only one Harijan minister, whereas Brahmins who made up only 2 per cent of the population might command two-thirds of the seats in the Cabinet. Khandekar suggested that despite the public commitment of the Congress, 'except for Mahatma Gandhi and ten or twenty other [upper-caste] persons there is none to think of the uplift of the Harijans in the true sense'.

This member eloquently defended the extension of reservation to jobs in government. He alluded to the recent recruitment to the Indian Administrative Service, the successor to the ICS. Many Harijans were interviewed but all were found unsuitable on the grounds that their grades were not good enough. Addressing his upper-caste colleagues, Khandekar insisted that

> You are responsible for our being unfit today. We were suppressed for thousands of years. You engaged in your service to serve your own ends and suppressed us to such an extent that neither our minds nor our bodies and nor even our hearts work, nor are we able to march forward. This is the position. You have reduced us to such a position and then you say that we are not fit and that we have not secured the requisite marks. How can we secure them?[40]

The argument was hard, if not impossible, to refute. But some members warned against the possible abuse of the provisions. One thought that 'those persons who are clamouring for these seats, for reservation, for consideration, represent a handful of persons, constituting the cream of Harijan society'. These were the 'politically powerful' among these groups.[41] For the left-wing congress politician Mahavir Tyagi, reservation did not lead to real representation. For 'no caste ever gets any benefit from this reservation. It is the individual or family which gets benefits'. Instead of caste, perhaps there might be reservation by class, such that 'cobblers, fishermen and other such classes send their representatives through reservation because they are the ones who do not really get any representation'.[42]

VIII

The first report on minority rights, made public in late August 1947, provided for reservation for Untouchables only. Muslims were denied the right, which in the circumstances was to be expected. However, one member of the Assembly regretted that 'the most needy, the most deserving group of adibasis [tribals] has been completely left out of the picture'.[43]

The member was Jaipal Singh, himself an adivasi, albeit of a rather special kind. Jaipal was a Munda from Chotanagpur, the forested plateau of South Bihar peopled by numerous tribes all more-or-less distinct from caste Hindu society. Sent by missionaries to study in Oxford, he made a name there as a superb hockey player. He obtained a Blue, and went on to captain the Indian team that won the gold medal in the 1928 Olympic Games.

On his return to India Jaipal did not, as his sponsors no doubt hoped, preach the Gospel, but came to invent a kind of gospel of his own. This held that the tribals were the 'original inhabitants' of the subcontinent – hence the term 'adibasi' or 'adivasi', which means precisely that. Jaipal formed an Adibasi Mahasabha in 1938 which asked for a separate state of 'Jharkhand', to be carved out of Bihar. To the tribals of Chotanagpur he was their *marang gomke*, or 'great leader'. In the Constituent Assembly he came to represent the tribals not just of his native plateau, but of all India.[44]

Jaipal was a gifted speaker, whose interventions both enlivened and entertained the House. (In this respect, the Church's loss was unquestionably politics' gain.) His first speech was made on 19 December 1946 when, in welcoming the Objectives Resolution, he provided a masterly summation of the adivasi case. 'As a jungli, as an adibasi', said Jaipal,

I am not expected to understand the legal intricacies of the Resolution. But my common sense tells me that every one of us should march in that road to freedom and fight together. Sir, if there is any group of Indian people that has been shabbily treated it is my people. They have been disgracefully treated, neglected for the last 6,000 years. The history of the Indus Valley civilization, a child of which I am, shows quite clearly that it is the newcomers – most of you here are intruders as far as I am concerned – it is the newcomers who have driven away my people from the Indus Valley to the jungle fastness . . . The whole history of my people is one of continuous exploitation and dispossession by the non-aboriginals of India punctuated by rebellions and disorder, and yet I take Pandit Jawahar Lal Nehru at his word. I take you all at your word that now we are going to start a new chapter, a new chapter of independent India where there is equality of opportunity, where no one would be neglected.[45]

Three years later, in the discussion on the draft constitution, Jaipal made a speech that was spirited in all senses of the word. Bowing to pressure by Gandhians, the prohibition of alcohol had been made a directive principle. This, said the adivasi leader, was an interference 'with the religious rights of the most ancient people in the country'. For alcohol was part of their festivals, their rituals, indeed their daily life itself. In West Bengal 'it would be impossible for paddy to be transplanted if the Santhal does not get his rice beer. These ill-clad men . . . have to work knee-deep in water throughout the day, in drenching rain and in mud. What is it in the rice beer that keeps them alive? I wish the medical authorities in this country would carry out research in their laboratories to find out what it is that the rice beer contains, of which the Adibasis need so much and which keeps them [protected] against all manner of diseases.'[46]

The Constituent Assembly had convened a sub-committee on tribal rights headed by the veteran social worker A. V. Thakkar. Its findings, and the words of Jaipal and company, sensitized the House to the tribal predicament. As a member from Bihar observed, 'the tribal people have been made a pawn on the chessboard of provincial politics'. There had been 'exploitation on a mass scale; we must hang down our heads in shame'.[47] The 'we' referred to Hindu society as a whole. It had sinned against adivasis by either ignoring them or exploiting them. It had done little to bring them modern facilities of education and health; it had colonized their land and forests; and it had brought them under a regime of usury and debt. And so, to make partial amends, tribals would also have seats in the legislature and jobs in government 'reserved' for them.

IX

The most controversial subject in the Assembly was language: the language to be spoken in the House, the language in which the constitution would be written, the language that would be given that singular designation, 'national'. On 10 of December 1946, while the procedures of the House were still being discussed, R. V. Dhulekar of the United Provinces moved an amendment. When he began speaking in Hindustani, the chairman reminded him that many members did not know the language. This was Dhulekar's reply:

> People who do not know Hindustani have no right to stay in India. People who are present in this House to fashion a constitution for India and do not know Hindustani are not worthy to be members of this Assembly. They had better leave.

The remarks created a commotion in the House. 'Order, order!' yelled the chairman, but Dhulekar continued:

> I move that the Procedure Committee should frame rules in Hindustani and not in English. As an Indian I appeal that we, who are out to win freedom for our country and are fighting for it, should think and speak in our own language. We have all along been talking of America, Japan, Germany, Switzerland and House of Commons. It has given me a headache. I wonder why Indians do not speak in their own language. As an Indian I feel that the proceedings of the House should be conducted in Hindustani. We are not concerned with the history of the world. We have the history of our own country of millions of past years.

The printed proceedings continue:

> The Chairman: Order, order!
>
> Shri R. V. Dhulekar (speaking still in Hindustani): I request you to allow me to move my amendment.

The Chairman: Order, order! I do not permit you to proceed further.
The House is with me that you are out of order.[48]

At this point Jawaharlal Nehru went up to the rostrum and persuaded Dhulekar to return to his seat. Afterwards Nehru told the errant member of the need to maintain discipline in the House. He told him that 'this is not a public meeting in Jhansi that you should address "Bhaio aur Behno" [brothers and sisters] and start lecturing at the top of your voice'.[49]

But the issue would not go away. In one session members urged the House to order the Delhi government to rule that all car number plates should be in Hindi script.[50] More substantively, they demanded that the official version of the Constitution be in Hindi, with an unofficial version in English. This the Drafting Committee did not accept, on the grounds that English was better placed to incorporate the technical and legal terms of the document. When a draft constitution was placed before the House for discussion, members nevertheless asked for a discussion of each clause written in Hindi. To adopt a document written in English, they said, would be 'insulting'.[51]

It is necessary, at this point, to introduce a distinction between 'Hindustani' and 'Hindi'. Hindi, written in the Devanagari script, drew heavily on Sanskrit. Urdu, written in a modified Arabic script, drew on Persian and Arabic. Hindustani, the *lingua franca* of much of northern India, was a unique amalgam of the two. From the nineteenth century, as Hindu–Muslim tension grew in northern India, the two languages began to move further and further apart. On the one side there arose a movement to root Hindi more firmly in Sanskrit; on the other, to root Urdu more firmly in the classical languages from which it drew. Especially in the literary world, a purified Hindi and a purified Urdu began to circulate.[52]

Through all this, the language of popular exchange remained Hindustani. This was intelligible to Hindi and Urdu speakers, but also to the speakers of most of the major dialects of the Indo-Gangetic plain: Awadhi, Bhojpuri, Maithili, Marwari and so on. However, Hindustani, as well as Hindi and Urdu, were virtually unknown in eastern and southern India. The languages spoken here were Assamese, Bengali, Kannada, Malayalam, Oriya, Tamil and Telugu, each with a script and sophisticated literary tradition of its own.

Under British rule, English had emerged as the language of higher education and administration. Would it remain in this position after the British left? The politicians of the north thought that it should be replaced by Hindi. The politicians and people of the south preferred that English continue as the vehicle of inter-provincial communication.

Jawaharlal Nehru himself was exercised early by the question. In a long essay written in 1937 he expressed his admiration for the major provincial languages. Without 'infringing in the least on their domain' there must, he thought, still be an all-India language of communication. English was too far removed from the masses, so he opted instead for Hindustani, which he defined as a 'golden mean' between Hindi and Urdu. At this time, with Partition not even a possibility, Nehru thought that both scripts could be used. Hindustani had a simple grammar and was relatively easy to learn, but to make it easier still, linguists could evolve a Basic Hindustani after the fashion of Basic English, to be promoted by the state in southern India.[53]

Like Nehru, Gandhi thought that Hindustani could unite north with south, and Hindu with Muslim. It, rather than English, should be made the *rashtrabhasha*, or national language. As he put it, 'Urdu diction is used by Muslims in writing. Hindi diction is used by Sanskrit pundits. Hindustani is the sweet mingling of the two.'[54] In 1945 he engaged in a lively exchange with Purushottamdas Tandon, a man who fought hard, not to say heroically, to rid Hindi of its foreign elements. Tandon was vice-president of the All-India Hindi Literature Conference, which argued that Hindi with the Devanagari script alone should be the national language. Gandhi, who had long been a member of the Conference, was dismayed by its chauvinist drift. Since he believed that both the Nagari and Urdu scripts should be used, perhaps it was time to resign his membership. Tandon tried to dissuade him, but, as Gandhi put it, 'How can I ride two horses? Who will understand me when I say that *rashtrabhasha* = Hindi and *rashtrabhasha* = Hindi + Urdu = Hindustani?'[55]

Partition more or less killed the case for Hindustani. The move to further Sanskritize Hindi gathered pace. One saw this at work in the Constituent Assembly, where early references were to Hindustani, but later references all to Hindi. After the division of the country the promoters of Hindi became even more fanatical. As Granville Austin observes, 'The Hindi-wallahs were ready to risk splitting the Assembly and the country in their unreasoning pursuit of uniformity.'[56] Their crusade provoked some of the most furious debates in the House. Hindustani was not acceptable to south Indians; Hindi even less so.

Whenever a member spoke in Hindi, another member would ask for a translation into English.[57] When the case was made for Hindi to be the sole national language, it was bitterly opposed. Representative are these remarks of T. T. Krishnamachari of Madras:

> We disliked the English language in the past. I disliked it because I was forced to learn Shakespeare and Milton, for which I had no taste at all . . . [I]f we are going to be compelled to learn Hindi . . . I would perhaps not be able to do it because of my age, and perhaps I would not be willing to do it because of the amount of constraint you put on me . . . This kind of intolerance makes us fear that the strong Centre which we need, a strong Centre which is necessary will also mean the enslavement of people who do not speak the language of the Centre. I would, Sir, convey a warning on behalf of people of the South for the reason that there are already elements in South India who want separation . . ., and my honourable friends in U.P. do not help us in any way by flogging their idea [of] 'Hindi Imperialism' to the maximum extent possible. Sir, it is up to my friends in U.P. to have a whole-India; it is up to them to have a Hindi-India. The choice is theirs . . .[58]

The Assembly finally arrived at a compromise; that 'the official language of the Union shall be Hindi in the Devanagari script'; but for 'fifteen years from the commencement of the Constitution, the English language shall continue to be used for all the official purposes of the Union for which it was being used immediately before such commencement'.[59] Till 1965, at any rate, the notes and proceedings of the courts, the services, and the all-India bureaucracy would be conducted in English.

X

Mahatma Gandhi had once expressed his desire to see an Untouchable woman installed as the first president of India. That did not happen, but some compensation was at hand when an Untouchable man, Dr B. R. Ambedkar, was asked to serve as the chairman of the Drafting Committee of the Constituent Assembly.

On 25 November 1949, the day before the Assembly wound up its proceedings, Ambedkar made a moving speech summing up their work.[60] He thanked his fellow members of the Drafting Committee, thanked their support staff, and thanked a party of which he had been a lifelong opponent. Without the quiet work in and out of the House by the Congress bosses, he would not have been able to render order out of chaos. 'It is because of the discipline of the Congress Party that the Drafting Committee was able to pilot the Constitution in the Assembly with the sure knowledge as to the fate of each article and each amendment.'

In a concession to patriotic nostalgia, Ambedkar then allowed that some form of democracy was not unknown in ancient India. 'There was a time when India was studded with republics.' Characteristically he invoked the Buddhists, who had furthered the democratic ideal in their Bhikshu Sanghas, which applied rules akin to those of Parliamentary Procedure – votes, motions, resolutions, censures and whips.

Ambedkar also assured the House that the federalism of the constitution in no way denied states' rights. It was mistaken, he said, to think that there was 'too much centralization and that the States have been reduced to Municipalities'. The constitution had partitioned legislative and executive authority, but the Centre could not on its own alter the boundary of this partition. In his words, 'the Centre and the States are co-equal in this matter'.

Ambedkar ended his speech with three warnings about the future. The first concerned the place of popular protest in a democracy. There was no place for bloody revolution, of course, but in his view there was no room for Gandhian methods either. 'We must abandon the method of civil disobedience, non-cooperation and *satyagraha* [popular protest]'. Under an autocratic regime, there might be some justification for them, but not now, when constitutional methods of redress were available. *Satyagraha* and the like, said Ambedkar, were 'nothing but the grammar of anarchy and the sooner they are abandoned, the better for us'.

The second warning concerned the unthinking submission to charismatic authority. Ambedkar quoted John Stuart Mill, who cautioned citizens not 'to lay their liberties at the feet of even a great man, or to trust him with powers which enable him to subvert their institutions'. This warning was even more pertinent here than in England, for

in India, Bhakti or what may be called the path of devotion or hero-worship, plays a part in its politics unequalled in magnitude by the part it plays in the politics of any other country in the world. Bhakti in religion may be the road to the salvation of a soul. But in politics, Bhakti or hero-worship is a sure road to degradation and to eventual dictatorship.

Ambedkar's final warning was to urge Indians not to be content with what he called 'mere political democracy'. India had got rid of alien rule, but it was still riven by inequality and hierarchy. Thus, once the country formally became a republic on 26 January 1950, it was

> going to enter a life of contradictions. In politics we will have equality and in social and economic life we will have inequality. In politics we will be recognizing the principle of one man one vote and one vote one value. In our social and economic life, we shall, by reason of our social and economic structure, continue to deny the principle of one man one value. How long shall we continue to live this life of contradictions? How long shall we continue to deny equality in our social and economic life? If we continue to deny it for long, we will do so only by putting our political democracy in peril.

XI

Eight months before the Constituent Assembly of India was convened a new constitution had been presented for approval to the Japanese Parliament, the *Diet*. However, this document had been almost wholly written by a group of foreigners. In early February 1946 twenty-four individuals – all Americans, and sixteen of them military officials – met in a converted ballroom in Tokyo. Here they sat for a week before coming up with a constitution they thought the Japanese should adopt. This was then presented as a *fait accompli* to the local political leadership, who were allowed to 'Japanize' the draft by translating it into the local tongue. The draft was also discussed in Parliament, but every amendment, even the most cosmetic, had to be approved beforehand by the American authorities.

The historian of this curious exercise writes that 'no modern nation ever has rested on a more alien constitution'.[61] The contrast with the Indian case could not be more striking. One constitution was written in the utmost secrecy; the other drafted and discussed in the full glare of the press. One was finalized at breakneck speed and written by foreigners. The other was written wholly by natives and emerged from several years of reflection and debate. In fairness, though, one should admit that, despite their different provenances, both constitutions were, in essence, liberal humanist credos. One could equally say of the

Indian document what the American supervisor said of the Japanese draft, namely, that 'it constitutes a sharp swing from the extreme right in political thinking – yet yields nothing to the radical concept of the extreme left'.[62]

Granville Austin has claimed that the framing of the Indian Constitution was 'perhaps the greatest political venture since that originated in Philadelphia in 1787'. The outlining of a set of national ideals, and of an institutional mechanism to work towards them, was 'a gigantic step for a people previously committed largely to irrational means of achieving other-worldly goals'. For this, as the title of the last section of Austin's book proclaims, 'the credit goes to the Indians'.[63]

Part Two

NEHRU'S INDIA

7

The Biggest Gamble in History

We are little men serving great causes, but because the cause is great, something of that greatness falls upon us also.

JAWAHARLAL NEHRU, 1946

India means only two things to us – famines and Nehru.
American journalist, 1951

I

IN THE FIRST YEARS of freedom, the ruling Congress Party faced threats from without, and within. As rebels against the Raj the nationalists had been sacrificing idealists, but as governors they came rather to enjoy the fruits of office. As a veteran Madras journalist put it, 'in the post-Gandhian war for power the first casualty is decency'.[1] *Time* magazine commented that after independence was achieved, the Congress 'found itself without a unifying purpose. It grew fat and lazy, today harbors many time-serving office-holders [and] not a few black-marketeers'.[2] An influential Bombay weekly remarked that 'from West Bengal to Uttar Pradesh, along the Gangetic Valley, the Congress is split. The old glamour of the premier political organization is fading, factions are becoming more acute and the party's unpopularity is increasing.'[3]

There were party factions at the district level, as well as at the provincial level. However, the most portentous of the cleavages was between the two biggest stalwarts, Pandit Jawaharlal Nehru and Sardar Vallabhbhai Patel. These two men, prime minister and deputy prime minister respectively, had major differences in the first months following Independence. Gandhi's death made them come together again. But in 1949 and 1950 the differences resurfaced.

In character and personality Nehru and Patel were certainly a study in contrast. The prime minister was a Brahmin from an upper-class background whose father had also been a prominent figure in the nationalist movement. His deputy, on the other hand, was from a farming caste, and a descendant of a sepoy mutineer of 1857. Nehru loved good food and wine, appreciated fine art and literature and had travelled widely abroad. Patel was a non-smoker, vegetarian, teetotaller, and, on the whole, 'a hard task master with little time for play'. He got up at 4 a.m., attended to his correspondence for an hour and then went for a walk through the dimly lit streets of New Delhi. Besides, 'a grave exterior and a cold and cynical physiognomy [made] the Sardar a really tough personality'. In the words of the *New York Times*, he was 'leather tough'.

There were also similarities. Both Nehru and Patel had a daughter as their housekeeper, companion and chief confidante. Both were politicians of a conspicuous integrity. And both were fierce patriots. But their ideas did not always mesh. As one observer rather delicately put it, 'the opposition of the Sardar to the leftist elements in the country is one of the major problems of political adjustment facing India'. He meant here that Patel was friendly with capitalists while Nehru believed in state control of the economy; that Patel was more inclined to support the West in the emerging Cold War; and that Patel was more forgiving of Hindu extremism and harsher on Pakistan.[4]

In late 1949 Nehru and Patel had a major disagreement. In the New Year, India would transform itself from a 'dominion', where the British monarch was head of state, to a full-fledged republic. Nehru thought that when the governor generalship became a presidency, the incumbent, C. Rajagopalachari, should retain the job. 'Rajaji' was an urbane scholar with whom the prime minister then got along very well. Patel, however, preferred Rajendra Prasad, who was close to him but who also had wider acceptance within the Congress Party. Nehru had assured Rajaji that he would be president, but much to his annoyance, and embarrassment, Patel got the Congress rank-and-file to put Prasad's name forward instead.[5]

The original date of Indian independence, 26 January, was chosen as the first Republic Day. The new head of state, Rajendra Prasad, took the salute in what was to become an annual and ever more spectacular parade. Three thousand men of the armed forces marched before the president. The artillery fired a thirty-one-gun salute while Liberator planes of the

Indian air force flew overhead. Gandhi's India was announcing itself as a sovereign nation-state.[6]

Round one had gone to Patel. A few months later commenced round two, the battle for the presidency of the Indian National Congress. For this post Patel had put forward Purushottamdas Tandon, a veteran of the Congress from the United Provinces, indeed, from the prime minister's own home town of Allahabad. Tandon and Nehru were personal friends, but hardly ideological bedfellows, for the presidential candidate was 'a bearded, venerable orthodox Hindu . . . who admirably represented the extreme communalist wing of the [Congress] party'. He was, in sum, 'a personification of political and social anachronisms', an 'anti-Muslim and pro-caste Hindu' who stood for 'the resurrection of a dead culture and a long extinct system of society'.[7]

Nehru had previously criticized Tandon for his desire to impose Hindi on regions of India which did not know the language. He was particularly upset when his fellow Allahabadi addressed a conference of refugees and spoke of revenge against Pakistan. India, believed Nehru, needed the healing touch, a policy of reconciliation between Hindus and Muslims. The election of Tandon as the president of the premier political party, the prime minister's own party, would send all the wrong signals.

When the election for the Congress presidency was held in August 1950 Tandon won comfortably. Nehru now wrote to Rajagopalachari that the result was 'the clearest of indications that Tandon's election is considered more important than my presence in the Govt or the Congress . . . All my instincts tell me that I have completely exhausted my utility both in the Congress and Govt'. The next day he wrote again to Rajaji, saying, 'I am feeling tired out – physically and mentally. I do not think I can function with any satisfaction to myself in future.'[8]

Rajaji now tried to work out a compromise between the two factions. Patel was amenable, suggesting a joint statement under both their names, where he and Nehru would proclaim their adherence to certain fundamentals of Congress policy. The prime minister, however, decided to go it alone. After two weeks of contemplation he had decided to exchange resignation for truculence. On 13 September 1950 he issued a statement to the press deploring the fact that 'communalist and reactionary forces have openly expressed their joy' at Tandon's victory. He was distressed, he said, that the 'spirit of communalism and revivalism has gradually invaded the Congress, and sometimes affects Government policy'. But, unlike Pakistan, India was a secular state.

'We have to treat our minorities in exactly the same way as we treat the majority,' insisted Nehru. 'Indeed, fair treatment is not enough; we have to make them feel that they are so treated.' Now, 'in view of the prevailing confusion and the threat of false doctrine, it has become essential that the Congress should declare its policy in this matter in the clearest and most unambiguous terms.'[9]

Nehru felt that it was the responsibility of the Congress and the government to make the Muslims in India feel secure. Patel, on the other hand, was inclined to place the responsibility on the minorities themselves. He had once told Nehru that the 'Muslims citizens in India have a responsibility to remove the doubts and misgivings entertained by a large section of the people about their loyalty founded largely on their past association with the demand for Pakistan and the unfortunate activities of some of them.'[10]

On the minorities question, as on other matters of philosophy and policy, Nehru and Patel would never completely see eye to eye. Now, however, in the aftermath of the bitter contest for the Congress presidency, the older man did not press the point. For Patel knew that the destruction of their party might very well mean the destruction of India. He thus told Congress members who visited him to 'do what Jawaharlal says' and to 'pay no attention to this controversy'. On 2 October, while inaugurating a women's centre in Indore, he used the occasion of Gandhi's birth anniversary to affirm his loyalty to the prime minister. He described himself in his speech as merely one of the many non-violent soldiers in Gandhi's army. Now that the Mahatma was gone, 'Jawaharlal Nehru is our leader', said Patel. 'Bapu [Gandhi] appointed him as his successor and had even proclaimed him as such. It is the duty of all Bapu's soldiers to carry out his bequest . . . I am not a disloyal soldier.'[11]

Such is the evidence placed before us by Patel's biographer, Rajmohan Gandhi. It confirms in fact what Nehru's biographer (Sarvepalli Gopal) had expressed in feeling: that what forestalled 'an open rupture [between the two men] was mutual regard and Patel's stoic decency'.[12] Patel remembered his promise to Gandhi to work along with Jawaharlal. And by the time of the controversy over the Congress presidency he was also a very sick man. It was from his bed that he sent a congratulatory handwritten letter to Nehru on his birthday, 14 November. A week later, when the prime minister visited him at his home, Patel said: 'I want to talk to you alone when I get a little strength . . . I have a feeling that you are losing confidence in me.' 'I have been losing confidence in myself,' answered Nehru.[13]

Three weeks later Patel was dead. It fell to the prime minister to draft the Cabinet Resolution mourning his passing. Nehru singled out his devotion to a 'united and strong India', and his 'genius' in solving the complicated problem of the princely states. To Nehru, Patel was both comrade and rival; but to their compatriots he was 'an unmatched warrior in the cause of freedom, a lover of India, a great servant of the people and a statesman of genius and mighty achievement'.[14]

II

Vallabhbhai Patel's death in December 1950 removed the one Congress politician who was of equal standing to Nehru. No longer were there two power centres within India's ruling party. However, the prime minister still had to contend with two somewhat lesser rivals; the president of the Congress, Purushottamdas Tandon, and the president of the republic, Rajendra Prasad. Nehru's biographer says of Prasad that he was 'prominent in the ranks of medievalism'.[15] That judgement is perhaps excessively harsh on a patriot who had sacrificed much in the cause of Indian freedom. Nonetheless, it was clear that the prime minister and the president differed on some crucial subjects, such as the place of religion in public life.

These differences came to a head in the spring of 1951 when the president was asked to inaugurate the newly restored Somnath temple in Gujarat. Once fabled for its wealth, Somnath had been raided several times by Muslim chiefs, including the notorious eleventh-century marauder Mahmud of Ghazni. Each time the temple was razed it was rebuilt. Then the Mughal emperor Aurangzeb ordered its total destruction. It lay in ruins for two and a half centuries until Sardar Patel himself visited it in September 1947 and promised help in its reconstruction. Patel's colleague K. M. Munshi then took charge of the rebuilding.[16]

When the president of India chose to dignify the temple's consecration with his presence, Nehru was appalled. He wrote to Prasad advising him not to participate in the 'spectacular opening of the Somnath temple [which] . . . unfortunately has a number of implications. Personally, I thought that this was no time to lay stress on large-scale building operations at Somnath. This could have been done gradually and more effectively later. However, this has been done. [Still] I feel that it would be better if you did not preside over this function.'[17]

Prasad disregarded the advice and went to Somnath. To his credit, however, his speech there stressed the Gandhian ideal of inter-faith harmony. True, he nostalgically evoked a Golden Age when the gold in India's temples symbolized great wealth and prosperity. The lesson from Somnath's later history, however, was that 'religious intolerance only foments hatred and immoral conduct'. By the same token, the lesson of its reconstruction was not to 'open old wounds, which have healed to some extent over the centuries', but rather to 'help each caste and community to obtain full freedom'. Calling for 'complete religious tolerance', the president urged his audience to 'try to understand the great essence of religion', namely, 'that it is not compulsory to follow a single path to realize Truth and God'. For 'just as all the rivers mingle together in the vast ocean, similarly different religions help men to reach God'.[18]

One does not know whether Nehru read the speech. In any case, he would have preferred Prasad not to go at all. The prime minister thought that public officials should never *publicly* associate with faiths and shrines. The president, on the other hand, believed that it should be equally and publicly respectful of all. Although he was a Hindu, said Prasad at Somnath, 'I respect all religions and on occasion visit a church, a mosque, a *dargah* and a *gurdwara*'.

Meanwhile, the growing Hindu tint of the Congress had led to the departure of some of its most effervescent leaders. Already in 1948 a group of brilliant young Congress members had left to start the Socialist Party. Now, in June 1951, the respected Gandhian J. B. Kripalani left to form his Kisan Majdoor Praja Party (KMPP), which, as its name indicated, stood for the interests of farmers, workers and other toiling people. Like the Socialists, Kripalani claimed that the Congress under Purushottamdas Tandon had become a deeply conservative organization.

As it happened, the formation of the KMPP strengthened Nehru's hand against Tandon. The Congress, he could now say, had to move away from the reactionary path it had recently adopted and reclaim its democratic and inclusive heritage. In September, when the All-India Congress Committee met in Bangalore, Nehru forced a showdown with Tandon and his supporters. The rank and file of the party was increasingly concerned with the upcoming general election. And, as a southern journalist pointed out, it was clear that the AICC would back the prime minister against Tandon, if only because 'the Congress President is no vote-getter'. By contrast, 'Pandit Nehru is unequalled as a vote-catcher. On the eve of the general elections it is the votes that count and Pandit Nehru has a value to the Congress which none else possesses'.[19]

That indeed, is what happened in Bangalore, where Tandon resigned as president of the Congress, with Nehru being elected in his place. As head of both party and government, 'Nehru could now wage full war against all communal elements in the country'.[20] The first battle in this war would be the general election of 1952.

III

India's first general election was, among other things, an act of faith. A newly independent country chose to move straight into universal adult suffrage, rather than – as had been the case in the West – at first reserve the right to vote to men of property, with the working class and women excluded from the franchise until much later. India became free in August 1947, and two years later set up an Election Commission. In March 1950 Sukumar Sen was appointed chief election commissioner. The next month the Representation of the People Act was passed in Parliament. While proposing the Act, the prime minister, Jawaharlal Nehru, expressed the hope that elections would be held as early as the spring of 1951.

Nehru's haste was understandable, but it was viewed with some alarm by the man who had to make the election possible. It is a pity we know so little about Sukumar Sen. He left no memoirs and few papers either. Born in 1899, he was educated at Presidency College and at London University, where he was awarded a gold medal in mathematics. He joined the Indian Civil Service (ICS) in 1921 and served in various districts and as a judge before being appointed chief secretary of West Bengal, from where he was sent on deputation as chief election commissioner.

It was perhaps the mathematician in Sen which made him ask the prime minister to wait. For no officer of state, certainly no Indian official, has ever had such a stupendous task placed in front of him. Consider, first of all, the size of the electorate: 176 million Indians aged twenty-one or more, of whom about 85 per cent could not read or write. Each one had to be identified, named and registered. The registration of voters was merely the first step. For how did one design party symbols, ballot papers and ballot boxes for a mostly unlettered electorate? Then, sites for polling stations had to be identified, and honest and efficient polling officers recruited. Moreover, concurrent with the general election would be elections to the state assemblies. Working with Sukumar Sen in this regard were the election commissioners of the different provinces, also usually ICS men.

The polls were finally scheduled for the first months of 1952, although some outlying districts would vote earlier. An American observer justly wrote that the mechanics of the election 'present a problem of colossal proportions'.[21] Some numbers will help us understand the scale of Sen's enterprise. At stake were 4,500 seats – about 500 for Parliament, the rest for the provincial assemblies. 224,000 polling booths were constructed, and equipped with 2 million steel ballot boxes, to make which 8,200 tonnes of steel were consumed; 16,500 clerks were appointed on six-month contracts to type and collate the electoral rolls by constituency; about 380,000 reams of paper were used for printing the rolls; 56,000 presiding officers were chosen to supervise the voting, these aided by another 280,000 helpers; 224,000 policemen were put on duty to guard against violence and intimidation.

The election and the electorate were spread over an area of more than a million square miles. The terrain was huge, diverse and – for the exercise at hand – sometimes horrendously difficult. In the case of remote hill villages, bridges had to be specially constructed across rivers; in the case of small islands in the Indian Ocean, naval vessels were used to take the rolls to the booths. A second problem was social rather than geographical: the diffidence of many women in northern India to give their own names, instead of which they wished to register themselves as A's mother or B's wife. Sukumar Sen was outraged by this practice, a 'curious senseless relic of the past', and directed his officials to correct the rolls by inserting the names of the women 'in the place of mere descriptions of such voters'. Nonetheless, some 2.8 million women voters had finally to be struck off the list. The resulting furore over their omission was considered by Sen to be a 'good thing', for it would help the prejudice vanish before the next elections, by which time the women could be reinstated under their own names.

Where in Western democracies most voters could recognize the parties by name, here pictorial symbols were used to make their task easier. Drawn from daily life, these symbols were easily recognizable: a pair of bullocks for one party, a hut for a second, an elephant for a third, an earthenware lamp for a fourth. A second innovation was the use of multiple ballot boxes. On a single ballot, the (mostly illiterate) Indian elector might make a mistake; thus each party had a ballot box with its symbol marked in each polling station, so that voters could simply drop their paper in it. To avoid impersonation, Indian scientists had developed a variety of indelible ink which, applied on the voter's finger, stayed there for a week. A total of 389,816 phials of this ink were used in the election.[22]

Throughout 1951 the Election Commission used the media of film and radio to educate the public about this novel exercise in democracy. A documentary on the franchise and its functions, and the duties of the electorate, was shown in more than 3,000 cinemas. Many more Indians were reached via All-India Radio, which broadcast numerous programmes on the constitution, the purpose of adult franchise, the preparation of electoral rolls and the process of voting.[23]

IV

It is instructive to reflect on the international situation in the months leading up to India's first general election. Elsewhere in Asia the French were fighting the Viet-Minh and UN troops were thwarting a North Korean offensive. In South Africa the Afrikaner National Party had disenfranchised the Cape Coloureds, the last non-white group to have the vote. America had just tested its first hydrogen bomb; Maclean and Burgess had just defected to Russia. The year had witnessed three political assassinations: of the king of Jordan, of the prime minister of Iran and of the prime minister of Pakistan, Liaqat Ali Khan, shot dead on 16 October 1951, nine days before the first votes were cast in India.

Most interestingly, the polls in India were to coincide with a general election in the United Kingdom. The old warhorse Winston Churchill was seeking to bring his Conservatives back into power. In the UK the election was basically a two-party affair. In India, however, there was a dazzling diversity of parties and leaders. In power was Jawaharlal Nehru's Indian National Congress, the chief legatee and beneficiary of the freedom movement. Opposing it were a variety of new parties formed by some greatly gifted individuals.

Prominent among parties of the left were J. B. Kripalani's KMPP and the Socialist Party, whose leading lights included the young hero of the Quit India rebellion of 1942, Jayaprakash Narayan. These parties accused the Congress of betraying its commitment to the poor. They claimed to stand for the ideals of the old 'Gandhian' Congress, which had placed the interests of workers and peasants before those of landlords and capitalists.[24] A different kind of critique was offered by the Jana Sangh, which sought to consolidate India's largest religious grouping, the Hindus, into one solid voting bloc. The party's aims were well expressed in the symbolism of its inaugural meeting, held in New Delhi on 21 September 1951. The session began with a recitation from the Vedas and a singing of the patriotic hymn 'Vande Matram'. On the rostrum, the party's founder, Syama Prasad Mukherjee, sat along with other leaders, behind them a

> white background [with] pictures of Shivaji, Lord Krishna persuading the remorse-striken Arjuna to take up arms to fight the evil forces of the Kauravas on the battle-field of Kurukshetra, Rana Pratap Singh and of an earthen deepak [lamp], in saffron. From the Pandal was hung banners inscribed with 'Sangh Shakth Kali Yuge', a dictum taken from [the] Mahabharata, professing to tell the people who attended the convention that in the age of Kali there was force only in [Jana] Sangh.[25]

The imagery was striking: taken from the Hindu epics but also invoking those Hindu warriors who had later fought the Muslim invader. But who, one wonders, represented the evil enemy, the Kauravas? Was it Pakistan, the Muslims, Jawaharlal Nehru or the Congress Party? All figured as hate objects in the speeches of the Sangh's leaders. The party stood for the reunification of the motherland through the absorption (or perhaps conquest) of Pakistan. It suspected the Indian Muslims as a problem minority, which had 'not yet learnt to own this land and its culture and treat them as their first love'. The Congress Party was accused of 'appeasing' these uncertainly patriotic Muslims.[26]

S. P. Mukherjee had once been a member of the Union Cabinet. So had B. R. Ambedkar, the great Untouchable lawyer who, as the

Union's law minister, helped draft the Indian Constitution. Ambedkar had resigned from office to revive the Scheduled Caste Federation in time for the election. In his speeches he sharply attacked the Congress government for doing little to uplift the lower castes. Freedom had meant no change for these peoples: it was 'the same old tyranny, the same old oppression, the same old discrimination . . .' After freedom was won, said Ambedkar, the Congress had degenerated into a *dharamsala* or rest-home, without any unity of purpose or principles, and 'open to all, fools and knaves, friends and foes, communalists and secularists, reformers and orthodox and capitalists and anti-capitalists'.[27]

Still further to the left was the Communist Party of India. As we have seen, in 1948 many activists of the CPI had gone underground to lead a peasant insurrection that they hoped would fructify into a countrywide revolutionary upsurge on the Chinese model. But the police and in some places the army had cracked down hard. So the communists came overground in time to fight the election. The Telengana struggle, said the party's general secretary, had been withdrawn 'unconditionally'. A temporary amnesty was granted and the militants put away their arms and went seeking votes. This abrupt change of roles produced dilemmas no text by Marx or Lenin could help resolve. Thus a woman communist standing for a seat in Bengal was not sure whether to wear crumpled saris, which would certify her identity with the poor, or wash and iron them, to better appeal to the middle-class audience. And a parliamentary candidate in Telengana (where the peasant revolt had been at its most intense) recalled his confusion at being offered a drink by a senior official: he said 'yes', and gulped down the offering, only to be hit by a 'reeling sensation' in his head as it turned out to be whisky rather than fruit juice.[28]

The election campaign of 1951–2 was conducted through large public meetings, door-to-door canvassing, and the use of visual media. 'At the height of election fever', wrote a British observer, 'posters and emblems were profuse everywhere – on walls, at street corners, even decorating the statues in New Delhi and defying the dignity of a former generation of Viceroys'. A novel method of advertising was on display in Calcutta, where stray cows had 'Vote Congress' written on their backs in Bengali.[29]

Speeches and posters were used by all parties, but only the communists had access to the airwaves. Not those transmitted by All-India Radio, which had banned party propaganda, but of Moscow Radio, which relayed its programmes via stations in Tashkent. Indian listeners could, if they wished, hear how the non-communist parties in the election were 'corrupt stooges of Anglo-American imperialists and oppressors of the workers'.[30] For the literate, a Madras weekly had helpfully translated an article from *Pravda* which called the ruling Congress 'a government of landowners and monopolists, a government of national betrayers, truncheons and bullets', and announced that the alternative for the 'long-suffering, worn-out Indian people' was the Communist Party, around which 'all progressive forces of the country, everyone who cherishes the vital interests of his fatherland, are grouping'.[31]

Adding to the list (and interest, and excitement) were regional parties based on affiliations of ethnicity and religion. These included the Dravida Kazhagam in Madras, which stood for Tamil pride against north Indian domination; the Akalis in Punjab, who were the main party of the Sikhs; and the Jharkhand Party in Bihar, which wanted a separate state for tribal people. There were also numerous splinter groupings of the left, as well as two Hindu parties more orthodox than the Jana Sangh: the Hindu Mahasabha and the Ram Rajya Parishad.

The leaders of these parties all had years of political service behind them. Some had gone to jail in the nationalist cause; others in the communist cause. Men like S. P. Mookerjee and Jayaprakash Narayan were superb orators, with the ability to enchant a crowd and make it fall in line behind them. On the eve of the election the political scientist Richard Park wrote that 'the leading Indian parties and party workers are surpassed by those of no other country in electioneering skill, dramatic presentation of issues, political oratory, or mastery of political psychology'.[32]

Some might celebrate this diversity as proof of the robustness of the democratic process. Others were not so sure. Thus a cartoon strip in *Shankar's Weekly* lampooned the hypocrisy of the vote-gathering exercise. It showed a fat man in a black coat canvassing among different groups of voters. He told an emaciated farmer that 'land for peasants is my aim'. He assured a well-dressed young man that 'landlords' rights will be protected'. At one place he said that he was 'all for nationalization'; at another he insisted that he would 'encourage private enterprise'. He told a lady in a sari that he stood for the Hindu Code Bill (a reform aimed principally at enhancing the rights of women), but said to a Brahmin with a pigtail that he would 'safeguard our Ancient Culture'.[33]

V

These varied parties all had one target: the ruling Congress. Its leader, Jawaharlal Nehru, had just survived a challenge to his leadership of the party. With the death of Vallabhbhai Patel he was also the dominant presence within the government. But he faced problems aplenty. These included angry refugees from East and West Pakistan, not yet settled in their new homes. The Andhras in the south and the Sikhs in the north were getting restive. The Kashmir question was, in the eyes of the world, still unresolved. And Independence had not as yet made any dent in the problems of poverty and inequality: a state of affairs for which, naturally, the ruling party was likely to be held responsible.

One way of telling the story of the election campaign is through newspaper headlines. These make interesting reading, not least because the issues they flag have remained at the forefront of Indian elections ever since. 'MINISTERS FACE STIFF OPPOSITION' read a headline from Uttar Pradesh. 'CASTE RIVALRIES WEAKEN BIHAR CONGRESS', read another. From the north-eastern region came this telling line: 'AUTONOMY DEMAND IN MANIPUR'. From Gauhati came this one: 'CONGRESS PROSPECTS IN ASSAM: IMPORTANCE OF MUSLIM AND TRIBAL VOTE'. Gwalior offered 'DISCONTENT AMONG CONGRESSMEN: LIST OF NOMINEES CREATES WIDER SPLIT'. A Calcutta headline ran: 'W. BENGAL CONGRESS CHIEF BOOED AT MEETING' (the hecklers being refugees from East Pakistan). 'NO HOPES OF FREE AND FAIR ELECTION', started a story datelined Lucknow: this being the verdict of J. B. Kripalani, who claimed that state officials would rig the polls in favour of the ruling party. And the city of Bombay offered, at three different moments in the campaign, these more-or-less timeless headlines: 'CONGRESS BANKS ON MUSLIM SUPPORT'; 'CONGRESS APATHY TOWARDS SCHEDULED CASTES: CHARGES REITERATED BY DR AMBEDKAR'; and 'FOURTEEN HURT IN CITY ELECTION CLASH'. But there was also the occasional headline that was of its time but emphatically not of ours – notably the one in the *Searchlight* of Patna which claimed: 'PEACEFUL VOTING HOPED [FOR] IN BIHAR'.

Faced with wide-ranging opposition from outside, and with some dissidence within his own party, Jawaharlal Nehru took to the road – and on occasion the plane and the train as well. From 1 October he commenced a tour which a breathless party functionary later described as comparable to the 'imperial campaigns of Samudragupta, Asoka and Akbar' as well as to the 'travel[s] of Fahien and Hieun Tsang'. In the space of nine weeks Nehru covered the country from end to end. He travelled 25,000 miles in all: 18,000 by air, 5,200 by car, 1,600 by train, and even 90 by boat.[34]

Nehru kicked off his party's campaign with a speech in the Punjab town of Ludhiana on Sunday 30 September. The choice of venue was significant: as was the thrust of his talk, which declared 'an all-out war against communalism'. He 'condemned the communal bodies which in the name of Hindu and Sikh culture were spreading the virus of communalism as the Muslim League once did'. These 'sinister communal elements' would if they came to power 'bring ruin and death to the country'. He asked his audience of half a million to instead 'keep the windows of our mind open and let in fresh breeze from all corners of the world'.

The sentiment was Gandhi-like, and indeed Nehru's next major speech was delivered in Delhi on the afternoon of 2 October, the Mahatma's birthday. To a mammoth crowd he spoke in Hindustani about the government's determination to abolish both untouchability and landlordism. Once more he identified communalists as the chief enemies, who 'will be shown no quarter', and 'overpowered with all our strength'. His 95-minute speech was punctuated by loud cheers, not least when he made this ringing declaration: 'If any person raises his hand to strike down another on the ground of religion, I shall fight him till the last breath of my life, both at the head of the Government and from outside.'

Wherever he went Nehru spoke out strongly against communalism. In S. P. Mookerjee's native Bengal he dismissed the Jana Sangh as the 'illegitimate child of the RSS and the Hindu Mahasabha'. To be sure, he touched on other themes as well. In Bihar he deplored the 'monster of casteism'. In Bombay he reminded his audience that a vote for Congress was also a vote for its foreign policy of principled neutralism. In Bharatpur and Bilaspur he deplored the impatience of his left-wing critics, whose ends he shared but not their means: as he put it, 'we can build the edifice of Socialism brick by brick only'. In Ambala he asked the women to cast off their purdahs and 'come forward to build the country'. In many places he expressed his admiration for the best among his opposition: for men such as Ambedkar, Kripalani, and Jayaprakash Narayan, who had once been his colleagues in the party or in government.

'We want a number of [such] men with ability and integrity,' he said. 'They are welcome. But all of them are pulling in different directions and doing nothing in the end.' He was particularly sorry to find himself in opposition to the Socialist Party, which, he said, 'contains some of my old intimate friends whom I admire and respect'. These sentiments were not shared by his daughter, Indira Gandhi, who in her own speeches alleged that the socialists were funded by American dollars.[35]

In the course of his campaign Nehru 'travelled more than he slept and talked more than he travelled'. He addressed 300 mass meetings and myriad wayside ones. He spoke to about 20 million people directly, while an equal number merely had his *darshan*, eagerly flanking the roads to see him as his car whizzed past. Those who heard and saw Nehru included miners, peasants, pastoralists, factory workers and agricultural labourers. Women of all classes turned out in numbers for his meetings. Sometimes there was a sprinkling of hostiles among the crowd. In parts of northern India Jana Sangh supporters shouted out at Nehru's rallies that he was not to be trusted because he ate beef. Coming across a group of communists waving the hammer and sickle, Nehru asked them to 'go and live in the country whose flag you are carrying'. 'Why don't you go to New York and live with the Wall Street imperialists?' they shot back.[36]

But for the most part the people who came to hear Nehru were sympathetic, and often adulatory. This summation by a Congress booklet exaggerates, but not by very much:

[At] almost every place, city, town, village or wayside halt, people had waited overnight to welcome the nation's leader. Schools and shops closed: milkmaids and cowherds had taken a holiday; the kisan and his helpmate took a temporary respite from their dawn-to-dusk programme of hard work in field and home. In Nehru's name, stocks of soda and lemonade sold out; even water became scarce . . . Special trains were run from out-of-the-way places to carry people to Nehru's meetings, enthusiasts travelling not only on foot-boards but also on top of carriages. Scores of people fainted in milling crowds.[37]

The independent press provided many instances of the popular mood. When Nehru spoke in Bombay, a procession, mainly of Muslims, marched to Chowpatty to the accompaniment of pipes and cymbals. It was headed by a pair of bullocks and a plough (the Congress symbol).

Everywhere, crowds started collecting from early morning for talks scheduled for the afternoon; almost everywhere, barricades were broken in 'the enthusiasm to catch a glimpse of Mr Nehru'. After he finished his speech in Delhi, Nehru was met as he came off the dais by a famous wrestler, Massu Pahalwan, who offered him a gold chain and remarked, 'This is only a token. I am prepared to give my life for you and the country.' The media was much taken with a Telugu-speaking woman who went to listen to Nehru speak in the railway town of Kharagpur. As the prime minister lectured on she was consumed by labour pains. Immediately, a group of fellow Andhras made a ring around her: the baby was safely delivered, no doubt while the midwives had an ear cocked to hear what their hero was saying.

The extraordinary popular appeal of the Indian prime minister is best captured in the testimony of the confirmed Nehru-baiter D. F. Karaka, editor of the popular Bombay weekly, the *Current*. He was in the vast crowd at Chowpatty beach, one of 200,000 people gathered there, many standing in the sea. Karaka noted – no doubt to his regret – 'the instant affinity between the speaker and his audience'. This is how the editor reported Nehru's speech:

He had come to Bombay after a long time, he told them. Many years.

He paused and looked at them with that wistful look he specialises in. In that pause, ominous for his political opponents, a thousand votes must have swung in his favour.

Yes, he felt a personal attachment to the city.

Pause.

Two thousand votes.

It was like coming home.

Pause.

Five thousand votes.

In Bombay he had passed some of the happiest moments in his life. Yes, the happiest.

Five thousand votes . . .

He remembered those great moments so vividly. And some of the saddest moments too – the sad, hard days of the [freedom] struggle.

Ten thousand votes for the Congress.

Pause. 'By looking at the people who have struggled together with me in the fight for freedom, I derive freedom and strength,' he said.

The affinity was complete.

Twenty thousand votes!

Pause.

A deep, sorrowful, soulful look in the fading twilight hour; with the air pregnant with emotion . . . He told the gathering that he had taken upon himself the role of a mendicant beggar. Amidst cheers, he said: 'If at all I am a beggar, I am begging for your love, your affection and your enlightened co-operation in solving the problems which face the country.'

Thirty thousand votes were sure for Nehru.

Pause.

A stir in the audience. A tear on the face of the man or woman sitting on the beach or standing on the shore. Two tears, a *sari*-end wiping them gently off a woman's face. She would give her vote to Nehru no matter what anyone else said. Memories of Gandhi came back to the people – the days when Nehru stood beside the Mahatma. Nehru . . . was the man he left to us as his political heir.

Fifty thousand votes! a hundred thousand! Two hundred thousand![38]

The crowds were moved by Nehru; and he, in turn, was moved by them. His own feelings are best captured in a letter he wrote to one who with both delicacy and truth can be referred to as his closest lady friend, Edwina Mountbatten:

Wherever I have been, vast multitudes gather at my meetings and I love to compare them, their faces, their dress, their reactions to me and what I say. Scenes from past history of that very part of India rise up before me and my mind becomes a picture gallery of past events. But, more than the past, the present fills my mind and I try to probe into the minds and hearts of these multitudes. Having long been imprisoned in the Secretariat of Delhi, I rather enjoy these fresh contacts with the Indian people . . . The effort to explain in simple language our problems and our difficulties, and to reach the minds of these simple folk is both exhausting and exhilarating.

As I wander about, the past and the present merge into one another and this merger leads me to think of the future. Time becomes like a flowing river in continuous motion with events connected with one another.[39]

VI

One place even Nehru didn't get to was the *tahsil* of Chini in Himachal
Pradesh. Here resided the first Indians to cast votes in a general election,
a group of Buddhists. They voted on 25 October 1951, days before the
winter snows shut their valleys from the world. The villagers of Chini
owed allegiance to the Panchen Lama in Tibet, and were ruled by rituals
administered by local priests. These included *gorasang*, a religious service
to celebrate the completion of a new house; *kangur zalmo*, a ceremonial
visit to the Buddhist library at Kanam; *menthako*, 'where men, women,
and children climb hills, dance and sing'; and *jokhiya chug simig*, the
interchange of visits between relatives. Now, although they didn't as yet
know it, was added a new ritual, to be performed at five-year intervals:
voting in a general election.[40]

Polling began in the UK general election on the same day, although
there the first voters were not Buddhist peasants in a Himalayan valley
but 'milkmen, charwomen and all-night workers returning home from
work'.[41] However, in those small islands the results of the election were
known the following day – Labour had been swept out of power and
Winston Churchill returned as prime minister. In India, the first voters
had to wait months, for the rest of the country did not go to the polls
until January and February 1952.

The highest turnout, 80.5 per cent, was recorded in the parliamentary
constituency of Kottayam, in present-day Kerala; the lowest, 18.0, was
in Shahdol in what is now Madhya Pradesh. For the country as a whole,
about 60 per cent of registered voters exercised their franchise, this
despite the high level of illiteracy. A scholar from the London School of
Economics described how a young woman in Himachal walked several
miles with her frail mother to vote: 'for a day, at least, she knew she was
important'.[42] A Bombay-based weekly marvelled at the high turnout in
the forest districts of Orissa, where tribals came to the booths with bows
and arrows. One booth in the jungle reported more than 70 per cent
voting; but evidently Sukumar Sen had got at least some things wrong,
for the neighbouring booth was visited only by an elephant and two
panthers.[43] The press highlighted the especially aged: a 110-year-old man
in Madurai who came propped up on either side by a great-grandson, a
95-year-old woman in Ambala, deaf and hunchbacked, who still turned
up to vote. There was also the 90-year-old Muslim in rural Assam who
had to return disappointed after being told by the presiding officer that

'he could not vote for Nehru'. A nonagenarian in rural Maharashtra cast his vote for the Assembly election, but fell down and died before he could do the same for Parliament. And there was a vindication of Indian democracy in the electoral roll of Hyderabad, where among the first who voted was the Nizam himself.

One place in which there was especially brisk polling was Bombay. Delhi was where the rulers lived, but this island metropolis was India's financial capital. It was also a very politically aware city. Altogether, 900,000 residents of Bombay, or 70 per cent of the city's electorate, exercised their democratic right on election day. The workers came in far greater numbers as compared to the fashionable middle class. Thus, reported the *Times of India*, 'in the industrial areas voters formed long queues long before the polling stations opened, despite the particularly cold and dewy morning. In contrast to this, at the WIAA Club [in Malabar Hill], which housed two polling stations, it appeared as if people straggled in for a game of tennis or bridge and only incidentally to vote.'

The day after Bombay went to the polls it was the turn of the Mizo hills. With regard to both culture and geography there could not have been a greater contrast. Bombay had a great density of polling stations: 1,349 in all, packed into just 92 square miles; the Mizo, a tribal area bordering East Pakistan and Burma, required a mere 113 booths spread over more than 8,000 square miles of territory. The people who lived in these hills, said one scribe, 'have not known any queues hitherto except those in battle arrays'. But they had nonetheless 'taken a strong fancy' to the exercise, reaching their booths after walking for days on 'perilous tracks through wild jungles, camping at night on the way amid song and community dances around the fire'. And so 92,000 Mizos, who 'have through the centuries decided an issue with their arrows and spears, came forward to give their decision for the first time through the medium of the ballot'.

An American woman photographer on assignment in Himachal Pradesh was deeply impressed by the commitment shown by the election officials. One official had walked for six days to attend the preparatory workshop organized by the district magistrate; another had ridden four days on a mule. They went back to their distant stations with sewn gunny sacks full of ballot boxes, ballots, party symbols and electoral lists. On election day the photographer chose to watch proceedings at an obscure hill village named Bhuti. Here the polling station was a school-house which had only one door. Since the rules prescribed a different entry and exit, a window had been converted into a door, with improvised steps on either side to allow the elderly and ailing to hop out after voting.[44]

At least in this first election, politicians and the public were both (to quote the chief election commissioner) 'essentially law-abiding and peaceful'. There were only 1,250 election offences reported. These included 817 cases of the 'impersonation of voters', 106 attempts to take ballot papers out of a polling station and 100 instances of 'canvassing within one hundred yards of a polling station', some of these last offences doubtless committed unknowingly by painted cows.[45]

VII

Polling for the general election ended in the last week of February 1952. When the votes were counted, the Congress had won comfortably. The party secured 364 out of 489 seats in Parliament and 2,247 out of 3,280 seats in the state assemblies. As critics of the Congress were quick to point out, the first-past-the-post system had produced a far from representative result. More than 50 per cent of the electorate had voted for non-Congress candidates or parties. For Parliament as a whole, Congress had polled 45 per cent of the vote and won 74.4 per cent of the seats; the corresponding figures for the states were 42.4 per cent and 68.6 per cent. Even so, twenty-eight Congress ministers had failed to win a seat. These included such men of influence as Jai Narayan Vyas, in Rajasthan, and Morarji Desai, in Bombay. More striking still was the fact that it was a communist, Ravi Narayan Reddy – he who drank his first glass of whisky during the campaign – who achieved the largest majority, larger even than Jawaharlal Nehru's.

One of the more notable defeats was that of the Scheduled Caste leader B. R. Ambedkar. Opposing him in his Bombay constituency was an obscure milkman named Kajrolkar. The gifted Marathi journalist P. K. Atre popularized a slogan which went:

> Kuthe to Ghatnakar Ambedkar,
> Aani Kuthe ha Lonivikya Kajrolkar?

which, roughly translated, means:

> Where is the (great) constitution-maker Ambedkar
> And where the (obscure) butter-seller Kajrolkar?[46]

Yet, in the end, the prestige and hold of the Congress, and the fact that Nehru made several speeches in Bombay, carried Kajrolkar to victory. As one wag remarked, even a lamp-post standing on the Congress ticket could have been elected. Or, as a political scientist more dispassionately put it, the election was won on 'Nehru's personal popularity and his ability to express the aspirations of a newly independent India in a vivid and forceful manner'.[47]

On the eve of the polls Sukumar Sen suggested they constituted 'the biggest *experiment* in democracy in human history'. A veteran Madras editor was less neutral; he complained that 'a very large majority [will] exercise votes for the first time: not many know what the vote is, why they should vote, and whom they should vote for; no wonder the whole adventure is rated as the biggest *gamble* in history'.[48] And a recently dispossessed maharaja told a visiting American couple that any constitution that sanctioned universal suffrage in a land of illiterates was 'crazy'. 'Imagine the demagoguery, the misinformation, the dishonesty possible', said the maharaja, adding, 'The world is far too shaky to permit such an experiment.'[49]

Sharing this scepticism was Penderel Moon, a Fellow of All Souls College, and an ex-ICS man who had chosen to stay on in India. In 1941, Moon had spoken to the graduating students of Punjab University about the unsuitability of Western-style democracy to their social context. Now, eleven years later, he was the chief commissioner of the hill state of Manipur, and had to depute election officers and supervise the polling and the counting. As the people of Manipur went to the polls on 29 January, Moon wrote to his father that 'a future and more enlightened age will view with astonishment the absurd farce of recording the votes of millions of illiterate people'.[50]

Just as sceptical as the All Souls man was the *Organiser*, a weekly published by the revanchist Hindu group, the RSS. This hoped that Jawaharlal Nehru 'would live to confess the failure of universal adult franchise in India'. It claimed that Mahatma Gandhi had warned against 'this precipitate dose of democracy', and that the president, Rajendra Prasad, was 'sceptical about this leap in the dark'. Yet Nehru, 'who has all along lived by slogans and stunts, would not listen'.[51]

There were times when even Nehru had second thoughts about universal franchise. On 20 December 1951 he took a brief leave of absence from the campaign to address a UNESCO symposium in Delhi. In his speech Nehru accepted that democracy was the best form of government, or self-government, but still wondered whether the quality of men who are selected by these modern democratic methods of adult franchise gradually deteriorates because of lack of thinking and the noise of propaganda . . . He [the voter] reacts to sound and to the din, he reacts to repetition and he produces either a dictator or a dumb politician who is insensitive. Such a politician can stand all the din in the world and still remain standing on his two feet and, therefore, he gets selected in the end because the others have collapsed because of the din.

This was a rare confession, based no doubt on his recent experiences on the road. A week later Nehru suggested that it might be better to have direct elections at the lower levels – say within the village and district – and indirect elections for the highest levels. For, as he put it, 'direct election for such a vast number is a complicated problem and the candidates may never come into touch with the electorate and the whole thing becomes distant'.[52]

Nehru had an unusual capacity – unusual among politicians, at any rate – to view both sides of the question. He could see the imperfections of the process even while being committed to it. However, by the time the final results were in, and the Congress had emerged as the unchallenged party of rule, the doubts in Nehru's own mind had disappeared. 'My respect for the so-called illiterate voter,' he said, 'has gone up. Whatever doubts I might have had about adult suffrage in India have been removed completely.'[53]

The election itself also comprehensively set to rest the doubts of the new American ambassador to India, Chester Bowles. This representative of the world's richest democracy assumed his post in Delhi in the autumn of 1951. He confessed that he was 'appalled at the prospect of a poll of 200 million eligible voters, most of whom were illiterate villagers'. He 'feared a fiasco', even (as the *Madras Mail* put it), 'the biggest farce ever staged in the name of democracy anywhere in the world'. But a trip through the country during polling changed his mind. Once, he had thought that poor countries needed a period of rule by a benevolent dictator as preparation for democracy. But the sight of many parties contesting freely, and of Untouchables and Brahmins standing in the same line, persuaded him otherwise. He no longer thought literacy was a test of intelligence, no longer believed that Asia needed a 'series of Ataturks' before they would be ready for democracy. Summing up his report on the election, Bowles wrote: 'In Asia, as in America, I know no grander vision than this, government by the consent of the governed.'[54]

A visiting Turkish journalist focused on the content of the election rather than its form. He admired Nehru's decision not to follow other Asian countries in taking 'the line of least resistance' by developing 'a dictatorship with centralisation of power and intolerance of dissent and criticism'. The prime minister had 'wisely kept away from such temptations'. Yet the 'main credit', according to the Turkish writer, 'goes to the nation itself; 176,000,000 Indians were left all alone with their conscience in face of the polling box. It was direct and secret voting. They had their choice between theocracy, chauvinism, communal separatism and isolationism on the one side; secularism, national unity, stability, moderation and friendly intercourse with the rest of the world on the other. They showed their maturity in choosing moderation and progress and disapproving of reaction and unrest.' So impressed was this observer that he took a delegation of his countrymen to meet Sukumar Sen. The chief election commissioner showed them samples of ballot boxes, ballot papers and symbols, as well as the plan of a polling station, so that they could work to resume the interrupted progress of democracy in their own country.[55]

In one sense the Turkish journalist was right. There were indeed 176 million heroes; or, at least 107 million – those among the eligible who actually took the trouble to vote. Still, some heroes were more special than others. As the respected Lucknow sociologist D. P. Mukerji pointed out, 'great credit is due to those who are in charge of this stupendous first experiment in Indian history. Bureaucracy has certainly proved its worth by honestly discharging the duties imposed on it by a honest prime minister.'[56]

The juxtaposition is important, and also ironical. For there was a time when Nehru had little but scorn for the bureaucracy. As he put it in his autobiography, 'few things are more striking today in India than the progressive deterioration, moral and intellectual, of the higher services, more especially the Indian Civil Services. This is most in evidence in the superior officials, but it runs like a thread throughout the services.'[57] This was written in 1935, when the objects of his derision had the power to put him and his like in jail. And yet, fifteen years later, Nehru was obliged to place the polls in the hands of men he would once have dismissed as imperialist stooges.

In this respect, the 1952 election was a script jointly authored by historical forces for so long opposed to one another: British colonialism and Indian nationalism. Between them these forces had given this new nation what could be fairly described as a jump-start to democracy.

8

HOME AND THE WORLD

Pandit Nehru is at his best when he is not pinned down to matters of detail.

Economic Weekly, 28 July 1951

I

NOT LONG AFTER THE 1952 election the Indian writer Nirad C. Chaudhuri produced an essay on Jawaharlal Nehru for a popular magazine. The writer was by this time moderately well known, but his subject still towered over both him and everybody else. Nehru's leadership, remarked Chaudhuri, 'is the most important moral force behind the unity of India'. He was 'the leader not of a party, but of the people of India taken collectively, the legitimate successor to Gandhiji'. As he saw it,

> Nehru is keeping together the governmental machine and the people, and without this nexus India would probably have been deprived of stable government in these crucial times. He has not only ensured co-operation between the two, but most probably has also prevented actual conflicts, cultural, economic, and political. Not even Mahatmaji's leadership, had it continued, would have been quite equal to them.
>
> If, within the country, Nehru is the indispensable link between the governing middle-classes and the sovereign people, he is no less the bond between India and the world. [He serves as] India's representative to the great Western democracies, and, I must add, their representative to India. The Western nations certainly look upon him as such and expect him to guarantee India's support for them, which is why they are so upset when Nehru takes an anti-Western or neutral line. They feel they are being let down by one of themselves.[1]

Through his long tenure as prime minister, Nehru served simultaneously as foreign minister of the government of India. This was natural, for among the Congress leadership he alone had a genuinely internationalist perspective. Gandhi had been universalist in outlook but had hardly travelled abroad. The other Congress leaders, such as Vallabhbhai Patel, were determinedly inward-looking. Nehru, on the other hand, 'had always been fascinated by world trends and movements'.[2]

Through the inter-war period Nehru remained a close observer of and occasional participant in European debates. In 1927 he visited Soviet Russia, and in the next decade travelled widely over the Continent. In the 1930s he played an active part in mobilizing support for the Republican cause in Spain. He became a pillar of the progressive left, speaking often on public platforms in England and France. His name and fame in this regard were aided by the publication and commercial success of his autobiography, which appeared in London in 1936.[3]

Representative of Nehru's ideas is a speech he delivered on 'Peace and Empire' at Friends House, Euston, in July 1938. This began by speaking of 'fascist aggression' but went on to see fascism as merely another variant of imperialism. In Britain the tendency was to distinguish between the two. But in Nehru's mind there was little doubt that those who 'sought complete freedom for all the subject peoples of the world' had to oppose both fascism and imperialism.

The crisis of the times, said Nehru, had promoted a 'growing solidarity of the various peoples' and a 'feeling of international fellowship and comradeship'. His own talk ranged widely around the hot spots of the world. He spoke of Spain, of Abyssinia, of China, of Palestine, and most sensitively, of Africa. The 'people of Africa deserve our special consideration', he pointed out, for 'probably no other people in the world have suffered so much, and have been exploited so much'.[4]

In the late summer of 1939 Nehru planned a trip to India's great Asian neighbour, China. He had been in friendly correspondence with Chiang Kai-shek, for, as he told a colleague, 'more and more I think of India and China pulling together in the future'. He hoped to go by air to Chungking, spend three weeks travelling in the hinterland and to return home via the Burma Road. Sadly, the war in Europe put paid to the tour.[5]

Nehru was jailed for his part in the Quit India movement of 1942. When he was released in July 1945 his energies were devoted to the endgames of empire. But after it became clear that India would soon be free, his thoughts turned once more to foreign affairs. In a radio broadcast of September 1946 he singled out the United States, the Soviet Union and China as the three countries most relevant to India's future. The next year he spoke in the Constituent Assembly on how India would be friends with both the US and the USSR, rather than become camp followers of one power 'in the hope that some crumbs might fall from their table'. As he put it, 'we lead ourself'.[6]

An early articulation of what came to be known as 'non-alignment' is contained in a letter written by Nehru to K. P. S. Menon in January 1947, as the latter prepared to take up his assignment as India's first ambassador to China:

> Our general policy is to avoid entanglement in power politics and not to join any group of powers as against any other group. The two leading groups today are the Russian bloc and the Anglo-American bloc. We must be friendly to both and yet not join either. Both America and Russia are extraordinarily suspicious of each other as well as of other countries. This makes our path difficult and we may well be suspected by each of leaning towards the other. This cannot be helped.[7]

Nehru saw Indian independence as part of a wider Asian resurgence. Past centuries might have belonged to Europe, or to the white races in general, but it was now time for non-white and previously subordinated peoples to come into their own.

A remarkable initiative in this regard was the Asian Relations Conference, held in New Delhi in the last week of March 1947. Twenty-eight countries sent representatives – these included India's close neighbours (Afghanistan, Burma, Ceylon and Nepal), the still colonized nations of Southeast Asia (such as Malaya, Indonesia and Vietnam), China and Tibet (the two sent separate delegations), seven Asian 'republics' of the Soviet Union and Korea. The Arab League was also represented and there was a Jewish delegation from Palestine. As a Western journalist covering the event recalled, for a week the city of Delhi 'was filled with the most intricate variety of people, strange in costume and countenance – brocades from South-East Asia, bell-bottoms from the Eastern Soviet Republics, braided hair and quilted robes from Tibet . . . dozens of curious languages and poly-syllabic titles. One way and another, as we kept reminding one another, this multitude represented nearly half the population of the world.'[8]

The conference was held in the Purana Qila, a large, somewhat rundown yet still majestic stone structure built by Sher Shah Suri in the sixteenth century. The opening and concluding sessions were open to the public, and attracted large crowds – 20,000, by one estimate. The official language was English but interpreters were provided for the delegates. Speakers spoke on a podium; behind them was mounted a huge map of the continent, with ASIA written atop it in neon lights. The inaugural address was by Nehru. 'Rising to a great ovation', he talked of how, 'after a long period of quiescence', Asia had 'suddenly become important in world affairs'. Its countries could 'no longer be used as pawns by others'.[9] However, as the journalist G. H. Jansen recalled, Nehru's speech 'was not directly or strongly anti-colonial. "The old imperialisms are fading away", he said. With an almost contemptuous wave of the hand he did something worse than attack them; he pronounced a valediction.'[10]

After Nehru had his say, each participating country, in alphabetical order, sent a speaker to the podium. This took two whole days, after which the meeting broke up into thematic round-tables. There were separate sections on 'national movements for freedom'; 'racial problems and inter-Asian migration'; 'economic development and social services'; 'cultural problems'; and 'status of women and women's movements'.

The conference concluded with a talk by Mahatma Gandhi. He regretted that the conference had not met in the 'real India' of the villages but in the cities that were 'influenced by the West'. The 'message of Asia', insisted Gandhi, was 'not to be learnt through the Western spectacles or by imitating the atom bomb . . . I want you to go away with the thought that Asia has to conquer the West through love and truth.'[11]

Gandhi made his appearance, but this was really Nehru's show. His admirers saw it as confirmation of his status as the authentic voice of resurgent Asia. His critics were less generous. In its account of the conference, the Muslim League newspaper, *Dawn*, complained of how 'skilfully he [Nehru] has worked himself into some sort of all-Asian leadership. That is just what this ambitious Hindu leader had intended – to thrust himself upon the Asian nations as their leader and through his attainment of that prestige and eminence to further the expansionist designs of Indian Hinduism.'[12]

II

Nehru had often been to Europe before Independence. His first trip to the United States, however, took place two years after he had assumed office as prime minister. The US had not loomed large in Nehru's political imagination. His *Glimpses of World History*, for example, devotes far less space to it than to China or Russia. And what he says is not always complimentary. The capitalism of the American kind had led to slavery, gangsterism, and massive extremes of wealth and poverty. The American financier J. Pierpont Morgan owned a yacht worth £6 million, yet New York was known as 'Hunger Town'. Nehru admired Roosevelt's attempts at regulating the economy, but he was not hopeful that FDR would succeed. For 'American Big Business is held to be the most powerful vested interest in the modern world, and it is not going to give up its power and privileges merely at the bidding of President Roosevelt'.[13]

Before Nehru's trip to America in late 1949, an enterprising reporter at *Time* magazine went through his writings. The exercise revealed that he had 'simply never given the subject [of America] much thought. As a British university man, he has perhaps looked down snobbishly at American deficiency in culture. As a sentimental socialist, he has ticked off the U.S. as unrivalled in technology but predatory in its capitalism.'[14]

Nehru's feelings were widely shared. Like British aristocrats, the Indian elite tended to think of America and Americans as uncouth and uncultured. Representative are the views of P. P. Kumaramangalam, scion of an illustrious south Indian family. His father, Dr P. Subbaroyan, was a rich landlord and an influential politician – he later served in Nehru's Cabinet. The son studied at Sandhurst – his siblings in Oxford and Cambridge. These, a brother named Mohan and a sister named Parvathi, went on to become leading lights of the Communist Party of India. This predisposed them to a dislike of America. But in this respect the brother who was an army officer outdid them. After Indian independence he was sent for training to the artillery school at Fort Sill in Oklahoma. From here he wrote to a Madras mentor of how

This country is not one that I will ever get fond of. I have not got
a very high opinion of them. The people that I have to deal with are
very kind, hospitable and have been very good to the two of us. But
somehow I feel there is a trace of artificiality in that and also it is the
result of trying to impress one. They I think are very jealous of the old
world and its background and culture and this results in an aggressive
inferiority complex. As for their state of morality, there is none. People
seem to delight in trying to outwit each other by any means, mainly
crooked. The politicians are racketeers and big business has a tight
grip on everything in the country. The small country tradesman and
the farmer I think have their hands pretty securely tied by the big men.
I do hope our country proceeds with caution and doesn't get entirely
under the influence of the [United] States.[15]

Americans, for their part, had their own prejudices about India.
They admired Gandhi and his struggle for national independence,
but their knowledge of the country itself was scant. As Harold Isaac
once pointed out, for the postwar American there were really only
four kinds of Indians. These were: (1) the *fabulous* Indians, the
maharajas and magicians coupled with equally exotic animals such as
tigers and elephants; (2) the *mystical* Indians, a people who were 'deep,
contemplative, tranquil, profound . . .'; (3) the *benighted* Indians, who
worshipped animals and many-headed gods, living in a country that was
even more heathen than China; and (4) the *pathetic* Indians, plagued
by poverty and crippled by disease – 'children with fly-encircled eyes,
with swollen stomachs, children dying in the streets, rivers choked with
bodies . . .' Of these images perhaps the last two predominated. It was
no accident that the book on the subcontinent best known in America
was Katherine Mayo's *Mother India*, a book that Gandhi had described
as a 'drain inspector's report'.[16]

Nehru in part shared the prejudices of Indians, and he was sensible
of the American ones. But for this first high-level encounter between
the youngest and richest democracies he was prepared to put them
on hold. In August 1949, as he prepared for his trip, Nehru was
uncharacteristically nervous. 'In what mood shall I address America?'
he asked his sister Vijayalakshmi. 'How shall I address people etc.? How
shall I deal with the Government there and businessmen and others?
Which facet of myself should I put before the American public – the

Indian or the European . . . I want to be friendly with the Americans but always making it clear what we stand for.'[17]

Nehru spent three weeks in America, delivering a speech a day to audiences as diverse as the United States Congress and a congregation in a Chicago chapel. He was awarded an honorary doctorate by Columbia University and listened to by a crowd of 10,000 at the University of California at Berkeley. He displayed the common touch, being photographed with a taxi driver in Boston, but also made clear his membership of the aristocracy of the intellect, as in a much-publicized visit to Albert Einstein in Princeton.

Addressing Congress, Nehru spoke respectfully of the founders of America, but then counterposed to them a great man from his own country. This was Gandhi, whose message of peace and truth had inspired independent India's foreign policy. The Mahatma, however, 'was too great for the circumscribed borders of any one country, and the message he gave may help us in considering the wider problems of the world'. For what the world most lacked, said Nehru, was 'understanding and appreciation of each other among nations and peoples'.

This was diplomatically put, but elsewhere Nehru spoke more directly. At Columbia University Nehru deplored the desire to 'marshal the world into two hostile camps'. India, he said, would align with neither, but pursue 'an independent approach to each controversial or disputed issue'. In his view, the main cause of war was the persistence of racialism and colonialism. Peace and freedom could be secured only if the domination of one country or one race over another was finally brought to an end.[18]

The American press was impressed with the Indian prime minister. The *Chicago Sun Times* went so far as to say that 'in many ways Nehru is the nearest thing this generation has to a Thomas Jefferson in his way of giving voice to the universal aspirations for freedom of people everywhere'.[19] The *Christian Science Monitor* described him as a 'World Titan'. When he left, a columnist in the *St. Louis Post Dispatch* observed that 'Nehru has departed from us, leaving behind clouds of misty-eyed women'.[20] Even *Time* magazine admitted that, while Americans were still not sure what Nehru stood for, 'they sensed in him, if not rare truth, a rare heart'.[21]

There was, however, one set of people who did not warm to the visitor from India – the mandarins of the State Department. Nehru had several long discussions with the secretary of state, Dean Acheson, but these went nowhere. In his memoirs Acheson wrote dismissively and with some despair about Nehru's visit. In their talks he found him 'prickly', arrogant ('he talked to me . . . as though I was a public meeting'), and too ready to pick on the faults of others (notably the French and Dutch colonialists) without recognizing any of his own. When Acheson broached the subject of Kashmir, he got 'a curious combination of a public speech and flashes of anger and deep dislike of his opponents'. Altogether, he found Nehru 'one of the most difficult men with whom I have ever had to deal'.[22]

Other American officials were more sympathetic to Nehru. One such was Chester Bowles, who was ambassador in New Delhi from 1951–3. Witnessing Nehru at work in his own environment, Bowles was visibly impressed by his commitment to democracy and democratic procedure, and to the rights of minorities. Dean Acheson, and many other Americans, divided the world into two categories: friends and foes.[23] That was not a reading that Bowles endorsed. He insisted that 'it is immature and ridiculous for us [Americans] to jump to the conclusion that because he [Nehru] is not 100 per cent for us, he must be against us'.[24]

During Bowles's tenure India and the United States drew closer. The US sent experts and equipment to help with Indian programmes of agricultural development. But the popular mistrust persisted. A writer from Delaware, touring the subcontinent in the early fifties, came across many educated Indians for whom the United States was a country 'isolated by gross faults, stewing alone in the unthinkable sins of materialism, imperialist ambitions, war mongering, political corruption, spiritual and cultural poverty, racial discrimination and injustice'.[25]

The mutual distrust deepened after 1953, when the Republicans found themselves back in power after twenty years out of it. Towards the end of that year William F. Knowland, the Republican leader in the Senate, undertook a six-week world tour. After he returned home he told the US News and World Report that Jawaharlal Nehru did not represent all the nations or peoples of Asia. Said Senator Knowland emphatically: 'Certainly Nehru does not speak for the Republic of Korea, for Japan, for Free China or Formosa, for Thailand, Viet Nam, Laos or Cambodia. He certainly does not speak for Pakistan. The only countries he might be able to speak for with some authority, or at least represent their views, would be India itself, Indonesia which is also neutralist in outlook, and perhaps Burma . . .'.[26]

These views were shared by the new secretary of state, John Foster Dulles. Dulles was the coldest of cold warriors, whose foreign policy was dominated by his obsession with communism. In the battle against the Soviet Union, Dulles was prepared to disregard the internal political systems of other nations. Generally speaking, dictators who toed the American line were to be preferred to democrats who didn't: 'If he is a bastard, at least he is our bastard', as he is famously supposed to have said.

Dulles and Nehru disliked each other from the start. The American claimed that 'the concept of neutrality is obsolete, immoral, and shortsighted'. Those who professed it were, in effect, crypto-communists. Nehru, naturally, did not take kindly to this interpretation. As the Australian diplomat Walter Crocker wrote, the Indian prime minister did not miss the irony that,

> as regards the sanctity of the Free World and the Free Life proclaimed by Dulles, he, damned by Dulles, was carrying India through a gargantuan effort towards Parliamentary Democracy, the rule of law, freedom and equality for all religions, and social and economic reforms, while among the countries which Dulles praised and subsidized because they were 'willing to stand up and be counted' as anti-Communist were effete or persecuting tyrannies, oligarchies and theocracies, sometimes corrupt as well as retrograde.[27]

Dulles further offended Indian sensibilities when he suggested that Portugal – a trusted US ally – could keep its colony of Goa as long as it chose to. However, the secretary's decisive contribution to wrecking Indo-US relations was the military pact he signed with Pakistan in February 1954. As one historian drily remarked, 'Mr Dulles wanted pacts . . . Pakistan wanted money and arms.'[28]

Almost from the time of Independence the United Kingdom had seen Pakistan as a potential ally in the Cold War; as, in fact, a 'strong bastion against Communism'. By contrast, India was seen as being soft on the Soviets. Winston Churchill himself was much impressed by the argument that Pakistan could be made to stand firm on Russia's eastern flank, much as that reliable Western client, Turkey, stood firm on the west. The brilliant young Harvard professor Henry Kissinger endorsed this idea – in his view, the 'defense of Afghanistan [from the Soviets] depends on the strength of Pakistan'.[29]

For Republicans like Dulles, the fight against communism was paramount. Hence the tilt towards Pakistan, which he saw as a key member of a defensive ring around the Soviet Union. From bases in Pakistan American planes could strike deep into Soviet central Asia. Dulles's view was seconded by Vice-President Richard Nixon and their combined efforts ultimately prevailed over President Eisenhower, who was worried about the fall-out in India following any formal alliance with Pakistan.[30]

American military aid to Pakistan ran to about $80 million a year. The US also encouraged the Pakistanis to join the anti-Soviet military alliances in central and Southeast Asia known as CENTO and SEATO. Two months before Dulles signed his pact with the Pakistanis an American missionary who had worked for years in the subcontinent warned that 'to weigh Pakistan militarily over and against India would alienate India'.[31] That it certainly did, although there were other strains on Indo-American relations as well. In the ongoing conflicts of the Cold War – as in Korea and Indo-China – India was seen as being too neutral by far. Nehru's vigorous canvassing of the recognition of the People's Republic of China, and his insistence that it be given the permanent seat in the UN Security Council then occupied by Taiwan, was also not taken to kindly by Washington. There were an increasing number of Americans who felt that Nehru had 'entered the arena of world politics as a champion challenging American wisdom'.[32]

As perhaps he had. For, as Nehru wrote to the industrialist G. D. Birla in May 1954, 'I do not think that there are many examples in history of a succession of wrong policies being followed by a country as by the United States in the Far East during the past five or six years. They have taken one wrong step after another . . . They think that they can solve any problem with money and arms. They forget the human element. They forget the nationalistic urges of people. They forget the strong resentment of people in Asia against impositions.'[33]

The industrialist himself was rather keen that the two countries forge better relations. In October 1954 Birla visited the United States and spoke to a cross-section of influential people. He even had half an hour with John Foster Dulles, who complained about how India 'misrepresented them as war-mongers and so on and so forth'.[34] In February 1956 Birla visited the United States again on a bridge-building mission. He asked Nehru for advice, and got a sermon. 'Dulles's statement about Goa has angered everybody here', said the prime minister. 'Indo-American relations are much more affected by this kind of thing than by the aid they may give. Then there is the American military aid to Pakistan, which is a constant and growing threat to us and, in effect, adds to our burdens much more than the actual aid they give to us.'[35]

The next month John Foster Dulles made so bold as to visit New Delhi. The record of his talks with the Indian government is still classified, but we do have the proceedings of a press conference he addressed. Here, the secretary of state was subject to a series of hostile questions. He was asked why he had said that Goa was an integral part of Portugal. Dulles did not deny this, but clarified that he was for a 'peaceful solution' of the controversy. Then the talk turned to military aid to Pakistan, and the possibility that it might lead to an escalation of the conflict in Kashmir. Dulles defensively answered that 'the arms supply to Pakistan is not designed in any way to be a threat to India'. When the questioner persisted, Dulles angrily remarked that 'we do not feel that because there is a dispute over Kashmir . . . Pakistan should be unarmed so that it could not resist Soviet Communist aggression'. The secretary of state then threatened to walk out if any more questions were asked on Goa or Kashmir.[36]

India and the United States did seem to have much in common – the democratic way of life, a commitment to cultural pluralism, and (not least) a nationalist origin myth that stressed struggle against the British oppressor. But on questions of international politics they resolutely differed. America thought India soft on communism; India thought America soft on colonialism. In the end, that which divided seemed to overwhelm that which united; in part because of the personal chemistry – or rather, lack thereof – between the key players on either side.[37]

III

Jawaharlal Nehru visited the Soviet Union two decades before he toured North America. Arriving by train from Berlin, he reached the Russian frontier on 7 November 1927, the tenth anniversary of the Bolshevik seizure of power. 'Lenin worship' was abundantly on display. There were red flags and busts of the Bolshevik hero everywhere. Nehru went on to Moscow, a city which impressed him both with its physical grandeur and its apparent social levelling. 'The contrasts between extreme luxury and poverty are not visible, nor does one notice the hierarchy of class or caste.'

Nehru wrote a travelogue on his trip; its tone is unfailingly gushing, whether speaking of peasant collectives, the constitution of the USSR, the presumed tolerance of minorities, or economic progress. A visit to Lenin's tomb prompted a reverie on the man and his mission, ending with a ringing endorsement of Romain Rolland's claim that the Bolshevik leader was 'the greatest man of action in our century and at the same time the most selfless'. He was taken to a model prison, which he thought illustrative of the 'better social order and humane criminal law' of the socialist system.

As compared to bourgeois countries, concluded Nehru, the Soviet Union treated its workers and peasants better, its women and children better, even its prisoners better. The credulousness of the narrative is made complete by the epigraph to the book of his travels – Wordsworth on the French Revolution: 'Bliss was it in that dawn to be alive / But to be young was very heaven.'[38]

Nehru's biographer points out that he visited 'the Soviet Union in the last days of its first, halcyon period. If his reaction was idealistic, it was partly because there was still some idealism in the air.'[39] This is true, after a fashion; for there was still a glow about Lenin (whose own intolerance was not yet widely known outside Russia); while the extermination of kulaks and the Siberian death camps lay in the future. And of course there were other such endorsements provided by Western fellow-travellers of the 1920s. Like them, Nehru had come intending to be impressed; and he was.[40]

It was, above all, the Soviet economic system which most appealed to Nehru. As a progressive intellectual of his time, he thought state ownership more just than private property, state planning more efficient than the market. His *Glimpses of World History* contains an admiring account of the Soviet five-year plans. Yet at no time was he attracted by the Bolshevik model of armed revolution or by the one-party state. His training under Gandhi predisposed him towards non-violence, and his exposure to Western liberalism made him an enthusiast for electoral democracy and a free press.

After Independence, relations with the Soviet Union were at first frosty. This was because the Communist Party of India, with Moscow's blessing, had attempted to overthrow the state. But the insurrection failed, and the Soviets also thawed. Now they sought to woo India away from the Western camp. In 1951, while the American Congress debated a request for food aid from India, the Soviets – unencumbered by democratic procedure – offered to send 50,000 tons of wheat at once. Indian efforts in mediating in the Korean conflict were also appreciated by Moscow. Previously, Asian states had been judged by their suitability for communism; but (as with Dulles's America) the Cold War made ideology more flexible. It no longer mattered if a country was socialist; what was crucial was whether it was on one's side.[41]

The consummation of this change was the reception given to Jawaharlal Nehru when he visited the Soviet Union in 1955. 'Wherever Nehru went in the Soviet Union', wrote one observer, 'there were large crowds to greet him. In all the factories workmen gathered in thousands to have a glimpse of him.' At Moscow University 'the students left their classes and gave him a great ovation'. (One of the students was Mikhail Gorbachev; years later, he was to recall in his memoirs the impact made on him by Nehru and his idea of a moral politics.[42]) On the last day of his stay the Indian prime minister was due to speak at a public meeting in Gorky Park. But the crowd turned out to be far larger than anticipated, so the venue was shifted to the stadium of the Dynamo Moscow football team.[43]

Six months later the Soviet leaders Bulganin and Khrushchev came for a return visit. The Indians in turn pulled out all the stops. Before the visitors arrived in Delhi, loudspeakers exhorted the people to turn out in numbers, in grateful response to the reception the Russians had given Nehru. In the event there were spectacular turnouts in all the cities the duo visited. There were several reasons for this enthusiasm: the curiosity for the exotic and foreign, the Indian love of a good show and, not least, the deep vein of anti-Western feeling which took vicarious pride in Russia's challenge to the USA. The crowds were biggest in radical, anti-imperialist Calcutta, where students and factory workers made up a good proportion of the half a million who came out to cheer the Soviet leaders. But even New Delhi was ablaze with illumination. 'The brightly lit Delhi Stock Exchange vied with the Communist Party office in a challenge of festive lights.'[44]

In their three weeks in India Bulganin and Khrushchev visited steel mills and hydroelectric plants, and spoke at public meetings in no fewer than seven state capitals. The most significant of these, without question, was Srinagar, the capital of Jammu and Kashmir state. Here they made clear that they accepted the Valley as being part of the Indian Union, and the Kashmiris as being one of the 'talented and industrious peoples of India'.[45] Nothing could have sounded sweeter to Indian ears.

IV

On the eve of Nehru's departure for Moscow in 1955 an Indian critic had worried that he would be taken in by his hosts. For 'like many another sensitive nature, accustomed in its late twenties and early thirties to regard the Soviet Union as truly Progressive, the Prime Minister seems never to have quite got over the vision of those days. Despite all that has happened since then, the Soviet [Union] still retains for him some of that enchantment. To its virtues he continues to be very kind, to its vices and cruelties, he is almost blind.'[46]

The writer was A. D. Gorwala, a Western-oriented liberal. There were others like him, Indians who believed that India should ally more strongly with the democracies in the Cold War.[47] But these were most likely outnumbered, and certainly outshouted, by those Indians who suspected the United States and favoured the Soviet Union. One reason for this was that while the Americans were loath to ask their European allies to disband their empires in Asia and Africa, the Russians spoke frequently about the evils of racialism and colonialism.[48]

Nehru at first tried hard to avoid taking sides in the Cold War. But, as he often said, this non-alignment was not mere evasion; it had a positive charge to it. A third bloc might come to act as a salutary moderating effect on the hubris of the superpowers. We have spoken already of the Asian Relations Conference in 1947. Another such effort, in which Nehru played an important part, was the Afro-Asian conference, held in the Indonesian city of Bandung in 1955.

Only countries that had independent governments were invited to Bandung. Twenty-nine sent delegations, including India and China. Four African nations were represented (the others still lay under the colonial yoke); but delegates from Iran, Iraq, Saudi Arabia and Syria all came. The meeting discussed methods of cultural and economic co-operation, and committed itself firmly to the end of colonial rule. For, as President Sukarno of Indonesia observed, 'how can we say that colonialism is dead so long as vast areas of Asia and Africa are unfree?'[49]

Nehru considered the Bandung Conference 'a great achievement'; it 'proclaimed the political emergence in world affairs of over half the world's population. [But] it presented no unfriendly challenge or hostility to anyone . . .' As he told the Indian Parliament on his return, the historic links between Asian and African countries had been sundered by colonialism; now, as freedom dawned, they could be revived and reaffirmed.[50]

This last protestation was in answer to the charge that Bandung and the like were, in essence, anti-Western. How 'non-aligned', in fact, was non-alignment? In India, its ideals were put sternly to the test in the second half of 1956. In July of that year Gamal Abdel Nasser nationalized the company that managed the Suez Canal. Britain (whose strategic interests were most threatened by the action) reacted by asking for international control over the Canal. Nehru, who knew both parties well, tried hard to mediate. But he failed, and ultimately, in late October, the British, in collusion with the French and the Israelis, undertook a military invasion of Egypt. This act of neocolonial aggression drew worldwide condemnation. Finally, under American pressure, the Anglo-French alliance was forced to withdraw.[51]

Close on the heels of the invasion of Egypt, Soviet tanks rolled into Budapest. This followed a popular revolt which had overthrown the Soviet client regime in favour of a more representative government. Moscow reacted in brutal fashion to restore the *status quo ante*. Their action, like that of the British and the French in the Middle East, was viewed as an unacceptable infringement of national sovereignty.

Indian commentators saw the invasions of Egypt and Hungary as wholly comparable. Both were 'acts of international brigandage' by powers that commanded permanent seats in the UN Security Council – both had 'spread a wave of cynicism throughout the world'. As a Madras journal pointed out, while the independence of Egypt threatened the oil resources of Britain and France, 'the independence of Hungary would not only threaten the supply of uranium so essential for the maintenance of the Red Army in top form, but would cause a dangerous rift in the Soviet empire. London could not countenance the first and Moscow could not tolerate the second. Hence their acts of naked aggression which amount to a savage exhibition of the predatory animal instinct.'[52]

Nehru had criticized the Anglo-French intervention as soon as it happened.[53] But now, when the United Nations met to discuss a resolution calling upon the Soviet Union 'to withdraw all of its forces without delay from Hungarian territory', India, represented by V. K. Krishna Menon, abstained. This caused great resentment in the

Western world, and exposed the Indian government to the charge of keeping double standards.[54]

There was also much domestic criticism of India's stand. There was an angry debate in Parliament, and sections of the press deplored 'our shameful sycophancy to the Soviet rulers . . .' 'By kowtowing to Russia we have abdicated our moral pretensions', wrote one journalist. It was speculated that the government may have been influenced by its uncertain hold over Kashmir, since one of the UN resolutions it had abstained from asked for an internationally supervised plebiscite in Hungary.[55]

Later research has revealed that Nehru was actually deeply unhappy about the Soviet invasion. He had sent several private messages to Moscow urging it to withdraw its troops. Afterwards, India spoke out in public too, but the damage had been done. It was compounded when Nehru stood by Krishna Menon's original abstention, on the grounds that insufficient information was available at the time.[56]

The fiasco over Hungary undermined Nehru's international credibility. Non-alignment was seen by some as meaning 'fierce condemnation of the Western bloc when its actions are wrong', but 'equivocal language when the Soviet bloc goes off the rails'.[57] The episode also exposed the prime minister to the charge of putting personal loyalty above national purpose. For while he privately deplored what Krishna Menon had done, he stood by him in public.

Krishna Menon was an old friend of Nehru, and in his own way a remarkable man. Educated at the London School of Economics, he was also the first editor of Penguin's prestigious non-fiction imprint, Pelican Books. In the 1930s he had worked tirelessly in canvassing British support for Indian independence. But he also found time to act as an unofficial spokesman and literary agent for Nehru. He was rewarded with the High Commissioner's job in London after Independence. Here he worked very hard, but also made enemies, through his arrogance and by frequently advertising his friendship with the prime minister.[58]

After returning from London, Krishna Menon was made a Cabinet minister without portfolio. He became a sort of roving ambassador, representing India at the UN and at disarmament meetings in Geneva. A man of forceful opinions, he was controversial both in his homeland and out of it. The 'lucidity of his intellect', wrote one journalist who knew him well, 'is sometimes clouded by passions and resentments'. Since his 'likes and dislikes are stronger than would seem quite safe for a man in his position', it did seem 'strange that a man who carries such a storm around with him should have been used for delicate diplomatic missions'.[59]

Even before Hungary there had been adverse comment about the prime minister's reliance on Krishna Menon. Within the Congress, there were many who were uncomfortable with his pro-communist leanings.[60] And the Western press cordially hated him, a New York paper speaking of the 'lack of loveableness' in this 'least tactful of diplomats'.[61]

But Nehru would stand by Menon. As early as 1953 it was being noticed in Delhi that the prime minister 'turns blue when anyone criticises his diplomatic pet, Mr Krishna Menon'. This blindness was to cost Nehru dearly over Hungary in 1956. But he still would not discard him. Why? A helpful answer is provided by Alva Myrdal, who was Sweden's ambassador in India at the time, and knew Nehru well. The prime minister, concluded Myrdal, 'knew Menon's shortcomings but kept listening to him because of his brilliance. Menon was the only genuine intellectual foil Nehru had in the government', the only man with whom he could discuss Marx and Mill, Dickens and Dostoevsky.[62]

V

Let us now turn to India's relationship with its larger and even more populous neighbour, China. The two civilizations had long been linked by ties of trade and culture. More recently, each had keenly watched the other's struggle against European domination. The Congress, and Nehru, had a particular regard for the Kuomintang leader Chiang Kai-shek, who had urged the Americans to in turn urge the British to grant the Indians independence.

In 1949, however, the Kuomintang were overthrown by the communists. What would relations now be like? To indicate continuity, India retained their serving ambassador to Beijing, who was the historian K. M. Pannikar. In May 1950 Pannikar was granted an interview with Mao Zedong, and came away greatly impressed. Mao's face, he recalled later, was 'pleasant and benevolent and the look in his eyes is kindly'. There 'is no cruelty or hardness either in his eyes or in the expression of his mouth. In fact he gave me the impression of a philosophical mind, a little dreamy but absolutely sure of itself.' The Chinese leader had 'experienced many hardships and endured tremendous sufferings', yet 'his face showed no signs of bitterness, cruelty or sorrow'. Mao reminded Pannikar of his own boss, Nehru, for 'both are men of action with dreamy, idealistic temperaments', and both 'may be considered humanists in the broadest sense of the term'.[63]

This would be laughable if it were not so serious. Intellectuals have always had a curious fascination for the man of power; George Bernard Shaw wrote about Lenin in much the same terms. Yet Shaw was an unaffiliated writer, responsible only to himself. Pannikar was the official representative of his government. What he said and believed would carry considerable weight. And here he was representing one of history's most ruthless dictators as a dreamy, soft, poetic kind of chap.

In October 1950, not long after Mao met Pannikar, China invaded and annexed Tibet. They had long claimed suzerainty over that country, and in the past had often exercised control over it. But there had also been periods when Tibet was genuinely independent, as in the four decades before the communist invasion. Tibet and China, after all, had sent separate, independent delegations to the Asian Relations Conference in 1947.

Nehru was now placed in an unenviable position. India had close relations with Tibet, economic as well as cultural. But a newly free and still vulnerable India could scarcely go to war on Tibet's behalf. Speaking in Parliament a few weeks after the Chinese action, Nehru hoped that the matter would be resolved peacefully. He clarified that he believed that while China had historically exercised some kind of 'suzerainty' over Tibet, this did not amount to 'sovereignty'. He also added that he did not see how Tibet could at all be a 'threat' to China.[64]

Privately, Nehru thought 'the Chinese acted rather foolishly' in annexing Tibet. There was 'a strong feeling here [in India] of being let down by them'. Still, thought the prime minister, 'we have to be careful not to overdo' criticisms of a neighbouring country that was also emerging from the shadows of European domination.[65]

Other members of the government urged a stronger line. Vallabhbhai Patel, for instance, was convinced that the Chinese had made a dupe out of Pannikar. They had lulled him into a 'false sense of confidence' which led the ambassador to overlook completely the plans for the invasion. But now that the deed was done, it behoved India to be vigilant. Writing to Nehru on 7 November, Patel warned that 'China is no longer divided. It is united and strong.' 'Recent and bitter history', said the home minister,

also tells us that communism is no shield against imperialism and that the Communists are as good or as bad imperialists as any other. Chinese ambitions in this respect not only cover the Himalayan slopes on our side but also include important parts of Assam . . . Chinese irredentism and Communist imperialism are different from the expansionism or imperialism of the Western Powers. The former has a cloak of ideology which makes it ten times more dangerous. In the guise of ideological expansion lies concealed racial, national or historical claims.

Patel urged Nehru to be 'alive to the new danger' from China, and to make India 'defensively strong'. He then outlined a series of steps to enhance security. He thought that in view of the 'rebuff' over Tibet, India should no longer advocate China's case for entry into the UN. Finally, he argued that the latest developments should prompt a fresh reconsideration of 'our relationship with China, Russia, America, Britain and Burma'. Patel seemed here to be hinting that India should reconsider its policy of non-alignment in favour of an alliance with the West.[66]

This latter shift was advocated more vigorously by the journalist D. F. Karaka. Like Patel, Karaka was appalled by Pannikar's carelessness. (Apparently, the ambassador did not hear about the Chinese invasion until it was announced on All-India Radio.) The annexation of Tibet had shown that the Himalaya was no longer impregnable. And the Indian army lacked the equipment or training to take on a determined and focused enemy. Thus, concluded Karaka, 'whatever may be our past unhappy relations with Britain, however much may be our fear of American imperialism spreading in Asia, we have to decide now whether we will continue with this policy of neutrality and endanger our frontiers, or whether we will take the lesser risk and make a military pact with the United States and with Great Britain.'[67]

Nehru would not deign to take notice of journalists such as Karaka. But he did answer Patel, in a note on the subject circulated to the Cabinet. He thought it a pity that Tibet could not be 'saved'. Yet he considered it 'exceedingly unlikely' that India would now face an attack from China; it was 'inconceivable' that they would 'undertake a wild adventure across the Himalayas'. He thought that 'the idea that communism inevitably means expansion and war, or to put it more precisely, that Chinese communism means inevitably an expansion towards India, is rather naive'. Regardless of the happenings in Tibet, India should still seek 'some kind of understanding' with Beijing, for 'India and China at peace with each other would make a vast difference to the whole set-up and balance of the world'.[68]

A month later Patel died. Now there existed no real opposition to a policy of 'understanding' with China. The two countries shared vast borders – thousand of miles of mostly unmarked and unsurveyed territory. On India's west, the border ran along the Buddhist-dominated district of Ladakh in Jammu and Kashmir state, which touched the Chinese provinces of Tibet and Sinkiang. On the east, the border was defined by the McMahon Line, drawn on the crest of the Himalaya, as a result of a treaty signed by the British and Tibet in 1914. In the middle, the two countries touched each other near the watershed of the river Ganga, which divided Tibet from the Indian state of Uttar Pradesh.

The border in the centre was relatively uncontentious, whereas in the two extremes the situation was more problematic. The Chinese regarded the McMahon Line in particular as an imperialist imposition. For the moment they let the matter pass, and focused on getting India's goodwill, necessary at this time as a bridge to the Western world. In the summer of 1952 a government delegation led by Mrs Vijayalakshmi Pandit visited Beijing. Mrs Pandit had served as India's ambassador to Moscow; more to the point, she was Nehru's adored younger sister. She met Mao once and Chou En-lai twice, and was profoundly impressed by both. Mao, wrote Mrs Pandit to her brother, was 'quiet [and] precise', with a 'great sense of humour'. His appearance in public called Gandhi to mind. As with the Mahatma, 'the public doesn't just applaud him, they worship him. There is both love and adoration in the glances of those who look at him. It is moving to see.' As for Chou En-lai, he 'is a great statesman and possesses abundant vitality and charm. He is polished and has a sense of humour which is terribly infectious. One has to join in his laughter – and he laughs often. He makes one feel at home in a moment and his conversation loses nothing in translation.'

The letter did strike the odd ambivalent note. 'We have been wined and dined', wrote Mrs Pandit, 'and have spoken of friendship and culture and peace until I am getting a little tired.' And she wasn't sure whether the Great Helmsman reminded her more of Gandhi or of Stalin. For while 'Mao gives the impression of being kind and tolerant and wise', the 'tolerant part struck me almost as if it might be a pose as it is reminiscent of the Russian leaders particularly Stalin. He uses the same gesture in greeting and has the same technique with the public.' Still, what stood out was 'the great vitality of the people and the dedicated manner in which they are working. The oppression one feels in Moscow is absent here. Everybody seems happy and determined to make the country prosperous'.[69]

Mrs Pandit seems to have reacted to China in 1952 much as her brother had reacted to Russia in 1927. Perhaps this dawn might not turn out to be a false one after all. So Nehru was inclined to think, too. Soon, romanticism was to be reinforced by realpolitik. The United States began to tilt markedly towards Pakistan, giving New Delhi one more reason to befriend Beijing. In a wide-ranging agreement signed in April 1954, India officially recognized Tibet as being part of China. The joint declaration outlined five principles of peaceful co-existence (*panch sheel*), which included mutual non-aggression and mutual respect for each other's territorial integrity.[70]

One person who did not welcome this agreement was the former secretary general of the Foreign Ministry, Sir Girija Shankar Bajpai. Writing to a colleague, Bajpai warned that communist China was no 'different from Russian Communism in its expansionist aims . . .' The current thinking in New Delhi was of 'the naturalness of indefinite continuance of indefinite peace and friendship between China and us'. Bajpai feared that 'those on whom the P[rime] M[inister] now relies most for advice completely and vehemently reject any possibility of a change in what appears to be China's present policy of peace with its Asian neighbours'.[71]

It is unlikely that this warning reached Nehru, and even if it had he would most likely have disregarded it. Towards the end of 1954 he visited China for the first time. As in Russia six months later, huge crowds were mobilized to greet the visitor, who appreciated this 'tremendous emotional response from the Chinese people'. Nehru had discussions with Chou En-lai about border questions, and with Mao about the world situation. He also pressed the case for Tibetan autonomy, the Chinese assuring him in the Dalai Lama's presence that the Buddhist state would enjoy a status which 'no other province enjoyed in the People's Republic of China'.[72]

On his return from China Nehru addressed a mammoth public meeting on the Calcutta Maidan. A million people heard him affirm that 'the people of China do not want war'; they were too busy uniting their country and getting rid of poverty. He spoke admiringly of the spirit of unity in China, the absence of the provincial and sectarian interests that bedevilled India. As for the 'mighty welcome' he had received in the People's Republic, this was 'not because I am Jawaharlal with any special ability, but because I am the Prime Minister of India for which the Chinese people cherish in their hearts the greatest of love and with which they want to maintain the friendliest of relations'.[73]

Two years later the compliment was returned when Chou En-lai visited India. With him were the Dalai and Panchen Lamas, who had been invited as part of the celebrations of the 2500th birth anniversary of the Buddha. On a drive through the countryside the Dalai Lama escaped his Chinese minders and travelled with Nehru. A revolt was brewing in Tibet against the occupiers, he said; he himself was strongly tempted to seek asylum in India. If that was not possible, at least India could send a consul to Lhasa who was not pro-Chinese or pro-communist. When Nehru asked Chou about the situation in Tibet, the Chinese leader conceded that there had been 'unfortunate incidents' there, and promised to look into them.[74]

So there the matter rested. The Dalai Lama went back to Lhasa, and India and China continued to be brothers-in-arms; as the slogan of the time went, *Hindi-Chini bhai-bhai*. The man most responsible for this was the charming Chou. He impressed Nehru, of course, but also a man more cynical by far, the veteran politician C. Rajagopalachari. 'Rajaji' had lunch with the Chinese prime minister and later wrote to a friend that, 'frankly my impression was very favourable. Apart from the general thawing of all communists the Chinese Premier is I believe a good type of man and trustworthy.'[75]

In public India and China expressed undying friendship, but on the ground each was working to protect its strategic interests. India was more concerned with the eastern sector; China with the western one. The British had drawn the McMahon Line to protect the prosperous tea estates of the province of Assam from a putative raid down the Himalaya. There was an 'Inner Line' at the foot of the hills, beyond which no one could venture without a permit. Between this and the border lay some 50,000 square miles of densely forested territory, inhabited by many self-contained and self-administered tribes, each too small to form a separate state, each too remote to be subservient to any existing one. Some of the tribes were Buddhist, and there was also an old Buddhist monastery at Tawang. This paid tribute to Tibetan authorities and was 'ecclesiastically subject' to Lhasa.

Under the treaty of 1914, the British persuaded the Tibetans to relinquish control over Tawang. For, as one colonial official argued, it was necessary to get this 'undoubtedly Tibetan territory' into British India, 'as otherwise Tibet and Assam will adjoin each other and, if Tibet should again come under Chinese control, it will be a dangerous position for us'.[76]

Other tribes living between the Inner and Outer Lines were beyond Tibetan influence. These, like the Buddhists, became Indian citizens by default in August 1947, when the new government inherited the borders bequeathed it by the British. Slowly, New Delhi moved to fill in the administrative vacuum that the British had left behind. In February 1951 a small force accompanied by a political officer visited Tawang, and instructed the lamas that they need no longer pay tribute to Lhasa. Officials also began to fan out into what was now called the North-East Frontier Agency, or NEFA. An Indian Frontier Administrative Service (IFAS) was formed, whose recruits were coached on how best to deal with the sometimes truculent tribes by the British-born anthropologist Verrier Elwin, who was now an Indian citizen and a confidant of Nehru.[77]

The Chinese, for their part, focused on expanding their footprint in the western sector. Here, too, the adjoining Indian territory, known as Ladakh, was Buddhist in its religious colouring. However, it had been an independent state as early as the tenth century. And for the past 150 years it had been part of the principality of Kashmir, whose own allegiances were all to the Indian side of the border.

Between north-east Ladakh and Sinkiang, on the Chinese side, lay an elevated table-land named Aksai Chin, 'absolutely bare' for the most part, with occasional patches of 'scant herbage'.[78] In the past, Ladakhi pastoralists had used Aksai Chin for grazing and salt collection. By an agreement of 1842 this area was identified as being part of Kashmir. This was confirmed by the British, who were worried that the Russians, their adversary in the 'Great Game', might use the plateau to advance heavy artillery into British India.

That didn't happen, but after 1950 the Chinese saw in the same flat terrain a route to their troublesome province of Tibet from the Sinkiang town of Yarkand. Peking sent surveyors to scout the land, and in 1956 began building a road across Aksai Chin. By October 1957 the road was ready, equipped to carry 10-ton military trucks with arms and personnel from Yarkand to Lhasa.

We owe this information to accounts published much later. At the time, however, the Chinese activities in the west, and the Indian activities in the east, were carried on out of each other's gaze. To the world at large, and to their own citizens, the two Asian neighbours were bound by an exemplary relationship of friendship and co-operation.

VI

'If there were ever two countries where every prospect promised brotherly understanding and friendship', wrote a Bombay newspaper in January 1952, 'these two are India and Pakistan. Every possible kind of tie exists between them; the tie of race, the ties of language, of geography, economy and culture.'[79]

Yet India's relations with Pakistan were poisoned from the start. The country had been divided against a backdrop of violence; and the mutual suspicion and hostility persisted. In the winter of 1949–50 there was a wave of communal riots in East Pakistan. Several hundred thousand Hindus crossed over the border into India. Nehru now suggested to his Pakistani counterpart, Liaqat Ali Khan, that they together visit the affected areas to bring about peace. His offer was declined; but Khan agreed to come to Delhi and sign an agreement binding both countries to the humane treatment of their respective minorities. However, the 'Nehru–Liaqat' pact failed to stem the tide of refugees. There was much anger among Hindus in West Bengal, some of whom even wanted the government to go to war with Pakistan on their behalf.[80]

The two main conflicts, however, were about those elemental human needs, land and water. The first, which this book has already alluded to and to which it will return, related to the unresolved status of Kashmir. The second pertained to the fair use of the Indus and its five main tributaries. These rivers ran from east to west, that is, from India towards Pakistan. The Indus and the Jhelum entered Pakistan before any major extraction was possible, but the other four rivers ran for many miles in Indian territory. This made it possible for India to regulate their flow and impound water before the rivers reached the other country.

After Partition, the governments of East and West Punjab signed a 'Standstill Agreement' whereby water continued to flow uninterrupted. When this lapsed, in April 1948, India stopped the waters of the Ravi and the Sutlej from flowing west. They claimed that no fresh agreement had been signed, but it was widely believed that the action was revenge for the Pakistan-backed invasion of Kashmir. Anyhow, the drying up of their canals created panic among the farmers of West Punjab. Within a month a new agreement was signed, and water supply restored. However, the building of the Bhakra-Nangal dam, on the Indian side of the Sutlej river, prompted fresh protests by Pakistan.

Both sides now sought a more permanent solution to the problem. Pakistan asked for the matter to be referred to international arbitration, which India at first refused. The World Bank stepped in to play the role of peacemaker. Knowing the recalcitrance of both sides, the Bank offered a surgical solution – the waters of three rivers would go to Pakistan, the waters of the other three rivers to India. This proposal was tabled in February 1954; it took another six years for the two sides to finally sign it.[81]

With the Indus, as with Kashmir or any other topic under the subcontinental sun, agreement was made more difficult by domestic politics. An Indian or Pakistani head of government who promoted dialogue was inevitably accused of selling out to the other side. An early example of this was the trade war of 1949–51, prompted by the devaluation of the Indian rupee. Pakistan stopped the shipment of jute in protest; India retaliated by refusing to supply coal.[82] The conflict was resolved only when, in February 1951, Nehru agreed to recognize the par value of the Pakistani rupee. His decision was welcomed by chambers of commerce, but bitterly opposed by politicians of all stripes. The general consensus in New Delhi was that 'India has been completely defeated'. One Congress member reported that the feeling in the party office was that 'such a humiliation could not have been possible if Sardar Patel were alive'. A refugee leader remarked, 'The real question to be considered now is to find out the next issue on which Jawaharlal will surrender to Pakistan – Kashmir, or more probably Evacuee Property'. A spokesman of the Hindu Mahasabha said, 'In order to become a world leader, Nehru can go to the extent of surrendering the whole of India to Pakistan.' And an RSS organizer claimed, 'This shows what is to come next. More appeasement and surrenders if the masses do not check Nehru.'[83]

On the Pakistani side, any concession to India was likewise seen by opposition politicians as appeasement of the enemy. At the popular level, however, the feelings about the other side were distinctly mixed. Nationalist ideology drove them apart; but mass culture brought them back together again. It was not just that they ate the same food and lived in the same kinds of homes. They also had the same sense of fun. Indian film stars were widely admired in Pakistan; and Pakistani cricketers given a rousing reception when they played in India.

This ambivalence is captured in an exchange printed by the Karachi newspaper *Dawn* in 1955. A lady who had recently visited her relatives in

India wrote of her experiences while travelling by train from Amritsar to Ambala. When they heard she was from Pakistan, she was set upon by passengers who were refugees from Sindh and West Punjab. Apparently, 'some of the non-refugee Hindu passengers remonstrated, but the refugee Hindus and Sikhs brushed aside their remonstrance, saying that the non-refugees could not realise the suffering of the refugees from Pakistan'. This account of Indian animosity provoked several letters recounting the warmth and hospitality on offer on the other side of the border. A man advised any future traveller to India to 'indulge in Amroods and Pans [guavas and betel-leaf] which are at their best these days instead of indulging in such talks as tend to injure the growing Indo-Pak accord'. A woman correspondent complained that such 'mis-statements' created bitterness and precluded 'amity between India and Pakistan'. This last ideal was then endorsed by the original letter-writer, with this telling caveat: 'I wish, however, that as a Pakistani, which I suppose she is, she had the delicacy of stating "Pakistan and India" instead of "India and Pakistan".'[84]

VII

Indian foreign policy was opposed to the continuance of colonial rule anywhere. This, naturally, meant reclaiming the pieces of the motherland that were still under the control of foreigners. When the British left in 1947, the Portuguese stayed on in Goa and their other possessions in India while the French remained in control of three slivers of land in the south – most importantly the port of Pondicherry – as well as the eastern enclave of Chandernagore.

In June 1949 the population of Chandernagore voted by an overwhelming majority to merge with India. The election had witnessed a resounding display of patriotism, with posters representing a mother in Indian dress reaching out to reclaim a child clad in Western apparel. A year later the territory was transferred. But the French hung on to their slices of south India. In the spring of 1954 the situation became 'increasingly tense'; there was a vigorous pro-merger movement afoot in Pondicherry, and daily demonstrations in front of the French consulate in Madras. On 1 November the French finally handed over their territories, which the Indians celebrated with a spectacular display of fireworks. The following January's annual Republic Day parade for the first time featured a float from Pondicherry, with young girls singing French songs.[85]

In welcoming back these fragments, Jawaharlal Nehru praised the governments of both countries for their 'tolerance, good sense and wisdom', thus solving the problem of French India 'with grace and goodwill'.[86] These remarks were intended above all for the Portuguese, who, however, were not listening. They were determined to hang on to Goa for as long as they could. As the transfer of Pondicherry was being finalized, the Portuguese dictator Antonio de Oliveira Salazar spoke on national radio of their Indian colonies as belonging to 'the Portuguese Nation by injunction of History and force of Law'. 'Goa constitutes a Portuguese community in India', he insisted: 'Goa represents a light of the West in lands of the Orient.' It had to be retained, so that it might 'continue to be the memorial of Portuguese discoveries and a small hearth of the spirit of the West in the East'.[87]

A Goa Congress Committee had been in operation since well before Independence; its activists included resident Goans as well as exiles in Bombay. They argued that the conditions in Goa were far worse than in British India; racial prejudice was rife and human rights wholly absent. In 1946 the left-wing Congress politician Ram Manohar Lohia visited the territory and exhorted the people to rise against the rulers. A wave of strikes and protests followed; these were crushed by the authorities. On 15 August 1947 the Indian tricolour was hoisted here and there, but the protesters were quickly taken away by the police.[88]

Apart from Goa, the Portuguese also held several smaller territories up the Konkan coast. One was Daman, which had a garrison of 1,500 African soldiers from Portuguese East Africa. This abutted the Indian province of Bombay, which after Independence had imposed prohibition. There was now a flourishing trade in the smuggling of liquor. On Sunday evenings the frontier between Daman and Bombay was 'strewn with pilgrims to Bacchus, wending their way back to the land where they belong, back to Bharat, land of scarcity and austerity'.[89]

Alcoholics apart, most politically conscious Indians were outraged by the Portuguese attitude over their colonies. Nehru at first moved slowly, hoping that the matter would be resolved by dialogue. But his hand was being forced by radicals of the Socialist Party, who began a series of satyagrahas to compel Goa to join the union. In July 1954 a group of activists from Bombay seized the tiny enclave of Dadra. The next month the somewhat bigger enclave of Nagar-Haveli also fell without a fight. Then 1,000 volunteers attempted to cross over to Daman on Independence Day. They were stopped by the Indian police, whereupon they wired the prime minister for support. Nehru wired back saying that such a showdown would not 'help our cause'.[90]

The socialists were only temporarily deterred. A year later a group led by N. G. Goray entered Goa shouting slogans. They walked several miles into the territory before being attacked by the police. Several protesters were badly injured. The *satyagrahis* were put in Fort Aguada prison, where they spent twenty months before being released. During these protests in 1954 and 1955, the Portuguese arrested more than 2,000 people.[91]

VIII

For Jawaharlal Nehru, foreign policy was a means of making India's presence felt in the world. After Independence he personally supervised the creation of the Indian Foreign Service (IFS), transferring to its cadre able officers of the ICS and making fresh selections from the young. A job in the IFS had a nearly unique combination of idealism and glamour; it also offered the chance of personal contact with the prime minister. One IFS officer recalled how, early in 1948, Nehru called him to his room and showed him a map of the world. The prime minister's eyes ranged over the globe, and his fingers pointed to places north, south, east and west. 'We will have forty embassies!' he exclaimed. 'We will have forty missions!'[92]

Five years later, when India did have forty missions, Nehru wrote them all a letter of self-congratulation. The 'prestige of India has greatly increased' since Independence, he said, for 'we have always avoided playing a flashy role in international affairs . . . Gradually, an appreciation has grown in other countries of our own sincerity of purpose even though there has been disagreement.' He asked all those representing India abroad – 'from the Head of the Mission to the humblest employee' – to 'feel and work as a happy family, cooperating with each other . . . We are all partners in a great adventure, and are all partners and comrades in the same undertaking.'[93]

Although presented and carried out as a collective enterprise, this particular adventure had 'made by the prime minister' stamped all over it. In 1950, one of his most intelligent and least sycophantic cabinet ministers spoke of how Nehru was becoming 'the biggest man in the world, overtopping the USA men, the UK men and every other man'. Through its leader, a country 'without material, men or money – the three means of power' – was 'now fast coming to be recognized as the biggest moral power in the civilized world . . . her word listened to with respect in the councils of the great'.[94] Even opposition politicians appreciated what Nehru had done for India's international standing. Non-alignment seemed to them to be a creative application of Gandhian principles in world affairs. Confidence in its viability was strengthened when India was called upon to play an important mediatory role in the conflicts and civil wars of the time.

Intelligent foreigners also praised Nehru's non-alignment. When that now great publishing firm, Feltrinelli of Milan, began operations in 1955, one of the first two books it published was Nehru's autobiography, which it celebrated both for its 'consistent and coherent anti-fascism' and as an authentic voice of 'the countries that were emerging from colonial domination . . . to take their place forcefully in the global political system'.[95] And from her post in the Swedish embassy in New Delhi, Alva Myrdal wrote to her husband Gunnar of how Nehru was 'naturally playing an authoritative, not to say world-historical role without the slightest tendency to Caesarism. Isn't it true that he is perhaps the only person we have seen reach a high and powerful position without taking on new self-importance?'[96]

Such was Nehru's standing among the people of the front-line states in the Cold War, those who stood between the United States and the Soviet Union. In 1955 non-alignment still had a glow and moral halo about it. The next year was the Hungary fiasco, and the beginning of the Western disillusionment with Nehru. It took longer for him to lose the enchanted support of his countrymen.

9

REDRAWING THE MAP

Some want to revive the tradition of Shivaji and to hoist the Bhagwa Jhanda in Samyukta Maharashtra; others wish to extend the economic empire of the Bombay and Ahmedabad millionaires all over Maha-Gujarat. Provincial prejudices, rivalries and jealousies are being revived on all sides and everyone seems anxious to separate from, rather than unite with, the others. The Assamese want this bit of land cut off from Bengal, the Bengalis want a slice of Bihar, the Telugus are discontented in Orissa, the Tamilian minority wants to cut itself off from Travancore . . .

K. A. ABBAS, left-wing writer, January 1951

I

THE LEADING INDIAN NATIONALISTS had long been sensible of the power of the mother tongue to rouse and move. This was a land of many languages, each with its distinct script, grammar, vocabulary and literary traditions. Rather than deny this diversity, the Congress sought to give space to it. As early as 1917 the party had committed itself to the creation of linguistic provinces in a free India. A separate Andhra circle was formed in that year, a separate Sindh circle the following year. After the Nagpur Congress of 1920, the principle was extended and formalized with the creation of provincial Congress committees (PCCs) by linguistic zones: the Karnataka Pradesh PCC, the Orissa PCC, the Maharashtra PCC, etc. Notably these did not follow, and were often at odds with, the administrative divisions of British India.

The linguistic reorganization of the Congress was encouraged and supported by Mahatma Gandhi. When Independence finally came Gandhi thought that the states of the new nation should be defined on the basis of language. Shortly afterwards, on 10 October 1947, he wrote to a colleague: 'I do believe that we should hurry up with the

reorganization of linguistic provinces . . . There may be an illusion
for the time being that different languages stand for different cultures,
but there is also the possibility [that with the creation] of linguistic
provinces it may disappear. I shall write something [about it] if I get
the time . . . I am not unaware that a class of people have been saying
that linguistic provinces are wrong. In my opinion, this class delights
in creating obstacles.'[1]

Jawaharlal Nehru was also appreciative of the linguistic diversity of
India. In an essay of 1937, he wrote that 'a living language is a throbbing,
vital thing, ever changing, ever growing and mirroring the people who
speak and write it'. And 'our great provincial languages are no dialects
or vernaculars, as the ignorant sometimes call them. They are ancient
languages with a rich inheritance, each spoken by many millions of
people, each tied up inextricably with the life and culture and ideas
of the masses as well as the upper classes. It is axiomatic that the masses
can only grow educationally and culturally through the medium of
their own language.'[2]

That was Nehru's view in 1937, but by 1947 he was having other
thoughts. The country had just been divided on the basis of religion:
would not dividing it further on the basis of language merely
encourage the break-up of the Union? Why not keep intact the existing
administrative units, such as Madras, which had within it communities
of Tamil, Malayalam, Telugu, Kannada, Urdu and Konkani speakers, and
Bombay, whose peoples spoke Marathi, Gujarati, Urdu, Sindhi, Gondi
and other tongues? Would not such multilingual and multicultural
states provide an exemplary training in harmonious living? In any case,
should not the new nation unite on the secular ideals of peace, stability
and economic development, rather than revive primordial identities of
caste and language?

Nehru gave voice to these reservations in a speech to the Constituent
Assembly three months after Independence. While the Congress had
once promised linguistic provinces, he said, the country now faced
'a very critical situation resulting from partition'. Now 'disruptionist
tendencies had come to the fore'; to check them, one had to underline
'the security and stability of India . . . The first essential therefore is for
India as a whole to be strong and firmly established, confident in her
capacity to meet all possible dangers and face and meet all problems. If
India lives, all parts of India also live and prosper. If India is enfeebled,
all her component elements grow weak.'[3]

The creation of linguistic provinces, then, had to be deferred until such time as India was strong and sure of herself. Nehru seems to have persuaded even Gandhi of this, for in November 1947 the Mahatma was writing that 'the reluctance to enforce linguistic redistribution is perhaps justifiable in the present depressing atmosphere. The exclusive spirit is ever uppermost. No one thinks of the whole of India.' Gandhi now thought that the reorganization of provinces should be postponed until a calmer time, when communal strife had died out and been replaced by 'a healthy atmosphere, promoting concord in the place of discord, peace in the place of strife, progress in the place of retrogression and life in the place of death.'[4]

As ever, Gandhi extolled the need to take 'one step at a time'. But the principle itself he would not surrender. In a prayer meeting held on 25 January 1948 Gandhi returned to the subject of linguistic states. 'The Congress had decided some twenty years ago', he recalled, 'that there should be as many provinces in the country as there are major languages.' Now it was in power, and in a position to execute that promise. Gandhi thought that if new provinces were formed on the basis of language, and if

> they are all placed under the authority of Delhi there is no harm at all. But it will be very bad if they all want to be free and refuse to accept central authority. It should not be that Bombay then will have nothing to do with Maharashtra and Maharashtra with Karnataka and Karnataka with Andhra. Let all live as brothers. Moreover if linguistic provinces are formed it will also give a fillip to the regional languages. It would be absurd to make Hindusthani the medium of instruction in all the regions and it is still more absurd to use English for this purpose.[5]

Within a week Gandhi was dead. And the men in power had other, and more urgent, matters to attend to. Millions of refugees from East and West Pakistan had to be found homes and gainful employment. An undeclared war was taking place in Kashmir. A new constitution had to be decided upon. Elections had to be scheduled, economic policies framed and executed. For now, and perhaps indefinitely, the creation of new provinces had to wait.

Nehru's reluctance to superimpose divisions of language on the recent division by religion had the support of both Vallabhbhai Patel and C. Rajagopalachari. The latter insisted that 'further fissiparous forces' had to be checked forthwith.[6] And Patel worked hard within the Constituent Assembly to reverse the official Congress position. Under his direction, the Assembly appointed a committee of jurists and civil servants to report on the question. This recognized the force of popular sentiment – the 'strong appeal' that the demand for linguistic sentiments made on 'many of our countrymen' – but concluded that in the prevailing unsettled conditions 'the first and last need of India at the present moment is that it should be made a nation . . . Everything which helps the growth of nationalism has to go forward and everything which throws obstacles in its way has to be rejected or should stand over. We have applied this test to linguistic provinces also, and judged by this test, in our opinion [they] cannot be supported.'[7]

This verdict caused dismay among large sections of the Assembly. For most Congress members who spoke Marathi insisted on a separate Maharashtra state. Party members who claimed Gujarati as a mother tongue likewise wanted a province of their own. Similar were the aspirations of Congress members who spoke Telugu, Kannada, Malayalam or Oriya. To calm the clamour, a fresh committee was appointed. Both Nehru and Patel served on it; the third member was the party historian and former Congress President, Pattabhi Sitaramayya.

This committee, known as the 'JVP Committee' after the initials of its members, revoked the seal of approval that the Congress had once put on the principle of linguistic provinces. It argued that 'language was not only a binding force but also a separating one'. Now, when the 'primary consideration must be the security, unity and economic prosperity of India', 'every separatist and disruptive tendency should be rigorously discouraged'.

II

To quote one authority, Robert King, the JVP Committee report was a 'cold-water therapy'. It 'slowed things for a while'.[8] But the fires soon started up again. In 1948 and 1949 there was a renewal of movements aimed at linguistic autonomy. There was the campaign for Samyukta (Greater) Karnataka, aiming to unite Kannada speakers spread across the states of Madras, Mysore, Bombay and Hyderabad. Complementing this was the struggle for Samyukta Maharashtra, which sought to bring together Marathi speakers in a single political unit. The Malayalis wanted a state of their own, based on the merger of the princely states of Cochin and Travancore with Malabar. There was also a Mahagujarat movement.

In a class of its own was the struggle for a Sikh state in the Punjab. This brought together claims of language as well as religion. The Sikhs had been perhaps the main sufferers of Partition. They had lost their most productive lands to Pakistan. Now, in what remained of India, they had to share space and influence with the Hindus.

Circa 1950 the Hindus comprised roughly 62 per cent of the population of the Indian Punjab, with Sikhs being about 35 per cent. However, these figures marked a major regional divide. The eastern half of the province was a chiefly Hindi-speaking region, with Hindus comprising about 88 per cent of the population. The western half was a Punjabi-speaking region, with Sikhs constituting a little over half the population.

The division by religion did not perfectly map division by language. Where all Sikhs had Punjabi as their first language, so did many Hindus. However, the Hindus were prone to view Punjabi as merely a local dialect of Hindi, whereas the Sikhs insisted it was not just a language in its own right, but also a holy one. The Sikhs wrote and read Punjabi in the Gurmukhi script, whose alphabet they believed to have come from the mouth of the Guru.[9]

Since the 1920s the interests of the politically conscious Sikhs had been represented by the Akali Dal. This was both a religious body and a political party. It controlled the Sikh shrines, or *gurdwaras*, but also contested elections. The long-time leader of the Akali Dal was a man named Master Tara Singh, an important, intriguing figure, who (like so many such figures in Indian history) has yet to find his biographer.

Tara Singh was born in June 1885, as a Hindu. This fact should not unduly surprise us since the first-generation convert is often the most effective – not to say fundamentalist – of religious leaders. He studied at the Khalsa College in Amritsar, excelling in studies and also on the football field, where his steadfastness as a defender earned him the sobriquet 'Patthar', the rock. Rather than join the colonial government, he became headmaster of a Sikh school in Lyallpur, acquiring the title of 'Master'.[10]

In the 1920s Tara Singh joined the movement to rid the Sikh shrines of the decadent priests who then ran them. In 1931 he became the head of the Shiromani Gurdwara Prabandhak Committee, a post with vast authority and influence, not least over money. For the next thirty years he was the most resolute and persistent defender of the Sikh community, or *panth*. He was successfully able to project himself as 'the only consistent and long-suffering upholder of the Panth as a separate political entity, as the one Sikh leader who relentlessly pursued the goal of political power territorially organized for the Sikh community, and as a selfless leader without personal ambition'.[11]

Before 1947 Tara Singh insisted that the Sikh *panth* was in danger from the Muslims and the Muslim League. After 1947 he said it was in danger from the Hindus and the Congress. His rhetoric became more robust in the run-up to the general election of 1951–2. He inveighed against Hindu domination, and proclaimed that 'for the sake of religion, for the sake of culture, for the sake of the Panth, and to keep high the flag of the Guru, the Sikhs have girded their loins to achieve independence'.[12]

Tara Singh was arrested several times between 1948 and 1952, for defying bans on public gatherings and for what were seen as 'inflammatory' speeches. Hundreds of his supporters went to jail with him. He had strong support among the Sikh peasantry, particularly among the upper-caste Jats. Tara Singh's use of the term 'independence' was deliberately ambiguous. The Jat peasants wanted a Sikh province within India, not a sovereign nation. They wanted to get rid of the Hindu-dominated eastern Punjab, leaving a state where they would be in a comfortable majority. But by hinting at secession Tara Singh put pressure on the government, and simultaneously convinced his flock of his own commitment to the cause.

Not all Sikhs were behind Tara Singh, however. The low-caste Sikhs, who feared the Jats, were opposed to the Akali Dal. Some Jats had joined the Congress. And in a tendentious move, many Punjabi-speaking Hindus returned Hindi as their mother tongue in the 1951 census.

But the biggest blow to Tara Singh was the general election itself. In the Punjab Assembly, which had 126 seats, the Akalis won a mere 14.

III

Without question the most vigorous movement for linguistic autonomy was that of the Telugu speakers of the Andhra country. Telugu was spoken by more people in India than any other language besides Hindi. It had a rich literary history, and was associated with such symbols of Andhra glory as the Vijayanagara Empire. While India was still under

British rule, the Andhra Mahasabha had worked hard to cultivate a sense of identity among the Telugu-speaking peoples of the Madras presidency who, they argued, had been discriminated against by the Tamils. The Mahasabha was also active in the princely state of Hyderabad.

After Independence the speakers of Telugu asked the Congress to implement its old resolutions in favour of linguistic states. The methods they used to advance their case were various: petitions, representations, street marches and fasts. In a major blow to the Congress, the former Madras Chief Minister T. Prakasam resigned from the party in 1950 on the issue of statehood. Cutting across party lines, the Telugu-speaking legislators in the Madras Assembly urged the immediate creation of a state to be named Andhra Pradesh. In the monsoon of 1951 a Congress-politician-turned-swami named Sitaram went on hunger strike in support. After five weeks the fast was given up, in response to an appeal by the respected Gandhian leader Vinoba Bhave.[13]

The case for Andhra was now put to the test of universal adult suffrage. During his campaign tour in the Telugu-speaking districts, Jawaharlal Nehru was met at several places by protesters waving black flags and shouting 'We want Andhra'.[14] The official party paper wrote in dismay that 'the Congress President witnessed demonstrations by protagonists of an Andhra State, with slogans, placards and posters. At some places he smiled at them, at others he was enraged by their behaviour.'[15] The signs were ominous, and indeed despite its successes elsewhere the Congress did very poorly here. Of the 145 seats from the region in the Madras Legislative Assembly, the party won a mere 43. The bulk of the other seats were won by parties supporting the Andhra movement. These included the communists, who returned an impressive 41 members.

The election results encouraged the revival of the Andhra movement. Towards the end of February 1952 Swami Sitaram began a march through the Telugu-speaking districts, drumming up support for the struggle. He said the creation of the state 'could not wait any longer'. Andhras 'were ready to pay the price to achieve the same'. The swami urged all Telugu-speaking members of the Madras Assembly to boycott its proceedings till such time as the state of their dreams had been carved out.[16]

The agitating Andhras had two pet hates: the prime minister and the chief minister of Madras, C. Rajagopalachari. Both had gone on record as saying that they did not think that the creation of Andhra was a good idea.

Both were clear that even if, against their will, the state came into being, the city of Madras would not be part of it. This enraged the Andhras, who had a strong demographic and economic presence in the city, and who believed that they had as good a claim on it as the Tamils.[17]

On 22 May Nehru told Parliament how 'for some years now our foremost efforts have been directed to the consolidation of India. Personally, I would look upon anything that did not help this process of consolidation as undesirable. Even though the formation of linguistic provinces may be desirable in some cases, this would obviously be the wrong time. When the right time comes, let us have them by all means.'

As K. V. Narayana Rao has written, 'this attitude of Nehru appeared too vague and evasive to the Andhras. Nobody knew what the right time was and when it would come.' Impatient for an answer, the Andhras intensified their protest. On 19 October 1952 a man named Potti Sriramulu began a fast-unto-death in Madras. He had the blessings of Swami Sitaram, and of thousands of other Telugu speakers besides.[18]

Born in Madras in 1901, Sriramulu had studied sanitary engineering before taking a job in the railways. In 1928 he suffered a double tragedy when his wife died along with their newly born child. Two years later he resigned his post to join the salt *satyagraha*. Later he spent some time at Gandhi's Sabarmati ashram. Later still he spent eighteen months in jail as part of the individual *satyagraha* campaign of 1940–1.

A hagiographic study published in 1985 by the Committee for History of Andhra Movement claimed that Potti Sriramulu's stay at Mahatma Gandhi's ashram 'was epoch-making. For here was a seeker full of love and humility, all service and all sacrifice for his fellow-humanity; and here also was a guru, the world-teacher, equally full of affection, truth, *ahimsa* and kinship with *daridra narayana* or the suffering poor. While at Sabarmati, [Sriramulu] . . . did his tasks with cheer and devotion, and won the affection of the intimates and the approbation of the Kulapati [Gandhi].'[19]

Gandhi did regard Sriramulu with affection but also, it must be said, with a certain exasperation. On 25 November 1946 the disciple had begun a fast-unto-death to demand the opening of all temples in Madras province to Untouchables. Other Congress representatives, their minds more focused on the impending freedom of India, urged him to desist. When he refused they approached Gandhi, who persuaded him to abandon the fast. The Mahatma then wrote to T. Prakasam that he was 'glad that the fast of Sreeramulu ended in the happy manner you describe. He had sent me a telegram immediately he broke his fast. I know he is a solid worker, though a little eccentric.'[20]

That fast of 1946 Potti Sriramulu had called off at Gandhi's insistence; but in 1952 the Mahatma was dead. In any case, Andhra meant more to Sriramulu than the Untouchables once had. This fast he would carry out till the end, or until the government of India relented.

On 3 December Nehru wrote to Rajagopalachari: 'Some kind of fast is going on for the Andhra Province and I get frantic telegrams. I am totally unmoved by this and I propose to ignore it completely.' By this time Sriramulu had not eaten for six weeks. As his ordeal went on, support for the cause grew. Hartals (strikes) were called in many towns. The sociologist André Béteille, travelling to Madras from Calcutta at this time, recalls having his train stopped at Vizag by an angry mob shouting slogans against Rajaji and Nehru.[21]

Nehru was now forced to recognize the force of popular sentiment. On 12 December he wrote again to Rajaji, suggesting that the time had come to accept the Andhra demand. 'Otherwise complete frustration will grow among the Andhras, and we will not be able to catch up with it.' Two days later Rajaji cabled the prime minister in desperation: 'We might prevent more mischief if you summon repeat summon Swami Sitaram to Delhi. He is now in Madras hanging round the fasting gentleman, Sriramulu. The entire mischief starts from this focus, as the Andhra boys are highly emotional and prone to rowdyism. If you invite Sitaram for a talk, the atmosphere may change and probably the mischief may dwindle away.'[22]

By now it was too late. On 15 December, fifty-eight days into his fast, Potti Sriramulu died. Now all hell broke loose. 'The news of the passing away of Sriramulu engulfed entire Andhra in chaos.' Government offices were attacked; trains were halted and defaced. The damage to state property ran into millions of rupees. Several protesters were killed in police firings.[23] Nehru had once claimed that 'facts, not fasts' would decide the issue. Now, faced with the prospect of widespread and possibly uncontrollable protest, the prime minister gave in. Two days after Sriramulu's death, he made a statement saying that a state of Andhra would come into being.

Over the course of the next few months the Telugu districts of Madras province were identified for separation. The division of the province, wrote the chief minister, was 'accompanied by a lot of bad language, bad behaviour and distrust and anger'.[24] Suppressing his feelings, Rajagopalachari attended the inauguration of the new state of Andhra at Kurnool on 1 October 1953. Also in attendance, and as the chief guest no less, was that other erstwhile enemy of the Andhras, Prime Minister Jawaharlal Nehru.

IV

The formation of Andhra Pradesh grated with the prime minister of the day. 'You will observe', wrote Jawaharlal Nehru grimly to a colleague, 'that we have disturbed the hornet's nest and I believe most of us are likely to be badly stung.'[25]

As Nehru had feared, the creation of Andhra led to the intensification of similar demands by other linguistic groups. Somewhat against its will, the government of India appointed a States Reorganization Commission (SRC) to 'make recommendations in regard to the broad principles which should govern the solution of this [linguistic] problem'. Through 1954 and 1955 members of the Commission travelled across India. They visited 104 towns and cities, interviewed more than 9,000 people and received as many as 152,250 written submissions.

One of the longer and more interesting submissions was from the Bombay Citizens Committee. This was headed by a leading cotton magnate, Sir Purushottamdas Thakurdas, and had within its ranks other prominent industrialists such as J. R. D. Tata. On its masthead were many of the city's most successful lawyers, scholars and doctors.

The Bombay Citizens Committee had a one-point agenda – to keep the city out of the state of Maharashtra. To make the case they printed an impressive 200-page book replete with charts, maps and tables. The first chapter was historical, showing how the city was settled by successive waves of settlers from different linguistic communities. It claimed that there had been little Maharashtrian immigration before the end of the nineteenth century and that Marathi speakers comprised only 43 per cent of the city's current population. The second chapter spoke of Bombay's importance in the economic life of India. It was the premier centre of industry and finance, and of foreign trade. It was India's window to the world: more planes flew in and out of it than all the other Indian cities combined. The third and fourth chapters were sociological, demonstrating the multilingual and multicultural character of the city. To quote a European observer, it was 'perhaps the most motley

Major language movements, 1950s

Punjabi Speakers

Marathi Speakers

Telugu
Speakers

Arabian Sea

Bay of Bengal

Indian Ocean

| 0 | 100 | 200 | 300 | 400 miles |
| 0 | 200 | 400 | 500 kms |

assemblage in any quarter of this orb'; to quote another, it was 'a true
centre of the diverse varieties and types of mankind, far surpassing the
mixed nationalities of Cairo and Constantinople'. The fifth chapter was
geographical, an argument for Bombay's physical isolation, with the sea
and the mountains separating it from the Marathi-speaking heartland.

The first settlers were Europeans; the chief merchants and capitalists
Gujaratis and Parsis; the chief philanthropists Parsis. The city was
built by non-Maharashtrians. Even among the working class, Marathi
speakers were often outnumbered by north Indians and Christians.
For the Bombay Citizens Committee, it was clear that 'on the grounds
of geography, history, language and population or the system of law,
Bombay and North Konkan cannot be considered as a part of the Mahratta
region as claimed by the protagonists of Samyukta Maharashtra'.[26]

Behind the veneer of cosmopolitanism there was one language group
that dominated the 'save Bombay' movement: the Gujaratis. If Bombay
became the capital of a greater Maharashtra state, the politicians and
ministers would be mostly Marathi speakers. The prospect was not
entirely pleasing to the Gujarati-speaking bourgeoisie, whether Hindu
or Parsi. It was they who staffed, financed, and basically ran the Bombay
Citizens Committee.[27]

Nehru himself was somewhat sympathetic towards the idea of
keeping Bombay out of the control of a single language group. So was
the Marathi-speaking M. S. Golwalkar, this a rare meeting of minds
between the prime minister and the RSS supremo. Both thought that
the creation of linguistic states would 'lead to bitterness and give rise to
fissiparous tendencies endangering the unity of the country'.[28] In May
1954 Golwalkar spoke in Bombay at the invitation of the Anti-Provincial
Conference, which saw linguistic demands as a manifestation of 'the
menace of provincialism and sectionalism'. 'Multiplicity breeds strife',
thundered Golwalkar: 'One nation and one culture are my principles.'
To see oneself as Tamil or Maharashtrian or Bengali was to 'sap the
vitality of the nation'. He wished them all to use the label 'Hindu',
which is where he departed from Nehru, who of course wished them
all to be 'Indian'.[29]

But just as some in the Congress Party did not see eye-to-eye with
Nehru on this question, there were RSS cadres who departed from their
leader. From as early as 1946 there was a Samyukta Maharashtra Parishad
in operation. Within its ranks were Maharashtrians of all political
persuasions, left and right, secular and communal, Brahmin, Maratha

and Harijan. The Parishad sought a state that would unite Marathi speakers dispersed across many different political units. In their minds, however, there was no doubt that such a state could have only one capital: Bombay.

The president of the Samyukta Maharashtra Parishad was the veteran Congress man Shankarrao Deo, while its secretary and chief theoretician was the celebrated Cambridge-educated economist D. R. Gadgil. In Gadgil's opinion, while Bombay could still be the major port and economic centre of Maharashtra, there must be a 'compulsory decentralization' of the city's industries. Another ideologue, G. V. Deshmukh, was more blunt. Unless Bombay city became part of their state, he said, Maharashtrians would have to remain content with 'playing the part of secondary brokers to brokers, secondary agents to agents, assistant professors to professors, clerks to managers [and] hired labourers to shopkeepers'.[30]

To answer the Citizens Committee of the Gujaratis, the Samyukta Maharashtra Parishad prepared an impressive 200-page document of its own. The first part mounted a theoretical defence of the principle of linguistic states. These, it argued, would deepen federalism by bringing together speakers of the same language in one consolidated, cohesive unit. Thus, 'a linguistic province with its administration in the language of the common people, would make it possible for the people to feel and understand the working of democracy and the need to participate in it'.

Coming specifically to their own state, the document claimed that 'society all over the Marathi country is remarkably homogeneous'. There was the same configuration of castes, the same deities and saints, the same folklore and legends. That the Marathi speakers were presently spread out over three political units – Hyderabad, Bombay state, and the Central Provinces – was an accident of history that needed urgently to be undone.

A new and unified state of Maharashtra had to be created, argued the Parishad, with Bombay as its capital. For the land on which this island city stood had long been inhabited by speakers of the Marathi language. While the sea lay to Bombay's west, the territory to its north, south and east was dominated by Marathi speakers. The city itself was the main centre of the Marathi press, of publications in the Marathi language and of Marathi culture. Economically, Bombay depended heavily on its Marathi hinterland, from where it drew much of its labour and all its water and power. Its ways of communication all lay through Maharashtra. In sum, it was 'unthinkable to form a State of Maharashtra which has not Bombay as its capital and it would render impossible the working of a State of Maharashtra, if any attempt was made to separate the city of Bombay from it'. To the argument that the city did not have a Marathi-speaking majority, the Parishad answered that there were more people speaking this language than any other. In any case, it was in the nature of great port cities to be multilingual. In Burma's capital, only 32 per cent of the population spoke the national language, but 'nobody yet dared to suggest that Rangoon should be considered as non-Burmese territory'.[31]

Bombay was surrounded by Marathi-speaking districts; it must be the capital of a new state of Maharashtra. So argued the Samyukta Maharashtra Parishad. But the Citizens Committee claimed that Bombay had been nurtured mostly by non-Maharashtrians, and must therefore be constituted as a separate city-state. Could the two sides ever agree? In June 1954 Shankarrao Deo visited Sir Purushottamdas Thakurdas to discuss a compromise. Deo said that there was no negotiation possible on their core demand – Bombay as capital of Maharashtra – but said that they could work together to retain 'the same autonomous character of the metropolitan city, ensuring its cosmopolitan life; its trade, commerce and industry, etc.'. Sir Purushottamdas, for his part, was willing to give up the city-state idea in favour of a composite bilingual province of Marathi and Gujarati speakers.[32]

The meeting was civil, but inconclusive. The matter of Bombay was referred to the States Reorganization Commission, the hottest of the many hot potatoes it became their misfortune to handle.

V

The members of the States Reorganization Commission were a jurist, S. Fazl Ali, a historian and civil servant, K. M. Pannikar, and a social worker, H. N. Kunzru. Notably, none had any formal ties, past or present, with the Congress. After eighteen months of intensive work, the trio submitted their report in October 1955. The report first carefully outlined the arguments for and against linguistic states. It urged a 'balanced approach' which recognized 'linguistic homogeneity as an important factor conducive to administrative convenience and efficiency' yet not 'as an exclusive and binding principle, over-riding all other considerations'.

Among these other considerations were, of course, the unity and security of India as a whole.[33]

Next, in nineteen chapters, the report outlined their specific proposals for reorganization. With respect to the southern states, it seemed easy enough to redistribute areas according to the major language zones: Telugu, Kannada, Tamil and Malayalam. Districts and *taluks* (sub-districts) were reallocated with regard to which linguistic group was in a majority. Four compact states would replace the melange of territories deriving from the British period.

With regard to north India, the SRC likewise sought to divide the huge Hindi-speaking belt into four states: Bihar, Uttar Pradesh, Madhya Pradesh and Rajasthan. In the east, the existing provinces would stay as they were, with minor adjustments. The Commission rejected the demand for tribal states to be carved out of Bihar and Assam.

The SRC did not agree to the creation of a Sikh state. And it refused to allocate Madras city to Andhra. However, its most contentious recommendation was not to permit the creation of a united Maharashtra. As a sop, the Commission proposed a separate state of Vidarbha, comprising the Marathi-speaking districts of the interior. But Bombay state would stay as it was, a bilingual province of Gujarati and Marathi speakers. They respected the arguments of the Samyukta Maharashtra movement, said the Commission, but they could 'not lightly brush aside the fears of the other communities'.

VI

The SRC's recommendation that Bombay be the capital of a bilingual state was discussed in Parliament on 15 November 1955. The ambitious Bombay MP S. K. Patil thought the Commission should have gone further. He thought the government should create a city-state of Bombay; no doubt hoping that it might come to be managed by himself. The prospective city-state, he argued, had a 'cosmopolitan population in every respect'; it had been 'built upon the labour of everybody'. If left to govern itself, Bombay would 'be a miniature India run on international standards . . . [A] melting pot which will evolve a glorious new civilisation . . . And it is an extraordinary coincidence that the population of the city should be exactly one per cent of the population of the whole country. This one per cent drawn from all parts of the country will set the pace for other states in the practice of secularism and mutual understanding.'

Patil, like the SRC itself, asked the Maharashtrians to give up their claim on Bombay in the spirit of compromise. But it soon became clear that he did not speak for his fellow Maharashtrians. Speaking immediately after Patil in the Lok Sabha was the Congress MP from the city of Puné, N. V. Gadgil. Gadgil insisted that while he was in favour of compromise, 'there is a limit. That limit is, nobody can compromise one's self-respect, no woman can compromise her chastity and no country its freedom'. Everywhere the principle of language had been recognized, except in this one case. The report of the Commission had caused great pain throughout the Marathi-speaking world. The reports of protest meetings should make it clear 'that anything short of Samyukta Maharashtra with the city of Bombay as capital will not be acceptable'. If these sentiments went unheeded, warned Gadgil, then the future of Bombay would be decided on the streets of Bombay.

The SRC urged the Maharashtrians to accept the loss of Bombay in the name of national unity. Gadgil protested against this attempt at blackmail. The last 150 years, he said, had seen Maharashtrians contributing selflessly to the growth of national feeling. Marathi speakers founded the first Indian schools and universities, and helped found the Indian National Congress. The Mahrattas were 'the pioneers of violent action' against the British. Later, in the early twentieth century, when the Congress Party languished, 'who was it that brought in new life? Who propounded the new tenets and new philosophy? It was Lokmanya Tilak. In the Home Rule movement he led and in the 1920 movement we were behind none and ahead of many provinces . . . I will merely quote the certificate given to us by no less a person than Mahatma Gandhi that Maharashtra is the beehive of [national] workers.' Even now, in independent India, it was a Maharashtrian, Vinoba Bhave, who was 'carrying the flag of Gandhian philosophy and spreading his message from place to place'.

In the matter of Bombay, the Maharashtrians were being lectured on the need to 'work for the unity and safety and good of the country'. But, said the Puné MP bitterly, all these years 'we have done nothing else'. Gadgil's was a moving peroration – and the last line was the best: 'To ask us to serve the nation is to ask *chandan* [sandalwood] to be fragrant.'[34]

The matter now shifted, as Gadgil had warned, from the chamber to the streets. These, as one Bombay weekly warned, were 'literally seething with an unrest that may possibly erupt into something terrifyingly coercive, making ordered life impossible for some time to come'.[35] The discontent was being stoked by politicians of both left and right. The prominent communist S. A. Dange had thrown his weight behind Samyukta Maharashtra; so had the leading low-caste politician B. R. Ambedkar. With them were the Jana Sangh, and the Socialist Party, who were perhaps the most active of all. Many dissident Congress Party members had also joined, making this a comprehensively representative coalition of angry and disillusioned Maharashtrians.

This capacious inclusiveness was reflected in an amended name: the Samyukta Maharashtra Parishad had become the Samyukta Maharashtra Samiti.[36] 'Parishad' is best translated as 'organization', thus implying the central role of office-bearers; 'samiti' as 'society', this connoting a more co-operative and participatory endeavour.

Fearing trouble, in the early hours of 16 January the Bombay police swooped down on the leaders and activists of the newly constituted All-Party Action Committee for Samyukta Maharashtra. They made nearly 400 arrests in all. This prompted a call for a general strike on the 18th. That day shops and factories were closed, and buses and trains didn't run. Processions were made through the streets, burning effigies of Nehru and of the Gujarati-speaking chief minister of Bombay state, Morarji Desai. When a European journalist stopped to take a photograph of Nehru's portrait smashed and trampled at the roadside, 'tremendous cheers rose from the balconies and the roofs. "Take it, take it and show the world what we think of Nehru," they shouted.'[37]

Two days earlier, on the afternoon of the 16th, the first clashes between police and protesters had been reported. Mobs went on the rampage, looting shops and offices. For nearly a week the city was brought to a complete standstill and 15,000 policemen were called out to battle the rioters. When the smoke lifted, there were more than a dozen people dead, and property worth billions of rupees destroyed. It had been the worst riot in living memory.[38]

Jawaharlal Nehru was deeply shaken by the events in Bombay. The linguistic question, he wrote to a colleague, 'is more serious than even the situation created by the Partition and we have to give a positive lead'.[39] Meeting in Amritsar in the third week of January, the All-India Congress Committee deplored the violence by which 'Bombay and India were disgraced and dishonoured'. Under Nehru's direction, the party urged its members to discourage forces of 'disruption, separatism and provincialism', and instead work for 'the integration of all parts of this great country'. The Congress chief ministers of Bihar and West Bengal issued a joint statement proposing that their two states be merged into one. This union, they hoped, would quell 'separatist tendencies', aid economic progress and, above all, be 'a significant example of that positive approach to the problem of Indian unity' that the party bosses had called for.[40]

Among Nehru's allies were the home minister, G. B. Pant, and his fellow-in-effigy Morarji Desai. The intention of the protesters, said Desai, was to 'overturn Government practically and to take possession of the City by force. It was also their purpose in overawing the non-Maharashtrian elements in the City into submission and into agreeing that Bombay City should go to Maharashtra.'

This interpretation was vigorously contested by N. V. Gadgil. He believed the administration had overreacted. Gadgil wrote to both Nehru and Pant of how the firing and *lathi*-charges by the police had been 'on a scale which will make even the ex-British officials in England blush'. Back in 1919 the British had termed a peaceful meeting in Amritsar's Jallianawala Bagh a 'rebellion against the government', to justify the slaughter by General Dyer. In the same way, Morarji Desai had now exaggerated the protests in Bombay to 'justify police atrocities'. When 'the choice was between Morarji and Maharashtra', wrote Gadgil bitterly, Delhi had chosen Morarji on the grounds that 'one who shoots is a good administrator'. But the costs to the party were huge. For 'in Bombay indiscriminate firing by the police and other atrocities have resulted in complete alienation of Maharashtrian people from the Congress and the Government of India'.[41]

Meanwhile, the resentment smouldered on. The slogan on (almost) every Maharashtrian's lips was 'Lathi goli khayenge, phir bhi Bambai layenge' (We will face sticks and bullets, but get our Bombay in the end).[42] On 26 January, Republic Day, black flags were flown in several working-class districts of Bombay. When Jawaharlal Nehru planned a visit to the city in February, the Samyukta Maharashtra people organized a petition signed by 100,000 children, to be presented to the prime minister with the slogan 'Chacha Nehru, Mumbai dya' (Uncle Nehru, hand over Bombay). Nehru came, but amid tight security; he did not meet the press, let alone the children.[43]

In June 1956 the annual session of the Congress was to be held in Bombay. Nehru was met with black flags at the airport and all along the route. The atmosphere outside the meeting hall was tense. On the second day of the Congress a crowd threw stones at the members. Several were hurt, prompting a volley of tear-gas shells by the police.

Nehru's problems were compounded by the now open disaffection among the Maharashtrian section of the Congress Party. The Union's finance minister C. D. Deshmukh, MP for the coastal district of Kulaba, resigned in protest against the city not being allotted to Maharashtra. Other resignations followed.

Through the summer of 1956 both sides waited anxiously for the centre's decision on Bombay. While the Cabinet had accepted the other recommendations of the SRC, it was rumoured that both Nehru and the home minister, Pant, were inclined to make Bombay city a separate union territory. In the prevailing climate this was deemed unfeasible. On 1 November the new states based on language came into being. Joining them was a bilingual state of Bombay. The only concession to the protesters was the replacement of Morarji Desai as chief minister by the 41-year-old Maratha Y. B. Chavan.[44]

VII

The creation of linguistic states was, among other things, a victory of the popular will. Jawaharlal Nehru did not want it, but Potti Sriramulu did. Sriramulu's fast lasted fifty-eight days, during the first fifty-five of which the prime minister ignored it completely. In this time, according to one journalist, he criss-crossed India, delivering 132 speeches on all topics other than language.[45] But once Nehru conceded Andhra, and set up the States Reorganization Commission, it was inevitable that the country as a whole would be reorganized on the basis of language.

The movements for linguistic states revealed an extraordinary depth of popular feeling. For Kannadigas and for Andhras, for Oriyas as for Maharashtrians, language proved a more powerful marker of identity than caste or religion. This was manifest in their struggles, and in their behaviour when the struggle was won.

One sign of this was official patronage of the arts. Thus great effort, and cash, went into funding books, plays and films written or performed in the official language of the state. Much rubbish was funded as a result, but also much work of worth. In particular, the regional literatures have flourished since linguistic reorganization.

Another manifestation was architecture. To build a new capital, or at least a new legislative assembly, became a *sine qua non* of the new states. In Orissa, for example, two architects were commissioned to design and plan a wide range of government buildings. These, the architects were told, had to 'represent Orissan culture and workmanship'. The final product made abundant use of indigenous motifs: columns, arches, and sculpted images of gods. The architecture of new Bhubaneshwar, writes its historian, 'is an architecture which has risen from the native soil, sacred and pure'.[46]

A more spectacular exhibition of provincial pride was the new assembly-cum-secretariat of the state of Mysore. This was built opposite the Bangalore High Court, a fine columned building in red which remains perhaps the city's prettiest structure. However, the Mysore chief minister, Kengal Hanumanthaiya, saw the High Court as a colonial excrescence. He first sought permission to demolish it; when this was denied, he resolved that the new Vidhan Souda would dwarf and tame it. It had to convey an 'idea of power and dignity, the style being Indian, particularly of Mysore and not purely Western'.

The end product drew eclectically from the architecture of the great kingdoms of the Carnatic plateau. Hanumanthaiya gave very specific instructions to the builders, asking them to copy pillars from a particular room in the Mysore palace, doors from a particular old temple he named. The building as it came up was, as it were, a mighty mishmash. Yet it has served its central purpose, which was to stand, 'measure for measure, in triumph over the colonial Attara Kacheri [High Court]', thus to 'successfully function as a distilled essence of Kannada pride'.[47]

When it began, the movement for linguistic states generated deep apprehensions among the nationalist elite. They feared it would lead to the Balkanization of India, to the creation of many more Pakistans. 'Any attempt at redrawing the map of India on the linguistic basis', wrote the *Times of India* in early February 1952, 'would only give the long awaited opportunity to the reactionary forces to come into the open and assert themselves. That will lay an axe at the very root of India's integrity.'[48]

In retrospect, however, linguistic reorganization seems rather to have consolidated the unity of India. True, the artefacts that have resulted, such as Bangalore's Vidhan Souda, are not to everybody's taste. And there have been some serious conflicts between states on the sharing of river waters. However, on the whole the creation of linguistic states has acted as a largely constructive channel for provincial pride. It has proved quite feasible to be peaceably Kannadiga – or Tamil, or Oriya – as well as contentedly Indian.

An early illustration of this was the assembly elections in Andhra in 1955. Three years earlier, the Congress had done disastrously in the region. They were suspect on account of their prevarication on the question of statehood. By contrast, the communists had successfully ridden the bandwagon on *vishal* (greater) Andhra. But in 1955, with Andhra Pradesh firmly established, the Congress won in a landslide. Their main rivals, the communists, were comprehensively routed. Now, wrote one relieved commentator, 'Andhra Desa will no longer be suspect as the potential Yenan of India'.[49]

The Andhras would not secede from India, but they did redefine what it means to be Indian. Or at least one Andhra did. Potti Sriramulu is a forgotten man today. This is a pity, for he had a more than minor impact on the history, as well as geography, of his country. For his fast and its aftermath were to spark off a wholesale redrawing of the map of India according to linguistic lines. If Jawaharlal Nehru was the Maker of Modern India, then perhaps Potti Sriramulu should be named its Mercator.

10

THE CONQUEST OF NATURE

[The Indian people] have to choose whether they will be educated or remain ignorant; whether they will come into closer contact with the outer world and become responsive to its influences, or remain secluded and indifferent; whether they will be organized or disunited, bold or timid, enterprising or passive; an industrial or an agricultural nation, rich or poor; strong and respected or weak and dominated by forward nations. Action, not sentiment, will be the determining factor.

M. VISVESWARAYA, engineer, 1920

The Indian commitment to the semantics of socialism is at least as deep as ours to the semantics of free enterprise . . . Even the most intransigent Indian capitalist may observe on occasion that he is really a socialist at heart.

J. K. GALBRAITH, economist, 1958

I

Mahatma Gandhi liked to say that 'India lives in her villages'. At Independence, this was overwhelmingly a country of cultivators and labourers. Nearly three-quarters of the workforce was in agriculture, a sector which also contributed close to 60 per cent of India's gross domestic product. There was a small but growing industrial sector, which accounted for about 12 per cent of the workforce, and 25 per cent of GDP.

The peasant was the backbone of the Indian nation, and of the Indian economy. There existed enormous variations in agricultural practices across the subcontinent. There was, for instance, a broad division between the wheat regions of the north and west, where women generally did not participate in cultivation, and the rice regions of the south and east, where women's work was critical to the raising of seedlings. Large parts of peninsular India grew neither rice nor wheat: here, the chief cereals were an array of drought-resistant millets. Besides grain, peasants grew a wide range of fruit crops, as well as market-oriented produce such as cotton and sugar cane.

These variations notwithstanding, everywhere in India agriculture was largely empirical, based on knowledge and traditions passed down over the generations, rather than on ideas from books. Everywhere it was chiefly based on local inputs. The water, the fuel, the fodder, the fertilizer; these were all gathered in the vicinity of the village. The land was tilled with a plough pulled by a pair of bullocks. The homes were built of wood and thatch fetched by hand from the nearby forests.

Everywhere, those who worked on the land lived cheek-by-jowl with those who didn't. The agriculturists who made up perhaps two-thirds of the rural population depended crucially on the service and artisanal castes: on blacksmiths, barbers, scavengers and the like. In many parts there were vibrant communities of weavers. In some parts there were large populations of nomadic pastoralists.

On the social side, too, there were similarities in the way in which life was lived across the subcontinent. Levels of literacy were very low. Caste feelings were very strong, with villages divided into half a dozen or more endogamous *jatis*. And religious sentiments ran deep.

Rural India was pervaded by an air of timelessness. Peasants, shepherds, carpenters, weavers, all lived and worked as their forefathers had done. As a survey of the 1940s put it, 'there is the same plainness of life, the same wrestling with uncertainties of climate (except in favoured areas), the same love of simple games, sport and songs, the same neighbourly helpfulness, and the same financial indebtedness'.[1]

To the Indian nationalist, however, continuity was merely a euphemism for stagnation. Agricultural productivity was low; hence also levels of nutrition and health. About the only thing that was rising was population growth. From the late nineteenth century, as medical services expanded, the death rate rapidly fell. Consequently, since the birth rate remained constant, there was a steady rise in population. Between 1881 and 1941 the population of British India rose from 257 to 389 million. But (or hence) the per capita availability of food grains declined from an already low level of 200 kilograms per person per year to a mere 150.

Almost from the time the Congress was founded in 1885, Indian nationalists had charged the British with exploitation of the peasantry.

They resolved that when power came to them, agrarian reform would be at the top of their agenda. Three programmes seemed critical. The first was the abolition of land revenue. The second was the massive expansion of irrigation, both to augment productivity and reduce dependence on the monsoon. The third was the reform of the system of land tenure. Particularly in north and east India, the British had encouraged a system of absentee landlordism. In many other districts too, those who tilled the land usually did not own it.

While tenants did not have security of tenure, agricultural labourers had no land to till in the first place. Inequalities in the agrarian economy could be very sharp indeed. The forms of exploitation were manifold and highly innovative. Thus, apart from land tax, zamindars (landowners) in the United Provinces levied an array of additional cesses on their peasants such as *motorana* (to pay for the zamindar's new car) and *hathiana* (to pay for his elephants).[2] The landlord was prone to treat his animals and his vehicles far better than he did his labourers. Two weeks before Independence a progressive weekly from Madras ran a story about distress in rural Malabar. This profiled a large landlord who owned seven elephants, for which he needed some 25,000 kilograms of paddy. His own tenants, meanwhile, were given three days' ration for the whole week.[3]

The socialist elements in the Indian National Congress pushed the organization to commit itself to thoroughgoing land reform, as in the abolition of large holdings, the promotion of the security of tenants and the redistribution of surplus land. They also advocated an expansion in the provision of credit to overcome the widespread problem of rural indebtedness.[4]

But, as the nationalists also recognized, agrarian reform had to be accompanied by a spurt in industrial growth. The nation needed more factories to absorb the surplus of underemployed labourers in the countryside. It also needed factories to prove to itself that it was modern. To enter the comity of nations, India had to be educated, united, outward looking and, above all, industrialized.

In colonial times there had existed a sharp divide between factories owned by British firms and those owned by Indians. Jute, for instance, was largely in the hands of the foreigner; cotton textiles in the hands of the native. The Raj was frequently (and for the most part, justly) accused of deliberately discouraging Indian enterprise, and of distorting the tariff and trade structure to favour British firms. While some Indian capitalists were studiously apolitical, others had been vigorous supporters of the Congress. They naturally hoped that when freedom came, the biases would be reversed, placing foreign capitalists at a disadvantage.[5]

If India had to be industrialized, which model should it follow? To the leaders of the national movement, 'imperialism' and 'capitalism' were both dirty words. As John Kenneth Galbraith pointed out, 'until recent times a good deal of capitalist enterprise in India was an extension of the arm of the imperial power – indeed, in part its confessed *raison d'être*. As a result, free enterprise in Asia bears the added stigmata of colonialism, and this is a formidable burden.'[6]

What, then, were the alternatives? Some nationalists wrote admiringly of the Soviet Union, and of 'the extraordinary use they have made of modern scientific knowledge in solving their problems of poverty and want', thus passing in a mere two decades 'from a community of half-starved peasants to well-fed and well-clad industrial workers'. This had been accomplished by 'eliminating the profit motive from her industries which belong to and are being developed in the interest of the nation'; by feats of engineering that had made rivers into 'mighty sources of electric power'; and by a system of planning by disinterested experts which had increased production nine-fold and where 'unemployment and anarchy of production are unknown'.[7]

Another much admired model was Japan. Visiting that country during the First World War, the prominent Congress politician Lala Lajpat Rai marvelled at the transformation it had undergone, moving from (agrarian) primitivism to (industrial) civilization in a mere fifty years. Japan, he found, had built its factories and banks by schooling its workers and keeping out foreign competition. The role of the state was crucial – thus 'Japan owes its present and industrial prosperity to the foresight, sagacity and patriotism of her Government'. Once as backward as India, Japan had 'grown into a teacher of the Orient and a supplier of all the necessaries and luxuries of life which the latter used to get from the Occident'.[8]

II

In 1938 the Congress set up a National Planning Committee (NPC), charged with prescribing a policy for economic development in a soon-to-be-free India. Chaired by Jawaharlal Nehru, the committee had some thirty members in all – these divided almost equally between the worlds of science, industry and politics. Sub-committees were allotted specific subjects: such as agriculture, industry, power and fuel, finance, social services and even 'women's role in planned economy'. The NPC outlined 'national self-sufficiency' and the doubling of living standards in ten years as the main goals. Planning itself was defined as 'the technical co-ordination, by disinterested experts, of consumption, production, investment, trade, and income distribution, in accordance with social objectives set by bodies representative of the nation'.[9]

From Japan and Russia the NPC took the lesson that countries that industrialized late had to depend crucially on state intervention. This applied with even more force to India, whose economy had been distorted by two centuries of colonial rule. As one NPC report put it, planned development upheld the principle of 'service before profit'. There were large areas of the economy where the private sector could not be trusted, where the aims of planning could be realized only 'if the matter is handled as a collective Public Enterprise'.[10]

Notably, the private sector concurred. In 1944 a group of leading industrialists issued what they called *A Plan of Economic Development for India* (more commonly known as the Bombay Plan). This conceded that 'the existing economic organization, based on private enterprise and ownership, has failed to bring about a satisfactory distribution of the national income'. Only the state could help 'diminish inequalities of income'. But the state was necessary for augmenting production too. Energy, infrastructure and transport were sectors where the Indian capitalists themselves felt the need for a government monopoly. In the early stages of industrialization, they argued, it was necessary that 'the State should exercise in the interests of the community a considerable measure of intervention and control'. Indeed, 'an *enlargement* of the positive as well as preventative functions of the State is *essential* to any large-scale economic planning'.[11]

Now largely forgotten, the Bombay Plan gives the lie to the claim that Jawaharlal Nehru imposed a model of centralized economic development on an unwilling capitalist class. One wonders what free-market pundits would make of it now. They would probably see it as a *dirigiste* tract, unworthy of capitalism and capitalists. In truth, it should be seen simply as symptomatic of the *Zeitgeist*, of the spirit of the times.[12]

That spirit was all in favour of centralized planning, of the state occupying what was called the 'commanding heights' of the economy. Thus the Constitution of India directed the government to ensure that 'the ownership and control of the material resources of the community are so distributed as best to subserve the common good'; and that 'the operation of the economic system does not result in the concentration of wealth and means of production to the common predicament'. Within a month of the adoption of the constitution, the government set up a Planning Commission to carry out these 'directive principles'. Chaired by Nehru, the Commission included high Cabinet ministers as well as experienced members of the Indian Civil Service.

In the summer of 1951 the Planning Commission issued a draft of the first five-year plan. This focused on agriculture, the sector hardest hit by Partition. Besides increasing food production, the other major emphases of the plan were on the development of transport and communications, and the provision of social services. Introducing the proposals in Parliament, Jawaharlal Nehru praised the plan as the first of its kind to 'bring the whole of India – agricultural, industrial, social and economic – into one framework of thinking'. The work of the Commission, he said, had 'made the whole country "planning conscious"'.[13]

The expectations of the Planning Commission ran high. As one columnist wrote, 'one drawback of democracy is that it works slower than other political systems. But the people of India will not tolerate undue delay in their economic advancement.'[14] After the first general election the urgency intensified. Critics from left and right lambasted the first five-year plan as lacking in vision and ambition. True, food-grain production increased substantially, but output in other sectors failed to reach their targets.[15]

While introducing the first plan, Nehru had said that 'it was obvious to me that we have to industrialise India, and as rapidly as possible'. That objective was given pride of place in the second five-year plan. Its drafting was the handiwork of Prasanta Chandra Mahalanobis, a Cambridge-trained physicist and statistician who was steeped in Sanskrit philosophy and Bengali literature – in sum, 'an awesome polyglot, the kind of man for whom Nehru was guaranteed to fall'.[16]

Mahalanobis was, among other things, the man who brought modern statistics to India. In 1931 he set up the Indian Statistical Institute (ISI) in Calcutta. Within a decade, he had made the ISI a world-class centre of training and research. He was also a pioneer of inter-disciplinary research, innovatively applying his statistical techniques in the fields of anthropology, agronomy and meteorology.

In February 1949, Mahalanobis was appointed honorary statistical adviser to the Union Cabinet. The next year he helped establish the National Sample Survey (NSS) and the year following, the Central Statistical Organization (CSO). These were set up to collect reliable data on changing living standards in India – on wages, employment, consumption and the like. The NSS and the CSO are two reasons why India has a set of official statistics more reliable than those found anywhere else in the non-Western world.[17]

Such are the uncontentious aspects of Mahalanobis's legacy. Perhaps more important, and certainly more controversial, are his contributions to the theory and practice of planning. In 1954 Nehru committed his party, and by extension his country, to the creation of a 'socialistic pattern of society'. The same year, the ISI was asked by the government to study the problem of unemployment. Mahalanobis wrote a note on the subject, which seems to have impressed Nehru enough for him to assign the ISI responsibility for drafting the second five-year plan itself.

Mahalanobis took the task very seriously indeed. In the late summer of 1954, he set off for a long tour of Europe and North America. He had, he confessed, an 'inferiority complex about economic matters'. This trip abroad was thus educational – to improve his own knowledge about the subject – but also frankly propagandist. By cultivating foreign economists, he hoped to bring their Indian counterparts around to his own point of view. As he told a friend, 'at the back of everything is one single aim in my own mind – what effective help can we secure in making our own plans and in implementing them'.[18]

Mahalanobis first went to the United States of America, where he collected information on input–output coefficients, these maintained in a deck of 40,000 Hollerith punched cards. He talked to the man who had done the work (Wassily Leontief, a future Nobel laureate), before crossing the Atlantic to meet the dons of Cambridge. The 'most brilliant' of these was Joan Robinson, then just back from a trip to China (where she was 'much impressed by the progress they are making'.) She thought that the export–import sector in India needed more government control. Mahalanobis agreed, and in turn asked Joan Robinson to visit India as a guest of the ISI. This, he told her, 'might be of very great help to us because her support may carry conviction that our approach to development planning is not foolish. She smiled and said – "Yes, I think I would be able to knock some sense into the heads of the economists in your country."'

Mahalanobis now crossed the Channel, to converse with the French Marxists. Then it was time to shift to the other side of the Iron Curtain. He reached Moscow via Prague, and was at once impressed by the 'amazing' pace of construction work: buildings far bigger, and built much faster, than any he had ever seen. He had long talks with Soviet academicians, who said that if India wanted 'to do any serious planning we must have the active help of, not scores, but hundreds of technologists and scientists and engineers'. Mahalanobis agreed, and invited them to visit his country, so urgently in need of 'specialists and experts in the economics of planning'.[19]

These travels and talks finally bore fruit in a long paper presented to the Planning Commission in March 1954. Here Mahalanobis outlined eight objectives for the second five-year plan. The first of these was 'to attain a rapid growth of the national economy by increasing the scope and importance of the public sector and in this way to advance to a socialistic pattern of society'; the second, 'to develop basic heavy industries for the manufacture of producer goods to strengthen the foundation of economic independence'. Other (and we may presume lesser) objectives included the production of consumer goods by both the factory and household sector, the increasing of agricultural productivity and the provision of better housing, health and education facilities.

The emphasis on capital goods was justified in two principal ways. The first was that it would safeguard this former colony's economic, and hence political, independence. The second was that it would help solve the pressing problem of unemployment. 'Unemployment is chronic because of [the unavailability of] capital goods', argued Mahalanobis; it occurs 'only when means of production become idle'. The quickest way to create jobs was to build dams and factories.[20]

Mahalanobis's draft plan was submitted to a panel of expert economists. With one exception, all endorsed the emphasis on capital goods and the role of the public sector. To be sure, there were a number of specific caveats. Some economists urged a greater complementarity of agricultural and industrial production; others worried about where the funds for the plan would come from. Increasing taxes would not by themselves suffice, while deficit financing might lead to high inflation.

Table 10.1 – Sectoral outlays in the first two five-year plans

Sector	Outlay in first plan		Outlay in second plan	
	Total *	%	Total *	%
Agriculture and community development	372	16	530	11
Irrigation	395	17	420	9
Power	266	11	445	10
Industries and minerals	179	7	1075	24
Transport and communications	556	24	1300	28
Social services, housing, etc.	547	25	830	18

* In crores of rupees (1 crore = 10 million).

SOURCE: Compiled from A. H. Hanson, *The Process of Planning: A Study of India's Five-Year Plans, 1950 –1964* (London: Oxford University Press, 1966), table 7, p. 134.

But, on the whole, the leading economists of India were behind what was already being called 'the Mahalanobis Model of Planning'.[21]

This model was, among other things, an evocation of the old nationalist model of *swadeshi*, or self-reliance. Once, Gandhian protesters had burnt foreign cloth to encourage the growth of indigenous textiles; now, Nehruvian technocrats would make their own steel and machine tools rather than buy them from outside. As the second plan argued, underdevelopment was 'essentially a consequence of insufficient technological progress'.[22] Self-reliance, from this perspective, became *the* index of development and progress. From soap to steel, cashew to cars, Indians would meet their material requirements by using Indian land, Indian labour, Indian materials and, above all, Indian technology.

Table 10.1 compares the sectoral outlays for the first and second plans. In proportional terms the sectors of power, transport and communications, and social services, retained broadly the same importance. The decisive shift was from agriculture to industry, this compounded by a decline in the importance of irrigation.

While the heavy industries would be owned by the state, there was still plenty of room for private enterprise. For in 'an expanding economy the private sector would have an assured market'. Their main contribution would come in the form of consumer goods, these to be produced by units large as well as small.[23]

A government resolution of 1956 classified new industries into three categories. Class I would be the 'exclusive responsibility' of the state; these included atomic energy, defence-related industries, aircraft, iron and steel, electricity generation and transmission, heavy electricals, telephones, and coal and other key minerals. Class II would witness both public and private sector participation; here fell the lesser minerals, chemicals, pharmaceuticals, fertilizers, pulp and paper, and road transport. Class III consisted of all the remaining industries, to be undertaken 'ordinarily through the initiative and enterprise of the private sector'.[24]

Would the Mahalanobis model succeed? Many Indians thought so, most Indians certainly hoped so. So did their sympathizers worldwide. Representative here are the views of J. B. S. Haldane, the great British biologist who was then planning to move to India and the ISI. When shown the draft plan by Mahalanobis, Haldane commented that

> Even if one is pessimistic, and allows a 15 per cent chance of failure through interference by the United States (via Pakistan or otherwise), a 10 per cent chance of interference by the Soviet Union and China, a 20 per cent chance of interference with civil service traditionalism and political obstruction, and a 5 per cent chance of interference by Hindu traditionalism, that leaves a 50 per cent chance for a success which will alter the whole history of the world for the better.[25]

III

If Mahalanobis was the chief technician of Indian planning, then Nehru was its chief missionary. The prime minister believed that, in the Indian context, planning was much more than rational economics. It was good politics as well. While the plan was based on the work of economists and statisticians, to realize its goal the 'people must have the sensation of partnership in a mighty enterprise, of being fellow-travellers towards the next goal that they and we have set before us'. Popular participation was the only way to make 'this Plan, which is enshrined in cold print, something living, vital and dynamic, which captures the imagination of our people'.[26]

Planning was thus a 'mighty co-operative effort of all the people of India'. Nehru hoped that the new projects would be a solvent to dissolve the schisms of caste and religion, community and region. Introducing the first plan to his chief ministers, he wrote that 'the more we think of this balanced picture of the whole of India and of its many-sided activities, which are so interrelated with one another, the less we are likely to go astray in the crooked paths of provincialism, communalism, casteism and all other disruptive and disintegrating tendencies'. Introducing the second plan, he called it a 'brave effort to fashion our future', that will 'require all the strength and energy that we possess'. He believed that 'ultimately this is the only way to deal with the separatism, provincialism and sectarianism that we have to combat'.[27]

On the economic side, Nehru singled out two activities as providing the 'essential bases' for planning: the production of power and the production of steel.[28] At Independence, India had only two steel plants, both privately owned, which produced just over a million tonnes a year. This was inadequate for an expanding economy, more so one that had committed itself to the building of heavy industries.

The private sector was barred from starting new enterprises in steel, which, along with coal, shipbuilding, atomic energy and aircraft production, was deemed too important to be subject to the profit motive. The forest belt that runs across central India was rich in iron ore and coal, and it had plenty of rivers too. At once a lively competition began between the states that comprised this belt, each seeking to have the first public-sector steel plant within its borders. This was paralleled by a competition between the industrialized countries of the West, each of whom wanted the contract to build the first plant.[29]

The second plan had set a target of 6 million tonnes of steel. The output was needed to provide inputs to other planned industries. But it was also a way of promoting forced savings. As one economist famously put it, 'you can't eat steel'. While the second plan was being finalized, the Indian government signed three separate agreements for the construction of steel plants. The Germans would build one in Rourkela in Orissa, the Russians one in Bhilai in Madhya Pradesh, the British one in Durgapur in West Bengal. The Americans, much to their sorrow, had lost out. That the war-ravaged countries of Europe had grabbed two contracts was bad enough, that their hated Cold War rivals had taken the third was worse. Years later an American friend remembered how the decision that Bhilai was going to the Russians was communicated

over the radio in tones of palpable sadness by the fabled broadcaster
Ed Murrow.[30]

The Russians, of course, were delighted. Nikita Khrushchev visited
Bhilai and called it the 'Magnitogorsk of India'. *Pravda* ran lavish photo
features hailing Bhilai as a symbol of Indo-Soviet co-operation.[31] The
Indians were more enthusiastic still. A Bengali chemist who worked
in Bhilai recalled how his Russian boss had, over the years, become an
intimate friend as well. When the time came for the foreign expert to
leave, the Indian could not contain his tears. The Russian was stoic,
but his wife had sympathetic drops tricking down her cheeks. For the
bereft Bengali, those tears 'were nothing to me but the drops of the holy
water of the Volga, which pervasively mingled with the stream of our
Ganges, and inundated our fraternity and imperishable friendship'.

In Bhilai, Russian and Indian worked shoulder to shoulder, clearing
the land, building the roads and houses, erecting the plant. Those
who were part of this effort remembered it with warm affection. It
was, recalled one participant, 'a frenzy without panic, a tempo with
a plan. The construction team glowed with pride and satisfaction at
the newborn plant they had brought to life, the operation team was
anxiously eager to nurture it to its full stature . . . Each of us were
helping build the future – a future one could almost see, touch, and
feel.' Finally, in February 1959, under the benign eyes of the president of
India, the first flush of molten iron came out of a blast furnace in Bhilai.
All around there were tears of joy and rejoicing. Those who were there
long remembered them as 'the most exciting moments of [their] life'.[32]

The Indian steel industry was described by a senior official as 'at once
a school of technique and the mainspring of other industrial activities'.[33]
In fact it was more. The steel factory was a living refutation of the belief
that Indians were non-productive and pre-scientific – in a word, *backward*.

IV

In the economic modernization of India, large dams occupied a rather
special place. They would, on the one hand, emancipate agriculture from
the tyranny of the monsoon and, on the other, provide the electric power
to run the new industries mandated by the five-year plans. Jawaharlal
Nehru was enchanted by dams, which he called 'the temples of modern
India'. His fascination was shared by millions of his countrymen, who

too came to venerate these towering new monuments built in mud and concrete.

Indian intellectuals greatly admired the Tennessee Valley Authority, the integrated project that was a cornerstone of Franklin Roosevelt's New Deal. But they also admired the massive multipurpose projects undertaken in the Soviet Union. In the 1940s, anticipating Independence, scientists and engineers made trips to America and Russia to acquaint themselves at first hand with how dams were built. They were deeply impressed with what they saw.[34] On either side of the Iron Curtain, these projects represented 'the triumph of science, technology, foresight and centralized government over politics, petty local authorities and powers, ignorance, superstition, and backwardness'. They represented, indeed, 'the salvation of the nation through rationality and strength'.[35]

Like North America and Russia, the subcontinent had numerous large rivers. Damming and taming these rivers would kill three birds with one stone; generating electricity, providing water for irrigation and preventing flooding. After a particularly lethal bout of flooding on the Godavari in the monsoon of 1953, a leading engineer wrote to a leading politician that this was a river

> with enormous potential for good. The destruction caused by floods of this year has, however, demonstrated that if these flood waters are not harnessed for beneficial use, they will constitute a potential threat to the well-being of the people. Properly conserved, these flood waters will satisfy all the needs of the Godavari basin and leave ample reserves, which integrated with the Krishna waters will enable irrigation and power benefits to be extended right down to Madras and further south . . . No effort should therefore be spared in harnessing of the Godavari waters, in optimum integration with the Krishna, nor extraneous reasons permitted to delay or jeopardise their consummation.[36]

Here was a proselytizing technocrat speaking to the already converted. For while the Godavari was still undammed, most of the other major rivers had already come under the hand of man. Among the massive dam projects under way were those on the Mahanadi, Rihand, Tungabhadra, Damodar and Sutlej rivers.

In the mid-1950s the political scientist Henry Hart wrote a lyrical account of the transformation of 'New India's Rivers'. For Hart, these projects were 'the greatest of the monuments of free India'; to them 'men and women come, in a pilgrimage growing season by season, to see for themselves the dams and canals and power stations'.

In the book, there is a particularly fine description of the construction of the Tungabhadra dam. When finished, the dam would embody 32 million cubic feet of masonry; these laid at the rate of 40,000 cubic feet a day, every day for five years. The sheer scale could properly be conveyed only by means of analogy. 'Imagine the masonry in Tungabhadra Dam', wrote Hart, 'being laid as a highway, 20 feet wide, 6 inches thick. It would extend from Lucknow to Calcutta, or from Bombay to Madras.'[37]

Without question the most prestigious of all these schemes was the Bhakra–Nangal project in northern India. Again, its scale is best narrated in numbers. At 680 feet, the Bhakra dam was the second highest in the world; only the Grand Coulee Dam, on the Colorado river, was higher. The concrete and masonry that would finally go into it was estimated at 500 million cubic feet, 'more than twice the cubic contents of the seven great pyramids of Egypt'. The project would generate nearly a million kilowatts of electricity, while the water from the reservoir would irrigate 7.4 million acres of land, this carried in canals for whose excavation 30 million cubic yards of mud and stone had to be removed.[38]

This project was a form of compensation for the refugee farmers from West Punjab, a substitute for the canal colonies they had left behind on the other side of the border. These peasants, predominantly Sikh, had 'a martyr-like yearning to recreate within their own lifetimes the prosperity of which they have been cruelly deprived'. Bhakra–Nangal gave them 'the field and the resources from which they can rebuild and resettle themselves'. In fact, it gave them more – for in addition to the water there was power, from which the Punjabis could, if they so chose, for the first time build an industrial future for themselves.

The Bhakra–Nangal project was described in minute detail in a special issue of the *Indian Journal of Power and River Valley Development*. The issue opened with a set of four most revealing photographs. The first showed the densely wooded site before work began – it carried the caption, 'River Sutlej at Bhakra in its primeval splendour – the site as it was'. The second showed crane-like structures in the water and a low bridge slung across the gorge: this was 'Exploratory drilling in river bed with drills mounted on pontoons – the first invasion'. The third photo, taken apparently in the dry season, showed hillsides by now quite bare, with trucks and bulldozers on the river bed. Thus 'Concreting of the

Dam begins – man lays the foundation for changing nature'. In the last photo, the dam had begun to rise, aided by machines of a shape and size never before seen in India. This was 'Excavation with heavy machines in progress in pit-area – the struggle with nature'.[39]

The men and women who worked at Bhakra were all Indian, with one exception. This was an American, Harvey Slocum. Slocum had little formal education; starting out as a labourer in a steel mill, he had risen to the position of construction superintendent on the Grand Coulee dam. Slocum joined the Bhakra team as chief engineer in 1952 and imprinted upon it his own distinctive style of working. Officers and workers of all levels were mandated to dress uniformly. Slocum himself was at the site at 8 a.m. sharp, staying there until late evening. A stern disciplinarian, he could not abide the sloth and inefficiency that was rampant around him. Once, when the telephone system broke down, he wrote to the prime minister informing him that 'only God, not Slocum, could build the Bhakra Dam on schedule'.[40]

In the first week of July 1954 Nehru visited Bhakra to formally inaugurate the project. As he flicked on the switch of the power house, Dakotas of the Indian air force dipped their wings overhead. Next he opened the sluice gates of the dam. Seeing the water coming towards them, the villagers downstream set off hundreds of home-made crackers. As one eyewitness wrote, 'For 150 miles the boisterous celebration spread like a chain reaction along the great canal and the branches and distributaries to the edges of the Rajasthan Desert, long before the water got there.'[41]

V

In the push to industrialize India, a key role had to be played by technology and technologists. Since his days as a student at Cambridge, Jawaharlal Nehru had been fascinated by modern science. 'Science is the spirit of the age and the dominating factor of the modern world', he wrote. Nehru wished that what he called 'the scientific temper' should inform all spheres of human activity, including politics. More specifically, in an underdeveloped country like India, science must be made the handmaiden of economic progress, with scientists devoting their work to augmenting productivity and ending poverty.[42]

At the time of Indian independence a mere 0.1 per cent of GNP was spent on scientific research. Within a decade the figure had jumped to 0.5 per cent; later, it was to exceed 1 per cent. Under Nehru's active direction, a chain of new research laboratories was set up. These, following the French model, were established independently, outside of the existing universities. Within the ambit of the Council for Scientific and Industrial Research were some two dozen individual institutes. There was a strong utilitarian agenda at work, with scientists in these laboratories encouraged to develop new products for Indians rather than publish academic papers in foreign journals.[43]

An Indian scientist whom Nehru patronized early and consistently was the brilliant Cambridge-educated physicist Homi Bhabha. Bhabha founded and directed two major scientific institutions. The first was the Tata Institute of Fundamental Research in Bombay whose work, as its name implies, was aimed mostly at basic research. It had world-class departments of physics and mathematics and also, in time, housed India's first mainframe computer. The second was the Atomic Energy Commission, mandated to build and run India's nuclear power plants. This was handsomely funded by the government with an annual budget, in 1964, of about Rs100 million.[44]

Many new engineering schools were also started. These included the flagship Indian Institutes of Technology (IITs), five of which were inaugurated between 1954 and 1964. Like the new laboratories, the new colleges were intended to augment indigenous technical capability. Both Nehru and Bhabha were determined to lessen India's dependence on the West for scientific materials and know-how. They believed that 'if an item of equipment was imported from abroad, all one got was that particular instrument. But if one built it oneself, an all-important lesson in expertise was learnt as well'.[45]

VI

The industrial bias of Indian planning was tempered by a range of programmes promoting agrarian uplift. On the morning of 2 October 1952 (Mahatma Gandhi's birthday), the president of India inaugurated a nationwide series of community development programmes with a broadcast over the radio. Fifty-five projects were launched across India that day, these funded jointly by the governments of India and the United States. Among the schemes to be promoted by community development were roads and wells, cattle welfare and improved methods of cultivation.

The projects were launched by ministers, chief ministers, and commissioners. These dignitaries helped remove earth for building roads and laid foundation stones for schools and hospitals. In Alipur village, twelve miles out of Delhi on the road to Karnal, Jawaharlal Nehru dug into the earth to help prepare a road. 'With verve and vigour he plunged into the work, having taken his jacket off.' His companion, the American ambassador, also carried some baskets of earth. Not everyone was as agile as these two. When a well-dressed official attempted to emulate the prime minister the villagers shouted 'Sar par! Sar par!' – meaning, 'Carry the baskets on your head, you fool, not with your hands!' Speaking to the villagers, Nehru said that community development would bring about a rural revolution by peaceful means, not, as in other places, by the breaking of heads.[46]

How did these schemes work in practice? Two years after they began, the anthropologist S. C. Dube studied a community development project in western Uttar Pradesh. He looked at the project from the viewpoint of the village-level worker (VLW), the government functionary mandated with taking new ideas to the peasants.

By Dube's account, these 'agents of change' certainly had energy and enterprise. They got up at the crack of dawn, and worked all day. Among their duties were the demonstration to the villagers of the merits of new seeds and chemical fertilizers. These were tried on sample plots, the peasants looking on as the VLW explained scientific methods of dibbling. Different crops were sown, and different combinations of fertilizers used. The VLW also offered the villagers free *angrezi khad* (English manure) for use on their fields.

It appears that the peasants of the UP were somewhat ambivalent about the new techniques. Here is a conversation between the VLW and a farmer known only by his initials, 'MS':

VLW: What do you think of the new seed?
  MS: What can I think? If the government thinks it is good, it must be good.
VLW: Do you think it is better than the local variety?
  MS: Yes. It resists disease much better. It can stand frost and rain, and there is more demand for it in the market.

VLW: What about yield?

  MS: I cannot say. Some people say it is more, others say it is not.

VLW: Some people say it is not as good in taste.

  MS: They are right. It is not half as good. If the *roti* [bread] is served hot it is more or less the same, but if we keep it for an hour or so it gets as tough as hide. No, it is not as good in taste. People say that we all get very weak if we eat this wheat.

VLW: What is your experience?

  MS: Many more people suffer from digestive disorders these days. Our children have coughs and colds. Perhaps it is because of the new seed and sugar cane. It may be that the air has been spoilt by the wars.

VLW: And what about the new fertilizer?

  MS: They increase the yield; there is no doubt about it. But they probably destroy the vitality of the land and also of the grain.[47]

Indian peasants had mixed feelings about the new seeds and fertilizers. But they unambiguously welcomed fresh supplies of water. At the same time as S. C. Dube was studying community development in the UP, the British anthropologist Scarlett Epstein was living in Wangala, a village in southern Mysore lately the beneficiary of canal irrigation. Till the water came, this was like any other hamlet in the interior Deccan, growing millet for its own consumption. With irrigation came new crops such as paddy and sugar cane. These were sold outside the village for a handsome return. Paddy gave a profit after expenses of Rs136 per acre; sugar cane as much as Rs 980 per acre. These changes in local economics fostered changes in lifestyle as well. Before the canals arrived, the residents of Wangala wore scruffy clothes and rarely ventured outside the village. But 'Wangala men now wear shirts and a number also wear dhotis; their wives wear colourful saris bought with money and they all spend lavishly on weddings. Wangala men pay frequent visits to Mandya [town], where they visit coffee shops and toddy shops; rice has replaced ragi as their staple diet.'

These and other changes were made possible only by the extension of irrigation. As Epstein found, the coming of canal water was the turning point in the history of the village. Events of note, such as weddings, deaths and murders, were dated by whether they happened before or after irrigation.[48]

VII

Assured irrigation and chemical fertilizers increased agricultural productivity. But they could not solve what was a fundamental problem of rural India: inequality in access to land. Therefore, landless peasants were encouraged to settle in areas not previously under the plough. In the first decade of Independence, close to half a million hectares of land were colonized, principally from malarial forests in the northern Terai, the central Indian hills, and the Western Ghats. Previously these areas had been inhabited only by tribes genetically resistant to malaria. With the invention of DDT it became possible for the state to clear the forests. These lands were naturally fertile, rich in calcium and potassium and organic matter (if poor in phosphates). In any case, there was no shortage of peasants who wanted them.[49]

A second way of tackling landlessness was to persuade large landholders to voluntarily give up land under their possession. This was a method pioneered by a leading disciple of Gandhi, Vinoba Bhave. In 1951 Bhave undertook a walking tour through the then communist-dominated areas of Telengana. In Pochempelli village, he persuaded a zamindar named Ramchandra Reddi to donate a hundred acres of land. This encouraged Bhave to make this a countrywide campaign, known as the 'Bhoodan' movement. The saint trudged through the Indian heartland, giving speeches wherever he went. He must have walked perhaps 50,000 miles, while collecting in excess of 4 million acres. At first his mission was reckoned a success – like community development, a noble Gandhian alternative to violent revolution. But later assessments were less charitable. Like some other saints, Bhave preferred the grand gesture over humdrum detail. Critics pointed out that the bulk of the land donated to Bhave had never been distributed to the landless; over the years it had slowly returned to the hands of the original owners. Besides, much of the land that stayed under Bhoodan was rocky and sandy, unfit for cultivation. In few places were the intended beneficiaries organized to work the land they had been gifted. On balance, the Bhoodan movement must be reckoned a failure, albeit a spectacular one.[50]

A third way of ending landlessness was to use the arm of the state. Land reform legislation had long been on the agenda of the Congress. After Independence, the different states passed legislation abolishing the zamindari system which, under the British, had bestowed effective

Table 10.2 – Access to land in India, 1953 –1960

Size class (in hectares)	Percentage of holdings		Percentage of total area	
	1953 – 4	1959 – 60	1953 – 4	1959 – 60
less than 1	56.15	40.70	5.58	6.71
1 to 2	15.08	22.26	10.02	12.17
2 to 4	14.19	18.85	18.56	19.95
4 to 10	10.36	13.45	29.22	30.47
more than 10	4.22	4.74	36.62	30.70

SOURCE: Nripen Bandyopadhyaya, 'The Story of Land Reforms in Indian Planning', in Amiya Kumar Bagchi, ed., *Economy, Society and Polity: Essays in the Political Economy of Indian Planning in Honour of Professor Bhabatosh Datta* (Calcutta: Oxford University Press, 1988)

rights of ownership to absentee landlords. The abolition of zamindari freed up large areas of land for redistribution, while also freeing tenants from cesses and rents previously exacted from them.

After the end of zamindari, the state vested rights of ownership in their tenants. These, typically, came from the intermediate castes. Left unaffected were those at the bottom of the heap, such as low-caste labourers and sharecroppers. Their well-being would have required a second stage of land reforms, where ceilings would be placed on holdings, and excess land handed over to the landless. This was a task that the government was unable or unwilling to undertake.[51]

Even after a decade of planning, access to land remained very unequal. Table 10.2 indicates the percentages in five size classes of both the absolute number of holdings and the combined operational area of those holdings.

If we define those who own less than four hectares as 'small and marginal' farmers, and those who own more than four hectares as 'medium and large farmers', then Table 10.2 can be compressed into Table 10.3. This reveals a slight diminution in inequality, with a 3.6 per cent drop in the numbers of small / marginal farmers and a 4.6 per cent increase in the land held by them. The operative word is 'slight'; so slight as to be almost imperceptible, and, in a democracy committed to the 'socialistic pattern of society', simply unacceptable.

	Percentage of holdings		Percentage of total area	
Class of farmer	1953–4	1959–60	1953–4	1959–60
Small and Marginal	85.42	81.81	34.16	38.83
Medium and Large	14.58	18.19	65.84	61.17

Table 10.3 – Changes in land inequality in India, 1953 – 60

VIII

The Nehru–Mahalanobis model emphasized heavy industrialization, state control, and ultimately, a subsidiary role for the private sector. Behind it rested a wide consensus – and not merely in India. That in a complex modern economy the state must occupy the 'commanding heights' was a belief then shared by governments and ideologues all over the world.

In the United States, purposive government intervention had brought the country out of the horrors of the Great Depression. In Britain, Keynesian economics had been energetically applied by the Labour government that came to power in 1945. An appreciation of the state as a positive agent in economic change was also heightened by the recent achievements of the Soviet Union. At the time of the first war Russia was a backward peasant nation; by the time of the second, a mighty industrial power. Particularly impressive were its military victories against Germany, which had a far longer history of technological and industrial development. For the Western democracies, the feats of the Soviets only underlined the importance of the state direction of economic development.[52]

To be sure, there were dissenters. In the West there was Friedrich Hayek, who advocated a retreat of the state from economic activity. His ideas, however, were treated with benign – and sometimes not-so-benign – contempt. (He could not even get a position in the Department of Economics in the University of Chicago, being placed instead in the 'Committee on Social Thought'.) And in India there was B. R. Shenoy, the sole economist in the panel of experts who disagreed with the basic approach of the second five-year plan. As one commentator wrote, Shenoy 'appeared to be committed to laissez-faire methods in so doctrinaire a manner that no one, outside certain business circles, took much note of his criticisms'.[53]

In truth, Shenoy's arguments went beyond a mere belief in laissez faire. While he opposed the 'general extension of nationalisation on principle', his main criticism of the plan was that it was overambitious. It had, he thought, seriously overestimated the rate of savings in the Indian economy. The shortfall in funds would have to be made up by deficit financing, contributing to greater inflation.[54]

Another dissenter was the Chicago economist Milton Friedman. Visiting India in 1955 at the invitation of the government, he wrote a memorandum setting out his objections to the Mahalanobis model. He thought it too mathematical: obsessed by capital–output ratios, rather than by the development of human capital. He deplored the emphasis in industrial policy on the two extremes – large factories that used too little labour and cottage industries that used too much. As he saw it, the 'basic requisites' of economic policy in a developing country were 'a steady and moderately expansionary monetary framework, greatly widened opportunities for education and training, improved facilities for transportation and communication to promote the mobility not only of goods but even more important of people, and an environment that gives maximum scope to the initiatives and energy of farmers, businessmen, and traders'.[55]

Independently of Friedman, a young Indian economist had taken up one aspect of this critique – the neglect of education. The constitution mandated free and compulsory schooling for children up to the age of fourteen. But the sums allocated for this by the second plan, wrote B. V. Krishnamurti, were 'absurdly low'. He called for a 'substantial increase' in the allotment for education, the budget being balanced by an 'appropriate curtailment in the outlay on heavy industries'. Attention to detail was also crucial – to the enhancement of the social prestige of the schoolteacher, to higher salaries for them, to better buildings and playgrounds for the children. As Krishnamurti argued:

> A concerted effort on these lines to educate the mass of the population, specially in the rural areas, would undoubtedly have far-reaching benefits of a cumulatively expansionist character. This would greatly lighten the task of the Government in bringing about rapid economic development. For in a reasonable time, one could expect that the ignorance and inertia of the people would crumble and an urge to improve one's

material conditions by utilising the available opportunities would develop. If this were to happen, the employment problem would take care of itself. The people of the country would begin to move along the lines of those in the advanced democratic countries such as Great Britain and Switzerland.[56]

If B. V. Krishnamurti had been a professor in the centre of power, Delhi, rather than a lowly lecturer in Bombay, he might have got a hearing. In Friedman's case, his high position and prestige were offset by foreign economists of equal distinction but of opposing views. He was to them what B. R. Shenoy was to Indian economists – a lone free-marketeer drowned out by a chorus of social democrats and leftists.[57]

A critique of a different kind came from the Marxists. They thought that the Mahalanobis model gave not too little importance to the market, but too much. The second plan, they felt, should have mandated a thoroughgoing process of nationalization, whereby the state would not merely start new industries, but take under its wing the private firms already in operation. They wanted the working class to be involved with planning, on the model of the 'people's democracies' of Eastern Europe.[58]

Then there were the Gandhians, who provided a precocious ecological critique of modern development. In the vanguard of this 'early environmentalism' were two of the Mahatma's closest disciples, J. C. Kumarappa and Mira Behn (Madeleine Slade). Through the 1950s they pungently dissented from the conventional wisdom on agricultural policy. They argued that small irrigation systems were more efficacious than large dams; that organic manure was a cheap and sustainable method of augmenting soil fertility (when compared to chemicals that damaged the earth and increased foreign debt); that forests should be managed from the point of view of water conservation rather than revenue maximization (by protecting natural multispecies forests rather than the monocultural stands favoured by the state). These specific criticisms were part of a wider understanding of the world of nature. As Mira Behn wrote in 1949:

The tragedy today is that educated and moneyed classes are altogether out of touch with the vital fundamentals of existence – our Mother Earth, and the animal and vegetable population which she sustains. This world of Nature's planning is ruthlessly plundered, despoiled and disorganized by man whenever he gets the chance. By his science and machinery he may get huge returns for a time, but ultimately will come desolation. We have got to study Nature's balance, and develop our lives within her laws, if we are to survive as a physically healthy and morally decent species.[59]

One modern technology the Gandhians had deep reservations about were large dams. They thought them costly and destructive of nature. But, as Indians were soon finding out, dams were destructive of human community as well. By the early 1950s reports began appearing of the sufferings of those displaced by dams. In the summer of 1952, when the Hirakud authorities issued eviction notices to the residents of the 150 villages the project would submerge, they met with stiff resistance. A reporter on the spot concluded that 'the prosperity of Hirakud will be built on the sacrifice of such people who are now being destituted [sic] by the Government of Orissa without compensation and rehabilitation'. Three years later, a similar tale surfaced of villagers in Himachal Pradesh, who had to make way for the reservoir of the Bhakra dam. A full year had passed since Nehru had inaugurated the power house; yet 'complacency and indifference seem to be guiding the counsels of the Bhakra Control Board, particularly the Rehabilitation Committee'. Even 'the basic question of compensation, and the where, why and how of it remains to be decided to the satisfaction of the people concerned'.[60]

IX

The free-market critique; the human capital critique; the ecological critique – these make for fascinating reading today. But at the time these notes of dissent were scattered, and they were politically weak. There was then an overwhelming consensus in favour of a heavy industry-oriented, state-supported model of development. This was a consensus among intellectuals; no fewer than twenty-three of the twenty-four expert economists asked to comment on the Mahalanobis plan agreed with it in principle.[61]

This consensus was shared by large sections of the ruling class as well. In their Bombay Plan the leading industrialists had asked for an 'enlargement of the positive functions of the State'. They approvingly quoted the Cambridge economist A. C. Pigou's view that freedom and planning were entirely compatible. Indeed, these big businessmen went so far as to state that 'the distinction between capitalism and socialism has lost much of its significance from a practical standpoint. In many respects there is now a large ground common to both and the gulf between the two is being steadily narrowed further as each shows signs of modifying itself in the direction of the other. In our view, no economic organization can function effectively or possess lasting qualities unless it accepts as its basis a judicious combination of the principles associated with each school of thought'.[62]

For a final word on the romance and enchantment of Indian planning, we turn to an anonymous journalist covering one of its showpiece projects. This was Bokaro, site both of a thermal power project and a large reservoir. Visiting the place in September 1949, the reporter found that 'Bokaro stood in the midst of barren, rocky land, overlooking the confluence of two sandy rivers. The only habitation there was the office of the Executive Engineer manned by half-a-dozen persons, without any living or other facilities. One could reach Bokaro only by jeep and we had to carry our own food.'

Three and a half years later the journalist went back to Bokaro to see the prime minister inaugurate the power plant and the dam. 'What a different sight met my eyes', he exulted. Approaching the Bokaro valley on a 'first-class tarmac road', he saw 'the three sturdy stacks of the Power Station against the grey background of the hills'. What had been 'a dry river bed in 1949 has been turned into a fair-sized lake' with a concrete barrage thrown across it. For those who worked in dam and plant, there was now 'a modern residential area with tarred roads, electric lighting, a high school, hospital, filtered water supply and all the amenities one expects in the present day'.[63]

'Whenever I see these great engineering works', wrote Jawaharlal Nehru, 'I feel excited and exhilarated. They are visible symbols of building up the new India and of providing life and sustenance to our people'.[64] It appears the excitement and exhilaration were felt by plenty of other Indians as well.

11

THE LAW AND THE PROPHETS

Some of these progressive movements have a great fascination for Nehru. He always likes to be looked upon as a modern; he wants to be a Picasso hung up in the Royal Academy, looking upon the classical forms around him with a supercilious air.

D. F. KARAKA, journalist, 1953

It is a settled fact that every country and every nation has its own character. It is inborn and instinct with it. It cannot be changed. Shakespeare and Kalidas are both great poets and dramatists . . . India . . . could not produce a Shakespeare [nor] similarly England a Kalidas. I ask the sponsors of the reform, with all force and self-confidence, where is the necessity of *Europeanisation of Hindu* Law? . . . In codifying it there is danger of hurting seriously the susceptibilities and devotional feelings of millions of people.

Hindu lawyer, 1954

I

THE FRENCH WRITER ANDRÉ Malraux once asked Jawaharlal Nehru what had been his 'greatest difficulty since Independence'. Nehru replied: 'Creating a just state by just means'. Then he added, 'Perhaps, too, creating a secular state in a religious country'.[1]

Secularism was, indeed, an idea that underlay the very foundations of free India. The Indian national movement refused to define itself in religious terms. Gandhi insisted that the multiple faiths of India can and must co-exist peaceably in a free nation. This was a belief shared by Gandhi's most prominent follower, Nehru, and by his acknowledged mentor, Gopal Krishna Gokhale.

Congress nationalism suffered a body blow at Independence. Freedom came not, as Gandhi and his colleagues had hoped, to one nation, but to two. Secularism now faced a fresh set of challenges. One pertained to the domain of personal laws. In colonial times, the whole of India had come under a common penal code, drafted in the 1830s by the historian Thomas Babington Macaulay. But there was no attempt to replace the personal laws of various sects and religions with a common civil code. Here, as the British saw it, the colonial state's role was restricted to adjudicating between different interpretations of religious law.

After Independence, among those favouring a common civil code were the prime minister, Jawaharlal Nehru, and the law minister, Dr B. R. Ambedkar. Both were of a modernist cast of mind, and both were trained in the Western legal tradition. For both, the reform of personal laws became an acid test of India's commitment to secularism and modernization.

II

Article 44 of the Constitution of India reads: 'The State shall endeavour to secure for the citizens a uniform civil code throughout the territory of India.'

When this article was discussed in the Constituent Assembly, it provoked much agitation, particularly among Muslim members. During the two centuries of their rule, the British interfered little with personal laws; why could not the successor state follow their example? One member pointed out that 'as far as the Mussalmans are concerned, their laws of accession, inheritance, marriage and divorce are *completely dependent* upon their religion'. A second felt that 'the power that has been given to the state to make the civil code uniform is in advance of the time'. A third believed that the clause contravened another clause in the constitution: the freedom to propagate and practise one's religion.[2]

These arguments were forcefully refuted by B. R. Ambedkar. As he saw it, 'if personal laws are to be saved, . . . in social matters we will come to a standstill'. In traditional societies, religion presumed to hold a 'vast, expansive jurisdiction so as to cover the whole of life'. But in a modern democracy this licence had to be curtailed, if only 'in order to reform our social system, which is so full of inequities, so full of inequalities, discriminations and other things, which conflict with our fundamental rights'. To assuage the misgivings, Ambedkar said that the state might choose to apply a uniform civil code by consent, that is, only to those who chose voluntarily to submit to it.[3]

As it happened, during the last years of their rule the British had belatedly initiated the framing of a uniform code for Hindus. This sought to reconcile the prescriptions of the two principal schools of law – the Mitakshara and the Dayabhaga – and their numerous local variations. A committee had been set up in 1941 chaired by Sir B. N. Rau, who was also to play a crucial role in drafting the Indian Constitution. The committee toured India, soliciting a wide spectrum of Hindu opinion on the changes they proposed. Their progress was interrupted by the war, but by 1946 they had prepared a draft of a personal law code to be applied to all Hindus.[4]

That the Hindus were singled out was in part because they were the largest community, and in part because there was a vigorous reform movement among them. Mahatma Gandhi, in particular, had challenged the discriminations of caste and gender, by seeking the abolition of untouchability and bringing women into public life. Although there remained an influential orthodox section, modernist Hindus had campaigned strongly for laws that would make caste irrelevant and enhance the rights of women.

In 1948 the Constituent Assembly formed a Select Committee to review the draft of a new Hindu code. It was chaired by B. R. Ambedkar, the law minister. The code drafted by the Rau Committee was revised by Ambedkar himself, and then subjected to several close readings of the Select Committee.

Despite its name, the 'Hindu' Code Bill was to apply to Sikhs, Buddhists and Jains as well as all Hindu castes and sects. Introducing the new bill, Ambedkar told the Assembly that its aim was to 'codify the rules of Hindu Law which are scattered in innumerable decisions of the High Courts and of the Privy Council, [and] which form a bewildering motley to the common man and give rise to constant litigation'. The codification had a dual purpose: first, to elevate the rights and status of Hindu women; second, to do away with the disparities and divisions of caste. Among the notable features of the proposed legislation were:

1. The awarding, to the widow and daughter, of *the same share as the son(s)* in the property of a man dying intestate (which in the past had passed

only to his male heirs). Likewise, a Hindu woman's estate, previously limited, was now made absolute, to be disposed of as she wished.

2. The granting of maintenance to the wife who chose to live separately from the husband if he had a 'loathsome disease', was cruel to her, took a concubine, etc.

3. Abolition of the rules of caste and sub-caste in sanctifying a marriage. All marriages between Hindus would have the same sacramental as well as legal status, regardless of the castes to which the spouses belonged. An inter-caste marriage could now be solemnized in accordance with the customs and rites of *either* party.

4. Allowing either partner to file for and obtain divorce on certain grounds, such as cruelty, infidelity, incurable disease, etc.

5. Making monogamy mandatory.

6. Allowing for the adoption of children belonging to a different caste.

These changes went very far in the direction of gender equity. Later, much later, feminist scholars were to argue that they did not go far enough, that they exempted agricultural properties from their provisions, for example, or that the advantages conferred on female heirs by the new laws were greater in the case of self-acquired property as compared to property that was inherited.[5] But from the viewpoint of Hindu orthodoxy the changes had already gone far enough. They constituted radical departures from the main body of Hindu law, where the son had a much larger claim on his father's property as compared to the wife and daughter, where marriage was considered a sacrament and hence indissoluble, where the man was allowed to take more than one wife, and where marriage was governed strictly by the rules of caste.

In defending these changes, Ambedkar was at times rather defensive. Thus he argued that the Shastras, the Hindu holy texts, did not give the husband 'an unfettered, unqualified right to polygamy'. The 'right to marry a second time has been considerably limited by the [ancient law maker] Kautilya'. Again, the customary law of the various low castes, or *shudras*, had always allowed divorce. As for the woman's right to property, some schools allowed her a quarter share in her father's property; all Ambedkar had done was to 'raise [the daughter] up in the share of heirs', by making her share full and equal to that of the son.[6]

Ambedkar was here putting the best possible, or most liberal, spin on Hindu texts and traditions. But alternative interpretations were possible, and certainly more plausible. Not surprisingly, Ambedkar's proposals provoked 'loud denunciations' from the orthodox, who viewed them as 'a complete abrogation of the Hindu customs and traditions', an unacceptable interference with the rules of caste and the traditional relations between the sexes.[7]

A doughty opponent of the bill was the Constituent Assembly's own president, Rajendra Prasad. In June 1948, shortly after the Select Committee had been set up, Prasad warned the prime minister that to introduce 'basic changes' in personal law was to impose the 'progressive ideas' of a 'microscopic minority' on the Hindu community as a whole. Nehru answered that the Cabinet had declared itself in favour of the bill, that 'personally, I am entirely in favour of the general principles embodied in it'. To scrap the legislation now would be to give rise to the suspicion that the Congress was 'a reactionary and a very conservative body'; nor would it go down well 'in the mind of foreigners outside India'. Prasad shot back that the opinions of the 'vast bulk of [the] Hindu public' were more important than the views of foreigners.[8]

Within the Assembly there were other opponents as well. They stalled and thwarted the proceedings until Nehru, in high dudgeon, told them that to him the passing of the bill had become a matter of prestige. Prasad, in response, drafted a letter warning the prime minister that this would be 'unjust and undemocratic', as this 'fundamental and controversial legislation' had never been considered by the Indian electorate. Fortunately for him, Prasad consulted Vallabhbhai Patel before sending Nehru the letter. The timing is crucial here, for it was now December 1949, and soon the Congress would choose the first president of India from a shortlist that comprised Rajendra Prasad and C. Rajagopalachari. With this in view, Patel told Prasad not to send the prime minister his criticisms of the Hindu code, lest it 'prejudice your position within the party'.[9]

So Prasad kept quiet (and was duly elected the first president of the Indian Republic). But outside the Council House the cries grew louder. Already, in March 1949, an All-India Anti-Hindu-Code-Bill Committee had been formed. This held that the Constituent Assembly had 'no right to interfere with the personal laws of Hindus which are based on Dharma Shastras'. Sixty (male) members of the Delhi Bar issued a statement objecting to the codification of Hindu law, on the grounds that 'the mass of the Hindus believe in the Divine Origin of their personal laws'.

The Anti-Hindu-Code-Bill Committee was supported by conservative lawyers as well as by conservative clerics. The influential Shankaracharya of Dwarka issued an 'encyclical' against the proposed code. Religion, he said, 'is the noblest light, inspiration and support of men, and the State's highest duty is to protect it'.

The Anti-Hindu-Code-Bill Committee held hundreds of meetings throughout India, where sundry swamis denounced the proposed legislation. The participants in this movement presented themselves as religious warriors (*dharmaveer*) fighting a religious war (*dharmayudh*). The Rashtriya Swayamsevak Sangh threw its weight behind the agitation. On 11 December 1949, the RSS organized a public meeting at the Ram Lila grounds in Delhi, where speaker after speaker condemned the bill. One called it 'an atom bomb on Hindu society'. Another likened it to the draconian Rowlatt Act introduced by the colonial state; just as the protests against that act led to the downfall of the British, he said, the struggle against this Bill would signal the downfall of Nehru's government. The next day a group of RSS workers marched on the Assembly buildings, shouting 'Down with Hindu code bill' and 'May Pandit Nehru perish'. The protesters burnt effigies of the prime minister and Dr Ambedkar, and then vandalized the car of Sheikh Abdullah.

The leader of the movement against the new bill was one Swami Karpatriji Maharaj. We know little of this swami's antecedents, except that he was from north India and appeared to be knowledgeable in Sanskrit. His opposition to the Bill was coloured and deepened by the fact that it was being piloted by Ambedkar. He made pointed references to the law minister's caste, suggesting that a former Untouchable had no business meddling in matters normally the preserve of the Brahmin.

In speeches in Delhi and elsewhere, Swami Karpatri challenged Ambedkar to a public debate on his interpretations of the Shastras. To the law minister's claim that the Shastras did not really favour polygamy, Swami Karpatri quoted Yagnavalkya: 'If the wife is a habitual drunkard, a confirmed invalid, a cunning, a barren or a spendthrift woman, if she is bitter-tongued, if she has got only daughters and no son, if she hates her husband, [then] the husband can marry a second wife even while the first is living.' The swami supplied the precise citation for this injunction: the third verse of the third chapter of the third section of Yagnavalkya's *smriti* (scripture) concerning marriage. He did not, however, tell us whether the injunction also allowed the wife to take another husband if the existing one was a drunkard, bitter-tongued, a spendthrift, etc.

For Swami Karpatri, divorce was prohibited in Hindu tradition, while 'to allow adoption of a boy of any caste is to defy the Shastras and to defy property'. Even by the most liberal interpretations, the woman's inheritance was limited to one-eighth, not a half as Ambedkar sought to make it. The bill was altogether in violation of the Hindu scriptures. It had already evoked 'terrible opposition', and the government could push it through only at its peril. The swami issued a dire warning: 'As is clearly laid down in the Dharmashastras, to forcibly defy the laws of God and Dharma very often means great harm to the Government and the country and both bitterly rue the obstinate folly.'[10]

III

In December 1949, having agreed upon a constitution, the Constituent Assembly made way for a provisional Parliament, which was to be in place until the first general election. Through 1950 and 1951, Nehru and Ambedkar made several attempts to get the Hindu Code Bill passed into law. But the opposition was considerable, both within Parliament and outside it. To quote J. D. M. Derrett, 'every argument that could be mustered against the project was garnered, including many that cancelled each other out'. The 'offer of divorce to all oppressed spouses became the chief target of attack, and the cry that religion was in danger was raised by many whose real objection to the Bill was that daughters were to have equal shares with sons'.[11]

Within the provisional Parliament, orthodox members claimed that the Hindu laws had stayed unchanged from time immemorial. 'The rules of conduct and duties of men in our country are determined by the Vedas', said Ramnarayan Singh. Despite the challenges down the ages – posed by Buddhism, Islam and Christianity – 'the Vedic religion did not perish . . . [the] Vedic religion is still there'. But now, complained Ramnarayan Singh, 'we have Pandit Nehru's administration whose representative Dr Ambedkar wants to abrogate with a single stroke all those rules which have existed since the beginning of the world'.

Some parliamentarians argued that the government should frame and have passed an Indian code rather than a specifically Hindu one. 'I do not believe that only Hindu women are oppressed', said Indra Vidyavachaspati. By passing the bill in its present form, the state would 'give encouragement to [the] evil of communalism'. If it was not made applicable to all sections of the populations, insisted Vidyavachaspati, then 'the feeling of communalism will arise and what should have been a boon will turn into a curse'.

Other members were happy enough with the bill as it was. 'While I admire those who want to have one Civil Code for the whole of India', said Thakur Das Bhargava, 'I do not think that it would be a practical proposition to have one Civil Code for Muslims, Christians, Jews, etc.'. For Muslim members had already expressed their opposition to any tampering with their personal code, which they believed to be the revealed word of Allah himself. To ask at this stage for a uniform code was seen as a stalling tactic, diverting attention from the reform so urgently required within the majority community. As Dr Ambedkar put it, 'those who until yesterday were the greatest opponents of this Code and the greatest champions of the archaic Hindu Law as it exists to-day', now claimed that they were 'prepared for an All-India Civil Code'. This was because they hoped that while it had already taken 'four or five years to draft the Hindu Code [it] will probably take ten years to draft a Civil Code'.

Ambedkar knew that while there were enough influential Hindus – such as Jawaharlal Nehru – who were behind progressive legislation, among the Muslims the liberal contingent was nowhere near as strong. The government, he said, could not be so 'foolish' as 'not to realize the sentiments of different communities in this country'. That was why the code at present dealt only with the Hindus.[12]

Of course, not all Hindus were of the liberal party either. The reservations of the orthodox, as expressed in Parliament, were carried forward in the streets by the cadres of the Rashtriya Swayamsevak Sangh. They brought batches of volunteers into New Delhi, to shout slogans against the Hindu Code Bill and court arrest. Among their larger aims were the dismemberment of Pakistan and the unseating of Jawaharlal Nehru – as they shouted, 'Pakistan tod do', 'Nehru Hakumat Chhod Do'.

The main speaker at these RSS-organized shows was usually Swami Karpatriji Maharaj. Addressing a meeting on 16 September 1951, the swami challenged the prime minister to a debate on the proposed bill. 'If Pandit Nehru and his colleagues succeed in establishing that even one section of the proposed Hindu Code is in accordance with the Shastras', said Karpatri, 'I shall accept the entire Hindu Code'. The next day, in pursuance of this challenge, the swami and his followers marched on Parliament. The police prevented them from entering. In the ensuing scuffle, reported a Hindu weekly, 'police pushed them back [and] Swamiji's *danda* [stick] was broken, which is like the sacred thread, [the] religious emblem of the sannyasis'.[13]

Coincidentally, just two days before Swami Karpatriji's march, the president had written the prime minister a long letter of protest against the bill. As in 1948 and 1949, now too Rajendra Prasad felt that the present Parliament, based like its predecessor on a restricted franchise, was 'not competent to enact a measure of such a fundamental nature'. The bill, argued the president, was 'highly discriminatory', for it applied to only one community, the Hindus. Either the same laws governing marriage and property should be applied to all Indians, or else the existing customary laws of the different communities should be left untouched. Prasad wrote ominously that 'he proposed to watch the progress of the measure in Parliament from day to day'. If the bill was still passed, he would insist on his 'right to examine it on its merits . . . before giving assent to it'.[14]

Nehru wrote back saying that in his view there was 'a very widespread expression of opinion in the country in favour of the Bill'. But the president's opposition had him worried, for it presaged a possible stand-off between the government and the head of state. He showed Prasad's letter to several experts on the constitution. They assured him that the president was bound to act with 'the aid and advice of the Council of Ministers and cannot act independently of that advice'. As they saw it, the position of the president of India was even weaker than that of the British monarch.[15]

Despite this advice, Nehru chose not to challenge the president. In any case, the progress of the bill in the provisional Parliament had been painfully slow. An immense number of objections and amendments had been tabled. It took the better part of a year to have a mere four clauses passed. In the end 'the session ended, the bill was virtually talked out, and it lapsed'.[16]

The man who was most hurt by this failure was the law minister. Dr Ambedkar had staked his reputation on the bill, meeting criticism and calumny with equal resolution. That Nehru had finally chosen to give in to the opposition pained him deeply. In October 1951 he resigned from the Union Cabinet. He intended to announce his decision in the House, but when the Deputy Speaker asked for a copy of his speech beforehand, he walked out in a huff and released it to the press instead.

Ambedkar gave several reasons for his decision to resign. He had been in poor health, for one. For another, the prime minister had failed to repose adequate trust in him. Despite having a PhD in economics (from the London School of Economics, no less) he had been left out of discussions on planning and development. A third reason was his growing reservations about the government's foreign policy, particularly with regard to Kashmir. A fourth reason was that the condition of his fellow Scheduled Castes continued to be wretched. Despite the coming of political independence, and a constitution protecting their rights, they faced the 'same old tyranny, the same old oppression, the same old discrimination'.

Ambedkar came in the end to the issue which had finally provoked him to resign. He had, he said, set his cap on having the Hindu Code Bill passed before the end of the Parliament. He had tried hard to convince the prime minister about the urgency of the matter. But Nehru did not give him the kind of support he had hoped for. Facing opposition within his own party, the prime minister, complained Ambedkar, had not 'the earnestness and determination' required to overcome it.[17]

IV

In the first months of 1952 the recent debates on the Hindu Code Bill cast their shadow as India held its first general election. Feeling let down by the Congress, Dr Ambedkar had founded his own Scheduled Caste Federation in opposition to it. As for the prime minister, in his own constituency of Allahabad he was opposed by a leader of the now notorious Anti-Hindu-Code-Bill Committee.

This was Prabhu Dutt Brahmachari. He was an ascetic and celibate, to signal which he wore saffron. Brahmachari's candidature was supported by the Jana Sangh, the Hindu Mahasabha and the Ram Rajya Parishad. His campaign was run on a single-item agenda – no tampering with Hindu tradition. He printed pamphlets detailing the prime minister's attempts to interfere with that tradition, challenging him to an open debate on the subject.[18]

Nehru sensibly refused. He won his seat with a massive margin, while the Congress got a comfortable majority overall. Nehru saw this, in part, as a mandate for his campaign against communalism. Soon after the Parliament was convened he resurrected the Hindu Code Bill.

Keeping the earlier protests in mind, the original bill was now broken up into several parts. There were separate bills dealing with Hindu marriage and divorce, Hindu minority and guardianship, Hindu succession, and Hindu adoptions and maintenance. These component parts retained the rationale and driving force of the original unified proposal. The main thrust was to make caste irrelevant to Hindus with regard to marriage and adoption, to outlaw polygamy, to allow divorce and dissolution of marriage on certain specified grounds and to greatly increase a woman's share of her husband's and her father's property.[19]

The prime minister was in the vanguard of the pro-reform movement, telling Parliament that 'real progress of the country means progress not only on the political plane, not only on the economic plane, but also on the social plane'. The British had allied themselves with 'the most conservative sections of the community they could find'. The conjoining of tradition and colonialism meant that 'our laws, our customs fall heavily on the womenfolk'. Thus 'different standards of morality are applied to men and women'. Men were allowed more than one wife, but when a woman wished for a divorce she was challenged by men, only 'because men happen to be in a dominant position. I hope they will not continue in that dominant position for all time.'

Hindu customs and laws were hypocritical as well as unjust. Women were urged to model themselves on mythic figures of devotion and fidelity but, said Nehru, 'I do not seem to remember men being reminded in the same manner of Ramachandra and Satyavan, and urged to behave like them. It is only the women who have to behave like Sita and Savitri; the men may behave as they like.'[20]

Nehru worked hard to convince his colleagues of the importance of these measures. He wrote to one of his senior ministers, a Brahmin who tended towards the orthodox, that 'we have to remember that in the acknowledged social code and practice of India, as it has existed thus far, there was no lack of moral delinquency as well as extreme unhappiness. There were two codes, one for the man and the other for the woman. The woman got the worst of it always.' To a young first-time MP Nehru wrote that 'we should concentrate on the passage through Parliament of the Marriage and Divorce Bills and the Succession Bill. These are the really important ones. The bills dealing with adoption and guardianship, etc. are relatively unimportant.'[21]

By now the Anti-Hindu-Code-Bill Committee had lost its momentum. After the 1952 election the names of Swami Karpatriji Maharaj and

Prabhu Dutt Brahamachari do not appear in the newspapers or police records. There were no longer any protests on the streets, but there were still criticisms aplenty in Parliament. The orthodox MPs saw the new bills as designed to destroy Hindu culture. For them, the laws of Manu and Yagnavalkya were immutable and unchangeable, as relevant in 950 BC as in AD 1950.[22]

But there was also an opposition that was less vulgar and more considered; representing what we might call Hindu conservatives rather than Hindu reactionaries. Consider thus the views of the distinguished historian Radha Kumud Mookerji. He felt that the new proposals, particularly the provisions allowing divorce, were

> against the very spirit of Hindu civilization . . . The Bill is inspired by the western view of life which attaches more value to the romance of marital relations and married life than to parenthood in which marriage attains its fruition. The Hindu system conceives of parenthood as something that is permanent, unchangeable, and inviolable . . . The Bill seeks to change popular psychology as to the sanctity of marriage and family and loosen the ties of family as the very foundations of society. It thinks more of husband and wife than the father and mother in whom they are to be permanently merged to protect the child and the future of the race.[23]

This argument did not go uncontested. A woman member felt that 'the effect of a broken home is less injurious than that of a disharmonious home. Children are of a very receptive mind and the scenes that they may see of neglect and quarrel between the parents . . . are bound to leave their mark.' If 'the home has lost peace', remarked another member, there was no point 'forcing [husband and wife] to live together'; it was better to allow 'separation in a respectable fashion'.[24]

In the Lok Sabha the opposition to the reforms was led by the brilliant Hindu Mahasabha lawyer N. C. Chatterjee. If this was indeed a secular state, argued Chatterjee, what was the need for a 'Hindu' Marriage and Divorce Act? Why not make the same law apply for all citizens? Thus, if the government honestly believed in the virtues of monogamy, that 'this is a blessing and polygamy is a curse, then why not rescue our Muslim sisters from that curse and from that plight?' 'You have not the courage', Chatterjee told the law minister, 'to be logical and to be consistent.'[25]

The socialist J. B. Kripalani likewise felt that by prescribing monogamy only for the Hindus, the government was being hypocritical. 'You must bring it also for the Muslim community,' said Kripalani. 'Take it from me that the Muslim community is prepared to have it but you are not brave enough to do it.' But his own wife, the Congress MP Sucheta Kripalani, thought that the Muslims were not yet ready. For 'we know the recent past history of our country. We know what trouble we have had over our minority problem. That is why I think the Government today is not prepared to bring one Uniform Civil Code. But I hope the day will soon come in the future when we shall be able to have one.'[26]

The election of 1952 had returned to Parliament an array of articulate and confident women Congress MPs. These, naturally, saw the opposition to the legislation as the work of reactionaries. Subhadra Joshi, speaking in Hindi, launched a broadside against the custom of arranged marriages, which virtually sold women into *sharm ki zindagi*, a life of shame and degradation. Shivrajvati Nehru noted that, while male politicians talked grandly of economic and political reform, they were not willing to make a single change in the sphere of social life and custom. In Hindu society the man was free and sovereign (*purn swatantra*); but the woman was bonded – to him. Even now, the husband was prone to treat his wife as a pair of slippers on his feet, to be discarded at will.[27]

In support of the reforms were several Scheduled Caste members, who knew better than anyone else how Hindu 'custom' masked a multitude of sins. One MP said that if the orthodox had their way, they would

> start amending the Constitution so as to do away with all the mischief done by this Congress Government, and certain new fundamental rights will be added. The first of them will be that all Hindu women will have the wonderful and glorious right of burning themselves on the funeral pyres of their husbands. The second fundamental right would be that the cow will be declared a divine being, . . . and all Indians, including Muslims, Christians and so on will be compelled to worship the cow.[28]

The communists, for their part, thought the new laws were not radical enough. In the Lok Sabha, B. C. Das termed them 'a mild, moderate attempt at social reform with all the hesitancy and timidity characteristic of all social measures sponsored by this Government'. Still, those who opposed this 'moderate measure' had 'seventeenth-century minds'. In the Rajya Sabha, Bhupesh Gupta noted the delay in introducing the legislation owing to the fact that 'the Congress Party . . . functions on many occasions like a Rip Van Winkle'.[29]

Finally, one must take account of those Muslim members who were effusive in their thanks to government. One, speaking in Hindustani, praised it for keeping their laws intact and not allowing the slightest change in it. Another thanked the government 'for showing their great consideration to the views and the feelings of the Muslim community, and for having exempted them from the operations of this [Marriage] Bill, because there is the personal law for them, based on, and part of, their religion, and they hold religion as the most sacred and valuable thing in their life'.[30]

V

After a bruising battle extending over nearly ten years, B. R. Ambedkar's Hindu Code Bill was passed into law; not, as he had hoped, in one fell swoop, but in several instalments: the Hindu Marriage Act of 1955 and the Hindu Succession, Minority and Guardianship, and Adoptions and Maintenance Acts of 1956.

These acts were piloted through Parliament by the new law minister, H. V. Pataskar. He lacked both the stature of his predecessor and his scholarship. Once, when he suggested that the Hindu sacramental marriage permitted divorce, N. C. Chatterjee remarked that there was no basis for that statement, adding: 'If Shri Pataskar had sat for a Hindu Law examination in any University he would have been ploughed and he would have got zero.'[31]

This might have been accurate, but was anyway irrelevant. For, as one dissenter recognized, the new bills constituted a 'direct attack on the Hindu *shastras* and Hindu customs'.[32] The right of a woman to choose her partner or to inherit property were 'un-Hindu'; but not undemocratic, since the men had those rights all along. As Pataskar observed, the new laws were based on the constitutional recognition of 'the dignity of person, irrespective of any distinction of sex'.[33]

Another member of the Congress Party put it more eloquently. Women must have the right to choose (and discard) their husbands, he said, because 'we [Indians] were fighting for freedom. After liberating our country, our motherland, it is our responsibility to liberate our mothers, our sisters, and our wives. That will be the greatest culmination of the freedom that we have attained.'[34]

Towards that end the new laws were indeed a notable contribution. Sixty million Hindu women came under its purview. But the changes were significant in moral as well as numerical terms. As a leading American expert on Indian law has written, this was a 'wholesale and drastic reform' which 'entirely supplants the *shastra* as the source of Hindu law'. A leading British scholar of the subject goes further: 'For width of scope and boldness of innovation', he says, the series of acts considered here 'can be compared only with the Code Napoléon.'[35]

The radical changes in the Hindu law pertaining to marriage and property were principally the work of two men: Jawaharlal Nehru and B. R. Ambedkar. Sadly, in the last, crucial stages of the struggle Ambedkar was a bystander. Having failed to win his seat in the direct elections to Parliament in 1952, he then entered the Upper House. There he observed, silent, as the bills were discussed and passed between 1954 and 1956.[36] He was already a very sick man, with chronic diabetes and complications thereof, and in December 1956 he passed away. His sometime colleague Jawaharlal Nehru spoke in tribute in Parliament. Ambedkar, said the prime minister, would be remembered above all 'as a symbol of the revolt against all the oppressive features of Hindu society'. But he 'will be remembered also for the great interest he took and the trouble he took over the question of Hindu law reform. I am happy that he saw that reform in a very large measure carried out, perhaps not in the form of that monumental tome that he had himself drafted, but in separate bits.'[37]

This was a generous tribute, especially when we consider the bitterness that lay behind Ambedkar's resignation in 1951. Then, Ambedkar thought that Nehru was too weak to fight the opposition within and outside his party. From his point of view the prime minister was going too slowly, but, of course, from the point of view of the orthodox Hindu he was going too fast. In 1949 and 1950, when the bill was first introduced, Nehru was not even in effective control of the Congress. It was only after Vallabhbhai Patel's death that he really took charge, overcoming the conservatives in the Congress and leading his party to a convincing victory in the general election. With the party, and country, now behind him, he was prepared to introduce, and steer through, the legislation once proposed by Ambedkar.[38]

Nehru was determined to effect changes in the laws of his fellow Hindus, yet prepared to wait before dealing likewise with the Muslims. The aftermath of Partition had left the Muslims who remained in India vulnerable and confused. At this stage, to tamper with what they considered hallowed tradition – the word of Allah himself – would make them even less secure. Thus, when he was asked in Parliament why he had not brought in a uniform civil code immediately, Nehru answered that, while such a code had his 'extreme sympathy', he did not think that 'at the present moment the time is ripe in India for me to try to push it through. I want to prepare the ground for it and this kind of thing is one method of preparing the ground.'[39]

Others viewed this caution more cynically. As Dr Syama Prasad Mookerjee pointed out in the provisional Parliament, 'it is nobody's case that monogamy is good for Hindus alone or for Buddhists alone or for Sikhs alone'. Why not then have a separate bill prescribing monogamy for all citizens? Having asked the question, Dr Mookerjee supplied this answer: 'I am not going to tread on this question because I know the weaknesses of the promoters of the bill. They dare not touch the Muslim minority. There will be so much opposition coming from throughout India that government will not dare to proceed with it. But of course you can proceed with the Hindu community in any way you like and whatever the consequences may be.'

At this point C. Rajagopalachari interjected: 'Because we are the community'.[40] 'We' were the Congress, particularly its reformist wing, represented by Nehru and rather ably by Rajagopalachari as well. One can appreciate their hesitancy to take on people of faiths other than their own. For it had taken them the better part of ten years to 'proceed with the Hindu community in any way' they liked; that is in a way that would help bring their personal laws somewhat in line with modern notions of gender justice.[41]

12

SECURING KASHMIR

Do we believe in a national state which includes people of all religions and shades of opinion and is essentially secular . . ., or do we believe in the religious, theocratic conception of a state which considers people of other faiths as something beyond the pale? This is an odd question to ask, for the idea of a religious or theocratic state was given up by the world some centuries ago and has no place in the mind of the modern man. And yet the question has to be put in India today, for many of us have tried to jump back to a past age.

JAWAHARLAL NEHRU

I

THE REFORM OF PERSONAL laws was one test of Indian secularism. Another and greater test was with regard to the future of Kashmir. Could a Muslim majority state exist, without undue fuss or friction, in a Hindu-dominated but ostensibly 'secular' India?

As we have seen in Chapter 4, by 1949 Sheikh Abdullah was in firm control of the administration of Jammu and Kashmir. But the status of the territory was still under dispute. The United Nations had called for a plebiscite and was trying to get India and Pakistan to meet the conditions for holding it.

In February 1950 the UN Security Council asked both countries to withdraw their armies from the state. As before, both sides stalled. India asked for the Pakistanis to take their troops out first while Pakistan demanded that the National Conference government be removed from office. India had begun to regret taking the matter to the United Nations in the first place. By 1950 it was quite prepared to hold on to its part of the disputed state, and let Pakistan take the hindmost. The Indian Constitution, which came into effect in January 1950, treated Kashmir as part of the Indian Union. However, it guaranteed the state a certain autonomy; thus Article 370 specified that the president would consult the state government with regard to subjects other than defence, foreign affairs, and communications.[1]

As for Pakistan, politicians there held that their claim needed no certification from a popular vote. In September 1950 a former prime minister insisted that 'the liberation of Kashmir is a cardinal belief of every Pakistani . . . Pakistan would remain incomplete until the whole of Kashmir has been liberated'. Two weeks later, a serving prime minister observed that 'for Pakistan, Kashmir is a vital necessity; for India it is an imperialistic adventure'.[2]

On both sides of the border the governmental positions were echoed and amplified by the press. In the summer of 1950 the British broadcaster Lionel Fielden visited the subcontinent. As a former head of All-India Radio, Fielden had many friends in both India and Pakistan. Visiting them and speaking also to their friends, he found that on either side of the international boundary 'the visitor is assailed by arguments and harangues to prove that the other country is not only wrong but diabolically wrong, and mischievously to boot'. He observed that 'the tone of the Indian Press tends to be a little patronizing, sweetly reasonable but nevertheless obstinate, and rather consciously self-righteous'. On the other hand, 'the tone of the Pakistan Press and Pakistan leaders tends to be resentful, arrogant and sometimes aggressive'. Pakistani hostility was compounded by the fear that powerful forces in India wanted to reconquer or reabsorb their land in a united Akhand Bharat.

Fielden summarized the respective points of view: 'In clinging to Kashmir, India wants to weaken Partition; in claiming it, Pakistan wants to make Partition safe.' On the issue of Kashmir both sides were absolutely rigid. Thus, 'to fight to the last ditch for [Kashmir] is the slogan of all Pakistanis; not to give way on it is rapidly becoming the fixed idea in India.'

Fielden ended his analysis with a warning. In the long run, he pointed out, 'the most important thing' about the Kashmir conflict was 'the expense in armaments in which both countries are getting involved. This means that social services in both countries are crippled, and since both countries, apart from their refugees, have millions of the poorest people in the world, it is easy to see how this can lead to disaster.'[3]

The United Nations had tried and failed to solve the dispute. Could another 'third party' succeed? In January 1951, at a meeting at

10 Downing Street, the Australian Prime Minister Sir Robert Menzies suggested that a plebiscite be held under Commonwealth auspices. The British prime minister, Clement Attlee, appeared to favour the idea, but Nehru said any settlement must have the concurrence of the state government of Sheikh Abdullah. The Pakistani prime minister dismissed that government as 'puppets appointed by Nehru [whom] he could change any time'. In reply, Nehru noted that 'the Pakistan press was full of this religious appeal and calls for Jehad. If this was the kind of thing that was going to take place during a plebiscite, then there would be no plebiscite but civil upheaval, not only in Kashmir, but elsewhere in India and Pakistan.'[4]

II

In 1950, the maps of the government of India claimed the entire state of Jammu and Kashmir as part of its territory. New Delhi's claim to the whole rested on the fact that in October 1947 Maharaja Hari Singh had signed a document acceding to India. Meanwhile, its claim to the part actually held by it rested on the secularist sentiments of Sheikh Muhammad Abdullah, by now often referred to as simply 'the Sheikh'.

Abdullah was anti-Pakistan, but was he for India? That was a question to which the man himself would not give a straight answer. His vacillation is captured in a series of frustrated letters written by Nehru to his sister Vijayalakshmi Pandit:

10 May 1950. I am sorry to say that Sheikh Abdullah is behaving in a most irresponsible manner. The most difficult thing in life is what to do with one's friends.

18 July 1950. Meanwhile, Sheikh Abdullah has been behaving very badly in Kashmir in regard to domestic affairs and he appears to be bent on securing a conflict with us. He has gone to wrong hands there and is being misled.

10 August 1950. Sheikh Abdullah has come round a little and is in a more amenable frame of mind. I wonder how long this will last, because there are too many forces at play in Kashmir, which pull him in different directions.[5]

The note of scepticism in this last letter was warranted. For very soon Abdullah had once more begun behaving in a 'most irresponsible manner'; that is to say, had begun thinking of ways to detach Kashmir from India. On 29 September 1950 he met the American ambassador, Loy Henderson. In discussing the future of Kashmir, Abdullah told Henderson that

> in his opinion it should be independent; that overwhelming majority of the population desired their independence; that he had reason to believe that some Azad Kashmir leaders desired independence and would be willing to cooperate with leaders of National Conference if there was reasonable chance such cooperation would result in independence. Kashmir people could not understand why UN consistently ignored independence as possible solution for Kashmir. Kashmir people had language and cultural background of their own. The Hindus by custom and tradition widely different from Hindus in India, and the background of Muslims quite different from Muslims in Pakistan. Fact was that population of Kashmir homogeneous in spite of presence of Hindu minority.[6]

Abdullah went on to ask the ambassador whether the US would support an independent Kashmir. Unfortunately, the published records of the State Department do not reveal the US response. Did the United States ever seriously contemplate propping up Kashmir as a client state, given that its location could be of immense value in the struggle against communism?

We still can't say, and it seems Abdullah was equally unsure at the time, for he now went back to the Indian government to negotiate with them the terms of Kashmir's autonomy. The state, it was decided, would have its own constituent assembly, where the terms by which it would associate with India would be finalized. In January 1951 Abdullah wrote to the minister of states that, as he understood it, the Jammu and Kashmir Constituent Assembly would discuss 'the question of accession of the State, the question of retention or abolition of the Ruler as the Constitutional Head of the State and the question of framing a Constitution for the State including the question of defining the sphere of Union jurisdiction over the State'. He added that the Assembly would 'take decisions on all issues specified above', decisions the government of India must treat as 'binding on all concerned'. This suggested that even Kashmir's accession to India was not final. As an alarmed minister of states noted in the margins of the letter, the Sheikh's interpretation was 'perhaps going beyond what we said'.[7]

The Sheikh, as ever, presumed to speak for the state of Jammu and Kashmir as a whole. In truth, while he was still revered in the Valley, he was becoming quite unpopular among the Hindu of the Jammu region, who were keen to merge their part of the state with the Indian Union as quickly as possible. In 1949 a Praja Parishad (Peoples' Party) was formed to represent the interests of the Jammu Hindus. It was led by a seventy-year-old veteran, Prem Nath Dogra. Characteristically, Sheikh Abdullah dismissed the opposition in Jammu as a bunch of 'reactionaries'.[8]

In October 1951 elections were held to the Kashmir Constituent Assembly. The Praja Parishad had decided to contest but, early on, the nomination papers of several of their candidates were found to be invalid. In protest they chose to boycott the election. All seventy-five seats were won by Abdullah's National Conference. All but three of their candidates were returned unopposed.[9]

Sheikh Abdullah's opening speech in the Constituent Assembly ran for a full ninety minutes. Reading from a printed English text, the Sheikh discussed, one by one, the options before the people of Kashmir. The first was to join Pakistan, that 'landlord-ridden' and 'feudal' theocracy. The second was to join India, with whom the state had a 'kinship of ideals' and whose government had 'never tried to interfere in our internal autonomy'. Admittedly, 'certain tendencies have been asserting themselves in India which may in the future convert it into a religious State wherein the interests of the Muslims will be jeopardized'. On the other hand, 'the continued accession of Kashmir to India' would promote harmony between Hindus and Muslims, and marginalize the communalists. 'Gandhiji was not wrong', argued the Sheikh, 'when he uttered words before his death which [I] paraphrase: "I lift up mine eyes unto the hills, from whence cometh my help".'

Abdullah came, finally, to 'the alternative of making ourselves an Eastern Switzerland, of keeping aloof from both States, but having friendly relations with them'. This was an attractive option, but it did not seem practical. How would a small, landlocked country safeguard its sovereignty? As the Sheikh reminded his audience, Kashmir had once been 'independent' of both India and Pakistan; between 15 August and 22 October 1947, when its independence had been destroyed by the tribal invasion. What was the guarantee that a sovereign Kashmir 'may not be victim of a similar aggression'?[10]

Thus, the Sheikh rejected the option of independence as impractical, and the option of joining Pakistan as immoral. They would join India, but on terms of their own choosing. Among these terms were the retention of the state flag and the designation of the head of government as prime minister. Neither was acceptable to the Praja Parishad of Jammu. Asking for the complete integration of Kashmir into India, they had adopted the slogan: 'Ek Vidhan, ek Pradhan, ek Nishan' (One Constitution, One Head of State, One Flag).

In January 1952, shortly before Abdullah was due to speak in Jammu town, Hindu students protested against the National Conference flag being flown alongside the Indian tricolour. They were arrested and later expelled from their college. This sparked a wave of sympathy protests culminating in a march on the Secretariat, where demonstrators entered the offices, broke furniture and burnt records. The police cracked down hard, imposing a seventy-two-hour curfew and arresting hundreds of Parishad members. Also jailed was their aged leader, Prem Nath Dogra, although he had not participated in the protests himself.

The government in Delhi, fearful of a countrywide Hindu backlash, persuaded the Kashmir government to release the Parishad leaders. Abdullah agreed, if reluctantly. On 10 April he made a speech in which he said his party would accept the Indian Constitution 'in its entirety once we are satisfied that the grave of communalism has been finally dug'. He darkly added: 'Of that we are not sure yet.' The Sheikh said that the Kashmiris 'fear what will happen to them and their position if, for instance, something happens to Pandit Nehru'.[11]

Both the timing and venue of Abdullah's speech were significant. It was made in Ranbirsinghpura, a town only four miles from the border with Pakistan. And India had just come through a general election the result of which appeared to vindicate Jawaharlal Nehru and his policies. The speech was widely reported, and caused considerable alarm. Why was the man who had often issued chits complimenting India for its secularism suddenly turning so sceptical?

The Sheikh's change of mind coincided with a visit to Kashmir by the veteran British journalist Ian Stephens. Stephens, who had been editor of the Calcutta *Statesman* during the troubles of 1946–7, was known to be a strong supporter of Pakistan. He thought that the Kashmir Valley, with its majority Muslim population, properly belonged to that country. Still, he was sensitive to the dilemmas of its leader. He had long talks with Abdullah, whom he saw as 'a man of pluck and enlightenment, standing for principles good in their way; a victim, like so many of us, of the unique scope and speed and confusion of the changes in 1947, and now holding a perhaps uniquely lonely and perplexing post'. His was a regime upheld by 'Indian bayonets, which meant mainly Hindu bayonets'. Admittedly, 'in many ways it was a good regime: energetic, full of ideas, staunchly non-communal, very go-ahead in agrarian reform'. But, concluded Stephens, 'to the eye of history it might prove an unnatural one'.[12]

III

Once, Abdullah had been Nehru's man in Kashmir. By the summer of 1952, however, it was more that Nehru was Abdullah's man in India. The Sheikh had made it known that, in his view, only the prime minister stood between India and the ultimate victory of Hindu communalism.

Meanwhile, discussions continued about the precise status of Kashmir vis-à-vis the Indian Union. In July the Sheikh met Nehru in Delhi and also had a round of meetings with other ministers. They hammered out a compromise known as the Delhi Agreement, whereby Kashmiris would become full citizens of India in exchange for an autonomy far greater than that enjoyed by other states of the Union. Thus the new state flag (devised by the National Conference) would for 'historical and other reasons' be flown alongside the national flag. Delhi could not send in forces to quell 'internal disturbances' without the consent of Srinagar. Where with regard to other states residuary powers rested with the centre, in the case of Kashmir these would remain with the state. Crucially, those from outside the state were prohibited from buying land or property within it. This measure was aimed at forestalling attempts to change the demographic profile of the Valley through large-scale immigration.[13]

These were major concessions, but the Sheikh pressed for greater powers still. In a truculent speech in the state's Constituent Assembly he said only the state could decide what powers to give away to the Union, or what jurisdiction the Supreme Court would have in Kashmir. Then he told Yuvraj Karan Singh, the formal head of state, that if he did not fall into line he would go the way of his father, the deposed Hari Singh. The young prince, said the Sheikh, must 'break up with the reactionary elements', and instead identify with the 'happiness and sorrow of the common man'. For 'if he is under the delusion that he can retain his office with the help of his few supporters, he is mistaken'.[14]

The 'reactionary elements' referred to here were the Hindus of Jammu. They had restarted their agitation, with an amended if equally catchy slogan: 'Ek Desh mein Do Vidhan, Do Pradhan, Do Nishan – nahin chalenge, nahin chalenge' (Two Constitutions, Two Heads of State, Two Flags – these in one State we shall not allow, not allow). Processions and marches, as well as clashes with police, became frequent. Once more the jails of Jammu began to fill with the volunteers of the Praja Parishad.

The Hindus of Jammu retained a deep attachment to the ruling family, and to Maharaja Hari Singh in particular. They resented his being deposed and were displeased with his son for being 'disloyal' by agreeing to replace him. But their apprehensions were also economic – namely, that the land reforms recently undertaken in the Kashmir Valley would be reproduced in Jammu. In the Valley, zamindars had been dispossessed of land in excess of the ceiling limit. Since this was fixed at twenty-two acres per family, their losses were substantial. The land seized by the state had been vested chiefly in the hands of the middle peasantry. The agricultural proletariat had not benefited to quite the same extent. Still, the land reforms had gone further and been more successful than anywhere else in India.[15]

As it happened, the large landlords in the Valley were almost all Hindu. This gave an unfortunate religious hue to what was essentially a project of socialist redistribution. This was perhaps inevitable; despite the sincerity of the Sheikh's secularist professions, they could not nullify the legacies of history. At one time the state had been controlled by the Dogras of Jammu, who happened to be Hindu; now it was controlled by the National Conference, which was based in the Valley and whose leader and most of its members were Muslim.[16]

IV

Through the years 1950–2, as the rest of India became acquainted with its new constitution and had its first elections, Jammu and Kashmir was beset by uncertainty on two fronts. There were the unsettled relations between the state and the Union, and there was the growing conflict between the Muslim-majority Kashmir Valley and the Hindu-dominated Jammu region. Here was a situation made to order for a politician in search of a cause. And it found one in Dr Syama Prasad Mookerjee, who was to make the struggle of the Dogras of Jammu his own.

Dr Mookerjee had left Jawaharlal Nehru's Cabinet to become the founder-president of the Bharatiya Jana Sangh. His new party fared poorly at the general election of 1952 – only three of its members were elected to Parliament. The troubles in Kashmir came at an opportune time for Dr Mookerjee and the Jana Sangh. Here was a chance to lift the dispirited cadres, to forget the disappointments of the election and reinvent the party on the national stage.

Dr Mookerjee began his charge with a series of blistering attacks on the government in Parliament. 'Who made Sheikh Abdullah the King of Kings in Kashmir?' he asked sarcastically. The Sheikh had apparently said that they would treat both the provincial and national flags 'equally'; this, said the Jana Sangh leader, showed a 'divided loyalty' unacceptable in a sovereign country. Even if the Valley wanted a limited accession, Jammu and the Buddhist region of Ladakh must be allowed to integrate fully if they so chose. But a better solution still would be to make the whole state a part of India, without any special concessions. This would bring it on par with all the other princely states, which – despite earlier promises made to them as regards autonomy – had finally to agree to be subject to the provisions of the constitution *in toto*. Abdullah himself had been a member of the Indian Constituent Assembly, yet 'he is asking for special treatment. Did he not agree to accept this Constitution in relation to the rest of India, including 497 States. If it is good enough for all of them, why should it not be good enough for him in Kashmir?'[17]

In the autumn of 1952 Dr Mookerjee visited Jammu and made several speeches in support of the Praja Parishad movement. Their demands, he said, were 'just and patriotic'. He promised to 'secure' the Constitution of India for them. He then went to Srinagar, where he had a most contentious meeting with Sheikh Abdullah.[18]

The support of a national party and a national leader had given much encouragement to the Dogras. In November 1952 the state government moved to Jammu for the winter. As head of state, Karan Singh arrived first. Years later he recalled the 'derisive and hostile slogans' and black flags with which he was received by the Praja Parishad. Although 'the

National Conference had tried to lay on some kind of reception it was swamped by the deep hostility of the Dogra masses'. Writing to the government of India, he noted that 'an overwhelming majority of the Jammu province seem to me to be emphatically in sympathy with the agitation . . . I do not think it will be a correct appraisal to dismiss the whole affair as merely the creation of a reactionary clique.'[19]

Which, of course, is what Sheikh Abdullah was disposed to do. Through the winter of 1952/3 the Praja Parishad and the state government remained locked in conflict. Protesters would remove the state flag from government buildings and place Indian flags in their stead. They would be arrested, but others would soon arrive to replace them. The movement got a tremendous fillip when a Parishad member, Mela Ram, was shot by police near the Pakistan border. In Jammu, at least, Abdullah's reputation was in tatters. He had made his name representing the people against an autocratic monarch. Now he had become a repressive ruler himself.[20]

In January Dr Syama Prasad Mookerjee wrote a long letter to Jawaharlal Nehru in support of the Parishad and their 'highly patriotic and emotional' struggle to 'merge completely with India'. He added a gratuitous challenge with regard to the 'recovery' of the part of the erstwhile undivided state now in the possession of Pakistan. How was India 'going to get this [territory] back'? asked Mookerjee. 'You have always evaded this question. The time has come when we should know what exactly you propose to do about this matter. It will be nothing short of national disgrace and humiliation if we fail to regain this lost portion of our own territory.'

Nehru ignored the taunt. As for the Praja Parishad, he thought that they were 'trying to decide a very difficult and complicated constitutional question by methods of war'. Abdullah (to whom Mookerjee had written separately) was more blunt; as he saw it, 'the Praja Parishad is determined to force a solution of the entire Kashmir issue on communal lines'.

Mookerjee asked Nehru and Abdullah to release the Praja Parishad leaders and convene a conference to discuss the future of Kashmir. Mookerjee again challenged Nehru to go to war with Pakistan: 'Please do not sidetrack the issue and let the public of India know how and when, if at all, we are going to get back this portion of our cherished territory.'[21]

Eventually the exchange ran aground on a matter of pride. Nehru thought the Parishad should call off the movement as a precondition to talks with the government; Mookerjee wanted the government to offer talks as a precondition to the movement calling off the struggle. When the government refused to bend, Mookerjee decided to take the matter to the streets of Delhi. Beginning in the first week of March, Jana Sangh volunteers courted arrest in support of the demands of the Praja Parishad. The protesters would collect outside a police station and shout slogans against the government and against the prime minister, thereby violating Section 188 of the Indian Penal Code.

The *satyagraha* was co-ordinated by Dr Mookerjee from his office in Parliament House. Participating were members of what the authorities were calling the 'Hindu communal parties': the Jana Sangh, the Hindu Mahasabha and the Ram Rajya Parishad. By the end of April 1953 1,300 people had been arrested. Intelligence reports suggest that they came from all parts of India, yet were overwhelmingly upper caste: Brahmins, Thakurs, Banias.[22]

It was now summer, tourist season in the Valley. Among the first visitors to arrive, in late April, was the American politician Adlai Stevenson. He had come to Kashmir to sail on the Dal lake and see the snows, but also to meet Sheikh Abdullah. They met twice, for upwards of two hours each time. The content of these conversations were not revealed by either side, but some Indians assumed it was all about independence. A Bombay journal otherwise known to be sympathetic to the United States claimed that Stevenson had assured Abdullah of much more than moral support. A loan of $15 million would be on hand once Kashmir became independent; besides, the US would ensure that 'the Valley would have a permanent population of at least 5,000 American families, that every houseboat and hotel would be filled to capacity, that Americans would buy up all the art and craft output of the dexterous Kashmiri artisans, that within three years every village in Kashmir would be electrified and so on and so forth'.[23]

Stevenson later denied that he had encouraged Abdullah. When the Sheikh offered the 'casual suggestion that independent status might be an alternative solution', Stevenson stayed silent; he did not, he claimed, give 'even unconscious encouragement regarding independence, which did not seem to me realistic . . . I was listening, not talking'.[24]

So the Sheikh was once more contemplating independence. But independence for what? Not, most likely, the whole of the state of Jammu and Kashmir. One part (the north) was in Pakistani hands; another part (Jammu) was in the grip of a prolonged agitation. Abdullah's own papers are closed to scholars and he is silent on the subject in his memoirs, but we can plausibly speculate that it must have been the Valley, and the Valley alone, for which he was seeking independence. Here he was in control, with the population largely behind him; and it was here that the tourists would come to nurture his dreams of an 'Eastern Switzerland'.[25]

V

Not long after Stevenson, another politician came seeking to fish in troubled waters. On 8 May Dr Syama Prasad Mookerjee boarded a train to Jammu, en route to Srinagar. He had planned to take his *satyagraha* deep into enemy territory. Anticipating trouble, the state government issued orders prohibiting him from entering. Mookerjee disregarded the order and crossed the border on the morning of the 11th. The police requested him to return, and when he refused arrested him and took him to Srinagar jail.

Before the Praja Parishad movement, Dr Mookerjee had been a lifelong constitutionalist. A Bengali *bhadralok* of the old school, he was comfortable in a suit and tie, sipping a glass of whisky. During the entire nationalist movement he never resorted to *satyagraha* or spent a single night in jail. Indeed, he had long held, in the words of his biographer, that 'legislatures were the only forum for giving vent to diverse viewpoints on Government policies'. That belief sat oddly with Dr Mookerjee's support for the protests of the Praja Parishad. And now he was sanctioning and leading a street protest himself.

Why then did Dr Mookerjee resort to methods with which he was unfamiliar? He told his follower (and future biographer) Balraj Madhok that he was convinced that this was the only language the prime minister understood. 'As a man who had been [an] agitator all his life, Pandit Nehru, he felt, had developed a complex for agitational methods. He would bow before force and agitation but not before right or reason unless backed by might.'[26]

Now, in Srinagar jail, while charges were being compiled, Dr Mookerjee spent his time reading Hindu philosophy and writing to friends and relatives.[27] In early June he fell ill. Pain in one of his legs was accompanied by fever. The doctors diagnosed pleurisy. Then on 22 June he had a heart attack and died the following day.[28]

On 24 June an Indian air force plane flew Mookerjee's body back to his home town, Calcutta. Sheikh Abdullah had laid a shawl on the body, while his deputy, Bakshi Ghulam Mohammed, helped load the stretcher onto the plane. In Calcutta huge crowds lined the thirteen-mile route from Dum Dum airport to the family home in Bhowanipur. Nehru wrote to a friend in Madras that 'we are having a great deal of trouble as a result of Dr Mookerjee's death. The atmosphere in Delhi is bad. It is worse in Calcutta.'[29]

And worse still in Jammu. When the news reached the town an angry mob attacked and looted a government Arts emporium and set fire to government offices.[30] In Delhi, meanwhile, a crowd gathered at Ajmeri Gate, wearing black badges, waving black flags and shouting, 'Khoon ka Badla Khoon sé laingé' (Blood will be avenged by blood). The anger persisted for days. On 5 July a portion of Dr Mookerjee's ashes arrived in the capital; these were carried in a massive procession by the Jana Sangh through the old City, with the marchers shouting slogans of revenge and insisting that 'Kashmir hamara hai' (Kashmir shall be ours).[31]

In late June posters appeared in parts of Delhi warning Sheikh Abdullah that he would be killed if he came to the capital. These calls could not be taken lightly, for it had been in a similarly surcharged atmosphere that Mahatma Gandhi had met his end. Now, again, it appeared that 'in Delhi the entire middle class is in the hands of the [Hindu] communalists'. It was feared that not just the Sheikh, but also 'Mr Nehru may meet the fate . . . of Gandhiji due to the intense propaganda of the communalists'. The police were instructed to look out for 'any propaganda of a serious nature, or any plans or designs these groups of parties may have against the Prime Minister'.[32]

VI

The popular movement led by Dr Mookerjee planted the seed of independence in Sheikh Abdullah's mind; the outcry following his death seems only to have nurtured it. Sensing this, Nehru wrote two long emotional letters recalling their old friendship and India's ties to Kashmir. He asked Abdullah to come down to Delhi and meet him. The Sheikh did not oblige. Then Nehru sent Maulana Abul Kalam Azad (the most senior member of the Cabinet) to Srinagar, but that did not help either. The Sheikh now seemed convinced of two things: that he had the support of the United States and that 'even Nehru could not subdue [Hindu] communal forces in India'. On 10 July he addressed party workers at Mujahid Manzil, the headquarters of the National Conference in Srinagar. After outlining Kashmir's, and his own, grievances against the government of India, he said that 'a time will, therefore, come when I will bid them good-bye'.[33]

The Sheikh's turnabout greatly alarmed the prime minister. Writing to a colleague, Nehru said the developments in Kashmir were particularly unfortunate, for 'anything that happens there has larger and wider consequences'. For the 'problem of Kashmir [was] symbolic of many things, including our secular policy in India'.[34]

By now the government of Kashmir was divided within itself, its members (as Nehru observed), liable 'to pull in different directions and proclaim entirely different policies'. This was in good part the work of the government of India's Intelligence Bureau. Officers of the Bureau had been working within the National Conference, dividing the leadership and confusing the ranks. Some leaders, such as G. M. Sadiq, were left-wing anti-Americans; they disapproved of the Sheikh's talks with Stevenson. Others, like Bakshi Ghulam Mohammed, had ambitions of ruling Kashmir themselves.[35]

There was now an open rift within the National Conference between the pro-India and pro-independence groups. The latter were led by the Sheikh's close associate Mirza Afzal Beg. The former were in close touch with the sadr-i-riyasat, Karan Singh. It was rumoured that Sheikh Abdullah would declare independence on 21 August – the day of the great Id festival – following which he would seek the protection of the United Nations against 'Indian aggression'.[36] Two weeks before that date Abdullah dismissed a member of his Cabinet. This gave the others in the pro-India faction an excuse to move against him. Led by Bakshi Ghulam Mohammed, they wrote the Sheikh a letter accusing him of encouraging sectarianism and corruption. A copy of the letter was also sent to Karan Singh. He, in turn, dismissed Abdullah and invited Bakshi Ghulam Mohammed to form a government in his place.

Abdullah was served his walking papers in the early hours of the morning. When he was woken up and handed the letter of dismissal, the Sheikh flew into a rage. 'Who is the sadr-i-riyasat to dismiss me?', he shouted. 'I made that chit of a boy sadr-i-riyasat.' The police then told him that he had not just been dismissed, but also placed under arrest. He was given two hours to say his prayers and pack his belongings before being taken off to jail.

Why was Abdullah humiliated so? Did he have to be dismissed in the dead of night, and did he then have to be placed under detention? Karan Singh later recalled that this was done because 'Bakshi Ghulam Mohammed made it quite clear that he could not undertake to run the Government if the Sheikh and Beg were left free to propagate their views'. In other words, he was safe and quiet in jail, whereas as a free man, put out of office, he would quickly mobilize popular sentiment in his favour.[37]

Then, and later, it was widely believed that the arrest of Abdullah was masterminded by Rafi Ahmad Kidwai. Kidwai was a left-leaning member of the Cabinet, and a close friend of Nehru's. In Delhi it was thought that his desire to humiliate the Sheikh had its roots in the fact that Abdullah was currying favour with the Americans. In Kashmir, however, it was held that this was a plain, if misguided, act of revenge. Back in 1947 Kidwai's brother had been murdered by a Kashmiri in the hill station of Mussoorie. Deposing the Sheikh was a way of settling accounts.[38]

Did Jawaharlal Nehru himself sanction the arrest of his friend Sheikh Abdullah? Nehru's biographer thinks he did not know beforehand, whereas his chief of intelligence suggests he did. One thing is clear, however: once the deed was done he did nothing to countermand it.[39]

Like his predecessor, the new prime minister of Kashmir was a larger-than-life figure. He was known commonly as the Bakshi, much as his predecessor was known as the Sheikh. Born in 1907 in modest circumstances, Ghulam Mohammed began his political career by organizing a union of carriage drivers in Srinagar. That, and four terms in Hari Singh's jails, gave him sterling nationalist credentials. However, by temperament and orientation he was quite different from the Sheikh. One was a man of ideas and idealism, the other a man of action and organization. When the raiders attacked in October 1947, it was Abdullah who gave the rousing speeches while the Bakshi placed volunteers in position and watched out for potential fifth-columnists. After 1947, while Abdullah dealt with Nehru and Delhi, the Bakshi 'kept the structure of the State intact, at a time when the whole Government had collapsed and was non-existent'. As two Kashmiri academics wrote in 1950, 'being a strict disciplinarian himself, he can brook no indiscipline and dilly-dallying tactics. He is no lover of formal government routine and red-tapism. He believes in quick but right action.' The conclusion, in the India of the time, was inescapable: 'In fact, Bakshi is to Abdullah what Sardar [Patel] is to Nehru.'[40]

The analogy, though attractive, was inexact. For Patel did not covet his boss's job. And having got that job, the Bakshi intended to keep it. This meant, as he well understood, keeping Delhi on his side. Ten days after he had assumed power he visited Jammu, where he spoke to a large crowd, assuring them that 'the ties between Kashmir and India are irrevocable. No power on earth can separate the two.' Next, speaking in Srinagar to a meeting of National Conference workers, the Bakshi argued that 'Sheikh Abdullah played directly into the hands of foreign invaders by entertaining the idea of an independent Kashmir'. That, he said, was 'a dangerous game, pregnant with disastrous consequences for Kashmir, India, and Pakistan'. Since Kashmir lacked the resources to defend itself, independence was a 'crack-brained idea', calculated only to make the state a centre of superpower intrigue. It was an idea 'which can devastate the people'.[41]

As prime minister, Bakshi Ghulam Mohammed adopted a populist style, holding a *darbar* (court) every Friday, where he heard the grievances of the public. An early move was to raise the procurement price of paddy. Next, he made school education free, sanctioned new engineering and medical colleges and abolished customs barriers between Jammu and Kashmir and the rest of India.

In October 1954 the All-India Newspaper Editors Conference was held in Srinagar. The state government pulled out all the stops, placing the guests in the best hotels and throwing parties at which the finest Kashmiri delicacies were served. A grateful editor wrote that, although the new regime had been in place only for a year, 'it can be safely said that the Bakshi Government has in some fields, brought in more reforms than did Sheikh Abdullah's in its six years of existence'. After the public and the press it was the turn of the president. In October 1955 Dr Rajendra Prasad arrived in Srinagar amid 'carefully whipped-up mass enthusiasm' – crowds lining the road from the airport, a procession of boats on the Jhelum. The president had come to inaugurate a hydroelectric project, one of several development schemes begun under the new dispensation.[42]

All the while Sheikh Abdullah was cooling his heels in detention. He was first housed in an old palace in Udhampur, in the plains, before being shifted to a cooler bungalow in the mountains, at Kot. He was raising poultry and reported to have become 'very anti-Indian'.[43]

Within and outside Kashmir the Bakshi was viewed as something of a usurper. Relevant here are the contents of two secret police reports on Friday prayers in Delhi's Jama Masjid. On 2 October 1953 the prayers were attended by two members of Parliament from Kashmir. When they were asked by a Muslim cleric to organize a meeting on the situation in Kashmir, the MPs answered that the time was not right, for they were working behind the scenes for the release of Sheikh Abdullah. The MPs said that 'all Kashmiris would remain with India and die for it', but if the Sheikh continued to be held in jail, the state might then, in anger, 'go to Pakistan, for which the responsibility would not be theirs'.

Three months later Bakshi Ghulam Mohammed himself attended prayers in the Jama Masjid. This was a way of claiming legitimacy, for the mosque, built by Shah Jahan in the seventeenth century, was the subcontinent's grandest and most revered. The keepers of the shrine, sensible of the Bakshi's proximity to the ruler of Delhi, received him respectfully enough. But, as a police report noted, 'the Muslims who had congregated there, including some Kashmiris, were talking against Bakshi Ghulam Mohammed in whispering tones. They said that he had become the Prime Minister of Kashmir after putting his "guru" – Sheikh Abdullah – behind bars.'[44]

VII

In the 1950s, as in the 1940s, the Valley of Kashmir was troubled and unsettled. Behind the troubles of the 1940s lay the indecision of the Maharaja – who refused to accede to either Pakistan or India while there was still time – and the greed and fervour of the tribal raiders who invaded the state. Behind the troubles of the 1950s were the ambitions of Sheikh Abdullah and S. P. Mookerjee. Neither was willing to play within the rules of constitutional democracy. Both raised the political stakes and both, tragically, paid for it.

The developments in Kashmir were worrisome not just to Indians. The British general who had been in charge of the Indian army in 1947 thought that they might very well 'result in a worsening of Indo-Pak relations'. In the defence of Kashmir he had come to know both the Sheikh and the Bakshi very well. The Sheikh, though 'never a great man', was nonetheless 'sincere, in my opinion, in his love for his own country'. On the other hand, the Bakshi was 'quite insincere'; he was 'an individual without calibre'.[45]

In fact, the Bakshi did have a certain talent for organization, and for feathering his nest. He used his closeness to Delhi to get a steady flow of central funds into his state. These were used to pay for dams, roads, hospitals, tunnels and hotels. Many new buildings rose up in Srinagar, including a new Secretariat, a new sports stadium, and a new tourist complex. However, in the development projects undertaken by Bakshi's government there was always 'a percentage for family and friends'. His regime soon became known as the BBC, or the Bakshi Brothers Corporation.[46]

The developments of 1952–3 had raised sharp questions about India's moral claim to the Valley. Six years had elapsed since the invasion of 1947 – enough time for the world to forget it, and to remember only that the Valley was Muslim and so was Pakistan. Besides, the Kashmiri leader so long paraded as India's own had now been put into jail by the Indian government.

Could things have turned out otherwise? Perhaps if Sheikh Abdullah and Syama Prasad Mookerjee had acted with responsibility and restraint. And perhaps if Jawaharlal Nehru and the Indian government had listened to an obscure journalist of English extraction then editing a low-circulation liberal weekly out of Bangalore. In 1952–3, while Dr Mookerjee was demanding that Nehru should invade Pakistan and thus 'reclaim' northern Kashmir, Philip Spratt was proposing a radically different solution. India, he said, must abandon its claims to the Valley, and allow the Sheikh his dream of independence. It should withdraw its armies and write off its loans to the government of Jammu and Kashmir. 'Let Kashmir go ahead, alone and adventurously, in her explorations of a secular state', he wrote. 'We shall watch the act of faith with due sympathy but at a safe distance, our honour, our resources and our future free from the enervating entanglements which write a lie in our soul.'

Spratt's solution was tinged with morality, but more so with economy and prudence. Indian policy, he argued, was based on 'a mistaken belief in the one-nation theory and greed to own the beautiful and strategic valley of Srinagar'. The costs of this policy, present and future, were incalculable. Rather than give Kashmir special privileges and create resentment elsewhere in India, it was best to let the state go. As things stood, however, Kashmir 'was in the grip of two armies glaring at each other in a state of armed neutrality. It may suit a handful of people to see the indefinite continuance of this ghastly situation. But the Indian taxpayer is paying through the nose for the precarious privilege of claiming Kashmir as part of India on the basis of all the giving on India's side and all the taking on Kashmir's side.'[47]

That material interests should supersede ideological ones was an argument that came easily to a former Marxist (which Spratt was). It was not, however, an argument likely to win many adherents in the India of the 1950s.

13

TRIBAL TROUBLE

> [T]hese tribes . . . not only defend themselves with obstinate resolution,
> but attack their enemies with the most daring courage . . . [T]hey possess
> fortitude of mind superior to the sense of danger or the fear of death.
>
> British official commenting on the Nagas, circa 1840

I

THROUGH THE 1950s, while the government of India was seeking to maintain its hold on the Valley of Kashmir, its authority and legitimacy were also being challenged at the other end of the Himalaya. This was New Delhi's 'Naga problem', much less known than its Kashmir problem, even though it was as old – even older, in fact – and easily as intractable.

The Nagas were a congeries of tribes living in the eastern Himalaya, along the Burma border. Secure in their mountain fastness, they had been cut off from social and political developments in the rest of India. The British administered them lightly, keeping out plainsmen and not tampering with tribal laws or practices, except one – headhunting. However, American Baptists had been active since the mid-nineteenth century, successfully converting several tribes to Christianity.

At this time the Naga hills formed part of Assam, a province very diverse even by Indian standards, sharing borders with China, Burma and East Pakistan, divided into upland and lowland regions and inhabited by hundreds of different communities. In the plains lived Assamese-speaking Hindus, connected by culture and faith to the greater Indian heartland. Among the important groups of tribes were the Mizos, the Khasis, the Garos, and the Jaintias, who took (or gave) their names to the mountain ranges in which they lived. Also in the region were two princely states, Tripura and Manipur, whose populations were likewise mixed, part Hindu and part tribal.

Among the tribes of north-east India the Nagas were perhaps the most autonomous. Their territory lay on the Indo-Burmese border – indeed, there were almost as many Nagas in Burma as in India. Some Nagas had contact with Hindu villages in Assam, to whom they sold rice in exchange for salt. Yet the Nagas had been totally outside the fold of the Congress-led national movement. There had been no *satyagraha* here, no civil disobedience – in fact, not one Gandhian leader in a white cap had ever visited these hills. Some tribes had fiercely fought the British, but over time the two sides had come to view each other with mutual respect. For their part, the British affected a certain paternalism, wishing to 'protect' their wards from the corrosive corruptions of the modern world.

The Naga question really dates to 1946, the year the fate of British India was being decided in those high centres of imperial power, New Delhi and Simla. As elections were held across India, as the Cabinet Mission came and went, as the viceroy went into conclave with leaders of the Congress and the Muslim League, in their own obscure corner of the subcontinent some Nagas began to worry about their future. In January 1946 a group who were 'educated Christians and spoke expressive English' formed the Naga National Council, or NNC. This had the classic trappings of a nationalist movement in embryo: led by middle-class intellectuals, their ideas were promoted in a journal of their own, called *The Naga Nation*, 250 copies of which were mimeographed and distributed through the Naga country.[1]

The NNC stood for the unity of all Nagas, and for their 'self-determination', a term which, here as elsewhere, was open to multiple and sometimes mutually contradictory meanings. The Angami Nagas, with their honourable martial tradition and record of fighting all outsiders (the British included), thought it should mean a fully independent state: 'a government of the Nagas, for the Nagas, by the Nagas'. On the other hand, the Aos, who were more moderate, thought they could live with dignity within India, so long as their land and customs were protected and they had the autonomy to frame and enforce their own laws.

The early meetings of the NNC witnessed a vigorous debate between these two factions which spilled over into the pages of the *Naga Nation*.

A young Angami wrote that 'the Nagas are a nation because we feel ourselves to be a nation. But, if we are a Nation, why do we not elect our own sovereignty? We want to be free. We want to live our own lives . . . We do not want other people to live with us.' An Ao doctor answered that the Nagas lacked the finances, the personnel and the infrastructure to become a nation. 'At present', he wrote, 'it seems to me, the idea of independence is too far off for us Nagas. How can we run an independent Government now?'

Meanwhile the moderate wing had begun negotiations with the Congress leadership. In July 1946 the NNC general secretary, T. Sakhrie, wrote to Jawaharlal Nehru, and in reply received an assurance that the Nagas would have full autonomy, but *within* the Indian Union. They could have their own judicial system, said Nehru, to save them from being 'swamped by people from other parts of the country who might go there to exploit them to their own advantage'. Sakhrie now declared that the Nagas would continue their connection with India, 'but as a distinctive community . . . We must also develop according to our own genius and taste. We shall enjoy home rule in our country but on broader issues be connected with India.'[2]

The radicals, however, still stood out for complete independence. In this they were helped by some British officials, who were loath to have these tribes come under Hindu influence. One officer recommended that the tribal areas of the north-east be constituted as a 'Crown colony', ruled directly from London, and not linked in any way to the soon-to-be independent nation of India.[3] Others advised their wards that they should strike out for independence, as the state of India would soon break up anyway. As the Superintendent of the Lushai hills wrote in March 1947,

> My advice to the Lushais, since the very beginning of Lushai politics at the end of the War, has been until very recently not to trouble themselves yet about the problem of their future relationship to the rest of India: nobody can possibly foretell what India will be like even two years from now, or even whether there will be an India in the unitary political sense. I would not encourage my small daughter to commit herself to vows of lifelong spinsterhood; but I would regard it as an even worse crime to betroth her in infancy to a boy who was himself still undeveloped.[4]

In June 1947 a delegation of the NNC met the governor of Assam, Sir Akbar Hydari, to discuss the terms by which the Nagas could join

India. The two sides agreed that tribal land would not be alienated to outsiders, that Naga religious practices would not be affected and that the NNC would have a say in the staffing of government offices. Next, an NNC delegation went to Delhi, where they met Nehru, who once more told them that they could have autonomy but not independence. They also called on Mahatma Gandhi, in a meeting of which many versions have circulated down the years. In one version, Gandhi told the Nagas that they could declare their independence if they wished; that no one could compel them to join India; and that if New Delhi sent in the army, Gandhi himself would come to the Naga hills to resist it. He apparently said, 'I will ask them to shoot me first before one Naga is shot.'[5] The version printed in the *Collected Works of Mahatma Gandhi* is less dramatic; here, Gandhi is reported as saying, 'Personally, I believe you all belong to me, to India. But if you say you don't, no one can force you.' The Mahatma also advised his visitors that a better proof of independence was economic self-reliance; they should grow their own food and spin their own cloth. 'Learn all the handicrafts', said the Mahatma, 'that's the way to peaceful independence. If you use rifles and guns and tanks, it is a foolish thing.'[6]

The most vocal spokesmen for independence were the Angamis from Khonomah, a village which, back in 1879–80, had fought the British army to a standstill and whose residents were 'known and feared' across the Naga hills.[7] A faction styling itself the Peoples' Independence League was putting up posters calling for complete independence, in terms borrowed (with acknowledgement) from American freedom fighters: 'It is my living sentiment, and by the blessing of God it shall be my dying sentiment – Independence now and Independence forever' (John Adams); 'This nation, under God, shall have a new birth of freedom' (Abraham Lincoln); 'Give me liberty, or give me death!' (Patrick Henry).[8]

Meanwhile, the British Raj departed from New Delhi and the new Indian state began to consolidate itself. The secretary to the governor of Assam told the Nagas that they were too few to successfully rebel against a nation of 300 million. Writing in the *Naga Nation* he related the story of the dog with a bone in his mouth who looked into the water to see a dog with a bigger bone staring back at him; he chased after the mirage, dropping and losing what he had. Concluded the official: 'Why lose the bone of "autonomy" to try to get the bone of "independence" which it is not possible to get.'

The parable did not go down well with the educated Nagas. 'Bones, bones,' remarked one angry NNC member. 'Does he think that we are dogs?' However, the same warning was issued in more palatable form by Charles Pawsey, the departing deputy commissioner and an official whom the Nagas both loved and admired. Also writing in the *Naga Nation*, Pawsey underlined that autonomy within the Indian Union was the more prudent course to follow. For, 'Independence will mean: tribal warfare, no hospitals, no schools, no salt, no trade with the plains and general unhappiness.'9

II

As the Naga intelligentsia was struggling to define its 'independence', the Constituent Assembly of India was meeting in New Delhi. Among the topics for discussion was the place of tribals in a free and democratic India. On 30 July 1947 Jaipal Singh informed the Assembly of 'some very unhappy developments' which were brewing in the Naga hills. Jaipal had been receiving 'a telegram per day', the 'latest telegram becoming more confounded than the previous one. Each one seems to go one step further into the wilderness.' As he saw it, the Nagas had been 'misguided' into the belief that their status was akin to that of the princes, and that like them they could reclaim their sovereignty once the British left. When the Naga delegation had come to Delhi to meet Nehru and Gandhi, they had also met Jaipal, who apprised them of the 'blunt fact' that 'the Naga Hills have always been part of India. Therefore, there is no question of secession.'10

Jaipal Singh was, of course, a tribal himself, one of several million such whose homes lay in the hilly and forest belt that ran right across the heart of peninsular India. Known as 'adivasis' (original inhabitants), the central Indian tribals were somewhat different from those that dwelt in the north-east. Like them, they were chiefly subsistence agriculturists who depended heavily on the forests for sustenance. Like them, they had no caste system and were organized in clans; like them, they manifested far less gender inequality than in supposedly more 'advanced' parts of the country. However, unlike the Nagas and their neighbours, the tribes of central India had long-standing relations with Hindu peasant society. They exchanged goods and services, sometimes worshipped the same Gods and had historically been part of the same kingdoms.

These relations had not been uncontentious. With British rule, the areas inhabited by tribes had been opened up to commercialization and colonization. The forests they lived in suddenly acquired a market value; so did the rivers that ran through them and the minerals that lay beneath them. Some parts remained untouched, but elsewhere the tribals were deprived of access to forests, dispossessed of their lands and placed in debt to moneylenders. The 'outsider' was increasingly seen as one who was seeking to usurp the resources of the adivasis. In the Chotanagpur plateau, for example, the non-tribal was known as *diku*, a term that evoked fear as well as resentment.[11]

The Constituent Assembly recognized this vulnerability, and spent days debating what to do about it. Ultimately, it decided to designate some 400 communities as 'scheduled tribes'. These constituted about 7 per cent of the population, and had seats reserved for them in the legislature as well as in government departments. Schedule V of the constitution pertained to the tribes that lived in central India; it allowed for the creation of tribal advisory councils and for curbs on moneylending and on the sale of tribal land to outsiders. Schedule VI pertained to the tribes of the north-east; it gestured further in the direction of local autonomy, constituting district and regional councils, protecting local rights in land, forests and waterways and instructing state governments to share mining revenues with the local council, a concession not granted anywhere else in India.

Jaipal Singh thought that these provisions would have real teeth only if the tribals could come to forge a separate state within the Union. He called this putative state Jharkhand; in his vision it would incorporate his own Chotanagpur plateau, then in Bihar, along with contiguous tribal areas located in the provinces of Bengal and Orissa. The proposed state would cover an area of some 48,000 square miles and have a population of 12 million people.[12] The idea caught the imagination of the youth of Chotanagpur. Thus, in May 1947, the Adivasi Sabha of Jamshedpur wrote to Nehru, Gandhi and the Constituent Assembly urging the creation of a Jharkhand state out of Bihar. 'We want Jharkhand Province to preserve and develop Adivasi Culture and Language', said their memorandum, 'to make our customary law supreme, to make our lands inalienable, and above all to save ourselves from continuous exploitation.'[13]

In February 1948 Jaipal Singh delivered the presidential address to the All-India Adivasi Mahasabha, an organization that he had led since its inception a decade previously. He spoke here of how, after Independence,

'Bihari imperialism' had replaced 'British imperialism' as the greatest problem for the adivasi. He identified the land question as the most crucial, and urged the speedy creation of a Jharkhand state. Notably, he simultaneously underlined his commitment to the Indian Union by speaking with feeling about the 'tragic assassination of Gandhiji', and by raising a slogan that combined local pride with a wider Indian patriotism: 'Jai Jharkhand! Jai Adivasi! Jai Hind!'[14]

The Adivasi Mahasabha was now renamed the Jharkhand Party, and after several years of steady campaigning fought under that name in the first general election of 1952. With its symbol of a fighting cock, the party met with success beyond its own imaginings, winning three seats to Parliament and thirty-three to the state's Assembly. These victories all came in the tribal regions of Bihar, where it comprehensively trounced the ruling Congress Party. At the polls at any rate, the case for Jharkhand had been proved.

III

Jaipal Singh and his Jharkhand Party offered one prospective path for the tribals: autonomy within the Indian Union, safeguarded by laws protecting their land and customs and by the creation of a province in regions where the tribals were in a majority. The Naga radicals offered another: an independent, sovereign state carved out of India and quite distinct from it. Among the Nagas this view was upheld most insistently by the Angamis and, among them, by a certain resident of Khonomah village, yet another of those remarkable makers of Indian history who is still to find his biographer.

The man in question was Angami Zapu Phizo, with whose name the Naga cause was to be identified for close to half a century. Born in 1913, Phizo was fair and slightly built, his face horribly twisted following a childhood paralytic attack. Educated by the Baptists, and a poet of sorts – among his compositions was a 'Naga National Anthem' – he sold insurance for a living before migrating to Burma. He was working on the docks in Rangoon when the Japanese invaded. Phizo joined the Japanese on their march to India, apparently in return for the promise of Naga independence should they succeed in winning their war against the British.[15]

After the end of the war, Phizo returned to India and joined the Naga National Council. He quickly made his mark with his impassioned appeals for sovereignty, these often couched in a Christian idiom. He was part of the NNC delegation that met Mahatma Gandhi in New Delhi in July 1947. Three years later he was elected president of the NNC and committed the Nagas to 'full Independence'. He quelled the doubters and nay-sayers, who wanted an accommodation with India. Many young Nagas were willing to go all the way with Phizo. Travelling in the area in December 1950, the Quaker Horace Alexander met two NNC members whose 'minds are obsessed with the word "independence", and I do not believe that any amount of argument or appeals to the [Indian] constitution, still less any threat, will shake them out of it'.[16]

Phizo was a man of great energy and motivational powers. Through 1951 he and his men toured the Naga hills obtaining thumbprints and signatures to a document affirming their support for an independent Naga state. Later it was claimed that the bundle of impressions weighed eighty pounds, and that it was a comprehensive plebiscite which revealed that '99.99 per cent had voted in favour of the Naga independence'.[17] These figures call to mind similar exercises in totalitarian states, where, for example, 99.99 per cent of the Russian people are said to have endorsed Stalin as Supreme Leader. Still, there is no doubt that Phizo himself wanted independence, and so did numerous of his followers.

By now India itself had been independent for four years. The British officers had been replaced by Indian ones, but otherwise the new state had not had much impact on the Naga hills. Busy with healing the wounds of Partition, settling refugees, integrating princely states and drafting a constitution, the political elite in New Delhi had not given these tribes much thought. However, in the last week of 1951 the prime minister was in the Assam town of Tezpur, campaigning for his party in the general election. Phizo came down with three compatriots to meet him. When the NNC president said the Nagas wanted independence, Nehru called it an 'absurd' demand which attempted 'to reverse the wheels of history'. He told them that 'the Nagas were as free as any Indian', and under the constitution they had 'a very large degree of autonomy in managing their own affairs'. He invited Phizo and his men to 'submit proposals for the extension of cultural, administrative and financial autonomy in their land'. Their suggestions would be considered sympathetically, and if necessary the constitution could also be changed. But independence for the Nagas was out of the question.[18]

The NNC's response was to boycott the general election. After the elected Congress government was in place, Phizo sought another meeting with the prime minister in New Delhi. In the second week of February 1952 he and two other NNC leaders met Nehru in Delhi. The prime minister once more told them that, while independence was not an option, the Nagas could be granted greater autonomy. But Phizo remained adamant. At a press conference he said, 'we will continue our struggle for independence, and one day we shall meet [Nehru] again for a friendly settlement' (as representatives of a separate nation). The free state he had in mind would bring together 200,000 Nagas in India, another 200,000 in what he called 'no-man's land', and 400,000 who were presently citizens of Burma.[19]

Afterwards the Jharkhand leader Jaipal Singh hosted a lunch for Phizo and his group. A journalist present found the NNC president to be a 'short, slim man with [a] Mongolian look, with spectacles that hide the fires of dedicated eyes'. He also heard Jaipal say that, while he sympathized with the Naga cause, he 'abhorred any further fragmentation of India in the form of a new Pakistan'. He advised Phizo not to ask for a separate sovereign state, but to fight for a tribal province in the north-east, a counterpart to the Jharkhand he himself was struggling for. His guest answered that 'Nagas are Mongoloid and thus they have no racial affinity with the people of India'. Phizo said he hoped to unite the Nagas on this side with the Nagas on the Burmese side to form a country of their own. But, as the journalist on the spot observed, 'according to the official view in Delhi, such a State cannot be viable, and as those haunting hills form a strategic frontier between nations, it would be dangerous to let the Nagas loose'.[20]

IV

In October 1952 the prime minister spent a week touring the North East Frontier Agency (NEFA). He already had some acquaintance with the tribes of the peninsula, whose artistic traditions and zest for life he greatly admired. That past June, addressing a conference of social workers in New Delhi, Nehru had condemned those who wished to make tribals 'second-rate copies of themselves'. He thought the civilized world had much to learn from the adivasis, who were 'an extremely disciplined people, often a great deal more democratic than most others in India. Above all they are a people who sing and dance and try to enjoy life, not people who sit in stock exchanges, shout at one another and think themselves civilized.'[21]

Nehru's first extended exposure to the north-east renewed this appreciation of the tribals. As he wrote to a friend in government, his visit had been 'most exhilarating'. He wished these areas 'were much better known by our people elsewhere in India. We could profit much by that contact.' Nehru found himself 'astonished at the artistry of these so-called tribal people', by their 'most lovely handloom weaving'. However, there was the danger that this industry would come into competition with uglier but cheaper goods made by factories in the plains. Nehru came back with 'a most powerful impression that we should do everything to help these tribal folk in this matter'.[22]

The prime minister wrote a long report on his trip, which he sent to all chief ministers. There was, he noted here, a movement for 'merging . . . the tribal people into the Assamese'. Nehru thought that the effort rather should be 'on retaining their individual culture', on making the tribals feel 'that they have perfect freedom to live their own lives and to develop according to their wishes and genius. India to them should signify not only a protecting force but a liberating one.'

The NEFA adjoined the Naga district and indeed had many Nagas within it. While dismissing the demand for an independent Naga nation as 'rather absurd', Nehru 'had the feeling that the situation in the Naga Hills would have been much better if it had been handled a little more competently by the local officers and if some officers who were notoriously unpopular had not been kept there. Also, any attempt to impose new ways and customs on the Nagas merely irritates and creates trouble.'[23]

Even as Nehru was urging the officials to behave more sympathetically towards the Nagas, the NNC was issuing him with an ultimatum. This was carried in a letter dispatched to New Delhi on 24 October, while the prime minister was still in NEFA. In it, Phizo and his men insisted that 'there is not a single thing that the Indians and the Nagas share in common . . . The moment we see Indians, a gloomy feeling of darkness creeps into our mind.'[24]

Six months later Nehru visited the Naga capital, Kohima, in the company of the Burmese prime minister U Nu. When a Naga delegation wished to meet Nehru to present a memorandum, local officials refused to allow them an audience. Word spread of the rebuff, so that when the prime minister and his Burmese guest turned up to address a public meeting in their honour they saw their audience walking out as they arrived. In one account the Nagas bared their bottoms as they went. In another, Nehru's daughter, Indira Gandhi, said into a live microphone: *'Papa, wo jaa rahe hain'* (Father, these people are all leaving), to which he answered, wearily, *'Haan beti, main dekh raha hoon'* (Yes, child, I can see them go).[25]

The Kohima walkout, it was said later, hardened Nehru against the Nagas. In truth, Phizo and the NNC had set their minds on independence anyway. They were already collecting arms and organizing groups of 'home guards' in the villages. The state, for its part, was moving platoons of the paramilitary Assam Rifles into the district.

By the summer of 1953 the top NNC leadership had gone underground. Searching for them, the police raided Angami strongholds, further alienating the villagers. Apart from local knowledge and local support, the rebels had one great advantage – the terrain. It was indescribably beautiful: 'The scenery was the loveliest I have seen,' remarked one British visitor. 'Range upon range of forested hills which change their grouping continually as we climb and climb. The tops rise out of the mist like islands in a white sea.'[26] It was also perfectly suited for guerrilla warfare: as a veteran of the Japanese campaign observed, this was 'a country where a platoon well dug in can hold up a division, and a company can hold up an Army Corps'.[27]

This was a war conducted completely out of the vision of the wider world. No outsiders were allowed into the district, and journalists least of all. Reconstructing its history is a difficult task, relying as it must mostly on narratives gathered later by reporters and scholars. From these it appears that in 1954 things took a turn decidedly for the worse. In the spring of that year an army officer riding a motorcycle in Kohimah accidentally knocked down a passer-by. A crowd collected in protest, whereupon the police fired in panic, killing a respected judge and NNC member.

This incident created great resentment among the Nagas; it 'increased the depth of their hatred of the "unwanted Indians" and precipitated the revolt'. The extremists gained control of the NNC; petitions and demonstrations were abandoned, and preparations made for an armed uprising. The rebels began transporting weapons to a safe haven in the

Tuensang area. In June 1954 the Assam Rifles attacked a village believed to be sympathetic to the guerrillas. In September some rebels declared the formation of a 'federal government of Nagaland'.

By now killings and counter-killings were occurring with fair regularity. There were villages loyal to the government which were targeted by the rebels; villages sympathetic to the freedom struggle which were attacked by the authorities. A division of the Indian army was called in to quell the revolt, reinforcing the thirty-five battalions of the Assam Rifles already in action. In March 1955 a bitter battle broke out in Tuensang; when the firing ended and the smoke cleared, sixty houses and several granaries were found to have been burnt down.[28]

Despite the civil war, some channels of communication were still open. In September 1955 Phizo himself went with two colleagues to meet the Assam chief minister. No details of the meeting are available and after it was over the Naga leader returned to the jungle. However, one of his key aides, T. Sakhrie, had come round to the view that the Nagas could not ever hope to defeat the Indian army. Having made their point, the NNC guerrillas should lay down their weapons and their leaders seek an honourable settlement with the government in New Delhi.

Phizo, on the other hand, had pledged himself to a 'war that would not admit of truces, retreats or compromises'. The suggestion that he negotiate offended him greatly; not least because Sakhrie was, like him, an Angami from Khonomah, indeed from the same *khel* or clan of Merhuma. 'Phizo was absolutely furious with Sakhrie's softening posture', which came when many young men were flocking to the rebel cause, with the guerrilla army at an all-time high of 15,000 members. But Sakhrie was convinced that they still stood no chance against the mighty Indian nation. He began touring the villages, preaching against Phizo's extremism and warning that violence would only beget more violence.[29]

In January 1956 T. Sakhrie was dragged out of bed, taken to the jungle, tortured, then killed. It was widely believed that Phizo had ordered the murder, although he denied it. In any event, the message had gone home – this is how betrayers to the cause would be treated. In March a fresh announcement of a federal government of Nagaland was made. A national flag was designed and commanders appointed for the different regions of the designated homeland. Then, in July, occurred a killing that hurt India's image as much as Sakhrie's murder had hurt the NNC. A group of soldiers, having just beaten off a rebel ambush, were returning to Kohima. The town was under curfew; no one was supposed to be out on the streets. Catching sight of a solitary old man, the soldiers ordered him off the road. When the man protested the *jawans* beat him with rifle-butts and finally pushed him off a cliff.

The walker that the soldiers had so callously killed was a doctor named T. Haralu. He was, in fact, the first allopathic practitioner in the Naga hills and, as such, known and revered in and around Kohima. His killing dissipated any propaganda advantage the Indians might have received from Sakhrie's murder. For if that death had 'intensified defections from [the NNC] to New Delhi, exactly the reverse happened by the killing of Dr Haralu'.[30]

Meanwhile, the army presence had increased considerably. The newly named Naga Hills Force consisted of one regiment of mountain artillery, seventeen battalions of infantry and fifty platoons of Assam Rifles. The rebels also had their own military structure – headed by a commander-in-chief (a brilliant strategist named Kaito) with four commanders under him, their troops grouped into battalions and companies. The Nagas were equipped with British and Japanese rifles, and with Sten guns and machine guns, all part of the massive debris left behind after the Second World War. The rebels also used locally made muzzle-loaders and, in hand-to-hand combat, the traditional Naga sword or *dao*.

To add to the regular Naga forces there were highly effective bands of irregulars, divided into 'volunteer parties', 'courier parties' and 'women's volunteer organizations'. The last-named were nurses who could, when called upon, fight very well indeed. And there was also the silent support of the ordinary villager. As part of their counter-insurgency operations, the Indian army brought isolated hamlets together in 'grouped villages'; the residents had to sleep here at night, going out in the morning to work in the fields. Intended to break the chain of information from peasant to rebel, this tactic merely increased the army's unpopularity among the Nagas.[31]

By the middle of 1956 a full-scale war was on in the Naga hills. In a statement to Parliament in the last week of July, the home minister, Govind Ballabh Pant, admitted that the Indian army had lost 68 men while killing 370 'hostiles'. Pant accused Phizo of murdering Sakhrie – whom he called the 'leader of the sensible and patriotic group' – and of 'leading them [the Nagas] to disaster'. The talk of Naga independence he dismissed as 'mere moonshine'. Pant expressed the hope 'that good sense will prevail on the Nagas and they will realize that we all belong to India'.[32]

The Indian (and international) press was not covering the conflict, but we can get a sense of its scale from letters written by a Naga doctor to the last British deputy commissioner of the Naga hills, Charles Pawsey. A letter of June 1956 describes a tour in the interior where 'every night we looked up and saw villages burning in the hills – set alight by either the rebels or the army, no one knows.' As for the rebel leader,

> Phizo is being absolutely horrible to any Naga Government servant he catches, and even more so to any Naga who was on his council and has left him, as many have, because of his extreme methods . . . Many dobashis [headmen] have vanished and no one knows whether they are in hiding or Phizo's got them. Of course, their position is very difficult, for if they go about Government business Phizo gets them, and if they don't, the Government gets them.

Two months later, the Naga doctor wrote to Pawsey that

> As I see it, .5 per cent of the Nagas are with Phizo; 1 per cent are more moderate, and want to break away from Assam and come under Delhi, and 98.5 per cent just want to be left alone . . . Of course the way the army has behaved and is behaving means that now voluntary co-operation between the Nagas and any Government is beyond hope.

The methods of the army, he added, were such that they 'will affect Naga/Indian relations for the next 50–100 years'.[33]

In August 1956 there was an extended debate in the Lok Sabha on the situation in the Naga hills. A Meitei member from Manipur recounted how, on a recent visit to the region, the convoy of vehicles he was travelling in was attacked by the rebels. Based on his enquiries, it appeared that 'it is very difficult to bring them round to our way of thinking and ways of life; more especially, Phizo is a hard nut to crack'. He agreed that the Nagas could not 'have separate independence', yet thought that they should immediately be granted a separate state within the Indian Union.

The next speaker was the Socialist MP Rishang Keishing, who mounted a fierce attack on the army for burning villages and killing

innocent people (Keishing was himself a Tangkhul Naga from Manipur).
'The army men have shown an utter disregard for the sentiments of the
local Nagas, for, they have tried to terrify them by carrying the naked
corpses of the Nagas killed by them.' When Phizo had met Nehru in
1951 and 1952, said Keishing, 'the parties did not try to understand
each other's mind and the atmosphere was soon vitiated and tempers
lost'. He wished 'that the prime minister had displayed here the same
amount of patience and psychological insight for which he is famous in
the field of international diplomacy'. In the years since, brutal methods
had been used by both sides. 'Who can boast of an untarnished record?'
asked Keishing. 'Who can dare fling the first stone and assert that
they are not sinners? I ask this of the hostile Nagas as well as of the
government.' He recommended 'an immediate declaration of general
amnesty', the sending of an all-party delegation of parliamentarians
to the disturbed region and a meeting between the government and
the Naga National Council. He also appealed to Phizo's men to agree
to a truce, 'because the continuation of hostilities means the ruins of
innocent citizens'.

The prime minister, in reply, admitted that there had been some
killings – including that of Dr Haralu, 'which has distressed us
exceedingly' – but claimed 'that by far the greater part of the burning is
done by the Naga hostiles'. He argued that the government was seeking
the co-operation of the Nagas and that, as he had several times told
Phizo, New Delhi was always willing to consider suggestions to improve
the working of the Sixth Schedule, which allowed tribal areas great
autonomy in the management of their land and resources. He did not,
however, think the time ripe for sending a delegation of parliamentarians
to the Naga hills. And he insisted that 'it is no good talking to me about
independence [for the Nagas] . . . I consider it fantastic for that little
corner between China and Burma and India – a part of it is in Burma – to
be called an independent state'.[34]

In December 1956 a publication issued by the Indian High Commission
in London reported the 'success' of army operations in the Naga hills.
It claimed that the military had broken the back of the rebel resistance
and was now 'engaged in mopping-up operations'. The news appears to
have been swallowed whole, for weeks later the *Manchester Guardian* ran
an item with the headline: 'Naga Rebellion Virtually Over'. The Indian
government, it said, was taking steps 'to arrive at some understanding
with the Naga moderates, whose ranks are swelling steadily'. There

was, however, no evidence of any independent confirmation of this new dawn said to be emerging.[35]

V

Through the 1950s the Jharkhand movement carried on its campaign for a province within India run for and by adivasis. When the States Reorganization Commission visited the area in January 1955, they were met everywhere by processionists shouting '*Jharkhand alag prant!*' (Jharkhand must be a separate state). As one participant in the protests recalled, the 'Jharkhand demand was writ large on every Adivasi face'.[36]

Across the country, in Manipur, a struggle was afoot to have that former chiefdom declared a full-fledged state of the Indian Union. Back in 1949 a popular movement had forced the Maharaja to convene an assembly elected on the basis of universal adult franchise. But the assembly was dissolved when Manipur merged with India. The territory was now designated a 'Part C' state, which meant that it had no popularly elected body and was ruled by a chief commissioner responsible directly to Delhi.

Manipur covered an area of 8,600 square miles. There was a mere 700 square miles of valley, inhabited by 380,000 Meiteis owing allegiance to the Vaishnava traditions of Hinduism. The larger, hilly section was home to 180,000 Naga and Kuki tribals. It was one such tribal, the aforementioned Rishang Keishing, who in 1954 began a movement for representative government in Manipur. Keishing and his fellow socialists daily picketed the office of the chief commissioner in Imphal. Thousands of *satyagrahis* courted arrest, many of them women. But the government would not yield. Speaking in Parliament, the home minister said that the time was not ripe for the creation of legislative assemblies in Part C states such as Manipur and Tripura. 'These states', he said, 'are strategically situated on the borders of India. The people are still comparatively politically backward and the administrative machinery in these States is still weak.'[37]

One does not know whether the Naga National Council took cognizance of the struggles for Jharkhand and Manipur, and of New Delhi's reluctance to give in to them. In any case, Phizo and his men were holding out for something much more ambitious – not just a province within India, but a nation outside it. The demand might have been 'absurd', yet it inspired numerous Nagas to abandon their villages and join the guerrillas.

At this time, the mid-1950s, there were roughly 200,000 Nagas in the district that bore their name. There were a like number in the adjoining districts of NEFA, with another 80,000 in Manipur. Half a million Nagas in all, with perhaps just 10,000 of them participating full time in the struggle. However, weakness in numbers was amply compensated by strength of will. A small community of rebels had forced the Indian state to send in large contingents of military to suppress it.

Few Indians outside the north-east knew of the Naga conflict at the time, and virtually no foreigners. Yet the conflict had serious implications for the unity of the nation, for the survival of its democracy and for the legitimacy of its government. For nowhere else in the country, not even in Kashmir, had the army been sent in to quell a rebellion launched by those who were formally citizens of the Indian state.

In its first decade, this state had faced problems aplenty – among them oppositional movements based on class, religion, language and region. These had been handled by reason and dialogue or, in very rare instances, by the use of regular police. The conflict in the Naga hills, on the other hand, would not admit of such resolution. There was a fundamental incommensurability between what the NNC was demanding and what the government of India was willing to give them. This was an argument which, it seemed, could be ended only by one party prevailing, militarily, over the other.

Jawaharlal Nehru keenly understood the uniqueness of the Naga situation. Writing to his Cabinet colleagues in March 1955, he alerted them to 'the rather difficult problem in our tribal areas of the North East . . . [where] we have not succeeded in winning the people of these areas. In fact, they have been drifting away. In the Naga Hills district, they have non-cooperated for the last three and a half years and done so with great discipline and success.'[38]

A year later, Nehru wrote to the chief minister of Assam that while the army would be deployed so long as the rebels had arms and were willing to use them, 'there is something much more to it than merely the military approach'. While 'there can be no doubt that an armed revolt has to be met by force', said Nehru, 'our whole past and present outlook is based on force by itself being no remedy. We have repeated this in regard to the greater problems of the world. Much more must we remember this when dealing with our own countrymen who have to be won over and not merely suppressed.'[39]

Hidden away from the eyes of the world, unknown even to most Indians, the Naga rebellion was withal a serious headache for the government of India. Otherwise, Nehru's regime seemed secure and stable. It had been democratically elected, with a comfortable majority, while behind its foreign and domestic policies rested a wide national consensus. Soon, however, other challenges were to arise, these not in the peripheries, but in regions considered to be solidly part of India.

Dividing up British India: Lord Mountbatten *(centre)*, Jawaharlal Nehru *(far left)*, and Mohammad Ali Jinnah *(right)*, discussing the terms of independence and partition, New Delhi, May 1947. *(The Hindu)*

Jawaharlal Nehru in conversation with Lord and Lady Mountbatten, New Delhi, circa November–December 1947. *(Nehru Memorial Museum and Library)*

A group of unknown Indians marching to join Gandhi's funeral procession,
New Delhi, 31 January 1948. *(Henri Cartier-Bresson/Magnum)*

Vallabhbhai Patel (1875–1950), the "Iron Man of India," the integrator of
the princely states, and a key player in the framing of the Indian Constitution.
(Nehru Memorial Museum and Library)

The lawyer-economist B. R. Ambedkar (1892–1956), inspirational leader of the low castes and the chairman of the Drafting Committee of the Indian Constitution. *(The Hindu)*

FACING PAGE, TOP: A tent city of partition refugees from East Punjab, Kingsway Camp, Delhi, circa 1948. *(Press Information Bureau)*

FACING PAGE, BOTTOM: A street protest by Bengali refugees in Calcutta, circa 1950. *(Ananda Bazar Patrika)*

Potti Sriramulu (1901–1952), whose death by fasting led to the creation of the state of Andhra Pradesh and, ultimately, to the redrawing of the map of India on linguistic lines. *(The Hindu)*

Master Tara Singh (1885–1967), preacher, agitator, institution builder, and institution breaker, whose long struggle for a Sikh province came to fruition only after his death, photographed in Simla, circa 1946. *(The Hindu)*

The controversy over the reform of Hindu personal laws, circa 1949–1950, as captured by the doyen of Indian cartoonists, R. K. Laxman. *(R. K. Laxman)*

M. S. Golwalkar (1906–1973), chief organizer of the Rashtriya Swayamsevak Sangh, mentor and teacher to generations of extremists who have carried forward his struggle for a Hindu nation. *(Ananda Bazar Patrika)*

Jawaharlal Nehru and the Kashmiri leader Sheikh Mohammed Abdullah in days when they were still friends, in Srinagar, circa 1949. *(Nehru Memorial Museum and Library)*

Jawaharlal Nehru addressing a public meeting in Srinagar, 1952. Sheikh Abdullah, who is seated immediately to the right, was to be jailed by Nehru's government a year later. *(Press Information Bureau)*

A group of mostly Muslim women queueing up to vote in the first general elections in the old city of Delhi, February 1952. *(Press Information Bureau)*

FACING PAGE: An election poster issued by the Congress Party in 1952, featuring its president and chief campaigner, Jawaharlal Nehru. The poster was issued in several sizes, colours, and languages—altogether 750,000 copies were printed and distributed. *(Author's collection)*

for a
stable
secular
progressive
state

VOTE
CONGRESS

This Poster (No. 1) issued by the Central Publicity Board became the most popular election poster throughout India and was eagerly sought after by millions. Printed in three colours in sizes 30″×40″, 20″×30″ and 15″×20″, about 7½ lakhs copies were consumed.

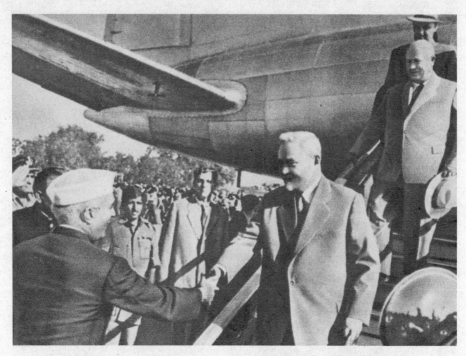

One side of non-alignment: Jawaharlal Nehru greeting the Soviet leaders
Nikolai Bulganin and Nikita Khrushchev at Delhi airport, 1955. *(Author's collection)*

Hindi-Chini bhai bhai: Nehru and Chinese Premier Chou En-lai in days
when they were still friends if not brothers, New Delhi, 1956.
(Nehru Memorial Museum and Library)

Jawaharlal Nehru with the scholar-statesman Chakravarti Rajagopalachari, New Delhi, circa 1959. Once a stalwart Congressman, "Rajaji" at age eighty founded and led the Swatantra party to oppose the policies of Nehru and the Congress. *(Author's collection)*

Nehru with the legendary beauty Maharani Gayatri Devi of Jaipur, New Delhi, circa 1955. Gayatri Devi was later to join Rajaji's Swatantra party and, still later, to be jailed by Indira Gandhi. *(Nehru Memorial Museum and Library)*

FACING PAGE, TOP: The tiny Lal Bahadur Shastri, admiring a bust of the giant of a man whom he succeeded as prime minister. In a brief tenure, Shastri more than held his own. *(Press Information Bureau)*

FACING PAGE. BOTTOM: Lal Bahadur Shastri with the Tibetan leader, the Dalai Lama, who sought and was granted refuge by India, New Delhi, 1965. *(Press Information Bureau)*

V. K. Krishna Menon (1897–1974), Nehru's confidant and a controversial defence minister in the years leading up to the war with China in 1962. *(Nehru Memorial Museum and Library)*

Menon's bête noire J. B. Kripalani, veteran of many battles with the British Raj and with successive governments of free India. *(Nehru Memorial Museum and Library)*

Angami Zapu Phizo, the unforgiving, unyielding leader of the Naga movement for freedom from Indian rule. *(Ananda Bazar Patrika)*

Martyrs memorial in Phizo's home village, Khonoma. *(Ananda Bazar Patrika)*

THESE MEN AND WOMEN OF KHONOMA GAVE THEIR LIVES FOR THE VISION OF A FREE NAGA NATION WE REMEMBER AND SALUTE THEM AND STILL HOLD FAST TO THEIR VISION

1956 – 1992

1. PELESATO CHASE
2. PERHIZO "
3. NIVISIE "
4. NIJULHU "
5. DOLHUCHA "
6. ARUNO "
7. VILAU DOLIE
8. NITO "
9. VISOLENO "
10. KIYAWHESIE "
11. MEGOVOR MERU
12. MHIASILIE "
13. KHRIETO SAVINO
14. RUDO-U "
15. LAVITO TERHUJA
16. KRUHELIE "
17. AHUNO "
18. NILELIE KHATE
19. KONIU "
20. VIVOLHUTO THO-U
21. MIAVIU KENIAU
22. DIALHUU "
23. KHRIEVOTSO "

24. LOKHRIETO IRALU
25. JUNO PFULISE
26. JALHULIE KOTSO
27. ULAU "
28. NILHUTUU "
29. THINOKHRIELIE "
30. THAVI CHASIE
31. NGUNYUNO PUNYU
32. CHABIZO SEYIE
33. RUYAHULIE "
34. MENEHENO "
35. HIEPIA VUPRU
36. NURHIU "
37. TISO-U JHUNYU
38. ZAPUNILIE SECHU
39. UVITO RATSA
40. DIEZELHUBIU MOR
41. THEKRUKIETO VIYIE
42. ZAKIESOLIE VAKHA
43. ROKOLALIE "
44. THIYIECHA "
45. RIATO "
46. NIPIELIE CHUCHA

PART THREE

SHAKING THE CENTRE

THE SOUTHERN CHALLENGE

Jawaharlal derives strength from the people. He likes vast crowds. Personal popularity leads him to believe that the people are satisfied with his administration: this conclusion, however, is not always justified.
NARENDRA DEVA, socialist, 1949

As the years rolled by, the very foundations on which Nehru's prestige and reputation rested began to weigh him down. At one time, he had a solution to every difficulty; today, he faces a difficulty in every solution.
R. K. LAXMAN, cartoonist, 1959

I

THE YEARS 1757 AND 1857 ARE much memorialized in Indian history. In the first, the East India Company defeated the ruler of Bengal in the battle of Plassey, thus gaining the British their first bridgehead on the subcontinent. In the second, the British faced, and eventually overcame, the massive popular uprising known to some as the 'Sepoy Mutiny' and to others as the 'First War of Indian Independence'.

Like 1757 and 1857, 1957 was also a year of momentous importance in the history of modern India. For it was in that year that India held its second general election. After the end of the Second World War, dozens of African and Asian nations won freedom from their European colonizers. From their inception, or very soon afterwards, most of these new nations became autocracies ruled by communists, the military or unaffiliated dictators. India was one of the very few exceptions and, because of its size and social complexity, the really remarkable one. Before and after the great gamble of 1952 a series of provincial elections were held, in which the verdict of the ballot was honoured. Still, for India to certifiably join the league of democracies there had to be a second general election to follow the first. This was held over a period of three weeks in the spring of 1957.

Sukumar Sen still served as chief election commissioner. Though fortuitous, the continuity was important, because the man who had designed the systems could test afresh how well they worked. The evidence suggests that they did so quite well: this general election cost the exchequer Rs45 million less than the previous one. The prudent Sen had safely stored the 3.5 million ballot boxes used the first time round and only half a million additional ones were required.

Before the election, the Ministry of Information and Broadcasting distributed a film called *It Is Your Vote*. Dubbed in thirteen languages, the film – which took 'scrupulous care . . . to avoid any matter which might be construed as propaganda in favour of any political party' – was screened in 74,000 cinema halls around the country. Among the viewers were many women who, the chief election commissioner noted, 'have come to value their franchise greatly'. Ninety-four per cent of adult women were now registered voters.

In all, 193 million Indians were registered to vote; of which slightly less than half actually did. The ballots they marked collectively consumed 197 tonnes of paper. Keeping them in line were 273,762 policemen, aided by 168,281 village *chowkidars* (watchmen).

The Election Commission had recommended that liquor stalls be kept shut on the days of polling, so that 'no alcoholic beverages might be available to the rowdy elements in the locality'. But there was plenty of colour nonetheless. A candidate in New Delhi insisted on filing his nomination in the name of 'Lord Jesus Christ'; a voter in Madras refused to exercise his franchise in favour of any person other than 'Shri Sukumar Sen, Election Commissioner'. In Orissa a dwarf, only two and a half feet tall, carried a stool with him to the polling booth. Everywhere ballot boxes were found to contain much else besides ballot papers: abusive notes addressed to candidates in one place, photographs of film actors in another. Some boxes were even found to have cash and change, which 'of course, [was] credited to the Treasury'.[1]

II

As in 1952, the 1957 election was in essence a referendum on the prime minister and his ruling party. Nehru was, again, the chief ideologue,

propagandist and vote-catcher for the Congress. Helping him behind
the scenes was his only child, Indira Gandhi. Estranged from her
husband Feroze, she and her two sons stayed with her widowed father
in his spacious official residence, Teen Murti House.[2] Mrs Gandhi
was often the last person the prime minister saw in the evening and
the first he saw in the morning. Serving as his official hostess, she met
and mixed with the high of this land and of many others. Her health,
previously frail, had noticeably improved. Contemporary photographs
show her once sickly frame to have filled out; the improvement
obvious not just in her appearance, but in her manner as well. A recent
biographer has linked this improvement to the new antibiotic drugs
then entering the market, which cured the tuberculosis she was thought
to suffer from.[3]

What we know of Mrs Gandhi's medical condition is based on
intelligent speculation. However, there is also hard evidence that
between the first and second elections she became more of a personality
in her own right. In March 1955 she was appointed to the Congress
Working Committee to 'represent the interests of women'. Following
this appointment she began touring the country speaking to women
about their rights and responsibilities. Her interests were not restricted
to her own gender; she presided over meetings held in Bombay to hasten
the liberation of Goa from Portuguese rule.

To those who knew her in her pre-political days, Indira Gandhi
sometimes affected a disdain for her new role. 'Mera sara samay
kumaitiyon thatha dusron kamon mein lag jata hai', she complained to
a friend: All my time now goes in committees and suchlike.[4] But
other evidence suggests that she rather liked it. The man who knew
her best of all wrote thus of her energetic participation in the election
campaign of 1957:

When voting finished today, large numbers of our Congress workers
turned up at Anand Bhawan, including many women. Indu has specially
shaken up the women, and even Muslim women came out. Indu has
indeed grown and matured very greatly during the last year, and
especially during these elections. She worked with effect all over India,
but her special field was Allahabad City and District which she organized
like a general preparing for battle. She is quite a heroine in Allahabad
now and particularly with the women.[5]

III

Back in 1952 the most powerful ideological challenges to Nehru and his Congress Party had come from the Jana Sangh on the right; and from the socialists on the left. Both those parties were now in disarray, caused in part by the departure of their charismatic leaders. S. P. Mookerjee was dead and Jayaprakash Narayan had abandoned politics for social service. Across northern India the Congress was virtually unchallenged. It won 195 seats in the north out of 226 it contested, this dominance contributing handsomely to its overall tally of 371 seats, which gave it a comfortable majority in Parliament.[6]

Its overall triumph notwithstanding, there were worrying signs for a party that had led the freedom struggle and since guided the Indian state. Outside the Indo-Gangetic plain a variety of challenges were taking shape. In Orissa the Congress was opposed by the Ganatantra Parishad – a grouping of local landlords – which, with the parties of the left, reduced it to a tally of 7 seats out of 20. In Bombay province, once the heartland of Indian nationalism, the Congress won 38 seats out of a total of 66. Most of the others went to the Samyukta Maharashtra Samiti or the Mahagujarat Parishad, each fighting for a separate state. (In what was effectively a plebiscite on the creation of a Marathi-speaking state with Bombay as its capital, the Samyukta Maharashtra Samiti garnered 5.5 million votes to the Congress's 5.3 million.) These losses were reproduced in the local elections which followed, with the Samiti capturing the municipalities of the great historic cities of Poona and Bombay.

A regional challenge was also brewing in the south. This took the shape of the Dravida Munnetra Kazhagam (or DMK), a party which grew out of the Dravidian movement started by E. V. Ramaswami Naicker. Known as 'Periyar' (great man), Ramaswami was a fervent opponent of the northern domination of Indian politics, culture and religion. He stood for a creation of a separate nation in south India, to be called Dravida Nadu. The DMK was started by a group of his former followers, who sought to use the vehicle of parliamentary politics for articulating their secessionist demands. The 1957 election was the first they took part in. Although they won but a handful of seats – these mostly in the assembly polls – their creeping successes were worrying, since the party stood not merely for a new province based on ethnicity or language, but for a separate nation-state altogether.[7]

It was, however, in the southernmost state of the Union that the Congress's claim to represent all of India was most gravely undermined. The state was Kerala, where a resurgent Communist Party of India had emerged as a strong popular alternative to the ruling party. In the parliamentary election the CPI won 9 seats out of the 18 fought for (the Congress won only 6). In the assembly polls, which were held at the same time, the communists won 60 seats out of 126, the support of five independents assuring it a slim majority.

The communist victory in the Kerala assembly election was a spectacular affirmation of the possibilities of a path once dismissed by Lenin as 'parliamentary cretinism'. A town in Italy had recently elected a Red mayor, but here was something qualitatively new; a first chance for communists to govern a full-fledged province of a very large country. With the Cold War threatening to turn hot, what happened in Kerala was of worldwide interest. But it also posed sharp questions for the future of Indian federalism. There had, in the past, been a handful of provincial ministries led by opposition parties or Congress dissidents. What New Delhi now faced was a different matter altogether; a state ruled by a party which was underground till the day before yesterday, which still professed a theoretical allegiance to armed revolution, and whose leaders and cadres were known to have sometimes taken their orders from Moscow.

IV

Located on the south-western tip of India, Kerala is a very beautiful state, with a long coastline and high mountains. The monsoon is both early and abundant, the vegetation gorgeously diverse; no part of India is greener. And no part is as culturally diverse. Hindus constitute about 60 per cent of the population; Muslims and Christians, the remaining 40 per cent. Crucially, these minority communities have a very long history indeed. The 'Syrian' Christians of Kerala claim to have been converted by St Thomas in the first century of the Christian era. More recently, Protestant and Catholic missionaries had also enjoyed conspicuous success. The first Muslims were a product of trade with the Arabs, and go back to at least the eighth century. These are the oldest communities of Christians and Muslims in the subcontinent. Like the Hindus of Kerala they spoke the local tongue, Malayalam. However, their relative

Table 14.1 – Religious composition of Kerala
vis-à-vis that of India as a whole

| | Percentage of total population | | |
	Hindu	Christian	Muslim
Kerala	60.83	21.22	17.91
India	83.51	2.44	10.69

SOURCE: K. G. Krishna Murthy and G. Lakshmana Rao, *Political Preferences in Kerala* (New Delhi: Radha Krishna, 1968), p. 10.

abundance in the population lent the state a certain distinctiveness, as Table 14.1 indicates.

From the late nineteenth century Kerala had been in a state of social ferment. These changes were being directed by four kinds of actors. First, there were the missionaries who, because of the Christian influence, found it easier to work here than in other parts of British India. Their Churches promoted modern education through a vast, interconnected network of schools and colleges. Second, there were the successive Maharajas of Cochin and (especially) Travancore, more progressive than most of their counterparts, and challenged by the missionaries to open decent schools of their own. Third, there were energetic caste associations, such as the Nair Service Society, which represented the dominant landed caste; and the Sree Narayana Dharma Paripalana (SNDP), named for Narayana Guru, the legendary leader of the Ezhavas, the caste of toddy-tappers ranked low in the ritual hierarchy. These too ran their educational institutions, as well as societies devoted to welfare and charity. Finally, there were the political parties, which included the Congress, of course, and also the Communist Party of India.[8]

The Kerala unit of the CPI was strongly rooted in the local soil. Its most influential leaders had started life in the Congress, then graduated leftwards. They started peasant unions to demand security for tenants and labour unions to demand better wages and working conditions for the landless. They instituted 'reading rooms' where intellectuals communicated radical ideas to their underprivileged audiences. Theatre and dance were also pressed into the service of left-wing propaganda. Through the late 1930s and beyond the communists made steady gains, their ideas and manifest idealism appealing to a divided society further hit by depression and war.

In a country generally riven by inequality, Kerala still stood out for the oppressiveness of its caste system. Here, the lowest of the low were not merely 'untouchable', but even 'unseeable'. When a Namboodiri Brahmin approached, a Paraiya labourer had to cry out in advance, lest the sight of him pollute his superior. Yet the combined efforts of the missionaries, the princes, the caste societies and the communists had seriously undermined traditional structures of authority. In a mere half-century, between 1900 and 1950, defiance had replaced deference as the idiom of social exchange in the Kerala countryside.[9]

When, after 1947, universal suffrage came to the state, the communists were in a very good position to exploit it. But instead they went underground, following orders from Moscow. They resurfaced in time for the 1952 election, and made a decent showing. Through the 1950s they worked steadily at expanding their influence. In February 1956, less than a year before the Indian general election, the Communist Party of the Soviet Union had its 20th Congress. Here Khrushchev famously denounced Stalin, and in passing also endorsed the possibility of a peaceful transition to socialism. In the general secretary's words, 'The winning of a stable parliamentary majority backed by a mass revolutionary movement of the proletariat and of all the working people could create for the working class of a number of capitalist and former colonial countries the conditions needed to secure fundamental social changes.'[10]

There would, of course, be no elections in the Soviet Union, but Big Brother now did not mind, indeed perhaps approved of, participation in elections by comrades elsewhere. (This shift was caused in part by imperatives of foreign policy – competing with their fellow superpower for allies, the Russians had to cultivate ex-colonial regimes that were often unsympathetic to revolutionary communism.) The communists in Kerala could now throw themselves more energetically into their campaign. Their manifesto declared that they wished only to make this a 'democratic and prosperous state', by starting new industries, increasing food production, raising wages of workers in factories and farms, nationalizing plantations, building houses and streamlining schools. The party of protest sought to become a party of governance; a transition which, it told the voter, its stewardship of local bodies had prepared it for. As the manifesto declared, the people also know that the administration of many municipalities and of the Malabar District Board under the leadership of the Communist Party is better than before, and that both the *panchayats* [village councils] which won awards from Prime Minister Nehru for good administration are under the leadership of the Communist Party. These experiences have made it clear that the Communist Party is capable not only of uniting the people for conducting agitation, but that it can also take over and run the administration successfully.[11]

V

The newly elected Communist chief minister of Kerala was E. M. S. Namboodiripad. 'EMS', as he was known to foe and friend alike, was a small man, barely five feet tall, but with a deep commitment to his credo, this allied to a fierce intelligence. Born in a Brahmin family, he had donated his ancestral home to the party. He read widely and wrote prodigiously – among his many works was an authoritative history of Kerala. Like Sheikh Abdullah, Master Tara Singh and A. Z. Phizo, EMS was, in this huge country, considered a mere 'provincial' leader. Yet he remains a figure of considerable historical interest, because of both the size of his province and the distinctiveness of his politics.[12]

Virtually the first act of the new government was to commute the sentences of prisoners on death row. Next, cases were withdrawn against those involved in labour disputes or other such 'political struggles'. More substantive measures were to follow, such as the opening of thousands of 'fair price' shops, to aid the distribution of food to the needy in a food-deficient state.[13]

The communist ministers made an impression with their efficiency, this a stark contrast with the sloth of their Congress counterparts. A liberal monthly praised EMS for his 'enviable record of public service', and for choosing as his colleagues 'people with the sovereign quality of throwing their minds into joint stock in the hour of deliberation. They will not be simple feeders at the public trough.'[14] They weren't; thus an otherwise congenitally anti-Red weekly was deeply impressed when the irrigation minister, V. R. Krishna Iyer, responded immediately to a call from a remote hamlet where a bund had been breached. The minister 'at once cut through his tour programme, and personally visited the place. He issued orders on the spot for immediate repairs, and personally supervised the carrying out of the job.' Further, he promised an enquiry into the conduct of those officials whose negligence had endangered the paddy crop.[15]

By taking office the communists had pledged to work within the framework of the Indian Constitution; by accepting central funds, to abide by the recommendations of the Planning Commission. But there was plenty they could still do within these constraints. For one, they could reform the archaic, inefficient and grossly inequitable system of landholding. Here they had the sanction not just of the Planning Commission and the constitution, but of successive policy documents of the Congress Party itself. These stated a commitment to land reform; a commitment which, as Ronald Herring has noted, 'did not become operative under any Congress regime but was closely approximated by the reforms of the Communist Party of India in Kerala'.[16]

The aims of the Agrarian Relations Bill introduced by EMS's government were modest: not the socialization or collectivization of land, not even the bestowing of land titles to the landless, merely the providing of stability of tenure to the mass of small peasants who cultivated holdings owned by absentee landlords. The bill sought to curb the wide powers of eviction previously enjoyed by landlords, to reduce rates of rent and waive arrears, and to fix a ceiling on ownership and redistribute the surplus land thus garnered. These were important measures, helping hundreds of thousands of poor peasants, but still somewhat short of what the Red catechism prescribed. The contradiction was resolved by recourse to the 'stages' theory of classical Marxism. It was argued that rural India was still 'semi-feudal'. All non-feudal classes were to be rallied around the proposed reforms which, when in place, would unleash agrarian capitalism, the next, necessary stop in the high road to socialism.[17]

The standard history of Kerala communism is subtitled 'a study in political adaptation' (to bourgeois democracy). Reformism in agriculture was one manifestation of this; a second, which must surely have confused the cadres more, was the encouragement of private enterprise. The party's manifesto had threatened the nationalization of plantations, many of them foreign-owned. After the election this was quietly abandoned. Then, within its first few months in office, the Kerala government invited India's largest capitalist house, the Birlas, to set up a rayon factory in Mavoor. The entrepreneurs were assured subsidized supplies of bamboo – to be gifted to the Birlas at one rupee per tonne, when the prevailing market price was perhaps a thousand times as much. This project constituted, on the capitalist's side, a breaking of ranks, for the Indian industrial class detested the communists. Their hope was that the central government would be likewise exercised by the Red menace; that 'Home Minister Pant and his New Delhi group [of Congress politicians] comes down on the Kerala Communists with a heavy hand and knocks them out of office'.[18] The pragmatic Birlas, however, were responding to the fact that the CPI controlled trade unions in important industrial centres outside Kerala. To start a plant here was to buy peace here – as well as elsewhere. As one columnist archly commented, it was hard to believe that the clan's patriarch, Ghanshyamdas Birla, had succumbed to the 'superlative charm of Chief Minister Namboodiripad'; it was more likely that he was 'getting ready for a Communist triumph in Bengal, where his interests are concentrated'.[19]

In office, as in opposition, the communists attracted a wide range of interested comment, this ranging from the warmly approbatory to the viciously hostile. There were those who wrote of an emerging new dawn, in terms reminiscent of the opening pages of George Orwell's *Homage to Catalonia*, with its sincere salute to the soul of man under socialism. On the first anniversary of the assumption of office by EMS's government, a journalist went to a tea shop where

> the central figure was the boy serving tea. Most of the discussions were based on rumours. But the boy was always sure of his facts as retailed by 'Janayugam', the Communist daily. It was a delight to watch this lad of sixteen arguing with a school-teacher on the wrong side of forty, a NGO (non-gazetted officer) in his twenties and the others in the presence of his boss, the tea-shop owner, and at the same time performing his own duties uninterrupted by the discussion. This can happen only in Kerala.[20]

On the other side, there was talk of Red terror, with a Kerala newspaper writing in apocalyptic mode of a class war to the finish, with the state taking the side of the lower orders:

> If there is a conflict arising between labourers and company managements woe betide the company managements, the police will side with the labour.

If a jenmi [landlord] is so ill-advised as to pick a quarrel with his agricultural labourers, woe unto the jenmi. The police will know what to do . . .

If a howling mass besiege a college or a bishop's palace, it will be termed as a popular, peaceful and constitutional agitation of aggrieved students . . .[21]

VI

In the winter of 1957–8 the Hungarian writer George Mikes travelled through India. As a refugee from communism – by then settled comfortably in London – he found 'the Kerala affair' most intriguing. 'What is a democratic Central Government to do with a Communist state?' he asked. 'What would the American administration do if California or Wisconsin suddenly – and I admit, somewhat unexpectedly – turned Communist? And again, how is a Communist government itself to behave with democratic overlords sitting on its neck?'[22]

One cannot say how an American president would have behaved in a similar situation – would he have sent in the Marines? – but in India the prime minister of the day was inclined to wait and watch. For the land reforms proposed by EMS's government were merely those promised by Congress governments. And the personal integrity of the Kerala ministers was not absent in the best of the Congress Party, such as Jawaharlal Nehru.

More controversial by far were the educational initiatives of the Kerala government. In the summer of 1957 it introduced an Educational Bill aimed at correcting the abuses in privately owned schools and colleges. These were the norm in Kerala, with schools managed by the Church, the Nair Service Society and the SNDP. The bill sought to enhance the status of teachers by checking the powers of the management to hire and fire at will, by setting norms for recruitment, and by prescribing salaries and humane working conditions. It also gave the state the powers to take over schools that did not abide by the bill's provisions.[23]

The opposition to the bill was led by the Church, whose own powers – moral as well as material – depended crucially on its control of educational institutions. The clergy was deeply anti-communist, a sentiment it managed successfully to instil in its flock. In the 1957 election, for example, the CPI had won only 3 out of 18 seats in Kottayam District, the Syrian Christian heartland.[24]

As it happened, the minister of education, Joseph Mundaserry, had spent decades teaching in a Catholic college in Trichur. He knew the corruptions of the system, and his bill was in some respects a brave attempt to correct them. However, his government sought to go further than modernize the management; it wanted also to introduce changes in the curriculum. New textbooks were prepared which sought subtly – and not so subtly – to present history through communist lenses. The lenses used by Christian pedagogues were ground to a very different specification. Consider these alternative versions of the Russian Revolution, in circulation in the schools of Kerala in these years:

New version: A republican Government was established under George Lavoff, a member of the Royal Family. It failed to secure popular support and proved incapable of ending the war or of effecting social and economic reforms. At this time, Lenin arrived in Russia and this gave impetus to the Russian people. A new Government with Lenin as President was evolved. First, Lenin made the Treaty of Brest-Litovsk with Germany. Then land and other capital goods were nationalised. All agricultural land was taken away from the landlords and divided among the peasants. All factories became the property of the State. The privileges of the clergy and the nobility were abolished. Mines, railways and banks were taken over by the Government. And thus to the astonishment of all, a new world, based upon Socialism, took shape in Russia and the dreams of Karl Marx were realized in this way.

Old version: Lenin established a Workers' Government. But the first election showed that the Bolsheviks had no majority. However, to maintain themselves in power, they dissolved the Duma on the ground that it was reactionary. Local Soviets who did not support the Bolsheviks were also disbanded. Private schools were forbidden and education was taken over by the State. Voting right was denied to the nobility and the clergy. Communism encourages violence, and does not believe in an omnipotent God. The Communists forget that man has a soul. It is a one-party Government that prevails in Communist Russia. There is neither freedom of opinion nor of religion. Many other defects in the System may also strike the eye of an observant critic.[25]

Here were two alternative visions of the kind of society Kerala should become; masquerading as two alternative readings of the Russian Revolution. One can see how the Christian version would enrage the Communists, and vice versa. In any event, the textbook row added fuel to an already well-burning fire. For by this time the Christians opposing the bill had been joined by the Nairs, the other community that loomed large in the economic life of Kerala. Where the Christians had always supported the Congress, the Nairs were split down the middle; about half of them had voted for the communists, the other half against. However, since the Nair Service Society also ran schools and colleges, the new bill helped tilt them against the communists and into a somewhat opportunistic alliance with the Christians.[26]

More opportunistic still was the local Congress Party. Defeated in the election, it saw in the resentment against the Educational Bill a chance to regain power. Its leaders proposed an anti-communist popular front, an idea attractive to 'the reactionary Catholic Church, landlords, planters and the other disgruntled elements', but a seeming betrayal of the socialistic philosophy of its leaders at the centre.[27] Through the latter part of 1958 there were a series of strikes and protest marches in Kerala. In one incident in Trichur the police fired on a crowd of Congress Party members, killing six.[28]

Feeling besieged, E. M. S. Namboodiripad was compelled to state his case through the pages of the country's most popular English-language weekly. Their 'opponents were scandalised', he said, because his government sometimes sought to act against the landlords, even if it did so strictly within the framework of the constitution. A Congress leader answered back, writing in the same columns about the growing 'lawlessness and insecurity in Kerala', caused by the tendency of communists to raise themselves above the law while acting vindictively against those who did not agree with them.[29] After the Supreme Court rejected an appeal in February 1959, the Kerala Education Bill received the assent of the president of India. In the same month Mrs Indira Gandhi was elected president of the Indian National Congress. She was the first woman to hold the post since Nellie Sen Gupta in 1933. Asked whether her domestic duties would suffer, Mrs Gandhi answered with asperity: 'My household work takes ten minutes only.'[30]

At this time the Congress was 'speaking with three voices: the members in Kerala active in violent agitation, the central leadership permitting such activity without approving of it, and Nehru disapproving of it but taking no action to curb it'.[31] Meanwhile the agitation intensified with the entry of the Nair doyen Mannath Padmanabhan. A founder of the Nair Service Society, long active in its schools and colleges, Mannath was an austere, *dhoti*-clad man who spoke only Malayalam. It was said that he had turned against the communists when they refused permission for him to start an engineering college in Palghat. Now he intended to dispatch 'these Communists, bag and baggage, not merely from Kerala, but from India and driv[e] them to their fatherland – Russia'. When an interviewer asked whether his age was not against him (he was eighty), Mannath reminded them of Bhishma Pitamah, the octogenarian warrior who had led the Pandavas into their own *dharma yuddh*, or holy war.[32] The clash in Kerala is perhaps best understood in terms of the political theorist W. H. Morris-Jones's characterization of the three 'idioms' of Indian politics. The first of these idioms was the 'modern', basing itself on universal ideas of freedom and justice, and expressed in Parliament, the law courts, and the English-language press. The second was the 'traditional', which emphasized primordial loyalties, the interests of one's caste or religion.

In its first phase the Education Bill controversy was, like so much else in modern India, simply a clash between the modern and traditional idioms of politics. But Mannath Padmanabhan brought with him yet a third idiom: the 'saintly'. Morris-Jones himself saw this idiom as operating 'at the margin' of Indian politics – as in the social work of Vinoba Bhave. Mannath, however, brought this idiom into a direct engagement with the other two – as, long before, and to even more spectacular effect, had Mahatma Gandhi. The people of Kerala followed him in part for the same reasons that the people of India had followed Gandhi; namely, that his personal integrity was unimpeachable, and that he had never sought or held political office.[33]

Mannath's arrival gave a huge boost to the movement, which soon contained, in the patriarch's words, 'everyone in Kerala who is not a Communist'. On 1 May 1959 a conference of community organizations met at Changanacherry to form a Vimochana Samara Samiti, or Liberation Committee, under Mannath's leadership. Over the next month its members carried their message into schools and colleges, churches and temples, into the homes of fisherfolk, peasants, merchants and workers.

By early June thousands of volunteers were ready to court arrest. Now commenced a series of *hartals*, or shut-down strikes, leading to the closure of schools, hospitals, public offices and factories. Large processions were taken out, often headed by Mannath, who – belying his saintly pretensions – allowed himself to be carried on a white horse with a silk umbrella held over him. Nair youths with swords walked menacingly in front of him.

The communists 'replied with organized brutality'. By one estimate there were 248 lathi-charges by police; also many bullets fired, leaving at least twenty dead and many more wounded, children and women among them. Each lathi-charge served only to swell further the ranks of the protesters. Some 150,000 protesters were jailed; a quarter of these were women.[34]

VII

It is hard to say who found the situation more distasteful – E. M. S. Namboodiripad, as the head of a 'people's government' which was now ordering daily lathi-charges and incarcerating thousands of ordinary folk; or Jawaharlal Nehru, the constitutional democrat who watched as his party took to the streets to dislodge a lawfully elected government. In Nehru's case the agony was compounded by the fact that he largely approved of the agrarian and educational policies of the Kerala government.[35]

Buoyed by the success of the agitation, Congress politicians in Kerala were pressing for the centre to invoke Article 356 of the constitution, whereby the president could dismiss a state government on account of a breakdown in law and order. The article had been used four times in the past, usually to call mid-term elections when a ruling party had lost its majority on account of a split or defections.

To see the situation for himself, Nehru visited Kerala in the last week of June 1959. He was alarmed at the 'thick walls of group hatred'; the two sides, he thought, were almost like two hostile countries at war.[36] But he remained reluctant to ask the president to dismiss EMS's government. His hesitancy was not shared by his daughter Indira, who thought the action was long overdue: 'When Kerala is virtually on fire', said Mrs Gandhi in a speech in Delhi, 'it becomes the centre's duty to go to the aid of the people; the misrule of the communist rulers of the state has created a situation which is unparalleled in the history of our country. *Such a situation does not brook legal quibbling.*'[37]

Mannath and his warriors were now preparing for a final showdown. The Muslim League had joined the struggle, lending it more legitimacy still. Through the month of July there were daily marches, with the protesters provoking the police into violence. In one particularly gruesome incident the police entered a fishing hamlet and fired on bystanders, killing a pregnant woman and two others near her.[38]

The Vimochana Samara Samiti had declared 9 August 'Zero Day', when 50,000 volunteers, representing all classes and communities, would descend on Trivandrum to paralyse the administration. On 26 July groups started marching on the capital from all parts of the state, gathering momentum and men along the way. 'The hour was approaching when the Communists must choose between massacre and defeat.'[39] A letter from the state governor, pleading with the centre to intervene, strengthened the hand of the Congress president, Indira Gandhi. Her prime minister (and father) finally succumbed, writing to Namboodiripad on 30 July that an order of dismissal was on the way, since 'it is no longer possible to allow matters to deteriorate, leading to continuing conflicts and human suffering. We have felt that, even from the point of view of your government, it is better for Central intervention to take place now'.[40]

Six months later Kerala went to the polls again. The Congress, allied with the Socialist Party and the Muslim League, asked the voter to choose between 'democracy and communism'. Nehru led a band of stalwarts in a campaign which featured posters of Flory Mata, the pregnant fisherwoman shot by the police during the 'liberation struggle'. A record 84 per cent of the adult population turned out to vote. In a House of 127 the communists won only 26 seats. The Congress won 60; their allies a further 31.[41] The results appeared to vindicate the dismissal of Namboodiripad's government. But, as Sarvepalli Gopal points out, that decision had 'tarnished Nehru's reputation for ethical behaviour in politics and, from a long-term view, weakened his position'.[42]

VIII

Recall that in the early years of Independence, circa 1947–9, the Congress had faced challenges from the extremism of left and right. The communists, claiming that this was a false freedom, had launched a bloody revolution against the nascent Indian state. On the other side, the RSS was mobilizing the forces of reaction in an attempt to create a Hindu Pakistan. The centre had held, and the Congress had successfully tamed these threats; by drafting a democratic constitution, winning a democratic election and putting in place the rudiments of a modern pluralist state.

Now, a decade later, the Congress was once more under attack from the far edges of the political spectrum. The left's challenge this time was democratic, and hence potentially more dangerous. For if EMS's government was to bring about social reform successfully, by redistributing land to the poor and creating schools for all, it might create a domino effect, that is, the victory of non-Congress parties in other states of the Union.

As it happened, there was also a new challenge from the right. This came from C. Rajagopalachari, 'Rajaji', the veteran Congress politician who had previously served as governor of Bengal, governor general of India and Union home minister. In 1952 the Congress asked Rajaji to take over as chief minister of Madras province. He stayed in that post until April 1954, when his party indicated that they wanted the powerful backward-caste leader K. Kamaraj to replace him. Now Rajaji settled down in a small house to spend his days, he said, reading and writing. (He was an accomplished short-story writer in his native Tamil, and had also written masterful versions of the Ramayana and the Mahabharata.)

However, philosophy and literature proved inadequate substitutes for public affairs. Thus Rajaji was moved to comment from time to time on the nuclear arms race between Russia and America, with regard to which he took a line not dissimilar to Nehru's. Then, when the second five-year plan committed the government of India to a socialist model of economics, he began commenting on domestic affairs too. Here, however, he came to be increasingly at odds with the prime minister.

The differences were in part political. Rajaji felt that the Congress had become complacent in the absence of a strong opposition. In October 1956 he made public his belief that there should be an opposition group *within* the Congress, without which – so he feared – the party 'would simply degenerate into a hunting ground for every kind of ambition and self-seeking'.[43] The proposal was rejected; so the veteran turned to promoting an opposition outside the Congress instead. In May 1958 he published an article with the provocative title 'Wanted: Independent Thinking'. This argued that 'probably the main cause for the collapse of independent thinking' in India was 'the long reign of popular favourites without any significant opposition'. However, a healthy democracy required 'an opposition that thinks differently and does not just want more of the same, a group of vigorously thinking citizens which aims at the general welfare, and not one that in order to get more votes from the so-called have-nots, offers more to them than the party in power has given, an opposition that appeals to reason . . .'[44]

The differences between Nehru and Rajaji were also economic. Rajaji worried that the second five-year plan would lead to an excessive centralization of state power. He was disturbed by the massive increases in taxation, conceived in the interests of the public sector, but which might only serve to 'discourage and deject citizens and wither the private sector'. In his view, the plan must 'be conceived as a supplement to rather than a substitute for the market economy'.[45]

In May 1959, and touching eighty, Rajaji launched a new political party, the Swatantra Party. This party focused its criticisms on the 'personality cult' around the prime minister, and on the economic policies of the ruling Congress. Its founding statement asked for a 'proper decentralized distribution of industry' through the nurturing of 'competitive enterprise' and, in agriculture, for the encouragement of the 'self-employed peasant proprietor who stands for initiative and freedom'. It rejected the 'techniques of so-called socialism' and the 'bringing into being of "Statism".'[46]

A democracy run by a single party automatically becomes a tyranny; such was Rajaji's rationale for starting Swatantra. For 'the Congress Party has so far run without a true Opposition. It has run with accelerators and no brakes.'[47] This party started by an octogenarian quickly gathered momentum. Those who joined up included captains of industry, naturally, but also peasant leaders worried by Congress threats to promote 'co-operative farming'. Although conventionally described as 'conservative', the party was in fact a curious amalgam of free-market liberals and agrarian leaders seeking an alternative to the Congress.[48]

Congress cheerleaders dismissed Swatantra as a party of 'right reaction'. The prime minister himself affected an airy disdain. When asked at a press conference about Rajaji's new party, he merely joked, 'He likes the Old Testament. I like the New Testament.'[49]

IX

The challenges posed by the communists on the left and the Swatantra Party on the right were compounded by serious accusations of financial malfeasance against the government in New Delhi. In September 1957 questions were raised in Parliament about the propriety of large investments made by the state-owned Life Insurance Corporation of India (LIC) in a private firm in Kanpur owned by an industrialist named Haridas Mundhra. When the finance minister, T. T. Krishnamachari, gave an equivocal reply, dissident Congress MPs began to ask sharper questions. Prominent in the debate was the prime minister's estranged son-in-law, Feroze Gandhi. He claimed that the Mundhra shares had been bought to boost their price well above their true market value. He wondered how 'the Life Insurance Corporation became a willing party to this questionable transaction with the mystery man of India's business underworld'. There was, Feroze Gandhi concluded, 'a conspiracy to beguile the [state-owned] Corporation of its funds'.[50]

Bowing to the criticism, the government announced a Commission of Inquiry into the affair. In fact there were two separate and successive enquiries, each headed by an eminent judge. Their findings were not complimentary to the Congress government. The LIC had a publicly stated 'blue-chip' policy, which committed it to investing money only in firms of high reputation and sound management. The Mundhra companies were neither; yet the Corporation had seen fit to make its largest ever investment in its stock. The officials quizzed by the judges could not satisfactorily explain their decision; nor could their minister.

The proceedings of these Commissions were held in Delhi and Bombay, and kept open to the public. They attracted great attention, most of it critical. People flocked to the hearings, there to see the minister and his officials fumble under questioning or contradict one another. The final reports of the judges were damning, and exacted a price: both the minister and his secretary were forced to demit office.[51]

The judicial probe into the LIC investment in the Mundhra companies, wrote the *Hindustan Times*, 'had the effect of an overall political shake-up, the like of which has not been experienced since Independence'. What 'looked like a molehill when the issue was first ventilated in Parliament', had 'assumed the proportion of a mountain'.[52] Known initially as the Mundhra Affair, it was soon promoted to become the Mundhra Scandal. Until it erupted, the ministers of Nehru's government were widely held to be fond of power, yet above financial impropriety. A halo of Gandhian austerity still hung around them. The Mundhra Affair made the first serious dent in this image. It was a dent as deep, and as damaging, as those made by political parties of left or right.

15

The Experience of Defeat

A divided India augurs ill not only for the Indian people but also for all Asia and world peace.

AUNG SAN, Burmese nationalist leader, June 1947

I

ON THE LAST DAY of March 1959 the Dalai Lama crossed the McMahon Line into the territory of the Republic of India. For years the Tibetan god-king had sat uncomfortably on his throne in Lhasa's Potala Palace, while the Chinese tightened their hold on his country. One contemporary source claimed that there were half a million Chinese troops in Tibet. In their wake had come perhaps ten times as many Han settlers.[1]

This was certainly an over-estimate. Even so, there were far too many Chinese for the Tibetans' liking. In 1958 the Khampas of eastern Tibet launched an armed uprising against the occupiers. After some initial successes, the revolt was put down by the Chinese. The reprisals which followed threatened to touch the Dalai Lama himself. When New Delhi agreed to grant him political asylum, he fled Lhasa under cover of darkness and with a small group of carefully chosen escorts.

The Dalai Lama spent his first night on Indian soil at the Buddhist monastery at Tawang. Then he made his way down to the plains, to the Assam town of Tezpur, where Indian officials 'debriefed' him. Three weeks later he was taken to New Delhi to meet the prime minister himself.

The conversation began with the Dalai Lama telling Nehru about the Khampa rebellion. The fighting had been bitter, and heavy losses had been incurred by both sides. Across Tibet there was deep resentment against the anti-religious propaganda of the communists. When the Chinese invited the Dalai Lama to Peking to attend a 'cultural function', his advisers warned that this was a plot to capture and confine him.

When he refused to go the Chinese issued threats. So he decided to leave for India.

The Dalai Lama told Nehru that any reforms in Tibet should be undertaken by the Tibetans in keeping with their religion and traditions. The Chinese way would leave them 'a people without their souls'. His own hope now was to bring about Tibet's independence with Indian help. His old tutor Heinrich Harrer (author of the classic *Seven Years in Tibet*) was also encouraging him to canvass support in the West.

In reply, Nehru told his visitor that India could not start a war with China for Tibet's freedom. Indeed, 'the whole world cannot bring freedom to Tibet unless the whole fabric of the Chinese state is destroyed'. Were he to go to the West, Nehru told the Dalai Lama, he would 'look like a piece of merchandise'. The Americans or Europeans had no real sympathy with his people or his cause: 'all they want is to exploit Tibet in their cold war with the Soviet Union'.

An 'independence or nothing' attitude, Nehru felt, would get the Tibetans nowhere. They must keep the door open for a negotiated settlement with the Chinese. India could help here, but only after it had mended its own broken fences with Peking. As he put it, 'at the moment our relations with China are bad. We have to recover the lost ground. By threats to China or condemnation of China we do not recover such ground.'[2]

II

By the time of the Dalai Lama's flight, Indian relations with China were very bad indeed. In the summer of 1957 the Ladakhi *lama* and parliamentarian Kushak Bakula had visited Tibet and noticed evidence of intensive road building towards Sinkiang. Then, in July 1958, an official magazine named *China Pictorial*, published in Peking, printed a map that showed large parts of NEFA and Ladakh as Chinese territory. On 21 August a counsellor in the Chinese embassy was called to the Indian Foreign Office, where a deputy secretary handed over a note of protest about the map. The correspondence became more concerned as the correspondents grew more elevated, and the stakes grew higher too.[3] On 18 October the foreign secretary wrote to the Chinese ambassador protesting about the section of the Sinkiang–Tibet highway that passed 'across the eastern part of the Ladakh region of the Jammu and Kashmir

State, which is part of India'.[4] And by the end of 1958 the prime ministers of the two nations, Jawaharlal Nehru and Chou En-lai, were writing to each other in an exchange that was to carry on for the next few years, this marked at first by pain and bewilderment, but in the end by anger and resentment.

The letters between Nehru and Chou remain a key source for understanding the border dispute. They may have been drafted by officials, but we can be sure that they were carefully checked by their signatories for tone as well as content. These were two politicians deeply interested in history. Both were imbued with – one might say carried by – a sense of mission, by the desire to take their long-subjected countries to a place of the first rank in the modern world.

In the hierarchy of contemporary Chinese nationalism, Chou En-lai occupied second place to Mao. In most matters he, like some 800 million others, deferred to the will, not to say whim, of the Great Helmsman. But when it came to foreign policy he was given a free hand. Among the top Chinese leadership, only he had lived and studied in the West. Coming of age, intellectually speaking, in Paris, Chou spoke French fluently and also had some English. He affected a cosmopolitan manner; when asked what had been the impact of the French Revolution, he answered, 'It is too early to tell.'

As Stuart Schram writes, by the time of the Bandung Conference of 1955 Chou En-lai had made his mark as 'an urbane and skilful diplomat', appearing 'side by side with Nehru as one of the two principal representatives of the non-European world, divided by ideology, but united by the fact that they were Asian'.[5]

In 1955 Chou and Nehru might have been divided only by political ideology. By 1958 they were divided also by national interest. In December of that year the Indian prime minister wrote the first of a long series of letters to Chou. Nehru began by expressing admiration for China's economic progress before turning, gingerly and gently, to the question of the border. When they met in 1956, recalled Nehru, the Chinese leader had indicated that he thought the McMahon Line was a legacy of British imperialism, but 'because of the friendly relations' between China and India, his government would, after consulting with the local Tibetan authorities, give it recognition. Chou had then confirmed Nehru's impression that 'there was no major boundary dispute between China and India'. But now came this map in *China Pictorial*, whose borderline 'went right across Indian territory'.

A month later Chou En-lai replied, stating that 'historically no treaty or agreement on the Sino-Indian boundary has ever been concluded'. The McMahon Line was 'a product of the British policy of aggression against the Tibet Region of China'. Juridically speaking, 'it cannot be considered legal'. The Indians had protested about a road in an area which, in Chou's opinion, 'has always been under Chinese jurisdiction'. 'All this shows that [contrary to Nehru's claim] border disputes do exist between China and India'. That was the context in which the *China Pictorial* map should be viewed. Chou suggested that both sides temporarily maintain the status quo, pending a final 'friendly settlement' on the border question.

On 22 March 1959 Nehru wrote back. He was 'somewhat surprised' to hear that the frontier between India and the 'Tibet Region of China' was not accepted by Peking, for it had the sanction of several specific agreements. These included those forged between Kashmir and Lhasa in 1842 and, in the east, the McMahon Line agreed upon in 1913–14. Besides, there were clear natural features, watersheds and mountain tops, that defined the borders between the two countries. There might be gaps here and there, but, said Nehru, for 'much the larger part of our boundary with China, there is sufficient authority based on geography, tradition as well as treaties for the boundary as shown in our published maps'. The letter ended with the hope that 'an early understanding in this matter will be reached'.

Before Chou En-lai could reply, the Dalai Lama fled to India. This greatly complicated matters, as the Chinese were deeply resentful of the popular welcome given him by large sections of the Indian public. For this they blamed New Delhi. Had not the granting of an audience by Nehru himself given an unfortunate legitimacy to the Tibetan leader? Peking's position was that the Tibetan revolt, far from being a popular uprising, was the product of 'fugitive upper-class reactionaries' aided by the 'American imperialists' and the 'Chiang Kai-shek clique'. Sections of the Chinese media went so far as to claim that the Indian town of Kalimpong was the 'commanding centre of the revolt', that the Delhi government was being influenced by 'imperialist propaganda and intrigues' and that 'Sino-Indian friendship was being destroyed from the Indian side'.[6]

There was some propaganda activity by Tibetan refugees in Kalimpong, the import of which was, however, greatly exaggerated by the Chinese. In fact, much louder protests had emanated from Indian sources, in particular the politician turned social worker Jayaprakash Narayan. 'JP' was a fervent advocate for Tibetan independence, a cause also supported by other, less disinterested elements in Indian politics, such as the Jana Sangh, which wanted New Delhi openly to ally with the United States in the Cold War and seek its assistance in 'liberating' Tibet.[7] But, as the foreign secretary assured the Chinese ambassador a month after the Dalai Lama's flight into exile, 'India has had and has no desire to interfere in internal happenings in Tibet'. The exiled leader 'will be accorded respectful treatment in India, but he is not expected to carry out any political activities from this country'. This was the government's position, from which some Indians would naturally dissent. For, as the foreign secretary pointed out, 'there is by law and Constitution complete freedom of expression of opinion in Parliament and the press and elsewhere in India. Opinions are often expressed in severe criticism of the Government of India's policies.'

This was not a nuance Peking could easily understand. For, at least in public, there could not be any criticism of the government's policies within China. The difference between these two political systems – call them 'totalitarianism' and 'democracy' – was most strikingly reflected in an exchange about an incident that took place in Bombay on 20 April. According to the Chinese version – communicated to New Delhi by Peking in a letter dated 27 April – a group of protesters raised slogans and made speeches which

> branded China's putting down of the rebellion in her own territory, the Tibetan Region, as [an] imperialist action and made all sorts of slanders. What is more serious is that they pasted up a portrait of Mao Tse-tung, Chairman of the People's Republic of China, on the wall of the Chinese Consulate-General and carried out wanton insult by throwing tomatoes and rotten eggs at it. While these ruffians were insulting the portrait, the Indian policemen stood by without interfering with them, and pulled off the encircling spectators for the correspondents to take photographs . . .

This incident in Bombay constituted, in Peking's view, 'a huge insult to the head of state of the People's Republic of China and the respected and beloved leader of the Chinese people'. It was an insult which 'the masses of the six hundred and fifty million Chinese people absolutely cannot tolerate'. If the matter was 'not reasonably settled', said the complaint, in case 'the reply from the Indian Government is not satisfactory', the 'Chinese side will never come to a stop without a satisfactory settlement of the matter, that is to say, never stop even for one hundred years'.

In reply, the Indian government 'deeply regret[ted] that discourtesy was shown to a picture of Chairman Mao Tse-tung, the respected head of a state with which India has ties of friendship'. But they denied that the policemen on duty had in any way aided the protesters; to the contrary, they 'stood in front of the [Mao] picture to save it from further desecration'. The behaviour of the protesters was 'deplorable', admitted New Delhi, but

> the Chinese Government are no doubt aware that under the law in India processions cannot be banned so long as they are peaceful . . . Not unoften they are held even near the Parliament House and the processionists indulge in all manner of slogans against high personages in India. Incidents have occurred in the past when portraits of Mahatma Gandhi and the Prime Minister were taken out by irresponsible persons and treated in an insulting manner. Under the law and Constitution of India a great deal of latitude is allowed to the people so long as they do not indulge in actual violence.

III

In the first week of September 1959 the government of India released a White Paper containing five years of correspondence with its Chinese counterpart. The exchanges ranged from those concerning trifling disputes, occasioned by the straying by armed patrols into territory claimed by the other side, to larger questions about the status of the border in the west and the east and disagreements about the meaning of the rebellion in Tibet.

For some time now opposition MPs, led by the effervescent young Jana Sangh leader Atal Behari Vajpayee, had been demanding that the government place before Parliament its correspondence with the Chinese. The release of the White Paper was hastened by a series of border incidents in August. Chinese and Indian patrols had clashed at several places in NEFA. One Indian post, at Longju, came under sharp fire from the Chinese and was ultimately overwhelmed.

Unfortunately for the government, the appearance of the White Paper coincided with a bitter spat between the defence minister and his chief of army staff. The minister was Nehru's old friend V. K. Krishna Menon, placed in that post in 1957 as compensation for drawing him away from diplomatic duties. The appointment was at first welcomed within the army. Previous incumbents had been lacklustre; this one was anything but, and was close to the prime minister besides. But just as he seemed well settled in his new job, Menon got into a fight with his chief of staff, General K. S. Thimayya, a man just as forceful as he was.

The son of a coffee planter in Coorg, standing 6' 3" in his socks, Thimayya had an impressive personality and a more impressive military record. When a young officer in Allahabad, he had met an elderly gentleman in a cinema who asked him, 'How does it feel to be an Indian wearing a British army uniform?' 'Timmy' answered with one word: 'Hot'. The old man was Motilal Nehru, father of Jawaharlal and a celebrated nationalist himself. Later, when they had become friends, Thimayya asked him whether he should resign his commission and join the nationalist movement. Motilal advised him to stay in uniform, saying that after freedom came India would need officers like him.[8]

Thimayya fought with distinction in the Second World War before serving with honour in the first troubled year of Indian freedom. He oversaw the movement of Partition refugees in the Punjab and was then sent to Kashmir, where his troops successfully cleared the Valley of raiders. Later, he headed a United Nations truce team in Korea, where he supervised the disposition of 22,000 communist prisoners of war. His leadership was widely praised on both sides of the ideological divide, by the Chinese as well as the Americans.

'Timmy' was the closest the pacifist Indians had ever come to having an authentic modern military hero.[9] However, he did not see eye to eye with his defence minister. Thimayya thought that his troops should be better prepared for a possible engagement with China, but Krishna Menon insisted that the real threat came from Pakistan, along whose borders the bulk of India's troops were thus deployed. Thimayya was also concerned about the antiquity of the arms his men currently carried. These included the .303 Enfield rifle, which had first been used in the First World War. When the general suggested to the minister that India should manufacture the Belgian FN4 automatic rifle under licence, 'Krishna Menon said angrily that he was not going to have NATO arms in the country'.[10]

India – China Boundary Dispute: Western and Middle Sectors

SINKIANG

Karakoram Pass

Karakash R.

AKSAI CHIN

Shyok River

Kongka Pass

Lanak Pass

Leh

LADAKH

Khurnak

Indus River

Rudok

TIBET

Demchok

Part of Spiti

Shipki Pass

Sutlej River

Gartok

Simla

PUNJAB

Nilang

Jadha

Pulamsumda

Niti Pass

Barakoti

Lapthal

Taklakot

UTTAR PRADESH

NEPAL

Sinkiang–Tibet highway

Areas claimed by Chinese

| 0 | 25 | 50 | 75 | 100 miles |
| 0 | | 50 | 100 | 150 kms |

In the last week of August 1959 Thimayya and Menon fell out over the latter's decision to appoint to the rank of lieutenant general an officer named B. M. Kaul, in supersession of twelve officers senior to him. Kaul had a flair for publicity – he liked to act in plays, for example. He had supervised the construction of a new housing colony, which impressed Menon as an example of how men in uniform could contribute to the public good. In addition, Kaul was known to Jawaharlal Nehru, a fact he liked to advertise as often as he could.[11]

Kaul was not without his virtues. A close colleague described him as 'a live-wire – quick-thinking, forceful, and venturesome'. However, he 'could also be subjective, capricious and emotional'.[12] Thimayya was concerned that Kaul had little combat experience, for he had spent much of his career in the Army Service Corps, an experience which did not really qualify him for a key post at Army Headquarters. Kaul's promotion, when added to the other insults from his minister, provoked General Thimayya into an offer of resignation. On 31 August 1959 he wrote to the prime minister conveying how 'impossible it was for me and the other two Chiefs of Staff to carry out our responsibilities under the present Defence Minister'. He said the circumstances did not permit him to continue in his post.[13]

The news of the army chief's resignation leaked into the public domain. The matter was discussed in Parliament, and in the press as well. Opposing Thimayya were communists such as E. M. S. Namboodiripad, who expressed the view that the general should be courtmartialled, and crypto-communist organs such as the Bombay weekly *Blitz*, which claimed that Thimayya had unwittingly become a tool in the hands of the 'American lobby'. Those who sided with him in his battle with the defence minister were *Blitz*'s great (and undeniably pro-American) rival, the weekly *Current*, as well as large sections of the non-ideological press. The normally pro-government *Hindustan Times* said that 'Krishna Menon must go', not Thimayya. It accused the minister of reducing the armed forces to a 'state of near-demoralization' by trying to create, at the highest level, a cell of officers who would be personally loyal to him.[14]

Some hoped that the outcry over Thimayya's resignation would force Krishna Menon to also hand in his papers. Writing to the general, a leading lawyer called the minister an 'evil genius in Indian politics', adding, 'If as a result of your action, Menon is compelled to retire, India will heave a sigh of relief, and you will be earning the whole-hearted gratitude of the nation.' Then Nehru called Thimayya into his office and over two long sessions persuaded him to withdraw his resignation. He assured him that he would be consulted in all important decisions regarding promotions. An old colleague of Timmy's, a major general now retired to the hill town of Dehradun, wrote to his friend saying he should have stuck to his guns. For 'the solution found is useless as now no one has been sacked or got rid of. The honeymoon cannot last long as you will soon find out.'[15]

The release of the White Paper on China, against the backdrop of the general's resignation drama, intensified the feelings against the defence minister. For even members of Parliament had not known of the extent of China's claim on Indian territory. That the Chinese had established posts and built a paved road through what, at least on their maps, was India was seen as an unconscionable lapse on the part of those charged with guarding the borders. Opposition politicians naturally went to town about China's 'cartographic war against India'. As a socialist MP put it, New Delhi might still believe in 'Hindi-Chini Bhai Bhai', but Peking followed Lenin's dictum that 'promises, like piecrusts, are meant to be broken'.[16]

Perhaps the prime minister should have been held accountable, but for the moment the fingers were pointed at his pet, Krishna Menon. If the country was 'woefully unprepared to meet Chinese aggression', said the *Current*, the fault must lie with the person 'at the helm of India's Defence Forces', namely, the defence minister. Even Congress Party members were now calling for Menon's head. The home minister, Govind Ballabh Pant, an old veteran of the freedom struggle and a longtime comrade of Nehru's, advised the prime minister to change Menon's portfolio – to keep him in the Cabinet, but allot him something other than Defence.[17] The respected journalist B. Shiva Rao, now an MP, wrote to Nehru that he was 'greatly disturbed by your insistence on keeping Krishna Menon in the Cabinet. We are facing a grave danger from a Communist Power. As you are aware, there are widespread apprehensions about his having pro-Communist sympathies'. It was 'not easy for me to write this letter', said Shiva Rao, and 'I know it will be a very difficult decision for you to make'. However, 'this is an emergency whose end no one can predict'.[18]

Nehru, however, stuck to his guns – and to Krishna Menon. Meanwhile the 'diplomatic' exchanges with China continued. On 8 September 1959 Chou En-lai finally replied to Nehru's letter of 22 March that had set out the Indian position. Chou expressed surprise that India

India–China Boundary Dispute:
Eastern Sector

Area claimed
by Chinese

BHUTAN

TIBET

Khinzemane
Tawang

McMahon Line

Longju

Tsangpo River

NORTH EAST
FRONTIER
AGENCY

Pre-1914 Outer Line

Brahmaputra River

Dihang or Siang River

McMahon Line

ASSAM

Walong

Rim

MYANMAR

0   25   50   75   100 miles

0   50   100   150 kms

wished the Chinese to 'give formal recognition to the situation created by the application of the British policy of aggression against China's Tibet region'. The 'Chinese Government absolutely does not recognise the so-called McMahon Line'. It insisted that 'the entire Sino-Indian boundary has not been delimited', and called for a fresh settlement, 'fair and reasonable to both sides'. The letter ended with a reference to the increasing tension caused by the Tibet rebellion, after which Indian troops started 'shielding armed Tibetan bandits' and began 'pressing forward steadily across the eastern section of the Sino-Indian boundary'.

Nehru replied almost at once, saying that the Indians 'deeply resent this allegation' that 'the independent Government of India are seeking to reap a benefit' from British imperialism. He pointed out that between 1914 and 1947 no Chinese government had objected to the McMahon Line. He rejected the charge that India was shielding armed Tibetans. And he expressed 'great shock' at the tone of Chou's letter, reminding him that India was one of the first countries to recognize the People's Republic and had consistently sought to befriend it.[19]

By this time, the India–China exchange comprised bullets as well as letters. In late August 1959 there was a clash of arms at Longju, along the McMahon Line in the eastern sector. Then in late October 1959 an Indian patrol in the Kongka Pass area of Ladakh was attacked by a Chinese detachment. Nine Indian soldiers were killed, and as many captured. The Chinese maintained that the Indians had come deliberately into their territory; the Indians answered that they were merely patrolling what was their own side of the border.

These clashes prompted New Delhi to review its frontier policy. Remarkably, till this time responsibility for the border with China had rested not with the army but with the Intelligence Bureau. Such border posts as existed were manned by paramilitary detachments, the Assam Rifles in the east and the Central Reserve Police in the west. Regular military forces were massed along the border with Pakistan, which was considered India's main and perhaps sole military threat. But after the Longju and Kongka Pass incidents, the 4th Division was pulled out of Punjab and sent to NEFA. This was a considerable change; trained for tank warfare in the plains, the 4th would now have to operate in a very different terrain altogether.

Through this new 'forward policy', the Indian government aimed to inhabit no-man's-land by siting a series of small posts along or close to the border. The operation was much touted in Delhi, where maps sprung up in Defence Ministry offices with little blue pins marking where these posts had been located. Not to be found on these maps were the simultaneous attempts by the Chinese to fill in the blanks, working from their side of what was now a deeply contested border.[20]

IV

By 1959, at least, it was clear that the Indian and Chinese positions were irreconcilable. The Indians insisted that the border was, for the most part, recognized and assured by treaty and tradition; the Chinese argued that it had never really been delimited. The claims of both governments rested in part on the legacy of imperialism; British imperialism (for India), and Chinese imperialism (over Tibet) for China. In this sense, both claimed sovereignty over territory acquired by less-than-legitimate means.

In retrospect, it appears that the Indians underestimated the force of Chinese resentment against 'Western imperialism'. In the first half of the twentieth century, when their country was weak, it had been subject to all sorts of indignities by the European powers. The McMahon Line was one of them. Now that, under the communists, China was strong, it was determined to undo the injustices of the past. Visiting Peking in November 1959, the Indian lawyer Danial Latifi was told by his Chinese colleagues that 'the McMahon Line had no juridical basis'. Public opinion in China appeared 'to have worked itself up to a considerable pitch' on the border issue. Reporting his conversations to Jawaharlal Nehru, Latifi tellingly observed, 'As you know, probably too well, it is difficult *in any country* to make concessions once the public has been told it [the territory under dispute] forms part of the national homeland.'[21]

It is also easy in retrospect to see that, after the failure of the Tibetan revolt, the government of India should have done one or both of the following: (i) strengthened its defences along the Chinese border, importing arms from the West if need be; (ii) worked seriously for a fresh settlement of the border with China. But the non-alignment of Nehru precluded the former and the force of public opinion precluded the latter. In October 1959 the *Times of India* complained that the prime minister had shown 'an over-scrupulous regard for Chinese susceptibilities and comparative indifference towards the anger and dismay with which the Indian people have reacted'.[22] Another newspaper observed that

Nehru was 'standing alone against the rising tide of national resentment against China'.[23]

As Steven Hoffman has suggested, the policy of releasing White Papers limited Nehru's options. Had the border dispute remained private the prime minister could have used the quieter back-channels of diplomatic compromise. But with the matter out in the open, sparking much angry comment, he could only 'adopt those policies that could conceivably meet with approval from an emotionally aroused parliament and press'. The White Paper policy precluded the spirit of give and take, and instead fanned patriotic sentiment. The Kongka Pass incident, in particular, had led to furious calls for revenge from India's political class.[24]

After the border clashes of September and October 1959, Chou En-lai wrote suggesting that both sides withdraw twenty kilometres behind the McMahon Line in the east, and behind the line of actual control in the west. Nehru, in reply, dismissed the suggestion as merely a way of legitimizing Chinese encroachments in the western sector, of keeping 'your forcible possession intact'. The 'cause of the recent troubles', he insisted, 'is action taken from your side of the border'. Chou now pointed out that, despite its belief that the McMahon Line was illegal, China had adhered to a policy of 'absolutely not allowing its armed personnel to cross this line [while] waiting for a friendly settlement of the boundary question'. Thus,

> the Chinese Government has not up to now made any demand in regard to the area south of the so-called McMahon line as a precondition or interim measure, and what I find difficult to understand is why the Indian Government should demand that the Chinese side withdraw one-sidedly from its western frontier area.

This was an intriguing suggestion which, stripped of its diplomatic code, read, 'You keep your (possibly fraudulently acquired) territory in the East, while we shall keep our (possibly fraudulently acquired) territory in the West.'[25]

Writing in the *Economic Weekly* in January 1960, the Sinologist Owen Lattimore astutely summed up the Indian dilemma. Since the boundary with China was self-evidently a legacy of British imperialism, the 'cession of a large part of the disputed territory . . . would not involve Indian national pride had it not been for the way the Chinese have been trying to draw the frontier by force, without negotiation'. For 'what Mr Nehru might concede by reasonable negotiations between equals he would never concede by abject surrender'.[26]

In the same issue of the journal a contributor calling himself 'Pragmatist' urged a strong programme of defence preparedness. The Peking leadership, he wrote acidly, 'may not think any better of the armed forces of India than Stalin did of those of the Vatican'. The Chinese army was five times the strength of its Indian counterpart, and equipped with the latest Soviet arms. Indian strategic thinking, for so long preoccupied with Pakistan, must now consider seriously the Chinese threat, for the friendship between the two countries had 'definitely come to an end'. Now, the 'first priority in our defence planning' must be 'keeping Chinese armies on the northern side of the border'. India should train mountain warfare units, and equip them with light and mobile equipment. Waiting in support must be a force of helicopters and fighter-bombers. For 'the important thing', said 'Pragmatist', is to 'build up during the next two or four years, a strong enough force which will be able to resist successfully any blitzkrieg across our Himalayan borders'.[27]

The political opposition, however, was not willing to wait that long. 'The nation's self-interests and honour', thundered the president of the Jana Sangh in the last week of January 1960, 'demand early and effective action to free the Indian soil from Chinese aggression'. The government in power had 'kept the people and Parliament entirely ignorant in respect of the fact of aggression itself', and now 'it continues to look on helplessly even as the enemy goes on progressively consolidating its position in the occupied areas'.[28]

Suspicion of the Chinese, however, was by no means restricted to parties on the right. In February 1960 President Rajendra Prasad commented on the 'resentment and anger' among the students of his native Bihar. These young people, he reported, wanted India to vacate 'the Chinese aggression' from 'every inch of our territory'. They 'will not tolerate any wrong or weak step by the government'.[29]

With positions hardening, New Delhi invited Chou En-lai for a summit meeting on the border question. The meeting was scheduled for late April, but in the weeks leading up to it there were many attempts to queer the pitch. On 9 March the Dalai Lama appealed to the world 'not to forget the fight of Tibet, a small but independent country occupied by force and by a fanatic and expansionist power'. Three days later a senior Jana Sangh leader urged the prime minister to 'not compromise the sentiments of hundreds of millions of his countrymen', and 'to take all necessary steps against further encroachment by the Chinese'. Less expected was a statement of the Himalayan Study Group of the Congress Parliamentary Party, which urged the prime minister to take a 'firm stand on the border issue'.[30]

In the first week of April the leaders of the non-communist opposition sent a note to the prime minister reminding him of the 'popular feeling' with regard to China. They asked for an assurance that in his talks with Chou En-lai 'nothing will be done which may be construed as a surrender of any part of Indian territory'.[31] Hemmed in from all sides, the prime minister now sought support from the Gandhian sage Vinoba Bhave, then on a walking tour through the Punjab countryside. Nehru spent an hour closeted with Bhave in his village camp; although neither divulged the contents of their talks, these became pretty clear in later speeches by the sage. On 5 April Bhave addressed a meeting at Kurukshetra, the venue, back in mythical time, of the great war between the Pandavas and the Kauravas. On this blood-soaked battlefield he offered a prayer for the success of the Nehru–Chou talks. 'Distrust belonged to the dying political age,' said the Gandhian. 'The new age was building itself around trust and goodwill.' The conversations with the Chinese visitor, hoped Bhave, would be free of anger, bitterness and suspicion.

It was not a message that went down well or widely. Five days before Chou En-lai was due, the Jana Sangh held a large demonstration outside the prime minister's residence. Protesters held up placards reminding Nehru not to forget the martyrs of Ladakh and not to surrender Indian territory. The next day, the non-communist opposition held a mammoth public meeting in Delhi, where the prime minister was warned that if he struck a deal with the Chinese his 'only allies would be the Communists and crypto-Communists'. In this climate, the respected editor Frank Moraes thought the talks were doomed to failure. The gulf between the two countries was 'unbridgeable', he wrote, adding: 'If Mr Chou insists on maintaining all the old postures, all that Mr Nehru can tell him politely is to go back to Peking and think again.'

Nehru, however, insisted that the Chinese prime minister 'would be accorded a courteous welcome befitting the best traditions of this country'. Chou was then on a visit to Burma; an Indian viscount went to pick him up and fly him to Delhi. When he came in 1956, he had been given a stirring public reception; this time – despite the Indian prime minister's hopes – he arrived 'amidst unprecedented security arrangements', travelling from the airport in a closed car. The Hindu Mahasabha organized a 'black flag' demonstration against Chou, but his visit was also opposed by the more mainstream parties. Two jokes doing the rounds expressed the mood in New Delhi. One held that 'Hindi-Chini Bhai Bhai' had become 'Hindi-Chini Bye Bye'; the other asked why Krishna Menon was not in the Indian delegation for the talks, and answered, 'Because he is in Mr Chou En-lai's party.'[32]

Chou En-lai spent a week in New Delhi, meeting Nehru every day, with and without aides. A photograph reproduced in the *Indian Express* after the second day of the talks suggested that they were not going well. It showed Chou raising a toast to Sino-Indian friendship, by clinking his glass with Mrs Indira Gandhi's. Mrs Gandhi was stylishly dressed, in a sari, but was looking quizzically across to her father. On the other side of the table stood Nehru, capless, drinking deeply and glumly from a wine glass while avoiding Chou En-lai's gaze. The only Indian showing any interest at all was the vice-president, S. Radhakrishnan, seen reaching across to clink his glass with Chou's.

Chou En-lai and Nehru spent nearly twenty hours in conversation. The transcripts of their talks are still officially secret, but copies kept by a vigilant (or rule-breaking) official have been consulted by this writer. These highlight vividly the hurt and hostility that pervaded the discussion. Nehru began by recalling all that India had done for China, such as introducing its leaders to the Asia–Africa conference at Bandung and pushing its case in the United Nations. In the light of these good turns, the Chinese 'infringement' of India's frontiers 'came as a great shock'. Chou answered with a complaint of his own, which was that in view of the friendship, ancient and modern, between India and China, 'the activities of the Dalai Lama and his followers have far exceeded the limits of political asylum'.

For two days Nehru and Chou traded charges and counter-charges. If the Indian insisted that the Himalaya had long been considered his country's natural as well as demographic frontier, then the Chinese dismissed the McMahon Line as a pernicious legacy of imperialism. Both prime ministers showed an excellent grasp of detail, each defending his case with impressive exactitude, each mentioning specific villages, valleys, hilltops, rivers, posts and treaties to make or advance his country's claims. Finally, Chou suggested that they try to 'seek a solution' rather than 'repeat arguments'. A suitable settlement, in his view, would be that 'neither side should put forward claims to an area which is no longer under its administrative control'. Some hours later he became more explicit, when he said that 'in the eastern sector, we acknowledge that what India considers its border has been reached by India's actual administration. But, similarly, we think that India should accept that China's administrative personnel has reached the line which it considers to be her border in the western sector.'

Again, suitably decoded, this meant – your case is stronger in the west, but our needs are greater there. And while our case is stronger in the east, perhaps more of your interests are at stake there. Please keep Tawang and its environs, Chou was saying, for all we want is Aksai Chin and the road linking Sinkiang and Tibet.

Chou advocated the retention and recognition of the status quo, but as Nehru pointed out in reply, that term was itself disputed. 'The question is, what is status quo?' said the Indian Prime Minister. For 'the status quo of today is different from the status quo of one or two years ago. To maintain today's status quo would be very unfair if it is different from a previous status quo.' The solution suggested by Chou would justify what, in Nehru's (and India's) view, were gains made illegally and by stealth by China.[33]

Chou En-lai also met the home minister, G. B. Pant, and the vice-president, Dr S. Radhakrishnan, both of whom complained, more in sorrow than in anger, of China's lack of appreciation for all India had done to gain its communist government legitimacy in the eyes of the world. Chou was more combatively challenged by the brilliant and opinionated finance minister, Morarji Desai. When the Chinese leader asked how the Indians could have allowed their soil to be used by Tibetan dissidents, Desai answered that 'in our country everybody holds conventions; the Algerians do so and so do the Indians sometimes [against their Government]'. Then he cleverly (or perhaps mischievously) added: 'The Chinese Prime Minister is aware that Lenin sought asylum in the UK but nobody restricted his political activities. We in India do not encourage anyone to conspire against China but we cannot prevent people from expressing their opinions. Freedom of speech is the basis of our democracy.'[34]

Reporting on his talks with Chou En-lai to the Indian Parliament, Nehru drily noted that 'the significant sentence in the [joint] communiqué [issued by the two sides] is that in spite of all these efforts no solution was found'. An apt epitaph to Chou's visit was also provided by Frank Moraes: 'Like Charles II the Sino-Indian talks seem a long time dying'. They did indeed. For the failed summit was followed by talks between lesser officials, these held in Peking in June–July 1960, in New Delhi in August–October, and finally in the Burmese capital Rangoon in November–December. Each side put forward masses of notes, maps, documents and letters to buttress their arguments. A contemporary commentary on this mountain of evidence remarks that 'it is quite evident that as far as consistency is concerned – and the length of time the claims have been advanced – the advantage lies with the Government of India'. No official Chinese maps showed Aksai Chin as part of China before the 1920s, and a Sinkiang map of the 1930s showed the Kunlun rather than the Karakoram to have been the customary boundary – which had been the Indian claim all along. At least in the western sector (where the Chinese transgressions had taken place) India seemed to have the stronger case. 'The Indian Government was both thorough and careful in presenting its case', whereas the Chinese presentation was marked by a 'maze of internal inconsistencies, quotations out of context, and even blatant and easily discernible falsehoods'.[35]

Even if the Indians had the better of this argument overall, there remained a basic incompatibility of positions. Any evidence emanating from Western sources – even from unaffiliated travellers and itinerant Jesuit priests – was dismissed as tainted by 'imperialism'. The Chinese would, up to a point, present counter-evidence, but in the end they would back off, saying that the border had not been delimited between the two countries as sovereign nations, that India could not claim the (ill-gotten) legacy of British India and that communist China did not stand by any treaties negotiated by anyone presuming to represent Tibet or China before the year of the revolution, 1949.[36]

It is noteworthy that the Chinese wished to maintain their gains in the western sector, where their historical position was weak. In exchange, they were willing to forfeit their much stronger claims in the east. This was clearly because of their need to have speedy access to Tibet. In October 1960, after his own summit with Nehru had failed and the officials' meetings were going nowhere, Chou En-lai vented his frustrations in this regard to the American journalist Edgar Snow. He claimed that the boundary dispute 'came to the fore' only after 'the Dalai Lama had run away and democratic reforms were started in Tibet'. He accused India of wanting to 'turn China's Tibet region into a "buffer zone"'. 'They don't want Tibet to become a Socialist Tibet, as had other places in China', he complained. And then he drew this somewhat far-fetched conclusion: 'The Indian side . . . is using the Sino-Indian boundary question as a card against progressive forces at home and as capital for obtaining "foreign aid".'[37]

V

The territorial map of India was being challenged from the outside by the Chinese. There was also pressure for the map to be redrawn from within, by various linguistic groups left dissatisfied by the recommendations of the States Reorganization Commission of 1956. The Maharashtrians continued to press the centre to give them the city of Bombay. Their case was artfully presented by the dynamic young chief minister, Y. B. Chavan, who argued that this was the way the Congress could make up the losses of the 1957 election, when the Samyukta Maharashtra Samiti had made a serious dent in its vote and seat shares. Eventually, on 1 May 1960, the states of Gujarat and Maharashtra came into being, with Bombay allotted to the latter.

The creation of Maharashtra quelled resentment in the west of India, while giving a boost to unfulfilled expectations in the north. For the one major language group that still didn't have a state of their own were the Punjabis. Their demand had been refused on the grounds that here language was dangerously allied with religion; that what was presented as 'Punjabi Suba' was in fact a 'Sikh Suba', a pretext for what could even become a separate nation of the Sikhs. Anyway, throughout 1960 and 1961 the evergreen Master Tara Singh launched a series of agitations for a Punjabi-speaking state. With him was another Sikh holy man, Sant Fateh Singh, a deputy who would later become a rival of the Master. Led by these two men, the Akali Dal volunteers began to court arrest in groups. Meanwhile, the Master and the Sant would go on periodic fasts, each announced as being 'unto death', each called off before making that supreme sacrifice.[38]

Against the Akalis, Nehru stood firm; the Congress chief minister of Punjab, Pratap Singh Kairon, firmer still. He came down hard on the Akali agitation, putting thousands of protesters in jail. Educated in America, Kairon was a man of drive and ambition, characteristics somewhat lacking in the other chief ministers of the day. Nehru thought this also translated into popular appeal. As he wrote to a friend, 'Sardar

Pratap Kairon's strength in the Punjab is that he represents, and is largely trusted by, the rural people. Those who criticize him are usually city people, whether Sikh or Hindu. During the recent fast of Master Tara Singh, it is extraordinary how the rural areas were not affected by it. They were busy with the Panchayat elections and other activities.'[39]

Kairon was the uncrowned king of Punjab for the eight years he was in power. He had dash and vision; he started an agricultural university, pioneered the tube-well revolution and persuaded peasants to diversify into such remunerative areas as poultry farming. He drew out the Punjabi women, persuading them to study, work, and even – given their athleticism – participate in competitive sports. He mingled easily with the common folk; anyone could walk into his office at any time. On law and order, his dispensation of justice was rough and ready. Thus he instructed his police to fine rather than imprison a peasant protester, who didn't mind becoming a martyr in the off-season but 'can't bear losing his earnings'. But a townsman who broke the law must be jailed, 'for he can't stand separation from the sweet lubricants of family'.[40]

As it happened, these were lubricants that Kairon could not be easily separated from himself. His two sons ran amok during his chief ministership, building huge business empires with the help of the state machinery, flouting property laws and zoning clauses. The chief minister was accused of the 'gross abuse of office to promote the business interests of his sons who have minted crores of rupees in the last few years'. Civil servants were instructed to turn a blind eye to these transgressions. Tough questions were asked in Parliament. Several Congress leaders, among them Indira Gandhi, urged the prime minister to replace Kairon. But Nehru stood by his man, expressing admiration for his drive and his stalwart stand against Punjabi Suba. However, he did agree to constitute a Commission, headed by a Supreme Court judge, to enquire into the allegations against Kairon.[41]

As the historian A. G. Noorani has written, 'in very many ways Sardar Pratap Singh Kairon [of Punjab] and Bakshi Ghulam Mohammed [of Kashmir] were alike'. Both men 'were blunt in speech, direct in approach, impatient with bureaucratic delays and disdainful of the proprieties of public life. Each did a hatchet man's job.' And 'both enjoyed the patronage of Prime Minister Nehru'.[42]

There was bad publicity for the prime minister in one border state, the Punjab, owing to the Akali agitation and the malfeasance of the state administration. And there was worse publicity in another border area, the Naga hills, owing to the dramatic appearance in London of the rebel leader A. N. Phizo. Sometime in 1956 Phizo had hopped across into Burma and then into East Pakistan, from where he continued to direct the Naga resistance movement. After three years of long-distance generalship he decided his case needed the backing of the Western world. Travelling under a forged El Salvadorean passport, he reached Switzerland, where he made contact with Reverend Michael Scott, a radical Anglican priest who had previously worked with the anti-apartheid movement in South Africa. With Scott's help he reached the United Kingdom.[43]

In London Phizo called a series of press conferences where, flanked by Michael Scott, he charged the Indian army with genocide against the Naga people. Also with Scott's help, he printed a pamphlet which spoke of how 'our age-old freedom has been and is being systematically destroyed by the Indian Army . . . They have tried to subjugate our nation and to annihilate it.' The army's campaign was dubbed 'a plan of racial extermination in the worst manner of the European fascists'. Indian troops, claimed Phizo, were 'shooting Christian pastors and church leaders, burning men and women alive, burning churches'. His pamphlet demanded an end to the 'slaughter', and the recognition by the government of India of 'the sovereign and independent state of Nagaland'. Phizo said that an independent Nagaland would 'wish to remain within the fold of the Christian nations, and the Commonwealth . . . [T]iny Nagaland is happy to be a follower of Jesus Christ, whom we have come to believe in as our Saviour'.[44]

Phizo was here simultaneously appealing to the British love of the underdog, to memories of the still recent war against fascism (with the Nagas placed in the role of the Jews, and the Indian government as the Nazis) and to the Christian sentiments of his audience. The rhetoric was somewhat artless, and yet surprisingly successful. His cause was taken up by David Astor, the liberal owner of the *Observer* newspaper who had played a stellar role in the fight against the Nazis. Phizo's charges were given wide play by the paper, and by several other journals too.[45]

Always sensitive to the opinions of the British press, the government of India answered with a propagandist tract of its own. This said that while the prime minister had assured the Nagas of 'maximum autonomy', under Phizo's leadership, 'the Naga movement began to assume a violent character'. The extent of violence and the suffering of civilians was not denied, but the blame for this was placed on the insurgents. The government's stand remained that 'they are prepared to concede the largest possible autonomy to the Nagas in their internal affairs in addition to all the privileges of Indian citizenship, such as representation in Parliament, but they could not agree to an independent state for them'.

This was reasonably put, but the effect was spoilt by an appendix which cast Phizo as a villain motivated merely by frustration and failure:

> Phizo's mental attitude has been conditioned by a series of frustrations and setbacks. He failed in the Matriculation examination. His attempts to establish himself first in motor-parts business and then as an insurance man did not meet with success. He was attacked by paralysis, which disfigured his face and as a result he acquired a strong complex . . . He has been known to have been suffering from a strong feeling of guilt for having misled his co-tribesmen into a path of hostility and violence, resulting in many deaths and reducing many of them to a state of misery.[46]

However, between the government of India and the leader of the Naga National Council stood a number of 'moderate' Nagas. These had banded together in a Naga Peoples' Convention which, from 1957 onwards, had begun seeking a peaceful settlement to the problem. The Aos were prominent among these peacemakers, but there were representatives of other tribes too. On 30 July 1960 the Naga Peoples' Convention presented a memorandum to the prime minister demanding a separate state of Nagaland within the Indian Union. This would have its own governor, chief minister, council of ministers, and legislative assembly, and the Union Parliament would not have the power to interfere with Naga religion, social practices or customary law.[47]

The demand for a Naga state within India was resisted by the Assamese elite, loath to let go of any part of their province. But with the Naga question now successfully internationalized, Nehru thought it prudent to make the concession. In the first week of August 1960 he announced in Parliament that a state of Nagaland was to be carved out of Assam. The decision to create this, the smallest state of the Union, gave rise to a series of responses that were interesting, varied and yet utterly predictable. The right-wing Jana Sangh saw the creation of Nagaland as 'an act fraught with explosive possibilities'; it was a concession to terror, 'tantamount to putting a premium on violence and rebellion', a wanton encouragement to 'regionalism and parochialism' which would endanger 'the unity and integrity of the country'. Some other tribes in Assam, the Khasis, the Garos and the Jaintias, resolved to fight for a state of their own, to be called 'Eastern Frontier'.[48]

Also predictable was the response of Phizo's men. Some Naga intellectuals thought that the granting of statehood within India was 'not only all they can hope to get but all they need to protect their social and political identity'. But how was one to convince the ordinary villager of this? For, as one newspaper noted, the 'armed rebels can emerge from the jungle any night with arguments that the statehood party are Quislings, and with bullet or bayonet correct any who disagree.'[49]

VI

After a decade in which it had seemed confidently in control, Jawaharlal Nehru's government suddenly looked very shaky indeed. There was dissent in the south, in Kerala and Tamil Nadu, and in the border zone, in Punjab and the Naga hills. Meanwhile a Ford Foundation report warned of the 'stark threat' of an 'ominous crisis' in the agricultural sector. Unless food production was tripled in the next decade, it claimed, there would be mass starvation and famine in India.[50]

More worrying, at least to Nehru, was the resurgence of communal conflict after a decade of comparative social peace. In June 1960 virulent anti-Bengali riots broke out in Assam. The victims were post-Partition refugees from East Bengal, who were accused of taking jobs from the Assamese and not speaking their language. Thousands of homes were destroyed and many Bengalis killed. Others fled across the border into refugee camps in West Bengal. The home minister, Lal Bahadur Shastri, flew to Assam to forge an uneasy peace which endorsed Assamese as the official state language while permitting the use of Bengali in the district where the migrants were in a majority.[51]

Then, in January 1961, a religious riot broke out in the central Indian city of Jabalpur. A Hindu girl had committed suicide; it was alleged that she took her life because she had been assaulted by two Muslim men. The claim was given lurid publicity by a local Jana Sangh newspaper, whereupon Hindu students went on a rampage through the town, attacking Muslim homes and burning shops. In retaliation a Muslim group torched a Hindu neighbourhood. The rioting continued for days, spreading also to the countryside. It was the most serious such incident since Partition, its main sufferers being poor Muslims, mostly weavers and *bidi* (cigarette) workers.[52]

The troubles on the border with China and the intensification of social conflict within the country gave rise to fresh concerns about the future of democratic India. In 1960 an American scholar published an impressively learned book with a simple title – *India* – but a portentous subtitle: *The Most Dangerous Decades*. The chapter and section titles were also revealing – 'Will the Union Survive?' was one, 'Totalitarian Equilibrium?' another. The writer was disturbed by the divisions of caste, region, religion and language, and by the rise of Indian communism. There were, he felt, 'seemingly irresistible compulsions of totalitarian experiments of one sort or another in the nature of the Indian Union'.[53]

The following year, 1961, the writer Aldous Huxley visited India after a gap of thirty-five years. He was overwhelmed by what he found, namely, 'the prospect of overpopulation, underemployment, growing unrest'. 'India is almost infinitely depressing', he wrote to a friend, 'for there seems to be no solution to its problems in any way that any of us [in the West] regard as acceptable.' Writing to his brother Julian, Huxley expressed the view that 'when Nehru goes, the government will become a military dictatorship – as in so many of the newly independent states, for the army seems to be the only highly organized centre of power'.[54]

The verdict of the British intellectual was echoed by the workaday journalist. Visiting India soon after Huxley, a reporter for the London *Daily Mail* thought that 'until now Nehru alone has been the unifying, cohesive force behind India's Government and foreign policy'. But after he was gone, 'the powers of caste and religion, of Rightism and Leftism . . . could eventually split this country from top to bottom and plunge it back 100 years'.[55]

VII

During 1960 and 1961, as some Indians rioted and others protested, their government continued its correspondence with its Chinese counterpart. No longer were these statesmanlike, or even conducted by statesmen; rather they consisted of notes exchanged by anonymous functionaries accusing the other party of transgressions of one kind or another. A Chinese note listed fifteen violations of their air space by Indian aircraft;

an Indian note listed various incidents of ill-treatment of Indian citizens in Tibet.[56]

These exchanges, published in successive White Papers by the government of India, led to a renewed call for Krishna Menon's head. Leading the charge was J. B. Kripalani, the Socialist Party MP from Sitamarhi in Bihar. Scholar, teacher, *khadi* worker and rebel, Kripalani was an authentic hero of the Indian freedom struggle. His moral authority derived in part from the fact that he had come close to Gandhi while aiding him in the Champaran *satyagraha* of 1917, years before Nehru himself made the acquaintance of the Mahatma. Kripalani had also been president of the Congress and, of course, spent many years in jail for his cause.

On 11 April 1961 Kripalani delivered what was described at the time as 'perhaps the greatest speech that has been made on the floor of that House since Independence'. This was a blistering attack on the defence minister. Under Krishna Menon's stewardship, said Kripalani, 'we have lost 12,000 square miles of our territory without striking a single blow'. Army promotions, he claimed, were based not on merit but 'according to the whims and fancies of the defence minister or what will suit his political and ideological purposes'. Menon had 'created cliques [and] lowered the morale of our [armed] forces'. In a stinging indictment, Kripalani charged the minister with 'wasting the money of this poor and starving nation', with 'the neglect of the defence of the country', and with 'having lent his support to the totalitarian and dictatorial regimes against the will of the people for freedom'.

Kripalani ended his speech with an appeal to the conscience of the members of the ruling party. Recalling how, back in 1940, the Conservative members of the British Parliament had compelled their prime minister, Neville Chamberlain, to resign, he appealed to those 'Congressmen who were not afraid of the British bullets and bayonets to place the good of the nation above the good of the party'. With this parting shot Kripalani sat down, to vigorous applause from the opposition benches.[57]

Throughout the second half of 1961 the Indian Parliament witnessed a series of bitter debates about the dispute with China. The prime minister himself was harried and hurt by a group of terriers at his heels. Three in particular nipped hard: Atal Behari Vajpayee of the Jana Sangh, Hem Barua of the Praja Socialist Party and N. G. Ranga of the Swatantra Party. Nehru was accused of turning a blind eye to Chinese 'occupation' of Indian territory and of placing himself magisterially above the fray. 'In regard to border disputes', said one member, 'the prime minister has a tendency to act like an umpire in a cricket match rather than as one whose interests are involved'. The criticisms had a personal, polemical, edge. For Nehru also served as foreign minister, and the policy of friendship with China was known to be his particular project. Unaccustomed to such hostility, the prime minister became increasingly irritable, on one occasion going so far as to refer to his critics as 'childish and infantile'.[58]

By now, there were elements in his own party who had made known their view that the prime minister should take a stronger line on China. When an opposition member taunted Nehru with regard to his remark that Aksai Chin was barren land, with no grass growing on it, a Congress MP added this telling supplement: 'No hair grows on my head. Does it mean that the head has no value?' This was widely viewed as a dig at Nehru who, of course, was completely bald himself.[59]

VIII

In the third week of December 1961 a detachment of the Indian army moved up to the borders of the Portuguese colony of Goa. For a decade now New Delhi had sought, by persuasion and non-violence, to convince Portugal to give up that territory. With those measures failing, Nehru's government decided to 'liberate' Goa by force.

On the morning of 18 December Indian troops entered Goa from three directions: Sawantwadi in the north, Karwar in the south and Belgaum in the east. Meanwhile, aeroplanes dropped leaflets exhorting the Goans to 'be calm and brave' and to 'rejoice in your freedom and strengthen it'. By the evening of the 18th the capital, Panjim, had been encircled. The troops were helped by the locals, who pointed out where the Portuguese had laid mines. The colonists fired a few shots before withdrawing. In the smaller enclaves of Daman and Diu the resistance was somewhat stiffer. In all, some fifteen Indian soldiers lost their lives, and perhaps twice as many Portuguese. Thirty-six hours after the invasion began, the Portuguese governor general signed a document of unconditional surrender.[60]

The Western press had a field day with this display of 'Indian hypocrisy'. Exposed for so long to lectures by Nehru and Krishna

Menon, they now hit back by attacking the use of force by a nation that professed 'non-violence'. The action was also represented as a breach of international law and, more absurdly, as a threat to Christians and Christianity in Goa.[61] In fact, 61 per cent of Goa was Hindu, while prominent Goan Christians, such as the journalist Frank Moraes and the Archbishop Cardinal Gracias, had an honoured place in Indian public life. There had long been an indigenous freedom movement within Goa and many, perhaps most, Goans welcomed the Indian action. In any case, the Goans were now at liberty to choose their own leaders, something always denied them by the Portuguese.

That Goa was legitimately part of India was not in dispute. That India had waited long enough before acting was also evident. Still, the timing of what was called 'Operation Vijay' was open to question. Why did it take place in December 1961 rather than December 1960 or December 1962? Nehru perhaps thought he had waited long enough for the Portuguese to leave; fourteen whole years. And he was under pressure from both left and right on the issue; the Jana Sangh and the communists, in a rare show of agreement, were urging him to use the army to liberate the colony. Still, the suspicion lingered that the precise timing of the invasion was determined by the electoral needs of his colleague Krishna Menon. Before the troops went in, the defence minister inspected them on the border. As the *New York Times* reported, he was here 'conducting a double campaign': one for the war that was about to commence, the other for the general election that had been scheduled for February 1962.[62]

In that election, Krishna Menon would be opposed by his parliamentary *bête noire*, Acharya Kripalani, who had announced that he would shift from the safe seat of Sitamarhi and take on the defence minister in the constituency he represented, North Bombay. All the opposition parties (the communists excepted) announced that they would support him. A battle of prestige was brewing; since the prime minister had refused to drop Menon from the Cabinet, the opposition now hoped that he would be removed via the ballot box.

Less than two months after his troops marched into Goa, Menon was in Bombay to fight his corner of the 1962 general election. Batting for him were the powerful Maharashtra chief minister Y. B. Chavan and senior members of the Union Cabinet. Even Menon's known critics in government, such as Morarji Desai and Jagjivan Ram, were commanded to go out and campaign on his behalf. Speaking on Kripalani's side were such stalwarts as C. Rajagopalachari, as well as many distinguished non-party men – lawyers, intellectuals and industrialists.

The contest was, among other things, a tribute to the cosmopolitan character of Bombay, with a Malayali and a Sindhi competing for the affections of the people of a state not their own. The constituency was very heterogeneous indeed – many Marathi and Gujarati speakers, but also many Bhaiyyas from UP, Goans, Sindhis and Tamilians. These various segments were wooed by both contestants, with the campaign manifesting an intensity commensurate to the stature of the disputants, and the importance of their dispute.

In the rich and by now very extensive history of Indian elections, there has perhaps been no single contest so loudly trumpeted as this one. The journal *Link*, sympathetic to Menon, called it 'the most important election in the history of our democracy'. The social worker Jayaprakash Narayan, a friend of Kripalani's, said that in this contest 'the future of Indian democracy and our spiritual values are at stake'.

The campaign was colourful, replete with evocative posters and savage slogans. The left-wing weekly *Blitz* ran a blistering campaign against a man they chose to refer to as 'Cripple-loony'. On the other side, Menon was lampooned by versifiers in several languages. One ditty went: *Chini hamla hoté hain/ Menon Saab soté hain/ Sona hai tho soné do/ Kripalani ji to aané do.* (As China advances, Menon sleeps/ Let him sleep if he must/ But call Kripalani to be with us.) An English verse advanced the same sentiments, if more elegantly: I do not hold with all these cracks and mockery/ At Krishna Menon./ It is his virtues I would rather pin on./ For instance, consider his skill with crockery:/ What could be finer/ Than the loving care with which he handles china?

The prime minister took the challenge to Menon as a challenge to himself. Nehru inaugurated the Congress campaign in Bombay, and found reason to support his man in other places as well. In Sangli, in Poona, in Baroda, he said that a defeat for Menon would signal a defeat for his own policies of socialism and non-alignment. His mentor's support helped Menon immeasurably. So did the liberation of Goa, which resonated well with the public of North Bombay, and not just with the Goans among them.

In the event, Kripalani's campaign was undone by Nehru's speeches, the action in Goa and the strength of the Congress Party machinery. He lost by more than 100,000 votes.[63]

IX

In the general elections of 1952 and 1957 the Congress had made much of its being the party of the freedom struggle. In 1962, however, its campaign focused more on what it had done since. Its policies, it said, had increased agricultural and industrial production, enhanced education and life expectancy and promoted the unity of the country. Never having held power, the opposition could not match these claims with counter-claims of their own.[64] In the event, the Congress comfortably retained its majority in Parliament, winning 361 seats out of 494 all told. The communists secured 29 seats, while the new opposition party, Swatantra, put up a decent show, returning 18 MPs. In the state of Madras there was a challenge from the quasi-secessionist DMK, which won 7 parliamentary seats (to go with 50 in the Legislative Assembly). But on the whole the Congress Party was confirmed in its pre-eminence, and Jawaharlal Nehru entered into his fourth term as prime minister.

The opposition within had been shown its place, but the opposition without remained. Throughout the spring and summer of 1962 clashes on the border continued. In July the Delhi journal *Seminar* ran a symposium on India's defence policy. One contributor insisted that 'the People's Republic of China does not pose any military threat to our country'. Another contributor was not so sure. This was General Thimayya, now retired, who noted that there were threats from both Pakistan and China. Where the country was moderately well placed to meet an attack from the former, Thimayya could not 'even as a soldier envisage India taking on China in an open conflict on its own. China's present strength in manpower, equipment and aircraft exceeds our resources a hundredfold with the full support of the USSR, and we could never hope to match China in the foreseeable future. It must be left to the politicians and the diplomats to ensure our security.' The 'present strength of the army and air forces of India', said the general, 'are even below the "minimum insurance" we can give to our people'.[65]

The implications were clear: either the diplomats should seek a treaty deal with China, or the politicians should canvass for military help from the Western bloc. But the rising tide of patriotic sentiment ruled out the first; and the non-alignment of the prime minister, strengthened by the anti-Americanism of his defence minister, ruled out the second.

In the third week of July 1962 there were clashes between Indian and Chinese troops in the Galwan valley of Ladakh. Then, in early

September, a conflict arose over the Dhola/Thag La ridge, in the valley of the Namka Chu river, some sixty miles west of Tawang. The region was where the borders of India, Tibet and Bhutan all met; the exact alignment of the McMahon Line was in dispute here. The Indians claimed the ridge fell south of the Line; the Chinese argued that it was on their side.[66]

It was back in June that a platoon of the Assam Rifles had established a post at Dhola, as part of the still continuing forward policy. On 8 September the Chinese placed a post of their own at Thag La, which overlooked (and threatened) Dhola. Peking and New Delhi exchanged angry letters. On the ground, Indian commanders were divided as to what to do. Some said that the Chinese must be shifted from Thag La. Others said that it would be too difficult, since the terrain was disadvantageous to the Indians (Thag La lay some 2,000 feet above Dhola). Meanwhile, at the site itself, the Chinese troops took to addressing homilies in Hindi via a megaphone. 'Hindi-Chini bhai bhai', they shouted: 'Ye zamin hamara hai. Tum vapas jao' (Indians and Chinese are brothers-in-arms, but this land is ours, so you may please vacate it).

The stalemate continued for three weeks, troops of the two nations facing each other across a narrow river, not knowing whether their leaders were making peace or about to go to war. Finally, on 3 October, Lieutenant General Umrao Singh, who had counselled prudence, was replaced as corps commander by B. M. Kaul, who flew in from Delhi to take command in NEFA. Those who recommended caution were overruled. 'To all objections Kaul gave sweeping and unrealistic assurances, based on the assumption of Delhi's future logistical support for any gamble he might now take.'[67] To dislodge the Chinese from Thag La, he now moved two battalions up from the plains. The troops had light arms and only three days of rations, no mortars or rocket launchers and only promises that supplies would catch up with them.

Indian soldiers reached the Namka Chu valley on the afternoon of 9 October, after a march through 'mud, mountains and rain'. 'Exhausted by days of marching over massive heights and appalling weather conditions, [these were] troops badly in need of a breather and the tools for war.'[68] That same evening they set up a post in a herder's hut from where they would, when reinforcements arrived, try to uproot the enemy. They were not given the chance. On the morning of the 10th the Chinese attacked. The jawans fought hard, but they had been drained by the long march up. They were also outnumbered and outgunned, their light arms proving no match to the heavy mortar used by the Chinese.

From 1959, in both Ladakh and NEFA, the Chinese and Indians had played cat-and-mouse, sending troops to fill up no-man's-land, clashing here and there, while their leaders exchanged letters and occasionally even met. Now things escalated to unprecedented levels. The Indian siting of Dhola was answered by the Chinese coming to Thag La, directly above it; this in turn provoked an attempt by the Indians to shift them. When this failed, Nehru, back in Delhi, told the press that the army had been given instructions to once more try and push out the 'enemy'.

In the event it was the enemy who acted first. A phoney war, which had lasted all of three years, was made very real on the night of 19–20 October, when the Chinese simultaneously launched an invasion in both the eastern and western sectors. The 'blitzkrieg' across the Himalaya had come, as 'Pragmatist' had predicted it would. And, as he had feared, the Indians were unprepared. That night, wrote the *New York Times*, a 'smouldering situation burst into flame' as 'heavy battles broke out in both of the disputed areas. Masses of Chinese troops under the cover of thunderous mortar fire drove the Indians back on each front'. Both sides had built up forces on the border, but 'independent observers laid the onslaught to the Chinese'. The Chinese attacked in waves, armed with medium machine guns backed by heavy mortars. Two Chinese divisions were involved in the invasion, these using five times as many troops as had the Indians.[69]

The Indians were 'taken by surprise' as the Chinese quickly overran many positions, crossed the Namkha Chu valley and made for the monastery in Tawang. Another detachment made for the eastern part of NEFA. Chinese troops moved deeper and deeper into Indian territory. Eight posts were reported to have fallen in Ladakh; almost twenty in NEFA. Tawang itself had come under the control of the Chinese.[70]

The ease with which the Chinese took Indian positions should not have come as a surprise. Their troops had been on the Tibetan plateau in strength from the mid-1950s, fighting or preparing to fight Khampa rebels. Unlike the Indians, they were well used to battles in the high mountains. Besides, access was much easier from the Tibetan side, the relatively flat terrain conducive to road building and troop movement. The geographical advantage was all to the Chinese. From Assam up to the McMahon Line the climb was very steep, the hills covered with thick vegetation and the climate often damp and wet. The Indian forward posts were hopelessly ill equipped; with no proper roads, they 'lived from air-drop to air-drop', dependent on supplies and for survival on sorties by helicopters.[71]

The Indian problems were compounded by a vacuum of leadership. On 18 October General Kaul had come down with acute chest pains. He was evacuated to Delhi and his corps was left leaderless for five days, by which time Tawang had fallen.

On 24 October the Chinese halted their advance, while Chou En-lai wrote to Nehru seeking a way to 'stop the border clashes' and 'reopen border negotiations'. Over the next fortnight they wrote each other two letters apiece, these achieving nothing. Chou said that China and India shared a common enemy, 'imperialism'. The current conflict notwithstanding, he thought it possible for both of them to 'restore Sino-Indian relations to the warm and friendly pattern of earlier days and even improve on that pattern'. His solution was for each side to withdraw twenty kilometres behind the line of actual control, and disengage.

Nehru's replies displayed his wounds for all to see. 'Nothing in my long political career has hurt me more and grieved me more', he said, than 'the hostile and unfriendly twist given in India–China relations' in recent years, culminating in 'what is in effect a Chinese invasion of India', in 'violent contradiction' of the claim that China wanted to settle the border question by 'peaceful means'. Peking had taken 'a deliberate cold-blooded decision' to 'enforce their alleged boundary claims by military invasion of India'. Chou's offer, he wrote, was aimed at consolidating and keeping the gains of this aggression. The solution he proposed was for Chinese troops to get behind the McMahon Line in the east, and to revert in the west to their position as of 7 November 1959, thus cancelling out three years of steady gains made by establishing posts in territory under dispute.[72]

Meanwhile, a casualty in Delhi had been added to all those suffered on the front. Now that Indian weaknesses had been so comprehensively exposed, V. K. Krishna Menon was finally removed as defence minister. (He was first shifted to the Ministry of Defence Production, then dropped from the Cabinet altogether.) Menon's exit was accompanied by a call by Delhi for Western arms. On 28 October the American ambassador went to see the prime minister. Nehru 'was frail, brittle and seemed small and old. He was obviously desperately tired.' India must have military aid from the West, he said.[73] Soon Britain and America were sending transport planes with arms and ammunition. France and Canada had also agreed to supply weapons.[74]

On 8 November the prime minister moved a resolution in Parliament deploring the fact that China had 'betrayed' the spirit of Panchsheel and India's 'uniform gestures of goodwill and friendship' by initiating 'a massive invasion'. The hurt was palpable; that 'we in India, who have . . . sought the friendship of China . . . and pleaded their cause in the councils of the world should now ourselves be victims of new imperialism and expansionism by a country which says that it is against all imperialism'. China may call itself 'communist', said Nehru, but it had revealed itself as 'an expansionist, imperious-minded country deliberately invading' another.

Nehru's speech might be read as a belated acknowledgement of the correctness of Vallabhbhai Patel's warning of 1950: that communism in China was an extreme expression of nationalism, rather than its nullification. The debate that followed took a full week; 165 members spoke, apparently a record.[75]

Back on the borders, the lull in the fighting was broken by a second Chinese offensive on 15 November. A 500-mile front was attacked in NEFA. There was a bitter fight in Walong, where soldiers from the Dogra and Kumaon regiments, hardy hill men all, fought heroically and almost wrested control of a key ridge from the Chinese.[76] There was also some spirited resistance in Ladakh, where the field commander was not subject to conflicting signals from Delhi. Here the troops stood their ground, and 'forced the Chinese to pay dearly for the territory they won'.[77]

But across most of NEFA it had been a very poor show indeed. Here the Indians simply disintegrated, with platoons and even whole regiments retreating in disarray. When the Chinese swept through there was much confusion among the Indian commanders. Where should they make their first, and perhaps last, stand? The option of Tawang was considered and abandoned. One general advocated Bomdi La, a good sixty miles to the south, where supplies could be easily sent up from plains. Finally, it was decided to stop the Chinese advance at Se La, a mere fifteen miles from Tawang.

The decision to make the stand at Se La was Kaul's. When he fell ill, his place had been taken by Lieutenant General Harbaksh Singh, a highly regarded commander with much field experience. But before Singh could adequately reorganize the defences, Kaul had flown back from Delhi to resume charge once more.

The Chinese had occupied Tawang on 25 October. When they halted there, the Indians were deceived into inaction. In fact, the Chinese were working on improving the road to Se La. On 14 November the Indians began a proposed counter-attack, choosing as their target an enemy post near Walong. Meanwhile, battles broke out north of Se La, the Chinese again with the advantage. The garrison commander, in panic, ordered withdrawal, and his brigade began retreating towards Bomdi La. There they found that the Chinese had already skirted Se La and cut off the road behind them. Large sections were mown down in flight, while others abandoned their arms and fled singly or in small groups. Se La was easily taken, and Bomdi La fell soon afterwards.[78]

The fall of Bomdi La led to panic in Assam. An Indian reporter, reaching Tezpur on 20 November, found it a 'ghost town'. The administration had pulled back to Gauhati, after burning the papers at the Collectorate and the currency notes at the local bank. Before leaving, 'the doors of the mental hospital [were] opened to release the bewildered inmates'.[79]

Back in Delhi and Bombay, young men were queuing up to join the army. The recruiting centres were usually sleepy places, open one or two days a week, with 90 per cent of the boys who showed up failing the first examination. Now their compounds were 'besieged by thousands of would-be recruits'. Some were labourers and factory hands; others, unemployed graduates. They all hoped that in this emergency 'the army will lower its physical requirements and give them food and lodging and a purpose in life'.[80]

It seems unlikely that these men would have made a better showing than those who had already fought, and lost. In any case, they did not get the chance. Poised to enter the plains of Assam, the Chinese instead announced a unilateral ceasefire on 22 November. In NEFA they pulled back to north of the McMahon Line. In the Ladakh sector they likewise retreated to positions they had held before the present hostilities began.

Why did the Chinese pack up and go home? Some thought they were deterred from coming further by the rallying of all parties, including the communists, around the government. The Western powers had pledged support, and were already flying in arms and ammunition.[81] As important as these considerations of politics were the facts of nature. For winter was setting in, and soon the Himalaya would be snowbound. And by pressing deep into India, the Chinese would make their supply lines longer and more difficult to maintain.

While the end of the war can be thus explained, its origins are harder to understand. There were no White Papers issued from the Chinese side, and their records are not open – and perhaps never will be. All one can say is that behind such a carefully co-ordinated attack there must have been several years of preparation. As for its precise timing, a speculation offered at the time – and which still seems plausible – was that the two superpowers, the Soviet Union and the United States, were preoccupied with the Cuban missile crisis, allowing Peking its little adventure without fear of reprisal.

The border war had underlined Chinese superiority in 'arms, communications, strategy, logistics, and planning'.[82] According to Defence Ministry statistics, 1,383 Indian soldiers had been killed, 3,968 were taken prisoner, while 1,696 were still missing.[83] These losses were small by the standards of modern warfare, yet the war represented a massive defeat in the Indian imagination. Naturally, the search began for scapegoats. Over the years, a series of self-exculpatory memoirs were published by the generals in the field. Each sought to shift the blame away from himself and towards another commander, or towards the politicians who had neglected their warnings and issued orders that were impossible to carry out. In his own contribution to the genre, Major General D. K. Palit – director general of military operations at the time of the war – notes that in these memoirs 'there are striking inconsistencies; each had his own wicket to defend'. Then he adds: 'Hindsight tends to lend rationality to events that in fact are innocent of coherence or logical sequence.'[84]

Among the Indian public, the principal sentiment was that of betrayal, of being taken for a ride by an unscrupulous neighbour whom they had naively chosen to trust and support. In his letters to Chou En-lai, Nehru expressed these feelings as well as anyone else. But for the deeper origins of the dispute one must turn to his earlier writings, in particular to an interview in which he spoke not as India's leader but as a student of world history. Back in 1959, Nehru had told Edgar Snow that 'the basic reason for the Sino-Indian dispute was that they were both "new nations", in that both were newly independent and under *dynamic nationalistic leaderships*, and in a sense were "meeting" at their frontiers for the first time in history'. In the past, 'there were buffer zones between the two countries; both sides were *remote* from the borders'. Now, however, 'they were meeting as *modern nations* on the borders'. Hence it 'was natural that a certain degree of conflict should be generated before they can stabilize their frontiers'.[85]

The India–China conflict, then, was a clash of national myths, national egos, national insecurities and – ultimately and inevitably – national armies. In this sense, however unique (and uniquely disturbing) it must have seemed to Indians, it was very representative. For competing claims to territory have been an all too common source of conflict in the modern world. Nehru's comments to Edgar Snow said as much. However, let us give the last word to an unlikely authority, the beat poet Allen Ginsberg. In March 1962 Ginsberg began a two-year trip around the subcontinent, bumming and slumming in the search for nirvana. In August, just as the clashes on the border began to intensify, he made an entry in his diary which set the India/China border conflict properly in perspective:

The Fights 1962:

US vs Russia in General / China vs Formosa over possession / India vs China over border territory / India vs Pakistan over possession Kashmir – Religious / India vs Portugal over possession Goa / India vs Nagas over Independence / Egypt vs Israel over possession of territory and Religion / E. Germany vs W. Germany sovereignty / Cuba vs USA – Ideas / N. Korea vs So. Korea – Sovereignty / Indonesia vs Holland – Territory / France vs Algeria – Territory / Negroes vs whites – US / Katanga vs Leopoldville / Russian Stalinists vs Russian Kruschevists / Peru APRA vs Peru Military / Argentine Military versus Argentine Bourgeois / Navajo Peyotists vs Navajo Tribal Council – Tribal / W. Irian? / Kurds vs Iraq / Negro vs Whites – So. Africa – Race / US Senegal vs Red Mali – Territory / Ghana vs Togo – Territory / Ruanda Watusi vs Ruanda Bahutu – Tribe power / Kenya Kadu vs Kenya Kana – Tribe power / Somali vs Aethopia, Kenya, French Somali / Tibet Lamas vs Chinese Tibetan secularists / India vs E. Pak – Assam Bengal over Border & Tripura / Algeria vs Morocco over Sahara.[86]

16

PEACE IN OUR TIME

Here we are having a grudging time, both with the weather and the problems which are arising; Kashmir, in particular, is giving us a severe headache.

VALLABHBHAI PATEL to G. D. BIRLA, May 1949

I

APART FROM THE SEVERAL thousand Indian soldiers dead or injured, the casualties of the China war included the chief of army staff, General P. N. Thapar (who resigned, citing ill health), the failed strategic thinker Lieutenant General B. M. Kaul (who was retired prematurely) and the defence minister, V. K. Krishna Menon (who was sacked). A greater casualty still was the reputation of Jawaharlal Nehru. The border war was Nehru's most consequential failure in fifteen years as prime minister. The inability to bring about radical land reform affected the rural poor; the dismissal of the Kerala communists angered many people in that state; other sections likewise had their own grievances against the government. But the failure to protect the nation's territory was a different matter altogether. The humiliation that resulted was felt, as military defeats invariably are, by the nation as a whole.

Krishna Menon and the army brass had been sacrificed, yet the prime minister knew that deep down he was ultimately responsible for the disaster, in a general sense, as the head of government, and in a very specific sense, as one who had guided and determined India's attitudes and policies towards China.

Those attitudes and policies now had to be rethought. Nehru could at last see what Vallabhbhai Patel had sensed long ago: that communism in China was merely a more bellicose form of nationalism. The border war provoked a reluctant tilt towards the United States, who had come forth with arms while Soviet Russia stayed neutral. A key player in this shift was the American ambassador in New Delhi, John Kenneth Galbraith. A Harvard economics professor who was sceptical of the free market, a scholar of art history, a noted *bon vivant* and wit, Galbraith was, to Indian eyes, a very untypical American indeed. (In fact, he was by birth Canadian.) Things were changing, back in Washington, where a new young president, John F. Kennedy, was seeking to reverse the American government's image as uncaring at home and arrogant abroad. It was these winds of liberalism that carried Galbraith along to India.

From the time he took charge in April 1961, the ambassador got on famously with Nehru. They discussed art and music and literature; this, on the Indian's part, a welcome diversion from the daily grind but on the American's a shrewd softening-up of a mind long prejudiced against his country. In March 1962 the First Lady, Jacqueline Kennedy, arrived for a trip through India, where she saw the Taj Mahal and Rajput forts and had extended conversations with the prime minister.

Nehru was charmed by Mrs Kennedy's beauty, as he had been by her envoy's brains. But the thaw would not have become a *tilt* had it not been for the war with China. On 9 November, after the first wave of attacks, Galbraith was called in to meet the prime minister. He found him 'deathly tired and I thought a little beaten'. (Earlier in the day, Nehru had made a speech in Parliament which was 'a good deal less than Churchillian'.) A request was made for arms from America. This came at a cost that could never be measured in money alone. For, as Galbraith wrote to President Kennedy, all his life Nehru had

> sought to avoid being dependent upon the United States and the United Kingdom – most of his personal reluctance to ask (or thank) for aid has been based on this pride . . . Now nothing is so important to him, more personally than politically, than to maintain the semblance of this independence. His age no longer allows of readjustment. To a point we can, I feel, be generous on this.[1]

By late November the arms began arriving, carried in planes that also contained soldiers in uniform. As an American journalist wrote, this meant the 'collapse of his [Nehru's] non-alignment policy'; to many those dark blue uniforms carried 'a special meaning', contained in one single word: 'failure'.[2] For the American ambassador, however, those uniforms spelt the word 'opportunity'. This might be the beginnings of an entente to contain a communist power potentially more threatening than Soviet Russia itself. As Galbraith wrote to President Kennedy,

> the Chinese are not quarreling with the Soviets over some academic points of doctrine. They are, one must assume, serious about their revolution. The natural area of expansion is in their part of the world. The only Asian country which really stands in their way is India and *pari passu* the only Western country that is assuming responsibility is the United States. It seems obvious to me [that] there should be some understanding between the two countries. We should expect to make use of India's political position, geographical position, political power and manpower or anyhow ask.[3]

II

In response to the Indian request, President Kennedy sanctioned the supply of a million rounds for machine guns, 40,000 land mines and 100,000 mortar rounds.[4] This fell far short of the Grand Alliance that his ambassador was recommending; yet it was far in excess of what other Americans thought New Delhi deserved. A bitter opponent of arms supply to India was Senator Richard B. Russell of Georgia, the long-serving chairman of the Senate Armed Forces Committee. A crusty old reactionary – doughtily opposed to desegregation and the like – Russell had previously termed India an 'unreliable friend' and called Nehru a 'demagogue and a hypocrite'. Now he told the Associated Press that he was 'against giving India any of our modern weapons for the principal reason that we would be just giving them to the Chinese Communists'. The Indians, said the senator, had 'put on a disgraceful exhibition in permitting themselves to be driven out of what should have been impregnable strongholds in the border mountains. They seem incapable of fighting and if we supply them with weapons they will just fall into the hands of the Communists'. While he was at present opposed to giving 'one dime of weapons to India', Russell said he might have a rethink if India's old rulers, the British, were prepared to 'take over the matter of re-organizing and re-training their military forces'.[5]

Russell's remarks were widely reported in the United States as well as in India. The storm of correspondence that it generated is a unique prism through which one can view US–India relations. One would expect the two countries to have been allies, if only because both were large and culturally diverse democracies. However, their relations had been clouded by suspicion on both sides – suspicion of India's non-alignment on one side, and of American military aid to Pakistan on the other. It did not help that these were both preachy peoples, whose foreign policy and diplomacy were invariably accompanied by an unctuous self-righteousness. Where democratic ideals sought to bring the two countries closer together, pride and patriotism pulled them further apart.

Thus, while Kennedy and Galbraith might have deplored Senator Russell's stand, he received much support from across Middle America. A correspondent from Wichita, Kansas, thanked the senator for warning that it was 'very dangerous for the US to make a doormat of itself to a country whose leaders have shown little interest or support to the US except to take our money and aid and then vilify us at every turn'. A lady from Loomis, California, agreed that 'nothing should be sent to that pro-Communist hypocrite and political actor Nehru and his Communist ministers'. A man from Plantation, Florida, thought that India's troubles were 'of their own consequences and making'; namely, the 'Neutralist Policy' which they followed even while 'the Communists have swallowed millions of people' the world over. An 85-year-old Democrat from South San Gabriel endorsed Russell's 'objection to this country saddling its taxpayers with the upkeep of four hundred million ignorant, starving people of India, whose leaders including Nehru and others are strikingly procommunist and hostile to our form of government . . . Nehru's so-called neutralism . . . should teach this nation to let India stew in its own superstitious and ignorant juices.'

From his compatriots, Senator Russell received dozens of letters of congratulation, but only one of dissent. This was written by a Fulbright scholar based in Madras, who said it was time to undo the American policy of arming Pakistan while denying aid to India. India, said the scholar, was a 'popular democracy', whereas Pakistan was a military dictatorship which 'exists as a political entity solely on its emotional antagonism to India'. Besides, it was not true that the Indian troops had simply fled. They had fought hard in parts, and had they been better armed, could have held their own. Now, 'India is seeing to the recruitment of more troops; I should think that it would be in our best interests to see that they are properly armed.'

There were also letters by Indians to the senator, these naturally angry and hurt. A correspondent from Bombay agreed that Nehru 'used foggy thinking with regard to the Chinese intentions', but refused to accept Russell's insinuation that 'courage and defiance [were] a monopoly of white skins' alone. The Indian *jawan* matched the American GI in grit as well as guts, as manifest in his heroism in the crucial battles of the two world wars. But this time the 'War machinery was just not good enough (thanks to Mr Menon). Our boys did without the luxury of air cover, automatic rifles, ear muffs, K-Rations and Bob Hope to cheer them up on the frigid front lines.'

Russell's biliousness was answered in kind by the novelist and scriptwriter Khwaja Ahmad Abbas, one of India's most prominent fellow-travelling intellectuals. Abbas said that while there was a long history of stupid remarks by Westerners about India, Russell's interview 'takes the cake for unwarranted slander and unmitigated mischief'. 'But surely, Senator Russell', wrote Abbas, 'if you are looking for "disgraceful exhibitions" of military debacles, you will find ample material nearer home' – in Pearl Harbor, in the early reverses in the Korean War, in the Bay of Pigs. He referred the American to General Eisenhower's praise for the Indian soldier, who had thwarted Rommel at El Alamein and, in other sectors across Europe and Africa, had fought 'to save Senator Russell and his "free world" from the menace of Hitler'.

Senator Russell's remarks brought to the fore the mutual misunderstandings between Indians and Americans as they had been up to 1962 – and beyond. Behind these lay different perceptions of foreign policy and national interest, and also a certain incompatibility of cultures. The two peoples ate, drank, sang, dressed and thought differently. As an admirer in Jacksonville wrote to the Senator: 'This Nehru, technically Caucasian, politically nothing of the sort . . . How can there be a "meeting of minds" with a man who stands on his head?' The reference was to Jawaharlal Nehru's love of yoga, a form of therapy then completely alien to the American way of life.[6]

III

The defeat by China caused the prime minister a certain loss of face in the international arena. It also undermined his position at home. Criticism of his leadership grew more strident. In the summer of 1963 the Congress lost a series of important by-elections, which put into

Parliament three opposition stalwarts: Minoo Masani, J. B. Kripalani and Ram Manohar Lohia.

In June 1963 Nehru held a press conference, his first in many months. The meeting lasted ninety minutes, and was notable for the anger the prime minister directed at the Chinese. He spoke of the 'dark spate of falsehoods emanating from Peking', and of their 'high record in vituperation'. Explaining the war, and India's defeat therein, Nehru claimed that 'the Chinese are a military-minded nation, always laying stress on military roads and preparedness . . . Right from the beginning of the present regime there, they have concentrated on the military apparatus being stronger. It is a continuation really of the past civil wars. So, they are normally strong.'[7]

Nehru also said that in attacking him personally, the Chinese 'have something in common with some of our opposition leaders here'. He then added, gratuitously: 'As for our opposition leaders, they have the habit of combining with anybody and everybody regardless of principle and a time may come when some of them may for the purpose combine with the Chinese'. Soon, the opposition leaders did formally combine among themselves to introduce a 'no-confidence' motion in Parliament, an act of daring that would have been inconceivable at any time between August 1947 and November 1962. The Congress had the numbers to easily defeat the vote, but the debate lasted all of four days, during which a series of telling points were made against the prime minister, his party, and his government.[8]

The criticisms in and out of Parliament prompted a serious rethink among the Congress leadership. Fifteen years in power had made the party complacent, somewhat out of touch with happenings on the ground – as evidenced in the recent by-election defeats and the growing strength of regional parties like the Dravida Munnetra Kazhagam (DMK). The chief minister of Madras, K. Kamaraj, was himself most threatened by the DMK; now, to check its rise and stem the rot within, he recommended that senior Congress ministers leave their posts to help rejuvenate the party. Under the 'Kamaraj Plan' six chief ministers resigned to work for the party – these included Bakshi Ghulam Mohammed of Kashmir and Kamaraj himself. Six senior Union ministers also resigned – among them Jagjivan Ram, Morarji Desai and Lal Bahadur Shastri.[9]

The prime minister stayed in his job. But he was noticeably weakened, in body as well as mind. In September 1963 the Socialist MP

H. V. Kamath saw Nehru walking in to take his seat in Parliament: 'an old man, looking frail and fatigued, with a marked stoop in his gait, coming down the gangway opposite with slow, faltering steps, and clutching the backrests of benches for support as he descended'. Kamath's mind went back to his own early visions of a man he had once venerated: at a Congress session in Madras, where Nehru stood 'sprightly, slim and erect'; at his home in Allahabad, where Nehru 'jumped two steps at a time, with me emulating him, as I followed him upstairs'.[10]

Where Indians would not speculate openly about Nehru's death, Western observers were under no such inhibition. In 1963 the American journalist Wells Hangen published a book with the title *After Nehru, Who?* This listed eight possible successors, each of whom was allotted a separate chapter. Six were from the Congress Party: Morarji Desai, V. K. Krishna Menon, Y. B. Chavan, Lal Bahadur Shastri, S. K. Patil and the sole female candidate, Indira Gandhi. A seventh possibility was the social worker and sometime socialist revolutionary Jayaprakash Narayan. The last listed was a general – B. M. Kaul.[11]

The question now being asked was not just 'After Nehru, Who?', but also 'After Nehru, What?' Shortly after the publication of Hangen's book, a reporter from the *Sunday Times* of London spent several weeks travelling through India. He met the prime minister, to find that 'old Nehru has gone downhill so fast recently'. The decay of the man mirrored the decay of his country. In contrast to the 'intensity and unfathomable ambition of a wild young China', India was a land of 'indescribable poverty' and a 'will-less Government'. What would happen after Nehru passed on? The reporter thought that the battle 'will lie between the Communists and the new generation of political bandits emerging in the States . . .'. A third contender was the army; thus far, the generals had stayed aloof from politics, but would they 'stand aside while India collapsed into disorder or was swept into Communism'? Such were the prospects for the future; meanwhile, 'the free world must grow accustomed to its most populous member being without coherent leadership, swallowing aid and arms without significant effect, a tempting prey to the predatory-minded, an indictment of the free and democratic method of advancement in Afro-Asian eyes, where mature authority is so deeply needed'.[12]

Contemporary photographs confirm that Nehru was in physical decline – sunken shoulders, a tired, even doped look on his face, an unfamiliar bulge around his waist. In the first week of September 1963

Indira Gandhi wrote to a friend that her father now had to have weekly readings taken of his blood pressure, weight and urine. 'The strain, physical, mental and emotional, is tremendous and he is bound to look tired', wrote Mrs Gandhi. 'The only medicine that can help is rest and relaxation.'[13]

Of which, of course, he got none. He had still to undertake the duties of prime minister and foreign minister, and to contribute his mite to the revival of the Congress. As the single recognizable face of party and government, Nehru continued to maintain a punishing schedule, going to the four corners of India to address public meetings, open schools and hospitals and speak to party workers. In the month of December 1963, for example, he visited Madras, Madurai, Chandigarh, Calcutta, Bihar and Bombay (twice).[14]

One place that the prime minister could have gone to, but chose not to, was Nagaland. For a state of that name had finally come into existence on 1 December 1963. In other circumstances Nehru would have been keen to inaugurate it himself. But the journey to Kohima was long and arduous, and perhaps he also remembered the hostile reception he had got there back in 1953. In the event, the honours were done by the new president of the Republic, Sarvepalli Radhakrishnan. However, the new chief minister and his fellow ministers were dismissed as 'traitors' by the underground, whose writ still ran across large parts of the state.[15]

In January 1964 Nehru crossed the country again, to attend the annual meeting of the Congress, held that year in the Orissa capital of Bhubaneshwar. He collapsed on the stage and had to be helped to his feet and rushed back to Delhi. The diagnosis was that he had suffered a mild stroke. As one headline put it: 'Mr Nehru's Illness Casts Gloom over Bhubaneshwar Meet'.[16]

IV

The China war had weakened Nehru's position not just in India or the world, but within the Congress Party itself. The locus of decision-making had now shifted from the prime minister's home to the Congress Parliamentary Party. Unlike in the past, Nehru could no longer get the party to always do his bidding in matters big and small.[17] For instance, he had not welcomed the Kamaraj plan, on the grounds that it would deplete his government of experience and talent.

After his illness, Nehru was able to persuade the party to return Lal Bahadur Shastri to the Cabinet. Shastri was officially called 'minister without portfolio', but in fact functioned as the *de facto* deputy to the prime minister. The two shared a language, a home state and a history of being in the same jails at around the same time. Nehru trusted and liked Shastri, whose own quiet, understated personality was in such marked contrast to his own.

The first assignment entrusted to Shastri pertained to the state of Jammu and Kashmir. On 27 December 1963 a major crisis had been sparked by the theft of a holy relic, a hair of the Prophet Mohammed, from the Hazratbal mosque in Srinagar. A week after it vanished, the relic mysteriously reappeared in the mosque. No one knew how it came back, just as no one knew how it had vanished in the first place. And no one knew whether the relic now in place was the genuine article, or a fake.

Through the month of January there were protests and demonstrations in the Valley. The ripples spread through the Muslim world. In distant East Pakistan there were religious riots aimed at the minority Hindu community, hundreds of thousands of whom fled to India. Now there was the danger of retaliatory riots targeting Muslims in India itself.

In the last week of January Nehru dispatched Lal Bahadur Shastri to Kashmir. After speaking to officials, and consulting local politicians, Shastri decided to hold a special showing, or *deedar*, to certify whether the returned relic was genuine. A panel of senior clerics was constituted to view the relic. They did so on 3 February, and to palpable relief all round decided that this was the real article. Calm returned to the Valley. To keep the peace going the government of India appointed, as chief minister, G. M. Sadiq, a politician known for his left-wing views, but also for his integrity.[18]

The Hazratbal incident brought home, once more, the fact that trouble in Kashmir had its repercussions on life in the subcontinent as a whole. The China fiasco had made Nehru more alert to the need to seek a final resolution of the Kashmir dispute. For India could not afford to have two hostile fronts. He was encouraged in this line of thinking by his old friend Lord Mountbatten. In April 1963 Mountbatten had told Nehru that 'if his glory had at one time, brought India credit' in the world, the country, and he, now had a 'tarnished image', principally owing to the failure to settle the question of Kashmir. The Englishman felt that this could be 'rectified' by a 'heroic gesture by India', such as the 'granting of independence to the [Kashmir] valley regardless of the Pakistani attitude'.[19]

In fact, during 1962 and 1963 there were several rounds of talks with Pakistan on the issues that divided the two countries. Here, the government of India was represented by the experienced Sardar Swaran Singh, while Pakistan was represented by the young and ambitious Zulfiqar Ali Bhutto. At these talks no one represented Kashmir. But, as the Hazratbal incident showed, it was not prudent to neglect the feelings of the people at the centre of the dispute. And who better to take their pulse than Sheikh Abdullah? By the end of 1963 Nehru was already thinking of releasing the Sheikh, who by this time had been in jail for ten years. The stroke at Bhubaneshwar, with its intimations of mortality, made him think further in this regard. Why not release Abdullah and have a last shot at solving the Kashmir problem before he was gone?

V

Sheikh Abdullah, we may recall, had been arrested by the government of India in August 1953. No charges were brought against him, but in January 1958 he was suddenly released. He made his way to the Valley, where he met with a spectacular reception. He addressed well-attended public meetings in Srinagar, including one at the Hazratbal mosque. This seems to have unnerved his enemies in the administration. Towards the end of April he was arrested once more. This time he was shifted to a jail in Jammu, and charged with plotting with Pakistan to break up India. He was accused, among other things, of attempting 'to facilitate wrongful annexation of the territories of the state by Pakistan; create communal ill-feeling and disharmony in the state and receive secret aid from Pakistan in the shape of money, bombs, etc.'.[20]

The charges were, to put it politely, trumped up. While the Sheikh contemplated independence, he never wanted to join Pakistan. And while the idea of being the ruler of a free Kashmir appealed to him, he saw as his subjects all the people of the state, regardless of religion. As even his political opponents conceded, he had not a communal bone in his body.

Speaking at his trial, the Sheikh said that he stood for a single objective: the right of self-determination for the people of Jammu and Kashmir, who, he insisted, were 'not a flock of sheep and goats to be driven by force one way or another'. Even so, he repeatedly underlined his commitment to secularism, his admiration for Mahatma Gandhi and his once-strong friendship with Jawaharlal Nehru. He recalled that Nehru himself had conceded that 'the people of the state are the final arbiters of their fate', significantly adding: 'He does not, I believe, deny this right to us even now.'[21]

Two months after the Sheikh's first arrest, in 1953, Nehru had written that 'the mere fact of his detention is of course a matter which troubles me greatly'.[22] The months turned into years, deepening the guilt. One way of sublimating the guilt was to take a close interest in the education of his friend's children (which, by some accounts, he even helped pay for). In July 1955 Nehru was visited by Abdullah's eldest son, Farooq, then studying in a medical college in Jaipur. Farooq told the prime minister that his classmates routinely referred to his father as a 'traitor'. This prompted Nehru to write to a minister in the Rajasthan state government, asking him to ensure that the boy had 'proper living quarters and some friendly companionship', so that he did not develop any 'complexes and the like'. As Nehru put it, 'Some people foolishly imagine that because we have had differences with Sheikh Abdullah, therefore we are not favourably inclined towards his son and his family. This, of course, is not only absurd but is just the reverse of how we feel. Personally, because Sheikh Abdullah is in prison, I feel rather a special responsibility that we should try to help his sons and family.'[23]

In 1964, woken up by the China war, and put on high alert by his own fading health, Nehru decided to put an end to the matter. He spoke to the chief minister of Jammu and Kashmir, and after obtaining his consent, decided to release Sheikh Abdullah. The news was conveyed to the world by Nehru's confidant Lal Bahadur Shastri. Abdullah's detention, said Shastri, had been 'a matter of pain to the government, and particularly to the prime minister'.[24]

On the morning of 8 April the Sheikh stepped out of Jammu jail, a free man once more. He drove in an open car through the streets of the town, accepting garlands and bouquets. The next day he gave his first public speech. According to a newspaper report, 'Sheikh Abdullah said the two pressing problems facing the subcontinent – communal strife and Kashmir – should be solved during Prime Minister Nehru's lifetime. He described Mr Nehru as the last of the stalwarts who had worked with Gandhiji and said that after him a solution of these problems would become difficult.'

Nehru had invited Abdullah to come and stay with him in New Delhi. The Sheikh said he would first go to the Valley, consult his friends and supporters, and meet the Prime Minister after the Id festival (which fell on 23 April). On the 11th he set off by car to Srinagar, a journey that normally would take a few hours. But the Sheikh travelled leisurely, stopping at towns and villages on the way. Wherever he halted, he also spoke. Thousands turned up to see and hear him, trudging miles from their own isolated hamlets. In these gatherings, women outnumbered men.

In his speeches, Abdullah described his state as a bride cherished by two husbands – India and Pakistan – neither of whom 'cared to ascertain what the Kashmiris wanted'. He said he would meet Jawaharlal Nehru with an open mind, and asked the Indians not to make up their minds beforehand either. As a journalist who interviewed him noted, the Sheikh had 'no personal bitterness, no rancour' – rather, he was imbued with 'a strong sense of mission', a compelling desire to seek a solution to Kashmir. At one meeting he was asked what he now felt about Nehru. Abdullah answered that he bore no ill will, for 'misunderstandings do occur even among brothers. I shall not forget the love Mr Nehru has showered on me in the past . . . I will meet him as an old friend and comrade.'

On 18 April – a week after he had left Jammu – the Sheikh drove in an open jeep from Anantnag to the Kashmiri capital Srinagar. The thirty-mile route was lined by a 'near-hysterical crowd' of half a million people. The road was covered with freshly plucked daisies and tulips and festooned with arches and bunting. When he finally entered the town, 'Srinagar's entire population . . . jammed the labyrinth of streets which were so richly decorated that even the sun did not penetrate the canopy of Kashmir silks, carpets and shawls'.

Meanwhile, back in Delhi, the prospect of talks between Nehru and Abdullah alarmed many members of the ruling Congress Party. Senior Cabinet ministers issued statements insisting that the question of Kashmir was 'closed'; the state was, and would stay, an integral part of India. More combative still were members of the Jana Sangh. The party's general secretary, Deen Dayal Upadhyaya, deplored the Sheikh's recent speeches, where he seemed to have 'questioned even the axiomatic facts of the Kashmir question' (such as its final accession to India). 'Instead of stabilizing the political situation of the state', complained Upadhyaya, 'Sheikh Abdullah has tried to unsettle every issue.'

The opposition from the Hindu right was predictable. As it happens, the left was also suspicious of Abdullah and his intentions. The Communist Party thought he was in danger of falling into an 'imperialist trap', designed to detach Kashmir from India. Among the Indian political establishment, it seems, only Nehru's mind remained open. But he was to receive unexpected support from two old stalwarts who had also worked with Mahatma Gandhi. One was Jayaprakash Narayan, popularly known as 'JP', the former radical socialist who for the past decade had been a leading light of the Sarvodaya movement. JP was an old friend of the Sheikh; he had also been a vocal advocate of better relations with Pakistan. In 1962 he had set up an India–Pakistan Conciliation Group which, among other things, sought to find an 'equitable and honourable' solution to the Kashmir dispute.[25]

Now, welcoming Sheikh Abdullah's release in a signed article in the *Hindustan Times*, JP deplored the insinuations against Abdullah by politicians inside and outside the Congress. These had threatened that he would be put back in jail if he went 'too far'. 'It is remarkable', commented JP acidly, 'how the freedom fighters of yesterday begin so easily to imitate the language of the imperialists.'

What alarmed politicians in Delhi was the Sheikh's talk about ascertaining afresh the wishes of the Kashmiri people. JP thought this eminently reasonable, for the elections in Jammu and Kashmir in 1957 and 1962 were anything but free and fair. In any case, if India was 'so sure of the verdict of the people, why are we so opposed to giving them another opportunity to reiterate it?' A satisfactory settlement of the Kashmir question would greatly improve relations between India and Pakistan. JP hoped that the leaders of India would display 'the vision and statesmanship that this historic moment demands'. He added, 'Happily, the one sane voice in the ruling party is that of the Prime Minister himself.'[26]

More unexpected perhaps was the endorsement received by Nehru from C. Rajagopalachari ('Rajaji'), the veteran statesman who had once been an intimate associate of the prime minister but had latterly become a political opponent. As the founder of the Swatantra Party, Rajaji had savaged the prime minister's economic policies. These criticisms sometimes had a sharp personal edge. Now, to the surprise of his followers, he came out strongly in favour of Nehru's initiative in releasing Abdullah. Like JP, he deplored the threats to put the Sheikh back in jail, thus to 'force him into silence and submission'. Fortunately, 'the Prime Minister may be ill but he preserves his balance, and has evidently refused to take any foolish step and degrade India'.

The freeing of Abdullah, argued Rajaji, should act as a prelude to allowing 'the people of Kashmir [to] exercise their human right to rule themselves as well as they can'. Indeed, solving the Kashmir tangle would pave the way for a larger resolution of the Indo-Pak dispute itself. Thus, Rajaji wrote of the need to

> try and think fundamentally in the present crisis. Are we to yield to the fanatical emotions of our anti-Pakistan groups? Is there any hope for India or for Pakistan, if we go on hating each other, suspecting each other, borrowing and building up armaments against each other – building our two houses, both of us on the sands of continued foreign aid against a future Kurukshetra? We shall surely ruin ourselves for ever if we go on doing this . . . We shall be making all hopes of prosperity in the future a mere mirage if we continue this arms race based on an ancient grudge and the fears and suspicions flowing from it.[27]

VI

In Kashmir, meanwhile, Sheikh Abdullah was talking to his colleagues and associates. He discovered that while he had been in jail, he had come to be associated with the Pakistan party. At his trial Abdullah had insisted that he never expressed a desire for Kashmir to join Pakistan. India or independence – those were the only two options he had countenanced. But the trial proceedings never reached the common people of the Valley. They knew only that he was being tried for conspiracy against the Indian nation. Would not that make him, by default, a friend of Pakistan?

The common people were strengthened in their beliefs by the propaganda of Bakshi Ghulam Mohammed's government, which had painted the Sheikh as an agitator for a plebiscite, and hence anti-Indian. Moreover, the chicanery and corruption of the Bakshi regime had greatly tarnished the image of India among the Kashmiris. Abdullah found that the pro-Pakistani elements were now perhaps in a majority. This did not please him. But, sensing the mood on the ground, he worked to gradually win over the people to his point of view. He met the influential priest Maulvi Farooqui and urged him to support a 'realistic' solution, rather than claim that Kashmir should accede to Pakistan in pursuance of the two-nation theory.[28]

On 23 April, two weeks after he was released, Sheikh Abdullah addressed a prayer meeting in Srinagar. A solution to the Kashmir dispute, he said, must take into account its likely consequences for the 50 million Muslims in India, and the 10 million Hindus in East Pakistan. Three days later, in his last speech before leaving for Delhi, he urged the Kashmiris to maintain communal peace, to thus set an example for both India and Pakistan. 'No Muslim in Kashmir will ever raise his hand against the minorities,' he proclaimed.

On 28 April, the day before Abdullah was due to arrive in Delhi, the Jana Sangh held a large procession in the capital. The marchers shouted anti-Abdullah and anti-Nehru slogans and demanded that the government of India abrogate Article 370 and declare Kashmir to be an 'integral and indivisible' part of India. At a public meeting held the same day, A. B. Vajpayee demanded that the prime minister tell Abdullah that Jammu and Kashmir had 'already been integrated with the Indian Union and that there was no scope for discussion on this matter'.

On the 29th Abdullah flew into Palam airport with his principal associates. The party drove on to Teen Murti House, where the prime minister was waiting to receive Abdullah. It was the first time the two men had seen one another since Nehru's government had locked up the Sheikh in August 1953. Now, as one eyewitness wrote, 'the two embraced each other warmly. They were meeting after 11 years, but the way they greeted each other reflected no traces of embarrassment, let aside bitterness over what happened in the intervening period'. The duo posed for the battery of press photographers before going inside.

This was a reconciliation between the leader of the nation and a man till recently regarded as a traitor to it. It anticipated, by some thirty years, the similarly portentous reconciliation between the South African president and his most notorious political prisoner. But even F. W. De Klerk did not go so far as to ask Nelson Mandela to stay with him.

On this visit, Abdullah stayed five days with Nehru in Teen Murti House. They met at least once or twice a day, usually without aides. While the prime minister was otherwise occupied, the Sheikh canvassed a wide spectrum of Indian opinion. He spoke to Congress ministers, to leaders of the opposition and to prominent non-political figures such as Jayaprakash Narayan. He placed a wreath on Gandhi's tomb in Rajghat and addressed a prayer meeting at Delhi's greatest mosque, the Jama Masjid.

That Nehru was talking to Abdullah was not to the liking of the Jana Sangh. Notably, it also caused disquiet among members of his own Cabinet, who worried that the Kashmir question would now be 're-opened'. To pre-empt the possibility, a senior minister told Parliament that the 'maintenance of the status quo [in Kashmir] was in the best interests of the subcontinent'. And twenty-seven Congress MPs issued a statement arguing that 'you can no more talk of self-determination in the case of Kashmir than in the case of, say, Bombay or Bihar'.

Within his party, the only senior man who appeared sympathetic to Nehru's efforts was Lal Bahadur Shastri. There were, however, some opposition politicians who saw the point of speaking seriously with Abdullah. Thus the Swatantra Party leader Minoo Masani urgently wired Rajaji:

> Understand Nehru and Lal Bahadur endeavouring to find solution with Sheikh Abdullah but are up against confused thinking within Congress Party alongside of Jan Sangh communist combination. If you think telegram or letter to Jawaharlal from yourself encouraging him [to] do the right thing and assuring your personal support would help please move in the matter.[29]

Rajaji chose not to write to Nehru, perhaps because he was too proud or feared a rebuff, but he did write to Lal Bahadur Shastri urging that Kashmir be given some kind of autonomous status. As he saw it, 'self-determination for Kashmir is as far as we are concerned a lesser issue than the aim of reducing Indo-Pak jealousy'. He thought that 'the idea that if we "let Kashmir go", we shall be encouraging secessions everywhere is thoroughly baseless'. 'I hope you and Jawaharlalji', wrote Rajaji to Shastri, 'will be guided by Providence and bring this great opportunity to a good result.'[30]

Shortly after his release Abdullah had expressed his wish to 'pay my respects personally to Rajaji, and have the benefit of his mature advice'.[31] Now, after his conversations with Nehru, he set off south to meet the prime minister's friend turned rival turned ally. He planned to stop at Wardha en route, to pay his respects to the Gandhian leader Vinoba Bhave. As he jokingly told a journalist, he would discuss 'spirituality' with Vinoba and 'practical politics' with Rajaji.

On 4 May Lal Bahadur Shastri wrote to Rajaji urging him 'to suggest to Sheikh Saheb not to take any extreme line . . . Sheikh Saheb has just come out [of jail] and it would be good for him to give further thought to the different aspects of the Kashmir question and come to a judgement after full and mature introspection and deliberation. It will be most unfortunate if things are done in a hurry or precipitated'.[32]

This was an airmail letter, but one does not know whether it reached Madras before the 5th, on which day Abdullah finally met Rajaji. They spoke for a full three and a half hours, provoking this front page headline in the *Hindustan Times*: 'Abdullah, CR, Evolve Kashmir Formula: Proposal to Be Discussed with Prime Minister'. Rajaji did not say a word to the press, but Abdullah was slightly more forthcoming. Speaking to the wise old man, he said, 'had helped clear his mind about what would be the best solution which would remove this cancer from the body politic of India and Pakistan'. Pressed for details, the Sheikh said these would have to await further talks with the prime minister. He did let on, however, that Rajaji and he had worked out 'an honourable solution which would not give a sense of victory either to India or Pakistan and at the same time would ensure a place of honour to the people of Kashmir'.

While Abdullah was in Madras, word reached him that President Ayub Khan had invited him to visit Pakistan. On returning to Delhi on 6 May he went straight to Teen Murti House. He spent ninety minutes with Nehru, apprising him of what was being referred to, somewhat mysteriously, as 'the Rajaji formula'. The prime minister next directed Abdullah to an informal committee of advisers. This consisted of the foreign secretary, Y. D. Gundevia, the high commissioner to Pakistan, G. Parthasarathi, and the vice-chancellor of the Aligarh Muslim University, Badruddin Tyabji.

Over two long days, Abdullah and the prime minister's men discussed the Kashmir issue threadbare. All kinds of alternatives were mooted. These included a plebiscite for the entire, undivided state of Jammu and Kashmir as it existed before 1947; the maintenance of the status quo; and a fresh division of the state, such that the Jammu and Ladakh regions went to India, Azad or northern Kashmir went to Pakistan, with a plebiscite being held in the Valley alone to decide its future. Abdullah told the officials that while they could work out the specifics of the solution, it must (1) promote Indo-Pakistani friendship; (2) not weaken the secular ideal of the Indian Constitution; (3) not weaken the position of the minorities in either country. He asked them to give him more than one alternative, which he could take with him to Pakistan.

The Sheikh's conditions more or less ruled out a plebiscite, the result of which, whatever it might be, would leave one country dissatisfied and minorities on both sides more vulnerable. What about the Rajaji formula? This, it appears, was for a condominium over Kashmir between India and Pakistan, with defence and external affairs being the joint responsibility of the two governments. (The model here was Andorra, a tiny but autonomous enclave whose security was guaranteed by its two large neighbours, France and Spain.) Another possibility was of creating a confederation among India, Pakistan and Kashmir.[33]

The trinity advising Nehru were selected for their ability and knowledge; it is noteworthy nonetheless that they came from three different religious traditions. It is noteworthy too that all were officials. Recall that when there was a chance to settle the dispute with China, the jingoism of the politicians compelled Nehru to take positions more hardline than he otherwise might have done. Now, in seeking a settlement with Pakistan, Nehru sought to work with his officials, rather than his ministers. The wisdom of this approach was made clear in a letter written to Rajaji by the writer and parliamentarian B. Shiva Rao. This noted that

> There is a clear attempt both from within the Cabinet and in Parliament to prevent the Prime Minister from coming to terms with Sheikh Abdullah if it should mean the reopening of the issue of accession. Many of these Ministers have made public statements while the discussions between the two are going on. It's a sign of the diminishing prestige and influence of the PM that they can take such liberties.

This was interesting, but the reply was more interesting still. This gave more flesh to the 'Rajaji formula', while locating Nehru's predicament in proper perspective. Thus, wrote Rajaji,

> Asking Ayub Khan to give a commitment in advance about Azad Kashmir now will break up the whole scheme. He will and cannot give it. He is in a worse situation than Nehru in regard to public pressures and emotional bondage . . . Any plan should therefore leave the prizes of war untouched . . . Probably the best procedure is for Sheikh to concentrate

on the valley leaving Jammu as a counterpoise to Azad Kashmir, to be presumed to be integrated to India without question.

This reduced shape of the problem is good enough, if solved as we desire, to bring about an improvement in the Indo-Pakistan relationship. And being of reduced size, would be a fitting subject for UN trusteeship partial or complete.[34]

On the Indian side, the best hope for peace was Jawaharlal Nehru. Sheikh Abdullah appears to have thought that Nehru was also the *last* hope. On 11 May the Sheikh told reporters that 'I do not want to plead for Nehru but he is the symbol of India in spite of his weakness. You cannot find another man like him.' He added that 'after Nehru he did not see anyone else tackling [the problems] with the same breadth of vision'.

For his part, Nehru was also quite prepared to give his old comrade and sometime adversary a sterling certificate of character. Speaking to the All-India Congress Committee in Bombay on the 16th, the prime minister said that the Sheikh was wedded to the principles of secularism. Nor did he believe in the two-nation theory. Both Nehru and he hoped that 'it would be possible for India, holding on to her principles, to live in peace and friendship with Pakistan and thus incidentally to put an end to the question of Kashmir'. 'I cannot say if we will succeed in this', said the prime minister, 'but it is clear that unless we succeed India will carry the burden of conflict with Pakistan with all that this implies.'

VII

On 20 May, Sheikh Abdullah returned to Delhi, to stay at Teen Murti House and have a final round of talks with Nehru before travelling to Pakistan. At a press conference on the 22nd, Nehru declined to disclose the details, saying that he did not want to prejudice the Sheikh's mission. But he did indicate that his government was 'prepared to have an agreement with Pakistan on the basis of their holding on to that part of Kashmir occupied by them'.[35]

Nehru's own papers on this subject are closed to scholars, but a letter written by his foreign secretary gives a clue to his thinking at the time. The prime minister had apparently asked legal experts to explore the implications of a confederation between India, Pakistan and Kashmir, 'as a possible solution to our present troubles'. Such an arrangement would not imply an 'annulment' of Partition. India and Pakistan would remain separate, sovereign states. Kashmir would be part of the confederation, with its exact status to be determined by dialogue. There might be a customs union of the three units, some form of financial integration and special provisions for the protection of minorities.[36]

To keep the discussion going, India was prepared to concede Pakistan's hold over Azad Kashmir and Gilgit, the two parts of the state that it had lost in the war of 1947–8. Would Pakistan concede anything in turn? As Abdullah prepared to depart for Rawalpindi, Minoo Masani wrote to A. K. Brohi, sometime Pakistani high commissioner to India and now a leading Karachi lawyer, a certified member of the Pakistani Establishment who had the ear of President Ayub Khan. 'The nature of the response which he [the Sheikh] is able to evoke from President Ayub', said Masani to Brohi, would 'have a decisive influence in strengthening or weakening the hands of those who stand for Indo-Pakistan amity here'. Nehru's Pakistan initiative was bitterly opposed from within his party and outside it. For it to make progress, for there to be a summit meeting between the prime minister and President Ayub Khan, it was 'of the highest moment that Sheikh Abdullah should come back with something on which future talks could be based'. Masani urged Brohi to use his influence with Ayub and other leaders, so that their talks with Abdullah might 'yield fruitful results in the interests of both countries'.[37]

Meanwhile, Abdullah proceeded to Pakistan. He hoped to spend two weeks in that country, beginning with the capital, Rawalpindi, moving on to Azad Kashmir and ending with East Pakistan, where he intended, among other things, to check on the feelings of the Hindu minority. On 24 May he touched down in Rawalpindi to a tumultuous reception. He drove in an open car from the airport to the town, the route lined by thousands of cheering Pakistanis. The welcome, said one reporter, 'surpassed in intensity and depth that given to Mr Chou En-lai in February'.[38]

Later, talking to newsmen, Abdullah called his visit 'a peace mission of an exploratory nature'. He appealed to the press to help cultivate friendship between India and Pakistan. 'He said he had come to the definite conclusion that the armed forces of both the countries facing each other on the ceasefire line must be disengaged and that the edifice of a happy and prosperous Kashmir could be built only on permanent friendship between India and Pakistan'. As in New Delhi, here too he emphasized that any solution to the dispute must not foster a sense of defeat for either India or Pakistan; must not weaken India's secularism or the future of its 60 million Muslims; and must satisfy the aspirations of the Kashmiris themselves.

The next day, the 25th, Abdullah and Ayub Khan held a three-hour meeting. The Sheikh would not touch on the details, saying only that he found in Rawalpindi 'the same encouraging response as in Delhi. There is an equal keenness on both sides to come to a real understanding.'

Later that day Abdullah addressed a mammoth public meeting in Rawalpindi. He was 'cheered repeatedly as he spoke for two hours, bluntly warning both Indians and Pakistanis from committing wrongs which would endanger the lives of the minorities in both countries'. The time had come, said Abdullah, for India and Pakistan to bury the hatchet. For if 'the present phase of tension, distrust and misunderstanding continued, both countries would suffer and their freedom be imperilled'.

On the 26th Abdullah met Ayub Khan again, for four hours this time, and came out beaming. The Pakistani president, he told a crowded news conference, had agreed to a meeting with Prime Minister Nehru in the middle of June. The meeting would take place in Delhi, and Abdullah would also be in the city, available for consultation. 'Of all the irritants that cause tension between India and Pakistan', said the Sheikh, 'Kashmir is the most important. Once this great irritant is removed, the solution of other problems would not present much difficulty.'

By this time the enchantment with the Sheikh was wearing thin among the Pakistani elite. Their representative voice, the *Dawn* newspaper, wrote of how Abdullah's statements, 'especially his references to India's so-called secularism, have caused a certain amount of disappointment among the public in general and the intelligentsia in particular'. *Dawn* thought that the Sheikh had been 'lured by the outward show of Indian secularism, obviously forgetting the inhumane treatment meted out to 60 million Muslims in the so-called secular state'. But the newspaper had a more fundamental complaint, that Abdullah had taken up the role of an apostle of peace and friendship between Pakistan and India, rather than that of the leader of Kashmir, whose *prime objective should be to seek their freedom from Indian bondage*'.[39]

On the 27th Abdullah proceeded to Muzaffarabad, a town he had not seen since Kashmir was divided in 1947. He had no idea of how the Kashmiris this side of the ceasefire line would react to his proposals. Before he could find out, news reached him that, back in New Delhi, Nehru had died. Abdullah at once 'broke into tears and sobbed'.

In a muffled voice he told the reporters gathered around him, 'He is dead, I can't meet him'. When asked for more reactions he retired to a room, to be alone with his grief.

Abdullah drove down to Rawalpindi and got on the first flight to Delhi. When he reached Teen Murti and saw the body of Nehru, 'he cried like a child'. It took him some time to 'compose himself and place the wreath on the body of his old friend and comrade'. To this account of a newsman on the spot we must add the witness of a diplomat who accompanied Nehru's body to the cremation ground. As the fire was burning the body to ashes, buglers sounded 'The Last Post': 'thus was symbolized the inextricability of India and England in Nehru's life'. Then, before the fire finally died down, 'Sheikh Abdullah leapt on the platform and, weeping unrestrainedly, threw flowers onto the flames; thus was symbolized the inextricability of the Muslim world in Nehru's life and the pathos of the Kashmir affair'.[40]

VIII

The events of April–May 1964 have unfortunately been neglected by scholars, whether biographers of Nehru or analysts of the Kashmir dispute.[41] If I have rehabilitated them here, it is because they provide fresh light on this most intractable of political problems – this 'severe headache' as Vallabhbhai Patel put it, this 'cancer [in] the body politic of India and Pakistan' in the words of Sheikh Abdullah – and because they provide a peculiarly poignant coda to the life and work of Jawaharlal Nehru.

The question remains – how serious were the three campaigners for peace in April–May 1964? The one who did not reveal his mind at all, at least not in the public domain, was Field Marshal Ayub Khan. We know nothing about what he really thought at the time, whether he was indeed serious about a negotiated settlement on Kashmir, and whether he could then, so to say, 'sell' an agreement with India to his people. Sheikh Abdullah, on the other hand, was forthcoming with his views, expressing them to the press and in countless public meetings and orations. Some thought his words a mere mask for personal ambition. Writing in the Economic Weekly, one commentator claimed that 'even a superficial study of his political behaviour convinces [one] that he is embarked on a most ramified plan to win an independent State by skilfully exploiting the hates and the prejudices, conscious and unconscious, and the power political tangles which provide the background to Indo-Pakistan relations'.[42]

This seems to me to be too cynical by far. For Abdullah's words, and still more his actions, make manifest his commitment to secularism, his concern for the minorities in both India and Pakistan. He was ambitious, certainly, but while in 1953 he seems to have fancied himself as the uncrowned king of Kashmir, in 1964 he saw himself rather as an exalted peacemaker, the one man who could bring tranquillity and prosperity to a poor and divided subcontinent.

About Jawaharlal Nehru's motives there should be no doubt at all. He felt guilty about Abdullah's long incarceration, worried about the continuing disaffection in Kashmir, sensible of the long-term costs of the dispute to both India and Pakistan. The question was not then of his motives, but of his influence. Would his colleagues listen to him? Had he and Ayub Khan, with a little help from Abdullah, actually worked out a settlement, would it have passed muster with the Congress Party, or the Indian Parliament?

Possibly not. But even if it did, would it have worked in the long run? The legal expert consulted by Nehru's office on the idea of a confederation delicately pointed out that 'historically, confederations have been dominated by one member or united under stress'.[43] In sheer size India swamped both Pakistan and Kashmir. Would it then have behaved like Big Brother? Relevant here is a cartoon by Rajinder Puri that appeared in the *Hindustan Times* the day Abdullah met Ayub Khan. It showed the Field Marshal standing ruminatively, finger on chin, with the Sheikh expansively gesticulating, and saying: 'You're afraid Delhi will try to dominate Pindi? My dear chap, when Delhi can't dominate Lucknow or Chandigarh . . .'.[44]

Here then were a host of imponderables – Ayub's motives, Abdullah's beliefs, Nehru's strength, the viability of a condominium or a confederation. In the end it was Nehru's strength that gave way – literally. And, as a Pakistani newspaper noted, his passing away meant 'the end of a negotiated settlement of the Kashmir issue'. For whoever succeeded Nehru would not have 'the stature, courage and political support necessary to go against the highly emotional tide of public opinion in India favouring a status quo in Kashmir'.[45]

17

Minding the Minorities

The first law of decency is to preserve the liberty of others.
FRIEDRICH SCHILLER

I

ON THE AFTERNOON OF 27 May 1964, as the news of Jawaharlal Nehru's death spread through New Delhi, one of the people it reached was an American graduate student named Granville Austin. Austin was writing a thesis on the making of the Indian Constitution, and thus had a more than ordinary interest in what Nehru stood for. He made his way to Teen Murti House, there to join an already large crowd of Indian mourners. As Austin wrote in his diary the next day, 'all wanted to go in, but they were prepared to wait'. The crowd stood, 'orderly and not noisy', as diplomats and ministers were ushered in by the prime minister's staff. Among the VIPs was Dr Syed Mahmud, a veteran freedom fighter who had been with Nehru at Cambridge and in jail. Like the others, he had to disembark from his car and walk up the steeply sloping lawn that fronted the prime minister's residence. Austin saw a weeping Mahmud given a helping hand by Jagjivan Ram, a senior Congress politician and Cabinet minister of low-caste origin. This was truly 'a scene symbolic of Nehru's India: a Muslim aided by an Untouchable coming to the home of a caste Hindu'.[1]

Between them, Muslims and Untouchables constituted a quarter of the population in free India. Before 1947, two leaders had most seriously challenged the Congress's claims to represent all of India. One was a Muslim, M. A. Jinnah, who argued that the party of Gandhi and Nehru represented only the Hindus. The other was a former Untouchable, B. R. Ambedkar, who added the devastating rider that the Congress did not represent all Hindus, but only the upper castes among them.

These claims were stoutly resisted. Gandhi himself had struggled against untouchability from long before Ambedkar had entered politics. And he had given his life in the cause of Hindu–Muslim harmony. For the Mahatma, *swaraj* (freedom) would have meaning only if it came to all Indians, regardless of caste or creed (or gender).

These were commitments Jawaharlal Nehru shared with Gandhi. In other matters, he might have been a somewhat wayward disciple. With his fellow intellectuals he chose to take India down the road of industrial modernization, rather than nurture a village-centred economy (as Gandhi would have wanted). But when it came to preserving the rights of minorities he stood shoulder-to-shoulder with the Mahatma. His was likewise a nationalism that was both composite as well as egalitarian.

Inspired by Gandhi, and guided by Nehru, the Indian Constitution both abolished untouchability and proclaimed the state neutral in matters of religion. Such was the law; how was the practice? Among all the tests faced by the new state this, perhaps, was the sternest. Since Hindus were both in a numerical majority and in positions of political pre-eminence, the idea of India would stand scrutiny only if they respected the rights and liberties of Indians different from themselves.

II

The idea of Pakistan had as its justification the need for minorities to be free of the fear of Hindu domination. Paradoxically, though, the state of Pakistan was created out of Muslim majority areas where this problem did not exist in the first place.

After 1947 there were large populations of Muslims scattered all over peninsular India – as they had been before that date. Several million Muslims migrated across the borders to East and West Pakistan, but many more than this elected to stay behind in India. The creation of Pakistan had made their position deeply vulnerable. This was the view, ironically, of two men who had played critical roles in the making of Pakistan: the Bengali Muslim Leaguer H. S. Suhrawardy and his United Provinces counterpart Chaudhry Khaliquzzaman. On 10 September 1947 – less than a month after Independence and Partition – Suhrawardy wrote to Khaliquzzaman in horror that 'the Muslims in the Indian Union have been left high and dry'. The antagonism caused by the formation of Pakistan had been heightened by the flight into India of Hindu and Sikh refugees. Suhrawardy now feared that 'there may be a general conflagration which can well destroy the Muslim minority in the Indian Union'. As for Khaliquzzaman, he had reached the melancholy conclusion that 'the partition of India [had] proved positively injurious to the Muslims of India, and on a long-term basis for Muslims everywhere'.

To protect their interests – and their lives – Suhrawardy drafted 'a declaration of co-operation and mutual assistance between the two Dominions', committing both to protecting their minorities and to not making provocative statements against each other. Suhrawardy got Gandhi to endorse the declaration, but failed to get Jinnah to consent, despite begging him to do so, 'for the sake of the helpless and hapless Muslims of the Indian Union'.[2]

As we have seen, the creation of Pakistan provided a fillip to the forces of Hindu communalism. The RSS and its ilk could now argue that the Muslims were betrayers who had divided the nation. In the view of the extremist Hindu, these Muslims should either go to Pakistan or face the consequences. The RSS grew in strength immediately after Partition, and although the murder of Gandhi in January 1948 stemmed its rise, the organization continued to exercise considerable influence in northern and western India.

Truth be told, there were chauvinists within the ruling Congress itself, men who were not completely convinced of the loyalty of Muslims to the new nation. Some were in positions of high authority. The governor of Bihar warned the owners of the great steel mill in Jamshedpur that their Muslim employees would leave for Pakistan, but destroy the machinery before going. There were other such rumours floating around the town, but the factory owners stayed steadfast, issuing a notice that they had no intention of dismissing their Muslim employees or of promoting communal disunity among the workforce.[3]

The deep insecurity of the Indian Muslim was foregrounded in a survey conducted by an American psychologist in 1950. His Muslim interviewees – who were from towns in north and west India – were beset by fear and suspicion. 'We are regarded as Pakistani spies,' said one. 'It is dangerous to live in a Hindu locality because they may abduct and rape our women,' said a second. 'Hindus charge heavy black market prices for goods they sell to Muslims,' said a third.[4]

III

Among those who did not wholly trust the Muslims was Vallabhbhai Patel, Home Minister of India. Patel remembered that the majority of Muslims had voted for the League in 1946, even in areas which would not form part of Pakistan. After the two states were created he remained suspicious of those who had stayed behind. In a speech at Lucknow in early January 1948 he reminded his audience that it was in that town that 'the foundation of the two-nation theory was laid'. For it was the UP intellectuals who had claimed that 'Muslims were a separate nation'. Now, for those who had chosen not to go to Pakistan, it was not enough to give 'mere declarations of loyalty to the Indian Union', they 'must give *practical proof* of their declarations'.[5]

Later that year, the secretary of Patel's Home Ministry wrote to the secretaries of all other departments, drawing their attention

to one aspect of security which has assumed urgency and importance in the present context of relations with Pakistan. There is growing evidence that a section of Muslims in India is out of sympathy with the Government of India, particularly because of its policy regarding Kashmir and Hyderabad, and is actively sympathetic to Pakistan. Such Government servants are likely to be useful channels of information and would be particularly susceptible to the influence of their relatives.

It is probable that among Muslim employees of Government there are some who belong to these categories. It is obvious that they constitute a dangerous element in the fabric of administration; and it is essential that they should not be entrusted with any confidential or secret work or allowed to hold key posts. For this purpose I would request you to prepare lists of Muslim employees in your Ministry and in the offices under your control, whose loyalty to the Dominion of India is suspected or who are likely to constitute a threat to security. These lists should be carefully prepared and scrutinised by the Heads of Departments or other higher authority, and should be used for the specific purposes of excluding persons from holding key posts or handling confidential or secret work.

I need scarcely add that I am sure you will see that there is no witch hunting; and that only genuine cases are included in the lists. Those who are loyal and whose work is satisfactory should of course be given every cause to feel that their claims are no less than those of men belonging to the majority community.[6]

This was an extraordinary letter, which sparked, if not a witch-hunt, an energetic attempt to seek out traces of disloyalty among the Muslim employees of the government of India. Consider the case of the Archaeological Survey of India (ASI), which had numerous Muslim employees, these entrusted with the upkeep of the great buildings of medieval India. When passed this letter by the education secretary, the ASI's director general wrote to his circle heads asking them to furnish lists of Muslim employees, those loyal to the Dominion of India, and those 'likely to constitute a danger to security'. The circle heads then commenced secret investigations among their staff, the results of which were communicated back to headquarters. Half a century later, their reports make for interesting and in some cases chilling reading.

Several heads wrote back saying that they did not personally distrust any of their employees. However, they were pressured to transfer those likely to be in a position of vulnerability. The major of an infantry unit in Bijapur had advised the ASI that the custodian of the Gol Gumbuz was 'not considered reliable'; he, apparently, had relatives in Hyderabad, a state which was refusing to join the Union. The custodian was then transferred to the Kanheri Caves in Bombay.

The most detailed report came from the superintendent of the northern circle, headquartered in Agra, and which had within its purview the Taj Mahal and Fatehpur Sikri. He listed twenty-eight employees whose relatives had migrated to Pakistan. Of these, he identified five 'as persons whose loyalty to the Dominion of India may not be above suspicion', who 'may constitute a danger to security if they get a favourable opportunity'. One was a booking clerk in Agra Fort, with a brother, son and mother in Hyderabad (Sindh); another a watchman at the Taj Mahal with a wife in Karachi. Another Taj watchman had two sons and a daughter in Karachi. The superintendent listed another seven employees who 'do not seem mischievous by nature, but may prove a useful channel for communicating information under the influence of their relations in Pakistan'.

On 20 October the home secretary sent a follow-up letter, targeting officials who had close relatives in Pakistan. Now that several months had passed since Partition, he said, 'there was no longer any reason [for]

Government servants to keep their families in Pakistan. On the contrary, having regard to the strained relations between the two Dominions that would be *prima facie* evidence of disloyalty to the Dominion of India'. Employees with families in Pakistan would have to bring them back within a month. The Home Ministry asked for lists of delinquents; it would then decide, case by case, whether 'the interests of the country' required disciplinary action against them.

Once more, the home secretary's instructions were passed on by the director general of the ASI to all his circle heads. Once more, the most detailed report came from the superintendent of the Agra circle, who did seem to regard this, with some relish, as a sort of witch-hunt. His ire was reserved particularly for the *khadims*, or hereditary watchmen, of the Taj Mahal, eighteen in all, whose posts were created by Emperor Shah Jahan in the seventeenth century, and later confirmed by the British. In the eyes of the superintendent they seemed all to be enemy agents, 'unwilling to tell the whole truth about themselves'. At least six still had families in Pakistan. One *khadim* had overstayed with his relatives across the border; he had been suspended, and ordered to 'hand over both summer and winter liveries and all other Government articles in his possession'. The superintendent wanted to suspend a second *khadim*, whom he suspected of wanting only to sell his property in Agra before migrating 'to Pakistan surreptitiously'. He had also targeted a third, who 'appears to have made efforts though not energetic enough to bring back the members of his family to India'.

Agra lay in the United Provinces, whose Muslims were very deeply divided indeed. The Muslims of the Punjab had migrated en masse across the border. From Bombay and the south, many intellectuals had voluntarily migrated to Pakistan, but the working-class Muslims had stayed behind. Pakistan was too far and too alien for them to consider making a new life in a new place. However, the UP Mussalman spoke Urdu – the official language of Pakistan – and also lived close enough to be able to jump aboard a train and go there. Many went; many others stayed where they were.

Almost every Muslim family in the UP was divided, and the employees of the ASI were no exception. The superintendent of the Agra circle, however, had no sympathy for employees with kin in what he considered 'enemy' territory. Bring them back, he told his subordinates, or face the consequences. A *khadim* named Shamsuddin had excited his boss's suspicion by selling his house when his entire family was in Pakistan.

In a somewhat pathetic petition dated 8 December 1948, Shamsuddin said that he had 'not the least idea of ever going to Pakistan'. There were four reasons why he had disposed of his house: (1) to pay back a debt he owed his relatives; (2) as 'my daughters are to be married, and I have to invest money in this peon's duty of mine'; (3) as the refugee tenants who had been allotted his house were misusing it, and it was best to sell it before its condition further deteriorated; (4) as 'I have to make arrangements for the last ceremonies of my life as my sons have deserted me'.

The superintendent was not convinced, demanding more positive proof of Shamsuddin's loyalty to the Union of India. A note of 13 June 1949 tells us that the *khadim* had travelled to Pakistan, and brought back with him his two unmarried daughters, and two grandchildren of a deceased daughter 'over whom he could exercise control'.[7]

Were the records of the government of India ever to be thrown open for those years, one might find that such loyalty oaths, extracted under pressure by senior officials, were very nearly ubiquitous. One scholar has recently found a statement issued in 1951 by Muslim pastoralists of Kachchh, the semi-arid part of Gujarat state which bordered the Sindh province of Pakistan. This assured the chief commissioner that 'we are loyal to the Government of India, and if [the] Pakistan government attacks the Indian government, we will sacrifice our lives for the security of India'.[8]

IV

It is not clear whether the prime minister approved of the attempts to ascertain the loyalty of certain select employees of the government of India. But we do know that his view of the Muslim situation was somewhat different from that of his deputy. As he wrote to Patel, he deplored the 'constant cry for retaliation and of vicarious punishment of the Muslims of India, because the Pakistanis punish Hindus. That argument does not appeal to me in the slightest. I am sure that this policy of retaliation and vicarious punishment will ruin India as well as Pakistan.'[9] Where the home minister demanded that the Muslims prove their loyalty, the prime minister placed the onus on the Indian state, which had a constitutional obligation to make all its citizens, but the Muslims especially, feel secure.

Nehru expressed these views both to Patel and in a series of letters he wrote to the chief ministers of various provinces.[10] Three months after Partition he reminded them that

> we have a Muslim minority who are so large in numbers that they cannot, even if they want, go anywhere else. That is a basic fact about which there can be no argument. Whatever the provocation from Pakistan and whatever the indignities and horrors inflicted on non-Muslims there, we have got to deal with this minority in a civilized manner. We must give them security and the rights of citizens in a democratic State. If we fail to do so, we shall have a festering sore which will eventually poison the whole body politic and probably destroy it.

Later in the same letter, he drew attention to 'the paramount importance of preserving the public services from the virus of communal politics'.[11]

This was a subject to which Nehru had necessarily to return. One provocation was quarrels about property, for in some places Muslims were being asked by over-energetic officers to give up their homes in favour of Hindu and Sikh refugees. The prime minister used the occasion of Gandhi's birthday to warn against 'creating an atmosphere of uncertainty and lack of security in the minds of large numbers of our Muslim fellow-countrymen'. For this had 'far-reaching consequences not only in India but also in Kashmir. It affects our reputation abroad. A few houses or shops attached or taken possession of do not make very much difference. But, if wrongly done, they do affect our reputation and thus injure us.'

The prime minister acknowledged that 'Pakistan is pursuing a policy of utter callousness in this matter'. However, he insisted that 'we cannot copy the methods or the ideals of Pakistan. They have declared themselves openly to be an Islamic State believing in the two-nation theory. We reject the theory and call ourselves a secular State giving full protection to all religions. We have to live up to our ideals and declarations. More especially on this day, Gandhi Jayanti, it is for us to remember what Gandhiji taught us and what he died for.'[12]

Nehru had made communal organizations his principal target during the election campaign of 1951–2. That election was fought and won on the plank of not making India a 'Hindu Pakistan'. However, Nehru continued to be worried about the rights of those Indians whose culture and faith demarcated them from the majority. A particular concern was the very low proportion of Muslims in positions of authority. There were hardly any Muslim officers left in the defence services, and not very many in the secretariat. This, he sensed, was the consequence of a failure in creating a proper 'sense of partnership in every group and individual in the country, a sense of being a full sharer in the benefits and opportunities that are offered'. If India was to be 'a secular, stable and strong state', he told his chief ministers, then 'our first consideration must be to give *absolute fair play* to our minorities, and thus to make them feel *completely at home* in India'.[13]

V

The acknowledged political leader of the Muslims left behind in the Indian Union was Maulana Abul Kalam Azad. Unlike his great rival Mohammad Ali Jinnah, Azad believed that non-Hindus could live with peace and honour in a united India. In Nehru's characteristically eloquent formulation, Maulana Azad was 'a peculiar and very special representative in a high degree of that great composite culture which has gradually grown in India'. He embodied that 'synthesis of various cultures which have come one after another to India, rivers that have flowed in and lost themselves in the ocean of Indian life'.[14]

Azad was deeply damaged by Partition. Seeing it as the failure of his life's mission, he retreated from the world of party politics (though in any case his orientation was always more of the scholar than that of the mass leader). He served as education minister in the Union Cabinet, and in that capacity helped promote new academies for the nurturing of Indian literature, dance, music and art. His age and temperament, however, confined him for the most part to Delhi.

A younger member of the Congress Party seeking a more active political role was Saif Tyabji, scion of a famous nationalist family. Grandson of an early president of the Congress, and himself an engineer educated at Cambridge, Tyabji was well placed to be a modernist bridge between the Congress and the Muslim masses. In 1955 he wrote a series of essays in the influential Urdu newspaper *Inqilab*, these later published in English translation under the title *The Future of Muslims in India*. In the 1952 election Muslims had voted in large numbers for the Congress, a party which, under Nehru's leadership, they felt they could trust more than its rivals.[15] Tyabji, however, felt that the Muslims should do more than vote for India's dominant party – they should join it, and influence its policies.

Saif Tyabji pointed out that the Congress was a democratic institution, with its national council made up of elected representatives sent from the states, these in turn chosen from district and *taluk* committees. All it cost to become a member of the Congress was a subscription fee of four annas (a quarter of a rupee). Spread out across India, the Muslims could enrol in numbers in all the districts, thus to influence the selection of Congress leaders at the higher levels of the organization. Such was Tyabji's political strategy, but he also urged his co-religionists to engage more fully with the cultural life of the country. As a 'patriotic Indian', he wished that the 'new Indian Culture' that was arising 'be as rich and varied and vigorous as possible, and this can only be so if it draws its nourishment from all possible sources'. Like other kinds of Indians, Muslims had to 'take an active part in its formation'. But 'if the Muslims sit back with folded arms, we can rest assured that the new Indian Culture will have little to do with the achievements in this country between the 11th century and the coming of the British. By this all Indians will suffer, but the responsibility for the loss will lie heavily on those Indians who are Muslims.'

Among Tyabji's other suggestions were that Muslims ask for technical and commercial education, rather than merely study the humanities and join the ranks of the educated unemployed. Even as regards humanistic learning, he deplored the attempts to 'keep our Islamic culture . . . in a state of fossilized purity'. Rather than mourn the decline of their language, Urdu, the Muslims should recognize that Hindi in the Devanagari script was here to stay. Urdu would be made more contemporary by making its literature available in Devanagari, and by suggesting appropriate words and idioms to enrich the new, emerging modern Hindi.[16]

Where the likes of Maulana Azad and Saif Tyabji sought to make Muslims into Congress Party MPs, there were others who argued that the community could better represent itself through its own organizations. In October 1953 a group of intellectuals and professionals met in Aligarh to discuss the founding of a political party to 'protect the minority rights of Muslims, and to enable them to lead an honourable life in this country'. Among their concerns were the low proportion of Muslims in the legislatures, and in the higher civil service.[17] Presiding over the convention was a former mayor of Calcutta, who claimed that, if present trends continued, the future held only 'economic paralysis, cultural death or disintegration and political helotage for Muslims'.[18] Six months later, in a speech at Delhi's Jama Masjid, the secretary of the UP Jamiat attacked the government of India as anti-democratic and pro-Hindu. 'It is high time', he said, 'for Muslims of India to unite and organise themselves under one leadership to face the eventualities in future'.[19]

Meanwhile, in southern India more concrete steps were being taken in this regard. In September 1951 the 'Indian Union Muslim League' (IUML) came into being in Madras, both its name and its charter marking it out from the pre-Partition party some might think it resembled. It sought to 'secure, protect, and maintain' the religious, cultural, economic and other 'legitimate rights and interests of the Muslims and other minorities', but also pledged itself to upholding and defending 'the independence, freedom and honour' of the Indian Union.[20] Several years later, a party was formed in Hyderabad to represent the city's Muslims – the Majlis Ittihad-ul-Musilmin. The Majlis put up several candidates in the 1957 elections, but won only a single assembly seat. The IUML was more successful in its own bastion of Kerala, where it won ten seats in the mid-term election of 1960.[21]

VI

Writing in 1957, W. C. Smith observed that in the history of Islam, Indian Muslims were unique in that they were very numerous and yet did not live in a state of their own. Unlike the Muslims of Iran, Iraq, Pakistan or Turkey, they shared their citizenship in the new Indian republic 'with an immense number of other people. They constitute the only sizable body of Muslims in the world of which this is, or ever has been, true.'[22]

The Muslims of India were a large minority, as well as a vulnerable one. They were under threat from Hindu communalism, and from the provocation of Pakistan. The leaders of that nation tended to deride Indian secularism, and 'to presume and encourage a disloyalty of Indian Muslims to their state'. Muslims were hostage to India–Pakistan relations in general, and to Pakistan's treatment of its own minorities in particular. Thus 'each new Hindu discontent fleeing from East Pakistan, and each new border incident or exacerbation of canal-water dispute or refugee-property question, has had repercussions on Muslim life within India.'[23]

Another problem, also linked to Partition, was the lack of a credible middle class. At or shortly after Partition, large numbers of Muslim civil servants, lawyers, scholars, doctors and entrepreneurs migrated to the new Islamic state, there to carve out careers unimpeded by Hindu competition. The Muslims who remained were the labouring poor, the peasants, labourers and artisans who were now seriously in want of an enlightened and liberal leadership. As one perceptive British official wrote, it was 'one of the curses of Partition' in Bengal that the Muslim officers had all opted for Pakistan, so that 'the Muslim minorities in West Bengal will be without representation in the services or anywhere else where they could look for help or protection'.[24] A partial exception was Kashmir, where under Sheikh Abdullah's regime between 1947 and 1953 Muslims were encouraged to own land, take to the professions and, above all, to educate themselves. Among the more far-sighted reforms were the creation of schools and colleges for girls, with the Women's College in Srinagar justly winning a countrywide reputation for excellence.[25] Elsewhere, Muslims continued to labour in menial jobs while being under-represented in education, in the professions, in the legislatures and in the administration.[26]

On the other side, there was the effort of the Indian political leadership to create a secular state, and to instil a feeling of belonging among the minorities. Nehru was the key figure here, but he was aided by other Congress members who had studied in the school of Gandhi. When street clashes threatened to escalate into a major riot in Ahmedabad in 1956, the chief minister, Morarji Desai, went on an indefinite fast to bring back the peace.[27] Such acts were prompted in part by genuine belief, and in part by diplomatic exigencies – the need to put one's best face outwards while making the case for Kashmir. Attacks on Muslims would make India's claim for the Valley more fragile.[28] Still, it was 'no small matter that the Hindu leaders of the nation, in the name of secularism and humanity, restrained the natural and potentially ferocious impetus of the Hindu majority to wreak vengeance on the Muslim group'.[29]

Immediately after Partition some had feared a conflagration that would destroy the Muslim minority in India. Instead, as Mushirul Hasan has noted, 'the communal temperature in the 1950s remained relatively low. There was a lull after a violent storm, a clear and downward trend in communal incidents.'[30] There was suspicion and tension on the ground, and occasional violent incidents, but no riots of the scale witnessed during the 1920s, 1930s or 1940s. The conflicts of the 1950s were rooted in language, ethnicity, class and caste, rather than in religion.

The lull was broken by the Jabalpur riots of early 1961, in which some fifty Indians, mostly Muslims, lost their lives. But this was a minor affray in comparison with what happened in the winter of 1963–4 when the theft of the Prophet's hair from the Hazratbal mosque in Srinagar prompted a series of attacks on Hindus in distant East Pakistan. Thousands of refugees fled into India, their stories leading to a rise in the communal temperature and to retributory violence against Muslims. In and around Calcutta 400 people died in religious rioting, three-quarters of them Muslims. Some of the violence was motivated by speculators seizing the chance to obliterate squatter colonies and re-develop them for sale. There was also serious rioting in the steel towns of Jamshedpur and Rourkela, in which perhaps as many as 1,000 people perished, most of them Muslims.[31]

By this time Partition was almost two decades in the past, yet its residues remained. For, as a Muslim leader in Madras bitterly remarked, the violence of 1963 – 4 only reinforced the 'fear that anything happening in Pakistan will have its repercussions on Muslims in India, particularly when exaggerated reports appear in the Indian Press, and people and parties inimical to Muslims are ready to seize the opportunity'.[32]

VII

Like the Muslims, the Untouchables were spread all across India. Like them, they were also poor, stigmatized and often on the receiving end of upper-caste violence. They worked in the villages, in the lowliest professions, as farm servants, agricultural labourers, cobblers and scavengers. By the canons of Hindu orthodoxy their touch would defile the upper castes, and in some regions their very sight too. They were denied access to land and to water sources; even their homes were set apart from the main village.

Under British rule, opportunities had arisen for some Untouchables to escape the tyranny of the village. These gained employment in the army, or worked in factories and urban settlements. Here too they were usually assigned the most menial jobs, as well as the most degrading.

Gandhi had redesignated the Untouchables as 'Harijans', or children of God. The Constitution of India abolished untouchability and listed the erstwhile Untouchable communities in a separate schedule – hence their new, collective name, 'Scheduled Castes'. However, village ethnographies of the 1950s confirmed that the practice of untouchability continued as before. The Scheduled Castes still owned little or no land, and were still subject to social and in some cases sexual abuse. But these ethnographies also revealed that at the bottom things were changing, albeit slowly. In some parts the low castes were refusing to perform tasks that they considered demeaning. No longer would they carry loads for free, or submissively allow upper-caste males to violate their women. More daringly, they were beginning to ask for higher wages and for land to cultivate, sometimes under the aegis of communist activists.[33]

In the cities, lower-caste assertion took a more organized form. Under the encouragement of the Communist Party of India, the municipal sweepers of Delhi – who belonged to the Balmiki caste – formed a union of their own. In October 1953 this union presented a charter of eleven demands to the municipal corporation, focusing on better pay and work conditions. The sweepers held processions and public meetings, and marched to the town hall in a show of strength. There were also a series of hunger strikes, and at least one major confrontation with the police. The historian of these protests notes that they were 'not just about wages, but also about dignity and the value of the labour of the Balmikis'.[34]

VIII

The burgeoning genre of Untouchable autobiographies also shows the 1950s to be a time of flux. Caste prejudice and caste discrimination were rampant, but no longer were they accepted so passively. There was an incipient stirring which became manifest in social protest and was aided by the new avenues of social mobility.[35]

The first such avenue was education. After Independence there was a great expansion in school and college education. By law, a certain portion of seats were reserved for the Scheduled Castes. By policy, different state governments endowed scholarships for children from disadvantaged homes. Where they could they took advantage, spawning an entire generation of first-generation learners. According to one estimate, while the school population doubled in the first decade of Independence, the number of ex-Untouchables in schools swelled eight-

or tenfold. There were also many more Scheduled Caste students at university than ever before.[36]

A second avenue was government employment. By law, 15 per cent of all jobs in state and state-aided institutions were reserved for the Scheduled Castes. Again, there was a massive expansion after 1947, with new positions available in the Secretariat and in government-run schools, hospitals, factories and infrastructure projects. Although exact figures are hard to obtain, it is likely that several million jobs were created for Scheduled Castes in the state sector in the first two decades after Independence. These were permanent positions, to be retained until retirement, and with pension and health benefits. In theory, such reservation existed at all levels of government; in practice, it was the reserved posts at the lower levels that tended to be filled first and fastest. As late as 1966, while only 1.77 per cent of senior administrative posts were occupied by Indians of low-caste origin, 8.86 per cent of clerical jobs were, and as many as 17.94 per cent of posts of peons and attendants.[37]

There was also reservation in Parliament and state assemblies, where 15 per cent of all seats were filled by Scheduled Caste candidates. Besides, universal franchise meant that they could influence the outcome of elections in the 'unreserved' category as well. In many parts, Scheduled Castes were quick to seize the opportunities the vote presented them. As one low-caste politician in Agra observed, his constituents 'may not understand the intricacies of politics', but they did 'understand the power of the vote and want to use it'.[38] And they understood it in all contexts – national, provincial and local. Already in the early 1950s, cases were reported of Scheduled Castes forging alliances to prevent upper-caste landlords from winning elections to village *panchayats* (councils).[39] The vote was quickly perceived as a bargaining tool; for instance, in a UP village, the shoemakers told an upper-caste candidate they would support him if he agreed to shift the yard for the disposal of dead animals from their compound to a site outside the village.[40]

For a fair number of Scheduled Castes, affirmative action did bring genuine benefits. Now, children of farm labourers could (and did) become members of Parliament. Those who joined the government as lowly 'class IV' employees could see their children become members of the elite Indian Administrative Service. But affirmative action also brought with it a new kind of stigma. Intended to end caste discrimination, it fixed the beneficiaries ever more firmly in their own, original caste. There was suspicion and resentment among the upper castes, and sometimes a tendency among the beneficiaries to look down upon, or even forget, their fellows. As one scholar somewhat cynically wrote, reservation had created 'a mass of self-engrossed people who are quickly and easily satisfied with the small gains they can win for themselves'.[41]

A final avenue of mobility was economic development in general. Industrialization and urbanization meant new opportunities away from the village, even if – as in the state sector – the Scheduled Castes came to occupy only the less skilled and less lucrative positions. Living away from home helped expand the mind, as in the case of a farm labourer from UP who became a factory worker in Bombay and learnt to love the city's museums, its collections of Gandhara art especially.[42] And sometimes there were economic gains to be made. Consider the Jatavs of Agra, a caste of cobblers and shoemakers whose world changed with the growth of a market for their products in the Middle East and the Soviet Union. The Jatavs became an 'urban yeomanry', now able to build and buy their own houses. While many continued as self-employed shoemakers, some Jatavs were able to open factories of their own, where the wages paid to their workers were considerably in excess of what they themselves had once hoped to earn. In 1960 a master craftsman took home about Rs250 a month, a factory worker about Rs100 – even the lesser figure was many times what an unskilled labourer earned. Although the distribution of gains was by no means even, the market had helped enhance their economic as well as social status. The present state of affairs was 'a far cry from the pre-1900 days, when most Jatavs were little more than labourers and city servants'.[43]

IX

As with the Muslims, the Scheduled Castes formed an important 'vote bank' for the Congress. They too tended to trust the party of Mahatma Gandhi more than its rivals. In the 1957 election, for example, the Congress won 64 out of the 76 seats reserved for Scheduled Castes in Parliament, and as many as 361 out of the 469 reserved for them in the legislative assemblies.

When the seats reserved for Scheduled Tribe members were added, nearly one in four MPs came from underprivileged backgrounds. Yet the ministers in Jawaharlal Nehru's Cabinet were overwhelmingly upper caste. This worried him. 'One of my greatest difficulties', he told a senior colleague, 'is to find suitable non-Brahmins.' Nehru asked the colleague to suggest candidates, but then found one himself: a Mrs Chandrasekhar from Madras, an educated Scheduled Caste whom he inducted as deputy minister.[44]

The ranking Scheduled Caste minister in the Union Cabinet was Jagjivan Ram from Bihar. Born into a Chamar (cobbler) home, he became the first such boy from his village to go to high school, and from there to the Banaras Hindu University. On graduation he joined the Gandhian movement, his steady work rewarded after 1947 by a series of Cabinet appointments. Among the Ministries he ran were those of Labour, Communications, Mines, and Railways. Jagjivan Ram had the reputation of being a first-class administrator, although he did not live the kind of squeaky-clean life his Gandhian background perhaps demanded of him.[45]

The most charismatic Scheduled Caste leader, however, remained outside the Congress. This was B. R. Ambedkar, who had joined Nehru's Cabinet as an Independent, leaving the government in 1951 to restart his Scheduled Caste Federation. His party fared disastrously in the 1952 election, although Ambedkar himself was later elected to the Upper House. By now this longtime foe of Hinduism was seeking to find a way of leaving the ancestral fold. He had contemplated converting to Sikhism, then to Islam, then to Christianity. Ambedkar finally settled on Buddhism, a faith of Indian origin that seemed best suited to his own rationalist and egalitarian temperament.

After he left the Cabinet, Ambedkar immersed himself in literature on or about the Buddha. He became a member of the Mahabodhi Society and travelled through the Buddhist countries of south-east Asia. At a public meeting in Bombay in May 1956, Ambedkar announced that he would convert to Buddhism before the end of the year. His mammoth study *The Buddha and his Dhamma* was already in the press. Ambedkar considered holding the conversion ceremony in Bombay – where the publicity would be immense – or in the ancient Buddhist site of Sarnath. In the event he chose Nagpur, a city in the centre of India where he had a large and devoted following. Many joined him in embracing Buddhism, in a colourful and well-attended ceremony that took place on 15 October 1956. Six weeks later Ambedkar died suddenly. He was cremated in Bombay, with an icon of the Buddha placed under his head. A million people participated in the funeral procession.[46]

Shortly before he died Ambedkar had decided to float a new party, the Republican Party of India. This formally came into being in 1957. Its leaders and cadre were, like Ambedkar himself, from the Mahar caste. It was also mostly Mahars who had followed their leader into Buddhism. Ambedkar was a figure of reverence among the Mahars of the Nagpur area. In his lifetime they celebrated his birthday with gusto, taking out processions holding his photograph aloft. When he came to town to speak, the factory workers would crowd in to hear him; even the 'women went to these parades as to a wedding'. Under his inspiration the Mahars formed troupes that performed plays parodying Hindu ritual and the behaviour of the upper castes. They also sang songs in his honour: 'From the moment that the glance of Bhim[rao Ambedkar] fell upon the poor', began one song, 'From that day our strength grew . . .'.[47]

But it was not merely in Mahar strongholds that Ambedkar was respected. All across northern India he was admired for his scholarship – he had doctoral degrees from Columbia and London universities – and for his political achievements – notably his drafting of the Constitution of India. For members of the Scheduled Castes who had a glimmer of learning themselves, for those who had been to high school or travelled outside their home village, Ambedkar was both exemplar and icon, the man who had breached the upper-caste citadel and encouraged his fellows to do likewise.

Ambedkar's slogan for his followers was: 'Educate, Agitate, Organize'. He set up a People's Education Society that ran schools and at least two good colleges. Scheduled Caste members who went to these or other schools came inevitably to regard Ambedkar as their mentor. Among the Scheduled Caste intelligentsia, books or pamphlets by Ambedkar became required reading, lovingly passed on from hand to hand.[48] Thus the son of a dock worker, sent by government scholarship to the Siddharth College in Bombay, began contributing to magazines and participating in debates – where 'the topic of all these writings and speeches was always Babasaheb [Ambedkar] and his Dalit movement'.[49]

The presence of B. R. Ambedkar underlines a quite profound difference between the Scheduled Castes and the other minority with whom I have here compared them. For the Muslims had no seats reserved for them in the Secretariat or in Parliament. Nor, in independent India, did they have a leader of Ambedkar's stature to inspire and move them – while he was alive or long after he was gone.

X

In March 1949 a group of Scheduled Caste members from the villages around Delhi walked to Mahatma Gandhi's memorial in the city. They had been thrown out of their homes by Jat landowners angered that these previously bonded servants had the cheek to take part in local elections and graze their cattle on the village commons. There, in the very heart of the capital, these outcasts began a hunger strike. By sitting on a memorial to the Father of the Nation, and by using the methods of protest forged by him, they attracted wide attention, including solicitous visits by prominent Gandhians and Cabinet ministers.[50]

Turn next to a case from urban India, to a newly elected Scheduled Caste MP who applied for membership of the Bar Association in his home town, Sitapur. His application was kept pending for four months, after which he was told that he could join but not use the washroom, and be served only by a Muslim servant. The MP brought the matter to the attention of the prime minister, who intervened to have him admitted without any preconditions.[51]

Elsewhere, the Scheduled Castes who asserted themselves were not so fortunate. The sociologist N. D. Kamble collated hundreds of examples of 'atrocities' perpetrated on Scheduled Castes in independent India. Here are a few choice – if that is the word – instances taken from Kamble's research:

April 1951: A labour camp in Matunga, Bombay.
A group of factory workers stages a play on Ambedkar's birthday. Upper-caste young men break up the performance, assault the actors, and damage the stage.

June 1951: A village in Himachal Pradesh.
A conference of Scheduled Castes is attacked by Rajput landlords. The SCs are beaten up with sticks, their leaders tied up with ropes and confined to a cattle pound.

July 1951: A rural school in the Jalgaon district of Bombay State.
A Brahmin teacher abuses Ambedkar for introducing the Hindu Code

Bill in Parliament. A SC boy protests, whereupon he is beaten and removed from the school.

June 1952: A village in the Madurai district of Madras State.
A SC youth asks for tea in a glass at a local shop. Tradition entitles him only to a disposable coconut shell. When he persists, he is kicked and hit on the head by caste Hindus.

June 1957: A village in the Parbani district of Madhya Bharat.
Newly converted Buddhists refuse to flay carcasses of dead cattle. They are boycotted by the Hindu landlords, denied other work, and threatened with physical reprisals.

May 1959: A village in the Ahmednagar district of Bombay State.
A Buddhist marriage party is not allowed to enter the hamlet through the village gates. When they persist, caste Hindus attack them with stones and swords.

October 1960: A village in the Aurangabad District of Maharashtra.
Caste Hindus enter the Scheduled Caste hamlet and break a statue of the Buddha into tiny pieces.[52]

What these cases – and the many more like them – reveal is a system that was in quite profound turmoil. All across India the winds of democratic politics had made the Scheduled Castes more willing to demand their rights. Aided by reservation in schools, offices, factories, and legislatures, inspired by the example of their great leader B. R. Ambedkar and encouraged by the constitutional provisions in favour of social equality, many among them were inclined to abandon the old road of deference in favour of the more rocky path of defiance. This in turn provoked a sometimes nasty reaction from those who persisted in thinking of themselves as social superiors.

XI

In the winter of 1925–6, the writer Aldous Huxley went on a long trip through British India. He attended the Kanpur session of the Indian National Congress and heard declamatory speeches asking for freedom. Huxley had some sympathy with these aspirations, yet worried that they represented only the upper-caste Hindu interest. As he wrote in the book of his travels,

> That the lower-caste masses would suffer, at the beginning, in any case, from a return to Indian autonomy seems almost indubitable. Where the superiority of the upper castes to the lower is a matter of religious dogma, you can hardly expect the governing few to be particularly careful about the rights of the many. It is even something of a heresy [for them] to have rights.[53]

Two decades later India became independent, and the constitution bestowed rights of equality on all citizens, regardless of caste, creed, age or gender. The lower castes were in fact granted special rights, special access to schools and jobs, in compensation for the discrimination they had suffered down the centuries. But, as a Scheduled Caste member of the Constituent Assembly pointed out, state law was one thing, social practice quite another. For the prejudices of caste had been opposed by reformers down the centuries, from Gautama Buddha to Mahatma Gandhi, yet they had all 'found it very difficult to get rid of this ghost of untouchability'. Laws had been enacted removing strictures against Untouchables, with regard to temple entry for example. 'What is the effect of these laws?' asked the member, before supplying this answer: 'Not an inch of untouchability has been removed by these laws ... If at all the ghost of untouchability or the stigma of untouchability from India should go the minds of these crores and crores of Hindu folks should be changed and unless their hearts are changed, I do not hope, Sir, that untouchability will be removed. It is now up to the Hindu society not to observe untouchability in any shape or form.'[54]

There was pessimism about the position of Untouchables in free India, and pessimism also about the future of that other large and insecure minority, the Muslims. Travelling through India and Pakistan in 1951, the Aga Khan – the influential leader of the Ismaili sect – found 'a horrible fear' among Muslims on both sides of the border, but in India especially. He wrote to Jawaharlal Nehru of 'the fear amongst Muslims which I myself share to a great extent' – this being that 'five or ten years hence there may be a [Hindu] Mahasabha government who openly make the union of what is now Pakistan – both East and West – with Bharat [India] the main purpose of foreign policy and high politics'.

The Muslim leader thought that a Hindu chauvinist party, once in power, would use atomic blasts to divert the rivers flowing through Kashmir into Pakistan, thus bringing that state to its knees. He drew a parallel with the situation in the Arab world, where – so he claimed – Sudan was preparing to stop the flow of the Nile into Egypt. In the Aga Khan's view, Hindu India was to Muslim Pakistan as Christian Sudan was to Muslim Egypt. As he put it, 'I have felt that this atmosphere of doom [which] prevails amongst Muslims on account of this very water question . . . is a replica of the similar fear in Egypt'.[55]

This letter is notable for at least three reasons. First, as an early illustration of the now widespread fear that Muslims were being persecuted worldwide. Second, for its easy equation of the interests of Indian Muslims with the welfare of Pakistan. Finally, and perhaps most tellingly, for its prediction that the Republic of India would become a Hindu state within ten years.

The Aga Khan and Aldous Huxley were both right and wrong in their scepticism – right with regard to the continuing social prejudice, wrong with regard to the intentions of the top political leadership. For the 'governing few' were in fact very careful of the rights of the many. Writing in 1959 – a decade and more after Independence – an Indian editor who was bitterly opposed to Nehru was constrained to recognize his two greatest achievements – the creation of a secular state and the granting of equal rights to Untouchables. Recalling the 'reactionary forces which came into play after partition', the editor remarked that 'had Nehru shown the slightest weakness, these forces would have turned this country into a Hindu state in which the minorities . . . could not have lived with any measure of safety or security'. It was also to Nehru's 'everlasting credit' that he insisted that Untouchables be granted full rights, such that 'in public life and in all government action, the equality of man would be scrupulously maintained in the secular state of India'.[56]

To be sure, there remained a slippage between public policy and popular practice. The laws promoting secularism and social equality were on the statute books, but most Muslims, and most Scheduled Castes, remained poor and marginalized. The threat of violence was never far away. Still, given the bloody birth of the nation, and the continuing provocation from Pakistan, it was no small matter that the Indian government refused to merge faith with state. And given the resilience of social institutions in general, and the ancient and sanctified history of this one in particular, it was remarkable that the caste system changed as much as it did. The progress made in abolishing untouchability or in assuring equal rights to all citizens was uneven, and – by the standards of understandably impatient reformers – very slow. Yet more progress had probably been made in the first seventeen years of Indian independence than in the previous seventeen hundred.

PART FOUR

THE RISE OF POPULISM

18

WAR AND SUCCESSION

> There is no question of Nehru's attempting to create a dynasty of his
> own; it would be inconsistent with his character and career.
>
> FRANK MORAES, political columnist, 1960

I

JAWAHARLAL NEHRU DIED ON the morning of 27 May 1964. The news was conveyed to the world by the 2 p.m. bulletin of All-India Radio. Two hours later the home minister, Gulzarilal Nanda, was sworn in as acting prime minister. Almost immediately the search commenced for a more permanent successor.

The central figure in the choice of a new prime minister was the Congress president, K. Kamaraj. Born in 1903, in a low-caste family in the Tamil country, Kamaraj dropped out of school to join the national movement. He spent close to eight years in jail, this spread out over two decades and six prison sentences. His status among the people was consolidated by his lifestyle – he lived austerely, and never married. He climbed steadily up the party hierarchy, and served as president of the Tamil Nadu Congress as well as chief minister of Madras before heading the party at the national level.[1]

Kamaraj was a thick-set man with a white moustache – according to one journalist, he looked 'like a cross between Sonny Liston and the Walrus'. Like the boxer (but unlike the Lewis Carroll character) he was a man of few words. The press joked that his answer to all questions put by them was one word in Tamil: 'Parkalam' (We shall see). His reticence served him well, never better than after Nehru's death, when he had to listen to what his party men had to say. From 28 May Kamaraj began consulting his chief ministers and party bosses (the 'Syndicate', as they were called) on the best person to succeed Nehru. An early name to consider was Morarji Desai, the outstanding administrator from Gujarat who had made it clear that he wanted the job.

In four days Kamaraj met a dozen chief ministers and as many as 200 members of Parliament. From his conversations it became clear that Desai would be a controversial choice: his style was too abrasive. The person most MPs seemed to prefer was Lal Bahadur Shastri, also a fine administrator, but one who was more accessible, and from the Hindi heartland besides. It helped that Nehru had come increasingly to rely on Shastri in his last days. These factors all weighed heavily with Kamaraj, who was concerned that the succession should signal a certain continuity.

Desai was persuaded to withdraw his candidature. On 31 May the Congress Working Committee approved the choice of Lal Bahadur Shastri. The next day the appointment was ratified by the Congress Parliamentary Party and the day following, Shastri was sworn in as prime minister. Very soon the new incumbent was asserting his authority. Desai was dropped from the Cabinet because he insisted on the number two position. There was a clamour to include Nehru's daughter, Indira Gandhi; Shastri complied, yet gave her the insignificant Information and Broadcasting portfolio. Mrs Gandhi, in turn, forestalled any move by Shastri to move into Teen Murti House (where Nehru had lived as prime minister) by proposing that it be made into a memorial to her father.[2]

Announcing Shastri's elevation to the press, Kamaraj had said that the undisputed rule of a great man would now be replaced by a form of collective leadership. Shastri had other ideas. An early innovation was the creation of a separate Prime Minister's Secretariat, where a band of carefully chosen officials would prepare papers on matters of policy. This was to fill in the gaps in the prime minister's learning – gaps larger by far than was the case with Nehru – but also to provide him with an independent, non-partisan source of advice, freeing him of excessive dependence on the Cabinet.[3]

Not long before Nehru's death, the United Kingdom had its own 'succession' drama, with the Conservatives deeply split on the choice of Harold Macmillan's successor. The left-wing *Guardian* newspaper gleefully remarked that the 'new Prime Minister of India, in spite of all forebodings, has been named with more dispatch, and much more dignity, than was the new Prime Minister of Britain'.[4] The paper's New Delhi correspondent met Nehru's successor, whom he found 'rock-sure of himself ', a 'very strong man indeed' who spoke in short and sharp sentences – 'no words wasted'.[5]

Old colonial hands were less optimistic. Nehru's death, wrote one ICS man to another, had made India's future fraught with uncertainty. For 'I can't imagine S[h]astri has the stature to hold things together, and all the trouble-makers from Kashmir to Comorin will work to fish in troubled waters, to say nothing of China and Pakistan. Cyprus on a big scale? What revolting times we live in!'[6]

II

With his death, Nehru's Kashmir initiative also died. However, on the other side of the country, moves were afoot to resolve the dispute between the Naga rebels and the government of India. Pained by a decade of bloodshed, the Baptist Church of Nagaland had constituted a 'peace mission' of individuals trusted both by the underground movement and the government of India. The three members agreed upon were the chief minister of Assam B. P. Chaliha, the widely respected Sarvodaya leader Jayaprakash Narayan and the Anglican priest Michael Scott, who had helped secure refuge in London for the Naga leader A. Z. Phizo.

Through the summer of 1964 this peace mission travelled through the territory, meeting members of the state government as well as of the 'Federal Republic of Nagaland'. A ceasefire agreement was signed by both sides; it came into effect on 6 September, signalled by the pealing of church bells. Two weeks later the first round of talks began between the government of India and the rebels.[7]

From Kohima, Jayaprakash Narayan wrote to a friend that, although the situation was still unpredictable, 'the strongest desire of almost every Naga at the present time seems to be for a lasting peace. The Naga people are dreading nothing more than the resumption of hostilities'. Then he added, less optimistically: 'However, it has to be said that as far as the talks between the Government of India and the underground leaders are concerned, very little progress so far has been made.'[8]

The records of the talks between the government and the rebels do reveal a fundamental incommensurability of positions. The NNC leader, Isak Swu, began by saying that 'today we are here as two nations – Nagas and Indians, side by side'. The foreign secretary, Y. D. Gundevia, answered that 'we are not living as two nations side by side. History tells us that Nagaland was a part and parcel of India.' Between these two

opposed positions, B. P. Chaliha and Jayaprakash Narayan tried valiantly
to locate common ground. Chaliha praised the Nagas as 'a people of
rare and high qualities', and hoped that 'both parties will find a way
to remove the gulf' between them. Narayan argued that 'compromise
is possible because we think that both sides have part of the truth. If
one were 100 per cent right, or 100 per cent wrong, there could be no
question of compromise.'[9]

The demand for Naga independence presented a powerful challenge
to the idea of India. Another somewhat different challenge was presented
by the testing of a nuclear device by China in October 1964. Immediately
there were calls for India to develop an atom bomb of its own. On
24 October the director of India's Atomic Energy Commission,
Dr Homi J. Bhabha, gave a talk on All-India Radio on the nuclear
question. He spoke of the need for universal nuclear disarmament, yet
hinted that, pending that eventuality, India might develop a nuclear
deterrent of its own. There was no means of successfully stopping a
nuclear thrust in mid-flight, said Dr Bhabha, adding: 'The only defence
against such an attack appears to be a capability and threat of retaliation.'
Further, 'atomic weapons give a state possessing them in adequate
numbers a deterrent power against attack from a much stronger state'.
Later in his talk, Dr Bhabha examined the cost of constructing an atomic
stockpile. By his calculations, fifty bombs would cost about Rs100
million, an expenditure that was 'small compared with the military
budgets of many countries'.[10]

The scientist's talk was grist to the mill of those politicians – mostly
from the Jana Sangh – who had long advocated that India test its own
atom bombs. The MP from Dewas, Hukum Chandra Kachwai, moved
a resolution in the Lok Sabha to this effect. In an eloquent speech he
identified China as India's main *dushman* (enemy). 'Whatever weapons
the enemy possesses, we must possess them too,' he thundered. Evoking
memories of the war of 1962, he said that the nation should not rest
until it had reclaimed every inch of land lost to or stolen by China. The
possession of an atomic stockpile would, he argued, also increase India's
prestige in the wider world.

A lively debate ensued, with some members endorsing Kachwai,
others opposing him in the name of India's reputation as a force
for peace. In his own intervention the prime minister claimed that
the promoters of the bomb had misread Dr Bhabha's intentions. The
scientist was calling for disarmament, while the production costs referred

to the United States, whose developed atomic infrastructure made the manufacture of additional bombs possible at little expense. In India, the costs would be prohibitive, said Shastri; in any case, to manufacture these deadly weapons would be to depart from the tradition of Gandhi and Nehru. Notably, the prime minister spoke not in narrow nationalistic terms but from the perspective of the human race. These bombs, he said, were a threat to the survival of the world, an affront to humanity (*manushyata*) as a whole.

Shastri's speech was somewhat defensive, and certainly less stirring than that of the chief speaker on the other side. But the large Congress majority in the House ensured that the resolution asking India to go the nuclear route was comfortably defeated.[11]

III

India's Republic Day, 26 January, is annually celebrated in New Delhi by a government-sponsored march down Rajpath (formerly Kingsway), with gaily decorated floats representing the different states competing with tanks and mounted submarines for attention. In 1965, Republic Day was to be more than a symbolic show of national pride – it would also signal a substantial affirmation of national unity. Back in 1949 the Constituent Assembly had chosen Hindi as the official language of the Union of India. The constitution which ratified this came into operation on 26 January 1950. However, there would be a fifteen-year 'grace period', when English was to be used along with Hindi in communication between the centre and the states. Now this period was ending; henceforth, Hindi would prevail.

Southern politicians had long been worried about the change. In 1956 the Academy of Tamil Culture passed a resolution urging that 'English should continue to be the official language of the Union and the language for communication between the Union and the State Governments and between one State Government and another'. The signatories included C. N. Annadurai, E. V. Ramaswami 'Periyar', and C. Rajagopalachari. The organization of the campaign was chiefly the work of the Dravida Munnetra Kazhagam (DMK), which organized many protest meetings against the imposition of Hindi.[12]

In the wake of the China war the DMK had dropped its secessionist plank. It no longer wanted a separate country; but it did want to protect the culture and language of the Tamil people. The DMK's acknowledged leader was C. N. Annadurai. Known universally as 'Anna' (or elder brother), he was a gifted orator who had done much to build his party into a credible force in the state. In Anna's opinion Hindi was merely a regional language like any other. It had no 'special merit'; in fact, it was less developed than other Indian tongues, less suited to a time of rapid advances in science and technology. To the argument that more Indians spoke Hindi than any other language, Anna sarcastically answered: 'If we had to accept the principle of numerical superiority while selecting our national bird, the choice would have fallen not on the peacock but on the common crow.'[13]

Jawaharlal Nehru had been sensitive to the sentiments of the south; sentiments shared by the east and north-east as well. In 1963 he piloted the passing of an Official Languages Act, which provided that from 1965 English 'may' still be used along with Hindi in official communication. That caveat proved problematic; for while Nehru clarified that 'may' meant 'shall', other Congress politicians thought it actually meant 'may not'.[14]

As 26 January 1965 approached, the opponents of Hindi geared up for action. Ten days before Republic Day, Annadurai wrote to Shastri saying that his party would observe the day of the changeover as a 'day of mourning'. But he added an interesting rider in the form of a request to postpone the day of imposition by a week. Then the DMK could enthusiastically join the rest of the nation in celebrating Republic Day.

Shastri and his government stood by the decision to make Hindi official on 26 January. In response, the DMK launched a statewide campaign of protest. In numerous villages bonfires were made to burn effigies of the Hindi demoness. Hindi books and the relevant pages of the constitution were also burnt. In railway stations and post offices, Hindi signs were removed or blackened over. In towns across the state there were fierce and sometimes deadly battles between the police and angry students.[15]

The protests were usually collective: strikes and processions; *bandhs*, *hartals* and *dharnas*. The headlines in the *Hindu* newspaper tell part of the story:

TOTAL HARTAL IN COIMBATORE

ADVOCATES ABSTAIN FROM WORK

STUDENTS FAST IN BATCHES

PEACEFUL STRIKE IN MADURAI

LATHI-CHARGE IN VILLUPURAM

TEAR-GAS USED IN UTHAMAPALYAM

There was one form of protest that was individual, and disturbingly so: the taking of one's life. On Republic Day itself, two men set themselves on fire in Madras. One left a letter saying he wanted to sacrifice himself at the altar of Tamil. Three days later a twenty-year-old man in Tiruchi poisoned himself with insecticide. He too left a note saying his suicide was in the cause of Tamil. These 'martyrdoms', in turn, sparked dozens more strikes and boycotts.

There is a vivid account of the revolt by a police officer asked to quell it. When a party of constables entered the town of Tiruppur, they found that the rioting was over but crowds still hung around, curious or sullen. Police lorries and jeeps lay burnt and smouldering on the streets and in the *taluk* office compound. The police station was in a shambles, a spare transmitter overturned, all the glass broken and the verandah fence torn down. Injured constables were resting inside and the inspector lay on his back with a stomach injury. Dead bodies of rioters were strewn about, one on the station steps, another on a street behind. A third, shot clean through the navel, lay on a river bank close by, an abusive crowd behind it still being held at bay by a rifle party.

The 'real mistake', writes this officer, was in 'the failure to appreciate the depth of feeling' evoked by the imposition of Hindi. What some in New Delhi saw as 'an exhibition of mere parochial fanaticism' was in fact 'a local nationalist movement'.[16]

The intensity of the anti-Hindi protests alarmed the central government. Soon it became clear that the ruling Congress Party was split down the middle on the issue. On the last day of January a group of prominent Congress Party members met in Bangalore to issue an appeal to 'the Hindi-loving people not to try to force Hindi on the people of non-Hindi areas'. The hustling of Hindi in haste, they said, would imperil the unity of the country.

The signatories to this appeal included S. Nijalingappa (Chief Minister of Mysore), Atulya Ghosh (the boss of the Bengal Congress), Sanjiva Reddy (a senior Union minister), and K. Kamaraj (the Congress president). On the same day, they were answered by the high-ranking Congress leader Morarji Desai. Speaking to the press in Tirupati, Desai claimed that by learning Hindi the Tamil people would only increase their influence within India as a whole. The Congress leaders in Madras, he said, should 'convince the people of their mistake [in opposing Hindi] and get them around'. Desai regretted that Hindi had not been made official in the 1950s, before the protests against it had crystallized. Only Hindi could be the link language in India, for the alternative, English, 'is not our language'. 'No regional sentiments', insisted Desai, 'should come in the way of this move of the Government to forge the integration of the country further'.[17]

The prime minister, Lal Bahadur Shastri, was now placed in the hot seat. His heart was with the Hindi zealots; his head, however, urged him to listen to other voices. On 11 February the resignation of two Union ministers from Madras forced his hand. The same evening the prime minister went on All-India Radio to convey his 'deep sense of distress and shock' at the 'tragic events'. To remove any 'misapprehension' and 'misunderstanding', he said he would fully honour Nehru's assurance that English would be used as long as the people wanted. Then he made four assurances of his own:

First, every state would have complete and unfettered freedom to continue to transact its own business in the language of its own choice, which may be the regional language or English.

Secondly, communications from one state to another would be either in English or accompanied by an authentic English translation.

Thirdly, the non-Hindi states would be free to correspond with the central government in English and no change would be made in this arrangement without the consent of the non-Hindi states.

Fourthly, in the transaction of business at the central level English would continue to be used.

Later, Shastri added a crucial fifth assurance – that the All-India Civil Services Examination would continue to be conducted in English rather than (as the *Hindiwallahs* wanted) in Hindi alone.[18]

A week after the prime minister spoke on the radio there was a long and very heated discussion in Parliament on the riots in the Tamil country. Proponents of Hindi insisted that those who opposed the language were against the constitution and in effect anti-national; they also claimed that by giving in to violence the government would encourage more outbreaks of violence. Tamil members answered that they had 'already sacrificed enough for the Hindi demon'. They were supported by two stalwarts from Bengal – Hiren Mukherjee from the left, who accused the Hindi zealots of a 'contemptuous disregard' for those who did not speak their language, and N. C. Chatterjee from the right, who pointed out that 'the greatest integrating force today is the juridical and the legal unity of India', this enabled by the fact that the Supreme Court and the High Courts functioned in English. The Anglo-Indian member, Frank Anthony, deplored the 'increasing intolerance, increasing obscurantism, increasing chauvinism of those who purport to speak on behalf of Hindi'. J. B. Kripalani, speaking in a lighter vein, thought that the Hindi chauvinists had no hope at all. Even Indian babies, he noted, now 'do not say: Amma or Appa, but mummy and papa. We talk to our dogs also in English.' Kripalani remarked that 'Mr Anthony is very unnecessarily excited about the fate of his mother tongue. In England it [English] may disappear, [but] in India it will not disappear.'[19]

The parallels with the language question of the 1950s are uncanny. Then, too, a popular social movement led the prime minister of the day to reconsider both the stated official position and his own preferences. Nehru opposed linguistic states; Shastri believed Hindi should be the sole official language of the Union. But when protest spilled out into the streets, and when protesters were willing to offer their lives – Potti Sriramulu in 1953, a dozen Tamil young men in 1965 – the prime minister was forced to reconsider. Strikingly, in each case the Congress rank and file seemed to side with the opposition rather than with their own government. As with Nehru, Shastri's change of heart was occasioned as much by considerations of preserving party unity as by the unity of the nation itself.

IV

From south India, let us move back to that old trouble spot in the north, Kashmir. In March 1965 Sheikh Abdullah set out on a pilgrimage to Mecca. He took the long route, via London, where one of his sons was based. The Sheikh had been told by Shastri, via Sudhir Ghosh – a Rajya Sabha MP and a one-time associate of Mahatma Gandhi – that the best he could hope for was an autonomous Valley within the Indian Union. Ghosh thought the Lion of Kashmir was coming around to the idea, if slowly. He wrote to Horace Alexander, a Quaker and an old friend of India, asking him to keep a watch on Abdullah in London; the solution being charted for Kashmir would 'be ruined if, under pressure from over-zealous British newspaper men, Sheikh Abdullah makes a few

unwise statements in London . . . A few wrong remarks will give those
elements in the Congress Party who are anxious to push their knives into
Sheikh the necessary handle to upset the possibility of any settlement.'[20]

Abdullah seems not to have said anything indiscreet in the United
Kingdom. He proceeded to Mecca and stopped in Algiers on his way
home. There he did something far worse than speak carelessly to
a British journalist; he met with the Chinese prime minister, Chou
En-lai, who also happened to be in the Algerian capital. The content
of their conversations was not disclosed, but it was enough that he had
supped with the enemy. It was assumed that (as in 1953, when he met
Adlai Stevenson) Sheikh Abdullah had discussed the possibility of an
independent Kashmir. Back then it took four months for the Sheikh
to be jailed. Now he was placed under arrest as he got off the plane at
New Delhi's Palam Airport. He was taken to a government bungalow
in the capital and, a little later, transported across the country to the
southern hill town of Kodaikanal. Here he was given a charming cottage,
with fine views of hills not nearly as grand as those in Kashmir, but
forbidden to travel outside municipal limits or meet visitors without
official permission.

The news of the Sheikh's arrest was greeted with loud cheers in
both Houses of Parliament. He was seen as having betrayed India not
just by talking to a Chinese leader, but by doing so while the other foe,
Pakistan, was nibbling away at the borders. For while Abdullah was on
pilgrimage a conflict broke out over the Rann of Kutch, a salt marsh
claimed both by Pakistan and India. In the first week of April troops
exchanged fire in the Rann. The Pakistanis used their American tanks
to shell enemy positions – successfully, for the Indians had to withdraw
some forty miles to dry land. Angry telegrams were exchanged before
the two sides agreed to international arbitration under British auspices.[21]

One person dismayed by the rise of jingoism was Horace Alexander.
He wrote to Mrs Indira Gandhi and received a reply putting the inflamed
sentiments in perspective. 'What Sheikh Sahib does not realize', said
Mrs Gandhi, 'is that with the Chinese invasion and the latest moves in
and by Pakistan, the position of Kashmir has completely changed.' For
the frontiers of the state touched China and the USSR as well as India and
Pakistan. And 'in the present world situation, an independent Kashmir
would become a hot-bed of intrigue and, apart from the countries
mentioned above, would also attract espionage and other activities
from the USA and UK.'[22]

Abdullah's arrest and the clash in Kutch had put an idea into the head of the Pakistani president, Ayub Khan. This was to foment an insurrection in the Indian part of Kashmir, leading either to a war ending with the state being annexed to Pakistan, or in international arbitration with the same result. In the late summer of 1965 the Pakistan army began planning 'Operation Gibraltar', named for a famous Moorish military victory in medieval Spain. Kashmiri militants were trained in the use of small arms, with their units named after legendary warriors of the Islamic past – Suleiman, Salahuddin, and so on.[23]

In the first week of August, groups of irregulars crossed the ceasefire line into Kashmir. They proceeded to blow up bridges and fire-bomb government installations. The intention was to create confusion, and also to spark unrest. Radio Pakistan announced that a popular uprising had broken out in the Valley. In fact, the local population was mostly apathetic – some intruders were even handed over to the police.[24]

When the hoped-for rebellion did not materialize, Pakistan launched its reserve plan, codenamed 'Operation Grand Slam'. Troops crossed the ceasefire line in the Jammu sector and, using heavy artillery and mortar, made swift progress. The Indians fought back and, in the Uri sector, succeeded in capturing the pass of Haji Pir, a strategic point from where they could look out for infiltrators.[25]

On 1 September the Pakistan army launched a major offensive in Chhamb. An infantry division with two regiments of American Patton tanks crossed the border. Catching the Indians by surprise, they occupied thirty square miles within twenty-four hours. Their aim was to capture the bridge at Akhnoor, thus to sever links between Jammu and Kashmir and the state of Punjab. The defenders now called in their air force, with some thirty aircraft raining down bombs on the enemy. The Indian Vampires were answered by Pakistani Sabre jets.

By the 5th the Indian position was getting desperate, with the Pakistanis pressing hard on Akhnoor. To relieve the pressure, New Delhi ordered the army to open a new front. On the morning of the 6th, several tank regiments, supported by infantry, crossed the international border that divided the Punjab. They were heading straight for Pakistan's first city, Lahore. Pakistani troops and tanks were hastily redeployed from the Kashmir operation. Now commenced perhaps the most bitter tank battle seen anywhere since the end of the Second World War. The two sides fought each other inch for inch, sometimes in barren soil, at other times in the middle of sugar-cane fields. The Indians routed the

Pakistanis around Asal Uttar but then, attempting to recapture Khem Karan, were badly mauled in turn. The Indian commander, a veteran of the Second World War, said that he had 'never seen so many tanks destroyed, lying there in the battlefield like abandoned toys'.[26]

Overhead, the aeroplanes screamed en route to attack the enemy's bases. A large tonnage of bombs was dropped by both sides, but – as an Indian chronicler later wrote – 'luckily or unluckily some of the bombs failed to explode – they were old and had been supplied to the contending parties mostly by the same source'.[27]

As the battles raged, the Chinese weighed in with words in support of the Pakistanis. On 4 September Marshal Chen Yi, visiting Karachi, condemned 'Indian imperialism for violating the Cease-Fire Line', and endorsed 'the just actions taken by the Government of Pakistan to repel India's armed provocations'. Three days later Peking issued a statement claiming that India was 'still entrenched' over large sections of Chinese territory. The next day Chou En-lai stated that 'India's acts of aggression pose a threat to peace in this part of Asia'.[28]

Back in New Delhi, a surge of patriotic sentiment had overcome the population. At the daily press briefing, newsmen would ask the government spokesman: 'Has Lahore airport fallen?' 'Is the radio station under our control?' Lahore never fell, although why this was so remained a matter of dispute. The Indians argued that capturing the city was never on the agenda – why get into a house-to-house operation with a hostile population? The Pakistanis claimed that the Indian chief of army staff had bragged that he would have his evening drink at the Lahore Gymkhana – but the brave defenders of the city never allowed him to.[29]

The escalation of hostilities alarmed the superpowers, and on 6 September the United Nations Security Council met to discuss the matter. The UN secretary general, U Thant, flew to the subcontinent, and after meeting leaders in both capitals got them to agree to a ceasefire. The decision was made easier by the fact that in the Punjab the two sides had fought themselves to a stalemate. On 22 September hostilities were finally called off.

The battles took place principally in two sectors in the north-west – Kashmir and the Punjab. There were some exchanges in Sindh, but the eastern border – dividing the two halves of Bengal – stayed quiet. As is common in such cases, both sides claimed victory, exaggerating the enemy's losses and understating their own. In truth, the war must be declared a draw. As a reasonably independent authority had it, the

Pakistanis lost 3,000 to 5,000 men, about 250 tanks and 50 aircraft, whereas the casualties on the Indian side were 4,000 to 6,000 men, about 300 tanks, and 50 aircraft. With their much larger population, and bigger army, the Indians were better able to absorb these losses.[30]

For the Western public, the *Reader's Digest* magazine provided this colourful summary of the war far away: 'The blood of Pakistani and Indian soldiers stained the wheat-lands of the Punjab and the stony ridges of Kashmir; vultures hung over corpses on the Grand Trunk Road, the immortal highway of Kipling's *Kim*; and refugees huddled against tilting bullock carts, hesitant to start the journey home.'[31]

V

Before the war Shastri and Ayub Khan had met once, at Karachi in October 1964, when the Indian leader stopped there on his way home from Cairo. There is a photograph of the two together, the army man dressed in a suit, towering over the little Gandhian in his *dhoti*. Ayub was deeply unimpressed by the Indian, telling an aide: 'So this is the man who has succeeded Nehru!'[32]

There is little question that the Pakistani leadership seriously underestimated the Indian will to fight. Operation Gibraltar was conceived in 'the euphoric aftermath' of the Kutch conflict, which had 'shown the Indians in a poor light'.[33] In the first week of June 1965 the *Dawn* newspaper carried an essay written pseudonymously by a high official, which analysed Indian troop deployment before recommending that Pakistani strategy should 'obviously be to go for a knock-out in the Mohamed Ali Clay style'.[34] An army directive confidently stated that 'as a general rule Hindu morale would not stand more than a couple of hard blows delivered at the right time and place'.[35]

There was, indeed, an unmistakably religious idiom to an operation initiated by Pakistani Muslims on behalf of their brethren in Kashmir. Memories of wars fought and won ten centuries ago were evoked. The radicals in Pakistan believed that the *kafir* would be vanquished by the combination of Islamic fervour and American arms.[36] The hope was that after the Kashmiris had arisen, their brothers would cut off enemy communication, and 'start the long expected tank promenade down the Grand Trunk Road to Delhi', forcing a humiliating surrender.[37] The song on the lips of the warriors was: '*Hus ke liya hai Pakistan, ladh ke lenge Hindustan*' (We achieved Pakistan laughing, we will take India fighting).

As it happened, the attack united the Indians. Many Kashmiris stood with the army against the invaders. A Muslim soldier from Kerala won India's highest military honour, the Param Vir Chakra. Another Muslim, this time from Rajasthan and ironically named Ayub Khan, knocked out a couple of Pakistani tanks. All across India Muslim intellectuals and divines issued statements condemning Pakistan and expressing their desire to sacrifice their lives for the motherland.[38]

Ayub and company were encouraged by the debacle against China in 1962. But that was in the wet and slippery Himalaya, whereas this was terrain the Indians knew much better. The army commanders in 1965 had won their first spurs fighting tank battles on flat land in the Second World War. Besides, in the years since the Chinese disaster they had been provided with more (and better) equipment. The new defence minister, Y. B. Chavan, had gone on an extensive shopping spree in 1964, visiting Western capitals and the Soviet bloc to buy the tanks, planes, rifles and submarines that his forces required.[39]

This defence minister was more respected by his troops than his counterpart in 1962. Chavan was no Krishna Menon and, when it came to the conduct of war, Shastri was no Nehru either. He certainly preferred peace, writing to a friend after the Kutch conflict that in his view the problems between India and Pakistan should be settled amicably, step by step. He hoped that 'our fights and disputes do not take a form that makes battle inevitable'.[40] But when war came he was decisive, swift to take the advice of his commanders and order the strike across the Punjab border. (In a comparable situation, in 1962, Nehru had refused to call in the air force to relieve the pressure.) And when the conflict ended he was happy to be photographed – *dhoti* and all – atop a captured Patton tank, a gesture that would not have come easily to his predecessor.

However, in one respect Shastri was indeed like Nehru – in his refusal to mix matters of state with matters of faith. Days after the ceasefire, with patriotic feelings riding high, he spoke at a public meeting at the Ram Lila grounds in Delhi. Here he took issue with a BBC report that claimed that 'since India's Prime Minister Lal Bahadur Shastri is a Hindu, he is ready for war with Pakistan'. Shastri said that while he was a Hindu, 'Mir Mushtaq who is presiding over this meeting is a Muslim. Mr Frank Anthony who has addressed you is a Christian. There are also Sikhs and Parsis here. The unique thing about our country is that we have Hindus, Muslims, Christians, Sikhs, Parsis and people of all other religions. We have temples and mosques, *gurdwaras* and churches. But we do not bring this all into politics . . . This is the difference between India and Pakistan. Whereas Pakistan proclaims herself to be an Islamic State and uses religion as a political factor, we Indians have the freedom to follow whatever religion we may choose [and] worship in any way we please. So far as politics is concerned, each of us is as much an Indian as the other.'[41]

VI

During the Pakistan war, the prime minister coined the slogan 'Jai Jawan, Jai Kisan' (Hail the Soldier, Hail the Farmer). To salute the ordinary *jawan* in a nation given birth by Gandhian pacifism was distinctive, but so was the invocation of the humble *kisan*, in a nation taught to admire blast furnaces and high hydroelectric dams.

In fact, one of Shastri's first acts as prime minister was to increase budget allocations to agriculture. He was deeply concerned about the shortfalls in food production in recent years. The rate of increase of food grain had just about kept pace with the growth of population. If the rains failed, panic set in, with merchants hoarding grain and the state desperate to move stocks from surplus to deficit areas. There had been a drought in 1964, and another in 1965. Seeking a long-term solution, Shastri appointed C. Subramaniam to head the Ministry of Food and Agriculture. Born in 1910 into a family of farmers, Subramaniam had degrees in science and the law, and practised as an advocate before joining the freedom struggle. He had been a member of the Constituent Assembly, and was a widely admired minister in Madras before he joined the Union Cabinet. Subramaniam was known to be intelligent and a go-getter, which is why Nehru had placed him in charge of the prestigious Ministry of Steel and Mines. To shift him from Steel to Agriculture signalled a major change indeed.[42]

Subramaniam took to his new job with vigour. He focused on the reorganization of agricultural science, improving the pay and working conditions of scientists and protecting them from bureaucratic interference. The Indian Council for Agricultural Research, previously a somewhat somnolent body, acquired a new life and identity. Besides reviving the ICAR, Subramaniam also encouraged the states to set up agricultural universities, whose research focused on crops particular to that region. He began experimental farms, and set up a Seed Corporation of India to produce, in bulk, the quality seeds that would be needed for the proposed programmes of agricultural intensification.

Two of Subramaniam's key aides were, like him, from the Tamil country. One was the able secretary of agriculture, B. Sivaraman; the other was the scientist M. S. Swaminathan, who was directing the research teams adapting Mexican wheat to Indian conditions. It was around this crop that the new strategy revolved. Notably, while wheat is grown principally in the north of the country, these three architects of India's agricultural policy were all from the (very deep) south.[43]

Meanwhile, Subramaniam prevailed upon the United States to provide food aid till such time as the Indians were able to augment their own production. He met with and impressed the American president, Lyndon Johnson, and forged a close partnership with the US secretary of agriculture, Orville Freeman. In December 1965 Subramaniam and Freeman signed an agreement in Rome whereby India committed itself to a substantial increase in investment in agriculture, to a reform of the rural credit system, and to an expansion of fertilizer production and consumption. In return, the Americans provided a series of soft loans and agreed to keep wheat supplies going to tide over the shortages at the Indian end.[44]

While Subramaniam was signing what was informally called 'The Treaty of Rome', his prime minister was preparing to go to Moscow to sign a treaty of his own. This was with his Pakistani counterpart, Ayub Khan. After the war had ended, the Soviets offered their help in working out a peace settlement. In the first week of January 1966 Shastri and Ayub met in Tashkent, with the Soviet prime minister Alexei Kosygin as the chief mediator. After a week of hard bargaining the two sides agreed to give up what they most prized – international arbitration of the Kashmir dispute for Pakistan, the retention of key posts captured during the war (such as the Haji Pir pass) for India. The 'Tashkent Agreement' mandated the withdrawal of forces to the positions they held before 5 August 1965, the orderly transfer of prisoners of war, the resumption of diplomatic relations and the disavowal of force to settle future disputes.[45]

The agreement was signed on the afternoon of 10 January 1966. That night Shastri died in his sleep of a heart attack. On the 11th his body was flown to New Delhi on a Soviet aircraft. The next morning the body was placed on a gun carriage and taken in procession to the banks of the Jamuna, to be cremated not far from where Gandhi and Nehru had been. *Life* magazine made the event a cover story – as they had done with the death of Shastri's predecessor twenty months before. There were vivid pictures of the million-strong crowd, come to honour a man 'with whom many [Indians] felt a closer affinity than with Nehru'. What Shastri gave India, said *Life*, 'was mainly a mood – a new steeliness and sense of national unity'. The Chinese war had brought the country to a state of near collapse, but this time, when war came, 'everything worked – the trains ran, the army held fast, there was no communal rioting. The old moral pretentiousness, the disillusion and drift, the fear and dismay were gone.'[46]

This was a handsome tribute, but more notable perhaps were the compliments paid by those predisposed by ties of kin to see Shastri as an interloper. In the first months of the new prime minister's tenure, Mrs Indira Gandhi had complained that he was departing from her father's legacy. Within a year she was constrained to admit that 'Mr Shastri is, I think, feeling stronger now and surer of himself '.[47] Then there was Vijayalakshmi Pandit, who was even more fanatically devoted to her brother's memory. In July 1964 she thought that the morale of the government of India was at 'an unbelievably low level' – and 'there is now no Jawaharlal Nehru to stand up and restore confidence in the minds of the people'. On Shastri's death, however, she felt 'very sad', for 'he had begun to grow and we all thought he would put India on the right road'.[48] The condescension was characteristic, but when we consider who was writing this and when, this must be considered very high praise indeed.

Lal Bahadur Shastri may perhaps be seen as being in relation to Jawaharlal Nehru as Harry Truman was to Franklin Delano Roosevelt. Nehru and FDR both came from upper-class backgrounds, enjoyed long periods in power, undertook fundamental changes in their society and nation and were greatly venerated for doing so. Shastri, like Truman, was a smalltown boy of modest background, whose lack of charisma concealed a firm will and independence of mind. As with Truman, his background had endowed him with a keen practical sense, this in contrast to the more consciously intellectual – not to say ideological – style of his predecessor. Where the comparison breaks down is with regard to length of service. Whereas Truman had a full seven years as president of the United States, Shastri died less than two years after being sworn in as prime minister of India.

VII

On Shastri's death, Gulzarilal Nanda was once more sworn in as interim prime minister, and once more Kamaraj went in search of a permanent successor. Once more, Morarji Desai threw his hat in the ring. Once more, Kamaraj rejected him in favour of a more widely acceptable candidate.

The person whom the Congress president had in mind to succeed Shastri was Mrs Indira Gandhi. She was young – having just turned forty-eight – attractive, known to world leaders, and the daughter of the best-loved of Indians. To soothe a nation hit by two quick losses, she seemed the most obvious choice. True, Mrs Gandhi had little administrative experience, but this time the Congress 'Syndicate' would ensure that hers would be a properly 'collective' leadership.

The chief ministers consulted by Kamaraj quickly endorsed Mrs Gandhi's name. So far, so good – except that Morarji Desai decided he would contest for the leadership. So New Delhi now 'became the cockpit of concerted canvassing, large-scale lobbying, and hectic horse-trading'. Mrs Gandhi and Morarji Desai met with major leaders, while their seconds stalked the rank and file.[49]

In terms of experience as well as ability Desai should have been the favourite. Jawaharlal Nehru had once written of him that there 'were very few people whom I respect so much for their rectitude, ability, efficiency and fairness as Morarji Desai'.[50] It is doubtful whether he would have written about his own daughter in quite that fashion – certainly, he had no hope that Indira Gandhi would ever succeed him as prime minister. However, the words I have quoted are from a private letter; neither Desai nor his supporters were privy to it. Even if they had been, it is unlikely that it would have helped. With Kamaraj and the Syndicate so solidly backing Mrs Gandhi, and others in the Congress Party having their own reservations regarding Desai, Nehru's daughter commanded majority support in the Congress Parliamentary Party. When that body voted to choose a prime minister on 19 January 1966, she won by 355 votes to 169. Kamaraj had 'lined up the State satraps behind Mrs Gandhi', wrote one Delhi journal somewhat cynically, because 'the State leaders would accept only an innocuous person for Prime Minister at the Centre'.[51]

VIII

Mrs Gandhi was the second woman to be elected to lead a free nation (Sirimavo Bandaranaike of Ceylon having been the first); and the second member of her own family to become prime minister of India. Her first months in office were, if anything, as troubled as her father's. Nothing much happened in February, but in March a major revolt broke out in the Mizo hills. A tribal district bordering East Pakistan, these jagged hills were home to a population of a mere 300,000 people. But, as in Nagaland, among them were some motivated young men determined to carve out a homeland of their own.

The origins of the Mizo conflict go back to a famine in 1959, when a massive flowering of bamboo led to an explosion in the population of rats. These devoured the grain in the fields and in village warehouses, causing a scarcity of food for humans. A Mizo National Famine Front was formed, which found the state's response wanting. The first 'F' was then dropped, leading to the creation of the Mizo National Front (MNF). This asked first for a separate state within the Indian Union and then for a separate country itself.

The leader of the MNF was a one-time accountant named Laldenga. Deeply affected by the famine, he sought succour in books – the detective stories of Peter Cheyney to begin with, graduating in time to the works of Winston Churchill and primers on guerrilla warfare. In the winter of 1963–4 Laldenga made contact with the military government of East Pakistan, who promised him guns and money, and a base from which to mount attacks. The arms so obtained were cached in forests along the border.[52]

After years of patient planning, during which he recruited many young Mizos and trained them in the use of modern weaponry, Laldenga launched an uprising on the last day of February 1966. Groups of MNF soldiers attacked government offices and installations, looted banks, and disrupted communications. Roads were blocked to prevent the army moving troops into the area. In early March the MNF announced that the territory had seceded from the Indian Union and was now an 'independent' republic.[53]

The MNF captured one main town, Lungleh, and pressed hard on the district capital, Aizawl. The Indian response was to call in the army, and also the air force. Lungleh was strafed to force the rebels out, this the first time air power had been used by the Indian state against its own citizens. As in Nagaland, the rebels took refuge in the jungle, visiting the villages by night. After a fortnight caught up in the fierce fighting, a Welsh missionary working in the area managed to smuggle out this report to a friend in England:

> On Saturday morning we packed as many of our things as we could into trunks . . . and packed [a bag] to carry to go to Durlang through the jungle . . . Five minutes before we were due to start an aeroplane came overhead machine gunning . . . They were not firing at random, but trying to aim at the rebels' position as it were . . . We were there all day and the men were digging a trench, and we sheltered in it every time the jets came over firing. Pakhlira saw his house go up in flames. We prepared a meal of rice in a small house, but decided that it wasn't safe to sleep there and we all slept out in a terrace in the jungle where there was a sheltering bank. Not much sleep. We rose in the night and saw the whole Dawrupi go into flames from the furthest end to the Republic Road. They say that it was an effort by Laldenga's followers to burn the Assam Rifles out of the town.

The letter vividly captures the frightening position of ordinary Mizos caught in the cross-fire between the insurgents and the state. It goes on to speak, in more reflective vein, of how the conflict

> will be a very serious setback for the country . . . The government had to send in an army such as this so as to put a stop to this thing from the beginning in case it turns out to be like the country of the Nagas. We can only hope that the rebels will surrender so that things can get back to normal as soon as possible, but education will be in a complete mess for some time. The Matric[ulation] Exam is supposed to start next week. A very great responsibility rests on the shoulders [of rebel leaders] like Laldenga and Sakhlawliana for reducing the country to this sad condition . . .[54]

Far from surrendering, the rebels fought on, the conflict running for the rest of the year and into the next. Meanwhile, in Nagaland, the Peace Mission had collapsed. In the last week of February 1966 Jayaprakash Narayan resigned from the mission, saying that he had lost the confidence of the Nagas. 'JP' had told the underground that in the aftermath of the Indo-Pakistan war they should drop their demand for independence, and settle for autonomy within the Indian Union instead. In the federal system, foreign affairs and defence were in the hands of the centre, but the things that most mattered – education, health, economic development, culture – were in the control of the states. So JP advised Phizo's men to shed their arms and contest elections, thus to take over the administration by peaceful means.[55]

At the same time as JP became disenchanted with the rebels, Michael Scott had lost the confidence of the Indian government. They accused him of seeking to 'internationalize' the Naga issue by approaching the United Nations. Scott had suggested that likely models for Nagaland were Bhutan and Sikkim – nominally independent countries each with its own flag, currency and ruler, but militarily subordinated to India. In May 1966 New Delhi asked Scott to leave the country, making it clear that he was not welcome to return.[56]

There was no question that Michael Scott was deeply committed to the Naga cause. Between 1962 and 1966 he must have visited India a dozen times on Phizo's behalf. Sadly, he could not see that political independence for the Nagas was unacceptable to the Indian government. They were prepared to grant Phizo amnesty, safe passage into Nagaland, even the chief ministership of the state if he so desired. But the old rebel doggedly held out for more; and Scott supported him. Thus it was that another Englishman with long experience of India, the journalist Guy Wint, was constrained to comment that 'the main obstacle to peace [in the Naga hills] lies in the fanaticism of such people as Michael Scott and David Astor; both of whom allow themselves to be used by Phizo. Neither has any conception of what is at stake in accepting the Naga claim for complete secession.'[57]

The breakdown of the peace talks was signalled by a wave of attacks on civilian targets. On 20 April a bomb went off in a train in upper Assam, killing fifty-five passengers. Three days later a similar explosion claimed a further forty lives. The Naga radicals were now making contact with Peking, whose help they sought in renewing their struggle.[58]

Tribes were restive on the borders, and in parts of the heartland as well. Food scarcity in the district of Bastar, in central India, had sparked a popular movement led by the deposed Maharaja, Pravi Chandra Bhanj Deo. Pravi Chandra and his followers claimed that prosperity would return only when he, the rightful heir, was returned to the throne. The Maharaja was traditionally regarded as quasi-divine, as the key intermediary between the people and their gods. A man whose eccentricity bordered on lunacy – the reason the government had replaced him with his brother – Pravi Chandra was nonetheless revered by his people. There were a series of protests asking for his restoration and then, on 25 March, a several-thousand-strong march on the old capital, Jagdalpur. A battle broke out between the tribals, using bows and arrows, and the police, using tear-gas and bullets. When the smoke cleared about forty people were dead, one policeman and the rest tribals. Among those killed was Pravi Chandra. This was, to quote the chief minister of Madhya Pradesh – writing to the home minister in New Delhi – a 'tragic incident', 'shocking and regrettable'.[59]

From these rebellions the new prime minister turned with relief to the creation of a separate state for the Sikhs. In the war against Pakistan, Sikh commanders as well as *jawans* had distinguished themselves in large numbers. So had the ordinary Punjabi. Farmers opened stalls on the roadside to feed troops with the choicest delicacies. Others offered their homes; yet others nursed the wounded. As the general in command remembered, 'the whole province was electrified to a man. There were no reservations in offering help for the cause.'[60]

Their bravery in the war impelled the government of India to concede a longstanding demand of the Sikhs. In March 1966 a committee of MPs recommended a threefold division of the existing state, with the hill districts going to Himachal Pradesh and the eastern, Hindu-majority areas coming to constitute a new state of Haryana. What these deletions left behind was a Punjab that, finally, was both Punjabi-speaking as well as dominated by Sikhs.[61]

IX

Also in March the prime minister left for her first foreign tour. She stopped at Paris and London, but her main destination was the United States, a country whose goodwill (and grain) was greatly desired by India, for it would be some time before the new agricultural strategy would take effect. C. Subramaniam had ploughed up the lawns of his bungalow in Delhi to plant a new high-yielding variety of wheat, one of a series of experiments to test these new seeds in local conditions. Meanwhile, American farmers had perforce to help put food in Indian mouths.[62]

'New Indian Leader Comes Begging', was how one Alabama paper headlined Mrs Gandhi's visit. She made a more positive impression on the East Coast, handling the press well and impressing the public with the elegance of her dress and the dignity of her manner. Lyndon Johnson seems also to have quite warmed to her.[63] But after her return LBJ chose to keep his supplicants on a tight leash. Whereas the Indians had asked for an annual commitment of food aid, the American president released ships month by month. The American ambassador in New Delhi privately described LBJ's attitude as a 'cruel performance. The Indians must conform; they must be made to fawn; their pride must be cracked.' Despairing of the Indians ever getting their act together, at one stage Johnson suggested sending 1,000 extension workers to teach them how to farm. His ambassador found the thought 'appalling'; not only would these Americans know nothing about agriculture in Asia, they would bring with them '950 wives, 2,500 children, 3,000 air-conditioners, 1,000 jeeps, 1,000 electric refrigerators (many of which won't work), 800 or 900 dogs and 2,000 or 3,000 cats'.[64]

In both 1965 and 1966 India imported 15 million tonnes of American wheat under a public loan scheme known as PL-480, this going to feed 40 million mouths. A memorandum prepared in the US Department of Agriculture stated baldly that 'India was destitute'. When the rains failed again in 1966 the prospect for India was 'one more drought, one more year of acute dependence on PL-480 imports, one more year of exposure to the world as paupers'.[65]

Sections of the Washington establishment thought the Indians hypocritical, asking for aid with one hand while attacking American foreign policy with the other. New Delhi's criticisms of the Vietnam War rankled deeply. Lyndon Johnson was not pleased when the Indian president, S. Radhakrishnan, sent a message urging that 'the United States unilaterally and without any commitments cease bombing North Vietnam', adding that when that happened, 'the rest of the world would, through the force of world opinion, bring about negotiations'.[66]

X

The purchase of arms and grain from abroad, along with the import of machinery and materials for industrial development, caused a dangerous dip in India's foreign exchange reserves, which were down to $625 million in March 1966. To counter this, the government decided to devalue the rupee in June. Earlier pegged at Rs4.76 to the US dollar, the exchange rate now became Rs7.50.[67]

The World Bank and the International Monetary Fund had both recommended devaluation, though its magnitude exceeded even their expectations. However, in India the action was greeted by a storm of protest from the left. The communist MP Hiren Mukherjee claimed that devaluation had been forced on India 'by the cloak and dagger aid givers of America'. A communist trade union called it 'a shameful act of national betrayal'.

Large sections of Mrs Gandhi's own party were opposed to devaluation. Kamaraj, for one, saw it as undermining the policy of national self-reliance. But the action was supported by the free-market Swatantra Party, whose main spokesman in Parliament, Minoo Masani, said that 'if devaluation constituted a first step in a policy of economic realism in place of the doctrinaire policies pursued by the Congress government, it would have some desirable results in boosting the exports and promoting the inflow of foreign capital'.

Writing to a friend, the prime minister said that the devaluation was a 'most difficult and painful decision', taken only 'when various other palliatives which had been tried for the last two years did not produce satisfactory results'.[68] The liberal Delhi journal *Thought* went further – this, it said, was 'the hardest decision the Government of India has taken since this country became independent'. The weekly hoped that it would lead to a redirection of economic policy, towards producing goods for export and strengthening India's trading position. Devaluation, said *Thought*, should 'logically mean the end of giganticism in our efforts to develop the nation's economy'.[69]

In the end, though, devaluation was not accompanied by a liberalization of the trade regime. Controls on the inflow of capital remained in place, and there was no push to increase exports. It appears that the criticisms from within and outside her party inhibited Mrs Gandhi from promoting more thoroughgoing reform. The support from Swatantra would not have helped either – if anything, it would have tended to push Nehru's daughter back towards the left.

XI

Throughout 1966, one place that had been unusually quiet was the Valley of Kashmir. The war of 1965 had put secessionists on the back foot. The chief minister, G. M. Sadiq, was providing an efficient and clean administration, conspicuously so in comparison to Bakshi Ghulam Mohammed's. The tourist trade was booming, as was the market for Kashmiri handicrafts.

In the late summer of 1966 Jayaprakash Narayan wrote Mrs Gandhi a remarkable letter seeking a permanent solution to a problem that had 'plagued this country for 19 years'. 'Kashmir has distorted India's image for the world as nothing else has done', said JP. Even now, while peace reigned on the surface, beneath there was 'deep and widespread discontent among the people'. The only way to get rid of this was to release Sheikh Abdullah after promising 'full internal autonomy, i.e., a return to the original terms of the accession'. A settlement with Abdullah, believed JP, 'may give us the only chance we may have of solving the Kashmir problem'. For 'the Sheikh is the only Kashmiri leader who could swing Muslim opinion in the valley towards his side'.

His talks with Chou En-lai led to Sheikh Abdullah being dubbed a 'traitor', but in JP's view that act, though indiscreet, was certainly not treasonous. In any case, the Sheikh had come back to India to answer his detractors. JP's associate Narayan Desai met the Kashmiri leader in Kodaikanal and found him amenable to the idea of full autonomy. In the aftermath of the recent war with Pakistan, Abdullah saw quite clearly that an independent Kashmir was out of the question. So Narayan now suggested that the government release Abdullah and permit him to contest the upcoming 1967 general election, to assure the Kashmiris that 'they would be rid of the overbearing Indian police and enjoy full freedom to order their lives as they liked'. If the Sheikh fought and won in the election, if 'it could be shown that they [the Kashmiris] had taken that decision freely at an election run by their own genuine leaders . . ., Pakistan will have no ground left to interfere in their affairs'.

To 'hold a general election in Kashmir with Sheikh Abdullah in prison', remarked Narayan, 'is like the British ordering an election in India while Jawaharlal Nehru was in prison. No fair-minded person would call it a fair election.' This was a point that should have counted with Mrs Gandhi, but in case it didn't, JP offered this melancholy prediction:

> If we miss the chance of using the next general election to win the consent of the [Kashmiri] people to their place within the Union, I cannot see what other device will be left to India to settle the problem. To think that we will eventually wear down the people and force them to accept at least passively the Union is to delude ourselves. That might conceivably have happened had Kashmir not been geographically located where it is. In its present location, and with seething discontent among the people, it would never be left in peace by Pakistan.[70]

The prime minister wrote a brief note back, thanking JP 'for sharing your views on Kashmir and Sheikh Sahib'.[71] But no action was taken on his letter, and Sheikh Abdullah remained in confinement. However, in October 1966 the prime minister visited the Kashmir Valley for the first time since assuming office. Speaking at the sports stadium in Srinagar, she spoke of her 'special love' for Kashmir and Kashmiris. A large crowd turned out to hear her; in fact, wherever Mrs Gandhi went in the Valley, the people milled along the roads to see her.[72]

XII

For now, Kashmir appeared quiet – and its people quiescent. But down south, in Andhra Pradesh, an agitation was gathering ground. The protest was led by students, who demanded that a Planning Commission proposal for a steel plant in Vishakapatnam (Vizag) be implemented forthwith. The plant had been sanctioned several years earlier, but the fiscal crisis besetting the government had led to its being put on the shelf.

The decision to delay the Vizag steel plant caused an outcry in the Andhra country. For the young, a massive state-run factory still carried enchantment – and the hope of productive employment. Protesters blockaded roads, halted trains, and attacked shops and offices. The movement spread through the state – 'The entire student community of Guntur seems to be on the streets', said one report. The police were mobilized in several cities, while in Vizag itself the navy stood guard over key installations. A railway station was set ablaze in one place, a crowd fired upon by the police in another. Students damaged the lighthouse in Vizag and forced the radio station to go off the air. All trains running through the state were cancelled.[73]

Meanwhile, to the north, a famine loomed in Bihar. The tribal areas were worst hit; in Monghyr district, the adivasis were reduced to eating roots. There were acute shortages of water and fodder. The poor had looted grain here and there; the upper classes in the countryside now lived in fear of a more generalized rebellion.[74]

To striking students and starving peasants was added a more curious group of dissidents – Hindu holy men, or *sadhus*. The Hindu orthodoxy had long called for an end to the killing of the sacred cow; now, with the help of the Jana Sangh, the call had been converted into a social movement.

On 6 November a huge procession was taken through the streets of the capital. Among the 100,000 marchers were many *sadhus* brandishing tridents and spears. The march culminated in a public meeting outside Parliament House, where the first speaker was Swami Karpatri (of Anti-Hindu Code Bill fame). The crowd were further warmed up by Swami Rameshwaranand, a Jana Sangh MP recently suspended from the Lok Sabha for unruly behaviour. He asked the *sadhus* to *gherao* (surround) Parliament. The 'excited crowd made a beeline for the building, shouting "*Swami Rameshwaranand ki jai*" '. At this point the Jana Sangh leader Atal Behari Vajpayee appealed to the swami to withdraw his call. It was too late. As the *sadhus* surged towards Parliament's gates, they were turned back by mounted police. A ding-dong battle ensued: tear-gas and rubber bullets on the one side, sticks and stones on the other. As thick columns of smoke rose over the Houses of Parliament, the crowd retreated, only to vent its anger on what lay in its way. The security kiosk of All-India Radio was gutted, and the house of K. Kamaraj, the Congress president, set on fire. Also destroyed were an estimated 250 cars, 100 scooters and 10 buses. By the evening the army was patrolling the streets, for the first time since the dark days of 1947.

An agitation led by holy men, commented one journal acidly, had resulted in an 'orgy of violence, vandalism and hooliganism'. A. B. Vajpayee issued a statement deploring the fact that 'the undesirable elements, who resorted to violent activities in the demonstration against cow-slaughter, had done a great harm to the pious cause'.[75]

XIII

There was a line of thinking, widely prevalent in the West, which held that only the personality and example of Jawaharlal Nehru had kept India united and democratic. The quick changes of guard since his death, the successive droughts, the countless small rebellions and the major war with Pakistan – these, taken together, seemed only to confirm these fears. In December 1965 the *Sydney Morning Herald* worried for the future of democracy in India. The paper saw a 'sweeping upsurge of nationalistic spirit' in the country, which was 'in danger of turning into chauvinism, with increasing bitterness towards the Western powers'. This intolerance seemed also to be directed inwards: 'What many foreign observers are finding particularly perturbing is that free expression of liberal views by Indians seems to be in danger.'[76]

The same year, 1965, the writer Ronald Segal published a major study titled 'The Crisis of India'. On a tour of the country he found it on 'the economic precipice', with the 'ground . . . crumbling beneath her'. Meanwhile, 'her international stock was low and falling'. With poverty, scarcity, regional conflicts and corruption all rampant, India reminded Segal at times of Weimar Germany, at other times of Kuomintang China. He held little hope of democracy surviving. Among the 'authoritarian alternatives' on offer were 'Communism on the left' and 'militant communalism on the right', one or other of which was likely to prevail before too many years had passed.[77]

Also despairing of the country's future was Reverend Michael Scott. A friend who met him in May 1966 found him

> very depressed, not about his failure in regard to the Naga settlement, but about India in general. His view is that the older and abler generation is now dying off and being replaced by little, corrupt and wholly inefficient men. He has a strong feeling that sooner or later India is going to disintegrate and that the whole thing may sink into a Vietnam-type morass into which Britain and America may be drawn.[78]

When the monsoon failed again in 1966, the predictions were of mass starvation rather than of the break-up of India or the abrogation of democracy. To many Western environmentalists, India seemed to provide striking proof of Malthus's prophecy that human population growth would one day outstrip food supply. The respected Stanford biologist Paul Ehrlich wrote that while he had 'understood the population explosion intellectually for a long time', he 'came to understand it emotionally one stinking hot night in Delhi a couple of years ago'. As his taxi crawled through the streets, he saw around him 'people eating, people washing, people sleeping. People visiting, people arguing and screaming. People thrusting their hands through the taxi window, begging. People defecating and urinating. People clinging to buses. People herding animals. People. People. People.'[79]

The same year Ehrlich was writing this, two other American biologists were finishing a book which argued that 'today, India is the first of the hungry nations to stand at the brink of famine and disaster'. Tomorrow, 'the famines will come', and 'riding alongside will surely be riots and other civil tensions which the central government will be too weak to control'. They predicted 1975 as the year by which 'civil disorder, anarchy, military dictatorships, runaway inflation, transportation breakdowns and chaotic unrest will be the order of the day'.[80]

In truth, even some knowledgeable Indian observers had begun to fear for the fate of their country. In the first week of November 1966 a traditionally pro-Congress paper published a leading article entitled 'The Grimmest Situation in 19 Years'. The student strikes and the food scarcities were attributed to a 'virtual breakdown of authority'. The article predicted that 'the wave of violence will grow in intensity', with 'many other parts of the country being turned into Bihars'. 'The future of the country is dark for many reasons', said the *Hindustan Times*, 'all of them directly attributable to 19 years of Congress rule.'[81]

19

LEFTWARD TURNS

Never, never underestimate a politician's need to survive ... I will not make the mistake of underestimating the political instinct of a Kashmiri, who is, additionally, Jawaharlal Nehru's daughter.

Anonymous Indian columnist, May 1966

I

The general election scheduled for early 1967 would be the fourth since Independence, and the first since Jawaharlal Nehru's death. In the last weeks of 1966, an American magazine sent a reporter to assess the lie of the land. He was struck by 'the bizarre range of India's seething problems of religious fanaticism, language barriers, regional feuds'. Adding to the unrest were food shortages and inflation, and 'a continuing population explosion [which] impedes almost all progress'. These varied forms of violence had 'raised speculation that the elections [of 1967] may not be held'. The reporter thought it possible that 'the breakdown of law and order will be so complete that the Army will take power, as happened in neighbouring Pakistan and Burma'. And there was a more dismal prospect still – namely, that the 'collapse of the present regime [in India] would add a grim new element to the job the US has taken on in Vietnam – the effort to assure political stability and economic strength in Asia.'[1]

To the average Western visitor, India was – and remains – a strange, even overwhelming, place. This particular journalist was on his first – and so far as one can tell, last – visit. But as it happened, his prognosis was endorsed by another who doubtless knew India much better, having already lived there for six years at the time.

This was Neville Maxwell of the London *Times*, who in the first weeks of 1967 wrote a series of articles on 'India's Disintegrating Democracy'.

As Maxwell saw it, 'famine is threatening, the administration is strained and universally believed to be corrupt, the government and the governing party have lost public confidence and belief in themselves as well'. These various crises had created an *emotional readiness for the rejection of Parliamentary democracy*'. The 'politically sophisticated Indians' to whom Maxwell spoke expressed 'a deep sense of defeat, an alarmed awareness that the future is not only dark but profoundly uncertain'.

Maxwell's own view was that 'the crisis is upon India' – he could discern 'the already fraying fabric of the nation itself', with the states 'already beginning to act like sub-nations'. His conclusion was unequivocal: that while Indians would soon vote in 'the fourth – and *surely last* – general election', 'the great experiment of developing India within a democratic framework has failed'.

The imminent collapse of democracy in India, thought Maxwell, would provoke a frantic search for 'an alternative antidote for the society's troubles'. As he saw it, 'in India, as present trends continue, within the ever-closing vice of food and population, maintenance of an ordered structure of society is going to slip out of reach of an ordered structure of civil government and the army will be *the only alternative source* of authority and order. That it will be drawn into a civil role seems inevitable, the only doubt is how?'

Maxwell thought that 'a mounting tide of public disorder, fed perhaps by pockets of famine', would lead to calls for a strengthening of the office of the president, who would be asked 'to assert a stabilizing authority over the centre and the country'. Backing him would be the army, which would come to exercise 'more and more civil authority'. In this scenario, the president would become 'either the actual source of political authority, or a figure-head for a group composed possibly of army officers and a few politicians'.[2]

II

There are some fine ethnographic accounts of the 1967 Indian general election, field studies of different constituencies by scholars familiar with their culture and social composition. These show that elections were no longer a top-dressing on inhospitable soil; they had been fully indigenized, made part of Indian life, a festival with its own unique set of rituals, enacted every five years. The energy and intensity of this particular iteration was manifest in the large turnout at rallies and leaders' speeches, and in the colourful posters and slogans used to glorify parties or debunk their opponents. The rivalries were intense, at the state as well as the national level. Opposing the ruling Congress were parties to its left, such as the various communist and socialist fragments; and parties to the right, such as Jana Sangh and Swatantra. In some states the Congress's competition came from regional groupings – such as the Akali Dal in the Punjab and the DMK in Madras.

As these ethnographies reveal, twenty years of economic development had deepened and complicated the process of political competition. Often, rival candidates had cut their teeth running schools, colleges and co-operatives before contesting a legislative or parliamentary election. Those institutions were vehicles of prestige and patronage, their control valuable in itself and a means of mobilizing voter support.[3]

The election of 1967 is the first I have any personal memories of. What I remember best is this slogan, shouted with vigour along the streets of the small sub-Himalayan town in which I lived: *'Jana Sangh ko vote do, bidi peena chhod do/ Bidi mein tambaku hai, Kangresswala daku hai'*.

The Congress Party was full of thieves, and the cheroot contained that dangerous substance, tobacco: by rejecting both and embracing the Jana Sangh – the leading opposition party in town – the voter would purify himself as well as the government. Such was the slogan's message, which apparently resonated with many citizens. So found a survey of voters in thirteen states, conducted by the country's pioneer pollster, E. P. W. da Costa of the Indian Institute of Public Opinion. Conducted just before the polls, this survey found that the Congress had 'lost a great deal of its charisma'; it approached the election 'for the first time, as a political loser not as a guaranteed victor'.

The survey suggested that while the Congress would retain power in the centre, it would drop its vote share by 2–3 percentage points and lose perhaps fifty seats in the Lok Sabha. But it would lose even more heavily in the states. According to da Costa, non-Congress governments would be formed in the states of Kerala, Madhya Pradesh and Rajasthan, and perhaps also in Orissa, West Bengal, Bihar, Uttar Pradesh and Punjab.

Why had support for the Congress declined? The survey found that the minorities, once a loyal vote bank, were disenchanted with the party, as were large sections of the young and the less educated. On the other side, the opposition was more united than before. In most states, non-Congress parties had made seat adjustments – which meant that, unlike

Table 19.1 – *Performance of the Congress in Indian elections, 1952 – 67*

	LOK SABHA		STATE ASSEMBLIES	
	Percentage of total		Percentage of total	
Year	Votes	Seats	Votes	Seats
1952	45.0	74.4	42.0	68.4
1957	47.8	75.1	45.5	65.1
1962	44.5	72.8	44.0	60.7
1967	40.7	54.5	40.0	48.5

in the past, the Congress could not so easily benefit from a three- or four-way division of the vote.

As da Costa saw it, this fourth general election would inaugurate a 'second Non-Violent Revolution in India's recent history'. The first was begun by Mahatma Gandhi in 1919, and culminated in Independence in 1947. Since then, the Congress had held power in the centre as well as all the states, except for a very brief spell in Kerala. Now, this election would signal 'the disintegration of the monolithic exercise of power by the Congress Party'. Da Costa's conclusion is worth quoting: 'To the candidates this is, perhaps, a struggle for power; to the political scientist it is, as nearly half a century ago, the beginning of a break with the past. It is by no means yet a revolt; but it may in time be a revolution.'[4]

Poll predictions are notorious for being unreliable – in India perhaps even more than elsewhere. But when the actual results came in, da Costa must have felt vindicated. In the Lok Sabha the Congress's seat tally had dropped from 361 to 283, while its losses in the state assemblies were even greater. The party's decline is summed up in Table 19.1.

III

The most humiliating defeat suffered by the Congress was in the southern state of Madras. Here, the Dravida Munnetra Kazhagam (DMK) swept the polls, winning 138 seats out of a total of 234 in the Assembly. The Congress won a mere 50. The DMK leader C. N. Annadurai was sworn in as chief minister.

Madras had long been a Congress stronghold; many national leaders, past and present, hailed from the state. Now, even the venerable K. Kamaraj was washed away in the landslide. He lost in his home town, Virudhunagar, to a 28-year-old student activist named P. Srinivasan. When the news reached Madras, jubilant DMK cadres found a namesake of the victor, placed him on a horse and paraded him through the city. Of the Congress president's defeat, a respected weekly wrote that 'in terms of political prestige, here and abroad, it was beyond any doubt, the worst blow ever suffered by Mr. Kamaraj's party, before or after independence'.[5]

The Congress had a fairly good record in the state; its administration was known to be clean and efficient. Some commentators thought that the DMK rode to victory on the back of the anti-Hindi agitation of 1965. However, that movement itself was made possible by patient organizational work over the past decade. The DMK had fanned out into the towns and villages, creating local clubs and party branches. Crucial here were its links with the hugely popular Tamil film industry. One of its main leaders, M. Karunanidhi, was a successful scriptwriter. More important, it had the support – moral as well as material – of the great popular film hero M. G. Ramachandran (MGR).

Originally from Kerala, but born to a family of plantation labourers in Sri Lanka, MGR had a fanatical following in the Tamil countryside. In his films he vanquished the forces of evil, these variously represented by policemen, landlords, foreigners and the state. The movies he starred in played to packed houses, with viewers seeing them over and over again. Many of his most devoted fans were women.

All across Madras, MGR *manrams* (fan clubs) had been established. These discussed his films and also his politics. For MGR was a longtime supporter of the DMK. He gave money to the party, and was always at hand to speak at its rallies and conferences.

A month before the 1967 elections, MGR was shot and wounded by a rival film star named M. R. Radha (the two, apparently, had fallen out over what men in general, and Indian film stars in particular, usually fall out over). Photographs of the wounded hero were abundantly used in the election campaign. MGR himself decided to stand – he won his seat in a canter, and his party did the same.[6]

In power, the DMK practised what one scholar has called an 'assertive and paternalist populism'. Where the Congress brought large industrial projects to the state, the DMK focused on schemes that might win it immediate support. Thus it increased the percentage of government jobs reserved for the lower castes who were its own chief source of support. Greater control was exercised over the trade in cereals, and food subsidies granted to the urban poor. Meanwhile, to foster regional pride, the government organized an international conference on Tamil culture and language, in which scholars from twenty countries participated, and where the chief minister expressed the hope that Tamil would become the link language for the whole of India.[7]

IV

The Congress also lost in Kerala, to an alliance of the left. In 1963 the Communist Party of India (CPI) had split into two fractions, the newer one called the Communist Party of India (Marxist), or CPM. It was the CPM which had the more dynamic leaders, including E. M. S. Namboodiripad. Now the CPM won 52 out of the 133 seats in the Kerala State Assembly; the Congress 30, and the CPI 19. The communists came together to form the government, with EMS being sworn in for his second term as chief minister.

The Congress had previous experience of losing in Kerala but, to its distress, it also lost power in West Bengal, where the party had held undisputed sway since 1947. The winners in that state were the United Front–Left Front alliance, its main members the Bangla Congress (as its name suggests, a breakaway from the mother party), and the CPM. In the assembly elections the Congress won 127 seats out of a House of 280. On the other side, the CPM had 43 and the Bangla Congress 34; joined by an assortment of left-wing groups and independents, they could just about muster a majority.

The Bangla Congress leader Ajoy Mukherjee became chief minister. The deputy chief minister was Jyoti Basu, an urbane, London-educated lawyer who had long been the civilized face of Bengali communism. Basu and some others thought that their party could shape the government's policies from within. Other CPM members, notably its chief organizer Promode Dasgupta, thought that the party should never have joined the government at all.[8]

Whole books have been written on doctrinal disputes within the Indian communist movement. Here, we need know only that the Communist Party of India split in 1963 on account of two differences:

one external to the country, the other internal to it. The two issues were connected. The parent party, the CPI, was closely tied to the apron strings of the Communist Party of the Soviet Union; one consequence of this was that it had forsworn armed revolution, if only because the Soviets wanted good relations with the government of India. The breakaway CPM believed in fraternal relations with both the Russian and Chinese communist parties. It saw the Indian state as run by a bourgeois–landlord alliance and parliamentary democracy as mostly a sham; to be used when it suited one's purposes, and to be discarded when it didn't.[9]

The decision of the CPM to join the government was preceded by a bitter debate, with Jyoti Basu speaking in favour and Promode Dasgupta against. Ultimately the party joined, only to create a great sense of expectation among the cadres. An early gesture was to rename Harrington Road after a hero of the world communist movement, so that at the height of the Vietnam War the address of the United States Consulate was 7 Ho Chi Minh Sarani, Calcutta.

That was easy enough; but henceforth the decisions became harder. In the spring of 1967 a land dispute broke out in Naxalbari, in the Darjeeling district, where India's borders touched Nepal on the west and Pakistan on the east, with Tibet and the semi-independent kingdoms of Bhutan and Sikkim not far away. The economy in these Himalayan foothills was dominated by tea plantations, many run by British-owned companies. There was a history of land scarcity, and of conflicts over land – with plantation workers seeking plots of their own, and indigenous sharecroppers seeking relief from usurious landlords.

In the Naxalbari area, the rural poor were mobilized by a *krishak samiti* (peasants' organization) owing allegiance to the CPM. Its leader was a middle-class radical named Kanu Sanyal, whose rejection of his social milieu in favour of work in the villages had won him a considerable following. From late March 1967 the *samiti* organized a series of demonstrations against landlords who had evicted tenants and/or hoarded grain. These protests became more militant, leading to skirmishes with the police, which turned violent. A constable was killed; in retaliation, the police fired on a crowd. The peasant leaders decided to take to arms, and soon landlords were being beheaded.

The protests had their roots in the deeply inequitable agrarian structure of northern Bengal. But they may not have taken the form they did had the CPM not joined the government. Some activists, and perhaps many peasants, felt that now that their party was in power, they were at liberty to set right the feudal structure on their own. To their surprise, the party reacted by taking the side of the forces of law and order. By the late summer of 1967 an estimated 1,500 policemen were on duty in Naxalbari. Kanu Sanyal and his fellow leaders were in jail, while other rebels had taken refuge in the jungle.[10]

Naxalbari quickly came to enjoy an iconic status among Indian revolutionaries. The village gave its name to the region and, in time, to anyone anywhere who would use arms to fight the Indian state on behalf of the oppressed and disinherited. 'Naxalite' became shorthand for 'revolutionary', a term evoking romance and enchantment at one end of the political spectrum and distaste and derision at the other.[11]

Among those who approved of the Naxalites were the leaders of communist China. In the last week of June 1967 Radio Peking announced that

A phase of peasants' armed struggle led by the revolutionaries of the Indian Communist Party has been set up in the countryside in Darjeeling District of West Bengal State in India. This is the front paw of the revolutionary armed struggle launched by the Indian people under the guidance of Mao Tse-tung's teachings. This represents the general orientation of the Indian revolution at the present time. The people of India, China and the rest of the world hail the emergence of this revolutionary armed struggle.[12]

While the first sparks of revolution were being lit in Naxalbari, another group of Maoists were preparing for action in Andhra Pradesh. The Andhra 'Naxalites' were active in two regions: Telengana, where there had been a major communist insurgency in 1946–9, and the Srikakulam district, bordering Orissa. In both regions the areas of dispute were land and forests. In both the main agents of exploitation were the state and landlords, the main victims peasants and (especially) tribals. And in both, communist mobilization focused on free access to forest produce, better wages for labourers and the redistribution of land.

In Srikakulam the struggle was led by a schoolteacher named Vempatapu Satyanarayana. He led the tribals in a series of labour strikes, and in seizing grain from the fields of rich farmers and redistributing it to the needy. By the end of 1967 the landlords had sought the help of the police, who came in and arrested hundreds of protesters. Satyanarayana and his men now decided to take to arms. The houses of landlords and moneylenders were raided and their records and papers burnt. The state's response was to send in more police; by early 1969 there were as many as nine platoons of Special Armed Police operating in the district.

The struggle in Telengana was led by Tarimala Nagi Reddy. He was a veteran of the communist movement who had spent years organizing peasants and also served several terms in the state legislature. Now, he proclaimed the futility of the parliamentary path; resigning from the assembly as well as from the CPM, he took once more to the villages. He linked up with grass-roots workers in mobilizing peasants to ask for higher wages and for an end to corruption among state officials. Young militants were trained in the use of arms. The district was divided into zones; to each were assigned several *dalams* or groups of dedicated revolutionaries.[13]

Back in West Bengal, the coalition government had fallen apart in less than a year. President's Rule was imposed before fresh elections in early 1969 saw the CPM substantially increase its tally. It won 80 seats; making it by far the biggest partner in a fresh alliance with the Bangla Congress and others. Ajoy Mukherjee once more became chief minister, the CPM preferring to keep the key Home portfolio and generally play Big Brother.

These were years of great turmoil in the state, as captured in the titles of books written about the period such as *The Agony of West Bengal* and *The Disinherited State*. One axis of conflict was between the centre and the state. The government of India was worried about the law-and-order situation, the ruling Congress peeved about its own loss of power in West Bengal. The governor became a key player, communicating the concerns of the centre (and, less justifiably, of the Congress) to the local politicians. The assembly was disrupted regularly; on one occasion, the governor was physically prevented from delivering his customary opening address, having to flee the premises under police escort.[14]

A second axis of conflict was between the two main parties in the state government. Where Ajoy Mukherjee and his Bangla Congress tried weakly to keep the machinery of state in place, the CPM was not above stoking street protest and even violence to further its aims. In factories in and around Calcutta, workers took to the practice of *gherao* – the mobbing of their managers to demand better wages and working conditions. Previously the management had been able to call in the police; the new government, however, insisted that any such stoppage of work had to be referred first to the labour minister (a CPM man). This was an invitation to strike: according to one estimate, there were more than 1,200 *gheraos* in the first six months of the first UF–LF government.[15]

These stoppages created a ripple in the British press, in part because many of the great Calcutta firms were British owned, in part because this had once been the capital of the Raj. 'West Bengal expects more law-lessness' ran one headline; 'Riot stops opening of West Bengal Assembly', ran another. The response of many factory owners, Indian as well as European, was to shut down their units. Others shifted their business elsewhere, in a process of capital flight that served to displace Calcutta as the leading centre of Indian industry.[16]

Apart from capitalists worried about their profits, the prevailing lawlessness also disturbed the chief minister of West Bengal. He saw it as the handiwork of the CPM, whose ministerial portfolios included Land and Labour – where the trouble raged – and Home – where it could be controlled but wasn't. So in protest against the protests that old Gandhian Ajoy Mukherjee decided to organize a *satyagraha* of his own. He toured the districts, delivering speeches that railed against the CPM for promoting social discord. Then, on 1 December, he began a seventy-two-hour fast in a very public place – the Curzon Park in south Calcutta. In the rich history of Indian *satyagrahas*, this must surely be counted as the most bizarre: a chief minister fasting against his own government's failure to keep the peace.[17]

A third axis of conflict was between the CPM and the Naxalites. The latter had now formed a new party, called the Communist Party of India (Marxist-Leninist). In district after district, cadres left the parent party to join the new kid on the block; just as, back in 1963 – 4, they had left the CPI to join the CPM. The rivalries between the two parties were intense; and very often violent. The leader of the CPI(ML), Charu Mazumdar, urged the elimination of landlords, who were 'class enemies', as well as of CPM cadres, who were 'right deviationists'. On its part, the CPM raised a private army (euphemistically termed a 'volunteer force') to further their version of the 'people's democratic revolution'.[18]

As in British times, it is the reports of the Intelligence Bureau that best capture the contours of political unrest. One IB report listed 137 'major cases of lawlessness in West Bengal'; this over a mere six-week period between 19 March and 4 May 1970. These were classified under different headings. Several pitted two parties against each other: 'CPM vs CPI',

'CPM vs Congress', 'CPM vs CPML'. Sometimes the ire was directed against the state: 'CPM vs Police Party', for example, or 'Extremists vs Constables', this a reference to an attack on a police station in Malda district in which Naxalites speared a constable to death and looted the armoury. Then there was a case listed as 'Extremist Students vs Vice Chancellor', which dealt with an incident in Calcutta's Jadavpur University, where radical students kept the vice-chancellor captive for several hours before damaging the furniture and scribbling Maoist slogans on the walls of his office.[19]

In the villages, Naxalites had hoped to catalyse unrest by beheading landlords; in the city, they thought that the same could be achieved by random attacks on policemen. Kipling had once called Calcutta the 'City of Dreadful Night'; now the citizens lived in dread by day as well. The shops began closing in the early afternoon; by dusk the streets were deserted.[20] 'Not a day passes in this turbulent and tortured city', wrote one reporter, 'without a few bombs being hurled at police pickets and patrols'. The police, for their part, raided houses and college hostels in search of the extremists. In one raid they seized explosives sufficient to make 3,000 bombs.[21]

V

Tamil pride was resurgent in the south; class warfare on the rise in the east. But the Congress consensus was crumbling elsewhere as well. In the state of Orissa the Congress had been routed by a partnership between Swatantra and the party of the local landed elite. Their election campaign had targeted two leading Congress figures, Biju Patnaik and Biren Mitra, for their alleged corruption and opulent lifestyles. It was alleged that, while in power in the state, Patnaik and Mitra had taken bribes from businessmen and allotted lucrative government contracts to their friends and relatives.[22] A popular slogan, a local variant, so to say, of the one shouted in distant Dehradun, was 'Biju Biren kauthi/ mada botal jauthi ' (Where there are liquor bottles, there you will find Biju and Biren). On coming to power, the Swatantra–Jana–Congress alliance immediately constituted a commission of inquiry to look into the corruption of the previous government.[23]

Challenged by parties of left and right, the Congress also found itself bleeding from inside. In most states in northern India it had won

slender majorities. These became prey to intrigue, with the formation
of factions by ambitious leaders seeking to become chief minister. In the
states of Uttar Pradesh, Madhya Pradesh, Haryana and Bihar, Congress
governments were formed, only to fall when a group of disgruntled
defectors moved across to the other side. In a political lexicon already
rich in acronyms a new one entered: 'SVD', Samyukta Vidhayak Dal,
or the United Legislators Party – as the name suggests, a Rag, Tag and
Bobtail outfit, a coalition of legislators left, right and centre, united
only by the desire to grab power.

These SVD governments were made up of the Jana Sangh, socialists,
Swatantra, local parties and Congress defectors – this last often the key
element that made a numerical majority possible. At one level the SVD
phenomena signalled the rise of the lower castes, who had benefited
from land legislation but been denied the fruits of political power. In the
north, these castes included the Jats in Haryana and UP, the Kurmis and
Koeris in Bihar, the Lodhs in MP and the Yadavs in all these states. In
the south, they included the Marathas in Maharashtra, the Vokkaligas
in Mysore, the Vellalas in Madras and the Reddys and Kammas in Andhra
Pradesh. These castes occupied an intermediate position in the social
hierarchy, below the Brahmins but above the Untouchables. In many
areas they were the 'dominant caste', numerically significant and well
organized. What they lacked was access to state power. The DMK was
chiefly fuelled by such castes, as were the socialists who had increased
their vote share in the north. Notably, many of the Congress defectors
also came from this strata.

At another level, the SVD governments were simply the product of
personal ambition. Consider the state of Madhya Pradesh. Here, the
Congress's troubles started before the election, when the Rajmata (queen
mother) of Gwalior left the party because she had not been consulted
in the choice of candidates. With her son Madhavrao she campaigned
energetically against the Congress. An intelligence report claimed the
Rajmata spent Rs3 million during the election. Although the Congress
came back to power, in the Gwalior region the party was wiped out.
Now, claimed the report, the Rajmata was planning to spend more
money 'to subvert the loyalties of some Congress legislators . . . [and]
bring about the downfall of the new Congress Ministry'.[24]

The chief minister, a canny operator named D. P. Mishra, was
quite prepared for this. He was wooing defectors from other parties
himself – as he wrote to the Congress president, he had 'to open the door

for all who wish to join the Party'.[25] Eventually, though, the Rajmata was successful, when the prominent Congress defector Govind Narain Singh got twenty-eight others to leave the party with him. Before the crucial vote in the House, Singh kept his flock sequestered in his home, watching over them with a rifle in case they be kidnapped or otherwise seduced.

Not sure how long their tenure would last, the SVD government had to make every day count. Or every order, rather. Ministers specified a fee for sanctioning or stopping transfers of officials. Thus 'orders, particularly transfer orders, were issued and cancelled with bewildering rapidity'. Characteristically, the Jana Sangh wanted the Education portfolio, so that 'they could build up a permanent following through the primary schools'. They eventually got Home, where they maintained the communal peace by keeping their followers in check, yet took great care 'to see that no key post in any department went to a Muslim'.[26]

Despite the defections and the corruptions they engendered, what transpired after the 1967 elections was indeed what E. P. W. da Costa had called it – India's second non-violent revolution. One could now take a train from New Delhi to Calcutta, a journey of 1,000 miles right through the country's heartland, and not pass through a single Congress-ruled state.

VI

The late 1960s saw a fresh assertion of regionalist sentiment. Parts of the old Hyderabad state, merged with Andhra Pradesh in 1956, now wanted out. The movement was led by students of the Osmania University, who complained that Andhra was run for the benefit of the coastal elite. The new state they demanded would centre on the neglected inland districts. To be named Telengana, it would have Hyderabad as its capital. Strikes and processions were held, trains stopped and claims advanced of 'colonization by Andhras' and 'police *zulm*' (terror).[27]

Across the country a new state had in fact been created, out of the tribal districts of Assam. The movement here had a long history. An Eastern Indian Tribal Union was formed in 1955 to represent the inhabitants of the Khasi, Jaintia and Garo hills. Five years later it was renamed the All-Party Hill Leaders Conference (APHLC). In the 1967 elections the Congress was routed in the hills by the APHLC. This, along with the fear of stoking an insurgency on the Naga and Mizo pattern, prompted the centre to create a new province in December 1969. The state was called Meghalaya, meaning abode of the clouds.[28]

In Punjab, meanwhile, an existing state was in search of a capital of its own. After the state's division in 1966, Chandigarh served as the capital of both Punjab and Haryana. The Sikhs believed, with reason, that the city should be reserved to them – indeed, the centre had indicated that it would. Now the Punjabis were urging the government to make good their promise. Through 1968 and 1969 there were popular demonstrations to this effect. In October 1969 the veteran freedom fighter Darshan Singh Pherumal died after a fast aimed at making New Delhi hand over Chandigarh. The prime minister issued an anodyne note of sympathy: she hoped that Pherumal's death would 'move the people of Punjab and of Haryana towards bringing their hearts and minds together in an act of great reconciliation'.[29]

Just as the Sikhs wanted Chandigarh exclusively for themselves, so, with regard to Bombay, did some Maharashtrians. The city had a new political party, named the Shiv Sena after the great medieval Maratha warrior Shivaji. In some ways this was a continuation of the old Samyukta Maharashtra Samiti – albeit in a more extreme form. Instead of 'Bombay for Maharashtra' the call now was 'Bombay for Maharashtrians'. The Shiv Sena was the handiwork of a cartoonist named Bal Thackeray, whose main target was south Indians, whom he claimed were taking away jobs from the natives. Thackeray lampooned *dhoti*-clad 'Madrasis' in his writings and drawings; while his followers attacked Udupi restaurants and homes of Tamil and Telugu speakers. Another target were the communists, whose control of the city's textile unions the Shiv Sena sought to undermine by making deals with the management.

Bombay was India's *urbs prima*; its financial and industrial capital, and the centre of its entertainment industry. In this most cosmopolitan of cities, a nativist agenda proved surprisingly successful, being especially attractive to the educated unemployed. In 1968 the Sena won as many as 42 seats in the Bombay municipal elections, standing second only to the Congress.[30]

These calls for greater autonomy in the heartland were accompanied by stirrings in the periphery among groups and leaders who had never been entirely reconciled to being part of India in the first place. In March 1968 Sheikh Abdullah was freed from house arrest in Kodaikanal and allowed to return to his Valley. This was a year after the 1967 elections which, in Kashmir at any rate, had not really been free and fair: in twenty-two out of seventy-five constituencies the Congress candidate was returned unopposed when his rivals' nomination papers were rejected.[31] Her own advisers now prevailed upon Mrs Gandhi to free Abdullah. Their information was that the Sheikh was 'gradually adapting himself' to the fact that the accession of Kashmir to India was irrevocable.[32]

As in 1964, the Lion of Kashmir returned home to a hero's welcome, driving in an open jeep into the Valley, accepting garlands from the estimated half-million admirers who had lined the roads to greet him. As ever, his statements were amenable to multiple meanings, with him saying at one place that he would discuss 'all possibilities' with the Indian government, at another that he would never compromise on the Kashmiri 'right to self-determination'. To a British newspaper he offered a three-way resolution: Jammu to go to India, 'Azad' Kashmir to Pakistan, with the Valley – the real bone of contention – to be put under UN trusteeship for five years, after which it would vote on whether to join India or Pakistan, or be independent. Ambivalent on politics, the Sheikh was, just as characteristically, direct in his defence of secularism. When a dispute between students threatened to escalate into a Hindu–Muslim riot, Abdullah pacified the disputants, then walked the streets of Srinagar urging everyone to calm down. He made his associates take a pledge that they were 'prepared to shed their blood to protect the life, honour and property of the minorities in Kashmir'.[33]

Meanwhile, the rebels in Nagaland were seeking a fresh resolution of their own. With Phizo in London, the movement was passing into the hands of younger radicals, such as Isak Swu and T. Muivah. Where the older man had opposed seeking help from communist China – owing to its hostility to the Christian faith – these men had no such inhibitions. Reports came that 1,000 Nagas had crossed into Yunnan via Burma, there to receive Chinese machine guns, mortars and rocket launchers, as well as instruction on how to use them. Back in Nagaland, there were violent clashes between the Indian army and the rebels.[34]

Endorsing the move towards Peking was that longtime supporter of the Naga cause, David Astor of the *Observer*. Astor predicted that Nagaland would follow the course set by Ireland – where a colonial government had reluctantly to grant independence to the southern part of the island. Since the Nagas were as stubborn as the Irish, the magnate thought that they 'can now use the leverage of Chinese support . . . to survive successfully'. Astor hoped that 'friendly British voices would point out to Delhi the relevance of the lesson we had to learn when similarly challenged by the Irish'.[35] The advice rested on a serious, not to say tragic, underestimation of the powers of the Indian state.

VII

Disturbingly, the late 1960s also witnessed a rise in violence between Hindus and Muslims. According to figures released by the National Integration Council, there were 132 incidences of communal violence in 1966, 220 in 1967 and as many as 346 in 1968 (the upward trend continued during 1969 and 1970). These conflicts often had their origins in petty disputes, such as the playing of music before a mosque or the killing of a cow near a temple. Sometimes attacks on women or fights over property sparked the trouble. In terms of number of incidents, the states of Bihar and Uttar Pradesh were the worst hit.[36]

One reason for this sudden upsurge in violence was the weakness of state governments. Particularly culpable were the SVD regimes, who vacillated in using force to quell riots or rioters. Another reason was that, in the aftermath of the war of 1965, feelings against Pakistan ran high. These could easily be turned against Indian Muslims, seen (unfairly) as fifth columnists working on behalf of the enemy. 'Jana Sangh-inspired Hindus' were particularly prone to taunting Muslims in this fashion. Now, when a dispute broke out, to the old, religiously inspired slogans – 'Har Har Mahadev' and 'Allah O Akbar' – was added a new one on the Hindu side: 'Pakistan ya Kabristan' (Go to Pakistan, or else we will send you to your grave).[37]

One of the worst riots took place in Ahmedabad, the Gujarati city that Mahatma Gandhi had once called home. Ironically, it took place on the eve of the centenary of Gandhi's birth, and was thus a deep source of embarrassment to the government, which had planned a lavish celebration, with dignitaries coming in from all over the world. On 12 September 1969 a procession commemorating a Muslim saint ran into a group of *sadhus* walking back to their temple with cows. Hot words were exchanged, whereupon Muslim youths entered the temple and smashed a few idols. A Muslim delegation, led by a respected lawyer, went immediately to apologize, but the priests were not to be pacified. As word spread of the desecration, crowds of Hindus began collecting, looking for targets to attack. Qurans were burnt in one place, Muslim shops attacked in another. With the Muslims fighting back, the trouble spread through the city and, in time, to towns near Ahmedabad as well. As the police looked mutely on, gangs battled each other in the narrow streets of the old town. After a week of fighting, the army was called in to restore the peace. More than 1,000 people had lost their lives. Thirty times that number had been rendered homeless. A majority in both cases were Muslim.[38]

There was a very serious riot in Ranchi, in Bihar, in the summer of 1967; a very bad one in Jalgaon, in Maharashtra, three years later. In between, numerous other towns in north and west India had witnessed intercommunal violence. The writer Khushwant Singh bitterly noted that the Indian adolescent was now learning the geography of his country through the history of murder. Aligarh and Ranchi and Ahmedabad were no longer centres of learning or culture or industry, but places where Indians butchered one another in the name of religion. As Singh pointed out, in these riots 'nine out of ten killed are Muslims. Nine out of ten homes and business establishments destroyed are Muslim homes or enterprises.' Besides, the majority of those rendered homeless, and of those apprehended by the police, were also Muslim. 'Is it any great wonder', asked the writer, 'that an Indian Muslim no longer feels secure in secular India? He feels discriminated against. He feels a second-class citizen.'[39]

In 1967–8, when the communal temperature began to rise, India had a Muslim president (Dr Zakir Hussain) as well as a Muslim chief justice of the Supreme Court (M. Hidayatullah). However, as a Delhi journal pointed out, this was by no means representative of 'the position of Muslims in the totality of Indian life'. They were seriously under-represented in professions such as engineering and medicine, and in industry, trade and the armed forces. This was in part because of the flight of the Muslim upper crust to Pakistan, yet subtle social prejudice also contributed. The Muslims had long stood solidly behind the Congress, but in the elections of 1967 they voted in large numbers for other parties as a way of showing their disillusionment. The Muslim predicament was a product of bigotry and communal politics on the Hindu side, and of an obscurantist leadership on their own.[40]

VIII

To the historian, the late 1960s are reminiscent of the late 1940s, likewise a time of crisis and conflict, of resentment along lines of class, religion, ethnicity and region, of a centre that seemed barely to hold. I wonder if these parallels occurred to the Indians who lived through these times, to people in authority in particular, and to the prime minister most of all.

The resonances were not merely national or sociological, but also familial. With the Raj in its death throes, Jawaharlal Nehru became prime minister of an interim government in 1946; the next year, the post became more substantial when India became independent. Indira Gandhi was unexpectedly thrust into office in 1966; the next year, the job was confirmed formally when she led her party to an election victory. Like Nehru, she was in control in Delhi; like him, she could not be certain how far her government's writ ran beyond it. He and she had both to contend with communist insurrection and communal conflict; he was additionally faced with the problem of the princely states, she with the problem of a dozen anti-Congress state governments.

Here the parallels end. Seeking to unite a divided India, Nehru articulated an ideology that rested on four main pillars. First, there was democracy, the freedom to choose one's friends and speak one's mind (and in the language of one's choice) – above all, the freedom to choose one's leaders through regular elections based on universal adult franchise. Second, there was secularism, the neutrality of the state in matters of religion and its commitment to maintaining social peace. Third, there was socialism, the attempt to augment productivity while ensuring a more egalitarian distribution of income (and of social opportunity). Fourth, there was non-alignment, the placement of India beyond and above the rivalries of the Great Powers. Among the less compelling, but not necessarily less significant, elements of this worldview were the conscious cultivation of a multiparty system (notably through debate in Parliament), and a respect for the autonomy of the judiciary and the executive.

Although rearticulated in the context of a newly independent India, these beliefs had been developing over a period of more than twenty years. Nehru was a well-read and widely travelled man. Through his travels and readings, he arrived at a synthesis of socialism and liberalism that he thought appropriate to his country. In other words, the political beliefs he came to profess – and invited the people of India to share – were his own.

With Mrs Gandhi one cannot be so sure. She had neither read nor travelled extensively. She was unquestionably a patriot; growing up in the freedom movement, and with its leaders, she was deeply committed to upholding India's interests in the world. How she thought these could best be upheld was less certain. In all the years she had been in politics her core beliefs had not been revealed to either party or public. They knew not what she really thought of the market economy, or the Cold War, or the relations between religions, or the institutions and processes of democracy. The many volumes of Nehru's *Selected Works* are suffused with his writings on these subjects – subjects on which Mrs Gandhi, before 1967, spoke scarcely a word.

The prime minister was, so to say, *non*-ideological – an attribute not shared by her advisers. The chief among these was her principal secretary, P. N. Haksar. Educated at the London School of Economics, he was called to the Bar in the UK before returning to practise law in Allahabad. At Independence he joined the Foreign Service and served as India's ambassador to Austria and its first high commissioner to Nigeria. In 1967 he was deputy high commissioner in London, when Mrs Gandhi asked him to join her Secretariat. Haksar and she shared a home town, a common ancestry – both were Kashmiri Pandits – and many common friends.

Haksar was a kind of polymath: a student of mathematics, he was also keenly interested in history, particularly diplomatic and military history. Among his other interests were anthropology – he had attended Bronislaw Malinowski's seminar at the LSE – and food (he was a superb cook). Haksar tended to overpower friends and colleagues with the range of his knowledge and the vigour of his opinions. However, in this case intellectual force was not necessarily matched by intellectual subtlety. His political views were those of the left wing of the British Labour Party, circa 1945 – pro-state and anti-market in economic affairs, pro-Soviet and anti-American in foreign policy. He was also – it must be added – a man of an unshakeable integrity.[41]

This book owes a great deal to P. N. Haksar, whose papers, all 500 files of them, provide a privileged window into the history of the times. But the prime minister of the day owed him even more. For, as Katherine Frank writes, 'Indira trusted Haksar's intelligence and judgement implicitly and completely. From 1967 to 1973, he was probably the most influential and powerful person in the government.'[42] Haksar shared his influence and power with the career diplomat T. N. Kaul, the politician turned diplomat D. P. Dhar, the economist turned mandarin P. N. Dhar and the policeman turned security analyst R. N. Kao. Collectively they were known (behind their backs) as the 'Panch Pandava', after the five heroic brothers of the Mahabharata. Coincidentally, all were Kashmiri Brahmins. There was also an outer core of advisers, these likewise officials or intellectuals rather than politicians *per se*.

This was not accidental. Even more so than Lal Bahadur Shastri, Mrs Gandhi needed to assert her independence of the Congress 'Syndicate' which had chosen her. Socially, she shared little with the party bosses – her own friends came from a more rarefied milieu. She could not be certain when they might try to unseat her. Thus she came to rely on the advice of the mandarins around her, who had no political ambitions themselves. But they did have political views to which, in time and for her own reasons, she came to subscribe.

IX

After the elections of 1967, Morarji Desai once more made manifest his desire to become prime minister. A compromise was worked out under which he would serve as finance minister and deputy prime minister – the latter a post that no one had held since the death of Vallabhbhai Patel.

Hemmed in by the Syndicate, and threatened by Desai, the prime minister now sought to mark out her own identity by presenting herself as a socialist. This was done on the advice of P. N. Haksar. In a note he prepared for her in January 1968, the mandarin advised his mistress to clip Desai's wings, perhaps by appointing one or two other 'deputy' prime ministers in addition. While choosing ministers loyal to her, the prime minister had also to forge 'wider progressive alliances under [her] more effective personal lead'. For this, she needed to 'project more assertively [her] own ideological image directly to the people over the heads of [her] colleagues and party men'.[43]

Mrs Gandhi had rarely invoked the word 'socialist' before 1967, although it was one of the four pillars of her father's political philosophy. Notably, it was the pillar that was propped up most enthusiastically by her mandarins. In part, the appeal was negative, stemming from a Brahmanical distaste for business and businessmen. But there was also a positive identification with the idea of socialism. A greater role for the state in the economy, they believed, was necessary to ensure social equity as well as promote national integration. The public sector, wrote one mandarin, was 'a macrocosm of a united India'. In the private sector, Punjabis employed Punjabis, Marwaris trusted only Marwaris, but in the

Indian Railways and the great steel factories Tamils worked alongside Biharis, Hindus with Muslims, Brahmins with Harijans. Whether or not socialism was economically feasible, it was a 'social necessity'. For, 'socialism and a large public sector . . . are effective weapons for forging a united and integrated India'.[44]

There was a strong moral core to the socialism of P. N. Haksar and his colleagues. For the prime minister, however, the appeal was pragmatic, a means of distinguishing herself from the Congress old guard. In May 1967 she presented a ten-point programme of reform to the party, which included the 'social control' of banking, the abolition of the privy purses of princes and guaranteed minimum wages for rural and industrial labour. The Syndicate was unenthusiastic, but the programme appealed to the younger generation, who saw the party's recent reverses as a consequence of the promises unfulfilled over the years.[45]

Speeches made by Mrs Gandhi after her re-election show her identifying explicitly with the poor and vulnerable. Speaking to the Lok Sabha in February 1968, she stressed the problems of landless labour, expressed her 'concern for all the minorities of India' and defended the public sector from criticisms that it was not making profit (her answer that it did not need to, since it was building a base for economic development). Speaking to the Rajya Sabha in August, she asked for a 'new deal for the down-trodden', in particular, the Scheduled Castes and Scheduled Tribes, pledging her 'unceasing attention and effort to this cause'. A few days later, in her Independence Day address from the ramparts of the Red Fort, she singled out 'industrialists and businessmen' who had the nerve to talk of worker indiscipline while continuing to 'make big profits and draw fat salaries'.[46]

These views resonated with the so-called 'Young Turks' in the Congress, who had started a socialist ginger group within the party. This used the pulpit of Parliament to ask embarrassing questions of the more conservative ministers. The Young Turk Chandra Shekhar raised charges of corruption against Morarji Desai's son Kanti. He also insinuated that the finance minister had issued licences out of turn to a large industrial house. It was believed that he was speaking as a proxy for the prime minister – at any rate, she refused to censure him.[47]

Throughout 1968 and 1969, writes one biographer, Mrs Gandhi was a 'frustrated leader. She was not strong enough to defy the [Congress] organization and not rash enough to quit.'[48] Her chance came in the summer of 1969, when Dr Zakir Hussain died half-way through his term as president of the republic. The Syndicate wished to replace him with one of their own: N. Sanjiva Reddy, a former Lok Sabha Speaker and chief minister of Andhra Pradesh. Mrs Gandhi, however, preferred the vice-president, V. V. Giri, a labour leader with whom her own relations were very good.

In the first week of 1969 the All-India Congress Committee (AICC) met in Bangalore. Before she left for this meeting, the prime minister was apparently told by P. N. Haksar that 'the best way to vanquish the Syndicate would be to convert the struggle for personal power into an ideological one'.[49] In Bangalore, Mrs Gandhi openly showed her hand on the side of the Young Turks by proposing the immediate nationalization of the major banks. She also opposed Sanjiva Reddy's candidature for president, but was overruled by a majority in the Working Committee.

On returning to Delhi Mrs Gandhi divested Morarji Desai of the Finance portfolio. He was a known opponent of bank nationalization, once telling Parliament that it would 'severely strain the administrative resources of the government while leaving the basic issues untouched'. The state takeover of banks, believed Desai, would reduce the resources available for economic development, and increase bureaucracy and red tape.[50]

After relieving Desai of the Finance Ministry, Mrs Gandhi issued an ordinance announcing that the state had taken over fourteen privately owned banks. Explaining the action over All-India Radio, she said that India was 'an ancient country but a young democracy, which has to remain ever vigilant to prevent the domination of the few over the social, economic or political systems'. This mandated that 'major banks should be not only socially controlled but publicly owned', so that they could give credit not just to big business but to 'millions of farmers, artisans, and other self-employed persons'.[51]

In a statement to the press, the prime minister claimed that there was 'a great feeling in the country' regarding the nationalization: 95 per cent of the people supported it, with only big newspapers representing commercial interests opposing it. However, a small weekly, independently owned, suggested that this might be an individual quest masquerading as an ideological battle. Mrs Gandhi had 'chosen to adopt a radical stance suddenly as a tactic in the personal strife for dominance within the Congress party', said Thought; she now wished to 'project herself as a national figure who needs the Congress less than it needs her'.[52]

The nationalization of banks was challenged in the Supreme Court; the challenge was upheld, but the judgement was immediately nullified by a fresh ordinance brought in by government, signed this time by the president. In the first six months of state control there was a massive expansion in the banking sector – with as many as 1,100 new branches opened, a large proportion of them in remote rural areas that had never before been serviced by formal credit.[53]

X

Attention now shifted to the election of a new president, in which all members of Parliament and state assemblies would vote. The official Congress candidate was Sanjiva Reddy. V. V. Giri had decided to contest as an independent, while the opposition had put up C. D. Deshmukh, a former civil servant and Cabinet Minister. In violation of party practice and party discipline, the prime minister decided she would support V. V. Giri. This decision was not made public, but it was conveyed to her followers, who went around canvassing the younger Congress MPs to vote for Giri. The Congress president, S. Nijalingappa, now pressed the prime minister to issue a public declaration of support for Reddy. When she wouldn't, he spoke to the Jana Sangh and Swatantra leaders asking them to shift their own allegiance from Subba Rao to Reddy. This move was seized upon by Mrs Gandhi's camp, who accused Nijalingappa of hobnobbing with the enemy. They 'requisitioned' a meeting of the AICC to discuss the matter. The request was refused.

Four days before the presidential elections – due on 20 August 1969 – Mrs Gandhi finally spoke. She asked for a 'vote of conscience'. This was a call to Congress Party members to defy their organization and vote for the rival candidate. Which they did, in fairly large numbers. Many of the older party men voted for Reddy, but in the end Giri won, on the second count. Now commenced a bitter exchange of letters between the Congress president and the prime minister. Finally, on 12 November, Mrs Gandhi was expelled from the Congress for 'indiscipline'. By this time many MPs had thrown in their lot with her. In December rival Congress sessions were held, the parent body meeting in Ahmedabad and its new challenger in Bombay. The parties were becoming known as Congress (O) and Congress (R). The letters stood in one version for 'Organization' and 'Requisitionist', in another for 'Old' and 'Reform'.[54]

In expelling Mrs Gandhi from the Congress, Nijalingappa accused her of fostering a cult of personality, of promoting herself above party and nation. The history of the twentieth century, he pointed out,

> is replete with instances of the tragedy that overtakes democracy when a leader who has risen to power on the crest of a popular wave or with the support of a democratic organisation becomes a victim of political narcissism and is egged on by a coterie of unscrupulous sycophants who use corruption and terror to silence opposition and attempt to make public opinion an echo of authority. The Congress as an organisation dedicated to democracy and socialism has to combat such trends.[55]

Nijalingappa was a lifelong Congressman, a man from peasant stock who joined the freedom movement when he was very young. He built up the party in Mysore, later serving three terms as the state's chief minister.[56] About his commitment to the party and to democracy there could be no question. But 'socialism' was another matter. The nationalization of banks had strengthened his rival's claim to that label, while Nijalingappa's wooing of the Jana Sangh and Swatantra had weakened his own. This contrast was assiduously developed in the speeches and letters that bore Mrs Gandhi's name, but were the handiwork of P. N. Haksar and his colleagues. Here, the prime minister was presented as standing for socialism in economics and secularism in matters of religion, as being pro-poor and for the development of the nation as a whole. The Party president, on the other hand, was said to be promoting capitalism in economics and communalism in religion.[57]

The presentation was markedly successful. Of the 705 members of the AICC, as many as 446 attended the Congress (R) session; of the 429 Congress MPs (in both Houses), 310 joined the prime minister's camp. Of these, 220 were from the Lok Sabha, leaving the Congress (R) some forty-five seats short of a majority. To make up the numbers it turned to independents and to the Communist Party of India. The CPI was delighted to join up, seeing Mrs Gandhi's left turn as an opportunity for expanding its own influence. In August 1969, writing of the battle within the Congress, an influential journalist close to the CPI crowed that 'the Syndicate pretensions have been torn to pieces'. 'A tide has come in the affairs of the nation', he wrote, 'and there is little doubt that . . . Indira Gandhi is taking it at the flood . . . The tide is symbolised by the enthusiastic crowds from different walks of life that have been flocking to the Prime Minister's House every day. This is no ordinary craving for *darshan* of a beautiful face; they represent a new assertion of the power of the *demos*.' The journalist now looked forward to the 'implementation of a radical economic agenda and [a] firm stand against communalism'.[58]

In a comparable situation, back in 1950–2, Jawaharlal Nehru had bided his time. Faced with the conservative challenge of Tandon and company, he had worked to get his way with the party rather than divide it in two. But here, as one knowledgeable observer remarked, Mrs Gandhi had 'displayed a militancy foreign to Congress tradition'. In contrast to the incremental approach of Nehru and Shastri, she 'represented something ruthless and new. She had astonished people with her flair for cold assessment, shrewd timing, and the telling theatrical gesture; above all, with her capacity for a fight to the finish, even to bringing the eighty-four-year-old party of liberation to rupture'.[59]

XI

With the banks nationalized, Mrs Gandhi now turned to the abolition of the privileges of the princes. When their states merged with the Union, the princes were given a constitutional guarantee that they could retain their titles, jewels and palaces, be paid an annual privy purse in proportion to the size of their states and be exempt from central taxes and import duties. With so many Indians so poor, it was felt that these privileges were 'out of place and out of time' – these the words of P. N. Haksar, but widely endorsed within and outside his circle.[60]

As early as July 1967 the AICC passed a resolution asking for an end to titles and privy purses. The Home Ministry prepared a detailed note, recommending action via legislation rather than executive action. The home minister, Y. B. Chavan, was asked to commence negotiations with the princes, represented in these talks by the Maharaja of Dhrangadhara. It was hoped the princes would be amenable to the change; if not, a constitutional amendment would have to be brought.[61]

Chavan and Dhrangadhara had several long meetings in 1968, but no compromise could be reached. In any case, the power struggle within the Congress ruled out hasty action. There were many MPs who were either princes or under their control, and their votes were needed to

see Mrs Gandhi's candidate for president through. After Giri's election
the government and the princes continued to talk, each side proving as
obdurate as the other. At this stage, in December 1969, the Jam Saheb of
Nawanagar sent New Delhi an intriguing proposal. This criticized both
parties, the princes for adopting 'a most adamantly uncompromising
stand', the government for 'going back on their [constitutional]
commitments and assurances'. The Jam Saheb suggested, as a way out
of the impasse, that the government abolish the princes' privileges,
but pay them twenty years' worth of privy purses: 25 per cent in cash,
25 per cent in bonds to be redeemed after twenty years, and 50 per cent
to a public charitable trust headed by the ruler. This trust's aims would
be the promotion of sport, the education of backward classes and, above
all, the protection of 'our fast-disappearing wildlife'.[62]

The Jam Saheb thought this a scheme that 'would befit the dignity
of the nation'. Mrs Gandhi passed it on to the home minister, noting
that it was 'animated by a constructive purpose'. But nothing came of
it. On 18 May 1970 – the last day of the summer session of Parliament –
Y. B. Chavan introduced a bill calling for a constitutional amendment
annulling the privileges of the princes. The bill was taken up in the
next session, when Mrs Gandhi described it as an 'important step in
the further democratization of our society'.

The Lok Sabha adopted the bill by the necessary two-thirds margin – 336
for, 155 against. However, in the Rajya Sabha the motion failed to be
carried by a single vote. The prime minister had apparently anticipated
this adverse vote in the Upper House, for soon afterwards a presidential
order was issued derecognizing the princes.

Four days later, on 11 September 1970, a group of Maharajas moved
the Supreme Court against the order. The case was heard by a full
bench, headed by the chief justice. On 11 December the bench ruled
that the order was arbitrary and against the spirit of the constitution.
Some legal scholars viewed the judgement as a victory for democracy,
whereas left-wing radicals saw it as consistent with the 'tendency of the
Supreme Court to protect the vested interests'.

With regard to bank nationalization, too, the Court had put a spanner
in the works. This fresh challenge to her authority prompted the prime
minister to dissolve Parliament and call for a fresh mandate from the
people. The House still had a year to run. Explaining the decision over
All-India Radio, Mrs Gandhi said that while her government had sought

to 'ensure a better life to the vast majority of our people and satisfy their aspiration for a just social order . . . reactionary forces have not hesitated to obstruct [this] in every possible way'.[63]

XII

On one front, at least, there was very good news for Mrs Gandhi's government – the new agricultural strategy had begun paying dividends. In 1967 there was a bad drought, which particularly affected the state of Bihar, but the next year saw a bumper crop of food grains, 95 million tonnes (mt) in all. Much of this increase was accounted for by Punjab and Haryana, whose farmers had planted the new dwarf varieties of wheat developed by Indian scientists from Mexican models. However, the new varieties of rice had also done quite well, as had cotton and groundnuts.

C. Subramaniam's strategy had been to identify those districts where irrigation was available, and those farming communities most likely to take to the new seeds, and the heavy doses of fertilizers that went with them. The results were sensational. Between 1963 and 1967, before the new methods had been tried, the annual production of wheat in India was between 9 and 11 mt. Between 1967 and 1970 it ranged from 16 to 20 mt. The corresponding figures for rice were 30 – 37 mt for the earlier period and 37– 42 mt for the latter.[64]

These figures masked enormous variations by region. There remained large areas where agriculture was rain-fed, and where only one crop could be grown per year. Still, there was a feeling that endemic scarcity was a thing of the past. Modern science was laying the ghost of Malthus. In August 1969 a British journalist who was an old India hand wrote that 'for the first time in all the years I have been visiting the country, there is a coherence in the economic picture, for the first time an absence of feeling that the economy rested almost wholly on the simple success or failure of the monsoon'.[65]

The food problem was solved, but India might still fall apart – on account of, as Neville Maxwell and others had claimed, simply being too diverse. In an editorial marking twenty years of India's existence as a republic, the New York Times called it a 'remarkable achievement', then went on to say that 'both Union and democracy are under increasing strain these days, with the future of both in doubt'.[66] However, most Indians were by now comfortable with the diversity within. They could see what bound the varied religions, races and regions: namely, a shared political history (from the national movement onwards), a pluralistic constitution and a tradition of regular elections. Nor did they think the challenges of states a threat to national unity. As one commentator wrote – in rebuttal of doomsayers such as Maxwell – 'a strong centre is not necessarily conducive to democracy'. Federalism and rule by regional parties could help sustain democracy in India, in contrast to (say) Indonesia and Ghana, where the efforts of Sukarno and Nkrumah to impose a strong centre had only led to dictatorship.[67]

Among thinking Indians then, there was little fear that the events of the late sixties would presage the break-up of the country, or the replacement of elected politicians by soldiers in uniform. Army rule was out of the question, but there was yet the prospect of an armed communist movement engulfing large parts of the country. The Green Revolution could turn Red, for agricultural prosperity had also created social polarities. And the location of Naxalbari was significant: a thin strip of India wedged between East Pakistan and Nepal that was not far from China and provided the only access to the states of the north-east. This was an 'ideal operational field' for beginning a revolution, to escape into Pakistan or Nepal when one wished, to get arms from China if one wanted. So the worry grew in New Delhi that these pro-Peking Reds would 'fan out from Naxalbari to link up with their cells in Bengal, till they come right into the heart of Calcutta. Behind them will be the Chinese army menacing the Himalayan border.'[68]

On the other side, there were some who looked forward to the revolution in the making. These were the Naxalites, of course, but also their Western fellow-travellers. In the winter of 1968/9 the Marxist anthropologist Kathleen Gough – originally American but then teaching in Canada – wrote an article which saw, as 'the most hopeful way forward for India', a 'revolutionary movement that would root itself in the countryside' where the bulk of the poor were located. Taking heart from the progress, here and there, of the Naxalites and their ideology, Gough said that 'parliamentarianism seems doomed to failure, and the rebel Communists' path the only hopeful alternative'.[69]

Gough was not alone in seeing revolutionary communism as India's main hope, perhaps its only hope. That same winter, a young Swedish couple animated by the spirit of '68 travelled through the Indian countryside. They covered the land from tip to toe, from the parched fields of eastern Uttar Pradesh to the rich rice paddies of the southern

Cauvery delta. They saw a new critical awareness among the oppressed, manifest in 'growing antagonisms in Indian society'. Caste conflict was turning into class conflict (as Marxist theory said, and hoped, it would). Among the intellectuals, they saw a (to them welcome) scepticism about parliamentary democracy. As one left-wing student leader remarked, 'We must not let ourselves be fooled by the hocus-pocus of elections every fifth year.'

These changes, predicted the Swedish sociologists, 'will have widespread consequences for India's future'. Blood was being spilt (as Marxist theory said it must). 'The antagonisms are sometimes so violent that they are hard to imagine.' Fortunately, 'the new revolutionary movement . . . was growing in India today'. The authors were clear that 'only when these millions of poor people take their future in their own hands will India's poverty and oppression be brought to an end'. They left their readers with this hope: 'Perhaps Naxalbari does stand for the Indian revolution.'[70]

20

THE ELIXIR OF VICTORY

Gungi gudiya [dumb doll]
Ram Manohar Lohia on Indira Gandhi, circa 1967

I

IN NOVEMBER 1969 THE Delhi weekly *Thought* commented that 'the Congress seems to have written itself off as a nationally cohesive force'. The once-mighty party was now split into disputatious parts. When the next general election came, said *Thought*, 'Congressmen will be fighting Congressmen to the obvious advantage of regional or sectarian groups'. Consequently, 'Mrs Gandhi's party may not secure more than one-third of the seats in Parliament. The chances of the other group seem to be even slimmer.'[1]

A year later the prime minister called an election, fourteen months ahead of schedule. Her party – Congress (R) – wanted a popular mandate to implement the progressive reforms it had initiated, now held up by the 'reactionary' forces in Parliament. Its manifesto offered a 'genuine radical programme of economic and social development', upholding the interests of the small farmer and the landless labourer, and of the small entrepreneur against the big capitalist. It stood for the betterment of the lower castes, and for the protection of the minorities. Particular mention was made of the Urdu language, which 'shall be given its due place which has been denied to it so far'. It promised a 'strong and stable government', and asked for support in the fight against the 'dark and evil forces of right [wing] reaction', which were 'intent upon destroying the very base of our democratic and socialist objectives'.[2]

The position in which Indira Gandhi found herself in 1971 was in many ways reminiscent of her father's in 1952. Like Nehru then, Mrs Gandhi went to the polls having fought a bruising battle with members of her own party. Like him, she offered to the people a fresh, progressive-sounding mandate. And, like him, she was her party's chief campaigner and spokesperson, the very embodiment of what it said it stood for.

In calling an early poll, the prime minister had astutely dissociated the general election from elections to the various state assemblies which in the past had always taken place concurrently. That meant that parochial considerations of caste and ethnicity got mixed up with wider national questions. In 1967 this had proved to be detrimental to the Congress. This time, Mrs Gandhi made sure she would separate the two by calling a general election in which she could place a properly national agenda before the electorate.

The opposition, meanwhile, was seeking to build a united front against the ruling party. Urging it on was C. Rajagopalachari, now past ninety years of age. A common leader could not be agreed upon so, said 'Rajaji', the fight had to be conducted 'on the pattern of guerrilla warfare. Indira's candidates . . . must be opposed everywhere on the single ground that we oppose the conspiracy to tear up the constitution and to extinguish the people's liberties and put all power in the hands of the state'.[3]

The opposition constructed a 'Grand Alliance', bringing together Jana Sangh, Swatantra, Congress (O), the socialists, and regional groupings. The idea was to limit the number of multiway contests. A copywriter came up with the slogan 'Indira Hatao' (Remove Indira). This prompted the telling rejoinder, offered from the lips of the prime minister herself: 'Wo kehte hain Indira Hatao, hum kehte hain Garibi Hatao' (They ask for the Removal of Indira, whereas we want an End to Poverty itself).

Whether the work of the prime minister or one of her now forgotten minions, 'Garibi Hatao' was an inspired coinage. It allowed Congress (R) to take the moral high ground, representing itself as the party of progress, against an alliance of reaction. Personalizing the election was to backfire badly against the opposition, whose agenda was portrayed as negative in contrast to the forward-looking programme of the ruling party.

Mrs Gandhi worked tirelessly to garner votes for her party. Between the dissolution of Parliament, in the last week of December 1970, and the elections, held ten weeks later, she travelled 36,000 miles in all. She addressed 300 meetings and was heard or seen by an estimated 20 million people. These figures were recounted, with relish, in a letter written by Mrs Gandhi to an American friend. She clearly enjoyed the experience; as she remarked, 'it was wonderful to see the light in their [the people's] eyes'.[4]

The prime minister's speeches harped on the contrast, perceived and real, between the party she had left behind and the party she had founded. The 'old' Congress was in thrall to 'conservative elements' and 'vested interests', whereas the 'new' Congress was committed to the poor. Did not the nationalization of banks and the abolition of the privy purses show as much? The message struck a resonant chord, for, as one somewhat cynical journalist wrote:

> The man lying in a gutter prizes nothing more than the notion pumped into him that he is superior to the sanitary inspector. That the rich had been humbled looked like the assurance that the poor would be honoured. The instant 'poverty-removal' slogan was an economic absurdity. Psychologically and politically, for that reason, it was however a decisive asset in a community at war with reason and rationality.[5]

Her travels within India had made the prime minister far better known than she had been in 1967. In asking for votes, she exploited her 'charming personality', her 'father's historical role' and, above all, that stirring slogan 'Garibi Hatao'. The landless and low castes voted en masse for the Congress (R), as did the Muslims, who had been lukewarm the last time round. The new party's organizational weakness was remedied by its young volunteers, who went around the countryside amplifying their leader's words. The massive turnout on election day suggested that 'the people had been fired with a new hope of redemption'.[6]

Back in 1952 it had been said that even a lamp-post could win if it ran on the Congress symbol. It turned out that Mrs Gandhi's victory was even more spectacular than her father's. Congress (R) won 352 out of 518 seats; the next highest tally was that of the CPM, which won a mere 25. Both victor and vanquished agreed that this was chiefly the work of one person. As the writer Khushwant Singh commented, 'Indira Gandhi has successfully magnified her figure as the one and only leader of national dimensions'. Then he added, ominously: 'However, if power is voluntarily surrendered by a predominant section of the people to one person and at the same time opposition is reduced to insignificance, the temptation to ride roughshod over legitimate criticism can become irresistible. The danger of Indira Gandhi being given unbridled power shall always be present.'[7]

Among the consequences of the 1971 election was a change in the name of the ruling party. The Congress (R) now became known as Congress (I), for 'Indira'; later, even this was dropped. By the margin of its victory, Indira's Congress was confirmed as the real Congress, requiring no qualifying suffix.

Her success at the polls emboldened Mrs Gandhi to act decisively against the princes. Throughout 1971, the two sides tried and failed to find a settlement. The princes were willing to forgo their privy purses, but hoped at least to save their titles. But with her massive majority in Parliament, the prime minister had no need to compromise. On 2 December she introduced a bill seeking to amend the constitution and abolish all princely privileges. It was passed in the Lok Sabha by 381 votes to 6, and in the Rajya Sabha by 167 votes to 7. In her own speech, the prime minister invited 'the princes to join the élite of the modern age, the élite which earns respect by its talent, energy and contribution to human progress, all of which can only be done when we work together as equals without regarding anybody as of special status'.[8]

II

The statistics of the fifth general election were printed in loving detail in the report of the Chief Election Commissioner (CEC). The size of the electorate was 275 million, a 100 million up from the first edition in 1952. Yet no Indian had to walk more than two kilometres to exercise his or her franchise. There were now 342,944 polling stations, up 100,000 from 1962; each station was supplied with forty-three different items ranging from ballot papers and boxes to indelible ink and sealing wax; 282 million ballot papers were printed, 7 million more than the number of eligible voters (to allow for accidents and errors); 1,769,802 Indians were on polling duty – for the most part, these were officials of the state and central governments.

The CEC then turned, with less pleasure, to electoral malpractices. A study of the 1967 elections had found 375 cases of electoral violence of all kinds; of these, 98 were in Bihar.[9] In 1971 the Election Commission reported 66 instances of 'booth-capturing', where ballot boxes were seized by force and stuffed with ballots in favour of one candidate. In Anantnag in the Kashmir Valley a woman took away a ballot box under her burqa before returning it, now heavier by several hundred ballots.

Again, the most violations were in Bihar – the state accounted for 52 of 66 booths captured by hooligans hired by leaders of caste factions. The CEC believed this was 'perhaps the most caste-ridden State in the whole [of] India and this bane of excessive casteism vitiates in no mean degree the political atmosphere'.

These disfigurements notwithstanding, the holding of its fifth general election was a matter on which the country could congratulate itself. So wrote the CEC, in a preface whose lyricism sat oddly with the hardnosed numerical analysis that followed. For in between the last poll and this one, 'India was in the middle of the deepest and darkest woods and was groping for a way out'. Factionalism was rife; SVD governments came and went, and the president of the republic died, making 'the already dark political situation . . . darker'. Then the mighty Congress Party split; this, in the CEC's view, was comparable only to 'the Great Schism in the Whig Party in Great Britain in the year 1796'. In this 'state of tension, stress, confusion and flux, the prophets of doom, both inside and outside the country, started expressing serious misgivings and doubts as to the very survival of democracy in this Great Land'.

These doomsayers, said the chief election commissioner, had not reckoned with Bharata Bhagya Vidhata (The Supreme Dispenser of India's Destiny), which from 'ancient times' had thwarted 'adverse and hostile circumstances', by blowing 'into the soul of India that elixir-giving inspiration which imparted rejuvenated vigour to her vital, moral and spiritual forces'. Others might have disagreed, seeing the holding of this election not as a victory for Indian spiritualism but as a vindication of that very modern political form, electoral democracy.[10]

III

Three months before India held its fifth general election, Pakistan held its first ever election based on adult franchise. The poll had been called by General Yahya Khan, Ayub Khan's successor as president and chief martial law administrator.

Two parties dominated the campaign; Zulfiqar Bhutto's Pakistan People's Party in West Pakistan, and the National Awami League of Sheikh Mujibur Rahman ('Mujib') in East Pakistan. The son of a large landowner, educated at Oxford and Berkeley, Bhutto sought to declass himself, at least rhetorically, by promising every Pakistani *roti*, *kapda aur makaan* (food, clothing and a roof over your heads). Mujib's campaign was based on East Pakistan's sense of victimhood, its anger at the suppression of the Bengali language and the exploitation of its rich natural resources by the military rulers of the western half of the country.[11]

Yahya Khan appears to have called for elections in the hope that Bhutto's PPP would win, and allow him to continue as president. The polls were held in the third week of December 1970. The PPP won 88 out of the 144 seats in West Pakistan, whereas the Awami League swept the more populous East, winning 167 of its 169 seats. These results surprised Mujibur Rahman, and shocked Yahya Khan. For the president had intended that the newly elected assembly would frame a democratic constitution; the worry now was that the Awami League, with its majority, would insist on a federation where the eastern wing would manage its own affairs, leaving only defence and foreign policy to the central government. Mujib had already indicated that he would like East Pakistan to have control over the foreign exchange its products generated, and perhaps issue its own currency as well.

Yahya's reservations were reinforced by the ambitions of Bhutto. For the relationship between Pakistan's two wings had always been a colonial one, with West dominating East militarily, economically and even culturally. For both general and patrician, the prospect of having a Bengali decide their destinies was too horrible to contemplate. For the Bengali Muslim was regarded by his West Pakistani counterpart as effete and effeminate, and too easily corrupted by proximity to Hindus (over 10 million of whom still lived within their midst). Among these Hindus were many professionals – lawyers, doctors, university professors. The fear of the West Pakistani elite was that, if Mujib's Awami League came to form the government, 'the constitution to be adopted by them will have Hindu iron hand in it'.[12]

On the other side, the East Pakistani Muslims looked upon their West Pakistani counterparts as 'the ruling classes, as foreign ruling classes and as predatory foreign ruling classes'. They resented the rulers' dismissal of their language, Bengali; they complained that their agricultural wealth was being drained away to feed the western sector; and they noted that Bengalis were very poorly represented in the upper echelons of the Pakistani bureaucracy, judiciary and, not least, army. The feeling of being discriminated against had been growing over the years. By the time of the elections of 1970, 'the politically minded' East

Bengali had become 'allergic to a central authority located a thousand miles away'.[13]

In January 1971 Yahya Khan and Bhutto travelled separately to the East Pakistani capital, Dacca. They held talks with Mujib, but found him firm on the question of a federal constitution. The president then postponed the convening of the National Assembly. The Awami League answered by calling an indefinite general strike. Throughout East Pakistan shops and offices put down their shutters; even railways and airports closed down. Clashes between police and demonstrators became a daily occurrence.

The military decided to quell these protests by force. Troop reinforcements were flown in or sent by ship to the principal eastern port, Chittagong. On the night of 25/26 March, the army launched a major attack on the university, whose students were among the Awami League's strongest supporters. A parade of tanks rolled into the campus, firing on the dormitories. Students were rounded up, shot and pushed into graves hastily dug and bulldozed over by tanks. There were troop detachments at work in other parts of the city, targeting Bengali newspaper offices and homes of local politicians. That same night Mujibur Rahman was arrested at his home and flown off to a secret location in West Pakistan.[14]

The Pakistan army fanned out into the countryside, seeking to stamp out any sign of rebellion. East Bengali troops mutinied in several places, including Chittagong, where one major captured a radio station and announced the establishment of the Independent People's Republic of Bangladesh.[15] To combat the guerrillas the army raised bands of local loyalists, called Razakars, who put the claims of religion – and hence of a united Pakistan – above those of language. Villages and small towns, even the odd airport, fell into rebel hands, then were recaptured. The reprisals grew progressively more brutal. As an American consular official reported, 'Army officials and soldiers give every sign of believing that they are now embarked on a Jehad against Hindu-corrupted Bengalis.'[16]

One soldier later wrote a vivid recollection of the counter-insurgency operations, of the 'reassertion of state power' and the capture of those 'places [which] had been occupied by anti-state elements'. As he remembered, 'there was more resistance offered by the terrain than by the miscreants. Extensive damage to land communications and free intermingling of hostiles with the general populace made progress tedious.'[17]

After the first swoop, foreign correspondents were asked to leave East Pakistan, but later in the summer some were allowed to return. A German journalist saw signs of the civil war everywhere: in bazaars burnt in the cities and homesteads razed in the villages. There was 'a ghostly emptiness in settlements once bubbling with life and energy'. An American reporter found Dacca 'a city under the occupation of a military force that rules by strength, intimidation and terror'. The army was harassing the Hindu minority in particular; the authorities were 'demolishing Hindu temples, regardless of whether there are any Hindus to use them'. A World Bank team visiting East Pakistan found a 'general destruction of property in cities, towns, and villages', leading to an 'all-pervasive fear' among the population.[18]

The army action in Dacca sparked a panic flight out of the city. The repression in the hinterland magnified this flight, directing it across the border into India. By the end of April 1971 there were half a million East Pakistan refugees in India; by the end of May, three and a half million; by the end of August, in excess of 8 million. Most (though by no means all) were Hindus.[19] Refugee camps were strung out along the border, in the states of West Bengal, Tripura and Meghalaya. To distribute the burden, camps were also opened in Madhya Pradesh and Orissa. The refugees were housed in huts made of bamboo and polythene; the luckier ones in the verandahs of schools and colleges. The food came from Indian warehouses – not as bare as they would have been before the Green Revolution – and from supplies provided by Western aid agencies.[20]

From the beginning, the Indian government had followed an 'open door' policy; anyone who came was allowed in. Significantly, the responsibility for the camps vested with the centre, not the states. In fact, from the beginning of the conflict New Delhi had taken a very keen interest in the future of what was already being referred to in secret official communications as the 'struggle for Bangladesh'. On the other side, Islamabad spoke darkly of 'an Indo-Zionist plot against Islamic Pakistan'.[21] This was an exaggeration; for the origins of the problem were internal to Pakistan, while Israel was nowhere in the picture at all. Still, once the dispute presented itself, India was not above stoking it for its own ends.

A key player here was the Research and Analysis Wing (RAW), an intelligence agency set up in 1968 on the model of the CIA, its aims the pursuit of Indian interests worldwide, its activities screened from parliamentary enquiry, its orders to report directly to the Prime Minister's Office. The head of RAW was (perhaps inevitably) a Kashmiri Brahmin, R. N. Kao, while its officers were taken from the police and, on occasion, the army. No sooner had the Pakistani elections been called than RAW was being kept busy writing reports on that country. A memorandum of January 1971 presented a somewhat alarmist picture of Pakistan's armed strength: listing numbers of troops, tanks, aircraft and ships, it claimed that the country had 'achieved a good state of military preparedness for any confrontation with India'. It thought the 'potential threat' of an attack on India 'quite real, particularly in view of the Sino-Pakistan collusion'. Besides, the constitutional crisis might encourage the generals to undertake a diversionary adventure, to begin, as in 1965, with an 'infiltration campaign in Jammu and Kashmir'.[22]

Whether Yahya Khan had any such plans in January 1971 only the Pakistani archives can reveal. The archives on the Indian side tell us that India had certain designs of its own, aimed naturally at Pakistan. Thinking through these designs were P. N. Haksar and his colleague D. P. Dhar, then Indian ambassador to the Soviet Union. In April 1971 Dhar wrote to Haksar expressing pleasure that India was winning the propaganda war with Pakistan – chiefly by providing succour to the victims of its repression. Some analysts wanted swift military action but, advised Dhar, instead of 'policies and programmes of impetuosity', what India had to plan for 'is not an immediate defeat of the highly trained [army] of West Pakistan; we have to create the whole of East Bengal into a bottomless ditch which will suck the strength and resources of West Pakistan. Let us think in terms of a year or two, not in terms of a week or two.'[23]

IV

By the summer of 1971, along with the hundreds of camps for refugees, India was also hosting training camps for Bengali guerrillas. Known as the Mukti Bahini, these fighters numbered some 20,000 in all; regular officers and soldiers of the once united Pakistani army, plus younger volunteers learning how to use light arms. The instruction was at first in the hands of the paramilitary Border Security Force, but by the autumn the Indian army had assumed direct charge. From their bases in India, the guerrillas would venture into East Pakistan, there to attack army camps and disrupt communications.[24]

In April 1971 the Chinese prime minister wrote to the Pakistani president deploring the 'gross interference' by India in the 'internal problems' of his country. He dismissed the resistance as the work of 'a handful of persons who want to sabotage the unification of Pakistan'. He assured Yahya Khan that 'should the Indian expansionists dare to launch aggression against Pakistan, the Chinese Government and people will, as always, support the Pakistan Government and people in their just struggle to safeguard state sovereignty and national independence'.[25]

Chou En-lai's letter was reproduced in the Pakistani press, and must certainly have been read across the border as well. Meanwhile, New Delhi dispatched senior Cabinet ministers to countries in Europe and Africa, to speak there of the unfolding tragedy, and India's efforts to manage it. The prime minister wrote to world leaders urging them to rein in the Pakistani army. In the first week of July 1971 Dr Henry Kissinger – at the time national security adviser to President Nixon – met Mrs Gandhi in New Delhi, where he was acquainted for the first time with 'the intensity of feelings on the East Bengal issue'. The refugee influx had placed a great burden on India – 'we were holding things together by sheer will-power', said the prime minister. The crisis could be resolved only when 'a settlement which satisfied the people of East Bengal was reached with their true leaders'. America was asked to press such a settlement on the military rulers of West Pakistan.[26]

From New Delhi, Kissinger proceeded to Islamabad, and from there – in secret – to the Chinese capital, Peking. Pakistan had brokered this breaking of the ice between two countries long hostile to one another. Their help with China was another reason for the United States to stand solidly behind the generals in Islamabad. Thus Kissinger had carried a letter from Nixon to Mrs Gandhi, asking her to help in the peaceful return of the refugees and the maintenance of Pakistan as a united entity. In a combative reply, the prime minister lamented the fact that arms supplied by the Americans to Pakistan, directed in 1965 against India, were now 'being used against their own people, whose only fault appears to be that they took seriously President Yahya Khan's promises to restore democracy'. The president had asked for UN observers to supervise refugee repatriation but, asked Mrs Gandhi, 'would the League of Nations observers have succeeded in persuading the refugees who fled from Hitler's tyranny to return even whilst the pogroms against the Jews and political opponents of Nazism continued unabated?'[27]

Recently declassified documents point to a distinct difference of perspective between President Nixon and his chief adviser. The historian in Kissinger could foresee that 'there will some day be an independent Bangla Desh'. He also sensed – as he told the Indian ambassador to Washington – that while 'India was a potential world power, Pakistan would always be a regional power'.

Nixon, however, laid hopes on a military solution to the East Bengal problem. He had a deep dislike of one country – 'the Indians are no goddamn good', he told Kissinger – and a sentimental attachment to the leader of the other. In Nixon's opinion, Yahya Khan was 'a decent and reasonable man', whose loyalty to the US had to be rewarded by supporting his suppression of the East Bengal revolt. When, in April 1971, Kissinger prepared a note suggesting that the future for East Pakistan was 'greater autonomy and, perhaps, eventual independence', the president scribbled on it: 'Don't squeeze Yahya at this time'.

As Kissinger somewhat despairingly told a colleague, 'the President has a special feeling for President Yahya. One cannot make policy on that basis, but it is a fact of life.' Nixon expressed his prejudices forcefully: speaking to his staff in August 1971 he said that, while the Pakistanis were 'straightforward', if 'sometimes extremely stupid', the 'Indians are more devious, sometimes so smart that we fall for their line'. The president insisted that the US 'must not – cannot – allow India to use the refugees as a pretext for breaking up Pakistan'.[28]

As India drew apart from one superpower, it was coming closer to the other.[29] Moscow concurred with New Delhi's assessment that the 'twains of East and West Pakistan are not likely to meet again'. The USSR and India were now contemplating closer economic co-operation, through a greater flow of raw materials and finished goods between the two countries. As an inducement, the Russians offered to sell the Indian air force a number of their TU-22 bombers. Recommending the proposal, the Indian ambassador, D. P. Dhar, admitted that while these were inferior to Western models, to buy the planes from a NATO country would involve conditions that were both 'politically unacceptable and financially prohibitive'.[30]

In June 1971 the Indian foreign minister, Sardar Swaran Singh, was due to visit Moscow. On the eve of his arrival the Soviet Foreign Ministry approached D. P. Dhar with the suggestion that the USSR and India sign a treaty of friendship, which would 'act as a strong deterrent to force Pakistan and China to abandon any idea of military adventure'.

Dhar was told that 'India need not be worried about Pakistan, but should take into account the unpredictable enemy from the North' (i.e. China).[31] Later, when the two foreign ministers met, the common suspicion of China figured high on the agenda. Swaran Singh remarked that China was the only country to give 'all out, full and unequivocal support' to the Pakistani military regime. Andrei Gromyko answered that 'the Chinese are always against whatever the USSR stands for. Any cause which we support invites their opposition and anything which we consider unworthy of our support secures their support. I cannot think of any particular exception to this general rule.'[32]

Indian hostility to China dated back to the border conflict of 1959–62. Soviet hostility was more recent, a product of rivalry for leadership of the world communist movement. Mao Zedong had spoken sneeringly of 'Russian revisionism'; the armies of the two sides had clashed on the Uri river in 1969. India and the Soviet Union did not touch one another at any point, but each had a very long border with China. A closer alliance was in the interest of both. The secret documents quoted above, however, reveal that, contrary to the received wisdom, the alliance was first suggested not by the poor underdeveloped country but by the powerful superpower.

After meeting Gromyko, Swaran Singh discussed a possible treaty with the chairman of the USSR Praesidium, Alexei Kosygin. Drafts were exchanged before a final document was signed in New Delhi on 9 August 1971 by the foreign ministers of the two sides. For the most part, the Treaty of Peace, Friendship and Co-operation between the Republic of India and the Union of Soviet Socialist Republics was pure boilerplate: declarations of undying friendship between the 'High Contracting Parties'. The crux lay in a single sentence of Article IX, to wit:

> In the event of either Party being subjected to an attack or a threat thereof, the High Contracting Parties shall immediately enter into mutual consultations in order to remove such threat and to take appropriate effective measures to ensure peace and the security of their countries.[33]

By the late summer of 1971, the axes of alliance on the subcontinent were pretty clear: on the one side, there was (West) Pakistan with China and the United States; on the other, (East) Pakistan with India and the Soviet Union.

V

In the last week of September 1971 the prime minister travelled to the Soviet Union. The next month she visited a series of Western cities, ending in the capital of the free world. Everywhere, she spoke of the deepening crisis in East Pakistan. As she told the National Press Club in Washington, this was 'not a civil war, in the ordinary sense of the word; it is a genocidal punishment of civilians for having voted democratically'. 'The suppression of democracy is the original cause of all the trouble in Pakistan,' she said, adding, 'If democracy is good for you, it is good for us in India, and it is good for the people of East Bengal.'[34]

On her November visit Mrs Gandhi had two meetings with President Nixon. Kissinger had the impression that this was 'a classic dialogue of the deaf'. Nixon said that the US would not be a party to the overthrow of Yahya Khan, and warned India that 'the consequences of military action were incalculably dangerous'. Mrs Gandhi answered that it was the Pakistanis who spoke of waging a 'holy war'. She also pointed out that while the West Pakistanis had 'dealt with the Bengali people in a treacherous and deceitful way and . . . always relegated them to an inferior role', India, 'on the other hand, has always reflected a degree of forbearance toward its own separatist elements'.[35]

While Mrs Gandhi was away, the conflict had intensified. From the end of October the shelling along the border became more fierce, encouraged by the Indian army, which saw the exchanges as a cover for insurgents to creep in and out. By the third week of November heavy artillery was in action. In a battle on the 21st the Pakistanis were said to have lost up to thirteen tanks.[36] Reporting this to Nixon, Yahya Khan complained that India had 'chosen the path of unabashed and unprovoked aggression'. Twelve Indian divisions were massed near East Pakistan, seeking to turn 'localized attacks to open and large-scale warfare'.[37]

At this time in their history, the armies of the two sides were grossly mismatched. In the past decade the Indian armed forces had augmented its equipment, modernized its organization and laid the foundations of an indigenous weapons industry. While Indian intelligence had exaggerated Pakistani strength, a study by the International Institute of Strategic Studies showed that India in fact had twice as many tanks and artillery guns as its neighbour. Further, the morale of the Pakistan army had been deeply affected by the civil war, by the defection of

Bengali officers and the effect of having to fight those presumed to be one's own people.[38]

In the event it was the weaker side that sought to seize the initiative. On the afternoon of 3 December Pakistani bombers attacked airfields all along the western border. Simultaneously, seven regiments of artillery attacked positions in Kashmir.

The Indians retaliated with a series of massive air strikes. In Kashmir and Punjab they answered back on the ground while, in the seas beyond, the navy saw action for the first time, moving towards Karachi. The eruption of conflict in the west provided the perfect excuse for India to move its troops and tanks across the border into East Pakistan, turning a shadowy struggle into a very open one.[39]

Yahya Khan's decision to attack India from the west was, at first and subsequent glance, somewhat surprising; a military historian has even described it as 'barely credible'.[40] Perhaps the Pakistanis hoped to effect quick strikes, calling for UN or American intervention before the conflict got out of hand. Some generals in Islamabad also believed that succour would come from the Chinese. Thus, on 5 December, the commander of the Pakistani troops in East Pakistan, Lieutenant General A. A. K. Niazi, received a message from Army Headquarters informing him that there was 'every hope of Chinese activities very soon'.[41]

Such help may not have come anyway, but in December it was made impossible by the snows that covered the Himalaya. This, indeed, was the perfect season for the Indians to effect their march on Dacca. Three months earlier the rains from the monsoon would have made the ground soft underfoot; three months later the Chinese would have had the option of crossing into the border area they shared with India and East Pakistan. The weather was in favour of the Indians, as was the support of the local population; this to add to an overwhelming superiority in numbers.

The Indian army moved towards Dacca from four different directions. The delta was criss-crossed by rivers, but the Mukti Bahini knew where best to lay bridges, and which town housed what kind of enemy contingent. The Bahini was in turn helped by their civilian comrades: as the Pakistani Commander was to recall later, 'the Indian Army knew of all our battle positions, down to the last bunker, through the locals'.[42] Their path thus smoothed, the Indians made swift progress. Communications were snapped between Dacca and the other main city, Chittagong. Vital railheads were captured, rendering the defenders immobile.[43]

On 6 December the government of India officially revealed an intention it had long nurtured – namely, to support and catalyse the formation of a new nation-state to replace the old East Pakistan. On this day it formally recognized 'The Provisional Government of the Peoples' Republic of Bangladesh'. In Mujibur Rahman's absence, Syed Nazrul Islam served as acting president of the new state; he had a full-fledged Cabinet in tow. These men were to the Indians as de Gaulle's Free French forces had been to the Allies; waiting, not very patiently, while Big Brother recaptured their beloved city and handed it over to them. Within a week of war the Indian troops were within striking distance of Dacca. Artillery fire rained down on the city, with troops advancing from the north, south and east. A temporary hiccup was provided by an aircraft carrier of the American 7th Fleet, which moved into the Bay of Bengal, by means – to quote Henry Kissinger – of 'registering our position'.[44]

The threat was an idle one. Tied down in Vietnam, the Americans could scarcely jump into another war which might – given the Indo-Soviet Treaty – get horribly out of hand. As the collapse of Dacca became imminent, an argument broke out between East Pakistan's civilian governor, who wanted to surrender, and the general in command of the besieged troops, who wanted to fight on. On 9 December, the governor sent a telegram to Islamabad asking them to sue for an 'immediate ceasefire and political settlement'. Otherwise, 'once Indian troops are free from East Wing in a few days even West Wing will be in jeopardy'. He considered the 'sacrifice of West Pakistan meaningless', noting that 'General Niazi does not agree as he considers that his orders are to fight to the last and it would amount to giving up Dhaka'.[45]

The governor's views were independently confirmed by Pakistan's two main allies, China and the United States. On the 10th, Kissinger met ambassador Huang Hua in Washington. The Chinese diplomat bitterly remarked that the creation of Bangladesh would create a 'new edition of Manchukuo', an Indian puppet regime on the model of the one the Japanese had once run in China. Kissinger replied that 'it is our judgement, with great sorrow, that the Pakistan army in two weeks will disintegrate in the West as it has disintegrated in the East'. 'We are looking for a way to protect what is left of Pakistan,' he said, adding by way of consolation, 'We will not recognize Bangla Desh. We will not negotiate with Bangla Desh.'[46]

On the night of the 13th, the Indians bombed the house of the governor in Dacca. The same night Niazi received a message from

Yahya Khan advising him to lay down arms, as 'further resistance is not humanly possible'. The general waited a full day before deciding he had no choice but to obey. On the morning of the 15th he met the American consul general, who agreed to convey a message to New Delhi. The next day, the 16th, Lieutenant General J. S. Aurora of the Indian army's Eastern Command flew into Dacca to accept a signed instrument of surrender.[47] That same evening the prime minister made an announcement in the Lok Sabha that 'Dacca is now the free capital of a free country'. 'Long Live Indira Gandhi' shouted the Congress members, while even an opposition MP was heard to say that 'the name of the prime minister will go down in history as the golden sword of liberation of Bangla Desh'.[48] From Parliament Mrs Gandhi went to the studios of All-India Radio, where she announced a unilateral ceasefire on the western front. Twenty-four hours later General Yahya Khan spoke over the radio, saying he had instructed his troops to cease firing as well.[49]

The war had lasted a little less than two weeks. The Indians claimed to have lost 42 aircraft against Pakistan's 86, and 81 tanks against their 226.[50] But by far the largest disparity was in the number of prisoners. In the western sector, each side took a few thousand POWs, but in the east the Indians had now to take charge of around 90,000 Pakistani soldiers.

Less than pleased with the outcome of the war was President Richard Nixon. 'The Indians are bastards anyway', he told Henry Kissinger. 'Pakistan thing makes your heart sick', he said. 'For them to be done so by the Indians and after we had warned the bitch.' Nixon wondered whether, when Mrs Gandhi had visited Washington in November, he had not been 'too easy on the goddamn woman' – it seems to have been a mistake to have 'really slobbered over the old witch'. By this time even Kissinger had been turned off the Indians. He was cross with himself for having underestimated their military strength – 'The Indians are such poor pilots they can't even get off the ground,' he had claimed in October. His hope now was that 'the liberals are going to look like jerks because the Indian occupation of East Pakistan is going to make the Pakistani one look like child's play.'[51]

As for the American press, *Time* magazine even-handedly blamed both sides; Yahya's 'murderous rampage against rebellious Bengalis', along with Indira's launching of 'full-scale warfare', had together 'brought more suffering to the sub-continent'. However, the influential *New York*

Times columnist James (Scotty) Reston took a more partisan line, writing a brooding, almost conspiratorial piece which saw the Soviet Union as the real beneficiary from 'this squalid tragedy'. Its new ally India would 'provide access to Moscow's rising naval power to the Indian Ocean, and a base of political and military operations on China's southern flank'. 'The Soviet Union now has the possibility of bases in India', claimed Reston. He thought this country's experiment with democracy was in peril, wondering whether 'India will be able to encourage independence for one faction in Pakistan without encouraging independence for other factions in India itself, including the powerful Communist faction in the Indian state of Kerala'.[52]

VI

The victory over Pakistan unleashed a huge wave of patriotic sentiment. It was hailed as 'India's first military victory in centuries',[53] speaking in terms not of India the nation, but of India the land mass and demographic entity. In the first half of the second millennium a succession of foreign armies had come in through the north-west passage to plunder and conquer. Later rulers were Christian rather than Muslim, and came by sea rather than overland. Most recently, there had been that crushing defeat at the hands of the Chinese. For so long used to humiliation and defeat, Indians could at last savour the sweet smell of military success.

On the other side of the border the view was all too different. After the news came that their troops had surrendered, an Urdu newspaper in Lahore wrote that 'today the entire nation weeps tears of blood . . . Today the Indian Army has entered Dacca. Today for the first time in 1,000 years Hindus have won a victory over Muslims . . . Today we are prostrate with dejection.' Within days, however, the Urdu press was seeking consolation from the lessons of history. While the defeat was certainly 'a breach in the fortress of Islam', even the great Muhammad of Ghori had lost his first war in the subcontinent. But as another Lahore newspaper reminded its readers, Ghori had come back 'with renewed determination to unfurl the banner of Islam over the Kafir land of India'.[54]

In India, credit for the victory was shared by countless mostly unnamed soldiers and a single specific politician – the prime minister.

Mrs Gandhi was admired for standing up to the bullying tactics of the United States, and for so coolly planning the dismemberment of the enemy. Her parliamentary colleagues went overboard in their salutations, but even opposition politicians were now speaking of her as 'Durga', the all-conquering goddess of Hindu mythology. The intellectual and professional classes, usually so sceptical of politics and politicians, were also generous in their praise of the prime minister.

Representative of this mood of all-round admiration was a symposium on the Bangladesh liberation organized by the Gandhi Peace Foundation in New Delhi. This began with the editor of the *Times of India*, Girilal Jain, speaking of how 'India's self-esteem and image in the world have improved considerably as a result of the revival of the fortunes of the Congress Party under Mrs Indira Gandhi's leadership'. It continued with the RSS ideologue K. R. Malkani terming 1971 'a watershed in the political evolution of India'. With the events of that year, 'the old image of peace is being replaced by the new one of power. The old image only elicited patronizing smiles; the new image commands attention, and respect.' Then the diplomat G. L. Mehta claimed that 'the people have a new sense of self-confidence and not an unreasonable pride over its newly won prestige in the world'. The left-wing journalist Romesh Thapar concurred: the 'success of the Bangla Desh policy', he remarked, had given 'the thinking Indian a sense of achievement and power'. The left-wing jurist V. R. Krishna Iyer saw in the recent events a progressive maturation of Indian leadership: 'What in Gandhian days was a vague creed was spelt out in Nehru's time as an activist social philosophy, and became, under Mrs Gandhi's leadership, a concrete and dynamic programme of governmental action.'[55]

Away from India, Mrs Gandhi's calmness in a crisis was also admired by a woman who had seen some history in her time, the philosopher Hannah Arendt. In early November Arendt met the prime minister at the home of a mutual friend in New York. A month later, with Indian troops advancing on Dacca, she wrote to the novelist Mary McCarthy of how, at that party, she saw Mrs Gandhi, 'very good-looking, almost beautiful, very charming, flirting with every man in the room, without chichi, and entirely calm – she must have known already that she was going to make war and probably enjoyed it even in a perverse way. The toughness of these women once they have got what they want is really something!'[56]

VII

The prime minister, and her party, naturally sought to make political capital of what the soldiers had accomplished. In March 1972 fresh elections were called in thirteen states, some of which had opposition governments; others, uneasy Congress-led coalitions. In all thirteen, the Congress won comfortably. These included such crucial states as Bihar, Madhya Pradesh and Maharashtra. As the Jana Sangh leader Atal Behari Vajpayee ruefully remarked, while the opposition had put up 2,700 separate candidates, the ruling party had in effect fielded the same person in every constituency – Indira Gandhi.[57]

However, in at least one state the presence and example of the prime minister was not enough. This was West Bengal, where the Congress won only with resort to a mixture of terror, intimidation and fraud. Gangs of hooligans stuffed ballot boxes with the police idly looking on. There was 'mass-scale rigging' in Calcutta; as one activist recalled, *goondas* paid by the Congress told voters assembled outside polling stations that they might as well go home, since they had already cast all the registered votes.[58] Now in alliance with the CPI, the Congress captured 251 out of the 280 seats in the assembly, ending five years of political instability and bringing the state firmly within the ambit of New Delhi.

Her domestic rule secured, the prime minister turned her attention to a settlement with Pakistan. Yahya Khan had resigned, and Zulfiqar Ali Bhutto stepped in to take his place. Bhutto told the former British prime minister Sir Alec Douglas-Home that he was keen to forge 'an entirely new relationship with India', beginning with a summit meeting with Mrs Gandhi. The message was passed on, with the advice that in view of Pakistan's wounded pride, the invitation should come from India.[59]

The Indians were at first apprehensive, given Bhutto's unpredictability and history of animosity against India. Confidants of the Pakistani president rushed to assure them of his good intentions. The economist Mahbub ul Haq told an Indian counterpart that Bhutto was now 'in a very chastened and realistic mood'.[60] The journalist Mazhar Ali Khan, editor of *Dawn*, told his fellow ex-communist the Indian Sajjad Zaheer that Bhutto was honestly trying to forget the past. New Delhi should work to strengthen his hand, otherwise the army and the religious right would gang up to remove him, an outcome that would be disastrous for both India and Pakistan.[61]

Zaheer and Khan had worked together in pre-Partition days as fellow activists of the Student Federation of India. Now, encouraged by their former fellow-traveller P. N. Haksar, they met in London in the third week of March 1972 to discuss the terms of a possible agreement between their two national leaders. Khan's suggestions included a return of all Pakistani POWs in return for its recognition of Bangladesh, troop withdrawal to positions held before the conflict, and a joint declaration of peace. Coming finally to Kashmir, Khan said that the dispute should 'not be mentioned at all in the declaration as this will open a Pandora's box'. Zaheer answered that 'India must get an assurance that there will be no more attack, infiltration, subversion, anti-India propaganda in Kashmir by Pak[istan]'. Khan agreed, but said that this 'should be demanded by India *in practice*. He said we should realise that no Government in Pak[istan] can survive if it renounces, outright, its support to Kashmiris' right of self-determination.'[62]

Khan reported on these talks directly to Bhutto, while Zaheer conveyed them via P. N. Haksar to Mrs Gandhi. The Pakistani president was invited for a summit to be held in the old imperial summer capital of Simla in the last week of June 1972. He came accompanied by his daughter Benazir and a fairly large staff. First the officials met, and then their leaders. The Indians wanted a comprehensive treaty to settle all outstanding problems (including Kashmir); the Pakistanis preferred a piecemeal approach. At a private meeting Bhutto told Mrs Gandhi that he could not go back to his people 'empty-handed'. The Pakistanis bargained hard. The Indians wanted a 'no-war pact'; they had to settle for a mutual 'renunciation of force'. The Indians asked for a 'treaty'; what they finally got was an 'agreement'. India said that they could wait for a more propitious moment to solve the Kashmir dispute, but asked for an agreement that the 'line of control shall be respected by both sides'. Bhutto successfully pressed a caveat: 'Without prejudice to the recognised position of either side'.[63]

One of Mrs Gandhi's key advisers, D. P. Dhar, wanted her to insist on 'the settlement of the Kashmiri issue as an integral and irreducible content of a settlement with Pakistan', and to make this a precondition for the repatriation of POWs.[64] Dhar was a *cent per cent* Kashmiri, born and raised in the Valley. The prime minister, Kashmiri by distant origin only, felt less strongly on the subject; she was also more conscious of world opinion, and (as Mazhar Ali Khan had warned) mindful of Bhutto's precarious position within Pakistan. The agreement they finally signed – shortly after noon on 3 July – spoke only of maintaining the line of control. However, on Indian insistence, a clause was added that the two countries would settle all their differences 'by peaceful means through bilateral negotiations or by any other peaceful means mutually agreed upon' – this, in theory, ruling out either third-party mediation or the stoking of violence in Kashmir.[65] However, Bhutto had apparently assured Mrs Gandhi that, once his position was more secure, he would persuade his people to accept conversion of the line of control into the international border.

The ink had hardly dried on the Simla Agreement when Bhutto reneged on this (admittedly informal) promise. On 14 July he spoke for three hours in the National Assembly of Pakistan, his text covering sixty-nine pages of closely printed foolscap paper. He talked of how he had fought 'for the concept of one Pakistan from the age of 15'. He blamed Mujib, Yahya, and everyone but himself for the 'unfortunate and tragic separation of East Pakistan'. Then he came to the topic that still divided Pakistan and India – the future of Jammu and Kashmir. As the victor in war, said Bhutto, 'India had all the cards in her hands' – yet he had still forged an equal agreement from an unequal beginning. The Simla accord was a success, he argued, because Pakistan would get back its POWs and land held by Indian forces, and because it did 'not compromise on the right of self-determination of the people of Jammu and Kashmir'. He offered the 'solemn commitment of the people of Pakistan, that if tomorrow the people of Kashmir start a freedom movement, if tomorrow Sheikh Abdullah or Maulvi Farooq or others start a people's movement, we will be with them'.[66]

The Indians complained that Bhutto had gone back on his word.[67] They should perhaps have thought of how they had themselves felt in the last days of 1962. The Chinese had then inflicted a humiliation on the nation, affecting both leaders and citizens of all shades and stripes. That is also how the Pakistanis felt in 1972, having suffered a comparable defeat at the hands of the Indians. In truth, they felt even worse, for while the Chinese had merely seized some (mostly useless) territory from India, the Indians had, by assisting in the creation of Bangladesh, blown a big hole in the founding ideology of the Pakistani nation. To this there could be only one effective answer – to assist in the separation of Kashmir from India, thus to blow an equally big hole in the founding idea of Indian secularism.

21

THE RIVALS

Indira is India, India is Indira.
D. K. BAROOAH, Congress president, circa 1974

I

ON 15 AUGUST 1972 India celebrated the twenty-fifth anniversary of Independence. A special midnight sitting was held in the Lok Sabha where the prime minister recalled the struggle for freedom from the 1857 rebellion to the present, marking the major landmarks along the way. The Indian quest, said Mrs Gandhi, 'has been friendship with all, submission to none'.[1] The next morning she addressed the nation from the ramparts of the Red Fort. 'India is stronger today than it was twenty-five years ago', said the prime minister. 'Our democracy has found roots, our thinking is clear, our goals are determined, our paths are planned to achieve the goals and our unity is more solid today than ever before.' 'Nations march ahead', insisted Mrs Gandhi, 'not by looking at others but with self-confidence, determination and unity.'[2]

It is noteworthy that Mrs Gandhi's speech did not touch on economics. Since Independence, the Indian economy had grown at a rate of 3 – 4 per cent per year. The output of the factory sector increased by some 250 per cent, the rise being more marked in heavy industry as compared to consumer goods. A new class of entrepreneurs sprung up, who located units away from the old centres of industry. The state augmented infrastructural facilities: 56 million kilowatt hours of power were generated in 1971 (as against 6.6 million in 1950), while the extent of surfaced roads more than doubled, and the freight carried by the railways almost tripled.[3]

These developments helped rural producers as well as urban ones. Where irrigation was available – through dams or tube wells – farmers increased their production of both cereals and crops such as cotton, chillies and vegetables. Previously isolated villages were now integrated with the outside world. New roads allowed vehicles to take out crops and bring in commodities; they also transported villagers to the city and back, exposing them to new ideas. Within the village there was a slow spread of innovations such as the bicycle, the telephone and, above all, the school.[4]

These aggregate improvements masked significant regional variations. The Green Revolution had touched less than one-tenth of the districts in rural India. Most areas of farming were still rain-fed. Thus, despite the rise in industrial growth and agricultural production, there was still widespread destitution in the countryside. The year before the prime minister's anniversary speech, two economists in Poona, V. M. Dandekar and Nilakantha Rath, published a major study entitled, simply, *Poverty in India*. Drawing on countrywide surveys, this concluded that 40 per cent of the rural population and 50 per cent of the urban population did not enjoy even a 'minimum level of living' – defined as a per capita annual expenditure of Rs324 in the villages and Rs489 in the cities. The incidence of poverty had increased over the decade. At the beginning of the 1960s 33 per cent of the rural and 49 per cent of the urban population lived below this 'poverty line'. In or around 1970, estimated Dandekar and Rath, some 223 million Indians were poor, just over 40 per cent of the total population of about 530 million.

Other economists made other estimates: some put the percentage of the really poor even higher than Dandekar and Rath, others said it was slightly lower. The economists disputed exactly how many poor people there were in India, but all agreed that there were too many – close to 200 million by even the most conservative reckoning. These studies found that the poor in rural India spent roughly 80 per cent of their income on food and another 10 per cent on fuel, leaving a mere 10 per cent for clothing and other items.[5]

Another very great failure was education. There had been an enormous growth in the number of colleges offering instruction in the sciences and the humanities. An even greater expansion was in professional courses, such as engineering and medicine. But basic education had done poorly. There were more illiterates in 1972 than there had been in 1947. While thousands of new schools opened, there had been scarcely any attempt to bring literacy to the millions of adults who could not read or write. And even among those who entered school only a small proportion graduated; the drop-out rates were alarmingly high, especially for girls and children in low-caste families.[6]

A few months after Mrs Gandhi's Red Fort address the economist Jagdish Bhagwati spoke to a rather more select audience in the southern city of Hyderabad. Independent India presented itself as a mixed economy, partaking of both socialism and capitalism. But, argued Bhagwati, it had failed on both counts. It had grown too slowly to qualify as a 'capitalist' economy, and by its failure to eradicate illiteracy or reduce inequalities had forfeited any claims to being 'socialist'.[7]

II

The prime minister claimed that democracy had struck 'roots' in India. In some crucial ways it certainly had. Five general elections had been successfully conducted, plus close to a hundred elections in states the size of European countries. In addition to free elections there was also the unrestricted movement of people and ideas, the last expressed most vigorously in a very free press.

In other respects the democratic foundations of the nation were not so secure. The All-India Congress Committee had once elected representatives from the states, these in turn sent up by Congress bodies at the taluk and district levels. More significantly, the chief ministers of Congress-ruled states were chosen by the local legislators alone. However, after the Congress split in 1969, Mrs Gandhi was able to place her own candidates in key positions. This centralizing process was confirmed after her spectacular victory in the elections of 1971. Later in the year she sacked, in quick succession, the chief ministers of Rajasthan and Andhra Pradesh, replacing them with her own favourites. As one journal remarked, it mattered little who would be the new man in Andhra. For 'he that ascends the gaddi [seat of power] will have to look for his survival to the lady in Delhi rather than to the Legislators in Hyderabad or the Constituents in Andhra at large'.[8]

After the elections of 1971 the prime minister's second son, Sanjay, became more visible in public life. Expelled from his first Indian school, and graduating with difficulty from the second, he had served a brief apprenticeship with Rolls-Royce in the UK before returning home to start a car factory of his own. While he looked for land for that project he took his first steps in politics. In May 1971 he was sent by his mother to inaugurate the Congress campaign in the Delhi municipal polls. The next month he gave an interview to a widely read weekly, where he struck his questioner as not 'particularly keen on discussion or prolonged dialogue. He seems to be keen on results . . .' Sanjay also offered the opinion that 'the Indian youth are lily-livered. They have no guts. In their thinking they are dovetailed to the mental framework of their parents.'[9]

The prime minister's firstborn son, Rajiv, was a trained pilot working for Indian Airlines. She worried more about Sanjay, writing to a colleague in February 1971 that 'Rajiv has a job but Sanjay doesn't and is also involved in an expensive venture. He is so much like I was at that age – rough edges and all – that my heart aches for the suffering he may have to bear.'[10] As it happened, Sanjay's car project was cleared with undue haste. Eighteen applications were received for a licence to make small cars; only that of the prime minister's son was approved, despite his having no past experience in this regard. The Congress chief minister of Haryana, Bansi Lal, gave Sanjay's Maruti car company 300 acres of land at a giveaway price.[11]

Questions were asked by opposition MPs in Parliament. These Mrs Gandhi dismissed, but even her closest adviser, P. N. Haksar, expressed reservations. According to one report, he 'advised the Prime Minister to dump [the] Maruti project and extricate herself from her son Sanjay's doings'.[12] The advice was disregarded; Sanjay came to be seen more and more by his mother's side, while Haksar's own influence declined within the Secretariat.

By 1972 the Congress was subject to a creeping nepotism, and to galloping corruption as well. In June 1971 Haksar drew the prime minister's attention to the 'deeply entrenched and institutionalized corruption' in Congress-ruled Rajasthan.[13] Ministers were in collusion with civil servants, taking cuts on government projects. At the central level too, such practices were growing. One Union minister from Assam had mysteriously acquired a great deal of property; another from Madhya Pradesh was alleged to be working hand-in-glove with a French arms dealer, promising contracts in exchange for commissions.[14]

III

On the social front, one indicator of India's distinction was that it had a woman prime minister. What, however, of Indian women in general?

While Mrs Gandhi was winning elections and a war, the Indian Council of Social Science Research (ICSSR) had commissioned seventy-five separate studies on the status of women – with regard to the law, the economy, employment, education, health, and so forth.[15] The results were not altogether uplifting. In many ways, the processes of modernization promoted since Independence had increased the gender divide. For instance it was chiefly men who had taken advantage of the improvement in health facilities. This aggravated the sex ratio, which, in 1971, stood at 931 women for 1,000 men. Again, the proportion of women in the industrial labour force had declined, from 31.53 per cent in 1961 to 17.35 per cent in 1971. Factories had once recruited couples, but technical improvements had rendered redundant unskilled jobs previously undertaken by women.

The vast majority of women laboured away in the countryside. Among families of peasant cultivators there were 50 women workers to every 100 male ones; among families that owned no land this figure rose to 78. The most hazardous operations were often the preserve of women, such as the transplantation of rice, which left them vulnerable to intestinal and parasitical infections. To these hazards were added the burdens of child-rearing and fuel and fodder collection, tasks reserved for women and girls alone.[16]

The literacy rate was dismal in general and dire for women: 39.5 per cent of males could read and write in 1971, but only 18.4 per cent of females. A mere 4 per cent of women in rural Bihar were literate. The poverty in states such as Bihar and Orissa had led to the mass migration of males in search of work, placing even greater burdens on the women.

The ICSSR reported that 'what is possible for women in theory, is seldom within their reach in fact'. Their studies indicated 'that society has failed to frame new norms and institutions to enable women to fulfil the multiple roles expected of them in India today. The majority do not enjoy the rights and the opportunities guaranteed by the Constitution. Increasing dowry and other phenomena, which lower women's status further, indicate a regression from the norms developed during the Freedom Movement'.

The forces of social reform had an impact only in the cities, among high-caste, English-literate families, who educated their girls and sent them to professional colleges. Among this select section, there was an increase in the number of women doctors, professors, civil servants, even scientists. On the other hand many lower-class and farming communities

Table 21.1 – Number of girls per 100 boys enrolled in
educational establishments, 1947 and 1971

	Primary school	Middle school	High school	University
1947	36	22	14	19
1971	62	43	36	31

had changed from offering a brideprice to demanding a dowry, this a clear indication of the declining status of their women. Rapid urbanization and male migration had also led to an increased traffic in sex workers.

A heartening sign was an increase in the percentage of eligible women voting in elections: from 46.6 per cent in 1962 to 55.4 per cent in 1967 and 59.1 per cent in 1971. In the early seventies there were also signs of an incipient feminist movement, with the first organizations being formed to protect the rights of women workers and labourers, and to protest against rising prices.[17]

As with low castes, there were two ways to look at the question. From one perspective women were still grievously exploited; from another, there had indeed been progress, given the pitifully low baseline at Independence and the accumulated history of women's oppression, legitimized by both history and tradition. Thus, while the literacy rate remained shockingly low, given what it was before 1947 the development since had 'been phenomenal', as Table 21.1 indicates.

The most visible gains were in India's southernmost state, Kerala. Here, the sex ratio of women to men was 1.019, comfortably the highest (indeed, it was the only state to have more women than men). It ranked first in female life expectancy (60.7 years), in women's education (over 60 per cent, against a national average of less than 20 per cent), in expenditure on health care per capita, and in the proportion of births attended by trained midwives. Kerala also had the lowest infant mortality rate for girls: 48.5 for every 1,000 births.[18]

Kerala was an exception not merely for women. Here, men too were better educated, and had access to better health facilities. The statistics represented a more substantive social equality. There had been a remarkable assertion of the lower castes – untouchability had been more or less extinguished – as well as of the lower classes – the Kerala trade union movement was the most highly developed in India.

Why was Kerala so different? As explained in Chapter 14, it had a history of progressive Maharajas and missionaries, and of major social movements oriented around both caste and class. These reforming traditions were picked up by the first communist administration in 1957–9, and renewed further in the early seventies, when the state was ruled by a CPI–Congress alliance under the chief ministership of the communist C. Achuta Menon. This government transferred large amounts of land from absentee owners to cultivating tenants, and passed a new Agricultural Workers Act to enhance the wages and living conditions of the landless. Although these reforms fell short of what was demanded by radical intellectuals, they were much in advance of what was on offer elsewhere, furthering Kerala's reputation as, if not exactly egalitarian, certainly the least unjust state in India.[19]

IV

In March 1973 the government appointed a new chief justice of the Supreme Court. In the past, once a chief justice retired, the most senior member of the bench took his place. This time, Justice A. N. Ray was elevated while three colleagues were ahead of him. The choice was politically motivated, a manifestation of the government's increasing desire to control the judiciary. The law minister, H. R. Gokhale, had, in Parliament no less, spoken with contempt of the Court's recourse to 'the now archaic and long-past dead theories of Blackstone who regarded property as a natural right'. This attitude, he warned, stood in the way of the government's commitment to restructure 'the entire socio-economic fabric of our country [through] greater and greater State intervention'.[20]

In recent years the Supreme Court had been critical of attempts to disturb the basic structure of the Indian Constitution. Recent judgements in two recent cases concerning bank nationalization and the privy purse had been unfavourable to the government, forcing it to use the power of Parliament to amend the constitution. Meanwhile, in a public lecture in Bombay, Justice K. S. Hegde had expressed concern that the 'political exigencies and self-interest of individual leaders [had] perverted the working of the administrative machinery'. He thought that 'the centre has encroached on the powers reserved to the states, by recourse to extra-constitutional methods'. And he commented on the growing corruption, of 'too much hankering after pelf and patronage'.[21]

In the first weeks of 1973 the Supreme Court heard a petition challenging a new law which gave Parliament greater powers to amend the constitution. A full bench heard the case – with six judges voting to restrict Parliament's power, seven upholding them. Among those voting on the government's side was Justice A. N. Ray; among those on the other side, Justice Hegde. Ray's elevation was linked to this particular case, as well as to a more general view, held by P. N. Haksar most forcefully, that judges as well as civil servants should be 'committed' to the policies and philosophy of the government in power.

Among the critics of the appointment of A. N. Ray was the veteran Sarvodaya leader Jayaprakash Narayan. He wrote to the prime minister asking whether these out-of-turn promotions were intended to make the Supreme Court 'a creature of the government of the day'. She answered that the 'dismal conclusion' was unwarranted, adding that a mechanical adherence to the 'seniority principle had led to an unduly high turnover of chief justices'.[22] Another critic was the constitutional expert A. G. Noorani, who in a thoughtful essay deplored both the politicization of judges – many of whom had begun speaking on matters well outside their purview – and of the judiciary, as manifested in the elevation of A. N. Ray and other professedly 'progressive' judges. Noorani worried that neither the press nor the Bar was sufficiently alert to the threats to judicial independence. Unless these challenges were met, he warned, 'we might as well resign ourselves to the loss of individual liberty in India'.[23]

In fact, even before the new chief justice was chosen, many key jobs in government had been assigned to bureaucrats who shared the socialist ideology of Mrs Gandhi and her advisers.[24] By 1973 this ideology had extended out into ever newer areas. There was now a Monopoly and Restrictive Trade Practices Commission, which sought to curb the growth of big business houses and instead encourage small-scale enterprise. There was a continuing expansion of the public sector and a fresh nationalization of private industry. Those key resources, coal and oil, were now under government ownership. The oil crisis of April 1973 hit India nevertheless; when it came, the prime minister, in a spectacular and much-publicized show of nonchalance, rode from her home to Parliament in a horse-drawn buggy.

Half-way into her third term in office, Indira Gandhi looked in control, so much so that she had even begun negotiations with Sheikh Abdullah. The position of the Kashmir Valley, long and bitterly contested, had been altered by India's emphatic victory in the war of December

1971. Now, it was reported, there was a 'measure of disillusionment' in the secessionist camp. Even radicals in the Valley were talking of a settlement within the framework of the Indian Constitution.[25]

In his own recent statements, the Sheikh had left it unclear what he meant by 'self-determination': was it autonomy, or was it independence? Throughout 1971 he had been living in Delhi, so had witnessed at first hand Mrs Gandhi's emergence as a national leader. The war made him less confused; it now appeared that independence for his people was quite out of the question. In June 1972 he met the prime minister. The contents of the talks were kept secret, but shortly afterwards he was allowed back into Kashmir. As ever, he was greeted with large and mostly cheering crowds. But there were also some dissenters holding up placards saying 'No Bargaining on Kashmir' and 'We Want Plebiscite'.[26]

Back in 1964, by sending Abdullah to meet Ayub Khan, Jawaharlal Nehru had apparently accepted that Pakistan was a party to the Kashmir dispute. Now, after that country's bifurcation, Mrs Gandhi made it clear that this was no longer the case. After his return to the Valley, Abdullah told his people that they should not look towards Islamabad for help; instead, they should work out an honourable accommodation with New Delhi. In September, while speaking at a function to mark his sixty-seventh birthday, the Sheikh went so far as to say that 'I am an Indian and India is my homeland'.[27]

Abdullah hoped now to return as chief minister, and from that position work for greater autonomy for the state. He wanted the government to hold mid-term elections, which he was confident his National Conference would win. However, this was resisted by the state Congress leaders, who would not give up their posts so easily.

During 1972 and 1973 there were many rounds of talks between Mirza Afzal Beg, representing the Sheikh, and G. Parthasarathi, representing the prime minister. These discussed the means by which Abdullah could be reinstated without damaging either Kashmiri sentiments or Congress ambitions.[28]

At the other end of the Himalaya there were signs that more Nagas, too, were thinking of living within India. From its creation in 1963, Nagaland had been ruled by a faction at ease with the Indian Constitution. There remained insurgents in the jungle, and the occasional attacks on army convoys and mainstream politicians. But there were signs of normality as well. For example, in November 1972 the evangelist Billy Graham came to preach in Kohima, and 25,000 Nagas came to hear him, being bussed in from all parts of the state. Graham gave three sermons in as many days, praising the beauty of the hills, deploring the ramshackle condition of the local churches and asking the Nagas to 'commit everything to God'. A year later, India's leading football club, Mohun Bagan, came and played a series of exhibition matches in Kohima. In the first match, 'amidst great excitement and shouts from a jubilant crowd of about fifteen thousand', a Kohima XI beat the visitors by one goal. The next day, India's honour was restored when Mohun Bagan won the return match by five goals to nil.

On 1 December 1973 Indira Gandhi visited Kohima to mark the tenth anniversary of Nagaland becoming a full-fledged state of the Indian Union. In her speech – heard by an estimated 15,000 people – she urged the underground to 'come out and shoulder the responsibilities of building up Nagaland'. Several hundred rebels had already surrendered, and more came overground before the state elections of February 1974. For good or ill, the Nagas were getting a taste of Indian democracy. Thus, when the polls came, the streets were overrun by young men yelling '"Vote for . . ." at full blast', for 'a plate of rice and meat, and a sip of wine and a few currency [notes] are all that is needed to set a canvaser [sic] go ashouting for any prospective candidate'. Meanwhile, 'promises, particularly from ministers, are flowing generously. A club, dispensary, a school building for long neglected schools, a road where no road was . . . are promised even though for the past ten years there had been nothing done for them.'[29]

These elections brought a coalition government to power. It included several former rebels, who said they wanted to work for 'a final, negotiated settlement', to be brought about by 'faith, not guns'. A Delhi journal wrote hopefully that 'by and large the Nagas have been reconciled and if the Government of India diverts more funds for education, employment and economic development, the "hard core" will crack in the course of time, and there will be peace which is so urgently and vitally required in this border state'.[30]

V

In its time as an independent nation, India had faced conflicts aplenty – conflicts around land, language, region, religion. Of these the troubles in Kashmir and Nagaland had perhaps been the most serious. Ever since 1947 there had been charismatic leaders in both places, seeking a free state of their own. Their message had resonated widely among the people. Were they given the option, a majority of the inhabitants of the Naga hills as well as the Kashmir Valley might very well have chosen independence rather than statehood within India.

In 1973–4, however, Sheikh Abdullah was preparing to rejoin the system in Kashmir, and many rebel Nagas had come overground and taken part in elections. The once turbulent extremities were quiet. As if to compensate, there was now trouble in the heartland, in parts of the country which, for reasons of history, politics, tradition and language, had long considered themselves integral parts of the Republic of India.

The trouble began in Gujarat, the land of Gandhi, the Father of the Nation. The state was run by a Congress regime notorious for its corruption; the chief minister, Chimanbhai Patel, was popularly known as Chiman *chor* (thief). In January 1974 students led a movement demanding the dismissal of the state government. It called itself Nav Nirman, the Movement for Regeneration. The protests turned violent, with buses and government offices being burnt. Chiman *chor* was compelled to resign, and Gujarat came under President's Rule.[31]

The events in Gujarat inspired students in Bihar to launch a struggle against misgovernance in their own state. Bihar had witnessed a great deal of political instability, with defections galore and governments made and unmade. A Congress regime came to power in 1972, but within it corruption was rife. There was deep discontent in the countryside, where land was very unequally held; and in the cities, where there had been a steep rise in the prices of essential commodities. Left-wing groupings, led by the Communist Party of India, had formed a front with simple aims and a complicated name – Bihar Rajya Mahangai Abhaab Pesha Kar Virodhi Mazdur Swa Karamchari Sangharsha Samiti (The Bihar State Struggle Committee of Workers and Employees against Price Rise and Professional Tax). In the last week of 1973 the front organized a series of mass demonstrations, where the call was heard, '*Pura rashan pura kam, nahin to hoga chakka jam*' – 'Give us work and give us food, or else we will bring life to a standstill'. Which is exactly what they did.

These protests by the left sparked a competitive rivalry with the Akhil Bharatiya Vidyarthi Parishad (ABVP), the student union linked to the Jana Sangh. The ABVP and other, non-communist student groups came together in a united front of their own, the Chatra Sangharsh Samiti (CSS). This grew rapidly, and soon had branches in most towns of the state. Campus life was in turmoil, and classroom instruction came to an abrupt halt.

On 18 March 1974 the CSS marched on the state assembly in Patna. When police pushed them back, the retreating mob set fire to government buildings, a warehouse of the Food Corporation of India and two newspaper offices. The police clashed with protestors in several parts of the city; several students were badly hurt, and at least three died. The news of the trouble spread, provoking clashes between students and the police across the state.[32]

After the incidents of 18 March the students asked Jayaprakash Narayan to step in and lead their movement. 'JP' was now seventy-one, a veteran of movements militant as well as peaceful, the upholder or instigator of a hundred mostly worthy causes. In recent years he had worked for reconciliation in Nagaland and Kashmir, sought sympathetically to understand the Naxalites and persuaded the notorious bandits of the Chambal valley to lay down their arms. The call from the students was one he found impossible to refuse. For, long ago, he had started out as a student radical himself. But that had been in the American state of Wisconsin; this was in his own native state of Bihar.

In Jawaharlal Nehru's lifetime, Narayan had many exchanges with India's prime minister. The older man tried to get him to join his Cabinet, but JP preferred to stay outside. From there he chastised and scolded Nehru, but he was withal devoted to him, and devastated by his death. Through their friendship he knew the daughter, too. He was one of the first to congratulate Mrs Gandhi on her elevation to prime minister and, in years following, frequently offered her (unsolicited) advice. He applauded her leadership during the Bangladesh war, but was less approving of her conduct during the presidential election and (as we have seen) with regard to the supersession of the judges of the Supreme Court.[33]

When the Chatra Sangharsh Samiti asked him to lead their movement, JP agreed, on two conditions – that it should be scrupulously non-violent, and that it should not be restricted to Bihar. On 19 March, immediately after the clashes in Patna, Narayan said he could no longer 'remain a silent spectator to misgovernment, corruption and the rest, whether in Patna, Delhi or elsewhere'. 'It is not for this that I had fought for freedom', he continued. He had now 'decided to fight corruption and misgovernment and blackmarketing, profiteering and hoarding, to fight for the overhaul of the educational system, and for a real people's democracy'.[34]

Narayan was a figure of great moral authority, a hero of the freedom struggle who, unlike so many others of the ilk, had not been sullied by the loaves and fishes of office. His entry gave the struggle a great boost, and also changed its name; what was till then the 'Bihar movement' now became the 'JP movement'. He asked students to boycott classes, to leave their studies for a year and work at raising the consciousness of the people. All across Bihar there were clashes between students seeking to shut down schools and colleges, and policemen called in by the authorities to keep them open. In the towns, at least, the support for the struggle was widespread. In Gaya, for example, the courts and offices were closed as a consequence of 'housewives of respectable families of the town who were rarely seen out of [purdah] sitting on [picket lines] with small boys'. The authorities tried to clear the streets, but this provoked violence, with students raining bottles and sticks on the police and being answered by bullets. The riot left three people dead and twenty grievously injured.[35]

The Gaya incident took place in the middle of April 1974. The call was now renewed for the dissolution of the state assembly, for the imposition of President's Rule following the example of Gujarat. On 5 June Narayan led a massive procession through the streets of Patna. The march culminated in a meeting at the Gandhi Maidan, where JP called for a 'total revolution' to redeem the unfulfilled promises of the freedom movement. India had been free for twenty-seven years, said JP, yet 'hunger, soaring prices and corruption stalk everywhere. The people are being crushed under all sorts of injustice'.

Addressing himself to the students in the crowd, he warned that the road ahead would be a rocky one: 'You will have to make sacrifices, undergo sufferings, face lathis and bullets, fill up jails. Properties will be attached.' Yet, he was convinced that, in the end, the struggle would be worth it: 'Gandhiji spoke of Swaraj [freedom] in one year. I speak today of real people's government in one year. In one year the right form of education will emerge. Give one year to build a new country, a new Bihar.'[36]

It was in this meeting that JP spoke of 'total revolution' for the first time. The term, the struggle and the struggle's chosen agents all recall the activities a decade previously of the chairman of the Chinese Communist Party. In the late evening of his life, Mao had called upon the youth – in his case, the Chinese Red Guard – to rid society of its accumulated corruptions, to stamp out revisionists and capitalist-roaders who stood in the way of the creation of the perfect society. Robert Jay Lifton has suggested that the Cultural Revolution in China was impelled by its leader's frustrations at the gap between expectations and reality, by his impatient desire to transform his country before he left this earth. I find the argument persuasive, not least because it also helps explain the events in Bihar and India in 1974, this sudden turn towards radical politics by a man who, for so many years past, had disavowed politics altogether. Throughout the 1950s and 60s JP had been a social worker, a reconciler, a bridge-builder. Now, like Mao, he turned to the students, to what he called *yuvashakti* (youth power), to bring about the total revolution he had dreamed about in his own younger days.[37]

In between the Gaya firings and JP's Patna speech, the country was paralysed by a railway strike. Led by the socialist George Fernandes, the strike lasted three weeks, bringing the movement of people and goods to a halt. As many as a million railwaymen participated. Western Railways, which serviced the country's industrial hub, was worst hit. There were militant demonstrations in many towns and cities – in several places, the army was called out to maintain the peace.[38]

While the strike was on, India exploded a nuclear device. For several years now scientists had been pressing the government to conduct an atomic test. When the prime minister finally agreed, in May 1974, it was because the test helped to divert attention from the challenges posed by the railwaymen and the students in Bihar. Among certain sections the blast led to a surge of patriotic pride. There was, a reporter wrote, an 'unmistakable air of excitement in Delhi' when the news of the explosion came through. MPs gathered in the Central Hall of Parliament to congratulate one another – for them, 'the railway strike and the country's numerous economic problems had suddenly disappeared from view'.[39]

Others were less impressed, pointing out that membership of the elite nuclear club could not wish away the fact that India ranked 102nd among the nations of the world in terms of per-capita income. The test was also deplored in Pakistan, as a setback to the normalization of relations between the two countries.[40]

Following the nuclear test, Mrs Gandhi and Jayaprakash Narayan exchanged a series of letters, the exchange beginning on a civil note but ending in acrimony. On 22 May the prime minister wrote to JP expressing concern about his health, and hoping that, in view of the long friendship between the two families, their political disagreements could be expressed 'without personal bitterness or questioning of each other's motives'. Narayan answered that Mrs Gandhi was being disingenuous, for in a recent speech in Bhubaneshwar she had alluded to JP keeping the company of the rich and 'living in the posh guest-houses of big businessmen'. Those remarks, he said, had 'hurt and angered me'. He added that her recent utterances seemed 'not only to misunderstand me profoundly but also to miss – and to do so at the risk of tragic consequences – the meaning of the upsurge that is welling up from below'.

Mrs Gandhi replied immediately, clarifying that, in those remarks about the corruption of Sarvodaya leaders, 'I did not take your name or make any references personally derogatory to you. I cannot help if some newspapers added their own interpretation.' (This *was* disingenuous – the interpretation of the newspapers was the only one possible in the circumstances.) She suggested that even if he was incorruptible perhaps his associates were not. That was why some of his ideas, 'which appear rather utopian to me, could perhaps work if the whole population consisted of Jayaprakashs'. Mrs Gandhi also challenged his claim to be the nation's moral conscience. As she wrote, 'May I also, in all humility, put to you that it is possible that others, who may not be your followers, are equally concerned about the country, about the people's welfare, and about the need to cleanse public life of weakness and corruption.'

The exchange was concluded by JP six weeks after it began. He had hoped, he said, that she would have the grace to clarify *publicly* that in making those remarks in Bhubaneshwar she was not casting aspersions on his probity or character. That she would not do this hurt him; as he put it, 'I am only a private citizen but I do have my self-respect.' What seemed clear was that 'misunderstanding is growing and not lessening by correspondence between us'.[41]

It was time to return to the movement. In August JP toured the Bihar countryside to a rapturous reception. 'JP is driven in procession . . . cheering onlookers line the roads', wrote the journalist Ajit Bhattacharjea in his diary. 'Arches every hundred yards or so. The cars inch through the crowd to the podium – JP helped up the steps, pausing at every one.' After his tour, Narayan called for a conference of all opposition parties – the CPI excluded – to 'channel the enthusiasm among the people into the nation-wide people's movement'. The Bihar struggle, wrote JP, had 'acquired an all-India importance and the country's fate has come to be bound up with its success and failure'. He appealed to trade unions, peasant organizations and professional bodies to come aboard.[42]

At least one opposition party was already present in the JP movement – the Jana Sangh. Its student wing, the ABVP, had been there from the beginning, and older cadres were now moving into key roles. A Gandhian associate of JP wrote to him in alarm that 'the leadership of the movement, at least at local levels, is passing into the hands of the Jana Sangh'. He also worried that 'the common man has yet to be educated into the ways and values of our movement, whose appeal to him continues to be more negative than constructive'.[43]

A more detailed critique of JP's movement was offered by R. K. Patil, a former ICS officer who had later become an admired social worker in rural Maharashtra. At JP's invitation, Patil spent two weeks in Bihar, travelling through the state and talking to a wide cross-section of people. In a long (and remarkable) letter he wrote to Narayan – dated 4 October 1974 – he conceded that 'there can be no doubt about the tremendous popular enthusiasm generated by the movement'. He saw 'unprecedented crowds attending your meetings in pin-drop silence'. However, when they were on their own these crowds were less disciplined, as in the attacks on the state assembly and the forcible prevention of the Bihar governor from delivering his annual address.

Patil wondered whether the modes of protest being adopted in Bihar conformed strictly to Gandhian standards. But he went further, asking the question: 'What is the scope for Satyagraha and direct action in a formal democracy like ours . . . ?' By demanding the dismissal of a duly elected assembly, argued Patil, 'the Bihar agitation is both unconstitutional and undemocratic'. True, the electoral process had to be reformed, made more transparent and purged of the influence of power and money. Yet once an election was held its verdict had to be honoured. For 'there is no other way of ascertaining the general opinion of the people in a Nation-State, except through free and fair elections'.

Patil wrote, in conclusion, that he was 'well aware of the patent drawbacks of the Government presided over by Indira Gandhi'. But he still wasn't certain that it was 'wise to substitute for the law of "Government by Discussion", the law of "Government by Public Street Opinion"'. 'Today you are a force for good', wrote Patil to JP, 'but History records that the crowds can produce a Robespierre also. Hence perhaps my instinctive aversion to the Bihar type agitation.'[44]

On 1 November 1974 Mrs Gandhi and JP had a long meeting in New Delhi. The prime minister agreed to dismiss the Bihar ministry on condition that the movement drop its demand for the dissolution of

other state assemblies. The compromise was rejected. The meeting was
acrimonious, although it ended on a poignant note, with JP handing
over to Mrs Gandhi the letters written by her mother, Kamala Nehru,
to Narayan's recently deceased wife, Prabhavati.[45]

Three days later Narayan was manhandled by the police while on
his way to a public meeting in Patna. While warding off a baton, he
stumbled to the ground; the picture was splashed across the newspapers
the next day. He was an old man as well as a sick one (he suffered from
diabetes), and although the injuries were slight the indignity provoked
much outrage. The Bihar administration was compared to its colonial
predecessor – as one journal somewhat hyperbolically wrote, 'JP was,
for the first time in free India, a victim of police repression.'[46]

VI

In September 1974 the Republic of India acquired a chunk of territory
that previously constituted the quasi-independent state of Sikkim. While
Sikkim had its own flag and currency, and was ruled by its hereditary
monarch – known as the Chogyal – it was economically and militarily
dependent on New Delhi. In 1973 some citizens of the kingdom had
begun asking for a representative assembly. The Chogyal asked the
government of India for help in taming the rebellion. Instead, New
Delhi stoked it further. When an assembly was proposed and elections
held, the pro-India party won all but one seat. The Chogyal was forced
to abdicate, and the Indian Constitution was amended to make Sikkim
an 'associate state', with representation in Parliament.[47]

Sikkim was a very beautiful state, and also shared a border with
China. At another time, the prime minister would have drawn comfort
from this augmentation of the nation's territory. As it happened,
the Sikkim annexation provided Mrs Gandhi with only a temporary
diversion from her battle with Jayaprakash Narayan. For by the end of
1974 the Bihar movement was poised to become a truly national one.
Letters of support for JP were streaming in from all over the country,
as in a communication from an advocate in Andhra Pradesh which
saluted JP for 'breaking new ground at an age where people retire', and
professed 'admiration and respect at the movement you are directing'.[48]
Prominent politicians would come visiting Bihar, and promise to take
the ideas of the struggle back to their own states. In the last week of

November JP convened a meeting of opposition parties in New Delhi, where he expressed the view that the lesson of Bihar was that one needed 'radical changes all round, on institutional as well as moral planes, involving drastic changes in Government policies in the centre as well as in the States'.[49]

It is tempting to see the JP movement as being a reprise, at the all-India level, of the popular struggle against the communist government in Kerala in 1958–9. The parallels are uncanny. On the one side was a legally elected government suspected of wishing to subvert the constitution. On the other side was a mass movement drawing in opposition parties and many non-political or apolitical bodies. Like Mannath Padmanabhan, JP was a leader of unquestioned probity, a saint who had been called upon to save politics from the politicians. His behaviour was, or was perceived to be, in stark contrast to that of his principal adversary – for, like E. M. S. Namboodiripad in 1958–9, Mrs Gandhi had no desire to accede to her opponents' demand and voluntarily demit power.

This was a political rivalry, but also a personal one. As a veteran of the freedom struggle, and as a comrade of her father's, Jayaprakash Narayan would regard Mrs Gandhi as something of an upstart. For her part, having recently won an election and a war, the prime minister saw JP as a political naïf who would have been better off sticking to social work.

By the end of 1974 the polarization was very nearly complete. There were many Indians who were not members of the right-wing Jana Sangh, and yet thought the Congress too corrupt and Mrs Gandhi too insensitive to criticism. Some went so far as to hail JP's movement as a 'second freedom struggle', completing the business left unfinished by the first. There were many other Indians, not necessarily members of the Congress yet pained by JP making common cause with the Jana Sangh, who saw his movement as undermining the institutions of representative democracy. The first kind of Indian criticized Indira Gandhi, and with much force; the second kind criticized JP, albeit with less enthusiasm.[50]

In the first week of January 1975, a key aide of the prime minister was assassinated in JP's home state of Bihar. This was L. N. Mishra, who had held various Cabinet appointments under Mrs Gandhi and, more crucially, was a major fundraiser for the Congress party. A politician wholly *sans* ideology, Mishra had collected large sums of money from both the Soviets and the Indian business class. It was not clear who murdered him – whether a personal rival, or a trade unionist bitter about his role in the suppression of the railway strike of 1974. The prime minister blamed it on the 'cult of violence' allegedly promoted by Jayaprakash Narayan and his movement.[51]

Mishra's death did not impede JP's plans to march on Parliament in the spring, when the weather would be more hospitable to protesters from across the country. During January and February he travelled across India to drum up support.[52] In his speeches JP urged the people to remain non-violent; any untoward incidents, he said, would prompt the prime minister to assume dictatorial powers. At several places he claimed that Mrs Gandhi was looking for an excuse to arrest him. That, he predicted, would only make the movement more widespread, as in 1942, when the jailing of Mahatma Gandhi had led to an intensification of the Quit India movement.

JP compared himself to Gandhi implicitly and, more explicitly, the Congress regime to the colonial state. These were comparisons the prime minister naturally rejected. In an interview given to a Japanese journalist she said that, while she was not certain what the JP movement was for, 'it is clear what it is against. It is against my party, it is against me personally and all that I have stood for and stand for today.'

In fact, there were by now some members of Mrs Gandhi's party who had some sympathy for the other side. Among them were the erstwhile 'Young Turks' Chandra Shekhar and Mohan Dharia. Shekhar and Dharia called for a national dialogue on questions of rising prices, corruption and unemployment – issues, they said, that were so conspicuously flagged in the Congress's own 1971 manifesto.

Another man caught betwixt and between was Sheikh Muhammad Abdullah. The government and he had finally come to an agreement, by which the Congress Legislature Party of Jammu and Kashmir would elect him as their leader, and hence also as their chief minister. Two days before his installation he went to the Gandhi Peace Foundation in Delhi to seek the blessings of his old friend and supporter Jayaprakash Narayan. The newspapers carried a photograph of the two in a bear hug, the Kashmiri towering above the Gandhian.

JP told the press that he welcomed the Sheikh's return to Kashmir; the state, he said, needed him at its helm. But his friends in the Jana Sangh attacked the accord which had brought the Lion of Kashmir back to power. The party President, L. K. Advani, claimed that Abdullah still 'wanted to use the instrument of power to pursue his ambition of an independent Kashmir'. Others saw the matter very differently. After the Sheikh was sworn in as chief minister on 25 February, the *Indian Express* called it an 'epochal event in the history of free India'. Abdullah's return to his old post, twenty-three years after he had been forced to leave it, was 'a tribute to the resilience and maturity of Indian democracy, for it is only in a true democratic set-up that even the most serious differences can be harmonised and reconciliations effected within the framework of common loyalty to the country'.

The Kashmir chapter seemed, finally, closed. Jayaprakash Narayan was delighted that Sheikh Abdullah had rejoined the mainstream. On this, and perhaps this alone, Mrs Gandhi and he saw eye to eye. For on the very day that Abdullah was reading the oath in Jammu, JP called for a 'national stir' to oust the 'corrupt Congress leaders from power'. The Jana Sangh joined him here even as they opposed him on Kashmir – such were the contradictions of Indian politics.

On 2 March, four days before the planned march on Parliament, Mrs Gandhi dropped Mohan Dharia from her council of ministers. His mistake had been to request that she resume talks with Narayan. JP's response was to ask senior ministers such as Y. B. Chavan and Jagjivan Ram to resign in protest, thus to 'save their party from destruction', and restore its 'traditional values'.

On 3 March Delhi's inspector general of police convened a meeting on how to handle the coming influx of protesters. As many as 15,000 policemen would be on duty. To inhibit the marchers, the administration forbade the entry of trucks and buses from neighbouring states.

Despite the ban on buses, people began streaming into the capital. They were housed in a tented camp outside the Red Fort, now named 'Jayaprakash Nagar'. On the morning of the 6th they began walking towards the venue of the public meeting, the Boat Club lawns, adjacent to the Houses of Parliament. Leading them, in an open jeep, was Jayaprakash Narayan. JP was cheered by the crowds assembled along the way, who offered garlands and showered him with petals. The slogans on display were chiefly addressed to his rival. 'Vacate the Throne, the People are Coming', said one, in English, with a Hindi variation reading: *'Janata Ka Dil Bol Raha Hai, Indira Ka Singhasan Dol Raha Hai'* (The Heart of the People Is Singing, Indira's Regime Is Sinking). Behind JP came jeeps bearing leaders of the opposition parties. Altogether, it was one of the largest processions ever seen in Delhi, drawing in an estimated 750,000 participants. There were representatives from all over India, but much the largest contingents came from the states of Uttar Pradesh and Bihar.

At the Boat Club lawns JP spoke in an 'emotion-charged voice'. He compared the day's events to Gandhi's historic Salt March, and asked the crowd to be prepared for a long struggle. After the meeting he led a delegation to Parliament, where he presented the Speaker with a list of the movement's demands, which included the dissolution of the Bihar assembly, electoral reforms and the setting up of tribunals to investigate allegations against the Congress of rampant corruption.

Mrs Gandhi answered JP two days later, when in a speech at the steel town of Rourkela, she said that the agitators were bent on destroying the fabric of Indian democracy. Without mentioning her antagonist by name, she claimed his movement was nourished by foreign donations.

On 18 March JP led a march in Patna to mark the first anniversary of the movement. There was much singing and dancing, and the throwing of colour, this also being the day of the Holi festival. In his speech Narayan urged the formation of a single opposition party or, at the very least, of a common front to fight the Congress in all future elections.

JP's movement was strongly rooted in the northern states. He had supporters in the west, in Gujarat particularly, but the south was territory so far mostly untouched. So he now commenced a long tour of the states south of the Vindhyas, drawing decent but by no means massive crowds. In Tamil Nadu people warmly recalled that he had been against the imposition of Hindi.[53]

VII

While the JP movement was gaining ground, the prime minister was facing another kind of challenge, a challenge offered not through passionate sloganeering in the streets but in the cold language of the law. The scene here was the Allahabad High Court, which was hearing a petition filed by Raj Narain, the socialist who had lost to Mrs Gandhi in the Rae Bareilly parliamentary election of 1971. The petition alleged that the prime minister had won through corrupt practices, in particular by spending more money than was allowed, and by using, in her campaign, the official machinery and officials in government service. Throughout 1973 and 1974 the case dragged on, arguments and counter-arguments being presented before the judge, Justice Jag Mohan Lal Sinha.[54]

On 19 March 1975 Mrs Indira Gandhi became the first Indian prime minister to testify in court. She was in the witness box for five hours, answering questions about her election. In coming to Allahabad, the prime minister had left her son Sanjay behind in Delhi. With her instead was her elder son Rajiv, who, while his mother spoke in court, 'took his Italian wife, Sonia, to see the ancestral home of the Nehrus'.[55]

In April, Morarji Desai – an even older rival of Mrs Gandhi than JP – began a fast in Gujarat in protest against the continuation of President's Rule. New Delhi backed down, ordering fresh elections for June. The opposition parties began the process of forming a common front to fight the Congress.

As Gujarat went to the polls in the second week of June, L. K. Advani said the campaign had 'accelerated the polarisation of political parties and the Jana Sangh would try to further this process'. He looked forward to his party increasing its strength 'manifold'.[56]

While the votes were being counted, attention shifted to the High Court in Allahabad. On the morning of 12 June, in Room No. 15 of a court in which Mrs Gandhi's father and grandfather had both practised, Justice Sinha read out his judgement in the case brought before him three years previously by Raj Narain. He acquitted the prime minister on twelve out of fourteen counts. The charges he found her guilty of were, first, that the UP government constructed high rostrums to allow her to address her election meetings 'from a dominating position'; and second, that her election agent, Yashpal Kapoor, was still in government employment at the time the campaign began. By the judgement, her election to Parliament was rendered null and void. However, the justice allowed Mrs Gandhi a stay of twenty days on his order, to allow an appeal in the Supreme Court.[57]

The 12th of June was a very bad day for Mrs Gandhi. Early in the morning she was told that her old associate D. P. Dhar had died during the night. A little later came the news from Gujarat, which was also grim – the Janata Front was heading for a majority in the state elections. Then, finally, came this last and most telling blow, from her own home town, Allahabad.

The judgement sparked much prurient interest in the intentions of the judge. Educated in Aligarh, Justice Sinha had practised in Bareilly for fourteen years before becoming a district judge. He had been elevated to the bench in 1970. Some claimed that his judgement was biased by the fact that he and JP came from the same Kayasth caste: Others believed that in the days before the judgement the prime minister's men had offered him a seat on the Supreme Court were he to rule in their mistress's favour.[58]

Mrs Gandhi's election had been overturned on a quite minor charge, yet Justice Sinha's verdict also concentrated the popular mind on the more serious accusations levelled against her by JP's movement. The day after the judgement, opposition politicians began a *dharna* outside Rashtrapati Bhavan, demanding that the president dismiss the 'corrupt' prime minister. In Patna, JP issued a statement saying it would be 'shameful and cynical' were Mrs Gandhi to listen to the 'yes-men' around her and stay on in office. He also noted that the Gujarat election results suggested that the 'Indira wave' and 'Indira magic' were matters of the past.

On the other side, the yes-men were very busy indeed. On the 13th itself, the Congress chief minister of Haryana, Bansi Lal, began ferrying supporters into Delhi, publicly to proclaim their loyalty to Mrs Gandhi. The roads outside the prime minister's house were choked with her admirers. These shouted slogans in her favour and burnt effigies of Justice Sinha. Mrs Gandhi came out to address them, speaking of how foreign powers were conspiring with her domestic opponents to get rid of her. Her adversaries, she claimed, had 'lots of money at their disposal'.

Every day a fresh cadre of supporters would assemble outside Mrs Gandhi's house; every day she would come out and speak to them. Some Congress members privately deplored these populist demonstrations. Others publicly encouraged them. Addressing a Congress rally in Delhi, the party president, Dev Kanta Barooah, said that 'laws are made by people and the leader of the people is Mrs Gandhi'. Judges and lawyers, including the eminent legal luminary M. C. Chagla – once a member of Mrs Gandhi's own Cabinet – thought the prime minister was morally bound to resign, at least until her appeal was heard and disposed of. On the other side, 516 party MPs signed a resolution urging her to stay on. Ten thousand Congress members from Karnataka signed a similar appeal, in blood. In the middle of the debate a voice spoke from across the border – it was Zulfiqar Ali Bhutto, who worried that Mrs Gandhi would find a way out of her difficulties through 'an adventurist course against Pakistan'.

On 20 June Mrs Gandhi addressed a huge rally on the Boat Club lawns. A million people were said to have attended, even more than had heard JP at the same venue three months previously. The prime minister claimed the opposition was bent on liquidating her physically. Speaking after her, D. K. Barooah read out a couplet he had specially composed for the occasion:

Indira tere subah ki jai, tere sham ki jai,
Tere kam ki jai tere naam ki jai

Or, to render it in less expressive English:

Indira, we salute your morning and your evening too
We celebrate your name and your great work too.

Two days later the opposition answered with a rally of its own. It rained heavily, yet hundreds of thousands came. JP was the featured speaker, but his flight from Calcutta was cancelled at the last minute ('mechanical trouble', according to Indian Airlines). Representatives of the main opposition parties spoke, with Morarji Desai calling for a 'do or die' movement to get rid of the Indira Gandhi regime.

On 23 June the Supreme Court began hearing Mrs Gandhi's petition. The next day Justice V. R. Krishna Iyer issued a conditional stay on the Allahabad judgement: the prime minister could attend Parliament, he said, but could not vote there until her appeal was fully heard and pronounced upon. The *Indian Express* thought this meant that Mrs Gandhi 'must resign forthwith in the nation's and her interests'.

By now, at least some senior figures in the Congress Party thought that resignation would also be in the party's interests. If she couldn't vote in Parliament, she could scarcely lead her government to any purpose. She was advised to step down temporarily, to let one of her Cabinet colleagues – the uncontroversial Swaran Singh perhaps – keep the seat warm until the Supreme Court upheld her appeal (as her lawyers were confident it would), allowing her to return as prime minister.

Urging Mrs Gandhi not to resign were her son Sanjay and the chief minister of West Bengal, Siddhartha Shankar Ray, a well-trained barrister who had come from Calcutta to be at hand. Their advice was readily accepted. As Mrs Gandhi later told a biographer, 'What else could I have done except stay? You know the state the country was in. What would have happened if there had been nobody to lead it? I was the only person who could, you know.'[59]

Once the decision was taken, it was executed with remarkable swiftness. On the 25th, S. S. Ray helped draft an ordinance declaring a state of internal emergency, which a pliant president, Fakhruddin Ali Ahmad, signed as soon as it was put in front of him. That night the power supply to all of Delhi's newspaper offices was switched off, so that there were no editions on the 26th. Police swooped down on the opposition leaders, taking JP, Morarji Desai and many others off to jail. The next day the public of Delhi, and of India as a whole, was told by state-controlled radio that an emergency had been declared, and all civil liberties suspended.

At the time, and later, it was thought that the reaction far exceeded the original provocation. Justice Sinha had indicted Mrs Gandhi of two quite trifling offences. The Supreme Court was less likely to construe the height of a rostrum as an 'election malpractice'. As for the second charge, Yashpal Kapoor had resigned from service before joining the campaign, except that there was some dispute about the date on which his resignation was accepted. Most lawyers believed that the Supreme Court would reverse the Allahabad judgement. Yet, as one respected Delhi jurist put it, the prime minister forsook 'the advantages of the ordinary judicial remedy of appeal and resorted instead to the extraordinary, undemocratic and unconstitutional measures of Emergency'.[60]

A mere four months before the emergency was declared, the *Indian Express* had paid tribute 'to the resilience and maturity of Indian democracy', of how it allowed 'even the most serious differences [to] be harmonised and reconciliations effected'. The paper could now eat its words. Indian democracy, circa 1975, could reconcile the Valley of Kashmir to the Union of India, but not Indira Gandhi with Jayaprakash Narayan.

22

Autumn of the Matriarch

Future generations will not remember us by how many elections we had, but by the progress we made.

SANJAY GANDHI, December 1976

I

AT 6 A.M. ON 26 JUNE 1975, a meeting of the Union Cabinet was convened. The ministers, unthinking and bleary-eyed, were informed of the state of emergency, in effect since midnight. Their formal consent was obtained before Mrs Gandhi proceeded to the studios of All-India Radio (AIR) to convey the news to an equally unsuspecting nation. 'The President has proclaimed Emergency', she announced: 'There is nothing to panic about.' This, she said, was a necessary response to 'the deep and widespread conspiracy which has been brewing ever since I began to introduce certain progressive measures of benefit to the common man and woman of India.' 'Forces of disintegration' and 'communal passions' were threatening the unity of India. 'This is not a personal matter,' she claimed. 'It is not important whether I remain Prime Minister or not.' Still, she hoped that conditions would 'speedily improve to enable us to dispense with this Proclamation as soon as possible'.[1]

The disclaimers betray a certain defensiveness. For the fact was that the emergency had come hot on the heels of the Supreme Court order forbidding her from voting in Parliament. When the emergency was declared, the prime minister's closest friend, the designer Pupul Jayakar, was away in the United States. On the 27th Mrs Gandhi sent Mrs Jayakar a long note, explaining that the action was taken in response to the 'increasing violence' caused by a 'campaign of hate and calumny'. The number of arrests, she claimed, were a mere 900, most detainees kept not in jail but 'comfortably, in houses'. The 'general public reaction' was 'good', and there was 'tranquillity all over the country'. The emergency, the prime minister told her friend, was 'intended to enable a return to normal democratic functioning'.[2]

Across India people were being picked up and put into jails. These included leaders and legislators of parties other than the Congress, student activists, trade unionists, indeed, anyone with the slightest connection to the Jana Sangh, the Congress (O), the Socialists, or other groups opposed to the ruling party. Some of the detainees, such as Jayaprakash Narayan and Morarji Desai, were placed in government rest houses in the state of Haryana, not far from Delhi. However, the majority were sent to already overcrowded jails. And Mrs Gandhi's arithmetic was soon shown to be wildly off the mark. Thousands were arrested under MISA – the Maintenance of Internal Security Act, known by its victims as the Maintenance of Indira and Sanjay Act. And there were other legal instruments at hand. The Rajmatas of Gwalior and Jaipur, old political opponents of Mrs Gandhi, were jailed under an act supposedly meant for black-marketeers and smugglers.[3]

In the first few months of the emergency, the prime minister gave a flurry of interviews defending its proclamation. These too displayed a deep defensiveness. 'It is wholly wrong to say that I resorted to Emergency to keep myself in office,' she told the *Sunday Times* of London. 'The extra-constitutional challenge [of the JP movement] was constitutionally met.' The emergency was 'declared to save the country from disruption and collapse'; it had 'enabled us to put through the new economic programme', and led to 'a new sense of national confidence'. 'What has been done', she told the *Saturday Review* of New York, 'is not an abrogation of democracy but an effort to safeguard it'. In these interviews she attacked the Western press for 'India-baiting', for picking on her country in preference to more visibly authoritarian nations such as Pakistan and China.[4]

In her interviews and broadcasts the prime minister spoke of the need to infuse a 'new spirit of discipline and morale'. The government's copywriters were put to work, coining slogans such as 'Discipline Makes the Nation Great', 'Talk Less, Work More', 'Be Indian, Buy Indian', 'Efficiency is our Watchword'. Other exhortations were less impersonal, such as 'She Stood between Order and Chaos' and 'Courage and Clarity of Vision, Thy Name is Indira Gandhi'. Rendered in Hindi as well as English, these slogans were painted on the sides of buses, across bridges and on outsize hoardings erected outside government buildings.

These were the signs of a creeping dictatorship. Like military men who seize power via a coup, Mrs Gandhi claimed to have acted to save the country from itself. And, like them, she went on to say that, while she had denied her people freedom, she would give them bread in exchange. Within a week of the emergency she was offering a 'Twenty Point Programme for Economic Progress'. This promised a reduction in prices of essential commodities, the speedy implementation of land reforms, the abolition of indebtedness and of bonded labour, higher wages for workers and lower taxes for the middle class.[5]

Female dictators are altogether rare – in the twentieth century Mrs Gandhi may have been the only such. However, as a woman autocrat, she could use images and symbols denied to her male counterparts. On 11 November, four and a half months into the emergency, the prime minister came to the microphone to 'meet' and 'have a heart-to-heart talk' with her countrymen. She spoke for over an hour, on the need for discipline, on her economic programme, on the glories of ancient India and the duties of its modern citizens. 'Our opponents' wanted to 'paralyse the work of the Central Government', said the Prime Minister, and thus

> we found ourselves in a serious situation. And we took certain steps. But many of the friends in the country were rather puzzled as to what has Indiraji done? What will happen to the country now? But we felt that the country has developed a disease and, if it is to be cured soon, it has to be given a dose of medicine even if it is a bitter dose. However dear a child may be, if the doctor has prescribed bitter pills for him, they have to be administered for his cure . . . So we gave this bitter medicine to the nation.
>
> . . . Now, when a child suffers, the mother suffers too. Thus we were not very pleased to take this step . . . But we saw that it worked just as the dose of the doctor worked.[6]

II

On 15 August 1975 *The Times* of London carried a full page advertisement taken out by the 'Free JP Campaign'. The ad had been paid for by individuals: the first person to contribute being Bishop Trevor Huddleston, the last Dame Peggy Ashcroft. The other signatories to the appeal included such long-standing friends of India as the socialist Fenner Brockway, the economist E. F. Schumacher and the political scientist W. H. Morris-Jones, as well as celebrities with no specific connection to India, such as the actress Glenda Jackson, the historian A. J. P. Taylor and the critic Kenneth Tynan. On the page were printed photographs of Mahatma Gandhi and Jayaprakash Narayan. Aside from the long list of names, the text showcased a testament to JP's character and patriotism from the Mahatma himself.

'Today is India's Independence Day', said the ad. 'Don't Let the Light Go Out on India's Democracy'. The signatories called upon Mrs Gandhi to release all political prisoners, and Jayaprakash Narayan especially. The singling out of one person was not just in deference to his leadership of the oppositional movement in India. The prime movers of the 'Free JP Campaign' had known him from long before he launched his 'Total Revolution'. The left-wing Labourites, such as Brockway, had known him from the 1930s, as a great hero of the independence movement. The environmentalists, such as E. F. Schumacher, had known him from the 1950s, as a like-minded votary of decentralized development. The political scientists had known him from before and after Independence, as an ever-present, always influential exemplar of what Morris-Jones had called the 'saintly idiom' in Indian politics.

These foreign friends of India's freedom were old enough to have seen how close Jawaharlal Nehru and Jayaprakash Narayan had once been. They were appalled that Nehru's daughter had jailed JP, and hoped that an appeal to history would take him out of prison. So did that great group of pacifists, the Quakers, who did not put their name to the Times advertisement but tried the back-channels of reconciliation instead. The group had an old and honourable connection with India. Quakers such as Agatha Harrison and Horace Alexander had played crucial intermediary roles between British colonialists and Indian nationalists. More recently, they had worked with JP in attempting reconciliation between India and Pakistan and between the Naga rebels and the government in New Delhi.

In August, a month after the emergency was declared, the sociologist Joe Elder was sent by his fellow Quakers on a fact-finding mission to India. He met many people; JP's followers, Congress politicians and the prime minister. He found himself 'decreasingly prone to condemn one side or the other'. JP had erred in launching a mass movement without a cadre of disciplined, non-violent volunteers. His ideas had 'struck many as naïve, untested, or unconvincing'. His movement's credibility was weakened by the presence within it of extremists of left and right. On the other hand, the prime minister had clearly over-reacted in imposing the emergency. This had created fear in the minds of the people, and undermined the democratic process and democratic institutions.[7]

As Elder's account suggests, the emergency was a script jointly authored by JP and Mrs Gandhi. Both had shown too little faith in representative institutions: JP by asking for the premature dismissal of elected governments, Mrs Gandhi by jailing legally elected members of Parliament and legislative assemblies. Neither properly appreciated the role of the state in a modern democracy. JP wished simply for the state to disappear, for the police and army to 'disobey immoral orders'. On the other hand, Mrs Gandhi sought to make the state's functionaries ultimately dependent on the will of a single person at the helm.

The clash was made poignant by the fact that the adversaries had once been friends, bound by ties of history and tradition and by intimate personal relationships stretching across generations. One does not know how Mrs Gandhi felt about jailing JP. We do know that her staff had deeply ambivalent feelings. The prime minister's Information Adviser, H. Y. Sharada Prasad, was an old patriot and freedom fighter himself. He had been jailed in 1942, in the same Quit India campaign that first made JP a national figure. Unlike Joe Elder, he could not bring himself to admit that the prime minister had over-reacted. Yet, as he wrote to a friend, he grieved that a man like JP, 'at a moment of crucial ethical importance, decide[d] that RSS and CPM are more acceptable than the Congress. This is an excursion in reasoning that I have not been able to understand, much less excuse. I can only console myself with the thought that he would not have been so desperate if [his wife] Prabhavatiji had been alive.'[8]

Also unhappy about JP's incarceration was the economist P. N. Dhar, who had succeeded P. N. Haksar as the prime minister's principal secretary. He sent several emissaries to JP to see whether a conciliation could be effected, with prisoners released and the emergency lifted, in time for the next parliamentary elections, due in early 1976. The emissaries found JP willing to negotiate. A flood in his native Bihar had made him impatient to go and work among the sufferers. Talk that his irresponsibility had caused the emergency had reached his ears. He said he had no desire to revive the popular movement, but when elections were called would ask for a combined front to oppose the Congress, and canvass for its candidates.[9]

JP was keen that his old friend Sheikh Abdullah, now also a part of the Indian establishment as chief minister of Jammu and Kashmir, be the mediator between him and Mrs Gandhi. He had read a report quoting the Sheikh as saying that he was in favour of 'conciliation at All-India level', and that the prime minister was 'more than keen to end the emergency'. JP now wrote to Abdullah offering him his 'full co-operation' in any move he might make to resolve the differences between the opposition and the government. That said, the letter betrayed signs of wounds still not healed, as in JP's reference to himself being portrayed as 'the villain of the piece, the arch-conspirator, the culprit number one', and in his concluding challenge that 'the first test of [the prime minister's] keenness [to end the emergency] will be whether this letter is allowed to be delivered to you and whether you are permitted to see me'.[10]

The prime minister failed the test. The letter was not passed on to the Sheikh, and the moves to effect a reconciliation died with it. However, in November 1975 JP's health took a turn for the worse. With his kidneys failing, he was taken to a hospital in Chandigarh and, when the doctors there proved unequal to the task, released on parole and shifted to the Jaslok Hospital in Bombay, to be placed under the care of the nephrologist M. K. Mani. The government's action was hastened by the realization that all hell might break loose if JP were to die in jail.[11]

Although JP lay in a Bombay bed, chained to a dialysis machine, there was no general parole of political prisoners. An estimated 36,000 people were in jail under MISA, detained without trial. These were rather ecumenically spread across the states of the Union, 1,078 from Andhra Pradesh, 2,360 from Bihar and so on down the letters of the alphabet, until one reached 7,049 from Uttar Pradesh and 5,320 from West Bengal.[12]

These victims of political vengeance were housed, fed and clothed like common criminals – in fact, made to share their cells with them (prompting the witticism that Mrs Gandhi's much vaunted socialism was at least practised in the jails). Older prisoners looked nostalgically back to the days of the Raj, when the jails had been cleaner and the jailers altogether more humane. It seemed that women prisoners were singled out for special treatment. The Rajmatas of Gwalior and Jaipur were now living in conditions of unaccustomed austerity and filth. The socialist Mrinal Gore, more used to the simple life, was asked to share a toilet with the woman in the adjoining cell – who happened to be a leper. In the cell opposite was a lady lunatic who wore no clothes and shrieked day and night.[13]

III

Writing to a friend in January 1963, Indira Gandhi complained that democracy 'not only throws up the mediocre person but gives strength to the most vocal howsoever they may lack knowledge and understanding'.[14] Three years later, when she had just become prime minister, Mrs Gandhi told a visiting journalist that 'the Congress has become mori-bund', adding, 'Sometimes I feel that even the parliamentary system has become moribund.' Besides, the 'inertia of our civil service is incredible'; 'we have a system of dead wood replacing dead wood'. 'Sometimes I wish', said the newly elected prime minister of the world's most populous democracy, that 'we had a real revolution – like France or Russia – at the time of independence.'[15]

The impatience with democratic procedure had been manifested early, as for instance with the packing of the civil service, the judiciary and the Congress Party with individuals committed to the prime minister. But the process was taken much further with the emergency. Now, with opposition MPs locked away, a series of constitutional amendments were passed to prolong Mrs Gandhi's rule. The 38th Amendment, passed on 22 July 1975, barred judicial review of the emergency. The 39th Amendment, introduced two weeks later, stated that the election of the prime minister could not be challenged by the Supreme Court, but only by a body constituted by Parliament. This came just in time to help Mrs Gandhi in her election review petition, where the Court now held that there was no case to try, since the new amendment retrospectively rendered her actions during the 1971 elections outside the purview of the law.[16]

Some months later the Supreme Court did the prime minister a greater favour still. Lawyers representing the thousands jailed under MISA argued that the right of habeas corpus could not be taken away by the state. Judgements in the lower courts seemed to favour this view, but when the case reached the Supreme Court it held that detentions without trial were legal under the new dispensation. Of the five-member bench only one dissented: this was Justice H. R. Khanna, who pointed out that 'detention without trial is an anathema to all those who love personal liberty'.[17]

It was suggested that the judgement was influenced by extralegal considerations – by the hope of three of the judges that they might one day become chief justice, by the fear inspired by the punitive transfers of officials that had commenced with the emergency. In a despairing editorial entitled 'Fading Hopes in India', the *New York Times* remarked that 'the submission of an independent judiciary to an absolutist government is virtually the last step in the destruction of a democratic society'.[18]

In fact, there were other steps still to be taken. These included the 42nd Amendment, a twenty-page document whose clauses gave unprecedented powers to Parliament. It could now extend its own term – which it immediately did. The amendment gave laws passed by the legislature further immunity from judicial scrutiny, and further strengthened the powers of the centre over the states. All in all, the 42nd Amendment allowed Parliament 'unfettered power to preserve or destroy the Constitution'.[19]

In January 1976 the term of the DMK government ended in Tamil Nadu. Rather than call fresh elections, the centre ordered a spell of President's Rule. Two months later the same medicine was applied to Gujarat, where the Janata Front had lost its majority owing to defections.

Mrs Gandhi, and the Congress, were now supreme all over the land. When the art historians Mildred and W. G. Archer went to meet her in March 1976, the prime minister expressed satisfaction with the progress of the emergency. The new regime, she told them, 'had made the State Ministers shake in their shoes'. This was 'long over-due and was excellent', for 'too much devolution [was] fatal to India'. 'I have to keep India together', insisted Mrs Gandhi. 'That is an absolute must.'[20]

IV

Among the casualties of the emergency was the freedom of the press. Within its first week the government had instituted a system of 'pre-censorship', whereby editors had to submit, for scrutiny and approval, material deemed to be critical of the government or its functionaries. Guidelines were issued on what did and did not constitute 'news'. There could be no reports on processions or strikes, or of political opposition, or of conditions in the jails. Reports of open dissidence were naturally *verboten*, but in fact even stories mildly critical of the administration were not permitted.[21] As a newspaper in the Punjab was to recall, items 'killed' by the censor included

> reports about the closure of shops in Chandigarh's Bajwara market to protest against the arrest of shopkeepers, the six-year absence of a health officer and observations about the town's sanitation, especially the open drains; ... three letters to the editor about pay anomalies and inadequate salary scales of college lectures in Himachal Pradesh; an unsatisfactory bus service; a Chandigarh report about the rise in the price of tomatoes; the death of two persons while patrolling the rail tracks near Amritsar; and a brief item about black-marketing in essential drugs.[22]

The space had to be filled; and it was, by the words of the prime minister or by stories in praise of her government. (Editors who tried to print the liberty-loving essays of Tagore, Gandhi and Nehru instead were quickly brought to book.) 'Our newspapers, of course, give world news all right', wrote a reader in Simla to an English friend, 'but hardly any other news pertaining to the country itself, except the speeches of the PM . . . I have decided to forgo the pleasures of reading a newspaper.'[23] In truth, the disgust was shared by the journalists themselves. As a reporter for the Bombay weekly *Blitz* told *his* English friend: 'My paper is a supporter of the Emergency. But if we only sing the praises of the Government, what will our readers think of us?'[24]

Jokes tinged with satire were especially forbidden. The Tamil humorist Cho Ramaswamy failed to sneak in a cartoon showing the prime minister and her son Sanjay talking above the caption: 'A national debate on the Constitutional Amendments'. When a reader asked the question, 'Who is Indira Gandhi', Cho answered: 'She is the granddaughter of Motilal Nehru, the daughter of Jawaharlal Nehru, and the mother of Sanjay Gandhi'. This, too, was cut. The censors were vigilant, but the odd joke or two escaped their eye. Thus V. Balasubramanyam was able to print an article in the *Eastern Economist* on 'Livestock Problems in India', which began with the line: 'There are at present 580 million sheep in the country', and an anonymous democrat was able to place an ad in the *Times of India* announcing the 'death of D. E. M. O'Cracy, mourned by his wife T. Ruth, his son L. I. Bertie, and his daughters Faith, Hope, and Justice'.[25]

As the emergency proceeded, the government tightened its hold over the dissemination of information. The independent news agencies, the United News of India (UNI) and the Press Trust of India (PTI), were amalgamated with two lesser agencies into a single state-controlled news service called Samachar. The Press Council, an autonomous watchdog body, was abolished. A law granting immunity to journalists covering Parliament was repealed. And as many as 253 journalists were placed under arrest. These included Kuldip Nayar of the *Indian Express*, K. R. Sunder Rajan of the *Times of India* and K. R. Malkani of the *Motherland*.[26]

Some freedom-loving journalists resisted, but their newspapers' owners were mostly compliant, fearing the government might shut down their presses or seize their properties. They feared the stick, but were happy to bite at the carrot. This took the shape of government announcements paid for by the Directorate of Audio-Visual Publicity (DAVP). While 'liberally granting advertisements to so-called "friendly" periodicals', the DAVP withdrew their favours from those deemed critical of the government. More than one newspaper, and editor, and owner, was happy to change its tune in response to the inducements on offer.[27]

Among the major newspapers that willingly complied with the new regulations were the *Hindu*, the *Times of India* and, especially, the *Hindustan Times*. The editor of the last-named newspaper, the hugely respected B. G. Verghese, was sacked by its owner, the industrialist K. K. Birla, merely to please Mrs Gandhi. (Birla was a devoted acolyte of the prime minister – after the Allahabad High Court judgement of 12 June, he had taken a delegation of 500 businessmen to plead with her to stay on in office.[28]) Among the newspapers that struggled nobly to maintain their independence were the *Indian Express* and the *Statesman*. Both refused to toe the government line, resisting threats and blandishments alike. When their power was cut they got the courts to restore it. When their own stories were censored, they chose to leave white spaces rather than fill them with propaganda material. And they artfully reproduced, without comment, reports on the Indian situation in the foreign press, under such neutral headings as 'News Digest' or 'What our Contemporaries Say'.[29]

The mass-circulation newspapers were hardest hit, but the government did not spare the high-quality and slow-selling journals of opinion either. Two esteemed Delhi journals, the weekly *Mainstream* and the monthly *Seminar*, closed rather than submit to the censor's scrutiny. The Bombay weekly *Himmat* fought the censor doggedly, but finally shut down when asked to pay a prohibitively high deposit as a guarantee of good behaviour, the fine imposed for a piece that quoted, among other people, the Mahatma. Literary magazines also closed down, finding the curbs on their independence impossible to live with.

In some ways the government feared the little magazines even more. Their owners could not be bought; so they had to be coerced or bankrupted instead. Among the chosen targets was *Opinion*, a four-page newsletter brought out in Bombay by the former ICS officer A. D. Gorwala. A man of legendary integrity, Gorwala focused on attacks on the individual by the agencies of the state. He had also fought a long battle against corruption. A year into the emergency, *Opinion* was ordered to shut down, but Gorwala was able to print one last issue in which he observed that

> the current Indira regime, founded on June 26, 1975, was born through lies, nurtured by lies, and flourishes by lies. The essential ingredient of its being is the lie. Consequently, to have a truth-loving, straight-thinking journal examine it week after week and point out its falsehoods becomes intolerable to it.[30]

V

The day after the emergency was declared, a British reporter found the streets of Delhi to be 'uncannily normal'. The city's 'jingling flotilla' of cyclists set off for work in the morning. 'No angry crowds gathered. Shops and factories opened as usual. Beggars begged. The sleek race-horses of the rich had their daily exercise . . .'[31] As the veteran journalist Inder Malhotra wrote, 'in its initial months at least, the Emergency restored to India a kind of calm it had not known for years'.[32]

This calm was in sharp contrast to the strife-filled decade that preceded it; one reason why the emergency was widely welcomed by the middle class. The crime rate had come down and the trains ran on time. A good monsoon in 1975 meant that prices also fell. A visiting American journalist was told by an official in Delhi that it was only foreigners who cared for such things as the freedom of expression. 'We are tired of being the workshop of failed democracy,' said the official. 'The time has come to exchange some of our vaunted individual rights for some economic development.'

The journalist found that the business community were especially pleased with the emergency. A Delhi hotel owner told him that life now was 'just wonderful. We used to have terrible problems with the unions. Now when they give us any troubles, the government just put them in jail.' In Bombay, the journalist met J. R. D. Tata, arguably India's most respected industrialist. Tata too felt that 'things had gone too far. You can't imagine what we've been through here – strikes, boycotts, demonstrations. Why, there were days I couldn't walk out of my office into the street. The parliamentary system is not suited to our needs.'[33]

One fact is conclusive proof of the quiescence of the middle class – that hardly any officials resigned in protest against the emergency. Back in the days of British rule, Gandhi's call to 'non-cooperate' with the rulers led to thousands of resignations of teachers, lawyers, judges, even ICS officers. Now, the abrogation of democracy was protested by only a handful of people in state employment. These included Fali Nariman, who resigned as additional solicitor general, M. L. Dantwala, who declined to continue as an adviser to the Reserve Bank, and Bagaram Tulpule, who left his high position in a public-sector undertaking.

There was, however, some resistance offered in the Indian Parliament. On 23 July the House met to ratify the emergency. The Congress commanded a comfortable majority; and 34 MPs were in jail. Those opposition MPs at liberty to attend made speeches of protest before walking out. The CPM member A. K. Gopalan said the arrests had reduced Parliament to a 'farce and an object of contempt'. A Jana Sangh MP accused Mrs Gandhi of betraying the motherland for 'the sake of personal ends'.[34]

The opposition MPs later boycotted the House (or were jailed), but an independent member who continued to attend was P. G. Mavalankar of Ahmedabad, a political scientist by vocation and the son of the first Speaker of the Lok Sabha. His lineage made it difficult for the government to arrest him. So he stayed and, when given the chance, quoted the Holy Trinity of Indian nationalism, Tagore, Gandhi and Nehru – quoted them on the merits and virtues of liberty and freedom. Their views were contrasted with the 'draconian' MISA, used to further 'the political purpose of a vindictive government', an act which was 'the most obnoxious piece of legislation ever enacted in the recent history of India'.[35]

There was also resistance in the streets. On 14 November 1975 – the birthday of Jawaharlal Nehru – a body styling itself the Lok Sangharsh

Samiti (People's Struggle Committee) began a *satyagraha* in Bombay. Every day a group of protesters would stand at a busy intersection and shout slogans such as 'Down with Dictatorship' and 'JP Zindabad'. Within a month 1,359 people had been arrested – including 146 women. The protests spread to other states, where bus stands, railway stations and government offices became the theatre of slogan shouting and the courting of arrest. One report claimed that in the first three months of the *satyagraha* as many as 80,000 people had been put behind bars.[36]

On 15 August 1976 (Independence Day) another *satyagraha* commenced in Ahmedabad. It was led by Manibhen Patel, daughter of India's first home minister, Vallabhbhai Patel. Raising slogans such as 'Remove Emergency' and 'Release Political Prisoners', the fifty marchers proceeded on the road to Dandi, the same route that Gandhi had taken to break the colonial salt laws forty-six years previously. Manibhen Patel was arrested a mile down the road, but the next day a judge ordered her release. She continued the march to the sea, accompanied by a handful of policemen in plain clothes.[37]

One of those arrested in the Bombay *satyagraha* was the distinguished Marathi writer Durga Bhagwat. Other members of her fraternity protested in ways more congenial to their profession. A group of Kannada writers circulated, in *samizdat* form, poems satirizing the emergency and its prime mover. Consider these stanzas from G. S. Shivarudrappa's poem *In this Country*:

> In this country
> Hero worship, family pride
> Should all go. But
> Concessions to my family deity
> Should stay untouched.
> In this country
> Everybody should shut their mouth
> And remain quiet.
> But
> They better keep their ears open
> For my words.[38]

Other writers expressed their dissent in other ways. Bengali essayist Annada Sankar Ray announced that he would 'stop writing altogether in a fit of non-cooperative pique'. He refused to 'put pen to paper so long as the state of emergency continues'. The cartoonist K. Shankar Pillai, who had once sarcastically compared the loquacious Nehru to the Niagara Falls (and been cheered by his victim for it), now closed down his magazine before the state did so. 'Dictatorships cannot afford laughter', he remarked mournfully. 'In all the years of Hitler, there never was a good comedy, not a good cartoon, not a parody, or a spoof.' The Hindi novelist Phanishwaranath Renu returned the Padma Shri bestowed upon him by the government of India, the act recalling Tagore's disavowal of his knighthood after the Jallianwala Bagh massacre. And the Kannada polymath Shivarama Karanth gave back an even higher honour, the Padma Bhushan. Back in the 1920s he had entered the freedom movement under the inspiration of Gandhi; now, after fifty years of striving to uphold its values, Karanth felt 'impelled to protest against such indignities done to the people of India'.[39]

Finally, there was resistance that was carried on underground. The key figure here was George Fernandes, the firebrand socialist who had led the railway strike of 1974. When the emergency was declared Fernandes was in the Orissa town of Gopalpur-on-Sea. He lay low for a few weeks, in which time he had grown a beard and come to disguise himself as a Sikh. Then he travelled from town to town, meeting comrades and planning the sabotage of state installations. Dynamite was collected and stored, and young men trained in the act of blowing up bridges and railway tracks. From his ever-shifting hiding place, Fernandes sent out letters attacking 'the dictator', 'that woman', and 'the Nehru dynasty', and urging the people to rise against the regime.

No dynamite was actually detonated, yet the government of India was visibly angry that it could not capture Fernandes. His brother Lawrence was picked up from his home in Bangalore and brutally beaten and tortured. His friend, the actress Snehalata Reddy, was also imprisoned. Placed in a damp cell and denied proper food, her asthma was seriously aggravated; released on parole, she died a few weeks later. George Fernandes's wife and child fled the country, fearing persecution if they stayed behind. Fernandes himself was finally arrested in Calcutta on 10 June 1976, nearly a year into the emergency.[40]

In the summer of 1976 one of the few opponents of the regime still at large was the nonagenarian J. B. Kripalani. He complained that he had been left out while all his friends were given the privilege of imprisonment. Then he recalled a Sindhi proverb: 'When a witch goes through a street destroying everything, she leaves one house untouched.'[41] On 2 October 1975, Gandhi's birthday, he led a prayer meeting at the Mahatma's memorial in New Delhi – speeches were made and several people arrested, but not him. It was not so much his age as his sheer stature which kept him at large. Not Shivarama Karanth, not Morarji Desai, not even JP, had patriotic credentials as good as Kripalani's. He had joined the Mahatma in the Champaran *satyagraha* of 1917; several years before Jawaharlal Nehru did. He had been president of the Congress when freedom came three decades later. Later, three different states had sent him as their representative to the Indian Parliament. In sum, his CV was such that even the prime minister would have been embarrassed to arrest him on account of activities deemed a threat to the 'unity and stability' of the country.

In April 1976 Kripalani dared the government to print the names of those it had put in jail. Then he fell seriously ill. He was taken to hospital, where all manner of tubes and wires were put into him. When a friend came visiting he had a fresh complaint: 'I have no Constitution – all that is left are Amendments'.[42]

VI

The emergency revived the debate as to whether India could, should, or ever would be reliably democratic. In October 1975 a reporter from *Time* visited the country, and was much impressed by what he saw. He thought that press freedom and the like were 'of no great interest to the majority of India's 600 million people', who were 'more concerned' with the rate of inflation (down 31 per cent in the past year). 'The Prime Minister', he wrote, 'has won widespread support for seizing a rare opportunity to ram through a score of social reforms. These days India is engrossed in a frenzied campaign to encourage discipline, punctuality, cleanliness, courtesy.'[43]

So at least someone was taking the slogans seriously. Where the *Time* reporter thought that democracy was unsuited to India, the *Sydney Morning Herald* despaired that it had died out in a country which had been 'the main hope of democracy in Asia, indeed in the developing world'. If India had 'relapsed into traditional Asian autocracy', said the paper, the blame must be shared between 'Empress Indira' and her father, who had fostered 'heavy industrialization and nationalized bureaucracies upon the Indian entrepreneur, Soviet style, in the name of "socialism". To make his "socialism" work his daughter has merely added the complementary Soviet-style political dictatorship.'[44]

The 'India and/vs democracy' question was, as one might expect, most vigorously discussed in the British press. The political class in the United Kingdom was divided; while some MPs signed the 'Free JP appeal', Mrs Gandhi's regime was endorsed by, among others, Labour's Michael Foot (on the grounds that Nehru's daughter could do no wrong) and Jennie Lee, and the Tory Margaret Thatcher. Both of the last named visited India and concluded that the emergency was, on balance, beneficial to its people. After travelling to India and speaking to Congress leaders, a Conservative MP named Eldon Griffith wrote to *The Times* protesting that the regime was 'far less oppressive' than that paper reported it to be. He also suggested that the Westminster model was unsuited to non-Western contexts. In a spirited rejoinder, W. H. Morris-Jones observed that such denigration was 'a sport in which high imperial Tory and revolutionary Marxist could find common enjoyment'. As Morris-Jones pointed out, a 'growing number of Indians had begun to make the habit of liberal democracy indigenous'. Five elections had been successfully conducted, and a free press and autonomous institutions forged, before the emergency came to bring 'massive damage' to 'a way of political life which in two decades had already converted into citizens so many who had been subjects beyond the political pale'.[45]

What was the prospect for the future? In an assessment on the emergency's first anniversary, the *Observer* claimed to see a stirring beneath the calm. A bad monsoon could shatter the fragile economy, leading to inflation, and 'igniting the mass discontent that smoulders beneath the surface. The resulting explosion might well produce a political crisis more serious than that of June 1975.' Among the possible outcomes, in the *Observer*'s view, one could discount a return to democracy. For 'the most likely successor to Congress remains the Army'.[46]

VII

The *Observer* made the mistake of focusing on institutions rather than individuals. For, within India, what was being witnessed was not the army rising behind the façade of Congress rule, but the prime minister's second son emerging as the most likely successor to her office.

Recall that it was Sanjay Gandhi who had warned his mother against resigning, and he who had most strongly endorsed the emergency. In its first months he acquired a higher public profile. He was often to be seen by Mrs Gandhi's side, and was even advising her on Cabinet appointments. When the liberal I. K. Gujral was seen as being too soft on the press, he was replaced at the Ministry of Information and Broadcasting (I&B) by the more hard-line V. C. Shukla. When the experienced Swaran Singh (once a senior member of Nehru's Cabinet) was less than enthusiastic about the emergency, he was replaced as defence minister by Sanjay's friend Bansi Lal.[47]

Six weeks into the emergency Sanjay Gandhi gave a long interview to the Delhi magazine *Surge*. He spoke there of his personal life – he didn't drink, or smoke – and of his relationship to his mother ('yes, she obviously listens to my views', he said in answer to one question; 'She listened to them even when I was five years old'). He spoke of his work – he claimed to spend twelve to fourteen hours a day at his Maruti factory – and of the car he would soon produce, which would 'outcorner either the Fiat or the Ambassador' (the two cars that dominated the Indian market). He expressed himself in favour of free enterprise – 'the quickest way to grow' – and thought that the government should remove all controls on where, how and in what manner industries were established. Asked his idea of democracy, he said that it 'doesn't mean the freedom to destroy everything there is in a country. Democracy means the freedom to build a country.' Asked about the Congress, he said it should become a 'cadre-based party'. When the interviewer pointed out that both the Jana Sangh and the communists were based on cadres, Sanjay dismissed the first as 'a favour-based party'. As for the latter, he commented that 'if you take all the people in the Communist Party, the big wigs – even the not-so-big wigs – I don't think you will find a richer or more corrupt people anywhere'.[48]

Surge was a new magazine, and the interview was a scoop. The editor quickly sold the story to the agencies, who in turn passed it on to newspapers both Indian and foreign. These chose to highlight Sanjay Gandhi's views on free enterprise – so at odds with his mother's professed socialism – and his characterization of her loyal allies, the communists, as 'corrupt'. When these excerpts were published, the prime minister sent a panic-stricken note to her secretary, P. N. Dhar. Sanjay's comments were 'exceedingly stupid', she wrote. It would 'not only grievously hurt those who have helped us', but create 'serious problems with the entire Socialist Bloc'. Dhar was able to contain the damage – no more snippets appeared in the press, and *Surge* was prevented from printing the interview. Sanjay himself was persuaded to issue a statement clarifying that leaders in the Jana Sangh and Swatantra parties were even more 'corrupt', and that the CPI must be saluted for its support to 'progressive policies, specially those affecting the poor people'.[49]

Sanjay was not deterred from giving more interviews, though. When the *Illustrated Weekly of India* asked him about curbs on the press, he answered that the papers 'constantly told blatant, malicious lies. Censorship was the only way to put an end to this.' Asked to provide a balance sheet of the emergency, he said that 'the greatest gain is a sense of discipline and the speeding up of work'. And 'what has the country lost? Smuggling, black-marketing, hoarding, bus burning and the habit of coming late to work.'[50]

The editor of the *Weekly*, Khushwant Singh, emerged as the chief cheerleader and trumpeter of the rising son. Sanjay was termed as 'The Man Who Gets Things Done' and chosen as the 'Indian of the Year'. The magazine ran lavish features on Sanjay and his young wife, Maneka, pages and pages of photographs accompanied by an invariably fawning text. (Samples: 'He has determination, a sense of justice, a spirit of adventure and a total lack of fear'. 'Sanjay Gandhi has added a new dimension to political leadership: he has no truck with shady characters or sycophants; he is a teetotaller, he lives a simple life, . . . his words are not hot air but charged with action.')[51]

Less surprising perhaps was the attention paid to the prime minister's son by All-India Radio and the state-run television channel, Doordarshan. In a single year, 192 news items were broadcast about Sanjay Gandhi from the Delhi station of AIR. In the same period Doordarshan telecast 265 items about Sanjay's activities. When he made a twenty-four-hour trip to Andhra Pradesh, the Films Division shot a full-length documentary called *A Day to Remember*, with commentary in three languages.[52]

The surest sign of Sanjay Gandhi's growing importance in Indian politics was the deference paid him by Union ministers and chief ministers. Before deciding on which admiral to promote, the defence minister, Bansi Lal, took the two candidates to be questioned by Sanjay. When the young man visited Rajasthan, the state's chief minister came to the airport to receive him; on his drive into Jaipur city, Sanjay passed 501

arches erected in his honour. A similar show was organized when he
visited Uttar Pradesh; at Lucknow airport, when Sanjay stumbled on
the tarmac and lost his slipper, it was picked up and reverentially handed
back by the UP chief minister himself.[53]

VIII

The prime minister had once chastised the Indian princes for promoting
birth over talent. Now she had succumbed to that temptation herself.
The elevation of her son followed a notably feudal route. Just as an heir
apparent is given a title at an early age – a duke of this or the prince of
that – Sanjay was given charge of the Congress's youth wing. (He was
in theory merely a member of the Executive Council, but in practice
the Youth Congress's president took orders from him.) And just as sons
of Mughal emperors were once given a *suba* (province) to run before
taking over the kingdom itself, Sanjay was asked to look after affairs in
India's capital city. Within a few months of the emergency, the word
had got around: 'the PM herself wanted all matters pertaining to Delhi
to be handled by her son'.[54]

By now, Sanjay Gandhi had formulated a five-point programme
to complement his mother's twenty-point one. These dealt with,
respectively, family planning, afforestation, abolition of dowry, the
removal of illiteracy and slum clearance. Of these the focus was on
the first, nationally, and on the fifth, when it came to Delhi. The
capital was dotted with slums that had spontaneously arisen to house
the migrants who did the low-paying jobs in residential colonies and
government offices. Here lived sweepers, rickshaw-pullers, domestic
servants, office boys and their families. There were almost a hundred
such settlements in the city, housing close to half a million people.[55]

Sanjay Gandhi wanted these slums demolished and their inhabitants
settled in farmland across the river Jumna. Here, his ideas coincided
with those of Jagmohan, the ambitious vice-chairman of the Delhi
Development Authority (DDA). Jagmohan's great hero was Baron
Haussmann; he hoped to do for Delhi what that town planner had
once done for Paris. By clearing the slums and building boulevards, the
baron had transformed the French capital. Once 'an ugly and despicable
town', it had become a 'seat of vigorous and vibrant culture'. However,
Jagmohan's admiration for autocratic methods was catholic. He praised

what the Chinese communists had accomplished in Shanghai, for example: this a 'result of firm national policy and commitment', when 'in India, on the other hand, we are still in a state of drift'. The DDA vice-chairman once lamented that he was

> No Haussmann reborn
> No Lutyens with a chance
> Nor Corbusier with Nehru's arms
> I am a little fellow
> An orphan of these streets

Still,

> With all the millstones
> Around my neck
> I stand erect
> Restless and keen
> Willing to fight
> Willing to dream . . .[56]

This was written in 1974, before the emergency. A year later Sanjay Gandhi arrived, to free Jagmohan's arms, to remove the millstones from round his neck. The town planner had long been disturbed by slums, signs of a 'sick and soulless city'. Impatient to clean and clear them, he had been impeded by the messiness of democratic procedure – the need to obtain consent, to provide proper resettlement, to deal with political activists purporting to represent the people.

Jagmohan was a key member of a coterie that had sprung up around Sanjay Gandhi. Others included Naveen Chawla, who was secretary to the lieutenant governor, and the senior police officer P. S. Bhinder. Among the women who worked with Sanjay were the president of the Youth Congress, Ambika Soni, and a socialite-cum-social worker, Ruksana Sultana, who was seen as his unofficial representative to the slum dwellers. Every morning the group met in Sanjay's office to take orders and provide reports. Also in attendance was the prime minister's stenographer, R. K. Dhawan, who provided the link between this Delhi cabal and the doings of the government of India. Preceptor to the lot was Dhirendra Brahmachari, a long-haired swami who first entered the Gandhi home as Indira's yoga teacher, but stayed on to become a favourite of her son. Dressed and trained as a Hindu holy man, Brahmachari was yet modern enough to own and run a firearms factory in Kashmir.

The names of this coterie became known in the city, their doings discussed in hushed whispers. It was said that the surest way to have the government act in your favour was to speak to (and please) one of the above. Businessmen seeking licences or tax exemptions rushed to them; so did MPs hoping for a Cabinet appointment. Contrasts were drawn between Sanjay's largely 'Punjabi mafia' and his mother's once-powerful Kashmiri lobby. The brashness of the former was compared with the sophistication of the latter. However, the differences were not so much of style as of intent. Where the Kashmiris were 'committed' to their shared socialist ideology as much as to their leader, Sanjay's gang was committed only to Sanjay himself.[57]

The exception to this general rule was Jagmohan. He had already identified the tidying-up of Delhi as his life's mission – and was delighted to find it endorsed by the prime minister's son. Now, Sanjay's support and the emergency's cover gave legitimacy to the DDA vice-chairman's preference for coercion over persuasion. The bulldozers could move into the slums, free even of the probing eye of the press. In the fifteen years preceding the emergency the DDA had moved a mere 60,000 families; in the fifteen months following it the number more than doubled.[58]

Jagmohan's operations focused on the old city, where Mughal monuments and mosques nested cheek-by-jowl with damp houses and dark streets. On the morning of 13 April 1976 a bulldozer moved into the Turkman Gate area, behind Asaf Ali Road, the street that divides Old Delhi from New. In two days it had demolished a slum of recent origin, housing forty families. Then it moved towards a set of *pucca* houses of uncertain antiquity. The residents contacted their MP, a Congress Party member and old associate of Mrs Gandhi named Subhadra Joshi. Mrs Joshi in turn contacted the officials of the DDA; Jagmohan himself was appealed to.

The negotiations stalled the operations temporarily, but in a couple of days they had resumed. Three bulldozers were at work, acting, they said, on Jagmohan's orders. They had demolished more than a hundred houses when, acting in desperation, a group of women and children squatted on the road and defied the bulldozers to run over them. When they refused to move, the DDA called for the police. In sympathy with the protesters, shops in the vicinity began to close.

The police tried to shift the squatters with sticks and, when that failed, with tear-gas. The retaliation came in the form of stones. The fighting escalated and spread into the narrow lanes. The numbers of the mob grew; the police progressed from using tear-gas to using bullets. It took the better part of a day before order was restored. Estimates of the number who died in the fighting range from 10 to 200. Curfew was imposed in the Old City; it was a full month before it was lifted.[59]

The offices of India's leading newspapers are on Bahadur Shah Zafar Marg, less than a mile away from Turkman Gate. Yet in the conditions of the emergency none could write about the incident. However, the underground picked it up and played it up. The news reached Sheikh Abdullah, who was 'terribly distressed' by the shootings. He complained to the prime minister, who agreed that he could visit the area. Accompanied by a leading Congress politician, Abdullah toured the Old City, speaking to people about their recent experiences.[60] There he learnt that aside from the natural reluctance to leave their houses, the protesters had been hurt by being subject to the first of Sanjay Gandhi's five points – family planning. In June 1976 the underground newspaper *Satya Samachar* reported that the Sheikh had told a group of Congress MPs that 'the whole trouble began when young, old and even invalid people were dragged off to the sterilization camps. Nobody has any quarrel with the economic policies of the Prime Minister, but the way in which they are being implemented, I am sure, will lead to an explosion.'[61]

IX

In fairness, Sanjay Gandhi was not the only person concerned about his country's large and still growing population. The Malthusian spectre had long haunted India, as the pages of this book should have made clear already. Western journalists feared large-scale famine; Western biologists had written off the country altogether. Many Indians also worried that a rising population would put paid to the other achievements of their nation. Between 1857 and 1947 gross national product stagnated; there were periods in which it even declined. After Independence, GNP grew at 3 per cent per annum. However, with the high increase in human numbers, the per capita income grew at a mere 1 per cent a year.

The debates on India's population size dated from the earliest days of Independence. Social workers had set up a Family Planning

Association of India in 1949. The Planning Commission had spoken of the importance of family planning since its inception in 1950–1. However, culture and economics worked in favour of large families. The biases in educational development meant that girls were still valued more as child-bearers than as wage-earners. The continuing dependence on agriculture placed a premium on children. Indian Muslims and Catholics were enjoined by their clergy to abjure family planning. And Hindu couples greatly preferred sons to daughters, trying and trying again until they had one.

In 1901 the population of India stood at about 240 million; by 1971 it had reached close to 550 million. In this period, birth rates had fallen slightly, from nearly 50 births per 1,000 Indians to about 40. However, the decline in death rates had been far steeper, from 42 per 1,000 at the turn of the century down to 15 by the 1970s. Advances in medical care and more nutritious food allowed all Indians, including infants previously liable to early death, to live longer. But since the birth rate and average family size did not decline at a comparable rate, the population continued to rise.[62]

It is difficult precisely to date Sanjay Gandhi's own interest in family planning. His *Surge* interview of August 1975 does not mention the subject at all. Yet a year later, the *Illustrated Weekly of India* was speaking of how 'Sanjay has given a big impetus to the Family Planning Programme throughout the country'. He claimed that if his programme was implemented, '50 per cent of our problems will be solved'. He expressed himself in favour of compulsory sterilization, for which facilities should be provided 'right down to the village level'.[63]

Of Sanjay Gandhi's five points, writes his biographer, the other four were humdrum, unglamorous, 'hardly the stuff to build charismatic leadership credentials on'. But 'family planning was. Here was a Herculean project, the solving of which, everyone acknowledged, was vital if the nation hoped to survive, let alone prosper'. And so, 'family planning became the lynchpin of Sanjay Gandhi's Emergency activities'.[64]

In his tours around India, Sanjay Gandhi catalysed a competitive process between the states of the Union. Sanjay would tell one chief minister of what another had claimed to have done – '60,000 operations in two weeks' – and encourage him to exceed it. These targets were passed down to district officials, who were rewarded if they met or exceeded them and transferred otherwise. The process led to widespread coercion. Lower government officials had to submit to the surgeon's knife before arrears of pay were cleared. Truck drivers would not have their licences renewed if they could not produce a sterilization certificate. Slum dwellers would not be allotted a plot for resettlement unless they did likewise.[65]

The hand of the state fell heavily in the towns, but the villagers were not spared either. An anthropologist doing fieldwork in Maharashtra's Satara district reported that the emergency had little impact in its first year. A few homes were built for the landless under the twenty-point programme. A few slogans were painted denouncing the dictatorship. Then, in September 1976 – shortly after Sanjay Gandhi's visit to the state – a campaign for compulsory sterilization began in the villages. Local officials prepared lists of 'eligible men', that is, of those who already had three or more children. Police vans would come and take them off to the nearest health centre. Some men fled into the hills to escape the marauders. Those who had undergone a vasectomy were too embarrassed to talk about it.[66]

As with slum demolition, here too there was resistance. In September 1976 an underground newspaper reported a 'wave of protests' against family planning in Delhi and Uttar Pradesh. There were clashes between health officials and shopkeepers refusing to be sterilized. Resistance was reported from many towns in UP – Sultanpur, Kanpur, Bareilly. There was great resentment among school teachers, who had been asked to conduct house-to-house surveys in pursuance of the sterilization campaign. As many as 150 teachers were arrested for defying orders.

The worst incident, the Turkman Gate of family planning so to speak, took place in the town of Muzaffarnagar, seventy miles north-west of Delhi. The district magistrate here was notorious for his zeal, and for his communalism – under his orders, the chiefly Hindu police had gone with particular relish for Muslim artisans and labourers. On 18 October a scuffle broke out between officials promoting sterilization and their potential victims. Their pent-up anger released, the mob torched the health clinics and threw bottles and stones. The police were called in, and resorted very quickly to firing, in which more than fifty people died. A delegation of opposition MPs rushed to the town but were prohibited from speaking to the residents. However, reports leaked into the foreign press, and the prime minister was constrained to admit in Parliament that there had been an 'incident' in Muzaffarnagar.[67]

An incidental victim of Sanjay Gandhi's family planning drive was the great popular singer Kishore Kumar. Other film stars and musicians agreed to perform in a programme to raise money for sterilization, but Kishore refused. As a consequence, his songs were banned from Vividh Bharati, the AIR channel that exclusively broadcast film music. The Film Censor Board was instructed to hold up the release of movies in which Kishore acted or sang. Sanjay's men also warned record companies against selling Kishore's songs. It was an act of petty vindictiveness in keeping with the times.[68]

X

That the prime minister chose, at a time of crucial political importance, to rely on Sanjay Gandhi rather than P. N. Haksar and company – this was an excursion in reasoning that even her close friends found difficult to understand. Various theories were offered – that it was the manifestation of the guilt of a working mother and single parent, that she was paranoid about assassination and hence could trust only her family, that Sanjay knew her darkest secrets and hence had a hold over her, that she was grateful for his support when the emergency was declared. However appealing to the biographer, to the historian such speculation is nearly useless. For what matters here is not intent but consequence – not why Mrs Gandhi chose to rely so much on her younger son but on what this reliance meant for India and Indians.

It is tempting to view Mrs Gandhi's political career as being divided into two phases, with the emergency and Sanjay Gandhi providing the dividing line. Before Sanjay, it might be said, she won elections, created Bangladesh, reformed the Congress Party and made bold attempts to reorganize the economy. Under Sanjay's malign influence she turned her back on these larger social goals and became obsessed with the preservation of herself and her family.[69]

However, when one views the prime minister's career in the round, Sanjay and the emergency should be said to mark not a radical departure from past practice, but a deepening of it. From the time of the Congress split, Mrs Gandhi had worked to place loyal individuals in position of authority, and to make public institutions an instrument of her will. Institutions such as the bureaucracy, the judiciary, the presidency and the Congress Party had been eroded well before the emergency. Sanjay's arrival took the process further – some would argue much further. It also vulgarized and corrupted it, and made it more violent. But the process itself antedated his entry into Indian politics.

By June 1975 Mrs Gandhi had been prime minister of India for a little less than a decade. When one compares her tenure with that of her father, one is struck by a striking paradox – that Nehru's halting yet honest attempts to promote a democratic ethos in a hierarchical society were undone by his own daughter, and in decisive and dramatic ways. The grievously mistaken dismissal of the communist government in Kerala aside, Nehru took seriously the idea of an opposition. But Mrs Gandhi paid other political parties scant respect. She attended Parliament less regularly than Nehru, and spoke much less when in it. Nehru forged abiding friendships with politicians of other parties – something quite inconceivable in the case of Mrs Gandhi. Then there was the contrast with how they treated their own party. In Nehru's time the Congress was a decentralized and largely democratic organization. Even had he been so inclined, he would not have been able to impose a chief minister against the will of a state's own politicians.

The contrast is reinforced when one considers the other, non-political aspects of democratic life in India. Nehru respected the freedom of the press, and allowed it to flourish. Nehru respected the autonomy of the bureaucracy and the judiciary: there are no known cases of his having intervened to favour or act against a particular official.

At least from the time of the Congress split in 1969, Mrs Gandhi had begun to depart from the political traditions of India's founding premier. The departures became more marked over the years, and became fully apparent only with the enactment of the emergency and the repression that followed. For partisan reasons of their own, opposition politicians could not posit a contrast between the first and third prime ministers of India. Because they had once opposed Nehru, and because the Congress was now led by his daughter, they could scarcely praise one and diminish the other.

Unbound by such constraints, Western writers who knew both leaders could see quite clearly how Indira Gandhi had departed from Jawaharlal Nehru. A year into the emergency, two British friends of Nehru made the contrast the focus of their criticisms of the regime. Writing in the *Times*, Fenner Brockway deplored the conversion of 'the world's greatest democracy' into a 'repressive dictatorship'. Himself 'a son of India', Brockway 'appeal[ed] to Mrs Gandhi in memory of the principles of her distinguished father, to end these denials of freedom and liberty'.[70] Writing in the *Spectator*, John Grigg recalled Nehru's commitment to free elections and a free press. India's first prime minister was 'a true patriot because he was a true democrat . . . During his long premiership he made many mistakes but on the vital libertarian issue he never broke faith with the Indian people.' But now, noted Grigg sadly, 'Nehru's tryst with destiny seems to have been turned into a tryst with despotism – and by his own daughter.' Mrs Gandhi 'should have been the proudest upholder of India's democratic experiment, which was proving to the whole world that people did not have to be rich or educated to enjoy civil liberties'. Yet by her actions she had 'spuriously confirmed' the view of 'old-fashioned imperialists' that 'only authoritarian methods can work in a country like India'. Grigg asked the prime minister to free herself from her son's influence and return to the values of her father's generation. Indeed, he 'implore[d] her – at whatever cost in power, "face", and mother-love – to restore the freedoms she has taken away'. To do so, he wrote, 'would be the hardest act of her career but it would also be the bravest and best'.[71]

Other British friends wrote privately to Mrs Gandhi, urging her to end the emergency. One such was the old Quaker Horace Alexander, who had once mediated between Mahatma Gandhi and the British Raj, and also first introduced the current prime minister to the delights of birdwatching in the Indian countryside.[72] There was also impersonal yet very public criticism, offered in the then widely respected *Times* newspaper by the even more widely respected columnist Bernard Levin. In October 1976 Levin wrote two long articles on the recent attacks on democracy in India. Speaking of the suspension of habeas corpus, and the curbs on the press, he warned that Mrs Gandhi was turning her country into a 'tin-pot dictatorship'. In the first week of January 1977 he wrote two more essays, criticizing the constitutional amendments passed to emasculate the presidency and the judiciary. These 'tyrannous provisions' were 'entirely unnecessary except to one who wants total power and the ability to use it without check'. These latest changes, said Levin, had confirmed the 'transformation of India into a fully authoritarian regime under its seedy dictator, Mrs Indira Gandhi'.[73]

On 18 January 1977 the prime minister announced that Parliament was to be dissolved and fresh elections held. This came as a surprise to her political opponents, who were let out of their cells even as the announcement was being made on All-India Radio. And, from all accounts, it came as a shock to her son Sanjay, who too had not been informed beforehand. The term of the present Parliament could have been extended, year after year. The underground resistance had been fully tamed. And yet Mrs Gandhi decided, suddenly and without consulting anyone, to return India to democracy.

There was much speculation as to why the prime minister had turned her back on emergency rule. In the Delhi coffee houses, the gossip was that her intelligence chief had assured her that the Congress would be re-elected with a comfortable majority. Some felt that it was the consequence of competitive one-upmanship. President Bhutto had just announced elections in his usually autocratic Pakistan; could Mrs Gandhi delay elections in her unnaturally autocratic India? Her secretary, writing long after the event, offered yet a third explanation. The emergency, he noted, had cut Mrs Gandhi off from the public contact that previously nourished her. 'She was nostalgic about the way people reacted to her in the 1971 campaign and she longed to hear again the applause of the multitudes.'[74]

Perhaps all these factors contributed. So did the criticism from Western observers and (especially) friends. Aside from those already quoted, the emergency was strongly condemned by the former German chancellor Willy Brandt and the Socialist International ('all socialists must now feel a great sense of personal tragedy at what is happening in India'); by the World Council of Churches in Geneva ('a very serious abridgement of human rights'); and by the leading American trade union organization, the AFL/CIO ('India has become a police state in which democracy has been smothered').[75]

What, finally, persuaded Mrs Gandhi to end the emergency? One cannot say for certain, but it does seem that she was stung by the comments of those foreign observers impossible to dismiss as enemies of India. Fenner Brockway and John Grigg were not Richard Nixon and the CIA. Nor were they sceptics who had sneered at India, who had hoped that its democracy would fail. These, rather, were very old friends of India's freedom. While the Raj lasted they had pressed the British to leave, and after Independence had saluted the installation of a democratic regime. We do not know whether Mrs Gandhi read their essays, or indeed the articles by Bernard Levin. Yet it is more likely than not that she did. They might have been placed before her without comment by a member of her own staff, or of her intimate circle, himself less than enamoured of the emergency. It is a striking coincidence that the elections were called two weeks after Levin's second series in *The Times* – just enough time for them to be air-mailed to India, seen by someone in the PM's office, clipped and passed on to her.

But coincidence it may be. We shall never know for sure, one reason being that Mrs Gandhi's papers remain closed (and shall probably always be so). Still, it is appropriate to end this chapter with a fragment underlining how the dictatorship imposed by India's third prime minister was so much at odds with the democratic legacy of her father. Visiting New Delhi during the emergency, the *New York Times*'s A. M. Rosenthal – who had once served as his paper's correspondent in India – concluded that, had Jawaharlal Nehru lived while Indira Gandhi reigned, the two would have been political opponents rather than allies. An Indian friend of Rosenthal's captured that imagined scenario in this way: 'Indira is in the Prime Minister's house, and Jawaharlal is back to writing letters to her from jail again.'[76]

The allusion was to a series of letters written to Indira Gandhi by Nehru in the early 1930s, while lodged in a British jail. These presented his thirteen-year-old daughter with a panoramic sweep of world history. Starting with the Greeks, and ending with the Indian freedom struggle, the story as told by the father unfolded the (oft-interrupted) progress of the human animal towards greater sociability and freedom. The later letters explored how 'democracy, which was for a century and more the ideal and inspiration of countless people, and which can count its martyrs by the thousands,' was now 'losing ground everywhere'. The last letter, sent to Indira on 9 August 1933 – three years after the first – ended with the stirring paean to freedom contained in Rabindranath Tagore's great poem *Gitanjali*.

When published in book form, the letters sold briskly, and in time the author was persuaded by his publisher to bring out an expanded edition. A freshly written postscript, dated 14 November 1938, outlined the major political developments of the latter part of the decade. 'The growth of fascism during the last five years and its attack on every democratic principle and conception of freedom and civilization' wrote Jawaharlal to Indira, 'have made the defence of democracy the vital question today.' Unfortunately, 'democracy and freedom are in grave peril today, and the peril is all the greater because their so-called friends stab them in the back'.[77]

23

LIFE WITHOUT THE CONGRESS

All my father's works have been written in prison. I recommend prison
life not only for aspiring writers but for aspiring politicians too.

INDIRA GANDHI, 1962

I

IN JANUARY 1977, WHILE announcing fresh elections, the prime minister
recalled that 'some eighteen months ago, our beloved country was on
the brink of disaster'. The emergency had been imposed 'because the
nation was far from normal'. Now that it 'is being nursed back to health',
elections were permissible.

Even as Mrs Gandhi spoke over the radio, her opponents were
being released from jails across the country. The next day, 19 January,
the leaders of four parties met at the residence of Morarji Desai in
New Delhi. These parties were the Jana Sangh, the Bharatiya Lok Dal
(a party principally of farmers, led by the veteran Charan Singh), the
Socialist Party and Morarji's own Congress (O). The following day
Desai told the press that they had decided to fight the elections under
a common symbol and a common name. On the 23rd, the 'Janata (Peoples)
Party' was formally launched at a news conference in the presence of
Jayaprakash Narayan.[1]

Ten days after the formation of the Janata Party, Jagjivan Ram announced
that he was leaving the Union government. Known universally as
'Babuji', Ram was a lifelong Congressman, a prominent minister
in Nehru's and Indira Gandhi's Cabinets and – most crucially – the
acknowledged leader of the Scheduled Castes, the former Untouchables
who made up some 15 per cent of the electorate. It was Ram who had
moved the resolution in the Lok Sabha endorsing the emergency. His
resignation came as a shock to the Congress, and as a harbinger of things to

come. For Babuji was renowned for his political acumen; that he chose to leave the Congress was widely taken as a sign that this ship was, if not yet sinking, then leaking very badly indeed. In resigning from his old party Ram formed a new one: the Congress for Democracy. The CFD, he said, would collaborate with the Janata Party regarding candidates in order to avoid the Congress gaining from a split opposition vote.

The elections had been scheduled for the third week of March. The opposition campaign kicked off with a mass rally at New Delhi's Ramlila Grounds on Sunday 6 March. In a desperate measure to stem the crowds the government chose to telecast a popular romantic film, *Bobby*, at the same time as the rally. There was only one TV channel in 1977, this run by the state, and in normal circumstances half of Delhi's adult population would have been huddled around their screens. But, as one pro-Janata paper gleefully reported, on this day Babuji had won over *Bobby*. A million people heard JP and Jagjivan Ram speak, along with the leaders of the other opposition parties, all now pledged to a common fight against Indira Gandhi and the Congress.[2]

In India's commercial capital, Bombay, the same day saw the city's most popular weekly hit the stands containing interviews with Indira Gandhi and Jayaprakash Narayan, a veritable double scoop. The prime minister told the interviewer that the Janata men 'are only united against me, but not on any positive programme'. The new name could not hide the 'same old aim, which is to get rid of Indira Gandhi'. In his interview, JP claimed that 'the Janata Party is no greater hotchpotch than the Congress'. For the ruling party had within it 'all types of vested interests and it is seething with internal differences'. Asked for a message to the weekly's readers, Narayan said they should vote without fear, and remember that 'if you vote for the Opposition you will vote for Freedom. If you vote for the Congress you will vote for Dictatorship.'[3]

The chief protagonists of the conflicts of 1973–5 were also the chief campaigners in the elections of 1977. Despite his age and indifferent health, JP hit the road. Between 21 February and 5 March he spoke at Patna, Calcutta, Bombay, Chandigarh, Hyderabad, Indore, Poona and Ratlam – pausing only to spend time with his dialysis machine. Everywhere, he warned the audience that 'this is the last free election if the Congress is voted back to power'; then, 'nineteen months of tyranny shall become nineteen years of terror'.[4] In her speeches Mrs Gandhi denied that her party was the monopoly of one family. In any case, 'few families in the world' had a comparable record of service and sacrifice.

She admitted that there had been some excesses during the emergency, yet defended the regime as necessary at the time. 'We don't care who criticises us', she insisted. 'We have to proceed on the right path guided by sound policies, programmes and principles.'[5]

At least in northern India, the elections were inevitably seen as a referendum on those policies and programmes; and on one programme in particular, that of compulsory sterilization. There was, reported one journalist, a 'burning hatred against forced vasectomies'; this 'extremely emotive and explosive issue' had 'become the focus of all pent-up frustrations and resentment'. Voters told Congress candidates to show their own sterilization certificates; when they couldn't, they were simply asked to leave. Opposition election slogans also harped on the issue; these dismissed the Congress as a *sarkari khasi kendra*, the official castration centre, and warned that to re-elect the party would be to bring back forced sterilization. Other slogans targeted the programme's chief promoter: *Gandhi Nehru ke desh main kaun hai ye Sanjay Gandhi?* asked one – In the land of Gandhi and Nehru, who is this impostor Sanjay Gandhi? Particularly active in the election campaign were school-teachers and lower officials, those who had their promotions stopped or were punitively transferred for not having met the 'quotas' (of males to be sterilized) assigned them by the administration.[6]

On the night of 20 March 1977 the election results were posted outside newspaper offices in Delhi as they came in. The next day's papers reported that the crowds 'were partisan and loudly pro-Janata', cheering as 'the kingpins of the Congress Party tumbled one after another'. When news of Mrs Gandhi's defeat in her previously safe seat of Rae Bareilli was announced, 'the people in high spirits thronging the streets began shouting slogans and bursting crackers'. The news of Sanjay Gandhi's defeat was followed by louder cheers and more prolonged celebrations still. Mrs Gandhi had lost to her old foe and litigant Raj Narain; in the adjoining constituency of Amethi, Sanjay had been defeated by an obscure student leader.[7]

The defeats of mother and son were part of a wider washout of the Congress in Uttar Pradesh. They lost all 85 seats in the state, and all 54 seats in neighbouring Bihar, to the Janata–CFD alliance. In Rajasthan the Congress won one seat out of 25; in Madhya Pradesh one out of 40. These losses were partly offset by a robust performance in southern India, where the emergency had rested lightly. In Andhra Pradesh the

Congress won 41 seats out of 42; in Karnataka, 26 out of 28; in Kerala, 11 out of 20; in Tamil Nadu, 14 out of 39. The Janata surge had scarcely dented the south; still, given the higher population densities and seat shares of the northern states, in the aggregate the Congress fell far short of a majority. They won 153 seats in a house of 540, down more than 200 from the 1971 elections. On the other side, as many as 298 Janata and CFD candidates were successful.[8]

The elections had revealed a manifest regional divide, and also a divide by caste and religious affiliation. Two groups in particular, long considered to be loyal 'vote banks' of the ruling party, had this time deserted the Congress. One was the Scheduled Castes, many of whom were swayed into voting for Janata by the defection of Jagjivan Ram. The other was the Muslims, who had suffered grievously at the hands of Sanjay's pet programmes. When elections were called, the influential Imam of Delhi's greatest mosque, the Jama Masjid, asked Muslims to vote against the Congress. This they mostly did, contributing in good measure to the party's disastrous showing in northern India.[9]

Sober commentators spoke of a 'Janata wave'; less sober ones, of a 'revolution'. For the first time in the nation's thirty-year history, a party other than the Congress would govern at the centre. No Indian alive in 1977 knew what it was like not to have the Congress as the country's dominant and ruling political party. Few knew what it was like not to have Nehru or Indira Gandhi as its dominant and ruling political figure.

The results of the elections delighted many, angered some and surprised all. In a letter to a friend Mrs Gandhi attributed her defeat to malign forces. 'People have always thought that I was imagining things and overreacting', she wrote, 'but there has been a deep conspiracy and it was bound to overtake us.'[10] One editor who had been among her most steadfast supporters took the long and more hopeful view. Like Winston Churchill, Indira Gandhi had led her nation to victory in war; like him, she had been cheered for it; and like him she had been thrown out of power by an ungrateful people. There was consolation here for Mrs Gandhi, as well as a lesson for those who had replaced her. Thus the Janata–CFD regime 'will soon learn that promises are like lollipops, but performance is like a dose of bitter medicine. And the people are as mercurial as quicksilver. The cheering crowds of yesterday may turn into a jeering mob tomorrow.'[11]

II

Unlike the Congress, the Janata Party had not fought the elections under a single leader. After the results were in, a controversy arose as to who should be chosen prime minister. The supporters of Charan Singh felt that the sweep in northern India made him the logical choice. Jagjivan Ram's men argued that since his defection had been decisive he should be considered. Then there was Morarji Desai, who had almost become prime minister in 1964 and again in 1967.

The last week of March saw hectic canvassing on behalf of the three candidates. Finally, it was decided that the Grand Old Men behind Janata, Jayaprakash Narayan and J. B. Kripalani would make the choice. They settled on Desai, who had unparalleled administrative experience as well as a spotless personal record. Jagjivan Ram was offered the prestigious Defence portfolio, Charan Singh the powerful Home Ministry. Finance went to the old civil servant H. M. Patel, External Affairs to the Jana Sangh leader Atal Behari Vajpayee.

What would be the policies of the new government? It was hard to predict, since within both party and Cabinet there was a veritable mishmash of ideologies: 'some baiting Nehru, others praising him, some talking about the commanding heights of the public sector, and others brashly championing the Japanese and American models, some asserting the need for heavy industries, other clamouring for a "return to the villages" '.[12] The importance of Charan Singh signalled an anti-urban bias, and the Planning Commission was now dominated by economists who specialized in agriculture rather than industry. The importance of the socialists signalled a hard time for foreign capital; indeed, the industries minister, the fiery trade union leader George Fernandes, announced that the American multinationals Coca-Cola and IBM would both be made to quit India (which, in due course, they were).

Among the more pragmatic ministers was Madhu Dandavate, who was put in charge of the railways. This was the branch of government which serviced more Indians than any other, and none too well either. Dandavate too was a socialist, but his socialism eschewed rhetoric against the rich in favour of policies for the poor. As he put it, 'what I want to do is not degrade the first class but elevate the second class'. Dandavate initiated the computerization of railway reservations, which reduced corruption among booking clerks and uncertainty among passengers. He set in motion the repair or replacement of 5,000 kilometres of worn-out tracks. But his most far-reaching measure was to place two inches of foam on the hard wooden berths that passed for second-class 'sleepers', thus bringing their comfort levels closer to that prevailing in the first-class section of trains. Introduced at first on the major trunk lines, this change was in time effected on all trains, cumulatively benefiting hundreds of millions of travellers.[13]

In the government's early months observers waited with keen anticipation for a shift in foreign policy. The day after the election results were announced, the *New York Times* wrote that, whereas the attitude of the Congress towards the West had 'varied from a self-righteous edginess' to 'a chilliness bordering on hostility', 'all indications' from the Janata alliance were that 'a friendly attitude can be expected towards the United States, with a noticeable cooling of feelings for the Soviet Union'. American strategists were salivating at the prospect of a China–India–US alliance against the Soviet Union. The Janata victory, they thought, 'represent[ed] something of a windfall for Washington'.[14]

The mistake being made here was to equate one family with the nation as a whole. Washington believed it was only the personal choices of Jawaharlal Nehru and his daughter that explained the alliance with the Soviets. In truth, this had also to do with a more general scepticism regarding American intentions, caused both by its support of Pakistan and by the Indian intellectual's distaste for unbridled capitalism. Besides, the threat from China meant that New Delhi could scarcely turn its back on Moscow.

The Janata leaders did not want to reject the Soviets for the Americans, but to move towards a principled equidistance from the superpowers. As the influential editor (and JP biographer) Ajit Bhattacharjea remarked, the challenge for the new regime was 'to correct the tilt non-alignment had acquired over the years towards the Soviet Union without, if possible, antagonising Moscow'.[15] Thus in October 1977 Morarji Desai and A. B. Vajpayee together visited the Soviet Union to underline that the relationship between the two countries was much more than a familial one.

At the same time, overtures were also made to the other side. The jurist Nani Palkhivala, known for his pro-Western and free-market orientation, was sent as ambassador to Washington. In reciprocation, Jimmy Carter came to India in January 1978, the first American president to do so since Eisenhower. In a moving address to the Indian Parliament he spoke of the 'commonality of our fundamental values', and of how both countries had recently passed through 'grave crises' (namely, Watergate and the emergency) yet come through with their commitment to democracy intact. Then, in a spontaneous coda to his prepared text, he spoke of the debt owed by Martin Luther King's civil rights struggle to the ideas of Mahatma Gandhi.[16]

The Janata government also sought to mend fences with India's neighbours. In November 1977 India and Bangladesh signed an agreement for the sharing of the Ganga waters, which gave the former 20,500 cubic feet of water during the lean season, and the latter 34,500 cubic feet. The accord was signed over the protests of the state government of West Bengal, which claimed that Calcutta port would silt up if denied adequate water.[17] In February 1978 Foreign Minister Vajpayee visited Pakistan, where he charmed his hosts, the dictator General Zia-ul-Haq included, who had assumed that a man reared in the Jana Sangh would exhibit a fanatical hatred towards Muslims.[18] A year later Vajpayee visited China, the highest-ranking Indian to do so since the border war of 1962. On this occasion, however, the trip was marred by the Chinese attack on Vietnam, launched in arrogant disregard of India's long friendship with the country being invaded.

On economic policy the Janata government was less than unified; on foreign policy a little more so. The greatest consensus was on the new regime's treatment of the former prime minister. The Janata leaders were determined to make Mrs Gandhi pay for having imposed the emergency. As many as eight Commissions of Enquiry were appointed, each headed by a retired judge. Several dealt with the corruption of Congress chief ministers, one with the treatment of JP in jail and one, absurdly, with the possible maltreatment in a government hospital back in 1967 of the socialist leader (and founder of 'anti-congressism') Ram Manohar Lohia. There was also a commission set up to enquire into the affairs of Sanjay Gandhi's Maruti company.

The enquiry with the widest ambit was the Shah Commission, set up to punish those guilty of the excesses of the emergency. It was headed by a former chief justice of the Supreme Court, Justice J. C. Shah. It met in a courtroom of Patiala House, in central Delhi, where the white-haired judge sat on a raised platform flanked by two assistants. Below him, on a table with a microphone, sat the witness of the day, his testimony heard by a crowd composed mostly of journalists.[19]

In its first few months the Shah Commission examined scores of witnesses: bureaucrats, police officers, municipal officials, members of Mrs Gandhi's Cabinet. But the lady herself refused to testify. Three times she was called to the witness box; three times she came, and chose not to answer questions, claiming she was bound by the oath of Cabinet secrecy. A journal victimized during the emergency saw this as 'an outrageous attempt to make a mockery of the proceedings of the Commission'.[20] A journalist more sympathetic to the other side sarcastically commented that the 'Shah Commission was supposed to be a sort of Nuremberg Trial. Instead it has become a tamasha in which the heroine (or vamp) is constantly absent, and minor villains or comedians hold the stage. It is even losing its publicity value, as people have got bored with the commentaries on TV and radio and switch it off, just as the name of the Shah Commission is mentioned.'[21]

III

The change of government at the centre presaged changes of regime in the provinces as well. Following Mrs Gandhi's lead in 1971, Janata dismissed state governments across northern India, claiming that the results of the general election showed that these had 'lost the confidence of the people'. In fresh elections held to the state assemblies, Janata won easily in Uttar Pradesh, Madhya Pradesh, Rajasthan and Bihar.

In other states too changes were afoot. In West Bengal a coalition of left-wing parties came to power with a comfortable majority. The CPM itself won 178 seats out of 294 at stake with its allies winning a further 52. Back in 1967 and 1969 the CPM had shared power in Bengal with non-communist parties, in unstable coalitions easily undone by Machiavellian governors sent from New Delhi. Now they faced no such problem, and could set about effecting reform within the bourgeois system.[22]

The new chief minister was Jyoti Basu, the Middle Temple lawyer who had been the number two in those UF–LF governments of the 1960s. Others in his Cabinet were less genteel, coming from a background of work with farmers and labourers. Their top priority was agrarian reform. This focused on legalizing the rights of the *bargadars* (sharecroppers) who cultivated the bulk of the land in rural Bengal. The new government's Operation Barga set about recording their rights, and enhancing the share of the crop they could keep. Previously, the landlord would take half or more of the crop from the tenant; after the reforms, this share was reduced to 25 per cent, with 75 per cent being retained by the *bargadar*. More than a million poor peasants benefited from the reforms.

Meanwhile, the Left Front also conducted elections to village *panchayats*. *Panchayati Raj*, or local self-government, was a stated policy of the government, mandated by the constitution, but honoured mostly in the breach. The *panchayat* elections of 1977 in West Bengal were the first conducted with such seriousness and on such a wide scale. As many as 55,000 seats were contested for, with Left Front candidates winning two-thirds of them. Notably, most of those elected on the communist ticket were not sharecroppers but small landholders, teachers and social workers, members of what, in classical Marxist parlance, would be termed the 'petty bourgeoisie'. But they were party members or sympathizers withal. Along with Operation Barga, the *panchayat* elections helped deepen the hold of the Left Front over the Bengal countryside.[23]

There was also a change of regime in Tamil Nadu. Here the DMK had ruled for a decade before being dismissed on spurious grounds during the emergency. In the elections now called, their main rivals were the AIADMK, a breakaway from the parent party led and completely identified with the legendary film star M. G. Ramachandran. In the polls, the superior organizational machine of the DMK proved no match for the charisma and appeal of MGR. The AIADMK won 130 seats to its rival's 48. MGR quickly made it clear that the old slogans of 'Northern/ Hindi imperialism' were now out of date; he wanted, he said, good relations with the centre. Within Tamil Nadu the government instituted a slew of populist schemes in keeping with the chief minister's image, on the silver screen, of being a friend to the poor and needy. Among them was a 'midday meal' provided at state schools, in the hope that this would induce girl children to come to class and stay there.[24]

In the east, communists were becoming reconciled to bourgeois democracy; in the south, erstwhile secessionists to making their peace with the Indian nation-state. And there were also hopeful developments in regions and among peoples traditionally more truculent still. In the summer of 1977 Morarji Desai met the Naga leader A. Z. Phizo in London; although no settlement was reached, the fact that the two met, and in a foreign country, was seen as a significant concession by the Indian Government. Later in the year assembly elections were held in Nagaland. The 82-year-old Desai went to campaign, braving the risks of landing in mist-covered valleys. His visit, commented one newspaper, was 'testimony to the importance' he attached to the polls, which New Delhi hoped would 'end once and for all the sectional claims of Mr Phizo and his followers'.[25]

There were also fresh polls conducted at the other and equally troublesome end of the Indian Himalaya. Before the emergency Sheikh Abdullah had come to power in Kashmir at the head of a Congress regime, as part of an accord he had signed with Mrs Gandhi. Morarji Desai was keen that elections be held to test the legitimacy of a piece of paper signed by two individuals. The assembly was dissolved and the Sheikh re-established his National Conference. The revival of the party stoked great enthusiasm; as one Kashmiri recalled, 'the entire valley was red with N. C. flags. Every house and every market stood decorated with bunting.'[26] The National Conference won 46 out of 75 seats, a comfortable majority, this a little distorted by the fact that whereas the Sheikh's men had swept the Muslim-dominated Kashmir Valley, in the Hindu-majority Jammu region it won only 7 seats out of 32 at stake. That said, this was still the first 'truly fair and free' elections in the state since Independence, 'proving to the people of Kashmir that they too have the same fundamental rights which the people in the rest of the country enjoy and exercise'.[27]

IV

In the winter of 1978/9 the Swiss economist Gilbert Etienne travelled through the Indian countryside, visiting villages he had studied a decade and a half previously. He found a marked contrast between, on the one hand, 'dynamic' areas such as western Uttar Pradesh and the Cauvery delta of Tamil Nadu and, on the other, 'slow or no growth' areas such as eastern Uttar Pradesh and Orissa. What seemed crucial to rural prosperity was water management. Where irrigation facilities had been extended, productivity had risen, and incomes and lifestyles with it. Apart from water, a key input was chemical fertilizers, the consumption of which had increased fourfold in the 'Green Revolution' districts.

The gains from agricultural growth, discovered Etienne, had accrued chiefly to the rising 'backward' castes – such as the Jats in UP, the Kurmis and Yadavs in Bihar, the Marathas in Maharashtra and the Vellalas in Tamil Nadu. The upper or 'forward' castes, who once owned much land, had relocated to the cities. It was their space that these backward castes sought to fill. However, the position of those below them remained lamentable. The Scheduled Castes, who were at the bottom of the ritual hierarchy, had gained little from such rural development as had taken place in the 1960s and 70s. Representative here were the Musahars of Bihar. Etienne found that 'their children were malnourished and the caste generated an air of acute misery'.[28]

Etienne reported that 'one of the most dynamic schemes' in rural India sought to increase the production of milk by producers' co-operatives. This had its origins in a project started in the 1940s in the village of Anand, in central Gujarat. In the 1950s the co-operatives came to cover the whole of the Kaira district in which Anand fell. The milk they produced went to the city of Bombay, five hours away by express train. The success of this scheme (known as 'AMUL', with the first letter standing for the village where it began) prompted a countrywide extension, given the evocative name Operation Flood. At the beginning of the decade there were 1,000 co-operatives involving 240,000 farmers and producing 176 million litres of milk each year; by its end, 9,000 co-operatives with a million members all told were producing and selling nearly 500 million litres of milk annually.

These figures led some enthusiasts to speak of a White Revolution that had complemented the Green one. In truth, like that other revolution the gains from this one were very unevenly distributed. The scheme worked well in Tamil Nadu, a state with good rail and road facilities and a large urban population. In states with poorer infrastructure the results were disappointing. And everywhere it was the middle and rich farmers who had gained most; that is, those who had access to more fodder (in the shape of crop residues from their lands), more space to keep cows and buffaloes, and better access to credit.[29]

The commercialization of agriculture and milk production had benefited a significant section of farmers in rural India. Crucially, economic gains had converted themselves into political ambition. In the 1960s it was these rising rural castes who came to dominate the state governments in northern India. By the 1970s they had made their presence felt in national politics. In the Janata dispensation the force of rural assertion was 'dramatically represented in the personality and ideology of Charan Singh'. But it ran deeper than that of one man. After the 1977 Lok Sabha elections, 36 per cent of all members of Parliament came from farming backgrounds, up from 22 per cent in 1952. Their impact was felt in the rural orientation of the government's economic policies, as in the ever higher procurement price paid by the state for wheat and rice.[30]

V

Some commentators interpreted this rising rural power in class terms. They saw 'urban–rural struggles' and a sharpening of the conflict between factory owners and farmers. The terms of trade between industry and agriculture, once so heavily weighted in favour of the former, were now tilting towards the latter.[31] But this was also, and perhaps more significantly, a conflict that ran along the lines of caste.

In fact, when viewed in terms of caste rather than class, one could identify two distinct axes of conflict. The first was in the sphere of politics and administration, where the backwards sought to contest the pre-eminence previously enjoyed by the forward castes such as Brahmins, Rajputs, Kayasths and Banias, who had historically enjoyed a monopoly over literacy, scholarship, commerce and the exercise of political power.

The national movement had been dominated by the forward castes so, when Independence came, government both at the centre and in the states was dominated by them too. Slowly the pressures of representative democracy pushed forward the claims of those lower in status but more substantial in numbers. More chief ministers in the states came now from the backward castes. So did an increasing number of Cabinet ministers at the centre. One citadel remained unconquered: the office of prime minister. Like Nehru and Indira before him, Morarji Desai was from the highest-ranked Brahmin caste. (Although not a Brahmin, Lal Bahadur Shastri was a Kayasth, from an elite caste of scribes.)

In south India, a system of affirmative action, first instituted under colonial rule, had restricted the proportion of state jobs that the forwards castes could fill. Now the Janata regime sought to extend this system to their own strongholds in the north. In Bihar a commission set up in the early 1970s had recommended that 26 per cent of all posts in the administration be reserved for the backward castes. The report had been buried during the emergency. After the victory of the Janata Party in Bihar in 1977, the new chief minister, Karpoori Thakur, disinterred the report and decided to implement its recommendations.

Thakur's decision led to a storm of protest from the forward castes. Rajput and Bhumihar students burnt buses and trains and vandalized government buildings. The backward caste leaders were unyielding. Their resolve was strengthened by their strong representation in the state legislature, where nearly 40 per cent of the members came from castes that would benefit from the extension of reservation. As one politician put it, 'our movement is not only for reservation, it is for capturing political power in north India and in Delhi'. Indeed, under pressure from the backward-caste lobby within Janata, Morarji Desai had appointed a commission to examine whether reservation should be extended to central government jobs too. As mandated by the constitution, 15 per cent of these jobs went to Scheduled Castes and 7.5 per cent to Scheduled Tribes; now the backwards wanted a share as well. The commission that would look into this matter was headed by a Bihar politician, B. P. Mandal.[32]

Beyond the backward/forward divide, Bihar had become a metaphor for all that was wrong in India. Leading articles complained about the 'deteriorating law and order in the districts', of the corruption and inefficiency of government officials, of the instability of the state's politics (as many as nine chief ministers had been sworn in since 1967), all of which made Bihar 'a pitifully poor state'. Its present condition was contrasted with the halcyon days of yore, when Bihar had produced the Buddha, the emperor Ashoka and the great Mauryan Empire. Now, alas, 'the only time Bihar ever manages to hit the headlines is either when it is devastated by floods and famine or, when nature takes a respite, there are reports about coalmine tragedies, atrocities on Harijans, and corruption'.[33]

VI

Those atrocities were a consequence of the sharpening of a second kind of caste conflict – that between the backwards on the one side and the Scheduled Castes or Harijans on the other. This conflict too had a material basis; it was the former who mostly owned the land, and the latter who mostly laboured on it. Beyond disputes about wages and working conditions, this was also a dispute about dignity. The backwards slipped easily into the shoes of the forwards whose land they had gained. Like them, they treated the Harijans with disdain and often violated their women. At one time the lowest castes had had no option but to suffer in silence. However, the expansion of education, and the spaces opened up by political representation, meant that the younger Harijans were 'no longer ready to put up with contempt, abuse, beating and other forms of insult which were accepted by earlier generations as a matter of course'.[34]

There had been a dramatic increase in the number of attacks on Harijans since the new government assumed power in New Delhi. In the ten years that Mrs Gandhi was in power the number of reported incidents was 40,000. Between April 1977, when Janata assumed office, and September 1978, 17,775 cases of 'atrocities against Harijans' were reported. It was estimated that two-thirds of these reports were from the north, in states where Janata regimes were in power.[35]

The most serious conflict, however, took place in Marathwada, the arid, interior districts of Maharashtra that had once formed part of the Nizam's dominions. Here the Scheduled Castes were deeply influenced by the example of Dr B. R. Ambedkar. Many had converted to Buddhism, and many others had chosen to replace Gandhi's name for them – Harijan, meaning 'children of God' – with the more assertive Dalit, meaning 'oppressed'. A group of writers and poets calling themselves the Dalit Panthers demanded that the university in the region's main town of Aurangabad be named after their great leader. It was on 27 July 1978 that this request was finally acceded to, with the state government passing a resolution to rename Marathwada University as Dr Babasaheb Ambedkar University.

The renaming was bitterly opposed by the dominant Maratha caste. Students declared a *bandh* in the region's towns, closing schools, colleges, shops and offices. Then they spread into the villages, attacking and sometimes burning Dalit hamlets. An estimated 5,000 people, almost all low caste, were rendered homeless. The order to rename the university was withdrawn.[36]

Three months before the Marathwada riots there had been a violent clash between Dalits and upper castes in the UP town of Agra. Once again it was public admiration of Dr Ambedkar that sparked the trouble. Agra had a strong community of Jatavs, cobblers who had made money in the shoe trade. On 14 April 1978, Ambedkar's birthday, they held a procession, led by an elephant with a garlanded portrait of their hero atop it. That a means of transport traditionally associated with Hindu kings was being used by Dalits was too much for the upper castes to abide. The procession was attacked. In retaliation, the Jatavs stormed into shops owned by the upper castes. Two weeks of sporadic fighting ensued. Finally, the army was called in to restore order.[37]

VII

Of the 10,000 and more episodes of caste violence reported in the first year of Janata rule, one was to have an impact far beyond its place of origin. This was the incident at Belchi, a village in Bihar where, on 27 May 1977, nine Harijans were burnt to death by an upper-caste mob. Y. B. Chavan, leader of the opposition in Parliament, announced that he would go to the spot to conduct an inquiry. When Chavan failed to honour his promise, his party colleague and erstwhile prime minister chose to go instead.

In the months between her defeat in the elections and her visit to Belchi Mrs Gandhi had been very depressed. She (and Sanjay) both contemplated retirement from politics; settling in a cottage in the Himalaya was an option being considered. But the killings in Bihar drove her into action. Her political instinct told her that this might be the start of a possible comeback. So, while Chavan prevaricated, Mrs Gandhi flew to Patna and proceeded to Belchi. The roads had been washed away in the rains; she had to exchange her car for a jeep, then this for a tractor, then – when the mud got too deep – that for an elephant. It was via this mode of transport that the former prime minister reached Belchi to console the families of those killed in the violence.[38]

This dramatic gesture brought Indira Gandhi decisively back to the centre of the political stage. As one of her opponents later recalled, her visit to Belchi 'served several purposes. It helped damn the Janata Government as being indifferent to the fate of the poor and the Harijans. The ride refurbished Indira Gandhi's image as a friend of the poor and the lowly. It also showed to the average member of the Congress Party that Indira Gandhi was a woman of action and she alone could be trusted to lead the fight back to power.'[39]

The visit to Belchi was her own initiative, but Mrs Gandhi's revival was also helped by a less inspired initiative of the government in power. In the first week of October 1977 the home minister, Charan Singh, decided that he must arrest the former prime minister. Acting on his instructions, the Central Bureau of Intelligence prepared a charge sheet

accusing her of corruption. Armed with this piece of paper, the police
went to Mrs Gandhi's house and took her into custody. Their plan was
to drive her to a rest house in the neighbouring state of Haryana. On
the way they were forced to stop at a railway crossing. Mrs Gandhi got
out and sat down on a culvert. Her lawyers, meanwhile, told the police
their warrant did not permit them to take their client out of Delhi.
An argument ensued, conducted in the presence of many interested
bystanders. Eventually the police conceded the point, and the party
drove back to the capital.

Mrs Gandhi was kept overnight by the police, but when they
produced her before a magistrate the next morning, he threw out the
charge sheet as flimsy and insubstantial. The bungled 'arrest' redounded
badly on the Janata government, and helped redeem the reputation of
their hated opponent. She began making combative speeches against the
new regime, singling out the increase in crime and inflation (running
at double-digit levels), and the profiteering of hoarders and black-
marketeers. The deposed prime minister, commented the *New York Times*
in the last week of October, 'has been speaking more and more boldly
lately, trying to assume once more the posture of a national leader'.[40]

Mrs Gandhi's resurgence alarmed Janata, as well as many leaders in
her own party. Some Congress ministers had already testified against
her before the Shah Commission. In January 1978 the Congress formally
split into two factions, those who stayed with Mrs Gandhi forming the
'Congress (Indira)'. The next month this party easily won state elections
in Andhra Pradesh and Karnataka. The former prime minister had been
the chief campaigner; as the results showed, at least in the south her
image as a saviour of the poor, the adivasi, the Scheduled Castes and
women was firmly intact.[41]

Mrs Gandhi now began looking around for a safe seat via which to
re-enter Parliament. Eventually she chose the constituency of Chikmaglur,
in the coffee belt of Karnataka. The state's chief minister, Devaraj Urs,
had a high reputation for efficiency; among his achievements was the
bestowing of ownership rights to hundreds of thousands of tenant-
cultivators. The work of Urs and her own, largely unimpaired, standing
in south India persuaded Mrs Gandhi to seek election at the other end
of the country from her native Uttar Pradesh.[42]

Standing against the former prime minister was a former (and much
respected) chief minister of Karnataka, Veerendra Patil. Leading Patil's
campaign was Mrs Gandhi's old emergency-era adversary George

Fernandes, now minister for industries in the Janata government. 'I will not stir out of the constituency till the polling is over,' declared Fernandes to a reporter. 'We must defeat her.' Mrs Gandhi took the challenge seriously; as the same journalist reported, she 'smiles graciously at the women and children, accepts garlands at hundreds of roadside meetings, makes detours to visit numerous places of worship, calls on saints of all denominations'.[43]

In the event, Mrs Gandhi won easily. No sooner had she re-entered the Lok Sabha than she had to face a 'privilege motion' against her. A Parliamentary Committee, stacked with Janata members, reported that back in 1974, when she was prime minister, Mrs Gandhi had obstructed an inquiry into Sanjay's Maruti factory, and deliberately misled Parliament while doing so. Her punishment was left to the 'wisdom of the House'. The Janata majority decided that she must be sent to jail for a week. The spell in prison, ruled the election commissioner, meant that she would have to resign her seat. This precipitated another by-election in Chikmaglur; once again Mrs Gandhi contested, and won.[44]

VIII

Janata's attempts to humiliate the former prime minister were seriously misjudged. The stoicism with which Mrs Gandhi bore her sufferings was much admired, and the two brief arrests allowed her to acquire a halo of martyrdom. Admittedly, the men now in power had been victimized during the emergency, but that they chose to focus on taking revenge against an individual when they should really have been running a government spoke of a certain narrowness of vision.

Behind the attempts to arrest the former prime minister lay personal rivalries within the Janata camp. The home minister, Charan Singh, was not reconciled to being number two in the Cabinet. His move against Mrs Gandhi was a move to steal the thunder from Morarji Desai. He opened another flank in the same battle when he wrote to the prime minister complaining about the growing influence of Desai's son Kanti. Kanti lived with his father, and handled his appointments. Unflattering comparisons were made with the role once played by Sanjay Gandhi.

Through the first half of 1978 Charan Singh and Morarji Desai, home minister and prime minister respectively, exchanged a series of angry letters. Eventually, in June 1978, Desai was compelled to sack Singh from the Cabinet, along with his chief lieutenant Raj Narain. Others within Janata tried to broker a peace, but to no avail. In December, Singh emerged from months of seclusion to organize a massive farmers' rally in the capital. Some 200,000 peasants, mostly from northern India, and many from Charan Singh's own Jat caste, came to Delhi in their tractors and lorries to hear their leader speak.

This show of strength forced Desai to recall Charan Singh to the Cabinet. In February 1979 he was appointed finance minister. He was now also one of two deputy prime ministers, the other being Jagjivan Ram. Singh's first budget offered sops to farmers, as in an increased fertilizer and irrigation subsidy. But the patch-up proved short lived. One important Janata constituent, the Socialist Party, mostly sided with Singh; another, the Jana Sangh, decided to back Desai. Deepening the rift was the question of 'dual membership', the growing feeling that the Jana Sangh members of the Janata Party owed their primary allegiance to the Rashtriya Swayamsevak Sangh. Back in March 1977, Atal Behari Vajpayee had proclaimed that his old party was 'dead and buried'. But the feeling persisted that it was the RSS that directed the actions of Janata MPs and ministers who had a Jana Sangh background. They were asked to disavow their ties with the RSS, which they refused to do on the grounds that the Sangh was merely a 'cultural' body.

In the third week of July 1979 the Socialists chose to sit in a separate group in Parliament. This catalysed a split in Janata, a loss of majority for Morarji Desai's government and his own resignation. In his bid to construct a fresh majority, Desai wooed one Congress faction while Jagjivan Ram wooed another. The third leader in the fray, Charan Singh, now constructed an opportunistic alliance with his old nemesis Indira Gandhi. With the help of a letter of support from the Congress Party, Charan Singh was able to convince the president that he enjoyed majority support in the House. He was sworn in just in time to deliver the prime minister's annual Independence Day speech from the Red Fort, the first farmer to do so.[45]

The disintegration of the Janata Party proceeded against a background of despairing letters written by Jayaprakash Narayan to his protégés. In October 1979 JP died, a broken man. The liberal editor A. D. Gorwala paid tribute to Narayan as 'the great moral force of the country, the touchstone of right and wrong'. His 'last great effort', wrote Gorwala, was the formation and victory of the Janata Party, whose 'narrow, stupid partisan men . . . absorbed in their own self-interest and self-importance, failed him badly'.[46] Those self-absorbed men – Morarji Desai, Charan Singh, Jagjivan Ram – all came to JP's funeral in Patna, as, more strikingly, did Sanjay Gandhi and his mother. 'Poor old J. P.!', wrote Mrs Gandhi to a friend afterwards. 'What a confused mind he had leading to such a frustrated life!' She attributed his twists and turns to 'Gandhian hypocrisy', to the vow of celibacy extracted from him when he married the Mahatma's disciple Prabhavati. 'That and jealousy of my father probably conditioned the rest of his life', she remarked, adding: 'It is nonsense to say that he did not want office. One part of him did, very much so. He was torn between that and the desire to be regarded as a martyr and a saint.'[47]

There is a certain spitefulness in this assessment, and also a certain loftiness of tone. For Mrs Gandhi was having the last laugh, with regard not just to her old friend turned rival but also to the party he had created. Back in July, when Morarji Desai had resigned and his successor was being chosen, the journal *Himmat* presciently remarked that 'Mrs Gandhi is the only one who would like to have a mid-term poll – and would gain from it in the present climate. It is in her interest to have Mr Charan Singh installed as Prime Minister but only for two to three months.'[48]

Charan Singh was sworn in as prime minister in the last week of July 1979; a month later the Congress (I) informed the president that they were withdrawing support. It took the president a further month to explore and reject the alternatives. When he decided that a mid-term poll was the only solution, the Election Commission still needed time to prepare for it. So Charan Singh stayed on as prime minister until the end of the year, two full months more than *Himmat* had given him.

IX

The Janata Party came to power on a wave of hyperbole, with talk of a second freedom from authoritarian rule and a resounding restoration of democracy. Almost from its first weeks in office, the party seemed determined to squander this goodwill. It was soon noticed that in both the centre and the states Janata ministers were grabbing the best government bungalows, raiding the Public Works Department for air-conditioners and carpets, organizing lavish parties and weddings for their relatives, running up huge telephone and electricity bills, travelling abroad at the slightest pretext (or on no pretext at all).[49] Even traditionally anti-Congress journals were writing about the 'death of idealism' within Janata, of how it had so quickly become a 'political party of the traditional type', its members 'interested more and more in positions and perquisites and less and less in affecting society'. It was being said that while it had taken the Congress thirty years to abandon its principles, Janata had lost them within a year of its formation.[50]

Looking back on the three years of the Janata regime, one analyst remembered it as 'a chronicle of confused and complex party squabbles, intra-party rivalries, shifting alliances, defections, charges and counter-charges of incompetence and the corruption and humiliation of persons who had come to power after the defeat of Mrs Gandhi'.[51] Most Indians who lived through those years would make the same assessment, if more succinctly; the Janata Party, they would say, were merely a bunch of jokers. It takes a distinguished foreign observer to remind us that, beyond the fighting and squabbling, the Janata government made a notable contribution to Indian democracy. This, in the words of Granville Austin, was its 'remarkable success in repairing the Constitution from the Emergency's depredations, in reviving open parliamentary practice through its consultative style when repairing the Constitution, and in restoring the judiciary's independence'.[52]

The initiative here was taken by Morarji Desai. In an interview on the eve of the 1977 election, he remarked that during the emergency, democracy itself had been 'vasectomised'. If his party won, they would 'work for the removal of fear which has enveloped the people'. Then they would undertake 'to rectify the Constitution'. Morarji was clear that 'we will have to ensure that Emergency like this can never be imposed. No Government should be able to do so.'[53]

After Janata's victory, the job of repairing the constitution was supervised by the hard-working law minister Shanti Bhushan. The key amendment to be overturned was the 42nd. To replace its 'defiling' provisions, two fresh amendments were drafted, which reverted the term of Parliament and state assemblies to five years, restored the right of the Supreme Court to adjudicate on all election matters (that of the prime minister included), limited the period of President's Rule in the states, made mandatory the publication of parliamentary and legislative proceedings and made the promulgation of a state of emergency much more difficult. Any such act had now to be approved by a two-thirds majority in Parliament, had to be renewed every six months after a fresh vote on it, and had to be in response to an 'armed rebellion' (rather than a mere 'internal disturbance', as was previously the case). These changes were intended to curb the arbitrary powers of the executive and to restore the rights of the courts; in effect, to restore the constitution to what it was before Mrs Gandhi's emergency-era amendments.

The drafting of these amendments took time, because of the demands of legal precision and the need to ensure the kind of cross-party support that would make their passing in both Houses of Parliament possible. As these restorations were being debated, the press was reporting avidly on the Shah Commission, while a string of books and memoirs documenting the excesses of the emergency were being published. In this climate of opinion, even the Congress was in no mood to defend the changes in the constitution that its leaders had wrought. That damage was now undone by the freshly drafted 44th Amendment. When this was passed by a comfortable majority on 7 December 1978, among those voting for it were those two old enemies, Morarji Desai and Indira Gandhi.[54]

X

Although it failed to last its full term, the victory of the Janata Party was a watershed in Indian politics. For the first time since Independence a party other than the Congress came to govern at the centre. In the states too the landscape of politics became more variegated, with the victory of the communists in West Bengal, and that of the AIADMK in Tamil Nadu.

The Indian political system was being *decentred*, and not just in party terms. For the late 1970s also witnessed the flowering of numerous 'new' social movements. In 1978 there was a major conference of 'socialist-feminists' in Bombay, which focused on the growing violation of women's rights. Campaigns were launched against dowry and rape, against male alcoholism and the sexual abuse it frequently resulted in, and for better working conditions for women labouring in factories and household units. This new wave of feminism was widespread as well as wide ranging, with groups active in many states, mobilizing support through public rallies, street theatre, poster campaigns and house-to-house canvassing.[55]

The late seventies also saw the assertion of a vigorous environmental movement. Peasants launched struggles in defence of their forest rights, tribals protested against their displacement by large industrial projects and artisanal fisherfolk opposed trawlers that were depleting the fish stocks of the ocean. In these protests two things stood out: the leading role of women, who themselves bore the brunt of ecological degradation, and the fact that, unlike in the West, where the concern for nature was couched in aesthetic terms and voiced by the middle class, this was an 'environmentalism of the poor', driven by rural communities for whom access to the gifts of nature was linked to their very survival.[56]

Both the feminist movement and the environmental movement actually started in the early 1970s. Their progress was interrupted by the emergency, but when that ended they emerged once more and with renewed vigour. The same was the case with the civil rights movement. This had its origins in the treatment of Naxalite activists incarcerated in Calcutta jail. When these prisoners began a *bidi-chitti andolan*, a struggle for access to cigarettes and letters (denied them by their jailers), a retired engineer named Kapil Bhattacharya decided to form an Association for the Protection of Democratic Rights. The emergency inspired the formation of other such groups, based in Delhi, Bombay, Hyderabad and elsewhere. Some focused on 'civil liberties', the violation by the state of the basic human rights of its citizens. Others worked with a broader concept of 'democratic rights', which took the right to life and liberty guaranteed by the constitution also to mean the right to better wages and working conditions, and to gainful employment itself. The first kind of group took up jail reform and the abuse of power by state authorities (and the police in particular); the second kind also looked at the impact of state policies on the lives and livelihoods of the less privileged, the low castes and tribals in particular. These groups produced dozens of reports on the violations of civil liberties and democratic rights by the state, drawing on field investigations, often in remote parts of the country, conducted by public-spirited intellectuals based in the cities.[57]

These movements were described as 'new' because they took up issues neglected by the old, class-based social movements of peasants and workers. However, the late 1970s also saw those older concerns expressing themselves in new forms. Thus the trade union movement, which had historically focused on the factory sector, now began working among miners and labourers in household and cottage industries. Among the more notable initiatives was the Chhattisgarh Mineworkers Shramik Sangh (CMSS), whose leader Shankar Guha Niyogi sought to blend the ideas of Gandhi and Marx. The mines where the CMSS was active serviced the great public-sector steelworks at Bhilai. Working with miners of a chiefly tribal background, Niyogi campaigned for equal pay for women workers and against alcohol abuse by men, set up schools for children, and struggled to make the mine owners pay as much attention to health and safety as to a decent living wage.[58]

Accompanying and complementing these movements was a new kind of Indian press. For the end of the emergency unleashed the energies of journalists as only the struggle for national independence had done before it. Censorship was dead; there were now no limits to what reporters and editors could write about, or to the length of their stories. It also helped that the first offset presses arrived in India in the 1970s. No longer had type to be laboriously set in hot metal; no longer had journals to be printed in the bigger towns and cities alone.

The historian Robin Jeffrey has authoritatively tracked 'India's Newspaper Revolution' which began in 1977 and has gathered pace ever since. Among the components of this revolution we may single out five. Two were enabled by the new technology: the simultaneous printing of multiple editions of the same paper in towns far distant from one other and the enhancement of print quality and, especially, of the production of pictures and other visual material. Other innovations were a product of changes in society and politics: the end of censorship facilitated the rise of investigative journalism, of hard-hitting stories on crime and political corruption. The spread of education and the expansion of the middle class gave an enormous fillip to Indian-language journalism. A national readership survey, conducted in 1979 and restricted to the towns and cities, estimated that as many as 48 million urban Indians regularly read a periodical of some kind. The fastest increase was in the smaller towns and among Indian languages. In 1979, for the first time, those who read newspapers in Hindi (a language spoken by 40 per cent of Indians) numbered more than those who read them in English (a language spoken by a mere 3 per cent of Indians). The new journalism substituted a colloquial and demotic prose for the stiff, formal style once preferred by editors and reporters. Idioms and phrases derived from the classical Sanskrit, once *de rigueur*, were now abandoned in favour of the rhythms and cadences of everyday speech.[59]

Two somewhat contradictory trends were apparent in the India of the late 1970s. On the one hand there was an increasing fragmentation of the polity, as manifest in the rapid turnover of governments. With ever fewer exceptions, politicians and parties had abandoned ideology for expediency, and principle for profit. On the other hand there were new forms of social assertion among historically subordinated groups such as low castes, women and unorganized workers. There was now, for the first time, an active civil liberties movement. The press, which during the emergency had mostly been cowed without a fight, had become livelier than ever before.

Viewed from the more formal, purely political side, it appeared that Indian democracy was being corroded and degraded. If one took a more 'social' view, however, it appeared that Indian democracy was, in fact, being deepened and enriched.

24

DEMOCRACY IN DISARRAY

Not every individual or party is always disposed to use our democratic framework to further constructive purposes. It seems that the exercise of the democratic right sometimes takes the form of freedom even to destroy.

INDIRA GANDHI TO JAYAPRAKASH NARAYAN, May 1968

I

WRITING SHORTLY AFTER THE 1977 elections, the *Guardian* correspondent in India thought that the return to democracy might be short lived. 'Democracy can only survive if there is economic progress and reform,' he wrote. 'Already, the new [Janata] government faces an economic crisis; inflation rampant again, an explosion of wage demands, and a wave of strikes. If it is overwhelmed by protest, the cycle of repression could start all over again.'[1]

Altogether more optimistic was the old India hand Horace Alexander, now eighty-seven and living in retirement in a Quaker home in Pennsylvania. In a letter published in the *New York Times* Alexander said that 'the astonishing Indian elections' showed that 'the common people of India have political courage', this derived from Gandhi and the heritage of the freedom movement. In a letter to a fellow Quaker he likewise called the poll verdict 'a triumph for the common people of India', adding: 'Let none ever say that "democratic liberty" is a bourgeois conception, which is only meaningful to a small number of left-wing intellectuals.'[2]

The indefatigable Alexander also wrote to Mrs Gandhi. During the emergency he had peppered her with anxious letters about the fate of freedom and of the men she had detained. Now he remembered his old friend Jawaharlal Nehru saying that he wished he could have had a spell away from politics, to read and simply relax. He wondered whether Nehru's daughter, out of power, would 'spend some time enjoying birds, up in the Himalaya, or in Kashmir'. There was some chit-chat about art and literature, and then the letter concluded: 'We shall try to keep up with the news from India, and perhaps in five years from now, you will be in office once again with the biggest majority ever. Such is democracy!'[3]

Actually, it took less than three years for Mrs Gandhi to return to power. Her Congress Party won 353 seats in the 1980 elections, one more than in the 'Garibi Hatao' campaign of 1971. It did very well in the south, as before, while in the north it benefited hugely from a division of the vote between the two rival Janata factions, here contesting as separate parties. In the key state of Uttar Pradesh, for example, the Congress obtained 36 per cent of the popular vote, yet won 60 per cent of the parliamentary seats. One Janata faction got 22.6 per cent of the vote, the other 29 per cent; between them, they won 32 seats in the state to the Congress's 50.[4]

The 1980 elections, notes the editor Prabhas Joshi, marked the 'end of ideology' in Indian politics. Previous polls were fought and won on the planks of democracy, socialism, secularism and non-alignment. In 1980, however, Mrs Gandhi spoke not of the abolition of poverty but of her ability to rule. Janata could not hold together a government, she told the voters; whereas she could and had. Their bickerings apart, there were other factors that went against Janata. There were shortages of basic consumer goods, attributed naturally to the party in power. As one election cry went: '*Janata ho gayi fail, Kha gayi chini aur mitti ka tel*' (The Janata party has failed, Eaten up sugar and paraffin on the way).[5]

The Janata Party had thoroughly discredited itself. As a reporter covering the elections found, while Indira Gandhi had a 'tarnished image', her opponents were 'all tarnish and no image'.[6] Meanwhile, the rash of attacks on Scheduled Castes turned this very numerous voting segment back towards the Congress. Sanjay Gandhi had apologized to the Muslims for the excesses of the emergency; sections of this 'vote bank' returned to the fold as well.[7]

In most of India the elections were moderately free. In parts of Bihar and Uttar Pradesh, however, where roads were poor and telephone lines non-existent, the Election Commission was unable to monitor or check the capturing of booths by armed gangs. Here, there was a 'free enterprise militia' operating, such that 'adult franchise ha[d] been replaced by vicarious franchise', where the candidate with the most guns at his command could 'perform the function of "mass voting" on behalf of the electorate'.[8]

II

Not long after Mrs Gandhi returned to power, a veteran political scientist with Congress sympathies advised the prime minister to remake the party as 'the palpably real institution that the Congress was under Nehru'. For it was 'essential that a sharing of power replace its personalisation, that a leadership drawing its power from the grassroots rather than above should be allowed to emerge'. Mrs Gandhi's 'restored charisma' could then be used 'in the service of shoring-up and reinforcing the institutions of an open polity before it dissipates again as in the past'.[9]

These sentiments were at once noble and naive. For it was not just the Congress Party that Mrs Gandhi believed she embodied, but the Indian nation itself. In May 1980 she told a visiting journalist how, 'for many long years, I have been the target of attack [from] individuals, groups and parties', these either 'Hindu and Muslim fanatics', or 'old feudal interests', or 'sympathetic to foreign ideologies'. Where she stood 'for India's unfettered independence of action, self-reliance and economic strength', those 'who are against self-reliance, or secularism or socialism find some reason or other to malign me'.[10]

'Paranoia' may be the most appropriate word here. Anyway, in this frame of mind Indira Gandhi was in no mood to share power except with her son Sanjay, who was now both a member of Parliament and the general secretary of the Congress Party. Indeed, as one Delhi journal remarked, Sanjay was once more 'the most vital factor in Indian politics'. When Mrs Gandhi dismissed nine state governments after the 1980 elections it was Sanjay who allotted the Congress tickets for the assembly seats, Sanjay who decided who would be chief minister when and if Congress won. The newly appointed chief minister of Uttar Pradesh, Vishwanath Pratap Singh, spoke for many when he told the press that 'Sanjay is a leader in his own right and he is my leader too'.[11]

Mrs Gandhi was now sixty-three, and thoughts of the succession were not far from her mind. However, on 23 June 1980 Sanjay was killed while flying a single-engined plane for fun, as he was wont to do. He did three loops in the air, tried a fourth but lost control. The plane crashed a mere 500 yards from the home he shared with his mother. Both Sanjay and his co-pilot died instantly.[12]

Mrs Gandhi returned to work four days later. She was desperately lonely, one reporter remarking on her 'total and inviolable aloofness'.[13] By the end of August she had persuaded her elder son to fill the breach. Rajiv Gandhi had shown little previous interest in politics. He was a family man, devoted to his Italian wife Sonia and their two small children. He worked as a pilot with the sole domestic carrier, Indian Airlines. He flew Avros to Lucknow and Jaipur, and his main professional ambition was to be allowed to pilot Boeings between Delhi and Bombay.

Now, however, there was increasing pressure on him to enter politics, most of it coming from the prime minister herself. Speaking to an interviewer in August 1980, Rajiv Gandhi said that there was 'no question of my stepping into [Sanjay's] shoes'. Asked whether he would take up a party post or contest elections, Rajiv answered that he 'would prefer not to'. He added that his wife was 'dead against the idea of my getting into politics'.[14]

Nine months later Rajiv Gandhi was elected an MP from his brother's old constituency, Amethi. When asked why he had changed his mind, Rajiv answered: 'The way I look at it is that Mummy has to be helped somehow.' His entry into politics, wrote one *very* sympathetic journalist, 'surreptitious though it is, may be Mrs Gandhi's concept of giving India stability in leadership and continuity in government'. With the 'lack of leadership of any kind on the horizon', being a member of the Nehru family gave him a 'high identification quotient' and 'a head start'.[15]

Recognizing the signs – or bowing to the inevitable – Congress members and ministers all across the country queued up to *salaam* Rajiv. He was asked to lay foundation stones for medical colleges, open plants generating electricity for Harijan colonies and give speeches to Congress clubs on Nehru's birthday.[16]

As Rajiv Gandhi took his first steps in Indian politics, his mother was at work on the world stage, rebuilding bridges torn down during the emergency. Mrs Gandhi was deeply concerned about the battering her image had taken in the West. Now that she had been returned to power via the ballot box, she was determined to repair the damage. For a full eight months in 1982 the United Kingdom hosted a Festival of India, featuring exhibitions of Indian art at the Victoria and Albert Museum, concerts by Ravi Shankar and M. S. Subbulakshmi at the Royal Festival Hall and much else. The performers ran the gamut from the high and classical to the earthy and folk. Thus a high school in Worcestershire was turned into a 'miniature Rajasthan', with dancers and storytellers from that state camping for a week, their performances repaid in kind by the school putting on a performance of Kipling's *Jungle Book*.

The festival was promoted and part-funded by the government of India. The Indian prime minister visited the UK at its beginning and end, emerging as the 'star of the show'. During the emergency, sections of the British press had portrayed Mrs Gandhi as an ogress; now, commented one columnist, 'she must welcome the somewhat more flattering attention she is receiving'. At one function, where she and the British prime minister were the chief guests, Mrs Gandhi said that 'India was committed to democracy and socialism', adding that 'in respect of the latter we differ from Mrs Thatcher'. Meeting a group of newspaper editors, she tartly remarked: 'I hope you will give up calling me Empress of India now'.

The Festival of India was deemed a great success by its organizers; encores were to follow in the United States, the Soviet Union and France. The last word on the *tamasha* might rest with the cartoonist R. K. Laxman, who portrayed two half-naked men on an Indian street, with one reading a newspaper and saying to the other: 'But for such a festival we wouldn't know how great we and our achievements are!'[17]

III

Cartoonists are professionally obliged to mock the mighty, but in Laxman's case his comments might also have had something to do with the fact that he lived in Bombay, a city where the extremes of wealth and poverty were more strikingly manifest than anywhere else in India. As it happened, the festival in London coincided with an indefinite strike by the textile workers of Bombay. They were led into action by Datta Samant, a medical doctor whose political ideology was uncertain but who possessed sufficient charisma to allow him to supplant the socialists and communists who had hitherto led the city's trade unions.

Datta Samant's career in Bombay began with a unit called Empire Dyeing, where he was able to get the workers a salary increase of Rs200 a month. His success encouraged him to move into other factories; soon, the bulk of the workers in Bombay's vast textile industry owed their allegiance to him. Their wages had grown incrementally over the years;

inadequately protected against inflation, they sought an overhaul of the salary structure. Samant asked that the minimum wage be increased from Rs670 to Rs940 a month; when the demand was rejected out of hand, he called for a strike. Beginning on 18 January 1982, the strike was to last almost two years. More than 200,000 workers participated, and more than 22 million man-days of work were lost.

This was a genuine mass movement, the ripples from which were felt throughout the city and beyond. Thousands of workers courted arrest; others clashed with blacklegs seeking to break the strike. The truculent mood affected other sectors of the city's labour force. Underpaid police constables sought to form a union of their own; their protests spilled out into the streets. Eventually, the policemen had to be disarmed and jailed by the paramilitary Border Security Force.[18]

In the countryside too there were stirrings along class lines. Naxalite activists, detained during the emergency but released afterwards, were making their presence felt in the tribal areas of Andhra Pradesh among communities oppressed by the state's forestry department and by Hindu moneylenders. Other Naxalite groups were at work in the plains of central Bihar, organizing Harijan labourers against their upper-caste landlords. Some sympathizers, such as the Swedish writer Jan Myrdal, saw in these stirrings the possibility, and hope, that the Chinese revolution might one day find its Indian counterpart.[19]

The early 1980s saw fresh mobilization on the lines of ethnicity as well. The movement for a tribal state of Jharkhand had taken new and more militant forms. By official figures, some Rs30,000 million had been spent on 'tribal development' in the Chotanagpur plateau. Where this money had gone it was hard to say, for the people still lived in 'a primeval darkness'; without schools, hospitals, roads or electricity, with their lands seized by outsiders and their forests closed to them by the state. 'The Jharkhand demand is set against such a background', reported the writer Mahasweta Devi. 'Tales of woe and exploitation on the one hand; the pulse of resistance on the other.'[20]

The protests in Jharkhand were led by Shibu Soren, a young man with long black locks who quickly became a folk hero. He organized the forced harvest of paddy in lands 'stolen' from the adivasis by *dikus* (outsiders), as well as the invasion of forest lands that they claimed as their own. In September 1980 the police fired on a crowd of protesting tribals at Gua, killing at least fifteen people. The incident served only to intensify the demand for Jharkhand.[21]

There were also demands, if not as actively expressed as in Jharkhand, for two new states: Chhattisgarh, to be carved out of the tribal areas of Madhya Pradesh, and Uttarakhand, constituting the Himalayan districts of Uttar Pradesh. These too were regions rich in timber, water and minerals, in resources increasingly exploited by and for the benefit of the larger national economy, yet dispossessing the local inhabitants in the process.[22]

The 1980s also saw a renewal of Naga militancy. During the emergency the government of India had been able to persuade many members of Phizo's Naga National Council to lay down their arms and come out of hiding. Some in the administration hoped that this 'Shillong Accord' (named for the town where it was signed) would signal the end of the rebellion. However, the accord was seen as a sell-out by Naga radicals such as T. Muivah. Muivah was a Tangkhul Naga who, in the 1960s, had been one of the first to seek the help of China. Muivah had stayed four years in Yunnan, being trained by the People's Liberation Army. Deeply impressed by the Cultural Revolution, he sought to blend its ideals with the faith he was born into, thus to combine evangelical Christianity with revolutionary socialism.

In 1980 Muivah and Isak Swu set up the National Socialist Council of Nagaland (NSCN). By now Chinese aid had dried up, so Muivah instead built up links with other insurgent groups in India's north-east and in Burma. A journalist who met him in his jungle hideout reported Muivah's view that 'the only hope the Nagas had to achieve their independence would be if India itself broke up'. The Naga leader had his contacts among Sikh militants and Kashmiri separatists, and 'he fervently hoped a similar movement would emerge among the Tamils of southern India – which would indeed plunge the country into the anarchy he desired'.[23]

Muivah's strongest following was among his fellow Tangkhuls, who lived in the upland areas of Manipur. Were an independent Naga nation ever formed these hills would be part of it, but as things stood the Tangkhuls were less than happy to be ruled by the Meitei Hindus who were Manipur's dominant community. Worried by the birth of the NSCN, the Indian government increased troop deployment in the Ukhrul district of Manipur. On 19 February 1982 the insurgents ambushed a convoy on the Imphal–Ukhrul road, killing twenty-two soldiers of the Sikh Regiment, some officers among them. The army's answer was to go on a rampage, searching every village in the district, abusing the men and attacking the women. A civil liberties team visited the area, recording the testimonies of the victims. They found that 'even though only a few people supported the underground they were all suspects in the eyes of the army'.[24]

IV

There were movements for separate or new states within or outside the Union, and movements for greater autonomy within existing states. In the old Congress stronghold of Andhra Pradesh there was growing resentment at the centre's tendency to 'impose' chief ministers. Between 1978 and 1982 Mrs Gandhi changed the state's chief minister no fewer than four times. In February 1982 the new incumbent, T. Anjaiah, went to Hyderabad airport to welcome Rajiv Gandhi, accompanied by a huge posse of supporters with garlands. Rajiv chastised the chief minister for bringing a crowd, and in such strong words that there were tears in Anjaiah's eyes.[25]

The humiliation was felt personally, and collectively, with the Telugu media portraying it as an insult to the pride of the Andhras. Among those provoked into action was the great film star N. T. Rama Rao, who was to Telugu cinema what M. G. Ramachandran had been to its Tamil counterpart – its acknowledged hero and superstar. (By one reckoning he had acted in 150 movies; by another, 300. A third source chose to be much more precise, putting the number at 292.)

Unlike MGR, 'NTR' had no political past. Nor did his films usually carry a social message (they were mostly based on mythological themes). Now, on the eve of his sixtieth birthday, he formed a new regional party, Telugu Desam, which stood for 'the honour and self-respect of the 60 million Telugu speaking people'. No longer, he said, would the great state of Andhra Pradesh be treated as a 'branch office' of the Congress Party.[26]

The new party was formed in March 1982; elections to the state assembly were due at the end of the year. In preparation for the polls, NTR toured the districts of the state, speaking out against the 'corrupt' administration of the Congress. He travelled in a van remodelled to look like a chariot. At public meetings he would emerge dramatically from the vehicle, atop a platform raised with the help of a generator. He usually wore saffron, the colour of renunciation, indicating that he had given up his film career to serve the people. He was the mythological hero made real, come to rid the world of greed and corruption and bring justice for all. Women flocked to his meetings – he, in turn, offered them universities of their own and the preferential allotment of jobs in the state sector.[27]

While the national press was sceptical of NTR's chances, the major Telugu daily *Eenadu* threw its considerable weight behind him. Its confidence was rewarded when the Telugu Desam won a comfortable two-thirds majority in the assembly. In the second week of January 1983 Rama Rao was sworn in as chief minister at the Fateh Maidan in Hyderabad, with 200,000 cheering Andhras crowded into the grounds.[28]

One of NTR's first acts on assuming power was to instruct his food department to sell rice at two rupees a kilogram, to redeem a promise made before the polls. In general he acted as if he was the party as well as government, in this respect emulating his friend MGR as well as his rival Indira Gandhi. 'If the Prime Minister thinks that she is India', commented one socialist, then 'NTR behaves as if he is the sole representative of six and half crores of Telugu people. Telugu Desam MLAs have no voice in shaping the policies and programmes of the Government. NTR runs the show both as Chief Minister and also as the President of his party.'[29] Like Mrs Gandhi again, NTR was prone to nepotism, as when he allowed a film studio to be built by his son on unauthorized land.[30]

V

Another, more serious, movement for autonomy was taking shape in the state of Assam; 'more serious' because it was driven by a groundswell of grass-roots opinion rather than by individual charisma, and because this state was located not in the Indian heartland but in its long-troubled extremities.

Assam shared borders with West Bengal and several states of the north-east, as well as with the countries of Bangladesh and Bhutan. Assamese was the state language, but Bengali was also widely spoken. There was a long history of hostility between the speakers of the two languages. Bengalis had dominated the middle and lower rungs of the colonial administration. As officials, teachers and magistrates they exercised great authority and power over the local Assamese, treating them with condescension and even contempt. Beginning in the late nineteenth century, land-hungry Bengali peasants had begun to move into the forests and lowlands of Assam. After Independence this migration continued, accelerating whenever political instability or economic crisis affected East Bengal or, as it later became, Bangladesh. In the decade of the 1970s, for example, the number of registered voters in Assam jumped from 6.2 million to almost 9 million, the increase accounted for chiefly by immigrants from Bangladesh.[31]

The Assamese feared cultural subordination at the hands of the Bengali middle class, and demographic conquest at the hands of the Bengali peasantry. There were episodic riots in the 1950s and 1960s aimed at driving the immigrants back to where they came from. However, it was only from the late 1970s that these sentiments were transmuted into a widespread social movement.[32]

The key organization in this transformation was the All-Assam Students Union (AASU). Its network extended throughout the state; all student unions in schools and colleges were affiliated to it. Beginning in 1979 and carrying on over the next five years, the AASU led hundreds of strikes and processions intended to press the central government to clear their homeland of the infiltrators.

Assamese nationalists had based their arguments on culture and demography. AASU added a third leg to the stool: economics. The economy of Assam was manifestly dominated by outsiders. The rich tea plantations of the state were mostly owned by firms based in London or Calcutta. Assam had India's most productive oil fields, yet the liquid was pumped up by public-sector firms that employed few locals (and none at the top level of management). Worse, the oil was then sent to refineries located in other states. Local trade and commerce was controlled by Marwaris from Rajasthan. All in all, Assam was an 'internal colony', supplying cheap raw materials for metropolitan India to process and profit from.

The Assam movement's larger demand was for a new economic policy, where the state's residents could obtain income and employment from the best use of the state's natural resources. Its more immediate demand, however, was for the deletion of immigrants from the voters' list preparatory to their deportation from the state. This led to an unfortunate but perhaps inevitable polarization on communal lines. For many of the more recent immigrants were, in fact, Muslims. The Congress Party, then ruling in the centre and long dominant in the state, was accused of protecting the immigrants as a captive vote bank. Also hastening the polarization was the formation of an All-Assam Minorities Students Union (AAMSU).[33]

Visiting Assam in the summer of 1980, a Delhi journalist found that the 'movement had undoubtedly acquired gigantic proportions'. No longer was it confined to the literate or articulate. The Assamese people as a whole felt 'increasingly frustrated, driven to the wall. Aside from the anti-foreigner sentiment, the movement has developed other dangerous strains – anti-Bengali, anti-Left, anti-Muslim, anti-non-Assamese, and slowly but discernibly, even anti-Indian.'[34] Bengalis were being attacked and their homes burnt. But the central government was also targeted. Railway tracks were uprooted by individual saboteurs, while the AASU stopped the export of plywood and jute from the state. They were even successful in blocking the flow of oil, forcing the government to declare the pipeline and the land extending up to half a kilometre on either side of it a 'protected area'. Ultimately the army had to be called in to restore oil supplies from Assam to a refinery in distant Bihar.[35]

In the last week of July 1980 the prime minister warned the AASU leaders that their actions could lead to retribution. 'Suppose other states refused to supply Assam with steel?' she asked. 'How would the Assamese develop their industry?' Indian federalism was based on interdependence. For 'it was only in the shadow of a bigger unit that each unit can survive; otherwise outside pressures will be too great to bear'.[36]

Even as this warning was issued, however, the central government had begun negotiations with the AASU leaders. The talks were to continue for the next three years, on and off, sparking fresh strikes and protests whenever they broke down. Officially the negotiators were the AASU on one side and the Home Ministry on the other. But numerous interlocutors were also used, among them the Gandhi Peace Foundation and the Manipur chief minister R. K. Dorendra Singh. The real bone of contention was the cut-off date beyond which immigration could be considered 'illegal'. The AASU wanted all migrants who came in after 1951 to be removed from the voters' list and deported. The government of India thought this struck at the federal principle, violating the freedom of citizens to move from one part of the country to another. They were prepared, however, to recognize 1971 as the cut-off date, for it was then that the happenings in East Pakistan had provoked an unprecedented, so to say unnatural migration across the borders.

By one account, representatives of government and the agitation met on as many as 114 days in the calendar years 1980, 1981 and 1982. Various compromises were discussed: one, suggested by the Gandhi Peace Foundation, recommended that those who entered Assam between 1951 and 1961 be conferred rights of residence and voting (in effect, citizenship), those who came between 1961 and 1971 be dispersed to other states of India, and those who came after 25 March 1971 (the date on which Bangladesh declared itself a sovereign state) be deported.[37]

In the event, a solution proved intractable. The conflict resumed, taking ever uglier forms. In one particularly gruesome incident in February 1983 hundreds of Bengali Muslims were slaughtered by a mob of Assamese Hindus and tribals. Thus was fulfilled the grim prediction of the veteran journalist Devdutt, who, writing when the talks between the movement and the government were in their early stages, noted that if a resolution was not arrived at, 'like the turbulent Brahmaputra coursing along 450 miles in Assam, the seething discontent and disaffection will also wreak havoc'.[38]

VI

Contemporaneous with the Assam movement, there was a still more serious agitation for greater autonomy in the state of Punjab. I say 'still more serious' because Punjab bordered Pakistan, a country with which India had fought three wars. Besides, the majority community of the state were not Hindus but Sikhs. To the primordial attachments of language and region was thus added the potentially deadly element of religion.

As in Assam, the Punjab 'agitation', or 'movement', or 'crisis' (to give it three among its many names) had causes both distant and proximate. A section of the Sikh intelligentsia hoped for the renewal, in some shape or form, of the Sikh state ruled by Maharaja Ranjit Singh in the first half of the nineteenth century. Others looked only as far back as Partition, and the tragedies and losses suffered by the community then. It had taken twenty years of almost ceaseless struggle to compel New Delhi to constitute a Sikh majority province within India. However, even after the new Punjab was formed in 1966, the major Sikh political party, the Akali Dal, was unable authoritatively to *rule* the state. It rankled deeply that in 1967 and 1969 the Akalis had to form unstable coalitions with 'Hindu' parties such as the Jana Sangh, whereas in 1971 its old rival, the Congress, was able to come to power in the Punjab on its own.[39]

In October 1973 the Working Committee of the Akali Dal passed the 'Anandpur Sahib Resolution'. This asked the government of India to hand over Chandigarh to Punjab (it then shared the city with Haryana); to also hand over Punjabi-speaking areas then with other states; and to increase the proportion of Sikhs in the army. Asking for a recasting of the Indian Constitution on 'real federal principles', it said that 'in this new Punjab and in other States the Centre's interference would be restricted to defence, foreign relations, currency, and general administration; all other departments would be in the jurisdiction of Punjab (and other states) which would be fully entitled to frame [their] own laws on these subjects'.

By one reading, the Anandpur Sahib Resolution merely sought to make real the promise of states' autonomy hinted at by the constitution. But the Resolution was also amenable to more dangerous interpretations. The preamble spoke of the Akali Dal as 'the very embodiment of the hopes and aspirations of the Sikh *Nation*'. The 'political goal of the Panth [community]' was defined as 'the pre-eminence of the Khalsa [or Sikh brotherhood]', with the 'fundamental policy' of the Akali Dal being the 'realization of this birth-right of the Khalsa through creation of congenial environment and a political set-up'.[40]

Perhaps 1973 was not the best time to make these demands, with Mrs Indira Gandhi riding high on the wave of a war recently won and the centre more powerful than ever before. Its powers were increased still further with the emergency, when thousands of Akalis were put in jail. But in 1977 the emergency was lifted, elections called, and the Congress Party comprehensively trounced. With the Akalis now in power in the Punjab, the demands of the Anandpur Sahib resolution were revived, and new ones added. Among the losses at Partition were two of the five rivers that gave the state its name; if that was not bad enough, the Indian Punjab had to share the remaining three with the states of Haryana and Rajasthan. The Akalis claimed a greater share of these waters; to this economic demand was coupled a cultural one, the designation of Amritsar, home to the holiest Sikh shrine, the Golden Temple, as a 'Holy City'.[41]

In April 1978 there was a mass convention at Amritsar of a religious sect, the Nirankaris. The Nirankaris thought of themselves as Sikhs, but since they believed in a living Guru were regarded as heretics by the faithful. With the Akalis in power, some priests professed shame that the Holy City was being profaned thus. Leading the opposition to the Nirankari meeting was a hitherto obscure preacher named Jarnail Singh Bhindranwale. Born into a family of Jat Sikhs, Bhindranwale had left his wife and children to become head of a seminary called the Damdami Taksal. His was an impressive presence: over six feet tall, slim and athletic, with probing eyes and dressed in a long blue robe. He was an effective and even inspiring preacher, with a deep knowledge of the Sikh scriptures. He claimed that Sikhs 'were slaves in independent India', discriminated against by the Hindus. Bhindranwale wanted the Sikhs to purify themselves and return to the fundamentals of their faith. He spoke scathingly of the corrupt and effete Hindu, but mocked even more the modernized Sikh, he who had so far forgotten himself as to cut his hair and consume tobacco and alcohol.[42]

By some accounts, Bhindranwale was built up by Sanjay Gandhi and the Union home minister Zail Singh (himself a former chief minister of Punjab) as a counter to the Akalis. Writing in September 1982 the journalist Ayesha Kagal remarked that the preacher 'was originally a product nurtured and marketed by the Centre to cut into the Akali Dal's sphere of influence'.[43] The key word here is 'originally'. For whoever it was who first promoted him, Bhindranwale quickly demonstrated his own independent source of charisma and influence. To him were attracted many Jats of a peasant background who had seen the gains of the Green Revolution being cornered by the large landowners. Other followers came from the lower Sikh castes of artisans and labourers; they saw in the process of purification their own social advancement. Bhindranwale also benefited from the general increase of religiosity which, in the Punjab as in some other places, followed upon rapid and unexpected economic development.[44]

While the Nirankari convention was in progress at Amritsar in April 1978 Bhindranwale preached an angry sermon from the precincts of the Golden Temple. Moved by his words, a crowd of Sikhs descended upon the place where the heretics were meeting. The Nirankaris fought back; in the battle that ensued, fifteen people died.

Sikh pride took another blow in 1980, when the Akalis were dismissed and the Congress returned to power in Punjab. In June of that year a group of students met at the Golden Temple and proclaimed the formation of an independent Sikh republic. The republic had a name,

Khalistan, and a president, a Sikh politician based in London named Jagjit Singh Chauhan. Primarily it was Sikh émigrés who were behind this move; the pronouncement was made simultaneously in the United Kingdom, the United States, Canada and France.[45]

The government in Delhi was not unduly worried by these elements at the fringe. Its attention was focused on the Akalis, who, out of power, had chosen the path of confrontation. Their new leader, Sant Harcharan Singh Longowal, lodged himself in the Golden Temple, from where he would announce street protests on a variety of themes such as the handing over of Chandigarh, or the greater allocation of canal water. Bhindranwale was operating from another part of the temple. He had acquired a group of devoted gun-toting followers who acted as his acolytes and bodyguards and, on occasion, as willing and unpaid killers.

Through the early 1980s the politics of agitation co-existed uneasily with the politics of assassination. In April 1980 the Nirankari leader Baba Gurcharan Singh was shot dead in New Delhi. It was widely believed that Bhindranwale was behind the killing, but no action was taken. Then in September 1981 came the murder of Lala Jagat Narain, an influential editor who had polemicized vigorously against Sikh extremism. This time a warrant went out for the preacher's arrest. The police went to pick him up from a *gurdwara* in Haryana, but by the time they arrived Bhindranwale had returned to the safety of his own seminary in the Punjab. The chief minister, Darbara Singh, was all for pursuing him there, but he was dissuaded by the Union home minister, Zail Singh, who was worried about the political fall-out that might result. Bhindranwale then sent word that he was willing to turn himself in, but at a time of his choosing, and only so long as the arresting officers were Sikhs wearing beards. Amazingly, the Punjab government agreed to these humiliating terms. Two weeks after the murder the preacher gave himself up outside his seminary, even as a crowd of supporters chanted slogans and threw stones at the police. At several other places in the state his followers attacked state property, provoking the police to fire on them. According to one report, a dozen people died in the violence surrounding Bhindranwale's arrest.[46]

Three weeks later he was released for lack of evidence. Two chroniclers of the Punjab agitation write that 'Bhindranwale's release was the turning point in his career. He was now seen as a hero who had challenged and defeated the Indian government'. Another says that with the drama of his arrest 'Bhindranwale had transformed himself from a murder suspect [into] a new political force'.[47]

Throughout 1982 there were many rounds of negotiations between the centre and the Akalis. No agreement was reached, the sticking points being the areas Punjab would give up to Haryana in exchange for Chandigarh, and the sharing of river waters. On 26 January 1983, Republic Day, the Akali legislators in the state assembly resigned, the timing of their action suggesting perhaps an uncertain commitment to the Indian Constitution. The challenge of Bhindranwale was forcing them to become more extreme. The Akalis were now prone to comparing Congress rule to the bad old days of the Mughals. They began organizing *shaheed jathas* (martyrdom squads) to fight the new tormentors of the Sikhs.[48]

On 22 April 1983 a high-ranking Sikh policeman, A. S. Atwal, was killed as he left the Golden Temple after prayers. The man who shot him at close range coolly walked in afterwards. Atwal's murder further demoralized the Punjab police, itself overwhelmingly Sikh. A spate of bank robberies followed. Sections of the Hindu minority began fleeing the state. Those who remained organized themselves under a Hindu Suraksha Sangh (Defence Force). Centuries of peaceable relations between Hindus and Sikhs were collapsing under the strain.

In interviews, Bhindranwale described the Sikhs as a 'separate *qaum*', a word that is sometimes taken to mean 'community' but which can just as easily be translated as 'nation'. He had not asked for Khalistan, he said, but were it offered to him he would not refuse. The prime minister of India he mocked as a 'Panditain', daughter of a Brahmin, a remark redolent with the contempt that the Jat Sikh has for those who work with their minds rather than their hands. Asked whether he would meet Mrs Gandhi he answered, 'No I don't want to, but if she wants to meet me, she can come here.'[49]

To his followers, Bhindranwale could be even more blunt. 'If the Hindus come in search of you', he told them once, 'smash their heads with television antennas.' He reminded them of the heroic history of the Sikhs. When the Mughals had tried to destroy the Gurus, 'our fathers had fought them with 40 Sikhs against 100,000 assailants'. They could do the same now with their new oppressors. There was also a contemporary model at hand – that of Israel. If the few Jews there could keep the more numerous Arabs at bay, said Bhindranwale, then the Sikhs could and must do the same with the Hindus.[50]

On 5 October 1983, terrorists stopped a bus on the highway, segregated the Hindu passengers and shot them. The next day President's Rule was imposed in the state. In the last weeks of 1983 Bhindranwale took up residence in the Akal Takht, a building second in importance only to the Golden Temple. The latter, standing in the middle of a shimmering blue lake, is venerated by Sikhs as the seat of spiritual authority; the former, an imposing marble building immediately to its north, had historically served as the seat of temporal authority. It was from the Akal Takht that the great Gurus issued their *hukumnamas*, edicts that all Sikhs were obliged to follow and honour. It was here that Sikh warriors came to receive blessings before launching their guerrilla campaigns against their medieval oppressors.[51] That Bhindranwale chose now to move into the Akal Takht, and that no one had the courage to stop him, were acts steeped in the most dangerously profound symbolism.

VII

The rise of communal violence in the Punjab falsified numerous predictions made about the province and its peoples. In the 1950s it was claimed that the Sikhs would become increasingly 'Hinduized', indeed, become a sect of the great pan-Indian faith instead of standing apart as a separate religion. In the 1960s it was argued that, having tasted power, the Akali Dal would become 'secularized'; that its rhetoric and policies would henceforth be directed by economic rather than religious considerations. By the 1970s conflict had replaced consensus as the dominant motif of Punjab social science, except that the trouble, when it came, was expected to run along the lines of class, with the Green Revolution turning Red.

By the beginning of the next decade, however, the situation of the Sikhs in India was being compared to that of the Tamils in Sri Lanka. Here, as there, wrote the political scientist Paul Wallace in 1981, 'language, religion and regionalism combined into a potentially explosive context which political elites struggle to contain'.[52] Within the next year or two this mixture had been made still more deadly by the addition of a fourth ingredient: armed violence.

Hindu–Sikh conflict was, in the context of Indian history, unprecedented. While it was manifesting itself, other older and more predictable forms of social conflict were also being played out. Thus the journalist

M. J. Akbar, compiling his reports of the 1980s into a single volume, called the book *Riot after Riot* – a title that was melancholy as well as appropriate.[53]

One axis of this conflict was, naturally, caste. In January–February 1981 the state of Gujarat was convulsed by clashes between forward and backward castes. The issue under contention was the reservation of seats in engineering and medical colleges for those of low status. The Harijans in particular were very scantily represented, both as students and teachers. Of 737 faculty members in the medical colleges of Gujarat, only 22 were Harijan. However, their demands for greater representation were bitterly resisted. The conflict spread well beyond the students. Even the textile workers of Ahmedabad, long united under one banner, were soon divided on caste lines. At least fifty people died in the violence.[54]

A second axis of conflict, even more naturally, was religion. During the Janata regime the communal temperature had begun to rise alarmingly. With politicians allied to it in power in the centre and in the states, the Rashtriya Swayamsevak Sangh grew in strength and influence. In 1979 there was a major riot in the steel town of Jamshedpur; a judicial inquiry ordered by the government concluded that the RSS 'had a positive hand in creating a climate which was most propitious for the outbreak of communal disturbances'.[55]

After the Janata party's rout in the 1980 elections, its Jana Sangh members broke away to form a party of their own. They called it the Bharatiya Janata Party (BJP), but the new name did little to disguise a very old aim. There was once more a distinct political party to represent and advance the 'Hindu' interest. As it happened, the formation of the BJP heralded a wave of religious violence in northern and western India. There were major Hindu–Muslim riots in the Uttar Pradesh towns of Moradabad (August 1980) and Meerut (September– October 1982); in the Bihar town of Biharsharif in April–May 1981; in the Gujarat towns of Vadodara (September 1981), Godhra (October 1981) and Ahmedabad (January 1982); in Hyderabad, capital of Andhra Pradesh, in September 1983; and in the Maharashtra towns of Bhiwandi and Bombay in May–June 1984. In each case the riots ran on for days, with much loss of life and property, and were finally quelled only by armed force.[56]

From the plentiful literature on these numerous riots can be discerned some recurrent themes.[57] The riots were generally sparked by a quarrel that was in itself trifling. It could be a dispute over a piece of land claimed by both Hindus and Muslims, or over street space claimed by both Hindu and Muslim hawkers. It could be provoked by a pig straying into a mosque or a dead cow being found near a temple. Sometimes the cause was the coincidence of a Hindu and a Muslim festival leading to encounters on the street of large processions of both communities.

However, once begun, most disputes quickly escalated. The role of rumour was critical here, with the original incident being magnified in each retelling until a simple clash between two individuals had become a holy war between two simultaneously violated religions. Communal organizations helped this escalation, as did party rivalries, with local politicians identifying with one side or the other. Words gave way to blows, fisticuffs to sword fights, these in turn to firebombs and bullets. The police either looked on or were partisan. In the states of Bihar and Uttar Pradesh they invariably favoured the Hindus, encouraging and sometimes even participating in the looting of Muslim homes and shops.

Riots typically took place in towns where the Muslims constituted a significant proportion of the population – between 20 per cent and 30 per cent – and where some of them had lately climbed up the economic ladder, for example as artisans servicing a wider market. Whoever started the quarrel – and there were always claims and counter-claims – it was the Muslims and the poor who were the main sufferers: the Muslims because, even while numerous enough to fight their corner, they were in the end outnumbered by a factor of two or three to one; the poor because they lived in the crowded parts of town, in homes built from fragile or inflammable materials. A fire, once begun, would quickly engulf the whole locality. The middle class, on the other hand, lived in spacious residential colonies where it was easier to ensure personal as well as collective security.

In India, caste and communal conflict had usually run in parallel, but in the 1980s they began subtly influencing one another. A critical event here was the decision of an entire village of Harijans in Tamil Nadu to convert to Islam. On 19 February 1981 1,000 residents of Meenakshipuram became Muslims. With their religion and personal names, they even changed the name of their village; henceforth, they said, it would be known as 'Rehmatnagar'.

The Meenakshipuram incident provoked outrage among the RSS and its sister organizations. The cry was raised of 'Hinduism in danger', and the sinister hand of 'Gulf money' seen in the conversions. The Arab countries, it was claimed, were using their petrodollars to proselytize in the subcontinent, with Indian Muslims being willing accomplices.

Islamic preachers were indeed active in the area, but the Harijans were also reacting to the continuing oppression by upper-caste landlords, and to the discrimination they faced in entering schools and obtaining government jobs. Their hope was that they could escape social stigma by embracing a faith which preached equality for all its believers.[58]

VIII

To the historian, there are uncanny parallels between the first years of Mrs Gandhi's first term as prime minister and the first years of her second. These, like those, were years of trouble, and more trouble. Between 1966 and 1969 the Congress Party and the central government faced serious challenges from within the democratic system – as, for instance, the victories of the DMK in Madras and of the United Front in Bengal – and from without, such as the Mizo rebellion and the Naxalite insurgency. To add to all this, famine loomed large and there were serious scarcities of essential goods.

How Mrs Gandhi tackled that crisis we have already seen, our reconstruction aided by the colossal hoard of papers preserved by her principal secretary P. N. Haksar. By 1980 Haksar had left her, so there is no similar paper trail by which we can reconstruct the prime minister's response to this new crisis, caused by a fresh wave of ethnic and regional movements, and by the intensification of communal conflict.

In 1969 and 1970, the route taken by Mrs Gandhi was ideological: the reinvention of herself as the saviour of the poor and the forging of a new party and of new policies to go with it. What path might she have taken now, had she P. N. Haksar by her side? Or what path might she have taken if Sanjay Gandhi were still alive?

Such speculation is, of course, academic. What we do know is that from late 1982 or thereabouts the prime minister had begun thinking seriously about her re-election. She did not want a repeat of that 1977 defeat. To avert the possibility she decided that, when the polls came, she would present herself as the saviour of the nation, safeguarding its unity against the divisive forces that threatened it.[59]

The non-Congress parties, meanwhile, were equally sensible of the next election, and the need to build a common front. Leading the unity moves was N. T. Rama Rao, who convened a meeting of opposition parties in Vijayawada in May 1983. In attendance was the new chief

minister of Jammu and Kashmir, Farooq Abdullah, son of Sheikh
Abdullah, who had taken his father's job when the Sheikh passed away
in 1982.

The prime minister was irritated by the NTR's initiative, and angered
by Farooq's participation in it. When fresh elections were held to the
Jammu and Kashmir state in 1983 she campaigned vigorously for her
Congress Party. In speeches in the Hindu-dominated Jammu region she
portrayed Farooq as a quasi-secessionist. The divide between Jammu
and the Kashmir Valley had previously been presented in communal
colours, but never before by an Indian prime minister. It was a dangerous
gambit, and it didn't work – Farooq and his National Conference were
comfortably re-elected.[60]

Meanwhile, the conflict in the Punjab assumed dangerous proportions.
The attacks on Hindu civilians grew more frequent. On 30 April 1984
a senior Sikh police officer, a particular scourge of the terrorists, was
killed. Then, on 12 May, Ramesh Chander, son of the editor Jagat Narain
and inheritor of his mantle, was also murdered. By now Bhindranwale's
men had begun fortifying the Golden Temple, supervised by Shubeg
Singh, a former major general of the Indian army, a one-time hero
of the 1971 war who had trained the Mukti Bahini.

Under Shubeg's guidance the militants began laying sandbags on
turrets and occupying high buildings and towers around the temple
complex. The men on these vantage points were all in wireless contact
with Shubeg in the Akal Takht. An attack by government troops was
clearly anticipated. The defences were prepared in the hope that they
might hold out long enough to provoke a general uprising among Sikhs
in the villages, and a mass march towards the besieged temple. Enough
food was stocked to last the defenders a month.

The other side too was preparing for action. On 31 May Major General
R. S. Brar was summoned from Meerut, where he was in charge of an
infantry division, and told he would have to lead the operation to rid the
temple of terrorists. Brar was a Jat Sikh, whose ancestral village was but
a few miles from Bhindranwale's. And he knew Shubeg Singh well – the
latter had been Brar's instructor at the Indian Military Academy at
Dehradun and they had worked together in the Bangladesh operations.

Brar was briefed by two lieutenant generals, Sundarji and Dayal. The
government, he was told, believed that the situation in the Punjab had
passed out of control of the civil administration. The centre's attempts
to arrive at a settlement with Akalis had run aground. The Akalis had

failed to convince Bhindranwale to dismantle the fortifications and leave the temple. And they were themselves getting more militant. The Akali leader Sant Longowal had announced that on 3 June he would lead a movement to stop the passage of grain from the state. A siege was considered, and rejected, because of the fear of a rebellion in the countryside. The prime minister had thus decided, 'after much reluctance', that the militants had to be flushed out. Brar was asked to plan and lead what was being called 'Operation Bluestar', with the mandate that it should be finished in forty-eight hours if possible, with no damage to the Golden Temple itself and with minimum loss of life.[61]

Within twenty-four hours of this briefing the army began moving into Amritsar, taking over control of the city from the paramilitary. On 2 June a young Sikh officer entered the temple, posing as a pilgrim, and spent an hour walking around, carefully noting the preparations made for its defence. Patrols were also sent to study the vantage points occupied by the militants outside, which would have to be cleared before the assault.

On the night of the 2nd, the prime minister spoke on All-India Radio. She appealed to 'all sections of Punjab' not to 'shed blood, [but] shed hatred'. The call was disingenuous, since the army was already preparing for its assault. On the 3rd, Punjab's road, rail and telephone links were cut off, but in Amritsar itself the curfew was lifted to allow pilgrims to mark the anniversary of the martyrdom of Guru Arjun Dev.

The next day saw sporadic firing in the temple's perimeter as the army tried to knock out the towers occupied by the militants. That day and the next announcements were broadcast over loudspeakers asking pilgrims to leave the temple. The attack itself was launched on the night of the 5th. Brar's hope was that the peripheral parts of the temple would be seized by midnight, after which a lodgement would be placed within the Akal Takht, reinforcements sent up and the whole place cleared by the morning of the next day. His plan grievously underestimated the number of militants, their firepower, their skill and their resolve. Every window in the Akal Takht had been boarded up, with snipers placed to fire through cracks from within. Other militants with machine guns and grenades were scattered through the complex, using their knowledge of its narrow passages and verandahs to launch surprise attacks on the advancing troops.

By 2 a.m. on the 6th the troops were a fair way behind schedule. Brar writes that 'due to intense multi-directional fire of the militants, our forces were unable to get close enough [to the Akal Takht] to achieve any degree of accuracy'.[62] Finally, permission from Delhi was requested to use tanks to break the defences. By dawn, several tanks – the estimates range from five to thirteen – had broken through the temple's gates and taken up position. Through much of the day they rained fire on the Akal Takht. In the evening it was deemed safe to send troops into the building to capture any defenders who might still remain. They found Shubeg Singh dead in the basement, still clutching his carbine, with a walkie-talkie next to his body. Also found in the basement were the bodies of Bhindranwale and his devoted follower, Amrik Singh of the All India Sikh Students' Federation.

The government estimated the death toll at 4 officers, 79 soldiers and 492 terrorists. Other accounts place the number of deaths much higher; at perhaps 500 or more troops, and 3,000 others, many of these pilgrims caught in the cross-fire.

'Notwithstanding the fact that by converting the House of God into a battlefield, all the principles and precepts of the ten Sikh gurus were thrown overboard', remarks R. S. Brar, 'it must be admitted that the tenacity with which the militants held their ground, the stubborn valour with which they fought the battle, and the high degree of confidence displayed by them merits praise and recognition.'[63] It is impossible not to sympathize with the writer of these words, whose own job was, without question, the most difficult ever assigned to an Indian army commander in peacetime or in war. The Sikh general to whom both Brar and Shubeg reported during the liberation of Bangladesh had this to say about Operation Bluestar: 'The army was used to finish a problem created by the government. This is the kind of action that is going to ruin the army.'[64]

IX

The Golden Temple is ten minutes' walk from Jallianawala Bagh where, in April 1919, a British brigadier ordered his troops to fire on a crowd of unarmed Indians. More than 400 people died in the firing. The incident occupies a hallowed place in nationalist myth and memory; the collective outrage it provoked was skilfully used by Mahatma Gandhi to launch a countrywide campaign against colonial rule. Operation Bluestar differed in intent – it was directed at armed rebels, rather than a peaceable gathering – but its consequences were not dissimilar. It left a collective wound in the psyche of the Sikhs, crystallizing a deep suspicion of the government of India. The Delhi regime was compared to previous oppressors and desecrators, such as the Mughals, and the eighteenth-century Afghan marauder Ahmad Shah Abdali.[65] A reporter touring the Punjab countryside found a 'sullen and alienated community'. As one elderly Sikh put it, 'Our inner self has been bruised. The base of our faith has been attacked, a whole tradition has been demolished.' Now, even those Sikhs who had previously opposed Bhindranwale began to see him in a new light. For, whatever his past errors and crimes, it was he and his men who had died defending the holy shrine from the vandals.[66]

The view from outside the Punjab was quite different. Many people commended Mrs Gandhi for taking firm (if belated) action against terrorists claimed to be in the pay of Pakistan. The prime minister herself was now prompted to move against elements in other states who were opposed to her. For some time now she had been pressing for the dismissal of Farooq Abdullah's government in Jammu and Kashmir. When the state's governor, her own cousin B. K. Nehru, told her it would be unconstitutional, he was replaced by Sanjay Gandhi's old lieutenant Jagmohan. In July 1984 Jagmohan engineered a split in the ruling National Conference and declared the leader of the rump faction the new chief minister. Bags of money were sent by the Congress Party in Delhi to bribe Kashmiri legislators into deserting their leader. Farooq was not given the opportunity to test his majority on the floor of the House. Indeed, the dismissal order was served on him in the middle of the night, as it had been on his father who, back in 1953, had likewise been sent out of office on grounds of dubious legality and still more dubious morality. As B. K. Nehru wrote, the Kashmiris 'were convinced now at the second dethronement of their elected leader that India would never permit them to rule themselves.'[67]

A month later a change of regime was effected in Andhra Pradesh. Once more the governor, a former member of the Congress Party, played a malevolent role. A section of the Telugu Desam was induced to break away and, with Congress support, form a new government.[68] The dismissals of the J&K and Andhra chief ministers were in flagrant violation of democratic practice. These were not armed rebels but legally elected governments. One cannot rule out personal vindictiveness – it was NTR and Farooq, after all, who had first initiated the moves for opposition unity. The prime minister must also have calculated that it would help to have sympathetic regimes in place before the general election. Writing to a friend, she accused the opposition of having 'the single-minded objective of removing me'; their 'patchwork alliances', she claimed, were based on 'regionalism, communalism and casteism'.[69] It is tempting to turn the criticism on its head – certainly, many of Mrs Gandhi's own policies in 1983 and 1984 appear to have been dictated by the single-minded objective of winning the next general election.

In the aftermath of Operation Bluestar the prime minister had been warned by intelligence agencies of a possible attempt on her life. She was advised to change the Sikh members of her personal bodyguard. Mrs Gandhi rejected the suggestion, saying, 'Aren't we secular?'[70] On the morning of 31 October, while walking from her home to her office next door, she was shot at point-blank range by two of her security guards, Satwant Singh and Beant Singh. They were both Sikhs who had recently returned from a visit home, and been provoked by the hurt and anger they witnessed to take revenge for Operation Bluestar.

By the time the prime minister was admitted to hospital she was already dead. By early afternoon the foreign radio stations had put out the news, although All-India Radio made its own official announcement only at 6 p.m. Shortly afterwards her son Rajiv was sworn in as prime minister. When his mother was shot he was in Bengal; he rushed back to the capital, where a group of senior Cabinet ministers and Congress leaders unanimously decided that he should succeed his mother.

Later that night some incidents of arson and looting were reported in Delhi. The next morning the body of Mrs Gandhi was placed in Teen Murti House, where her father had lived as prime minister. All through that day, and the next, India's sole television channel, Doordarshan, showed the line of mourners streaming past the body. From time to time the cameras focused on the crowds outside, who were shouting slogans such as *Indira Gandhi amar rahe*' (Indira Gandhi shall be immortal) and, more ominously, *khoon ka badla khoon se lenge*' (Blood will be avenged by blood).

The violence that began on the night of 31 October spread and intensified through the first two days of November. The first serious episodes occurred in south and central Delhi; later, the action moved east across the river Yamuna, to the resettlement colonies located there. Everywhere it was Sikhs and Sikhs alone who were the target. Their homes were burnt, their shops looted, their shrines and holy books violated and desecrated. The mobs' deeds were accompanied by angry words: 'Finish off the Sardars', 'Kill the *gaddars* [traitors]', 'Teach a lesson to the Sikhs', were some of the slogans eyewitnesses reported hearing.

In Delhi alone more than a thousand Sikhs perished in the violence. Sikh males between eighteen and fifty years of age were particularly targeted. They were murdered by a variety of methods, and often in front of their own mothers and wives. Bonfires were made of bodies; in one case, a little child was burnt with his father, the perpetrator saying, '*Ye saap ka bachcha hai, isse bhi khatam karo*' (This offspring of a snake must be finished too).

The mobs were composed of Hindus who lived in and around Delhi: Scheduled Caste sweepers who worked in the city, and Jat farmers and Gujjar pastoralists from villages on the fringes. Often they were led and directed by Congress politicians: metropolitan councillors, members of Parliament, even Union ministers. The Congress leaders promised money and liquor to those willing to do the job; this in addition to whatever goods they could loot. The police looked on, or actively aided the looting and murder.[71]

Rajiv Gandhi's own comment on the riots was: 'When a big tree falls, the earth shakes'. Without question, the killing of Mrs Gandhi provoked strong feelings among her many admirers. Sections of the middle class venerated her for her conduct and leadership during the 1971 war; sections of the poor thought her the only Indian politician who empathized with their lot. And Hindus in general were dismayed at the happenings in the Punjab. The Khalistan movement, they believed, was aimed at tearing the country into pieces, and the fact that it was two Sikhs who had killed the prime minister seemed to confirm these fears. Immediately after Mrs Gandhi's killing rumours of other actions began to circulate. It was said that trains with dead bodies of Hindus were coming in from the Punjab, and that the capital's water supply had been poisoned by malcontents.

The public mood in Delhi was angry, distorted by happenings real and imagined. That said, Rajiv Gandhi's comment was still deeply insensitive. It was of a piece with the behaviour, overall, of the administration he was now asked to lead. By showing crowds baying for blood in Teen Murti House, state television was issuing a self-fulfilling prophecy. The police's indifference was shocking, the role played by Congress politicians positively immoral. But the lapse that perhaps signalled more than all the others was the unwillingness to call in the army. There is a large cantonment in Delhi itself, and several infantry divisions within a radius of fifty miles of the capital. The army was put on standby, but despite repeated appeals to the prime minister and his home minister P. V. Narasimha Rao, they were not asked to move into action. A show of military strength in the city on the 1st and 2nd would probably have quelled the riots – yet the order never came.

While Sikhs in the capital bore the brunt of the violence, there were also attacks on the community in other cities and towns of northern India. More than 200 Sikhs died in incidents in the state of Uttar Pradesh. Twenty Sikhs were killed in Indore, and as many as sixty in the steel town of Bokaro, where the mobs, as in Delhi, were led by local Congress politicians.

One city where the violence was minimal was Calcutta. There were 50,000 Sikhs resident in the city, many of them taxi-drivers, each one easily identified by his turban and beard. Very few were harmed; and not one died. The West Bengal chief minister, Jyoti Basu, had ordered the police to ensure that peace be maintained. The instructions were honoured, with the city's powerful trade unions keeping a vigilant eye. The example of Calcutta showed that prompt action by the administration could forestall communal violence; a lesson, alas, lost to the rest of the country.[72]

X

Mrs Gandhi's impact on the history of her country was definitive; as definitive, indeed, as her father's. Jawaharlal Nehru was prime minister of India for sixteen years and nine months. His daughter served in that post almost as long, albeit in two stretches: from January 1966 to March 1977, and then again from January 1980 to October 1984. These are the two figures of pre-eminent importance in the history of independent India. To compare one to the other is inevitable, and perhaps also necessary.

As a military leader Mrs Gandhi was immeasurably superior. Her decisiveness at the time of the Bangladesh crisis was in striking contrast to Nehru's wavering attitude towards the Chinese: now promising undying friendship, now issuing threats with no force to back them. So far as economic policies went, Nehru's stress on the public sector and self-reliance was in keeping with the spirit of the age, whereas in the 1960s, when the time had come to cautiously open up the economy to market forces, Mrs Gandhi instead further strengthened the hold of the state. Socially, both were genuinely non-parochial, seeking to represent all Indians, regardless of their gender or class, or religious and linguistic affiliation.

Where the advantage rests squarely with Nehru is with regard to the processes and procedures of democracy. This point was made, after Mrs Gandhi's death, by Krishna Raj, the editor of India's leading journal of public affairs, the *Economic and Political Weekly*. One point of contrast was how father and daughter treated the party to which both owed a lifelong allegiance. When Indira Gandhi took charge in 1966, wrote Krishna Raj, 'she found a reasonably well-organised Congress party, with several layers of responsive leadership across the length and breadth of the country'. But she then 'dismantled the party and she did so with a clear purposiveness. Because she did not trust anyone who would not play a subservient role to her and her family, she got rid of the intermediate leadership and re-built the party as a paper entity, without a democratic structure and with office-bearers personally selected and named by her.'

Tragically, it was not just the Congress Party that was made an extension of the prime minister's will. So was the government of India. Despite the ignominy of the China war, when Indira Gandhi came to power in January 1966 'India was a coherent nation, a nation marked by a quiet aura of social stability'. There was a set of socio-economic objectives around which it was united. The political class recognized the interconnection between means and ends. The 'faith was still widely shared that the paraphernalia of the state was never intended – at least not consciously intended – to be put to use for advancing private interests'. But by the time of Indira Gandhi's death there had been 'a qualitative transformation. India is a divided nation.' There were now 'deep wounds and deep dissensions'. The five-year plans, once acknowledged as 'an earnest statement of hopes and aspirations', now 'do not mean a thing'. Now, the 'apparatus of the state is all the time being manipulated for the sake of [the] fractional minority of the population at the top of the social hierarchy'. Now, 'the government at the centre is corrupt to the core and Indira Gandhi could not be absolved of direct responsibility for this state of affairs'.[73]

Sections of the Western press, meanwhile, saw dark days ahead for India. With Mrs Gandhi's death, wrote the *New York Times*, the country faced a 'period of prolonged uncertainty, with the potential for greater domestic instability and new tensions with its neighbours, particularly

Pakistan'. The New York *Sun* was even more pessimistic, writing that the prime minister's assassination 'has opened a bleak possibility that India may fly apart, internally, and become increasingly the catalyst for regional and global rivalries'. Some officials in Washington were worried that ethnic and religious rivalries would 'explode into general violence', that the country would fragment, and that 'a desperate leadership in India might look more and more to the Soviet Union for help'.[74]

This was not the first epitaph being written for the Union of India; nor would it be the last. Still, it is striking how, like the Congress sycophants, these Western observers appeared to think that Indira was, indeed, India. That this conclusion was reached provided further proof of the late prime minister's success in undermining the institutions that stood between her and the nation.

25

THIS SON ALSO RISES

In India the choice could never be between chaos and stability, but between manageable and unmanageable chaos, between humane and inhuman anarchy, and between tolerable and intolerable disorder.

ASHIS NANDY, sociologist, 1990

I

EVEN BY THE STANDARDS of Indian politics, 1984 was an especially turbulent year. The first week of June witnessed Operation Bluestar, an unprecedented attack by the state on a place of worship. The last day of October saw the assassination of Indira Gandhi, the first major political killing since that of Mahatma Gandhi. That murder had temporarily brought a halt to Hindu–Muslim violence; this one provoked a wave of violence by Hindus on Sikhs.

It was against this bloody backdrop that Rajiv Gandhi was sworn in as prime minister. A month after he took office, the country witnessed a tragedy that claimed as many lives as had the anti-Sikh riots. In the early hours of 3 December 1984 white smoke began filling the air of the central Indian city of Bhopal. Citizens asleep in their homes were woken up with fits of coughing, vomiting and a burning sensation in the eyes. In panic they got out of bed and went out into the street, the gas cloud following them. By dawn, 'the main thoroughfares of the city were jammed with an unending stream of humanity, plodding its way in search of safer surroundings'. Many fell down in the streets, overcome by dizziness and exhaustion. Others found their way, somehow, to the city's few modern hospitals, whose beds were rapidly filled to capacity.[1]

The deadly gas was methyl isocyanate (MIC), and it came from a pesticide plant owned and run by an American firm, Union Carbide. Stored in underground tanks, it was usually rendered harmless by a scrubber before being released into the atmosphere. However, on this night an unanticipated chemical reaction led to the release of MIC in its toxic state. The effects were devastating. Within hours of the leak, at least 400 people had died of exposure to the gas. The final tally was in excess of 2,000, making it the worst industrial accident in human history. The bulk of the victims lived in the slums and shanty towns which ringed the factory. Apart from those who died, another 50,000 would be affected for the rest of their lives by illness and injury caused by exposure to the gas.

In the wake of the tragedy came a wave of visitors to Bhopal, not all of them welcome. There were doctors who came to help, but also lawyers seeking an avenue of profit through a 'class action' suit on behalf of the victims to be filed in an American court of law. The CEO of Union Carbide came, was briefly arrested, then released on bail and flown back to New York. Ten days after the accident a team of Indian scientists came to neutralize the stocks of MIC that still lay in the Carbide factory. The project was named Operation Faith, but it inspired only distrust. Fearing a fresh leak, thousands of residents made to leave Bhopal, with 'the city bus terminal and the railway station present[ing] a chaotic scene . . . as fleeing people swarmed them carrying their essential belongings'.[2]

Investigations into the leak suggested a range of possible causes: that water had got into the tank; that the tank had not been properly cleaned; that the MIC was being stored at temperatures higher than recommended.[3] What was clear was that a potentially hazardous industry had no business to be in the city. Before the plant went into production in 1980, the town planner M. N. Buch recommended that Union Carbide choose a safer and less populated location. Indeed, as a report of June 1984 revealed, the history of the plant had been punctuated by gas leaks and burst pipelines – minor accidents, unacknowledged intimations of the major one that was waiting to happen.[4]

II

The accident in Bhopal occurred in the first week of December. At the end of the month, India witnessed its eighth general election. The polls were dominated by the murder and memory of Indira Gandhi. The Congress campaign, overseen by the advertising agency Rediffusion, presented Rajiv Gandhi as the logical heir to his mother's legacy, and the party itself as the only bulwark against the forces of secession. 'India could be your vote away from unity or separation', ran the punchline of one ad featuring Rajiv. 'Will the cast of '77 ever be united by a common ideology instead of a common greed for power?' ran another.[5] The Congress campaign, wrote one commentator, 'capitalized on the growing mass insecurities', whereby 'Mrs Gandhi's assassination was equated in the public mind with an assault on the Indian State and that perception was constantly reinforced.'[6]

When the results came in, the Congress had swept the polls, capturing almost 50 per cent of the popular vote and almost 80 per cent of the seats in Parliament. Under the leadership of a political novice, the Congress won 401 seats, far more than they ever had under Nehru or Indira Gandhi. However, as one of the prime minister's advisers admitted, 'the victory was as much his late mother's as his own'.[7]

The general election had been won by stoking the fear of secession: but now, with a comfortable majority in hand, the prime minister moved swiftly to make peace in the Punjab. The leaders of the Akali Dal were let out of jail and emissaries sent to talk to them. Sant Harcharan Singh Longowal seemed as keen as Rajiv Gandhi to put the past behind him. In July 1985 the two leaders signed an accord, agreeing to transfer Chandigarh to Punjab within a specified time frame, assuring Punjab a fair share of river waters and committing the government to a fresh review of centre–state relations in general. President's Rule was to be revoked and state elections held.

Following the agreement, Sant Longowal toured the Punjab, speaking at public meetings and preaching in *gurdwaras*. Everywhere he asked that the people support the moves for reconciliation. While addressing a congregation in Sangrur, Longowal was shot dead by two young men, who held him to have betrayed the Sikh cause by breaking bread with the rulers in New Delhi. The incident occurred on 20 August; bravely, the government chose to go ahead with assembly elections in late September. The Sant's death created a wave of popular support for his party. The Akali Dal won a comfortable majority, for the first time in the province's history. With two-thirds of the adult population casting their ballots, the polls were interpreted as a vote against extremism.[8]

Meanwhile, at the other end of the country, the government also clinched an agreement with the All-Assam Students Union. The two sides agreed on cut-off dates for 'infiltrators': those who had arrived after 1 January 1966 but before 25 March 1971 (when the civil war in

East Pakistan began) would be allowed to stay but not vote, while those who came later would be identified and deported. Here too President's Rule was ended and elections called. A student's union transformed itself into a political party, with AASU members creating the Asom Gana Parishad (AGP). When polls to the state assembly were held in December 1985 the AGP trounced the once-dominant Congress. The new chief minister, Prafulla Mahanta, was only thirty-two years of age; many of his legislators were even younger. As in Punjab, the result was hailed as a vindication of democracy. Senior Congress figures in Delhi argued that, while their party had lost, the Republic of India had won. 'Men who were distributing dynamite earlier were handling poll posters,' remarked one Union Minister: 'From a nationalistic point of view is that victory or defeat?'[9]

In June 1986 the government of India signed a peace agreement with Laldenga, leader of the Mizo National Front. By its terms, the MNF rebels laid down their arms and were granted an amnesty against prosecution. The government agreed to grant full statehood to Mizoram, and Laldenga himself assumed office as chief minister, taking over from the Congress incumbent. The model here was the Kashmir agreement of 1975, when Sheikh Abdullah had returned to power in a similar fashion.[10]

One journal remarked that Rajiv Gandhi 'had brought to the Mizos the goodwill of the nation'; as he had previously done to the Sikhs and the Assamese.[11] Although these agreements had actually been envisioned and drafted by officials – such as the veteran diplomat G. Parthasarathi – the credit accrued to the young prime minister, who was seen as standing above party rivalries in the interests of national reconciliation. In all three cases, parties or leaders opposed to the Congress had come to power through peaceful means.

III

That Rajiv Gandhi was an outsider in politics was to his advantage. In the popular mind, 'his name was not associated with any controversial issues, he was not aligned to any caucus, and he had not yet created a coterie of his own'. His appeal was enhanced by his youth – he was still under forty in 1984 – his good looks, and his open manner. Here was a 'fine gentleman, thoroughly well-meaning, earnest and honest . . . [H]is indulgent countrymen stuck the label "Mr Clean" on him'.[12]

Rajiv's main advisers also came from outside politics. They included Arun Singh and Arun Nehru, two friends from the corporate sector who were made ministers. Like him, they were young and English speaking. Like him, they were at ease with modern technology. They made manifest their intention to take India directly from the sixteenth century to the twenty-first, from the age of the bullock cart to the age of the personal computer. In some parts of the media the new recruits attracted derision or amusement, being known as 'Rajiv's computer boys'. In other parts they attracted approbation; here, Rajiv Gandhi was compared to John F. Kennedy, who had likewise 'symbolised youth and the hope of a new generation', assembling a 'team of the best and the brightest' to carve a new future for his land.[13]

In the first year of his term the prime minister was often on tour, making his acquaintance with parts of the country he had not previously seen. Rajiv Gandhi's 'Discovery of India' was appreciatively covered in the press, and on television. The 1980s had seen an enormous growth in the ownership of TV sets. With broadcasting still a state monopoly, the government channel, Doordarshan, shot and showed hundreds of hours featuring the young and handsome prime minister in the field: on a houseboat in Kashmir, in a remote tribal hamlet, among coconut trees in Kerala. Everywhere, he met ordinary Indians and received their petitions, passing them on to the district administration for action.[14]

The first crisis of the new regime was, in fact, caused by a petition. It had, however, been submitted not to the prime minister but to the Supreme Court of India. The petitioner was an elderly man named Mohammed Ahmed Khan, who wished to appeal against a lower court's decision demanding that he pay monthly maintenance to his divorced wife, Shah Bano. Khan contended that he had fulfilled his duties by paying Shah Bano an allowance for three months, the period specified (he claimed) under Islamic law. In rejecting Khan's appeal, the Supreme Court invoked Section 125 of the Criminal Procedure Code, whereby a divorced woman was entitled to claim an allowance from her ex-husband if he had taken another wife (as Khan had), and if she had not remarried and could not otherwise maintain herself (as was the case with Shah Bano). Section 125, noted the Court, 'was enacted in order to provide a quick and summary remedy to a class of persons who are unable to maintain itself. What difference would it then make as to what is the religion professed by the neglected wife, child or parent?' In their opinion, the explanations to the Criminal Procedure Code showed 'unmistakably, that Section 125 overrides the personal law, if there is any conflict between the two'.

M. A. Khan had first filed the appeal in 1981; it took four years for the case to come to judgement. Dismissing the appeal on 23 April 1985, the Supreme Court confirmed that Khan would have to continue to pay Shah Bano maintenance as fixed by the High Court (at the curious figure of Rs179.20 per month). Then the judges went beyond the specifics of the case to make some general remarks. They deplored the fact that Article 44 of the constitution, mandating a uniform civil code, 'has remained a dead letter'. They observed that 'a belief seems to have gained ground that it is for the Muslim community to take a lead in the matter of reforms of their personal law. A common civil code will help the cause of national integration by removing disparate loyalties to laws which have conflicting ideologies.'[15]

In some circles these remarks were taken as a gratuitous chastisement of the minority community as a whole. Muslims took exception to the judges, saying that 'it is alleged that the "fatal point in Islam is the degradation of women"'. (In fairness, they had also noted that the Hindu law-giver, Manu, believed that 'the woman does not deserve independence'.) Muslim clerics criticized the judgement as an attack on Islam. Mosques up and down the country 'resounded with the voices of mullahs and maulvis denouncing Shah Bano and the Supreme Court judgement'.[16] On the other hand, some Muslim scholars supported the verdict, or at any rate held it to be not inconsistent with scripture, where there existed 'ample and respectable Islamic authority' for the proposition that the divorcing husband must provide maintenance until his ex-wife's death or remarriage.[17]

Three months after the Supreme Court judgement an MP named G. M. Banatwala moved a private member's bill in Parliament seeking to exempt Muslims from the purview of Section 125. The bill was opposed in the House by the minister of state for home affairs, Arif Mohammed Khan, representing, so to say, the 'progressive' Muslim point of view. He defended the Court's judgement by quoting Maulana Azad, who was at once the most famous nationalist Muslim and an acknowledged authority on the scriptures. The Maulana had written that the 'Quran takes occasion to re-emphasize that proper consideration should be shown to the divorced woman in every circumstance'. This call 'was based on the reason that she was comparatively weaker than [a] man and her interests needed to be properly safeguarded'. Further, argued

Khan, 'we should have better practices these days and only if the down-trodden are uplifted, the Islamic tenets can be said to have been followed and justice done'.[18]

Arif Mohammed Khan had the support of the prime minister; with the Congress voting against it, the bill was defeated. However, the debate carried on outside the House. In her native Indore, the 75-year-old Shah Bano was denounced by conservatives as an infidel; demonstrations were held outside her house and neighbours were asked to ostracize her. On 15 November Shah Bano succumbed to the pressure, affixing her thumb impression to a statement saying that she disavowed the Supreme Court verdict, that she would donate the maintenance money to charity and that she opposed any judicial interference in Muslim personal law.[19]

Towards the end of 1985 the Congress Party lost a series of byelections in northern India. Commentators saw a 'Shah Bano factor' at work, with rivals of the Congress 'whipping up religious fervour' by attacking the Supreme Court in constituencies with large Muslim populations.[20] Reports of the alienation alarmed Rajiv Gandhi, who, within his party and Cabinet, began increasingly taking the advice of the conservative Z. A. Ansari rather than the liberal Arif Khan. In a three-hour speech in Parliament Ansari attacked the Supreme Court verdict as 'prejudiced, discriminatory and full of contradictions'. The judges, he added maliciously, were 'small men who were incompetent to interpret Islamic law'.[21]

By now, it was not merely Shah Bano who had succumbed to the pressure. The Congress itself had 'accorded recognition to fundamentalists as the sole spokesmen of their community'.[22] In February 1986 the government introduced a 'Muslim Women's Bill' in Parliament which sought to overturn the Supreme Court verdict, by taking Muslim personal law out of the purview of the Criminal Procedure Code. The bill placed the burden of supporting the divorced wife on her own relatives; all the husband was obliged to do was provide three months' maintenance. In May, the bill passed into law, with the Congress issuing a whip to its members to vote for it. Abandoned by his leader, his party and his government, Arif Mohammed Khan resigned, telling an interviewer that with this new legislation 'Indian Muslim women will be the only women to be denied maintenance anywhere in the world'.[23]

The controversy sparked by the Shah Bano case was in many ways a reprise of the debates over the reform of Hindu personal laws three decades previously. Then, too, attempts to enhance gender equity had been bitterly resisted by priests claiming to speak for the community as a whole. The claim was tested and found wanting, when Jawaharlal Nehru fought and won the 1952 elections on, among other things, the issue of the Hindu Code Bill.

Faced with a comparable situation in 1985–6, Rajiv Gandhi already had the support of 400 MPs. A reform of Muslim personal law to enhance the rights of women was comfortably within reach. So, even, was a gender-sensitive common civil code (as asked for by the constitution). What was lacking was a prime minister consistently committed to social reform. For as a high official in Rajiv Gandhi's government was to recall later, 'in the handling of the aftermath of the Shah Bano case the young P[rime] M[inister] was suddenly overwhelmed by the political system'. His initiatives in the Punjab and Assam had shown boldness and independence, but here, after first supporting the reformists, he had given way to the conservatives for fear of losing the Muslim vote. And so, 'Rajiv Gandhi the statesman started transforming himself into a politician'.[24]

IV

Ten months after the Supreme Court handed down its verdict in the Shah Bano case, a judgement by a lower court provoked a controversy more furious still. On 1 February 1986 the district judge of the town of Ayodhya, in Uttar Pradesh, ordered that the locks be opened to permit worship at a small Hindu shrine. Despite its modest size this was a rather special place. It was located inside a large mosque, built as far back as the sixteenth century by a general of the Mughal emperor Babar (and hence known as the Babri Masjid). Moreover, it was claimed that the site was the birthplace of the Hindu deity Ram, and that before the mosque was built, it had been home to a temple devoted to his worship.

There is no evidence that the hero of the epic Ramayan was a historical character, but Hindu sentiment and myth widely held that he was, and that he had been born in Ayodhya at the very spot where the mosque was later built. The site was known locally as Ram Janmabhoomi, literally, the piece of earth where Ram was born. Through the nineteenth century there were a series of clashes between rival groups claiming possession of the place. The British rulers then effected a compromise, whereby Muslims continued to worship inside the mosque, while Hindus made offerings on a raised platform outside.

Two years after India became independent in 1947 an official sympathetic to Hindu interests allowed an idol of the child Ram (Ram Lalla) to be placed inside the mosque. This was done under cover of darkness, and devotees were persuaded that it had appeared miraculously, a sign that the displaced deity wanted to reclaim his birthplace. Fresh tension broke out, defused only by an order allowing the worship of Ram Lalla on a single day in December. For the rest of the year, the idol was kept locked away from worshippers.

For three decades the status quo held until, in the early eighties, an organization named the Vishwa Hindu Parishad (World Hindu Council) began campaigning for the 'liberation of the spot where Ram was born'. The VHP brought under one banner hundreds of monks from the numerous old temples that dotted Ayodhya. Processions and public meetings were organized, where fiery speeches were made urging Hindus to free their god from 'a Muslim jail'. A local lawyer then filed a suit seeking public worship of the Ram idol. It was in response to this appeal that the district judge ruled that the locks be opened, and worship allowed.[25]

The judge's order was widely believed to have been directed from Delhi, from the Prime Minister's Office, no less. The local administration seemed to know of the judgement beforehand, for the locks were opened within an hour of the verdict. Remarkably, even the national TV channel was at hand to capture on camera the precise moment when devotees rushed into the newly opened shrine. There appeared to be a strong connection between the Muslim Women's Bill and the Ayodhya verdict. It was said that Rajiv Gandhi opened the locks on the advice of his colleague Arun Nehru, who thought the Congress now needed to compensate the chauvinists on the other side. A left-wing MP commented sarcastically that while the prime minister presented himself as a thoroughly modern man, striving to take India into the twenty-first century, in fact 'he has a mind as primitive as the *mullahs* and the *pandits*'.[26] Or, as the political analyst Neerja Chowdhury wrote, 'Mr Rajiv Gandhi wants both to run with the hare and hunt with the hounds'. If one act was aimed at the 'Muslim' vote, this other one seemed to target the far larger 'Hindu' vote. Chowdhury warned that 'a policy of appeasement of both communities being pursued by the government for electoral gains is a vicious cycle which will become difficult to break'.[27]

The opening of the locks emboldened the Vishwa Hindu Parishad. They now sought nothing less than the demolition of the mosque, and its replacement with a grand new temple dedicated to Ram. The VHP was working closely with the Rashtriya Swayamsevak Sangh, the older Hindu organization which was enjoying a fresh lease of life. The RSS and VHP held meetings across India demanding that the 'majority' stand up for their rights. The Muslim Women's Bill was adduced as yet another example of the Congress government seeking to placate the minority. Only Hindus, it was alleged, were asked to disown their faith in this mistakenly 'secular' state. A new slogan was coined and broadcast: *Garv se kaho hum Hindu hain!* (Say you are a Hindu, and say it with pride.)

This message, as the weekly *India Today* wrote in May 1986, 'struck a high-strung emotional chord. Slowly but surely, like a juggernaut gaining angry momentum, a palpable, resurgent, united and increasingly militant movement of Hindu resurgence is sweeping across the land'. Here was a movement that was 'revanchist', but which had also begun 'to smell the political power that comes with unity'.[28]

V

It is possible to view the Hindu faith as a river with many tributaries, some that feed into a main stream and others that leave it. Perhaps the image itself is mistaken, for in many respects there is no main river at all. This is a religion that was decentralized like no other. Each district has its own holy shrines, each run by its own, locally revered priest. Sometimes the allegiances are to caste as well as region; Madhava Brahmins of, say, the Uttara Kannada district have their own chosen temple, and their own religious preceptor.

It was the Ayodhya controversy that opened up the possibilities of bringing these far-flung traditions together into a unified movement. The Vishwa Hindu Parishad had formed a Dharam Sansad (Faith Council) composed of the major *dharmacharyas*, or leaders of Hindu sects. These in turn liaised with the lesser holy men, the thousands of *sants* and *sadhus* who each had a modest following of their own. Beyond the building of a Ram temple in Ayodhya, these moves towards a pan-Hindu unity had rich political possibilities. As one leading priest explained:

There are dozens of *dharmacharyas* [in] Hindu society and each has a vote bank of approximately twenty-five *lakhs* (or 2.5 million). For example, there is Gujarat's sant Sri Murari Bapu, Rajasthan's Sri Ramsukh Dasji Maharaj, UP's sant Sri Devrah Baba, RSS's Sri Deorasji, Ayodhya's Sri Nrittya Gopal Dasji Maharaj, etc. Besides them there are hundreds of *dharmacharyas* who wield a vote bank of at least one *lakh*. The Hindu society has about ten *lakh* strong team[s] of *sadhus*. If each mobilises a hundred people, the politics of this country would take a new turn and get hinduized.[29]

On the other side, the threats to the old mosque in Ayodhya had mobilized Muslim opinion in its defence. A Babri Masjid Action Committee was formed, which urged the state to prevent this and other Muslim shrines from being taken over by radical Hindus. In some sections of the community the mood was truculent. There were calls to allow worship in mosques controlled by the Archaeological Survey of India, and even a call to boycott the Republic Day celebrations if the government did not heed their demands.[30]

The growing Hindu consolidation was immeasurably helped by two contingent events. In September 1987 a young woman named Roop Kunwar committed ritual suicide in a village in Rajasthan, following her husband's death. Although sanctioned by Hindu tradition, *sati* had long been banned by law. While deplored by the state and, more actively, by feminist groups, Roop Kunwar's act inspired a groundswell of devotion in rural Rajasthan. A temple was built at the site of her self-immolation, attracting thousands of worshippers. Rallies were held hailing Roop Kunwar as an exemplar of Hindu womanhood in her devotion to her husband's memory.[31]

The other and more significant event was the telecast on Doordarshan of a new, spectacular production of the *Ramayan*. Episodes were shown every Sunday morning, beginning in January 1987 and ending in July 1988. There were seventy-eight episodes in all, with the series interrupted by a four-month break.

The *Ramayan* is a capacious epic, a story of love, sacrifice, heroism and betrayal, with plenty of blood and violence thrown in. It has a rich cast of minor and major characters, and lends itself well to soap-operatic treatment. And it was shown at a time when television viewership was rapidly increasing, with 3 million new sets being sold every year.[32] Still, the success of the show exceeded all expectations. With an estimated 80 million viewers, 'city streets and marketplaces were empty on Sunday mornings. Events advertised for Sundays were careful to mention: "To be held after Ramayan". Crowds gathered around every wayside television set.' Hotels, hospitals and factories reported large-scale absenteeism on Sunday mornings.[33]

As much as the numbers of viewers, it is the intensity of their experience that merits attention. Rising early on Sunday mornings, viewers would take a ritual bath and make their prayers. Before the show began, television sets were garlanded and smeared with sandalwood paste. Notably, the appeal of the serial cut across religious boundaries. Muslims watched it with pleasure and enchantment while churches rescheduled their services so as to avoid a clash.[34] As the anthropologist Philip Lutgendorf wrote, 'never before had such a large percentage of South Asia's population been united in a single activity, never before had a single message instantaneously reached so enormous [an] audience'.[35]

While Muslims and Christians watched the *Ramayana* for entertainment alone, for many Hindus delight was also mixed with devotion. By accident rather than design, the televised epic was introducing subtle changes in this pluralistic and decentralized religion, long divided into sects each worshipping different deities, lacking a holy book, a unique and singular god, or a single capital of the faith. Now, in front of their television sets, 'for the first time all Hindus across the country and at the same time listened to [and watched] the same thing: the serial in fact introduced a *congregational imperative* into Hinduism'.[36]

The *Ramayan* serial had been commissioned by state television independent of the happenings in Ayodhya. In the event, its appeal and influence contributed enormously to the VHP's movement to 'liberate' the birthplace of Ram. Hitherto one of many gods worshipped by Hindus, Ram was increasingly being seen, courtesy of the serial on television, as the most important and glamorous of them all.

VI

One of the new prime minister's more daring departures was on the economic front. Rajiv Gandhi appointed as his finance minister V. P. Singh, a low-key politician from Uttar Pradesh with a reputation for integrity. The government's first budget, introduced in March 1985, sought to remove some of the controls and checks in what was one of the most tightly regulated economies in the world. The trade regime was liberalized, with duties reduced on a variety of import items and incentives provided for exporters. The licensing regime was simplified, with key sectors such as machine tools, textiles, computers and drugs deregulated. Curbs on assets of individual companies were partially lifted, and rates of corporate and personal income tax reduced. These changes, it was argued, would result in increased production and greater competitiveness. The Indian economy, said the prime minister in February 1985, had got 'caught in a vicious circle of creating more and more controls. Controls really lead to all the corruption, to all the delays, and that is what we want to cut out.'[37]

Left-wing intellectuals attacked the budget as pandering to the rich. Freeing the trade regime would make India excessively dependent on foreign capital, they argued.[38] However, the new policies were welcomed by the business sector, and by the middle class.[39] This last sector of the population was by now quite large. Some estimates put their number as high as 100 million people. There was an expanding market for consumer durables, for items such as refrigerators and cars previously owned only by the select few. In 1984–5, the number of scooters and motorcycles sold increased by 25 per cent; the number of cars by as much as 52 per cent. New trades and businesses were opening all the time. There was a boom in the housing and real estate market and ever more restaurants and shopping complexes. The rising middle class, wrote one observer, had 'become the most visible sign of a rapidly progressing economy'.[40]

The latter half of the 1980s was a good time for Indian business. Industry grew at a healthy rate of 5.5 per cent per year, with the manufacturing sector doing even better, growing at 8.9 per cent per annum. Market capitalization rose from Rs68 billion in 1980 to Rs550 billion in 1989.[41] Naturally, some companies grew faster than others. The most spectacular rise was that of Reliance Industries, whose founder, Dhirubhai Ambani, had once been a lowly petrol pump attendant in Aden. Returning to India, he set himself up in the spice trade before branching out into nylon and rayon exports. Then he turned to manufacturing textiles, before adding petrochemical factories, engineering firms and advertising agencies to his ever growing portfolio of interests.

Reliance witnessed growth rates unprecedented in Indian industry, and seldom seen anywhere else in the world. Through the 1980s the company's assets grew at an estimated 60 per cent per year, its sales at more than 30 per cent per year, its profits at almost 50 per cent. Ambani was an innovator, using state-of-the-art technology (usually imported), and raising money from the growing middle class by public issue (something which other Indian family firms were loath to do). Yet his company's rise owed as much to his skilful networking as to pure business acumen. He kept politicians and bureaucrats in good humour, throwing them parties and gifting them holidays. As a result, he often knew of impending policy changes – in tariff rates, for example – well ahead of the competition.[42]

Reliance's proximity to men in power was only one sign of a growing nexus between politicians and businessmen. Every large business house maintained lobbyists in Delhi, their job to 'stealthily work on politicians and bureaucrats to advance company interests'. Nor were these doings confined to the national capital; state ministers and chief ministers were alleged to be handing favours to industrialists in exchange for money. A particularly lucrative source of corruption was transactions in real estate. The law of eminent domain allowed the state to take over farmland in the vicinity of towns at well below market rates, and then hand them over to favoured firms to build factories or offices. Hundreds of millions of rupees changed hand in these deals; some of the money going into the pockets of individual politicians, the rest into their party's treasury, to be used to fight elections.[43]

Their dealings with big money led to a profound change in the lifestyle of Indian politicians. Once known for their austerity and simplicity, they now lived in houses that were large and expensively furnished. Driving flashy cars and dining in five-star hotels, these were, indeed, the 'new maharajas'. The 'distance between Gandhi (Mahatma) and Gandhi (Rajiv)', remarked one observer, 'is a vast traverse in political ethic. The *dhoti* is out, so is the walking stick, wooden sandals and travelling in third-class railway compartments. Gucci shoes, Cartier sunglasses, bullet-proof vests, Mercedes Benz cars and state helicopters are in. Indian politics no longer smells of sweat, nor is it particularly clean and odourless – it reeks of aftershave.'[44]

VII

While industry and the middle class prospered, large parts of India were witness to endemic poverty and malnutrition. In the autumn of 1985 a series of starvation deaths were reported from the tribal districts of Orissa. When the rains failed and the crops with them, villagers were forced to eat a gruel made of tamarind seed and mango kernel, a mixture that led in many cases to stomach disease. In earlier times the forests had provided food and fruit in times of scarcity; but with rampant deforestation that form of insurance was no longer available. More than 1,000 deaths were reported from the districts of Koraput and Kalahandi alone.[45]

In 1987 there was another and more serious drought. The uplands of Orissa were once more hard hit, but also suffering were the semi-arid parts of western India, the states of Gujarat and Rajasthan in particular. In desperation, pastoralists ferried their animals by truck to the rich forests of central India in search of fodder not available in their own home range. The drought was believed to be the worst of the century. An estimated 200 million people were affected by it, their suffering vividly captured in press photographs of parched and cracked land with carcasses of cattle strewn across it.[46]

The scarcities of 1985 and 1987 underlined the continuing dependence of the economy on the monsoon. Yet even in areas of irrigated agriculture there was discontent. This was stoked by two newly formed farmers' organizations: the Shetkari Sanghatana, active in Maharashtra; and the Bharatiya Kisan Union, based in Haryana and Punjab. The former was led by a one-time civil servant named Sharad Joshi, the latter by a Jat farmer named Mahindra Singh Tikait. According to Joshi, the main axis of conflict was between 'India', represented by the city-based, English-speaking middle class, and 'Bharat', represented by the villagers. He argued that economic policies had consistently favoured 'India' over 'Bharat'. To reverse this bias, Tikait and he proposed higher prices for farm produce, and lower tariffs for electricity for farm use. Both their organizations commanded a large base; each could rustle up 50,000 or more farmers to march on the state capital to press their demands.[47]

Although Joshi and Tikait claimed to speak for the rural population as a whole, in truth they represented the middle and rich peasantry, those who used tractors and electrified pump-sets and had a surplus to sell in the market. The poor were mostly outside their purview. As studies conducted in the 1980s once more confirmed, class strongly overlapped with caste in village India, where the truly disadvantaged continued to be the Harijans or Scheduled Castes (SCs). A survey in Karnataka revealed that nearly 80 per cent of SCs living in the countryside, as well as more than 60 per cent of SCs in towns, were below the official poverty line, their monthly expenditure less than Rs50 a month. The picture was much the same in other parts of India.[48]

VIII

In his first year in office, Rajiv Gandhi had worked to resolve a series of ethnic conflicts – in Assam, in Mizoram, in the Punjab. By the end of his second year, however, his regime was confronted with fresh challenges based on the claims of ethnicity to add to the ongoing challenges based on religion and class.

As ever, a comprehensive coverage of social conflicts in this (or any other) decade in the history of independent India is beyond reach of a single chapter, book or scholar. One can only flag some of the more important ones. To begin with, there were conflicts between different groups in the same state. In Bengal, for instance, the Nepali-speaking population of the Darjeeling hills had begun asking for a state of their own. Their leader was a former soldier named Subhash Ghisingh. Among his cadre Ghisingh commanded total and unquestioning support; at a word from him they could shut down all the schools and shops in the district. His Gorkha National Liberation Front worked within the democratic process and outside it, sometimes petitioning Union ministers, at other times engaging in pitched battles with the police. Through the latter half of 1986 the clashes were particularly intense. Eventually, the prime minister met Ghisingh, persuading him to accept an autonomous hill council rather than a state for Nepali speakers.[49]

Across the border in Assam, the Bodo tribals were in revolt against the locally dominant Assamese. Their movement, mimicking their adversaries, was led by young men of the All-Bodo Students Union (ABSU). ABSU leaders wanted a separate state to be carved out of Assam, in pursuit of which they blockaded roads, burnt bridges and attacked non-Bodos. When the Assamese radicals retaliated the clashes became violent, claiming dozens of lives.[50]

In Tripura, meanwhile, tribal activists had launched a struggle against the Bengalis who had migrated in large numbers to the state after Partition. By some definitions the Tripura National Volunteers (TNV) qualified as 'terrorists', murdering and kidnapping civilians and ambushing police parties in pursuit of their ends. In 1986 TNV guerrillas killed more than a hundred people. In the next year their tally was even higher. However, in August 1988 the TNV leader Bijoy Hrangkhawl came out of hiding to sign an accord with the government. His volunteers laid down their arms in exchange for more seats for tribals in the local legislature and the provision of rice and cooking oil at subsidized rates in tribal villages.[51]

A second set of conflicts pitted residents of individual states against the Union government. Thus in Punjab, the euphoria generated by the Rajiv Gandhi–Longowal accord proved to be a highly temporary phenomenon. The *sant's* assassination was a harbinger of things to come, with a new generation of terrorists taking up the struggle for Khalistan. The injuries caused by Operation Bluestar and the anti-Sikh riots in Delhi had brought many fresh recruits to the cause. So had the failure of the central government to honour its commitment to transfer Chandigarh to Punjab. Militants were once more making their home in the Golden Temple. Statements in favour of Khalistan were being made by priests and, on occasion, by members of the ruling Akali Dal itself.[52]

To tackle the resurgence of terrorism the police force in Punjab was now 34,000 strong. To stiffen its morale a new chief was brought in: a plain-speaking Bombay policeman named J. F. Ribeiro. Also recruited, a little later, was K. P. S. Gill, a Sikh by extraction who had experience fighting extremism in the north-east. Ribeiro and Gill adopted a carrot-and-stick policy; meeting Sikh peasants in an extensive 'mass contact' programme on the one hand, forming vigilante groups to eliminate terrorists on the other. Police parties fanned out into the countryside, mounting search operations, firing at men on the run. Dozens of extremists were killed in these searches, but there was also much harassment of ordinary villagers.[53]

But the acts of terror continued. Buses were stopped on the highway, Hindu passengers separated from Sikhs and killed. In 1986 there were twice as many killings as there had been in 1984, when Bhindranwale was alive. In panic, many Hindus began fleeing across the border to Haryana.

To get rid of the minorities in the Punjab was indeed one of the terrorists' aims. Another aim was more sinister; to instil fear in Sikhs who lived *outside* the Punjab. To this end a series of bombs were set off in markets and bus terminals in Delhi and other towns of northern India. These were intended to provoke a fresh round of revenge killings against the Sikhs. Then the Sikhs who survived might come back to the Punjab, there to form a consolidated, unified, homogeneous community, the better to fight the battle for Khalistan. The model, apparently, was the successful struggle for Pakistan back in the 1940s, which had likewise been helped by creating panic among Muslims living outside the holy land.[54]

In a major operation in May 1988 commandos flushed out some fifty terrorists holed up in the Golden Temple complex. Unlike Operation Bluestar, this assault was launched in daylight, so that the adversaries could be pinpointed more clearly. In any case, these militants were not as well prepared or as motivated as Bhindranwale's men. They retreated into the Temple's *sanctum sanctorum*; denied access to food and water, they surrendered seventy-two hours later.[55]

The revival of terrorism in the Punjab coincided with renewed trouble in another border state, Jammu and Kashmir. Back in 1984, Mrs Gandhi had Sheikh Abdullah's son Farooq removed from office; now her son Rajiv restored the ties that once bound the two families and their respective parties, the Congress and the National Conference. In November 1986 they together formed a caretaker government in the state. Justifying the alliance, Farooq Abdullah said that 'the Congress commands the Centre. In a state like Kashmir, if I want to implement programmes to fight disease and run a government, I have to stay on the right side of the Centre.'[56]

In 1987 fresh elections were held to the Jammu and Kashmir assembly. To fight them, Kashmiri politicians seeking autonomy from the centre – rather than dependence or subservience – formed an umbrella grouping named the Muslim United Front (MUF). MUF workers were harassed by the administration; and the polls themselves were anything but free and fair. Although the National Conference–Congress alliance would probably have won anyway, their margin of victory was made much greater by the rigging of votes in their favour. Even the Intelligence Bureau conceded that as many as thirteen seats were lost by the MUF owing to 'electoral malpractice'.[57]

The way the 1987 elections were conducted led to deep disenchantment among political activists in Kashmir. Despairing of being treated fairly by New Delhi, they began looking to Pakistan for succour. Groups of young men crossed the border, joining training camps run by the Pakistani army. A year later they crossed back, to put into practice what they had learned. In the spring of 1989, the Kashmir Valley was witness to a series of shootings, bomb blasts and grenade attacks. This lovely valley was now home to 'Kalashnikovs, detonators, Molotov cocktails, gelatine fuses, mortars [and] masked militants'. Ninety-seven separate incidents of violence were recorded in the first half of 1989, in which at least 52 people were killed and 250 injured. Kashmir, commented one reporter grimly, 'appears to have the makings of another Punjab'.[58]

IX

Even as the Indian government was trying – with mixed success – to contain secession at home, it had embarked on an ambitious attempt to end ethnic strife in neighbouring Sri Lanka. That little island – as beguilingly beautiful in its own way as mountainous Kashmir – was caught in a bloody civil war between the Sinhala majority and the Tamil minority. The causes of the conflict were wearyingly familiar, to Indians at any rate, for they involved rival claims of language, ethnicity, religion and territory.

A detailed history of the Sri Lankan conflict would take us too far afield.[59] Suffice it to say that it really began when Sinhala was imposed as the sole 'official language' of the island nation. The Tamils asked for parity for their own tongue and, when this was denied, took to the streets in protest. Over the years, non-violent methods were thrown over in favour of armed struggle.

Of the several Tamil resistance organizations, the most influential and powerful were the Liberation Tigers of Tamil Eelam (LTTE). Led by a brutal fighter named Velupillai Prabhakaran, the LTTE had as its aim a separate nation, to be constituted from the north and east of the island, where the Tamils were in a majority. Throughout the early 1980s they mounted raids on Sri Lankan army camps and committed atrocities on civilians. The Sinhala response was, if anything, even more fierce. This was, in other words, a conflict of an almost unspeakable brutality and savagery.

LTTE fighters had long used the Indian state of Tamil Nadu as a safe haven. Their activities were actively helped by the state government, with New Delhi turning an indulgent blind eye. However, in the summer of 1987 Rajiv Gandhi was asked by the Sri Lankan President, J. R. Jayawardene, to help mediate in the conflict. Under an agreement signed between Colombo and New Delhi, an Indian Peace Keeping Force (IPKF) would be flown into the island. The Sri Lankan army would retreat to the barracks, and the LTTE militants persuaded – or forced – to disarm.

In late July 1987 Indian troops began going to Sri Lanka in batches of a few thousand. (Eventually, as many as 48,000 soldiers of the Indian army would be stationed there.) Their presence was unpopular among Sinhala nationalists, who saw it as an infringement of sovereignty, and among the Tamils, who had always thought that India was on their side. When asked to surrender their arms, the LTTE insisted on a series of preconditions, including the release of all Tamil prisoners in government custody and a halt to Sinhala colonization in the east of the island. Until October an uneasy peace held, broken when the IPKF moved against the militants. The LTTE headquarters in Jaffna was stormed and captured, but at an enormous cost. Popular opinion turned decisively against the Indians, who were now seen as an occupying force. The LTTE took to the jungles, from where they would snipe and harry the Indians. They made particularly effective use of land mines, blowing up convoys of soldiers as they travelled on the roads.

By the end of 1987 the press was writing of Sri Lanka as 'India's Vietnam'. For 'the Indian army had never seen a war like this: in an alien land, against a foreign enemy that wore no uniforms, knew no Geneva Convention on ethics of war, yet carried deadly modern weapons and fought routinely from behind the cover of women and children'.[60] An Indian commander was slightly more generous: while deploring the LTTE's 'senseless, mulish, destructive insistence' on armed struggle, he nonetheless saluted their 'discipline, dedication, determination, motivation and technical expertise'.[61]

As the bodies of dead soldiers were returned in bags to the mainland, pressure mounted to recall the living. From the summer of 1989 they began coming back, although the final pull-out was not accomplished until the spring of 1990. More than 1,000 Indian soldiers had died in the conflict.

The decision to send in troops to Sri Lanka was consistent with India's growing perception of itself as the 'rightful regional hegemon in South Asia'.[62] In demographic and economic terms it dominated the region, and it was now determined to express this dominance in terms of military preparedness as well. In January 1987 Indian infantry units mounted a large exercise on the Pakistan border, ostensibly to test new equipment but really to display to the old enemy a new-found power.[63] Then, in March 1988, India tested its first surface-to-surface missile, capable of attacking targets up to a distance of a hundred miles away. A year later it successfully tested a more sophisticated device, which could carry a load ten times more powerful and reach targets 1,500 miles away. Indian missile scientists had taken their country into an exclusive club whose only other members were the United States, the Soviet Union, the United Kingdom, France, China and Israel.[64]

These developments attracted apprehension in the smaller countries of South Asia. People were talking of the 'Ugly Indian', as they talked in other parts of the world of the 'Ugly American'. India, admitted a Calcutta weekly ruefully, 'is regarded as the bad boy of the region'.[65]

X

Rajiv Gandhi had come to power with a massive mandate in the polls held after his mother's death. As the general election of 1989 approached, however, the prospects for his party were decidedly uncertain. As in 1967 and 1977, now too the once regnant Congress was being hard pressed to maintain its position.

There was, first of all, the ever more serious challenge of regional parties. Through much of Rajiv Gandhi's tenure the Asom Gana Parishad had ruled in Assam, the Telugu Desam in Andhra Pradesh (where N. T. Rama Rao had come back to power in 1985), and the Akalis in the Punjab. In January 1989 the DMK was returned to power in Tamil Nadu. More robustly placed than all these parties was the CPM in West Bengal, which in 1989 had been in office for twelve years. In this time their leader and chief minister Jyoti Basu had 'grown phenomenally in stature'. Basu was held in great esteem in the countryside for the agrarian reforms his party had brought about. Unusually for a communist, he was also respected by industrialists, who admired his pragmatic approach to investment and his tempering of trade union militancy.[66]

A second challenge came from the Hindu right. The old Jana Sangh, since renamed the Bharatiya Janata Party (BJP), had won a mere two seats in the 1984 elections. But it had now hitched its wagon to the campaign for a Ram temple in Ayodhya. As that movement gathered popularity, so the party's fortunes rose. BJP cadres joined VHP and RSS workers in carrying out Ram *shila pujans*, ceremonies to worship and consecrate bricks which, they hoped, would be used in the construction of the Ram temple. To force the issue, the VHP announced that it would organize a formal *shilanyas* (foundation ceremony) at the disputed site in Ayodhya on 2 November. Bricks from different districts reached the site on the appointed day. The Congress government in Delhi was advised to stop the *shilanyas*, but eventually let it go ahead for fear of offending Hindus ahead of the general Election. The VHP chose a Dalit labourer from Bihar to lay the first brick of what they claimed would, one day soon, be a glorious temple dedicated to Lord Ram.[67]

The brick worship ceremonies led to religious conflict in several towns in northern India. The worst hit was the city of Bhagalpur, in Bihar, where Hindus and Muslims battled each other for a whole week in November. The conflict spilled over into the countryside, where RSS activists led groups in the smashing of looms and homes owned by the region's celebrated Muslim weavers. Several hundred Muslims died and many more were rendered homeless. These were gathered into relief camps run not by the government, but by Muslim merchants and Islamic relief organizations. The riots in Bhagalpur, and the aftermath of the Ram *pujans* generally, further polarized the communities. The Muslims felt betrayed by the Congress, while a large section of the Hindu middle class was drawn into an open support of the BJP.[68]

A third challenge to the prime minister came from his erstwhile Cabinet colleague V. P. Singh. As finance minister, Singh had conducted a series of raids on industrial houses accused of tax evasion. This was seen as exceeding his brief; he was shifted to the Defence portfolio, and later dropped from the Cabinet altogether. Not long afterwards a storm broke out over revelations that commissions had been paid to middlemen in a deal involving the sale of the Swedish Bofors gun to the Indian army. The news was first announced over Swedish radio in April 1987. Over the next two years the press and opposition politicians kept up the pressure on the government, demanding that it name and punish the offenders.

The government stonewalled, prompting speculation that the middlemen were somehow linked to the prime minister himself. The fact that there had been corruption in a defence transaction provoked widespread outrage, which was further intensified when it emerged that army experts had preferred a French gun to the Bofors, but had been overruled by the politicians.[69]

In the public mind, the Bofors controversy was, rightly or wrongly, linked to the departure of V. P. Singh from the Cabinet. The appellation 'Mr Clean' was transferred from Rajiv Gandhi onto him. Singh left the Congress, and in June 1988 stood and won as a candidate of the combined opposition in a parliamentary by-election in Allahabad. By now he had become the focal point of a growing anti-Congress sentiment. In October 1988 his Jan Morcha was merged with the old

Janata Party to form the Janata Dal. This new party then joined hands with regional groupings to create a National Front, launched at Madras's Marina Beach and hailed by one of its members, the ever-ebullient N. T. Rama Rao, as a chariot 'drawn by seven horses [that] will dispel the gloom and shadows that thickened through the passage of the last few decades of national history'.[70]

In the last year of his government's tenure Rajiv Gandhi embarked on four initiatives that aimed at reversing his declining popularity. In September 1988 he introduced a bill aimed at checking the freedom of the press. Under its terms, editors and proprietors could be sent to jail if they were guilty of 'scurrilous publication' or 'criminal imputation', terms whose definition would be the privilege of the state alone. The bill was evidently a response to the spate of recent stories on corruption; it was a 'belated preemptive strike before more damage could be done to the government's image'. It prompted a collective protest by editors across the country and a walk-out in Parliament, and was eventually dropped.[71]

Then, in January 1989, Rajiv Gandhi visited China, the first Indian prime minister to do so in more than three decades. This was, among other things, an attempt to recast himself as an international statesman. In talks with Chinese leaders the border question was delicately side-stepped. However, New Delhi ceded ground on Tibet, while Beijing for its part said it would not aid insurgents in India's north-east. Rajiv Gandhi had a ninety-minute conversation with the 84-year-old Deng Hsiao Ping, where he was told: 'You are the young. You are the future.'[72]

Next, in March 1989, Rajiv Gandhi reversed the outward-looking, growth-oriented economic policies of his first years in office. In the last budget tabled by his government he increased taxes on consumer durables and introduced fresh surcharges on air travel and luxury hotel bookings. At the same time, a new employment generation scheme was introduced for rural areas. With the elections beckoning, Rajiv Gandhi was 'going back to the kind of populism that his mother specialized in'.[73]

Finally, in the summer of 1989, the government launched a series of high-profile events to celebrate the birth centenary of Jawaharlal Nehru. Seminars, photo exhibitions, TV quizzes, poetry festivals, musical concerts, even skating competitions, were held in Nehru's name, all paid for by the state and publicized by state radio and television. On the face of it, these programmes merely honoured India's first prime minister, but 'at another, more subconscious level, the blitz repeatedly and subtly whispers the real but hidden message: that there has been no better guardian of the nation than the Nehru family and letting the family down would, in the ultimate analysis, amount to spurning a sacred legacy and inviting the forces of chaos'.[74]

Still, Rajiv Gandhi was leaving nothing to chance. In his campaign for re-election he addressed 170 meetings in different parts of the country. As in 1984, he was advised by Rediffusion to stress the threats to the country's unity, stoked and furthered by a sectarian opposition and to be overcome by the Congress alone.[75] This time, however, the message did not resonate nearly as widely. For one thing, the accusations of corruption had gravely hurt the government's credibility. For another, the opposition was far better organized. The three main groupings had co-ordinated their strategy so that in most constituencies the Congress candidate faced only one main opponent – from either the National Front, the BJP, or one of the communist parties.

The elections, held in November 1989, were a body blow to the Congress Party. They won only 197 seats, down more than 200 from their previous tally. On the other hand, the opposition couldn't quite claim victory either. The Janata Dal won 142 seats, the BJP 86, and the left a few more than fifty. V. P. Singh was sworn in as head of a National Front government, with the left and the BJP choosing to support it from outside. Thus, the second non-Congress prime minister of India was someone who, like the first (Morarji Desai), had spent the bulk of his political career in the Congress Party.

The general election of 1989 was the first in which no single party won a majority. That it constituted a watershed is not merely a retrospective reading; some observers had called it so at the time. 'India was in for a period of political instability', wrote Vir Sanghvi: 'The days of strong governments ruled by dictatorial Prime Ministers were over. This election was the inauguration of an era of uncertainty.'[76]

XI

Even by the standards of Indian history, the 1980s were an especially turbulent decade. The republic had always been faced with dissenting movements; but never so many, at the same time, in so many parts of India, and expressed with such intensity. Two challenges were especially worrying: the continuing insurgency in Punjab – the first such in a state considered part of the *heartland* of India (unlike those old trouble spots Nagaland and Kashmir) – and the unprecedented mobilization of radical Hindus across the country, which threatened the identity of the secular state. Adding to the violence, major and minor, was the growing political and administrative corruption, this highlighted but also made more troubling by an alert press. Outside the country's borders national prestige had been greatly damaged by the bloody nose given to the Indian army by the LTTE in Sri Lanka.

In the summer of 1985 the Calcutta weekly *Sunday*, then at the height of its importance and influence, ran a cover story on the 'uncontrollable wave of violence' in the country. 'Tension and frustration everywhere – social, economic and political', said the weekly, was 'giving way to sporadic terror and mass protests'. 'Acts of sabotage, arson, killings and destruction are breaking out all over India like an ugly rash.' Thirty-seven years after Independence, 'India finds itself at a crucial point in its history'.

Posing the question 'What is happening to the country and why?', *Sunday* asked a roster of eminent Indians to answer it. The editor Romesh Thapar remarked that the violence and anger showed that 'no one is in command at any level . . . [T]he fear is growing that we are moving beyond the point of no return, to use a phrase from the jargon of airline pilots. The breakdown is becoming too visible.' The columnist Kuldip Nayar reproduced a series of newspaper headlines on riots and killings, these recording 'trouble of varying intensity in areas thousands of miles apart', the work of people who 'for a long time lived on the edge of disaster' but whose 'discontent seems [now] to have reached a bursting point'. The policeman K. F. Rustomji noted grimly that Indian politics and administration were now captive to the 'fanatic and the demagogue', who 'claim the right to organise the deaths of thousands under the guise of democratic dissent'. 'Forget the dead, count the votes,' said Rustomji in a withering but not inaccurate characterization of the political purpose of those fanatics and demagogues. Then he added, 'In a few years even the votes may not be worth counting because we may have killed democracy by then.'[77]

These were recurrent themes in the press commentary of the period: that India would break up into pieces, or give up on democracy altogether. Writing in April 1987, *Sunday*'s own political editor Kewal Verma issued this dire warning:

If Rajiv Gandhi continues to slip and no alternative emerges (. . . none is in sight yet), it will lead to political destabilisation with disastrous consequences. For, Khalistan could become a reality. Already in the rural areas of Punjab, Sikh extremists are running a parallel administration. Also, the Rama Janmabhoomi–Babri Masjid issue could lead to large-scale communal war in north India. A prolonged state of political uncertainty and instability would be an invitation to adventurous forces to intervene in the situation. For instance, if the President dismisses the Prime Minister, it may be [the Chief of Army Staff] Gen. Sundarji who will decide who should stay.[78]

The writers quoted in this section were all Indians in their late fifties or early sixties, who had grown up in the warm glow of the Nehru years and remembered the hopes with which the new nation was forged. Their sentiments were no doubt coloured by nostalgia, at least some of which was merited. For the politicians of Nehru's day had worked to contain social cleavages rather than deepen or further them for their own interests. But in other ways the nostalgia was perhaps misplaced. The churning – violent and costly though it undoubtedly was – could be more sympathetically read as a growing decentralization of the Indian polity, away from the hegemony of a single region (the north), a single party (the Congress), a single family (the Gandhis).

One must reserve final comment on whether the gloom was really justified. For as the very many forecasts previously quoted in this book have shown, every decade since Independence had been designated the 'most dangerous' thus far. If there was a novelty about these latest predictions, it was merely that they came from Indians rather than foreigners.

XII

With the end of the present chapter, this book moves from 'history' to what might instead be called 'historically informed journalism'. Part Five, which follows, deals with the events of the last two-and-a-half decades, that is, with processes still unfolding.

Most archives around the world follow a 'thirty-year' rule, keeping closed documents written in the past three decades. That seems just about right, for once thirty years have passed any new 'disclosures' are unlikely to materially affect the lives of those still living.

In my experience, a historian also needs a generation's distance to write with any conviction or credibility about the past. That much time must elapse before one can place events and policies in a pattern, to see them away and apart from the din and clamour of the present. Once roughly three decades have gone by, much more material is at hand – not just archives that are now open, but also memoirs, biographies and analytical works that have since been published.

While writing about the very recent past one lacks the primary sources available for earlier periods. Besides, the historian is here writing about times that are close to him as well as his readers. He, and they, often have strong opinions about the politicians and policies of the day. In the chapters that follow, I have tried to keep my own biases out of the narrative, but my success in this respect may be limited – or at any rate, more limited than in other parts of the book. For these decades have been as rich in incident and controversy as any other time in the history of independent India.

PART FIVE

A HISTORY OF EVENTS

26

RIGHTS AND RIOTS

The language of the mob was only the language of public opinion
cleansed of hypocrisy and restraint.

HANNAH ARENDT

I

THROUGH THE 1970s AND 1980s, while state and national elections were
won and lost, the Indian political landscape had witnessed a steady rise
of the 'backward castes', of those groups intermediate between the
Scheduled Castes at the bottom and the Brahmins and Rajputs at
the top. Yadavs in UP and Bihar, Jats in Punjab and Haryana, Marathas
in Maharashtra, Vokkaligas in Karnataka and Gounders in Tamil
Nadu – these were all, in the phrase of the anthropologist M. N. Srinivas,
the 'dominant caste' in their localities: large in numbers, well organized,
exercising economic and social power. At election time – to use another
of M. N. Srinivas's concepts – they acted as a 'vote bank', lining up
solidly behind a politician of their caste.[1]

In Indian law, these groups are known as the 'Other Backward
Castes (or Classes)', to distinguish them from the Scheduled Tribes and
Scheduled Castes. It was these 'OBCs' who formed the social base
and provided the leadership of the parties that were to successfully
challenge the dominance of the Congress party. The DMK, which
came to power in Madras after the 1967 elections, as well as the SVD
governments of the states in the North, were in essence OBC parties.
Ten years later, these backward castes asserted themselves emphatically
on the national stage. At least two of the four components of the Janata
collective that came to power at the Centre in 1977 – the Lok Dal and
the Socialists – were also, effectively, OBC parties.[2]

Economic power had come to the OBCs through land reforms and the Green Revolution; political power through the ballot box. What was lacking was administrative power. It was thus that the Janata Government had, in 1977, appointed the 'Backward Classes Commission', known then, and ever after, as the 'Mandal' Commission after its proactive Chairman, the Bihari politician Bindeshwari Prasad Mandal. The Commission concluded that caste was still the main indicator of 'backwardness'. It identified, on the basis of state surveys, as many as 3,743 specific castes which were still 'backward'. These, it estimated, collectively constituted in excess of 50 per cent of the Indian population. Yet these castes were very poorly represented in the administration, especially at the higher levels. By the Commission's calculations, circa 1980, the OBCs filled only 12.55 per cent of all posts in the Central Government, and a mere 4.83 per cent of Class I jobs.

To redress this anomaly the Mandal Commission recommended that 27 per cent of all posts in the Central Government be reserved for these castes, to add to the 22.5 per cent already set apart for Scheduled Castes and Tribes. For 'we must recognise', said the Commission,

> that an essential part of the battle against social backwardness is to be fought in the minds of the backward people. In India government service has always been looked upon as a symbol of prestige and power. By increasing the representation of OBCs in Government services, we give them an immediate feeling of participation in the governance of this country. When a backward caste candidate becomes a Collector or Superintendent of Police, the material benefits accruing from his position are limited to the members of his family only. But the psychological spin off of this phenomenon is tremendous; the entire community of that backward class candidate feels elevated. Even when no tangible benefits flow to the community at large, the feeling that now it has its 'own man' in the 'corridors of power' acts as morale booster.[3]

By the time the Mandal Commission submitted its report the Janata Government had fallen. The Congress regimes that followed, headed by Indira and Rajiv Gandhi respectively, sought to give it a quiet burial. But when a 'National Front' government came to power in the general elections of 1989 the Report was disinterred. The new Prime Minister, V. P. Singh, was sensible of the rising political power of the OBCs, and of his less-than-solid position as head of a minority coalition. Seeking to outflank his critics by presenting himself as a spokesman for, if not the messiah of, the backward classes, in August 1990 Singh announced in Parliament that his Government would implement the Mandal Report. Henceforth, 27 per cent of all vacancies in the Government of India would be reserved for candidates from the 'Socially and Educationally Backward Classes' identified by the Commission.[4]

The Order sparked a lively debate in intellectual circles. Some scholars argued that the criteria for job reservation should be family income, rather than membership of a particular caste. Others deplored the extension of affirmative action in the first place; by allocating one job in two on considerations other than merit, the efficacy and reliability of public institutions was being put at risk. However, there were also scholars who welcomed the implementation of the Mandal Commission as a corrective to the dominance of upper castes, and especially Brahmins, in the public services. They pointed to the states of South India, where more than two-thirds of government jobs were allocated on the basis of caste, without (it was argued) affecting the efficiency of the administration.[5]

In September 1990, a case was brought before the Supreme Court of India, contesting the constitutional validity of the Mandal Commission's recommendations. Three principal arguments were made by the petitioner: that the extension of reservation violated the Constitutional guarantee of equality of opportunity; that caste was not a reliable indicator of backwardness; and that the efficiency of public institutions was at risk. While it deliberated on the case, the Bench issued a stay on the Government Order of 13 August.

As so often the case in India, arguments about public policy were conducted in newspapers and courts, and also spilled over into the streets. On the 19th of September, a Delhi University student named Rajiv Goswami set himself on fire in protest against the acceptance of the Mandal Commission report. He was badly burnt, but survived. Other students were inspired to follow his example. These self-immolators were all upper-caste, whose own hopes for obtaining a government job were now being undermined. Altogether, there were nearly 200 suicide attempts – of these, 62 students succumbed to their injuries.

Other protests were collective. Across northern India, groups of students organized rallies and demonstrations, shut down schools, colleges, and shops, attacked government buildings, and engaged in battle with the police. The guardians of the law sought to defend themselves, sometimes to deadly effect. There were incidents of police firing reported from as many as six states of the Union, these claiming more than fifty lives.[6]

The conflicts sparked by the Mandal Commission recommendations were far more intense in northern India. For one thing, affirmative action programmes had long been in existence in the South. For another, that region also had a thriving industrial sector; thus educated young men were no longer as dependent on government employment. Again, while in the South the upper castes constituted less than 10 per cent of the population, the figure in the North was in excess of 20 per cent. Since there was more at stake all round, the battles, naturally, were fiercer.

Among the strongest supporters of the Mandal Commission were two rising politicians. These were Mulayam Singh Yadav, who had become Chief Minister of Uttar Pradesh late in 1989; and Lalu Prasad Yadav, who became Chief Minister of Bihar early in 1990. Although unrelated, they had many things in common. Both were born in peasant households, both became politically active at university, joining the then still influential socialist movement. Both were jailed during the Emergency, and both joined the Janata Party after it was over.

As their common surname indicated, Mulayam and Lalu were from a caste of farmer-herders scattered across north and western India. In colonial times Yadavs had often acted as *lathials* (strongmen) of upper-caste landlords. After Independence, now with lands of their own, they had steadily gained in economic strength, social prestige, and political power. Both Mulayam and Lalu actively reached out to the Muslims, another very numerous (if much poorer) community in Uttar Pradesh and Bihar. The arithmetic of this move was electoral, for Yadavs and Muslims were each about 10 per cent of the population. In multi-cornered contests – the norm in India – 40 per cent of the vote was usually enough. So if a party or politician had sewn up both Yadavs and Muslims, and persuaded sections of other 'backward' groups to join them, then they had a very good chance of winning an election.[7]

As India's most populous states, Bihar and Uttar Pradesh together sent 139 members to Parliament. General elections were often decided here. In the first four elections the Congress won a majority of seats in UP and Bihar. In 1977, following the Emergency, the party was wiped out, but in 1980 and 1984 it recovered, winning 81 and 131 seats respectively. The last was an aberration, a consequence of the martyrdom of Indira Gandhi. In 1989 the Congress fared disastrously, winning a mere 19 seats in the two states. When mid-term elections were held two years later, it fared even worse, winning 5 seats in UP and only one in Bihar. The space vacated by the Congress in these crucial northern states was filled in part by the 'socialist' parties led by Lalu and Mulayam Singh Yadav, and in part by the Bharatiya Janata Party (BJP), whose axis of mobilization was religion rather than caste.

II

In 1984, the Bharatiya Janata Party, successor to the old Jana Sangh, won a mere two seats in the eighth General Elections. Five years later its tally went up to 86. A major reason for this rise was its involvement in the campaign to have a temple built in Ayodhya, to replace the medieval mosque that stood on the site, itself believed by many to have been the original birthplace of the mythical Lord Ram. The movement to construct the Ram temple was, as we saw in Chapter 25, led by a close affiliate of the BJP, the Vishwa Hindu Parishad.

Anxious to keep the Congress out of power, the BJP now supported V. P. Singh's National Front without joining the Government. However, Singh's decision to implement the Mandal Commission report, announced in August 1990, threw the party into a tizzy. Some leaders thought this a diabolical plan to break up Hindu society. Others argued that the extension of affirmative action was a necessary bow to the aspirations of the backward castes. Within the party, and within RSS shakhas, the debate raged furiously – should, or should not, the Mandal recommendations be endorsed?

Rather than take a position, the BJP chose to shift the terms of political debate, away from Mandal and caste and back towards religion and the Mandir/Masjid question. The party announced a yatra, or march, from the ancient temple of Somnath in Gujarat to the town of Ayodhya. The march would be led by L. K. Advani, an austere, unsmiling man reckoned to be more 'hardline' than his colleague Atal Behari Vajpayee. He would travel in a Toyota van fitted up to look like a 'rath' (chariot), stopping to hold public meetings on the way.

Commencing on 25 September 1990, Mr Advani's Rath Yatra planned to reach Ayodhya five weeks later, after travelling 10,000 kilometres through eight States. Activists of the Vishwa Hindu Parishad flanked the van, flagging it off from one town and welcoming it at the next.

At public meetings they were complemented by saffron-robed *sadhus*, whose 'necklaces of prayer beads, long beards and ash-marked foreheads provided a strong visual counterpoint' to these armed young men. The march's imagery was 'religious, allusive, militant, masculine, and anti-Muslim'. This was reinforced by the speeches made by Advani, which accused the government of 'appeasing' the Muslim minority, and of practising a 'pseudo-secularism' which denied the legitimate interests and aspirations of the Hindu majority. The building of a Ram temple in Ayodhya was presented as the symbolic fulfilment of these interests and aspirations.[8]

Advani's march through north-western India was a major headache for V. P. Singh's government. For the procession 'posed a provocation that could not be ignored. Growing disorder, riots, and a final destruction of the mosque loomed ahead. Yet there would be serious consequences to stopping it. Not only would Singh have to act against [the revered god] Rama, but he would also bring down his own ruling coalition and risk serious disorder'.[9] The *yatra* reached Delhi, where Advani camped for several days, daring the government to arrest him. The challenge was ducked, and the procession started up again. However, a week before it was to reach its final destination, the van was stopped and Advani placed under preventive detention. The arrest had been ordered by the Bihar chief minister Lalu Prasad Yadav, through whose state the march was then passing.

While L. K. Advani cooled his heels in a Bihar government guest house, his followers were making their way to Ayodhya. Thousands of *kar sevaks* (volunteers) were converging from all parts of the country. The Uttar Pradesh chief minister, Mulayam Singh Yadav, was like his Bihari namesake a bitter political opponent of the BJP. He ordered the mass arrest of the *kar sevaks*. Apparently as many as 150,000 were detained, but almost half as many still found their way to Ayodhya. 20,000 security personnel were already in the temple town; some regular police, others from the paramilitary Border Security Force (BSF).

On the morning of 30th October, a large crowd of *kar sevaks* was intercepted at a bridge on the river Sarayu, which divided Ayodhya's old town from the new. The volunteers pushed their way past the police and surged towards the Babri Masjid. There they were met by BSF contingents. Some *kar sevaks* managed to dodge them, too, and reach the mosque. One planted a saffron flag on the structure; others attacked it with axes and hammers. To stop a mass invasion the BSF *jawans* used tear gas and, later, live bullets. The *kar sevaks* were chased through narrow streets and into temple courtyards. Some of them resisted, with sticks and stones – they were supported by angry residents, who rained down improvised missiles on the police.[10]

The battle between the security forces and the volunteers raged for three whole days. At least twenty *kar sevaks* died in the fighting. Their bodies were later picked up by VHP activists, cremated, and the ashes stored in urns. These were then taken around the towns of northern India, inflaming passions wherever they went. Hindus were urged to take revenge for the blood of these 'martyrs'. The state of Uttar Pradesh was rocked by a series of religious riots. Hindu mobs attacked Muslim localities, and – in a manner reminiscent of the grisly Partition massacres – stopped trains to pull out and kill those who were recognizably Muslim. In some places the victims retaliated, whereupon they were set upon by the Provincial Armed Constabulary, long notorious for its hostility towards the minority community.[11]

As one commentator put it, L. K. Advani's *rath yatra* had, in effect, become a *raktyatra*, a journey of blood.[12]

III

Back in 1979, after the Janata Party split, Charan Singh had run a minority government for a few months. However, V. P. Singh was the first prime minister to head a minority government after a general election had thrown up a fractured verdict. He was weak and on unsure ground from the start, as reflected in the haste with which he implemented the Mandal Report to outflank rivals within his own party, and as reflected also in the open challenge to his government offered by L. K. Advani's *rath yatra*.

Nor were these the only conflicts V. P. Singh had to deal with. In the winter of 1990–1, a bitter dispute broke out between Karnataka and Tamil Nadu. The quarrel, over the waters from the Cauvery river, was an old one, now given fresh impetus by the failure of the monsoon and the growing demands for irrigation water among commercial farmers.

The Cauvery originates in Karnataka, flows through the state and into Tamil Nadu, from where it merges with the Indian Ocean. The lower parts of the delta have for centuries had a sophisticated irrigation network, allowing farmers to grow high-value paddy. In contrast, irrigation works in Karnataka are of recent origin; the first canals were built in the early twentieth century, with a further spurt in canal building after the 1970s.

In 1928, Cauvery waters irrigated 11 million acres of farmland in what is now Karnataka, and 145 million acres in what is now Tamil Nadu. By 1971 the gap had increased; the figures now were 44 million acres in Karnataka and 253 million acres in Tamil Nadu. However, by the 1990s the upper riparian state had virtually caught up with the lower one – the figures now were 213 million acres for Karnataka and 258 million acres for Tamil Nadu. This massive expansion of irrigation facilities had generated much wealth for the farmers of the Mandya and Mysore districts of Karnataka. Once dependent on a single harvest of a low-value crop (usually, millet), they could now enjoy two or even three harvests a year of high-value crops such as rice and sugar-cane.

Through the 1970s and 1980s, the central government convened a series of discussions to work out a mutually acceptable distribution of the Cauvery waters. Twenty-six ministerial meetings were held between 1968 and 1990; all failed to arrive at a consensus. Tamil Nadu feared that the frenetic canal building in the upper reaches threatened its farmers downstream. Karnataka argued that its late start should not preclude the fullest development of the waters in its territory.

In June 1990, by an order of the Supreme Court, a Cauvery Water Disputes Tribunal was constituted. Three, presumably impartial, judges were its members. On 25 June 1991, the tribunal passed an interim order, directing Karnataka to release 205 billion cubic feet of water per year to Tamil Nadu, pending final disposal of the matter. Ten days later, the Karnataka Assembly passed a unanimous resolution rejecting the tribunal's order. The Karnataka government then passed its own order, which mandated its officials to 'protect and preserve' the waters of the Cauvery for the State's farmers.

The matter went to the Supreme Court, which held that the Karnataka directive was *ultra vires* of the constitution. The central government now made the tribunal's interim order official by publishing it in the gazette. The Karnataka chief minister, S. Bangarappa, responded by declaring a *bandh* (general strike) in the State. All schools and colleges were closed and, with the administration looking on, protesters were allowed to go on the rampage in Tamil localities of the state capital, Bangalore. The violence continued for days, with an estimated 50,000 Tamils being forced to flee the state.

Karnataka's defiance sparked angry words from the chief minister of Tamil Nadu, J. Jayalalithaa. Her administration, in turn, encouraged the targeting of Kannada homes and businesses in Tamil Nadu. Altogether, property worth more than Rs200 million was destroyed.

While ordering the constitution of the Cauvery Water Disputes Tribunal, the chief justice of the Supreme Court noted that 'disputes of this nature have the potentiality of creating avoidable feelings of bitterness among the peoples of the States concerned. The longer the disputes linger, more the bitterness. The Central Government as the guardian of the interests of the people in all the States must, therefore, on all such occasions take prompt steps to set the Constitutional machinery in motion'.[13]

However, while the central government could set the machinery in motion, it no longer had the powers to compel the states to accept its recommendations. That there was now a minority government in Delhi added to the problems. Had Nehru or Indira Gandhi been prime minister, they would have convened a meeting of the respective chief ministers, and sought to hammer out a compromise. Lal Bahadur Shastri and even Morarji Desai would most likely have done the same. In that case a lasting solution may yet have been deferred, but at least the dispute might not have spilled over into the streets. This hostility, both official and popular, between two states of the Union was unprecedented in its ferocity, and boded ill for the future.[14]

IV

From conflicts in the heartland of India we now move to conflicts in the extremities. Pre-eminent here was that old sore spot, Kashmir. After a quiet decade or two, the Valley erupted in the first months of 1989. In November of that year, Rajiv Gandhi was replaced as Prime Minister by V. P. Singh. Singh appointed a 'mainstream' Kashmiri politician, Mufti Mohammad Sayeed, to the crucial post of Home Minister. This was a gesture meant to please the Muslims of India in general and the Muslims of the Valley in particular. With one of their kind in charge of law and order, surely the police would bear down less heavily than before?

The experiment was very soon put to the test. On 8 December 1989, a young woman doctor was kidnapped as she walked to work in Srinagar. But this was no ordinary medic; the lady was Rubaiya Sayeed, the daughter of the Union home minister. She had been abducted by militants of the Jammu and Kashmir Liberation Front (JKLF). They demanded that, in exchange for her release, five specified JKLF activists be freed from detention. The chief minister, Farooq Abdullah, did not want to yield to the threat. He was over-ruled by the prime minister in Delhi. On the 13th, the jailed militants were released; a large crowd welcomed them, and marched them triumphantly through the streets of Srinagar. Among the slogans they shouted, one was especially ominous: *'Jo kare khuda ka kauf, utha le Kalashnikov'* – If you wish to do God's work, go pick up a Kalashnikov. Later that day, Rubaiya Sayeed was reunited with her family.[15]

The government's capitulation was regarded as a major victory by the militants. Further kidnappings followed: of a BBC reporter, of a senior official, of another daughter of a prominent politician. There were also a series of assassinations: those killed included the Vice Chancellor of Kashmir University and the head of the local television station.[16]

At this stage, circa 1989–90, Indian intelligence reported as many as 32 separatist groups to be active in the Valley. Of these two were especially important. The first was the Jammu Kashmir Liberation Front (JKLF), which stood for an independent, non denominational state of Jammu and Kashmir, in which Hindus and Sikhs would have the same rights as Muslims. Its goal was captured in the popular cry: *'Hame kya chhaiye, azaadi, azaadi'* (What do we want? Freedom! Freedom!). The second was the Hizb-ul Mujahideen, which (as its name suggests) veered more towards an Islamic regime and was not averse to a merger of the state with Pakistan. The Hizb-ul was led by Syed Salauddin, the nom de guerre of a once democratic politician who had contested the 1987 elections but been denied victory by a blatant rigging of the votes. It was then that he turned to the gun, and to Pakistan, taking many other young men with him.[17]

Both the JKLF and Hizb-ul had collected a wide variety of arms. With these they killed soft and hard targets, looted banks and dropped grenades in front of police posts. Their acts grew more daring; in November 1990, they even launched a rocket at the broadcasting station of All India Radio. The government now decided to take a tougher stance, moving in paramilitary forces and some army units to help maintain order. By 1990, there were as many as 80,000 Indians in uniform in the Valley. Thus, 'the attempt to find a political solution was put aside in favour of a policy of repression'.[18]

The situation in Kashmir is tellingly reflected in this series of newspaper headlines, all from the year 1990:

YOUTH TO THE FORE IN SECCESSION BID

BLASTS ROCK KASHMIR

KASHMIRI MILITANTS HANG POLICEMAN IN SRINAGAR

PAKISTAN BLAMED FOR REBELLION IN JAMMU AND KASHMIR

ARMY JOINS BATTLE AGAINST MILITANTS IN KASHMIR

TROOPS CALLED OUT IN ANANTNAG, CURFEW IMPOSED

SECURITY FORCES KILL 81 MILITANTS

3 DIE IN FIRING ON J&K PROCESSION

TOTAL BANDH IN KASHMIR, HEADLESS BODIES FOUND

J AND K TROUBLE CLAIMS 1,044 [LIVES] TILL SEPT[EMBER]

'PEOPLE POWER' IN SRINAGAR: CURFEW LIFTED, SHOPS SHUT

TRICOLOUR BURNT AT UN OFFICE

5 LAKH ATTEND J&K 'FREEDOM' RALLY

INDEPENDENCE ALONE CAN HEAL KASHMIR'S WOUNDS[19]

The inhabitants of the Kashmir Valley were caught in the cross-fire, although, as the last few headlines suggest, their sympathies lay more with the militants than the security forces. Those who might have been neutral were persuaded to take sides following the murder in May 1990 of the respected cleric Mirwaiz Mohammed Farooq. A massive crowd of mourners accompanied his body to the burial ground. Somewhere, somehow – the details remain murky – they got into an altercation with a platoon of the Central Reserve Police Force (CRPF). The CRPF men, in panic, fired on the mourners, killing thirty and injuring at least three hundred others. The Mirwaiz's assassins were apparently in the pay of Pakistan; but by day's end the propaganda war had been decisively lost by India.[20]

The alienation of the Kashmiris was deepened by the behaviour of those sent apparently to protect them. Indian soldiers, and more particularly the CRPF men, were prone to treat most civilians as terrorist sympathizers. Their actions were documented by Amnesty International,[21] but also by Indian human rights activists. In the spring of 1990, a team led by the respected jurist V. M. Tarkunde travelled through the Valley, talking to government officials, militants and ordinary villagers. Many cases of police and army 'excesses' were reported: beatings (sometimes of children), torture (of men innocent of any crime), extra-judicial (or 'encounter') killings and the violation of women. 'It is not possible to list all the cases which were brought to our notice', commented Tarkunde's team:

> But the broad pattern is clear. The militants stage stray incidents and the security forces retaliate. In this process large numbers of innocent people get manhandled, beaten up, molested and killed. In some cases the victims were caught in [the] cross-fire and in many more cases they were totally uninvolved and there was no crossfiring. This tends to alienate people further. The Muslims allege that they are being killed and destroyed because they are Muslims.[22]

V

As a rule, the Muslims in India were poorer than the Hindus, as well as less educated. There were a few Muslim entrepreneurs, but no real Muslim middle class. They continued to be under-represented in the professions, and in government service. Forty per cent of Muslims in cities lived below the poverty line; the situation in the countryside was not much better. The literacy rate for Muslims was well below the national average, and the gap between them and the other communities was growing. Few Muslim girls were sent to school, while the boys were often placed in *madrasas* (Islamic schools) whose archaic curricula did not equip them for jobs in the modern economy. Meanwhile, the taunts of the Sangh Parivar had inculcated a defensive, almost siege-like mentality among the Muslim intelligentsia. The young men, especially, sought succour in religion, seeing in a renewed commitment to Islam an alternative to poverty and persecution in the world outside. Nor was this turn to faith always quietist. A Students Islamic Movement of India had arisen, whose leaders argued that threats from the rival religion could only be met through force of arms.[23]

The rise of Hindu fundamentalism in the 1990s put an already vulnerable minority further on the defensive. In the border state of Jammu and Kashmir, however, the roles were reversed. Here, the Muslim majority was increasingly expressing its aspirations in religious terms, with the Hindu minority suffering as a consequence.

The popular revolt that broke out in the Valley in 1989 was at first led by the JKLF. Within a year, however, the JKLF had ceded ground to the Hizb-ul Mujahideen, whose own commitment to a multi-religious Kashmir was much less certain. The cry of *azaadi* (freedom) was being replaced by the call of *jihad* (holy war). As a popular slogan of the Hizb-ul cadres went: '*Na guerilla jang, na qaumi jang: al jihad, al jihad*'. (This is neither a guerilla war nor a national liberation struggle; this is jihad, jihad.)[24]

One consequence of this turn to religion was that the community of Kashmiri Pandits became suspect in the eyes of the militants. They were Hindus, but in other respects akin to their Muslim brethren; speaking the same language, eating the same kind of food, partaking of the same syncretic culture of the Valley. In the past, there had been economic rivalry between Hindus and Muslims. Sheikh Abdullah, for example, had resented and then brought to an end Pandit control of cultivable land and of the state administration. But the social harmony was more-or-less complete. Even in the Partition riots of 1947 Kashmir was untouched, an oasis of peace lauded by Mahatma Gandhi himself.

In the winter of 1989–90, as the Hizb-ul supplanted the JKLF, the Pandits became a target of attack. Because they were Hindus, and for no other reason, they were seen as agents of a state that had for so long oppressed the Kashmiris. Several hundred Pandits were killed in 1989–90, and killed in ways that made the ones who survived deeply insecure. As a reporter who documented these murders later wrote:

> These women and men were not killed in the cross-fire, accidentally, but were systematically and brutally targeted. Many of the women were gang-raped before they were killed. One woman was bisected by a mill saw. The bodies of the men bore marks of torture. Death by strangulation, hanging, amputations, the gouging out of eyes, were not uncommon. Often their bodies were dumped with notes forbidding anyone – on pain of death – to touch them.[25]

In panic, Pandit families began leaving the Valley for the Hindu-majority Jammu region. Others fled further afield, to Delhi, and even to Bombay.

There were an estimated 200,000 Pandits living in the Kashmir Valley. By the summer of 1990, at least half had left. They lived in refugee camps, some run by the government, others by the RSS. At first, the state's hope, and their own, was that the migration was temporary, and that once peace returned they would return to the Valley. In the event, they stayed on, and on.[26]

Through the 1990s, there were further attacks on Pandits who had chosen to remain. Sometimes entire hamlets were set on fire. By the end of the decade, less than 4,000 Pandits were left in the Valley, a melancholy reminder of the centuries in which they had lived cheek-by-jowl with their compatriots.[27]

The growing militancy in Kashmir was actively aided by Pakistan. That country's Inter-Services Intelligence (ISI) ran camps where terrorists were trained in the use of arms and provided maps of the region. With the ISI's help, Kashmiri activists moved freely across the border, into India to kill or bomb, then back to Pakistan for rest and replenishment. By now, indigenous militants had been joined by foreign mercenaries – Arabs, Chechnyans, Uzbeks – who had cut their teeth in the war against the Soviet puppet regime in Afghanisthan. When that war ended, and Russian troops had returned, defeated, to their homeland, these fighters found another holy cause in the liberation of Kashmir.

VI

Among the casualties of L. K. Advani's *rath yatra* was Prime Minister V. P. Singh. In November 1990 he resigned, unable to sustain his minority government in the absence of BJP support. As in 1979 – when Morarji Desai demitted office – the Congress allowed a lame duck Prime Minister (in this case, Chandra Shekhar) to hold charge while they prepared for mid-term elections. These were held in the summer of 1991. In the middle of the campaign Rajiv Gandhi was assassinated, while speaking in a town in Tamil Nadu. The assassin, who was also blown up by the bomb she was carrying, was later revealed to be a representative of the Liberation Tigers of Tamil Eelam (LTTE). The killing was an act of vengeance, for the LTTE had not forgiven Rajiv Gandhi for sending troops against them in 1987.

Notwithstanding the murder of Rajiv Gandhi, the elections went ahead on schedule. Pollsters had predicted a hung Parliament, with no party anywhere near a majority. However, the sympathy generated by the killing allowed the Congress to win 244 seats. With support from independents, they were in a position to form a majority government. P. V. Narasimha Rao, a veteran Andhra Congressman who had held important positions in Rajiv Gandhi's Cabinet, was sworn in as prime minister.

Although he had been chief minister of Andhra Pradesh, Narasimha Rao was far from being a mass leader. A scholar and linguist, he was a loyal Congressman, who had faithfully served both Indira and Rajiv Gandhi. He had not fought the Lok Sabha elections in 1991, and may even have been contemplating retiring from active politics. But the assassination of Rajiv Gandhi changed everything. Rao was now nominated by the Congress as a compromise choice for prime minister, winning out over his ambitious rivals, Arjun Singh and Sharad Pawar.

On taking office, Narasimha Rao was immediately confronted with a major crisis, this linked to the growing external debt of the government. India had long taken aid from multilateral institutions such as the World Bank. In Rajiv Gandhi's regime borrowings from the market also increased rapidly. In the summer of 1991 the debt had reached $70 billion, of which 30 per cent was owed to private creditors. At one stage, foreign exchange reserves were down to two weeks of imports.

Apart from profligate borrowings by previous governments, two other factors had contributed to this crisis. The Gulf War had massively increased the price of oil, a key component of India's import bill. And the political uncertainty in India had led many non-resident Indians to withdraw dollar deposits from Indian banks.[28]

Till he became prime minister, Rao was known as a quiet, understated man who had lived and served in the shadow of Indira Gandhi and her elder son. But now he revealed a boldness altogether at odds with what was previously known of his character. He appointed as his finance minister Dr Manmohan Singh, an apolitical economist whose previous jobs included finance secretary and governor of the Reserve Bank. Moreover, Rao gave Singh the freedom to carry out economic reforms as he saw fit.

Before he became a public servant, Manmohan Singh had written an Oxford DPhil suggesting that India move towards a more open trade regime. His thesis was written in the 1960s; now, three decades later, he seized the chance to put its recommendations into practice. The rupee was devalued, quotas removed for imports, tariffs reduced, exports encouraged and foreign direct investment welcomed in. The domestic market was also freed; the 'licence-permit-quota-raj' was substantially done away with, and the public sector discouraged from expanding.

Finally, the reforms sought to curb the profligacy of the government. Measures were introduced to reduce the fiscal deficit, which was running at an alarming 8 per cent of gross domestic product.[29]

One of the first acts of the new Government was to devalue the rupee. As someone who had been in the Congress during the abortive 1966 devaluation, and seen a novice prime minister (in that case, Indira Gandhi) vilified for the act, Narasimha Rao was nervous about a fresh move in that direction. However, it was deemed necessary, and the rupee was made to depreciate by some 18 per cent of its value to encourage exports. This bold, not to say controversial, move was vigorously defended by the finance minister, who told the press that socialist countries like the Soviet Union and China had recently devalued their currencies, while Pakistan and South Korea (among other Asian nations) had also followed aggressive exchange rate policies to enhance their competitiveness. 'Our people – the economists, the journalists, the politicians', remarked Manmohan Singh, 'somehow believe that devaluation is sinful and dishonourable. It is nothing of the sort'. If the rupee was left as it was, the balance of payment situation, already precarious, would further worsen.[30]

Meanwhile, a new Industrial Policy, framed in July 1991, made it clear that 'industrial licensing will henceforth be abolished for all industries, except those specified, irrespective of levels of investment'. The exceptions were industries critical to the country's defence, or hazardous to the environment and to human health, such as cigarette and alcohol manufacture. This was a dramatic reversal of the existing policy, which had reserved many industries to the state, and many others to the small-scale sector.[31]

There was also a liberalization of the services sector, with private players being encouraged to invest in insurance, banking, telecommunications and air travel sectors previously under more or less complete state control. Some economists thought that the reforms did not go far enough, noting, for instance, that the labour laws remained rigid (making it almost impossible for managers to fire workers), and that, while barriers to entry had been removed, barriers to exit remained (thus, entrepreneurs still needed government permission to close down unprofitable units). The bureaucratic regime had been undermined but not completely dismantled. It still took weeks or months to start a business in India, where in China or Malaysia it took a matter of days.[32]

In supervising these (overdue) reforms Manmohan Singh was helped by some capable civil servants, but especially by his prime minister. The Congress Party was historically committed to the state occupying the 'commanding heights of the economy'. Both Nehru and Indira Gandhi saw themselves as socialists. How would the party rank and file, and of course its senior leaders, take to this radical overthrowing of this legacy? While giving his finance minister a free hand, Narasimha Rao assured him that he would persuade the party to come around. As Manmohan Singh was to later recall, 'there was a lot of opposition in the country and within the [Congress] party. But Prime Minister Rao's political management made it possible to overcome all that.'[33]

In fact, in the 1980s itself the government of India had lost some of its antipathy towards business. Greater encouragement was given to private enterprise, with key sectors being delicensed. These were 'pro-business' policies that enabled Indian industry to become more productive and profitable. However, they stopped short of being 'pro-market' policies that removed impediments to entry and exit by Indian or foreign firms, thus encouraging competition and expanding consumer choice.[34]

The changes introduced by Narasimha Rao and Manmohan Singh in 1991 constituted a major departure from past policies. Even a year or two before they were undertaken, such reforms were considered unlikely or even impossible. In a book published in 1989, a professor at the Harvard Business School identified the vested interests which kept the command economy going. They included politicians, bureaucrats and indigenous entrepreneurs. The apparently permanent hold of this alliance of interests, wrote the Harvard professor, had 'served to diminish prospects for fundamental reforms of the nation's economic policies'. In countries like South Korea, the discipline of the market and the openness to foreign capital had led to a surge of wealth and productivity. In India, however, the state was 'paralyzed', and local entrepreneurs 'blind' to the need for reform. The prospect was grim, namely, that 'the "miracle" growth achieved by these other industrializing countries will continue to elude India'.[35]

For years together, the Indian economy had expanded at what was derisively termed the 'Hindu Rate of Growth'. The pro-business reforms of the 1980s had increased the growth rate, and the pro-market reforms of the 1990s was to augment it further. The steadily improving performance of the Indian economy is captured in the following table:

Table 26.1

Period	Growth in Gross Domestic Product	Growth in Per Capita Income
1972–82	3.5%	1.2%
1982–92	5.2%	3.0%
1992–2002	6.0%	3.9%

Source: Vijay L. Kelkar, India: On the Growth Turnpike, K. R. Narayan Oration, Australian National University, Canberra, 2004.

VII

When V. P. Singh announced the implementation of the Mandal Report the Congress, then in Opposition, was lukewarm. The elections of 1991 then saw the party return to power at the Centre, despite its poor showing in Uttar Pradesh and Bihar, this compensated for by a strong performance in the South. But were the Congress ever to regain ground in the North, it had to woo back the backward castes. Accordingly, the new Congress prime minister, P. V. Narasimha Rao, issued a fresh government order on 26 September 1991, endorsing the Mandal Report but adding the rider that in allotting 27 per cent of jobs to OBCs 'preference shall be given to candidates belonging to poorer sections' among them.

Meanwhile, the Supreme Court continued its hearings on the petition placed before it. It finally gave its verdict on 16 November 1992. Seven judges dismissed the petition, upholding the Constitutional validity of the Mandal Commission and the orders which sought to implement it. Three others dissented. The judgements were characteristically prolix, filling nearly five hundred closely printed pages. The dissenting judges argued that 'caste-collectivity' was 'unconstitutional'; that in deciding on who was disadvantaged, impersonal criteria like income should be used instead. On the other side, speaking for the majority, Justice Jeevan Reddy referred to past judgements where caste had been used as a proxy for backwardness. He argued that

> it goes without saying that in the Indian context, social backwardness leads to educational backwardness and both of them together lead

to poverty – which in turn breeds and perpetuates the social and educational backwardness. They feed upon each other constituting a vicious circle. It is a well-known fact that till independence the administrative apparatus was manned almost exclusively by members of the 'upper' castes. The Shudras, the Scheduled Castes and the Scheduled Tribes and other similar backward social groups among Muslims and Christians had practically no entry into the administrative apparatus. It was this imbalance which was sought to be redressed by providing for reservation in favour of such backward classes.[36]

In upholding the government orders the Supreme Court added two caveats: that reservations should not in any circumstances exceed 50 per cent of the jobs in government; and that caste criteria would apply only in recruitment, not in promotions.

It was the Janata Party that had constituted the Mandal Commission in 1978; it was its new avataar, the Janata Dal, that implemented its recommendations in 1990. Its enthusiasm was not at first shared by rival parties. For the CPI and CPM traditionally saw class, not caste, as the major axis of political mobilization. The Bharatiya Janata Party (BJP) accorded pride of place to (the Hindu) religion. As for the Congress, it presumed to speak for the nation as a whole. However, by the time the Supreme Court passed its judgement in November 1992, these parties were all prepared to endorse it. For they very quickly realized the political implications of the Mandal Commission Report, and the political costs of opposing it.

The controversy surrounding the Mandal Commission is reminiscent in some ways of the debate, conducted back in the 1950s, around the report of the States Reorganization Commission. As a marker of identity, caste was as primordial as language – as likely to be deplored by modernizing intellectuals, as prone to be successfully used for social and political mobilization. Then, as now, the force of argument was found powerless when faced with the logic of numbers. Then, as now, what began as a contentious and many-sided debate ended with an all-party consensus.

Most reports commissioned by the government of India are read by few people and discussed by even fewer. The reports of the States Reorganization and Mandal Commissions were altogether exceptional. They were read by many, debated by many more, and actually even implemented. They may even be – if only because of the number of people they affected – the two most influential reports ever commissioned by a government anywhere in the world.

The influence exercised by the States Reorganization Commission was direct: it led to the redrawing of the administrative map of India on linguistic lines. The Mandal Commission's influence, however, was mostly indirect. By its terms only a few thousand government jobs came up for allotment to OBCs. But the debate the report sparked, and its eventual acceptance, provided a tremendous fillip to OBC pride and solidarity. Among the beneficiaries were the two Yadavs, Lalu and Mulayam. Both left the Janata Dal and set up their own parties, and very successfully too. Lalu's Rashtriya Janata Dal stayed in power in Bihar for more than a decade (until 2005); it is again, as I write, the leading party in a coalition government in the state. Mulayam's Samajwadi Party was episodically in power in Uttar Pradesh in the 1990s; it is once again in power as I write, with Mulayam's son Akhilesh Yadav serving as chief minister.

VIII

In the parliamentary elections of 1991, the BJP won 120 seats, up thirty-five from the last time. Meanwhile, it also won the assembly elections in Uttar Pradesh. It was now in power in four states in northern India: Madhya Pradesh, Rajasthan and Himachal Pradesh being the others. Clearly, the Ram campaign was paying political dividends. Riots were being effectively translated into votes. At the same time, these successes at the polls had led to a crisis of identity. Was the BJP a political party, or was it a social movement? Some leaders thought the party should now put the mosque-versus-temple controversy on the 'back-burner'. It should instead raise broader questions of economic and foreign policy, and work also to expand its influence in south India. On the other side, the VHP and the RSS were determined to keep the spotlight on that disputed territory in Ayodhya. In October 1991, they acquired the land around the mosque, and began levelling the ground, preparing for temple construction.

In July 1992, a team from the central government was sent to study the situation. They found that there had been 'large-scale demolition' on the disputed site, and the building of a 'large concrete platform', both in clear contravention of court orders asking for the status quo to be maintained. To their dismay, the Uttar Pradesh government, headed by the old RSS hand Kalyan Singh, had turned a blind eye to these activities. There was, in sum, 'the flagrant violation of the law in Ayodhya'.

Worried that the trouble would escalate, the Home Ministry in New Delhi had prepared a contingency plan, allowing for the imposition of President's Rule in Uttar Pradesh and a Central takeover of the mosque / temple complex. However, the prime minister, Narasimha Rao, still hoped for the matter to be resolved by dialogue. He had several meetings with VHP leaders, and also consulted with the opposing Babri Masjid Action Committee. The possibility of having the matter referred to the Supreme Court was also discussed.[37]

Meanwhile, the VHP announced that the 6th of December had been chosen as the 'auspicious' day on which work on the temple would commence. From the middle of November, volunteers began streaming into Ayodhya, encouraged by the fact that the state government was now in the hands of the BJP. The chief minister, Kalyan Singh, was summoned to New Delhi. The prime minister urged him to allow the Supreme Court to decide on the case. Singh answered that 'the only comprehensive solution to the Ayodhya dispute was to hand over the disputed structure to the Hindus'.[38]

Kalyan Singh had instructed his government to house and feed the thousands of volunteers coming in from outside the state. Reports of this large-scale influx alarmed the Home Ministry. They prepared a fresh contingency plan, under which paramilitary forces would be sent to Ayodhya. By the end of the month, some 20,000 troops had been stationed at locations within an hour's march of the town, ready to move in when required. This, claimed the Home Secretary at the time, 'was the largest mobilisation of such forces for such an operation since Independence'.[39]

On the other side, more than a hundred thousand *kar sevaks* had reached the temple town, 'complete with *trishuls* [tridents] and bows and arrows'. On the last day of November, at a press conference in Delhi where he announced his own departure for Ayodhya, L. K. Advani said that 'I cannot give any guarantee at the moment on what will happen on 6 December. All I know is that we are going to perform *kar seva*'.[40]

On the morning of the 6th, a journalist at the site found that 'straddling the security wall [around the mosque] were PAC constables armed with batons and RSS volunteers with armbands'. The Central forces stationed around Ayodhya had not been asked to move into the town. The job was left to the UP police and its constabulary. The VHP had planned to begin the prayers at 11.30, on a raised platform constructed beforehand. However, by this time some *kar sevaks* had begun making menacing moves towards the mosque. RSS workers and police constables tried to stop them, but were met instead by a hail of stones thrown by the crowd, which was getting more charged by the minute. '*Mandir yahin banayenge*', they shouted, pointing at the Babri Masjid – we will build our temple at this very spot. An intrepid youngster scaled the railing ringing the mosque and climbed on top of one of its domes. This was the signal for a mass surge towards the monument. The police fled, allowing hundreds of *kar sevaks* to charge the mosque, waving axes and iron rods.

By noon, volunteers were crawling all over the Masjid, holding saffron flags and shouting slogans of victory. Hooks attached to ropes were anchored to the domes, while the base was battered with hammers and axes. At 2 p.m., one dome collapsed, bringing a dozen men down with it. '*Ek dhakka aur do, Babri Masjid tor do!*' (Shove some more, and the whole thing will collapse) screamed the radical preacher Sadhvi Ritambara. At 3.30, a second dome also gave way. An hour later, the third and final one was also demolished. A building that had seen so many rulers and dynasties come and go, that had withstood the furies of four hundred and more monsoons, had in a single afternoon been reduced to rubble.[41]

Was the demolition of the Babri Masjid planned aforehand? Or was it simply the result of a spontaneous display of popular emotion and anger? To be sure, some BJP leaders were taken aback by the turn of events. Despite his threatening talk the week before, when he saw volunteers rushing the monument, L. K. Advani asked them to return. As the domes came crashing down, he got into an argument with the senior RSS functionaries H. V. Seshadri and K. S. Sudarshan. They thought that now the deed was done, the RSS and the BJP should claim credit for it. 'The course of history is not pre-determined', said Sudarshan to Advani. 'Accept what has happened'. Advani answered that he would instead 'publicly express regret for it'.[42]

In press conferences after the event, the term most often used by BJP spokesmen to describe the happenings at Ayodhya was 'unfortunate'. They knew that in a democracy ostensibly bound by the rule of law, an act of vandalism by the main Opposition party could scarcely be condoned. When he met the press at the party's Delhi headquarters on the evening of the 6th, the ideologue K. R. Malkani 'made it clear that we did want the old structure to go, but that we wanted it gone through due process of law. The regret was that it had been demolished in an irregular manner'. Seeking to distance the BJP from the act, he claimed that the *kar sevaks* who attacked the mosque were most likely from the Shiv Sena, since they had been heard speaking in Marathi.[43]

The radicals within the movement were less coy. One VHP leader boasted that, in September itself, engineers had been asked to identify the structure's weak spot, and volunteers trained on how best to bring it down. 'Without this planning how do you think we razed the masjid in six hours?', he told a reporter: 'Do you think a group of frenzied *kar sevaks* could have gone about it so systematically?'[44] And in a speech in Madras soon after the demolition, the polemicist Arun Shourie noted that 'while the BJP leaders tried to disown and distance themselves from what had happened, the Hindus of India appropriated the destruction; they owned it up'. The Ayodhya events, said Shourie, demonstrated 'that the Hindus have now realised that they are in very large numbers, that their sentiment is shared by those who man the apparatus of the state, and that they can bend the state to their will'. His own hope was that 'the Ayodhya movement has to be seen as the starting point of a cultural awareness and understanding that would ultimately result in a complete restructuring of the Indian public life in ways that would be in consonance with Indian civilisational heritage' – a somewhat roundabout way of saying that the demolition of the Babri Masjid should, and perhaps would, be a prelude to the reshaping of India as a Hindu state.[45]

One cannot be certain that all Hindus shared these sentiments – as Shourie presumed they did. But those Hindus who brought down the mosque on 6th December had certainly bent the Indian state to their will. The forces to stop them were at hand, yet the order asking them to act never came. Worried that it would be charged with being anti-Hindu, the government of Prime Minister Narasimha Rao 'came to perceive the lesser evil in the demolition of the mosque'. Only after the deed was done was action taken – in the shape of the dismissal of the Uttar Pradesh government and the imposition of President's Rule.[46]

When the domes of the Babri Masjid fell, they brought those atop them down too. More than fifty *kar sevaks* were injured, some very seriously. At least six deaths were reported. The aftermath of the event was, however, more deadly still. The main leaders of the BJP, such as L. K. Advani, were taken into protective custody; yet riots broke out in town after town, in an orgy of violence that lasted two months and claimed more than two thousand lives.

The troubles began in the vicinity itself. An influential local priest had expressed the desire that Ayodhya should become the 'Vatican of the Hindus'. To cleanse the town of the minorities was one step towards that larger goal. *Kar sevaks* celebrated the felling of the mosque by setting fire to Muslim homes and localities. In other towns, riots were a consequence of processions organized by the Vishwa Hindu Parishad. Elsewhere, it was Muslims who came out into the streets to protest the demolition, by attacking police posts and attempting to burn government buildings.

Sometimes sparked by triumphant Hindus, at other times by defiant Muslims, the riots covered large parts of northern and western India. 246 died in Gujarat, 120 in Madhya Pradesh, 100 in Assam, 201 in Uttar Pradesh, 60 in Karnataka. The weapons used by the mobs ranged from acid and sling-shot to swords and guns. Children were burnt alive, women shot dead by the police. In this epidemic of violence, 'every possible refinement in human unkindness ... [was] on display'.[47]

The city worst hit was India's commercial capital, Bombay. On the morning of 7th December, the Muslim locality of Muhammad Ali Road witnessed an outpouring of collective anger in which Hindu shops were raided, and effigies of BJP leaders set aflame. A temple was also razed to the ground. When a posse of constables arrived on the scene, the crowd were undaunted. 'Police in Ayodhya just stood by and let the mosque be demolished', they shouted: 'We're going to get you now'. Through that day and the next, mobs battled police in the area. At least 60 people died in the violence.

Meanwhile, to the north of the city, the shanty-town of Dharavi was suffering from an excess of Hindu triumphalism. A 'victory rally' organized by the BJP and Shiv Sena ended in attacks on Muslim homes and shops. In retaliation, Muslims stabbed a priest and set his temple on fire. In other places, anger was vented not on the rival community but on the state. Dozens of government buses were trashed or burnt, as were at least 130 bus shelters.[48]

On 9 December, the Shiv Sena and the BJP announced a city-wide strike to protest against the arrest of their leaders in Ayodhya. This, recalled a Bombay journalist, 'was a signal for their followers to go on the rampage. They attacked mosques and Muslim establishments. In one locality, the Shiv Sena put up a notice announcing an award of Rs50,000 to anyone pointing out a Muslim house'.[49]

The Shiv Sainiks were encouraged by their leader and mentor, Balasaheb Thackeray. In an editorial in the party newspaper, *Saamna*, published on 10th December, Thackeray insisted that the violence of the past few days was merely

> the beginning of an era of retaliatory war. In this era, the history and geography of not only this country but the entire world is going to change. The dream of the Akhand Hindu Rashtra [United Hindu State] is going to come true. Even the shadow of fanatical sinners [i. e., Muslims] will disappear from our soil. We will now live happily and die happily ... No revolution is possible by shedding tears. Revolution needs only one offering, and that is the blood of devotees![50]

Curfew was imposed, and the army called in. It still took ten days for the city to get back to normal, for the commuter trains to be up and running, for offices and factories to be working as before. For three weeks the peace held, but then in the beginning of January a fresh riot broke out. On the morning of the 5th, two Hindu dock workers were stabbed to death in a Muslim locality. The cause was not clear – it might have been a product of union rivalry – but the story that Hindus were killed in a Muslim area spread through the city, catalysing more violence. In Dharavi, angry Hindus looted shops and warehouses owned by Muslims. In another slum area, Jogeshwari, a Hindu family was burnt to death. For a week the fires raged, till Bal Thackeray announced in a *Saamna* editorial that the attacks could stop 'since the fanatics had been taught a lesson'. It was, indeed, the minorities who had borne the brunt of the violence. Of the nearly 800 people who died in the riots, at least two-thirds were Muslim, this when they constituted a mere 15 per cent of the city's population.

Once more the city limped back to normal. This time the peace held for two whole months. On 12 March 1993, a series of bombs went off in south Bombay; one set outside the Stock Exchange, others in front of or inside luxury hotels and corporate offices. The intention was to cause the maximum damage, for the explosions occurred in the early afternoon; the busiest time in the richest part of the city. More than three hundred people died in the blasts. The material used to blow them up was the powerful explosive, RDX. The operations had been directed by two Dubai-based mafia dons, both Muslims, in apparent revenge for the killings of their co-religionists earlier in the season.

The rise of the Shiv Sena had, over the years, somewhat dented Bombay's reputation as the most cosmopolitan and multi-cultural of cities. That image was dealt a body blow by the riots and bomb blasts of 1992–3. This was now a 'permanently altered city', a 'deeply divided city', even a 'city at war with itself'.[51]

The Babri Masjid demolition was depressing enough, but, as the columnist Behram Contractor wrote, 'the bigger tragedy, perhaps, is not that India is no longer a secular country, but that Bombay is no longer a cosmopolitan city. Whatever happens henceforth, whether the Ram Janmabhoomi issue is resolved, whether Hindus and Muslims relearn to live together, Bombay's reputation as a free-living and high-swinging city, absorbing people from all communities and all parts of India, is gone for ever'.[52]

The rise of the Hindu right in general, and the events at Ayodhya in particular, prompted a fresh wave of gloomy forebodings about the future of India. 'The secular fabric of the country has been seriously damaged', wrote the Madras fortnightly *Frontline*, adding: 'India will never be the same again'. For the 'events of December 6 and 7 gave India a taste of what things would be [like] if and when the Hindutva combine's Hindu Rashtra [Hindu State] comes into existence. It became clear ... [that] the minority communities would have no right to live, not to speak of social interaction; that freedom of expression would be non-existent; and that truth would be only what the rulers perceive'. 'In the week that followed [6 December 1992], India changed, perhaps forever', commented the Calcutta weekly *Sunday*. With the breakdown of authority and the rule of law, 'in the eyes of the world, India moved one step closer to being perceived as a tinpot African "republic"'. The 'forces let loose by the vandalism at Ayodhya', lamented the New Delhi magazine *India Today*, 'have begun not just to take a ghastly toll of human lives, but also to reduce to rubble the edifice of our hopes and aspirations as a people and as a nation.'[53]

These worries were shared by the Western press. 'Like the three domes that crowned the 464-year-old Babri mosque', wrote *Time* magazine, 'the three pillars of the Indian state – democracy, secularism and the rule of law – are now at risk from the fury of religious nationalism'.[54] The day after the mosque came down, *The Times* of London carried a story with the headline: 'Militants Bury Hope of Harmony in Rubble of Indian Mosque'. The next day's paper quoted the views of the Labour politician, Jack Straw, then on a visit to Bombay. Straw thought that there was a real danger that India would slide 'into the abyss of sectarianism'. The same issue carried a leading article by the Irish intellectual Conor Cruise O'Brien, which confidently proclaimed that 'India's history as a secular state appears to be coming to an end'. O'Brien now anticipated a mass flight of Muslims into Pakistan, and the emigration of educated Hindus into Europe and North America.[55]

These were the immediate, so to say knee-jerk, responses of excitable journalists and professional cynics (O'Brien had previously predicted that the fall of the Berlin Wall would lead to the revival of a cult of Hitler in Germany and of a party based on Nazi ideals). But writers trained to take the long view also echoed these fears. A British author who had written many affectionate books about the subcontinent remarked that 'all who care about that country must tremble for the future of its secular democracy'.[56] And an American scholar who had spent a lifetime studying India went so far as to compare the Sangh Parivar to the Nazis. 'It is past time to note', wrote Paul Brass, 'that Indian politics and society display many of the symptoms of a murderous pre-fascist stage which has already produced a multiplicity of localized Kristallnachts in numerous urban sites'. The 'spread of violence, lawlessness and disorder at the local level', thought Brass, might prompt the central government (then controlled by the Congress) into 'another venture into authoritarian practices'. And so the 'Indian state may yet disintegrate in this clash between secular opportunists and chauvinist nationalists equally tied to the pursuit of illusions and chimeras, "symbols and shadows" of national unity and greatness pursued by all the tyrannical regimes of the twentieth century'.[57]

These forecasts were dire, alarmist, as Western predictions had tended to be ever since India became independent in 1947. Once, it was thought that India would balkanize into many parts or experience mass famine. Now, it was said that India might become a tinpot dictatorship of the African kind or a fascist dictatorship modelled on European examples. These predictions also did not come to pass. That said, the destruction of the Babri Masjid and the riots that followed left deep scars, these felt by individuals, communities, and perhaps the nation itself.

27

A Multi-polar Polity

The current resurgence of identity politics, or the politics of caste and community, is but an expression of the primacy of the group over the individual. It does not augur well for liberal democracy in India.

ANDRÉ BÉTEILLE, sociologist, 2002

I

THE PREVIOUS CHAPTER ANALYSED the rise and impact of two kinds of identity-based mobilizations – that of the 'Other Backward Castes', organized by such parties as the Samjawadi Party and the Rashtriya Janata Dal, and that of Hindus, organized by the Bharatiya Janata Party. Notably, the 1990s also witnessed an upsurge by Dalits, as the formerly 'Untouchable' castes were now known. This was led by the Bahujan Samaj Party (BSP), which was founded by a brilliant political entrepreneur named Kanshi Ram.

After the death of Dr B. R. Ambedkar in 1956, the most prominent 'Untouchable' leader was Jagjivan Ram. He was in the Congress, and it was in good part because of him that the lowest castes were regarded as a captive 'vote bank' by the party. The claim was challenged only in Maharashtra, first by the Republican Party, founded shortly after Ambedkar's death, and later by the militant Dalit Panther organization. One consequence was that 'Dalit', meaning 'oppressed', replaced the official 'Scheduled Caste' or the Gandhian 'Harijan' as the preferred self-appellation for the low castes.

From the 1950s through the 1980s, Dalits mostly voted for the Congress. For decades, Jagjivan Ram had 'carried the banner of the downtrodden and stood for their interests'. His death in 1988, said an obituarist, 'left a void' which would be almost impossible to fill. 'Scattered, unorganised, leaderless and oppressed, the fate of the scheduled castes, who form 15 per cent of the country's population,... hangs precariously in the balance'.[1]

As it happened, by this time Kanshi Ram (no relation of Jagjivan) had been active for more than a decade. Born in 1932 in the Punjab, he joined government service after university, working in a laboratory in Maharastra where he was introduced to the writings of B. R. Ambedkar. Thus radicalized, he quit his job in 1971 and began an organization to represent government employees from a disadvantaged background. This was called the All India Backward and Minority Communities Employees Federation (BAMCEF). For the next decade Kanshi Ram travelled across India, building district and state chapters of the organization. By the early 1980s BAMCEF had a membership of 200,000, many of them graduates and postgraduates. This was a trade union of the Scheduled Caste élite, which, in the leader's words, would form the 'think tank', 'talent bank', and 'financial bank' for the depressed classes as a whole.[2]

BAMCEF's growth area was north India, and particularly Uttar Pradesh, where its rallies regularly attracted audiences of a hundred thousand and more. The organization's success emboldened Kanshi Ram to start a political party. Several names were tried, but finally it came to be called the Bahujan Samaj Party (BSP), 'bahujan' being a more inclusive category than 'Dalit'. Whereas the latter represented the Scheduled Castes or former Untouchables, the former contained within it backward castes and Muslims as well.

Four decades of affirmative action had created a strong and articulate middle class among the Scheduled Castes. In the beginning, the SCs were

Table 27.1 – Employment profile of Scheduled Castes in the government of India

Group	No. of Scheduled Castes employed		SC jobs as % of total jobs	
	1965	1995	1965	1995
Class I	318	6,637	1.64	10.12
Class II	864	13,797	2.82	12.67
Class III	96,114	378,172	8.88	16.15
Class IV	101,073	2,221,380	17.75	21.60
Total	198,369	2,619,986	13.17	17.43

SOURCE: Niraja Gopal Jayal, 'Social Inequality and Institutional Remedies: A Study of the National Commission for Scheduled Castes and Scheduled Tribes', paper presented at NETSAPPE Conference, Bangalore, June 2003.

mainly recruited at the bottom of the state machinery, filling menial jobs; over time, they came to be better represented at the higher levels, working as Class I magistrates and officers in the secretariat.

A government job provided both economic security and social prestige. By 1995, more than two million Dalits were thus advantaged. Of course, the majority of Dalits continued to live lives that were economically impoverished as well as socially degrading – working as agricultural labourers, sweepers and construction workers.[3] Still, there was now a sizeable middle class to take their case forward. This was the class which staffed BAMCEF, and which then assumed leading roles in Kanshi Ram's Bahujan Samaj Party. In this respect, the path they followed was very nearly the reverse of the OBCs. Having tasted political power, the OBCs sought to claim administrative power through the Mandal Report. The SCs, however, first acquired a stake in the administration, before seeking a greater role in party politics.

The BSP made its debut in the 1984 general elections. It garnered more than a million votes, but won no seats. It made a greater impression in state elections in Uttar Pradesh. Here, the party activists successfully wooed the Dalit masses, warning them that the Congress wanted only pliant *chamchas* (sycophants) from their ranks. The BSP, on the other hand, stood for 'social justice', even 'social transformation'. Only a party of their own could enhance the dignity, pride and prospects of the Dalits.[4]

The message was carried by Dalit lawyers, teachers and officers to their less privileged brethren. Apart from holding meetings and rallies, these intellectuals published a series of tracts providing the lower castes with a heroic history of their own. These were driven by the conviction that 'till now Indian history is mostly written by brahmins'. Now, an alternate narrative was constructed, which claimed that it was actually the Dalits who 'created cultures such as Harappa and Mohenjodaro'. But then the invading Aryans 'took away their land, alienated them forcibly, hijacked their culture, and subjected them to a state of slavery'. Throughout history this suppression had been stoutly resisted, by Dalit workers, peasants, singers and poets. Their deeds – real as well as mythic – were commemorated in booklets printed and distributed in the hundreds of thousands in the Uttar Pradesh of the 1990s.[5]

Political organization and social conscientization, working hand in hand, enabled the BSP to take impressive strides in Uttar Pradesh. In the 1993 state elections it won as many as sixty-seven seats. The BSP's gains were mostly at the expense of the Congress. This party powered by Dalits had emerged as one of the three major political groups in the state, the others being Mulayam Singh Yadav's Samajwadi Party and the Hindu-oriented Bharatiya Janata Party (BJP).

By this time, Kanshi Ram had been supplanted as the BSP's main leader by a one-time protegé. Her name was Mayawati. She was born in 1956 in New Delhi, the daughter of a government clerk. Her ambition was to join the prestigious Indian Administrative Service, but an encounter with Kanshi Ram at a BAMCEF rally made her enter politics instead. At public meetings she attracted attention with her oratorical skills, her slashing wit aimed mostly at the rival Congress party. By the early 1990s she had become the public face of the party. Realizing that the Dalits could never come to power on their own, she sought to build cross-caste and cross-party alliances. In 1995, she became chief minister, the first Dalit and only the second woman to hold that post in India's largest state. Her term in office was short; but she was to enjoy other and longer terms as chief minister of Uttar Pradesh.

Writing in the 1970s, the journalist and old India hand James Cameron pointed out that the prominent women in Indian public life all came from upper-class, English-speaking backgrounds. 'There is not and never has been a working-class woman with a function in Indian politics', remarked Cameron, 'and it is hard to say when there ever will be'. Within two decades there was an answer, or perhaps one should say a refutation, when a lady born in a Dalit home became chief minister of India's most populous state.[6]

In other parts of the country the Dalit voice was also being heard. The 'most significant feature of the Scheduled Castes in contemporary India', wrote the sociologist André Béteille, 'is their increased visibility'. They were 'still exploited, oppressed and stigmatized; but their presence in Indian society could no longer be ignored'.[7]

Once submissive as well as suppressed, the Dalits now knew of their rights under the Indian Constitution and were prepared to fight for them. Indeed, the man who piloted that Constitution, B. R. Ambedkar, had become the symbol and inspiration for Dalits everywhere. One anthropologist wrote that 'across Tamil Nadu, statues, portraits, posters and nameplates bearing the image of Dr Ambedkar proliferate. Halls, schools and colleges named after him abound and even his ideological opponents feel obliged to reproduce his picture and lay claim to his legacy'.[8] Pretty much the same was true of most other states of the Union. Wherever Dalits lived or worked, photographs of Ambedkar were ubiquitous: finely framed and lovingly garlanded, placed in prominent positions in hamlets, homes, shops and offices. Meanwhile, due to pressure from Dalit groups, statues of Ambedkar were put up at public places in towns and cities – at major road intersections, outside railway stations, in parks. The leader was portrayed standing proud and erect, clutching in his right hand a copy of the Constitution he had helped author.[9]

II

Against this background of lower-caste assertion and right-wing Hindu consolidation, P. V. Narasimha Rao continued as prime minister, albeit shakier than before. He was widely blamed for the demolition of the Babri Masjid, critics arguing that he should have asked the president to invoke Article 356 and dismiss Kalyan Singh's palpably partisan government in UP. Some senior Congressmen tried to have him removed and, when they failed, left the party to float political outfits of their own.

Despite his political weakness, and his apparently diffident personality, Narasimha Rao initiated radical reforms in economic policy. He also made bold moves in foreign policy. For instance, he took an active interest in forging better relations with the countries of South-east Asia. This was prompted by an awareness of the rising economic strength of the region, yet tactically justified as being a return to the 'pan-Asian' policies of Jawaharlal Nehru.[10] It was also under Rao that India first established diplomatic relations with Israel and, reversing decades of frosty relations between India and the United States, brought these two estranged democracies closer together.[11]

All through his political career Narasimha Rao had been a loyal follower, not to say sycophant, of the Nehru-Gandhi family. But when he became prime minister he began to show that he could be his own man. In his first months in office, he would regularly visit Sonia Gandhi, the widow of Rajiv. However, as time went on these visits became less frequent.

In 1994, India, and the world, observed the 125th anniversary of the birth of Mahatma Gandhi. To mark the occasion, Narasimha Rao announced the creation of a Gandhi Peace Prize. That Rao admired

Mahatma Gandhi was not in question. Yet in creating this prize, he was also perhaps dealing a subtle snub to an unrelated family carrying that surname. For one of Rajiv Gandhi's own first acts as prime minister had been to set up an award named after his mother, which his government claimed would become as prestigious as the Nobel Peace Prize. The Indira Gandhi Prize was worth 25 lakhs. Narasimha Rao now announced that the Gandhi Peace Prize would be worth four times that amount.

III

One of Narasimha Rao's initiatives was however owed directly to Rajiv Gandhi. These were the 73rd and 74th Amendments to the constitution, the first mandating the creation of local government institutions at the level of the village, *taluk* (county), and district; the second doing the same for towns and cities. Office-bearers were to be chosen on the basis of universal adult franchise. Everywhere, one-third of the seats were reserved for women, with additional reservation for Scheduled Castes and Scheduled Tribes.

Panchayati raj, or village self-governance, had been an abiding concern of Mahatma Gandhi's. However, both Jawaharlal Nehru and Indira Gandhi were hesitant to devolve power to lower levels, if for different reasons: the former because he felt it would be inimical to economic development, the latter because of a general preference for centralization. In the 1960s, Rajasthan and Maharashtra had both experimented with village and district councils. However, the first serious attempts to create village *panchayats* were in West Bengal, after the Left Front came to power in that state in 1977. The process was taken further by the Janata government in Karnataka, which between 1983 and 1987 devolved significant responsibilities to local institutions.

As prime minister between 1984–89, Rajiv Gandhi sought to create an all-India system of local self-governance. His interest was in part a genuflection to the rise of local autonomy movements, which called for a wider sharing of power and authority. But it was also based on political calculation – namely, the fact that while the Congress ruled at the centre, many state governments were dominated by parties hostile to it. *Panchayati raj* would allow New Delhi to bypass these parties and deal directly with the grassroots, allocating local bodies a portion of the funds previously transferred to the state administration.[12]

The process initiated by Rajiv Gandhi bore fruition after his death, when the Congress regained power at the Centre. During the discussions leading up to the amendments, state governments had expressed concern about the undermining of their authority. The legislation as finally passed gave individual states the discretion to specify the functions and powers of the *panchayats* in their territory. The provincial acts varied widely in intent and consequence. Some states gave *panchayats* responsibility over all aspects of development work – irrigation, education, health, road-building, etc. – and transferred funds appropriately. Other states upheld a more parsimonious view of the functions and finances of their local institutions.[13]

To begin with, West Bengal was in the forefront of *panchayati raj*; afterwards, the lead was taken by the other state with a strong Communist presence, Kerala. When it came to power in 1996, the 'Left Democratic Front' (LDF) decided to allocate 35–40 per cent of plan funds for programmes designed and executed by local institutions. Across the state, *panchayats* were encouraged to hold meeetings, where villagers interacted with officials and technical experts to set their own priorities. Hundreds of locality-specific plans were prepared, which tended to highlight the careful management of natural resources such as soil, water and forests.[14]

In Kerala, as in Bengal, the promotion of *panchayati raj* was based on an unstable mixture of idealism and opportunism. On the one hand, left-wing intellectuals and activists believed that by devolving power, villagers could spend public monies on projects relevant to their needs, instead of being subject to directives from above. There was also some evidence that decentralization reduced the leakages in the system, that there was less corruption and thus more money actually spent on development works. On the other hand, in the original Gandhian vision, *panchayati raj* was to be a 'party-less democracy', where the most respected (or able) villagers were elected regardless of political affiliation. In practice, the process was deeply politicized. In Kerala, and even more so in West Bengal, the CPI(M) saw in *panchayati raj* an instrument to deepen its hold over the countryside. The power of the *panchayat*, and its officials, was used not merely in and for themselves but, crucially, to mobilize votes during assembly and parliamentary elections.[15]

Panchayati raj had profound implications for relations between castes. In Uttar Pradesh, where the Dalits were vocal and organized, the dominant castes were now forced to share power at the local level with those historically less advantaged. In Orissa, where the Dalits were more submissive, they were excluded from participation in many *panchayats* (in violation of the law). In Tamil Nadu, the formation of village councils sharpened existing conflicts between the landed Thevars and the Dalits. About one-fifth of *panchayat* presidents had by law to be Dalits, but these often found their authority eroded by the upper castes. Likewise, while some women presidents acted autonomously, others were mere mouthpieces for the male members of their family or caste.[16]

IV

While Jawaharlal Nehru was alive, the Congress always ruled at the Centre. And of all the Opposition parties, only the Communists in Kerala had enjoyed power in the states. Beginning with the elections of 1967, the political landscape of India became more variegated. An increasing number of state governments fell into the hands of non-Congress parties. In 1977 the first non-Congress government came to power in New Delhi. The 1980s saw Congress regain power in the Centre, but at the end of the decade it lost power again.

This growing decentralization of the political system manifested itself in the rise of coalition governments. The Janata Party which came to power in 1977 was itself a coalition of four different parties. The next non-Congress government was the National Front that came to power in 1989. This had seven distinct components, and was yet a minority government.[17]

In 1991, in the elections held in the aftermath of Rajiv Gandhi's assassination, the Congress won 244 seats. It was by some distance the largest single party, but still fell nearly 30 seats short of a majority. However, the support – brought about by persuasion or other means – of independents and the Jharkhand Mukti Morcha allowed it to remain in power for a full five-year term.

In the elections of 1996 the tally of the Congress fell to 140 seats. P. V. Narasimha Rao resigned as prime minister and, shortly afterwards, as party president. The Bharatiya Janata Party won 161 seats, more than anyone else. Following established procedure, the president invited the BJP to form the government. The party's candidate for prime minister was Atal Behari Vajpayee. Vajpayee was considered more 'moderate' than the leader of the Ayodhya movement, Lal Krishna Advani. He had a warm and gregarious personality; was noted for his sense of humour; and had even gone so far as to praise the Hindu Right's pet aversion, Jawaharlal Nehru.

At 161 seats, the BJP was more than a hundred short of a majority of Parliament. It could not attract adequate numbers on this side, and after a mere thirteen days in office, Vajpayee's government fell. It was replaced by the United Front, a coalition of socialist and regional parties, including the Communist Party of India but not the larger Communist Party of India (Marxist). The Congress chose to support the party from outside, as did the CPI(M).

The United Front's nominee for prime minister was H. D. Deve Gowda, then serving as chief minister of Karnataka. He belonged to the UF's largest fragment, the Janata Dal. After ten months as Prime Minister Deve Gowda was replaced by Inder Kumar Gujral. India had now had twelve prime ministers; five were serving Congressmen, while six others had previously been, and for long periods, members of the Congress Party. The only prime minister of India thus far who had never been a Congressman was Atal Behari Vajpayee, who had held the job for thirteen days in 1996.

The UF Government was a fragile and unstable experiment. Lacking the numbers, or the will, it could not effect major policy changes, even if it had desired to make them. Meanwhile, after Rao's exit, the Congress had persuaded Rajiv Gandhi's widow Sonia to join the party. Born in Italy, a Catholic by upbringing, Sonia had married into India's top political family but had no political ambitions herself. In 1981, she had been deeply resistant to the idea of her husband entering politics. After his death ten years later, she retreated into her home and her family. But now she came back from the shadows, unable to resist the urge to restore her family to political pre-eminence.[18]

V

In the first years of Indian independence, the wounds of Partition had provided the excuse for a vigorous assertion by the Hindu Right. The RSS was particularly active. But when the Jana Sangh won a mere three seats in the 1952 elections, commentators were ready to write an epitaph for a party that, in a modern, secular, democratic state, dared to base its politics on religion. The socialist politician Asoka Mehta wrote that

Hindu communalism 'has proved to be weak twice, once in [the elections of] 1946 and again in 1951–2'. He was confident that 'its ghost is now laid for good'.[19] 'The Hindu is too tolerant', remarked the writer-couple Taya and Maurice Zinkin, themselves long resident in India. The election results had shown that 'Hindu communalism has been utterly defeated', indeed, that 'communalism has thus failed, probably finally'.[20]

Other observers were less sanguine. The Kashmiri leader Sheikh Abdullah thought that it was mostly Jawaharlal Nehru who kept the Indian state and Indian politics along the secular path. He worried about what would happen after Nehru was gone. Indeed, after Nehru's death the Jana Sangh slowly gained in influence. It won 25 seats to the Lok Sabha in 1967, and 22 in 1971, more or less holding its own despite the 'Indira wave' of that year. Later, its participation in the JP movement, its leaders' incarceration during the emergency, and its role in the Janata government substantially increased the party's profile and presence. Then it fell away again. As the freshly named Bharatiya Janata Party it won two seats in the elections of 1984. Even Atal Behari Vajpayee, who had been a member of parliament since 1957, failed to win re-election.

Once more, obituaries were written for a politics based on religion. Once more, it was claimed that the Hindu would not tolerate bigotry among his kind. 'The most striking feature of Indian politics is its persistent centrism', wrote two American political scientists. Apart from the natural Indian tendency towards moderation, the BJP had also to contend with the fragmentation of the electorate on lines of caste and region. Hence the conclusion that 'the support base for a national confessional party, [representing] the Hindu majority, is illusionary'.[21]

The events of the 1990s confounded these predictions. For the big political story of this decade was in fact the rise of Hindu communalism, as manifested most significantly in the number of seats won by the BJP in successive general elections. As the VHP leader Ashok Singhal remarked in 1994, the destruction of the Babri Masjid was 'a catalyst for the ideological polarization which is nearly complete'.[22]

Beyond the formal theatre of party politics, there was also a transformation occurring on the ground. In towns and villages across northern India, relations between Hindus and Muslims were being redefined. Once, members of the two communities had lived next to one another, traded with one another, even befriended and played with one another. True, there was also competition and conflict. Each community thought itself theologically superior, each had memories – real or imagined – of being scorned or victimized by the other. However, the compulsions of living together meant that these divisions were deflected or subsumed by activities conducted in common. But with the riots sparked by the Ayodhya movement, ambivalence had been replaced by an unambiguous animosity. Hostility and suspicion was now the governing – some would say sole – idiom of Hindu-Muslim relations.[23]

Fewer in numbers, and generally poorer in economic terms, the Muslims had more to lose from the souring of relations. In most riots, more Muslims died than Hindus, more Muslim homes were burnt than Hindu ones. The whole community had become prey to a deep insecurity. The taunts of Hindu chauvinists that they should move to Pakistan made them feel vulnerable and victimized. The sentiments of the ordinary Indian Muslim in the turbulent decade of the 1990s were movingly expressed by the Telugu poet Khadar Mohiuddin. On the one hand, he wrote, the Muslim is told by the Hindus to think that

> My religion is a conspiracy
> My prayer meetings are a conspiracy
> My lying quiet is a conspiracy
> My attempt to wake up is a conspiracy
> My desire to have friends is a conspiracy
> My ignorance, my backwardness, a conspiracy.

On the other hand, said Khadar,

> It's no conspiracy
> [for the Hindu] to make me a refugee
> in the very country of my birth
>
> It's no conspiracy
> to poison the air I breathe
> and the space I live in
>
> It's certainly no conspiracy
> to cut me to pieces
> and then imagine an uncut Bharat.

The Muslim was being continually asked to prove his loyalty to India. As Khadar Mohiuddin found, 'cricket matches weigh and measure my patriotism'. When India played Pakistan, it was demanded of Muslims that they display the national flag outside their homes, and that they loudly and publicly cheer for the national side. In the poet's words: 'Never mind my love for my motherland/What's important is how much I hate the other land'.[24]

The polarization of the two communities was a victory for the 'Sangh Parivar', the collective name by which the family of organizations built around the RSS and the BJP is known. Through the first five decades of Indian independence, the ideology of the Sangh Parivar had remained pretty much constant. To my knowledge, the best summation of this ideology appears in D. R. Goyal's authoritative history of the RSS. In Goyal's rendition, the core beliefs of what the Sangh Parivar calls 'Hindutva' are as follows:

> Hindus have lived in India since times immemorial; Hindus are the nation because all culture, civilisation and life is contributed by them alone; non-Hindus are invaders or guests and cannot be treated as equal unless they adopt Hindu traditions, culture etc.; the non-Hindus, particularly Muslims and Christians, have been enemies of everything Hindu and are, therefore, to be treated as threats; the freedom and progress of this country is the freedom and progress of Hindus; the history of India is the history of the struggle of the Hindus for protection and preservation of their religion and culture against the onslaught of these aliens; the threat continues because the power is in the hands of those who do not believe in this nation as a Hindu Nation; those who talk of national unity as the unity of all those who live in this country are motivated by the selfish desire of cornering minority votes and are therefore traitors; the unity and consolidation of the Hindus is the dire need of the hour because the Hindu people are surrounded on all sides by enemies; the Hindus must develop the capacity for massive retaliation and offense is the best defence; lack of unity is the root cause of all the troubles of the Hindus and the Sangh is born with the divine mission to bring about that unity.[25]

Goyal adds that 'without fear of contradiction it can be stated that nothing more than this has been said in the RSS shakhas during the past 74 years of its existence'.

While its ideology was unchanged, in time the organization of the RSS grew enormously in strength and influence. Once an all-male body, it opened a separate women's wing which both schoolgirls and housewives were encouraged to join. Once limited to northern India, it set up active branches in states where it previously had no presence at all. Everywhere, the core ideology of the Sangh was adapted to the local context. Thus in Gujarat the rebuilding of the ancient Somnath temple was celebrated as a manifestation of a united and assertive Hinduism. In Orissa, the focus was on the great Jagannatha temple, used by the RSS to build bridges between local and pan-Indian Hindu identities. There was a particular emphasis on work in tribal areas, on 'reclaiming' the adivasis and 'returning' them to the Hindu fold. Schools were opened where tribal youths were taught Sanskrit and acquainted with Hindu myths and legends. The RSS worked hard in times of natural calamity, bringing grain when the rains failed and rebuilding homes after an earthquake.[26]

As its organization grew, the RSS's ideology found even fuller expression through a new campaign strategy. M. S. Golwalkar had once thought that cow-slaughter was the issue on which the Sangh Parivar would launch a countrywide struggle.[27] That failed, but then the egregious mistakes of the Congress delivered an even more emotive issue into their lap. When Rajiv Gandhi's government appeased Muslim fanatics and overturned the Supreme Court verdict in the Shah Bano case, the Hindu radicals could claim, more convincingly than ever, that (pace D. R. Goyal's words above) the present rulers were 'motivated by the selfish desire of cornering minority votes', that to counter this 'the unity and consolidation of the Hindus is the dire need of the hour'. That 'non-Hindus are invaders or guests' was further proven by the stubborn reluctance of Muslims to hand over the Babri Masjid. The monument itself was a standing insult to Hindu pride, a nasty reminder of the slavery of past times that had not yet been fully overcome. That they were not allowed to construct a shrine to their beloved Lord Ram was only because 'the Hindu people are surrounded on all sides by enemies'; enemies within, as in the politicians who appeased Muslims, and enemies without, as in the malevolent Muslim nation (Pakistan) which had fought three wars against them. To build the Ram temple, but also to protect themselves more generally, the Hindus had to 'develop the capacity for massive retaliation', to realize that 'offence is the best defence'.

To the phrases already quoted from D. R. Goyal's summation, let us now add the critical last line: 'lack of unity is the root cause of all the troubles of the Hindus and the Sangh is born with the divine mission to bring about that unity'.

In the Ram movement, the RSS's mission was furthered by its sister organizations: in particular, the Vishwa Hindu Parishad, which had taken up the issue in the first place. Then there was the Bajrang Dal, named after Ram's great monkey devotee Hanuman (who was also called Bajrang Bali). This was composed of angry youths, equipped not so much to 'protect' their idol (as Hanuman is supposed to have done) but to beat up anyone who stood in their way. Finally, there was the Shiv Sena, actually another party altogether, and whose ideas and methods were even more extreme than the VHP and the Bajrang Dal. They were prone to calling Muslims 'poisonous snakes' and 'traitors', and advising them to move to Pakistan.[28]

By the 1980s, the RSS could no longer be called a male or north Indian body; it had reached out to women, and to other parts of the country. However, it was only through the Ram movement that it successfully overthrew the tag of being a 'Brahmin-Bania' organization, led and dominated by the élite, traditionally literate, Hindu castes. For the first sixty years of its existence it had been guided by a Maharashtrian Brahmin – first K. B. Hedgewar, then M. S. Golwalkar, finally Balasaheb Deoras. However, in March 1994 a non-Brahmin from Uttar Pradesh, Rajendra Singh, was appointed head of the organization. This was a bow not only to the Mandal debate, but also an acknowledgement of the major role played by the backward castes in the Ayodhya movement. The cadres of the Shiv Sena and the VHP were mostly drawn from the middle castes, and there were a fair number of Dalits as well.

Through this broadening of the base – in terms of region, gender and, above all, caste – was created what might justly be called the 'mother of all vote banks'. In the early days of the Ayodhya controversy, circa 1985–6, VHP leaders were prone to refer to the issue as one which affected the 'sentiments of sixty crore [six hundred million] Hindus'. As time went on, and the issue remained unresolved, demographic change caused a natural inflation in numbers: 'sixty crore' became 'seventy crore', even 'eighty crore'. This was of course a conceit. The VHP and the RSS did not speak for the majority of Hindus. But apparently, they spoke for enough Hindus to allow their political front, the Bharatiya Janata Party, to emerge as the largest single party in the Indian Parliament.

In the 1990s, the BJP came to define the political agenda in a way the Congress once did in the 1950s and 1960s. Now, the broader political discourse came to be obsessed with questions of religious identity rather than matters of economic development or social reform. Losing its hold on the government, winning ever fewer seats in Parliament, the Congress was now merely reacting to debates initiated by the BJP. After she took charge as Congress president in 1998, Sonia Gandhi worked overtime to dispel the image of her party as 'anti-Hindu'. She regularly visited temples, and even went so far as to participate in the great Kumbh Mela, a congregation held every twelve years in which tens of millions of Hindus take a dip in the Ganga at Allahabad.[29]

While the Ayodhya dispute remained its focus, the Sangh Parivar also took up other campaigns in the 1990s. More sites were identified where, it was alleged, Muslims had usurped a Hindu shrine – in Mathura, in Banaras, in the Madhya Pradesh town of Dhar, in the Baba Budan hills of Karnataka's Chikmagalur district. Movements were launched, with varying success, to 'reclaim' these places from the 'intruders'. Simultaneously, a series of attacks were launched on Christian missionaries, particularly those working in tribal areas. Churches were burnt and priests beaten up in both Gujarat and Madhya Pradesh. An Australian missionary was burnt alive in Orissa, along with his two sons, the arsonist later identified as a member of the Bajrang Dal named Dara Singh.[30] Hindus were a comfortable majority in India, yet the RSS insisted that their pre-eminence was threatened on the one hand by Christian proselytization and on the other by the larger family size of Muslims, this in turn attributed to the practice of polygamy.[31]

Occurring in different parts of India, sometimes led by the RSS, at other times initiated by the VHP or the Shiv Sena, there was nonetheless an underlying pattern to these campaigns. In every case, a religious minority – Muslim or Christian – was targeted, and accused of having hurt Hindu sentiment, or of being in the pay of a foreign power. The demonizing of the other was a necessary prelude to mobilizing one's own forces, thus to foster a collective spirit of solidarity in a long divided Hindu community.

VI

If Hindu militancy was on the rise in the heartland, in one crucial border state it was Islamic militancy that was in the ascendant. The state was, of course, Kashmir.

By the mid 1990s, Kashmiri militants had been joined by many hundreds of *mehmani mujahideen* (guest freedom fighters). These owed allegiance to different groups, all of which were headquartered in Pakistan, and all of which practised the austere, fundamentalist version of Islam taught in that country's many religious schools.

Through the 1980s, the Islamicization of Pakistani society had proceeded apace. At the nation's birth, in 1947, it had a mere 136 *madrasas*; by the late 1990s it had as many as 30,000. These *madrasas*, writes Tariq Ali, were 'indoctrination nurseries designed to produce fanatics'. Pakistan now boasted of as many as 58 Islamic political parties and 24 armed religious militias, peopled in the main by the products of the *madrasa* system.[32]

The intensification of religious sentiment in Pakistan deepened its commitment to the 'liberation' of Kashmir. Preachers in mosques and madrasas spoke repeatedly of Indian *zulm* (terror) in the Kashmir valley, urging their followers to join the *jihad* there. Youths so swayed entered groups like the Lashkar-i-Toiba, which was rapidly assuming a leading role in the armed struggle. The proximate aim was the uniting of Kashmir with the Pakistani nation; this 'a religious duty binding not only on the people of Pakistan, but, in fact, on the entire Muslim *ummat* [brotherhood]'. A wider ambition was to catalyze a civil war in India. As the chief of the Lashkar, Hafiz Mohammed Saeed boasted, they were aiming to 'set up a *mujahideen* network across India', which, when it was up and running, would spell 'the start of the disintegration of India'.[33] 'Revenge is our religious duty', said Saeed to an American journalist: 'We beat the Russian superpower in Afghanisthan; we can beat the Indian forces too. We fight with the help of Allah, and once we start jehad, no force can withstand us'. Speaking to a Pakistani reporter, the Lashkar chief claimed that 'our struggle will continue even if Kashmir is liberated. We still have to take revenge [against India] for [the loss of] East Pakistan'.[34]

This animosity and hatred was perhaps not unexpected. For the *jihadis*, India was the land of the *kafirs*, or unbelievers. But as it happened their wrath was being visited on some co-religionists as well. There were killings of activists from the National Conference, which wanted autonomy within India; of the JKLF, which wanted independence rather than merger with Pakistan; and of the Peoples Conference, which advocated non-violence.[35] The fundamentalists also came down hard on the pleasures of the people. Cinema halls and video parlours were closed, and drinking and smoking banned. Militant groups distributed leaflets ordering women to cover themselves from head to toe by wearing the long black veil, or *burqa*. The *burqa* was contrary to Kashmiri custom – here many women did not even wear head-scarves. Besides, they cost Rs2,000 apiece. Cynics suggested that tailors and cloth merchants were behind the move. There were, withal, savage attempts to enforce the ban, with acid being thrown on women who disregarded it.[36]

The main target of fundamentalist ire, however, was the Indian state and its symbols. Scarcely a week passed without a suicide attack on an army post or police camp, to stop or stem which even more troops were moved into the Valley. There were now bunkers on every street corner in Srinagar. The Indian army had become 'an imposing and ubiquitous presence' in Kashmir, a 'parallel government' even. It was charged not merely with the maintenance of law and order, but also with running hospitals, airports, bus stations and tourist centres. The state government had abdicated most of its duties. By 1995 or thereabouts, there were only two functioning institutions in Kashmir – the Indian Army on the one side and the network of *jihadi* groups on the other.[37]

As the Valley came to resemble a zone of occupation, popular sentiment rallied to the *jihadi* cause. Terrorists mingled easily with the locals, and were given refuge before or after their actions. When their men were killed in bomb attacks, the reprisals of the Indian security forces could be murderous. Soldiers dropped in unannounced in remote villages, searching for terrorists – when they did not find them, they beat up the peasants instead. A large number of custodial deaths were also reported.

The costs of this apparently unending war were colossal. According to one estimate, in the decade of the 1990s, some 12,000 civilians died unnatural deaths: three-fourths at the hands of militants, the rest in the cross-fire. Security forces claimed to have killed 13,400 militants, while losing 3,100 of their own. Given the low population densities, so many deaths in Kashmir was the equivalent of 4 million Indians being killed in the country as a whole.[38] The casualties were spread all across this lovely if increasingly desolate Valley. However, they were mostly of young men, of Kashmiris who came of age in this cursed decade. The journalist Muzamil Jaleel, who almost became a militant himself, later visited a graveyard near his native village. As many as twenty-one tombstones were of his friends and classmates.[39]

As James Buchan has written, in the years since 1990,

the Kashmiri Muslims and the Indian government conspired to abolish the complexities of Kashmiri civilization. The world [it] inhabited has vanished: the state government and the political class, the rule of law, almost all the ... Hindu inhabitants of the valley, alcohol, cinemas, cricket matches, picnics by moonlight in the saffron fields, schools, universities, an independent press, tourists and ... banks. In this reduction of civilian reality, the sights of Kashmir ... are redefined: not the ... lakes and Mogul gardens ..., or the storied triumphs of Kashmiri agriculture, handicrafts and cookery, but two entities that confront each other without intermediary: the mosque and the army camp.[40]

Through the 1990s, as Hindu fundamentalism gathered strength in the rest of India, Islamic fundamentalism was on the ascendant in Kashmir. The two processes began independently, yet each legitimized and furthered the other. With every communal riot sparked by the Ayodhya movement, radicals in the Valley could more easily portray India as a state run for and by Hindus. With every killing of innocent civilians or Indian soldiers in the Valley, the RSS could point to the hand of Pakistan in fomenting trouble within India. There were two critical events that, as it were, defined this epoch of competitive fundamentalisms: the destruction of the Babri Masjid, and the exodus of the Kashmiri Pandits. Would one trust a state that could not honour its commitment to protect an ancient place of worship? Would one trust a community that so brutally expelled those of a different faith? Such questions resonated across the subcontinent, asked by countless Indians not previously known to think along lines of religion and faith.

VII

Let us now move to that other historically troubled part of the Republic of India, the North-east. Here, there was some good news from the largest state in the region, Assam. This was that an accord had been reached with the Bodos, allowing for an 'autonomous council' to be formed in those districts where that community was in a majority.[41] The bad news was that the secessionist United Liberation Front of Assam (ULFA) was very active. Some parts of the state were securely under the control of the official administration; whereas in other parts it was the writ of ULFA that ran. Practically every tea garden paid an annual sum to the rebels, this based on the numbers of workers the estate employed, and on its profitability. To further augment their coffers the insurgents mounted raids on banks. Army units were sent in to restore order; they captured and killed some top ULFA cadres, while others crossed over the border into Bangladesh.[42]

The 1990s were also a turbulent decade for the state of Tripura. Armed groups fighting for tribal rights regularly attacked settlements of immigrant Bengalis. Here, too, insurgency was sometimes hard to distinguish from sheer criminality. As one researcher remarked, 'innocent deaths, kidnappings and extortions are a regular part of life in Tripura and have been for many years now'. Nearly 2,000 killings were reported between 1993 and 2000 – of security men, insurgents, but most of all, civilians.[43]

The gun was also ubiquitous in Manipur, another tiny state that had once been an independent chiefdom. The violence was chiefly a product of ethnic rivalries. The majority Meities, who lived in the valley, clashed with the tribals in the uplands. In the hills also there were divisions; principally, between the Tangkhul Nagas and the Kukis. In May 1992 Naga militants burnt Kuki villages, starting a deadly cycle of massacres and counter-massacres. While fighting among themselves, these groups were all opposed to the Indian state. Some Kukis, and more Tangkhuls and Meities, dreamt of forming independent nations of their own.[44]

VIII

The history of independent India was, from the start, a history of fires rising up in one place, yet being tamed in another. Thus, as Kashmir and Manipur smouldered in the 1990s, other once-turbulent regions and communities were making their peace with the Indian Union. In Mizoram, the leaders of the Mizo National Front (MNF) had made a spectacularly successful transition; once insurgents in the jungle, they were now politicians in the secretariat, put there by the ballot box. Peace had brought its own dividend in the form of water pipelines, roads and, above all, schools. In the latter part of the 1990s, Mizoram had overtaken Kerala as India's most literate state. The integration with the mainland was proceeding apace; Mizos were learning the national language, Hindi, and watching and playing the national game, cricket.

Since they spoke fluent English (the state's own official language), young Mizos, men as well as women, found profitable employment in the growing service sector, in hotels and airlines in particular. Mizoram's chief minister, Zoramthanga, was speaking of making his territory the 'Switzerland of the East'. In this vision, the tourists would come from Europe and the Indian mainland, while the economy would be further boosted by trade with neighbouring Burma and Bangladesh. The Mizos would supply these countries fruit and vegetables and buy fish and chicken in exchange. Zoramthanga was also canvassing for a larger role in bringing about a settlement between the government of India and the Naga and Assamese rebels. It was easy to forget that this visionary had once been a radical separatist, seeking independence from India when serving as the 'defence minister' and 'vice president' of the 'Mizo Government-in-Exile'.[45]

The troubles had also been resolved, more or less, in the state of Punjab. Here the process had been more tortuous. In 1987 President's Rule was imposed on the state, and repeatedly extended, for six months at a time. Without elected politicians to report to, the police energetically chased the militants, by means fair and foul. Gun battles were common, quite often around police posts but also in the countryside. In 1990 the Army was called in to help; a year later it was withdrawn. In 1992 elections were at last held to the State Assembly. The Akali Dal boycotted the polls; and the elected Congress chief minister, Beant Singh, was killed by a suicide bomber not long after he took office.

In 1993, however, the Akalis returned to democratic politics by taking part in elections to local village councils. Four years later they won an emphatic victory in the Assembly polls. By this time militancy was perceptibly on the wane. Some terrorists had become extortionists, squeezing money from Sikh professionals and from ordinary peasants. The popular mood had turned away from the idea of a separate state of Khalistan. Sikhs once more saw the advantages of being part of India. Agricultural growth had slowed down, but trade was flourishing, and the state's languishing industrial sector was being primed for revival.[46]

A sign of normalcy was that the Akalis, now in power, were fighting among themselves; individuals and factions vying for control of particularly prestigious or profitable ministries. The veteran chief minister, Prakash Singh Badal, sought to transcend these squabbles through a celebration of the 300th anniversary of the proclamation by the tenth Guru, Gobind Singh, of the Khalsa, or Sikh brotherhood.[47] His government alloted Rs3,000 million for the festivities, and the Centre chipped in with a further grant of Rs1,000 million. New memorials to Sikh heroes were built, along with new sports stadia, shrines and guest houses. At the great *gurdwara* of Anandpur Sahib, Sikh intellectuals and writers were honoured in a colourful ceremony attended by the chief minister and by the prime minister as well. One of those felicitated, the novelist and journalist Khushwant Singh, noted with satisfaction that this once 'alienated community' had 'regain[ed] its self-esteem and resume[d] its leading role in nation-building'.[48] The costs, however, had been heavy. By one reckoning, more than 20,000 lives were lost in the Punjab between 1981 and 1993 – 1,714 policemen; 7,946 terrorists; and 11,690 civilians.[49]

The troubles in the Punjab went back two decades, long enough for the residents of the state, but actually a fairly short period of time compared to other conflict-ridden states of the Union. Many Kashmiris had been rebelling against the Indians since the 1950s; many Nagas, from the 1940s itself. In the 1990s, the main insurgent group was the National Socialist Council of Nagaland. The NSCN had a solid core of several thousand well-trained fighters. They operated from bases in Burma, making raids across the border and engaging the Indian Army. Within Nagaland the rebels commanded support, respect, and perhaps also, fear. At any rate, they were sustained by collections made from the public. Even government officials paid a monthly 'tax' to the underground, this a curious if typically Indian paradox, the subsidizing by the state of a group committed to its destruction.

In the mid-1990s, however, a collective of church groups and civil society organizations called the Naga HoHo persuaded the rebels and the government to declare a ceasefire. In 1997 the guns fell silent, and the two sides began to talk. At first the conversations were held in Bangkok and Amsterdam, but eventually the two major NSCN leaders, T. Muivah and Isak Swu, agreed to visit India. They met the prime minister and travelled to the north-east, but failed to clinch an agreement. There were two stumbling blocks; the rebels' insistence that a settlement had to be outside the framework of the Indian Constitution; and their demand that parts of Manipur, Assam and Arunachal Pradesh, where Naga tribes lived, be merged with the existing state of Nagaland into a 'Greater Nagalim'.

IX

The year 1989 marks a watershed in Indian political history. Before that date, the Congress was a mighty colossus; after that date, single-party dominance gave way to a multi-polar system. In the past, some 40 per cent of the national vote had allowed the Congress to win some 60 per cent of the seats in Parliament. Now, behind the fall in the number of seats won by the Congress lay a steady decline in its vote share, as the following table makes clear:

Table 27.2

Vote share of	1989	1991	1996	1998
Congress	39.5	36.5	28.8	25.8
BJP	11.5	20.1	20.3	25.6

Between 1989 and 1998, the vote share of the Congress declined by more than 10 percentage points; over this period, the vote share of the BJP increased by roughly the same extent. However, in the four general elections in these years, these two major parties garnered a mere 50 per cent of the vote between them. Where did the other 50 per cent go? The Communist parties, concentrated in West Bengal and Kerala, generally won about 8 per cent of the vote. The backward caste and Dalit parties, strong in north India, together claimed about 16 per cent of the vote. The regionalist parties, which had a marked presence in southern and eastern India, got about 11 per cent of the vote.

The decline of the Congress had come in two phases. The first phase, which began in Kerala in 1957 and peaked in Andhra Pradesh in 1983, saw Congress hegemony challenged by parties based on the identities of region, language and class. The second phase, which began in north India in 1967 and peaked in the same region in the 1990s, saw the Congress losing ground to parties basing themselves on the identities of caste and religion. On the one hand, the upper castes in particular and Hindus in general deserted the party and gravitated towards the BJP. On the other hand, the lower castes preferred to throw their weight behind parties such as Mayawati's Bahujan Samaj Party and Mulayam's Samajwadi Party. Even the Muslims, traditionally among the Congress's strongest supporters, were turned off by the demolition of the Babri Masjid into voting for other parties.

Between 1947 and 1989, India had six different Prime Ministers. Between 1989 and 1998, India also had six different Prime Ministers. Governments now were more unstable, and also more variegated, tending to be multi-party rather than single-party affairs.

The rise of coalition or minority governments was a manifestation of the widening and deepening of democracy in India. Different regions and different groups had acquired a greater stake in the system; with parties that sought to represent them winning an increasing number of seats – usually at the expense of the Congress, which for the first two decades of Independence had claimed, rather successfully, to be a party that represented no section of India in particular but all in general.

This deepening of democracy had however come at a cost – that of a steady loss of coherence in public policy. The wide-ranging policies of economic and social development that Jawaharlal Nehru crafted in the 1950s – among them the boost to heavy industrialization, the reform of archaic personal laws and an independent foreign policy – would not have been feasible in the fragmented and divided polity of the 1990s. Even programmes focused on specific sectors, such as the thrust to agricultural development that Lal Bahadur Shastri and Indira Gandhi provided in the 1960s, would have been difficult to bring to fruition.

In the past, in allotting portfolios to ministers their relevant experience and abilities were taken into account. Now, the distribution of ministries was dictated more by the compulsions of having to please alliance partners, who demanded portfolios seen either as prestigious or profitable. And in the execution of their duties, cabinet ministers were prone to think more of the interests of their party or their state, rather than of India as a whole.

As the decade of the 1990s came to an end, the once unipolar polity came to have several distinct poles. There was the Congress, declining but still significant, and the BJP, rising but by no means dominant. These were the two so-to-say 'national' parties. Meanwhile, there was also a third pole, this constituted by a variety of caste- and region-based parties which neither the Congress nor the BJP could ignore. Now, before a general election, the smaller parties, each powerful in a single state, needed to be cajoled and placated before joining an all-India coalition. Thus, as one long-time observer of Indian politics put it, 'the two aspirants to be "national parties", the Congress and the BJP, now must behave like fast-food franchises. They sell their brand to local agents, who choose, reject, bargain or change sides on the basis of local conditions ...'.[50] Ideology played no part in this bargaining – it was all based on strategic calculation, on what one could extract from the national party by way of ministerships at the centre or subsidies to one's state.

Citizens waiting outside All India Radio to watch the general elections return, New Delhi, 1971. *(Press Information Bureau)*

Street graffiti in Bombay, circa 1970, mixing and matching India's two great popular passions: elections and films. *(Press Information Bureau)*

Indira Gandhi with U.S. president Richard Nixon, the foreign leader who most cordially disliked her, Washington, 1971. *(Press Information Bureau)*

Indira Gandhi's most doughty domestic opponent, the socialist and social worker Jayaprakash Narayan. *(The Hindu)*

Indira Gandhi and her favoured son, Sanjay Gandhi, circa 1975.
(Press Information Bureau)

Big Mother/Newspeak: Indira Gandhi at a conference on "democracy"
held during the emergency. *(Press Information Bureau)*

RIGHT: C. N. Annadurai, the gifted orator who led India's first successful regional party, the Dravida Munnetra Kazhagam. *(The Hindu)*

The London-educated lawyer-turned-communist Jyoti Basu being sworn in as the chief minister of West Bengal, Writers Building, Calcutta, 1977. Basu stayed in the job for twenty-three years, and his party, the Communist Party of India (Marxist), is in power yet. *(Ananda Bazar Patrika)*

FACING PAGE, BOTTOM: The great film star M. G. Ramachandran, a follower of Annadurai, who likewise became chief minister of Tamil Nadu. *(The Hindu)*

The cartoonist-turned-demagogue Balasaheb Thackeray, whose party, the Shiv Sena, has been episodically in power in Maharashtra and whose cadres have been responsible for a series of attacks on Muslims. *(The Hindu)*

The austere Morarji Desai, caught with a rare smile on his face, circa 1977. A Congressman for over four decades, Desai became the first non-Congress prime minister of India in 1977, after the ending of the emergency. *(The Hindu)*

Prime Minister Indira Gandhi inspecting the guard at Delhi's Red Fort on 15 August, Independence Day. The year is 1980; her son Sanjay's recent death seems marked on her face. *(Press Information Bureau)*

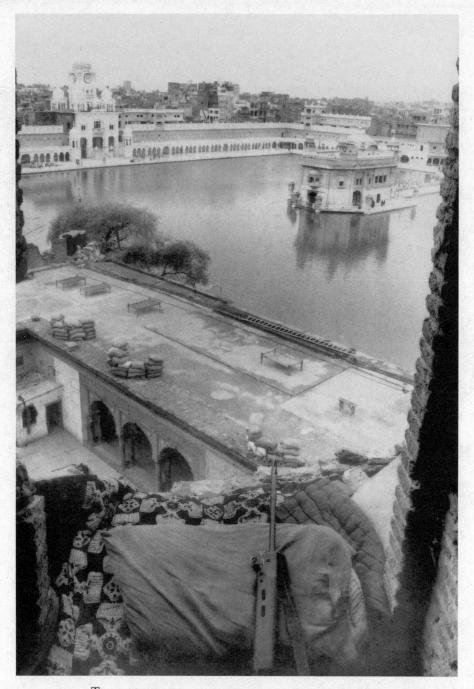

The Golden Temple in Amritsar photographed in May 1984,
shortly before the army attack. The fortifications being prepared by the Sikh
militants are clearly visible. *(The Hindu)*

Rajiv Gandhi, the third member of his family to become prime minister of India, the first to take the job not entirely willingly. *(The Hindu)*

Indian soldiers capturing a crucial vantage point during the Kargil conflict of 1999.
(Prashant Panjiar/Outlook)

Protests against the construction of a dam in Maheswar,
Madhya Pradesh, circa 2000. *(The Hindu)*

Atal Behari Vajpayee, the Hindu politician and orator, whose many decades in Opposition were finally rewarded by a full five-year term as prime minister of India. *(The Hindu)*

The Dalit politician Mayawati, celebrating her birthday as chief minister of Uttar Pradesh, with her mentor, Kanshi Ram *(to her right)*, looking on. *(The Hindu)*

Women in Manipur protesting atrocities committed by the Indian army, July 2004. *(Amrita Bazaar Patrika)*

Muslim separatists in Kashmir, circa 2000. *(Associated Press)*

A protester against caste quotas setting himself on fire, New Delhi, 1990.
(Associated Press)

Hindu radicals atop the Babri Masjid in Ayodhya, preparing to bring it down,
6 December 1992. *(The Hindu)*

Amitabh Bachchan in Manmohan Desai's 1977 film *Amar Akbar Anthony*,
a story of three brothers separated in childhood and brought up as Hindu, Muslim,
and Christian respectively. Naturally, the brothers are reunited in the end.
(Courtesy of Nasreen Munni Kabir)

The great classical singer M. S. Subbulakshmi (1916–2004), adorning the cover of a Madras magazine, which sees no need to introduce her. *(Author's collection)*

RULERS AND RICHES

Meet the pissed-off [American] programmer ... He's the guy – and, yeah, he's usually a guy – launching websites like yourjobisgoingtoindia.com and nojobsforindia.com. He's the guy telling tales – many of them true, a few of them urban legends – about American programmers being forced to train their Indian replacements.

Article in *Wired* magazine, February 2004

I

IN EARLY 1998, THE Congress withdrew support from the United Front government. When elections were called, the Bharatiya Janata Party improved its position further, winning 182 seats, forty-one more than the Congress. This time, the support of smaller parties and independents gave the BJP the numbers to govern. Among its allies were regional parties from Punjab, Tamil Nadu, Maharashtra, Haryana, West Bengal, Andhra Pradesh and Orissa, as well as a fragment of the old Janata Dal, led by the once-fiery socialist George Fernandes.

This collective partnership was known as the 'National Democratic Alliance'. The main party, the BJP, provided the prime minister, Atal Behari Vajpayee, while also holding the Home, Finance, and External Affairs portfolios. However, George Fernandes was made defence minister; he was also appointed convenor of the NDA, a not insignificant move, since Fernandes was a Christian by birth. The BJP under Vajpayee thereby wanted to signal that whatever the rhetoric it had recently used in the election campaign, once in power it would seek to moderate its hardline 'Hindutva' image.

The BJP had taken to coalition politics in the belief that it could never come to power on its own. With its roots so strongly in northern

India, its expansion depended heavily on alliances with other parties, each based in a particular state. With the exception of the Shiv Sena in Maharashtra, these parties did not subscribe to the 'Hindutva' (or Hindu-first) ideology. Thus, in forging alliances the BJP had to promise to put to one side such contentious issues as the Ram temple in Ayodhya and the abrogation of Article 370 (which accorded special status to the state of Jammu and Kashmir).[1]

II

Through the 1990s, Indian politics became more complex at the domestic level, with greater competition between parties and the introduction of a third tier of government. However, when it came to India's dealings with the rest of the world there was a noticeable convergence of views. Whether led by the BJP or the Congress, or indeed the various Third Fronts, the Union government was committed to enhancing the country's military capabilities, and to a more assertive foreign policy in general.[2]

One manifestation of this new strategy was a growth in the size and power of the military. India was rapidly moving 'from a defence dependent upon diplomacy to a diplomacy strengthened by a strong defence'.[3] Military expenditure rose steadily through the decade, from US $7,000 million to $12,000 between 1991 and 1999. Some of this money went on salaries – there were now more than one million Indians in uniform, working in the Army, Navy, or Air Force, with another million staffing the various paramilitary outfits.

Some of the money also went to buy state-of-the-art weaponry. And some went to manufacturing, indigenously, instruments of war that the richer Western countries were not prepared to sell to India. In addition to the Agni and Prithvi missiles developed in the 1980s, India now had an intercontinental ballistic missile named Surya (with a range of up to 12,000 kilometres), and a missile named Sagarika that could be launched from ships. Indian scientists had also developed a range of defensive options, designing shorter-range missiles to be aimed at any the enemy might throw at them.[4]

These missiles were designed by the Defence Research and Development Organization (DRDO), one of two scientific institutions that played a vanguard role in the defense sector. The other was the Atomic Energy

Commission (AEC), which had the responsibility for the production of nuclear power, as well as for the production of nuclear weapons. An atomic device had been tested in 1974, but in subsequent years the AEC scientists were able to considerably improve on its sophistication and destructiveness. From the early 1990s they pressed the government to allow them to test their improved bombs.

In his history of India's nuclear programme, George Perkovich tracks the persistent efforts of the scientists. Those who led the missile and nuclear programmes told successive prime ministers that in the absence of tangible results, talented young scientists would prefer high-paying jobs in the commercial sector to the service of the state. 'Without full-scale tests', they argued, 'morale would fall and the nation would not find replacements for the aging cohort that had produced the first device in 1974'. In late 1995, Prime Minister Narasimha Rao sanctioned tests, but backed off when American satellites revealed the preparations, provoking a strong warning from the US government. When a United Front Government came to power in 1996, the scientists urged the new prime minister, H. D. Deve Gowda, to give them the green signal. Gowda demurred; he didn't care about American opinion, he said, it was only that his priorities were economic development rather than a show of military strength.[5]

The BJP-led National Democratic Alliance assumed office in March 1998. The next month Pakistan tested a medium-range missile, provocatively named 'Ghauri', after a medieval Muslim warrior who had conquered and (according to legend) laid waste to much of northern India. A quick answer was called for, if only because 'the BJP's historic toughness on national security would have seemed hollow if the government did not respond decisively to the new Pakistani threat'.[6] The heads of the AEC and the DRDO insisted that a nuclear test would be the most fitting response. Their calls were endorsed by the atomic physicist Raja Rammana, who carried enormous prestige as the man who had 'fathered' the 1974 tests. Ramanna met Prime Minister Vajpayee, who assured him that he wanted 'to see India as a strong country and not as a soft one'. To this the physicist added a definitive caveat: 'Also, you can't keep scientists in suspended animation for twenty-four years. They will simply vanish'.[7]

In the second week of May 1998, the Indians blasted five nuclear devices in the Rajasthan desert. Three kinds of bombs were tested: a regular fission device, a thermonuclear bomb and a 'sub-kiloton' device.

Before and after the tests senior members of the NDA government made provocative statements aimed at India's neighbours. The defence minister, George Fernandes, described China as India's 'number one threat'. The home minister, L. K. Advani, said that India was prepared to give hot pursuit across the border to any terrorists that Pakistan may send to make trouble in Kashmir.

Opinion polls conducted immediately after the tests suggested that a majority of the urban population supported them. The most enthusiastic acclaim, however, came from the BJP's sister organizations, the VHP and the RSS. They announced that they would build a temple at the test site, and take the sand, contaminated by radioactivity but nonetheless 'holy' for them, to be worshipped across India. The Shiv Sena chief, Bal Thackeray, saluted the scientists for showing that Hindu men were 'not eunuchs'. The scientists themselves posed triumphantly in front of the news cameras, clad in military uniforms.[8]

Two weeks later this balloon of patriotic pride was punctured and deflated. On the 28th of May, Pakistan tested its own nuclear device. Their atomic programme had been built on the basis of designs and materials acquired in dubious circumstances from a Dutch laboratory by the scientist A. Q. Khan, supplemented by Chinese technical help. The Indian bomb was wholly indigenous. But these discriminations were made meaningless when six atomic blasts (deliberately, one more than the other side) disturbed the Chagai Hills in Balochistan province. The Pakistani public greeted the news by dancing and singing in the streets. The 'father' of this bomb, A. Q. Khan, told interviewers that 'our devices are more consistent, more compact, more advanced and more reliable than what the Indians have'.[9]

The Pakistani achievement was glossed as an 'Islamic' bomb, in part because at this time no other Muslim nation had one. In India, too, both supporters and opponents of the tests tended to see them as 'Hindu' inspired. In truth, although the BJP was in power in May 1998, the preparations had been laid under successive Congress regimes. The policy of nuclear ambiguity – we have the bomb, but we won't test it – was becoming unsustainable. Pressed by the West to sign the Comprehensive Test Ban Treaty, India decided to make its nuclear status a matter of public record.[10]

The BJP naturally tried to make political capital out of the tests, but faced with signing the CTBT and thus signing off on all nuclear ambitions, a Congress regime would have acted likewise. Indeed, it had been Congress prime ministers who had, in the past, most insistently laid claim to a 'great power' status for India. These claims became more persistent after the end of the Cold War. Indian leaders demanded that in deference to its size, democratic history and economic potential, the country be made a permanent member of the United Nations Security Council. That the claim was disregarded made the matter of nuclear tests all the more urgent. Across party lines, strategic thinkers argued that an open declaration of nuclear weapons would make the Western powers sit up and take notice. Reason and argument having failed, India had necessarily to 'blast' its way to world attention.[11]

III

The only countries to be officially acknowledged as nuclear powers were the five permanent members of the UN Security Council – the US, Russia, China, France and the UK. It was also known that Israel had nuclear bombs. When, in the summer of 1998, India and Pakistan simultaneously entered this exclusive club it created some disquiet among the older members. It was feared that the Kashmir dispute could spark the first atomic war in history. Pressure was put on both countries to sort out their differences on the negotiating table.

In February 1999, the Indian prime minister travelled by bus to Lahore to meet his Pakistani counterpart. Atal Behari Vajpayee and Nawaz Sharif spoke of increasing trade between the two countries, and of putting in place a more liberal visa regime. No progress was made on Kashmir, but the fact that the two sides were talking was, to subcontinental eyes as well as Western ones, a most reassuring sign.[12]

Barely three months after the Vajpayee-Sharif 'summit', Indo-Pak relations were once more on a short fuse. The provocation was the infiltration, into the Kargil district of Jammu and Kashmir, of hundreds of armed men, some Kashmiri in origin but others unambiguously citizens of Pakistan. The operation had been planned by the Pakistani army, who told their civilian prime minister about it only when it was well under way. The idea was to occupy the mountain tops that overlooked the highway linking Srinagar to Leh, the only all-weather road connecting two towns of crucial importance. The generals apparently believed that their nuclear shield provided protection, inhibiting the Indians from acting against the intruders.[13]

The Indian army was first alerted to the infiltration by a group of shepherds. Scanning the mountains with binoculars, in search of wild goats to hunt, they instead spotted men in Pathan dress digging themselves into bunkers. They conveyed the information to the nearest regiment. Soon, the army found that the Pakistanis had occupied positions across a wide swathe of the Kargil sector, from the Mushkoh Valley in the west to Chorbat La in the east. The decision was taken to shift them.[14]

The shepherds saw the Pathans on 3 May 1999. Two weeks later the Indians began the artillery bombardment of enemy positions. Air force planes screamed overhead, while on the ground jawans made their way laboriously up the mountain slopes. Men reared in tropical climes had now to battle in cold and treacherous terrain. 'In battle after decisive battle Indian infantry battalions clambered up near perpendicular cliffs the entire night in freezing temperatures before lunging straight into battle at first light against the intruders ...'.[15]

The exchanges were fierce and, on both sides, costly. Dozens of peaks, each defended by machine guns, had to be recaptured, one by one. A major victory was the taking of Tiger Hill, in the Drass sector. The battles raged all through June. By the end of the month, the Pakistanis had been cleared from 1,500 square kilometres of Indian territory. The areas reoccupied included all vantage points overlooking the Srinagar-Leh highway.[16]

In the last week of June 1999, the American president, Bill Clinton, received an unexpected phone call from the Pakistani prime minister. The two countries were close allies, and now the junior partner was asking to be bailed out of a jam of its own creation. More than 2,000 Pakistanis had already lost their lives in the conflict, and Nawaz Sharif was in search of a face-saving device to allow him to end hostilities. Clinton granted him an appointment on 4th July, American Independence Day. In that meeting, Sharif promised to withdraw Pakistani troops if America would put pressure on India to resolve the Kashmir dispute. Clinton agreed to take an 'active interest' in the question. With this assurance, Sharif returned to Islamabad and formally called off the operation.[17]

Approximately 500 Indian soldiers died in the Kargil conflict. They came from all parts of the country, and when their coffins returned home the grief on display was mixed with a large dose of pride. The bodies were kept in public places – schools, colleges, even stadiums – where friends, family and fellow townsmen came to pay their respects. A cremation or burial with full military honours followed, this attended by thousands of mourners and presided over by the most important dignitary on hand – often a chief minister or governor. The men being honoured included both officers and soldiers. Many hailed from the traditional catchment area of the Indian army (the north and the west of the country), but many others were born in places not previously known for their martial traditions, such as Ganjam in Orissa and Tumkur in Karnataka.[18] And some who died defending India came from regions long thought to be at odds with the very idea of India. A particularly critical role in recapturing the Kargil peaks was played by soldiers of the Naga regiment. Their valour at the other end of the Himalaya, hoped one army general, would allow the 'brave Nagas [to] finally get their Indian identity'. Their bravery was certainly saluted by their kinsmen; when the body of a Naga lieutenant returned home to Kohima, thousands thronged the airport to receive it.[19]

The Kargil clashes also furthered the reintegration of the Punjab and the Punjabis. Farmers along the border insisted that if the conflict became a full-fledged war, they would be at hand to assist the Indian army, providing food and shelter and even, if required, military help. 'We shall fight with the *jawans*', said one Sikh peasant, 'and teach the Pakistanis a bitter lesson for violating our territory'.[20]

Across India, the conflict with Pakistan unleashed a surge of patriotic sentiment. Thousands volunteered to join the lads on the front, so many in fact that in several places the police had to fire to disperse crowds surrounding army recruitment centres.[21] The war with China had likewise fuelled a similar response, with unemployed youth seeking to join the forces. Yet there was a significant difference. On that occasion, the intruders had overrun thousands of square miles before choosing on their own to return. This time they had been successfully thrown out by the use of force.

In this respect the Kargil war was a sort of cathartic experience for the men in uniform and, beyond that, for their compatriots as a whole. The Indian army had finally redeemed itself. It had removed, once and for all, the stigma of having failed to repulse the Chinese in 1962. At the same time, the popular response to the conflict bore witness to the birth of a new and more assertive kind of Indian nationalism. Never before had bodies of soldiers killed in battle been greeted with such an effusion of sentiment. It appeared as if each district was determined to make public its own contribution to the national cause. The mood was acknowledged and stoked further by reporters in print and on television, whose competitive jingoism was surprising even to those familiar with that profession's hoary record of making truth the first casualty of war.

IV

The successful repulsion of the invaders in Kargil encouraged the BJP to dissolve Parliament and call fresh elections. By claiming credit for the nuclear tests and the military victory, the ruling alliance hoped to consolidate patriotic pride behind it. The BJP's main rival, the Congress, was now led by Sonia Gandhi. In September 1998, while making her first formal speech as party president, Sonia Gandhi had urged that Dalits, adivasis and the youth be brought back into the Congress fold. The party, she said, should adopt a 'social justice' platform; as and when it returned to power, its policies would focus on the 'basic issues of health, education, food security, nutrition and family planning'.[22]

In May 1999, several major leaders, notably the Maratha strongman Sharad Pawar, left the Congress, citing the 'foreign origins' of the new leader. There were other and more weighty criticisms being made of Sonia Gandhi. In particular, she was an indifferent speaker, her Hindi grammatically correct but heavily accented (betraying that her first language was Italian).

Meanwhile, with the withdrawal of one of its major coalition partners, the AIADMK, the Vajpayee government lost a no-confidence vote in Parliament by a single vote. The Sonia Gandhi-led Congress sought to form an alternate government but failed to garner the required support. The president, K. R. Narayanan, now dissolved Parliament in preparation for fresh elections. When these were held, in September–October 1999, the Congress slipped to 114 seats in Parliament. The BJP got 182 seats, the same as in the last elections. However, the NDA as a whole had obtained 270 seats, just a few seats short of an overall majority. Now it was more or less assured of a full term in office.

As prime minister, Atal Behari Vajpayee took forward the economic reforms initiated by Narasimha Rao. Besides further encouraging entrepreneurship, Vajpayee's government gave a push to infrastructure development, seeking to modernize airports and to improve road connectivity. In March 2000 the government announced a 'Golden Quadrilateral' project, which aimed to link India's major cities with four lane highways, to facilitate the speedy transport of goods by trucks.

By the early 2000s, after a decade of market and trade liberalization, the Indian economy had finally escaped from what was mockingly referred to as 'the Hindu rate of growth'. Annual GDP growth rates were in excess of 6–7 per cent rather than hovering around the 2–3 per cent mark. The sector that had done best was that of services, which grew at an average of 8.1 per cent a year through the 1990s. Much of this was contributed by the software industry, whose revenues grew from a paltry $197 million in 1990 to $8,000 million in 2000. In some years the industry grew at more than 50 per cent a year. Much of this expansion was aimed at the overseas market. While in 1990 the Indian software industry's exports were valued at $100 million, by the end of the decade the figure had jumped to $6,300 million.

In the year 2000, there were 340,000 software professionals in India, with some 50,000 fresh engineering graduates being recruited annually. About 20 per cent of these professionals were women. In the first years of the twenty-first century the industry grew at an even faster rate. By 2004, it was employing 600,000 people, and exporting $13 billion worth of services.

In both India and abroad, the software industry was commonly acknowledged as the 'poster boy' of the reforms. The industry was a largely indigenous product, with firms big and small owned by Indian entrepreneurs, employing Indian engineers trained at Indian universities. Yet the work they did was mostly for foreign clients, who included many of the Fortune 500 companies. Some of this work was routine – maintaining accounts and employee records, for example. Other work was more innovative, such as designing new software which was then patented and sold overseas. (I-Flex, a financial package developed by an Indian company, was in use in more than 70 countries.) In its early years, the industry focused on 'body-shopping', sending engineers on short-term visas to work 'on-site' in European and American companies. However, with the development of satellite communications and the World Wide Web, and the increasing sophistication of the work being done, the emphasis shifted to 'outsourcing', to the codes being written within India and then sent back overseas.

Software firms such as Wipro, TCS and Infosys were now household names in India. But they were also known and widely respected in business circles abroad. They were listed on the New York Stock Exchange, and owned and operated subsidiary companies in many parts of the world. But there were also many small and medium-sized companies in the business, and the market share of the largest firms steadily declined.[23]

The software enterprises were clustered around a few major cities: Delhi, Madras, Hyderabad and above all, Bangalore, which acquired the sobriquet of 'India's Silicon Valley'. Bangalore was home to India's finest research university, the Indian Institute of Science, established in 1909. After Independence, the city became a hub of industrial units, with large, state-owned factories set up to manufacture machine tools, aircraft, telephones, and electronic equipment. When one added, to this rich scientific tradition, Bangalore's mild, Mediterranean climate and cosmopolitan culture, one understood why it emerged as such an attractive investment destination. Wipro and Infosys were both headquartered here, as were several other important players in the software industry.

To explain the rise of the software sector one must invoke factors both proximate and distant. Success, said John F. Kennedy, has many fathers. In this particular case, however, all the claimants had truth on their side. Some credit was certainly due to the reforms of 1991, which opened up the foreign market for the first time. But some credit also accrued to Rajiv Gandhi's government, which gave special emphasis to the then very nascent electronics and telecommunications industries. Moving back a decade further, the Janata government's expulsion of IBM allowed the development of an indigenous computer manufacturing and maintenance industry. But perhaps the story should really begin with Jawaharlal Nehru's government, which had the foresight to set up a chain of high-quality engineering schools, and the wisdom to retain English as the language of higher education and of inter-state and inter-national communication. For, as one respected analyst of the IT sector commented, 'India's greatest asset is a large, educated, English-speaking workforce that is willing to work at relatively low wages'.[24] This was a delicious irony: that this showpiece of market liberalization was made possible by a man committed to a state-sponsored path of economic development.[25]

In addition to these other factors, a geographical accident also contributed enormously to the boom – the fact that India is the other side of the globe from the United States, so that work done in the day was ready by the time the client got up the next morning.

The facility with English, and the luck to be five or ten hours ahead of the prosperous West, led to other forms of work being outsourced to India. At the higher end of the value chain, medical tests of patients in US hospitals were sent to be analysed by Indian radiologists and pathologists. At the lower end were the mushrooming 'call centres', where young Indians stayed up all night to take calls from holders of Western credit cards, or to book seats on Western planes and trains. Many of the employees in these centres were women, who could speak grammatical English in an accent of one's choice, and who worked harder than their American counterparts at one-tenth the cost. In 2002 there were more than 300 call centres in India, employing 110,000 people. The industry was growing at a staggering 71 per cent per year. It was estimated that by 2008 it would employ 2 million people, and generate $25 billion dollars, amounting to as much as 3 per cent of India's Gross Domestic Product (GDP).[26]

The outsourcing of Western work to Indian workers was now taking ever more varied forms. English teachers in Kerala tutored American kids over the Internet in grammar and composition. Catholic priests in the US and Canada sent prayer requests to their Indian counterparts. One could have a thanksgiving prayer said for Rs40 (roughly one dollar) in an Indian church, whereas in an American church it would cost five times that amount.[27]

If somewhat less spectacularly, the reforms initiated by Narasimha Rao's government and carried forward by Prime Minister Vajpayee also had an impact on the manufacturing sector. Increased competition and the entry of foreign firms led to greater productivity and lower prices, benefiting the domestic consumer. Some Indian industries seized on opportunities offered by the opening of international markets. Top clothing brands like Gap, Polo and Tommy Hilfiger increasingly had their products made in India. By the year 2000, India exported some half-a-million motor vehicles a year, as well as many sophisticated components used in vehicles assembled elsewhere (one out of every two American trucks now used an axle made by an Indian firm). Another growth area was pharmaceuticals. Medicines exported by Indian companies were valued at $1,000 million in 2003 – these included drugs made according to modern pharmacoepia as well as those following the indigenous 'Ayurveda' system.[28]

The opening of the economy also led to many foreign firms coming in to tap the Indian market. Between 1991 and 2000, the government approved more than ten thousand investment proposals by foreign companies; if all had fructified, they would be worth a staggering $20,000 million. They spanned the range from telecommunications to chemicals, and from food processing to paper products. Of the projects that actually got off the ground, the most visible brands were in the consumer sector: such as cars made by Ford and Honda, televisions by Samsung, phones by Nokia and drinks by Pepsi and Coca-Cola, whose advertisements and showrooms were now a noticeable presence in the major Indian cities. Less visibly, companies such as Philips, Microsoft and General Electric had also begun establishing research stations in India, which employed local as well as expatriate engineers in developing cutting-edge technologies for the global market.[29]

The importance of foreign trade to the Indian economy steadily grew through the 1990s. Exports increased from 4.9 per cent to 8.5 per cent of GDP, imports from 7.9 per cent to 11.6 per cent of GDP. Yet, in the aggregate, this remained a relatively closed economy. In 1980, India accounted for 0.57 per cent of world trade; twenty years later the figure had inched up to 0.71 per cent.[30]

V

One less noticed aspect of economic liberalization was the changes in the social composition of the entrepreneurial class. Once, the major capitalists in India came from the traditional business communities – Marwaris, Jains, Banias, Chettiars, Parsis. However, in recent years, a range of peasants castes had moved into the industrial sector. Some of the most successful entrepreneurs were now Marathas, Vellalas, Reddys, Nadars and Ezhavas – from castes who for centuries had worked the land. Again, some of the best-known software 'start-ups' – such as Infosys – were initiated by Brahmins, from families which traditionally served the state or the academy and regarded commerce with disdain. There were also a few successful Muslim entrepreneurs, such as Azim Premji of the software giant WIPRO.[31]

Meanwhile, the surge in economic growth had led to an expansion in the size and influence of the Indian middle class. The emergence of this stratum, wrote E. Sridharan, 'has changed India's class structure from one characterized by a sharp contrast between a small elite and a large impoverished mass, to one with a substantial intermediate class'.

How substantial it actually was remained a matter of definition and interpretation. Defined most broadly, to include all households with an annual income in excess of Rs70,000 rupees a year (at 1998–9 prices), the middle class consisted perhaps of as many as 250 million Indians. Defined most exclusively, to keep out all those who earn less than Rs140,000 a year, it consisted of only 55 million Indians.[32]

In the past, the middle class was dominated by those working in the state sector; as civil servants, public-sector managers, university teachers, and the like. Now, those working in private firms, as well as self-employed professionals, were becoming as, if not more, significant elements of the middle class.[33] A large number were first-generation members; the first people in their family to own homes, drive scooters or cars, or take holidays. This new middle class was likely to be vernacular rather than cosmopolitan, speaking Hindi or Marathi or Tamil or Assamese rather than English, thus far the language of the Indian elite.[34]

This new middle class was the prime target of the new products and services that had entered the Indian market in recent years. By the early 2000s, there were more than 50 million subscribers to cable television in India, and at least 100 million Indians who owned mobile phones. The spread of these services grew exponentially, as did the spread of that artefact most typical of the modern consumer economy, the motor vehicle.

In the early years of Indian independence, an ethic of Gandhian austerity hung heavily over the Indian middle class. In a poor country, one was not supposed to have much wealth, and certainly not supposed to display it. Even those inclined towards hedonism were stalled by the absence of choice. With the opening of the economy in the 1990s, the guilt formerly associated with consumerism rapidly disappeared. Whether it be cigarettes, cars, whisky or sunglasses, foreign brands previously unavailable in India now flooded the market. Commercial television carried appealing images of the goods on offer; and banks and credit card companies rushed in to help one buy – and consume – them.[35]

Although most characteristic of the big cities, the new consumption was not restricted to them. An ethnographic study of rural Kerala spoke of how consumers in this age of liberalization exercised their choices with care and discrimination, with one eye on their pocket and the other on their neighbour. Rural Kerala, of course, was anything but characteristic of rural India as a whole. For one thing, the villages blended seamlessly into the towns; for another, many villagers had spent time working in the Middle East, making the kind of money that took them straight into the middle class. Anyhow, among these new consumers, wrote two scholars,

> styles and tastes are hierarchically arranged, brand-names acting as markers of distinction: a Keltron (Kerala Electronics; a state enterprise) television confers less prestige than an Onida, Indian made, which, in turn, is not as good as a Sony made under licence in India, with maximum prestige attached to foreign-made, imported televisions ... Sometimes people leave their labels on consumer durables to emphasise their origins.[36]

As with televisions, so too with a whole range of products from facial creams to cars – the Indian consumer was now spoiled for choice. Once, the only automobiles locally available were a 1950s model Morris and a 1960s model Fiat; now, if one had the money one could buy the latest Mercedes Benz. Middle-class Indians, once very focused on saving for the future, were now much more present-minded. Twenty years ago, but a handful of Indians had credit cards; now several million did so. This was once a risk-averse culture, now millions of Indians invested in property and in the stock market.

These changes in production and consumption led to a fundamental transformation of the urban landscape. Modest homes gave way to grand apartment buildings, one-story offices were replaced by imposing structures in glass and concrete. There were still traditional bazaars, whose little stalls sold locally made pots and pans or locally grown fruits and vegetables; but there were now also large malls, which displayed, under one roof, such international brands as Levi, Estée Lauder, Sony and Baskin Robbins.

VI

A second consequence of the rapid economic growth of the 1990s was a decline in the percentage of Indians who lived below the official poverty line. There was a vigorous scholarly debate on precisely how many poor people there were in India. Some statisticians concluded that a mere 15 per cent lived below the poverty line, while the more pessimistic estimates put the figure as high as 35 per cent. While the precise numbers were in dispute, virtually all scholars accepted that in both absolute and relative terms poverty had declined in the 1990s. At the beginning of the 1990s, close to 40 per cent of Indians were 'poor'; by the end of the decade, the figure had dropped by 10 percentage points or more.[37]

Still, there were huge numbers of poor people in India – close to 300 million perhaps. For beyond the glitzy malls and spanking new office buildings lay the slums and shanty towns where the majority of urban residents lived. These were the people who serviced the middle class yet would never be part of it, who 'sell newspapers they will never read, sew clothes they cannot wear, polish cars they will never own and construct buildings where they will never live'.[38] Other slum dwellers laboured long hours at low wages, in jobs perilous to their health, such as cutting metal and separating chemicals. They were usually unorganized, liable to be laid off without notice and without insurance or pension benefits.[39]

The majority of the poor people in India, however, lived in the villages. For the fruits of economic liberalization had scarcely percolated into the countryside. Agricultural growth was painfully slow during the 1990s. There were some attempts at the diversification of crops, at growing fruits and vegetables for the domestic market, and flowers for export. Yet these moves were limited in their success, largely because of deficiencies in infrastructure, i.e., the lack of electricity to process crops or keep them in storage, and the lack of roads to take them to the market.[40]

Even when it came to that basic resource, food, the picture was less cheering than it might have been. Taking the country as a whole, there was a comfortable food surplus. 'Buffer stocks' of 40 to 50 million tonnes were being maintained in government godowns. Yet the distribution mechanisms in place were seriously inadequate; in times of scarcity, stocks did not move quickly enough to communities that needed them. The targeting was inefficient; grain from the Public Distribution System (PDS) more easily reached urban areas than rural ones, and rich states than poor ones. And there was terrific corruption; according to one estimate, only 20 per cent of the grain released through the PDS actually reached the intended recipients, the rest being sold on the black market. Hunger and malnutrition remained endemic in many parts, with starvation deaths reported when the rains failed.[41]

Through much of the country, life and livelihood remained dependent on the availability of water. Fifty years after Independence, less than

40 per cent of cultivated area was under irrigation. For most farmers, the uncertainties caused by the year-to-year fluctuation in rainfall were compounded by the pre-emption of perennial water sources by the cities. Delhi took its supplies from the Tehri dam, two hundred miles away; Bangalore from the Cauvery, a hundred miles distant. Home to the privileged and the powerful, the cities got the water they demanded at a highly subsidized rate. Scarcity and discrimination sometimes promoted desperate acts. Travelling in Tamil Nadu, the journalist P. Sainath saw his train stopped in the dead of night by peasants who then took all the water they could find. Ten years later, when a drought hit northern Rajasthan, herders in Bikaner had to buy water in the open market to save their livestock from dying. The price they paid was 166 times the price a Delhi consumer was paying for his water.[42]

In the last years of the twentieth century, the first farmers' suicides were reported. This was a disturbingly novel phenomenon, for while hunger and poverty had been a feature of the subcontinental landscape for centuries, never before had so many rural people gone so far as to take their own lives. Suicide, as the pioneering studies of the French sociologist Emile Durkheim had shown, was a product of the anomie and alienation caused by modern urban living. It increased in late-nineteenth-century France, among migrants to cities dislocated from the protective care of the family and community; and it also, as it happened, increased in late-twentieth-century Bangalore, among young software professionals stressed out by the long hours of work or the rapid success of their colleagues.

Indian anthropologists had previously reported high rates of suicide among some isolated mountain tribes.[43] But what was now happening among settled peasant communities was unprecedented. Between 1995 and 2005 there were at least 10,000 suicides by farmers, these occurring in states as dispersed as Andhra Pradesh and Rajasthan. Usually, it was the male head of the household who killed himself, most often by swallowing pesticides, at other times by hanging or electrocution. In many cases, he took this extreme step because of an inability to pay off debts accumulated over the years, these owed to banks, co-operatives, or private moneylenders. But indebtedness had also been a pervasive feature of rural life; why, now, did it lead so often to this tragic outcome? No systematic studies exist yet to answer this question, but some preliminary speculation might be in order. The rash of farmers' suicides was perhaps related to the rapidity of social change in contemporary India. The new consumer society, its images carried into the villages by television, placed a very high premium on success and failure. Thus, when crops failed, or a new crop did not give the yield it promised, the personal humiliation felt was greatly in excess of what it might have been in an earlier, more stable, and less acquisitive time.[44]

VII

One reason for the continuing poverty was the government's poor record in providing basic services such as education and health care. In 1991, the year the reforms began, only 39 per cent of Indian women could read and write; and only 64 per cent of the men. Here, India lagged behind not merely the developed nations of the West, but also some of its Asian neighbours. Thus Sri Lanka had educated 89 per cent of its women and 94 per cent of its men, while the corresponding figures for China were 75 per cent and 96 per cent respectively.

The inability – some would say unwillingness – to educate all or even most of its citizens counted as independent India's greatest failure.[45] In the 1990s, however, the government initiated a number of schemes to universalize education. First, there was the District Primary Education Programme, which focused on 250 districts where female literacy was less than the national average. A little later, this was superseded by a Sarva Shiksha Abhiyan (Programme to Educate All). The funds devoted to primary education from the public exchequer were increased, and there was also an inflow of money from foreign donors.

The government was pushed to be more proactive by an order of the Supreme Court directing all state governments to provide cooked midday meals in schools. Many children who entered primary school dropped out well before they got to high school. A high proportion of these 'dropouts' were girls, who were withdrawn by their families to help with household tasks such as cooking, cleaning and collecting firewood. In Tamil Nadu, where midday meals had first been introduced, they had helped considerably in increasing enrolment. It was hoped that a countrywide extension would encourage parents to send their children to school and keep them there.[46]

A number of innovative non-governmental organizations also entered the educational field in the 1990s. One NGO, active in the poorer districts of Andhra Pradesh, was able to place every child in 400 villages in school. The NGO ran a 'bridge course' for those who entered school late (most of whom were girls) – giving them six months of intensive coaching before placing them in the regular curriculum. Another NGO was following similar methods among the slum dwellers of India's largest city, Mumbai. They had opened 3,000 *balwadis* or playschools, where children between the ages of 3 and 5 were taught to read and write. In these densely crowded slums, with space at a premium, all kinds of sites were used as playschools: temple courtyards, school verandahs, public parks, even offices of political parties. From the *balwadis* these children were sent on to regular municipal schools. By 1998, some 55,000 children had passed through this process, which was now being extended to other cities and towns of northern and western India.[47]

Within the state system, there were considerable variations in implementation and effectiveness. Schools in Bihar and Uttar Pradesh were very badly run, with poor or non-existent facilities – no blackboards, no chairs, no toilets for girls. The teachers were disinterested – rates of absenteeism were high – and the parents apathetic. Among the better performing states were Kerala and Tamil Nadu in the south, and Himachal Pradesh in the north. The educational progress of this last state was both rapid and unexpected. Himachal was dominated by the Rajputs, a caste who had traditionally kept their women at home. It was also a hilly state, with widely dispersed hamlets, making schools hard to site and harder to get to. However, these natural and cultural disadvantages were overcome by the state's administration, led by Himachal's first chief minister, Dr Y. S. Parmar. After the state was carved out of Punjab in the late 1960s, Parmar made elementary education a pivotal element of public policy. Public expenditure on education was twice the national average, while the teacher-child ratio was far higher than in other parts of India. Parents were quick to realize the benefits of sending both their boys and girls to school. Concerned families and capable administrators worked to ensure that the schools were well maintained, and teachers properly motivated. The results were impressive: while, in 1961, only 11 per cent of girls in these hill districts were literate, by 1998 the figure had jumped to 98 per cent.[48]

Although no other state performed nearly as well as Himachal Pradesh, the data suggested that the education sector was not as somnolent as it had once been. By the end of the 1990s, the female literacy rate had risen from 39 per cent to 54 per cent; the male literacy rate, from 64 per cent to 76 per cent. Behind these changes in quantity lay a fundamental change in mentality. Once, many poor parents had chosen to put their children to work rather than send them to school. Now, they wished to place them in a position from which they could, with luck and enterprise, exchange a life of menial labour for a job in the modern economy. As the educationist Vimala Ramachandran wrote in 2004, 'the demand side had never looked more promising. The overwhelming evidence emanating from studies done in the last 10 years clearly demonstrates that there is a tremendous demand for education – across the board and among all social groups. Wherever the government has ensured a well-functioning school within reach, enrolment has been high'.[49]

Where developments in education called for a cautious optimism, the outlook in the health sector remained bleak. Hospitals owned and run by the central and state governments were in a pathetic state: crowded, corrupt, without basic facilities or qualified doctors. And the political class seemed unconcerned. In fact, public expenditure on health was on the decline. While in 1990 it constituted 1.3 per cent of GDP, by 1999 the figure had dropped to 0.9 per cent. At the same time, there was a tremendous expansion of privatized health care, which by 2002 accounted for nearly 80 per cent of all health expenditure. This, however, was aimed at servicing the growing middle class. In some areas the poor were served by committed NGOs, but for the most part they were left to their own devices, going to indigenous medicine men or village quacks to treat their illnesses.

Some statistics may be in order here. Average life expectancy in 2001 was a niggardly 64 years. In many states, infant mortality rates remained high. In Meghalaya, for example, it was 89 deaths per 1,000. India had 60 per cent of the world's leprosy cases (about half a million). 15 million Indians suffered from tuberculosis, a number that rose by 2 million every year. To these older diseases was added a new one – AIDS. By 2004, more than 5 million Indians were HIV positive.[50]

'India', wrote one knowledgeable observer, 'has stopped thinking about public health and has paid a very heavy price for that'.[51]

VIII

Economic liberalization had improved the lives of many million Indians, but left millions more untouched. And there were also some Indians who had been adversely affected by the freeing of the market and the opening of the economy to the outside world.

Among those who suffered from economic liberalization the adivasis, or tribals, of central India were perhaps foremost. They lived in the most resource-rich areas of the country – with the best forests, the most valuable minerals, and the freest-flowing rivers. Over the years, they had lost many of these resources to the state or to outsiders, and struggled hard to retain what remained.

A particular target of tribal ire was the Forest Department, which restricted their access to wood and to non-timber forest produce such as honey and herbs, which they collected and sold for a living. In the state of Madhya Pradesh, the trade in tendu leaves (used for making *bidis*, or cheroots) was particularly lucrative. The government had handed over the trade to private contractors, but the actual collection was done by the tribals. The rates were niggardly: Rs30 for 5,000 leaves. In the early 1990s, the tribals demanded higher rates; when this was denied, they stopped traffic on major highways in the state.[52]

According to one study, while adivasis constituted 8 per cent of the country's population, they constituted 40 per cent of the population displaced by dams, mines, steel mills and other such projects.[53] Another study documented how, with regard to access to education and health, adivasis were even worse off than Dalits. Surveys comparing the two communities showed that while 41 per cent of the Dalits lived under the official 'poverty line', the figure for adivasis was closer to 50 per cent. Likewise while the literacy rate of Dalits was low, at roughly 30 per cent, that of the adivasis was 6 percentage points lower still. As for public health facilities, one in six Dalits had no access to doctors and clinics, but one in four adivasis did. Only 43 per cent of adivasis had access to safe drinking water, as compared to 64 per cent of Dalits.[54]

A variety of activists were working in adivasi areas; some Gandhian in orientation, others Marxist. The issues they took up included access to land and forests, and the provision of decent schools and hospitals. These were, surely, the groups most neglected by the Indian state, and also the most condescended to. The colonial regime had designated an array of tribal communities as being 'criminal'; their crime being that they lived not in settled villages but moved around in search of a living. After Independence, these tribes had been formally 'denotified', but the prejudice against them remained. Officials posted in tribal districts were known for their disdain towards those whom they were paid to serve.

Once quiescent, under activist influence the tribals were now moved to protest; the consequence being a series of clashes with the police.[55]

The most celebrated of tribal assertions in the 1990s was the 'Narmada Bachao Andolan' (Save the Narmada Movement). Its leader was Medha Patkar, who was not herself a tribal, but a social worker raised and radicalized in Bombay. The movement aimed at stopping a massive dam on the Narmada river which would render homeless some 200,000 people, a majority of them adivasi in origin. Patkar organized the tribals in a series of colourful marches: to the dam site in Gujarat, to the city of Bhopal (capital of Madhya Pradesh, the state to which most of the oustees belonged), to the national capital, Delhi, there to demand justice from the mighty government of India. The leader herself engaged in several long fasts to draw attention to the sufferings of her flock.[56]

Patkar's struggle was unsuccessful in stopping this particular dam, but it did draw wide attention to the government's disgraceful record in resettling the millions displaced by development projects. Official acknowledgement of the long history of adivasi suffering, meanwhile, came through the creation in 2000 of two new states of the Union: named Jharkhand and Chhattisgarh, and carved out of the tribal districts of Bihar and Madhya Pradesh respectively. Also formed was the state of Uttarakhand, from the hill districts of Uttar Pradesh, likewise rich in natural resources, these likewise subject to exploitation by powerful external interests.

One state with a large tribal population was Orissa. The state was divided into a coastal region, dominated by caste Hindus; and a series of mountain ranges in the interior, where lived a variety of adivasi communities. In the state as a whole the Hindus were in a majority, and wielded most of the political and administrative power. In 1999 Orissa overtook – if that is the word – Bihar as India's poorest state. And among the residents of Orissa the upland tribals were the poorest and most vulnerable. Whether reckoned in terms of land, income, health facilities or literacy rate, they lagged behind the state as a whole. The tribals were heavily dependent on the monsoon and on the forests for survival. With the woods disappearing, and the rains sometimes failing, they plunged deeper into poverty, as manifested periodically in starvation deaths.[57]

The wealth in these highlands was mostly under the ground. Orissa had 70 per cent of the country's bauxite reserves, and also substantial deposits of iron ore. These minerals were concentrated in the tribal districts of Rayagada and Koraput. In the past, these ores were worked by

Indian public sector companies, but in the 1990s these were supplanted by private firms, domestic as well as foreign. The state government signed a series of leases, offering land at attractive prices to companies who wished to mine these hills.[58]

One of the more ambitious projects was floated by a consortium named Utkal Alumina, which brought together Canadian and Norwegian firms with the Aditya Birla Group. This had its eye on the Baphlimali hills of the Kashipur block of Rayagada district, under which lay a deposit of 200 million tonnes of bauxite. The proposal was to mine this ore and transport it to a newly built refinery, which would process the material and export the refined product.

Some of the land to be used for these operations was owned by the government; but some 3,000 acres were cultivated by tribals. These saw no benefit in the project, which would dispossess them of their fields and give them naught in return. A delegation of tribal activists met the chief minister and demanded that he cancel the lease. Their request was refused; instead, the government sent a team to survey the land preparatory to its acquisition. Over the next few years the tribals tried a variety of strategies to stop the project from getting off the ground. Employees of Utkal Alumina were prohibited from entering the villages. Roads were blockaded, and marches organized to raise consciousness of the environmental and social damage that mining would cause. When the company constructed a 'model' of the kind of house in which they intended to rehabilitate the tribals, the prospective beneficiaries simply demolished it.[59]

On the other side, the administration was determined to go ahead with the project. They saw it as a source of revenue for the exchequer, some of this intended also for the pockets of parties and politicians. In March 1999, a group of social scientists from Delhi visited Rayagada, and wrote a report warning the Orissa government 'that unless the popular discontent among local tribals over the acquisition of land was properly addressed this peaceful district may turn into a hotbed of Naxalite [Maoist] activity ...'.[60] A year-and-a-half later, the journalist Darryl D'Monte travelled from Mumbai to study the situation on the ground. He found the tribals resolute in their opposition. The mines, they told him, would 'destroy the ecosystem of the Baphlimali plateau'. One adivasi leader said they would stop all vehicles from entering the area. 'We are prepared for any consequences', he insisted, adding: 'In a conflagration, anyone ought to be prepared to get singed'. D'Monte noted that the government was equally determined to push the project through. 'Over the past five years the district administration, in tandem with the police and politicians, has almost acted like the advance guard of the companies ...'.[61]

The conflagration came two months later, and tragically it was the tribals who got singed. On the 15th of December, the ruling Biju Janata Dal organized a meeting in the area, to canvass support for the project. Angry villagers refused to allow them to hold the meeting. Three platoons of police arrived to disperse the protesters, but were held up by a group of women. When the police lathi-charged the women, the men arrived to help them. At some stage the police opened fire, killing three tribals. Among the first to express solidarity with the victims were Maoist revolutionaries.[62]

IX

To be sure, India had long been marked by sharp inequalities. Some regions and some social groups were noticeably less poor than others. However, the market-oriented reforms of the 1990s tended to accentuate these inequalities. The economies of the states that were poorest grew slowly during the decade, while those of the states that were already better off grew faster. Through the 1990s Bihar registered an annual growth rate of 2.69 per cent, Uttar Pradesh of 3.58 per cent, and Orissa of 3.25 per cent. On the other side, Gujarat had a growth rate of 9.57 per cent, Maharashtra of 8.01 per cent, and Tamil Nadu of 6.22 per cent. Broadly speaking, the states that did well were located in the south and west of the country, while the states that fared indifferently were in the north and east. At the very bottom were the massively populous states of Bihar and Uttar Pradesh. In 1993, these two states accounted for 41.7 per cent of India's poor; in 2000, for 42.5 per cent.[63]

It appeared that economic performance was crucially dependent on initial endowments of human capital and physical infrastructure. The states that had better schools and hospitals and hence a more skilled and healthy workforce were usually also the states that had better roads, more reliable electricity and less corrupt administrations.[64] Naturally, it was to these locations that investment and investors gravitated. In a pre-reform era, the central government often chose to site industries in areas deemed 'backward'. But private entrepreneurs were under no such obligation. They looked to where they would get the best return on their capital. These were the southern and western states, which surged further ahead as a consequence.

That said, even in the most prosperous states it was not the entire population that prospered. The capitals of Karnataka and Andhra Pradesh, Bangalore and Hyderabad respectively, were at the leading edge of the software boom, but their own hinterlands had been left far behind. Between 1994 and 2000, per capita consumption expenditure grew in rural Karnataka at 9.5 per cent annually, in urban Karnataka at 26.5 per cent. The corresponding figures for Andhra Pradesh were 2.8 per cent (rural) and 18.5 per cent (urban). Taking India as a whole, expenditure grew at 8.7 per cent per year in the countryside, but at 16.6 per cent in the cities.[65]

As the economist T. N. Srinivasan observed in 2000, these wide disparities meant that 'if one is poor in India', then

> one is more likely to live in rural areas, more likely to be a member of the Scheduled Caste or Tribe or other socially discriminated groups, more likely to be malnourished, sick and in poor health, more likely to be illiterate or poorly educated and with low skills, more likely to live in certain states (such as ... Bihar, Madhya Pradesh, Rajasthan and Uttar Pradesh, and also Orissa) than in others ...[66]

Across the country, prosperity co-existed with misery, technological sophistication with human degradation. The paradoxes of life in India were tellingly captured in a conversation between the prime minister and villagers in Orissa that took place in September 2001. From his home in New Delhi, Atal Behari Vajpayee spoke by satellite to tribals in Kashipur, whose kinsmen had died eating mango kernel because their crops had failed. 'It is extremely unfortunate that in today's world people die by eating poisonous material', said the head of a government that could speak to its citizens by videophone, yet not supply them with wholesome food.[67]

X

In 2004, the Indian economy became a subject of debate in the American presidential election. This was unprecedented; more striking still was the fact that it was not the poverty of Indians but their wealth that was being discussed. In several speeches on the stump, the Democratic challenger John Kerry stoked fears of more American jobs being shipped east if President Bush were re-elected. If he was chosen by the voters, promised Kerry, he would reinstate a protectionist regime to save American jobs from being 'Bangalored'. This too was another first; the first time that a Presidential candidate had singled out an Indian city by name as a threat to American interests.

Other American politicians had got into the act before Kerry. In 2002, a computer programmer from Florida ran for Congress on a one-point programme: an end to 'outsourcing'. The same year, a woman member of the New Jersey Senate introduced a bill forbidding the outsourcing of state contracts to foreign firms. Like her counterpart in Florida, her main complaint was against Indian computer firms and professionals. These politicians were responding sympathetically to the 'pissed off programmers', to the Americans who had lost their jobs to Indians and wanted them back.[68]

In December 2003, the influential *Business Week* magazine ran a cover story on 'The Rise of India'. It noted that there were now more IT engineers in Bangalore than in the whole of Silicon Valley. And they were mostly doing work for American clients, for giant corporations like GE who wanted complex engineering problems solved, as well as for Kansas farmers who wished merely to have their tax returns filled out. This 'techno take-off is wonderful for India', commented *Business Week*, 'but terrifying for many Americans'. The local workers laid off by foreign substitutes would face 'wrenching change'; few would ever land a job as well paid as the one they had just lost. 'No wonder India [was] at the centre of a brewing storm in America'. State legislatures were under pressure to ban outsourcing; some succumbed, like Indiana, which cancelled contracts awarded to Indian firms.[69]

Some commentators on India's economic rise wrote in paranoid terms; others out of admiration. In April 2004, *Newsweek* informed its readers that India was no longer a poor, benighted, Third World country; it was now 'a good place to do business', indeed, 'an investment-worthy partner' for Americans and American business.[70]

The predictions came thick and fast – that Indians would take away American and European jobs; that India, with China, would become the global superpower of the twenty-first century. Whether they stemmed from fear and paranoia, or from wonder and admiration, it was surely strange, if not a miracle, that such forecasts were made at all. For through most of India's history as an independent nation it had heard altogether different tunes being sung. With every communal riot it was said that India would break up into many different fragments. With every failure of the monsoon it was predicted that mass starvation and famine would follow. And with every death or killing of a major leader it was forecast that India would abandon democracy and become a dictatorship.

Those earlier prophecies also stemmed from a variety of motives – some were made with concern, others out of pity or contempt. They prompted anger and embarrassment among educated Indians. These newer predictions, however, led to a rising tide of self-congratulation. Indian newspapers and magazines now ran stories captioned 'Global Champs' and 'On the Way to Number One'. One Delhi columnist was so certain that India was becoming the world's titan that he worried that it would repeat the errors of those it had replaced. Where the West in its heyday had callously exploited its colonies, he urged 'Indian business to establish a loving and friendly relationship with other countries ...'. The important thing, he said, was 'to ensure that India is not seen as a cruel imperial power in the world of tomorrow'. That India would indeed soon be an imperial power was, however, taken for granted.[71]

Those older anticipations of India's demise were greatly exaggerated. For the constitution forged by the nation's founding fathers allowed cultural heterogeneity to flourish within the ambit of a single (and democratic) nation-state. However, these celebrations of India's imminent rise to power were premature as well. Despite the manifest successes of the new economy there remained large areas of poverty and deprivation. Only purposive state intervention could correct these imbalances; and the Indian state, circa 2000, was too corroded and corrupted to act with much purpose. It was mistaken, then, to see India as swiftly going down the tube; and it was mistaken, now, to see it as soon taking its place among the elect of the earth.

XI

In October 1999, Pakistan's brief flirtation with parliamentary democracy ended. Prime Minister Nawaz Sharif was deposed in a coup led by the chief of army staff, Pervez Musharraf. The Indians were not best pleased with these developments; for it was Musharraf who was believed to have masterminded the Kargil operations earlier that year.

In March 2000 President Clinton visited South Asia. He spent five days in India and five hours in Pakistan, in a historic reversal of the traditional American bias towards the smaller country. This was an acknowledgement of India's rising strength, but also a chastisement of Pakistan's return to military rule.

During the Cold War the United States had tilted markedly towards Pakistan. After the Soviet Union had collapsed, it moved towards a position of equidistance between India and Pakistan. Clinton's visit suggested that America had now in fact begun favouring India. The reasons for this were chiefly economic; the sense that here was a large market for American goods. In 1990, Indo-US trade was worth $5.3 billion; now it had nearly tripled. Thus, while for many decades Washington was prone to treat India as an 'insignificant pawn' in the Cold War, by the end of the twentieth century it had become a 'natural ally'.[72]

The day after President Clinton landed in New Delhi, terrorists dressed in Indian army uniforms descended upon the village of Chittisinghpora in Kashmir, pulled out Sikh men from their homes, and shot them. In a village of 300 homes, 'nearly every house ha[d] lost a relative, neighbour, or friend'. The tragedy was compounded when the security forces shot five men they claimed had committed the crime, but who were later found to be innocent.[73]

The Chittisinghpora killers were probably freelancers who did not have the sanction of the Pakistani government. Still, there was little question that it was the Kashmir issue which continued to most deeply divide the two nations. President Musharraf issued periodic reminders of Pakistan's undying commitment to the 'liberation struggle' of the Kashmiris. The Indian prime minister chastised his counterpart for adhering to the 'pernicious two-nation theory that brought about the partition'.[74]

Neither country was prepared to accept the other's position on Kashmir. However, a dialogue was recommenced, this motivated perhaps by the need to act as responsible nuclear powers in the eyes of the world. In July 2001 President Musharraf visited Agra at the invitation of the Indian government. He and his wife were put up in a luxury hotel overlooking the Taj Mahal. The general and Vajpayee talked for long hours, with and without aides. The meeting ended inconclusively, when a draft communique left both sides dissatisfied, with India wanting a greater emphasis to be placed on cross-border terrorism and Pakistan asking for a more explicit acknowledgement of the democratic aspirations of the Kashmiri people.

While General Musharraf was in Agra terrorists struck again in the Valley. In a dozen separate attacks at least eighty people were killed. This was becoming a pattern – whenever important dignitaries visited New Delhi the violence in Kashmir would escalate. When the US secretary of state Colin Powell came in October 2001, terrorists launched a grenade assault on the Jammu and Kashmir Assembly. Two months later, they undertook an even more daring action. Four suicide bombers entered the Indian Parliament in a car and attempted to blow it up. They were killed by the police, who later identified them as Pakistanis.[75]

The Assembly building in Srinagar was a symbol of the state's integration with India. The Parliament building in New Delhi was the symbol of Indian democracy itself. Within its portals met elected politicians representing a billion people. The attacks on these two places brought an end to the diplomatic dialogue. India accused Pakistan of abetting the terrorists. Appeals were made to the US government to rein in its old ally. While sympathizing with America after the incidents of 11 September 2001, India added that their sympathy was made the more sincere by the fact that they had long been victims of terrorist violence themselves.

In the spring of 2002 exchanges between Indian and Pakistani troops became more frequent. As spring turned to summer, and the troop build-up intensified, the concerns of 1998 returned – would the subcontinent be witness to the first ever nuclear exchange? A respected Nepali monthly thought that the region was 'poised on the cusp of war once again'. A leading American analyst believed that 'the crisis between India and Pakistan is the most dangerous confrontation since Soviet ships steamed towards the US naval blockade of Cuba in 1962'.[76]

In the end, war was averted; although perhaps it wasn't even planned. Within India, attention shifted to the coming assembly elections in Kashmir. The state had, as a Delhi newspaper squarely put it, a 'long history of rigged elections', the polls of 1977 being the exception to the rule.[77] In the past, the Election Commission had, in Kashmir at any rate, 'always appeared to be in the company of, and therefore in collaboration with, security forces and partisan state government functionaries ...'. Now it worked overtime to redeem its reputation. The chief election commissioner ordered a complete revision of the voters' list, which was unchanged since 1988. An extensive survey of all houses led to a new, comprehensive list, covering 350,000 pages in the elegant but hard-to-print Urdu script. Copies of the electoral rolls were then distributed to all political parties, and displayed in schools and hospitals and government offices across the state. A further precaution was the import of 8,000 electronic voting machines, to prevent booth-capturing and rigging.[78]

The assembly elections were held in September 2002. The militants killed a prominent moderate just before the polls, and urged the public to boycott them. Despite these threats, some 48 per cent of Kashmiris turned out to vote, somewhat less than was usual in other parts of India, but far in excess of what had been anticipated. International observers were at hand to confirm that the polls were fair. The ruling National Conference was voted out of power; the winners were an alliance comprising the Congress and the Peoples Democratic Party. The 2002 Jammu and Kashmir election, wrote two long-time students of the state's politics, could 'be seen as a reversal of [the] 1987 assembly elections which by eroding the democratic space had become [the] catalyst for separatist politics ... This election has brought about a change in the regime through the popular verdict and to that extent it has become instrumental in providing a linkage between the people and the government'.[79] The new chief minister, Mufti Mohammad Sayeed, expressed these sentiments more crisply, when he remarked that 'this is the first time since 1953 that India has acquired legitimacy in the eyes of the [Kashmiri] people'.[80]

XII

After the Babri Masjid came down in December 1992, Hindu radicals had hoped to build a grand temple in its place. Architects were commissioned to design an edifice in marble, and craftsmen engaged to cut the stone and polish it. However, the site itself remained in the custody of the state. Cases were being heard in the Allahabad High Court and the Supreme Court, to decide whether a Ram temple had ever existed here, and whether the VHP had (as it claimed) the legal rights to the land surrounding the old mosque. Attempts were also made to find a solution outside the courts. The influential Shankaracharya of Kanchi met with the Babri Masjid Action Committee, and urged them to hand over this one site, in exchange for which no further demands would be made on the Muslims.

The BJP remained committed to the construction of a temple in Ayodhya. When it came to power at the centre in 1998, it said it would forge a national consensus on the issue, failing which it would enact enabling legislation. The prime minister, Atal Behari Vajpayee, said that 'Rama occupies an exalted place in Indian culture', and claimed that 'the entire country wants a Rama temple at Ayodhya', the issue being 'how to make it and where'.[81]

However, at the site itself the status quo prevailed. The courts took their time disposing of the matter, and no compromise could be reached outside them either. Meanwhile, the Vishwa Hindu Parishad organized tours of Ayodhya by *kar sevaks* from all over the country. They also held religious ceremonies in anticipation of the building of the temple. One such *yagna*, held in the last week of February 2002, was attended by hundreds of volunteers from the state of Gujarat. On their way back home by train, these *kar sevaks* got into a fight with Muslim vendors at the Godhra railway station. The vendors were asked to chant slogans in homage to Lord Ram; when they refused, their beards were pulled. Word of the altercation spread; young men from the Muslim neighbourhood outside the station joined in. The *kar sevaks* clambered back into the train, which started moving even as stones were being thrown. However, the train stopped on the outskirts of the station, when a fire broke out in one of its coaches. Fifty-eight people perished in the conflagration.

Godhra was a town with a long history of communal violence; it had experienced serious riots in 1949, and again in 1981. That Hindus and Muslims had not always been on the best of terms, and that the Ayodhya problem had strained relations further, is clear. It is also beyond dispute that the incident at the station was sparked by *kar sevaks* taunting Muslim vendors. What remains unclear is the cause of the fire afterwards. The VHP claimed that it was the handiwork of a Muslim mob. On the other hand, forensic evidence suggested that it originated inside the bogey, and was probably the result of a gas cylinder or kerosene stove accidentally catching fire.[82]

Word that a group of *kar sevaks* had been burnt to death at Godhra quickly spread through Gujarat. A wave of retributory violence followed. This was at its most intense, and horrific, in the cities of Ahmedabad and Baroda. Once known for their philanthropic industrialists and progressive intellectuals, once centres of technical innovation and artistic excellence, both places had experienced a prolonged period of economic decline. With this came a deterioration in inter-community relations. Hindus and Muslims now rarely worked or played together, a separation that had in the recent past expressed itself in bouts of communal violence.[83]

These latest riots in Baroda and Ahmedabad were unprecedented in their savagery. Muslim shops and offices were attacked, mosques torched, and cars vandalized. Muslim women were raped, Muslim men killed and bonfires made of their bodies. The mobs were often led by activists of the VHP, with the local administration in collusion. Their weapons ranged from swords and guns to petrol bombs and gas cylinders. The vandals had voter lists, which allowed them to identify which homes were Muslim and which were not. Ministers of the state government were camped in police control rooms, directing operations. The police had been instructed to give 'free run of the roads to VHP and Bajrang Dal mobs'.[84]

Beyond Baroda and Ahmedabad, the violence also reached out into smaller towns and rural settlements. In the district of Sabarkantha, mobs roamed the countryside in tractors and jeeps, targeting properties owned by Muslims. The numerical record of their activities is available: 'altogether, 2161 houses, 1461 shops, 304 smaller enterprises, ... 71 factories, 38 hotels, 45 religious places, and 240 vehicles were completely or partially destroyed'.[85] What was true of Sabarkantha was broadly true of the state as a whole. The VHP had made it clear that it wanted to render the Muslims hopeless as well as homeless. Thus in Ahmedabad, weeks after the riots had subsided Muslims still found it difficult to get loans from banks, gas and phone connections and admission in school for their children. Muslims who had fled their villages were told they would have to drop charges against the rioters if they wished to return. Sometimes their safety was made conditional on their conversion to Hinduism.[86]

The chief minister of Gujarat at the time of the 2002 riots was Narendra Modi, a hard-line Hindutva ideologue who had grown up in the unforgiving school of the RSS. Now, he seemed to justify the violence on Muslims by pointing to the burning of the coach in Godhra, which, he said, had set in motion a 'chain of action and reaction'. In truth, the reaction was many times that of the original action. More than 1,000 Muslims were killed, and at least hundred times that number rendered homeless, living in refugee camps whose pitiable condition was noticed by the prime minister and president themselves.[87]

The Oxford English Dictionary defines 'pogrom' as 'an organized massacre of a particular ethnic group'. By this definition, while there have been hundreds of inter-religious riots in the history of independent India, there have been only two pogroms: that directed at the Sikhs in Delhi in 1984, and that directed at the Muslims of South Gujarat in 2002. There are some striking similarities between the two. Both began as a response to a single, stray act of violence committed by, as it were, members of the minority community. Both proceeded to take a generalized revenge on the minorities as a whole. The Sikhs who were butchered were in no way connected to the Sikhs who killed Mrs Gandhi. The Muslims who were killed by Hindu mobs were completely innocent of the Godhra crime.

In both cases, the pogroms were made possible by the willed breakdown of the rule of law. The prime minister in Delhi in 1984, and the chief minister in Gujarat in 2002, issued graceless statements that in effect justified the killings. And serving ministers in their government went so far as to aid and direct the rioters.

The final similarity is the most telling, as well as perhaps the most depressing. Both parties and leaders reaped electoral rewards from the violence they had legitimized and overseen. Rajiv Gandhi's party won the 1984 general elections by a very large margin. And, in December 2002, Narenda Modi was re-elected as chief minister of Gujarat after his party won a two-thirds majority in the Assembly polls.[88]

XIII

Visiting Gujarat in April 2002, Prime Minister Atal Behari Vajpayee announced a rehabilitation package for the victims of the recent riots. At a press conference in Ahmedabad, Vajpayee urged the state's chief minister to henceforth follow his *rajdharma* and not discriminate between citizens according to their caste or community.[89]

The prime minister was upset at the Gujarat government's mishandling of the riots, and the adverse international publicity that had resulted. He had wanted Modi removed as chief minister, but senior party men (including his deputy prime minister, L. K. Advani) dissuaded him, arguing that a public acknowledgement of this failure would cost the party dearly.

Vajpayee had been nominated as prime minister by the BJP in part because of his length of service (he was a member of parliament as far back as 1957), in part because of his oratorical skills, in part because he was seen as more acceptable to the BJP's allies than Advani. Aided by an able principal secretary, Brijesh Mishra, Vajpayee ran a fairly firm ship as prime minister, keeping the allies in check and moderating the extremists in his own party. Thus he became the first non-Congress prime minister to complete a full term in office, a not inconsiderable achievement. For the first three decades of Independence the Congress utterly dominated Indian politics. But now, at last, an Opposition capable of taking on and beating it had emerged. The BJP had once challenged the Congress at the level of ideology; then it had successfully challenged it at the polls; now, under Vajpayee's leadership, it had shown it could run a government too.

The term of the NDA government was to end only in October 2004; but, perhaps worried about the impact of an adverse monsoon, in February itself the prime minister dissolved Parliament. A campaign was crafted for re-election, featuring the slogan, 'India Shining'. The steady progress the economy had made under the NDA, and the perceived disarray of the Opposition, led most observers to predict a handsome victory for the ruling alliance. A poll conducted by the widely read *India Today* magazine estimated that the NDA would win between 330 and 340 seats, a comfortable majority. 'Everything in the road map', wrote the magazine, 'points right back to where it all began for Atal Bihari Vajpayee: 7 Race Course Road [the Prime Minister's residence] and another term in its fully groomed environs'. The NDA was 'enjoying the ride of its life'; on the other side, for the Congress, the magazine anticipated 'by far the worst drubbing the 119-year-old party will ever record in its history'.

India Today thought the general election whose results it was so certain of would throw up a question apiece for the leaders of the two major alliances. Thus 'for Vajpayee, the question may well be how long he wishes to stay as prime minister'; and for Sonia Gandhi, 'will she – should she – withdraw from the cut and thrust of electoral politics and make way for another leader?'[90]

29

PROGRESS AND ITS DISCONTENTS

[In India] the growth process is so biased, making the country look more and more like islands of California in a sea of sub-Saharan Africa.

JEAN DRÉZE and AMARTYA SEN

I

WHEN POLLING ENDED IN the 2004 general elections and the votes were counted, the results were contrary to what the pollsters had expected. They had predicted a comfortable victory for the ruling alliance; in the event, the National Democratic Alliance won a mere 189 seats, whereas the United Progressive Alliance (UPA), led by the Congress, secured 222. The president now asked the UPA to form the government. It was generally expected that the Congress president, Sonia Gandhi, would become prime minister.

In her early years in politics, Sonia Gandhi had not made much of an impact. But she worked extremely hard, and travelled extensively across the country. Her persistence was rewarded; although the BJP-led NDA was in power at the centre, as many as fifteen state governments were headed by the Congress.[1]

When, in May 2004, the time came for the UPA to take office at the centre, Sonia Gandhi chose to decline the post of prime minister. She instead nominated Dr Manmohan Singh, the self-effacing economist who had been finance minister in the 1990s and had since served three terms in the Upper House of Parliament. Sonia Gandhi did not reveal why she would not be prime minister herself; or why she had chosen Dr Singh above other Congress leaders. Perhaps she thought having a prime minister born and raised in Italy would raise unnecessary controversy; perhaps, never having worked in government, she was not sure how she would handle the complexities of the job.

The personal relationship between party president and prime minister was cordial. However, in terms of their economic policies they diverged. Manmohan Singh was a reformist, who would, left wholly on his own, have pushed for a further freeing of market forces, the reduction of subsidies, the removal of restrictive labour laws, and the full convertibility of the rupee. On the other hand, Sonia Gandhi was a populist who wished the state to restrict the role of the market, protect the interests of workers, and provide greater subsidies and social services to farmers and agricultural labourers.[2]

Sonia Gandhi had constituted a National Advisory Council, chaired by herself, and composed largely of social activists who shared her welfarist ideas. The NAC pressed its ideas on the prime minister. Among the schemes adopted by the government was a National Rural Employment Guarantee Act, which would guarantee to adult members of rural households one hundred days of paid employment a year. The programme would cost the state exchequer an estimated Rs 20,000 crores annually.[3] Another was a Right to Information Act, which would make it mandatory for details of government programmes, allocations and appointments to be placed when asked for in the public domain, excepting those matters pertaining to security, defence, or strategic national interests. A third was a Forest Rights Act, which sought to allot tribal families plots of land in state-owned forests.

Following the NDA model, the Congress kept the Finance, Home, and Foreign ministries, those assigned to these posts chosen by the party president rather than the prime minister. However, important economic ministries such as Information Technology and Agriculture were ceded to alliance partners.[4]

II

In March 2005, less than a year after coming to power, the UPA Government announced the setting up of a 'high-level' committee to study the socio-economic and educational status of Muslims in India. It was to be chaired by a retired judge of the Delhi High Court, Justice Rajinder Sachar.

The establishment of the Sachar Committee was shrewd politics. Muslims across India had voted in large numbers for the UPA in the general election of 2004. But it was also an honest acknowledgement of the palpable failure of the Indian state to fulfil the assurances that Gandhi and Nehru had given to those Muslims who had stayed behind in India after Partition. Six decades later, the community remained economically vulnerable, socially insecure and politically marginal.

To be sure, not all Muslims were poor. There were prosperous artisans in some towns in north India, making products for export. Gujarat and Maharashtra had many established Muslim traders. One large IT firm, and at least two large pharmaceutical firms, were owned by Muslims. Some of India's most celebrated film stars were Muslim. But, on the aggregate, Muslims were among the poorest communities in India. They were under-represented in Parliament, in state legislatures, in the all-India civil services, in the judiciary and in the professional classes more generally. The typical Muslim was a barber, tailor, rickshaw puller or peasant, making barely enough for subsistence. Literacy rates were low. Few Muslim women were in the work force.[5]

In the 1950s, there were far more Muslims with university degrees than Dalits. By the time the Sachar Committee had been set up, the situation had been reversed. Inspired by Ambedkar's example, Dalits had taken energetically to education. Affirmative action also helped Dalits obtain university admission and, in time, jobs as doctors, police officers, civil servants and engineers. Meanwhile, Muslims lagged behind, their situation made more precarious by their reactionary leadership, composed of *mullahs* who preferred to hark back to the glorious early days of Islam rather than engage with the complex challenges of the twenty-first century.[6]

Almost the only sphere of Indian life in which Muslims were over-represented was in the nation's cities. They constituted about 14 per cent of the country's population, but 18 per cent of the urban population. Here, too, their situation was far from happy. Some 37 per cent of urban Muslims lived below the poverty line, as against 22 per cent of urban Hindus. Their lowly economic status was compounded by their fragile social status. They lived in ghettoes, interacting mostly with members of their own community. When they ventured out into the city at large they were often met with prejudice and hostility, and sometimes outright ostracism. Hindu landlords would not rent apartments to Muslim tenants, even if these spoke English, had high-paying jobs and otherwise were cosmopolitan rather than stereotypical. Muslim children found it hard to get admission in non-denominational schools.[7]

The Sachar Committee drew on past surveys and its own investigations to compile its report, which was presented in November 2006. The report identified three crucial issues facing Indian Muslims. The first was the problem of identity. Six decades after Partition, Muslims were still blamed for the 'vivisection' of India, still seen as having an uncertain and wavering allegiance to the national flag. At the same time, they were demonized for having willy-nilly served as a vote bank for parties that, it was said, sought merely to 'appease' them.

The second generic problem faced by Muslims was that of security. In villages as well as towns, they were often subject to taunts, insults, and, not least, physical violence. Everyday life was harsh. In times of religious strife, life was horrific. Because they lived largely in segregated spaces, and because they were almost always in a minority, Muslims suffered disproportionately whenever communal riots broke out.

The third problem identified by the Sachar Committee was that of equity. The community was under-represented in institutions of higher learning, and in the professions. They had less than their share of government jobs. And they had little access to bank credit.

Having identified the problems, the Sachar Committee offered a range of recommendations to address them. They asked for the establishment of an Equal Opportunities Commission, to which grievances could be brought, and in time addressed. They urged the Government to work to increase the participation of Muslims in public bodies, increase their share of employment in the state sector, and recognize degrees granted in Muslim religious schools, *madrasas*.[8]

III

Some communities and regions lagged behind, but overall the macro-economic picture continued to be rosy. That an economist who was an architect of the 1991 reforms was now prime minister reassured investors. The Sensex, the key index of the stock exchange in India's financial capital, Mumbai, continued to do well. In the year 2004 the Sensex hovered around the 6,000 mark; by early 2007, it had exceeded 14,000. Among the major gainers were Indian automobile, IT and pharmaceutical firms, sectors that had benefited enormously from economic liberalization.[9]

In the last week of April 2007, India joined an elite club of nations with a trillion-dollar economy. It was the twelfth member of this group, its membership aided in part by a steady appreciation of the rupee against the dollar.[10] A week later, the world's largest passenger aircraft, the Airbus A380, made its maiden landing at New Delhi's Indira Gandhi International Airport, in a further sign of the country's (or economy's) arrival on the world stage. The plane's touchdown was greeted with loud cheers from a crowd specially assembled for the occasion.

In statistical as much as in symbolic terms, the Indian economy was marching along. In January 2007, the Sensex had crossed the 14,000 mark; by October of the same year, it had exceeded 20,000. Boosters compared the surge in the share index to India's recent victory in a major international cricket tournament. 'There are some similarities', wrote one business journalist, 'between the Twenty20 World Cup and Indian bourses. India won the cup, even ardent fans were surprised. The Sensex seems poised to cross the 20,000 mark despite the recent bearish assessments. Yuvraj Singh hit six sixes in one over; the Sensex zoomed from 16,000 to 17,000 points in six trading sessions. M.S. Dhoni proved he was cool and canny – a fine captain; Indian policymakers are being praised for their sound economic decisions.'[11]

The Indian economy was growing at home; and Indian entrepreneurs were eyeing pickings abroad. In June 2008, the Tatas announced the purchase of the British luxury brands Jaguar and Land Rover in an all-cash transaction.[12] In the same month as an iconic British brand became Indian-owned, a well-established Indian brand passed into Japanese hands. This was the pharmaceutical firm Ranbaxy, once a typical family firm that had passed from father to son, now to be run by the Japanese company Daiichi Sankyo, which had paid Rs15,000 crore (about $2.5 billion) for a controlling 35 per cent share.[13]

These transactions were symptomatic of a larger shift in Indian desires and aspirations. From the 1950s till the 1980s, policy-maker and entrepreneur alike had their horizons firmly fixed on the domestic market. Indian economic growth was then governed by the mottoes of self-sufficiency and self-reliance. The hope, and ambition, was that everything Indians consumed would be made by Indian firms alone. Back then, the state was supposed to occupy the 'commanding heights' of the economy. Now the state had retreated from the sphere of production and distribution; and the economy had slowly opened out to the world. Many Indians were now increasingly consuming goods made abroad; other Indians were making, in India, services consumed abroad. That some Indian companies would buy British plants – as the Tatas had done with Jaguar – and that other Indian companies would sell out to Japanese firms – as Ranbaxy had done with Daiichi Sankyo – was not something Jawaharlal Nehru or Indira Gandhi, or indeed the technocrats who ran the Planning Commission, could or would have anticipated.

IV

The rise of the Sensex and the strides made by Indian firms at home and abroad notwithstanding, the process of economic growth was not always smooth or without friction. Under the Land Acquisition Act of 1894 – framed when India was a British colony, but still on the statute books – the state could acquire land from peasants for what it deemed 'public purpose'. But those whose lands were forcibly acquired often resisted. In 2005, for example, when the government sought to site a nuclear plant in a rich and fertile tract of coastal Maharashtra, farmers and fishermen organized a series of protest meetings and demonstrations. The state came down hard, arresting many villagers, some even under the old colonial law of sedition.[14]

Nuclear energy was in the state sector, but the Land Acquisition Act was also often used, or misused, to transfer land from farmers to private industry. In West Bengal, for example, the Left Front government had long portrayed itself as a party of the countryside, opposed to the interests of the pampered middle class of Calcutta. Now, in an abrupt shift in policy, it invited an Indonesian conglomerate, Salim Group, to set up a Special Economic Zone in the Nandigram area of the Purbo Medinipur district. The process of land acquisition was set in motion, angering local villagers.

In January 2007, bitter clashes broke out between protesters and the police in Nandigram. Six people died. In this clash, CPI(M) cadres stood with the police, while the protesters were aided by cadres of the main opposition party in the state, the Trinamool Congress (TMC).

The countryside in Nandigram was now dotted with police camps. The combative leader of the TMC, Mamata Banerjee, demanded that the government withdraw all notices for the acquisition of land. Meanwhile, a prominent national politician, Sushma Swaraj of the Bharatiya Janata

Party, visited Nandigram and deplored the 'atrocities' being committed on farmers.[15]

Apart from inviting the Indonesian Salim Group, the West Bengal government had also asked the Tatas to set up an automobile plant in their state. The group's patriarch, Ratan Tata, had nurtured a dream – or fantasy – of manufacturing a 'people's car', to be called the Nano, and priced at less than Rs100,000, within reach of every middle-class family in the country. When offered land in Singur in West Bengal for the Nano plant the Tatas took it at once. But, as in Nandigram, the promise had been made without consulting the farmers whose land was to be acquired. This was a fertile agricultural tract, well irrigated and with bountiful rainfall too.

The protesting farmers of Singur were led and mobilized by Mamata Banerjee. Ms Banerjee organized many processions and demonstrations against the Tata project. She also undertook several fasts. In August 2008, after the protests had been underway for almost a year, the Tatas suspended work at Singur and announced that they would shift the plant and machinery outside West Bengal. They directly blamed the state administration for this retreat. As a company statement put it in the first week of September, 'the situation around the Nano plant continues to be hostile and intimidating. There is no way this plant could operate efficiently unless the environment became congenial and supportive of the project. We came to West Bengal hoping we could add value, prosperity and create job opportunities in the communities in the state.'[16]

In October 2008 – a month after they quit West Bengal – Tata Motors announced that they had found a new location for their Nano plant. This was in Gujarat, in a region called Sanand, where the government had alloted it 1,100 acres of land. This was a relief for the Tatas, whose chairman, Ratan Tata, had invested so much personal prestige in the Nano project. But it was also a shot in the arm for Gujarat's chief minister, Narendra Modi. Ever since the pogrom of 2002, Modi had been suspect in the eyes of the Indian intelligentsia. Large sections of the media were also less than sympathetic to his angular, abrasive, ways. On the other hand, sections of big business, such as the Ambanis, had maintained excellent relations with Modi. For Ratan Tata – the head of India's most respected industrial house – to now endorse him was a major victory for Modi. The endorsement came in the way of a public embrace, the two men hugging one another while appearing on stage to announce the new location of the Nano plant.

In fact, Modi's personal re-branding had been going on for some time. As the journalist Sheela Bhatt perceptively remarked in 2005, 'Narendra Modi thinks a detergent named development will wash away the memory of 2002.' While focusing on new infrastructure, energy, and industrial projects, Modi had launched what Bhatt called 'a massive self-publicity drive', publishing diaries, calendars, booklets and posters where his own photograph appeared prominently alongside words and statistics speaking of Gujarat's achievements under his leadership. 'Modi has made sure that in Gujarat no one can escape noticing him', remarked Bhatt.[17]

Now people outside Gujarat were noticing him too. Thus, as Ratan Tata put it at the inauguration of the Nano project, 'there is a good M and a bad M', the first being Narendra Modi, who had welcomed him in Gujarat after the second M, Mamata Banerjee, had him effectively exiled from West Bengal. For his part, Modi praised the 'nationalistic spirit' of the Tatas, while hoping that 'the coming of the Nano to Gujarat will begin a new chapter of partnership which will propel the state in a new direction of growth.'[18]

V

The software industry was, so to say, the benign face of liberalization in India, in that it used skilled labour and modern technologies to generate wealth. The brutal face was constituted by the mining sector, where politicians allocated contracts to entrepreneurs close to them, who gave back a share of the proceeds in return. Meanwhile, in their haste to make as much money as soon as possible, mining lessees ravaged the land, leaving a trail of social and environmental devastation in their wake.

In the first decade of the twenty-first century, international metal prices rose by more than 400 per cent. This sparked a mining boom across India, with massive amounts of forest land diverted to the extraction of iron, bauxite, coal and limestone. Thus in a single day, the government of Jharkhand cleared forty-seven mining leases, these among the thousand or more leases granted by state governments in these years.

Success in the mining sector owed little to technical or managerial innovation and creativity. What mattered far more was proximity to a particular politician or political party. In this classic form of crony capitalism, corruption took three principal forms. First, ministers or governments in charge of granting leases took a certain sum – usually in the range of Rs10 to Rs12 crores – upfront as a bribe. Second, by fixing royalty payable to the state at an implausibly low level, politicians allowed mining lords to make super-normal profits, a share of which was passed on to them. (For example, in 2008, when iron ore prices were between Rs5,000 to 10,000 a tonne, the royalty payable to the state was less than Rs30 per tonne). Third, under-invoicing was rampant, with far fewer trucks reported than those actually carrying ore from the mine to port or train station. So, for example, if thirty loaded trucks left the mine one day, only two would be recorded by the government's mining inspectors.[19]

The web of corruption extended far and wide. It included officials of the forest, mining, and transport departments, of the railways, and of the ports. However, the principal beneficiaries were the politicians on the one hand and the mining lords on the other. The nexus between these two classes was particularly intimate. Politicians came to own mines (sometimes under the names of their relatives); mining lords came to fight elections and become ministers. Politicians of the Congress, the BJP and various regional parties were all involved.

The mining boom corroded the political system through corruption and cronyism. And it also had devastating social and environmental impacts. Since the mining companies had political patronage, they did not care to observe environmental or labour regulations. The owners brought in labourers from outside the state, who, displaced from their families, were too weak to organize themselves for better working or housing conditions. The forest, water, wildlife and pollution controls in place were likewise ignored, these violations largely overlooked by the local administration, intimidated by the connections that mining lords had with ministers and even chief ministers.

Since mining was effectively unregulated, when the price of ore was high there was an incentive to extract as much as possible, as quickly as possible. This impulse towards over-extraction was shared both by mine-owners and by politicians, since the latter did not know how long they would be in power, and wanted a share of these galloping profits quickly too.

Moreover, since it was conducted with other than state-of-the-art technology, and since the law was rarely respected, mining in India led to massive environmental degradation. Forests were cut down, rivers and springs polluted, cultivable lands rendered infertile. This damage ran into hundreds of thousands of crores of rupees. Often, it was irreversible. It impacted wildlife and biodiversity, but, far more seriously, the local village economy, based on fertile soil, clean water and healthy forests which provided wood for fuel and house-building, as well as fruit, artisanal raw material (such as bamboo for basket-makers), and medicinal plants. With the forests gone, the lands damaged and the water scarce or polluted, villagers in mining areas suffered enormously.[20]

Finally, since those who lived in and around mining areas did not benefit, and were indeed often impoverished by its side-effects, this industry generated a great amount of discontent. It was no accident that Maoists were particularly active in states like Orissa and Chhattisgarh, where tribal communities had been displaced by the rush of mining leases granted to prospectors from outside. On the other side, the state had set up vigilante groups – such as the notorious 'Salwa Judum' militia in Chhattisgarh – that attacked and killed villagers who opposed mining and hounded journalists and human rights activists out of the districts where mining was taking place.

The criminality and lawlessness that ran through the mining districts of the Indian heartland sat poorly with the country's self-image as the 'world's largest democracy'. These districts were so far from being a modern, twenty-first century, rule-bound society that the closest comparison must be to the California of the nineteenth century or the Congo of the twentieth century, when a rush to loot precious metals likewise fuelled an escalating cycle of violence and brutality.[21]

VI

In the first decade of the twenty-first century India was, by any objective standard, an environmental basket case. Of the twenty cities in the world with the worst air pollution, as many as thirteen were in India. Six hundred and fifty million people – over half the country's population – lived in regions considered excessively polluted by India's own national standards. If air quality was improved to meet these standards, these 650 million Indians would, on an average, each live 3.2 years longer.[22]

The air was foul and the water filthy. The country's most loved river, the Ganga, was biologically dead for most of its course, killed by untreated sewage and toxic chemicals from factories and towns on its banks. (Some

144 towns, small and large, on the Ganga's banks collectively deposited an estimated 3,500 million litres of sewage every day into the river.) Half-burnt human corpses (it was considered auspicious to be cremated along the Ganga) polluted the river further. Hundreds of thousands of Indians died each year from diarrhoea and other diseases, contracted after drinking this contaminated water. Meanwhile, the decline of fish stocks put fisherfolk out of work.[23]

Other rivers were scarcely less polluted. In many states (including the country's grain bowl, the Punjab), groundwater aquifers were depleting at an alarming rate, threatening agricultural sustainability. Natural forests were being steadily destroyed or degraded, hurting village communities who depended on them for fuel, fodder and agricultural inputs.

The conventional wisdom among conventional economists was that India was 'too poor to be green'. Once it got rich it would clean up. But this wisdom – such as it was – was based on a mechanical, or perhaps unhistorical, extension of the development experience of Western Europe and North America to Asia and Africa. For industrialization and economic growth in Europe and North America was enabled in part – perhaps large part – by the access to the land and resources of the colonies that those countries controlled. Developing countries like India had no such colonies; and they had far higher population densities. Therefore, there was a case to be made that India had to be even more environmentally conscious than were England or the United States at a comparable stage of their development experience.

This case was strengthened by the evidence on the ground. For, all across India, it was the poor who most directly bore the burden of environmental degradation. Depleting forests deprived peasants of fuel and fodder. Polluted rivers deprived them of irrigation water (and sometimes of drinking water too). Open-cast mining brought debris to agricultural fields and dried up springs. In the cities, air pollution made the urban poor – already badly housed, over-worked and under-nourished – more vulnerable to respiratory and other diseases than their richer (and better-fed, better-protected) counterparts.

Arguments such as these, upending the conventional wisdom of development economics, had an honourable lineage in India. They were first made in the 1970s, by popular movements such as the Chipko Andolan, a struggle of poor peasants in the Himalaya against monocultural commercial forestry. Chipko was followed by movements around forest rights in other parts of India, and by movements against destructive mining and dam projects as well. Meanwhile, social workers, often of a Gandhian persuasion, had organized rural communities in reforestation drives and water conservation schemes across India.

Movements like Chipko challenged the reigning economic belief – or superstition – that India was too poor to be green. In fact, as these movements showed, sustainable management of water, soil, pasture and forests was absolutely critical to the livelihoods of the majority of Indians. These struggles led to the creation in 1980 of a Department of Environment at the centre (and in time in the states), and to new laws and regulations to forestall environmental abuse by industries whether in the public or private sector.[24]

The Environment Ministry was meant to be a regulatory as well as a prescriptive body. On the one hand, it had to frame laws to check environmental damage, monitor air and water pollution and assess the environmental impact of proposed new mines, highways, dams and factories. On the other hand, it was meant to fund scientific research to forge sustainable policies for forestry, wildlife, agriculture, energy management, etc.

Sadly, for much – if not most – of its existence, the Environment Ministry fulfilled neither objective. The ministers who headed it generally ignored or disregarded the advice of India's top scientists. Every major project was supposed by law to prepare an Environmental Impact Assessment (EIA). In other countries this was prepared by a group of independent experts. In India, in a naked display of crony capitalism, it was the project promoter who himself chose the consultant to write the EIA. Naturally, the ensuing report minimized or downplayed the negative impacts of the project.

The ideological climate of economic liberalization was deeply inhospitable to environmental concerns. With India (for the first time) experiencing high rates of economic growth, environmental activists were dismissed as party-poopers, as throwbacks to a discredited era of socialist economics, or as agents of foreign powers determined to keep India backward. Bowing to the mood, the press ran fewer (and fewer) stories on the degradation of the environment and the marginalization of the rural communities that it caused. A greater abdication was by the Ministry of Environment and Forests, which dismantled the existing safeguards and made the clearance of even the most destructive projects a mere formality.

In the India of the early twenty-first century, attacks on environmental activists were frequent and abrasive. A prominent politician claimed that 'in a developing country, environment standards laid down by developed countries can't be taken as the thumb rule.'[25] A free-market columnist attacked what he saw as 'the fundamentalist and irrationalist nature of the ecology movement', claiming that it had 'turned investors against India.'[26] One environmental journalist ruefully wrote that 'the editor of a leading media house, everytime I pitched a green story, would invariably complain: "Environmentalism is stalling growth; all I am interested in is double-digit growth for this country"'.[27]

In truth, environmental responsibility was absolutely necessary for sustaining economic growth in the long term. A group of ecological economists working at the World Bank computed the costs to Indian society – in the form of ill health, lost income and increased economic vulnerability – of specific forms of environmental abuse: among them air pollution, forest and pasture loss, degradation of crop lands, and poor sanitation and water supply. The study estimated that in the year 2009, the cost of environmental degradation in India was about Rs3.75 trillion, equivalent to 5.7 per cent of GDP. In other words, if the air had not been so polluted, if forests had not been so rapidly felled, if the soil had not become so toxic or saline due to over-use of chemicals, if water sources had remained uncontaminated – in that case, India would have added more than 5 percentage points to its annual growth rate.[28]

VII

Even where there were no new industrial or mining projects coming up, there could be violent clashes in the countryside. For the rising self-consciousness of the Dalits had brought them into conflict with castes ranked higher than them in the social hierarchy of rural India.[29]

One theatre of this conflict was the southern-most districts of the southern state of Tamil Nadu. The clashes here were between the Thevars, a rising middle caste of landowners, and the landless Dalits. They were sparked by disputes over wages, or pique that a community once condemned to scavenging was now sending members to the Indian Administrative Service. The Dalits, emboldened, were refusing to be served tea in a separate glass at village cafés (a long-standing custom). And for each statue build by the Thevars of their revered leader Muthuramalinga Thevar (1908–65), the Dalits would build a statue of Ambedkar in reply. (Indeed, some of the bloodiest clashes were provoked by the demolition by one side of a statue erected by the other.) The rows were material as well as ideological, they were frequent, and they were costly. In a single decade, caste conflicts in Tamil Nadu resulted in more than a hundred deaths.[30]

Nowhere were the Dalits as oppressed as in the state of Bihar; nowhere were they better organized to resist; nowhere were caste conflicts so frequent, so bitter, and so bloody. The agrarian system of eastern India had historically exhibited the grossest forms of feudalism. In neighbouring West Bengal these inequalities had been attenuated by land reforms, but in Bihar they persisted down into the present. The middle and upper castes owned the land, and the Dalits tilled it. From the 1970s, however, Maoist radicals had taken up their case. Although they had more or less disappeared from West Bengal, where their movement had begun, these 'Naxalites' had steadily gathered strength in the districts of central Bihar. They formed agricultural labour fronts, which demanded higher wages, shorter hours and an end to social coercion (which, in some areas, included the right of the landlord to a low-caste bride on her wedding night). They also demanded a share of village common land and access to natural resources such as freshwater fish, theoretically owned by the 'community' as a whole, but usually the preserve of the upper castes alone.[31]

Their mobilization by left-wing radicals had instilled a great deal of self-respect among the lowliest in central Bihar. Travelling through the state in 1999, the journalist Mukul noticed a new-found confidence among the Dalits. Visitors were treated as social equals, and met with the salutation 'Namaskar, bhaijee' (Greetings, brother). Unlike in the past, the Dalits 'do not fold their hands. They do not bend their body. They do not call anybody "huzur", "sahib", "sir", or anything like this. This new found word [Bhaijee], is heard repeated all over the region in village after village and haunts the heart'.[32]

The anthropologist Bela Bhatia writes that 'this sense of dignity is one of the principal achievements of the Naxalite movement'. Other achievements included an end to forced labour and a significant enhancement of the wage rate. Normally paid in kind, this had doubled; besides, the quality of the grain was much better than before. Once made to work twelve hours non-stop, labourers were now allowed regular breaks. And, for the first time in recorded history, women were paid (and treated) the same as men.

The long-term aim of these radicals, however, was the overthrow of the Indian state. Open and hidden, legal and illegal, activities were carried on side by side: processions and strikes on the one hand, the collection of weapons and attacks on their enemies on the other. The Naxalites had their own Lal Sena (Red Army), whose members were trained in the use of rifles, grenades and land mines. They also had their *safaya* (clean-up) squads, whose marksmen were trained to assassinate particularly oppressive landlords.[33]

In response, the ruling élites had formed *senas* of their own. Each of the landowning castes maintained its own private army. The Bhumihars had their Ranbir Sena, the Kurmis their Bhoomi Sena, the Rajputs their Kunwar Sena, the Yadavs their Lorik Sena. The modern history of Bihar was punctuated with gruesome massacres perpetuated by one caste/class group upon another. Sometimes, a Bhumihar or Yadav *sena* would round up and burn alive a group of Dalits. At other times, the Naxalites would raid an upper-caste hamlet and shoot its inhabitants.[34]

Behind this violence lay a savage hatred. '*Mera itihaas mazdooron ki chita par likhi hogi*', claimed one Bhumihar landlord – my biography will be written around the funeral pyres of [Dalit] labourers. '*Aath ka badla assi se lenge!*', shouted the Naxalites – if you kill eight of ours we will kill eighty in revenge.[35]

The growing power of the Naxalites in Bihar was spectacularly underlined by an attack on the town of Jehanabad in November 2005. Hundreds of armed gunmen stormed the town, rained down bombs on government offices and attacked the jail. They freed two hundred inmates, mostly of their own party, among them their area commander. The operation was made easier by the fact that a large chunk of the district police force was away on election duty. Still, the act underlined the fragility of the legally constituted state in Bihar. For Jehanabad is a mere sixty kilometres from the provincial capital, Patna.[36]

Atrocities against Dalits were by no means the preserve of caste Hindus alone. In the Punjab, the land-owning Jat Sikhs resented the growing self-confidence of the labouring and artisanal castes. From the early twentieth century, Dalit Sikhs had struggled for a share of the land and access to shrines (both controlled by Jats). Some Dalits sought escape in a religion of their own, named Adi-Dharm. More recently, the prosperity fuelled by the Green Revolution had opened up new possibilities for low castes: work in towns and factories, and opportunities to start their own businesses. There was also a growing Dalit Sikh diaspora, which sent money back to their kinsmen in the village.[37]

One conflict may be taken as representative. This was over control of a shrine in the village of Talhan, on the outskirts of the industrial city of Jalandhar. The shrine was in memory of an artisan-turned saint named Baba Nihal Singh. Sikhs of all castes worshipped there, and in such numbers that their offerings made the temple one of the richest in the whole district. (The collection was estimated at fifty million rupees annually.) However, the temple committee was controlled by the Jats. They decided how the money was to be spent, whether in the beautification of the shrine, or in building roads to the village, or on feasts. The Dalits had long asked, and long been denied, representation in the management committee. At last they decided to take the matter to court. In January 2003, while the case was being heard, the Jats announced a social boycott of the Dalits. They, in turn, organized a series of protest strikes. Six months later, the groups clashed violently at a village fair. The administration then intervened to work out a compromise; two Dalits were inducted into the management committee, but they had to maintain Sikh tradition by keeping their hair and beard unshorn.[38]

VIII

In the first years of the new millennium, Kashmir was relatively peaceful. After the 2002 assembly elections, tourists began returning to Kashmir, filling the hotels in the Valley and the houseboats in Dal Lake. In January 2005, civic polls were held in Jammu and Kashmir for the first time in almost three decades. An impressive 60 per cent of voters cast their ballots in these local elections, despite intimidating threats by terrorists and the assassination of several candidates. Those who voted said they wanted the new councillors to provide new roads, clean water and better sanitation. A shopkeeper in the town of Sopore – a stronghold of pro-Pakistani militants – was quoted as saying: 'We can't wait for civic amenities till azadi [independence]'.[39]

According to official figures, the number of 'violent incidents' in Jammu and Kashmir decreased from 3,505 in the year 2002 to fewer than 2,000 in 2005.[40] The state could by no means be said to be at peace. But, for the first time in many years, the claim of the Indian government over this territory did not seem altogether hollow. In talks with Pakistan, New Delhi could urge a series of 'confidence-building measures', such as a bus linking the two halves of Kashmir. The first bus was scheduled to leave from Srinagar for Muzaffarabad on 7 April 2005. On the afternoon of the 6th, terrorists stormed the tourist complex where the passengers were staying. They were repulsed, and the next day two buses left as planned. A reporter who travelled on one of the vehicles wrote of how, when it crossed the newly built Aman Setu (Peace Bridge) and entered Pakistani territory,

> divided families were reunited, tears and rose petals flecked their faces. The significance of this extraordinary moment lay perhaps in the ordinariness of the backdrop: two buses with 49 passengers had crossed over – and blurred a line that has divided Kashmir for over five decades in blood and prejudice.[41]

Meanwhile, across the country, the ceasefire called in Nagaland in 1997 held, albeit uneasily. However, a mutually satisfactory solution remained out of reach. The government of India said it would give the Nagas the fullest possible autonomy, but within the Indian Constitution. The NSCN insisted that any solution must acknowledge Naga sovereignty, for – it claimed – 'Nagaland was never a part of India either by conquest by India or by consent of the Nagas'.[42] It also asked for the retention of a separate Naga army. Anything less would be a betrayal of the memory of those who died for the cause.

Adjoining Nagaland was the state of Manipur, which was increasingly beset with violence, between insurgent groups and the Indian government, and between different communities within Manipur itself. Large-scale unemployment had led many young men to take up the gun. Among the majority Meities, who lived in the valley, there were several armed groups unreconciled to being part of India. Meanwhile, in the hills of Manipur, the Tangkhul Nagas wished to make common cause with their brethren in Nagaland. The violence was intensified by ethnic rivalries between Meities, Nagas and Kukis.[43]

In the Kashmir Valley, as well as in some parts of the North-east, the Indian security forces operated under the Armed Forces Special Powers Act (AFSPA), which gave officers and soldiers immunity from prosecution by civil courts, unless specifically permitted by the central government. Since the Act also granted permission to 'fire upon or otherwise use force even to the extent of causing death' on anyone suspected of breaching the law, it acted as an incentive to aggressive behaviour.

There was a massive military presence in the north-east. The states of the region variously bordered China, with whom India had fought a costly war; Bangladesh, with whom India had a profoundly ambivalent relationship; and Burma. But it is not merely for external security that the Indian army had so many men there. They were also needed to maintain the flow of essential goods and services, protect road and rail links, and, not least, suppress rebellion and insurgency. 'We have no say vis-à-vis the army', remarked a long-serving Manipur chief minister: 'They have their own way of working, they will not tell us or listen to us, although they are supposed to be aiding the civil administration'.[44]

For many years now, human rights groups had asked for the repeal of the AFSPA. In the lead were the women of Manipur, long active in opposing male violence of all kinds. The state had dozens of local groups called Meira Paibis, or Women Torch Bearers. These campaigned successfully against alcoholism, before turning their attention to the excesses of the security forces. The Meira Paibis demanded that troops leave schools and marketplaces, that they stop picking up young boys at will, and that they open up their prisons and detection centres to public scrutiny.[45]

In November 2000, a young Manipuri woman named Irom Sharmila went on a hunger fast demanding the repeal of AFSPA. Taken away to hospital – she still refused to eat – she was force-fed by the state because she said she would rather die than live under a regime run by the military.[46]

The anti-AFSPA movement was renewed in July 2004, when a Manipuri housewife was picked up from her home on the charge of abetting terrorism. She was tortured, raped and killed, and her body left to rot by the roadside. The incident sparked a wave of angry protests in the Manipur Valley. A group of women marched to the army base in Imphal, where they took off their clothes and covered themselves with a white banner carrying the legend: 'Indian Army, Take our Flesh'. A student leader set himself on fire on Independence Day, leaving a note which read: 'It is better to self-immolate than die at the hands of security forces under this Act. With this conviction I am marching ahead of the people as a human torch'.[47]

IX

In the 2000s, as in the five decades that had preceded it, some parts of India were peaceable and quiet; other parts, turbulent and disorderly. The economy grew and the middle class expanded, but poverty continued to be widespread. From New Delhi, the central government sought to manage and moderate conflicts as best, or as least badly, as it could.

The prime minister, Dr Manmohan Singh, was in matters of state policy not always his own man. He had to accommodate his party president's economic preferences even when they did not coincide with his own. He had to consult with her on all major appointments: ministers, governors, heads of commissions.

Dr Singh was a scholar and civil servant by background, not a politician. Back in 1991, when he was made finance minister, he publicly thanked Prime Minister Narasimha Rao for, as he put it, 'having given me an opportunity to serve the country at the fag-end of my career'.[48] This son of Punjabi refugees, this earnest, self-effacing, hard-working, professional economist could never have imagined being in a position of such responsibility. When, a decade and more later, his party president offered Dr Singh the top job itself, he was even more grateful. Thus his extreme deference to Sonia Gandhi on almost all matters of domestic policy and politics.

The one sphere in which the prime minister was given a relatively free hand was foreign policy. Here, he was determined to further strengthen ties with the United States. That country was now the sole superpower, and it was a major market for India's software industry. There was now a large and wealthy Indian diaspora in America, which could be used profitably in this regard. Indian strategic thinkers suspicious of China urged Dr Singh to forge an ever-closer partnership with Washington so that the two countries could together 'bear the burdens of ordering the Eastern Hemisphere in the twenty-first century'.[49]

Dr Singh got along well with the American president of the time, George W. Bush. This relationship helped the prime minister negotiate a special agreement, under which the United States would collaborate in enhancing the capacity of India's civil nuclear energy industry. Ever since the Pokharan blasts of 1998, India had not been allowed access to advanced Western technologies. Now, on the promise that this would be for energy generation alone, and that India would make its civil nuclear facilities open to inspection by international agencies, the US agreed to provide such technology and expertise as this industry would require.

The proposed Indo-US nuclear deal was debated in the Lok Sabha in November 2007. The government found its plans to forge a national consensus thwarted by an unlikely alliance of the right-wing BJP and the left-wing CPI(M). The BJP had always stood for closer relations with the United States, and had it been in power would surely have pushed for such a deal itself. But now, merely to spite the Congress and deny it any credit, it opposed the deal. The opposition of the Left was at least more consistent, based on a long-standing suspicion of the leading country of the capitalist world.

The prime minister, Dr Manmohan Singh, ran a minority government, which had stayed in power only through the support of the Communist parties. Indeed, even if they were not formally part of government, the Left had left their imprint on some of its policies, most notably the rural employment guarantee programme. But now India's growing rapprochement with the United States caused unease in the minds of party patriarchs, schooled during the Cold War to regard America as an enemy of socialism and of the 'working people'. The CPI(M) thus described the nuclear deal as a 'surrender' to Washington.[50]

Despite the opposition of the Left, Dr Manmohan Singh pushed forward with the tilt towards the United States. In January 2008, the two countries signed an agreement worth more than $1 billion, whereby the US would supply the sophisticated C-130J transport aircraft to India, along with spare parts and spare engines. These would greatly augment the capacity of the Indian Air Force, since these planes could fly in the most adverse weather conditions and could land on makeshift runways in deserts and mountains.[51]

Through the first half of 2008, the Congress and the Left parties held a series of informal meetings to seek to bridge their differences. In the end, a reconciliation proved impossible. In July, the CPI(M) and the CPI withdrew support from the Congress-led central government, chiefly on the question of the civilian nuclear deal with the United States. The Congress was unrepentant; a party spokesman remarking that the 'Left are isolated on this issue. They are not only isolated but in the exalted company of the BJP (Bharatiya Janata Party).' The ruling party were confident that they had the numbers to have the nuclear deal ratified in Parliament.[52]

The optimism was not misplaced. With the support of regional parties and independents, the UPA government won a trust vote in the Lok Sabha in July, with 253 members voting in favour of the government, 232 against. (There were claims that some non-Congress members of the House had been bribed to vote in favour of the government.) The result, said Prime Minister Singh, would 'send a message to the world at large that India is prepared to take its rightful place in the comity of nations'.[53]

In economic matters, the prime minister always had a global orientation, advocating an outward-looking trade policy early in his academic career and helping dismantle the licence-permit-quota-raj while serving as finance minister in the 1990s. What was new, and distinctive, was Dr Singh's determination to forge closer relations between India and the United States. He believed that India's rising economic might had to be accompanied by a corresponding rise in its global political influence. For that, he judged, India had to ally strongly with the world's sole remaining superpower.

While Sonia Gandhi would have liked to keep the alliance with the Left intact, Manmohan Singh was prepared to break it on the question of the nuclear deal, which he saw as vital to a wider India-US rapprochement. That Dr Singh was sincere in his belief that this policy was in India's larger interests was not in question; but his enthusiasm was such that it led him to a quite uncharacteristic display of hyperbole. On his next visit to the United States, in September 2008, Dr Singh told the American president, George W. Bush, that 'in the last four and half years that I have been prime minister, I have been the recipient of your generosity, your affection, your friendship'. Then he added: 'For 34 years, India has suffered from a nuclear apartheid. We have not been able to trade in nuclear material, nuclear reactors, and nuclear raw materials. And when this restrictive regime ends, I think a great deal of credit will go to President Bush. And, for this I am very grateful to you, Mr. President.'

We must take Dr Singh at his word that George W. Bush was affectionate and friendly towards him. We might also accept that the ending of India's nuclear isolation was a significant victory. But whether these facts had to be stated in such flattering terms must be open to question. More noteworthy still was a further, final, effusion, where, in the full glare of cameras and recorders, the Indian prime minister told the American president that 'the people of India deeply love you', an assertion far more problematic, and far harder to justify, than those that had preceded it.[54]

X

Through 2007 and 2008, as the high politics of the Indo-US nuclear deal was being played out in New Delhi and Washington, there had been a wave of terror attacks in different parts of the country. In February 2007, the Samjhauta Express that ran from New Delhi to the border with Pakistan was bombed, with sixty-seven people dying in the attack. The train was promoted as a symbol of peace and understanding; and those who attacked it were almost certainly Hindu fundamentalists, opposed to any reconciliation with Pakistan. The timing suggested as much, for the terror attack occurred a day before the Pakistani foreign minister was scheduled to visit New Delhi.[55]

Other terror attacks were the handiwork of Islamic terrorists, often based in or aided by elements in Pakistan. In May 2007 nine people were killed when a blast ripped through the historic Mecca Masjid in Hyderabad. A year later, at least sixty-four people were killed when a series of blasts rocked another old, historic, city, the Rajasthan capital, Jaipur. Then, in September 2008, twenty people were killed when five bombs were set off in a busy marketplace in New Delhi.[56]

India had been subject to terror attacks before. Over the years, dozens of bomb explosions had taken place in markets and suburban trains. In 2001 the Parliament in New Delhi had been stormed by a group of terrorists. In such attacks over the years, perhaps hundreds of security personnel, and certainly thousands of civilians, had been killed or maimed.

On 26 November 2008, India witnessed its most daring terror attack yet. That evening, a group of militants from Pakistan came by boat right up to the waterfront in south Mumbai, a much-visited tourist spot housing the iconic Gateway of India and the Taj Mahal Hotel. They had previously undergone weeks of training in camps run by the Islamist group Lashkar-e-Toiba, overseen by serving and retired officers of the Pakistan army. In the course of their training the Lashkar chief Hafiz Saeed had told the young militants: 'If you die waging jihad, your faces will glow like the moon. Your bodies will emanate scent. And you will go to paradise'.[57]

After landing in Mumbai, these terrorists, ten in all, went on a rampage through the city, attacking guests in the Taj Mahal Hotel, commuters in the city's main railway terminal, and any others who came in the way. The militants also attacked a Jewish centre, another target deliberately chosen, in view of India's growing closeness to Israel, and of the general demonization of Jews among Islamic radicals around the world.

News of the attack spread through Mumbai and India, provoking horror and amazement in equal measure. Television crews and cameras parked themselves outside the Taj, where the terrorists were setting off grenades as they went from room to room, from floor to floor. Mumbai had a large police force, but commandos trained to meet such attacks were not assigned to the city. These were instead concentrated in Delhi, to protect government installations and powerful politicians. By the time special forces were dispatched the terrorists had been on the rampage for more than twelve hours. It took four days in all for nine of the attackers to be killed, and a tenth, the sole survivor, to be captured. The captive confessed to having come from Pakistan, and to having been trained by the Lashkar-e-Toiba.[58]

More than two hundred people were killed by the terrorists in Mumbai. About twenty of them were foreigners. Large sections of the Taj Hotel were gutted from inside. But beyond the damage to men and materials the attack had left a deep emotional scar on the citizens of Mumbai and of India. These parts of the city were well loved and well visited. The Taj was arguably India's most famous hotel. The Chhattrapati Shivaji terminus was the busiest railway station in India. The shock was deepened by the ease with which these famous places were attacked – by a group of marauders coming in from the open sea in a small boat that they had hijacked.

The terror attack on south Mumbai swiftly acquired the label 26/11, to match the 9/11 that had ravaged that other great, buzzing, cosmopolitan, commercially vigorous and culturally vibrant city, New York. Looking back at the tragedy eight years on, three responses to the attack at the time it occurred strike one as especially significant. The first came from the Gujarat chief minister, Narendra Modi, who flew to Mumbai and based himself outside the Trident Hotel (another target of the terrorists) where he told eager reporters of how he would like the government to tackle attacks such as this one. Mumbai was not in his state, and he had thus no business to be speaking in public about such matters. This was an opportunistic bid to project himself as a leader with national ambitions and aspirations.

By calling a press conference in Mumbai, Narendra Modi was subtly contrasting his own preference for strong, quick, visible action with the rather more understated style of the prime minister, Dr Manmohan Singh. That commandos took so long to come to Mumbai was certainly a security lapse for which the government of India was responsible. Once the attack had subsided and the terrorists killed, a clamour grew for retributive action against the nation which had harboured and trained the attackers. Opposition politicians called for the bombing of terror camps in Pakistan. The prime minister resisted these pressures. The fact of the attack, and the way it had played out in public, had shamed Pakistan enough in the eyes of the world. To escalate matters now, with both countries in possession of nuclear weapons, was risky in the extreme. This restraint in the face of extreme provocation was both necessary and wise.

Restraint of another, and perhaps even more admirable, kind, was displayed by the ordinary citizens of Mumbai. The city had a long history of Hindu-Muslim violence, extending back a hundred years and more. Most recently in 1992–3, there had been savage attacks on Muslims by Hindu mobs celebrating the demolition of the Babri Masjid, followed by bomb attacks by Muslim extremists on the Stock Exchange and other buildings. Although one cannot be absolutely certain, it is overwhelmingly likely that one of the aims of the terrorists of 26/11 and of their handlers was to spark a fresh cycle of religious violence. Had Hindus been provoked into attacking Muslims within Mumbai, perhaps this would have spread to other cities, justifying the Islamist claim (or hope) that India was as much a 'Hindu' state as Pakistan was a 'Muslim' one. But this did not happen. The city mourned its own dead, peacefully and with dignity. The Hindus did not target innocent Muslims; on their part, the Muslim clerics of Mumbai declined to bury the bodies of their co-religionists from across the border since their acts were so plainly immoral.

XI

The year 2008 witnessed Islamic radicals launching terror attacks in different parts of India, culminating in the attack on Mumbai in

November. In these twelve months Hindutva extremists had not been entirely inactive either. There was the bombing of the Samjhauta Express, mentioned earlier. And in the autumn of 2008 there was a major episode of religious rioting in the tribal districts of Orissa. This was sparked by the killing of a VHP leader, Swami Laxmanananda, after an attack on his ashram at Jalespata in the Kandhamal district. The killers were most likely Maoists.

A product of the cow protection movement of the 1960s, Swami Laxmanananda had worked for many years in Kandhamal, seeking to assimilate the tribals to the Hindu fold, by urging them to worship Hindu gods and goddesses, and abjure alcohol. In 2006, to mark the birth centenary of the RSS patriarch M. S. Golwalkar, the Swami organized a massive congregration of tribals and non-tribals in Kandhamal. This was part of the general endeavour to bring tribals 'home' (ghar wapsi) to what the Swami perceived as their original and natural faith, namely, Hinduism.[59]

Swami Laxmanananda was not the only missionary active in these parts, however. In the tribal districts of Orissa, wrote one reporter, there was 'a volatile mix of Christian missionaries, Sangh Parivar activists ... and Maoists which is battling for the hearts and minds of the people.' The Christian missionaries had been successful in converting large numbers of a former Untouchable community, the Panos. The Hindu missionaries targeted the tribal Kandhas, who made up 52 per cent of the population. The Maoists, for their part, sought volunteers from both communities for their armed struggle against the state.

In this fragile, deeply contested space, the murder of Swami Lakshmanananda proved the proverbial fire in the haystack. The VHP leader from Gujarat, Praveen Togadia, an old hand in stoking sectarian violence, led the Swami's funeral procession, following which angry mobs torched Christian homes and churches. The violence continued for a full seven weeks. Tens of thousands of Christian Panos fled their villages into makeshift refugee camps.

Visiting the villages the Panos had abandoned, a reporter found their homes 'reduced to charred shells, their churches ransacked, their hard-earned worldly goods looted or destroyed, their grains burnt and their goats scattered. The manner in which the houses have been targeted show prior knowledge: as in Gujarat [in 2002], only the homes of the minorities have been torched.'[60]

The Kandhamal district had a mere thirteen police stations, with just five hundred constables tasked to maintain the peace in this vast and hilly terrain. The police were too few, they were poorly trained and they were under-equipped. Even if they had the will to contain the violence they had not the means. Indeed, at least two police stations were attacked by mobs, thousands of rioters surrounding a post with a few cowering cops inside.[61]

XII

As the next general elections approached, the political landscape was as complex and variegated as it had ever been. In May 2007, the BSP won a surprising, as well as striking, majority in Uttar Pradesh. Once implacably hostile to the upper castes, the party had now reached out to Brahmins and Muslims. As many as 139 of the seats contested by the BSP were allocated to upper castes.[62] As one commentator put it, by forging alliances with other communities, 'the BSP has turned the old Congress constituency – the Brahmin, Muslim, Dalit combine – on its head. Only, in Mayawati's brave new world, instead of the Brahmins being in the driver's seat, it is the Dalit: indeed, she has done what her mentor and creator of the BSP, Kanshi Ram, had dreamt of – she has turned the pyramid upside-down. And so, for the first time after 1991, when the BJP won an absolute majority in Uttar Pradesh, the state has voted for single-party rule and stability, ending 14 years of messy coalition governments.'[63]

A year later, in May 2008, the Bharatiya Janata Party formed a government in Karnataka. This was the first southern state in which the BJP, traditionally a party of the North and West, had won power. The Congress in Karnataka had been discredited by years of (mis)rule; while a group of powerful and wealthy mining lords had thrown their weight, and their cash, behind the BJP. A prominent BJP leader, Ananth Kumar, described this election as a 'semi-final', presaging what he hoped would be the party's victory in the general elections due to be held in a year's time.[64]

In December 2008, when state elections were held in Jammu and Kashmir, the National Conference emerged as the largest party. Omar Abdullah, the grandson of Sheikh Abdullah and the son of

Farooq Abdullah, became chief minister. The Congress once more joined the ruling coalition, as the junior partner. In elections held in other states in the same month, the Congress regained power in Rajasthan, but could not wrest back power from the BJP in Madhya Pradesh and Chhattisgarh.

The next general elections were due in May 2009. The Congress was in power at the centre, and in some key states. But the advent of the BJP in Karnataka indicated the growing pan-Indian appeal of the party. Meanwhile, regional parties were still robust in some states, whereas in the largest state of all, Uttar Pradesh, a party founded for and by Dalits was in power.

In January 2009 the prime minister underwent heart surgery. Some thought he would retire once his term was over. However, when the general elections were announced in early March, Manmohan Singh was presented as one of the three faces of the Congress. The others were the party president, Sonia Gandhi – the prime architect of the 2004 win – and her son Rahul, who in September 2007 had been made one of the Congress's general secretaries. Party posters featured portraits of all three leaders.

On the other side, with Atal Behari Vajpayee ailing, the BJP offered as its Prime Ministerial candidate his long-time colleague and some-time deputy, Lal Krishna Advani. Advani had waited many years for this opportunity. The prime mover behind the Ayodhya campaign that had effectively made his party a national force, he had, in 1996 and again in 1998, made way for Vajpayee when the BJP was in a position to form the central government.

At the time of the 2009 elections, Advani was eighty-one. Manmohan Singh was only five years younger, but he had kept his government going for a full term. The economy was doing well, for which sections of the middle class gave him credit, as they did for the nuclear deal with the United States. The prominence given to Rahul Gandhi was intended to attract first-time voters, while, as the architect of the UPA's social welfare schemes, Sonia Gandhi had an appeal among the underprivileged. The rural employment guarantee programme in particular had begun to show results. Scheduled Castes, Scheduled Tribes and women had benefited substantially from this scheme, while the building of roads and wells had helped the rural economy as a whole.[65]

Most observers (this writer included) expected a fragmented verdict, with both Congress and BJP falling well short of a majority, each side then scrambling for partners to make up the numbers. The possibility of a 'Third Front' (as in 1989 and 1996) forming the government was also in the air. In the event, the Congress increased its tally by more than 60 seats. It won as many as 206 seats in the Lok Sabha, the first time it had crossed the two hundred mark since 1991. With several regional parties already committed to an alliance with it, the Congress no longer needed the Left at all.

The incumbent prime minister, Manmohan Singh, would now emulate Jawaharlal Nehru and Indira Gandhi in serving two full terms in office. Speaking to his party after the results were out, Dr Singh said the five years to follow could be 'decisive' in India's history. 'If we can sustain the growth rates of the last five years', he said, 'we can reduce poverty, create new employment, accelerate rural development and industrialization and transform the lives of our people.' 'We must', said the prime minister, 'grasp the nettle firmly and forge ahead.'[66]

XIII

In the 2009 elections, the Congress had done particularly well in Andhra Pradesh, winning 33 out of 42 seats on offer. This was because of the energetic campaigning of the state's chief minister, Y. S. Rajasekhar Reddy. 'YSR', as he was popularly known, was a ruthless political operator, who ran both party and state with a firm hand. One of his achievements, such as it was, was to suppress the long-standing demand for a separate state of Telangana, to be carved out of the districts of Andhra that had been part of the erstwhile Hyderabad State.[67]

The parts of Andhra Pradesh once ruled directly by British had access to the coast, and were watered by large rivers. They were progressive and prosperous compared to those parts that lay in the interior, and had formerly been ruled by the Nizam. However, when the united state of Andhra Pradesh was formed in 1956, the princely capital of Hyderabad was chosen as its capital too.

The coastal Andhra/Telangana divide beset the state from its origins. The intellectuals of Telangana complained that the politicians and businessmen diverted public investment away from the hinterland towards the already pampered coastal districts. They produced figures showing that while Telangana had 42 per cent of the state's cultivated area, it was allotted 30 per cent of the state's expenditure on agriculture,

27 per cent of the allocation of fertilizers, and less than its fair share of canal waters and hydel power as well.

In the late 1960s a major movement broke out, led by students, demanding the creation of a separate state of Telangana. A pamphlet issued by the movement's leaders argued that 'smaller states can help [in] democratising our political process, which in turn will attract the larger sections into [the] developmental process ...' Indeed, 'smaller states may herald a new and promising era in the political and economic life of [the] nation'. These words were accompanied by massive street protests, which paralyzed road and rail links. The movement was suppressed only by the use of considerable force.[68]

In later decades the demand for Telangana never went away, with *dharnas* and strikes occurring from time to time. Before the general elections of 2004, the Congress party, then out of power, forged an alliance with the Telangana Rashtra Samithi (TRS). It made one particular promise and one general promise; support for the creation of a Telangana state, and the formation of a new States Reorganization Commission. Linguistic states had assured Indian unity; now it was perhaps time for a further reorganization, to break up large, unwieldy states such as Andhra, Maharashtra, West Bengal and, above all, Uttar Pradesh.

After it unexpectedly came to power, the Congress reneged on both promises: the first because it was opposed by the powerful Andhra chief minister, Y. S. Rajasekhara Reddy, the second because it was opposed by the Left parties, whose support was crucial to the new government's survival, and who vetoed a new SRC because Bengali communists did not want to give encouragement to the movement for a state of Gorkhaland.

The demand for Telangana revived after Y. S. Rajasekhar Reddy died in a helicopter crash in September 2009. YSR's successor lacked his authority, and his ruthlessness. On the other side, the Telangana movement was now led by K. Chandrasekhar Rao (known as KCR), a charismatic figure and powerful orator. In the last week of November 2009 KCR went on a fast unto death demanding the immediate constitution of a separate Telangana state. This drew tens of thousands of his followers into the streets, disrupting life in the state's capital, Hyderabad, which was now also a major centre of the IT and pharmaceutical industries.

Confronted by KCR's fast and the popular upsurge that it led to, the UPA panicked. On 9 December 2009, the Union home minister,

P. Chidambaram, issued a statement promising that 'the process of forming the state of Telangana will be initiated'. He urged KCR to abandon his fast (which he did), and asked the chief minister to withdraw all cases against those associated with the agitation.

The announcement led to anger and disappointment among the Congress MPs from coastal Andhra. But once the Union home minister had made his promise in public there was no going back. After a series of tortuous and prolonged negotiations, Andhra Pradesh was formally bifurcated. The two states would share Hyderabad as their capital for ten years, after which it would be exclusively Telangana's. The residual state, still called Andhra Pradesh but popularly known as Seemandhra, would be allocated Central funds to build a new capital.[69]

XIV

Two core principles of the Indian constitution were equality and pluralism. The constitution sought to bestow equal rights on women and Dalits, and recognize and respect different languages, religions and ways of life. There was, to be sure, a substantial slippage between theory and practice. Women and Dalits continued to be discriminated against. Hindutva radicals made Muslims and Christians feel vulnerable and insecure.

One area in which neither diversity nor equality was prescribed or recognized, even in theory, was sexual choice. The practice of homosexuality was held to be criminal, as defined by Section 377 of the nineteenth century Indian Penal Code. In August 2009 – shortly after the UPA was re-elected – the Delhi High Court struck down Section 377 of the IPC. A division bench, consisting of Chief Justice A. P. Shah and Justice S. Muralidhar, held that Section 377 violated the right to privacy and dignity. It traced the rise of progressive legislation in these matters in other countries, where sex between consenting adults in private had been decriminalized, and homosexuals given equal rights in the professional sphere, even in such bastions of conservatism as the army.

The original petition against Section 377 was filed by the Naz Foundation in 2001. It sought the legalization of gay sex between consenting adults. The petitioners were opposed by various religious groups, Hindu, Muslim and Christian, as well as by the Home Ministry of the government of India.

Those who argued for the retention of Section 377 claimed it was needed in the interests of a generalized and ostensibly universal notion of 'public morality'. Justices Shah and Muralidhar on the other hand, saw the section as specific in place and time; as they remarked, 'it was based on a conception of sexual morality specific to [the] Victorian era drawing on notions of carnality and sinfulness'. Section 377, said the High Court, 'targets the homosexual community as a class and is motivated by an animus towards this vulnerable class of people'. For as it stood, 'Section 377 IPC has the effect of viewing all gay men as criminals. When everything associated with homosexuality is treated as bent, queer, repugnant, the whole gay and lesbian community is marked with deviance and perversity. They are subject to extensive prejudice because of what they are or what they are perceived to be, not because of what they do. The result is that a significant group of the population is, because of its sexual non-conformity, persecuted, marginalised and turned on itself'.

Removing Section 377 would free this group of this stigma, and incidentally be a progressive public health measure as well. In any case, remarked the judges, it 'is not within the constitutional competence of the State to invade the privacy of citizens' lives or regulate conduct to which the citizen alone is concerned .... The criminalisation of private sexual relations between consenting adults absent any evidence of serious harm deems the provision's objective both arbitrary and unreasonable'.

The Delhi High Court held that Section 377 of the IPC violated Article 14 (equality before the law), Article 15 (prohibition of discrimination on grounds of religion, race, caste, sex or place of birth, the court accepting the petitioners' pleas that 'sex' included 'sexual orientation') and Article 21 (protection of life and liberty) of the constitution. The judges ended by observing that 'if there is one constitutional tenet that can be said to be the underlying theme of the Indian constitution, it is that of "inclusiveness". This court believes that [the] Indian constitution reflects this value deeply ingrained in Indian society, nurtured over several generations. The inclusiveness that Indian society traditionally displayed, literally in every aspect of life, is manifest in recognising a role in society for everyone. Those perceived by the majority as "deviants" or "different" are not on that score excluded or ostracised'.[70]

XV

The Delhi High Court judgement was widely welcomed by democrats, who saw it as the natural, logical, extension of the promises of equality and pluralism mandated by the constitution. However, even as pluralism was being extended in one direction, in theory, it was being denied in another direction, in practice. After several years of relative peace, there was now discontent once more in the Kashmir Valley.

In May 2008, some forty hectares of forest land were allotted to house pilgrim shelters on the route to Amarnath, a popular Hindu shrine in the mountains of Kashmir, inaccessible by motor road, and involving a long, arduous journey by foot or on horseback. When the diversion of land was made public, some feared that this was the thin edge of a wedge to carry out the proclaimed policy of Hindutva radicals to settle Hindus permanently in the Valley.

In the third week of June, protests erupted in the Valley against the transfer of land for the Amarnath yatra. This prompted a counter-stir in the Hindu-dominated Jammu region, where activists threatened to blockade the only road connecting the mainland to the Valley. After more protests and the killing of several Kashmiris in police firing, the land allotment order was reversed. The BJP and its associates now called for an all-India bandh. 'If there is no Amarnath yatra, there would be no Haj also,' declared the VHP's Praveen Togadia in Delhi. The VHP also called for a countrywide boycott of all products and goods from Kashmir.

The protests and counter-protests continued through the autumn of 2008. When winter came and the state's political class shifted to Jammu for the winter, the troubles had subsided. But they had left further and fresh wounds on the collective psyche of the Kashmiris of the Valley, new hurdles in the way of their being seen as, and seeing themselves as, full-fledged citizens of India.[71]

2009 was relatively quiet in Kashmir (and for Kashmiris) but 2010 was another year of discontent. In June a student was killed in police firing. This led to crowds of young men (and sometimes boys) coming out into the streets to protest, provoking more firing, and inevitably, more protest. The protesters threw rocks and stones at the police. The army was then called in to restore order. Troops marched through the narrow lanes of Srinagar and other towns, while Kashmiris watched, sullenly, from their homes.[72]

The protests resumed, and at episodic intervals, the police and protesters battled it out in the streets. Friday evenings were often the most tense, as, after hearing stirring sermons in mosques, young Kashmiris were in a militant mood. Occasionally, police posts were attacked, provoking fierce retaliation. Through July and August large parts of Srinagar and other towns were often under curfew. On several different occasions, police and paramilitary fired on crowds shouting 'azadi, azadi' (freedom, freedom), the deaths and the injuries mounting steadily.[73]

The protests further intensified in September, when copies of the Koran were burnt by a fundamentalist pastor in Florida. Angry Kashmiris torched a Christian school and fought with the police who had come out to contain them. The death toll for the summer of 2010 had now crossed seventy.[74] A journalist who had closely tracked Kashmir for many years urged the prime minister to take 'bold steps to demonstrate his willingness to address the grievances of ordinary Kashmiris.' Dr Singh, wrote this commentator, should not insult Kashmiri sentiments 'by talking of economic packages, roundtable conferences and all-party talks'. Rather, 'he should unreservedly express regret for the deaths that have occurred these past few weeks. He should admit, in frankness and humility, the Indian state's failure to deliver justice all these years. And he should ask the people of Kashmir for a chance to make amends. There is still no guarantee the lava of public anger which is flowing will cool.' For, wrote this journalist in August 2010, if the prime minister did not 'make an all-out effort to create some political space today, there is no telling where the next eruption in the valley will take us.'[75]

The advice was well meant, but unlikely to be heeded. For the Indian political establishment had increasingly ceded control of the Kashmir Valley to the army. The AFSPA continued to be deeply resented, but no prime minister was courageous enough to think of repealing it, even in districts away from the border where militancy was on the wane. If the central government was unable or unwilling to offer a hand of friendship and reconciliation, the Kashmiris for their part were now increasingly under the sway of a fundamentalist, Wahabbist, version of Islam. The Sufism that had once permeated the Valley was now in permanent retreat. What had begun as a freedom struggle had taken on the characteristics of a holy war.[76]

XVI

In August 2009, the Lok Sabha adopted The Right of Children to Free and Compulsory Education Bill, 2009, mandating free and compulsory education to children aged between six and fourteen. Although such a provision had been mandated in the constitution, the government had thus far failed to meet this obligation. Indeed, government schools were so poorly run that even peasant and working-class families preferred to put their children in private schools, often incurring debts to do so. Now, to make up for past failures by the state, all private schools, except those recognized as 'minority' institutions, would henceforth have to allot 25 per cent of their seats to children from disadvantaged backgrounds, who would pay no fees.[77]

Later the same month, the UPA government proposed that reservation for women at all tiers of the *panchayati raj* system be raised from 33 to at least 50 per cent. To become law, the proposal would however require an amendment to the constitution.[78] Some months later, the Cabinet approved an even more radical proposal, which was to have 33 per cent of seats in the national Parliament, and in State Assemblies, reserved for women. The Congress president, Sonia Gandhi, strongly backed this proposal.

In March 2010, the Women's Reservation was tabled in the Rajya Sabha, where it was bitterly opposed by some of the Congress's own alliance partners. The Rashtriya Janata Dal pulled its ministers out of the government in protest. The bill was then dropped, for fear of creating a further rift in the ruling coalition.[79]

These gestures towards an inclusive education policy and parliamentary reservation for women were aimed to consolidate the Congress's claim to represent or speak for the majority of Indians. However, from the end of 2009 the Union government found itself in the middle of one scandal after another. First, there was a controversy about the allocation of second and third generation (2G and 3G) telecom licences, which, said the Central Bureau of Investigation, were given to private companies 'on a first-come-first-served basis at the rates of 2001 – which were very low – without any competitive bidding'. The CBI estimated the loss to the exchequer as being about Rs22,000 crores.[80]

The minister in charge of the telecom sector was A. Raja of the DMK. However, the next scandal involved a senior Congress politician, Suresh Kalmadi, who was in charge of preparations for the Commonwealth Games (CWG), due to be held in New Delhi in 2010. Reports began to surface of large sums of money being paid to secure road and building contracts for these Games.[81]

These allegations were energetically taken up by newspapers and television. In a bid at damage control, the government appointed a

Committee to probe into the Commonwealth Games affair, while A. Raja resigned from the Cabinet. However, the corruption scandals were a blot on the reputation of the prime minister, who, despite his personal reputation for honesty, had allowed these alleged illegalities to happen.

In October 2010, a report by the Comptroller and Auditor General (CAG) was tabled in Parliament. This estimated the loss to the state exchequer as a result of the 2G allocation to be up to Rs 1.76 lakh crore.[82] The credibility of the prime minister and his government fell further when, in February 2011, the CBI felt it had enough evidence to arrest A. Raja.[83]

There were now a large number of television channels which energetically competed for viewers. Corruption was not unknown in the past; but never before had it been manifest in so many high places. That a central government headed by a prime minister who claimed to be personally incorruptible had its hand in the till – or several tills – made this an exciting story for journalists to follow. That state agencies such as the CBI and the CAG had themselves held that illegalities had occurred, that the real or putative sums of the money pilfered were so colossally large, and that Cabinet ministers had been arrested, made the story even more compelling. Through the winter of 2010–1 the 2G, 3G and CWG scandals dominated the headlines, on television and in print, and in both English and Hindi, with other language-media not far behind. That the prime minister and his party president stayed silent added to the intrigue and to the sense of their presumed complicity in the corrupt acts of their party colleagues. In the summer of 2011, within two years of its re-election, the United Progressive Alliance was facing a serious crisis of credibility.

30

The Rise of the 'BJP System'

The Congress is still, and is likely to be for a long time, the most organized political party in the country, with a nationwide following and considerable depth in the localities.

RAJNI KOTHARI, 1970

In Narendra Modi, the people of India see a dynamic, decisive and development-oriented leader who has emerged as a ray of hope for the dreams and aspirations of a billion Indians. His focus on development, eye for detail and efforts to bring a qualitative difference in the lives of the poorest of the poor have made Narendra Modi a popular and respected leader across the length and breadth of India. Narendra Modi's life has been a journey of courage, compassion and constant hard work.

The website of the Prime Minister of India,
as updated at 7 p.m. on 26 May 2014

I

AMONG THE REASONS THAT the Congress lost the 1989 general election was the Bofors scandal. And some assembly elections had also been won and lost on the question of corruption. However, it was only in the summer of 2011 that the misuse of public office for private gain became a major national issue, debated all over the country. The debate was sparked by a fast in New Delhi in April by the veteran social worker Anna Hazare.

In 2011, Hazare was seventy-three years of age. Born in a peasant family in Maharashtra, he worked for many years as a driver in the Indian army. After retirement, he settled in his ancestral village, Ralegan Siddhi, and designed and implemented an extremely successful model of sustainable agriculture. He motivated the peasants to conserve rainwater (by building check dams) and reforest barren hillsides. He also persuaded (by some accounts, coerced) them to give up alcohol. A decade after Hazare settled in the village, Ralegan Siddhi was a beacon of 'green development', visited by environmental activists from around India and the world.[1]

Hazare's given names were Kisan Baburao. However, through his work in Ralegan Siddhi he came to be called '*Anna*', elder brother. Once his village became well known, he expanded his theatre of action to the state of Maharashtra as a whole. He drew attention to corruption in the state's development programmes, and occasionally fasted to put pressure on Maharashtra's officials and politicians. Now, in April 2011, the telecom and Commonwealth Games scams, and the massive media attention they engendered, persuaded Hazare that he needed to move himself to the national stage.

Hazare's fast in New Delhi was conducted at Jantar Mantar, which had become the preferred venue for protests once the police had closed Rajpath to activists. Before starting his ordeal he visited Rajghat, the memorial to Mahatma Gandhi. Here he told the assembled reporters: 'I have come to request Gandhiji to give good sense to this government. So many sacrifices were made for this country. But everything is being destroyed. You [Gandhiji] gave direction to this country but these people are destroying it.'[2]

By 'these people', Hazare meant the politicians and officials who manned and ran the government of India. His fast had one general aim – to focus national attention on the problem of corruption – and one specific aim, to compel the government to pass a bill appointing a '*Lokpal*', or ombudsman, with the powers to detect and punish corrupt officials and politicians.

Hazare's fast was widely, and at times breathlessly, covered by the press. The government's failure to punish the guilty in the telecom and Commonwealth Games scams was imprinted on the public imagination. And more or less every Indian had at some stage of his or her life paid a bribe. There was, the television cameras sensed, an extremely receptive audience for the fast, so they positioned themselves at Jantar Mantar, reporting the event. Hazare sat on the stage, while anti-corruption activists made a series of stirring speeches, the national tricolour waving in the background. A stream of writers, retired judges, musicians and even the odd Bollywood actor trooped off to Jantar Mantar to visit

Hazare, each new celebrity endorsement adding to the excitement and the drama.

An umbrella organization called 'India Against Corruption' had been formed to support Hazare. Its prime movers included Arvind Kejriwal, an engineer-turned-civil servant-turned-activist, who had worked on the Right to Information campaign. India Against Corruption organized supportive vigils in cities across the country, where candles were lit and songs sung in solidarity with the protests in Delhi.[3]

Prominent among those who came out to support Hazare were college students and young professionals. They were moved by the sight of an old man come, as he proclaimed, to save the nation from those who had corrupted it. Hazare himself did not use a smartphone or the Internet, but these young admirers took his message energetically across social media. They suggested that, in terms of message and method, Anna Hazare was, so to say, Mahatma Gandhi reborn. 'Join Dandi March-II' and 'A Mahatma announces fast-unto-death' were among the taglines used on Twitter and Facebook. On 7 April 2011, two days into Hazare's fast, a tweet reading 'Earthquake named Anna Hazare lashes on corrupt Indian politicians, epicenter India, it measures 1.22 Billion Richter Hearts' was one of the top ten global trending topics on Twitter.[4]

Unnerved by the protests, and even more so by the widespread and entirely sympathetic coverage in the media, the government of India buckled in. On 9 April it announced that it would set up a committee of ten members to help prepare a Lokpal Bill. In this committee, five Cabinet ministers would work with five people nominated by India Against Corruption, an extraordinary concession placing an elected national government on par with one, and not entirely representative, section of civil society. On hearing of this, Hazare broke his fast, and said he hoped the new Lokpal Bill would be passed by Parliament before 15 August 2011, Independence Day.[5]

II

Through the summer of 2011, the national conversation was focused on corruption. In the last week of April, the CBI arrested Suresh Kalmadi, the chairman of the Commonwealth Games Organising Committee in New Delhi, for 'conspiracy' in awarding a contract to a Swiss firm at an inflated cost of Rs141 crore. Kalmadi was a prominent and influential

Congressman, and although the party now suspended him, it could not escape the odour from his arrest.[6]

Meanwhile, the ten-member committee set up to draft a new Lokpal Bill had run into rough weather. The Cabinet ministers and the social activists deeply distrusted one another; this distrust separately communicated by them every evening to reporters as soon as the sittings ended. India Against Corruption demanded that the sittings be telecast live; a demand the government found impossible to meet. The activists then chose to boycott the meetings, and the committee was disbanded.

In the first week of June, a fresh fast commenced in New Delhi, this one undertaken by Baba Ramdev, a yoga teacher with a substantial following in northern and eastern India. Ramdev was, in terms of personality, quite different from Hazare; earthy rather than earnest, and with large ambitions for himself, these both political – he was close to the BJP, and had contemplated forming a party himself – as well as commercial, the development of a line of food and medicinal products based on Ayurveda.

Ramdev had for some time demanded that the government act to bring back money stashed away in Swiss banks by rich Indians. Now, in June 2011, he sat on fast under a massive *pandal* at the Ramlila Maidan, the great open ground at the border of New and Old Delhi, which had witnessed many epic speeches and rallies from the time of the Independence struggle of the 1920s and 1930s to the movement led by Jayaprakash Narayan in the 1970s. When asked about the cost of the marquee, Ramdev answered (to quote the inadequate English translation of his richly flavoured Hindi): 'Making one such pandal is nothing big for me. Everyone knows I can get several like these built in a single day. All the people gathered here would be willing to pay for the cost'.[7]

Knowing of his mass appeal, the government had at first treated Ramdev with indulgence. Cabinet ministers had met him beforehand and urged him to postpone or abandon his fast. When he went ahead anyway, they sent emissaries to the Ramlila Maidan urging him to call it off. That didn't work either. They then chose to take a punitive line, with a large posse of police descending on the marquee and dispersing Ramdev's followers. Ramdev himself panicked, changing into a woman's dress and seeking to flee the scene. The police detained but did not arrest him. Instead, he was served an order externing him from Delhi.[8]

In the last week of July, the Union Cabinet approved a Lokpal Bill. However, the bill did not meet the approval of the activists, for it exempted the prime minister, the higher judiciary, and the conduct of members of Parliament from its purview. India Against Corruption termed the bill a 'cruel joke' and 'a deceit on the nation'.[9] Anna Hazare announced that he would go on a fresh fast to press for an improved bill that would be 'strong and effective'.[10]

On the 15th of August, Prime Minister Manmohan Singh delivered his Independence Day address from the ramparts of the Red Fort. Speaking from behind a bullet-proof screen, he acknowledged that corruption was 'a big obstacle' in the way of the country fulfilling its potential. But, he added, there was no 'magic wand' to eradicate it.[11]

The next day, Anna Hazare announced that he would go on a fresh fast for a Lokpal Bill that met his and his colleagues' approval. He was arrested, and taken to the capital's Tihar jail. He refused to seek bail, and instead began his fast in prison. His incarceration brought thousands of people out into the streets of Delhi, with parallel protests elsewhere in the country. The Opposition refused to allow Parliament to function, demanding Hazare's release. On the 20th of August, the government released him, whereupon Hazare continued his fast as a free man, albeit in the full glare of the public and the media. He moved to the Ramlila Maidan, where his supporters had erected a stage on which he sat, waving and occasionally speaking to the assembled crowds.[12]

Hazare was no Gandhi, but this second fast rivalled the Dandi March in attracting the nation's attention. That, unlike the Mahatma's march to the sea, it was conducted in the age of live, satelite, television added enormously to its appeal. Through the day, the people of Delhi – students, workers, and professionals – thronged the Ramlila Maidan, to see for themselves the spectacle as it unfolded. The leaders of India Against Corruption made exhortative speeches, volunteers waving the national tricolour as they spoke. In the morning and again in the evening, Hazare would emerge from behind a screen (where he was fasting, and resting) to promise the flock that he would continue his ordeal for 'ek aur din, desh ke liye, desh ke liye' (one more day, for the nation's sake).

At home, in Bangalore, I sat in front of the television, one among millions of Indians who had abandoned work to watch and take in this gripping political drama. The contrast between Hazare and the prime minister was particularly striking: two men in their seventies, one willing to stake his life to end corruption, the other unwilling to take action against the corrupt ministers in his government.[13]

With every passing hour the legitimacy of the Congress regime further crumbled. As the columnist C. P. Surendran wrote at the time, 'a party that can't argue its case against a retired army truck driver whose only strength really is a kind of stolid integrity and a talent for skipping meals doesn't deserve to be in power'.[14]

As Hazare fasted, the government sent emissaries to him, among them ministers and officials from his native Maharashtra. Then on 27th August, with Anna Hazare's fast well into its second week, both Houses of Parliament decided unanimously to pass a revised Lokpal Bill that would incorporate the ideas of Hazare and his colleagues. The next day, Hazare ended his fast, sipping from a glass of coconut water mixed with honey, offered to him by two little girls, a Dalit and a Muslim, the symbolism most likely not Hazare's own but chosen for him by his media-smart advisers. Across the country, tens of thousands of Indians poured into the streets, celebrating what India Against Corruption was calling 'a people's victory'.[15]

As 2011 came to a close, the UPA regime in New Delhi was suffering from a crisis of credibility. And worse was to follow. In February 2012, the Supreme Court ruled that the 122 telecom licences issued by the government were illegal as they were handed out without a proper and transparent process. Both the BJP and the Left welcomed the verdict, and said that although the minister who had issued the licences (A. Raja) was already in jail, the prime minister himself could not escape responsibility. There were calls for Dr Manmohan Singh to resign.[16]

The Congress was beset by corruption scandals at the centre, as well as in states where it was in power. In Maharashtra, the Congress government had diverted apartments meant for war widows to its own favoured politicians and bureaucrats. When this came to light, the chief minister, Ashok Chavan, was compelled to resign. In July 2012, the CBI filed a charge sheet against Chavan and his associates. The crimes they were accused of included cheating and criminal conspiracy.[17]

Perhaps even more so than in other parts of India, politicians in Maharashtra were remarkably quick to skim off government contracts. In 2012, the Union government's own annual economic survey noted that although some Rs70,000 crores had been spent on irrigation projects in the past decade, the irrigated area in Maharashtra increased by only 1 per cent. The irrigation portfolio had long been held by the Nationalist Congress Party (NCP), an ally of the Congress in both state and centre, and likewise a party known for its proximity to builders and contractors. Charged with misappropriating funds meant for irrigation, which, if properly used, could have forestalled drought in Maharashtra, a leading NCP politician remarked that he would urinate in the dams to help fill them. His callous remark intensified the criticism his party and government were facing.[18]

The next month, August, saw an even more severe blow to the image of the ruling alliance in New Delhi. The Comptroller and Auditor General (CAG), a high constitutional authority charged with overseeing the fiduciary conduct of the central government, tabled a report in Parliament charging that favouritism in the allocation of coal blocks had led to a loss to the exchequer of Rs1.86 lakh crore. These coal blocks were largely in forests owned by the state, which had here (mis)used its discretionary powers to allot them to entrepreneurs close to the Congress or to individual Congress leaders.[19]

Many of these (mis)allocations had taken place in the years 2006–9, when the Coal Ministry was directly under the control of the prime minister. Dr Manmohan Singh long had an image of being personally incorruptible; indeed, this reputation had played a part in swaying voters in favour of the Congress in 2009. While he had not personally benefited from these transactions, that they had occurred under his watch was a body blow to his reputation. The calls for the prime minister to resign became even louder.

III

In May 2011, the Left Front, which had ruled continuously in West Bengal since 1977, lost power to the Trinamool Congress, a party led, directed and controlled by Mamata Banerjee. Meanwhile, in Tamil Nadu, J. Jayalalithaa of the AIADMK, was sworn in as chief minister. With Mayawati in power in Uttar Pradesh, at this point in time three of India's largest and most important states were run by women politicians. Meanwhile, Sushma Swaraj was Leader of the Opposition in the Lok Sabha, and, of course, Sonia Gandhi was both president of the Congress party and chairperson of the United Progressive Alliance that ruled at the centre.

Some women were vastly influential in Indian politics. But on the whole the status of women in India was not something to boast about. The Constitution makers had hoped that in time women would become increasingly visible as workers, managers, doctors, lawyers, teachers and entrepreneurs. There was some progress in this direction in the first decades of Independence; however, from the 1980s onwards there was a patriarchal backlash. India's major religions, Hinduism and Islam, placed men in a superior position to women both in scripture and in social practice. Their prejudices clashed or competed with the ideals of the Indian Constitution, with unhappy results. In villages, caste *panchayats* placed all kinds of restrictions on what women could wear or do – in some places, even mobile phones were banned. Honour killings of girls who chose their own husbands became distressingly common. Meanwhile, in many Muslim families, girls were withdrawn from high school, not allowed to work outside the home and often compelled to wear the veil.[20]

Indeed, despite rising education levels among women, the percentage of females in the workforce was declining in India. It fell from 34 per cent to 27 per cent in the first decade of the twenty-first century, at a time of tremendous economic growth. And working women faced a great deal of discrimination in the workplace. Even in professedly forward-looking professions such as the media and the law, there were few women in leadership roles.[21]

A study of the six largest Asian economies judged India the worst in terms of biases against women. The age at marriage was the lowest in India. Even when they had well-paid jobs in the organized sector, Indian women were expected to bear the brunt of housework and child rearing, and set aside their own aspirations to please or satisfy their parents and parents-in-law.[22]

If the status of women was bad in the cities, in the countryside it was even worse. Over the previous century the sex ratio had been steadily falling – from 972 females to 1,000 males in the year 1901, it had dropped to 947 in 1951 and 933 in 2001. It rose to 940 in 2011, yet it remained adverse, revealing the fact that child mortality was highly variable by gender. In most Indian homes, boys were treated better than girls – provided more nutritious food, better access to health care and sent to school, while their sisters laboured in field and forest. From the 1980s, advances in medical technology had worked to make more lethal an already deadly prejudice. Thus, the new sex determination tests allowed parents to abort female foetuses. Although banned by law, these tests were widely available in clinics throughout India.[23]

Clinics aborting female foetuses were especially popular in the northern states of Haryana and Punjab, where the sex ratio was well under 900. This had led to what was being called a 'crisis of masculinity'. According to the traditional rules of marriage, one's spouse had to be from one's caste and linguistic group, though usually not from one's village. As boys grew into men, an increasing number found that brides were simply unavailable in the locality. So they contracted unions with girls from hundreds of miles away, belonging to other states, castes, and linguistic groups. Now, women from the states of Assam, Bihar and West Bengal were being sought – and, occasionally, bought – by men from Haryana and Punjab. These 'cross-region' liaisons were sometimes informal, at other times legalized through the rites of marriage. Questions remained about how the offspring of these highly unusual unions would be treated by a society still bound, in most other respects, by the ties of caste and kinship.[24]

There was violence against the female foetus, and even more violence against girls once they came into the world and grew into adulthood. There was a great deal of sexual abuse in the home, not just the beating and brutalizing of wives by husbands, but of female cousins by male cousins, of nieces by uncles, even, on occasion, of daughters by fathers. Sexual violence was quite common in the workplace too. The exploitation, threatened or actual, of younger women colleagues by their male bosses was a feature of newsrooms, corporate offices, even progressive, 'do-good' think tanks and activist groups.[25]

The depths of patriarchal prejudice in modern India were dramatically, shockingly, demonstrated in the gang-rape of a twenty-three-year-old woman named Jyoti Singh in Delhi in December 2012. Ms Singh was travelling with her boyfriend in a bus at night, with only four other passengers, all male, on board. These four men beat up the woman's companion (with iron rods), and forced themselves on her. The driver and conductor did nothing to stop them. While all this was taking place, the bus drove past several police check-posts. Finally, the men threw the couple out of the bus and on to the highway, where a passer-by saw them and called the police, who took them to hospital.[26]

As Jyoti Singh battled for her life, and her story became known, outraged citizens descended on the streets of Delhi. Students from the capital's universities led the protest, organizing demonstrations and candle-light vigils. The protesters marched on Rashtrapati Bhavan, the presidential palace, demanding the death penalty for the rapists. They had to be dispersed by the police. In many other cities in India, similar meetings and protests were held.[27]

Responding to the protests, the government constituted a committee, headed by Justice J. S. Varma (a former chief justice of the Supreme Court), to suggest measures for the speedier trial of, and more punitive punishment for, criminals 'committing sexual assault of extreme nature against women'. Meanwhile the victim (who had been given the name 'Nirbhaya', one without fear) had been shifted to Singapore, where she died on the 29th of December. Three weeks later, the Varma Committee submitted its report. It passed strictures on the tardiness of the judicial process and the apathy of civil society. And it had this to say about the professed guardians of law and order: 'The insensitivity of the police to deal with rape victims is well known. The police respect a patriarchal form of society, and have been unable to deal with extraordinary cases of humiliation and hardship ...'. The report went on to note that 'the police are involved in trafficking of children (including female children)'.

The Varma Committee asked for the police to be made more accountable, for the judiciary to be more vigilant, for the state to provide facilities for the education of abandoned or homeless children, for political parties not to allow candidates with criminal antecedents to contest elections. It also recommended 'the creation of a new constitutional authority akin to the Comptroller and Auditor General for education [and] non-discrimination in respect of women and children.'

The last line of the report read: 'We pay our tribute to the departed soul of Nirbhaya which has occasioned this exercise'.[28]

Following the tabling of the Varma Committee report, Parliament passed the Criminal Law (Amendment) Bill, 2013, which provided for more stringent punishment for crimes against women. Those who committed crimes such as rape could be sentenced to life imprisonment, while repeat offenders could even get the death penalty. The bill also defined stalking and voyeurism as non-bailable offences, and prescribed a ten-year jail term for those who threw acid on women (a not uncommon crime in some parts of India).[29] The law was in place; the more – far more – arduous task of transforming popular attitudes and undermining patriarchy in everyday life remained.

Indeed, in India, where progress and reaction, tradition and modernity were in complicated and contentious co-existence, one could not always trust the law to show the way to justice and reason either. In July 2009 the Delhi High Court had struck down Section 377 of the

Indian Penal Code, which criminalized gay sex. The judgement was challenged in the Supreme Court, with Hindu, Muslim and Christian conservatives coming together in a rare display of inter-religious solidarity. In December 2013 the Supreme Court restored Section 377 and criminalized adult gay sex again. Justices G. S. Singhvi and S. J. Mukhopadhyaya disagreed with the Delhi High Court that Section 377 violated the provisions of the constitution of India. They concurred with those who, back in the nineteenth century, had framed the IPC, and held that gay sex was 'against the order of nature'.[30]

In the court as the judgement was passed were many gays and lesbians. They wept as the judges (one of whom later confessed that he had never met a gay man in his life) read out their order restoring the status quo.[31] Those in same-sex relationships, who had begun to breathe freer after the 2009 judgement, would now once more face the threat of police persecution and social ostracism.

IV

In most democracies, a party in power gets anxious about re-election roughly a year-and-a-half before its term ends. The anxiety is manifest in, among other things, the things the ruling party's leader says or does, the concessions or promises she or he makes to the electorate. So it was with Indira Gandhi in 1983, with Rajiv Gandhi in 1987, and so it was with Sonia Gandhi as India entered the year 2013. In January, her son Rahul Gandhi was appointed vice president of the Congress at a party convention in Jaipur, with fireworks lighting up the sky and MPs telling journalists how they were dazzled by the dynamism of this latest member of the Nehru-Gandhi family. The sycophancy was not limited to ordinary MPs however; some months later, even the prime minister, Dr Manmohan Singh, told the press that he would 'be happy to work for the Congress party under the leadership of Rahul Gandhiji'.[32]

Even as she supervised the elevation of her son, Sonia Gandhi sought to reinforce her party's welfarist credentials. The UPA had proposed a food security scheme whereby two-thirds of the population would be provided grains free or at heavily subsidized rates. The scheme had been criticized as a likely drain on the exchequer, and as promoting corruption. There were other criticisms too; that the bill sought to promote an excessive dependence on carbohydrates at a time when

Indians were moving towards mixed diets and that it pampered farmers rather than consumers.

The bill mandating the food security scheme had not been passed in Parliament. Yet Mrs Gandhi was determined to see it through. She made the party's commitment public on 20 August, Rajiv Gandhi's birth anniversary. While speaking of her husband's professed commitment to the poor, she told the assembled reporters that the 'UPA government is following the ideals of [Mahatma] Gandhi and continuously marching forward to bring revolutionary changes in the lives of the aam admi.'[33]

In so far it promised more welfare schemes, the Congress strategy for the 2014 elections was akin to that in 2009. This time, however, the party posters had a single face, that of Rahul Gandhi. Their main rival, the BJP, had no strategy in place of their own. Their stalwarts A. B. Vajpayee and L. K. Advani were now too old to be plausible prime ministerial candidates. On the other hand, there were several younger BJP chief ministers in the states, as well as several BJP leaders in Parliament, all experienced enough and plausible enough. Which of these would it be?

Unlike the Congress, the BJP was a party that took decisions on the basis of discussion and debate, not through the whims of a single individual or family. Indeed, the party's mentoring organization, the RSS, had long been opposed to 'vyakti puja', the worship of individuals. But now, as the party and its councils considered their options, one of its members pressed his claims most forcibly on their attentions. This was Narendra Modi, who had been chief minister of Gujarat for a decade, and who was determined to make his own, independent, bid for prime minister.

Early in 2013 – with national elections still more than a year away – Narendra Modi began to project himself aggressively on the national stage. Recognizing the power (and numbers) of first-time voters, he spoke to student bodies in several cities. Here he spoke of the successes, real and imaginary, of what he called the 'Gujarat model'. He told his audiences of how he had nurtured industrial and agricultural growth in his state, of how he had cut down corruption and bureaucratic red tape, and generated hope among the young.[34]

In March, Narendra Modi was appointed to the BJP's Central Parliamentary Board. In June, he was appointed head of the election campaign committee. Finally, in September, he was officially nominated the BJP's prime ministerial candidate. His elevation was opposed by some party seniors who were nervous of his abrasive personality and controversial past. Each time, the clamour of the cadres forced the opposition to Mr Modi within the BJP to back down.[35]

On 15 August 2013 India celebrated its sixty-seventh Independence Day. The prime minister gave his customary address to the nation from the Red Fort in Delhi. In a daring bid to outdo him, Narendra Modi gave his own Independence Day speech in the town of Bhuj in north Gujarat, with a mock Red Fort erected on the podium. The speech itself taunted Dr Singh for the failures of his government. A chief minister mocking a serving prime minister on Independence Day was unprecedented. However, Modi's speech helped project himself as the alternative to a corrupt and corroding regime.[36]

In November 2013, assembly elections were held in the major states of Madhya Pradesh, Rajasthan and Chhattisgarh. The BJP won all three comfortably. The frailties of India's Grand Old Party, and of the government it ran in New Delhi, were increasingly visible.

Narendra Modi now began to campaign full-time for the general elections. Between January and May he gave several speeches a day, flying in to one venue in a chartered plane and flying on to the next after he had spoken. He addressed more than four hundred rallies across India, in large cities, small towns and rural locations.

In the eyes of many Indians the 2002 Gujarat pogrom remained a blot on Modi's reputation. However, in later years he had assiduously remade himself as a 'vikash purush', a man of development. Meanwhile, Manmohan Singh had ruled out a third term for himself. The Congress's election campaign would be led by Rahul Gandhi.

In 1984, Rajiv Gandhi, Rahul's father, was prime minister when there was a pogrom against Sikhs in New Delhi. Given India's painfully slow criminal justice system, perpetrators of the anti-Sikh violence had not yet been brought to book. Meanwhile, Congress leaders who led the mobs were renominated as MPs and, in at least one case, as a minister. And so, to those who pointed to Mr Modi's complicity in the violence against Muslims in Gujarat in 2002, the BJP pointed instead to the Congress-sponsored violence against Sikhs in north India in 1984.

One pogrom having cancelled out another, Modi now asked to be compared, as an administrator and politician, with Rahul Gandhi. In this contest there could be only one winner. Modi was an energetic and effective orator in his native Gujarati and in India's most widely spoken language, Hindi. On the other hand, Rahul Gandhi was an indifferent and unwilling speaker. Modi had vast resources of energy, travelling across the country to spread his message. Rahul Gandhi's political activities were erratic and episodic. He would spend a night in the home of a poor villager, then not be visible for weeks on end.

To make this contest presidential, man-to-man rather than party-versus-party, was an inspired move on the part of Narendra Modi. For he had been chief minister of an important Indian state for more than a decade. On the other hand, in ten years in Parliament Rahul Gandhi had made few speeches, and no memorable ones. He had declined to take up a post in the Cabinet. He had no administrative experience whatsoever.

Modi often compared his family background to that of the Congress heir-apparent's. The Gujarat chief minister claimed to have worked in a tea-shop as a young boy. The claim was unverified; but what was not in dispute was that he was born in a backward caste, in a family of modest means. Narendra Modi was entirely self-made. On the other hand, Rahul Gandhi was born to privilege, yet had made little of his good fortune. The contrast between him as a one-time *chaiwallah* and Rahul as a pampered princeling was relentlessly hammered home by Modi throughout his campaign.

Modi also took to referring to Rahul as *shehzada*, a Urdu word of Persian origin meaning 'crown prince'. That the Gandhis saw themselves as a hereditary dynasty destined to rule India far into the future was a charge easy to sustain, not least because, while in power, Sonia Gandhi had named dozens of government schemes after Nehru, Indira and Rajiv, and because as party president she had automatically chosen her son as vice president although he was by no means the most capable Congressman of his generation. Still, the choice of appellation was noteworthy; Modi deliberately did not choose the common Hindi word for crown prince, *yuvraj*, preferring a word that denoted foreign-ness, a barely concealed reference to Sonia's Italian origins as well as to the Congress's perceived 'appeasement' of Urdu-speaking Muslims. In his speeches, Modi mocked the *shehzada* for his laziness and incompetence, while asking voters to give him sixty months in office to undo all the harm the Congress was alleged to have done in the past sixty years.[37]

Mindful of his sectarian past, Narendra Modi did not foreground his party's Hindutva ideology in his speeches. Rather, he emphasized the importance of rapid economic development, and, in particular, job creation. In the two decades since the Indian economy had been freed from stifling state controls, it had made impressive strides, as witnessed by the rapid decline in poverty and a corresponding growth of the middle class. However, the sectors that had fuelled this growth, such as IT and pharmaceuticals, did not generate much employment. Noting this, Modi promised to pay more attention to manufacturing, to better satisfy the aspirations of the millions of young men entering the workforce every year.

The crowds that flocked to hear Narendra Modi everywhere were evidence of the excitement and hope he generated. Despite Rahul Gandhi being much younger than him, first-time voters were far more impressed by Modi, who exuded authority and decisiveness whereas his rival seemed weak, lazy and confused. A third-year college student in Mumbai, who would vote in a general election for the first time, told a reporter at a Modi rally that 'we need him. We need dictatorship in India. He is a dictator who can fight corruption and lack of unity and discipline in the country'.[38]

Narendra Modi's campaign was widely (and sometimes breathlessly) covered on television, a medium far more ubiquitous in India than it had ever been before. Back in 1996, only 19 per cent of Indians watched news shows on television. By 2014 this was up to 46 per cent. Tens of millions of voters watched and were impressed by Modi's speeches, and by his evident zest and energy. Surveys conducted in 2013–14, in the run-up to the elections, showed that among those who regularly watched television and read newspapers, potential BJP voters led potential Congress voters by as much as 20 percentage points.[39]

In reaching out to younger voters, Modi made good use of forms of communication even newer than television. He had an extensive website, which was regularly updated, as well as active Facebook and Twitter accounts. He tweeted often about the concerns of the young and of his own emphasis on development, with exhortative tweets about these subjects juxtaposed with sarcastic or derisive tweets about his opponents.[40]

Narendra Modi's election campaign was superbly orchestrated. He hired the country's top copywriters, who gave him two simple but tellingly effective lines: 'Abki baat Modi sarkar' (This time a Modi government, much more resonant in Hindi, where it rhymes); and 'Achche din aane wale hain' (The good times are about to come). His campaign was also extremely well funded. Money was raised from large corporations and from Indians living abroad. By one estimate, the money spent by the BJP on advertising alone was equivalent to £500 million.[41] A comparable amount would have been spent on busing people to rallies and on the leader's travel expenses.

Modi was advised by, among other people, young Indian professionals who had worked in the United States. They brought with them the latest techniques of campaigning, including the adroit use of social media. On the other hand, the Congress eschewed such methods, choosing to rely on old-fashioned appeals to the name and fame of their First Family.[42]

V

In December 2012, while campaigning in the Gujarat state elections, Narendra Modi used the phrase 'neo middle class', to describe the tens of millions of Indians who wished to climb out of poverty and enjoy the fruits of a middle-class life. This class helped him win re-election in Gujarat, and he now hoped it would propel him to national power too.

Mahatma Gandhi famously said that India lives in its villages. By the time the twenty-first century arrived, it had begun increasingly to live in its cities and towns too. In 1951, only five Indian cities had a population greater than 1 million. By 2011, as many as fifty-three cities did. The urban population now constituted some 31 per cent of the total population of India. Back in 1951, it was a mere 13 per cent. Close to four hundred million Indians now lived in urban centres.[43]

There had always been a great deal of migration in India, between villages and from village to city. This movement of people across the country became even more common after economic liberalization. One study estimated that inter-state migration increased by 53.6 per cent between 1991 and 2001. This was a consequence of uneven development, with some states and regions prospering more than others. Eastern India in particular was economically depressed, so it saw a large outflow of migrants going to work in the cities of the West and the South, and in the farms of Punjab and coffee estates of Kodagu as well. In 2001, three in five families in rural Bihar had migrants working outside the village. Their contribution to household income was substantial, especially among the lower castes.[44]

In the cities, the new migrants worked chiefly in the informal sector. With factories closing or laying off workers as they adopted labour-saving technologies, these villagers-turned-townsfolk took jobs as hawkers, vendors, construction workers, plumbers and security guards. An overwhelming majority of these migrants were male. Attracted by the vigour of the city, they made the urban economy more vigorous by their own labour. Thus the contribution of cities to India's Gross Domestic Product had increased from 29 per cent in 1950–1 to 62 per cent in 2007.[45]

Urbanization bred new desires and aspirations, with migrants to cities seeking to leave their old lives in the country behind. They wanted a pucca house, running water, access to entertainment and to such consumer goods as they could hope to buy. And they wanted to make their own way in life, rather than be patronized by welfare handouts by the state.[46]

Meanwhile, as the cities grew, the villages changed: socially, economically and politically. Once, upper castes such as Brahmins in south India and Rajputs in north India had dominated the countryside. Now, they had lost or sold their land, and were challenged on the ideological front as well. Integration with the outside world had once been a preserve of upper castes, but now many middle- and lower-caste men (less often women) were also going out of the village to study, or more often to work.

Increased mechanization of agriculture had led to a decrease in the demand for rural labour; but there had been a decline in supply too, as Dalits no longer wanted to work in the fields. They preferred employment outside the village because it paid them better and also freed them from the stranglehold of their locally dominant caste. The work they did now – for example, in construction, or the loading and unloading of trucks and railway carriages – was often physically demanding as well as hazardous to health. But it was much less demeaning.

Another, and perhaps even more fundamental, change was with regard to education. In one fairly representative village in northern India, the percentage of literate upper-caste Thakurs had increased from 38.6 per cent in 1958 to 82 per cent in 2008. In the same period, the percentage of educated lower-caste Jatavs (traditionally considered Untouchable) had increased from 3 per cent to 42.7 per cent. In 1958, less than one in ten Thakur women were literate; in 2008, more than four in ten. In 1958, no Jatav women in the village could read or write; in 2008, one in five could.

There was a strong interest, across castes, in educating one's children. Rajputs did not want their children to be farmers; Dalits did not want their children to be condemned to a life of agrestic serfdom. With young men across castes seeking jobs and fulfilment outside the village, a growing proportion of those who actually cultivated land were in their fifties or sixties, for whom it was too late to contemplate a change of profession or location.

Village life was changing profoundly across India. Yet in some spheres there was a marked continuity between past and present. Castes were still segregated in residential terms; and, at least within the village, in social terms too. An overwhelming majority of marriages (probably closer to 100 per cent than 95 per cent) in rural India were contracted within the same endogamous group, and were arranged by parents or relatives.[47]

There had, in recent decades, been a blurring of boundaries between town and country. Indians who lived in villages became increasingly familiar with city life, either because of their own experiences or of the influx of artefacts of modernity in their homes. Village patriarchs now wished to send their children to the nearest town to study in an English-medium school. They themselves rode motorcycles rather than cycles or bullock-carts. Many even worked part-time in the modern sector, in the small factories and workshops that had begun to be located along highways, where land was cheaper than in crowded cities.[48]

The ever-greater mobility that Indian villagers now enjoyed led to a weakening – though certainly not a severing – of the links between caste and occupation. Some Banias chose to abandon trade for teaching school teachers, some Yadavs preferred service in the army to herding cows. And, in a more radical break with tradition, some Dalits chose to venture into entrepreneurship. They built successful companies in the leather trade, a trade traditionally associated with their caste. Others ventured into altogether new areas; running automobile dealerships, construction companies and pharmaceutical factories. There was now even a Dalit Chamber of Commerce.[49]

To be sure, such success stories were rare and exceptional. A majority of Dalits continued with their old, lowly paid, stigmatized professions. They lived in separate quarters in villages and in towns. Upper castes would not eat with them, meet with them, marry amongst them. Yet seven decades of democracy and development had made dents in the edifice of tradition and prejudice. With affirmative action, some Dalits could become senior government officers. With elections based on universal adult franchise, some Dalits could become ministers and chief ministers. Now, with economic liberalization, some Dalits could become billionaires too.

VI

As the BJP, the Congress and the major regional parties campaigned for the next general elections, battles of a more elemental kind were being played out in some parts of the country. In July 2012, savage riots broke out in Assam between Bodo tribals and Muslims originally from Bangladesh, but settled for several decades in eastern India. Close to fifty people died in the violence, while more than 100,000 fled their homes to refugee camps. The majority of victims were Muslims. With the local police unwilling or incapable of stemming the violence, the army had to be called in to restore order.[50]

The epicentre of the violence was in the Kokrajhar and Baksa districts of lower Assam. Even after the riots had subsided, the mostly Muslim refugees were fearful of returning to their homes and villages. When, at last, they did, they faced fresh violence. In the first week of May 2014, Bodo militants killed 23 people in a single day. Once more, the army came out to conduct flag marches and seek to re-establish the authority of the state.[51]

The clash in Assam was between two vulnerable and insecure communities. The Bodos felt that they had been suppressed by the dominant Ahom community of Assam; after a long struggle, they had been granted autonomy in the districts in which they were a majority. Meanwhile, Muslims from densely populated Bangladesh had settled in their vicinity, sparking fresh resentment, and, in time, violence.[52]

A year after the troubles in Kokrajhar, riots broke out in India's most populous state, Uttar Pradesh. The Muslims here were authentically of the land. They had lived in the Indo-Gangetic plains as long as the Hindus, except that, some six or seven centuries ago, they had converted to Islam. From the late nineteenth century this part of northern India had been subject to periodic bouts of religious rioting. Hindus and Muslims had clashed in the 1940s, before and after Partition, and in the 1980s and 1990s, as a consequence of the Ramjanmabhoomi agitation.

Social peace in Uttar Pradesh was fragile, threatened on the one side by the hardline Hindutva elements of the Sangh Parivar and on the other by parties who canvassed support among the Muslim clergy. In power in UP in 2013 was the Samajwadi Party (SP), whose major leader, Mulayam Singh Yadav, was so known for cultivating the Muslim vote that he was referred to as 'Maulana Mulayam'. His young and inexperienced son, Akhilesh Yadav, was now chief minister.

In September 2013, riots between Hindus and Muslims broke out in western Uttar Pradesh. The trouble began after a young Muslim man was seen in conversation with a young Jat woman, whereupon he was killed by her brothers. The violence escalated, with BJP leaders asking Hindus (and the dominant Jats in particular) to teach Muslims a lesson and SP leaders urging Muslims to answer fire with fire. The call to action, and vengeance, was communicated through Facebook and WhatsApp, this perhaps the first time these new technologies were used to foment inter-communal hatred in India. More than fifty people perished in the riots, and tens of thousands were rendered homeless. As in Assam, as indeed in most parts of the country (outside of Kashmir), when such incidents took place, Muslims suffered disproportionately.[53]

VII

Through April and May 2014, some five hundred and fifty four million Indians voted in the country's sixteenth general election. This was, as in every previous Indian general election, the largest exercise of the popular will in human history. The election was conducted over nine phases. Some 800,000 soldiers and policemen were placed on election duty, with five hundred trains and even fifty helicopters commandeered to convey them from place to place.[54]

When the votes were counted, on 16 May, the Bharatiya Janata Party had got an impressive 282 seats, a clear majority. Its main rival, the Congress Party, had been comprehensively routed. Congress had won a meagre 44 seats, more than a hundred and fifty less than in 2009.

The BJP's most stunning victory was in Uttar Pradesh, India's largest state. Here, it won 71 seats out of 80, prevailing over the Congress as well as locally powerful caste-based parties. (In the 2009 elections the BJP had won a mere 10 seats in the state). It also did well in Bihar, Madhya Pradesh and Rajasthan, and, inevitably, in Narendra Modi's Gujarat. The BJP fared less well in the states of West Bengal and Odisha in the east, and in Tamil Nadu and Kerala in the south. In these states, a majority of the population do not speak or comprehend Hindi, and were not so easily swayed by the seductive powers of Narendra Modi's oratory.

Taking the country as a whole, the BJP increased its vote share from 19 per cent to 31 per cent. First-time voters in particular, and those under thirty-five in general, voted enthusiastically for the BJP, a striking reflection of Rahul Gandhi's incompetence as a vote-gatherer, since the young thought his far older rival much more likely to fulfil their expectations.[55]

The election was not won by Narendra Modi alone. Even so, there had been few instances in the past where a single individual left such an impress on an Indian election. Perhaps the only precedents were the elections of 1952 and 1971, where Jawaharlal Nehru and Indira Gandhi led and personified their party's successful campaign, just as Modi had now done.

Although schooled in the RSS, as chief minister of Gujarat Narendra Modi had kept the Sangh at a distance. He did not want an alternate centre of power. However, in the run-up to the general elections, the RSS and Modi were once more reconciled. After an initial hesitation, the Sangh endorsed him as the BJP's prime ministerial candidate, and RSS cadres canvassed energetically for Modi on the ground, particularly in the key state of Uttar Pradesh. Their reward was soon forthcoming; out of 23 members of the prime minister's Cabinet, seventeen were from the RSS.[56]

In July, Modi's close associate Amit Shah was elected president of the BJP. Shah was the one man the prime minister trusted completely. In Gujarat, he at one time held nine portfolios in Modi's Cabinet. However, Shah had a controversial past; he had even been externed by the Supreme Court from his home state for fear he might tamper with the evidence in cases of extra-judicial killings. Now, as president of the ruling party, he was the second most powerful man in India.[57]

VIII

In his first months in office, Narendra Modi announced a whole array of new schemes and programmes. There was the 'Swachh Bharat' mission, which promised to eliminate open defecation by 2 October 2019, the 150th birth anniversary of Mahatma Gandhi. The prime minister himself took a broom to the dirty riverside ghats of the holy city of Varanasi.[58] Then there was the 'Make in India' campaign, which promised to make the country a hub of manufacturing to match China.[59] Next came Modi's 'Beti Bachao Beti Padhao' mission, which sought to promote gender equality through the education of girls.[60] And there was also the 'Smart Cities Mission', whereby the prime minister sought to have one hundred urban centres developed as hubs of innovation and creativity.[61]

The prime minister also revealed a penchant for acronyms. While welcoming Foreign Direct Investment, he said that FDI must also stand for First Develop India. On New Year's Day 2015, the Planning Commission was abolished, being replaced by the Niti Aayog, the first word of which also spelt National Institution for Transforming India.[62] And in advocating better relations with the country's most powerful neighbour, Modi argued that we should INCH towards MILES, the first acronym joining India and China, the second joining Millennium with Exceptional Synergy.[63]

In its last year in power, the UPA government had brought about a new Land Acquisition Act, which made the consent of farmers mandatory before their land could be taken over for industrial or other projects. Narendra Modi had promised to repeal this with a new law, making it easier for entrepreneurs to acquire land to build factories that would generate employment as well as wealth. However, the law his advisers drafted was fiercely resisted within sections of his own party, nervous as being seen as excessively 'pro-business'.

Modi's election campaign had been handsomely funded by large corporates. He had himself promised faster industrial growth and the rapid generation of jobs. After his proposed land acquisition bill was stalled, he now promoted a new Goods and Services Tax (GST). This was originally an initiative of the previous prime minister, Dr Manmohan Singh, who had however failed to get it passed through Parliament.

The GST bill sought to eliminate the existing taxes, levies and duties that prevailed in different states, and replace them with a single Value Added Tax for all goods and services. When the UPA government had first proposed the GST, Modi had opposed it, saying it would infringe on states' rights. Most entrepreneurs, however, were strongly in favour of a GST; so were most economists, who argued that it would create a unified national market, spur growth and reduce corruption. In August 2016 a GST bill passed through Parliament; it had now to be ratified by a majority of state assemblies before it could become law.[64]

Modi's focus on energizing the domestic economy was expected. For the economic growth that India experienced in recent decades had not generated adequate employment. Between 2000 and 2010, India's total workforce had increased by 63 million. Of these, 44 million joined the unorganized sector, 22 million became informal workers in the organized sector, while the number of formal workers in the organized sector actually fell by 3 million. Despite its long history of industrial enterprise, and its many technical and engineering colleges, India had not been able to match the success of even Bangladesh and Vietnam (let alone China) in generating widespread employment in factories that produced goods for the world market.[65]

By the standards of most developing countries the unemployment rate in India was low. But it was increasing, a worrying sign for politicians and policy-makers. It stood at 6.8 per cent in 2001, and had climbed to 9.6 per cent a decade later. The export boom of the 1990s had tapered off. New manufacturing projects were inhibited by high (and rising) land and labour costs. The infrastructure promised by the state (better roads, ports and airports) to ease movement of raw materials as well as finished goods had not substantially materialized. It was thus that the BJP had claimed in its 2014 election manifesto that it would create ten million jobs a year, an extremely ambitious target which, once in power, it was finding increasingly hard to achieve.[66]

In 2015, the limitations of India's 'jobless growth' model were starkly shown up when some 2.3 million young men applied for 368 junior posts advertised for by the Uttar Pradesh government. The jobs were at the lowest level of the government hierarchy. They involved riding a bicycle to run errands for senior officers, keeping watch outside their offices, or serving them and their guests tea. Yet so scarce was private sector employment in this part of India that some 25,000 postgraduates and even 255 men with PhD's applied for these menial jobs in government.[67]

The prime minister's emphasis on such programmes as Make in India was a response to such anomalies in the development process. This push towards more rapid economic growth, however, led to a further dilution of environmental standards and safeguards. In October 2015, the Ministry of Environment and Forests made mining easier by deleting the hydrological value of forest cover as a constraint on new projects. Natural forests play a crucial role in sustaining rivers and lakes. The new policy encouraged forest destruction at the hands of new mining and industrial projects, imperilling the supply of fresh water to agriculture and rural households.[68]

The Ministry of Environment and Forests (which now had 'Climate Change' added on to its title) had its budget slashed by 50 per cent in the first year of Modi's prime ministership. Meanwhile, existing laws for wildlife and biodiversity protection were also relaxed, and fines levied on industries for causing pollution cancelled. The consent of tribal communities for new projects in their vicinity, previously mandatory, was now withdrawn.[69]

Industrial growth at all costs was the new mantra, regardless of what this dilution of environmental norms would mean for the provision of clean air and water to the ordinary citizen, or for the sustainability of the development process itself. The implications of these new policies soon revealed themselves, when, in April 2016, a global study reported that India led the world in environmental conflicts. Some 27 per cent of all nature-related conflicts in the country were related to the scarcity of water. Other conflicts pertained to the destruction of forests, the disposal of untreated garbage, and the impact of industrial pollution.[70]

IX

The economic policies Narendra Modi pursued as prime minister were consistent with his track record in Gujarat. What was more surprising was his keen interest in global affairs. In his first year in office, Modi travelled to as many as nineteen countries, these including Japan, China, Australia and the United States. In his second year, he travelled to another seventeen, while re-visiting some countries he had already been to.

Although he was not formally the Minister of External Affairs, Modi took complete charge of foreign policy, as only Jawaharlal Nehru among Indian prime ministers had done before him. He told an interviewer that he travelled so much since (so he claimed) the Indian media had painted an unflattering portrait of him, and he wanted world leaders to discover for themselves the real personality of the new prime minister of India.[71]

In his travels abroad, Modi made it a point to address members of the Indian diaspora, in public meetings held in such places as New York's Madison Square Gardens and London's Wembley football stadium, where large and delirious crowds cheered him on. His speeches were characteristically robust. To convey that, unlike past prime ministers, he was authentically Indian and proud of his heritage, he invoked religious thinkers such as Sri Aurobindo and Swami Vivekananda, presented the Bhagavad Gita to foreign dignitaries, and celebrated the gift, by India, of yoga to the world.[72]

In other countries, as in India, Modi seemed tireless. Yet it was not easy to discern a particular thread in his foreign policy initiatives. He visited Japan and made some unflattering remarks about another country (which many presumed to be China), but then, a few weeks later, entertained the Chinese president in Gujarat. Modi invited the Pakistani prime minister to his swearing-in ceremony in May 2014, and, a year-and-a-half later, dropped in to attend his grand-daughter's wedding in Lahore. Yet relations between Pakistan and India continued to be frosty, with official spokesmen trading barbs and innuendos, as they had long done. Modi's own Defence Minister said in public that 'going to Pakistan or going to hell is the same thing'.[73]

The one area where there was clear continuity was in India's relations with the United States. When Barack Obama visited New Delhi in January 2015, Modi spoke of there being a special 'chemistry' between him and the American president.[74] In truth, Modi was merely consolidating the work done by his two immediate predecessors, Vajpayee and Manmohan Singh, in bringing the world's two largest democracies, which had been alienated from one another during the Cold War, closer together once the Cold War had ended.[75]

X

In a book published in 1970, Rajni Kothari had spoken of the 'Congress system' of Indian politics. Unlike in Europe and North America, where two or more parties alternated in power, in India one party was dominant, if not hegemonic. It was solidly in power at the centre and in most of the states. For many years after Independence, the Congress was successful in presenting itself as the 'authoritative spokesman of the nation as well as its affirmed agent of criticism and change'.

Kothari was writing in the aftermath of the 1967 elections, the first time Congress's countrywide dominance was seriously threatened. The party retained power at the centre, but lost power in as many as eight states. But, as Kothari showed, in the ways that mattered, the Congress remained 'the preponderant political force in the country'. Indeed, in six of the states lost by the Congress in 1967, the government was led by a former Congressman. And so the Congress remained 'the ruling party and the overwhelming political force at the national level' – in addition, it 'control[led] various avenues for influencing state politics'.

One byproduct of the political dominance of the Congress was that it helped keep the country together in those first, fraught, fractious decades of Independence. Thus, as Kothari remarked, 'because the Congress managed to be in power continuously and there was no united or effective threat to its authority, the country's political process gained incomparable advantages of continuity and unity'.[76]

This 'Congress system' of which Kothari spoke held, more or less, for the first three decades after Independence. It was challenged in 1977, after the Emergency, but then re-asserted itself between 1980 and 1989.

The years 1989 to 1998 were a period of transition in Indian politics. Congress dominance weakened across India, as parties based on regional, religious, caste and class identities won elections and ran governments in state after state. A third phase was inaugurated in 1998, with the emergence of a bipolar polity. This was a consequence of the rise to national prominence of the Bharatiya Janata Party. The two poles were constituted by the Congress and the BJP respectively, around each of which smaller parties clustered.

The general elections of 2014 saw the Congress reduced to an all-time low. In December of that year, after state elections in Jammu and Kashmir and Jharkhand, a further and perhaps more definitive landmark was reached: the BJP now had more members of state assemblies than the Congress.

The rapid decline of the Congress was a consequence of, among other things, the fading appeal of its First Family. With an ever-younger electorate, fewer and fewer Indians remembered the contributions of Nehru, Indira or Rajiv. The party organization had crumbled in many parts of the country; once it lost power in a particular state, the Congress found it extremely hard to regain it. In Tamil Nadu it had not been in power since 1967; in West Bengal, since 1977; in Uttar Pradesh, since 1989. A third reason was the lacklustre leadership of Rahul Gandhi. He failed to inspire enthusiasm among voters; indeed, he was the first member of his family not to command the respect of even his party colleagues.[77]

While the Congress had lost ground across India, some regional parties remained robust. In the general elections of 2014 the BJP had done very well in Bihar. But when assembly elections were held there in 2015, Modi's party was crushed by an alliance of two Bihar-based parties. The next year, Mamata Banerjee and the TMC won comfortable re-election in West Bengal, and J. Jayalalithaa and her AIADMK did likewise in Tamil Nadu. The Communists remained strong in Tripura and Kerala, while in the city-state of Delhi, a new party, the Aam Admi Party – born out of the anti-corruption movement of 2011 – had humiliated both the BJP and the Congress.

As I write this, in October 2016, it is clear that the BJP has replaced the Congress as the principal pole of Indian politics. Another milestone in its march was the victory in the Assam state elections earlier this year, where the Congress had been in power since 2001. A combination of anti-incumbency, Narendra Modi's personal appeal and the subtle stoking of fears of further Muslim immigration from Bangladesh enabled the BJP to win a majority in Assam.[78] This was the party's first bridgehead in eastern India, perhaps presaging further inroads into the smaller north-eastern states, hitherto Congress strongholds.

As this book goes to press, BJP is in power at the centre, and in as many as thirteen states. Karnataka remains the only major state in which the Congress is in power. The BJP is today India's sole *national* party, with a major presence in a majority of the states of the Union. It is to national politics now what the Congress once was.

XI

At the height of its power and influence in the 1950s and 1960s, the Congress could count on comfortably winning the elections it fought. But it still faced protest and opposition from politicians in other parties, from intellectuals, from social movements and from insurgencies. There were criticisms of the Congress government's economic and foreign policies by scholars and by MPs, opposition to its social policies from popular movements (think the language struggle), and, not least, violent attempts to challenge the unitary idea of India it had promoted (think the Kashmiri, Naga and Mizo upsurges).

And so it has been with the BJP government too. In the Lok Sabha, the alliance led by the BJP enjoys a comfortable majority. However, whenever a state assembly election is held, what is now India's sole national party is strongly challenged by other parties. And, what might worry it as much, in between assembly and national elections the BJP faces intense pressure from popular movements conveying various forms of discontent with the government's policies.

One early source of discontent with Narendra Modi's government was the influence on its functioning of the Rashtriya Swayamsewak

Sangh. Between 1998 and 2004, when Vajpayee was prime minister, the RSS's hardline Hindutva agenda was largely kept in abeyance, in part because the BJP did not have the numbers to govern on its own. But now the party had a majority in the Lok Sabha, in whose making RSS cadres had played an important and perhaps determining role. The Sangh asked in return for control of key ministries (Education, Culture and Home among them), while also demanding that key appointments be cleared by it.

Meanwhile, some newly elected BJP Members of Parliament made provocative statements in public. One charged Muslims with promoting 'love jihad' by capturing Hindu girls and converting them. A second praised Mahatma Gandhi's assassin, Nathuram Godse. A third asked that all Christians and Muslims be 'reconverted' to Hinduism. A fourth used an extremely derogatory word, implying a complete lack of morals, to describe the Muslim community as a whole.[79]

The increasing visibility of the RSS, and its growing influence on government policy, sparked a torrent of criticism from scholars and writers on the Left, who had dominated intellectual discourse in India. They feared that the secular and plural character of education would be replaced by one emphasizing the ideals of Hindu supremacists. That the prime minister had stayed silent while these provocative, abusive, statements were made by his party MPs was seen as a sign that he agreed with them. Many writers, some very distinguished, returned state awards in protest.

Meanwhile, the BJP's student wing, the Akhil Bharatiya Vidyarthi Parishad (ABVP), sought to increase its influence in university politics. The ABVP urged MPs and ministers to throw their weight behind them, by, for instance, arresting or intimidating left-wing student activists. In Hyderabad University, pressured by the ABVP, the Union Ministry of Education had an Ambedkarite group banned and some of its members rusticated. This led to the death by his own hand of a young Dalit activist, a research scholar who in his suicide note wrote poignantly of his own intellectual ambitions, now to remain unfulfilled because of upper-caste hostility and prejudice.[80]

The protection of the cow, and a total ban on cow slaughter, had long been a key item in the Hindutva agenda. Now, with the BJP in power, it was sought to be made a major plank of public policy. BJP governments in Haryana and Maharashtra banned the sale and consumption of beef.

In other states, Hindutva vigilantes attacked and occasionally killed individuals suspected of selling cows or eating beef.[81]

The early victims of these attacks were Muslims, but then, in July 2016, four Dalits in Modi's home state of Gujarat were thrashed by upper-caste vigilantes for skinning dead cows. The leather trade was traditionally dominated by Dalits, and the skinning of dead cows was a ubiquitous phenomena in rural India. But in the heightened passions unleashed by the cow protection campaigners, this everyday practice was deemed blasphemous. Worse, the vigilantes in Gujarat filmed their beating of Dalits and uploaded it on social media.

The outrage sparked condemnation in the press, and, more significantly, massive protests across Gujarat. Dalits threw dead carcasses in front of government offices, and burnt government buses. They organized well-attended meetings in many towns, vowing not to submit to upper-caste persecution. The protests were so intense and prolonged that Anandiben Patel, Modi's handpicked successor as chief minister of Gujarat, was compelled to resign. The prime minister himself, who had previously stayed silent on the subject, was finally forced to speak out once cow vigilantism had manifested itself in his own home state.[82]

Not all of the protests against the BJP government were provoked by RSS or Hindutva policies, however. Others were a legacy of past policies by other parties and governments. Thus the extension by V.P. Singh of affirmative action beyond Scheduled Castes and Scheduled Tribes had prompted a manic rush to be included in the official list of 'Other Backward Castes'. Among the new and arguably spurious claimants to 'backward' status were the Jats of Haryana and the Patidars of Gujarat. These were both dominant castes, who controlled the village economy in these states, and were extremely influential in politics as well.

Both Patidars and Jats had a strong sense of, and pride in, their caste identity. Both resented the rise of castes lower than them in the social hierarchy, and now sought to re-establish their dominance by acquiring access to reserved seats in colleges and government offices.

In July 2015, the Patidars commenced a major agitation in Gujarat, blockading roads and bringing everyday life to a halt. They demanded immediate inclusion in the OBC list. In February 2016, the Jats of Haryana emulated them. Their protests were even more violent, with the burning of bus and train stations, and the torching of homes and government offices. At one stage, the water supply of the nation's capital, New Delhi, was imperilled.[83]

Both the Patidar and Jat agitations were led and staffed by men in their twenties and thirties. For the younger members of these castes no longer wanted to make a living by farming. In Patidar villages, young men drove around on their motorbikes, played cards or fiddled with their smartphones. Jat youngsters did all these things, and organized wrestling matches and drinking parties as well.[84] Turning their back on their past, unable to fully grasp or control the present, this new generation of Jats and Patidars channelled their anger and frustration into collective protests against the state on the question of reservation.[85]

In power in both Haryana and Gujarat was the BJP. The suddenness of the Jat and Patidar protests, their almost savage intensity, were a sign of how fragile the hold of the ruling party, of *any* ruling party, on the populace was. Democracy and development had brought both prosperity and discontent in their wake. What face would manifest itself when, and in what manner, was something no scholar or historian, or even a politician presumably more in touch with the 'grassroots', could accurately or properly anticipate.

XII

In December 2014, Assembly elections were held in Jammu and Kashmir. The results revealed a divided state, with the Peoples Democratic Party (PDP) getting 28 seats in the Muslim-dominated Valley but the BJP sweeping the Hindu-dominated Jammu region. Neither party enjoyed a majority. After weeks of uncertainty, the PDP and the BJP formed a coalition government.

Unlike the National Conference, which since Sheikh Abdullah signed his accord with Indira Gandhi had been solidly committed to making Kashmir part of India, the PDP had a more ambivalent stand. It fought elections and eschewed the gun, but sometimes expressed sympathy for the separatist movement. On the other side, the Jammu wing of the BJP had deep roots in the RSS, going back to the Praja Parishad movement of the 1950s which sought to completely 'integrate' Kashmir with India.

The PDP-BJP coalition was dictated by the fractured electoral verdict. It held the peace, uneasily, both between the two parties and in the Valley itself. In the summer of 2015 the tourist trade was brisk. However, an attempt to impose a beef ban on the Valley provoked resentment, as did the tardiness of the government in releasing funds to rebuild homes damaged or destroyed by floods the previous year.

In January 2016 the chief minister, the veteran Mufti Mohammad Sayeed, died. His daughter Mehbooba was sworn in as his successor. Then, in July, the always uneasy (and perhaps unnatural) peace was broken by the killing by the security forces of a young militant named Burhan Wani. It was said that Wani had gone underground after witnessing his brother being thrashed by army men. From his hideouts he posted videos of his speeches on social media, acquiring a cult-like status in the process.

The killing of Wani led to an outpouring of grief, followed by anger. There was a massive attendance at his funeral (estimates of the crowd range from 30,000 to over 100,000), following which young Kashmiris clashed with the police in many towns and villages. The police responded with pellet guns, these blinding many protesters, further intensifying the anger. For more than a month the Valley lay under curfew, with shops, schools, colleges and offices all shut. More than seventy people died in the violence.[86]

The troubles in Kashmir led to a tide of jingoism in the Indian media. Television channels competed with one another to term the protesters agents of Pakistan. Indians who deplored the excessive use of force and the blinding of youngsters were called Pakistani agents too. These media hounds juxtaposed, to the 'bad Kashmiris' on the streets of Srinagar, a 'good Kashmiri' named Shah Faesal, who had topped the prestigious Indian Administrative Service examination some years previously. This crude stereotyping prompted a public response by Shah Faesal, where he worried that the government he served 'had outsourced, or rather abdicated, communications to TV channels, which are only interested in provoking and alienating.' The Indian state, he continued, 'can't afford to leave the Kashmir project to intellectual renegades, political turncoats, opportunists, intelligence agencies, and most importantly, to self-appointed vigilantes of the national interest.' He warned that 'every hour of prime time TV news aggression pushes Kashmir a mile westward from India.'[87]

This was written in late July. In the third week of September 2016, terrorists coming into Kashmir from Pakistan attacked an army camp at the border town of Uri, killing eighteen Indian soldiers. There were fresh calls for retribution against Pakistan, for the bombing of training camps in that country. Some ideologues even demanded that India abrogate the Indus Waters Treaty, so as to starve Pakistan into submission. As the rhetoric escalated, the sufferings of the Kashmiris receded further into the background.

Back in May 1949, Vallabhbhai Patel had written to the industrialist G. D. Birla, then overseas, to fill him in on the news in India. 'Here we are having a grudging time', reported Patel, 'both with the weather and the problems which are arising; Kashmir, in particular, is giving us a severe headache.' By 'us' Patel meant the Indian state, the Indian establishment. Sixty-seven summers later, the headache was as severe as it had ever been.

Epilogue

A 50–50 Democracy

The Sikhs may try to set up a separate regime. I think they probably will and that will be only a start of a general decentralization and break-up of the idea that India is a country, whereas it is a subcontinent as varied as Europe. The Punjabi is as different from a Madrassi as a Scot is from an Italian. The British tried to consolidate it but achieved nothing permanent. No one can make a nation out of a continent of many nations.

GENERAL CLAUDE AUCHINLEK, 1948

Few people contemplating Indira Gandhi's funeral in 1984 would have predicted that ten years later India would remain a unity but the Soviet Union would be a memory.

ROBIN JEFFREY, 2000

I know that most Members of Parliament see the Constitution for the first time when they take an oath on it.

PRAMOD MAHAJAN, Union Minister, 2000

India is a halfway house where underperforming institutions coexist uncomfortably with overzealous ones, creating stress, conflict and loss – especially when venality or whimsicality in one is matched by self-righteousness in another.

T. N. NINAN, 2015

I

IN AN ESSAY SUMMARIZING a lifetime of thinking on the subject, Isaiah Berlin identified 'the infliction of a wound on the collective feelings of a society, or at least of its spiritual leaders', as a 'necessary' condition for the birth of nationalist sentiment. For this sentiment to transform itself into a political movement, however, required 'one more condition', namely, that the society in question 'must, in the minds of at least some of its most sensitive members, carry an image of itself as a nation, at least in embryo, in virtue of some general unifying factor or factors – language, ethnic origin, a common history (real or imaginary)'. Later in the same essay, Berlin commented on the 'astonishingly Europocentric' thought of nineteenth and early twentieth century political thinkers, where 'the people of Asia and Africa are discussed either as wards or as victims of Europeans, but seldom, if ever, in their own right, as peoples with histories and cultures of their own; with a past and present and future which must be understood in terms of their own actual character and circumstances ...'.[1]

Behind every successful nationalist movement in the Western world was a certain unifying factor, a glue holding the members of the nation together, this provided by a shared language, a shared religious faith, a shared territory, a common enemy – and sometimes all of the above. Thus, the British nation brought together those who huddled together on a cold island, who were mostly Protestant, and who detested France. In the case of France, it was language which powerfully combined with religion. For the Americans a shared language and mostly shared faith worked in tandem with animosity towards the colonists. As for the smaller East European nations – the Poles, the Czechs, the Lithuanians, etc – their populations have been united by a common language, a mostly common faith, and a shared and very bitter history of domination by German and Russian oppressors.[2]

By contrast with these (and other examples) the Indian nation does not privilege a single language or religious faith. Although the majority of its citizens are Hindus, India is not a 'Hindu' nation. Its constitution does not discriminate between people on the basis of faith; neither, more crucially, did the nationalist movement that lay behind it. From its inception the Indian National Congress was, as Mukul Kesavan observes, a sort of political Noah's Ark which sought to keep every species of Indian on board.[3] Gandhi's political programme was built upon harmony and co-operation between India's two major religious communities, Hindus and Muslims. Although, in the end, his work and example were unsuccessful in stopping the division of India, the failure made his successors even more determined to construct independent India as a secular republic. For Jawaharlal Nehru and his colleagues, if India was anything at all it was not a 'Hindu Pakistan'.

The story of Indian secularism is a story that combines success with failure. Membership of a minority religion is no bar to advancement in business or the professions. One of the richest industrialists in India is a Muslim. Some of the most popular film stars are Muslim. Many of the country's most prominent lawyers and doctors have been Christians and Parsis. At least three presidents and two chief justices have been Muslim. Indeed, between 2004 and 2007, the president of India was a Muslim, the prime minister a Sikh, and the leader of the ruling party a Catholic born in Italy, a fact that in those months and years was often spoken of with pride by Indians.

On the other hand, in everyday life minorities face prejudice and hostility. Muslims in particular remain one of the poorest and most vulnerable communities in India. Besides, there have been periodic episodes of religious rioting, in the worst of which (as in Delhi in 1984 and Gujarat in 2002) the minorities have suffered grievous losses of life and property. Still, for the most part the minorities appear to have retained faith in the secular ideal. Relatively few Indian Muslims have joined terrorist or fundamentalist organizations. Even more than their compatriots, Indian Muslims feel that their opinion and vote matters. One survey found that while 69 per cent of all Indians approved and endorsed the ideal of democracy, 72 per cent of Muslims did so.[4]

Nurturing religious pluralism in a land recently divided on the basis of faith was always going to be hard work. The creation of an Islamic state on India's borders was a provocation to those Hindus who themselves wished to merge faith with state. The Ayodhya movement of the 1980s saw Hindutva radicals greatly increase their political salience. More recently, the rise of Islamic fundamentalism across the globe, and especially in neighbouring Pakistan and Bangladesh, has given further fuel to Hindu fundamentalists. India is not yet a Hindu Pakistan but, for the foreseeable future, those who wish to make it so will be present and active in the country. In times of stability, or when the political leadership is firm, they will be marginal or on the defensive. In times of change, or when the political leadership is irresolute, they will be influential and assertive.

II

The pluralism of religion was one cornerstone of the foundation of the Indian republic. A second was the pluralism of language. Here again, the intention and the effort well predated Independence. In the 1920s, Gandhi reconstituted the provincial committees of the Congress on linguistic lines. The party had promised to form linguistic provinces as soon as the country was free. The promise was not redeemed immediately after 1947, because the creation of Pakistan had promoted fears of further balkanization. However, in the face of popular protest the government yielded to the demand.

Linguistic states have been in existence for sixty years now. In that time they have deepened and consolidated Indian unity. Within each state, a common language has provided the basis of administrative unity and efficiency. It has also led to an efflorescence of cultural creativity, as expressed in film, theatre, fiction and poetry. However, pride in one's language has rarely been in conflict with a broader identification with the nation as a whole. It has proved perfectly possible – indeed, desirable – to be Kannadiga and Indian, Malayali and Indian, Andhra and Indian, Tamil and Indian, Bengali and Indian, Oriya and Indian, Maharashtrian and Indian, Gujarati and Indian and, of course, Hindi-speaking and Indian.

That, in India, unity and pluralism are inseparable is graphically expressed in the country's currency notes. On one side is printed a portrait of the 'father of the nation', Mahatma Gandhi; on the other side a picture of the Houses of Parliament. The note's denomination – 5, 10, 50, 100, etc. – is printed in words in Hindi and English (the two official languages), but also, in smaller type, in all the other languages of the Union. In this manner, as many as seventeen different scripts are represented. With each language, and each script, comes a distinct culture and regional ethos, here nesting more-or-less comfortably with the idea of India as a whole.

Some Western observers – usually Americans – believed that this profusion of tongues would be the undoing of India. In their own country, English had been the glue binding the different waves of immigrants, who had, over time, to discard the languages they brought with them – German, Yiddish, Italian, etc – and speak and write English alone. Americans visiting or living in India thus tended to argue that a single language – be it Hindi or English – should be spoken by all Indians. Linguistic states they regarded as a grievous error. Thus, in a book published as late as in 1970, and at the end of his stint as the *Washington Post*'s man in India, Bernard Nossiter wrote despairingly that this was 'a land of Babel with no common voice'. The creation of linguistic states would 'further divide the states from each other [and] heighten the impulse toward secession ...'. From its birth the Indian nation had been 'plagued by particularist, separatist tendencies', wrote Nossiter, and 'the continuing confusion of tongues ... can only further these tendencies and puts in question the future unity of the Indian state'.[5]

That, to survive, a nation-state had necessarily to privilege one language was a view that the Soviet dictator Joseph Stalin shared with American liberals. Stalin insisted that 'a national community is inconceivable without a common language', and that 'there is no nation which at one and the same time speaks several languages'.[6] This belief came to inform the language policy of the Soviet Union, in which the learning of Russian was made obligatory. The endeavour, as Stalin himself put it, was to ensure that 'there is one language in which all citizens of the USSR can more or less express themselves – that is Russian'.[7]

The United States was a land made by successive waves of immigrants, who had perforce to learn English to speak to one another. The USSR, on the other hand, was a political formation constituted of many linguistic communities. In that respect it was closer to the Republic of India than the US. The Soviet promotion of Russian led eventually to the growth of subnationalist sentiments and the creation of many independent nations. In India, on the other hand, exactly the reverse has happened – that is, the sustenance of linguistic pluralism has worked to tame and domesticate secessionist tendencies.

A comparison with neighbouring countries might be helpful here. In 1956, the year the states of India were reorganized on the basis of language, the Parliament of Sri Lanka (then Ceylon) introduced an Act recognizing Sinhala as the sole official language of the country. The intention was to make Sinhala the medium of instruction in all state schools and colleges, in public examinations and in the courts. Potentially the hardest hit were the Tamil-speaking minority who lived in the north of the island, and whose feelings were eloquently expressed by their representatives in Parliament. 'When you deny me my language', said one Tamil MP, 'you deny me everything'. 'You are hoping for a divided Ceylon', warned another, adding: 'Do not fear, I assure you [that you] will have a divided Ceylon'. A left-wing member, himself Sinhala-speaking, predicted that if the government did not change its mind and insisted on the act being passed, 'two torn little bleeding states might yet arise out of one little state'.[8]

In 1971, two torn medium-sized states arose out of one large-sized one. The country being divided was Pakistan, rather than Sri Lanka, but the cause for the division was, in fact, language. For the founders of Pakistan likewise believed that their state had to be based on a single language as well as a single religion. In his first speech in the capital of East Pakistan, Dhaka, Mohammed Ali Jinnah warned his audience that they would have to take to Urdu sooner rather than later. 'Let me make it very clear to you', said Jinnah to his Bengali audience, 'that the State Language of Pakistan is going to be Urdu and no other language. Anyone who tries to mislead you is really the enemy of Pakistan. Without one State language, no nation can remain tied up solidly together and function.'[9]

In the 1950s, bloody riots broke out when the Pakistan government tried to force Urdu on recalcitrant students. The sentiment of being discriminated against on the grounds of language persisted, and ultimately resulted in the formation of the independent state of Bangladesh.

Pakistan was created on the basis of religion, but divided on the basis of language. And for more than two decades a bloody civil war raged in Sri Lanka, the disputants divided somewhat by territory and faith but most of all by language. The lesson from these cases might well be: 'One language, two nations'. Had Hindi been imposed on the whole of India the lesson might well have been: 'One language, twenty-two nations'.

III

Indian nationalism has not been based on a shared language, religion, or ethnic identity. Perhaps one should then invoke the presence of a common enemy, namely, European colonialism. The problem here is the methods used to achieve India's freedom. The historian Michael Howard claims that 'no Nation, in the true sense of the word, ... could be born without war ... no self-conscious community could establish itself as a new and independent actor on the world scene without an armed conflict or the threat of one'.[10] Once again, India must count as an exception. Certainly, it was the movement against British rule that first united men and women from different parts of the subcontinent in a common and shared endeavour. However, their (eventually successful) movement for political freedom largely eschewed armed struggle in favour of non-violent resistance. India emerged as a nation on the world stage without an armed conflict between oppressed and oppressor.

Gandhi and company have been widely praised for preferring peaceful protest to violent revolution. However, they should be equally commended for having the wisdom to retain, after the British left India, such aspects of the colonial legacy as might prove useful in the new nation.

The colonialists were often chastised by the nationalists for promoting democracy at home while denying it in the colonies. When the British finally left, it was expected that the Indians would embrace metropolitan traditions such as parliamentary democracy and Cabinet government. More surprising perhaps was their endorsement and retention of a quintessentially colonial tradition – the civil service.

The key men in British India were the members of the Indian Civil Service (ICS). In the countryside they kept the peace and collected the taxes, while in the Secretariat they oversaw policy and generally kept the machinery of state well-oiled. Although there was the odd rotten egg, these were mostly men of integrity and ability.[11] A majority were British, but there were also a fair number of Indians in the civil service.

When independence came, the new government had to decide what to do with the Indian members of the ICS. Nationalists who had been jailed by them argued that they should be dismissed or at least put in their place. The home minister, Vallabhbhai Patel, however, felt that they should be allowed to retain their pay and perquisites, and in fact be placed in positions of greater authority. In October 1949 a furious debate broke out on the subject in the Constituent Assembly of India. Some members complained that the ICS men still had the 'mentality [of rulers] lingering in them'. They had apparently 'not changed their manners', 'not reconciled themselves to the new situation'. 'They do not feel that they are part and parcel of this country', insisted one nationalist.

Now Vallabhbhai Patel had himself been jailed many times by ICS men. But this experience had only confirmed his admiration for them. He knew that without them the Pax Brittanica would, simply, have been inconceivable. And he understood that the complex machinery of a modern, independent nation-state needed such officers too. As he reminded the members of the Assembly, the new constitution could only be worked 'by a ring of Service which will keep the country intact'. He testified to the ability of the ICS men, but also to their sense of service. As Patel put it, the officers had 'served very ably, very loyally the then Government and later the present Government'. Patel was clear that 'these people are the instruments [of national unity]. Remove them and I see nothing but a picture of chaos all over the country'.[12]

In those first, difficult years of Indian freedom, the ICS men vindicated Vallabhbhai Patel's trust in them. They helped integrate the princely states, resettle the refugees, and plan and oversee the first general elections. Other tasks assigned to them were more humdrum but equally consequential – such as maintaining law and order in the districts, working with ministers in the Secretariat, and supervising famine relief. In 1950, Patel inaugurated a new cadre modelled on the ICS but with a name untainted by the colonial experience. This was the Indian Administrative Service, or IAS.

As of this writing there are some 5,500 IAS officers in the employment of the government of India. The IAS is complemented, as in British days, by other 'all India' services, among them the police, forest, revenue and customs services. These serve as an essential link between the centre and the states. Officers are assigned to a particular state; they spend half or more of their service career in that province, the rest in the centre. To the older duties of tax collection and the maintenance of law and order have been added a whole range of new responsibilities. Conducting elections is one; the supervising of development programmes another. In the course of his career an average IAS officer would acquire at least a passing familiarity with such different and divergent subjects as criminal jurisprudence, irrigation management, soil and water conservation and primary health care.[13]

It was an ICS man, Sukumar Sen, who laid the groundwork for elections in India, and it has been IAS men who have kept the machinery going. The chief election commissioners in the states are drawn from the service. Junior officers supervise polls in their districts; those in the middle rungs serve as election observers, reporting on violations of procedure. More generally, the civil services serve as a bridge between state and society. In the course of their work, these administrators meet thousands of members of the public, drawn from all walks of life. Living and working in a democracy, they are obliged to pay close attention to what people think and demand. In this respect, their job is probably even harder than that of their predecessors in the ICS.

However, in recent years IAS officers have become excessively subservient to the ministers they work with. The autonomy of the civil services, once so zealously guarded, has been undermined by unprincipled alliances between individual politicians and individual IAS officers furthering personal agendas, including taking illegal commissions on government projects. The IAS's hegemony on top jobs in government has also impeded the entry of qualified professionals. In the complex, fast-changing world of the twenty-first century, India needs experts rather than generalists to head government departments and regulatory institutions. It is past time for civil service reform; that said, the IAS and the allied services have played a crucial role in maintaining the unity of an often-divided country.

A colonial institution that has played an equally critical role is the Indian army. Its reputation took a battering after the China war of 1962, before it redeemed itself through its performance in successive wars with Pakistan. The blows inflicted by Tamil insurgents in Sri Lanka in 1987–8 dented the army somewhat, but then self-respect was restored by the successful ousting of the Kargil intruders a decade later. While its reputation as a fighting force has gone up and down, as an agency for maintaining order in peacetime the Indian army has usually commanded the highest respect. In times of communal rioting, the mere appearance of soldiers in uniform is usually enough to make the rioteers flee. And in times of natural disaster they bring succour to the suffering. When there is a flood, famine, cyclone or earthquake, it is the army which is often first on the scene, and always the most efficient and reliable actor around.

The Indian army is a professional and non-sectarian body. It is also apolitical. Almost from the first moments of independence, Jawaharlal Nehru made it clear to the army top brass that in matters of state – both large and small – they had to subordinate themselves to the elected politicians. At the time of the transfer of power the army was still headed by a British general, who had ordered that the public be kept away from a flag-hoisting ceremony to be held on the day after Independence. As prime minister, Nehru rescinded the order, and wrote to the general as follows:

> While I am desirous of paying attention to the views and susceptibilities of our senior officers, British and Indian, it seems to me that there is a grave misunderstanding about the matter. In any policy that is to be pursued, in the army or otherwise, the views of the government of India and the policy they lay down must prevail. If any person is unable to lay down that policy, he has no place in the Indian army, or in the Indian structure of government. I think this should be made perfectly clear at this stage.[14]

A year later, it was Vallabhbhai Patel's turn to put a British general in his place. When the government decided to move against the Nizam, the commander-in-chief, General Roy Bucher, warned that sending troops into Hyderabad might provoke Pakistan to attack Amritsar. Patel told Bucher that if he opposed the Hyderabad action he was free to resign. The general backed down, and sent the troops as ordered.[15]

Shortly afterwards Bucher retired, to be succeeded by the first Indian C-in-C, General K. M. Cariappa. At the beginning of his tenure Cariappa restricted himself to military matters, but as he grew into the job he began to offer his views on such questions as India's preferred model of economic development. In October 1952, Nehru wrote advising him to give fewer press conferences, and at any rate to stick to safe subjects. He also enclosed a letter from one of his Cabinet colleagues, which complained that Cariappa was 'giving so many speeches and holding so many Press Conferences all over the country', giving the impression that he was 'playing the role of a political or semi-political leader'.[16]

The message seems to have gone home, for when Cariappa demitted office in January 1953, in his farewell speech he 'exhorted soldiers to give a wide berth to politics'. The army's job, he said, was not 'to meddle in politics but to give unstinted loyalty to the elected government'.[17] Nehru knew, however, that the general was something of a loose cannon, who could not be completely trusted to follow his own advice. Within three months of his retirement, Cariappa was appointed high commissioner to Australia. The general was not entirely pleased, for, as he told the prime minister, 'by going away from home to the other end of the world for whatever period you want me in Australia, I shall be depriving myself of being in continuous and constant touch with the people'. Nehru consoled the general that as a sportsman himself he was superbly qualified to represent India to a sporting nation. But the real intention, clearly, was to send him as far away from the people as possible.[18]

As the first Indian to head the army, General Cariappa carried a certain cachet. However, by the time he came back from Australia, Cariappa was a forgotten man. Nehru's foresight was confirmed, however, by the statements the general made from time to time. In 1958 he visited Pakistan, where army officers who had served with him in undivided India had just effected a coup. Cariappa publicly praised them, saying that it was 'the chaotic internal situation which forced these two patriotic generals to plan together to impose Martial Law in the country to save their homeland from utter ruination'.[19] Ten years later, he sent an article to the *Indian Express*, which argued that the chaotic internal situation in

West Bengal demanded that President's Rule be imposed for a minimum of five years. The recommendation was in violation of the letter and spirit of the constitution. Fortunately, the piece was returned by the editor, who pointed out to the general that 'it would be embarrassing in the circumstances both to you and to us to publish this article'.[20]

The pattern set in those early years has persisted into the present. As Lieutenant General J. S. Aurora notes, Nehru 'laid down some very good norms', which ensured that 'politics in the army has been almost absent'. 'The army is not a political animal in any terms', remarks Aurora, and the officers especially 'must be the most apolitical people on earth!'[21] Aurora himself became a national hero after overseeing the liberation of Bangladesh, but neither he nor other officers have sought to convert glory won on the battlefield into political advantage.

To be sure, after retirement some senior army officers have served as ambassadors and governors. A few have entered party politics, with two serving as ministers in BJP-led governments. Further, in conflict-ridden zones such as Kashmir and the North-east, the army has sometimes forced its will on the civilian administration, most notably with regard to the AFSPA, whose withdrawal it will not countenance even when violence and terror have subsided. These exceptions notwithstanding, the Indian army has on the whole stayed away from politics, in contrast to Pakistan, where the military has actively intervened in the political process, deposing elected governments and supplanting them with martial law administrations.[22]

IV

The army, like the civil services, is a colonial institution that has successfully adapted itself to a democratic republic. The same may be said about the English language. In British times the intelligentsia and professional classes communicated with one another in English. So did the nationalist élite. Patel, Bose, Nehru, Gandhi and Ambedkar all spoke and wrote in their native tongue, and also in English. To reach out to regions other than one's own, its use was indispensable. Thus a pan-Indian, anti-British consciousness was created, in good part, by thinkers and activists writing in the English language.

After Independence, among the most articulate advocates for English was C. Rajagopalachari. The colonial rulers, he wrote, had 'for certain accidental reasons, causes and purposes ... left behind [in India] a vast body of the English language'. But now it had come there was no need for it to go away. For English 'is ours. We need not send it back to Britain along with Englishmen'. He humorously added that, according to Indian tradition, it was a Hindu goddess, Saraswati, who had given birth to all the languages of the world. Thus English 'belonged to us by origin, the originator being Sarawati, and also by acquisition'.[23]

On the other hand, there were some influential nationalists who believed that English must be thrown out of India with the British. They included the RSS leader M. S. Golwalkar and the socialist ideologue Ram Manohar Lohia. They put pressure on Nehru's government to replace English with Hindi as the language of inter-provincial communication. The pressure was resisted. Visiting India in 1961, the Canadian writer George Woodcock found that despite India's strangeness, its 'immense variety of custom, landscape and physical types', this was 'a foreign setting in which one's language was always understood by someone nearby, and in which to speak with an English accent meant that one was seen as a kind of cousin bred out of the odd, temporary marriage of two peoples into which love and hate entered with equal intensity'.[24]

After Nehru's death the efforts to extinguish English were renewed. Despite pleas from the southern states, on 26 January 1965 Hindi became the sole, official language of inter-provincial communication. As we have seen, this provoked protests so intense and furious that the order was withdrawn within a fortnight. Thus English continued as the language of the central government, of the superior courts and of higher education.

Over the years, English has confirmed, consolidated and deepened its position as the language of the pan-Indian élite. The language of the colonizers has, in independent India, become the language of power and prestige, the language of individual as well as social advancement. As the historian Sarvepalli Gopal observes, 'that knowledge of English is the passport for employment at higher levels in all fields, is the unavoidable avenue to status and wealth and is mandatory to all those planning to migrate abroad, has meant a tremendous enthusiasm since independence to study it'. But, as Gopal also writes, English 'may be described as the only non-regional language in India. It is a link language in a more than administrative sense, in that it counters blinkered provincialism'.[25]

Those, like Nehru and Rajaji, who sought to retain English, sensed that it might help consolidate national unity and further scientific advance. That it has done, but largely unanticipated has been its role in fuelling economic growth. For behind the spectacular rise of the software industry lies the proficiency of Indian engineers in English.

English is one of India's two main link languages. Hindi is the other. When imposed by fiat by the central government, Hindi was resisted by the people of the south and the east. However, when conveyed seductively by the medium of cinema and television, Hindi has been accepted by them.

The Hindi film is the great popular passion of the Indian people, watched and followed by Indians of all ages, genders, castes, classes, religions and linguistic groups. The most widely revered Indians are film stars. Yet cinema does not merely provide Indians with a common pantheon of heroes; it also gives them a common language and universe of discourse. Lines from film songs and snatches from film dialogue are ubiquitously used in conversations in schools, colleges, homes and offices – and on the street.

Hindi cinema provides a stock of social situations and moral conundrums which widely resonate with the citizenry as a whole. But, over time, it has also made the Hindi language more comprehensible to those who previously never spoke or understood it. In Bengaluru and Hyderabad, Hindi has become the preferred medium of communication between those who speak mutually incomprehensible tongues. Even in Chennai, where the language was once fiercely resisted, taxi drivers have picked up enough Hindi to converse with passengers from the north and the west.

The link languages of India are Hindi and English, sometimes working in combination. The English spoken in India today has moved far away from the Anglicized, Oxford-accented and BBC-inflected language once spoken by the country's elite. It has become indigenized, adopting words and idioms from Indian languages. Meanwhile, a hybrid tongue, called 'Hinglish', has also emerged, mingling the two link languages in different proportions, depending on the provenance of the speaker.

V

In 1888, John Strachey wrote that he could never imagine that Punjab and Madras could ever form part of a single political entity. But in 1947 they did, along with many other provinces Strachey regarded as distinct 'nations'. While in 1947 the unity might have been mostly political, in the decades since it has been shown also to be economic, cultural, and, it must be said, emotional.

The economic integration of India is a consequence of its political integration. They act in a mutually reinforcing loop. The greater the movement of goods and capital and people across India, the greater the sense that this is, after all, one country. In the first decades of independence, it was the public sector that did most to further this sense of unity. In plants such as the great steel mill in Bhilai, Andhras laboured and lived alongside Punjabis and Gujaratis, fostering appreciation of other kinds of tongues, customs and cuisine, while underlining the fact that they were all part of the same nation. As the anthropologist Jonathan Parry remarks, in the Nehruvian imagination 'Bhilai and its steel plant were seen as bearing the torch of history, and as being as much about forging a new kind of society as about forging steel'. The attempt was not unsuccessful; among the children of the first generation of workers, themselves born and raised in Bhilai, provincial loyalties were superceded by a more inclusive patriotism, a 'more cosmopolitan cultural style'.[26]

More recently, it has been the private sector which has, if with less intent, furthered the process of national integration. Firms headquartered in Tamil Nadu set up cement plants in Haryana; doctors born and educated in Assam establish clinics in Mumbai. Many of the engineers in Hyderabad's IT industry come from Bihar. The migration is not restricted to the professional classes; there are barbers from Uttar Pradesh working in the city of Bengaluru, as well as carpenters from Rajasthan. However, it must be said that the flow is not symmetrical. While the cities and towns that are 'booming' become ever more cosmopolitan, economically laggard states sink deeper into provincialism.

The Republic of India is a union of twenty-nine states. Of these, twenty-six are comfortable with being part of the Union. Yet discontent persists in parts of the other three states. Pre-eminent among these disaffected regions is the Valley of Kashmir. The Indian state's hold on the Valley and its people has been contested from the start, by Pakistan, which claims this territory as its own, and by many residents of the Valley themselves. The region is once more in the grip of mass protests as I write.

Pakistan has an interest in stoking and supporting armed insurgents in Kashmir. However, successive Indian governments have scored self-goals of their own, by jailing popular Kashmiri leaders, rigging elections, pressing for the abrogation of Article 370 which assures the state a special status, and, above all, through the repression by brute force of popular protests. There is a massive army presence in Kashmir, these troops complemented by hundreds of thousands of less-trained paramilitary forces. And so, as one thoughtful scholar writes, 'India's constitutional settlement, for all its other grandeur, has not yet passed the Kashmir test.'[27]

Back in the 1950s, a section of the Tamils wanted to secede from India. In the 1960s, a section of the Mizos launched an insurrection for an independent Mizoram. In the 1980s, a section of the Sikhs fought the Indian state with arms, seeking to create an independent Khalistan. Those rebellions are now all history, with Tamil Nadu, Mizoram and Punjab – and the overwhelming majority of the residents of these states – entirely content to be part of the Republic of India.

Even in Kashmir, the Jammu and Ladakh regions are not seeking secession. A significant section of the residents of the Valley, however, are. Meanwhile, in Nagaland, where the movement for an independent nation precedes that in Kashmir, the ceasefire called for in 1997 still holds, tenuously. Many rounds of talks have been held between the government of India and the most influential faction of the National Socialist Council of Nagaland. But no settlement is yet in sight.

There are two issues still outstanding. The first is that of sovereignty. The NSCN once wanted a solution outside the framework of the Indian constitution. Now, they may be willing to be part of India, so long as the distinctive history of the Naga people is given formal recognition. A way to do so in a manner that would satisfy the honour of both parties has not yet been found. The second, and even more complicated problem, is that of territoriality. The NSCN insists that the government of India create a unified and integrated state incorporating those parts of Arunachal, Assam and (above all) Manipur where Naga tribes live. This would involve a redrawing of boundaries, which those other states (and particularly Manipur, which stands to lose the most) are loath to agree to.

The perils involved in re-setting provincial boundaries were vividly manifest when, in 2010, the NSCN leader T. Muivah wished to visit his home village, which he had not seen in forty-seven years. Muivah was a Tangkhul Naga, and his village lay in the hill areas of Manipur state. The Manipur government saw the visit as a precursor to the demand that these areas be handed over to a Greater Nagaland. The state's police assembled in force on the border with Nagaland, to prevent Muivah's entry. In response, the Nagas in Nagaland organized a two month long blockade of the highway that connected the Manipur Valley to the outside world. This further soured relations between the two states, making the prospect of a permanent settlement of the Naga question recede further into the future.[28]

The third state of the Union where the hold of the Indian ideal is uncertain and fragile is Manipur itself. The dominant community here are the Meiteis, who live in the valley, with Nagas, Kukis and other tribes residing in the hills. The Meiteis fear the colonization of their fertile valley by outsiders, and resent the fact that (because they are technically Hindus) they do not enjoy the fruits of affirmative action (which Manipur's tribal communities do). They also harbour fond memories of the independent chiefdom they once had.

Many Meitei activists dislike and distrust the Indian state. Some nourish dreams of an independent nation. Meanwhile, the Nagas and Kukis distrust the Meiteis for their political and administrative stranglehold over the state of Manipur as it exists today. Some, perhaps many, of the Nagas in Manipur wish to make common cause with the Nagas in Nagaland in pursuit of their independent nation. And Kukis and Nagas have on occasion fought each other fiercely too.[29]

These multiple rivalries and animosities have generated a lot of violence and bloodshed. To control the situation in Manipur the central government has posted several army detachments, as well as tens of thousands of paramilitary forces. In Imphal town there are security check-points every few hundred yards; in the rural and mountain roads, every few miles. The Indian state's armed might is on intimidating display in Manipur; as it is in the Valley of Kashmir; and as it would be in Nagaland too, were there not a ceasefire in operation.

That said, if to the disturbed districts of Nagaland, Manipur and Kashmir one adds the territory under the control of Maoist revolutionaries in central India, this would amount to not more than 10 per cent of the total area of the Republic of India. Thus some 90 per cent of the population of the Republic of India, living in roughly 90 per cent of the country, palpably feel themselves to be part of a single nation. Across this vast and diverse terrain, the elected government enjoys a legitimacy of power and authority. Throughout this territory the citizens of India are free to live, study, take employment and invest in businesses.

There are perhaps only two other modern political experiments comparable in scale and size to the Republic of India, which have likewise sought to forge national unity amidst an astonishing diversity of languages, religions, ethnicities, and ways of life. These are the now deceased Union of Soviet Socialist Republics and the still flourishing United States of America. The USSR witnessed savage violence following its birth, this continuing through the famines and the death camps of the 1930s and beyond. The United States was founded on the backs of the genocide of the Native Americans, and consolidated by the enslavement of millions of Africans. Ninety years after its formation, it was torn by a civil war in which some 750,000 people perished.

European nations such as France, England and Spain also witnessed bloody civil wars at various points in their history. So too, as I have noted already, have the countries of Pakistan and Sri Lanka within South Asia itself. But India hasn't, at least thus far. Born through the mass violence of Partition, India has since escaped the kind of intense and often endemic strife that has beset so many other national experiments in Asia and Africa, not to speak of Europe and the Americas.

VI

The history of independent India has amended and modified theories of nationalism based on the experience of the West. However, it has even more frontally challenged theories of democracy emanating from the Western experience.

Ever since the 1952 elections were described as the 'biggest gamble in history', obituaries have been written for Indian democracy. It has been said, time and again, that a poor, diverse and divided country cannot sustain the practice of (reasonably) free and fair elections.

Yet it has. In those first general elections voter turnout was less than 46 per cent. Over the years this has steadily increased; from the late 1960s about three out of five eligible Indians have voted on election day. The voter turnout during the most recent general elections, in 2014, was 66.3 per cent, a record for India, and far higher than is the case in most Western democracies, including the United States.

In Assembly elections the voting percentage has tended to be even higher. When these numbers are disaggregated they reveal a further deepening. In the first two general elections, less than 40 per cent of eligible women voted; by 1998 the figure was in excess of 60 per cent. Besides, as surveys showed, they increasingly exercised their choice independently, that is, regardless of their husband's or father's views on the matter. Also voting in ever higher numbers were Dalits and tribals, the oppressed and marginalized sections of society. In north India in particular, Dalits turned out in far greater numbers than high castes. As the political analyst Yogendra Yadav points out, 'India is perhaps the only large democracy in the world today where the turnout of the lower orders is well above that of the most privileged groups'.[30]

Recent studies of voter behaviour suggest that while the middle and upper castes vote because they consider it a civic duty, the poor vote to assert their identity as, at least on this day, equal citizens of the land. A rickshaw puller in UP told a researcher that 'voting is important. If I don't vote, I am dead to the state'. A peasant in the same state put it even more emphatically: 'I am because I vote on Election Day. Otherwise, what is my stature in this society?' A respondent in Maharashtra remarked that 'the system may not work for us, but I can vote. It is still "Lokshahi" – rule by the people, not "Rajshahi" – rule by the King'. And a citizen in Tamil Nadu remarked that 'if the government does not work [for us], we will vote for someone else'.[31]

An ethnographic study of rural Bengal found that 'on election day, the village woke up earlier than usual and bustled around urgently with an air of suppressed excitement, like on important festivals'. Men preferred to vote as soon as the booth opened in the morning, with women going in the afternoon, after lunch. Both men and women chose to go in groups, seeing this as a convivial, social, occasion. Notably, the 'egalitarian mechanics of the poll afforded particular pleasure', the fact that on this day, this occasion, this ritual, the traditional hierarchies of caste, class and gender broke down completely.[32]

The Indian love of voting is well illustrated by the case of a cluster of villages on the Andhra/Maharashtra border. Issued voting cards by the administrations of both states, the villagers seized the opportunity to exercise their franchise twice over.[33] It is also illustrated by the peasants in Bihar who go to the polls despite threats by Maoist revolutionaries. Dismissing elections as an exercise in bourgeois hypocrisy, the Maoists have been known to blacken the faces of villagers campaigning for political parties, and to warn potential voters that their feet and hands would be chopped up. Yet, as an anthropologist working in central Bihar found, 'the overall effect of poll-boycott on voter turnout seems to be negligible'. In villages where Maoists had been active for years, 'in fact, election day was seen as an enjoyable (almost festive) occasion. Women dressed in bright yellows and reds, their hair oiled and adorned with clips, made their way to the polling booth in small groups'.[34] Likewise, in parts of the north-east where the writ of the Indian state runs erratically or not at all, insurgents are unable to stop villagers from voting. As one chief election commissioner wryly put it, 'the Election Commission's small contribution to the integrity of the country is to make these areas part of the country for just one day, election day'.[35]

These developments vindicate the faith in universal adult franchise placed by the framers of the Indian constitution. After the first such exercise, in 1952, Devadas Gandhi, the Mahatma's son and also the editor of the *Hindustan Times*, wrote to an American friend that 'the general elections are a very great event, greater than I had anticipated. Adult franchise has had a wonderful start. It has meant an awakening and education which could not have been achieved by any other means'.[36] And so it has turned out.

That elections have been successfully indigenized in India is demonstrated by the depth and breadth of their reach – across and into all sections of Indian society – by the passions they evoke, and by the humour that surrounds them. There is a very rich archive of electoral cartoons, poking fun at promises made by prospective politicians, their desperation to get a party ticket and much else.[37] At other times the humour can be gentle rather than mocking. Consider the career of a cloth merchant from Bhopal named Mohan Lal, who contested elections against five different prime ministers. Wearing a wooden crown, and a garland gifted by himself, he would walk the streets of his constituency, ringing a bell. He unfailingly lost his deposit, thereby justifying his own, self-inflicted sobriquet of *Dhartipakad*, or he who lies, humbled, on the ground. His idea in contesting elections, said Mohan Lal, was 'to make everyone realise that democracy was meant for one and all'.[38]

That elections allow all Indians to palpably feel part of India is also made clear by the experience of Goa. When it was united – or reunited – with India by force in 1961, there was much adverse commentary in the Western press. But where in four hundred years of Portuguese rule the Goans had never been allowed to choose their own leaders, within a couple of years of coming under the rule of New Delhi they were able to do so. The political scientist Benedict Anderson has tellingly compared India's treatment of Goa with Indonesia's treatment of East Timor, that other Portuguese colony 'liberated' by armed nationalists:

> Nehru had sent his troops to Goa in 1960 (sic) without a drop of blood being spilt. But he was a humane man and the freely elected leader of a democracy; he gave the Goanese their own autonomous state government, and encouraged their full participation in India's politics. In every respect, General Suharto was Nehru's polar opposite.[39]

VII

Considering the size of the electorate, it is overwhelmingly likely that more people have voted in Indian elections than voters in any other democracy. India's success in this regard is especially striking when compared to the record of its great Asian neighbour, China. That country is larger, but far less divided on ethnic or religious lines, and far less poor as well. Yet there has never been a single general election held there. In other ways, too, China is much less free than India. The flow of information is highly restricted – when the search engine Google set up shop in China in February 2006, it had to agree to submit to state censorship. The movement of people is regulated as well – the permission of the State is usually required to change one's place of residence.

India/China comparisons have long been a staple of scholarly analysis. Now, in a world that becomes more connected by the day, they have become ubiquitous in popular discourse as well. In this comparison China might win on economic grounds but will lose on political ones. Indians like to harp on their neighbour's democracy deficit, sometimes directly and at other times by euphemistic allusion. When asked to put on a special show at the World Economic Forum of 2006, the Indian delegation never failed to describe their land, whether in speech or in print or in posters, as the 'World's Fastest Growing Democracy'.

Is this self-congratulation merited? The one area in which India is reliably democratic is in the regular practice of free and fair elections. Indians also have considerable freedom of movement; they can travel or work anywhere they like in the Union, although in some areas, only local residents can buy or own property.

However, in other crucial respects India's democratic credentials are flawed, sometimes deeply so. One dark spot, arguably growing darker, has to do with political corruption. The great German sociologist Max Weber once remarked that 'there are two ways of making politics one's vocation: Either one lives "for" politics or one lives "off" it.'[40] The first generation of Indian leaders lived mostly for politics. They were attracted by the authority they wielded, but were also often motivated by a spirit of service and sacrifice. The current generation of Indian politicians, however, are more likely to enter politics to live off it. They are attracted by the power and prestige it offers, and also by the opportunities for financial reward. Control over the state machinery, they know, can give glittering prizes to those in charge.

Political corruption was not unknown in the 1950s, as the cases of the Mundhra scandal and the Kairon administration in the Punjab demonstrate. But it was restricted. Most members of Jawaharlal Nehru's Cabinet, and even Lal Bahadur Shastri's, did not abuse their position for monetary gain. Some Congress bosses did, however, gather money for the party from the business sector. In the 1970s, politicians began demanding a commission when contracting arms deals with foreign suppliers. The money – or most of it – went into the party's coffers to be used in the next elections. By the 1980s, however, political corruption had shifted from the institutional to the personal level – thus an increasing number of ministers at the centre and the states were making money from government contracts, from postings of officials, and by sundry other means.

The evidence of political corruption is, by its very nature, anecdotal rather than documentary. Those who take or give commissions rarely leave a paper trail. However, in the 1990s the Central Bureau of Investigation (CBI) laid charges against a number of prominent politicians for having assets 'disproportionate' to their position. The leaders so charged included the chief ministers of Bihar and Tamil Nadu, Lalu Prasad Yadav and J. Jayalalithaa. Each was accused of amassing hundreds of millions of rupees from the allocation of government contracts. In another case, the CBI raided the house of Sukh Ram, the Union minister for communications, and found 36 million rupees in cash. It was alleged that this represented the commission on licences awarded to private telecom companies.

In most of these cases, the charges were not converted into convictions, sometimes because of lack of evidence, at other times because of the timidity of the judiciary. There was also a sense of honour among thieves. In the run-up to an election the Opposition made a hue and cry about corruption in the ruling administration, but if it was elected it did not pursue cases against the previous regime, trusting that it would be similarly rewarded when it lost power.[41] Indeed, politicians from different parties and different states often exchanged favours. In one documented case, a Haryana chief minister sanctioned the sale of a plot of public land to the son of a Punjab chief minister – while the market value of the land was Rs500 million, the price actually paid was Rs25 million.[42]

A major source of corruption has been the state's control over land, forests, minerals, rivers, coastlines and the airwaves. The reforms of the 1990s had left these sectors untouched. Now, as the economy grew, and globalized, natural resources such as iron, spectrum and oil and natural gas (both offshore and terrestrial) acquired an ever increasing value. Rather than allot them through open auctions, both central and state governments chose to allot these resources to cronies, taking large, indeed massive, kickbacks in return. Likewise, environmental clearances, mandatory under the law, were rarely withdrawn or given on the basis of scientific evidence, but rather on the proximity of entrepreneurs to politicians. This was the case also with large loans made by public sector banks to private capitalists, these often, or even usually, decided on considerations other than creditworthiness.[43]

In the words of the political scientist Peter deSouza, corruption was Indian democracy's 'inconvenient fact'. Governments in power in New Delhi took kickbacks on purchases from abroad, on defence deals especially. The percentage taken on foreign contracts was in the region of 20 per cent. In most states the majority of ministers were on the take, skimming money off licences to companies, postings of top officers, land deals and much else. Economists estimated that 70 per cent to 90 per cent of rural development funds were siphoned off by a web extending up from the *panchayat* head to the local MP, with officials too claiming their share. One reason that city roads were in such poor shape was that the much of the money allocated to them was spent elsewhere. Of every Rs100 allocated to road-building by the Bangalore City Corporation, for example, Rs40 went into the pockets of politicians and officials, with another Rs20 being the contractor's profit margin. Only Rs40 were spent on the job, which was either done badly or not at all.[44]

Because being in power was so profitable, there was now an increasing trade in politicians. To make up the numbers and obtain a majority, legislators were bought and sold for a (usually high) price. In the era of minority and coalition governments the trade was especially brisk. Legislators routinely crossed the floor and changed parties. This had become so common that in times of political instability, the MLAs of a particular party were taken en masse for a 'holiday' in destinations such as Goa, lest they defect to the other side. Here these men – sometimes up to fifty of them – were kept in a hotel, drinking and playing cards, while armed guards watched out for furtive phone calls or unknown visitors. The holiday extended until the crisis has passed, which could take several weeks.

VIII

A second dark spot, also growing darker, is the growing criminality of the political class. As early as 1985, the weekly *Sunday* ran a cover story on 'The Underworld of Indian Politics', which spoke of how, in the states of Uttar Pradesh and Bihar especially, candidates with criminal records were contesting elections, sometimes winning them, and sometimes being made ministers as well. Among the crimes these men were charged with were 'murder, abduction, rape, molestation, gangsterism'.[45] Over the next decade, a greater number of criminals entered politics, so many in fact that a citizens group filed a Public Interest Litigation (PIL) in the Supreme Court demanding that parties release details of their candidates. In May 2002, the Court made it mandatory for those contesting state or national elections to make public their assets and their criminal record (if any).

The group that had filed the original PIL then set up 'Election Watch Committees' in the states, these comprising local lawyers, teachers, and students. The affidavits filed by candidates in five state elections held in 2002–3 were collated and analysed. In the major political parties – such as the BJP, the Congress, Uttar Pradesh's Samajwadi Party (SP) and Bihar's Rashtriya Janata Dal (RJD) – between 15 per cent and 20 per cent of candidates had criminal records. A detailed study of Rajasthan's 2003 Vidhan Sabha election showed that roughly half the candidates were very rich by Indian standards – they had a declared wealth of more than 3 million rupees each. And as many as 124 candidates had criminal records. 40 per cent of these were charged with crimes that qualified as 'serious' – which included armed robbery, attempt to murder, defiling a place of worship and arson.[46]

Equally revealing was an analysis made of the affidavits of the 541 MPs elected in the 2004 parliamentary polls. The Congress had the wealthiest candidates – their MPs each had, on the average, assets of Rs31 million. Most MPs had assets in excess of Rs10 million; those who ranked lowest on this scale were the Communists. On the question of criminal charges, the lead was taken by parties powerful in UP and Bihar: 34.8 per cent of RJD MPs had been charge-sheeted, 27.8 per cent of Bahujan Samaj Party MPs and nearly 20 per cent of SP MPs. The Congress and the BJP came out slightly 'cleaner', having 17 per cent and 20 per cent of their MPs charged with crimes respectively. However, the situation was reversed when it came to money owed to public financial institutions. Of all such debts, Congress MPs accounted for 45 per cent, and the BJP members for 23 per cent. Again, it was Communist MPs who came out best – they reported virtually no debts at all.[47]

In 2014, one of the founders of the group that filed the original PIL published a statistical analysis of the affidavits filed by candidates in all state and national elections over the past decade. This revealed that roughly 18 per cent had pending criminal charges against them. What was more disturbing was that 28 per cent of those with criminal records won the seats they contested. In every party except one, those with serious criminal records were more likely to win than those without. This suggested that, despite the secrecy and credibility of the voting process itself, candidates with money and muscle power could impress or intimidate citizens into casting votes in their favour.

This study further analysed the growth in assets (as declared in their affidavits) of those who won seats in Assemblies or in Parliament. The results revealed that, as in the case of criminal records, the Communists came out cleanest, the Congress and the BJP less clean, and the regional parties the dirtiest of all. The growth in assets of CPI(M) candidates who won was 64 per cent, the corresponding figure for Congress being 201 per cent, for the BJP 142 per cent, for the BSP 499 per cent, and for the Telugu Desam Party a staggering 1,069 per cent.[48]

Conducting research in a Bengali village, a Norwegian anthropologist found that the term most often used to describe politics was '*nungra*' (dirty). Politicians were described as those who promoted 'abusive exchanges' (*galagali*), caused 'fist-fights' (maramari) and promoted 'disturbances' (*gandagol*). In sum, politics served only to fill society with 'poison' (*bish*). This was not always so, said the villagers. Once, soon after Independence, politicians were honest, hardworking and dedicated, but now every party was peopled with 'scheming, plotting [and] unprincipled individuals'.[49]

The statements were fairly representative of matters in the country as a whole. A survey carried out by Gallup in sixty countries found that the lack of confidence in politicians was highest in India, where 91 per cent of those polled felt that their elected representatives were dishonest.[50]

Some consolation can perhaps be found in statements by scholars writing about other societies in other times. Thus, of his own country in the 1940s, Jorge Luis Borges writes that 'the State is impersonal; the Argentine can conceive only of personal relations. Therefore, to him, robbing public funds is not a crime. I am noting a fact; I am not justifying or excusing it'. And, speaking of his own continent, Europe, in centuries past, R. W. Southern remarks that 'nepotism, political bribery, and the appropriation of institutional wealth to endow one's family, were not crimes in medieval rulers; they were part of the art of government, no less necessary in popes than in other men'.[51]

IX

With corruption and criminalization, Indian politics has also increasingly fallen victim to nepotism. Once, most parties had a coherent ideology and organizational base. Now, they have degenerated into family firms.

The process was begun by and within that grand old party, the Indian National Congress. For most of its history, the Congress was a party run by and for democrats, with regular elections to district and state bodies. After splitting the Congress in 1969, Mrs Indira Gandhi put an end to elections within the party organization. Henceforth, Congress chief ministers and state unit presidents were to be nominated by the leader in New Delhi. Then, during the Emergency, Mrs Gandhi dealt a second and more grievous blow to Congress tradition, when she anointed her son Sanjay as her successor.

After Sanjay's death, his elder brother Rajiv was groomed to take over the party and, in time, government. When, in 1998, the Congress bosses asked Sonia Gandhi to head the party, it was an acknowledgement that the party had completely surrendered to the claims of the dynasty. Sonia, in turn, asked her son Rahul to enter politics in 2004, allotting him the safe family borough of Raebareli. Although his mother remains (as of this writing) Congress president, it was Rahul Gandhi who led the party into the 2014 general elections, and is likely to replace his mother soon as party president.

Apart from its corrosive effects on the ethos of India's pre-eminent political party, Mrs Indira Gandhi's embrace of the dynastic principle has served as a ready model for others to emulate. Many political parties in India have been converted into family firms. The DMK was once the proud party of Dravidian nationalism and social reform; its cadres are now resigned to the fact that M. Karunanidhi's son will succeed him. For all his professed commitment to Maharashtrian pride and Hindu nationalism, when picking the next Shiv Sena leader Bal Thackeray could look no further than his son Udhav. The Samajwadi Party and Rashtriya Janata Dal claim to stand for 'social justice', but Mulayam Singh Yadav made sure that his son Akhilesh would succeed him, while when Lalu Prasad Yadav was forced to resign as chief minister of Bihar (after a corruption scandal), his wife Rabri Devi was chosen to replace him, although her previous work experience was limited to the home and the kitchen. (More recently, Lalu has placed two of his sons in top ministerial posts in Bihar). Moreover, once a party has caught the disease of dynasticism, it cannot or will not return to the meritocratic or ideological principles by which it was founded or once run.

Nor is the dominance of a single family active only at the level of the top leadership of India's political parties. The practice has been extended down the system, so that if a sitting MP dies, his son or daughter is likely to be nominated in his place. The historian Patrick French has coined the term 'hereditary MPs' (abbreviated to HMPs) to describe a phenomenon little known in the West but of considerable significance in India. In an analysis of the Lok Sabha elected in 2009, he found that some 29 per cent of MPs were HMPs, who had entered politics through family connections, with one or more members of their family having previously been an MLA, an MP, or a minister. The phenomenon was especially pervasive among the regional parties and among the younger generation. Thus as many as two-thirds of MPs under the age of forty were from political families, but less than 10 per cent of those over seventy years of age.[52]

After the 2014 Lok Sabha elections, the proportion of HMPs fell from 30 per cent to 22 per cent, still a substantial figure. The practice is encouraged by political parties across the board; on the whole, 75 per cent of dynastic MPs were renominated by their respective parties, as against 65 per cent of non-dynastic MPs. Candidates often spoke proudly of their family background while campaigning, sons promising to carry on the work of the fathers who had gifted them their seat.[53]

The figures cited above come from analyses of successive Lok Sabhas. Studies of the constitution of state assemblies would most likely reveal a similar pattern. Notably, even the BJP, a party that prides itself on its cadre-based, ideology-driven, non-nepotistic nature, has increasingly fallen prey to family-based politics. Thus 15 per cent of the BJP MPs in 2014 were from political families (the corresponding figure for 2009 was 19 per cent). And in the states where the BJP has ruled, the relatives of ministers and chief ministers have become increasingly powerful. In 2011, the veteran BJP leader and former Himachal Pradesh Chief Minister Shanta Kumar remarked that 'the culture of parivar-tantra (family politics), replacing Loktantra (democracy) has arisen even in the BJP … BJP has been the party of workers but right from Himachal Pradesh to Karnataka, it is becoming a party of sons, daughters and relatives.' Kumar added that 'if we compromise with the corrupt to remain in power, we have no right to call ourselves a party with a difference.'[54]

Nepotism in Indian politics is by no means ubiquitous. However, it is now common enough to be worrying. In a mature democracy, anyone with any interest or ability should be able to enter a political party of one's choice, and, once there, to acquire more authority and responsibility on the basis of one's performance. Angela Merkel and Barack Obama came literally from nowhere, becoming German chancellor and American president respectively entirely on the basis of their own achievements. There was no family member to assist or inspire them in their political journey. Such is the case for the vast majority of lesser German and American politicians as well.

Interestingly, that the dynastic principle is at odds with democratic practice has been noticed, and taken advantage of, by some Indian politicians in recent years. In the campaign of 2014, Narendra Modi often stressed his own, lowly, non-political origins in contrast to the radically different background of his main rival, born into privilege in India's pre-eminent political family. Among chief ministers, both Nitish Kumar of Bihar and Arvind Kejriwal of Delhi owe their success in part to the fact they were the first, and remain the only, member of their family to be active in party politics.

X

A fourth area of democratic imperfection has to do with the provision of justice. This was brought vividly to light in April 2016, when, at a function in New Delhi with the Prime Minister Modi present, the chief justice of India spoke of the unconscionable delays in the process of dispensing justice. Addressing the prime minister in the name of the 'poor litigant' and 'people languishing in jails', the chief justice urged him 'to rise to the occasion and realise that it not enough to criticize'. At this point, the chief justice was so overwhelmed with the dimensions of the problem that he broke down, pulling out a handkerchief to wipe away his tears.

The failures to provide speedy justice were largely a consequence of the massive, chronic, under-staffing of India's courts. In 2016, the Supreme Court had a shortfall of 19 per cent of its assigned strength, the High Courts a shortfall of 44 per cent, and subordinate courts a shortfall of 25 per cent. The Allahabad High Court had as many as 88 unfulfilled vacancies; the Madras High Court, 40.

These shortfalls lead to major delays. In India's High Courts, once a case is filed, it takes, on the average, three years and one month to be disposed of. The person losing the case can then ask for a stay and appeal to the Supreme Court. Some cases, filed originally in a district court and contested all the way up to the highest court in the land, can take several decades to achieve finality, the litigants sometimes dying in the process.[55]

The judicial system in India is painfully slow. And it is also shockingly corrupt. In September 2010, Shanti Bushan – one of India's most respected lawyers who had served as law minister in the Union government – created a stir when he claimed in the Supreme Court that, of the sixteen chief justices of India he had served under, eight were corrupt. He listed their names in a sealed envelope which he submitted to the court, daring the judges to open it.[56]

The evidence for judicial corruption is even more anecdotal than that for political corruption. Yet, going by the perception of petitioners and lawyers, it does seem that the taking of bribes and inducements is fairly common among the lower judiciary, certainly prevalent among High Court judges, and not entirely absent even in the Supreme Court.

The justice system, at least as it operates in India, is biased in favour of the rich and influential. Thus, in many cases, when a politician, film star or businessman is the accused in a crime he was charged with committing, witnesses have been bought or threatened into changing their original statements. Or they might even be physically eliminated, as has happened in the case of an influential godman accused of sexual harassment, and that of a massive educational fraud in Madhya Pradesh in which senior politicians (of more than one party) were involved. In both cases multiple witnesses died, in mysterious circumstances.[57]

The autonomy of the judiciary has also been undermined by political interference. The first government to seek to make judges subservient to it was that led by Indira Gandhi. Her key advisers, such as P. N. Haksar, Mohan Kumaramangalam and H. R. Gokhale, vigorously pursued the idea of a 'committed judiciary'. They actively interfered in judicial appointments, most famously – or notoriously – by superceding several outstanding judges to make A. N. Ray the chief justice of India in 1973.

More recently, some Supreme and High Court judges may have been influenced in their working by the prospect of post-retirement sinecures. For example, a Congress government appointed a former Supreme Court judge to the Rajya Sabha, while a BJP government made a former chief justice the governor of a state. In both cases, the judge in question had passed judgements or conducted enquiries which exonerated controversial ruling party politicians. The eminent jurist Fali Nariman termed such appointments 'most improper and unfortunate'. Judges 'seeking jobs or a seat in Parliament from the Executive', he remarked, 'gravely affects the concept of independence of the judiciary, proudly and repeatedly proclaimed – alas only by sitting Judges of the Supreme Court – as a basic feature of the Constitution.'[58]

Then there is the problem of undertrials, whose percentage has been steadily increasing over the years. It now rests at just under 70 per cent. These men and women (most of whom are poor, and many from a low caste background) have merely been charged, not proven guilty. Yet they can languish for years in crowded, dark, dirty jails, eating undercooked and/or adulterated food, drinking contaminated water, and with no access to legal or medical aid.[59]

The state of Indian prisons is depressing. Meanwhile, in their regular, routine, duties of assuring public safety and security, the Indian police do not distinguish themselves either. There are too few of them in the first place. India has 130 policemen per 100,000 citizens, as against the global norm of 222.[60] Those that are there are often overweight, undertrained and corrupt. Like the courts they tend to favour the rich;

further, they can display a marked bias against religious minorities. In a rare moment of self-criticism, the Mumbai police admitted in July 2014 that they experienced a trust deficit among Muslims, who saw them as 'communal, biased and insensitive', as well as 'ill-informed, corrupt and lacking professionalism', the second part of which verdict all Indians regardless of religion would endorse.[61]

One study found that of all the government departments in the state of Karnataka, the police were the most corrupt. In the first eleven months of the year, citizens reported paying close to 9 crores as bribes to the men in khaki. The study surveyed 37 government agencies; the second most corrupt was the transport department, whose yearly takings were less than 10 per cent of that alleged to have been collected by the police department. It is extremely likely that in other states of the Union the same kind of situation prevails.[62]

The malfunctioning of the Indian police is a product of its increasing politicization over the years. An MLA or MP often decides who shall be posted as the superintendent of police in the district in which his constituency falls. The most prestigious and powerful jobs in the police are allocated, as often as not, on the basis of kin and caste. At other times they are bid for in the open market. In some states chief ministers are said to have demanded, and obtained, lakhs or even crores of rupees in return for posting an officer to a district or division of his choice.

Once the top jobs are decided on considerations other than competence, it hard to prevent lesser jobs being allocated in the same manner. So inspectors and station head officers and constables are also often chosen on the basis of caste, religion, favouritism or bribery. Down the line, this puts a premium on a police officer pleasing the man (or minister) who appointed him to his post, rather than focusing on his main job, which is the protection of the ordinary citizen. It also encourages corruption, the desire to make hay before one is suddenly divested of one's responsibilities when a government changes, an MP fails to win re-election, or the boss retires.

As the Supreme Court despairingly noted in 2006, 'many of the deficiencies in the functioning of the police have arisen largely due to a dose of unhealthy and petty political interference at various levels starting from transfer and posting of policemen of different ranks, misuse of police for partisan purposes and political patronage quite often extended to corrupt police personnel'.[63]

XI

Democracy is about, among other things, the enhancement of individual freedoms. Despite the corruption and corrosion of public institutions, are Indians, acting and thinking as individuals, freer than they were in 1947?

In many respects they are. Growing urbanization has meant a steady delinking of caste from occupation. Now, many more Indians are freer than they ever were to follow a profession of their choice, rather than that of their parents. Urbanization has also led to a lessening of the stranglehold of the family. Many more Indians can now fall in love with and marry a person of their choice (rather than one chosen for them by their parents). They can also more easily make friends across caste and religious boundaries.

Even in matters of sexual choice, Indians are perhaps freer than at any time since Independence. Despite the Supreme Court judgement of 2013 upholding Section 377 of the Indian Penal Code, gays and lesbians are relatively immune to ostracism and persecution, at least in the cities.

To be sure, the extent of these freedoms is heavily determined by class and gender. Gays who are middle class are less subject to social prejudice than those who are working class. Parents of all classes are more likely to accept a son's choice of career or spouse than a daughter's.

The place where Indians are most free, most able to act as individuals, may be the voting booth. Back in the 1950s, women often voted as their fathers or husbands or brothers did. Dalits often voted as the upper castes told them too. Now, while friends, family and caste fellows may be consulted before voting, the final decision is entirely one's own.

One area where Indians have become less free in recent decades relates to artistic and literary expression. Archaic colonial laws are too often invoked by courts or the state to ban books and censor films. The rise of identity politics has made it almost impossible to present a fair, unbiased, assessment of the life and work of Indian political figures revered by a particular caste, linguistic, or religious group. Attacks on independent writers and artists have become more frequent; occasionally, they are even murdered for their views. Since no politician or political party has ever taken a forthright stand in favour of freedom of expression, these attacks go unpunished. On the whole, Indian writers, artists and film-makers are probably less free, more vulnerable, than they have been at any time since the Emergency of 1975–7.[64]

XII

How democratic is India? When asked this question, I usually turn for recourse to an immortal line of the great Hindi comic actor Johnny Walker. In a film where he plays the hero's sidekick, Walker answers every query with the remark: *'Boss, phipty/phipty'*. When asked what prospect he has of marrying the girl he so deeply loves, or of getting the job he so dearly desires, the sidekick tells the boss that the chances are roughly even, 50 per cent of success, or 50 per cent of failure.

Is India a democracy, then? The answer is, well, *phipty-phipty*. It mostly is when it comes to holding elections and permitting freedom of movement and expression. It mostly is not when it comes to the functioning of institutions crucial to the everyday life of a democracy. Most political parties have become family firms. Most politicians are corrupt, and many come from a criminal background. India's law-makers are too often law-breakers as well. Meanwhile, civil servants have lost their autonomy of functioning, doing what their political bosses ask rather than what justice or reason demands. The courts are slow and over-burdened, and not always fair either. The police are corrupt in good days and venal in bad.

As the Republic turns seventy, the national experiment seems more robust than the democratic one. No part of India is likely to secede soon, if at all. The astonishing project of creating a nation without a common language, common religion or common enemy has, thus far at least, largely succeeded. However, the record when it comes to nurturing equality of citizenship is decidedly mixed.

In his famous last speech to the Constituent Assembly. B. R. Ambedkar noted that India would soon become a polity based on the principle of one person, one vote. He wondered when it could become a society based on the principle of one person, one value.

That question remains as pertinent as when it was first posed. For the Republic of India is in danger of becoming what I call an 'elections-only democracy'. Every election, whether to a state Assembly or to a national Parliament, is free and fair. The Election Committee is rightly praised as a model institution. Yet other instruments of democratic accountability remain deeply imperfect. Parliament meets rarely – when it does, it resembles a wrestling pit more than the stately chamber of discussion it was meant to be. The criminal justice system is in a state of near-collapse. The state is, on the one side, weak and incompetent when providing basic services such as education and health care; but, on the other, savage and brutal in its suppression of discontent.

In India today, Dalits, women, Muslims and tribals are perhaps not as persecuted as one might have feared when the nation was created. Many individual Dalits, women and Muslims (but fewer tribals) have overcome discrimination, becoming successful professionals, public servants, politicians and entrepreneurs. Yet these social groups remain, on the whole, less-than-equal citizens of the land. Seventy years after Independence, upper-caste Hindu males still command disproportionate privileges in the everyday life of the Republic.

In the first edition of this book, published in 2007, I argued that as a multi-lingual, multi-religious political experiment, the Republic of India anticipated the European Union by several decades. Ten years later, I might add that it seems likely to outlive the EU as well. But I do not write this in any spirit of triumphalism. For India, and Indians, could learn a lesson or two from some individual European countries in how to limit the influence of corruption and cronyism in politics; how to nurture impersonal, rule-round institutions; how to dispense justice fairly and speedily; how to train public officials to treat all citizens alike regardless of age or class or gender or ethnicity.

It is easy enough for Indian patriots to compare our democratic record with other ex-colonial nations in Asia and Africa; but tougher, and more necessary, to compare it with the countries of Western Europe and North America. I think that is what B. R. Ambedkar, Jawaharlal Nehru, and Vallabhbhai Patel (among other such figures) would have wanted us to do. For Indians today may be more free than when the British left these shores, but they are surely less free than what the framers of our Constitution hoped or wished them to be.

Acknowledgements

In close to five decades as a citizen of India I have had plenty of opportunity to discover that this is sometimes the most exasperating country in the world. However, it was only while working on its modern history that I found that it was at all times the most interesting. It was my friend Peter Straus who set me off on the journey, by suggesting that I write a book on independent India. And it was the selfless tribe of archivists and librarians who made the journey an adventure rich in thrills and unexpected discoveries.

The greatest thanks are owed to the staff of the Nehru Memorial Museum and Library, that capacious repository of private papers, periodicals, microfilms and books about modern India. For weeks on end I had as my kindly companions Shri Jeevan Chand and Shri Rautela of the Manuscripts Division, who brought file after file up from a large, dark corridor into the sunny reading room where I worked. Outside, in the Main Section, the library staff were unfailingly courteous. In sourcing manuscripts, I also received much help from the Library's Deputy Director, Dr N. Balakrishnan, and his sterling assistant Deepa Bhatnagar.

Next in order of importance is that other – and more famous – public repository, the British Library in London. My base here was the old India Office Library and Records, which – while I worked there – was called the 'Oriental and India Office Collections' (it now functions under the label of 'Asian and African Studies'). By any name it remains a happy place to work in, with its brisk and efficient staff, its close links to other collections, and – not least – the serendipitous meetings it allows with scholars from around the world.

Among the other libraries and archives where I collected material for this book are those maintained by the National Archives of India, New Delhi; the Centre for South Asian Studies, Cambridge; the University of California, Berkeley; Stanford University; Cornell University; the

University of Michigan, Ann Arbor; the University of Georgia, Athens; Friends House, Euston; the India International Centre, New Delhi; the National Library of Scotland, Edinburgh; the Imperial War Museum, London; Oslo University; the Madras Institute of Development Studies, Chennai; Tata Steel, Jamshedpur; and the Lal Bahadur Shastri National Academy of Administration, Mussoorie. A special thanks is owed to the Centre for Education and Documentation in Bengaluru, from whose fabulously comprehensive collection of news clippings I have extensively drawn.

Aside from private papers and periodicals, this book also draws on other books old and new, as well as pamphlets. Not many of these could I find in libraries (at least not the libraries in my home town, Bengaluru, which is a great centre of science but not, alas, of the humanities). The bulk were bought from bookshops known and unrecognized. I am grateful, in particular, to the Premier Bookshop, Bengaluru; the Select Bookshop, Bengaluru; Prabhu Booksellers, Gurugram; the New and Secondhand Bookshop, Mumbai; and Manohar Booksellers, New Delhi. As handy and helpful were the unnamed pavement stalls in Mumbai's Flora Fountain and Delhi's Daryaganj – from whom and where, over the past two decades and more, I have obtained so much of the material for my work as a historian.

The photographs that I have used here come principally from four collections: those maintained by the Press Information Bureau, the Nehru Memorial Museum and Library, and the *Hindu* and *Ananda Bazaar Patrika* group of newspapers. I thank these institutions for their assistance, and my wife Sujata for advice on the final selection.

For help of various kinds, I would like to thank Chinmayi Arun; Kanti Bajpai; Suhas Baliga; Rukmini Banerji; Nupur Basu; Millicent Bennett; Stanley Brandes; Vijay Chandru; Shruti Debi; Kanak Mani Dixit; Zafar Futehally; Amitav Ghosh; my parents S. R. D. and Visalakshi Guha; Supriya Guha; Wajahat Habibullah; Rajen Harshe; Radhika Herzberger; Trevor Horwood; Shreyas Jayasimha; Robin Jeffrey; Bhagwan Josh; Nasreen Munni Kabir; Devesh Kapur; Mukul Kesavan; Soumya Keshavan; Nayanjot Lahiri; Nirmala Lakshman; Edward Luce; Lucy Luck; Raghu Menon; Mary Mount; Rajdeep Mukherjee; Rudrangshu Mukherjee; Anil Nauriya; Nandan Nilekani; Mohandas Pai; Sriram Panchu; Prashant Panjiar; Shekhar Pathak; Srinath Raghavan; Nitya Ramakrishnan; Ramesh Ramanathan; Jairam Ramesh; my nephew Karthik Ramkumar; Mahesh Rangarajan; Anuradha Roy; Tirthankar

Roy; John Ryle; P. Sainath; Sanjeev Saith; Rajdeep Sardesai; Jalpa Rajesh Shah; Rajbhushan Shinde; K. Sivaramakrishnan; Arvind Subramanian; R. Sudarshan; Nandini Sundar; M. V. Swaroop; Shikha Trivedy; Siddharth Varadarajan; A. R. Venkatachalapathy; Rajendra Vora; Amy Waldman; and Francis Wheen.

Some friends deserve special mention, for their long-term help in matters professional and personal. These good souls are Rukun Advani, André Béteille, Keshav Desiraju, Gopal Gandhi, David Gilmour, Ian Jack, Sanjeev Jain and Sunil Khilnani. André and David also provided detailed comments on a draft of the book. And I was kept going by the memory of my friend Krishna Raj, editor for thirty-five years of the *Economic and Political Weekly*, the journal whose own life is so closely bound up with the life of the Republic – as the notes to this book testify.

I thank, for their support, encouragement, criticism and chastisement, my editors, Richard Milner of Macmillan and Dan Halpern of Ecco/ HarperCollins. I promise to be less tardy with the books that might follow! In fact, without my agent Gill Coleridge even this one would not have been finished. On more than one occasion I have been tempted to take an extended holiday, or drop the book altogether. Each time it was Gill who brought me back, showing me the ways in which it might be continued and, in the end, completed.

My greatest debt, as expressed in the dedication, is to the always interesting and occasionally exasperating Indians with whom I am privileged to share a home.

Postscript: In preparing this revised edition of *India after Gandhi*, I have got valuable research assistance from Sachin Arya. I am also grateful to Keshava Guha and T. N. Ninan for commenting on the new chapters, and to Diya Kar Hazra and Sushmita Chatterjee of Picador India for so expertly seeing the book through the press.

Notes

Prologue: Unnatural Nation

1 The translation is by Qurratulain Hyder.
2 See Ralph Russell and Khurshidul Islam, ed. and trans., *Ghalib, 1797–1869: Life and Letters* (1969: reprint Delhi: Oxford University Press, 1994), chapter 7.
3 John Strachey, *India* (London: Kegan, Paul, Trench and Co., 1888), pp. 2–5.
4 The best single-volume treatment remains Sumit Sarkar, *Modern India: 1885–1947* (London: Macmillan, 1985). For a more up-to-date account see Sekhar Bandopadhyay, *From Plassey to Partition* (Hyderabad: Orient Longman, 2004), an additional merit of which is its excellent bibliography.
5 Interview in the *Adelaide Advertiser*, November 1891, quoted in the 'NB' column of *The Times Literary Supplement*, 9 March 2001.
6 E. H. D. Sewell, *An Outdoor Wallah* (London: Stanley Paul and Co., 1945), p. 110, emphasis added. These words were written in 1934.
7 Winston Churchill, *India: Speeches and an Introduction* (London: Thornton Butterworth, 1931), pp. 38, 120, 125 etc.
8 These quotes are taken from Devesh Kapur, 'Globalization and the Paradox of Indian Democracy', mimeo, Department of Political Science, University of Texas at Austin, December 2005.
9 Don Taylor, 'This New, Surprising Strength of Mrs Gandhi', *Evening Standard*, 21 August 1969, emphasis in original.
10 *The Statesman* (New Delhi), 10 August 1998.
11 Adam Przeworski, Michael E. Alvarez, José António Cheibub and Fernando Limongi, *Democracy and Development: Political Institutions and Well-being in the World, 1950–1990* (Cambridge: Cambridge University Press, 2000), quoted in Kapur, 'Globalization'.
12 Sunil Khilnani, *The Idea of India* (New York: Farrar, Straus and Giroux, 1997), p. 4.
13 Krishna Kumar, *What is Worth Teaching?* 3rd edn (Hyderabad: Orient Longman, 2004), p. 109.
14 Tony Judt, *Postwar: A History of Europe Since 1945* (London: William Heinemann, 2005), p. xiii.
15 Marc Bloch, *French Rural History: An Essay on its Essential Characteristics* (1931; reprint London: Routledge and Kegan Paul, 1978), preface.

1. FREEDOM AND PARRICIDE

1 *Collected Works of Mahatma Gandhi* (New Delhi: Government of India, 1958– ; hereafter cited as CWMG), vol. 42, pp. 398–400.

2 Jawaharlal Nehru, *An Autobiography, with Musings on Recent Events in India* (1936; reprint London: The Bodley Head, 1949), p. 209.

3 *The Indian Annual Register, 1930*, part I (Jan.–June), p. 23.

4 This account of the ceremonies is based on Jim Masselos; ' "The magic touch of being free": The Rituals of Independence on 15 August', in Masselos, ed., *India: Creating a Modern Nation* (New Delhi: Sterling Publishers, 1990); Tai Yong Tan and Gyanesh Kudesia, *The Aftermath of Partition in South Asia* (London: Routledge, 2000), chapter 2; The *Statesman*, 15 August 1947; reports in Philip Talbot Papers, Centre for South Asian Studies, University of Cambridge (hereafter CSAS); reports and correspondence in Mountbatten Papers (Mss Eur F200), Tyson Papers (Mss Eur F341), and Saumarez Smith Papers (Mss Eur C409), all in the Oriental and India Office Collections, British Library, London (hereafter OIOC).

5 Actually, as Salman Rushdie once remarked, half the world had not yet gone to sleep, and the other half was already awake. This witticism did not stop Rushdie from including Nehru's speech in an anthology of Indian writing that he edited – the only piece of non-fiction to find a place in the volume.

6 As related in Rajmohan Gandhi, *The Good Boatman: A Portrait of Gandhi* (New Delhi: Viking, 1993).

7 This section on Gandhi and the run-up to independence draws on D. G. Tendulkar, *Mahatma: Life of Mohandas Karamchand Gandhi*, 2nd edn (1963; reprint New Delhi: Publications Division, 1990), vols 7 and 8; N. K. Bose, *My Days with Gandhi* (1953; reprint Hyderabad: Orient Longman, 1990); N. K. Bose and P. H. Patwardhan, *Gandhi in Indian Politics* (Bombay: Lalvani Publishing House, 1967); and relevant volumes of CWMG.

8 The words of the then viceroy, Lord Linlithgow, speaking on 8 August 1940.

9 B. R. Nanda, 'Nehru, the Indian National Congress and the Partition of India, 1935–47', in C. H. Philips and Mary Doreen Wainwright, eds, *The Partition of India: Policies and Perspectives* (London: George Allen and Unwin, 1970), p. 183.

10 The *Statesman*, 16 August 1947.

11 The new governor was R. F. Mudie, a British member of the Indian Civil Service who had elected to stay on and work for the government of Pakistan. The quote is from a typescript in the Mudie Papers, OIOC (Mss Eur F164/12).

12 Quoted in Gyanendra Pandey, *Remembering Partition: Violence, Nationalism and History in India* (Cambridge: Cambridge University Press, 2002), p. 98.

13 See L/P and J/8/575, OIOC.

14 Robin Jeffrey, 'The Punjab Boundary Force and the Problem of Order, August 1947', *Modern Asian Studies*, vol. 8, no. 4, 1974.

15 'Partition' (1968), in W. H. Auden, *Collected Poems*, ed. Edward Mendelson (New York: Vintage, 1991), pp. 803–4.

16 Quoted in Urvashi Butalia, *The Other Side of Silence: Voices from the Partition of India* (Delhi: Viking, 1998), p. 65.

Before he left India Radcliffe burnt all his notes and papers. He never wrote about his experiences in the subcontinent either. Auden was cynical about this silence, saying that 'he quickly forgot the case, as a good lawyer must'.

17 This and subsequent quotes from Rees are from his papers deposited in the OIOC (especially files Mss Eur F274/66 to Mss Eur F274/70).

18 Quoted in H. M. Seervai, *Partition of India: Legend and Reality* (Bombay: Emenem Publications, 1989), p. 148.

19 Nehru to Rees, 3/9/1947, Mss Eur F274/73, OIOC.

20 Baroo, 'Life in the Punjab Today', *Swatantra*, 4 October 1947.

21 See Mss Eur F200/129.

22 Donald F. Ebright, *Free India; the First Five Years: An Account of the 1947 Riots, Refugees, Relief and Rehabilitation* (Nashville: Parthenon Press, 1954), p. 28. Later estimates have pushed up the number of dead to a million or more.

23 Note by Major William Short dated 17 October 1947, in Mss Eur F200/129, OIOC.

24 As reported in Pyarelal, 'In Calcutta', *Harijan*, 14 September 1947.

25 This quote, and much of the preceding two paragraphs, draw from Denis Dalton, *Mahatma Gandhi: Nonviolent Power in Action* (New York: Columbia University Press, 1993), chapter 5, 'The Calcutta Fast'.

26 See Richard Symons, *In the Margins of Independence: A Relief Worker in India and Pakistan, 1942–1949* (Karachi: Oxford University Press, 2001).

27 The violence against the Meos is described in Shail Mayaram, *Resisting Regimes: Myth, Memory and the Shaping of a Muslim Identity* (New Delhi: Oxford University Press, 1997).

28 Tendulkar, *Mahatma*, vol. 8, pp. 112–31.

29 'To Members of the R.S.S.', *Harijan*, 28 September 1947.

30 Nehru to Patel, 30 September 1947, in Durga Das, ed., *Sardar Patel's Correspondence, 1945–50*, 10 vols (Ahmedabad: Navjivan Press, 1971–74), cited hereafter as SPC, vol. 4, pp. 297–9.

31 Entry dated 13 September 1947, in Alan Campbell-Johnson, *Mission with Mountbatten* (New York: E. P. Dutton and Co., 1953), p. 189.

32 'A.I.C.C. Resolutions', *Harijan*, 23 November 1947.

33 Golwalkar, *We, or Our Nation Defined* (1938; Nagpur: Bharat Prakashan, 1947), pp. 55–6, quoted in Mohan Ram, *Hindi against India: The Meaning of DMK* (New Delhi: Rachna Prakashan, 1968), p. 64.

34 *Hindustan Times*, 8 December 1947.

35 Tendulkar, *Mahatma*, vol. 8, pp. 246–66.

36 Robert Payne, *The Life and Death of Mahatma Gandhi* (New York: E. P. Dutton and Co., 1969), pp. 637–41; see also Ashis Nandy's fascinating essay on Gandhi and Godse in his *At the Edge of Psychology and other Essays* (New Delhi: Oxford University Press, 1980).

37 Patel spoke in Hindustani. The English translation used here is from *The Statesman*, 31 January 1948.

38 Quoted in Sucheta Mahajan, *Independence and Partition: The Erosion of Colonial Power in India* (New Delhi: Sage Publications, 2000), pp. 320–1.

39 See the correspondence between Nehru and Patel in SPC, vol. 6, pp. 8–31.

2. THE LOGIC OF DIVISION

1 Khizar Hayat Tiwana to Major Short, 15 August 1947, Short Papers, OIOC (Mss Eur. 189/19).

2 There is a massive literature on Partition, which includes: (i) memoirs by key
   civil servants and military officials who served in the government at the time;
   (ii) biographies of the important politicians involved in the negotiations – Nehru,
   Gandhi, Jinnah, Patel, Mountbatten et al.; (iii) regional studies of Partition in
   the Punjab and in Bengal; and (iv) wider analytical overviews. To this must be
   added the volumes of original documents published both in Britain (the Transfer
   of Power project) and in India (the Towards Freedom Project plus the published
   correspondence of Nehru, Patel, Gandhi et al.). A fine recent overview, with
   much of the relevant literature cited therein, is Sucheta Mahajan, *Independence
   and Partition: The Erosion of Colonial Power in India* (New Delhi: Sage Publications,
   2000). An earlier work representing most of the competing points of view is
   C. H. Philips and Mary Doreen Wainwright, eds, *The Partition of India: Policies
   and Perspectives* (London: George Allen and Unwin, 1970).

3 See the revealing portrait in the memoir of Jinnah's former junior, M. C. Chagla,
   Roses in December: An Autobiography (1973; reprint Bombay: Bharatiya Vidya
   Bhavan, 1994), chapter 5.

4 Lord Birkenhead to Lord Reading, quoted in John Grigg, 'Myths about the
   Approach to Indian Independence', in Wm. Roger Louis, ed., *More Adventures
   with Britannia: Personalities, Politics and Culture in Britain* (Austin: University of
   Texas Press, 1998), p. 211.

5 See Khalid bin Sayeed, *Pakistan: The Formative Phase, 1857–1948*, 2nd edn (Karachi:
   Oxford University Press, 1969), esp. chapter 6. Two magisterial treatments of
   Muslim consolidation during late colonial rule are C. S. Venkatachar, '1937–47 in
   Retrospect: A Civil Servant's View', in Philips and Wainwright, *The Partition of
   India*; and Hamza Alavi, 'Misreading Partition Road Signs', *Economic and Political
   Weekly*, 2–9 November 2002.

6 Kenneth O. Morgan, *Labour in Power, 1945–1951* (Oxford: Clarendon Press, 1984),
   p. 221.

7 'The Pakistan Nettle', in Moon Papers, OIOC (Mss. Eur F230/39).

8 This account of the 1946 elections is based largely on Sho Kuwajima, *Muslims,
   Nationalism and the Partition: 1946 Provincial Elections in India* (New Delhi:
   Manohar, 1998), supplemented by David Gilmartin, *Empire and Islam: Punjab
   and the Making of Pakistan* (Berkeley: University of California Press, 1988) and
   'A Magnificent Gift: Muslim Nationalism and the Election Process in Colonial
   Punjab', *Comparative Studies in Society and History*, vol. 40, no. 3, July 1998; and
   I. A. Talbot, 'The 1946 Punjab Election', *Modern Asian Studies*, vol. 14, no. 1, 1980.

9 See Peter Clarke, *The Cripps Version: The Life of Sir Stafford Cripps, 1889–1952*
   (London: Allen Lane, 2002), part V.

10 Faiz Ahmad Faiz, 'Subh-e-Azadi' (Freedom's Dawn), as translated from the Urdu
   by V. G. Kiernan in *Poems by Faiz* (1958; reprint Delhi: Oxford University Press,
   2000), pp. 123–4.

11 Humayan Kabir, 'Muslim Politics, 1942–7', in Philips and Wainwright, *The
   Partition of India*, p. 402.

12 Philip Ziegler, *Mountbatten* (London: Collins, 1985), p. 439.

13 Andrew Roberts, 'Lord Mountbatten and the Perils of Adrenalin', in his *Eminent
   Churchillians* (London: Weidenfeld and Nicolson, 1994).

14 Jenkins to Mountbatten, 3 May 1947, Mss Eur F200/125, OIOC.

15 Jenkins to Mountbatten, 30 July 1947, Mss Eur F200/127, OIOC.

16 J. D. Tyson to 'Dear Folk', 5 May 1946, Mss Eur E341/40, OIOC.
17 Note by Sir Francis Burrows, 14 February 1947, Mss Eur F200/24, OIOC.
18 See Malcolm Darling, *At Freedom's Door* (London: Oxford University Press, 1949).
19 Nicholas Mansergh, editor-in-chief, *Constitutional Relations between Great Britain and India: Transfer of Power, 1942–47*, 12 vols (London: Her Majesty's Stationery Office, 1970–1983), cited hereafter as TOP, vol. 12, items 200, 209, 389 and 489.
20 Quoted in Richard Symons, *In the Margins of Independence: A Relief Worker in India and Pakistan, 1924–1949* (Karachi: Oxford University Press, 2001), p. 3.

3. Apples in the Basket

1 Pothan Joseph, 'Mountbatten Quits India', *Swatantra*, 19 June 1948.
2 Brian Hoey, *Mountbatten: The Private Story* (London: Pan Books, 1995), pp. 3, 4, 201.
3 Denis Judd, ed., *A British Tale of Indian and Foreign Service: The Memoirs of Sir Ian Scott* (London: Radcliffe Press, 1999), p. 147.
4 See Penderel Moon, ed., *Wavell: The Viceroy's Journal* (London: Oxford University Press, 1973).
5 The books I have in mind are Alan Campbell-Johnson, *Mission with Mountbatten* (New York: E. P. Dutton and Co., 1951); H. V. Hodson, *The Great Divide: Britain–India–Pakistan* (London: Hutchinson, 1969); Dominique Lapierre and Larry Collins, *Freedom at Midnight* (New Delhi: Rupa, 1975); and Philip Ziegler, *Mountbatten: The Official Biography* (London: Collins, 1985). For an early revisionist view, see Leonard Mosley, *The Last Days of the British Raj* (New York: Harcourt, Brace and World, Inc., 1961).
6 Ziegler, *Mountbatten*, p. 424.
7 V. P. Menon, *Integration of the Indian States* (1956; reprint Hyderabad: Orient Longman, 1997). There have been some fine studies of individual princely states, and of British policy towards the Maharajas. However, no one since Menon has attempted an analytical overview of the demise of the princely order, with its (often profound) implications for the history of independent India.
8 For a brilliant brief survey of British relations with princely India, see K. M. Pannikar, *Indian States*, Oxford Pamphlet on Indian Affairs, no. 4 (Bombay: Oxford University Press, 1942). See also the essays in Robin Jeffrey, ed., *People, Princes and Paramount Power: Society and Politics in Indian Princely States* (Delhi: Oxford University Press, 1978).
9 Quoted in Mario Rodrigues, *Batting for the Empire: A Political Biography of Ranjitsinhji* (New Delhi: Penguin India, 2003).
10 Ian Copland, *The Princes of India in the Endgames of Empire* (Cambridge: Cambridge University Press, 1999), p. 227.
11 W. H. Morris-Jones, 'The Transfer of Power, 1947: A View from the Sidelines', *Modern Asian Studies*, vol. 16, no. 1, 1982, pp. 17–18.
12 S. Gopal, *Jawaharlal Nehru: A Biography*, vol. 1: *1889–1947* (London: Cape, 1975), p. 359.
13 See Rajmohan Gandhi, *Patel: A Life* (Ahmedabad: Navjivan Press, 1991), pp. 408–11; SPC, vol. 5, *passim*.
14 The phrase was coined by Pannikar, and is the underpinning of his classic *Asia and Western Dominance* (London: George Allen and Unwin, 1959).

15 'Maharaja of Bikaner's Appeal to the Princes', appendix 2 to SPC, vol. 5, pp. 518–24. This appeal was almost certainly drafted by K. M. Pannikar.

16 Penderel Moon to Major Billy Short, 29 March 1947, Mss Eur F179/16, Short Papers, OIOC.

17 A representative view is that of the last head of this department, Sir Conrad Corfield. See his 'Some Thoughts on British Policy and the Indian States, 1935–47', in C. H. Philips and Mary Doreen Wainwright, eds, *The Partition of India: Policies and Perspectives* (London: George Allen and Unwin, 1970), pp. 527–34.

18 Menon to Sir P. Patrick (under-secretary of state for India), 8 July 1947, in TOP, vol. 12, pp. 1–2.

19 SPC, vol. 5, pp. 536–8.

20 TOP, vol. 12, pp. 36, 51.

21 Campbell-Johnson, *Mission with Mountbatten*, p. 140.

22 'Press Communiqué of an Address by Rear-Admiral Viscount Mountbatten of Burma to a Conference of the Rulers and Representatives of Indian States', TOP, vol. 12, pp. 347–52.

23 See TOP, vol. 12, pp. 585–8; Hodson, *The Great Divide*, pp. 369f.

24 The words are those of Vallabhbhai Patel, from his statement to the princes of 5 July 1947. See SPC, vol. 5, p. 537.

25 'Satyagraha Movement in Mysore', *Swatantra*, 27 September 1947; H. S. Doreswamy, *From Princely Autocracy to People's Government* (Bangalore: Sahitya Mandira, 1993), chapter 9.

26 Menon, *Integration of the Indian States*, pp. 153–4, 179.

27 See E. M. S. Namboodiripad, 'Princedom and Democracy', *New Age*, August 1956 (a review article on V. P. Menon's *Integration of the Indian States*).

28 Robert Trumbull, *As I See India* (London: Cassell and Co., 1952), pp. 76–7.

29 See speeches at Jaipur, Gwalior and Bikaner in *Time Only to Look Forward: Speeches of Rear Admiral The Earl Mountbatten of Burma, as Viceroy of India and Governor-General of the Dominion of India, 1947–8* (London: Nicholas Kaye, 1949), pp. 76–8, 91–3, 102–4.

30 These paragraphs summarize a story told over several hundred pages in Menon, *Integration of the Indian States*.

31 Menon to V. Shankar (private secretary to Vallabhbhai Patel), 9 August 1949, in G. M. Nandurkar, ed., *Sardar's Letters – Mostly Unknown: Post-Centenary*, vol. 2 (Ahmedabad: Sardar Vallabhbhai Patel Smarak Bhavan, 1981), pp. 74–6.

32 As told to me by C. S. Venkatachar, who succeeded V. P. Menon as secretary of the Ministry of States.

33 Hodson, *The Great Divide*, pp. 367–8.

34 The Travancore story has been principally reconstructed here from TOP, vol. 12, pp. 76–7, 203–4, 232–3, 281–2, 298–9, 335–6, 414, 421–2, 453; supplemented by A. Sreedhara Menon, *Triumph and Tragedy in Travancore: Annals of Sir C. P.'s Sixteen Years* (Kottayam: Current Books, 2001), esp. pp. 231–53. But see also A. G. Noorani, 'C. P. and Independent Travancore', *Frontline*, 4 July 2003, and K. C. George, *Immortal Punnapra-Vayalar* (Thiruvananthapuram: Communist Party of India, 1975).

35 The best, presumably, was Jawaharlal Nehru.

36 Draft letter dated 18 July 1947 from Nawab of Bhopal to Lord Mountbatten, Mss Eur D1006 (Major A. E. G. Davy Papers), OIOC.

37 My account of the Bhopal case is based on TOP, vol. 12, pp. 144–5, 291–7, 436–8, 644, 671–2; Copland, *The Princes of India*, pp. 235–6, 253; Hodson, *The Great Divide*, pp. 365, 375; Menon, *Integration of the Indian States*, pp. 118–19.

38 TOP, vol. 12, pp. 603–4, 659–62, 767; Menon, *Integration of the Indian States*, pp. 116–18; K. M. Pannikar to Vallabhbhai Patel, undated, but probably from late July 1947, in G. M. Nandurkar, ed., *Sardar's Letters – Mostly Unknown, II: Birth Centenary*, vol. 5 (Ahmedabad: Sardar Vallabhbhai Patel Smarak Bhavan, 1978), pp. 55–6.

39 R. M. Lala, 'Junagadh', the *Current*, 27 September 1950; Campbell-Johnson, *Mission with Mountbatten*, pp. 191–2; Mosley, *Last Days*, pp. 181–3.

40 Shah Nawaz was the father of Zulfiqar Ali Bhutto and grandfather of Benazir Bhutto, both future prime ministers of Pakistan.

41 Patel's feelings on Junagadh are described in Malcolm Darling to Guy Wint, 7 December 1947, Box 60, Darling Papers, CSAS.

42 'Report by Secretary, Ministry of States, on Junagadh', in SPC, vol. 7, pp. 688–95.

43 This account is principally based on Menon, *Integration of the Indian States*, pp. 124–49; Hodson, *The Great Divide*, pp. 427–40.

44 Rafi Ahmed, 'Hyderabad Politics', *Swatantra*, 29 November 1947.

45 K. M. Munshi, *The End of an Era (Hyderabad Memoirs)* (Bombay: Bharatiya Vidya Bhavan, 1957), pp. 10–11.

46 TOP, vol. 12, pp. 31–2, 87; 'Viswamitra', 'Monckton and Mountbatten', *Swatantra*, 15 May 1948.

47 Coupland, quoted in V. B. Kulkarni, *K. M. Munshi* (New Delhi: Publications Division, 1983), p. 117; Patel, quoted in Munshi, *End of an Era*, p. 1.

48 Lucien D. Benichou, *From Autocracy to Integration: Political Developments in Hyderabad State (1938–1948)* (Hyderabad: Orient Longman, 2000), esp. chapter 5.

49 Amit Kumar Gupta, *The Agrarian Drama: The Leftists and the Rural Poor in India, 1934–51* (New Delhi: Manohar, 1996), pp. 291–317, 412–22 etc.

50 See Swami Ramananda Tirtha, *Memoirs of Hyderabad Freedom Struggle* (Bombay: Popular Prakashan, 1967), pp. 181–2.

51 Benichou, *From Autocracy to Integration*, p. 178.

52 See TOP, vol. 12, pp. 613–15.

53 Benichou, *From Autocracy to Integration*, pp. 230, 235; 'Viswamitra', 'Monckton and Mountbatten'.

54 See TOP, vol. 12, p. 121.

55 Benichou, *From Autocracy to Integration*, pp. 208–10.

56 'Conflict in Hyderabad', *The Times*, April 1948, clipping in Theodore Tasker Papers, Mss Eur D798/30–36, OIOC.

57 Wilfrid Russell, *Indian Summer* (Bombay: Thacker and Co., 1951), p. 210.

58 C. H. V. Pathy, 'A Close-up of Syed Kasim Razvi', *Swatantra*, 29 May 1948.

59 A vivid account of the society and politics of Hyderabad, c. 1947–8, is contained in Asokamitran's novel *The Eighteenth Parallel*, translated from the Tamil by Gomathi Narayanan (Hyderabad: Orient Longman, 1993).

60 O. V. Ranga Rao, 'Exodus of C. P. Muslims to Hyderabad', *Swatantra*, 11 October 1947; Lanka Sundaram, 'Nizam's Acts of War and India's Duty', *Swatantra*, 1 November 1947.

61 S. Gopal, *Jawaharlal Nehru: A Biography*, vol. 2: *1947–1956* (London: Cape, 1979), pp. 40–1; SPC, vol. 5, pp. 236–9; SPC, vol. 7, pp. 150–1, 186–7, 194 etc.

62 See Mirza Ismail, *My Public Life: Recollections and Reflections* (London: George Allen and Unwin, 1954), pp. 105–28.

63 Quoted in Munshi, *End of an Era*, p. 176.

64 Ibid., pp. 230–1; Gandhi, *Patel*, pp. 482–3; Benichou, *From Autocracy to Integration*, pp. 236–7.

65 Sri Prakasa, *Pakistan: Birth and Early Days* (Meerut: Meenakshi Prakashan, 1965), p. 122.

66 Pattabhi Sitaramayya, 'The Hyderabad Tangle', *Swatantra*, 12 June 1948.

67 Abbas, 'Three Days in Hyderabad', *Swatantra*, 24 June 1950.

68 P. J. Griffiths, 'India and the Future', *The Nineteenth Century*, August 1947.

69 See editorial in the *Economic Weekly*, 8 January 1955.

70 *Democracy on the March* (New Delhi: Publications Division, 1950), pp. 1, 9–10 etc.

71 Menon, *Integration of the Indian States*, p. 493.

4. A VALLEY BLOODY AND BEAUTIFUL

1 For an overview, see Alastair Lamb, *Kashmir: A Disputed Legacy, 1846–1990* (Karachi: Oxford University Press, 1992).

2 Karan Singh, *Autobiography*, revised edn (Delhi: Oxford University Press, 1994), pp. 18–19.

3 Quoted in Ajit Bhattacharjea, *Kashmir: The Wounded Valley* (New Delhi: UBS, 1994), p. 67.

4 V. K. Chinnammalu Amma, 'Sheikh Muhammad Abdullah', *Swatantra*, 22 May 1948; Trilok Nath Moza, 'Sher-i-Kashmir Sheikh Abdullah', *Swatantra*, 5 June 1948.

5 These paragraphs on Kashmir politics in the 1930s and 1940s draw largely from Bhattacharjea, *Kashmir*, pp. 65–76, and Lamb, *Kashmir*, pp. 89–95.

6 Malika Pukhraj, *Song Sung True: A Memoir*, ed. and trans. Saleem Kidwai (New Delhi: Kali for Women, 2003), pp. 200–1.

7 S. Gopal, *Jawaharlal Nehru: A Biography*, vol. 1: *1889–1947* (London: Cape, 1975), pp. 322–3.

8 SPC, vol. 1, pp. 13–15.

9 TOP, vol. 9, p. 71.

10 SPC, vol. 1, pp. 29–30; Hasan Zaheer, *The Times and Trials of the Rawalpindi Conspiracy, 1951: the First Coup Attempt in Pakistan* (Karachi: Oxford University Press, 1998), pp. 72–3.

11 Mountbatten to Sir Akbar Hydari (governor of Assam), 17 June 1947, Mountbatten Papers, Mss Eur F200/13, OIOC.

12 See Ramchandra Kak's note, 'Jammu and Kashmir in 1946–47', written in 1960 as a retrospective defence of the idea of independence. Copy in R. Powell Papers, Mss Eur D862, OIOC.

13 TOP, vol. 11, p. 592.

14 TOP, vol. 12, pp. 3–5, 368.

15 D. G. Tendulkar, *Mahatma: Life of Mohandas Karamchand Gandhi*, 2nd edn (1963; reprint New Delhi: Publications Division, 1990), vol. 8, pp. 67–8.

16 Michael Brecher, *The Struggle for Kashmir* (New York: Oxford University Press, 1953), pp. 23–4.

17 Rajmohan Gandhi, *Patel: A Life* (Ahmedabad: Navjivan Press, 1991), p. 439.

18 SPC, vol. 1, pp. 45–7.

19 See Josef Korbel, *Danger in Kashmir*, 2nd edn (Princeton: Princeton University Press, 1966), pp. 70–1.

20 SPC, vol. 1, pp. 56, 62.

21 Quoted in Prem Shankar Jha, *Kashmir, 1947: Rival Versions of History* (Delhi: Oxford University Press, 1998), pp. 32–3.

22 R. B. Batra, quoted in Sisir Kumar Gupta, *Kashmir: A Study in India–Pakistan Relations* (Bombay: Asia Publishing House, 1966), p. 106.

23 Lamb's *Kashmir: A Disputed Legacy* is the best case for Pakistan; Jha's *Kashmir, 1947* an answer from the Indian point of view.

24 See Richard Symons, *In the Margins of Independence: A Relief Worker in India and Pakistan, 1942–1949* (Karachi: Oxford University Press, 2001), pp. 78–9.

25 This and the next few paragraphs are based on Lamb, *Kashmir: A Disputed Legacy*, pp. 122–34; Brecher, *Struggle for Kashmir*, pp. 25–33; Gupta, *Kashmir*, pp. 110–15; Zaheer, *Rawalpindi Conspiracy*, pp. 82–7, 94–6 etc.

26 Lt. Gen. L. P. Sen, *Slender was the Thread: Kashmir Confrontation, 1947–48* (New Delhi: Orient Longman, 1969), pp. 34–8.

27 Stanley Wolpert, *Jinnah of Pakistan* (New York: Oxford University Press, 1984), p. 348.

28 Untitled typescript dated 3 November 1947 by Major J. E. Thomson, Powell Papers, Mss Eur D862, OIOC; extracts from report in *Daily Express*, 11 November 1947, in *White Paper on Jammu and Kashmir* (New Delhi: Government of India, 1948), pp. 24–5.

29 Lamb, *Kashmir: A Disputed Legacy*, p. 143.

30 Amar Devi Gupta, 'A 1947 Tragedy of Jammu and Kashmir State: The Cleansing of Mirpur', Mss Eur C705, OIOC.

31 Lord Birdwood, 'Kashmir', *International Affairs*, July 1952.

32 See the eyewitness accounts reproduced in Dewan Ram Prakash, *Fight for Kashmir* (New Delhi: Tagore Memorial Publications, 1948), pp. 34–9.

33 This account is based on V. P. Menon, *Integration of the Indian States* (1956; reprint Hyderabad: Orient Longman, 1997), pp. 397–400; Gandhi, *Patel*, pp. 442–4. However, Prem Shankar Jha (*Kashmir, 1947*, pp. 63–4) claims that the Instrument of Accession was signed by Maharaja Hari Singh in Srinagar on the night of the 25th/26th itself, that is before he fled to Jammu.

34 S. N. Prasad and Dharm Pal, *History of Operations in Jammu and Kashmir (1947–48)* (New Delhi: Ministry of Defence, 1987), pp. 28f., 379.

35 Major L. E. R. B. Ferris, quoted in Lt. Col. Maurice Cohen, *Thunder over Kashmir* (1955; reprint Hyderabad: Orient Longman, 1994), pp. 3–4.

36 Nehru to Vijayalakshmi Pandit, 28 October 1947, Vijayalakshmi Pandit Papers, Nehru Memorial Museum and Library, New Delhi (hereafter NMML).

37 As told by the veteran Punjab politician Khizr Hyat Tiwana to the ex-Punjab civil servant Malcolm Darling. See diary note of 9 January 1948, Box 60, Darling Papers, CSAS.

38 Baroo, 'Kashmir Interlude', *Swatantra*, 29 November 1947.

39 Bhattacharjea, *Kashmir*, pp. x–xii.

40 Lord Mountbatten, 'Note of a Discussion with Mr Jinnah in the presence of Lord Ismay at Government House, Lahore, on 1 November 1947', in SPC, vol. 1, pp. 73–81.

41 Prasad and Pal, *History of Operations*, pp. 39–40.

42 Ibid., p. 60; Sen, *Slender was the Thread*, pp. 111–12.

43 Nehru to Hari Singh, 13 November 1947, in S. Gopal, general ed., *Selected Works of Jawaharlal Nehru: Second Series* (New Delhi: Nehru Memorial Fund, 1984–), hereafter SWJN2, vol. 5, pp. 324–7.

44 CWMG, vol. 90, pp. 122–3.

45 C. Dasgupta, *War and Diplomacy in Kashmir, 1947–8* (New Delhi: Sage Publications, 2002), p. 78.

46 Nehru to Hari Singh, 1 December 1947, in SPC, vol. 1, pp. 100–6.

47 H. V. Hodson, *The Great Divide: Britain–India–Pakistan* (London: Hutchinson, 1969), pp. 466–7; Lamb, *Kashmir: A Disputed Legacy*, pp. 164–5.

48 Brecher, *Struggle for Kashmir*, pp. 55–75; *Reports of the United Nations Special Commission for India and Pakistan, June 1948 to December 1949* (New Delhi: Ministry of External Affairs, 1950), pp. 53f., 281f.

49 Josef Korbel, *Danger in Kashmir* (1954; revised edition Princeton: Princeton University Press, 1966), p. 109.

50 S. Gopal, *Jawaharlal Nehru: A Biography*, vol. 2: *1947–1956* (London: Cape, 1979), pp. 26–7; Dasgupta, *War and Diplomacy*, pp. 17, 111, 134. Cf. also Rajbans Krishen, *Kashmir and the Conspiracy against Peace* (Bombay: People's Publishing House, 1951).

51 H. V. Hodson to Philip Noel-Baker, 2 March 1948, copy in Short Papers, Mss Eur F189/1, OIOC.

52 See Hodson, *The Great Divide*, pp. 469–70.

53 Untitled note by Major General T. W. Rees, Rees Papers, Mss Eur F274/72, OIOC.

54 Dasgupta, *War and Diplomacy*, pp. 144–51, 167–8, 177–83.

55 Air Chief Marshal P. C. Lal, *My Years with the IAF* (New Delhi: Lancer International, 1987), pp. 58–67.

56 Sen, *Slender was the Thread*, p. 242; Prasad and Pal, *History of Operations*, pp. 276–7.

57 Penderel Moon to Major Billy Short, 18 October 1948, Short Papers, Mss Eur F189/22, OIOC, emphasis added.

58 Korbel, *Danger in Kashmir*, pp. 146–9. Korbel was the father of Madeleine Albright, who was to herself deal with the Kashmir question in the 1990s when she was secretary of state in President Clinton's administration.

59 See material in File 74, C. Rajagopalachari Papers, Fifth Instalment, NMML.

60 *Swatantra*, 14 August 1948.

61 Anon., 'South India and Kashmir', *Swatantra*, 25 February 1950.

62 Sheikh Abdullah to C. Rajagopalachari, 27 April 1948, C. Rajagopalachari Papers, Fifth Instalment, NMML.

63 J. K. Banerji, *I Report on Kashmir* (Calcutta: The Republic Publications, 1948), pp. 9–10.

64 Y. D. Gundevia, ed., *The Testament of Sheikh Abdullah* (Dehra Dun: Palit and Palit, 1974), pp. 90–1.

65 V. V. Prasad, 'New Delhi Diary', *Swatantra*, 9 October 1948.

66 P. N. Kaula and K. L. Dhar, *Kashmir Speaks* (Delhi: S. Chand and Co., 1950), p. 71.

67 K. A. Abbas, 'The Enchanted Valley', *Swatantra*, 23 April 1949.

68 'Marching through Kashmir', *Time*, 10 October 1949.

69 Korbel, *Danger in Kashmir*, p. 25.

70 Kingsley Martin, 'Kashmir and UNO', and 'As Pakistan Sees it', *The New Statesman and Nation*, 21 and 28 February 1948.

71 Quoted in Dewan Ram Parkash, *Fight for Kashmir* (New Delhi: Tagore Memorial Publications, 1948), p. 99.

72 A. Lakshmana Rao, 'Brigadier Usman', *Swatantra*, 10 July 1948.

73 Parkash, *Fight for Kashmir*, p. 174.

74 K. A. Abbas, 'Will Kashmir Vote for India?', the *Current*, 26 October 1949.

75 Wares Ishaq, 'Kashmir Will Vote for Pakistan', the *Current*, 2 November 1949.

76 Representative here are the interpretations in Dasgupta, *War and Diplomacy*.

77 On Gurdaspur see Lamb, *Kashmir: A Disputed Legacy*, esp. pp. 115–16; and, for a rebuttal, Jha, *Kashmir, 1947*, p. 81.

78 Zaheer, *Rawalpindi Conspiracy*, pp. 144–5.

79 The quotes that follow are taken from Brecher, *Struggle for Kashmir*, pp. ix–x.

5. REFUGEES AND THE REPUBLIC

1 Donald F. Ebright, *Free India, the First Five Years: An Account of the 1947 Riots, Refugees, Relief and Rehabilitation* (Nashville: Parthenon Press, 1954), pp. 46–7, 62–3 etc.

2 A. N. Bali, *Now it Can be Told* (Jullundur: The Kashvani Prakashan Ltd, 1949), esp. chapter 9.

3 V. V. Prasad, 'New Delhi Diary', *Swatantra*, 25 December 1947.

4 This account is principally based on M. S. Randhawa, *Out of the Ashes: An Account of the Rehabilitation of Refugees from West Punjab in Rural Areas of East Punjab* (Bombay: privately published, 1954); and Gyanesh Kudaisya, 'The Demographic Upheaval of Partition: Refugees and Agricultural Resettlement in India, 1947–67', *South Asia*, vol. 18, no. 1, 1995.

   Of the roughly 2.5 million farmers who came from West Punjab about 80 % were resettled in East Punjab. Others were given land in the Ganganagar area of the former Bikaner state, and in the Terai regions of Uttar Pradesh. In both places there are now flourishing communities of Sikh farmers.

5 Ian Stephen, 'A Day in Qadian', *The Statesman*, 9 January 1949. Mohammad Zafrullah Khan, Pakistan's eloquent spokesman in the UN on the Kashmir question, was an Ahmadiya. So was the physicist Abdus Salam, the only Pakistani to be awarded a Nobel Prize. In the 1980s, under the regime of General Zia-ul-Haq, the Ahmadiyas were declared as heretics (for their belief in a living Prophet), and have since faced discrimination and persecution.

6 See L. C. Jain, *The City of Hope: The Faridabad Story* (New Delhi: Concept Publishing Co., 1998), which also describes the corrosion of the co-operative spirit by the bureaucracy. See also 'Experiments in Living: Faridabad–Nilokheri–Etawah', *The Times of India*, 14 February 1952.

7 Dorothy Jane Ward, *India for the Indians* (London: Arthur Barker Ltd, 1949), pp. 187–9.

8 See V. N. Dutta, 'Punjabi Refugees and the Urban Development of Greater Delhi', in R. E. Frykenberg, ed., *Delhi through the Ages* (Delhi: Oxford University Press, 1993).

9 Anon., 'A Glimpse into Crowded Bombay', *Swatantra*, 7 August 1948.

10 H. L. Mansukhani, 'The Resettlement of Sind Refugees', *Swatantra*, 11 September 1948.

11 Anon., 'A Glimpse into Crowded Bombay'.

12 R. M. Lala, 'Kolwada: Landmark of Swaraj', the *Current*, 3 May 1950.

13 Gardner Murphy, *In the Minds of Men: The Study of Human Behavior and Social Tensions in India* (New York: Basic Books, 1953), pp. 170–5.

14 Taya Zinkin, *Reporting India* (London: Chatto and Windus, 1962), pp. 25–6, 31.

15 Prafulla K. Chakrabarti, *The Marginal Men: The Refugees and the Left Political Syndrome in West Bengal* (Calcutta: Naya Udyog, 1999), p. 33.

16 Joya Chatterji, 'Right or Charity? The Debate over Relief and Rehabilitation in West Bengal, 1947–50', in Suvir Kaul, ed., *The Partitions of Memory: The Afterlife of the Division of India* (Delhi: Permanent Black, 2001), p. 99.

17 Sir Jadunath Sarkar, 'Brothers from over the River: The Refugee Problem of India', *The Modern Review*, September 1948.

18 Chakrabarti, *Marginal Men*, chapter 3.

19 See letters and statements of 1948–50 in Voice of New India, *A Tale of Woes of East Pakistan Minorities* (Calcutta: D. R. Sen, 1966), pp. 13–51.

20 The *Current*, 4 February 1953.

21 'Squatters' Colonies', *Economic Weekly*, 5 June 1954.

22 See undated memorandum (c. 1954?) in File 6, Meghnad Saha Papers, Seventh Instalment, NMML.

23 See 'Report of a Tour of Inspection of some of the Refugee Homes in North-west India' (1955), reproduced in *Seminar*, no. 510, February 2002.

24 'Congress may Lose West Bengal – if Refugees Remain Unsettled', *Economic Weekly*, 10 July 1954.

    There is now a growing literature of memoirs written (or spoken) by Bengali refugees. For a sampling of works in English, see Jasodhara Bagchi and Subhoranjan Dasgupta, eds, *The Trauma and the Triumph: Gender and Partition in Eastern India* (Kolkata: Stree, 2003); Gargi Chakravartty, *Coming out of Partition: Refugee Women of Bengal* (New Delhi: Bluejay Books, 2005); Manas Ray, 'Growing Up Refugee', *History Workshop Journal*, no. 53, 2002.

25 See R. M. Lala, 'Refugees', the *Current*, 29 March 1950.

26 SWJN2, vol. 4, pp. 115–17. (The original broadcast was in Hindi.)

27 Aparna Basu, *Mridula Sarabhai: Rebel with a Cause* (Delhi: Oxford University Press, 1996), chapter 8.

28 Ritu Menon and Kamla Bhasin, *Borders and Boundaries: Women in India's Partition* (New Delhi: Kali for Women), pp. 91–3, 97–8. Cf. also Urvashi Butalia, *The Other Side of Silence: Voices from the Partition of India* (New Delhi: Viking, 1998), chapter 4.

29 See Chitra Bhanu, 'Food Situation Getting Worse in Malabar', *Swatantra*, 29 July 1947; 'Famine Conditions in East Godavari', *Swatantra*, 4 October 1947; P. V. C. Rao, 'The Food Debacle' and 'Lesson of Gujerat Famine', *Swatantra*, 7 August 1948 and 12 February 1949.

30 Clare and Harris Wofford, *India Afire* (New York: The John Day Co., 1951), pp. 105–6, 113–15; 'Communists in Hyderabad', *Swatantra*, 28 May 1949.

31 Ananth Rao Kanangi, 'Communists in Andhra', the *Current*, 3 May 1950.

32 Quoted in John H. Kautsky, *Moscow and the Communist Party of India* (New York: John Wiley and Sons, 1956), p. 49.

33 G. S. Bhargava, 'Balchandra Triambak Ranadive', *Swatantra*, 22 April 1950.

34 D. Jayakanthan, *A Literary Man's Political Experiences*, trans. M. S. Venkataramani (New Delhi: Vikas Publishing House, 1976), pp. 19–22.

35 Gene D. Overstreet and Marshall Windmiller, *Communism in India* (Berkeley: University of California Press, 1959), chapter 13.

36 Quoted in M. R. Masani, *The Communist Party of India: A Short History* (Bombay: Bhavan's Book University, 1967), pp. 78–9.

37 *Pravda*, 25 November 1949, quoted in Mahavir Singh, *Soviet View of the Indian National Congress* (New Delhi: Sanchar Publishing House, 1991), p. 22.

38 Penderel Moon to his father, 5 February 1949, Moon Papers, Mss Eur F230/23, OIOC.

39 Anon., 'Rounding up of Communists in Hyderabad', *Swatantra*, 4 June 1949; Wofford and Wofford, *India Afire*, pp. 118–19.

40 Amit Kumar Gupta, *The Agrarian Drama: The Leftists and the Rural Poor in India, 1934–51* (New Delhi: Manohar, 1996), pp. 464–5.

41 SWJN2, vol. 4, pp. 52–3.

42 See correspondence in G. M. Nandurkar, *Sardar's Letters – Mostly Unknown – Post-Centenary*, vol. 2 (Ahmedabad: Sardar Patel Smarak Bhavan, 1981), pp. 20–2, and vol. 3 (1983), pp. 42–3.

43 Baroo, 'Enter the Sangh', *Swatantra*, 10 September 1949. For a sympathetic contemporary portrait of the RSS, see Jagat S. Bright, *Guruji Golwalkar and R.S.S.* (Delhi: New India Publishing Co., 1951).

44 Letter quoted in the *Current*, 19 October 1949.

45 N. S. Muthana, 'Golwalkar's Climb on Congress Ladder', the *Current*, 9 November 1949.

46 News report in the *Current*, 16 November 1949.

47 Dewan Chaman Lall, quoted in Tai Yong Tan and Gyanesh Kudesia, *The Aftermath of Partition in South Asia* (London: Routledge, 2000).

48 R. G. Casey, *An Australian in India* (London: Hollis and Carter, 1947), p. 114.

49 Albert Mayer, *Pilot Project, India: The Story of Rural Development at Etawah, Uttar Pradesh* (Berkeley: University of California Press, 1958), p. 13.

6. IDEAS OF INDIA

1 *Hindustan Times*, 10 and 11 December 1946.

2 In the description of the independent Anglo-Indian member, Frank Anthony. *Constituent Assembly Debates: Official Report* (reprint New Delhi: Lok Sabha Secretariat, 1988), hereafter cited as CAD, vol. 8, p. 329.

3 K. Santhanam, quoted in Granville Austin, *The Indian Constitution: Cornerstone of a Nation* (1966; reprint New Delhi: Oxford University Press, 2002), p. 13. The varied ideologies and political trends represented in the Assembly are discussed in S. K. Chaube, *Constituent Assembly of India: Springboard of Revolution*, 2nd edn (New Delhi: Manohar, 2000), esp. chapters 8 to 10.

4 Winston Churchill quoted in CAD, vol. 2, pp. 267, 271.

5 See 'Summary of representations received in office regarding "Rights of Minorities" ', in File 37, C. Rajagopalachari Papers, Fifth Instalment, NMML.

6 Austin, *The Indian Constitution*, p. 71.

7 CAD, vol. 1, pp. 59–61. That Nehru would mention the Soviet Revolution alongside the other two may be considered by some characteristic of his broadmindedness, by others as characteristic merely of his lack of discrimination.

8 See CAD, vol. 4, pp. 737–62.

9 Cf. Austin, *The Indian Constitution*, pp. 314–15.

10 The words are those of Ambedkar. See CAD, vol. 9, p. 974. The contributions of Munshi, Aiyar and Rau to the making of the Indian Constitution were immense. They prepared dozens of notes and minutes on specific subjects, the more important of which are reproduced in B. Shiva Rao, ed., *The Framing of India's Constitution: Select Documents*, 4 vols (New Delhi: Indian Institute of Public Administration, 1968). On K. M. Munshi's role, see also N. H. Bhagwati, 'An Architect of the Constitution', in *Munshi at Seventy-Five* (Bombay: Dr K. M. Munshi's 76th Birthday Celebration Committee, 1962).

11 In the preface to the 1999 edition of his book, Austin amends this slightly, speaking of unity, social revolution and democracy as 'the three strands of a seamless web'. Austin's work is indispensable, but see also the long critique by Upendra Baxi, '"The Little Done, the Vast Undone" – Some Reflections on Reading Granville Austin's *The Indian Constitution*', *Journal of the Indian Law Institute*, vol. 9, 1967, pp. 323–430.

12 CAD, vol. 7, p. 39.

13 Ibid., vol. 7, pp. 219, 285, 350, 387 etc.

14 Ibid., vol. 7, p. 305.

15 For a good discussion of how this choice was made, see E. Sridharan, 'The Origins of the Electoral System', in Zoya Hasan, E. Sridharan and R. Sudarshan, eds, *India's Living Constitution* (New Delhi: Permanent Black, 2002). See also 'Report by the Constitutional Adviser on his Visit to U.S.A., Canada, Ireland and England', in Shiva Rao, *Select Documents*, vol. 3, pp. 217–26.

16 Nehru, quoted in Austin, *The Indian Constitution*, p. 121.

17 The phrase is Granville Austin's. See *The Indian Constitution*, p. 50.

18 An excellent discussion of the framing of the fundamental rights section is contained in B. Shiva Rao, ed., *The Framing of India's Constitution: A Study* (New Delhi: Indian Institute of Public Administration, 1968), chapter 7.

19 Austin, *The Indian Constitution*, p. 56.

20 CAD, vol. 4, p. 769.

21 CAD, vol. 11, pp. 711–13.

22 CAD, vol. 7, p. 360.

23 CAD, vol. 11, p. 616.

24 Intervention by Shibban Lal Saxena, CAD, vol. 11, pp. 705–6.

25 Ibid., p. 212.

26 Interventions by Loknath Misra and K. Hanumanthaiya, CAD, vol. 11, pp. 799, 617.

27 CAD, vol. 5, pp. 54–5.

28 Intervention by Balkrishna Sharma, CAD, vol. 5, pp. 74–6.

29 Speech of 17 December 1946, CAD, vol. 1, p. 102.

30 CAD, vol. 4, p. 546.

31 Ibid., vol. 4, p. 859.

32 CAD, vol. 5, pp. 211–13.

33 Ibid., vol. 5, p. 271.

34 CAD, vol. 7, p. 306; CAD, vol. 8, p. 300.

35 Intervention by Naziruddin Ahmad, CAD, vol. 8, pp. 296–7.

36 CAD, vol. 1, p. 138.

37 CAD, vol. 4, p. 668.

38 CAD, vol. 7, p. 356.

39 CAD, vol. 5, pp. 202–3; vol. 11, pp. 608–9.

40 CAD, vol. 9, p. 667–9.

41 Intervention by Brajeshwar Prasad, CAD, vol. 10, p. 239.

42 CAD, vol. 8, pp. 344–5.

43 CAD, vol. 5, p. 210.

44 Regrettably, there is no biography of Jaipal Singh. See, however, P. G. Ganguly, 'Separatism in the Indian Polity: A Case Study', in M. C. Pradhan et al., eds, *Anthropology and Archaeology: Essays in Commemoration of Verrier Elwin* (Bombay: Oxford University Press, 1969).

45 CAD, vol. 1, pp. 143–4.

46 CAD, vol. 7, pp. 559–60.

47 Intervention by Brajeshwar Prasad, CAD, vol. 9, p. 281.

48 CAD, vol. 1, pp. 26–7.

49 *Hindustan Times*, 11 December 1946.

50 CAD, vol. 8, p. 745.

51 CAD, vol. 7, pp. 20–31.

52 See Suniti Kumar Chatterji, *Languages and the Linguistic Problem*, Oxford Pamphlet on Indian Affairs, no. 11 (Bombay: Oxford University Press, 1943); Alok Rai, *Hindi Nationalism* (Hyderabad: Orient Longman, 2000).

53 Nehru, 'The Question of Language', in his *The Unity of India: Collected Writings, 1937–1940* (London: Lindsay Drummond, 1941), pp. 241–61.

54 Letter to Krishnachandra, 12 May 1945, in CWMG, vol. 80, p. 117.

55 See letters in CWMG, vol. 80, pp. 181, 317–18; vol. 81, pp. 33–4, 332.

56 Austin, *The Indian Constitution*, p. 267.

57 Cf. interventions by B. Pocker Sahib Bahadur and Jaipal Singh, CAD, vol. 4, pp. 553, 554.

58 CAD, vol. 7, p. 235.

59 Article 343 of the Constitution of India.

60 This section is based on Ambedkar's last speech to the Constituent Assembly – CAD, vol. 11, pp. 972–81.

61 John W. Dower, *Embracing Defeat: Japan in the Wake of World War II* (New York: W. W. Norton and Co., 1999), p. 347. The making of the Japanese constitution is discussed in chapters 12 and 13.

62 Courtney Whitney, quoted ibid., p. 373.

63 Austin, *The Indian Constitution*, pp. 308, 309–10, 328.

7. The Biggest Gamble in History

1 'Vignhneswara' (V. Raghunathan), *Sotto Voce: A Social and Political Commentary*, vol. 1: *The Coming of Freedom* (Madras: B. G. Paul and Co., 1951), p. 203.

2 Quoted in the *Current*, 18 July 1951.

3 'Disintegration of the Congress', the *Current*, 9 May 1951.

4 See S. H. Desai, 'Sardar Patel', the *Current*, 14 August 1948; A. S. Iyengar, *All Through the Gandhian Era: Reminiscences* (Bombay: Hind Kitabs Ltd, 1950), pp. 289–95 (section titled 'Nehru and Patel'); V. Shankar, *My Reminiscences of Sardar Patel*, vol. 2 (New Delhi: Macmillan, 1975), pp. 20–3.

5 Prasad had a greater following than Rajaji because he was a Hindi speaker from
   north India (like the majority of Congress politicians at the time) and because,
   unlike Rajaji, he had actively participated in the Quit India movement of 1942.
   See Rajmohan Gandhi, *The Rajaji Story, 1937–1972* (Bombay: Bharatiya Vidya
   Bhavan, 1984), pp. 190–4.
6 The *Statesman*, 26 January 1950. Left-wing critics complained of the pageantry,
   saying it was a colonial hangover. They were reminded that 'pomp and
   pageantry were Indian before they became British, and the British used them
   because they understood the Indian mentality'. See 'Shridharani in Delhi',
   Swatantra, 8 January 1950.
7 The verdicts, respectively, of Michael Brecher, *Nehru: A Political Biography* (London:
   Oxford University Press, 1959), p. 43; K. A. Abbas, 'Rajarshi Tandon – the New
   President', *Swatantra*, 9 September 1950; the *Current*, 13 September 1950.
8 Nehru to Rajagopalachari, letters of 26 and 27 August 1950, File 189,
   C. Rajagopalachari Papers, Fifth Instalment, NMML.
9 Nehru, 'Statement to the Press', 13 September 1950, copy in File 24,
   C. Rajagopalachari Papers, Fifth Instalment, NMML. I have failed to locate this
   statement in any volume of Nehru's selected works.
10 Letter of 28 March 1950, in SPC, vol. 10, p. 19.
11 Rajmohan Gandhi, *Patel: A Life* (Ahmedabad: Navjivan Press, 1991), pp. 526–7.
12 S. Gopal, *Jawaharlal Nehru: A Biography*, vol. 2: *1947–1956* (London: Cape, 1979),
   p. 309.
13 Gandhi, *Patel*, p. 530.
14 'Vallabhbhai Patel', in S. Gopal and Uma Iyengar, eds, *The Essential Writings of
   Jawaharlal Nehru*, vol. 1 (New Delhi: Oxford University Press, 2003), p. 633.
15 Gopal, *Nehru*, vol. 2, p. 155.
16 See K. Mukherjee, 'The Resurrection of Somnath', *Indian Review*, July 1951.
17 Nehru to Rajendra Prasad, 2 March 1951, copy in Subject File 46,
   C. Rajagopalachari Papers, Fourth Instalment, NMML.
18 Speech in Hindi at Somnath, 11 May 1951, in Valmiki Choudhary, ed., *Dr Rajendra
   Prasad: Correspondence and Select Documents*, vol. 14 (New Delhi: Allied Publishers,
   1991). I am grateful to Professor Bhagwan Josh of Jawaharlal Nehru University for
   this reference. This and other translations from the Hindi in this book are mine.
19 Editorial in *Swatantra*, 8 September 1951.
20 Gopal, *Nehru*, vol. 2, p. 155.
21 Richard L. Park, 'India's General Election', *Far Eastern Survey*, 9 January 1952.
22 This description of the mechanics of the election is based on Sukumar Sen, *Report
   on the First General Elections in India, 1951–52* (New Delhi: Election Commission,
   1955); supplemented by Park, 'India's General Election'; and Irene Tinker and
   Mil Walker, 'The First General Elections in India and Indonesia', *Far Eastern
   Survey*, July 1956.
23 *The Times of India* (Bombay – hereafter TOI), 5 November 1951.
24 See, for example, Asoka Mehta, *The Political Mind of India* (Bombay: Socialist
   Party, 1952).
25 News report in the *Searchlight* (Patna), 22 November 1951.
26 See Craig Baxter, *The Jana Sangh: A Biography of an Indian Political Party* (Bombay:
   Oxford University Press, 1971), pp. 87–8 etc.

27 Reports in *Hindustan Times* (Delhi – hereafter HT); 12 October 1951; TOI, 9 November 1951; Mehta, *The Political Mind*, p. 61.

28 TOI, 9 November 1951; Manikuntala Sen, *In Search of Freedom: An Unfinished Journey* (Calcutta: STREE, 2001), pp. 220–1; Ravi Narayan Reddy, *Heroic Telengana: Reminiscences and Experiences* (New Delhi: Communist Party of India), pp. 71–2.

29 Lord Birdwood, *A Continent Decides* (London: Robert Hale, 1953), p. 103; TOI, 22 January 1952 (news report headline 'Bovine Election Propaganda').

30 TOI, 1 January 1952.

31 S. Borzenko, 'Before the Elections in India', originally published in *Pravda*, 25 October 1951, translated in *Swatantra*, 1 December 1951.

32 Park, 'India's General Election'.

33 Prakash, 'Lalaji', *Shankar's Weekly*, 6 January 1952.

34 This and the following paragraphs on Nehru's all-India election tour are based on newspaper reports in TOI and HT, supplemented by Anon., *The Pilgrimage and After: The Story of how the Congress Fought and Won the General Elections* (New Delhi: All-India Congress Committee, 1952).

35 See Ajit Bhattacharjea, *J.P.: His Biography* (New Delhi: Orient Longman, 1975), pp. 254, 256. Mrs Gandhi based her allegations on the fact that one socialist leader, Ram Manohar Lohia, had recently returned from a speaking tour in the United States, while another, Jayaprakash Narayan, had once studied in that country.

36 Frank Moraes, *Jawaharlal Nehru: A Biography* (New York: Macmillan, 1956), p. 413.

37 Anon., *The Pilgrimage and After*, p. 23.

38 D. F. Karaka, *Nehru: The Lotus Eater from Kashmir* (London: Derek Verschoyle, 1953), pp. 96–8.

39 Nehru to Lady Mountbatten, 3 December 1951, quoted in Gopal, *Nehru*, vol. 2, p. 161.

40 This account of voting and voter behaviour is largely based on contemporary newspaper accounts, especially in TOI and HT.

41 HT, 26 October 1951.

42 Irene Tinker Walker, 'The General Election in Himachal Pradesh, India, 1951', *Parliamentary Affairs*, vol. 6, no. 3, summer 1953.

43 'General Elections', lead edit, *Economic Weekly*, 5 January 1952.

44 Jean Lyon, *Just Half a World Away: My Search for the New India* (London: Hutchinson, 1955), pp. 125–30.

45 Sen, *Report on the First General Elections*, p. 135.

46 Personal communication from Professor Rajen Harshe of Hyderabad University, 21 May 2002.

47 Park, 'India's General Election'.

48 C. R. Srinivasan, 'The Elections Are On', *Indian Review*, January 1952, emphasis added.

49 Clare Woodford and Harris Woodford, Jr., *India Afire* (New York: John Day, 1951), p. 25.

50 Letter in Mss Eur F230/26, OIOC.

51 *Organiser*, 7 January 1952, quoted in Margaret W. Fisher and Joan V. Bondurant, eds, *The Indian Experience with Democratic Elections*, Indian Press Digests, University of California, Berkeley, no. 3, December 1956, p. 60.

52 The *Tribune* (Ambala), 22 December 1951, and the *Hitavada*, 30 December 1951, both quoted ibid., pp. 56–7, 58.

53 This paragraph is based on press reports quoted ibid., pp. 61f; Nehru's remarks are quoted in W. H. Morris-Jones, 'The Indian Elections', *Economic Weekly*, 28 June and 5 July 1952.

54 Chester Bowles, *Ambassador's Report* (New York: Harper and Brothers, 1954), chapter 11.

55 Ahmed Emin Yalman, editor, *Daily Vatan* (Istanbul), writing in TOI, 21 February 1951.

56 D. P. Mukerji, 'First Fruits of General Elections', *Economic Weekly*, 26 January 1952.

57 Jawaharlal Nehru, *An Autobiography: With Musings on Recent Events in India* (1936; reprint London: The Bodley Head, 1949), p. 598 (quote taken from the postscript dated Badenweiler, 25 October 1935).

8. Home and the World

1 Nirad C. Chaudhuri, 'After Nehru, Who?', *Illustrated Weekly of India*, 10 May 1953.

2 Arthur Lall, *The Emergence of Modern India* (New York: Columbia University Press, 1981), p. 128. Lall was a high-ranking member of the Indian Foreign Service and had worked closely with Nehru.

3 The autobiography was Nehru's second book-length work. The first, whose title (*Glimpses of World History*) is testimony to his global outlook, was written initially as a series of letters to his daughter from jail. His third major book was published in 1946; its title is revealing – it was called *The Discovery of India*, suggesting that perhaps this man was an internationalist well before he became a patriot, that he had discovered the world before he had discovered India.

4 'Peace and Empire', in Jawaharlal Nehru, *Peace and India* (London: The India League, 1938).

5 See Nehru to S. K. Datta, letters of 20 June 1939 and 24 December 1941, Datta Papers, Mss Eur F178/28, OIOC.

6 See Jawaharlal Nehru, *India's Foreign Policy: Selected Speeches, September 1946–April 1961* (New Delhi: Publications Division, 1961), pp. 3, 24, 28–9, 31–2. It is important to remember here that Nehru wrote his speeches himself.

7 Quoted in K. P. S. Menon, 'India and the Soviet Union', in B. R. Nanda, ed., *Indian Foreign Policy: The Nehru Years* (Delhi: Vikas Publishing House, 1976), p. 134.

8 James Cameron, *Point of Departure* (London: Arthur Barker, 1967), p. 247.

9 *Asian Relations: Being a Report of the Proceedings and Documentation of the First Asian Relations Conference, New Delhi, March–April 1947* (New Delhi: Asian Relations Organization, 1948).

10 Quoted in Parsa Venkateshwar Rao, Jr., 'The Misty Origins of NAM', *New Sunday Indian Express*, 26 January 2003.

11 CWMG, vol. 87, pp. 190–3.

12 Quoted in 'The Asian Conference, 1947', in Diana Mansergh, ed., *Independence Years: The Selected Indian and Commonwealth Papers of Nicholas Mansergh* (New Delhi: Oxford University Press, 1999), p. 81.

13 Nehru, *Glimpses of World History* (1934; revised edition London: Lindsay Drummond, 1949), p. 930.

14 *Time*, 17 October 1949.

15 P. P. Kumaramangalam to C. Rajagopalachari, 22 December 1947, in File 82, Fifth Instalment, C. Rajagopalachari Papers, NMML. Kumaramangalam went on to become chief of army staff, the highest-ranking military officer in India.

16 Harold Isaac, *Images of Asia: American Views of China and India* (1958; new edition New York, Harper and Row, 1972), esp. Part III.

17 Quoted in S. Gopal, *Jawaharlal Nehru: A Biography*, vol. 2: *1947–1956* (London: Cape, 1979), p. 59.

18 These speeches are reproduced in Jawaharlal Nehru, *Visit to America* (New York: John Day, 1950).

19 Quoted in J. J. Singh, 'The Triumph of Nehru', *Indian Review*, January 1950.

20 See Gopal, *Nehru*, vol. 2, p. 61.

21 *Time*, 14 November 1949.

22 Acheson, *Present at the Creation: My Years in the State Department* (London: Hamish Hamilton, 1970), pp. 334–6.

23 Cf. Vijayalakshmi Pandit's comments on Dean Acheson in her *The Scope of Happiness: A Personal Memoir* (New Delhi: Orient Paperbacks, 1981), pp. 235–6.

24 Chester Bowles, *Ambassador's Report* (New York: Harper and Brothers, 1954), chapter 9.

25 Saunders Redding, *An American in India: A Personal Report on the Indian Dilemma and the Nature of her Conflicts* (Indianapolis: Bobbs-Merrill, 1954), p. 47.

26 Quoted in *The Hindu*, 30 October 1953.

27 Walter Crocker, *Nehru: A Contemporary's Estimate* (New York: Oxford University Press, 1966), p. 114.

28 Keith Callard, *Pakistan: A Political Study* (London: George Allen and Unwin, 1957), p. 321.

29 Untitled note enclosed with letter from Winston Churchill to Lord Mountbatten, 21 November 1947, in Mss Eur F200/39, OIOC; Kissinger, quoted in Aslam Siddiqi, *Pakistan Seeks Security* (Lahore: Longmans, Green and Co., 1960), p. 109.

30 See Baldev Raj Nayar, *Superpower Dominance and Military Aid: A Study of Military Aid to Pakistan* (New Delhi: Manohar, 1991); anon., 'US–Pak[istan] Pact: An American View', *Swatantra*, 27 February 1954.

31 E. Stanley Jones, quoted in *The Hindu*, 25 December 1953. Jones was the author of a number of books on Indian themes, among them a sympathetic study of Mahatma Gandhi.

32 Taya Zinkin, 'Indo-American Relations', *Economic Weekly* annual, January 1956.

33 Letter of 21 May 1954, Birla Papers, NMML.

34 'Interview with Hon. John Foster Dulles', ibid.

35 Letter of 6 February 1956, ibid.

36 *Dulles Press Conference in India* (New Delhi: United States Information Service, 1956).

37 Cf. Denis Kux, *India and the United States, 1941–1991: Estranged Democracies* (Washington, DC: National Defence University Press, 1993).

38 Jawaharlal Nehru, *Soviet Russia: Some Random Sketches and Impressions* (Allahabad: Allahabad Law Journal Press, 1928).

39 S. Gopal, *Jawaharlal Nehru: A Biography*, vol. 1: *1889–1947* (London: Cape, 1975), p. 108.

40 Cf. David Caute, *The Fellow Travellers* (New Haven: Yale University Press, 1987).

41 Robert H. Donaldson, *Soviet Policy Towards India: Ideology and Strategy* (Cambridge, Mass.: Harvard University Press, 1974), pp. 109–12.

42 Cf. Mikhail Gorbachev, *Memoirs* (London: Doubleday, 1996), pp. 52–3: 'Obviously, we [students] were still very far from understanding the principles of democracy. Yet, the simplified black-and-white picture of the world as presented by our propaganda was even then considered rather sceptically by the students. Jawaharlal Nehru's visit to Moscow in June 1955 was an unexpected stimulus for me in this respect . . . This amazing man, his noble bearing, keen eyes and warm and disarming smile, made a deep impression on me.'

43 K. P. Menon, *The Flying Troika* (London: Oxford University Press, 1963), pp. 110–19.

44 Anon., 'Soviet Leaders' Visit and After', *Economic Weekly*, 24 December 1955.

45 N. A. Bulganin and N. S. Khrushchev, *Visit of Friendship to India, Burma and Afghanistan: Speeches and Official Documents, November–December 1955* (Moscow: Foreign Languages Publishing House, 1955).

46 A. D. Gorwala, 'As Nehru Leaves for Moscow', the *Current*, 1 June 1955.

47 As for example, C. Parameswaran, *Nehru's Foreign Policy X-Rayed* (New Delhi: privately published, 1954).

48 See, for representative views, L. Natarajan, *American Shadow over India* (Bombay: People's Publishing House, 1952); Romesh Thapar, *India in Transition* (Bombay: Current Book House, 1956). Louis Fischer, travelling through India in 1953–4, commented that the prevailing understanding of non-alignment 'tended to close minds to criticisms of Russia while stimulating a less-than-friendly attitude towards the Western democracies'. Fischer, *This is Our World* (London: Cape, 1956), pp. 142–3.

49 'The Bandung Conference', in A. Appadurai, *Essays in Politics and International Relations* (Bombay: Asia Publishing House, 1969), pp. 79–113.

50 *Lok Sabha Debates*, vol. 4, 1955, cols 8962–74.

51 Gopal, *Nehru*, vol. 2, pp. 277–90.

52 'Aggression in Egypt and Hungary' (editorial), *Swatantra*, 10 November 1956.

53 See Nehru, *India's Foreign Policy*, pp. 534f.

54 See Escott Reid, *Envoy to Nehru* (Delhi: Oxford University Press, 1981), chapter 11.

55 'L. N. S.' 'Double-Think', *Swatantra*, 17 November 1956.

56 Gopal, *Nehru*, vol. 2, pp. 291–9.

57 Frank Moraes, *India Today* (New York: Macmillan, 1960), pp. 198–9.

58 See T. J. S. George, *Krishna Menon: A Biography* (London: Cape, 1964).

59 Vincent Sheean, *Nehru: The Years of Power* (London: Victor Gollancz, 1960), pp. 144–5.

60 See news report in the *Current*, 15 February 1956.

61 *United Nations World*, quoted in the *Current*, 21 April 1954.

62 Sisela Bok, *Alva Myrdal: A Daughter's Memoir* (Reading, Mass.: Addison-Wesley, 1991), p. 252.

63 K. M. Pannikar, *In Two Chinas: Memoirs of a Diplomat* (London: George Allen and Unwin, 1955), pp. 80–2.

64 Nehru, *India's Foreign Policy*, pp. 302–3.

65 Nehru to Vijayalakshmi Pandit, 1 November 1953, Vijayalakshmi Pandit Papers, NMML.

66 SPC, vol. 10, pp. 335–41. Cf. also Marc C. Feer, 'Tibet in Sino-Indian Relations', *India Quarterly*, vol. 9, no. 4, 1953.

67 D. K. Karaka, 'Nehru's Neutralism Brings Mao to our Frontier', the *Current*, 29 November 1950.

68 SPC, vol. 10, pp. 342–7.

69 Vijayalakshmi Pandit to Jawaharlal Nehru, 16 May 1952, copy in File 123, C. Rajagopalachari Papers, Fifth Instalment, NMML.

70 John Rowland, *A History of Sino-Indian Relations: Hostile Co-existence* (Princeton: D. Van Nostrand, 1967), chapter 7.

71 Bajpai to Subimal Dutt, 18 October 1954, letter in possession of Dr Supriya Guha. It has been claimed that Patel's famous letter to Nehru on Tibet was actually drafted by Bajpai (personal communication from his son, K. S. Bajpai).

72 Gopal, *Nehru*, vol. 2, pp. 227–30; Moraes, *India Today*, p. 191. Among the topics discussed by Nehru and Mao was the possibility of an atomic war between the superpowers. When the Indian said he dreaded the prospect, the Chinese leader answered that he welcomed it, because while Western imperialism would be destroyed the more populous socialist bloc would still have some men standing; these would then reproduce themselves, and in time 'the whole world would become socialist'. See Stuart Schram, *Mao Tse-tung* (Harmondsworth: Penguin, 1967), p. 291 and n.

73 News report in the *Times of India*, 3 November 1954.

74 Notes in File 6, Subimal Dutt Papers, NMML; George N. Patterson, *Tragic Destiny* (London: Faber and Faber, 1959), pp. 160–3.

75 Letters to 'R' dated 8 December 1956, in File 46, C. Rajagopalachari Papers, Fourth Instalment, NMML.

76 Sir Charles Bell, quoted in Dorothy Woodman, *Himalayan Frontiers: A Political Review of British, Chinese, Indian and Russian Rivalries* (London: Barrie and Rockcliff, 1969) p. 179. Woodman's book remains the best historical account of the origins of the border dispute between India and China. But see also Hsiao-Ting Lin, 'Boundary, Sovereignty, and Imagination: Reconsidering the Frontier Disputes between British India and Republican China, 1914–47', *Journal of Imperial and Commonwealth History*, vol. 32, no. 3, 2004.

77 On Elwin, the IFAS and their work in NEFA, see Ramachandra Guha, *Savaging the Civilized: Verrier Elwin, His Tribals, and India* (Chicago: University of Chicago Press, 1999), chapter 11.

78 Woodman, *Himalayan Frontiers*, p. 66.

79 'Indo-Pakistan Clash of Ideologies', *Times of India*, 26 January 1952.

80 Gopal, *Nehru*, vol. 2, pp. 82–8; Gargi Chakravartty, *Coming out of Partition: Refugee Women of Bengal* (New Delhi: Bluejay Books, 2005), pp. 15–25.

81 I have simplified and summarized a complex story told in detail in A. A. Michel, *The Indus Rivers: A Study of the Effects of Partition* (New Haven: Yale University Press, 1967).

82 See J. B. Das Gupta, *Indo-Pakistan Relations, 1947–1955* (Amsterdam: Djambatan, 1958), pp. 51–2.

83 'Feelings in the Capital about the Trade Pact with Pakistan', unsigned note dated 28 February 1951, in File 61, C. Rajagopalachari Papers, Fourth Instalment, NMML. A year before this, when Nehru signed his agreement with Liaqat Ali Khan, a critic complained that he 'represents the beatific school which believes

in self-flagellation in reconciliation [with] the enemy'. 'Shridharani from New Delhi', the *Current*, 12 April 1950.

84 *Dawn*, 19, 24, 25 and 28 January 1955.

85 N. V. Rajkumar, *The Problem of French India* (New Delhi: All-India Congress Committee, 1951); Governor of Madras to President of India, 16 April 1954, in File 215, C. Rajagopalachari Papers, Fifth Instalment, NMML; *Dawn*, 27 January 1955.

86 *Times of India*, 2 November 1955.

87 As quoted in *Goa and the Indian Union* (Lisbon: Secretariado Nacional Da Informação, 1954).

88 See *Portuguese India: A Survey of Conditions After 400 Years of Foreign Colonial Rule* (Bombay: Goa Congress Committee, 1939); Julião Menezes, *Goa's Freedom Struggle* (Bombay: privately published, 1947).

89 R. M. Lala, 'Report on Daman', the *Current*, 22 November 1950.

90 Aloysius Soares, *Down the Corridors of Time: Recollections and Reflexions*, vol. 2: *1948–70* (Bombay: privately published, 1973), pp. 45ff.; the *Current*, 25 August 1954.

91 Homer A. Jack, *Inside Goa* (New Delhi: Information Service of India, 1955); P. D. Gaitonde, *The Liberation of Goa: A Participant's View of History* (London: C. Hurst and Co., 1987).

92 Y. D. Gundevia, *Outside the Archives* (Hyderabad: Sangam Books, 1984), pp. 18–19.

93 Letter of 22 January 1953, in Nehru correspondence, Y. D. Gundevia Papers, NMML.

94 C. Rajagopalachari to Edwina Mountbatten, 5 September 1950, File 189, C. Rajagopalachari Papers, Fifth Instalment, NMML.

95 See Carlo Feltrinelli, *Secret Service* (London: Granta Books, 2002).

96 Bok, *Alva Myrdal*, p. 243.

9. Redrawing the Map

1 CWMG, vol. 89, pp. 312–13.

2 'The Question of Language' (1937), in Nehru, *The Unity of India: Collected Writings, 1937–1940* (London: Lindsay Drummond, 1941), pp. 232–3.

3 Quoted in Robert D. King, *Nehru and the Language Politics of India* (Delhi: Oxford University Press, 1997), p. 102.

4 CWMG, vol. 90, p. 86.

5 Ibid., p. 494.

6 See letter of 8 June 1948 to Tushar Kanti Ghosh, in Subject File 82, C. Rajagopalachari Papers, Fifth Instalment, NMML.

7 *Report of the Linguistic Provinces Commission* (New Delhi: Constituent Assembly of India, 1948), paras 146 and 147.

8 King, *Nehru and Language Politics*, pp. 107, 108.

9 See Baldev Raj Nayar, *Minority Politics in the Punjab* (Princeton: Princeton University Press, 1960), chapters 2 and 3.

10 Satindra Singh, 'Master Tara Singh: A Born Rebel', *Thought*, 9 December 1967.

11 Nayar, *Minority Politics*, p. 143.

12 Quoted ibid., p. 36.

13 The best account of the history of the Andhra movement, on which the preceding paragraphs largely draw, is K. V. Narayana Rao's *The Emergence of Andhra Pradesh* (Bombay: Popular Prakashan, 1973).

14 The *Current*, 2 January 1952. See also Selig Harrison, *India: The Most Dangerous Decades* (Princeton: Princeton University Press, 1960), pp. 234–5.

15 *Congress Sandesh*, quoted in Narayana Rao, *Emergence of Andhra Pradesh*, p. 241.

16 See *Times of India*, 24 February 1952.

17 See 'Kowshika', *The Boundaries of Andhra Province* (Pudukottai: Anbu Nilayam, 1947).

18 Narayana Rao, *Emergence of Andhra Pradesh*, p. 243.

19 *History of Andhra Movement*, vol. 2 (Hyderabad: Committee for History of Andhra Movement, 1985), p. 496.

20 Gandhi to T. Prakasam, 4 January 1947, in *History of Andhra Movement*, pp. 496–7; also CWMG, vol. 86, p. 242.

21 Interview with Professor Béteille, New Delhi, December 2001.

22 See Subject File 123, C. Rajagopalachari Papers, Fifth Instalment, NMML.

23 Cf. P. R. Rao, *History of Modern Andhra* (New Delhi: Sterling Publishers, 1984), p. 130.

24 Letter of 18 August 1953 to General Sir Roy Bucher, Subject File 124, C. Rajagopalachari Papers, Fifth Instalment, NMML.

25 S. Gopal, *Jawaharlal Nehru: A Biography*, vol. 2: *1947–1956* (London: Cape, 1979), p. 259.

26 *Memorandum Submitted to the States Reorganization Commission* (Bombay: Bombay Citizens Committee, 1954).

27 The activities of the Committee, including its strategies for fund-raising and public relations, can be followed through the massive material contained in File 383, Purushottamdas Thakurdas Papers, NMML.

28 M. S. Golwalkar, quoted in *Times of India*, 8 November 1951.

29 *Times of India*, 24 May 1954.

30 Gadgil and Deshmukh are both quoted in Robert W. Stein, *The Process of Opposition in India* (Chicago: University of Chicago Press, 1970), p. 46.

31 Samyukta Maharashtra Parishad, 'Memorandum to the States Reorganization Committee', May 1954, copy in the library of the Gokhale Institute of Politics and Economics, Puné. D. R. Gadgil was the chief draughtsman of this memorandum.

32 See report of meeting of 20 June 1954 in File 383, Purushottamdas Thakurdas Papers, NMML.

33 This section is based on *Report of the States Reorganization Commission* (Delhi: Manager of Publications, 1955).

34 See *Lok Sabha Debates*, vol. X, 1955.

35 The *Current*, 4 January 1956.

36 The change of name was affected towards the end of 1955.

37 Taya Zinkin, *Reporting India* (London: Chatto and Windus, 1962), p. 108.

38 The *Current*, 25 January 1956. See also V. M. Bhave, 'Struggle for Maharashtra', *New Age*, September 1956.

39 Letter of 23 January 1956, Subject File 68, C. D. Deshmukh Papers, NMML.

40 See papers in Subject File 67, C. D. Deshmukh Papers, NMML.

41 See letters and papers in Subject File 4, N. V. Gadgil Papers, NMML.

42 As reported in alarm to the Home Minister, G. B. Pant, by Sir Purushottamdas Thakurdas. See letter of 20 January 1956, in File 383, Purushottamdas Thakurdas Papers, NMML.

43 The *Current*, 15 and 29 February 1956.

44 Y. D. Phadke, *Politics and Language* (Bombay: Himalaya Publishing House, 1979), chapter 6.

45 See Baburao Patel, *Burning Words: A Critical History of Nine Years of Nehru's Rule from 1947 to 1956* (Bombay: Sumati Publications, 1956), pp. 106–8.

46 Ravi Kalia, *Bhubaneshwar: From a Temple Town to a Capital City* (Carbondale: Southern Illinois University Press, 1994).

47 Janaki Nair, ' "Past Perfect": Architecture and Public Life in Bangalore'. I am grateful to Dr Nair for showing me a copy of this ms prior to its publication in her history of Bangalore, *The Promise of the Metropolis: Bangalore's Twentieth Century* (New Delhi: Oxford University Press, 2005).

48 *Times of India*, 26 February 1952.

49 'Andhra Answers Dulles', *Economic Weekly*, 5 March 1955.

10. THE CONQUEST OF NATURE

1 W. Burns, ed., *Sons of the Soil: Studies of the Indian Cultivator*, 2nd edn (Delhi: Manager of Publications, 1944), introduction.

2 Gyanendra Pandey, *The Ascendancy of the Congress in Uttar Pradesh, 1926–34: A Study in Imperfect Mobilization* (Delhi: Oxford University Press, 1978); Peter Reeves, *Landlords and Governments in Uttar Pradesh: A Study of their Relations until Zamindari Abolition* (New Delhi: Oxford University Press, 1991).

3 Chitra Bhanu, 'Food Situation Getting Worse in Malabar', *Swatantra*, 29 July 1947.

4 See, for illuminating contemporary analyses, Z. A. Ahmad, *The Agrarian Problem in India: A General Survey* (Allahabad: All-India Congress Committee, 1936); S. Y. Krishnaswami, *Rural Problems in Madras* (Madras: Government of Madras, 1947). Valuable surveys of the economic history of colonial India include V. B. Singh, ed., *Economic History of India: 1857–1956* (Bombay: Allied Publishers, 1965); Dharma Kumar, ed., *The Cambridge Economic History of India*, vol. 2: *c. 1757–c. 1970* (Cambridge: Cambridge University Press, 1983); and Tirthankar Ray, *The Indian Economy, 1857–1947* (New Delhi: Oxford University Press, 2006).

5 See, *inter alia*, Dwijendra Tripathi, ed., *Business and Politics in India: A Historical Perspective* (Delhi: Manohar, 1991); Medha M. Kudaisya, *The Life and Times of G. D. Birla* (New Delhi: Oxford University Press, 2003).

6 J. K. Galbraith, 'Rival Economic Theories in India', *Foreign Affairs*, vol. 36, no. 4, 1958, p. 591.

7 See Meghnad Saha, 'The Problem of Indian Rivers' (1938) and 'Technological Revolution in Industry – How the Russians Did It' (1943), both in Santimay Chatterjee, ed., *Collected Works of Meghnad Saha*, vol. 2 (Bombay: Orient Longman, 1986).

8 Lajpat Rai, *The Evolution of Japan and Other Papers* (Calcutta: Modern Review, 1922).

9 K. T. Shah, 'Principles of National Planning', in Iqbal Singh and Raja Rao, eds, *Whither India?* (Baroda: Padmaja Publications, 1948). Shah was a Bombay

economist who served as Secretary of the NPC. See also R. Chattopadhyay, 'The Idea of Planning in India, 1930–1951', unpublished PhD dissertation, Australian National University, Canberra, 1985.

10 See, for example, *National Planning Committee: Report of the Sub-Committee on Power and Fuel* (Bombay: Vora and Co., 1949).

11 *Memorandum Outlining a Plan of Economic Development for India (Parts One and Two)* (Harmondsworth: Penguin Books, 1945), emphases added. The signatories to the Bombay Plan included G. D. Birla, Kasturbhai Lalbhai, Lala Shri Ram, J. R. D. Tata, and Purushottamdas Thakurdas.

12 The intellectual climate of the time, as it pertained to economic policy, is captured in Tirthankar Ray, 'Economic History and Modern India: Redefining the Link', *Journal of Economic Perspectives*, vol. 16, no. 3, 2002; Nariaki Nakatozo, 'The Transfer of Economic Power in India: Indian Big Business, the British Raj and Development Planning, 1930–1948', in Mushirul Hasan and Nariaki Nakatozo, eds, *The Unfinished Agenda: Nation-Building in South Asia* (Delhi: Manohar, 2001); Pranab Bardhan, 'A Note on Nehru as Economic Planner', in Milton Israel, ed., *Nehru and the Twentieth Century* (Toronto: University of Toronto Press, 1991).

13 Speech in Lok Sabha on 15 December 1952, in *Planning and Development: Speeches of Jawaharlal Nehru (1952–56)* (New Delhi: Publications Division, n.d.), pp. 7–8. See also R. Ramadas, 'Report on the Draft Five-Year Plan', *Swatantra*, 1 December 1951.

14 See *Times of India*, 4 November 1954.

15 Cf. A. H. Hanson, *The Process of Planning: A Study of India's Five-Year Plans, 1950–1964* (London: Oxford University Press, 1966), pp. 111–20.

16 Sunil Khilnani, *The Idea of India* (New York: Farrar, Straus and Giroux, 1997), p. 83. Mahalanobis was an intimate of Rabindranath Tagore – it was said that he had a better knowledge of Tagore's poems and plays than did the poet himself.

17 See, for details, Ashok Rudra, *Prasanta Chandra Mahalanobis: A Biography* (Delhi: Oxford University Press, 1996).

18 This and the following two paragraphs draw upon Mahalanobis's letters to Pitambar Pant, June–July 1954, Pitambar Pant Papers, NMML. See also Khilnani, *Idea of India*, pp. 83f.

19 Mahalanobis wrote that he was 'in favour of seeking the help of both USA and USSR (and of the UK and other countries) in developing the industrial production of India' (letter of 7 July 1954, in Pitambar Pant Papers, NMML). He was in this respect genuinely non-partisan. In the years to come his ISI played host to top economists from both sides of the Iron Curtain – to men such as Simon Kuznets, Oskar Lange, Charles Bettelheim, Jan Tinbergen and many, many others. For details see Rudra, *Prasanta Chandra Mahalanobis*, chapter 14.

20 'Recommendations for the Formulation of the Second Five-Year Plan', and 'The Approach of Operational Research to Planning in India', both written in 1955, both reprinted in P. K. Bose and M. Mukherjee, eds, *P. C. Mahalanobis: Papers on Planning* (Calcutta: Statistical Publishing Society, 1985). Along with these narrative papers, Mahalanobis also framed two mathematical models of economic growth. These are discussed in T. N. Srinivasan, 'Professor Mahalanobis and Economics', printed as chapter 11 in Rudra, *Prasanta Chandra Mahalanobis*.

21 Hanson, *Process of Planning*, pp. 128–30. See also K. N. Raj, 'Model-Making and the Second Plan', *Economic Weekly*, 26 January 1956.

22 Government of India, *The Second Five-Year Plan* (New Delhi: Planning Commission, 1956), p. 6.

23 P. C. Mahalanobis, 'Draft Plan Frame for the Second Five-Year Plan', *Economic Weekly*, special issue, 18 June 1955.

24 Hanson, *Process of Planning*, pp. 459–62.

25 Haldane to Mahalanobis, 16 May 1955, quoted in S. Gopal, *Jawaharlal Nehru: A Biography*, vol. 2: *1947–1956* (London: Cape), pp. 305–6.

26 Letter of 22 December 1952, in Jawaharlal Nehru, *Letters to Chief Ministers*, edited by G. Parthasarathi, 5 vols (New Delhi: Oxford University Press, 1985–9) hereafter cited as LCM, vol. 3, pp. 205–7.

27 Letter of 22 December 1952, LCM, vol. 3, p. 205; letter of 14 February 1956, LCM, vol. 4, p. 346.

28 Letter of 13 January 1955, LCM, vol. 4, p. 123.

29 'Triangular Contest for Steel Plant', *Economic Weekly*, 19 December 1953; Taya Zinkin, *Challenges in India* (New York: Walker and Co., 1966), chapter 7.

30 The friend was Joe Miller, the late and legendary librarian of the Yale School of Forestry and Environmental Studies.

31 See Subject File 5, K. P. S. Menon Papers, NMML.

32 Ved Mehta, *Portrait of India* (New York: Farrar, Straus and Giroux, 1970), pp. 285–97.

33 S. Bhoothalingam, 'Rourkela Steel Plant', *Indian Review*, April 1956.

34 For example Meghnad Saha, *My Experiences in Soviet Russia* (Calcutta: publisher unknown, 1945); K. L. Rao, *Cusecs and Candidates: Memoirs of an Engineer* (New Delhi: Metropolitan, 1978).

35 Daniel Klingensmith, 'One Valley and a Thousand: America, India and the World in the Image of the Tennessee Valley Authority, 1945–1970', unpublished PhD thesis, Department of History, University of Chicago, 1999, p. 228.

36 A. N. Khosla to C. Rajagopalachari, 30 August 1953, in Subject File 124, C. Rajagopalachari Papers, Fifth Instalment, NMML.

37 Henry C. Hart, *New India's Rivers* (Bombay: Orient Longman, 1956), pp. 97–100.

38 'India Marches on: Bhakra–Nangal Project', *MysIndia*, 28 November 1954. Much smaller was the complementary Nangal project, a low concrete dam located eight miles downstream of the Bhakra.

39 *Indian Journal of Power and River Valley Development*, Bhakra–Nangal special issue, 1956.

40 This portrait of Slocum is based on J. D. Sahi, *Odd Man Out: Exploits of a Crazy Idealist* (New Delhi: Gitanjai Publishing House, 1991), pp. 55–69, 133; M. S. Randhawa, *A History of Agriculture in India*, vol. 4: *1947–1981* (New Delhi: Indian Council of Agricultural Research, 1986), pp. 92–3.

41 Hart, *New India's Rivers*, p. 225; report in the *Current*, 14 July 1954.

42 Obaid Siddiqi, *Science, Society, Government and Politics: Some Remarks on the Ideas of Jawaharlal Nehru*, Zaheer Memorial Lecture, Indian Science Congress, Cochin, February 1990.

43 See Shiv Visvanathan, *Organizing for Science: The Making of an Industrial Research Laboratory* (New Delhi: Oxford University Press, 1985).

44 On Bhabha see Robert S. Anderson, 'Building Scientific Institutions in India: Saha and Bhabha', Occasional Paper, Centre for Developing-Area Studies, McGill University, 1975.

45 George Greenstein, 'A Gentleman of the Old School: Homi Bhabha and the Development of Science in India', *American Scholar*, vol. 61, no. 3, 1992, p. 417.

46 *Hindustan Times*, 3 October 1952. The Community Development programmes were inspired by, and to a great extent modelled upon, the work of Albert Mayer in eastern Uttar Pradesh in the late 1940s. See Alice Thorner, 'Nehru, Albert Mayer, and Origins of Community Projects', *Economic and Political Weekly*, 24 January 1981.

47 S. C. Dube, *India's Changing Villages* (London: Routledge and Kegan Paul, 1958), pp. 157–63, 192–216 etc.

48 T. S. Epstein, *Economic Development and Social Change in South India* (Manchester: Manchester University Press, 1962), esp. pp. 27–47.

49 For details see B. H. Farmer, *Agricultural Colonization in India Since Independence* (London: Oxford University Press, 1974).

50 See, *inter alia*, R. P. Masani, *The Five Gifts* (London: Collins, 1957); Hallam Tennyson, *Saint on the March: The Story of Vinoba* (London: Victor Gollancz, 1961); Geoffrey Ostergaard and Melville Currell, *The Gentle Anarchists: A Study of the Leaders of the Sarvodaya Movement for Non-violent Revolution in India* (Oxford: Clarendon Press, 1971). There is a characteristically acid portrait of Bhave in V. S. Naipaul's *A Wounded Civilization* (Harmondsworth: Penguin, 1977).

51 See Ronald J. Herring, *Land to the Tiller: the Political Economy of Agrarian Reform in South Asia* (New Haven: Yale University Press, 1983); 'Slow Pace of Land Reforms', *Economic Weekly*, 30 May 1953; S. K. Dey, *Power to the People? A Chronicle of India 1947–67* (Bombay: Orient Longman, 1969), pp. 232f.

52 The climate of economic policy in the postwar world is usefully sketched in Daniel Yergin and Joseph Stanislaw, *The Commanding Heights: The Battle for the World Economy* (New York: Simon and Schuster, 2002), chapters 2 and 3.

53 Hanson, *Process of Planning*, p. 128.

54 See 'A Note on Dissent on the Memorandum of the Panel of Economists' (1955), reprinted in Mahesh P. Bhatt and S. B. Mehta, *Planned Progress or Planned Chaos? Selected Prophetic Writings of Prof. B. R. Shenoy* (Madras: EastWest Books, 1996), pp. 3–24.

55 'A Memorandum to the Government of India, 1955', in *Friedman on India* (New Delhi: Centre for Civil Society, 2000), pp. 27–43.

56 Note of 10 October 1955, reprinted in V. N. Balasubramanyam, *Conversations with Indian Economists* (London: Macmillan, 2001), pp. 198–201.

57 It is noteworthy that the essays of Shenoy, Krishnamurti and Friedman were printed for public distribution only in the 1990s – by which time, of course, the political and intellectual climate was far more congenial to their views.

58 'Not a People's Plan', *Economic Weekly*, 18 June 1955.

59 I have written elsewhere, and at greater length, about these 'Green Gandhians'; as in Ramachandra Guha, *Environmentalism: A Global History* (New York: Addison-Wesley-Longman, 2000), pp. 23–4, 67–8, and 'Mahatma Gandhi and the Environmental Movement', Parisar Annual Lecture, Puné, 1992.

60 Reports in the *Current*, 11 June 1952 and 8 June 1955.

61 For the consensus among economists see I. G. Patel, *Glimpses of Indian Economic Policy: An Insider's View* (New Delhi: Oxford University Press, 2002), esp. chapter 2.

62 *Memorandum*, p. 92.

63 'A Correspondent', 'On Revisiting the Damodar Valley', *Economic Weekly*, 28 February 1953.

64 Letter of 2 October 1952, LCM, vol. 3, pp. 114–15. Nehru was speaking here of
the Tungabhadra dam, which he visited barely a month before coming to Bokaro.

11. THE LAW AND THE PROPHETS

1 André Malraux, *Antimemoirs*, trans. Terence Kilmartin (London: Hamish
Hamilton, 1968), p. 145. The conversation took place sometime in 1958.
2 CAD, vol. 8, pp. 543–6, 722–3 (emphasis added).
3 Ibid., pp. 551, 781.
4 For an analysis of the Rau Committee see Chitra Sinha, 'Hindu Code Bill
(1942–1956) and Feminist Consciousness in Bombay', unpublished PhD thesis,
Department of History, Mumbai University, 2003.
5 See for example, Bina Agarwal, 'A Bill of Her Own?', *New Indian Express*,
23 December 2004.
6 Ambedkar's speeches on the bill are reproduced in Valerian Rodrigues, ed.,
The Essential Writings of B. R. Ambedkar (New Delhi: Oxford University Press,
2002), pp. 495–516.
7 Dhananjay Keer, *Dr. Ambedkar: Life and Mission*, 3rd edn (1971; reprint, Bombay:
Popular Prakashan, 1995), p. 417.
8 The correspondence between Prasad and Nehru has been reproduced in SPC,
vol. 6, pp. 399–404.
9 SPC, vol. 9, pp. 109–11.
10 This account of the doings of the All-India Anti-Hindu-Code Bill Committee is
based on the reports and documents in Subject File 106, D. P. Mishra Papers,
Third and Fourth Instalments, NMML.
11 J. D. M. Derrett, *Hindu Law Past and Present* (Calcutta: A. Mukerjee and Co., 1957),
pp. 69–70. For a sampling of the conservative legal opposition to the code, see
K. S. Hajela, 'The Draft Hindu Code, its Exposition, Comment and Criticism',
All-India Reporter (Journal), 1949, pp. 64–7. For a modernist view, see Lahar Singh
Mehta, 'Some Implications of the Hindu Code Bill, 1948', *All India Reporter
(Journal)*, 1950, pp. 26–9.
12 The debates on the Hindu code in the provisional Parliament are reproduced
in Vasant Moon, ed., *Dr. Babasaheb Ambedkar: Writings and Speeches*, vol. 14
(Bombay: Government of Maharashtra, 1995).
13 See Files 422, 423, 424 and 430, Delhi Police Records, Ninth Instalment, NMML.
14 Rajendra Prasad to Nehru, 15 September 1951, copy in Subject File 189,
C. Rajagopalachari Papers, Fifth Instalment, NMML.
15 Nehru to Rajendra Prasad, 15 September 1951; secret note to Cabinet by Nehru,
dated 25 September 1951, both in Subject File 46, C. Rajagopalachari Papers,
Fourth Instalment, NMML.
16 Derrett, *Hindu Law*, p. 71.
17 The text of Ambedkar's resignation speech was reproduced in the *Hindustan Times*,
12 October 1951. Cf. also Vasant Moon, ed., *Dr. Babasaheb Ambedkar: Writings and
Speeches*, vol. 15 (Mumbai: Government of Maharashtra, 1997), pp. 825–8.
18 See File 127, Delhi Police Records, Sixth Instalment, NMML.
19 See *Lok Sabha Debates*, 26 April 1955.

20 The most significant of Nehru's parliamentary interventions on the subject
   are collected in *Jawaharlal Nehru's Speeches*, vol. 3: *March 1953–August 1957*
   (New Delhi: Publications Division, n.d.), pp. 438–54 (section entitled 'Changing
   Hindu Society').

21 Nehru to K. N. Katju, 13 June 1954; to R. Venkataraman, 30 September 1954;
   SWJN2, vol. 26, pp. 173, 180.

22 See, for example, the speeches of K. C. Sharma, B. D. Shastri and Nand Lal
   Sharma, *Lok Sabha Debates*, 29 April, 2 May and 13 December 1955, respectively;
   speech of H. C. Mathur, *Rajya Sabha Debates*, 11 December 1954.

23 *Rajya Sabha Debates*, 9 December 1954.

24 Interventions of Seeta Parmanand and M. P. N. Sinha, *Rajya Sabha Debates*, 8 and
   6 December 1954. To placate the orthodox, the law minister changed the title
   of the bill from the 'Hindu Marriage and Divorce Bill' to the 'Hindu Marriage
   Bill' – this to put the accent 'not on the dissolution of marriage' but on the
   'maintenance of marriage [which] is more important' (*Lok Sabha Debates*,
   26 April 1955). The change, needless to say, was purely cosmetic.

25 *Lok Sabha Debates*, 29 April 1955. Others opposed the clause out of not logic,
   but envy. As S. Mahanty sourly noted, 'it makes a discrimination in favour of
   the Muslims who may marry four wives under the Shariat law and not incur
   any of the offences under this Act' (*Rajya Sabha Debates*, 6 December 1954).

26 *Lok Sabha Debates*, 2 May 1955.

27 *Lok Sabha Debates*, 26 and 29 April 1955.

28 Intervention by Shri Khandekar, *Lok Sabha Debates*, 29 April 1955.

29 Ibid., *Rajya Sabha Debates*, 8 December 1954.

30 Intervention by M. Muhammad Ismail, *Rajya Sabha Debates*, 11 December 1954.

31 *Lok Sabha Debates*, 29 April 1955.

32 Intervention by Nand Lal Sharma, *Lok Sabha Debates*, 13 December 1955.

33 *Lok Sabha Debates*, 13 December 1955.

34 Intervention by S. S. More, *Lok Sabha Debates*, 2 May 1955.

35 Marc Galanter, *Law and Society in Modern India*, ed. by Rajeev Dhavan (Delhi:
   Oxford University Press, 1997), p. 29; J. D. M. Derrett, *Religion, Law and the State
   in India* (London: Faber and Faber, 1968), p. 326.

36 Cf. *Rajya Sabha Debates*, 11 December 1954, where Dr P. Subbarayan gave his
   'special meed of tribute to Dr. Ambedkar who is not here but who laboured hard
   to push through the Hindu Code before the last Parliament but circumstances
   did not permit of this measure going through'.

37 *Lok Sabha Debates*, 6 December 1956.

38 For a fine discussion of these questions see Lotika Sarkar, 'Jawaharlal Nehru and
   the Hindu Code Bill', in B. R. Nanda, ed., *Indian Women: From Purdah to Modernity*
   (New Delhi: Nehru Memorial Museum and Library, 1976).

39 Quoted in D. E. Smith, *India as a Secular State* (Princeton: Princeton University
   Press, 1963), p. 290.

40 See *Parliamentary Debates*, 17 September 1951, excerpted in Eminent
   Parliamentarians Series, Monograph Series, *Dr Syama Prasad Mookerjee* (New
   Delhi: Lok Sabha Secretariat, 1990), pp. 82f.

41 On the workings of the new laws in the several decades they have been in
   operation, see J. D. M. Derrett, *A Critique of Modern Hindu Law* (Bombay:

N. M. Tripathi, 1970); Satyajeet A. Desai, *Mulla's Principles of Hindu Law*, 18th edn (New Delhi: Butterworths India, 2001). The caveat 'somewhat' is in deference to feminist arguments that while the new bills removed many of the disadvantages suffered by Hindu women, they did not bestow 'radical equality' on them. See Archana Parashar, *Women and Family Law Reform in India* (New Delhi: Sage, 1992), pp. 79–134.

12. Securing Kashmir

1 Sisir Kumar Gupta, *Kashmir: A Study in India–Pakistan Relations* (Bombay: Asia Publishing House, 1966), p. 365.

2 See Michael Brecher, *The Struggle for Kashmir* (New York: Oxford University Press, 1953), p. 111.

3 Lionel Fielden, 'India Revisited: Indo-Pak Problems', *Indian Review*, May 1950.

4 Note by Nehru on Kashmir, dated 9 January 1951, in Subject File 62, C. Rajagopalachari Papers, Fourth Instalment, NMML.

5 See Jawaharlal Nehru Correspondence, Vijayalakshmi Pandit Papers, NMML.

6 Cable to State Department by Henderson, quoted in Ajit Bhattacharjea, *Kashmir: The Wounded Valley* (New Delhi: UBS, 1994), pp. 196–7.

7 See Abdullah to Gopalaswami Ayyangar, 16 January 1951, and note on file by latter, both in Subject File 62, C. Rajagopalachari Papers, Fourth Instalment, NMML.

8 See 'Leaderlessness of Jammu', article of March 1950, reprinted in Balraj Puri, *Jammu – A Clue to the Kashmir Tangle* (Delhi: privately published, 1966), pp. 20–3.

9 Baburao Patel, *Burning Words: A Critical History of Nine Years of Nehru's Rule from 1947 to 1956* (Bombay: Sumati Publications, 1956), pp. 147–8.

10 The Sheikh's speech is printed *in extenso* in Gupta, *Kashmir*, pp. 367–70.

11 Prem Nath Bazaz, *The History of Struggle for Freedom in Kashmir, Cultural and Political: From the Earliest Times to the Present Day* (New Delhi: Kashmir Publishing Co., 1954), pp. 569–71.

12 Ian Stephens, *Horned Moon: An Account of a Journey through Pakistan, Kashmir, and Afghanistan* (London: Chatto and Windus, 1953), pp. 212–13. From Stephens' book we learn that he was in the Valley in April 1952 – exact dates are not given, so we cannot say whether he talked to the Sheikh before or after his notorious Ranbirsinghpura speech. That speech had also hinted that perhaps Kashmir's place in India was 'unnatural'. This might have been a mere coincidence in thinking. On the other hand, if Abdullah met Stephens *before* Ranbirsinghpura, his speech might very well have been influenced by one who cynically saw 'an anti-Muslim substructure' in 'Pandit Nehru's new secular Republic' (*Horned Moon*, p. 267).

13 Gupta, *Kashmir*, pp. 371–2.

14 Speeches of 11 and 19 August 1952, copies in Subject File 4, Y. D. Gundevia Papers, NMML.

15 See Daniel Thorner, 'The Kashmir Land Reforms: Some Personal Impressions', *Economic Weekly*, 12 September 1953.

16 Cf. Richard L. Park, 'India Argues with Kashmir', *Far Eastern Survey*, 2 July 1952.

17 Eminent Parliamentarians Series, Monograph Series, *Dr Syama Prasad Mookerjee* (New Delhi: Lok Sabah Secretariat, 1990), pp. 18–19, 109–23.

18 Balraj Madhok, *Portrait of a Martyr: Biography of Dr Shyama Prasad Mookerjee* (Bombay: Jaico Publishing House, 1969), pp. 159–61.

19 Karan Singh, *Autobiography* (New Delhi: Oxford University Press, 1989), pp. 149–50.

20 The *Current*, 10 and 24 December 1952.

21 The letters exchanged between Mookerjee on the one side and Nehru and Abdullah on the other were later published by the Jana Sangh in *Integrate Kashmir: Mookerjee–Nehru and Abdullah Correspondence* (Lucknow: Bharat Press, 1953).

22 See Files 12, 127 and 164, Delhi Police Records, Eighth Instalment, NMML.

23 The *Current* (Bombay), 26 August 1953.

24 Quoted in S. Gopal, *Jawaharlal Nehru: A Biography*, vol. 2: *1947–1956* (London: Cape, 1979), p. 131, n. 65.

25 For a contemporary interpretation along these lines, see Sadiq Ali and Madhu Limaye, *Report on Kashmir* (New Delhi: Praja Socialist Party, 1953). This reports that the Sheikh 'was often heard to remark in his private talks that if Jammu wanted to go out of Kashmir it was welcome to do so; in fact it would be good riddance. Its merger in India would serve just the purpose he had in view, namely an Independent Kashmir' (p. 5).

26 Madhok, *Portrait of a Martyr*, pp. 147–65.

27 See correspondence between Mookerjee and Rajagopalachari in Subject File 124, C. Rajagopalachari Papers, Fifth Instalment, NMML.

28 Madhok, *Portrait of a Martyr*, pp. 240–2.

29 Letter of 2 July to Rajagopalachari, Subject File 123, Rajagopalachari Papers, Fifth Instalment, NMML.

30 The *Current*, 1 July 1953.

31 See File 164, Delhi Police Records, Eighth Instalment, NMML.

32 See reports and correspondence, File 166, Delhi Police Records, Ninth Instalment, NMML.

33 Gopal, *Nehru*, vol. 2, pp. 130–1, which also excerpts Nehru's letters to Abdullah.

34 Nehru to Rajagopalachari, 31 July 1953, Subject File 123, C. Rajagopalachari Papers, Fifth Instalment, NMML.

35 See B. N. Mullik, *My Years with Nehru: Kashmir* (Bombay: Allied Publishers, 1971), chapter 3.

36 The *Current*, 26 August 1953. Three years later a copy of the Id speech that Abdullah was to have made surfaced. This did not call directly for independence, but reopened the question of accession to India and also, for the first time, asked that Pakistan be made a party to the dispute. See Mridula Sarabhai, ed., *Sheikh–Sadiq Correspondence* (August to October 1956) (New Delhi: privately published, 1956), appendix I: 'Id Speech'.

37 Karan Singh, *Autobiography*, pp. 156–64.

38 See reports in File 73, Delhi Police Records, Sixth Instalment, NMML.

39 Gopal, *Nehru*, vol. 2, pp. 132–3; Mullik, *My Years with Nehru: Kashmir*, pp. 42–7.

40 P. N. Kaula and K. L. Dhar, *Kashmir Speaks* (Delhi: S. Chand and Co., 1950), pp. 189–90. An American journalist wrote of the Bakshi that he was a 'realist [who] can run a party machine and keep its joints oiled', adding that he seemed to be 'constituted chiefly of iron or steel' (Vincent Sheean, *Nehru: The Years of Power* (London: Victor Gollancz, 1960), pp. 109–10). This likewise brings Patel to mind; not least because he was known as the 'Iron Man of India'.

41 *The Hindu*, 25 August and 14 and 29 September 1953.

42 The *Current*, 31 March, 25 August and 6 October 1954 and 12 October 1955.
43 The *Current*, 14 November 1955. Cf. also Sheikh Abdullah, *Flames of the Chinar: An Autobiography*, abridged and trans. Khushwant Singh (New Delhi: Penguin India, 1993), chapter 18.
44 See File 73, Delhi Police Records, Sixth Instalment, NMML.
45 General Roy Bucher to Rajagopalachari, 14 August 1953, in Subject File 124, Fifth Instalment, C. Rajagopalachari Papers, NMML.
46 Bhattacharjea, *Kashmir*, p. 205.
47 See Spratt's unsigned column 'The World This Week', *MysIndia*, 13 July, 3 and 17 August, and 9 November 1952 respectively.

13. Tribal Trouble

1   This account of the early years of the Naga National Council is based on Mildred Archer, 'Journal of a Stay in the Naga Hills, 9 July to 4 December 1947', Mss Eur F236/362, OIOC. Archer, the wife of the last deputy commissioner in the Naga Hills, W. G. Archer, had interviewed a wide cross-section of the NNC membership and subscribed to the NNC journal. In later years she became an authority on British art in India.
2   Charles Chasie, *The Naga Imbroglio* (Kohima: Standard Printers and Publishers, 1999), pp. 33–6.
3   The Crown colony scheme is discussed in a forthcoming book by Professor David Syiemlieh of the North-eastern Hill University, Shillong.
4   A. R. H. Macdonald to P. F. Adams (secretary to the governor of Assam), 23 March 1947, copy in Mss Eur F236/76, OIOC. The 'Lushai hills' are now more familiarly known as the Mizo hills.
5   See A. Z. Phizo, *The Fate of the Naga People: An Appeal to the World* (London: privately published, July 1960).
6   CWMG, vol. 88, pp. 373–4. The context makes it clear that Gandhi was against the Nagas using guns and tanks though, of course, he would have opposed the Indian army's use of them too.
7   Cf. J. H. Hutton, *The Angami Nagas* (London: Macmillan, 1921), p. 11 and *passim*.
8   See entry for 30 August 1947 in Archer, 'Journal'. The invocation of God, and the recourse to American heroes, were a consequence of the deep influence on the Nagas of the Baptist missionaries who had converted them.
9   Entries for 27 September and 23 August 1947, in Archer, 'Journal'.
10 CAD, vol. 4, pp. 947–8.
11 Useful studies of the tribal predicament include G. S. Ghurye, *The Scheduled Tribes* (Bombay: Popular Prakashan, 1959; first published under a different title in 1943); C. von Fürer Haimendorf, *Tribes of India: The Struggle for Survival* (Berkeley: University of California Press, 1982); Verrier Elwin, *The Tribal World of Verrier Elwin: An Autobiography* (Bombay: Oxford University Press, 1964); and K. S. Singh, *Tribal Society in India* (New Delhi: Manohar, 1985). See also André Béteille, 'The Concept of Tribe with Special Reference to India', in his *Society and Politics in India: Essays in a Comparative Perspective* (London: Athlone Press, 1991).
12 See Agapit Tirkey, *Jharkhand Movement: A Study of its Dynamics* (New Delhi: Other Media Communications, 2002), chapter 2.

13 Memorandum dated 1 May 1947, in Subject File 37, C. Rajagopalachari Papers, Fifth Instalment, NMML.

14 Jaipal's speech is reproduced on pp. 2–14 of Ram Dayal Munda and S. Bosu Mullick, eds, *The Jharkhand Movement: Indigenous Peoples' Struggle for Autonomy in India* (Copenhagen: IWGIA, 2003).

15 This paragraph is based on an anonymous three-part report on the Naga situation in the *Current*, 4, 11 and 18 July 1956, and on Nirmal Nibedon, *Nagaland: The Night of the Guerillas* (New Delhi: Lancer, 1983), pp. 24–5.

16 Letter to Jairamdas Daulatram, governor of Assam, 11 December 1950, in Subject File 188, C. Rajagopalachari Papers, Fifth Instalment, NMML.

17 A. Lanunungsang Ao, *From Phizo to Muivah: The Naga National Question in Northeast India* (New Delhi: Mittal Publications, 2002), pp. 48–9.

18 'No Independence for Nagas: Plain Speaking by Mr Nehru', *Times of India*, 1 January 1952.

19 'Demand for Naga State: Delegation Meets Nehru', *Times of India*, 12 February 1952.

20 Report by Krishnalal Shridharani in the *Current*, 19 March 1952.

21 'The Tribal Folk', in *Jawaharlal Nehru's Speeches*, vol. 2 (New Delhi: Publications Division, 1954), pp. 576f.

22 Nehru to Rajagopalachari, 26 October 1952, in Subject File 107, C. Rajagopalachari Papers, Fifth Instalment, NMML.

23 The report on the NEFA tour is reprinted in LCM, vol. 4, pp. 147–65.

24 NNC letter of 24 October 1952, quoted in the *Current*, 15 April 1953.

25 Ramachandra Guha, *Savaging the Civilized: Verrier Elwin, His Tribals, and India* (Chicago: University of Chicago Press, 1999), p. 285.

26 Entry for 10 July 1947 in Archer, 'Journal'.

27 Arthur Swinson, quoted in Nibedon, *Nagaland*, p. 26.

28 Asoso Yonuo, *The Rising Nagas: A Historical and Political Study* (Delhi: Vivek Publishing House, 1974), pp. 210–13.

29 This account of the Phizo–Sakhrie rift is based on Nibedon, *Nagaland*, pp. 57–68.

30 Ibid., pp. 80–2.

31 Lt. Gen. S. P. P. Thorat, *From Reveille to Retreat* (New Delhi: Allied Publishers, 1986), chapter 15, 'The Nagas'. As the commanding officer of the Eastern Command, General Thorat was in charge of operations against the rebels.

32 See clippings in Mss Eur F158/239, OIOC.

33 Dr S. R. S. Laing to Charles Pawsey, letters of ? June 1956 and 13 August 1956, in Box I, Pawsey Papers, CSAS.

34 *Lok Sabha Debates*, 23 August 1956.

35 *India News*, 8 December 1956; *Manchester Guardian*, 18 December 1956; both in Mss Eur F158/239, OIOC.

36 Ignes Kujur, 'Jharkhand Betrayed', in Munda and Bosu Mullick, *The Jharkhand Movement*, pp. 16ff.

37 *Lok Sabha Debates*, 22 November 1954; the *Current*, 16 February 1955.

38 Letter of 9 March 1955, in T. T. Krishnamachari Papers, NMML.

39 Nehru to Bishnuram Medhi, 13 May 1956, reproduced as appendix VII in Udayon Misra, *The Periphery Strikes Back: Challenges to the Nation-State in Assam and Nagaland* (Shimla: Indian Institute of Advanced Study, 200), pp. 203–4.

14. THE SOUTHERN CHALLENGE

1 *Report on the Second General Elections in India, 1957* (New Delhi: Election Commission, 1958).

2 Feroze Gandhi was also from the Nehrus' home town, Allahabad. A Parsi by faith, he at first spelt his surname 'Ghandy'. However, after he joined the national movement as a young man, he changed the spelling to bring it in line with that of Mahatma Gandhi. That amended surname proved to be of incalculable significance to his wife; for most foreigners, and not a few Indians, assumed that she was in some way related to the Mahatma.

3 Cf. Katherine Frank, *Indira: A Life of Indira Nehru Gandhi* (London: HarperCollins, 2001), pp. 240–1.

4 Indira Gandhi to Brijkrishna Chandiwala, 11 November 1957, Chandiwala Papers, NMML.

5 Nehru to Vijayalakshmi Pandit, 12 March 1957, quoted in Nayantara Sahgal, *Indira Gandhi: Her Road to Power* (New York: Frederick Ungar, 1982), pp. 1–2.

6 The data in this and the subsequent paragraphs are chiefly derived from the excellent statistical supplement on Indian elections printed as an appendix to the *Journal of the Indian School of Political Economy*, vol. 15, nos 1 and 2, 2003.

7 For the rise of the DMK in the 1950s, see Marguerite Ross Barnett, *The Politics of Cultural Nationalism in South India* (Princeton: Princeton University Press, 1976).

8 The social history of modern Kerala has been treated with authority and insight in several books by Robin Jeffrey. See specially his *The Decline of Nair Dominance* (1975; 2nd edn New Delhi: Manohar, 2003) and *Politics, Women and Wellbeing: How Kerala Became a 'Model'* (New Delhi: Oxford University Press, 1992).

9 See Dilip M. Menon, *Caste, Nationalism and Communism in South India: Malabar, 1900–1948* (Cambridge: Cambridge University Press, 1994).

10 Nikita Khrushchev, quoted in *Communist Double Talk at Palghat* (Bombay: Democratic Research Service, 1956), p. 112.

11 'Communist Manifesto for Stable Government, Prosperous Kerala', quoted in Victor M. Fic, *Kerala: Yenan of India* (Bombay: Nachiketa Publications, 1970), pp. 68–9.

12 Sadly, like Abdullah, Phizo et al. EMS has yet to find a serious biographer.

13 E. M. S. Namboodiripad, *Twenty-Eight Months in Kerala* (New Delhi: People's Publishing House, 1959), esp. pp. 5–6, 22–3.

14 P. N. Sampath, 'Red Government in Kerala', *Indian Review*, July 1957.

15 The *Current*, 8 May 1957. Krishna Iyer was actually an independent member of the Kerala legislature, a fellow-traveller rather than a card-holding communist. He was later a judge of the Supreme Court.

16 Ronald J. Herring, *Land to the Tiller: The Political Economy of Agrarian Reform in South Asia* (New Haven: Yale University Press, 1983), p. 163.

17 This paragraph draws upon material in ibid., chapter 6, and T. J. Nossiter, *Communism in Kerala: A Study in Political Adaptation* (Delhi: Oxford University Press, 1982), pp. 149–57.

18 The *Current*, 24 April 1957.

19 'Letter from Kerala: Bloodsuckers still Thrive', *Economic Weekly*, 19 April 1958.

20 Ibid.

21 *Kerala Mail*, quoted in the *Current*, 28 August 1957.

22 George Mikes, *East is East* (London: André Deutsch, 1958), p. 153.

23 For a useful summary see S. C. Joseph, *Kerala: The 'Communist' State* (Madras: The Madras Premier Company, 1959), chapter 8.

24 See 'Who Supported the Communists in Kerala? An Analysis of the 1957 Election Results', *Economic Weekly*, 1 August 1959.

25 See 'Kerala Letter: Co-existence in Peril', *Economic Weekly*, special issue, July 1959. It is not clear whether these excerpts were originally in English or are translated here from the Malayalam.

26 Rajni Kothari, 'Kerala: A Post-mortem', *Economic Weekly*, 28 November 1959.

27 'Kerala Letter: Congress Misalliance with the Congress Church', *Economic Weekly*, annual issue, January 1958.

28 Nossiter, *Communism in Kerala*, p. 145.

29 'Red Rule in Kerala', statements by E. M. S. Namboodiripad and Panampilli Govinda Menon, *Illustrated Weekly of India*, 25 January 1959.

30 Kamla Chopra, 'Indira Gandhi: A Profile', *Illustrated Weekly of India*, 22 February 1959.

31 S. Gopal, *Jawaharlal Nehru: A Biography*, vol. 3: *1956–1964* (London: Cape, 1984), p. 66.

32 Profiles of Mannath in the *Illustrated Weekly of India*, 28 June 1959 and in the *Current*, 16 September 1959; Anon., *The Agitation in Kerala* (Trivandrum: Department of Public Relations, 1959), pp. 9–12.

33 W. H. Morris-Jones, 'India's Political Idioms', in C. H. Philips, ed., *Politics and Society in India* (London: George Allen and Unwin, 1963).

34 A good description of the protests is contained in George Woodcock's *Kerala: A Portrait of the Malabar Coast* (London: Faber and Faber, 1967), pp. 270ff.

35 See the letters from Nehru to the prominent Kerala Congress politician R. Sankar, quoted in Robin Jeffrey, 'Jawaharlal Nehru and the Smoking Gun: Who Pulled the Trigger on Kerala's Communist Government in 1959?', *Journal of Commonwealth and Comparative Politics*, vol. 29, no. 1, 1991.

36 See Gopal, *Nehru*, vol. 3, p. 68.

37 Quoted in 'Mrs Indira Gandhi's Election', undated, unsigned typescript in Pupul Jayakar Papers, held by Mrs Radhika Herzberger (emphasis added.) Cf. also *The Statesman*, 27 July 1959.

38 Kannikara Padmanabha Pillai, *The Red Interlude in Kerala* (Trivandrum: Kerala Pradesh Congress Committee, 1959), pp. 183ff.

39 Woodcock, *Kerala*, p. 272.

40 Nehru to Namboodiripad, 30 July 1959, quoted in Gopal, *Nehru*, vol. 3, pp. 71–2.

41 See K. P. Bhagat, *The Kerala Mid-Term Election of 1960* (Bombay: Popular Book Depot, 1962).

42 Gopal, *Nehru*, vol. 3, p. 73.

43 See correspondence and papers in Subject File 34, C. Rajagopalachari Papers, Fifth Instalment, NMML.

44 The article is reproduced in C. Rajagopalachari, *Satyam Eva Jayate* (The Truth Alone Shall Triumph) (Madras: Bharathan Publications, 1961), vol. 1, pp. 149–53. Cf. also 'Rajaji on Need for Strong Opposition', *Swarajya*, 9 March 1957.

45 C. Rajagopalachari, 'Some Thoughts on the Budget', the *Current*, 17 August 1957.

46 See 'Statement of Principles of the Swatantra Party', reproduced in *Economic Weekly*, special issue, July 1959, p. 894.

47　C. Rajagopalachari, 'The Case for the Swatantra Party', *Illustrated Weekly of India*, 16 August 1959.

48　See H. L. Erdman, *The Swatantra Party and Indian Conservatism* (Cambridge: Cambridge University Press, 1967).

49　Gopal, *Nehru*, vol. 3, p. 120.

50　See Tarun Kumar Mukhopadhyaya, *Feroze Gandhi: A Crusader in Parliament* (New Delhi: Allied Publishers, 1992), pp. 109–23.

51　A useful summary of the main aspects of the controversy is contained in M. C. Chagla, *Roses in December: An Autobiography* (1973; revised edn Bombay: Bharatiya Vidya Bhavan, 1994), pp. 203–11. Justice Chagla headed one of the commissions; Justice Vivian Bose the other. But cf. also A. D. Gorwala, *The Lies of T. T. K.* (Bombay: R. V. Pandit, 1959). Feroze Gandhi died in 1960, not long after his speeches about the Mundhra scandal in Parliament.

52　Quoted in Motilal C. Setalvad, *My Life: Law and other Things* (Bombay: N. M. Tripathi, 1970), p. 282.

15. THE EXPERIENCE OF DEFEAT

1　George N. Patterson, *Tragic Destiny* (London: Faber and Faber, 1959), p. 187.

2　'Record of Prime Minister's Talk with Dalai Lama' (24 April 1959), in File 9, Subimal Dutt Papers, NMML.

3　See Ramesh Sanghvi, *India's Northern Frontier and China* (Bombay: Contemporary Publishers, 1962), pp. 1–2.

4　*Notes, Memoranda and Letters Exchanged and Signed between the Governments of India and China, 1954–1959* (New Delhi: Ministry of External Affairs, 1959), pp. 46, 26–7. This was the first of nine similarly titled White Papers issued by the government of India between 1959 and 1962, subsequently referred to here as WP I, WP II etc. Unless otherwise stated, the rest of this section is based on the notes and correspondence in this first White Paper.

5　Stuart Schram, *Mao Tse-tung* (Harmondsworth: Penguin, 1967), p. 282.

6　George N. Patterson, *Peking versus Delhi* (London: Faber and Faber, 1963), pp. 162–3.

7　For JP's views see *The Tragedy of Tibet: Speeches and Statements of Jayaprakash Narayan* (New Delhi: Afro-Asian Committee on Tibet, 1959); for the Jana Sangh position, see 'India's Stake in Tibet's Freedom', *Organiser*, 27 April 1959, reprinted in Pandit Deendayal Upadhyaya, *Political Diary* (Bombay: Jaico Publishing House, 1968), pp. 97–101.

8　See Subject File 16, Thimayya Papers, NMML.

9　He was the first, and remains the last, Indian military man to be the subject of a biography by a Western author: Humphrey Evans, *Thimayya of India* (New York: Harcourt, Brace and Co., 1960).

10　Arthur Lall, *The Emergence of Modern India* (New York: Columbia University Press, 1981), p. 119.

11　Wells Hangen, *After Nehru, Who?* (London: Rupert Hart-Davis, 1963), chapter 9. Kaul's alleged closeness to Nehru is also extensively advertised in his memoirs, where he claims that he was a sort of confidant and sounding-board for the prime minister. See Lt. Gen. B. M. Kaul, *The Untold Story* (Bombay: Allied Publishers, 1967), pp. ix–x, 81–2, 86fn, 87, 97, 114, 118 etc.

12 Maj. Gen. D. K. Palit, *War in High Himalaya* (New Delhi: Lancer International, 1991), p. 76.

13 See Thimayya to Nehru, letters of 31 August and 3 September 1959, Thimayya Papers, NMML.

14 Press Clippings File 16, Thimayya Papers, NMML. This file has a cover note, almost certainly in the general's own hand, summarizing its contents thus: 'If a poll was to be taken outside Parliament, opinion both inside and outside would have found favour with Thimayya'.

15 Letters of Ashutosh Lahiri and Sheodatt, Subject File 15, Thimayya Papers, NMML.

16 H. V. Kamath, 'The Sino-Indian Border Dispute', *Illustrated Weekly of India*, 18 October 1959.

17 The *Current*, 14 and 28 October 1959.

18 Shiva Rao to Nehru, 3 December 1959, B. Shiva Rao Papers, NMML.

19 Chou to Nehru, 8 September 1959, and Nehru to Chou, 26 September 1959, in WP II, pp. 27–46.

20 The 'forward policy' is described in the memoirs of one of its chief architects, B. N. Mullik. See his *My Years with Nehru: The Chinese Betrayal* (Bombay: Allied Publishers, 1971), esp. chapters 14 and 19. Mullick was the chief of the Intelligence Bureau, and privy to most crucial decisions taken with regard to the border dispute.

21 Latifi to Nehru, 27 November 1959, copy in Subject File 423, P. N. Haksar Papers, Third Instalment, NMML (emphasis in original).

22 Quoted in Neville Maxwell, *India's China War* (Harmondsworth: Penguin, 1972), p. 152.

23 *The Hindu*, quoted in Dorothy Woodman, *Himalayan Frontiers: A Political Review of British, Chinese, Indian and Russian Rivalries* (London: Barrie and Rockcliff, 1969), p. 245.

24 Steven A. Hoffman, *India and the China Crisis* (Delhi: Oxford University Press, 1990), pp. 67, 73, 82–3 etc. The origins and trajectory of the India–China dispute are, as one can imagine, the subject of a huge and very motivated literature. On the one side are the various self-serving memoirs by Indian generals and officials, which seek to blame China for 'betraying' India's trust. These are collectively answered by Neville Maxwell's *India's China War*, a well-documented book but one that sees everything, big and small, from the Chinese point of view. Hoffman's is an admirably detached and comprehensive account of the dispute, perhaps the best there is.

25 Chou to Nehru, letters of 7 November and 17 December 1959; Nehru to Chou, letters of 16 November and 21 December 1959, in WP III, pp. 45–59.

26 Owen Lattimore, 'India–Tibet–China: Starting Principle for Frontier Demarcation', *Economic Weekly*, annual issue, January 1960. Steven Hoffman explains that Chou's 'barter' offer could not be acceptable to India because 'it was being asked to accept the clandestine and forceful seizure of parts of its territory [in the west], in return for a worthless assurance that another part of the frontier [in the east] would not be menaced' (*India and the China Crisis*, pp. 86–7).

27 'Pragmatist', 'The Political Economy of Defence', *Economic Weekly*, annual issue, January 1960.

28 Presidential address of Pitambar Das, reproduced in Girja Kumar and V. K. Arora, eds, *Documents on Indian Affairs, 1960* (Bombay: Asia Publishing House, 1965), pp. 22f.

29 See Gyanvati Darbar, *Portrait of a President: Letters of Dr Rajendra Prasad*, vol. 2 (New Delhi: Vikas Publishing House, 1976), pp. 85–6.

30 Unless otherwise stated, this and the following paragraphs are based on reports and comments in the *Indian Express*, various issues of 10 March to 27 April 1960.

31 Kumar and Arora, *Documents*, pp. 493–4. The signatories to this letter included J. B. Kripalani, M. R. Masani, A. B. Vajpayee, and N. G. Goray.

32 The *Current*, 27 April 1960.

33 'Record of Talks between Prime Minister of India and Prime Minister of China, 20th to 25th April 1960', in Subject File 24, P. N. Haksar Papers, First and Second Instalments, NMML. The transcripts of the talks run to over a hundred foolscap pages.

34 Copies of the transcripts of Chou En-lai's talks with Desai, Pant, Radhakrishnan and other leaders are in Subject File 26, P. N. Haksar Papers, First and Second Instalments, NMML. Desai was right in spirit if not in substance, for it was Karl Marx who sought asylum in the UK, whereas Lenin lived in exile in that other bourgeois nation, Switzerland.

35 This paragraph is based on Margaret W. Fisher, Leo E. Rose and Robert A. Huttenback, *Himalayan Battleground: Sino-Indian Rivalry in Ladakh* (London: Pall Mall Press, 1963), esp. chapter 11.

36 The transcripts of the talks are reproduced in Appendix XI of Parshotam Mehra, *Negotiating with the Chinese, 1846–1987* (New Delhi: Reliance Publishing House, 1989).

37 Interview in *Look* magazine, 18 October 1960, reproduced in Edgar Snow, *The Other Side of the River: Red China Today* (New York: Random House, 1963), pp. 762–3.

38 Baldev Raj Nayar, *Minority Politics in the Punjab* (Princeton: Princeton University Press, 1969), esp. pp. 248–60; the *Current*, 16 August and 23 August 1961; correspondence between Nehru, Rajaji and Tara Singh in Subject File 82, C. Rajagopalachari Papers, Fourth Instalment, NMML.

39 Nehru to Jayaprakash Narayan, 10 October 1961, Brahmanand Papers, NMML.

40 See E. N. Mangat Rai, *Commitment My Style* (Delhi: Vikas Publishing House, 1973), chapter 10. Mangat Rai was Kairon's chief secretary for five of his eight years in power.

41 The *Current*, 9 December 1959, 6 January 1960 and 14 September 1963.

42 A. G. Noorani, *Ministers' Misconduct* (Delhi: Vikas Publishing House, 1973), p. 42.

43 Nirmal Nibedon, *Nagaland: The Night of the Guerillas* (New Delhi: Lancer, 1983), pp. 88–90.

44 A. Z. Phizo, *The Fate of the Naga People: An Appeal to the World* (London: privately published, July 1960).

45 See, for example, the clippings in the W. G. Archer Papers, Mss Eur F236, OIOC.

46 Anon., *The Naga Problem* (New Delhi: Ministry of External Affairs, 1960). As many as 2,000 copies of this pamphlet were printed.

47 This memorandum is reproduced in Kumar and Arora, *Documents*, pp. 91–5.

48 Ibid., pp. 101–5.

49 Clipping from *The Times*, 21 September 1962, in Mss Eur F158/239, OIOC.

50 Daniel Thorner, 'Ploughing the Plan Under: Ford Team Report on Food "Crisis" ', *Economic Weekly*, special issue, July 1959.

51 See *Report of Non-Official Enquiry Commission on Cachar* (Calcutta: N. Chatterjee, 1961); L. P. Singh, *Portrait of Lal Bahadur Shastri: A Quintessential Gandhian* (New Delhi: Ravi Dayal, 1996), chapter 3.

52 The *Current*, 8 March 1961.

53 Selig S. Harrison, *India: The Most Dangerous Decades* (Princeton: Princeton University Press, 1960).

54 See Grover Smith, ed., *Letters of Aldous Huxley* (London: Chatto and Windus, 1969), pp. 926–7.

55 Arthur Cook, 'Nehru', *Daily Mail*, 20 February 1962.

56 For details, see WPs IV, V and VI, *passim*.

57 *Lok Sabha Debates*, 11 April 1961.

58 Ibid., 17 August and 28 November 1961, 14 August 1962.

59 Ibid., 5 December 1961.

60 P. D. Gaitonde, *The Liberation of Goa: A Participant's View of History* (London: C. Hurst and Co., 1987), chapter 18; *Illustrated Weekly of India*, special issue, 18 February 1962; D. R. Mankekar, *The Goa Action* (Bombay: The Popular Book Depot, 1962).

61 See clippings and papers in File 8, Box XVI.18, Richard B. Russell Papers, University of Georgia, Athens; File 29, Penderel Moon Papers, OIOC (Mss Eur F230/29).

62 *New York Times*, 18 and 19 December 1961. There is also a suggestion that sections within the Indian army welcomed the Goan adventure as a victory easily won. It was, recalled one officer, 'light relief from the gloom and foreboding of the general strategic scene' along the borders with China. See Maj. Gen. D. K. Palit, *Musings and Memories*, vol. 2 (New Delhi: Lancer, 2004), pp. 411–12.

63 My account of the election is based on Aloo J. Dastur, *Menon versus Kripalani: North Bombay Election, 1962* (Bombay: University of Bombay, 1967), supplemented by Norman D. Palmer, 'The 1962 Election in North Bombay', *Pacific Affairs*, vol. 30, no. 1, spring 1963. Cf. also A. D. Gorwala, *Krishna Menon: Danger to India* (Bombay: privately published, January 1962). The Hindi ditty was supplied by Nitya Ramakrishnan.

64 'Seminarist', 'Issues in the Election', *Seminar*, July 1962.

65 K. P. Subramania Menon, 'The Ramifications', and General K. S. Thimayya, 'Adequate "Insurance" ', both in *Seminar*, July 1962. That, even in retirement, Thimayya was seriously worried about the Chinese threat is also indicated by a book that he once owned and which is now in my possession; written by a retired major, it provides a historical conspectus of the NEFA region that had become so central to the border conflict. My copy of the book – Major Sitaram Johri, *Where India, China and Burma Meet* (Calcutta: Thacker, Spink and Co., 1962) – has 'K. S. Thimayya, 9 Feb. 62' written on its flyleaf; I found it in a second-hand store in Bangalore, once the general's home town, and now mine.

66 As the spark that fuelled the Chinese invasion, the Thag La conflict has been widely written about. My account is based on, among other sources, Brigadier J. P. Dalvi, *Himalayan Blunder* (Delhi: Hind Pocket Books, 1970),

chapters 7, 9–12; Maxwell, *India's China War*, pp. 357 ff.; Hoffman, *India and the China Crisis*, pp. 130ff.

67 Hoffman, *India and the China Crisis*, p. 149.

68 Dalvi, *Himalayan Blunder*, pp. 262–3.

69 *New York Times*, 21 October 1962.

70 *New York Times*, 24 October 1962.

71 Dalvi, *Himalayan Blunder*, pp. 80–1.

72 Chou to Nehru, 24 October and 4 November 1962, Nehru to Chou, 27 October and 14 November 1962, printed with enclosures in WP VIII, pp. 1–17.

73 John Kenneth Galbraith, *Ambassador's Journal* (Boston: Houghton Mifflin, 1969), p. 385.

74 *New York Times*, 28 and 30 October 1962.

75 *Lok Sabha Debates*, 8–14 November 1962. In his closing speech Nehru deplored the series of attacks on Chinese shopkeepers in New Delhi, which 'brutalizes us and gives us a bad name'. Like his mentor, Gandhi, he knew how easily nationalism could shade into jingoism. To take revenge on innocent shopkeepers was deeply wrong-headed, for 'we should always distinguish between governmental action and the people as a whole'.

76 The Walong battle is vividly described in G. S. Bhargava, *The Battle for NEFA* (Bombay: Allied Publishers, 1964), chapter 5.

77 Hoffman, *India and the China Crisis*, pp. 180–1.

78 Maxwell, *India's China War*, pp. 398ff. In his memoirs, Kaul argues that Se La was a well-positioned and well-fortified garrison that could have held out for a week or more; he blames its fall and the flight of the troops on the failure of nerve of the man in charge, Major General A. S. Pathania. See Kaul, *The Untold Story*, pp. 413ff.

79 As recalled in B. G. Verghese, 'Unfinished Business in the North-East', *Mainstream*, 15 June 2002.

80 A. M. Rosenthal, 'War Fever in India', *New York Times*, 3 November 1962.

81 D. R. Mankekar, *The Guilty Men of 1962* (Bombay: Tulsi Shah Enterprises, 1968), pp. 88–90.

82 Woodman, *Himalayan Frontiers*, p. 293.

83 Maxwell, *India's China War*, p. 465.

84 Palit, *War in High Himalaya*, pp. 225, 231.

85 As quoted in Snow, *Other Side of the River*, pp. 761–2 (emphases added).

86 Allen Ginsberg, *Indian Journals: March 1962–May 1963* (San Francisco: City Lights Books, 1970), p. 50.

16. Peace in Our Time

1 John Kenneth Galbraith, *Ambassador's Journal* (Boston: Houghton Mifflin, 1969), pp. 405–12.

2 Robert Sherrod, 'Nehru: The Great Awakening', *Saturday Evening Post*, 19 January 1963.

3 Galbraith to Kennedy, 29 January 1963, copy in Dean Rusk Papers, University of Georgia, Athens. Perhaps it was the economist in Galbraith that provoked him to identify China rather than Russia as the greater long-term threat to American interests.

4 Cf. Richard Parker, *John Kenneth Galbraith: His Life, His Politics, His Economics* (New York: Farrar, Straus and Giroux, 2005), p. 400.

5 See clippings in Files 9 and 10, Box XVI.18, Richard B. Russell Papers, University of Georgia, Athens. The rest of this section is likewise based on material contained in these files.

6 There was also a letter, too crazy to quote in the text perhaps, which urged a cheaper method of disposing of the Chinese threat than arming the Indians. S. B. Crowe of Sanford, Florida, recommended that the Americans drop boxes of atomic waste, each with an explosive charge, on the Chinese side of the Himalaya. The Reds would be told of this, so that they would 'stay out of Tibet and India'. However, 'if Mao wishes to conduct an experiment in genetics and send 150 million through this radiation hazard, it would be an interesting experiment'. Estimating that this would save the American taxpayer 'about a billion dollars', Mr Crowe signed off as follows: 'Yours for more economy in Government. The barrel isn't bottomless, in spite of Mr Keynes and his theories.'

7 'Transcript of Prime Minister's Press Conference held on June 15, 1963, in New Delhi', issued by Press Information Bureau, Government of India, copy in Subject File 189, P. N. Haksar Papers, Third Instalment, NMML. Cf. also *The Statesman*, 16 June 1963.

8 See Stanley Kochanek, *The Congress Party of India: The Dynamics of One-Party Democracy* (Princeton: Princeton University Press, 1968), pp. 79ff.

9 Ibid., pp. 78–80.

10 H. V. Kamath, *Last Days of Jawaharlal Nehru* (Calcutta: Jayashree Prakashan, 1977), pp. 1–2.

11 Wells Hangen, *After Nehru, Who?* (London: Rupert Hart-Davis, 1963).

12 These quotes are from an article by Tom Stacey, originally published in the *Sunday Times* of London and reprinted under a different title in the *Current*, 1 January 1964.

13 Indira Gandhi to Mridula Sarabhai, 4 September 1963, Reel 57, Mridula Sarabhai Papers, on microfilm, NMML.

14 Cf. Kanji Dwarkadas to Lord Scarborough, 16 January 1964, Mss Eur F253/53 (Lord Lumley Papers), OIOC.

15 For the different ways in which the creation of the state was received, see P. N. Luthra, *Nagaland: From a District to a State* (Shillong: Directorate of Information and Public Relations, 1974), pp. 1–16; A. Lanunungsang Ao, *From Phizo to Muivah: The Naga National Question in North-east India* (New Delhi: Mittal Publications), pp. 81–2.

16 The *Current*, 4 January 1964.

17 Cf. report in the *Current*, 20 April 1963.

18 C. P. Srivastava, *Lal Bahadur Shastri: A Life of Truth in Politics* (Delhi: Oxford University Press, 1995), pp. 71–4; Rajeshwar Prasad, *Days with Lal Bahadur Shastri: Glimpses from the Last Seven Years* (New Delhi: Allied Publishers, 1991), pp. 27–9.

19 Mountbatten's conversations with Nehru are reported in the correspondence contained in Subject File 52, T. T. Krishnamachari Papers, NMML.

20 Aparna Basu, *Mridula Sarabhai: Rebel with a Cause* (Delhi: Oxford University Press, 1996), chapter 9, 'Kashmir'; *Hindustan Times* (hereafter HT), 9 April 1964.

21 *Dawn*, 18 November 1960.

22 Nehru to Vijayalakshmi Pandit, 3 October 1953, Vijayalakshmi Pandit Papers, NMML.

23 Nehru to Tikaram Paliwal, 17 July 1955, in SWJN2, vol. 29, pp. 452–3.

24 These paragraphs on Abdullah's release and his triumphant return to the Valley are based principally on the HT, issues of 6–24 April 1964.

25 See letters and papers in Subject File 28 ('Indo-Pakistan Conciliation Group'), Brahmanand Papers, NMML.

26 Jayaprakash Narayan, 'Our Great Opportunity in Kashmir', HT, 20 April 1964.

27 C. Rajagopalachari, 'Am I Wrong?', *Swarajya*, 25 April 1964.

28 See report in HT, 23 April 1964. In the rest of this section, quotes not given specific attributions come from this newspaper.

29 Telegram dated 29 April 1964, in Subject File 92, C. Rajagopalachari Papers, Fourth Instalment, NMML.

30 Letter of 29 April 1964, ibid. As some other letters in this file show, most Swatantra Party members opposed Masani and Rajaji in their support of the Nehru–Abdullah talks. K. M. Munshi said that the Sheikh should be put back in jail. Dahyabhai Patel (son of Vallabhbhai Patel) said that the only solution to the Kashmir problem was to settle the Valley with Hindu refugees from East Pakistan.

31 Abdullah to Minoo Masani, 16 April 1964, ibid.

32 Shastri to Rajaji, 4 May 1964, ibid.

33 'Kashmir – Talk with Sheikh Abdullah on 8th May, 1964, at PM's House', Subject File 4, Y. D. Gundevia Papers, NMML.

34 Shiva Rao to Rajaji, 10 May 1964; Rajaji to Shiva Rao, 12 May 1964; both in Subject File 92, C. Rajagopalachari Papers, Fourth Instalment, NMML.

35 HT, 23 May 1964.

36 Y. D. Gundevia to V. K. T. Chari (Attorney-General, Madras), 13 May 1964, Subject File 4, Y. D. Gundevia Papers, NMML.
    The confederal solution to the Kashmir problem was apparently first proposed by the journalist Arthur Moore as early as January 1948. Moore believed that 'India, Pakistan and Kashmir should become a federated commonwealth state, with common foreign affairs, common defence, and such finance as concerned these subjects, but otherwise all three to be self-governing States'. He spoke about it to Mahatma Gandhi before he died, and later also appears to have broached the topic with the prime minister. Moore also wrote about the idea in a volume of tributes to Nehru on his 70th birthday, where he called this the 'greatest test for Nehru's statesmanship . . . [for] there will never be satisfactory relations between India and Pakistan till the Kashmir issue is settled'. See Arthur Moore, 'My Friend's Son', in Rafiq Zakaria, ed., *A Study of Nehru* (1959; 2nd edn Bombay: The Times of India Press, 1960), esp. pp. 175–6. It seems very likely, considering where it appeared, that Nehru had read Moore's article.

37 Letter of 20 May 1964, in Subject File 92, C. Rajagopalachari Papers, Fourth Instalment, NMML. Within Parliament, Masani was one of the fiercest critics of the prime minister. But, like his mentor Rajaji, he saw that in progress on Kashmir lay the future of the subcontinent. On this subject at least he was willing to bat for Nehru.

38 HT, 25 May 1964. Unless otherwise indicated, the rest of this section is based on HT, 25–30 May 1964.

39 *Dawn*, quoted in HT, 27 May 1964 (emphasis added).

40 Walter Crocker, *Nehru: A Contemporary's Estimate* (New York: Oxford University Press, 1966), p. 178.

41 In his magisterial three-volume biography of Nehru S. Gopal gives the matter three paragraphs; Nehru's most recent biographer, Judith Brown, allows it one. Recent works on the Kashmir dispute, as for instance by Schonfield, Bose and Ganguly, do not mention these events at all.

42 Romesh Thapar, 'Behind the Abdullah Headlines', *Economic Weekly*, 30 May 1964.

43 V. K. T. Chari to Y. D. Gundevia, 16 May 1964, in Subject File 4, Y. D. Gundevia Papers, NMML.

44 HT, 26 May 1964.

45 Quoted in HT, 29 May 1964.

17. MINDING THE MINORITIES

1 Austin's diary entry of 28 May 1968 was published thirty years later in *The Hindu*, 29 May 1994.

2 See correspondence between H. S. Suhrawardy, Chaudhary Khaliquzzaman, Jawaharlal Nehru, M. A. Jinnah and M. K. Gandhi, reproduced in A. G. Noorani, ed., *The Muslims of India: A Documentary Record* (New Delhi: Oxford University Press, 2003), pp. 40–52. See also Chaudhry Khaliquzzaman, *Pathway to Pakistan* (Lahore: Longmans, Green and Co., 1961).

3 Jawaharlal Nehru to J. R. D. Tata, 23 October 1947; Tata to Nehru, 4 November 1947, letters in Tata Steel archives, Jamshedpur.

4 Gardner Murphy, *In the Minds of Men: The Study of Human Behavior and Social Tensions in India* (New York: Basic Books, 1953), pp. 144–7.

5 See 'You Cannot Ride Two Horses', in *For a United India: Speeches of Sardar Patel* (1949; reprint New Delhi, Publications Division, 1982), pp. 49–52 (emphasis added).

6 'Top Secret' letter dated 17 July 1948 from HVR Iengar, Home Secretary, to Dr Tara Chand, Education Secretary, in File 6/228/48 ('Information regarding government servants whose family is still staying in Pakistan'), records of the Archaeological Survey of India, New Delhi. The rest of this section is based on this file, a copy of which was kindly passed on to me by Professor Nayanjyot Lahiri of the University of Delhi.

7 The superintendent was called Pandit Madho Sarup Vats. While we know no more of his biography, 'Vats' is a Punjabi Hindu surname, and it is possible that his vendetta was influenced by direct or indirect knowledge of the massacres in the Punjab.

8 Quoted in Farhana Ibrahim, 'Defining a Border: Harijan Migrants and the State in Kachchh', *Economic and Political Weekly*, 16 April 2005.

9 Nehru to Patel, 20 February 1950, SPC, vol. 10, p. 5.

10 E.g. Nehru's letters to Patel of 6 October and 21 November 1947, SPC, vol. 4, pp. 399–401, 362–4.

11 Letter of 15 October 1947, LCM, vol. 1, pp. 32–3.

12 Letter of 2 October 1949, ibid., pp. 478–9.

13 Letters of 29 September 1953 and 15 June 1954, LCM, vol. 3, pp. 375–6, 570 (emphases added).

14 Speech in Lok Sabha on Azad's death, reproduced in *Maulana Azad: A Homage* (New Delhi: Publications Division, 1958), pp. 30–1.

15 On Muslim support to the Congress in national and state elections through the 1950s, see Sisir K. Gupta, 'Moslems in Indian Politics, 1947–1960', *India Quarterly*, vol. 18, no. 4, 1962.

16 Saif Faiz Badruddin Tyabji, *The Future of Muslims in India* (Bombay: Writers' Emporium, 1956). Tyabji's forward-looking agenda makes an interesting contrast with the nostalgia-laden lament of the great Lucknow divine S. Abul Hasan Ali Nadwi. See his *Muslims in India*, trans. Mohammad Asif Kidwai (Lucknow: Academy of Islamic Research and Publications, 1961). Tyabji himself died shortly after making a speech in the Lok Sabha in 1958; his death, when only just forty, described to me (by the distinguished conservationist Zafar Futehally) as 'a great tragedy for the Muslims of India'.

17 See reports in Files 78 and 79, Delhi Police Records, Fifth Instalment, NMML.

18 Quoted in W. H. Morris-Jones, *Parliament in India* (London: Longmans, Green and Co., 1957), p. 27, fn.

19 'Daily Diary', 19 February 1954, in File 138, Delhi Police Records, Sixth Instalment, NMML.

20 See Noorani, *The Muslims of India*, pp. 99–100.

21 See, for details, Theodore P. Wright, Jr., 'The Effectiveness of Muslim Representation in India', in D. E. Smith, ed., *South Asian Politics and Religion* (Princeton: Princeton University Press, 1966).

22 W. C. Smith, *Islam in Modern History* (1957; reprint New York: Mentor Books, 1959), pp. 263–4.

23 Ibid., pp. 268–74.

24 J. D. Tyson to his family, 9 August 1947, in Mss Eur D341/40, OIOC.

25 See Farida Abdulla Khan, 'Other Communities, Other Histories: A Study of Muslim Women and Education in Kashmir', in Zoya Hasan and Ritu Menon, eds, *In a Minority: Essays on Muslim Women in India* (New Delhi: Oxford University Press, 2005).

26 See the essays and evidence in M. K. A. Siddiqui, *Muslims in Free India: Their Social Profile and Problems* (New Delhi: Institute of Objective Studies, 1998).

27 *The Current*, 5 September 1956.

28 D. E. Smith, *India as a Secular State* (Princeton: Princeton University Press, 1963), esp. pp. 412–13.

29 Smith, *Islam in Modern History*, p. 267.

30 Mushirul Hasan, *Legacy of a Divided Nation: India's Muslims Since Independence* (Delhi: Oxford University Press, 1997), p. 161.

31 Taya Zinkin, *Challenges in India* (New York: Walker and Co., 1966), pp. 147ff.

32 Mohamed Raza Khan, *What Price Freedom? A Historical Survey of the Political Trends and Conditions Leading to Independence and the Birth of Pakistan and After* (Madras: privately published, 1969), pp. 503f.

33 See the studies collected in M. N. Srinivas, ed., *India's Villages* (1955; reprint Bombay: Media Promoters and Publishers, 1985), pp. 28–9, 94, 100 etc.; and in McKim Marriot, ed., *Village India: Studies in the Little Community* (Chicago: The University of Chicago Press, 1955), pp. 45, 47, 51, 68, 70–2 etc.

34 Vijay Prashad, *Untouchable Freedom: A Social History of a Dalit Community* (New Delhi: Oxford University Press, 2000), pp. 156–63.

35 Among the autobiographies and memoirs available in English, see especially Omprakash Valmiki, *Joothan: A Dalit's Life*, trans. Arun Prabha Mukherjee (Kolkata: Samya, 2003); Narendra Jadhav, *Outcaste: A Memoir* (New Delhi: Viking, 2003); Vasant Moon, *Growing up Untouchable in India*, trans. Gail Omvedt (Lanham, Md.: Rowman and Littlefield, 2001); Siddharth Dube, *Words Like Freedom: The Memoirs of an Impoverished Indian Family, 1947–1997* (New Delhi: HarperCollins India, 1998); and the pioneering anthology edited by Arjun Dangle, *Poisoned Bread: Translations from Modern Marathi Dalit Literature* (Hyderabad: Orient Longman, 1992).

36 Harold R. Isaacs, *India's Ex-Untouchables* (New York: John Day, 1965), pp. 80–1.

37 This paragraph is based on three essays by Lelah Dushkin: 'The Backward Classes. I: Special Treatment Policy' and 'The Backward Classes. II: Removal of Disabilities', *Economic Weekly*, 28 October and 4 November 1961; and 'Backward Caste Benefits and Social Class in India, 1920–1970', *Economic and Political Weekly*, 7 April 1979. Cf. Marc Galanter, *Competing Equalities: Law and the Backward Classes in India* (Delhi: Oxford University Press, 1984).

38 Quoted in Owen M. Lynch, *The Politics of Untouchability: Social Mobility and Social Change in a City of India* (New York: Columbia University Press, 1969), p. 89.

39 See Bernard S. Cohn, 'The Changing Status of a Depressed Caste', in Marriot, *Village India*, esp. pp. 70–2.

40 J. Michael Mahar, 'Agents of Dharma in a North Indian Village', in J. M. Mahar, *The Untouchables in Contemporary India* (Tucson: University of Arizona Press, 1972), p. 29.

41 Isaacs, *India's Ex-Untouchables*, p. 126.

42 Dube, *Words Like Freedom*, p. 53.

43 Lynch, *The Politics of Untouchability*, chapter 3 and *passim*.

44 Nehru to Rajagopalachari, letters of 5 May and 25 June 1952, in Subject File 123, C. Rajagopalachari Papers, Fifth Instalment, NMML.

45 Oliver Mendelsohn and Marika Vicziany, *The Untouchables: Subordination, Poverty and the State in India* (Cambridge: Cambridge University Press, 1998), pp. 207–8, 252; Devendra Prasad Sharma, *Jagjivan Ram: The Man and His Times* (New Delhi: Indian Book Co., 1974).

46 This account of Ambedkar's last days is based on Vasant Moon, *Dr. Babasaheb Ambedkar*, trans. Asha Damle (New Delhi: National Book Trust, 2002), pp. 203–19. The best treatments of Ambedkar's thought (including his conversion to Buddhism) are Eleanor Zelliot, *Untouchable to Dalit: Essays on Ambedkar Movement* (Delhi: Manohar, 1992), and Jayashree Gokhale, *From Concessions to Confrontation: The Politics of an Indian Untouchable Community* (Bombay: Popular Prakashan, 1993). See also Valerian Rodrigues, ed., *B. R. Ambedkar: Essential Writings* (New Delhi: Oxford University Press, 2004).

47 Moon, *Growing up Untouchable*, pp. 52, 107–11, 127, 160–1 etc.

48 Cf. Valmiki, *Joothan*, p. 71f.

49 Jadhav, *Outcaste*, p. 231.

50 Rameshwari Nehru, *Gandhi Is My Star* (Patna: Pustak Bhandar, 1950), pp. 110ff.

51 The *Current*, 8 February 1956.

52 N. D. Kamble, *Atrocities on Scheduled Castes in Post-Independent India* (New Delhi: Ashish Publishing House, 1981), pp. 8–46. Kamble's sources were newspaper accounts in English, Hindi and Marathi. I have simplified and summarized his renditions.

53 Aldous Huxley, *Jesting Pilate: The Diary of a Journey* (London: Chatto and Windus, 1927), pp. 116–17.
54 Speech by H. J. Khandekar, 21 November 1949, in CAD, vol. 11, pp. 736–7.
55 Aga Khan to Jawaharlal Nehru, 25 January 1951, copy in Subject File 61, C. Rajagopalachari Papers, Fourth Instalment, NMML.
56 D. F. Karaka, writing in the *Current*, 11 November 1959. Karaka then went on to list Nehru's failures, among them the inability to root out corruption and nepotism, and the foolishness of trusting communist China.

18. WAR AND SUCCESSION

1 V. K. Narasimhan, *Kamaraj: A Study* (Bangalore: Myers Indmark, 1967); Duncan B. Forrester, 'Kamaraj: A Study in Percolation of Style', *Modern Asian Studies*, vol. 4, no. 1, 1970; J. Anthony Lukacs, 'Meet Kumaraswamy Kamaraj', *Illustrated Weekly of India*, 22 May 1966.
2 This account is based on Michael Brecher, *Succession in India: A Study in Decision Making* (London: Oxford University Press, 1966), chapters 2 and 3. But see also Stanley Kochanek, *The Congress Party of India: The Dynamics of One-Party Democracy* (Princeton: Princeton University Press, 1968) pp. 88f.
3 Cf. Brecher, *Succession*, pp. 115–17.
4 The *Guardian*, 3 June 1964 (editorial), clipping in Mss Eur F158/1045, OIOC.
5 Patrick Keatley, 'A Sparrow's Strength', reprinted in *The Bedside Guardian 13: A Selection from 'The Guardian' 1963–1964* (London: Collins, 1964), pp. 200–3.
6 J. H. Hutton to Charles Pawsey, 29 May 1964, in Box II, Pawsey Papers, CSAS.
7 M. Aram, *Peace in Nagaland: Eight Year Story, 1964–72* (New Delhi: Arnold-Heinemann (India), 1974), pp. 20–38: A. Paul Hare and Herbert H. Blumberg, eds, *A Search for Peace and Justice: Reflections of Michael Scott* (London: Rex Collings, 1980), chapter 11 ('Nagaland Peace Mission').
8 Narayan to J. J. Singh, dated Kohima, 11 September 1964, J. J. Singh Papers, NMML.
9 See V. K. Nuh, comp., *The Naga Chronicle* (New Delhi: Regency Publications, 2002), pp. 274ff.
10 Dr Bhabha's speech was quoted *in extenso* in the *Lok Sabha Debates*, 27 November 1964.
11 *Lok Sabha Debates*, 27 November and 11 December 1964. Both Kachwai and Shastri spoke in Hindi.
12 See K. S. Ramanathan, *The Big Change* (Madras: Higginbothams, 1967), chapter 6.
13 A. S. Raman, 'A Meeting with C. N. Annadurai', *Illustrated Weekly of India*, 26 September 1965.
14 See Robert D. King, *Nehru and the Language Politics of India* (New Delhi: Oxford University Press, 1997); Mohan Ram, *Hindi Against India: The Meaning of DMK* (New Delhi: Rachna Prakashan, 1968).
15 This account is principally based on news reports in *The Hindu*, 27 January–15 February 1965. But see also the four-page photo spread on 'Language Riots in Madras', in the *Illustrated Weekly of India*, 28 February 1965.
16 Eric Stracey, *Odd Man in: My Years in the Indian Police* (New Delhi: Vikas Publishing House, 1981), pp. 209–27.

17 Cf. Morarji Desai, 'National Unity through Hindi', the *Current*, 30 January 1965.

18 See *Selected Speeches of Lal Bahadur Shastri* (New Delhi: Publications Division, 1974), pp. 119–22.

19 *Lok Sabha Debates*, 18 February 1965.

20 Ghosh to Alexander, 3 March 1965, File 60, Horace Alexander Papers, Friends House, Euston.

21 Sir Morrice James, *Pakistan Chronicle* (London: Hurst and Co., 1993), pp. 123–6; G. S. Bhargava, *After Nehru: India's New Image* (Bombay: Allied Publishers, 1966), pp. 260–3, 276, 439–41. The Kutch ceasefire agreement was signed by officials representing the respective foreign ministries – both Muslims, they were, coincidentally, first cousins, one of whom had chosen to be a citizen of India.

22 Letter of 24 May 1965, in File 60, Horace Alexander Papers, Friends House, Euston.

23 James, *Pakistan Chronicle*, pp. 128–31.

24 See the then Jammu and Kashmir chief secretary's letters of August 1965 in Nayantara Sahgal and E. N. Mangat Rai, *Relationship: Extracts from a Correspondence* (New Delhi: Kali for Women, 1994), pp. 134–9.

25 This account of the hostilities is principally based on Brian Cloughley, *A History of the Pakistan Army: Wars and Insurrections* (Karachi: Oxford University Press, 1999), pp. 68–72, 84–5, 102–6; Air Chief Marshal P. C. Lal, *My Years with the IAF* (New Delhi: Lancer, 1987), pp. 126–34; Lt. Gen. Harbaksh Singh, *In the Line of Duty: A Soldier Remembers* (New Delhi: Lancer, 2000), pp. 334–53.

26 Singh, *In the Line of Duty*, p. 353.

27 Lal, *My Years*, p. 134.

28 See C. P. Srivastava, *Lal Bahadur Shastri: A Life of Truth in Politics* (New Delhi: Oxford University Press, 1995), pp. 273–5.

29 Cf. Bhargava, *After Nehru*, pp. 300–3.

30 Herbert Feldman, *From Crisis to Crisis: Pakistan, 1962–1969* (London: Oxford University Press, 1972), p. 146.

31 John Frazer, 'Who Can Win Kashmir?', *Reader's Digest*, January 1966.

32 As told to me by K. S. Bajpai, who was Indian consul general in Karachi at the time.

33 Lt. Gen. Jahan Dad Khan, *Pakistan Leadership Challenges* (Karachi: Oxford University Press, 1999), p. 51.

34 Quoted in Feldman, *From Crisis to Crisis*, pp. 139–40.

35 Quoted in Cloughley, *A History*, p. 71.

36 For a detailed analysis, see the untitled note on Kashmir by Prem Nath Bazaz dated 24 October 1965, in Subject File 46, C. Rajagopalachari Papers, Fourth Instalment, NMML.

37 Alastair Lamb, *Kashmir: A Disputed Legacy, 1846–1990* (Karachi: Oxford University Press, 1992), p. 263.

38 Nayantara Sahgal, 'What India Fights For', *Illustrated Weekly of India*, 3 October 1965; Anon., *The Fight for Peace* (New Delhi: Hardy and Ally (India), 1966), esp. pp. 260ff.

39 T. V. Kunhi Krishnan, *Chavan and the Troubled Decade* (Bombay: Somaiya Publications, 1971), pp. 99–115; R. D. Pradhan, *Debacle to Revival: Y. B. Chavan as Defence Minister* (Hyderabad: Orient Longman, 1999), pp. 182–7, 207–12, 238–42.

40 Shastri to Jayaprakash Narayan, 21 July 1965 (in Hindi), in Subject File 28, Brahmanand Papers, NMML.

41 The speech is reproduced in D. R. Mankekar, *Lal Bahadur: A Political Biography* (Bombay: Popular Prakashan, 1965), appendix 3. Unlike Nehru, Shastri was a practising Hindu. But when asked by an interviewer to speak about his faith, he answered that 'one should not discuss one's religion in public'. Interview in the *Illustrated Weekly of India*, 18 October 1964.

42 Singh, *Portrait of Lal Bahadur Shastri*, pp. 87–8.

43 A valuable discussion of the making of the new strategy is contained in the memoirs of B. Sivaraman – *Bitter Sweet: Governance of India in Transition* (New Delhi: Ashish Publishing House, 1987). See especially chapter 11, 'Green Revolution'.

44 John P. Lewis, *India's Political Economy: Governance and Reform* (Delhi: Oxford University Press, 1995), chapter 4; Gilles Boquérat, *No Strings Attached? India's Policies and Foreign Aid, 1947–1966* (Delhi: Manohar, 2003), chapter 15.

45 Srivastava, *Lal Bahadur Shastri*, chapter 31.

46 'Shastri's Last Journey', *Life*, 21 January 1966.

47 Letter to Dorothy Norman, 13 March 1965, in D. Norman, ed., *Indira Gandhi: Letters to an American Friend, 1950–1984* (San Diego: Harcourt Brace Jovanovich, 1985), p. 111.

48 Vijayalakshmi Pandit to A. C. Nambiar, letters of 31 July 1964 and 26 January 1966, copies in Pupul Jayakar Papers, in the possession of Radhika Herzberger, Mumbai.

49 Anand Mohan, *Indira Gandhi: A Personal and Political Biography* (New York: Meredith Press, 1967), pp. 20–37.

50 Nehru to C. D. Deshmukh, 16 April 1956, in Subject File 67, C. D. Deshmukh Papers, NMML.

51 'A Fitful Improvisation', *Thought*, 22 January 1966.

52 Nirmal Nibedon, *Mizoram: The Dagger Brigade* (New Delhi: Lancer, 1980), esp. pp. 30–51.

53 Sajal Nag, *Contesting Marginality: Ethnicity, Insurgency and Subnationalism in North-East India* (New Delhi: Manohar, 2002), pp. 217–24, and 'Tribes, Rats, Famine, State and the Nation', *Economic and Political Weekly*, 24 March 2001; see also reports in *Thought* (New Delhi), 2 April 1966 and 7 and 14 October 1967.

54 Unsigned, undated letter to I. A. Bowman, postmarked 13 March 1966, in Mss Eur F229/62, OIOC.

55 Jayaprakash Narayan to Marjorie Sykes, 24 February 1966, copy in J. J. Singh Papers, NMML. Narayan, *Nagaland Mein Shanti Ka Prayas* (The Quest for Peace in Nagaland) (Varanasi: Sarva Seva Sangh, 1966).

56 See clippings in Mss Eur F158/239, OIOC.

57 Guy Wint to I. A. Bowman, 16 September 1966, in Mss Eur F229/24, OIOC.

58 Nirmal Nibedon, *Nagaland: The Night of the Guerillas* (New Delhi: Lancer, 1983), pp. 137–45.

59 Subject File 136, D. P. Mishra Papers, Third and Fourth Instalments, NMML; Nandini Sundar, *Subalterns and Sovereigns: An Anthropological History of Bastar, 1854–1996* (Delhi: Oxford University Press, 1997), chapter 7.

60 Singh, *In the Line of Duty*, p. 357.

61 See clippings in Mss Eur F158/295. The creation of the new Punjab and Haryana states was approved in March 1966, but the decision finally came into effect only in November, after the borders were delimited. Cf. *Hindustan Times*, 2 November 1966.

62 Cf. C. Subramaniam, *Hand of Destiny: Memoirs*, vol. 2: *The Green Revolution* (Bombay: Bharatiya Vidya Bhavan, 1995), chapter 11 and *passim*.

63 Mrs Gandhi's US trip is described in K. A. Abbas, *Indira Gandhi: Return of the Red Rose* (Delhi: Hind Pocket Books, 1966), pp. 147–57.

64 Chester Bowles, *Promises to Keep: My Years in Public Life, 1941–1969* (New Delhi: B. I. Publications, 1972), pp. 525–35. Cf. also Howard B. Schaffer, *Chester Bowles: New Dealer in the Cold War* (New Delhi: Prentice-Hall India, 1994), pp. 280ff.

65 Anon., 'India's Food Crisis, 1965–67', in File 7, Box 32, Thomas J. Schonberg Files, Dean Rusk Papers, University of Georgia, Athens.

66 Memorandum to President Johnson from Orville Freeman, 19 July 1966, in File 6, Box 32, Thomas J. Schonberg Files, Dean Rusk Papers, University of Georgia, Athens.

67 This account of the 1966 devaluation is based on Rahul Mukherji, 'India's Aborted Liberalization – 1966', *Pacific Affairs*, vol. 73, no. 3, 2000, supplemented by Kuldeep Nayar, *Between the Lines* (Bombay: Allied Publishers, 1969), chapter 3.

68 Indira Gandhi to Jayaprakash Narayan, 7 June 1966, copy in J. J. Singh Papers, NMML.

69 *Thought*, 11 June 1966.

70 Jayaprakash Narayan to Indira Gandhi, 23 June 1966, Sarvodaya Ashram, Sokhodeora (Gaya), copy in J. J. Singh Papers, NMML.

71 Indira Gandhi to Jayaprakash Narayan, 6 July 1966, copy in J. J. Singh Papers, NMML.

72 *Thought*, 15 October 1966.

73 *Hindustan Times*, 31 October–5 November 1966.

74 Reports in *Hindustan Times*, 5 and 6 November 1966.

75 *Hindustan Times*, 7 November 1966; *Thought*, 12 November 1966.

76 'Indians Becoming Increasingly Hostile to West', *Sydney Morning Herald*, 13 December 1965.

77 Ronald Segal, *The Crisis of India* (Harmondsworth: Penguin, 1965), pp. 171, 227, 255–7, 272, 309–10.

78 Ursula Betts to Ian Bowman, 25 May 1966, Mss Eur F229/24, OIOC.

79 Paul Ehrlich, *The Population Bomb* (New York: Ballantine Books, 1968), Preface.

80 William and Paul Paddock, *Famine – 1975! America's Decision: Who Will Survive?* (Boston: Little, Brown and Co., 1968), pp. 60–1, 217–18.

81 S. Mulgaokar, 'The Grimmest Situation in 19 Years', *Hindustan Times*, 3 November 1966.

19. LEFTWARD TURNS

1 Sol W. Sanders, 'India: A Huge Country on the Verge of Collapse', *U.S. News and World Report*, 28 November 1966.

2 Neville Maxwell, 'India's Disintegrating Democracy', in three parts, *The Times*, 26 and 27 January and 10 February 1967 (emphases added).

3 Cf. Yogesh Atal, *Local Communities and National Politics* (Delhi: National, 1971); A. M. Shah, ed., *The Grassroots of Democracy* (New Delhi: Permanent Black, 2007).

4 E. P. W. da Costa, *The Indian General Elections 1967: The Structure of Indian Voting Intentions: January 1967. A Gallup Poll with Analysis* (New Delhi: Indian Institute of Public Opinion).

5   *Thought*, 4 March 1967.

6   These paragraphs on MGR and the DMK are based on Robert L. Hardgrave
    and Anthony C. Neidhart, 'Films and Political Consciousness in Tamil
    Nadu', *Economic and Political Weekly*, 11 January 1975; N. Balakrishnan, 'The
    History of the Dravidian Munnetra Kazhagam, 1949–1977', unpublished PhD
    dissertation, School of Historical Studies, Madurai Kamaraj University, 1985,
    esp. pp. 278–86.

7   Narendra Subramanian, *Ethnicity and Populist Mobilization: Political Parties,
    Citizens and Democracy in South India* (New Delhi: Oxford University Press, 1999),
    pp. 204–10; Sagar Ahluwalia, *Anna – the Tempest and the Sea* (New Delhi: Young
    Asia Publications, 1969), pp. 51–7, 82–4.

8   Jyoti Basu, *Memoirs: A Political Autobiography* (Calcutta: National Book Agency,
    1999), pp. 195–209.

9   Bhabani Sengupta, *Communism in Indian Politics* (New York: Columbia University
    Press, 1972).

10 Marcus F. Franda, *Radical Politics in West Bengal* (Cambridge, Mass.: MIT Press,
    1971), chapter 6.

11 Cf. Rabindra Ray, *The Naxalites and their Ideology* (New Delhi: Oxford University
    Press, 1992).

12 *Mainstream*, 8 July 1967, quoted in Franda, *Radical Politics*, p. 171.

13 Shanta Sinha, *Maoists in Andhra Pradesh* (New Delhi: Gyan Publishing House,
    1989), chapters 4–7; Sumanta Banerjee, *In the Wake of Naxalbari: A History of the
    Naxalite Movement in India* (Calcutta: Subarnarekha, 1980), chapter 5.

14 See clippings and papers in Subject File 3, Dharma Vira Papers, NMML.

15 Sankar Ghosh, *The Disinherited State: A Study of West Bengal, 1967–70* (Calcutta:
    Orient Longman, 1971), chapter 3.

16 Cf. clippings in Mss Eur F158/456, OIOC.

17 Ghosh, *The Disinherited State*, pp. 248ff.

18 See Subject File 99, P. N. Haksar Papers, Third Instalment, NMML.

19 See IB report in Subject File 212, P. N. Haksar Papers, Third Instalment, NMML.

20 See Ranjit Gupta, *The Crimson Agenda: Maoist Protest and Terror* (Delhi:
    Wordsmiths, 2004), pp. 105, 110–11, 157–9 etc.

21 Inder Malhotra, 'Naxalites Put City in Fear of Bombs', *Guardian*, 19 August 1970.

22 For the (very long) list of charges, see S. N. Dwivedy, *The Orissa Affair and the CBI
    Inquiry* (New Delhi: privately published, 1965).

23 Sunit Ghosh, *Orissa in Turmoil* (Bhubaneshwar: Bookland International, 1991),
    pp. 149–57; Sukadev Nanda, *Coalition Politics in Orissa* (New Delhi: Sterling
    Publishers, 1979), pp. 70–7.

24 Special Branch report marked 'Top Secret', 26 February 1967, Subject File 25,
    D. P. Mishra Papers, Second Instalment, NMML.

25 Mishra to Kamaraj, 21 June 1967, ibid.

26 See R. C. V. P. Noronha, *A Tale Told by an Idiot* (New Delhi: Vikas Publishing
    House, 1976), chapter 8.

27 Prem Shankar Jha, 'Telengana: Language is not Enough', *Illustrated Weekly of
    India*, 3 August 1969.

28 S. K. Chaube, *Hill Politics in North-East India* (Bombay: Orient Longman, 1973),
    chapters 7 and 8.

29 See letters and notes in Subject File 142, P. N. Haksar Papers, Third Instalment, NMML.

30 Dipankar Gupta, *Nativism in a Metropolis: The Shiv Sena in Bombay* (Delhi: Manohar, 1982), pp. 39–40, 82–3 etc.; Vaibhav Purandare, *The Sena Story* (Mumbai: Business Publications, 1999), pp. 22–4, 42–4 etc.

31 *Thought*, 11 February 1967.

32 See notes in Subject File 128, P. N. Haksar Papers, Third Instalment, NMML.

33 *Thought*, 16 March, 6 July and 19 October 1968; *Daily Telegraph*, 27 June 1968.

34 See news clippings in Mss Eur F158/239, OIOC.

35 See letters and papers in File 61, Alexander Papers, Friends House, Euston.

36 *Thought*, 7 June 1968.

37 A. G. Noorani, 'How Does a Riot Begin and Spread?', *Illustrated Weekly of India*, 9 November 1969; N. C. Saxena, 'The Nature and Origins of Communal Riots in India', in Asghar Ali Engineer, ed., *Communal Riots in Post-Independence India*, 2nd edn (Hyderabad: Orient Longman, 1991); K. D. Malaviya to Fakhruddin Ali Ahmad, 30 March 1967, in Subject File 128, P. N. Haksar Papers, Third Instalment, NMML.

38 Ghanshyam Shah, 'The 1969 Communal Riots in Ahmedabad: A Case Study', in Engineer, *Communal Riots*; untitled report on the Ahmedabad riots by a group of Congress MPs, 7 October 1969, in Subject File 142, P. N. Haksar Papers, Third Instalment, NMML.

39 Khushwant Singh, 'Learning Geography through Murder', *Illustrated Weekly of India*, 31 May 1970.

40 Editorial in *Thought*, 2 March 1968; cf. also S. E. Hassnain, *Indian Muslims: Challenge and Opportunity* (Bombay: Lalwani Publishing House, 1968).

41 This sketch is based on Bidyut Sarkar, ed., *P.N. Haksar: Our Times and the Man* (New Delhi: Allied Publishers, 1989), a conversation with Professor André Béteille, Delhi, February 2005 and the material in the P. N. Haksar Papers, NMML.

42 Katherine Frank, *Indira: A Life of Indira Nehru Gandhi* (London: HarperCollins, 2001), p. 314.

43 Note dated 21 January 1968, in Subject File 198, P. N. Haksar Papers, Third Instalment, NMML.

44 Speech by S. S. Dhawan, London, March 1969, copy in Subject File 197, P. N. Haksar Papers, Third Instalment, NMML.

45 Inder Malhotra, *Indira Gandhi: A Personal and Political Biography* (London: Hodder and Stoughton, 1989), pp. 108f.

46 *The Years of Challenge: Selected Speeches of Indira Gandhi, January 1966–August 1969*, 2nd edn (New Delhi: Publications Division, 1985), pp. 25–8, 34–9, 172–4, 268–9.

47 *Thought*, 8 and 29 March 1969.

48 Uma Vasudev, *Indira Gandhi: Revolution in Restraint* (Delhi: Vikas Publishing House, 1974), p. 502.

49 Malhotra, *Indira Gandhi*, p. 116.

50 *Thought*, 23 December 1967; Morarji Desai, *The Story of My Life*, vol. 2 (Delhi: Macmillan India, 1974), pp. 243f.

51 The speech is reproduced in A. Moin Zaidi, *The Great Upheaval, 1969–1972* (New Delhi: Orientalia India, 1972), pp. 103–6.

52 *Thought*, 19 July and 16 August 1969.

53 For details see Subject File 153, P. N. Haksar Papers, Third Instalment, NMML.

54 Trevor Drieberg, *Indira Gandhi: Profile in Courage* (Delhi: Vikas Publications, 1972), chapter 7.

55 S. Nijalingappa to Indira Gandhi, 11 November 1969, in Zaidi, *The Great Upheaval*, p. 231.

56 Sukumar Muralidharan and Ravi Sharma, 'A Congressman from Another Age: S. Nijalingappa, 1902–2000', *Frontline*, 1 September 2000.

57 Cf. drafts of speeches in Subject File 143, P. N. Haksar Papers, Third Instalment, NMML.

58 N(ikhil) C(hakravartty), 'Syndicate at Waterloo', *Mainstream*, 16 August 1969.

59 Nayantara Sahgal, *Indira Gandhi: Her Road to Power* (New York: Frederick Ungar, 1982), p. 53.

60 Note by P. N. Haksar dated 16 September 1967, Subject File 118, P. N. Haksar Papers, Third Instalment, NMML.

61 Subject File 121, P. N. Haksar Papers, Third Instalment, NMML; Rajinder Puri, *India 1969: A Crisis of Conscience* (Delhi: privately published, 1971), pp. 67–73.

62 See letters in Subject File 145, P. N. Haksar Papers, Third Instalment, NMML.

63 This account of the Parliamentary and judicial interventions in the privy purse controversy is based on D. R. Mankekar, *Accession to Extinction: The Story of Indian Princes* (Delhi: Vikas Publishing House, 1974), chapters 18 to 20.

64 For details see M. S. Randhawa, *A History of Agriculture in India*, vol. 4: *1947–1981* (New Delhi: Indian Council of Agricultural Research, 1986), chapters 30 to 32.

65 Don Taylor, 'This New, Surprising Strength of Mrs Gandhi', *Evening Standard*, 21 August 1969.

66 *New York Times*, 26 January 1970.

67 'Is India Cracking up?', editorial in *Thought*, 4 January 1967.

68 'The Meaning of Naxalbari', *Thought*, 17 June 1967.

69 Kathleen Gough, 'The Indian Revolutionary Potential', *Monthly Review*, February 1969 (based on an essay originally published in *Pacific Affairs*, winter issue, 1968–9).

70 Lasse and Lisa Berg, *Face to Face: Fascism and Revolution in India*, trans. Norman Kurtin (Berkeley: Ramparts Press, 1971), pp. 23–4, 28, 31, 56, 125, 162, 209–10.

20. The Elixir of Victory

1 *Thought*, 22 November 1969.

2 See *Election Manifestos 1971* (Bombay: Awake India Publications, 1971).

3 Rajaji to Minoo Masani, 2 January 1971, in Subject File 142, C. Rajagopalachari Papers, Fourth Instalment, NMML.

4 Indira Gandhi to Dorothy Norman, 23 April 1971, in D. Norman, ed., *Indira Gandhi: Letters to an American Friend, 1950–1984* (New York: Harcourt Brace Jovanovich, 1985), p. 132.

5 *Thought*, 20 May 1972.

6 'A Special Correspondent', 'The Making of Fifth Lok Sabha', *Thought*, 20 March 1971.

7 Khushwant Singh, 'Indira Gandhi', *Illustrated Weekly of India*, 14 March 1971.

8 See D. R. Mankekar, *Accession to Extinction: The Story of Indian Princes* (Delhi: Vikas Publishing House, 1974), chapter 21.

9 D. N. Dhanagare, 'Urban–Rural Differences in Election Violence', in S. P. Varma and Iqbal Narain, eds, *Fourth General Elections in India*, vol. 2 (Bombay: Orient Longman, 1970).

10 This section is based on Election Commission of India, *Report on the Fifth General Elections in India, 1971–72* (New Delhi: Manager of Publications, 1973), *passim*. The CEC was named S. P. Sen Varma; his report – the mystical preface apart – was clearly modelled on the first such, written by his great predecessor Sukumar Sen.

11 This and the following paragraphs are principally based on Herbert Feldman, *The End and the Beginning: Pakistan 1969–1971* (London: Oxford University Press, 1975), chapters 7 to 9. Cf. also D. R. Mankekar, *Pak Colonialism in East Bengal* (Bombay: Somaiyya Publications, 1971).

12 Lt. Gen. A. A. K. Niazi, quoted in Muntassir Mamoon, *The Vanquished Generals and the Liberation War of Bangladesh* (Dhaka: Somoy Prakashan, 2000), p. 159.

13 R. K. Dasgupta, *Revolt in East Bengal* (Calcutta: G. C. Ray, 1971), pp. 4, 7, 9, 21, 24–5, 29, 39, 52, 61 etc. For the colonial treatment of East Pakistan by the West Punjabi elite, see also Anthony Mascarenhas, *The Rape of Bangla Desh* (Delhi: Vikas Publications, 1971).

14 Cf. reports by eyewitnesses collected in Anon., *Bangla Desh Documents* (Madras: The BNK Press, 1972), chapter 6.

15 Jyoti Sen Gupta, *History of Freedom Movement in Bangladesh, 1943–1973* (Calcutta: Naya Prokash, 1974), pp. 314–16, 325–6. The major who made the announcement was Zia-ur-Rahman, later president of Bangladesh.

16 State Department telegram dated 2 July 1971, reproduced in Roedad Khan, comp., *The American Papers: Secret and Confidential India–Pakistan–Bangladesh Documents, 1965–1973* (Karachi: Oxford University Press, 1999), pp. 613–15.

17 Maj. Gen. Hakeem Arshad Qureshi, *The 1971 Indo-Pak War: A Soldier's Narrative* (Karachi: Oxford University Press, 2002), pp. 60, 71. The sentences quoted could as easily have been penned by an Indian army commander writing about Nagaland in 1957.

18 Werner Adam, 'Pakistan's Open Wounds', *Washington Post*, 6 June 1971; report in the *New York Times*, 25 June 1971; World Bank team report in Subject File 171, P. N. Haksar Papers, Third Instalment, NMML.

19 Anon., *Bangla Desh Documents*, chapter 7.

20 K. C. Saha, 'The Genocide of 1971 and the Refugee Influx in the East', in Ranabir Samaddar, ed., *Refugees and the State: Practices of Asylum and Care in India, 1947–2000* (New Delhi: Sage Publications, 2003).

21 Iqbal Akhund, *Memoirs of a Bystander: A Life in Diplomacy* (Karachi: Oxford University Press, 1997), p. 201.

22 25-page secret report entitled 'Threat of a Military Attack or Infiltration Campaign by Pakistan', RAW, January 1971, copy in Subject File 220, P. N. Haksar Papers, Third Instalment, NMML.

23 Dhar to Haksar, 18 April 1971, ibid.

24 Cf. reports in Subject File 169, P. N. Haksar Papers, Third Instalment, NMML.

25 The letter is reprinted in F. S. Aijazuddin, ed., *The White House and Pakistan: Secret Declassified Documents, 1969–1974* (Karachi: Oxford University Press, 2002), pp. 129–30.

26 'Record of PM's Conversation with Dr Kissinger', 7 July 1971, in Subject File 225, P. N. Haksar Papers, Third Instalment, NMML.

27 Indira Gandhi to Richard Nixon, 7 August 1971, copy in Subject File 220, P. N. Haksar Papers, Third Instalment, NMML.

28 See the documents in Louis Smith, ed., *Foreign Relations of the United States, 1969–1976*, vol. 11: *South Asia Crisis, 1971* (Washington, DC: Department of State, 2005), pp. 28, 35, 164, 167, 288–9, 303, 316, 324, 557 etc.; and the documents in Aijazuddin, *The White House*, pp. 242–6, 258–62.

29 For the broader context of India's changing relations with the superpowers in the early seventies, see T. V. Kunhi Krishnan, *The Unfriendly Friends: India and America* (New Delhi: Indian Book Co., 1974); Shashi Tharoor, *Reasons of State: Political Development and India's Foreign Policy under Indira Gandhi, 1966–1977* (New Delhi: Vikas Publishing House, 1982); and Linda Racioppi, *Soviet Policy towards South Asia since 1970* (Cambridge: Cambridge University Press, 1994).

30 This paragraph is based on letters and papers in Subject Files 163, 225 and 229, P. N. Haksar Papers, Third Instalment, NMML.

31 Top Secret Note of 5 June 1971 in Subject File 89, P. N. Haksar Papers, Third Instalment, NMML.

32 'Record of conversations between Foreign Minister and Mr A. A. Gromyko, Minister of Foreign Affairs, USSR, on 7th June 1971', in Subject File 203, P. N. Haksar Papers, Third Instalment, NMML.

33 The text of the treaty is reproduced in A. Appadorai, ed., *Select Documents on India's Foreign Policy and Relations, 1947–1972*, vol. 2 (Delhi: Oxford University Press, 1985), pp. 136–40.

34 Indira Gandhi, *India: The Speeches and Reminiscences of Indira Gandhi, Prime Minister of India* (London: Hodder and Stoughton, 1975), pp. 162–4.

35 See Aijazuddin, *The White House*, pp. 313, 336–9.

36 Robert Jackson, *South Asian Crisis: India–Pakistan–Bangla Desh* (London: Chatto and Windus, 1975), p. 102.

37 Letter of 23 November, in Aijazuddin, *The White House*, pp. 364–5.

38 Jackson, *South Asian Crisis*, pp. 106–7; Brian Cloughley, *A History of the Pakistan Army: Wars and Insurrections* (Karachi: Oxford University Press), pp. 148–9.

39 B. G. Verghese, *An End to Confrontation: Restructuring the Sub-Continent* (New Delhi: 1972), pp. 35–50.

40 Cloughley, *A History of the Pakistan Army*, p. 222.

41 Lt. Gen. A. A. K. Niazi, *The Betrayal of East Pakistan* (Delhi: Manohar, 1998), p. 132.

42 Ibid., p. 114.

43 D. R. Mankekar, *Pakistan Cut to Size* (New Delhi: Indian Book Co., 1972), pp. 54–63.

44 Jackson, *South Asian Crisis*, pp. 137–8.

45 Telegram quoted in Niazi, *Betrayal*, p. 180.

46 See Aijazuddin, *The White House*, pp. 447, 449–50.

47 Niazi, *Betrayal*, pp. 187ff.

48 *Lok Sabha Debates*, 16 December 1971.

49 Living not far from the border then, I heard Yahya's speech as it was delivered – he had (as Pakistani accounts also suggest) consumed a goodly amount of whisky before taking up the microphone.

50 Air Chief Marshal P. C. Lal, *My Years with the IAF* (New Delhi: Lancer International, 1986), p. 321.

51 Smith, *Foreign Relations*, pp. 439, 499, 594, 612, 674 etc. Cf. also the letters exchanged between Mrs Gandhi and Nixon after the end of the war, reproduced in Aijazuddin, *The White House*, pp. 476–80.

52 *Time*, 3 January 1972; James Reston, 'India's Victory a Triumph for Moscow', *New York Times*, undated (?20 December 1971) clipping in Subject File 217, P. N. Haksar Papers, Third Instalment, NMML.

53 *Thought*, 29 January 1972.

54 Quoted in C. M. Naim, *Ambiguities of Heritage: Fictions and Polemics* (Karachi: City Press, 1999), p. 139.

55 See 'India After Bangla Desh: A Symposium', *Gandhi Marg*, vol. 16, no. 2, 1972.

56 Letter of 8 December 1971, in Carol Brightman, ed., *Between Friends: The Correspondence of Hannah Arendt and Mary McCarthy, 1949–1975* (New York: Harcourt Brace and Co., 1995), p. 303.

57 A. B. Vajpayee quoted in *Thought*, 20 May 1972.

58 Ranajit Roy, *The Agony of West Bengal: A Study in Union–State Relations*, 3rd edn (Calcutta: New Age Publishers, 1973), pp. 3–4; Sajal Basu, *West Bengal – the Violent Years* (Calcutta: Prachi Publications, 1974), p. 78.

59 'Message to Mrs Gandhi from Sir Alec Douglas-Home', 20 March 1972, in Subject File 179, P. N. Haksar Papers, Third Instalment, NMML.

60 As quoted in S. R. Sen to I. G. Patel, letter dated 2 March 1972, in Subject File 225, P. N. Haksar Papers, Third Instalment, NMML.

61 Untitled note in Subject File 236, P. N. Haksar Papers, Third Instalment, NMML.

62 Sajjad Zaheer to P. N. Haksar, 23 March 1972, in Subject File 243, P. N. Haksar Papers, Third Instalment, NMML (emphasis in original). Mazhar Ali Khan was the father of the student radical, and later prolific author, Tariq Ali.

63 A. Raghavan, 'Five Days that Changed History', *Blitz*, 8 July 1972.

64 Note by Dhar dated 12 March 1972, in Subject File 235, P. N. Haksar Papers, Third Instalment, NMML.

65 The text of the Simla Agreement is reproduced in Appadorai, *Select Documents*, pp. 443–5.

66 The text of the speech is to be found in Subject File 93, P. N. Haksar Papers, Third Instalment, NMML.

67 Notes in ibid.

21. THE RIVALS

1 See Indira Gandhi, *India: The Speeches and Reminiscences of Indira Gandhi Prime Minister of India* (London: Hodder and Stoughton, 1975), pp. 215–16.

2 As reported in *The Hindu*, 16 August 1972.

3 A. Vaidyanathan, 'The Indian Economy since Independence (1947–70), in Dharma Kumar, ed., *The Cambridge Economic History of India*, vol. 2 (Cambridge: Cambridge University Press, 1983).

4 This paragraph summarizes several longitudinal studies of rural India, as in G. Parthasarathy, 'A South Indian Village after Two Decades', *Economic Weekly*, 12 January 1963; Kumudini Dandekar and Vaijayanti Bhate, 'Socio-Economic Change During Three Five-Year Plans', *Artha Vijnana*, vol. 17, no. 4, 1975; Robert W. Bradnock, 'Agricultural Development in Tamil Nadu: Two Decades of Land

Use Changes at Village Level', in Tim P. Bayliss-Smith and Sudhir Wanmali, eds, *Understanding Green Revolutions: Agrarian Change and Development Planning in South Asia* (Cambridge: Cambridge University Press, 1984).

5 These studies are usefully summarized in M. L. Dantwala, *Poverty in India: Then and Now* (Madras: Macmillan India, 1971); and M. Mukherjee, N. Bhattacharya and G. S. Chatterjee, 'Poverty in India: Measurement and Amelioration', in Vadilal Dagli, ed., *Twenty-Five Years of Independence – A Survey of Indian Economy* (Bombay: Vora and Co., 1973). The Dandekar–Rath study was first published in the *Economic and Political Weekly* in January 1971.

6 J. P. Naik, 'Education', in S. C. Dube, ed., *India since Independence: Social Report on India, 1947–1972* (New Delhi: Vikas Publishing House, 1977); Amrik Singh, 'Twenty-five Years of Indian Education; An Assessment', in Jag Mohan, ed., *Twenty-five Years of Indian Independence* (New Delhi: Vikas Publishing House, 1973).

7 'Indian Economic Policy and Performance: A Framework for a Progressive Society' (1973), reprinted in Jagdish N. Bhagwati, *Essays in Development Economics* (Cambridge, Mass.: MIT Press, 1985).

8 Anon., 'Mummy Knows Best', *Thought*, 2 October 1971.

9 *Thought*, 5 May 1971; D. R. Rajagopal, 'Sanjay Gandhi', *Illustrated Weekly of India*, 11 July 1971.

10 Letter of 2 February 1971, Indira Gandhi Correspondence, P. N. Haksar Papers, NMML.

11 The *Current*, 28 July 1973.

12 *The Star*, 12 August 1973, clipping in Subject File 93, P. N. Haksar Papers, Third Instalment, NMML.

13 Note of 29 June 1971, ibid.

14 See notes and correspondence in Subject Files 242 and 243, P. N. Haksar Papers, Third Instalment, NMML.

15 Unless otherwise stated, this section is based on the synthesis report of those studies: *Status of Women in India* (New Delhi: Indian Council of Social Science Research, 1974). Much of the data quoted there, and here, are taken from the 1971 Census of India.

16 D. R. Gadgil, *Women in the Working Force in India* (London: Asia Publishing House, 1965); Bina Agarwal, 'Women, Poverty and Agricultural Growth in India', *Journal of Peasant Studies*, vol. 13, no. 2, 1985–6.

17 Radha Kumar, *The History of Doing: An Illustrated Account of Movements for Women's Rights and Feminism in India, 1860–1990* (New Delhi: Kali for Women, 1993), chapter 6.

18 See, for more details, P. G. K. Pannikar and C. R. Soman, *Health Status of Kerala* (Trivandrum: Centre for Development Studies, 1984).

19 Ronald J. Herring, 'Abolition of Landlordism in Kerala: A Redistribution of Privilege', *Economic and Political Weekly, Review of Agriculture*, June 1980; P. Radhakrishnan, 'Land Reforms and Changes in Land System: Study of a Kerala Village', *Economic and Political Weekly, Review of Agriculture*, September 1982.

20 See *Lok Sabha Debates*, 30 November 1971.

21 Justice K. S. Hegde, 'Perspectives of the Indian Constitution', Rajendra Prasad Memorial Lecture, Bharatiya Vidya Bhavan Bombay, March 1972, copy in Subject File 220, P. N. Haksar Papers, Third Instalment, NMML.

22 See the letter from Indira Gandhi to Jayaprakash Narayan of 9 June 1973 and his reply of 27 June 1973, both in Jayaprakash Narayan Papers, NMML.

23 A. G. Noorani, 'Crisis in India's Judiciary', *Imprint*, January 1974.

24 Inder Malhotra, *Indira Gandhi: A Personal and Political Biography* (London: Hodder and Stoughton, 1989), pp. 152–3 etc.

25 *Thought*, 1 January 1972.

26 *Thought*, 8 July 1972.

27 The *Current*, 8 July 1972; *Thought*, 23 September 1972.

28 The minutes of these talks are unavailable, but for some clues of what might have been discussed see the material in Subject Files 183 and 235, P. N. Haksar Papers, Third Instalment, NMML.

29 These paragraphs on Nagaland in the early 1970s are based on reports in the Kohima weekly *Citizens Voice*, issues of which are in Box VIII, Pawsey Papers, CSAS.

30 *Thought*, 2 March 1974.

31 See Ajit Bhattacharjea, *Unfinished Revolution: A Political Biography of Jayaprakash Narayan* (New Delhi: Rupa and Co., 2004), pp. 193ff.

32 The previous three paragraphs draw upon Ghanshyam Shah, 'Revolution, Reform, or Protest? A Study of the Bihar Movement', in three parts, *Economic and Political Weekly*, 9, 16 and 23 April 1977.

33 The correspondence between Narayan and Mrs Gandhi, very rich and largely unexplored by biographers of either party, is in the Jayaprakash Narayan Papers, NMML. The correspondence between JP and Nehru – also less intensely mined than it might have been – is scattered between this collection and the Brahmanand Papers, also at the NMML.

34 Quoted in Bhattacharjea, *Unfinished Revolution*, pp. 205–6.

35 See reports in Subject File 272, Jayaprakash Narayan Papers, Third Instalment, NMML.

36 English translation of speech in *Everyman's Weekly*, 22 June 1974.

37 See Robert Jay Lifton, *Revolutionary Immortality: Mao Tse Tung and the Cultural Revolution* (Penguin: Harmondsworth, 1967). I offer this comparison knowing that it will be dismissed both by Marxists, who will see JP as a lily-livered reformist in comparison with the builder of the Chinese revolution, and by the Gandhians, who will profess shock at the lumping together of a man of non-violence with one known to have been responsible for so many deaths.

38 Anon., 'Railway Strike in Retrospect', *Economic and Political Weekly*, 18 January 1975.

39 S. Nihal Singh, *Indira's India: A Political Notebook* (Bombay: Nachiketa Publications, 1978), pp. 215–16.

40 George Perkovich, *India's Nuclear Bomb: The Impact on Global Proliferation* (Berkeley: University of California Press, 1999), pp. 170–80; *Thought*, 25 May 1974; Aziz Ahmad (Foreign Minister of Pakistan) to Horace Alexander, 15 June 1974, in Alexander Papers, Friends House, Euston.

41 These paragraphs are based on the letters between Mrs Gandhi and JP in the Jayaprakash Narayan Papers, NMML.

42 Bhattacharjea, *Unfinished Revolution*, pp. 211f.; *Everyman's Weekly*, 21 September 1974.

43 See correspondence between Acharya Ramamurti and JP in Subject File 273, Jayaprakash Narayan Papers, Third Instalment, NMML.

44 Letter of 14 October 1974, in Subject File 277, Jayaprakash Narayan Papers, NMML. Patil's letter – to which JP's reply, if there was one, is untraceable – is reminiscent of the warnings uttered along these lines in the Constituent Assembly by his great fellow Maharashtrian, B. R. Ambedkar.

45 Bhattacharjea, *Unfinished Revolution*, pp. 216–17.

46 *Everyman's Weekly*, 16 and 23 November 1974.

47 See B. S. Das, *The Sikkim Saga* (New Delhi: Vikas Publishing House, 1983).

48 Letter to JP dated 18 July 1974 from M. Shah, Adoni, Kurnool Dist., A. P., in Subject File 273, Jayaprakash Narayan Papers, Third Instalment, NMML.

49 See statements in Subject File 272, Jayaprakash Narayan Papers, Third Instalment, NMML.

50 For a sampling of the former view, see the pages of the *Everyman's Weekly* for 1974–5; for the latter, see the *Illustrated Weekly of India* for the same period.

51 Katherine Frank, *Indira: A Life of Indira Nehru Gandhi* (London: HarperCollins, 2001), p. 368; Christopher Andrew and Vasili Mitrokhin, *The World was Going our Way: The KGB and the Battle for the World* (New York: Basic Books, 2005), pp. 322–3.

52 Unless otherwise indicated, the rest of this section is based on reports and comments in the *Indian Express*, 1 February to 21 March 1975.

53 Anon., 'The South Poses a Problem for JP', *Everyman's Weekly*, 4 May 1975.

54 Granville Austin, *Working the Democratic Constitution: The Indian Experience* (New Delhi: Oxford University Press, 1999), pp. 314–16.

55 *Indian Express*, 20 March 1975.

56 Unless otherwise stated, the rest of this section is based on reports in the *Indian Express*, 10 to 28 June 1975.

57 Prashant Bhushan, *The Case that Shook India* (New Delhi: Vikas Publishing House, 1978), pp. 98ff.

58 Ibid., p. 94.

59 Quoted in Dom Moraes, *Indira Gandhi* (Boston: Little, Brown and Co., 1980), p. 220.

60 Danial Latifi, 'Indira Gandhi Case Revisited', undated typescript in Subject File 225, P. N. Haksar Papers, Third Instalment, NMML.

22. Autumn of the Matriarch

1 Indira Gandhi, *Democracy and Discipline: Speeches of Shrimati Indira Gandhi* (New Delhi: Ministry of Information and Broadcasting, 1975), pp. 1–2.

2 The note is reproduced in Pupul Jayakar, *Indira Gandhi: An Intimate Biography* (New York: Pantheon Books, 1993), pp. 202–3.

3 K. R. Malkani, *The Midnight Knock* (New Delhi: Vikas Publishing House, 1978), p. 37.

4 Gandhi, *Democracy and Discipline*, pp. 18–19, 61 etc. This volume prints eleven interviews given in the first three months of the emergency – almost one a week – by a prime minister never known to be over-fond of the press.

5 See D. V. Gandhi, comp., *Era of Discipline: Documents on Contemporary Reality* (New Delhi: Samachar Bharati, 1976), p. 254.

6 Indira Gandhi, *Consolidating National Gains: Speeches of Shrimati Indira Gandhi* (New Delhi: Ministry of Information and Broadcasting, 1976), p. 29. The speech was originally delivered in Hindi; I have used the official translation.

7 Joe Elder, 'Report on Visit to India, August 11–22, 1975', in File 78, Horace Alexander Papers, Friends House, Euston.

8 Sharada Prasad to S. K. De, 16 September 1975, ibid.

9 P. N. Dhar, *Indira Gandhi, the 'Emergency', and Indian Democracy* (New Delhi: Oxford University Press, 2000), pp. 307–11.

10 Narayan to Sheikh Abdullah, 23 September 1975, reprinted in M. G. Devasahayam, *India's Second Freedom – An Untold Saga* (New Delhi: Siddharth Publications, 2004), pp. 351–4.

11 For the circumstances of JP's release, see ibid., chapters 29 and 30.

12 See table reproduced in K. Gangadharan, P. J. Koshy, and C. N. Radhakrishnan, *The Inquisition: Revelations before the Shah Commission* (New Delhi: Path Publishers, 1978), p. 260.

13 Note of 14 January 1976, in 'Emergency File', Hari Dev Sharma Papers, NMML.

14 Indira Gandhi to Verrier Elwin, 14 January 1963, letter in the possession of the Elwin family, Shillong.

15 See Ved Mehta, *Portrait of India* (New York: Farrar, Straus and Giroux, 1970), pp. 545–6.

16 Granville Austin, *Working a Democratic Constitution: The Indian Experience* (New Delhi: Oxford University Press, 1999), pp. 319–24.

17 Ibid., pp. 334–41.

18 *New York Times*, 30 April 1976.

19 Austin, *Working a Democratic Constitution*, pp. 373–4. Cf. also Nani Palkhivala, 'Reshaping the Constitution', *Illustrated Weekly of India*, 4 July 1976.

20 'Notes on a Meeting with Indira Gandhi, 1, Safdarjung Road, 14th March 1976', in Mss Eur F236/269, OIOC.

21 See the detailed list of forbidden subjects printed in Sajal Basu, ed., *Underground Literature During Indian Emergency* (Calcutta: Minerva Associates, 1978), pp. 102–14.

22 Prakash Ananda, *A History of the Tribune* (New Delhi: The Tribune Trust, 1986), pp. 165–6.

23 Ram Krishan Sharma to Penderel Moon, 25 November 1975, in Mss Eur F230/36, OIOC.

24 Report in the *Guardian*, 2 August 1976.

25 John Dayal and Ajay Bose, *The Shah Commission Begins* (New Delhi: Orient Longman, 1978), p. 208; Michael Henderson, *Experiment with Untruth: India under Emergency* (Delhi: Macmillan India, 1977), p. 89.

26 G. S. Bhargava, *The Press in India: An Overview* (New Delhi: National Book Trust, 2005), p. 53 etc.

27 Dayal and Bose, *Shah Commission*, pp. 280–93; Henderson, *Experiment with Untruth*, p. 89.

28 See K. K. Birla, *Indira Gandhi: Reminiscences* (New Delhi: Vikas Publishing House, 1987), pp. 50–1.

29 Bhargava, *The Press in India*, pp. 65–6.

30 Quoted in Ved Mehta, *The New India* (Harmondsworth, Penguin, 1978), pp. 63–4.

31 Report by Jonathan Dimbleby in the *Sunday Times*, reproduced in Amiya Rao and B. G. Rao, eds, *The Press She Could not Whip: Emergency in India as reported by the Foreign Press* (Bombay: Popular Prakashan, 1977), pp. 20–1.

32 Inder Malhotra, *Indira Gandhi: A Personal and Political Biography* (London: Hodder and Stoughton, 1989), p. 182.

33 Report by J. Anthony Lukacs in the *New York Times*, reproduced in Rao and Rao, eds., *The Press She Could not Whip*, pp. 186–98.

34 See Basu, *Underground Literature*, pp. 7–11.

35 P. G. Mavalankar, '*No, Sir*': *An Independent MP Speaks During the Emergency* (Ahmedabad: Sannistha Prakashan, 1979), pp. 20–5, 29–30 etc.

36 *The Economist*, 24 January 1976. This is almost certainly an over-estimate, and based on the figures supplied by the underground newspaper *Satya Samachar*.

37 *Satya Samachar*, 20 September 1976, in 'Emergency File', Hari Dev Sharma Papers, NMML.

38 Translated by Sugata Srinivasaraju and reproduced as an epigraph to his translation of Chi Srinivasaraju's *Phoenix and Four other Mime Plays* (Bangalore: Navakarnataka Publications, 2005).

39 Basu, *Underground Literature*, pp. 27, 29, 65; Henderson, *Experiment with Untruth*, p. 21.

40 These paragraphs on George Fernandes's activities during the emergency are principally based on C. G. K. Reddy, *Baroda Dynamite Conspiracy: The Right to Rebel* (New Delhi: Vision Books, 1977); supplemented by material in 'Emergency File', Hari Dev Sharma Papers, NMML, and in Snehalata Reddy, *A Prison Diary* (Mysore: Karnataka State Human Rights Committee, 1977).

41 Henderson, *Experiment with Untruth*, p. 27.

42 I regret I cannot provide a precise reference for this story. I cannot remember where I first heard or read it; whether from a friend who knew Kripalani, or in an obituary printed in the papers when he died. Sadly, as with so many remarkable characters who figure in these pages, Kripalani is yet to find a biographer.

43 'The Emergency: A Needed Shock', *Time*, 27 October 1975.

44 *Sydney Morning Herald*, 1 September 1976.

45 Letters in *The Times*, 3 and 14 July 1976.

46 'Indira Gandhi's Year of Failure', editorial in the *Observer*, 27 June 1975.

47 The only serviceable biography of Sanjay Gandhi at the time of writing remains Vinod Mehta's *The Sanjay Story: From Anand Bhavan to Amethi* (Bombay: Jaico, 1978).

48 The interview is reproduced in full in Uma Vasudev, *Two Faces of Indira Gandhi* (New Delhi: Vikas Publishing House, 1977), pp. 193–208. Vasudev, who conducted the interview, was editor of *Surge*.

49 Ibid., pp. 108–10; Dhar, *Indira Gandhi*, pp. 325–9.

50 *Illustrated Weekly of India*, 25 January 1976.

51 *Illustrated Weekly of India*, 15 August, 14 October and 7 and 14 November 1976.

52 Dayal and Bose, *Shah Commission*, pp. 189, 229; Mehta, *The Sanjay Story*, p. 139.

53 Janardhan Thakur, *All the Prime Minister's Men* (New Delhi: Vikas Publishing House, 1977), p. 57; Satyindra Singh, 'Pleasing the Crown Prince', *Sunday Pioneer*, 25 June 2000; Mehta, *The Sanjay Story*, pp. 87, 97, 165.

54 Mehta, *The Sanjay Story*, p. 81.

55 Cf. Emma Tarlo, *Unsettling Memories: Narratives of India's 'Emergency'* (Delhi: Permanent Black, 2003), pp. 80–2, 98, and map after p. 148.

56 Jagmohan, *Island of Truth* (New Delhi: Vikas Publishing House, 1978), pp. 9–10, 182–3 etc.

57 Mehta, *The Sanjay Story*; Thakur, *All the Prime Minister's Men*; and Vasudev, *Two Faces*, all deal at some length with this coterie and its doings.

58 Tarlo, *Unsettling Memories*, p. 140.

59 This account of the Turkman Gate incident is principally based on John Dayal and Ajoy Bose, *For Reasons of State: Delhi under Emergency* (Delhi: Ess Ess Publications, 1977), chapter 2. But cf. also Mehta, *The Sanjay Story*, pp. 90–5; and Inder Mohan, 'Turkman Gate, Sanjay Gandhi and Tihar Jail', *PUCL Bulletin*, vol. 5, no. 8, August 1985. Dayal and Bose, as well as Mehta, write that Jagmohan's determination to clear Turkman Gate was in part motivated by the fact of the residents being Muslim – he saw them, apparently, as Pakistani fifth columnists. Jagmohan's own account of the incident is in *Island of Truth*, pp. 144–9.

60 Mohammad Yunus, *Persons, Passions and Politics* (New Delhi: Vikas Publishing House, 1980), pp. 251–2.

61 *Satya Samachar*, 12 June 1976, in 'Emergency File', Haridev Sharma Papers, NMML.

62 There is a very extensive literature on this subject, which this bare summary by no means does justice to. For an introduction to the complexity of issues involved, see Pravin Visaria, 'Population Policy', *Seminar*, March 2002.

63 *Illustrated Weekly of India*, 15 August 1976.

64 Mehta, *The Sanjay Story*, p. 112.

65 Ibid., pp. 117–29; Tarlo, *Unsettling Memories*, pp. 80–2, 98, 140, 150–1.

66 Lee I. Schlesinger, 'The Emergency in an Indian Village', *Asian Survey*, vol. 17, no. 7, July 1977.

67 *Satya Samachar*, 26 September 1976; news bulletin of Lok Sangharsh Samiti dated 23 November 1976, both in 'Emergency File', Hari Dev Sharma Papers, NMML.

68 Basu, *Underground Literature*, p. 36; Gangadharan et al., *Inquisition*, pp. 130–3.

69 The *locus classicus* of this view is the book written by her former Secretary P. N. Dhar on the Emergency. But shades of the argument haunt virtually all the biographies of Mrs Gandhi. See Dhar, *Indira Gandhi*, as well as the biographies by Jayakar, Malhotra, Moraes, and Vasudev cited above.

70 *The Times*, 26 August 1976.

71 John Grigg, 'Tryst with Despotism', *Spectator*, 21 August 1976.

72 See the correspondence between Alexander and Mrs Gandhi in File 78, Horace Alexander Papers, Friends House, Euston.

73 Levin's articles are reproduced in full in Rao and Rao, eds., *The Press She Could not Whip*, pp. 124–31, 268–76.

74 Dhar, *Indira Gandhi*, p. 344.

75 Henderson, *Experiment with Untruth*, p. 153; Kuldip Nayar, *The Judgement: Inside Story of the Emergency in India* (New Delhi: Vikas Publishing House, 1977), p. 55.

76 A. M. Rosenthal, 'Father and Daughter: A Remembrance', *New York Times*, 1 November 1984.

77 See Jawaharlal Nehru, *Glimpses of World History* (1934; 4th edn London: Lindsay Drummond, 1949).

23. LIFE WITHOUT THE CONGRESS

1 S. Devadas Pillai, ed., *The Incredible Elections; 1977: A Blow-by-Blow Document as Reported in the Indian Express* (Bombay: Popular Prakashan, 1977), pp. 19–22, 37–8, 43.

2 Ibid., pp. 74–6, 107–11.

3 *Illustrated Weekly of India*, 6 March 1977.

4 Ajit Bhattacharjea, *Unfinished Revolution: A Political Biography of Jayaprakash Narayan* (New Delhi: Rupa and Co., 2004), pp. 282–3.

5 Pillai, *The Incredible Elections*, pp. 196, 198, 237, 244–5, 247.

6 Inder Malhotra, 'The Campaign that Was', *Illustrated Weekly of India*, 20 March 1977; Javed Alam, *Domination and Dissent: Peasants and Politics* (Calcutta: Mandira, 1985), pp. 63, 65, 98, 168–9.

7 Reports in Pillai, *The Incredible Elections*, pp. 419–22.

8 S. L. M. Prachand, *The Popular Upsurge and the Fall of Congress* (Chandigarh: Abhishek Publications, 1977).

9 Cf. Theodore P. Wright, Jr., 'Muslims and the 1977 Indian Election: A Watershed?', *Asian Survey*, vol. 17, no. 12, December 1977.

10 Indira Gandhi to Fory Nehru, 17 April 1977, copy in Pupul Jayakar Papers, Mumbai.

11 Khushwant Singh, writing in his 'Editor's Page', *Illustrated Weekly of India*, 27 March 1977.

12 Janardhan Thakur, *All the Janata Men* (New Delhi: Vikas Publishing House, 1979), p. 148.

13 See *Himmat*, 30 June 1978.

14 *New York Times*, 22 March 1977, and *Washington Post*, 19 April 1977, both quoted in Baldev Raj Nayar, 'India and the Super Powers: Deviation or Continuity in Foreign Policy?', *Economic and Political Weekly*, 23 July 1977.

15 Ajit Bhattacharjea, 'Janata's Foreign Policy', *Himmat*, 30 December 1977.

16 Cf. press clippings on Carter's visit in File 77, Horace Alexander Papers, Friends House, Euston.

17 Report in *The Times*, 7 November 1977.

18 As recalled in 'When Zia Complimented Vajpayee', *New Indian Express*, 21 February 1999.

19 Cf. report in *Himmat*, 4 November 1977.

20 *Himmat*, 20 January 1978.

21 K. A. Abbas, *Janata in a Jam?* (Bombay: Jaico Publishing House, 1978), p. 84.

22 Ajit Roy, 'West Bengal: Not a Negative Vote', *Economic and Political Weekly*, 2 July 1977.

23 Sunil Sengupta, 'West Bengal Land Reforms and the Agrarian Scene', *Economic and Political Weekly, Review of Agriculture*, June 1981; Atul Kohli, *The State and Poverty in India: The Politics of Reform* (Cambridge: Cambridge University Press, 1987), chapter 3; Prabir Kumar De, *The Politics of Land Reform: The Changing Scene in Rural Bengal* (Calcutta: Minerva Associates, 1994).

24 Narendra Subramanian, *Ethnicity and Populist Mobilization: Political Parties, Citizens and Democracy in South India* (New Delhi: Oxford University Press, 1999), pp. 283–6; K. Mohandas, *MGR: The Man and the Myth* (Bangalore: Panther Publishers, 1992), pp. 11–12, 33–4.

25 *The Guardian*, 12 November 1977.

26 D. D. Thakur, *My Life and Years in Kashmiri Politics* (Delhi: Konark Publishers, 2005), p. 277.

27 Shamim Ahmed Shamim, 'Kashmir', *Seminar*, April 1978. Cf. also Mir Qasim, *My Life and Times* (New Delhi: Allied Publishers, 1992), pp. 154–5.

28 Gilbert Etienne, *India's Changing Rural Scene, 1963–1979* (Delhi: Oxford University Press, 1982).

29 Useful overviews of Operation Flood are contained in Martin Doornbos and K. N. Nair, eds, *Resources, Institutions and Strategies: Operation Flood and Indian Dairying* (New Delhi: Sage Publications, 1990); Shanti George, *Operation Flood: An Appraisal of Current Indian Dairy Policy* (Delhi: Oxford University Press, 1985).

30 Ashutosh Varshney, *Democracy, Development, and the Countryside: Urban–Rural Struggles in India* (Cambridge: Cambridge University Press, 1998), chapter 4.

31 Cf. ibid. and Ashok Mitra, *Terms of Trade and Class Relations* (London: Frank Cass, 1977).

32 Neerja Chowdhury, 'Sharpening the Battle Lines', *Himmat*, 23 March 1979; Harry W. Blair, 'Rising Kulaks and Backward Classes in Bihar: Social Change in the Late 1970s', *Economic and Political Weekly*, 12 January 1980.

33 Kalpana Sharma, 'Bihar – the Ungovernable State?', and Rajiv Shankar, 'Why Bihar Remains Poor', both in *Himmat*, 6 October 1978.

34 Sachidananda, 'Bihar's Experience', *Seminar*, November 1979.

35 Arun Sinha, 'Class War, Not "Atrocities" against Harijans', *Economic and Political Weekly*, 10 December 1977; Pravin Sheth, 'In the Countryside', *Seminar*, November 1979.

36 Atyachar Virodh Samiti, 'The Marathwada Riots: A Report', *Economic and Political Weekly*, 12 May 1979.

37 Owen M. Lynch, 'Rioting as Rational Action: An Interpretation of the April 1978 Riots in Agra', *Economic and Political Weekly*, 28 November 1981.

38 Pupul Jayakar, *Indira Gandhi: An Intimate Biography* (New York: Pantheon Books, 1993), pp. 253–4, 263–4.

39 Madhu Limaye, *Janata Party Experiment: An Insider's Account of Opposition Politics*, vol. 1 (Delhi: B. R. Publishing Corporation, 1994), p. 451.

40 *New York Times*, 30 October 1977.

41 Cf. *Himmat*, 10 March 1978.

42 Cf. James Manor, 'Pragmatic Progressives in Regional Politics: The Case of Devaraj Urs', *Economic and Political Weekly*, annual issue, February 1980.

43 Ramesh Chandran, 'The Battle for Chikmaglur', *Illustrated Weekly of India*, 5 November 1978.

44 Granville Austin, *Working a Democratic Constitution: The Indian Experience* (New Delhi: Oxford University Press, 1999), pp. 463–4.

45 This account of the conflicts within Janata and the party's split is based on Arun Gandhi, *The Morarji Papers: Fall of the Janata Government* (New Delhi: Vision Books, 1983); Limaye, *Janata Party Experiment*, vol. 2; Terence J. Byres, 'Charan Singh, 1902–87: An Assessment', *Journal of Peasant Studies*, vol. 15, no. 2, 1987–8; and issues of the *Himmat* weekly throughout 1978 and 1979.

46 Editorial in *Opinion*, 16 October 1979.

47 Indira Gandhi to Fory Nehru, 17 April 1977, in Jayakar Papers, Mumbai. In her own biography (Jayakar, *Indira Gandhi*, p. 303), she quotes this letter but leaves out the crucial last sentence.

48 *Himmat*, 20 July 1979.

49 Jag Parvesh Chandra, *Verdict on Janata* (New Delhi: Metropolitan Book Co., 1979),
    pp. 26, 96; Thakur, *All the Janata Men*, pp. 148–50.

50 *Himmat*, issues of 6 January and 10 February 1978.

51 Sharad Karkhanis, quoted in Gandhi, *The Morarji Papers*, pp. 97–8.

52 Austin, *Working the Democratic Constitution*, pp. 403–4.

53 *Illustrated Weekly of India*, 6 March 1977.

54 This account is based on Austin, *Working a Democratic Constitution*, pp. 409–30. But
    cf. also Soli Sorabjee, 'Repairing the Constitution: The Job Remains', *Himmat*,
    23 March 1979.

55 Radha Kumar, *The History of Doing: An Illustrated Account of Movements for Women's
    Rights and Feminism in India, 1860–1990* (New Delhi: Kali for Women, 1993), esp.
    chapters 6 to 8; Chhaya Datar, *Waging Change: Women Tobacco Workers in Nipani
    Organise* (New Delhi: Kali for Women, 1989).

56 For details see Ramachandra Guha, *How Much Should a Person Consume?
    Environmentalism in India and the United States* (Berkeley: University of California
    Press, 2006), chapter 2, 'The Indian Road to Sustainability'.

57 This account is based on my own interactions with these groups over the past
    three decades. Unfortunately, there is no history of the civil liberties movement
    in modern India, or studies of its most important groups: such as the People's
    Union for Civil Liberties and the People's Union for Democratic Rights, both
    based in Delhi; the pioneering Association for the Protection of Democratic
    Rights, based in Calcutta; the Committee for the Protection of Democratic
    Rights, based in Bombay; and the Andhra Pradesh Civil Liberties Committee,
    based in Hyderabad. Dr Sitarama Kakarala of the National Law School in
    Bangalore is currently completing a book on the last-named group.

58 Anil Sadgopal and Shyam Bahadur 'Namra', eds, *Sangharh aur Nirman: Shankar
    Guha Niyogi aur Unka Naye Bharat ka Sapna* (Struggle and Construction: Shankar
    Guha Niyogi and his Dreams for a New India) (Delhi: Rajkamal Prakashan,
    1993). Niyogi was murdered by an assassin – hired, most likely, by local
    industrialists – in 1992.

59 Robin Jeffrey, *India's Newspaper Revolution: Capitalism, Politics and the Indian-
    Language Press, 1977–99* (London: C. Hurst and Co., 2000).

24. DEMOCRACY IN DISARRAY

1 Walter Schwarz, 'Two-Party Democracy Faces a Test Run', *Guardian*, 14 May 1977.

2 Clipping from the *New York Times*, 4 April 1977; letter to S. K. De, dated
   17 June 1977, both in Temp Mss 577/81, Horace Alexander Papers, Friends
   House, Euston.

3 Horace Alexander to Indira Gandhi, 8 April 1977, ibid.

4 These figures on seats and vote shares come from the statistical supplement to the
   Journal of Indian School of Political Economy, vol. 15, nos 1 and 2, 2003, this part
   of a special issue on 'Political Parties and Elections in Indian States: 1990–2003',
   edited by Suhas Palshikar and Yogendra Yadav.

5 Prabhas Joshi, 'And Not Even a Dog Barked', *Tehelka*, 2 July 2005; *India Today*,
   1–15 January 1980.

6 See Mervyn Jones, *Chances: An Autobiography* (London: Verso, 1987), p. 271.

7 Moin Shakir, 'Election Participation of Minorities and Indian Political System', *Economic and Political Weekly*, annual issue, February 1980.

8 Nalini Singh, 'Elections as They Really Are', *Economic and Political Weekly*, 24 May 1980.

9 Bashiruddin Ahmad, 'Trends and Options', *Seminar*, April 1980.

10 Typescript of interview with Bobby Harrypersadh, dated 31 May 1980, in Jayakar Papers, Mumbai.

11 *India Today*, 16–31 May 1980.

12 *The Hindu*, 24 June 1980.

13 The *Tribune*, 27 October 1980, copy in Pupul Jayakar Papers, Mumbai.

14 *India Today*, 16–31 August, 1980.

15 M. V. Kamath, 'Why Rajiv Gandhi?', *Illustrated Weekly of India*, 31 May 1981.

16 *India Today*, 1–15 December 1981.

17 These paragraphs on the Festival of India are based on the clippings and correspondence in Mss Eur F215/232, OIOC.

18 Rajni Bakshi, *The Long Haul: The Bombay Textile Workers Strike* (Bombay: BUILD Documentation Centre, 1986); Meena Menon and Neera Adarkar, *One Hundred Years, One Hundred Voices: The Millworkers of Girangaon: An Oral History* (Calcutta: Seagull Books, 2004). The strike, in effect, killed the city's textile industry, with most units being declared 'sick' by the owners or the state. These mill lands are now the subject of much controversy in Bombay, with citizens asking that they be used for working-class housing or for parks, and property speculators hoping to turn them into luxury apartments and shopping malls.

19 Jan Myrdal, *India Waits* (Hyderabad: Sangam Books, 1984).

20 Mahasweta Devi, 'Contract Labour or Bonded Labour?', *Economic and Political Weekly*, 6 June 1981.

21 Darryl D'Monte, 'In Santhal Parganas with Sibu Soren', *Illustrated Weekly of India*, 8 April 1979, and 'The Jharkhand Movement' (in two parts), *Times of India*, 13 and 14 March 1979. For wider historical overviews of the Jharkhand question, see Sajal Basu, *Jharkhand Movement: Ethnicity and Culture of Silence* (Shimla: Indian Institute of Advanced Study, 1984); Susan B. C. Devalle, *Discourses of Ethnicity: Culture and Protest in Jharkhand* (New Delhi: Sage Publications, 1992); Nirmal Sengupta, ed., *Jharkhand: Fourth World Dynamics* (Delhi: Authors Guild, 1982).

22 See Shankar Guha Niyogi, 'Chattisgarh and the National Question', in *Nationality Question in India: Seminar Papers* (Hyderabad: Andhra Pradesh Radical Students Union, 1982).

23 Bertil Lintner, *Land of Jade: A Journey through Insurgent Burma* (Bangkok: White Lotus, 1990), pp. 83–4 and *passim*.

24 'Report of a Fact-Finding Team', chapter 21 in Luingam Luithui and Nandita Haksar, eds, *Nagaland File: A Question of Human Rights* (New Delhi: Lancer International, 1984).

25 Personal communication from P. Sainath, who was covering Andhra Pradesh politics at the time.

26 *Times of India*, 30 March 1982; *Sunday*, 16 January 1983.

27 See interview with NTR in *Sunday*, 12 December 1982.

28 *Times of India*, 10 January 1983.

29 M. Ramchandra Rao, 'NTR – Victim of His Own Charisma?', *Janata*, 24 April 1983.

30 *Indian Express*, 15 September 1983.

31 Myron Weiner, *Sons of the Soil: Migration and Ethnic Conflict in India* (Princeton: Princeton University Press, 1978), chapter 3; Alaka Sarmah, *Immigration and Assam Politics* (Delhi: Ajanta Books, 1999); Anindita Dasgupta, 'Denial and Resistance: Sylhet Partition Refugees in Assam', *Contemporary South Asia*, vol. 10, no. 3, 2001.

32 Amalendu Guha, 'Little Nationalism Turned Chauvinist: Assam's Anti-Foreigner Upsurge 1979–80', *Economic and Political Weekly*, annual issue, October 1980.

33 Sanjib Baruah, *India against Itself: Assam and the Politics of Nationality* (Philadelphia: University of Pennsylvania Press, 1999), esp. chapter 5; Tilotomma Misra, 'Assam and the National Question', in *Nationality Question in India*; Udayon Misra, *The Periphery Strikes Back: Challenges to the Nation-State in Assam and Nagaland* (Shimla: Indian Institute of Advanced Study, 2000), chapters 4 and 5.

34 Chaitanya Kalbagh, 'The North-East: India's Bangladesh?', *India Today*, 1–15 May 1980.

35 *Economic Times*, 3 November 1980.

36 Quoted in the *Times of India*, 30 July 1980.

37 See T. S. Murty, *Assam, the Difficult Years: A Study of Political Developments in 1979–83* (New Delhi: Himalayan Books, 1983).

38 Devdutt, 'Assam Agitation: It Is not the End of the Tunnel', *The Financial Express*, 8 October 1980.

39 A wide-ranging and still valuable collection of essays on Sikh political history is Paul Wallace and Surendra Chopra, eds, *Political Dynamics of Punjab* (Amritsar: Guru Nanak Dev University Press, 1981).

40 There are various versions of the Anandpur Sahib Resolution. I have here used the text as authenticated by Sant Harcharan Singh Longowal and printed in *White Paper on the Punjab Agitation* (New Delhi: Government of India Press, 1984), pp. 67–90.

41 This account of the Punjab dispute draws upon the following books and articles: Robin Jeffrey, *What's Happening to India: Punjab, Ethnic Conflict and the Test for Federalism*, 2nd edn (Basingstoke: Macmillan, 1994); Chand Joshi, *Bhindranwale: Myth and Reality* (New Delhi: Vikas Publishing House, 1984); Anup Chand Kapur, *The Punjab Crisis* (Delhi: S. Chand and Co, 1985); Ram Narayan Kumar, *The Sikh Unrest and the Indian State* (Delhi: Ajanta Publishers, 1997); Mark Tully and Satish Jacob, *Amritsar: Mrs Gandhi's Last Battle* (London: Pan Books, 1985); Satinder Singh, *Khalistan: An Academic Analysis* (New Delhi: Amar Prakashan, 1982); Harjot Oberoi, 'Sikh Fundamentalism: Translating History into Theory', in Martin E. Marty and R. Scott Appleby, eds, *Fundamentalisms and the State* (Chicago: University of Chicago Press, 1996); Hamish Telford, 'The Political Economy of Punjab: Creating Space for Sikh Militancy', *Asian Survey*, vol. 32, no. 11, November 1992.

42 Cf. the suggestive analysis of Bhindranwale's sermons in Mark Juergensmeyer, 'The Logic of Religious Violence: The Case of the Punjab', *Contributions to Indian Sociology*, new series, vol. 22, no. 1, 1988.

43 Ayesha Kagal, quoted in Paul Wallace, 'Religious and Ethnic Politics: Political Mobilization in Punjab', in Francine R. Frankel and M. S. A. Rao, eds, *Dominance and State Power in India: Decline of a Social Order*, vol. 2 (Delhi: Oxford University Press, 1990), p. 451.

44 See profile of Bhindranwale in *India Today*, 1–15 October 1981; Murray J. Leaf, *Song of Hope: The Green Revolution in a Panjab Village* (New Brunswick: Rutgers University Press, 1984), chapter 7, 'Religion'.

45 Clipping in Mss Eur F230/36, OIOC.

46 *Indian Express*, 21 September 1981.

47 The verdicts, respectively, of Tully and Jacob, *Amritsar*, p. 71, and Joshi, *Bhindranwale*, p. 90.

48 For an insightful contemporary account of the pressures on the Akalis to become more extreme, see Gopal Singh, 'Socio-economic Bases of the Punjab Crisis', *Economic and Political Weekly*, 7 January 1984.

49 Interview with Madhu Jain in *Sunday*, 4 September 1983; Rajinder Puri, 'Remembering 1984', *National Review*, November 2003.

50 Anne Vaugier-Chatterjee, *Histoire Politique du Pendjab de 1947 à nos Jours* (Paris: L'Harmattan, 2001), pp. 158f.

51 On the significance of the Akal Takht, see Madanjit Kaur, *The Golden Temple: Past and Present* (Amritsar: Guru Nanak Dev University Press, 1983), pp. 268–70.

52 Paul Wallace, 'Religious and Secular Politics in Punjab: The Sikh Dilemma in Competing Political Systems,' in Wallace and Chopra, *Political Dynamics of Punjab*, pp. 1–2.

53 M. J. Akbar, *Riot after Riot: Reports on Caste and Communal Violence in India* (New Delhi: Penguin India, 1988).

54 Achyut Yagnik, 'Spectre of Caste War', *Economic and Political Weekly*, 28 March 1981; Pradip Kumar Bose, 'Social Mobility and Caste Violence: A Study of the Gujarat Riots', *Economic and Political Weekly*, 18 April 1981.

55 Quoted in Moin Shakir, 'An Analytical View of Communal Violence', in Asghar Ali Engineer, ed., *Communal Riots in Post-Independence India*, 2nd edn (Hyderabad: Sangam Books, 1991), p. 95.

56 Individual studies of these riots are contained in Akbar, *Riot after Riot*; Engineer, *Communal Riots*; in the reports of civil liberties groups and in articles published in the *Economic and Political Weekly* during these years.

57 The following paragraphs, identifying and enumerating these themes, are based on my own reading of the literature; but see also Asghar Ali Engineer, 'An Analytical Study of the Meerut Riots', *PUCL Bulletin*, vol. 3, no. 1, January 1983.

58 George Mathew, 'Politicisation of Religion: Conversions to Islam in Tamil Nadu', *Economic and Political Weekly*, 19 June 1982.

59 See M. J. Akbar, *India: The Siege Within* (Harmondsworth: Penguin Books, 1985), pp. 197ff.

60 Cf. Balraj Puri, 'Who is Playing with National Interest?', *Economic and Political Weekly*, 11 February 1984.

61 Lt. Gen. K. S. Brar, *Operation Blue Star: The True Story* (New Delhi: UBS Publishers, 1987), pp. 35–7. Since he led the operation, and since all journalists had been evacuated beforehand, Brar's book is essential in any reconstruction of Operation Bluestar. However, it should be read alongside Tully and Jacob, *Amritsar*, this based on interviews with eyewitnesses and survivors.

62 Brar, *Operation Bluestar*, p. 91.

63 Ibid., pp. 126–7.

64 Lt. Gen. J. S. Aurora, 'If Khalistan Comes, the Sikhs will be the Losers', in Patwant Singh and Harji Malik, eds, *Punjab: The Fatal Miscalculation* (New Delhi: Patwant Singh, 1985), p. 133.

65 J. S. Grewal, *The Sikhs of the Punjab*, 2nd edn (Cambridge: Cambridge University Press, 1999), p. 227.

66 Shahnaz Anklesaria, 'Fall-out of Army Action: A Field Report', *Economic and Political Weekly*, 28 July 1984.

67 Sten Widmalm, 'The Rise and Fall of Democracy in Jammu and Kashmir, 1975–1989', in Amrita Basu and Atul Kohli, eds, *Community Conflicts and the State in India* (Delhi: Oxford University Press, 1988); B. K. Nehru, *Nice Guys Finish Second* (New Delhi: Viking, 1997), pp. 627–41.

68 *The Week*, 26 August 1984.

69 Indira Gandhi to Erna Sailer, 20 October 1984, copy in Jayakar Papers, Mumbai.

70 Pupul Jayakar, '31 October', typescript in ibid.

71 This account of the anti-Sikh riots in Delhi is based on two works deservedly regarded as classics: Anon., *Who are the Guilty? Report of a Joint Inquiry into the Cause and Impact of the Riots in Delhi from 31 October to 10 November* (Delhi: PUDR and PUCL, 1984); Uma Chakravarti and Nandita Haksar, *The Delhi Riots: Three Days in the Life of a Nation* (New Delhi: Lancer International, 1987). I have also drawn upon conversations with friends and colleagues who were active in providing relief after the riots.

72 'The Violent Aftermath', *India Today*, 30 November 1984.

73 'Indira Gandhi's Bequest', *Economic and Political Weekly*, 3 November 1984.

74 Daniel Sutherland, 'India Seen Facing Era of Uncertainty', *New York Times*, 1 November 1984; Henry Trewhitt, 'U.S. Fears Assassination may bring Chaos in India, Rivalry in South Asia', *The Sun*, 1 November 1984.

25. THIS SON ALSO RISES

1 *Times of India*, 4 December 1984.

2 *Times of India*, 14 December 1984.

3 Praful Bidwai, 'What Caused the Pressure Build-Up', *Times of India*, 26 December 1984.

4 Radhika Ramaseshan, 'Profit against Safety', *Economic and Political Weekly*, 22–29 December 1984; *Indian Express*, 5 December 1984. The Bhopal tragedy has had a tortured and still continuing afterlife, with the survivors and their families ranged against the government (accused of providing insufficient medical relief) and Union Carbide (accused of paying paltry amounts of compensation).

5 Hari Jaisingh, *India after Indira: The Turbulent Years (1984–1989)* (New Delhi: Allied Publishers, 1989), pp. 19–20; *Business India*, 17–30 December 1984.

6 Harish Khare, 'The State Goes Macho', *Seminar*, January 1985.

7 Mani Shankar Aiyar, *Remembering Rajiv* (Calcutta: Rupa and Co., 1992), p. 53.

8 Harish Puri, 'Punjab: Elections and After', *Economic and Political Weekly*, 5 October 1985; *India Today*, 15 September and 15 October 1985.

9 *India Today*, 15 September 1985 and 15 January 1986; *Sunday*, 29 December–4 January 1986.

10 See Lalchungnunga, *Mizoram: Politics of Regionalism and National Integration* (New Delhi: Reliance Publishing House, 2002), Appendix D; report in *Sunday*, 20–26 July 1986.

11 'Mizoram: Quest for Peace', *India Today*, 31 July 1986.

12 S. S. Gill, *The Dynasty: A Political Biography of the Premier Ruling Family of Modern India* (New Delhi: HarperCollins India, 1996), pp. 394–5.

13 *Business India*, December 31 1984–January 13 1985.

14 Shubhabrata Bhattacharya, 'Rajiv Gandhi's Discovery of India', *Sunday*, 22–28 September 1985.

15 See judgment in Criminal Appeal No. 103 of 1981, decided on 23 April 1985 (*Mohd. Ahmed Khan* v. *Shah Bano and Others*), *Supreme Court Cases* (1985), 2 SCC, pp. 556–74.

16 Hutokshi Doctor, 'Shah Bano: Brief Glory', *Imprint*, May 1986.

17 See Danial Latifi, 'Muslim Law', in Alice Jacob, ed., *Annual Survey of Indian Law*, vol. 21 (New Delhi: The Indian Law Institute, 1985).

18 *Lok Sabha Debates*, 23 August 1985.

19 Ritu Sarin, 'Shah Bano: The Struggle and the Surrender', *Sunday*, 1–7 December 1985.

20 E.g. editorial in *The Statesman*, 19 December 1985.

21 *Indian Express*, 21 December 1985.

22 Vasudha Dhagamwar, 'After the Shah Bano Judgement – II', *Times of India*, 11 February 1986.

23 See *Eve's Weekly*, issue of 29 March–4 April 1986.

24 R. D. Pradhan, *Working with Rajiv Gandhi* (New Delhi: HarperCollins India, 1995), pp. 130–1.

25 Peter Van der Veer, *Gods on Earth: The Management of Religious Experience and Identity in a North Indian Pilgrimage Centre* (London: The Athlone Press, 1988), especially chapter 1, and ' "God Must Be Liberated": A Hindu Liberation Movement in Ayodhya', *Modern Asian Studies*, vol. 21, no. 2, 1987. Ayodhya's sister town, Faizabad, gives its name to the district. The official who passed the verdict was technically the district judge of Faizabad.

26 Saifuddin Chowdhury, quoted in *Sunday*, 9–15 March 1986.

27 See articles by Neerja Chowdhury in *The Statesman*, 20 April and 1 May 1986, reproduced in A. G. Noorani, ed., *The Babri Masjid Question*, vol. 1 (New Delhi: Tulika Books, 2003), pp. 260–6.

28 Inderjit Badhwar, 'Hindus: Militant Revivalism', *India Today*, 31 May 1986.

29 Sant Ramsharaan Das of Banaras, writing in May 1989, quoted in Manjari Katju, *Vishwa Hindu Parishad and Indian Politics* (Hyderabad: Orient Longman, 2003), p. 73.

30 *India Today*, 15 March 1986; *Sunday*, 25–31 January 1987.

31 Cf. Rajni Bakshi, 'The Rajput Revival', *Illustrated Weekly of India*, 1 November 1987.

32 This figure comes from David Page and William Crawley, *Satellites over South Asia: Broadcasting, Culture and the Public Interest* (New Delhi: Sage Publications, 2001), p. 56.

33 Arvind Rajagopal, *Politics after Television: Religious Nationalism and the Reshaping of the Indian Public* (Cambridge: Cambridge University Press, 2001), p. 84.

34 Sevanti Ninan, *Through the Magic Window: Television and Change in India* (New Delhi: Penguin India, 1995), pp. 6–8.

35 Philip Lutgendorf, 'Ramayan: The Video', *Drama Review*, vol. 34, no. 2, 1990, p. 128.

36 Robin Jeffrey, 'Media Revolution and "Hindu Politics" in North India, 1982–99', *Himal*, July 2001, emphasis added.

37 Interview in *Financial Express*, quoted in Supriya Roychowdhury, 'State and Business in India: The Political Economy of Liberalization, 1984–89', unpublished PhD dissertation, Department of Politics, Princeton University, pp. 100–1. Cf. also Stanley A. Kochanek, 'Regulation and Liberalization in India', *Asian Survey*, vol. 26, no. 12, 1986.

38 H. K. Paranjape, 'New Lamps for Old! A Critique of the "New Economic Policy"', *Economic and Political Weekly*, 7 September 1985.

39 Cf. reports in *India Today*, 15 March and 15 April 1985.

40 T. N. Ninan, 'Rise of the Middle Class', *India Today*, 31 December 1985. See also 'The Rising Affluence of the Middle Class', *Sunday*, 29 October–1 November 1986.

41 Roychowdhury, 'State and Business in India', pp. 73, 122.

42 T. N. Ninan and Jagannath Dubashi, 'Dhirubhai Ambani: The Super Tycoon', *India Today*, 30 June 1985; T. N. Ninan, 'Reliance: Under Pressure', *India Today*, 15 August 1986; Perez Chandra, 'Reliance: The Man Behind the Legend', *Business India*, 17–30 June 1985; Paranjoy Guha Thakurta, 'The Two Faces of Dhirubhai Ambani', *Seminar*, January 2003.

43 'Crony Capitalism', *Sunday*, 2–8 October 1988; Teesta Setalvad, 'Pawar, Politics and Money', *Business India*, 10–23 July 1989; Sankarshan Thakur, 'How Corrupt Is Bhajan Lal?', *Sunday*, 21–27 July 1985.

44 Indranil Banerjie, 'The New Maharajahs', *Sunday*, 17–23 April 1988.

45 Niraja Gopal Jayal, *Democracy and the State: Welfare, Secularism and Development in Contemporary India* (Delhi: Oxford University Press, 1999), pp. 46ff.; 'The Wretched of Kalahandi', *Sunday*, 19–25 January 1986.

46 R. Jagannathan, 'Welcome to Hard Times', *Sunday*, 6–12 September 1987.

47 M. V. Nadkarni, *Farmers' Movements in India* (New Delhi: Allied Publishers, 1987); special issue on 'New Farmers' Movements in India', *Journal of Peasant Studies*, vol. 21, no. 2, 1993–4.

48 Vijay Naik and Shailaja Prasad, 'On Levels of Living of Scheduled Castes and Scheduled Tribes', *Economic and Political Weekly*, 28 July 1984.

49 Tanka B. Subba, *Ethnicity, State and Development: A Case Study of the Gorkhaland Movement in Darjeeling* (New Delhi: Har-Anand Publications, 1992); 'Peace in the Angry Hills?', *Sunday*, 24–30 July 1988.

50 *Sunday*, 27 August–2 September 1989; *India Today*, 15 September 1989; *Business India*, 26 June–9 July 1989.

51 *Sunday*, 25–31 January 1987 and 28 August–3 September 1988.

52 Shekhar Gupta, 'Punjab Extremists: Calling the Shots', *India Today*, 28 February 1986.

53 See *India Today*, issues of 30 April 1986 and 15 September 1988; *Sunday*, 3–9 January 1986. The violation of human rights by the police in Punjab throughout the 1980s and 1990s is extensively documented in Ram Narayan Kumar et al., *Reduced to Ashes: The Insurgency and Human Rights in Punjab* (Kathmandu: South Asia Forum for Human Rights, 2003).

54 Reports in *Sunday*, 19–25 May 1985, 19–25 July 1987 and 20–26 March and 1–7 June 1988 and in *India Today*, 15 June and 31 December 1986.

55 Shekhar Gupta and Vipin Mudgal, 'Operation Black Thunder: A Dramatic Success', *India Today*, 15 June 1988.

56 Interview in *India Today*, 30 November 1986.

57 Sten Widmalm, 'The Rise and Fall of Democracy in Jammu and Kashmir, 1975–1989', in Amrita Basu and Atul Kohli, eds, *Community Conflicts and the State in India* (Delhi: Oxford University Press, 1988), pp. 167ff.

58 *Sunday*, 9–15 July 1989.

59 For which see, among other works, A. Jeyaratnam Wilson, *Sri Lankan Tamil Nationalism: Its Origins and Development in the 19th and 20th Centuries* (London: C. Hurst and Co., 2000); Sankaran Krishna, *Postcolonial Insecurities: India, Sri Lanka, and the Question of Nationhood* (Delhi: Oxford University Press, 2000).

60 Shekhar Gupta, 'Operation Pawan: In a Rush to Vanquish', *India Today*, 31 January 1988.

61 Lt. Gen. S. C. Sardeshpande, *Assignment Jaffna* (New Delhi: Lancer, 1992), preface.

62 Krishna, *Postcolonial Insecurities*, p. 154 and *passim*.

63 See Gill, *Dynasty*, pp. 474–7.

64 See report in *India Today*, 15 June 1989.

65 Cover story on 'The Ugly Indian', *Sunday*, 12–18 July 1987.

66 See report in *Sunday*, 28 September–4 October 1988.

67 Nilanjan Mukhopadhyay, *The Demolition: India at the Crossroads* (New Delhi: HarperCollins India, 1994), pp. 260–2; Christophe Jaffrelot, *The Hindu Nationalist Movement and Indian Politics, 1925 to the 1990s* (New Delhi: Penguin India, 1999), pp. 383ff.

68 See People's Union for Democratic Rights, *Bhagalpur Riots* (New Delhi: PUDR, 1990).

69 Chitra Subramaniam, *Bofors: The Story Behind the News* (New Delhi: Viking, 1993).

70 *India Today*, 31 March and 15 October 1988; *Sunday*, 30 October–5 November 1988.

71 This 'Defamation Bill' is discussed in M. V. Desai, 'The Indian Media', in Marshall M. Bouton and Philip Oldenburg, eds, *India Briefing, 1989* (Boulder: Westview Press, 1989).

72 *India Today*, 15 January 1989.

73 *Sunday*, 12–18 March 1989.

74 Indranil Banerjie, 'Mera Dynasty Mahan', *Sunday*, 1–7 October 1989.

75 See *India Today*, 31 October 1989; *Sunday*, 12–18 November 1989.

76 Vir Sanghvi, 'A Vote for Change', *Sunday*, 3–9 December 1989.

77 *Sunday*, 16–22 June 1985.

78 Kewal Varma, 'The Politics of V. P. Singh', *Sunday*, 19–25 April 1987.

26. RIGHT AND RIOTS

1 M. N. Srinivas, Caste in Modern India and Other Essays (Bombay: Asia Publishing House, 1962).

2 The political assertion of the backward castes through the 1960s and 70s is usefully described in Christophe Jaffrelot, *India's Silent Revolution: The Rise of the Low Castes in North Indian Politics* (Delhi: Permanent Black, 2003). See also D. L. Sheth, 'Secularisation of Caste and Making of New Middle Class', *Economic and Political Weekly*, 21–28 August 1999.

3 Report of the Backward Classes Commission (Delhi: Controller of Publications, 1980), Volume I, p. 57.

4 Sanjay Ruparelia, *Divided We Govern: Coalition Politics in Modern India* (New Delhi: Oxford University Press, 2015), p. 117f.

5 André Béteille, 'Distributive Justice and Institutional Wellbeing', *Economic and Political Weekly*, Special Number, March 1991; Dharma Kumar, 'The Affirmative Action Debate in India', *Asian Survey*, volume 32, number 3, March 1992; Norio Kondo, 'The Backward Classes Movement and Reservation in Tamil Nadu and Uttar Pradesh: A Comparative Perspective', in Mushirul Hasan and Nariaki Nakazato, eds, *The Unfinished Agenda: Nation-Building in South Asia* (Delhi: Manohar, 2001).

6 Jaffrelot, *India's Silent Revolution*, pp. 345–7.

7 See Paranjoy Guha Thakurta and Shankar Raghuraman, *A Time of Coalitions: Divided We Stand* (New Delhi: Sage Publications, 2004).

8 Richard H. Davis, 'The Iconography of Rama's Chariot' in David Ludden, ed., *Making India Hindu: Religion, Community, and the Politics of Democracy in India* (second edition, New Delhi: Oxford University Press, 1996).

9 Ibid, p. 46.

10 Jaffrelot, *Hindu Nationalist Movement*, pp. 420–2.

11 See Paul Brass, *The Production of Hindu-Muslim Violence in Contemporary India* (New Delhi: Oxford University Press, 2003), pp. 110–23.

12 See Katju, *Vishva Hindu Parishad*, p. 65.

13 See, for more details, S. Guhan, *The Cauvery River Dispute: Towards Conciliation* (Chennai: *Frontline*, 1993).

14 As this book goes to press, the dispute over the Cauvery waters has intensified once more. The Supreme Court ordered that Karnataka release 15,000 cusecs of water each day to meet the demands of the summer crop in Tamil Nadu. Protests erupted in the southern districts of Karnataka, with strikes and bandhs in several towns, including the state capital, Bengaluru. Reports in *Times of India* (Bengaluru edition), 7 September 2016.

15 *India Today*, 31 December 1999.

16 Manoj Joshi, *The Lost Rebellion: Kashmir in the Nineties* (New Delhi: Penguin Books, 1999), Chapters 1 and 2. Cf. also Tavleen Singh, *Kashmir: A Tragedy of Errors* (New Delhi: Viking, 1995).

17 Smita Gupta, 'The Rise and Rise of Terrorism in Kashmir', *The Telegraph*, 21 April 1990.

18 Schofield, *Kashmir in Conflict*, p. 147.

19 These headlines are taken from various news reports filed in the Centre for Education and Documentation, Bangalore.

20 *The Telegraph*, 27 May 1990; Joshi, *The Lost Rebellion*, pp. 72–3.

21 See 'Urgent Action' reports of Amnesty International, numbers UA 102 and 108 of 1991, copies in the files of the Centre for Education and Documentation, Bangalore.

22 V. M. Tarkunde et al. 'Report on Kashmir Situation', in Asghar Ali Engineer, ed., *Secular Crown on Fire: The Kashmir Problem* (Delhi: Ajanta Publications), pp. 210–23.

23 This paragraph draws upon, among other works, M. K. A. Siddiqui, *Muslims in Free India: Their Social Profile and Problems* (New Delhi: Institute of Objective Studies, 1998); Abusaleh Shariff, 'On the Margins: Muslims in a State of Socio-Economic

Decline', *The Times of India*, 22 October 2004; Yogendra Sikand, 'Lessons of the Past: Madrasa Education in South Asia', *Himal*, volume 14, number 11, November 2001; *idem*, 'Countering Fundamentalism: The Ban on SIMI', *Economic and Political Weekly*, 6 October 2001; Arjumand Ara, 'Madrasas and Making of Muslim Identity in India', *Economic and Political Weekly*, 3 January 2004.

24 Navnita Chadha Behera, *State, Identity and Violence: Jammu, Kashmir and Ladakh* (New Delhi: Manohar, 2000), p. 179.

25 Sonia Jabbar, 'Spirit of Place', in *Civil Lines 5: New Writing from India* (New Delhi: IndiaInk, 2001), pp. 28–9. See also the vivid eye-witness account of a young Pandit who had to flee the valley with his family – Rahul Pandita, *Our Moon Has Blood Clots: The Exodus of the Kashmiri Pandits* (New Delhi: Random House India, 2013).

26 Cf. reports in *The Telegraph*, 1 April 1990; in *Frontline*, 14–27 April 1990; in *The Illustrated Weekly of India*, 17 June 1990; in the *Times of India*, 11 February 1991. See also Alexander Evans, 'A Departure from History: Kashmiri Pandits, 1990–2001', *Contemporary South Asia*, volume 11, number 1, 2002.

27 Cf. Praveen Swami, 'The Nadimarg Outrage', *Frontline*, 25 April 2003.

28 Vinay Sitapati, *Half Lion: How P. V. Narasimha Rao Transformed India* (New Delhi: Penguin, 2015), Chapters 6 and 7.

29 Anne O. Krueger and Sajjid Chinoy, 'The Indian Economy in Global Context', in Anne O. Krueger, ed., *Economic Policy Reforms and the Indian Economy* (New Delhi: Oxford University Press, 2002). For an overview of the Indian economy on the eve of the reforms, see Bimal Jalan, ed., *The Indian Economy: Problems and Prospects* (New Delhi: Viking, 1992).

30 See Jairam Ramesh, *To the Brink and Back: India's 1991 Story* (New Delhi: Rupa, 2015), pp. 35–7, 144–5, 184.

31 Arvind Panagriya, 'Growth and Reforms during 1980s and 1990s', *Economic and Political Weekly*, 19 June 2004.

32 Ashok V. Desai, *My Economic Affair* (New Delhi: Wiley Eastern, 1993); Kaushik Basu, 'Future Perfect?', *Hindustan Times*, 5 May 2005.

33 See http://indianexpress.com/article/india/india-news-india/manmohan-singh-opening-indian-economy-1991-economic-reforms-pv-narasimha-rao-rbi-indian-rupee-devaluation-2886876/ (accessed 1 July 2016).

34 See Dani Rodrik and Arvind Subramanian, From 'Hindu Growth' to *Productivity Surge: The Mystery of the Indian Growth Transition*, National Bureau of Applied Economic Research, Washington, March 2004.

35 Dennis J. Encarnation, *Dislodging Multinationals: India's Strategy in Comparative Perspective* (Ithaca, N. Y.: Cornell University Press, 1989), pp. 214–5, 225.

36 Surendra Malik, compiler, Supreme Court Mandal Commission Case, 1992 (Lucknow: Eastern Book Company, 1992), pp. 180, 196, 379, 387, 412, 424, etc.

37 Madhav Godbole, *Unfinished Innings: Recollections and Reflections of a Civil Servant* (Hyderabad: Orient Longman, 1996), pp. 344–53.

38 See P. V. Narasimha Rao, *Ayodhya: 6 December 1992* (New Delhi: Viking, 2006), pp. 99–100.

39 Godbole, *Unfinished Innings*, p. 363.

40 Quoted in *Sunday*, 6–12 December 1992.

41 This account of the demolition of the Babri Masjid is based, in the main, on Dilip Awasthi, 'A Nation's Shame', *India Today*, 31 December 1992. But see also

Harinder Baweja, 'Today, 10 Years Ago: What Really Happened', *The Asian Age*, 6 December 2002.

42 The conversation was reported in *Sunday*, 13–19 December 1992.

43 K. R. Malkani, *The Politics of Ayodhya and Hindu-Muslim Relations* (New Delhi: Har-Anand Publications, 1993), pp. 3–4.

44 Quoted in Venkitesh Ramakrishnan, 'The Wrecking Crew', *Frontline*, 1 January 1993.

45 Arun Shourie, 'The Buckling State', in Jitendra Bajaj, ed., *Ayodhya and the Future India* (Madras: Centre for Policy Studies, 1993), pp. 47–70.

46 Francine R. Frankel, *India's Political Economy, 1947–2004*: The Gradual Revolution (second edition, New Delhi: Oxford University Press, 2005), pp. 714–5.

47 See 'Bloody Aftermath', *India Today*, 31 December 1992.

48 Clarence Fernandez and Naresh Fernandes, 'The Winter of Discontent', in Dileep Padgaonkar, ed., *When Bombay Burned* (New Delhi: UBSPD, 1993), pp. 12–41.

49 Kalpana Sharma, 'Chronicle of a Riot Foretold', in Sujata Patel and Alice Thorner, *Bombay: Metaphor for Modern India* (Delhi: Oxford University Press, 1999), p. 277.

50 Translated from the Marathi and quoted in Purandare, *The Sena Story*, p. 369.

51 Clarence Fernandez and Naresh Fernandes, 'A City at War with Itself', in Padgaonkar, ed., *When Bombay Burned*, pp. 42–104; Sharma, 'Chronicle', pp. 278–86.

52 'Bombay Has Lost Its Character', *The Afternoon Dispatch and Courier*, 10 January 1993, reprinted in 'Busybee', *When Bombay was Bombed: Best of 1992–3* (Bombay: Oriana Books, 2004).

53 *Frontline*, 1 January 1993; Sunday, 13–19 December 1992; *India Today*, 31 December 1992.

54 Michael S. Serrill, 'India: The Holy War', *Time*, 21 December 1992.

55 *The Times*, 7 and 8 December 1992.

56 Geoffrey Morehouse, 'Chronicle of a Death Foretold', *The Guardian*, 10 March 2001.

57 Paul R. Brass, *The Politics of India Since Independence* (second edition, Cambridge: Cambridge University Press, 1994), pp. 353–4, 365–6, 348–9.

27. A MULTI-POLAR POLITY

1 'In Search of the Messiah', *Sunday*, 31 August–6 September 1988.

2 Jaffrelot, *India's Silent Revolution*, Chapter 11.

3 Cf. Ghanshyam Shah, ed., *Dalits and the State* (New Delhi: Concept Publishing Company, 2002).

4 For more on Kanshi Ram and the rise of the BSP, see Sudha Pai, *Dalit Assertion and the Unfinished Democratic Revolution: The Bahujan Samaj Party in Uttar Pradesh* (New Delhi: Sage Publications, 2002); Badri Narayan, *Kanshiram: Leader of the Dalits* (Gurgaon: Penguin India, 2014); Kanchan Chandra, *Why Ethnic Parties Succeed: Patronage and Ethnic Head Counts in India* (Cambridge: Cambridge University Press, 2004).

5 Badri Narayan, 'Heroes, Histories and Booklets', *EPW*, 13 October 2001.

6 James Cameron, *An Indian Summer* (London: Macmillan, 1974), p. 122.

7 André Béteille, 'The Scheduled Castes: An Inter-Regional Perspective', *Journal of Indian School of Political Economy*, volume 12, numbers 3 and 4, 2000.

8 Hugo Gorringe, *Untouchable Citizens: Dalit Movements and Democratisation in Tamil Nadu* (New Delhi: Sage Publications, 2005), p. 112.

9 The posthumous political importance of Ambedkar awaits a serious scholarly analysis. For clues to how important he is to the Dalit consciousness see, among other works: Chandra Bhan Prasad, *Dalit Diary: 1999–2003* (Chennai: Navayana Publishing, 2004); Fernando Franco, Jyotsna Macwan, and Suguna Ramanathan, *Journeys to Freedom: Dalit Narratives* (Kolkata; Samya, 2004); and the 'Margin Speak' column in the *EPW* written by the Ambedkarite intellectual Anand Teltumbde.

10 See V. Jayanth, 'Narasimha Rao and the Look East Policy', http://www.thehindu.com/2004/12/24/stories/2004122407541200.htm (accessed 1 July 2016).

11 See Sitapati, *Half Lion*, Chapter 13.

12 See D. Bandyopadhyay, Saila K. Ghosh and Buddhadeb Ghosh, 'Dependency versus Autonomy: Identity Crisis of India's Panchayats', *EPW*, 20 September 2003.

13 For details, see Mahi Pal, 'Panchayati Raj and Rural Governance: Experiences of a Decade', *EPW*, 10 January 2004.

14 See T. M. Thomas Isaac and Richard W. Franke, *Local Democracy and Development: People's Campaign for Decentralized Planning in Kerala* (New Delhi: LeftWord Books, 2000); Jos Chathukulam and M. S. John, 'Five Years of Participatory Government in Kerala: Rhetoric and Reality', *EPW*, 7 December 2002.

15 Rashmi Sharma, 'Kerala's Decentralisation: Idea in Practice', *EPW*, 6 September 2003; Pranab Bardhan and Dilip Mookherjee, 'Poverty Alleviation Efforts of Panchayats in West Bengal', *EPW*, 28 February 2004; Arild Engelsen Ruud, *Poetics of Village Politics: The Making of West Bengal's Rural Communism* (New Delhi: Oxford University Press, 2003); Nirmal Mukherji and D. Bandopadhyay, 'New Horizons for West Bengal Panchayats', in Amitava Mukherjee, ed., *Decentralization: Panchayats in the Nineties* (New Delhi: Vikas Publishing House, 1994).

16 There is a growing academic literature on these questions. See, inter alia, the essays by Niraja Gopal Jayal, Bishnu N. Mohapatra and Sudha Pai in the 'Democracy and Social Capital' special issue of *EPW*, 24 February 2001; S. Sumathi and V. Sudarsen, 'What Does the New Panchayat System Guarantee: A Case Study of Pappapatti', *EPW*, 20 August 2005.

17 Cf. M. P. Singh and Rekha Saxena, *India at the Polls: Parliamentary Elections in the Federal Phase* (Hyderabad: Orient Longman, 2003).

18 See Rasheed Kidwai, *Sonia: A Biography* (New Delhi: Viking Penguin, 2003).

19 Mehta, *The Political Mind of India* (Bombay: Socialist Party, 1952), p. 38.

20 Taya and Maurice Zinkin, 'The Indian General Elections', *The World Today*, volume 8, number 5, May 1952.

21 Susanne Hoeber and Lloyd I. Rudolph, 'The Centrist Future of Indian Politics', *Asian Survey*, volume 20, number 6, June 1980.

22 Quoted in Lise McKean, *Divine Enterprise: Gurus and the Hindu Nationalist Movement* (Chicago: The University of Chicago Press, 1996), p. 315.

23 Cf. the evidence and testimonies in Peter Gottshcalk, *Beyond Hindu and Muslim: Multiple Identities in Narratives from Village India* (New Delhi: Oxford University Press, 2001).

24 Khadar Mohiuddin, 'Birthmark', in Velcheru Narayana Rao, ed. and tr., *Twentieth Century Telugu Poetry: An Anthology* (New Delhi: Oxford University Press, 2002), pp. 221–7.

25 D. R. Goyal, *Rashtriya Swayamsewak Sangh* (second edition, New Delhi: Radhakrishna Prakashan, 2000), pp. 17–8. For a fuller exposition of this ideology, and from the horse's mouth as it were, see M. S. Golwalkar, *Bunch of Thoughts* (Bangalore: Vikrama Prakashan, 1966).

26 On the growth of the RSS since 1947, see, among other works, Tapan Basu et. al., *Khaki Shorts and Saffron Flags: A Critique of the Hindu Right* (Hyderabad: Orient Longman, 1993); Thomas Blom Hansen, *The Saffron Wave: Democracy and Hindu Nationalism in India* (New Delhi: Oxford University Press, 1999); Pralay Kanungo, 'Hindutva's Entry into a "Hindu Province": Early Years of RSS in Orissa', *EPW*, 2 August 2003; Nandini Sundar, 'Teaching to Hate: RSS' Pedagogical Programme', *EPW*, 17 April 2004.

27 Gowalkar, 'Total Prohibition of Cow-Slaughter', *The Hitavada*, 26 October 1952,

28 Cf. Thomas Blom Hansen, *Urban Violence in India: Identity Politics, 'Mumbai', and the Postcolonial City* (Delhi: Permanent Black, 2001), p. 85.

29 Neerja Chowdhury, 'Sonia Takes a Political Dip at the Kumbh', *The New Indian Express*, 20 January 2001.

30 On this last incident, see *The Telegraph*, 25 January 1999.

31 On the latter question, see P. N. Mari Bhatt and A. J. Francis Zavier, 'Role of Religion in Fertility Decline: The Case of Indian Muslims', *EPW*, 29 January 2005.

32 This paragraph is based on Hasan Abbas, *Pakistan's Drift into Extremism: Allah, the Army, and America's War on Terror* (Armonk, N. Y.: M. E. Sharpe, 2005), Chapters 9 and 10. The Tariq Ali quote comes from his *The Clash of Fundamentalisms: Crusades, Jihads, and Modernity* (London: Verso, 2002), p. 196.

33 Yoginder Sikand, 'Changing Course of Kashmiri Struggle: From National Liberation to Islamist Jihad', *EPW*, 20 January 2001.

34 Pamela Constable, 'Selective Truths', in *Guns and Roses: Essays on the Kargil War* (New Delhi: HarperCollins India, 1999), p. 52; Hafiz Mohammed Saeed, interviewed by Amir Mir in *Outlook*, 23 July 2001.

35 Cf. Anil Nauriya, 'The Destruction of a Historic Party', *Mainstream*, 17 August 2002; Praveen Swami, 'The Killing of Lone', *Frontline*, 21 June 2002.

36 Cf. news report in the *Times of India*, 24 January 1990; Joshua Hammer, 'Srinagar Dispatch', *The New Republic*, 12 November 2001.

37 Reeta Chowdhuri-Tremblay, 'Differing Responses to the Parliamentary and Assembly Elections in Kashmir's Regions, and State-Societal Relations', in Paul Wallace and Ramashray Roy, ed., *India's 1999 Elections and 20ᵗʰ Century Politics* (New Delhi: Sage Publications, 2003).

38 Prabhu Ghate, 'Kashmir: The Dirty War', *EPW*, 26 January 2002.

39 Jaleel, 'I Have Seen my Country Die', *The Telegraph*, 26 May 2002.

40 Buchan, 'Kashmir', *Granta*, number 57, Spring 1997, p. 66.

41 Chandana Bhattacharjee, *Ethnicity and Autonomy Movement: Case of Bodo-Kacharis of Assam* (New Delhi: Vikas Publishing House, 1996); Sudhir Jacob George, 'The

Bodo Movement in Assam: Unrest to Accord', *Asian Survey*, volume 34, number 10, October 1994.

42 Sanjoy Hazarika, *Strangers of the Night: Tales of War and Peace from India's Northeast* (New Delhi: Penguin Books, 1995), pp. 167–226. Cf. also Sanjib Baruah, 'The State and Separatist Militancy in Assam: Winning a Battle and Losing the War?', *Asian Survey*, volume 34, number 10, October 1994.

43 Anindita Dasgupta, 'Tripura's Brutal Cul de Sac', *Himal*, December 2001.

44 Bhagat Oinam, 'Patterns of Ethnic Conflict in the North-East: A Study on Manipur', *EPW*, 24 May 2003; U. A. Shimray, 'Socio-Political Unrest in the Region Called North-East India', *EPW*, 16 October 2004.

45 Anon., 'A Blueprint for Mizoram', *Grassroots Options*, Monsoon 1999; Sudipta Bhattacharjee, 'How to be Thirteenth Time Lucky', *The Telegraph*, 30 June 1999; Nitin Gokhale, 'Meghna Naidu in Aizawl', *Tehelka*, 9 October 2004.

46 Sarabjit Singh, *Operation Black Thunder: An Eyewitness Account of Terrorism in Punjab* (New Delhi: Sage Publications, 2002), especially Chapters 22 through 30.

47 Cf. Anne Vaugier-Chatterjee, 'Strains on Punjab Governance: An Assessment of the Badal Government (1997–1999)', *International Journal of Punjab Studies*, volume 7, number 1, 2000.

48 See 'The Dynamic Sikhs', cover story in *Outlook*, 29 March 1999.

49 Singh, *Operation Black Thunder*, p. 338.

50 Robin Jeffrey, '"No Party Dominant": India's New Political System', *Himal*, March 2002, p. 41.

28. Rulers and Riches

1 See E. Sridharan, 'Coalition Strategies and the BJP's Expansion, 1989–2004', *Commonwealth and Comparative Politics*, volume 43, number 2, 2005.

2 Cf. the critique of Nehru's views in Jaswant Singh, *Defending India* (Bangalore: Macmillan India, 1999), pp. 29, 39, 42–3, 57–8, etc.

3 Stephen P. Cohen, *India: Emerging Power* (New Delhi: Oxford University Press, 2001), pp. 144–5.

4 Anupam Srivastava, 'India's Growing Missile Ambitions: Assessing the Technical and Strategic Dimensions', *Asian Survey*, volume 40, number 2, 2000.

5 Perkovich, *India's Nuclear Bomb: The Impact on Global Proliferation* (Berkeley: University of California Press, 1999), pp. 364–76.

6 Ibid., p. 412.

7 Quoted in Raj Chengappa, *Weapons of Peace: The Secret Story of India's Quest to be a Nuclear Power* (New Delhi: HarperCollins India, 2000), pp. 51–2.

8 See Paul R. Dettman, *India Changes Course: Golden Jubilee to Millenium* (Westport, Conn.: Praeger, 2001), p. 41f.

9 Interview in *Newsline* (Karachi), June 1998.

10 Bhumitra Chakma, 'Toward Pokharan II: Explaining India's Nuclearisation Process', *Modern Asian Studies*, volume 39, number 1, 2005.

11 For the links between the 1998 tests and India's wider ambitions, see Hilary Synnott, *The Causes and Consequences of South Asia's Nuclear Tests*, Adelphi Paper 332 (London: The International Institute for Strategic Studies, 1999); Ashok

Kapur, *Pokharan and Beyond: India's Nuclear Behaviour* (New Delhi: Oxford University Press, 2001). The arguments of the critics of India's nuclear ambitions are collected in M. V. Ramanna and C. Rammanohar Reddy, eds, *Prisoners of the Nuclear Dream* (Hyderabad: Orient Longman, 2003).

12 Cf. cover story in *India Today*, 1 March 1999.

13 On why and how Pakistan planned the Kargil operation, see Abbas, *Pakistan's Drift into Extremism*, pp. 169–74; Owen Bennett Jones, *Pakistan: Eye of the Storm* (New Delhi: Viking, 2002), pp. 87ff; Aijaz Ahmad, 'The Many Roads to Kargil', *Frontline*, 16 July 1999.

14 Praveen Swami, *The Kargil War* (revised edition, New Delhi: LeftWord Books, 2000), pp. 10–1.

15 Rahul Bedi, 'A Dismal Failure', in *Guns and Roses: Essays on the Kargil War* (New Delhi: HarperCollins India, 1999), p. 142.

16 The course of the Kargil war is described in the works cited in footnotes 30 and 31 above, and in Srinjoy Chowdhury, *Despatches from Kargil* (New Delhi: Penguin Books, 2000).

17 Abbas, *Pakistan's Drift into Extremism*, p. 174; interview with Nawaz Sharif in *India Today*, 26 July 2004.

18 Cf. news reports in *The Asian Age*, 4 July 1999; *The Telegraph*, 9 July 1999; *The Hindu*, 19 July 1999.

19 *The Asian Age*, 6 July 1999; *The Hindu*, 4 July 1999

20 Sarabjit Pandher, 'Spirit of Nationalism Eclipses Memories of [Operation] Bluestar', *The Hindu*, 16 June 1999.

21 'Army Job Seekers Go Berserk', *The Hindu*, 18 July 1999.

22 See Venkitesh Ramakrishnan, 'A Debate without Direction', *Frontline*, 12–25 September 1998.

23 Nagesh Kumar, 'Indian Software Industry Development: International and National Perspective', *EPW*, 10 November 2001; Pradosh Nath and Amitava Hazra, 'Configuration of Indian Software Industry', *EPW*, 23 February 2002; Arun Shourie, 'Ensuring IT remains Indian Territory', *The New Indian Express*, 3 January 2004.

24 AnnaLee Saxenian, 'Bangalore: The Silicon Valley of Asia?', in Krueger, ed., *Economic Policy Reforms*, p. 175.

25 See, for more details, Dinesh C. Sharma, *The Long Revolution: The Birth and Growth of India's IT Industry* (New Delhi: HarperCollins India 2009).

26 Raj Chengappa and Malini Goyal, 'Housekeepers to the World', *India Today*, 18 November 2002; 'Outsourcing to India', *The Economist*, 5 May 2001.

27 Saritha Rai, 'Prayers Outsourced to India'; idem, 'US Kids Outsource Homework to India', both originally published in *The New York Times*, reprinted in *The Asian Age*, 14 June 2004 and 11 September 2005, respectively.

28 Shankkar Aiyar, 'Made in India', *India Today*, 1 December 2003.

29 R. Nagaraj, 'Foreign Direct Investment in India in the 1990s: Trends and Issues', *EPW*, 26 April 2003.

30 Arvind Virmani, 'India's External Reforms: Modest Globalisation, Significant Gains', *EPW*, 9 August 2003.

31 See Harish Damodaran, *India's New Capitalists: Caste, Business and Industry in a Modern Nation* (London: Palgrave Macmillan, 2008).

32 E. Sridharan, 'The Growth and Sectoral Composition of India's Middle Class: Its Impact on the Politics of Economic Liberalization', *India Review*, volume 3, number 4, 2004.

33 Surinder S. Jodhka and Aseem Prakash, *The Indian Middle Class* (New Delhi: Oxford University Press, 2016).

34 Devesh Kapur, 'The Middle-Class in India: A Social Formation or a Political Actor?', *Political Power and Social Theory*, volume 21, 2010.

35 Cf. William Mazzarella, *Shovelling Smoke: Advertising and Globalization in Contemporary India* (Durham, N. C.: Duke University Press, 2003), pp. 74–6, 240, 258, etc.

36 Filippo Osella and Caroline Osella, *Social Mobility in Kerala: Modernity and Identity in Conflict* (London: Pluto Press, 2000), p. 127.

37 See, among other works, the special issue on 'Poverty Reduction in [the] 1990s', of the *EPW*, dated 25–31 January 2003; K. Sundaram and Suresh D. Tendulkar, 'Poverty in India in the 1990s: An Analysis of Changes in 15 Major States', *EPW*, 5 April 2003; Angus Deaton, ed., *The Great Indian Poverty Debate* (New Delhi: Macmillan India, 2005).

38 The words of the novelist Eduardo Galeano, writing of the Latin American city, which in these respects is wholly of a piece with its Indian counterpart. Galeano, 'The Other Wall', *The New Internationalist*, November 1989.

39 Cf. special issue on 'Footloose Labour', *Seminar*, November 2003; Supriya RoyChowdhury, 'Labour Activism and Women in the Unorganised Sector: Garment Export Industry in Bangalore', *EPW*, 28 May-4 June 2005; and, for a more general overview, Ajit K. Ghose, 'The Employment Challenge in India', *EPW*, 27 November 2004.

40 P. K. Joshi, Ashok Gulati, Pratap S. Birthal, and Laxmi Tewari, 'Agriculture Diversification in South Asia: Patterns, Determinants and Policy Implications', *EPW*, 12 June 2004; M. S. Sidhu, 'Fruit and Vegetable Processing Industry in India: An Appraisal of the Post-Reform Period', *EPW*, 9 July 2005.

41 Ramesh Chand, 'Whithern India's Food Policy: From Food Security to Food Deprivation', *EPW*, 12 March 2005; Jean Drèze, 'Praying for Food Security', *The Hindu*, 27 October 2003; Madhura Swaminathan, *Weakening Welfare: The Public Distribution of Food in India* (New Delhi: LeftWord Books, 2000); Ashok Gulati, Satu Kåhkonen and Pradeep Sharma, 'The Food Corporation of India: Successes and Failures in Foodgrain Marketing', in Satu Kåhkonen and Anthony Lanyi, eds, *Institutions, Incentives and Economic Reforms in India* (New Delhi: Sage Publications, 2000); and, especially, P. Sainath, *Everybody Loves a Good Drought: Stories from India's Poorest Districts* (New Delhi: Penguin Books India, 1996).

42 P. Sainath, 'Trains Raided for Water in TN', *The Times of India*, 14 May 1993; Sowmya Sivakumar and Eric Kerbart, 'Drought, Sustenance and Livelihoods: "Akal" Survey in Rajasthan', *EPW*, 17 January 2004.

43 Cf. Verrier Elwin, *Maria Murder and Suicide* (Bombay: Oxford University Press, 1943).

44 Farmers' suicides were the subject of a remarkable series of field reports published by P. Sainath in *The Hindu*, too numerous to list individually, but easily tracked down on www.thehinduonnet.com
Cf. also R. S. Deshpande and Nagesh Prabhu, 'Farmers' Distress: Proof Beyond Question', *EPW*, 29 October 2005; *Tehelka*, special issue on the farming crisis, 6 March 2004.

45 Cf. Myron Weiner, *The Child and the State in India* (Princeton: Princeton University Press, 1990).

46 Jean Dréze and Aparajita Goyal, 'Future of Mid-Day Meals', *EPW*, 1 November 2003.

47 Sucheta Mahajan, 'MVF India – Education as Empowerment', *Mainstream*, 16 August 2003; Rukmini Banerji, 'Pratham Experiences', *Seminar*, February 2005.

48 See 'The PROBE Team', *Public Report on Basic Education in India* (New Delhi: Oxford University Press, 1999), Chapter 9.

49 Ramachandran, 'The Best of Times, the Worst of Times', *Seminar*, April 2004.

50 Subhadra Menon, *No Place to Go: Stories of Hope and Despair from India's Ailing Health Sector* (New Delhi; Penguin Books, 2004).

51 Pamela Philipose, 'India is Seriously Sick', *The New Indian Express*, 24 January 2006.

52 Peoples Union for Democratic Rights, *Satpura ki Ghati: People's Struggle in Hoshangabad* (New Delhi: PUDR, 1992).

53 Walter Fernandes, 'Development-induced Displacement and Tribal Women', in Govind Chandra Rath, ed., *Tribal Development in India: The Contemporary Debate* (New Delhi: Sage Publications, 2006).

54 Arup Maharatna, *Demographic Perspectives on India's Tribes* (New Delhi: Oxford University Press, 2005), Chapter 2 and passim.

55 Cf. Rahul, 'The Bhils: A People Under Threat', *Humanscape*, volume 8, number 8, September 2001; various issues of *Budhan: The Denotified and Nomadic Tribes Rights Action Group Newsletter*.

56 Cf. Amita Baviskar, *In the Belly of the River: Adivasi Battles over 'Development' in the Narmada Valley* (New Delhi: Oxford University Press, 1995); Jean Dreze, Meera Samson, and Satyajit Singh, eds, *The Dam and the Nation* (New Delhi: Oxford University Press, 1998).

57 Arjan De Haan and Amaresh Dubey, 'Poverty, Disparities, or the Development of Underdevelopment in Orissa', *EPW*, 28 May–4 June 2005; Sanjay Kumar, 'Adivasis of South Orissa: Enduring Poverty', *EPW*, 27 October 2001; Jean Dréze, 'No More Lifelines: Political Economy of Hunger in Orissa', *The Times of India*, 17 September 2001.

58 Meena Menon, 'The Battle for Bauxite in Orissa', *The Hindu*, 20 April 2005.

59 Anon., *The Struggle Against Bauxite Mining in Orissa* (Bangalore: Peoples Union for Civil Liberties, 2003); Anon., *How Wrong? How Right?* (Kashipur: Agragamee, 1999).

60 Quoted in Manash Ghosh, 'Sins of Development', *The Statesman*, 9 March 1999.

61 Darryl D'Monte, 'Another Look at "Backwardness"', *Lokmat Times*, 13 October 2000; idem, 'Recent Memories of Underdevelopment', posted on www.tehelka. com, 12 October 2000.

62 *The Struggle Against Bauxite Mining*, pp. 15–16; reports in *The Indian Express*, 18 and 19 December 2000.

63 Montek S. Ahluwalia, 'Economic Reform of States in Post-Reform Period', *EPW*, 6 May 2000; S. Mahendra Dev, 'Post-Reform Regional Variations', *Seminar*, May 2004.

64 Cf. K. P. Kannan, 'Shining Socio-Spatial Disparities', *Seminar*, May 2004; Jean Dréze, 'Where Welfare Works: Plus Points of the T[amil] N[adu] Model', *The Times of India*, 21 May 2003.

65 Angus Deaton and Jean Dréze, 'Poverty and Inequality in India: A Re-Examination', *EPW*, 7 September 2002.

66 Srinivasan, *Eight Lectures on India's Economic Reforms* (New Delhi: Oxford University Press, 2000), p. 31.

67 Report in *The Statesman*, 20 September 2001.

68 Daniel H. Pink, 'The New Face of the Silicon Age', *Wired*, February 2002 (http://www.wired.com/wired/archive/12.02/india_pr.html).

69 Manjeet Kripalani and Pete Engardio, 'The Rise of India', *Business Week*, 8 December 2003 (http://www.businessweek.com./magazine/content/03_49/b3861001_mz001.htm).

70 Ron Moreau and Sudip Mazumdar, 'An Indian Champion', *Newsweek*, 12 April 2004.

71 Bharat Jhunjhunwala, 'Gathering Storm of Indian Imperialism', *The New Indian Express*, 10 August 2005.

72 Cohen, *India*, pp. xv, 285–92.

73 Sonia Jabbar, 'Blood Soil: Chittisinghpora and After', in Urvashi Butalia, ed., *Speaking Peace: Women's Voices from Kashmir* (New Delhi: Kali for Women, 2002), pp. 226f.

74 See Atal Behari Vajpayee, 'Musings from Kumarakom', *The Hindu*, 2 January 2001.

75 Cf. the list of major terrorist strikes printed in *The Indian Express*, 7 April 2005.

76 *Himal South Asian*, June 2002; Michael Krepon, 'No Easy Exits', *India Today*, 10 June 2002.

77 See *Hindustan Times*, 19 May 2002.

78 James Michael Lyngdoh, *Chronicle of an Impossible Election: The Election Commission and the 2002 Jammu and Kashmir Assembly Elections* (New Delhi: Penguin Books, 2004), pp. 129, 141–2, 149–50, 180–81, etc.

79 Rekha Chowdhury and Nagendra Rao, 'Kashmir Elections 2002: Implications for Politics of Separatism', *EPW*, 4 January 2003.

80 Quoted in *The Times of India*, 26 September 2003.

81 See Noorani, ed., *The Babri Masjid Question*, Volume 2, pp. 197ff.

82 See Jyoti Punwani, 'The Carnage at Godhra', in Siddharth Varadarajan, ed., *Gujarat: The Making of a Tragedy* (New Delhi: Penguin Books, 2002).

83 Ashutosh Varshney, *Ethnic Conflict and Civic Life: Hindus and Muslims in India* (New Delhi: Oxford University Press, 2002), esp. pp. 229–30, 240–1, 275–7; Jan Breman, 'Ghettoization and Communal Politics: The Dynamics of Inclusion and Exclusion in the Hindutva Landscape', in Ramachandra Guha and Jonathan Parry, eds, *Institutions and Inequalities: Essays for André Béteille* (New Delhi: Oxford University Press, 1999); Udit Chaudhuri, 'Gujarat: The Riots and the Larger Decline', *EPW*, 2–9 November 2002.

84 Nandini Sundar, 'A License to Kill: Patterns of Violence in Gujarat', in Varadarajan, ed., *Gujarat*; Achyut Yagnik and Suchitra Sheth, *The Shaping of Modern Gujarat: Plurality, Hindutva and Beyond* (New Delhi: Penguin Books, 2005), Chapter 11; report by Ashis Chakrabarti in *The Telegraph*, 18 May 2002.

85 Bela Bhatia, 'A Step Back in Sabarkantha', *Seminar*, May 2002.

86 Anand Soondas, 'Gujarat's Children of a Lesser God', *The Telegraph*, 13 March 2002; 'Gujarat Villagers Set Terms for Muslims to Come Home', *The New Indian Express*, 6 May 2002.

87 Cf. Varadarajan, ed., *Gujarat*, p. 22f.

88 For a perceptive (and prescient) analysis of Narendra Modi's political style, see Sankarshan Thakur, 'An Architect of Fractures, or the Man Who Could be Prime Minister', first published in *Man's World*, December 2002, reproduced in https://sankarshanthakur.com/2013/09/14/an-architect-of-fractures-or-the-man-who-could-be-prime-minister/ (accessed 10 August 2016).

89 See Manas Dasgupta, 'Vajpayee's Advice to Modi', *The Hindu*, 5 April 2002.

90 Ajit Kumar Jha, 'Atal Wave', *India Today*, 9 February 2004, available online at http://indiatoday.intoday.in/story/vajpayee-bjp-set-for-landslide-win-in-forthcoming-2004-elections/1/197000.html (accessed 1 July 2016).

29. PROGRESS AND ITS DISCONTENTS

1 Harish Khare, 'Reloading the Family Matrix', *Seminar*, June 2003.

2 Cf. T. N. Ninan, 'Big Growth, Bigger Debates', *Seminar*, January 2006.

3 Cf. Jean Dréze, 'Bhopal Convention on the Right to Work: Brief Report and Personal Observations', *Social Action*, volume 54, number 2, 2004; Rinku Murgai and Martin Ravallion, 'Employment Guarantee in Rural India: What Would it Cost and How Much Would it Reduce Poverty', *EPW*, 30 July 2005.

4 E. Sridharan, 'Electoral Coalitions in 2004 General Elections: Theory and Evidence', *EPW*, 18 December 2004.

5 See the section of special articles on Indian Muslims, sparked by the Sachar Committee Report, in *EPW*, 10 March 2007.

6 Cf. Yoginder Sikand, *Muslims in India: Contemporary Social and Political Discourses* (Gurgaon: Hope India, 2007).

7 Laurent Gayer and Christophe Jaffrelot, eds, *Muslims in Indian Cities: Trajectories of Marginalisation* (New Delhi: HarperCollins India, 2012).

8 *Social, Economic and Educational Status of the Muslim Community in India: A Report* (New Delhi: Government of India, 2006).

9 *The Hindu*, 4 January 2007, http://www.thehindu.com/todays-paper/tp-business/sensex-crosses-14000mark/article1777806.ece (accessed 18 July 2016)

10 *The Hindu*, 27 April 2007, http://www.hindu.com/2007/04/27/stories/2007042708181700.htm (accessed 18 July 2016).

11 Alam Srinivas, 'Red Rag and the Matador', *Outlook*, 8 October 2007, http://www.outlookindia.com/magazine/story/red-rag-and-the-matador/235734 (accessed 18 July 2016).

12 http://news.bbc.co.uk/2/hi/7313380.stm ; http://www.reuters.com/article/us-tata-jaguar-idUSBMA00084220080602 (both accessed 18 July 2016)

13 *The Tribune*, 12 June 2008, http://www.tribuneindia.com/2008/20080612/main1.htm (accessed 18 July 2016).

14 See R. Karthikeyan, 'The Story of a Resistance', *Fountain Ink*, February 2015.

15 *The Hindu*, 11 January 2007, http://www.thehindu.com/todays-paper/salim-group-undeterred-by-the-violence-in-nandigram/article1781092.ece (accessed 18 July 2016).

16 *Economic Times*, 3 September 2008, http://articles.economictimes.indiatimes.com/2008-09-03/news/27712402_1_nano-plant-singur-factory-alternate-options (accessed 18 July 2016).

17 Sheela Bhatt, 'The Talented Mr Modi', http://ia.rediff.com/news/2005/
     jan/12spec.htm) and 'Why does Modi Look Invincible', http://www.rediff.com/
     news/2005/jan/13spec1.htm (accessed 9 August 2016).

18 Bloomberg News, 8 October 2008, http://www.bloomberg.com/news/
     articles/2008-10-08/india-modi-wins-as-gujarat-gets-tatas-nano-plantbusinessweek-
     business-news-stock-market-and-financial-advice (accessed 18 July 2016).

19 These paragraphs draw on two excellent investigative reports: Nitin Sethi, 'India
     Undermined', *The Times of India*, Crest Edition, 30 October 2010; Saikat Datta,
     'Miner Sins', *Outlook*, 23 November 2009.

20 Radhika Raj, 'Uphill Struggle', *Hindustan Times*, Mumbai, 31 October 2010.

21 There is now a growing literature on the social and environmental impact of
     mining on India. See, among other works, Hartman de Souza, *Eat Dust: Mining
     and Greed in Goa* (Noida: HarperCollins India, 2015); Felix Padel and Samarendra
     Das, *Out of This Earth: East India Adivasis and the Aluminium Cartel* (Hyderabad:
     Orient Blackswan, 2010); Nandini Sundar, *The Burning Forest: India's War in
     Bastar* (New Delhi: Juggernaut, 2016); Rohit Prasad, *Blood Red River: A Journey
     into the Heart of India's Development Conflict* (Gurgaon: Hachette India, 2016);
     *"When Land is Lost, Do we Eat Coal?": Coal Mining and Violations of Adivasi Rights
     in India* (Bangalore: Amnesty International India, 2016). This section also draws
     on my own travels in the mining districts of Uttarakhand, Goa, Chattisgarh, and
     Karnataka.

22 Michael Greenstone, Janhavi Nilekani, Rohini Pande, Nicholas Ryan, Anant
     Sudarshan and Anish Sugathan, 'Lower Pollution, Longer Lives: Life Expectancy
     Gains if India Reduced Particulate Matter Pollution', *EPW*, 21 February 2015;
     Amy Kazmin, 'Gasping for Air', *Financial Times*, 18 November 2015.

23 Victor Mallet, 'Holy river, deadly river', *Financial Times*, 14/15 February 2015,
     Gargi Parsai, 'Cleaning the Ganga', *Deccan Herald*, 20 July 2016.

24 Cf. the chapter 'The Indian Road to Sustainability', in Ramachandra Guha, *How
     Much Should a Person Consume? Environmentalism in India and the United States*
     (Berkeley: University of California Press, 2006).

25 Praful Patel, then Minister of Civil Aviation, quoted in the *Times of India*,
     13 December 2010.

26 Gurcharan Das, writing in the *Times of India*, 6 March 2011.

27 See Bahar Dutt, *Green Wars: Dispatches from a Vanishing World* (New Delhi:
     HarperCollins India, 2014).

28 Muthukumara Mani, ed., *Greening India's Growth: Costs, Valuations, and Trade-Offs*
     (New Delhi: Routledge, 2013).

29 For a broad overview of the changes in the position of Dalits in contemporary
     India, see Gilbert Etienne, *Dalits in Villages and Poverty Alleviation Policies,
     1963–2008*, Occasional Publication number 16, Institute of Rural Management,
     Anand.

30 See the reports authored by and collected in S. Viswanathan, *Dalits in Dravidian
     Land* (Chennai: Navayana Publishing, 2005). Cf. also Haruka Yanagisawa,
     A Century of Change: Caste and Irrigated Lands in Tamil Nadu, 1860s–1970s
     (New Delhi: Manohar, 1996), Chapter 7.

31 Shashi Bhushan Singh, 'Limits to Power: Naxalism and Caste Relations in a South
     Bihar Village', *EPW*, 16 July 2005.

32 Mukul, 'The Untouchable Present: Everyday Life of Musahars in North Bihar', *EPW*, 4 December 1999.

33 Bela Bhatia, *The Naxalite Movement in Central Bihar*, Ph D thesis, Faculty of Social and Political Studies, Cambridge University, 2000. Also Bhatia, 'The Naxalite Movement in Central Bihar', *EPW*, 9 April 2005.

34 See *Labour File*, volume 4, numbers 5 and 6, 1998, p. 39.

35 Bhatia, *The Naxalite Movement*, pp. 134, 87 (my translation).

36 See *The Hindu*, 14 November 2005.

37 Mark Juergensmeyer, *Religion as Social Vision: The Movement Against Untouchability in 20ᵗʰ Century Punjab* (Berkeley: University of California Press, 1982); Harish K. Puri, 'Scheduled Castes in Sikh Community: A Historical Perspective', *EPW*, 28 June 2003.

38 Ronki Ram, 'Limits of Untouchability, Dalit Assertion and Caste Violence in Punjab', in Harish K. Puri, ed., *Dalits in Regional Context* (Jaipur: Rawat Publications, 2004); Surinder S. Jodhka and Prakash Louis, 'Caste Tensions in Punjab: Talhan and Beyond', *EPW*, 12 July 2003.

39 *Hindustan Times*, 30 January 2005; *The New Sunday Express*, 30 January 2005.

40 Reported in *The Hindu*, 17 May 2005.

41 Muzamil Jaleel, writing in *The Indian Express*, 8 April 2005.

42 These quotes are from interviews with Muivah in *The Times of India*, 2 March 2005; and in *The Hindu*, 29 April 2005.

43 Bhagat Oinam, 'Patterns of Ethnic Conflict in the North-East: A Study on Manipur', *EPW*, 24 May 2003; U. A. Shimray, 'Socio-Political Unrest in the Region Called North-East India', *EPW*, 16 October 2004; 'Manipur Scenario', *Mint*, 25 November 2009; 'Manipur's merger with India was a forced annexation', *Tehelka*, 11 December 2010.

44 Rishang Keishing, quoted in Ved Marwah, *Uncivil Wars: Pathology of Terrorism in India* (New Delhi: HarperCollins India, 1995), p. 295.

45 N. Lokendra Singh, 'Women, Family, Society and Politics in Manipur (1970–2000)', *Contemporary India*, volume 1, number 4, 2002.

46 Irom Sharmilla's story is told in Anubha Bhonsle, *Mother, Where's My Country: Looking for Light in the Darkness of Manipur* (New Delhi: Speaking Tiger, 2015). She finally broke her fast only in July 2016, fifteen-and-a-half years after she had begun in, in the interim moving from hospital to court and back again, all the while being force-fed by the state.

47 Peoples Union for Democratic Rights, *Why the AFSPA Must Go* (New Delhi: PUDR, 2005); front-page photographs in *The Telegraph*, 16 July 2004; Sushanta Talukdar, 'Manipur on Fire', *Frontline*, 10 September 2004.

48 Quoted in Ramesh, *To the Brink and Back*, p. 186.

49 See C. Raja Mohan, 'The Return of the Raj', *The American Interest*, May–June 2010.

50 *The Hindu*, 29 November 2007, http://www.thehindu.com/todays-paper/123-agreement-with-us-is-unacceptable-to-us-advani/article1958019.ece (accessed 19 July 2016).

51 *The Hindu*, 8 February 2008, http://www.thehindu.com/todays-paper/article1195519.ece (accessed 19 July 2016).

52 News report by Press Trust of India, 8 July 2008, http://www.sify.com/news/left-withdraws-support-to-upa-govt-news-national-jegrS6biadc.html (accessed 19 July 2016).

53 *The Hindu*, 23 July 2008, http://www.thehindu.com/todays-paper/article1312488. ece (accessed 19 July 2016).

54 *The Hindu*, 27 September 2008, http://www.thehindu.com/todays-paper/ manmohan-to-bush-people-of-india-love-you/article1346764.ece (accessed 19 July 2016).

55 *Outlook*, 19 February 2007, http://www.outlookindia.com/website/story/ samjhauta-sabotaged/233930 (accessed 19 July 2016).

56 Reports in *The Hindu*, 19 May 200, and 14 May and 14 September 2008, http://www.hindu.com/2007/05/19/stories/2007051907990100.htm; http://www.hindu.com/2008/05/14/stories/2008051460640100.htm; http://www.hindu.com/2008/09/14/stories/2008091457120100.htm (all accessed 19 July 2016)

57 Quoted in Adrian Levy and Cathy Scott-Clark, *The Siege: The Attack on the Taj* (Gurgaon: Penguin Books, 2013), p. 127.

58 *The Observer*, 30 November 2008, https://www.theguardian.com/world/2008/ nov/30/mumbai-terror-attacks-india3 (accessed 19 July 2016).

59 Pralay Kanungo, 'Hindutva's Fury against Christians in Orissa', *EPW*, 13 September 2008.

60 Smita Gupta, 'Hounds and the Flock', http://www.outlookindia.com/magazine/ story/hounds-and-the-flock/238766 (accessed 20 July 2016).

61 http://www.thehindu.com/todays-paper/tp-national/article1339932.ece (accessed 20 July 2016).
Although this was the first major riot in the district, the tribal Kandhas and the 'untouchable' Panos had long had an uncomfortable, rivalrous relationship, as documented in 1950 by the anthropologist F. G. Bailey. See his *Tribe, Caste and Nation: A Study of Political Activity and Political Change in Highland Orissa* (Manchester: Manchester University Press, 1960).

62 See 'Maya's Magic', *India Today*, 21 May 2007.

63 Smita Gupta, 11 May 2007, in http://www.outlookindia.com/website/story/11- may-2007/234596 (accessed 19 July 2016)

64 *The Hindu*, 28 May 2008, http://www.thehindu.com/todays-paper/article1265436. ece (accessed 19 July 2016).

65 The impacts of NREGA have been analysed in a series of scholarly studies reproduced in Jean Dréze, ed., *Social Policy: Essays from EPW* (Hyderabad: Orient Blackswan, 2016), Section IV.

66 Quoted in http://news.bbc.co.uk/2/hi/south_asia/8062882.stm (accessed 20 July 2016).

67 Cf. K. Balagopal, 'Andhra Pradesh: Beyond Media Images', *EPW*, 12 June 2004.

68 Ramachandra Guha, 'Redrawing the Map, Again', *Hindustan Times*, 10 December 2009.

69 See Jairam Ramesh, *Old History, New Geography: Bifurcating Andhra Pradesh* (New Delhi: Rupa, 2016), Chapter 2 and passim.

70 See http://www.lawyerscollective.org/files/Naz per cent20Foundation per cent20Judgement.pdf (accessed 20 July 2016).

71 This account is based on http://www.rediff.com/news/amarnath08.html; http:// www.greaterkashmir.com/news/gk-magazine/amarnath-land-row-chronology- of-events/38658.html (both accessed 20 July 2016), as well as on my own recollection of the events as they unfolded at the time.

72 *The Christian Science Monitor*, 7 July 2010, http://www.csmonitor.com/World/
    terrorism-security/2010/0707/Indian-Army-deployed-to-quell-deadly-Kashmir-
    protests (accessed 20 July 2016).

73 http://www.ndtv.com/india-news/kashmirs-bloody-sunday-8-killed-valley-
    burns-425750; *The Hindu*, 6 September 2010, http://www.thehindu.com/
    news/national/other-states/3-killed-as-police-open-fire-on-mob-in-kashmir/
    article617495.ece (both accessed 20 July 2016).

74 Jim Yardley, 'Tensions High Across Kashmir After Koran Protests', *New York
    Times*, 14 September 2010, http://www.nytimes.com/2010/09/15/world/
    asia/15kashmir.html?_r=0 (accessed 20 July 2016).

75 Siddharth Varadarajan, 'The Only Package Kashmir Needs is Justice', *The Hindu*,
    20 August 2010, http://www.thehindu.com/opinion/lead/the-only-package-
    kashmir-needs-is-justice/article551897.ece (accessed 20 July 2016).

76 Cf. Yoginder Sikand, 'Jihad, Islam and Kashmir: Syed Ali Shah Geelani's Political
    Project', *EPW*, 2 October 2010.

77 http://www.thehindu.com/todays-paper/article197456.ece (accessed 20 July 2016).

78 http://www.livemint.com/Politics/PKcxtdYT03keXpSGaL7sCL/Cabinet-
    approves-50-women8217s-quota-in-panchayats.html (accessed 20 July 2016).

79 *The Hindu*, 9 March 2010, http://www.thehindu.com/todays-paper/article725434.
    ece (accessed 20 July 2016).

80 *India Today*, 5 August 2010, http://indiatoday.intoday.in/story/
    Raja+faces+heat+as+CBI+raids+DoT+on+2G+scam/1/67517.html (accessed
    20 July 2016).

81 http://indiatoday.intoday.in/story/cwg-officials-suspended,-sponsorship-deal-
    scrapped/1/107925.html (accessed 20 July 2016).

82 *Times of India*, 16 November 2010, http://timesofindia.indiatimes.com/
    india/2G-scam-Raja-ignored-PMs-advice-says-CAG-report/articleshow/6934810.
    cms?referral=PM (accessed 20 July 2016).

83 *The Hindu*, 2 February.
    http://www.thehindu.com/news/national/cbi-arrests-former-telecom-minister-a-
    raja/article1148712.ece (accessed 20 July 2016).

30. The rise of the 'BJP System'

1 Anil Agarwal and Sunita Narain, *Towards Green Villages: A Strategy for
   Environmentally-Sound and Participatory Rural Development* (New Delhi: Centre
   for Science and Environment, 1989); Mukul Sharma, *Green and Saffron: Hindu
   Nationalism and Indian Environmental Politics* (New Delhi: Permanent Black, 2011).

2 Quoted in Jiby Kattakayam, 'I will fight till joint panel is set up', *The Hindu*,
   5 April, http://www.thehindu.com/news/national/i-will-fight-till-joint-panel-is-
   set-up-hazare/article1601666.ece (accessed 1 August 2016).

3 David Lalmalsawma, 'Hunger strike over Lokpal Bill as thousands protest
   corruption', http://in.reuters.com/article/idINIndia-56135720110405, (accessed
   1 August 2016).

4 Debarshi Dasgupta, 'Beyond Clicktivism', *Outlook*, 18 April 2011, http://www.
   outlookindia.com/magazine/story/beyond-clicktivism/271256 (accessed
   1 August 2016).

5 Sandeep Joshi, 'Hazare ends fast, says fight has begun', *The Hindu*, 9 April 2011, http://www.thehindu.com/news/national/hazare-ends-fast-says-fight-has-begun/article1645213.ece (accessed 1 August 2016).

6 Vinay Kumar, 'Suresh Kalmadi arrested', *The Hindu*, 25 April 2011, http://www.thehindu.com/news/national/article1765899.ece (accessed 1 August 2016).

7 As reported by Jiby Kattakayam in *The Hindu*, 4 June 2011, http://www.thehindu.com/news/national/i-wont-sit-back-and-watch-if-attacks-are-made-on-me-ramdev/article2076204.ece (accessed 1 August 2016).

8 See http://www.firstpost.com/politics/crackdown-20504.html (accessed 1 August 2016).

9 See http://timesofindia.indiatimes.com/india/Cabinet-approves-draft-of-Lokpal-Bill-Team-Anna-calls-it-deceit-on-the-nation/articleshow/9394983.cms?referral=PM (accessed 1 August 2016).

10 Gargi Parsai, 'Cabinet approves Lokpal Bill', *The Hindu*, 28 July 2011, http://www.thehindu.com/news/national/cabinet-approves-lokpal-bill/article2302010.ece (accessed 1 August 2016).

11 http://tribune.com.pk/story/231812/indian-pm-warns-on-graft-on-independence-day/ (accessed 1 August 2016).

12 This paragraph is based on reports in *The Telegraph*, 17–21 August 2011.

13 Arati R. Jerath, 'Netas Shaken and Stirred', *Times of India*, Crest Edition, 27 August 2011; 'Middle Class Deserts Manmohan', cover story in *Outlook*, 29 August 2011.

14 See http://blogs.timesofindia.indiatimes.com/India-Circus/why-anna-hazare-should-not-win-this-battle/ (accessed 1 August 2016).

15 Gargi Parsai, 'Anna Hazare ends fast', *The Hindu*, 28 August 2011, http://www.thehindu.com/news/national/anna-hazare-ends-fast/article2405862.ece; Maseeh Rahman, 'Anna Hazare ends hunger strike after Indian government backs down', *The Guardian*, 28 August 2011, https://www.theguardian.com/world/2011/aug/28/anna-hazare-ends-hunger-strike (both accessed 1 August 2016).

16 Reports in *The Hindu*, 3 February 2012, http://www.thehindu.com/todays-paper/supreme-court-scraps-upas-illegal-2g-sale/article2855383.ece (accessed 2 August 2016).

17 Report in *The Hindu*, 4 July 2012, http://www.thehindu.com/news/national/cbi-chargesheets-ashok-chavan-12-others-in-adarsh-case/article3601723.ece (accessed 2 August 2016).

18 Reports in the *Business Standard*, 25 September 2012, http://www.business-standard.com/article/economy-policy/what-is-maharashtra-irrigation-scam-112092503026_1.html; and in *The Hindu*, 8 April 2013, http://www.thehindu.com/news/national/other-states/ajit-pawars-remark-on-drought-irresponsible-opposition/article4591859.ece (both accessed 2 August 2016).

19 Report in *The Hindu*, 17 August 2012, http://www.thehindu.com/news/national/now-coal-burns-rs186000crore-hole-in-exchequer/article3784709.ece (accessed 2 August 2016).

20 T. K. Rajalakshmi, 'Woman as victim', *Frontline*, 6 February 2015; Mohammad Ali, 'No smartphones for girls, rules Muzaffarnagar Jat panchayat', *The Hindu*, Bengaluru, 26 June 2016.

21 Purva Khera, *Macroeconomic Impacts of Gender Inequality and Informality in India*, IMF Working Paper, February 2016, available at http://www.imf.org/external/pubs/ft/wp/2016/wp1616.pdf

22 Malvika Chandran, 'Women in the Workplace: India ranks lowest in the diversity study', *Mint*, 7 September 2011.

23 Mahendra K. Premi, 'The Missing Girl Child', *EPW*, 26 May 2001; P. N. Mari Bhatt, 'On the Trail of "Missing" Indian Females', in two parts, *EPW*, 21 and 28 December 2002.

24 Ravinder Kaur, 'Across-Region Marriages: Poverty, Female Migration and the Sex Ratio', *EPW*, 19 June 2004; Prem Chowdhry, 'Crisis of Masculinity in Haryana: The Unmarried, the Unemployed, and the Aged', *EPW*, 3 December 2005.

25 Rupali Sharma, 'Beware of the Devil at Home', *Sunday Times of India*, Kolkata, 13 January 2013.

26 Report in *The Hindu*, 18 December 2012, http://www.thehindu.com/todays-paper/gangraped-in-moving-bus-23yrold-girl-fighting-for-life-in-delhi-hospital/article4211729.ece

27 Report in *The Hindu*, 23 December 2012, http://www.thehindu.com/todays-paper/waves-of-protest-slam-raisina-hill/article4230667.ece (accessed 2 August 2016).

28 http://www.thehindu.com/multimedia/archive/01340/Justice_Verma_Comm_1340438a.pdf (accessed 2 August 2016).

29 Press Trust of India report dated 19 March 2013, http://articles.economictimes.indiatimes.com/2013-03-19/news/37844331_1_acid-attacks-life-term-jail-term (accessed 2 August 2016).

30 See http://judis.nic.in/supremecourt/imgs1.aspx?filename=41070 (accessed 3 August 2016).

31 Report in the *Times of India*, 12 December 2013, http://timesofindia.indiatimes.com/india/Supreme-Court-makes-homosexuality-a-crime-again/articleshow/27230690.cms (accessed 3 August 2016).

32 Reports in *The Hindu*, 19 January and 7 September 2013, http://www.thehindu.com/news/national/congress-prince-crowned-vicepresident/article4323414.ece and http://www.thehindu.com/news/national/rahul-ideal-choice-for-pm-says-manmohan/article5104208.ece (both accessed 2 August 2016).

33 PTI report dated 20 August 2013, http://www.thehindubusinessline.com/news/national/sonia-gandhi-launches-food-security-programme-in-delhi/article5042041.ece (accessed 2 August 2016).

34 See http://indiatoday.intoday.in/story/gujarat-chief-minister-narendra-modi-srcc-college-delhi-university/1/249136.html; and, for a video recording of a representative speech, https://www.youtube.com/watch?v=SOJE59fwj_w (both accessed 2 August 2016). Modi's rebranding of himself from the late 2000s onwards has been well analysed in Nilanjan Mukhopadhyaya, *Narendra Modi: The Man, the Times* (Chennai: Westland, 2013).

35 See https://intpolicydigest.org/2013/06/12/can-congress-party-stop-narendra-modi/ (accessed 17 December 2016).

36 See http://www.ndtv.com/india-news/at-bhuj-college-narendra-modi-challenges-taunts-manmohan-singh-531714 (accessed 2 August 2014).

37 For a sampling of Modi's election speeches see https://www.youtube.com/watch?v=FPW8_53X_UQ ; https://www.youtube.com/watch?v=ayMIwPs_Oog; https://www.youtube.com/watch?v=dHiTiorePLA; and also, for those with infinite patience and a deeper interest in oratory, http://www.narendramodi.in/10-memorable-speeches-of-shri-narendra-modi-from-2014-lok-sabha-elections-campaign-3143

38 Vanshri Randive, quoted in http://timesofindia.indiatimes.com/city/navi-mumbai/Narendra-Modis-rally-Along-with-the-faithful-came-clueless-villagers/articleshow/27766164.cms (accessed 23 December 2013).

39 Rahul Verma and Shreyas Sardesai, 'Does Media Exposure Affect Voting Behaviour and Political Preferences in India?', *EPW*, 27 September 2014.

40 Joyojeet Pal, Priyank Chandra and V. G. Vinod Vydiswaran, 'Twitter and the Rebranding of Narendra Modi', *EPW*, 20 February 2016.

41 *Hindustan Times*, 20 April 2014, http://www.hindustantimes.com/india/bjp-s-advertisement-plan-may-cost-a-whopping-rs-5-000-cr/story-y8x34eYh26xwoAxeRuaCoO.html (accessed 2 August 2016).

42 For an excellent overview and analysis of the general election campaign, see Rajdeep Sardesai, *2014: The Election That Changed India* (Gurgaon: Penguin India, 2015).

43 Cf. http://iihs.co.in/wp-content/uploads/2013/12/IUC-Book.pdf

44 Amrita Datta, 'Migration, Remittance and Changing Sources of Income in Rural Bihar (1999–2011)', *EPW*, 30 July 2016.

45 R. B. Bhagat, 'Nature of Migration and Its Contribution to India's Urbanization', in Deepak K. Mishra, ed., *Internal Migration in Contemporary India* (New Delhi: Sage, 2016).

46 Pramit Bhattacharya, 'The rise of India's "neo middle class", *Mint*, 31 December 2012, http://www.livemint.com/Opinion/1bdWFKσ9ImvhFySfrCI3aJ/The-rise-of-Indias-neo-middle-class.html (accessed 6 August 2016).

47 These paragraphs draw on two excellent collections: Himanshu, Praveen Jha and Gerry Rodgers, eds, *The Changing Village in India* (New Delhi: Oxford University Press, 2016); and the special issue of *EPW*'s *Review of Rural Affairs*, 25 June–2 July 2016, both of which feature longitudinal analyses of villages in different parts of India that have been extensively studied and re-studied by economists and anthropologists since the 1950s.

48 Dipankar Gupta, 'The Importance of Being "Rurban",' *EPW*, 13 June 2015.

49 Lydia Polgreen, 'Destroying India's walls with success in business', *International Herald Tribune*, 21 December 2011; Devesh Kapur, D. Shyam Babu and Chandra Bhan Prasad, *Defying the Odds: The Rise of Dalit Entrepreneurs* (New Delhi: Random House India, 2014).

50 *The Hindu*, 25 July 2012, http://www.thehindu.com/news/national/other-states/article3678009.ece (accessed 2 August 2016).

51 Report in *Indian Express*, 3 May 2014, http://indianexpress.com/article/india/india-others/30-killed-in-36-hours-by-bodo-militants-in-assam-curfew-imposed/ (accessed 2 August 2016).

52 Sripad Motiram and Nayantara Sarma, 'The Tragedy of Identity: Reflections on Violent Social Conflict in Western Assam', *EPW*, 15 March 2014.

53 Deevakar Anand, 'How not to handle a riot's aftermath', *Tehelka*, 12 October 2013; 'Muzaffarnagar: Tales of death and despair in India's riot-torn town', http://www.bbc.com/news/world-asia-india-24172537 (accessed 2 August 2016); Jagpal Singh,'Communal Violence in Muzaffarnagar', *EPW*, 30 July 2016.

54 Report in *Outlook*, 18 May 2014, http://www.outlookindia.com/newswire/story/elections-2014-took-18-months-of-planning/841162 (accessed 2 August 2016).

55 E. Sridharan, 'Class Voting in the 2014 Lok Sabha Elections', *EPW*, 27 September 2014;

56 Rana Ayyub, 'The RSS Blueprint for Narendra Modi', *DNA*, 29 May 2014, http://www.dnaindia.com/analysis/analysis-the-rss-blueprint-for-narendra-modi-1992165 (accessed 3 August 2016).

57 See http://www.economist.com/blogs/banyan/2014/07/indian-politics (accessed 3 August 2016).

58 See http://indiatoday.intoday.in/gallery/when-modi-picked-up-spade-to-clean-varanasi-ghat/1/13353.html (accessed 3 August 2016).

59 Report in *The Hindu*, 26 September 2014, http://www.thehindu.com/business/Economy/make-in-india-campaign-industry-lines-up-behind-narendra-modis-pitch/article6447490.ece (accessed 3 August 2016).

60 Report in the *Times of India*, 23 January 2015, http://timesofindia.indiatimes.com/india/PM-Modi-launches-Beti-Bachao-Beti-Padhao-campaign-says-female-foeticide-is-a-sign-of-mental-illness/articleshow/45985741.cms (accessed 3 August 2016).

61 Report in *The Economic Times*, 26 June 2015, http://economictimes.indiatimes.com/news/economy/policy/pm-narendra-modi-launches-smart-cities-mission-says-centre-committed-to-urban-india/articleshow/47811630.cms (accessed 3 August 2016).

62 Report in *The Hindu*, 2 January 2015, http://www.thehindu.com/news/national/planning-commission-to-be-renamed-niti-ayog/article6744546.ece (accessed 3 August 2016).

63 See http://timesofindia.indiatimes.com/india/INCH-towards-MILES-Modis-China-mantra/articleshow/42670778.cms (accessed 3 August 2016).

64 Reports in *Times of India*, 4 August 2016.

65 See Vijay Joshi, *India's Long Road: The Search for Prosperity* (Gurgaon: Penguin India, 2015), Chapter 5.

66 Shweta Punj and M. G. Arun, 'Where are the Jobs', *India Today*, 2 May 2016.

67 Report in the *Financial Times*, 20 September 2015.

68 See http://scroll.in/article/761934/india-is-diluting-forest-protection-by-ignoring-this-one-vital-thing (accessed 3 August 2016).

69 See, among other reports, http://indiatogether.org/how-non-compliance-is-condoned-environment; http://www.business-standard.com/article/current-affairs/govt-cancels-rs-200-crore-green-fine-on-adani-116070101477_1.html; http://thewire.in/53410/compensatory-afforestation-bill-not-passed-current-flawed-form/ (all accessed 3 August 2016). Cf. also Ashish Kothari, 'A Hundred Days Closer to Ecological and Social Suicide', *EPW*, 27 September 2014.

70 See http://www.indiaspend.com/cover-story/india-leads-world-in-environmental-conflicts-10655 (accessed 3 August 2016).

71 See http://timesofindia.indiatimes.com/india/PM-Modis-exclusive-interview-with-Times-Now-Full-transcript/articleshow/52940908.cms (accessed 3 August 2016).

72 Kanti Bajpai, 'Modi's foreign policy of shanti and shakti', *Seminar*, January 2016.

73 http://www.ndtv.com/india-news/going-to-pakistan-is-same-as-going-to-hell-says-manohar-parrikar-1444813 (accessed 28 August 2016).

74 See http://www.dnaindia.com/india/report-we-share-a-good-chemistry-modi-on-barack-2055609 (accessed 3 August 2016).

75 Some analysts, however, worried that under Modi's leadership India was coming too close to the United States, and sacrificing its own strategic interests by allowing itself to be used by the US as a counterpoint to China. See Srinath Raghavan,

'Skidding Down the Strategic Slope: Indo-US Relations', *EPW*, issue of 25 June–2 July 2016.

76 Rajni Kothari, *Politics in India* (New Delhi: Orient Longman, 1970), pp. 156–7, 187, 192, 304, 307.

77 Ramachandra Guha, 'The Long Life and Lingering Death of the Indian National Congress', in *Democrats and Dissenters* (Gurgaon: Allen Lane, 2016).

78 Malini Bhattacharjee, 'Tracing the Emergence and Consolidation of Hindutva in Assam', *EPW*, 16 April 2016; Udayon Misra, 'Victory for Identity Politics, not Hindutva in Assam', *EPW*, 28 May 2016.

79 http://timesofindia.indiatimes.com/india/Yogi-Adityanath-Love-jihad-will-be-a-bypoll-issue-in-UP/articleshow/41164779.cms; http://timesofindia.indiatimes.com/india/BJP-MP-Sakshi-Maharaj-calls-Nathuram-Godse-a-patriot-retracts/articleshow/45484389.cms; http://indianexpress.com/article/india/india-others/aligarh-based-hindu-outfit-announces-mass-re-conversions-on-xmas-bjp-mp-welcomes-move/; http://indianexpress.com/article/india/india-others/union-minister-spells-out-choice-in-delhi-ramzada-vs-haramzada/ (all accessed 29 August 2016).

80 'Rohith's Living Legacy', *EPW*, 6 February 2016.

81 Ashwaq Masoodi, 'The rise of the Gau Rakshak', *Mint*, 26 July 2016; Arpit Parashar, 'The lynch mob and agenda 2017', *Fountain Ink*, December 2015; Parth M. N. 'Vigilante groups beat and kill to protect cows in India', http://www.latimes.com/world/asia/la-fg-cow-terror-snap-story.html (accessed 3 August 2016).

82 See http://scroll.in/article/812329/your-mother-you-take-care-of-it-meet-the-dalits-behind-gujarats-stirring-cow-carcass-protests (accessed 3 August 2016); Reports in the *Times of India*, 19 and 20 July 2016.

83 http://www.ndtv.com/india-news/the-real-story-of-what-hardik-patel-21-wants-and-why-1210424 (accessed 3 August 2016); Mahesh Langa, 'Gujarat on the boil', *The Hindu*, 27 August 2015; Arpit Parashar, 'Jats create new divisions', *Fountain Ink*, April 2016.

84 Prem Chowdhry, 'Masculine Spaces: Rural Male Culture in North India', *EPW*, 22 November 2014; Alice Tilche, 'Migration, Bacherlood and Discontent among the Patidars', *EPW*, *Review of Rural Affairs*, 25 June–July 2 2016.

85 As this book goes to press, in October 2016, the Marathas in Maharashtra, likewise the dominant caste in their state, have launched a major agitation demanding affirmative action for themselves, if need be at the expense of the Dalits.

86 *Sunday Times of India*, 10 July 2016; , Shujaat Bukhari, 'Wrath of Kashmir', *Frontline*, 19 August 2016.

87 Shah Faesal, 'Every hour of prime time TV news aggression pushes Kashmir a mile westward from India', *Indian Express*, 20 July 2016, http://indianexpress.com/article/opinion/columns/kashmir-protest-burhan-wani-killing-selective-indian-media-coverage-insensitive-residents-column-2922176/ (accessed 3 August 2016).

Epilogue: A 50–50 Democracy

1 Isaiah Berlin, 'Nationalism: Past Neglect and Present Power' (1979), in his *Against the Current: Essays in the History of Ideas*, edited by Henry Hardy (London: Pimlico, 1997), pp. 346–7, 353–4.

2 The modern literature on nationalism will fill a decent-sized library. For
   a sampling of relevant works, see Ernest Gellner, *Nations and Nationalism*
   (Oxford: Basil Blackwell, 1983); Benedict Anderson, *Imagined Communities:
   Reflections on the Origins and Spread of Nationalism* (London: Verso, 1983);
   Anthony D. Smith, *The Ethnic Origin of Nations* (Oxford: Basil Blackwell,
   1986); Liah Greenfeld, *Nationalism: Five Roads to Modernity* (Cambridge, Mass.:
   Harvard University Press, 1992); Eric Hobsbawm, *Nations and Nationalism
   Since 1780* (Cambridge: Cambridge University Press, 1993); Tom Nairn, *Faces
   of Nationalism: Janus Revisited* (London: Verso, 1997). Cf. also the classic early
   work of Hans Kohn: *Nationalism: Its Meaning and History* (Princeton, N. J.:
   Van Nostrand, 1955).
3 See Mukul Kesavan, *Secular Common Sense* (New Delhi: Penguin India, 2001).
4 Cf. Javeed Alam, *Who Wants Democracy?* (New Delhi: Orient Longman, 2004).
5 Bernard D. Nossiter, *Soft State: A Newspaperman's Chronicle of India* (New York:
   Harper and Row, 1970), pp. 119–23.
6 Joseph Stalin, *Marxism and the National Question* (London: Martin Lawrence, 1936),
   pp. 5–6.
7 Quoted in Peter A. Blitstein, 'Nation-Building or Russification? Obligatory Russian
   Instruction in the Soviet Non-Russian School', in Ronald Grigor Suny and Terry
   Martin, *A State of Nations: Empire and Nation-Building in the Age of Lenin and Stalin*
   (New York: Oxford University Press, 2001), p. 255.
8 See Neil DeVotta, *Blowback: Linguistic Nationalism, Institutional Decay and Ethnic
   Conflict in Sri Lanka* (Stanford, CA: Stanford University Press, 2004), pp. 89–91.
9 See S. M. Burke, ed., *Jinnah: Speeches and Statements 1947–1948* (Karachi: Oxford
   University Press, 2000), p. 150, emphasis added.
10 Howard, quoted in Samuel Huntingdon, *Who Are We? America's Great Debate*
   (Indian edition: New Delhi: Penguin India, 2004), pp. 28–9.
11 Cf. David Gilmour, *The Ruling Caste: Imperial Lives in the Victorian Raj* (London:
   John Murray, 2005).
12 *CAD*, Volume 10, pp. 43–51.
13 On the history and functioning of the IAS, see David C. Potter, *India's Political
   Administrators: From ICS to IAS* (New Delhi: Oxford University Press, 1996);
   K. P. Krishnan and T. V. Somanathan, 'Civil Service: An Institutional Perspective',
   in Devesh Kapur and Pratap Bhanu Mehta, eds, *Public Institutions in India* (New
   Delhi: Oxford University Press, 2004).
14 Nehru to General Lockhart, 13 August 1947, in Group XLIX, Part I, Cariappa
   Papers, National Archives of India, New Delhi.
15 See papers in Group XXI, Part II, Cariappa Papers.
16 Nehru to Cariappa, 13 October 1952, in Group XLIX, Part I, Cariappa Papers.
17 Report in *The Hindu*, 14 January 1953, reproduced in the same newspaper on
   14 January 2003.
18 See correspondence in Group XLIX, Part I, Cariappa Papers.
19 Note of 12 December 1958, Group XXXIII, Part I, Cariappa Papers. Cariappa went
   on to claim that for these Pakistani Generals 'war between India and Pakistan
   was simply unthinkable'.
20 Frank Moraes to General Cariappa, 19 December 1968, Group XLIX, Part I,
   Cariappa Papers.

21 J. S. Aurora, 'If Khalistan Comes, the Sikhs will be the Losers', Patwant Singh and Harji Malik, eds, *Punjab: The Fatal Miscalculation* (New Delhi: Patwant Singh, 1985), pp. 137–8.

22 Cf. Steven Wilkinson, *Army and Nation: The Military and Indian Democracy Since Independence* (Cambridge, Mass.: Harvard University Press, 2015).

23 C. Rajagopalachari, quoted in Guy Wint, *Spotlight on Asia* (Harmondsworth: Penguin Books, 1955), p. 130.

24 Woodcock, *Beyond the Blue Mountains: An Autobiography* (Toronto: Fitzhenry and Whiteside, 1987), p. 105.

25 S. Gopal, 'The English Language in India Since Independence', in John Grigg, ed., *Nehru Memorial Lectures, 1966–1991* (Delhi: Oxford University Press, 1992), pp. 202–3.

26 Parry, 'Nehru's Dream and the Village "Waiting Room": Long Distance Labour Migrants to a Central Indian Steel Town', *Contributions to Indian Sociology*, volume 37, 2003.

27 Pratap Bhanu Mehta, 'Playing the Baloch Card', *Indian Express*, 18 August 2016.

28 Sajal Nag, *In Search of the Blue Bird: Auditing Peace Negotiations in Nagaland*, NMML Occasional Paper, History of Society, New Series, number 60 (New Delhi: Nehru Memorial Museum and Library, 2014); N. K. Das, 'Naga Peace Parleys: Sociological Reflections and a Plea for Pragmatism', *EPW*, 18 June 2011.

29 Cf. Malem Ningthouja, '"Us", "them", and an elusive peace', *The Hindu*, 7 September 2015; Pradip Phanjoubam, 'In Northeast, lines of conflict', *Deccan Chronicle*, 4 September 2015.

30 Yadav, 'Understanding the Second Democratic Upsurge: Trends of Bahujan Participation in Electoral Politics in the 1990s', in Francine R. Frankel, Zoya Hasan, Rajeev Bhargava and Balveer Arora, eds, *Transforming India: Social and Political Dynamics of Democracy* (New Delhi: Oxford University Press, 2002), p. 133.

31 Amit Ahuja and Pradeep Chibber, 'Why the Poor Vote in India: "If I Don't Vote, I am Dead to the State"', *Studies in Comparative International Development*, volume 47, number 4, 2012.

32 Mukulika Banerjee, 'Sacred Elections', *EPW*, 28 April 2007.

33 Report in the *Deccan Herald*, 10 October 2004.

34 Bela Bhatia, *The Naxalite Movement*, pp. 114–20.

35 J. M. Lyngdoh, quoted in *The Times of India*, 3 December 2003.

36 Devadas Gandhi to Louis Fischer, 12 January 1952, Fischer papers, Princeton University Library.

37 See, for instance, the collected works of R. K. Laxman, published by Penguin India. Laxman is the most prolific and (by common consent) the most original of Indian cartoonists, but there have been many other gifted practitioners, who, like him, specialize in political satire.

38 Cf. obituary in *The Telegraph*, 2 January 2003.

39 Anderson, *The Spectre of Comparisons* (London: Verso, 1998), p. 132.

40 See 'Politics as a Vocation' in Hans Gerth and C. Wright Mills, eds, *From Max Weber: Essays in Sociology* (New York: Oxford University Press, 1946).

41 See, for a general overview of corruption in independent India, Shiv Visvanathan and Harsh Sethi, eds, *Foul Play: Chronicles of Corruption* (New Delhi: Banyan Books, 1998).

42 B. S. Nagaraj, 'Smokescreen Resort', *Indian Political Review*, July 2003.

43 For an excellent discussion of these issues, see T. N. Ninan, *The Turn of the Tortoise: The Challenge and Promise of India's Future* (Gurgaon: Penguin Books India, 2015), especially Chapters 2, 5 and 10.

44 Peter Ronald deSouza, 'Democracy's Inconvenient Fact', *Seminar*, November 2004; Prem Shankar Jha, 'Keep it Poll-ution Free', *Hindustan Times*, 2 January 2006; report in the *Times of India* (Bangalore edition), 21 January 2006.

45 *Sunday*, 2–9 March 1985.

46 Reetika Khera, 'Monitoring Disclosures', *Seminar*, February 2004. This account of the criminalization of politics also draws upon information supplied by Professor Trilochan Sastry, a founder member of the Association for Democratic Reforms, the group which filed the original PIL in the Supreme Court.

47 Samuel Paul and M. Vivekananda, 'Holding a Mirror to the New Lok Sabha', *Economic and Political Weekly*, 6 November 2004.

48 Trilochan Sastry, 'Towards Decriminalisation of Elections and Politics', *EPW*, 4 January 2014. The link between crime and politics is the subject of Milan Vaishnav's *When Crime Pays: Money and Muscle in Indian Politics* (New Delhi: HarperCollins 2017), published just as this book is going to press.

49 Arild Engelsen Ruud, 'Talking Dirty about Politics: A View from a Bengali Village', in C. J. Fuller and Veronique Bénéi, eds, *The Everyday State and Society in India* (New Delhi: Social Science Press, 2000), pp. 116–8.

50 Report in the *International Herald Tribune*, 19 November 2004.

51 Jorge Louis Borges, *The Total Library: Non-Fiction, 1922–1986*, edited by Elliot Weinberger and translated by Esther Allen, Jill Levine, and Elliot Weinberger (London: Penguin Books, 2001), p. 309; R. W. Southern, *Western Society and the Church in the Middle Ages* (Harmondsworth: Penguin Books, 1970), p. 154.

52 Patrick French, *India: A Portrait* (New York: Alfred A. Knopf, Jr. 2011).

53 Kanchan Chandra, ed., *Democratic Dynasties: State, Party and Family in Contemporary Indian Politics* (Cambridge: Cambridge University Press, 2016).

54 As reported in the *New Indian Express*, Coimbatore, 25/7/2011.

55 Damayanti Datta, 'What Makes him Cry: Why the Judicial System has Broken Down and how to Fix it'; Harish Narasappa, 'The Long, Expensive Road to Justice', both in *India Today*, 9 May 2016.

56 Report in the *Times of India*, 17 September 2010, http://timesofindia.indiatimes.com/india/Eight-chief-justices-were-corrupt-Ex-law-minister/articleshow/6568723.cms (accessed 19 August 2016).

57 See Mandira Nayar, 'License to Silence?', *The Week*, 11 October 2015.

58 As reported in the *Indian Express*, 4 September 2014, http://indianexpress.com/article/india/india-others/ex-cji-sathasivam-appointed-kerala-governor/ (accessed 29 August 2016).

59 Murali Karnam, 'Conditions of Undertrials in India', *EPW*, 26 March 2016

60 Ninan, *Turn of the Tortoise*, p. 120.

61 See http://indianexpress.com/article/india/maharashtra/muslims-think-we-are-communal-corrupt-police/ (accessed 17 July 2014).

62 Report in the *Times of India*, 27 November 2014, http://timesofindia.indiatimes.com/city/bengaluru/Police-most-corrupt-dept-in-state-says-portal/articleshow/45289327.cms (accessed 29 August 2016).

63 See http://humanrightsinitiative.org/old/programs/aj/police/india/initiatives/
prakash_singh_judgment.pdf (accessed 29 August 2016).

64 For a fuller analysis, see the essay 'Eight Threats to Freedom of Expression in
India', in Ramachandra Guha, *Democrats and Dissenters* (Gurgaon: Allen Lane,
2016).

Index

and the Sikhs 13, 182, 318–19
split 125, 137, 447
  1969 466, 513, 514, 775
  1978 518–19, 533
'Syndidate' in 386, 402–3, 433–5, 437
and tribals 259–60, 264, 266
unrepresentative nature 359
and the Untouchables 374–5, 378–9
and the West 523
youth wing 507, 508
Congress (R) (later Congress (I)) 436–7, 443–6
Congress Working Committee 281, 386
Conjeevaram temple 108
Connaught Circus, Delhi 88
Conservative Party (British) 28, 53, 133, 324,
  386, 504
Constituent Assembly 5, 6, 8, 21, 29, 39, 40,
  41, 52, 78, 150, 243, 245, 247, 399, 757, 782
  and the civil code 224, 227–8, 230
  and the Constitution 102, 103–6, 111–16,
    118–21, 229
  Drafting Committee 105, 110, 117, 119–20
  and linguistic diversity 116, 178, 180, 389
  proceedings of 102
  and the Scheduled Castes 379
  Select Committee 225, 227
  and tribals 262, 263–4
Constituent Assembly building 6, 228
Constitution of India xxvi–xxvii, 5, 39, 97,
  102–22, 133, 135, 144–5, 203, 219, 225, 229,
  231–2, 263,287, 291, 295, 303–4, 352, 376,
  389–90, 392, 439, 441, 444, 468, 470–2, 557
  Amendments 497–99, 503, 515, 537–8
  38th Amendment 495
  39th Amendment 495
  42nd Amendment 496, 537–8
  44th Amendment 538
  73rd Amendment 633–5
  74th Amendment 633–5
  Article 44 224
  Article 356 293
  Article 370 240, 350, 652, 765
  and caste 359–60, 371, 379, 603, 604, 618
  and the Communists 286
  Indira Gandhi and 472
  and Kashmir 179, 239, 242, 244, 246–7, 352
  and Sikkim 480
  and tribals 265–6
consumer goods 205, 207, 464, 543, 735
Contractor, Behram 626

Cooch Behar 37
corruption 87, 155, 252, 259, 290, 349, 412, 422,
  424, 426, 434, 437, 470, 474–6, 478, 484, 499,
  522, 530, 533, 537, 540, 550, 583, 584, 592–5,
  645, 665, 691, 692, 718–24, 729–30, 733, 740,
  745, 771–2, 775–6, 778, 780–1, 783,
cosmopolitanism 188, 190, 191, 301, 327, 427,
  626, 660, 663, 686, 706, 764
cotton 203
Council House 5, 227
Council of Ministers 231
Council for Scientific and Industrial Research
  213
Coupland, Reginald 52
cows xvi, 104, 108, 235, 411, 429, 640, 708, 746–7
crafts, craftsmen 59, 249, 374, 409, 679
cricket 172, 638–9, 645, 646, 688
Criminal Law (Amendment) Bill, 2013 728
Criminal Procedure Code 575–8
Cripps, Sir Stafford 28, 35
Crocker, Walter 156
Crown xx, 37, 41, 47, 51, 96
Cuban missile crisis 334
Cunningham, Sir George 67
Current (Bombay weekly) 80, 140, 307–8
Curzon Park, Calcutta 423

da Costa, E. P. W. 416–17, 426
Dacca 449–50, 456–8, 459, 460
Dadra 174
Dahl, Robert xxiv
Daily Mail (newspaper) 323
Dakota aircraft 68, 212
Dalai Lama 168, 169, 299–300, 302–3, 313,
  315, 317
Dalit Panthers 531, 628
Dalits 376, 531–2, 592, 628–35, 641, 649, 658,
  670, 686, 696–9, 709–10, 713, 724, 735–6,
  746–7, 768, 781, 783. *see also* Harijans;
  Untouchables
Daman 174–5, 325
Damodar River 210
dams 205, 209–12, 220, 221, 222, 399, 666
Dandavate, Madhu 522
Dandekar, V. M. 465
Dange, S. A. 193
Dantwala, M. L. 500
Darjeeling Hills 586
Das, B. C. 235–6
Dasguputa, Promode 419, 420